THE OXFORD HANDBOOK OF

EMPIRICAL LEGAL

RESEARCH

THE OXFORD HANDBOOK OF

EMPIRICAL LEGAL RESEARCH

Edited by

PETER CANE

HERBERT M. KRITZER

OXFORD
UNIVERSITY PRESS

OXFORD
UNIVERSITY PRESS

Great Clarendon Street, Oxford OX2 6DP
United Kingdom

Oxford University Press is a department of the University of Oxford.
It furthers the University's objective of excellence in research, scholarship,
and education by publishing worldwide. Oxford is a registered trade mark of
Oxford University Press in the UK and in certain other countries

© The Various Contributors 2010

The moral rights of the author have been asserted

First published 2010
First published in paperback 2012
Reprinted 2013

British Library Cataloguing in Publication Data
Data available

Library of Congress Cataloging in Publication Data
Data available

ISBN 978-0-19-965994-4

CONTENTS

PART I: SURVEYING EMPIRICAL LEGAL RESEARCH

LIST OF ABBREVIATIONS

ABA	American Bar Association
ABM	agent-based modeling
ADR	alternative dispute resolution
AFDC	Aid to Families with Dependent Children
AHRC	Arts and Humanities Research Council
ALRC	Australian Law Reform Commission
ANES	American National Election Study
ATE	after-the-event
BIT	bilateral investment treaty
BJS	Bureau of Justice Statistics
CAA	Clean Air Act
CAFA	Class Action Fairness Act 2005
CAPS	Chicago Alternative Policing Strategy
CAT	Convention against Torture and Other Cruel, Inhuman or Degrading Treatment or Punishment
CBA	cost-benefit analysis
CBP	Consumer Bankruptcy Project
CBR	Centre for Business Research
CEDAW	Convention on the Elimination of All Forms of Discrimination against Women
CEPEJ	European Commission for the Efficiency of Justice
CERD	International Convention on the Elimination of All Forms of Racial Discrimination
CESDIP	Centre de Recherches Sociologiques sur le Droit et les Institutions Pénales
CFA	conditional fee agreement
CI	confidence interval
CJRA	Civil Justice Reform Act
CLRP	Civil Litigation Research Project
COHRE	Center on Housing Rights and Evictions
CP	Community policing
CPS	Crown Prosecution Service
CRC	Credit Research Center
CRC	Convention on the Rights of the Child

CSCAA	Committee to Study Compensation for Automobile Accidents
CWA	Clean Water Act
DFID	Department for International Development
DPP	Director of Public Prosecutions
DWP	Department of Work and Pensions
ECHR	European Convention on Human Rights
ECtHR	European Court of Human Rights
ECJ	European Court of Justice
ECMH	efficient capital markets hypothesis
EEOC	Equal Employment Opportunity Commission
ELR	Empirical Legal Research
ELS	Empirical Legal Studies
ENM	*Ecole nationale de la Magistrature*
EPA	Environmental Protection Agency
EPI	employment protection index
EPL	employment protection legislation
ESRC	Economic and Social Research Council
EU	European Union
FJC	Federal Judicial Center
FSA	Financial Services Authority
GATT	General Agreement on Tariffs and Trade
GIS	Geographical Information Systems
ICC	International Chamber of Commerce
ICCPR	International Covenant on Civil and Political Rights
ICESCR	International Covenant on Economic, Social and Cultural Rights
ICJ	International Court of Justice
ICSID	International Centre for the Settlement of Investment Disputes
ICTY	International Criminal Tribunal for the former Yugoslavia
IDR	informal dispute resolution
IGO	international governmental organizations
INGO	international non-governmental organizations
IPO	initial public offering
IPPC	Independent Police Complaints Commission
IPSA	International Political Science Association
IR	international relations
IRS	Independent Review Service
ISA	International Sociological Association
ISFL	International Society for Family Law
J4P	Justice for the Poor
JSC	Judicial Services Commission
LCIA	London Court of International Arbitration
LLSV	La Porta, Lopez-de-Silanes, Shleifer, and Vishny

LSA	Law and Society Association
LSE	London School of Economics
LSP	Law and Society Program
MDL	multi-district litigation
MLAR	Market-Led Agrarian Reform
MNC	multi-national corporation
MNE	multi-national enterprise
NAS	National Academy of Sciences
NDNAD	National DNA database
NGO	non-governmental organization
NLRA	National Labor Relations Act
NP	Neighborhood Policing
NPIA	National Policing Improvement Agency
NPM	new public management
NRPP	National Reassurance Policing Program
OASDI	Old-Age, Survivors and Disability Insurance
ODR	online dispute resolution procedures
OECD	Organization for Economic Cooperation and Development
OSH	occupational safety and health
OSHA	Occupational Safety and Health Administration
PACE	Police and Criminal Evidence Act 1984
PACER	Public Access to Court Electronic Records
PICT	Project on International Courts and Tribunals
PIE	perceived injurious experience
PIL	public interest litigation
POP	problem-oriented policing
PSLRA	Private Securities Litigation Reform Act 1995
PSR	pre-sentence reports
RCCJ	Royal Commission on Criminal Justice
RCSL	Research Committee of the Sociology of Law
RAE	Research Assessment Exercise
SEC	Securities and Exchange Commission
SFI	Social Fund Inspector
SFO	Social Fund Officer
SSAT	Social Security Appeal Tribunals
SSDI	Social Security Disability Insurance
SSI	Supplemental Security Income
STS	Science & Technology Studies
TANF	Temporary Assistance for Needy Families
TAS	The Appeals Service
TRI	Toxics Release Inventory
UCL	University College, London

UCP	Uniform Customs and Practice for Documentary Credits
UNDP	United Nations Development Programme
UNIDROIT	International Institute for the Unification of Private Law
unPIE	unperceived injurious experience
VEP	voluntary environmental program
WARN	Worker Advance Notification and Retraining Act
WERS	Workplace Employment Relations Survey
WTO	World Trade Organization

CONTRIBUTORS AND EDITORS

Michael Adler is Emeritus Professor of Socio-Legal Studies and Leverhulme Emeritus Fellow at the University of Edinburgh.

Sharyn Roach Anleu is Professor of Sociology at Flinders University, South Australia.

Julia Black is Professor of Law at the London School of Economics and Political Science.

Anthony Bottoms is Emeritus Professor in the Institute of Criminology at the University of Cambridge.

Anthony Bradney is Professor of Law at Keele University.

Peter Cane is Distinguished Professor of Law at the Australian National University College of Law.

Cary Coglianese is Edward B Shils Professor of Law and Professor of Political Science at the University of Pennsylvania.

Catherine Courcy is a law clerk for Judge Susan N. Burke Hennepin County (Minnesota) District Court.

David Cowan is Professor of Law and Policy at the University of Bristol.

Fiona Cownie is Professor of Law at Keele University.

Margaret Davies is Professor of Law at Flinders University, South Australia.

Simon Deakin is Professor of Law at the University of Cambridge.

Gary Edmond is Professor of Law in the School of Law and Centre for Interdisciplinary Studies of Law at the University of New South Wales.

Lee Epstein is Provost Professor of Law and Political Science and the Roder Family Trustee Chair in Law at the University of Southern California.

Paul Fenn is Norwich Union Professor of Insurance Studies at Nottingham University Business School.

Denis Galligan is Professor of Socio-Legal Studies at the University of Oxford and Jean Monnet Professor of European Public Law at the University of Siena.

Bryant G. Garth is Dean and Professor of Law at Southwestern Law School.

James L. Gibson is the Sidney W. Souers Professor of Government in the Department of Political Science and Professor of African and African American Studies at Washington University in St. Louis. He is also the Director of the Program on Citizenship and Democratic Values and Weidenbaum Center on the Economy, Government, and Public Policy, and Professor Extraordinary in Political Science, and Fellow, Centre for Comparative and International Politics, Stellenbosch University, South Africa.

Tom Ginsburg is Professor of Law at the University of Chicago.

Linda Haller is Senior Lecturer in Law at the University of Melbourne.

Simon Halliday is Professor of Law at the University of Strathclyde and Conjoint Professor of Law at the University of New South Wales.

David Hamer is Associate Professor in Evidence and Proof at the Sydney Law School, University of Sydney.

Christine B. Harrington is Professor of Politics, Affiliated Faculty of Law, and a Core Faculty in the Institute for Law and Society at New York University.

Christopher Hodges is Head of the CMS Research Programme on Civil Justice Systems in the Centre for Socio-Legal Studies at the University of Oxford.

Jacqueline Hodgson is Professor of Law at Warwick University.

Bridget Hutter holds a Chair in Risk Regulation and is Director of the Centre for Analysis of Risk and Regulation at the London School of Economics.

Martin Innes is Professor in the School of Social Sciences and Director of the Universities' Police Science Institute at the University of Cardiff.

Linda Camp Keith is Associate Professor of Political Science at the University of Texas at Dallas.

Herbert M. Kritzer is Marvin J. Sonosky Chair of Law and Public Policy and Affiliated Professor of Political Science at the University of Minnesota.

David S. Law is Professor of Law and Professor of Political Science at Washington University in St Louis.

Robert M. Lawless is Professor of Law at the University of Illinois College of Law.

Roderick Macdonald is FR Scott Professor of Constitutional and Public Law at McGill University.

Kathy Mack is Professor of Law at Flinders University, South Australia.

Mavis Maclean is Senior Research Fellow at the Oxford Centre for Family Law and Policy, University of Oxford.

Andrew D. Martin is Professor of Law and Political Science at Washington University in St. Louis.

Stephen Meili is Professor of Clinical Instruction at the University of Minnesota.

Carrie J. Menkel-Meadow is Chancellor's Professor, University of California, Irvine Law School and A.B. Chettle Professor of Law, Dispute Resolution and Civil Procedure, Georgetown University Law Center.

Sally Engle Merry is Professor of Anthropology, Law and Society at New York University.

Richard Moorhead is Professor of Law at Cardiff Law School.

Laura Beth Nielsen is a Research Fellow at the American Bar Foundation and Associate Professor of Sociology and Director of Legal Studies at Northwestern University.

Martin Partington is Emeritus Professor of Law and Senior Research Fellow at the University of Bristol.

Neil Rickman is Professor of Economics at the University of Surrey and Director of the RAND Europe's Institute for Civil Justice.

Andrew Roberts is a Senior Lecturer in Law at the University of Melbourne.

David Robertson is Professor in the Department of Politics and International Relations at the University of Oxford.

Peter Russell is Professor Emeritus of Political Science at the University of Toronto.

Colin Scott is Professor of EU Regulation and Governance at University College, Dublin.

Gregory Shaffer is Melvin C Steen Professor of Law at the University of Minnesota.

Wesley Skogan is Professor of Political Science and Faculty Fellow in the Institute for Policy Research at Northwestern University.

Catalina Smulovitz is Professor of Political Science, Universidad Torcuato Di Tella, Buenos Aires, Argentina.

Neil Vidmar is Russell M Robinson II Professor of Law and Professor of Psychiatry at Duke University.

Andrew von Hirsch is Honorary Professor of Penal Theory and Penal Law at the University of Cambridge.

Elizabeth Warren is Leo Gottlieb Professor of Law at Harvard Law School.

Lisa Webley is Reader in Law at the University of Westminster.

Sally Wheeler is Professor of Law at Queen's University, Belfast.

INTRODUCTION

In the American legal academy, empirical research gained contemporary prominence in the late 1990s. The early years of the first decade of the twenty-first century saw the emergence and rapid development of a movement that labeled itself
"Empirical Legal Studies" (ELS). In the original proposal for this volume its title
referred to "empirical legal studies." However, as the project evolved we decided
against associating it with ELS in particular. We thought it important explicitly to
acknowledge the diversity of approaches to and sites of empirical investigation of
law, legal systems, and other legal phenomena. In particular, there are at least three
approaches and research groupings that predate the contemporary ELS movement,
which may be respectively identified as socio-legal/law and society (an interdisciplinary movement with strong roots in sociology but including scholars from a
wide range of traditional disciplines including law), empirically oriented law-and-
economics, and judicial behavior/politics. While some researchers working in these
traditions see themselves as part of the new ELS community, many others do not.
The phrase "empirical legal research" in the title, *The Oxford Handbook of Empirical
Legal Research*, is designed both to reflect and to celebrate the healthy pluralism of
empirical approaches to the study of law and legal phenomena.

American legal realists were, perhaps, the first to appreciate the value and importance
of, and to promote, study of "law in action" as opposed to "law on (or 'in') the books."
As described in Chapter 36 of this book, the earliest work in the United States included
crime surveys in the 1920s and 1930s, and studies in the 1930s of court dockets and auto
accident compensation. The genesis of empirically based studies of judicial behavior is
commonly traced to the pioneering work of C. Hermann Pritchett in the late 1940s. Jury
studies gained prominence through the Chicago jury project led by Harry Kalven and
Hans Zeisel in the 1950s. In Britain, a major event in the development of empirical legal
research was the establishment in 1972 of the ESRC-funded Oxford Centre for Socio-
Legal Studies. The *British Journal of Law and Society*, now simply the *Journal of Law and
Society*, first appeared two years later. At around the same time, the Royal Commission
on Civil Liability and Compensation for Personal Injury, popularly known as the
Pearson Commission, commissioned the first large-scale empirical investigation of the
civil justice system in England and Wales, and this was soon followed by the work of
the Royal Commission on Legal Services (the "Benson Commission"). The Socio-Legal
Studies Association (SLSA) was founded in 1990 to enable socio-legal scholars to meet
and disseminate their work, much of which is empirical. The UK Home Office (like
the U.S. Department of Justice) has been a major funder of research into the criminal

justice system since the 1970s. UK universities now host various multi-disciplinary empirical legal research centres. In the United States, early centers of contemporary empirically oriented legal research included the University of California at Berkeley, the University of Wisconsin at Madison, and the American Bar Foundation (with links to both Northwestern University and the University of Chicago). The Law and Society Association was founded in 1964, and the *Law & Society Review*, the journal of the Association, began publication in 1967. The Law and Courts section of the American Political Science Association was established around 1982. In recent years a growing number of U.S. law schools have attracted groups of empirically oriented scholars.

While empirical research on legal phenomena can be found throughout the twentieth century, in very recent years—as already noted—there has been a marked increase in the vibrancy of empirical legal research, particularly within the U.S. legal academy. In 2004 the *Journal of Empirical Legal Studies* was established, edited at Cornell Law School. This journal was designed specifically to appeal to legal academics doing or interested in empirical research. The First Annual Conference of Empirical Legal Studies was held at the University of Texas Law School in October 2006, and the ELS conference is now an annual event. The situation in the UK is somewhat different. November 2006 saw the publication of the Report of The Nuffield Inquiry on Empirical Legal Research entitled *Law in the Real World: Improving our Understanding of How Law Works* and written by Professor Dame Hazel Genn and Professors Martin Partington and Sally Wheeler. The motivation for the inquiry was a concern that despite high levels of activity in the empirical legal research community, there are not enough producers of empirical legal research in the UK to meet current and likely future demand, and that there may not be a "robust successor generation of trained empirical legal researchers" available to take the place of senior scholars likely to retire in the next decade or so. Although the report focused on research on the civil rather than the criminal side, it witnesses a perception of the growing importance of empirical legal research in all areas.

A lively interest in empirical legal research is by no means confined to the United States and the UK or to common law countries. There are active communities of empirical legal scholars in Australia and Canada. In the civil law world, empirical legal research conducted over the last 20 years or so can be found in a number of countries including the Netherlands, Belgium, Germany, Spain, Israel, Russia, and Japan. International organizations such as the World Bank have sponsored empirical legal research in various countries (e.g., Argentina, Bangladesh, Brazil, Dominican Republic, Ecuador, Georgia, Mexico, Peru, the Philippines, and Russia) in pursuit of the goal of improving legal systems as a means of encouraging economic investment and reducing poverty.

A feature of every truly successful intellectual movement is the ability to communicate its core ideas and methods, and the nature and significance of its achievements, to a wide audience beyond the movement's active practitioners. This is a task to which the broad community of empirical legal researchers has not so far devoted as much energy as it deserves. One of the important points made in the Nuffield Report is that there is no strong culture of empirical legal training and research in UK law schools. This is partly because there is a lack of empirical legal literature directed to "mainstream" legal scholars, many of whom remain more or less ignorant of the importance and value of empirical research and may find empirical legal scholarship difficult and somewhat mysterious. More generally, the lack of a widely appealing and accessible literature helps to explain why empirical legal research has a low profile in the UK legal academy and (except on the criminal side) is almost entirely absent from the law school curriculum. In the United States, law schools are just beginning to think about how empirical legal research activities can be integrated into the law school curriculum; and while texts on law and social science have been around since at least 1969, the first law school text intended specifically for courses on empirical legal studies, *Empirical Methods in Law* by Robert M. Lawless, Jennifer K. Robbennolt, and Thomas S. Ulen, appeared in late 2009.

Our aspiration is that this volume should make a significant contribution to informing and educating both scholars (whatever their disciplinary identification and in whatever research tradition they operate) and students—especially law students—about empirical legal research. It also aims to provide scholars who may be interested in undertaking empirical research about law with inspiration and resources for attempting the difficult transition from doctrinal or theoretical, library-based research to empirical research. More than that, we hope and expect that the book will find an audience beyond the academy in government, the public-policy sector and the wider community.

The Oxford Handbook of Empirical Legal Research has been designed to promote a prime aim of the *Oxford Handbook* series, which is to provide succinct discussions and analyses of debates, controversies, methods, and trends in scholarship that are original and searching but also easily accessible to readers who are less familiar with the particular subject area. *Handbooks* aspire to challenge and stimulate the experienced and knowledgeable while at the same time informing and inspiring the uninitiated and the less experienced. Of course, there is already a large body of empirical legal literature, but on the whole it reports the results of particular empirical research projects, and its typical target audience consists of other empirical scholars. There is little truly outward-looking literature that aims to educate and inform a wider audience and to encourage the development of empirical research skills and activity by celebrating the achievements of empirical legal scholarship. This *Handbook* is designed to start the process of filling this gap in the literature.

It is important to say something about how we understand the term "empirical." Many of those associated with the ELS movement that originated in the United States at the beginning of the twenty-first century equate empirical work with research that employs statistical and other quantitative methods. However, this understanding is by no means universal, and empirical legal research employing a mix of qualitative and quantitative social science methodologies long predates the contemporary

ELS movement. Interestingly, the strongest advocates of equating "empirical" with "quantitative" are scholars within law faculties, many of whom lack advanced training in social science. Among those with social science training, whether in law faculties or social science faculties, "empirical" is usually understood to include both quantitative and qualitative approaches. This is not to say that some scholars trained in social science do not have strong preferences as between qualitative and quantitative approaches. However, while social science departments have long included statistics and quantitative research methods courses in their curriculums, in the past 20 years the number of courses devoted to qualitative methods has increased significantly in U.S. social science departments, particularly in the fields of sociology and political science.

In this volume, we have adopted a broad perspective on what constitutes "empirical" legal research. Specifically, we have sought to include both quantitative and qualitative social science research within the label "empirical legal research." Nonetheless, readers of this *Handbook* will find that quantitative research dominates in many of the chapters (and that some chapters refer exclusively to quantitative research). To some extent, this dominance reflects the preferences of individual authors, but it is also a function of the nature of existing empirical research in particular areas.

For our purposes, "empirical" research involves the systematic collection of information ("data") and its analysis according to some generally accepted method. Of central importance is the *systematic* nature of the process, both of collecting and analyzing the information. The information can come from a wide range of sources including surveys, documents, reporting systems, observation, interviews, experiments, decisions, and events. While the data can be retained as text or images, systematic analysis will often involve coding or tagging units of text or images using symbols that may or may not have numeric properties (in the sense that they can be manipulated algebraically, or compared in terms of absolute or relative size). The analysis can involve simple counting, sophisticated statistical manipulation, grouping into like sets, identification of sequences (in some circumstances called "process tracing"), matching of patterns, or simple labelling of themes. Ultimately, the analyst engages in a process of interpreting the results of the analysis in order to link those results to the question motivating the research. In some instances the interpretation flows clearly from the results, but in others it is more fragile and reflects not only the results of the analysis but also other information that the analyst brings to the work.

We have deliberately omitted from the project two categories of work that some might argue fall within the concept of "empirical" research we have described above. The first category comprises traditional historical studies. We have omitted legal history from the *Handbook* simply because it is a discrete, long-established field of research with its own norms, methodologies, and standards. Some empirical legal researchers use historical materials and may employ historiographical methods, but they tend not to label what they are doing as "legal history". Typically such research begins with an hypothesis of the sort associated with social science and uses historical information as its data.

The second category of research we have omitted is traditional analysis of formal legal documents—primarily court decisions ("cases") and legislative materials. One reason for omitting such work is that scholars who work primarily with documentary legal materials typically describe what they do as "legal analysis" rather than "empirical legal research." Conversely, scholars who describe their research as "empirical" would typically not regard traditional legal analysis as empirical. Of course, this distinction between analytical and empirical legal research is not clear-cut, and there are many examples of scholarship that straddle the line between the two by going beyond the formal legal documents themselves to examine their broader social, economic and political context and operation. Conversely, formal legal documents may provide relevant data for empirical investigation of certain legal phenomena such as judicial behavior. If the relationship between analytical and empirical research is understood as a spectrum, this volume concentrates on work at the empirical end of that spectrum. Another reason for not including traditional analytical legal scholarship is that this genre of research is the subject matter of *The Oxford Handbook of Legal Studies* (2003).

In fairness to our authors, we need to say something about the brief they were given. They were asked to provide not surveys of the available research or literature reviews but rather concise, original, and critical discussions of work that they consider to have made a significant contribution to our understanding of the various topics covered in the *Handbook*. They were also asked to identify gaps in the extant body of research and possible topics for future research. Because this book is aimed at an international audience, our contributors were encouraged to cast their nets widely and not limit discussion to research done in their own country or concerned with their own legal system. That said, the common-law, English-speaking world has so far produced much more empirical legal research than the civil law world; and within the common law world, much more empirical research has been produced in the United States than anywhere else. These facts are reflected both in the list of contributors and in the substance of the various contributions. The reasons the United States dominates in this area (as in so many others) are, no doubt, various and complex. One may be that law is a graduate school in the U.S. tertiary education system, and the number of law faculty members holding both JDs and PhDs in some other discipline (particularly one of the social sciences) has risen sharply over the last 15 years. Another obvious explanation is that because courts in the United States are understood to be essentially political institutions, U.S. political scientists are much more interested in judges and judicial behavior than their counterparts in the rest of the common law world: Law and Courts is one of the largest Sections of the American Political Science Association. This general topic is one that deserves much more attention than it receives in this volume.

More technically, authors were asked to reduce the number of footnotes to an absolute minimum, and to write as accessibly as possible for the non-specialist reader. The *Handbook* is meant primarily not for established producers of empirical legal research but for consumers, potential consumers and aspiring producers. Contributors were expected to observe allocated word limits, which reflect arguably contestable editorial judgments about the relative quantity, significance and vibrancy of research in particular areas. It should also be emphasized that authors were asked to refer by name to no more than 50 pieces of scholarship. Some found this limitation irksome and challenging, although in the end all managed to work within or close to it. The rationales for the limit were to encourage contributors to give their own personal account of scholarship in their area and to relieve them of the need to be comprehensive or "balanced." We wanted them to identify themes and trends rather than to recount or focus on individual pieces of research. Inevitably, there will be considerable room for disagreement about the items that should or should not have been included in the lists of references in the various chapters, and also about the various authors' perspectives on the bodies of research they discuss. The lists of references should not be thought of as encapsulating the authors' answers to some question such as "what are the fifty most important pieces of empirical research in your area?" Rather, the references will most likely have been chosen for their aptness to support the particular argument an author has chosen to make about scholarship in the field.

In planning the *Handbook* we tried to ensure coverage of all areas and legal phenomena on which a significant amount of empirical legal research has been conducted and reported. Inevitably, however, there are topics that might have been included but which did not make it into the book, some as a result of a judgment on our part that there did not seem to be a sufficient body of empirical work to warrant extended treatment, some because we did not think of them at the time we planned the volume, and some simply because we could not include everything.

One topic omitted because of lack of a body of relevant empirical research is antitrust/competition law. Interestingly, this is an area where empirical research is regularly employed to assess whether violations of law have occurred and to determine damages for such violations. There is a small body of literature about how to conduct empirical analyses for such use. However, we were unable to locate a substantial body of empirical research on the application or impact of antitrust/competition law, and hence we decided not to include a chapter on this topic. A second topic, which in retrospect we might have included, is legal consciousness, perhaps coupled with the closely related topic of legal culture. Both topics make an appearance in several chapters, but none is devoted entirely to them even though there is probably a sufficient literature to have justified a chapter, as well as a growing interest in the study of legal consciousness and how it can yield insights into legal culture.

A third area that, with the benefit of hindsight, was a strong contender for inclusion is insurance and insurance law. In practice, insurance is central to the operation of the law of personal injury compensation (which receives some attention in the chapter on personal injury litigation). However, it is also important in various other areas including corporate malfeasance, professional regulation, social welfare law, and environmental law. Moreover, insurance companies are themselves heavily regulated, and hence research on the success or failure of such regulation is of considerable significance.

Other topics that might have been covered include election law; intellectual property (patents, copyright, and trademark), and, more broadly, the interface between law, and science and technology; and tax law. We planned a chapter on the use of empirical methodologies in program and policy evaluation, but in the end were not able to include it. Individual readers will, perhaps, be able to identify other significant omissions. We accept full responsibility for inclusions and omissions while reiterating that this volume is intended as a first contribution to the promotion and wider dissemination of empirical legal research rather than the last word.

Our sincere thanks are due to John Louth, who was extremely supportive in the early planning stages, and to Alex Flach, who took over responsibility from John in the course of the project. We owe very special thanks the Ros Wallington who, as ever, provided efficient and cheerful administrative support; and to all those involved in the production of this major undertaking. But above all, we are indebted to those without whom this volume could not have been produced—our authors—not only for their excellent contributions but also for their patient and flexible responses to our numerous editorial demands and high expectations.

Peter Cane and Herbert M. Kritzer
Canberra and Minneapolis
February 2010

PART I

SURVEYING EMPIRICAL LEGAL RESEARCH

1

THE ART, CRAFT, AND SCIENCE OF POLICING

MARTIN INNES

FOLLOWING on from the pioneering academic studies of the police conducted in the 1950s and 1960s, there has been a significant and ongoing expansion of empirical investigations into various aspects of the police and of policing. Differentiating between policing as an activity and the police as a state institution in this way is now an established conceptual convention that demarcates the progress and increasing sophistication of analysis in this area. "Policing" refers to a wide variety of social ordering and control practices that are performed by a plethora of social actors and institutions. Writing about "the police" focuses on agencies of the state whose remit gravitates around a set of interventions designed, as the sociologist Egon Bittner (1974) noted, to deliver "the emergency maintenance of social order," employing legally sanctioned, coercive power when required.

This conceptual distinction between policing and the police is a pivotal organizing motif for empirical research. A large number of studies have focused on the police as a public institution, grouped around a number of key topics, including: public attitudes to the police; processes of recruitment, training, and socialization; systems for dealing with complaints and corruption; the makeup of the police, in terms of their socio-demographic backgrounds, educational status, and norms and values; and changes in definition of the police "mission." Albeit there is some overlap, such concerns differ from those animating studies of the performance of the policing function. The study of policing is far more explicitly concerned with actions, practice, and the conduct of formal social control by both public and private actors. This Chapter concentrates more explicitly on the findings of this latter group of studies. The reason for adopting this focus is partly to do with considerations of space, but also because it is these latter studies that engage more directly with how the law informs what it is that police do. On this basis, this Chapter seeks to:

- provide a framework for understanding the varied ways that policing has been empirically studied;
- delineate the continuities and changes in the ideas that animate policing policy and practice;
- chart the key trajectories of development in how the policing function has been conceived and delivered.

The Chapter commences by establishing a broad framework for mapping and making sense of the key orientations of research on the policing function. This is followed by sections exploring three key dimensions of policing: order management, crime management, and security management. The Chapter concludes by identifying some emerging trends in the organization and conduct of police work as policing organizations seek to reconfigure their capacities and capabilities to meet new challenges.

The central thesis developed through this exploration is that effective policing synthesizes art, craft, and science. Aspects of this perspective were first developed by Reppetto (1978) in his research on police detectives. In this Chapter though, these ideas are considerably extended, developed, and refined in order that they can be applied to the conduct of policing more broadly. The "art" of policing refers to the creative and sometimes "intuitive" insights that inform how policing is performed. As a counterpoint to this, the Chapter also explores how contemporary policing is increasingly seeking to harness scientific knowledge and technology and, at least in part, adopt an avowedly more "scientific" approach. Positioned somewhere between these two poles is the sense that there is a particular "craft" of policing, dependent upon the acquisition of experiential competence and practical skill. The purpose of this Chapter is to show how empirical research has revealed that effective policing often integrates and depends upon an amalgam of art, craft, and science.

I. Mapping the Landscape

Drawing on intellectual resources originating within several academic disciplines including sociology, law, psychology, geography, management, and political science, the study of policing has benefited from its interdisciplinary base. Crudely speaking, we can divide the vast majority of enquiries between those designed to function as "mirrors" and those that operate as "motors" (Innes, 2010). Research cast as a mirror is intended to "reflect" and articulate aspects of the complex realities of contemporary policing policy and practice. Its role is to describe, account for, and explain how and why policing engages with social problems and social orders in particular ways. In contrast, research as a "motor" is more explicitly and deliberately undertaken with the intention of providing an engine for reform, improvement, and development. Of course, in reality it frequently happens that research originally envisaged as a mirror or a motor also performs the other function as a result of how it is interpreted and used by scholars and practitioners. Nevertheless, as a basic distinction of "ideal types," that between mirrors and motors is helpful in mapping the contours of the policing research landscape.

Beyond the mirror/motor distinction, we can further identify four key types of empirical policing research on the basis of the relationships that exist between researchers and their object of study. Four distinct relationships exist in policing research:

- *Research by the police* includes empirical studies undertaken by police organizations to inform their operational performance or strategic policy-making. This work is conducted "in-house" and involves no external professional research capacity.
- *Research on the police* is the counterpoint to the above, involving direct study of aspects of police organizations and their activities by a professional "outsider." In effect, the police are the object of study, and there is no explicit expectation that any findings should inform or shape the future conduct of policing. Such studies can either be undertaken independently by scholars and researchers, or they may be commissioned by non-police organizations.
- *Research for the police.* As the growth of policing studies has progressed, so policing organizations worldwide have emerged as important commissioners of research. Research for the police includes all studies where the police have set the research requirement, and the data collection and analysis is undertaken by research professionals.
- *Research with the police.* Reflecting the growing interest in action research methodologies more broadly, a recent area of development has been a more co-productive approach in which officers are frequently engaged directly in the process of research, and findings are continually fed back into the organization to try and leverage improvement. Major examples of this include the work of Skogan (2007) in Chicago and Innes et al. (2008) in the UK.

The following discussion draws on research conducted by, on, for, and with police organizations, to map out the key ideas and perspectives that have been established on the police and policing. In this literature, one finds two different sets of ideas. First, there are those that have had a "deep and wide" influence on the study of policing. Akin to axiomatic statements, these are fundamental truths that, although not always obvious, exhibit a persistent and ongoing influence, subtly configuring the perspectives and understandings developed in relation to a particular subject. The precise content of such ideas is frequently reconfigured and reworked across different contexts, but the ideas are significant because they provide a cross-cutting intellectual scaffolding that extends across specific topics. Second, and in contrast, there is a greater number of more narrowly and locally influential ideas that are more domain-specific, molding understanding of specific aspects of policing.

An example of the former is the general observation that police officers tend to under-enforce the law, preferring to seek compliance informally to solve conflicts and problems where this is judged possible and desirable. This disposition was perhaps the key finding of the foundational studies of policing completed in the 1960s. These studies (e.g., Skolnick, 1966; Banton, 1964) mainly focused on the uniformed patrol officer, seeking to illuminate their working methods. Informed largely by qualitative data, much of it observational, studies began to accumulate that challenged a number of popular preconceptions about who the police were, what they did, how and why. Thus, rather than accenting the notion that policing was action-packed and continually focused on solving crimes and catching "villains," these works detailed the more mundane realities of policing. This emphasis was neatly captured in the title of Reiner's (1978) book, *The Blue-Coated Worker,* which deliberately lacked any suggestion of the drama and sensationalism so often associated with police work. The uniqueness of the police role was located not in the specific tasks that police officers perform but, rather, in how they provide a generalized rapid response interface between the state and citizenry for situations where the social order is breached or threatened (Bittner, 1974). To this end, Rubinstein (1973) sought to detail aspects of the "street-craft" of the patrol officer, and the way officers negotiate solutions to the conflicting needs and wants of citizens in circumstances that are often emotionally charged.

Indeed, the overarching conceptual focus of these early studies was on the "craft" of police work. Positioning something as a craft emphasizes the value of a technical skill acquired through practice and experience, as opposed to the more creative and intuitive processes of an "art." It also occupies a different conceptual "space" from the more rationalized and procedurally governed notions associated with casting policing as an activity driven more by "science."

The craft base of street policing is particularly evident in Skolnick's (1966) discussion of discretion, and of the way police officers deploy it in dealing with conflicts and maintaining order. He found that law was often implemented by officers as a strategy of last resort, frequently only after other attempts to elicit compliance had failed.[1] Thus, although an agency of formal social control, police routinely sought to accomplish their aims through informal means. As will become evident, this remains one of the grounding truths of police research threaded through many empirical studies.

A variant of this disposition to under-enforce the law was evident in Manning's (1980) ethnography of police drug squads. This study teased out some of the complex judgments involved in police decisions about how to intervene in embedded social problems such as illicit drug markets. Manning showed that under certain conditions and in particular settings, police tended toward a studied process of under-enforcement rather than choosing to enforce the law in relation to all known infractions. This reflected an experientially grounded belief that a relatively stable drugs market, where the key actors were known and thus could be kept under surveillance, was preferable to creating instability by arresting large numbers of people which, in turn, could lead to greater levels of violence as other drug gangs fought for control of the available territory. Moreover, foregoing an arrest can, in the hands of a skilled officer, become a commodity to be traded for assistance in developing intelligence about other criminal activities of potential interest (ibid.; see also Marx, 1988).

Illuminating the workings of police discretion by tying it to police culture served to uncover a layer of complexity in how police interventions accomplished order. The result was the revelation of previously invisible decisions that clearly showed a distinction between the law as set out "in books" and its performance "in action." The contribution of police culture to the theoretical positions that were initially worked out and have subsequently shaped the overarching trajectory of development of policing studies, was that it suggested that police decision-making about when, how, and why to intervene through law was shaped by a variety of extra-legal factors. Among these factors were elements that collectively resulted in law being used more intensively and more frequently in relation to minority and relatively poor communities, whose members are over-policed as suspects and under-policed as victims (Fielding, 1981).

In an attempt to integrate these key findings and fashion an empirically informed and theoretically nuanced perspective on how policing shapes and is shaped by the interactional and institutional orders of contemporary society, Innes (2003a) posits that the police function can be understood as gravitating around three principal modes of intervention:

- *Order management*, in which the police role pivots around the management of social order (as discussed above). This concept can be refined by recognizing that the order-management functions of policing range from sustaining and

---

[1] For a more detailed exposition of the workings of discretion, see Chapter 3.

protecting social order in neighborhoods through to the kinds of tasks involved in the policing of mass public protests.

- *Crime management*, in which police undertake a range of activities proactively and reactively to both prevent and detect crime. This category of activity stretches across protecting the public from prolific and high-risk predatory offenders, investigating volume crime, and disrupting serious organized crime networks.

- *Security management*, in which the police engage in a diffuse array of actions intended to support the integrity of nation states, businesses, communities, and individuals. These are typically performed by both private and public policing providers, sometimes acknowledging the subjective harms of crime, such as fear generation, in addition to more objective concerns.

Casting the police role as one of "management" recognizes the limits and constraints on what policing interventions can practically achieve. This theme appears repeatedly in empirical studies of police work. As outlined above, patrol officers do not simply "enforce" the law; rather they craft judgments about how, when, why, and against whom to implement legal sanctions. Moreover, and as will be considered in more detail in the next section, many of the problems that police are called on to deal with are caused by factors that lie outside the police's direct sphere of influence. Consequently, labeling policing as fundamentally concerned with "crime control," accents a rather narrow aspect of what police officers do and misrepresents the impact that they can have on a range of social problems. Thus, pursuing the notion that police seek to "manage" a variety of social issues seems appropriate. The sections that follow assess in turn each of the three dimensions listed above.

II. ORDER MANAGEMENT

The preceding discussion introduced the idea that the essence of the police function in liberal democratic polities, albeit rhetorically often constructed around law enforcement, in reality lies in the management of social order. This order-management function ranges from the micro-management of public civility in neighborhoods, to controlling mass political protests where there is the potential for serious violence and disorder.

Echoing the idea that police frequently seek to accomplish their goals through informal means rather than through invocation of law, Waddington (1994) asserts that similar processes underlie their approach to mass public order events. They

seek to diffuse the risks of confrontation by securing compliance through negotiations with the organizers of protests. Several historically oriented studies have
argued that over the past three to four decades the spread of this approach has
been responsible for overall reductions in violence and arrests associated with the
policing of public protests (cf. Waddington, 1998). These "negotiated management"
strategies work by seeking to create a degree of predictability in both the conduct
of protesters and the police response to it. Noakes et al. (2005) examined the spatial
dynamics of protest policing in Washington, DC, concluding that the escalation of
coercive force by police correlated with their expectations for disorder. Relatedly,
Waddington (1994) contends that it is when they perceive that they are losing control
that police are liable to forego their reliance on "soft power" and react to "provoca-
tions" violently. This need to assure the maintenance of control and the consequent importance of the physical layout of spaces in which protests are situated are
reflected in the emphasis in police public-order training and strategy on the ability
to "take the ground" as a means of shaping the collective behavior of protestors.
Accordingly, Noakes et al. (2005) conclude that spatially contained protests tend to
be dealt with less aggressively by police than what they label "transgressive" ones
(by which they mean protests with no formal plan, or that depart from the plan
agreed between police and a protest's leaders). This is an important finding in that
it keys in to some of the ways in which the nature of mass political protests is changing and how police have to respond to those changes. Fundamentally, the order-
management function of policing has to accommodate citizens' lawful rights to
express their disquiet with the economic, social, and environmental consequences
of contemporary liberal democratic systems.

However, we should not overstate the homogeneity of the public order strategies used to accommodate these rights to protest. The general shift to negotiated
management approaches does not mean that all forces have moved this way or that
all protests are dealt with through negotiation. For example, Sheptycki's (2005)
analysis of the situation in Bolivia and of the response to anti-globalization protests in Canada suggests a continued use of authoritarian tactics in some settings
and circumstances. More subtly, Vitale (2005) provides a detailed account of the
New York Police Department's (NYPD) handling of a major anti-war rally in
2003. He argues that rather than negotiated management, the policing response
was in a "command and control" style—assertive and seeking to micro-manage
the demonstrations in an effort to prevent disorder and the disruption of everyday life. In this sense, he suggests that the policing of protest in New York was
subtly inflected with some basic principles underpinning the NYPD's "broken
windows" policing model (discussed below) that focuses on problems of neighborhood order.

Police involvement in the regulation of neighborhood order has tended to fall
largely under the umbrella of "community policing" (CP). Although it has lately
become one of the orthodoxies of policing liberal societies, CP was originally

presented in a more reactionary form. Its early proponents positioned it as a counter-point to the kinds of practices associated with what Mark Moore (1992) dubbed "the professional policing" movement. Driven by the new opportunities for deployment afforded by the adoption of technologies such as the patrol car, the police radio, and the systematic analysis of recorded crime data, the professional model of policing was thought to promise a more effective and efficient style of emergency policing, where officers could respond quickly and directly to calls for service from the pub-lic. In effect, it was a reform movement premised on a more "scientific" approach to policing. By the 1970s, however, a sense of creeping disillusionment was becoming evident, with a number of commentators charting some unintended consequences of this "professional" model.

The response from a number of students of the police was that a more community-oriented style of policing might prove more successful. Albeit ini-tially constituting a fairly loosely coupled set of ideas and principles, running through the various iterations propounded by individual authors was a sense that rather than focusing on crime control, police officers should be encouraged to use their discretion in order to respond to troubles and tensions emerging within localized communities. In effect, this represented a reassertion of the primacy of the "craft" of policing over the notion that it could be delivered solely on the basis of "science."

Arguably the most (in)famous rendition in this vein was a think-piece by James Q. Wilson and George Kelling published in 1982. Despite the lack of any real research evidence to support the claims made, the account of the street-craft of the fictitious Officer Kelly and the significance attached to repairing metaphorical "broken win-dows" in order to reduce the potential for a "decay spiral," chimed with the beliefs and "recipe knowledge" of a number of senior police. In New York, in the early 1990s, it was credited with inspiring and informing the reform program undertaken within the NYPD by Mayor Giuliani and Commissioner William Bratton. Although some empirical evidence to support the claims embedded within the broken windows the-sis has been produced, that evidence is at best partial, and has been strenuously con-tested (Harcourt, 2001). Certainly the claim, that the assertive policing style could be credited with making a major contribution to the significant drops in recorded crime seen in New York during the 1990s, has proven to be one of the most conten-tious issues in the international policing studies literature in recent years (see, for example, Bowling, 1999).

One of the most trenchant criticisms of this claim about the effect of New York's policing model is that it fails to provide a coherent explanatory account of how the reductions in crime were produced. The explanation proffered is that by vigor-ous enforcement of statutes and laws in relation to incivilities and quality-of-life crimes, more serious offending was discouraged. The trouble is that the accounts of New York's dramatic reductions in crime go little beyond simple description of what was actually done. As a consequence, more critical ripostes suggest alternative explanations of the crime reductions such as a significant increase in the number of police officers and the adoption of improved crime analysis processes in the form of what is known as COMPSTAT (Silverman, 1999).[2]

Such criticisms, that there is a lack of specificity in accounts of how CP, informed by the broken windows thesis, acts on the police's operating environment, are fairly common among those who are more skeptical of the claimed achievements of CP. However, some attempts have been made to derive more structured and systematic formulations of this style of policing, the most influential probably being Goldstein's (1990) "problem-oriented policing" (POP) approach. Goldstein's principal proposition is that, under the auspices of the professional policing model, police organizations increasingly self-defined their role as one of responding to individual calls for service in connection with discrete incidents. In so doing, Goldstein argued, police administrators failed to grasp the connections that frequently exist among different incidents and the contexts in which they are located. By working to identify and respond to "problems" rather than isolated incidents, Goldstein posited, police could increase their capacity and capability to reduce crime.

Goldstein's ideas and especially his SARA model,[3] which mirrors key aspects of the process of scientific investigation, have received significant levels of support in a number of U.S. police departments and have been widely publicized through the Home Office in the UK. And yet, while a number of research-based evaluations describe some successes achieved through this approach when used as a motor for police reform (Eck, 2006), the general consensus is that it has been less successful than might have been anticipated in effecting a radical step-change in the conduct of policing (Braga and Weisburd, 2006). For example, Cordner and Biebel (2005) provide a detailed evaluation of the results achieved in the San Diego Police Department, which has invested heavily in training officers in the POP approach. Cordner and Biebel distinguish between what they label a "problem-solving" and a "problem-oriented" disposition. Under the latter, the police organization concerned is strategically geared to tackling interlinked and connected issues in an integrated way. By contrast, problem-solving is a more delimited engagement with the process of scanning, analyzing, responding to, and assessing the impact of interventions. It is this latter disposition that they found most often in San Diego.

---

[2] COMPSTAT stands for 'Computerized Statistics' and is a management process directly informed by detailed analysis of crime data, whereby local police commanders are made accountable for local patterns and trends in crime. It was developed by the NYPD, but versions of it have since been taken up by many police agencies worldwide.

[3] SARA is a structured process for identifying and intervening with respect to problems, comprising four key phases of activity: Scanning—involves looking across available incident data to identify key clusters or series; Analysis—involves looking in more detail at the potential causes of these clusters or series; Response—is the action phase, where measures are introduced to address the identified problem; Assessment—this phase seeks to establish what difference the interventions have made.

Clarke (1998) attributes the limited uptake of genuinely "problem-orientated" work to a number of common flaws in terms of how police departments operationalize the POP approach:

- They fail to attend to the issue of "dosage" and whether variations in the scale and intensity of actions are related to variations in crime statistics.
- The assessment phase is either forgotten or rudimentary, and the inclusion of control data is omitted.
- They do not look for potential displacement of the problem to other areas, or into a different type of problem.

Although possessing certain affinities with CP, POP places less emphasis on the core values and ideas that served to animate some of the original calls for CP, particularly ideas such as being responsive to local needs, supporting communities by tackling the risks that assail them, and building their overall resilience so that they can mobilize their informal social control capacity to deal with minor problems in the future. More recently, though, there has been a significant revival in the fortunes of CP. In effect, these new iterations have sought to build on both the successes and failures of the earlier attempts to deliver CP and POP by stressing the need to deliver CP programs systematically, and to scientifically capture and measure the benefits of doing so.

In the United States, the key program of work has been the Chicago Alternative Policing Strategy (CAPS). The significance of CAPS is that it has been operationalized "at scale" across the whole of a major urban environment and over an extended period of time. Furthermore, it has been the subject of an intensive evaluation program conducted in partnership with Northwestern University. First introduced on a quasi-experimental basis in five prototype districts, accompanied by matched control sites, the initial successes indicated by the evaluation framework led to the program being expanded city-wide in 1995. Since that time, the evaluators have continued to monitor the progress of implementation and outcomes through a variety of qualitative and quantitative data streams and have used these findings to "drive" the impetus for further reform. Reporting the findings from across a ten-year period, Skogan (2007) details some intriguing outcomes. He found that the impacts of the deep and far-reaching reforms enacted by the Chicago Police Department were stratified across the city's ethnic communities. Overall, the groups who gained most from the changes tended to be African-American neighborhoods. White communities typically gained less, but as Skogan notes, on average they started in a better position. The least benefit was to Hispanic communities afflicted by entrenched multiple deprivation. These variations raise interesting questions about how police reform interacts with broader processes of social and economic change.

The CAPS approach was a direct and formative influence upon what eventually developed into the national Neighborhood Policing (NP) program in England and Wales. In 2008 every area of the country was assigned a dedicated Neighborhood Policing team or officer to provide locally tailored policing services. This significant development in the orientation of policing in England and Wales was underpinned by a program of empirical research undertaken by NP's more experimental predecessor, the National Reassurance Policing Program (NRPP).

The goal of the NRPP was to identify a structured process for delivering local policing services, built around three key components derived from intensive and extensive research into social reactions to crime, disorder, and policing (Innes et al., 2008):

- visible, accessible, familiar, and effective police staff;
- targeting the "signal crimes" and "signal disorders" that function as key sources of citizen insecurity; and
- co-producing responses through working with partner agencies and communities themselves.

This formulation was arrived at as a way of solving some of the problems that previous studies had identified as a cause of the limited impacts of earlier iterations of community policing. A Home Office scientific evaluation of the approach in sixteen trial sites, involving extensive surveying of local publics, found that it had produced statistically significant reductions in self-reported victimization and fear of crime, and increases in public confidence in the police (Tuffin et al., 2006). These findings provided a "motor" for subsequent investments in the national NP program.

While the recent initiatives in Chicago and England and Wales point to CP's potential, studies of programs in other locations are less positive in their assessment of CP's impact. For example, based on qualitative research in Seattle, Herbert (2006) concludes that a key problem for CP is the "weight of expectation" that is placed on communities to participate in developing their security by actively cooperating with police. Especially in those areas that most need CP, he maintains, there is simply a lack of community capacity and capability to do what is required by the principles of CP processes. But perhaps what Herbert's evidence shows is that producing the sorts of outcomes valued by CP is difficult but not impossible. A more optimistic tone is to be found in Carr's (2005) ethnographic study of neighborhoods in Chicago. He details how, in the wake of a series of youth-gang related homicides, the local community mobilized, supported by specific actions taken by the police, to improve their neighborhood security. The police contribution involved dealing creatively with incivilities and chronic quality-of-life problems as much as enforcing the law.

III. CRIME MANAGEMENT

In outlining the key ideas that form the foundation of policing studies, it was noted that one of the primary accomplishments of empirical research on the police has been to contrast the mundane realities of day-to-day police work with the rather more glamorous and dramatic representations found in mass-media accounts. Nowhere is this more evident than in relation to studies of detective work and the police role in investigating crime.

For most people, the principal function of the police is the prevention, investigation, and detection of crime—what can be helpfully summarized as crime management work. Despite the symbolic significance accorded to this aspect of policing by both the public and police officers alike, arguably the most significant finding of research into crime management is the limited influence that police officers have on overall crime levels. For example, a number of detailed empirical studies have concluded that the single most important determinant of whether or not a crime will be solved by the police is not any investigative action performed by them but rather the quantity and quality of information provided by members of the public.

In one of the most-cited pieces of empirical research on policing, the Kansas City Preventative Patrol Experiment, the impact of a crime management strategy of randomized uniform patrols was assessed by manipulating levels of police presence in an area (Kelling et al., 1974). It was famously concluded that randomized patrols had little effect on overall crime levels. But what about other interventions and their role in enabling police to investigate crimes? In their detailed assessment of American detectives, Greenwood et al. (1977) found that in those cases where a victim or witnesses were able to provide police with a description of what happened and who was involved, there was an increased likelihood of a suspect being identified and located; in contrast, in the absence of such intelligence, progress toward clearing the crime (identifying the perpetrator, with or without sufficient evidence for prosecution) was unlikely.

The notion that when dealing with crime police are fundamentally cast as "information workers" runs through all the major studies in this area. For instance, a similar pattern was also present in Ericson's (1993) study of Canadian detectives. Based on ethnographic data he found that rather than "crime-solving," the work of detectives was more akin to a "crime management," with significant emphasis placed on the bureaucratic tasks of maintaining and updating case files. A rather different emphasis, albeit one that further stresses the salience of information, is found in Dick Hobbs' (1988) account of the "art" and "craft" of detectives in London's East End. Rather than bureaucrats, his detectives are "legal entrepreneurs" using aspects of the criminal law as a resource to be artfully and creatively deployed in seeking to "work" cases and develop "snouts" (informants). What comes to the surface in Hobbs's rendering is a degree of "moral symmetry" between the police and many of those they are investigating.

Aspects of all three of these roles, (detectives as information workers, bureaucrats and legal entrepreneurs) are evident in Innes's (2003b) ethnographic study of police homicide detectives. In effect, the position that he arrives at is that the police role in responding to major crimes is part "art" and part "craft," but also increasingly shaped by the use of scientific methods and technologies. These UK data remind us that most fatal violence is fairly mundane in its origins and that the majority of homicides the police deal with are "hot," emotionally driven crimes, committed in a domestic setting or between people who are well known to each other. In such situations, the reality of the police's work on these "self-solving" cases has little to do with the ratiocinative search for an unknown offender so beloved of fictional dramas. Rather, in a direct echo of Ericson's account, it involves carefully and painstakingly piecing together a narrative on the basis of the evidence collated in preparation for the juridical component of the criminal justice process. However, sometimes hard-to-solve "whodunnit" cases do occur, where standard operating procedures and routine practices do not work. Confronted by such circumstances, detectives can and do invoke more creative and innovative approaches in an attempt to advance their inquiry. Police culture places high value on these "arts" of investigation, which tend to be explained as depending on "hunches" and intuition. Innes (2003b) argues that, in addition to finding creative ways around the procedural constraints of law, detectives' capacities to act "artfully" in an investigation can be explained on the basis of individuals' abilities to construct "abductive inferences." Abduction involves "reasoning to the best explanation" when confronted with incomplete information. It is this ability to reason abductively, to infer a compelling explanation for "who did what to whom and why" when confronted with limited information, that elevates the investigative "artists" within police occupational culture above those officers who practice a craft of investigation or depend on "science" to solve cases.

In recent years, development of technologies for processing and interpreting "contact trace materials" has been a significant motor driving reform of police investigative practice. As Cole's (2003) historical investigation of fingerprinting techniques shows, the capacity to identify people who do not wish to be known has been a recurrent concern for the police. Fingerprinting now constitutes one among a panoply of forensic technologies routinely used by police when seeking to determine who did what to whom, and to provide an evidenced narrative account of their preferred version of events. Of particular salience over the past two decades has been the role of DNA "fingerprinting," or "profiling," as it is more properly termed.

Williams and Johnson (2008) argue that DNA profiling is best conceived as a "socio-technical assemblage," based on a complex and densely woven web of embodied practices, discursive framings and technical infrastructure. They trace a pattern of mutual influence between recent developments in police investigative practice and the capabilities and capacities of DNA profiling. So rather than some grand strategy or narrative arc of reform that exploits the emergence of this new technology and its application within policing, the picture they outline is of a series of incremental innovations and adjustments.

Illustrating the relevance of research done *by* the police, the National Policing Improvement Agency (NPIA) (2009) has evidenced trends in the use in the UK of the largest DNA database (NDNAD) in the world. Since 1995 when it was first introduced, 5.76 million "subject profiles" have been uploaded onto the NDNAD, and in 2009 over 350,000 "crime scene profiles" were also being stored. In March of that year, compared with twelve months previously, there had been an 11% increase in the number of profiles held. This year-on-year increase and indeed the whole expansion program have taken place against a backdrop of falling recorded crime levels (Kershaw et al., 2008). However, we should not assume a causal relationship between falling crime and the increase in size and use of the database. For, as the report reveals, only 17% of all recorded crimes in England and Wales in 2007–8 were actually subject to a crime-scene examination; and, of course, a proportion of these do not yield any forensic materials.

Looking in more detail at these data, it emerges that in 2007–08 the NDNAD was employed to identify suspects in 155 criminal homicide cases. According to Home Office Statistics there were a total of 748 cases of homicide over that period (Kershaw et al., 2008). Thus we can infer that the NDNAD substantively contributed to police investigative solutions in 21% of criminal homicides. This is important in light of the rhetorical claims frequently made for, and the power imputed to, DNA profiling. For even in the most serious of cases, those subject to intensive and extensive crime-scene examination efforts (cf. Innes, 2003), the police rely primarily on traditional methods of suspect identification in the majority of investigations. Looking at a different crime type, there were 729,000 domestic burglaries in 2007–08 (Kershaw et al., 2008). The NPIA data show that in only 8,189 cases (or just over 1%) was the NDNAD used to link a suspect to a crime. These broad patterns are replicated by the Forensic Science Service's own data modeling which finds "that 'forensic activity'...leads to the detection of 0.9 per cent of recorded crime" (Williams and Johnson, 2008: 119).

In some of the journalistic representations accompanying recent developments in police use of forensic science, a certain "shock and awe" rhetoric has been exploited by the police and other commentators in their accounts of what harnessing the latest developments in forensic science enables them to do (Innes and Clarke, 2009). It is certainly the case that such technologies have enabled them to solve at least some otherwise intractable crimes. But, as the data reported above show, it is important that we do not overstate the real world impacts of forensic technologies. Arguably as significant as the improvements in investigative efficacy made possible by these technologies has been their use in revealing mistakes and errors made by the police that have resulted in miscarriages of justice (McCartney, 2006). The results have been overturned convictions and, in at least some cases, the actual perpetrators being brought to justice. On balance, the adoption and adaptation of these technologies have had complex consequences for the police crime-management function.

Although there is a growing empirical literature on how a variety of scientific technologies are deployed in support of police investigative practices, there remain significant gaps in our knowledge about the consequences of the use of these technologies. We do not have a good understanding of the relative and interactive contributions of these methods in terms of how they are used collaboratively by police. Nor is there much clarity about how much change they are inducing in terms of the ways police carry out their crime management functions. For example, there is some anecdotal evidence suggesting that, influenced by the rhetorical power of claims made about DNA profiling, police investigators are attending less carefully to other investigative strategies and tactics in the belief that such methods are relatively unimportant and that science can be relied on to "crack the case." Likewise, it is quite plausible that such technologies, rather than driving change, are simply absorbed into the established routines and practices of policing, as suggested by several studies of proactive policing.

Proactive investigation involves the prediction and prevention of criminal offending. While a considerable amount of effort has focused on trying to determine which individuals and groups are likely to engage in criminality of different kinds, arguably an even greater impact has been achieved by "hot-spotting" and crime-pattern analysis technologies, drawing on established social science methods. The idea that crimes and other associated social problems are not uniformly distributed across space but rather tend to cluster in particular places is one of the fundamental tenets of the "social science" of criminology. Based on empirical analysis of police data, Sherman (1992) found that around 3% of residential addresses are responsible for over half of all calls to the police. The practical relevance of this finding was demonstrated through an experimental research design in Minneapolis in which 110 crime hot spots were randomly assigned to treatment or control groups. For an eight-month period the treatment areas with higher levels of preventive police patrolling performed relatively well on measures of reported crime and observations of disorder. The researchers concluded that there were "clear, if modest, general deterrent effects of substantial increases in police presence in crime hot spots" (Sherman and Weisburd, 1995: 645). By demonstrating the extent to which crimes clustered around a comparatively small number of micro-locations, the elementary crime mapping employed established a way for police assets to be targeted on the criminogenic locales responsible for a disproportionate amount of police business. Moreover, this study is an example of how certain aspects of the policing-studies literature are increasingly designed explicitly as applied science, deliberately conceived to develop an evidence base to "drive" police reform.

Informed by these studies, crime mapping and analysis has been widely adopted, as police organizations have sought to align their resources more accurately with risky places and people. Utilizing systematic review techniques, Braga (2001) identified nine evaluations of focused police interventions at crime hot spots and noted crime reduction effects in seven of them. Moreover, data from four of these studies suggest the potential for the diffusion of benefits over an area beyond that targeted by the police intervention.

The establishment of a crime-mapping and analysis capacity within policing organizations has led some scholars to conclude that over the past two decades there has been a fundamental realignment in the balance of police crime-management work with a progressive move toward adopting a proactive investigative stance. Maguire (2000), summarizing the findings of a number of fieldwork studies in the UK, suggests police strategy is increasingly predicated on the identification of "risks and targets." Rather than seeking to investigate and prosecute after an offense has occurred, the preferred methodology is to utilize ongoing surveillance of populations "at risk," and "of risk" and to target interventions accordingly in order to suppress the occurrence of offences.

Critiques of this proactive disposition and its consequences have been featured in a number of recent research studies. Based upon ethnographic fieldwork in three American police departments, Manning (2008) developed a nuanced understanding of the transformative potential of this supposedly more evidence-based approach to the delivery of policing services. Looking across his three research sites he found that ultimately the impacts achieved by crime maps in shifting and changing police practice "on the ground" are limited. This is attributed to the way crime mapping creates tension with some of the fundamental cultural beliefs and understandings of "street cops" that theirs is a craft-based occupation. Similarly, Gill (2000) suggests that rather than altering policing "on the ground," these methods for generating intelligence actually tend to be absorbed and adapted into established routines, reinforcing a tendency to "round up the usual suspects."

IV. Security Management

The use of intelligence and surveillance methods by police has been of particular importance in responding to a criminal activity that has acquired much greater political and public prominence than it had previously—terrorism. As Brodeur (1983) notes, since their inception, the public police have always had a key role in "high policing" through their involvement in counter-subversion and counter-terrorism activities. Across most Western countries, such participation has taken on a far higher public profile since the attacks in the United States in 2001. However, compared with other areas of practice we know comparatively little about the art, craft, and science of high policing.

Seeking to map the basic contours of this relatively invisible and under-studied dimension, Bayley and Weisburd (2009) report results from an international survey. They found that in all countries surveyed, the police constitute only one node in a multi-agency counter-terrorism apparatus. Under such arrangements, police typically assume a particular role in supporting national security, while intelligence agencies perform other functions. As such, looking across the world, contemporary approaches to countering terrorist threats tend to combine elements that are both proactive and reactive, both offensive and defensive, involving both military and law-enforcement personnel and the use of both "hard" and "soft" power, shaped by the physical environment and social interactions, and delivered both locally and trans-nationally. In their approaches to counter-terrorism, individual nation-states have tended to balance these elements in different ways. Some have adopted a more offensive posture, prioritizing military capacity and emphasizing the role of coercive power. In contrast, other states have adopted a law-enforcement paradigm, seeking to influence and persuade using "soft power."

While many countries had significant experience of countering terrorism prior to 9/11, it is generally agreed that since that time there has been a global expansion in investment in counter-terrorism. This has led to expansion of the resources and legal powers of national domestic and overseas intelligence agencies; use of military assets against terrorism; a reconfiguring of the police mission with greater emphasis on the police role in national security; and a greater involvement of civil society organizations and institutions in the counter-terrorism apparatus. Innes (2006) suggests that police tend to be engaged in one or more roles:

- prospective search for offenders and preemptive targeting of high-risk individuals;
- retrospective search for offenders and securing perpetrators after an actual or attempted attack;
- prospective community protection through social and physical measures designed to create a "hostile environment" for potential assailants, while also affording resilience and reassurance to the public; and
- retrospective community protection by implementing measures following an attack (actual or attempted) that seek to minimize the attack's harmful effects.

Evidence from Northern Ireland has documented the complexities that attend police counter-terrorism interventions undertaken through these modes. Based on a period of observational fieldwork conducted in the Divis flats in Belfast, Slucka (1989) found that police actions were one of the principal determinants of social support for the Provisional Irish Republican Army. On those occasions where the police were seen to over-reach and act provocatively, the otherwise largely "soft" social support within the community for groups engaging in terrorist violence tended to "harden" and increase. Furthermore, in this battle for community "hearts and minds," one of the ways in which the dissident groups sought to buttress their legitimacy and social support was through the provision of basic social-control services. In a situation where policing had been fundamentally militarized and focused almost exclusively upon mitigating the violence of the paramilitary groups, something akin to a "policing vacuum" tended to arise. By providing a form of response to crimes such as burglary and drug dealing, the paramilitary groupings sought to secure a degree of local public legitimacy.

Recognizing the significance of social support in the continuance of terrorist campaigns, U.S. and UK responses to the contemporary threats posed by violent Islamists inspired by Al-Qaeda's ideologies have emphasized harnessing both "high" and "low" policing assets. This has had a marked impact upon the policing infrastructure generally. In the United States, Fosher (2009) has documented how the establishment of the Department of Homeland Security has led to a renegotiation of the relationships between local and federal policing agencies and central government. Thacher (2005) has augmented this understanding by providing a more focused account of the delivery of homeland security strategy through a joint task-force arrangement, supposedly integrating the resources of local police and national security agencies. His concern is that the focus on national security issues threatened to overwhelm the more "mundane" crime and disorder concerns of the local police. In particular, he worried that the co-optation of local policing into a national security effort possesses the potential to undermine levels of community trust in the broader policing mission. Echoing these findings, drawing upon semi-structured interviews with a number of key UK actors, Thiel (2008) examined attempts to connect the work of counter-terrorism specialists with the work of the more numerous and geographically dispersed Neighborhood Policing teams. He locates a number of tensions evident in the relationships between the various agencies involved, centering upon issues about sharing classified information and the problems that arise in reconciling short-term objectives of intercepting and disrupting potential threats with longer-term aims of building community cohesion. In a similar manner to that seen in the United States, the infrastructure of counter-terrorism in the UK has been fundamentally re-worked, with the London based anti-terrorism branch of the Metropolitan Police augmented by a network of Counter-Terrorism Units located throughout England and Wales, with police staff co-located with members of the Security Service.

In recent years, reforms aimed at protecting national security have not been only internal. A key movement has been to export policing models, techniques, and technologies from the West to post-conflict and developing countries. For Bayley (2006), the provision of policing assistance was effectively "industrialized" during the 1990s and established as a significant element of foreign policy in the United States and UK in particular. This expansion, and the expenditures underpinning it, have taken place in the absence of any real evidence that positive outcomes have been achieved (Marenin, 1998). Despite this lack of evidence, the trend is not abating, for as Greener (2009) identifies, there has recently been significant expansion in the UN

Department of Peacekeeping Operations, Police Division, which has acquired an elevated status and is no longer the "poor cousin" of the military.

Through the auspices of the Department for International Development (DFID) the UK has been a key actor in the provision of police-reform assistance. Evaluative studies commissioned to assess the achievements to date have not been particularly positive. For example, in their review of community policing reforms in Uganda, Raleigh et al. (2000) concluded that the reforms had failed to achieve any real traction. In part, such failures may be a symptom of a tendency for police and security-sector reform to remain divorced from wider efforts to change the life-prospects of those afflicted by poverty, as implied in a second DFID report,

…poorer communities are unable to play a significant part in community policing unless major efforts are made to provide them with the basic necessities of survival and development…Policing does not occur in a vacuum…(Clegg et al., 2000: 8–18).

The tenor of these conclusions is consistent with evidence from a number of countries where attempts to adopt and adapt CP have accomplished less than anticipated. Perhaps the most high-profile failure has been in South Africa, where reforms were undertaken as part of the deeper process of democratic change. The lack of success has been attributed to the fact that the police institution has neither the capacity nor the organizational infrastructure required to deliver Community Policing (Pelser and Louw, 2002). Pessimistically, Marks et al. (2009) have recently suggested that the ideal that police in South Africa will secure a monopoly over the delivery of coercive force is little more than a "dream." As such, the picture in South Africa is similar to that in many other countries on that continent, where state policing maintains a narrowly conceived public-order focus, and is primarily responsive to the demands of dominant elites (Hills, 2000).

Synthesizing the kinds of problems that have been identified with this policing export drive, Bayley (2006) lists a number of "inhibitors" to effective reform of the policing sector including a lack of accountability; absence of strategic planning; over-emphasis on the crime control needs of the United States relative to those of the country being assisted; uncritical promotion of deterrent law enforcement; over-reliance on training not embedded in programs of institutional change; failure to adapt programs to local circumstances; and under-appreciation of the importance of consulting and collaborating with local stakeholders.

Across a number of settings the common conclusion is that at least part of the problem in securing effective police reform is a failure to acknowledge the need to configure the "arts" and "crafts" of policing, as well as its organizational structures, in a form appropriate for the local settings and situations. Western models are implemented in a "de-contextualized" form, simply and unthinkingly transplanted with little consideration to how aspects of the practices and processes being implemented might interact with the needs, expectations, traditions, and customs of local people. These kinds of issues have been tellingly highlighted in studies of the Australian Federal Police's involvement in the Solomon Islands (Dinnen and Braithwaite, 2009) and Papua New Guinea (McLeod, 2009).

The internationalization of policing through a process of exports and imports reflects an increasingly prevalent sensibility that in a globalizing world populated by increasingly mobile communities, national security is contingent upon events and occurrences that lie beyond the boundaries of any one country. Consequently, intervening in post-conflict situations to promote regional stability is integral to many countries' national-security strategies. International policing assistance is therefore provided in support of both peace-making and peace-keeping, and subsequently as part of processes attempting to normalize democratic policing into the routines of fragile states.

Mapping the increasing participation of the police in security-management tasks in recent decades focuses attention on the increasing diversity of the work of the public police. However, some of the most important maneuvers in security management have lain outside the remit of public policing agencies and have involved the increasing use of private policing providers. It is not surprising, then, that a number of the most astute and insightful commentaries on policing in recent years have focused on the expanding role played by private policing in the provision of security. Johnston's (1992) historical study reminds us that until sometime around the middle of the twentieth century, the majority of policing services were in fact delivered by private as opposed to public police. As such, there is a greater degree of continuity with the current situation than some have supposed. Thus the widely agreed-upon fact that public police are now outnumbered by privately funded security staff marks a return to earlier arrangements. Jones and Newburn (1998) suggest that the key factor about the current situation is that private security staff have effectively replaced other kinds of authority figures (such as caretakers, bus conductors, park wardens and so forth), who, in the performance of their functions, acted as sources of surveillance and social control.

Based upon a review of the international literature, Mazerolle and Ransley (2006) suggest that privately provided—or what they label "third-party"—policing tends to be deployed in five main ways, controlling: drugs; violent crimes; property crime; youth problems; and criminogenic places. On the basis of seventy-seven studies providing some form of evaluative data, they suggest third-party policing appears to have some potential for controlling violent crime and dealing with young people, but is less effective at controlling property crime. Paradoxically, though, it is this latter problem that constitutes the predominant focus of much private security provision.

A more critical perspective on the role of private policing is to be found in Shearing and Stenning's (1987) exegesis of the ways in which instruments of policing, governance, and social ordering are woven into the fabric of the social environment. Through a case study of Disneyland they show how a combination of situational and social interventions are embedded in a "seen but unnoticed" way in the experience of the consumer such that the need for overt social control interventions to secure compliance is drastically reduced. In this sense, these developments in the supply of policing services resonate with broader theoretical debates about the securitization of social life (see Garland, 2001).

That the delivery of policing services takes place through multi-polar arrangements in which public police agencies are one among a number of providers, is a theme recurrent across a number of studies. Among the most influential of these accounts has been Ericson and Haggerty's (1997) treatise on "Policing the Risk Society." Based on work in Canadian police departments, they suggest that an increasing amount of public policing capacity is expended on acting as an "information hub," transmitting and receiving data from across the policing sector. For them, the public-facing aspects of policing that have preoccupied many studies are of less consequence than the more hidden "back-stage" transformations that have occurred in the social world of policing. However, Manning (2008) takes issue with their overarching conclusion. Based on his study of crime analysis, he suggests they have overstated the extent of change.

This sense of continuity is also present in Wakefield's (2003) observational study of private security guards and how they accomplish their aims of regulating social order in what she labels "mass private property." In findings echoing the orthodoxies of public policing, she documents how, in the "securitized space" of the shopping mall, private police surveillance is disproportionately directed toward lower class groups. The craft of the security staff is one of "impression management," regulating and protecting the visual order of the space in a way that communicates that it is part of the public realm even though it is in fact privately owned, controlled and manipulated. The social groups that are the principal focus for the "surveillance gaze" of private police are very similar to those identified by the earliest empirical studies as the main interest of the public police.

V. CONCLUSION: POLICING BY OPERATIONS, TASKFORCES, AND CAMPAIGNS

Empirical research on the conduct of the policing function has shown that it is an amalgam of an art, craft, and science. Certain aspects of the delivery of policing are increasingly predicated on "scientific" knowledge and expertise. This reflects how, particularly in relation to "managing" crime, policing has increasingly sought to harness scientific method and knowledge. Consequently it is not surprising that a more scientific and avowedly experimental orientation is evident in some of the studies that have sought to test the impact of particular technical and technological innovations on the police's ability to successfully manage crime problems.

Importantly though, research shows that the impact of science on policing is not restricted to the crime-management function. Through the structured process associated with the problem-oriented policing model and the more rationalized approaches underpinning the recent reinventions of community policing in the United States and UK, the ways in which police seek to manage order are also increasingly premised on scientific evidence. However, it is important that we do not overstate the influence of science on what it is the police do. For it remains the case that much of what counts as effective policing is more an "art" or "craft" than a science. Depicted as a craft, policing involves learning a particular set of practical skills and, through experience, acquiring the know-how to employ them in a manner appropriate to a particular situation in order to achieve a desired outcome. Distinctively, discussions of the "art" of policing place more emphasis on the ability of officers to act intuitively and creatively to circumvent problems that they encounter.

In developing this perspective on policing, it is vital not to misrepresent the situation and pretend that the relationships between art, craft, and science are frictionless. Tensions and conflicts do arise, especially when scientific knowledge is being deployed as a "motor" for reform and does not align with the "craft" base of frontline officers. When this occurs, significant resistance to change can be elicited and has to be overcome or circumvented.

Suggesting that policing combines aspects of art, craft, and science to undertake the order-management, crime-management, and security-management functions articulates a complex portrayal of policing and how it is enacted. This is appropriate and coheres with the fact that policing is increasingly complex, engaged simultaneously in the provision of both neighborhood and national security. Reflecting shifts in its operating environment, policing has been engaged not just in managing crime but also a more diffuse and "ambient" sense of insecurity that is, according to a number of leading commentators, inducing fundamental shifts in the makeup of society's institutional and interactional orders (see Garland, 2001). It is set against this backdrop that the police's roles in managing both "order" and "security" have acquired increasing salience. It also accounts for the fact that the suite of interventions that police have sought to engage with respect to various social problems has been expanded and elaborated, with increasing emphasis on prevention through a combination of prediction and preemption. Moreover, through CP, key aspects of the police mission have effectively been re-thought, with the police function increasingly predicated upon the provision of community support to build social cohesion and social capital.

What do these conditions portend for the future of policing, and what aspects of policing should be studied in the future? There is perhaps a growing acknowledgement that the police role in society should not be too narrowly defined. As articulated in this Chapter, police organizations must simultaneously deliver a range of outcomes covering the combination of order management, crime management, and security management. Thus they must investigate crime, prevent terrorism, secure local order, and sustain a degree of public support and legitimacy, all at the same time. It is the balancing of these varied, competing, and possibly conflicting demands that is the hallmark of modern policing. Such conceptualizations therefore demand sophisticated models of policing, both in terms of abstract theory and processes for "real world" delivery.

Responding to the kinds of pressures that such complexities generate, we may be starting to see a nascent trend for policing to be undertaken not by the generalist uniformed officers or investigators featured in the original pioneering studies, but increasingly by specialists according to a clearly demarcated division of labor. Individual aspects of the police function are increasingly cast as requiring domain expertise provided through specialist units. Accordingly, particular units specialize in the investigation and detection of particular crimes (such as homicide, burglary, fraud, and street robbery), while other officers adopt a more proactive orientation to high-risk people and places, and still others focus on public order tasks (see Roberts and Innes, 2009). Some of this provision of policing comes from public agencies and some from the private sector.

The establishment of such modes of organization poses new questions and challenges for researchers. These center upon how various components of the policing system are connected and how particular specialties are brought together and coordinated to deliver specific interventions and services. In his study of "Joint Terrorism Taskforces" in Michigan, Thacher (2005) catalogs both the potential benefits and unanticipated risks attached to such arrangements. In particular, he charts how the ultimate objectives of community policing and counter-terrorism may conflict. Reaching similar conclusions, Roberts and Innes (2009) examine the workings of Operation Trident, a long-running, dedicated anti-gun crime initiative of London's Metropolitan Police that applies a range of policing specialists and assets to a specific problem. A related development is the tendency for police to pursue campaigns around particular issues, such as domestic violence, street robbery, or drugs.

Policing by campaigns, operations, and taskforces appears to have been adopted across the sector as a way of focusing attention and resources on issues with political traction in situations where the police are being asked to perform a diffuse and diverse array of tasks. These forms of initiative-based policing afford the connectivity and coordination that is needed to overcome the increasing division of labor. However, it remains to be seen how effective these modes of organization are and what their longer-term consequences are for the art, craft, and science of policing.

REFERENCES

Banton, M. (1964). *The Policeman in the Community,* London: Tavistock.

Bayley, D. (2006). *Changing the Guard*, New York: Oxford University Press.

Bayley, D. and Weisburd, D. (2009). "Cops and Spooks: The Role of the Police in Counterterrorism," in D. Weisburd, L. Mock, I. Hakimi, T. Feucht, and S. Perry (eds.), *To Protect and to Serve: Policing in an Age of Terrorism,* New York: Springer Verlaag.

Bittner, E. (1974). "Florence Nightingale in Pursuit of Willie Sutton: A Theory of the Police," in H. Jacobs, (ed.), *The potential for reform of criminal justice,* Beverly Hills: Sage.

Bowling, B. (1999). "The Rise and Fall on New York Murder: Zero Tolerance or Crack's decline," *The British Journal of Criminology* 39(4): 531–4.

Braga, A. (2001). "The effects of hot spots policing on crime," *Annals of the American Academy of Political and Social Science* 578: 104–25.

Braga, A. and Weisburd, D. (2006) "Problem-oriented policing: the disconnect between principles and practice," in D. Weisburd and A. Braga (eds.), *Police Innovation: Contrasting Perspectives,* Cambridge: Cambridge University Press.

Brodeur, J. (1983). 'High Policing and Low Policing: Remarks about the Policing of Political Activities," *Social Problems* 30(5): 507–20.

Carr, P. (2005). *Clean Streets: controlling Crime, Maintaining Order and Building Community Activism,* New York: New York University Press.

Clarke, R. (1998). "Defining police strategies: Problem-solving, problem-oriented policing and community-oriented policing," in T. O'Connor Shelley and A.C. Grant (eds.), *Problem-Oriented Policing: Crime Specific Problems, Critical Issues and Making POP Work,* Washington, DC: Police Executive Research Forum.

Clegg, I., Hunt, R., and Whetton, J. (2000). *Policy Guidance on Support to Policing in Developing Societies,* Swansea: University of Wales.

Cole, S. (2003). *Suspect Identities,* Cambridge, MA: Harvard University Press.

Cordner, G. and Biebel, E. (2005). "Problem-Oriented Policing in Practice," *Criminology and Public Policy* 4(2): 155–81.

Dinnen, S. and Braithwaite, J. (2009). "Reinventing Policing Through the Prism of the Colonial Kiap," *Policing and Society* 19(2): 161–73.

Eck, J. (2006). "Science, Values and Problem-Oriented Policing: Why Problem-Oriented Policing," in D. Weisburd and A. Braga (eds.), *Police Innovation: Contrasting Perspectives,* Cambridge: Cambridge University Press.

Ericson, R. (1993). *Making Crime* (2nd edn.), Toronto: University of Toronto Press.

Ericson, R. and Haggerty, K. (1997). *Policing the Risk Society,* Oxford: Clarendon Press.

Fielding, N. (1981). *The Police and Social Conflict,* Athlone Press.

Fosher, K. (2009). *Under Construction: Making Homeland Security at the Local Level,* Chicago: University of Chicago Press.

Garland, D. (2001). *The Culture of Control,* Oxford: Oxford University Press.

Gill, P. (2000). *Rounding Up the Usual Suspects? Developments in Contemporary Law Enforcement Intelligence,* Aldershot: Ashgate.

Goldstein, H. (1990). *Problem-Oriented Policing,* New York: McGraw Hill.

Greener, B. (2009). "UNPOL: UN Police as peacekeepers," *Policing and Society* 19(2): 106–118.

Greenwood, P., Janet Chaiken, J., and Petersilia, J. (1977). *The Criminal Investigation Process,* Lexington, MA: D.C. Heath.

Harcourt, B. (2001). *Illusion of Order,* Cambridge, MA: Harvard University Press.

Herbert, S. (2006). *Citizens, Cops and Power: Recognizing the Limits of Community*, Chicago: Chicago University Press.

Hills, A. (2000). *Policing Africa: Internal Security and the Limits of Liberalization*, Boulder, CO: Lynne Rienner.

Hobbs, D. (1988). *Doing the Business: Entrepreneurship, Detectives and the Working Class in the East End of London*, Oxford: Clarendon Press.

Innes, M. (2003a). *Understanding Social Control: Deviance, Crime and Social Order*, Buckingham: Open University Press.

Innes, M. (2003b). *Investigating Murder: Detective Work and the Police Response to Criminal Homicide*, Oxford: Clarendon Press.

Innes, M. (2004). "Signal Crimes and Signal Disorders: Notes on Deviance as Communicative Action," *British Journal of Sociology* 55(3): 335–55.

Innes, M. (2006). "Policing uncertainty: countering terror through community intelligence and democratic policing," *Annals of the American Academy of Political and Social Science* (605): 222–41.

Innes, M. (2010). "A 'Mirror' and a 'Motor': Researching and Reforming Policing in an Age of Austerity," *Policing: A Journal of Policy and Practice* 4(2): 127–34.

Innes, M., Abbott, L., Lowe, T., and Roberts, C. (2008). "Seeing Like a Citizen: Field Experiments in Community Intelligence-led Policing," *Police Practice and Research* 10(2): 99–114.

Innes, M. and Clarke, A. (2009). "Policing the Past: Cold Case Studies, Forensic Evidence and Retroactive Social Control," *British Journal of Sociology* 60(3): 543–63.

Johnston, L. (1992). *The Rebirth of Private Policing*, London: Routledge.

Jones, T. and Newburn, T. (1998). *Private Security and Public Policing*, Oxford: Clarendon Press.

Kelling, G., Pate, A., Dieckman, D., Brown, C., et al. (1974). *The Kansas City Preventative Patrol Experiment*, Washington, DC: Police Foundation.

Kershaw, C., Nicholas, S., and Walker, A. (2008). *Crime in England and Wales 2007/08*, London: Home Office Statistical Bulletin

Maguire, M. (2000). "Policing by risks and targets: some dimensions and implications of intelligence-led crime control," *Policing and Society* 9: 315–36.

Manning, P. (1980). *The Narc's Game*, Cambridge, MA: MIT Press.

Manning, P. (2008). *The Technology of Policing*, New York: New York University Press.

Marenin, O. (1989). "The utility of community needs surveys in community policing," *Police Studies* 12(2): 73–81.

Marks, M., Shearing, C., and Wood, J. (2009). "Who Should the Police Be? Finding a New Narrative for Community Policing in South Africa," *Police Practice and Research* 10(2): 145–55.

Marx, G. (1988). *Undercover: Police Surveillance in America*, Berkeley: University of California Press.

Mazerolle, L. and Ransley, J. (2006). *Third Party Policing*, Cambridge: Cambridge University Press.

McCartney, C. (2006). *Forensic Identification and Criminal Justice: Forensic Science, Justice and Risk*, Cullompton: Willan.

McLeod, A. (2009). "Police Capacity Development in the Pacific: The Challenge of Local Context," *Policing and Society* 19(2): 147–60.

Moore, M. (1992). "Problem-Solving and Community Policing," in M. Tonry and N. Morris (eds.), *Modern Policing*, Chicago: University of Chicago Press.

National Policing Improvement Agency (2009). *The National DNA Database 2007–9*, London: NPIA.

Noakes, J., Klocke, B., and. Gillham, F. (2005). "Whose streets? Police and protester struggles over space in Washington DC 29–30 September 2001," *Policing and Society* 15(3): 235–54.

Pelser, E. and Louw, A. (2002). "Evaluating community safety forums," in E. Pelser (ed.), *Crime Prevention Forums*, Pretoria: Institute for Security Studies.

Raleigh, C., Biddle, K., Male, C., and Neema, S. (2000). *Uganda Police Project Evaluation, Evaluation Report FV591*, London: Department for International Development.

Reiner, R. (1978). *The Blue Coated Worker*, Cambridge: Cambridge University Press.

Reiner, R. (1992). *The Politics of the Police* (2nd edn.), Hemel Hempstead: Harvester Wheatsheaf.

Reppetto, T. (1978). "The Detective Task: The State of the Art, Science, Craft?," *Police Studies: The International Review of Police Development* 1(3): 5–10.

Roberts, C. and Innes, M. (2009). "The 'Death' of Dixon? Policing gun crime and the end of the generalist police constable in England and Wales," *Criminology and Criminal Justice* 9(3): 337–57.

Rubinstein, J. (1973). *City Police*, New York: Ballantine Books.

Shearing, C. and Stenning, P. (1987). *Private Policing*, Thousand Oaks, CA: Sage.

Sheptycki, J. (2005). "Policing Political Protest When Politics Go Global: Comparing public order policing in Canada and Bolivia," *Policing and Society* 15(3): 327–52.

Sherman, L. (1992). "Attacking crime: policing and crime control," in M. Tonry and N. Morris (eds.), *Modern Policing*, Chicago: University of Chicago Press.

Sherman, L. and Weisburd, D. (1995). "General Deterrent Effects of Police Patrol in Crime Hotspots: A randomized control trial," *Justice Quarterly* 12: 626–48.

Silverman, E. (1999). *NYPD Battles Crime: Innovative Strategies in Policing*, Boston: Northeastern University Press.

Skogan, W. (2007). *Police and Community in Chicago*, New York: Oxford University Press.

Skolnick, J. (1966). *Justice Without Trial: Law Enforcement in Democratic Society*, New York: Wiley.

Slucka, J. (1989). *Hearts and Minds, Water and Fish: Support for the IRA and INLA in a Northern Ireland Ghetto*, Greenwich, CT: JAI Press.

Thacher, D. (2005). "The Local Role in Homeland Security," *Law and Society Review* 39(5): 635–76.

Thiel, D. (2008). *Policing Terrorism: A Review of the Evidence*, London: Police Foundation.

Tuffin, R., Morris, J., and Poole, A. (2006). *An Evaluation of the Impact of the National Reassurance Policing Programme*, London: Home Office.

Vitale, A. (2005). "From Negotiated Management to Command and Control: How the New York Police Department polices protests," *Policing and Society* 15(3): 283–304.

Waddington, P.A.J. (1994). *Liberty and Order: Public Order Policing in a Capital City*, London: UCL Press.

Waddington, P.A.J. (1998). "Controlling protest in contemporary historical and comparative perspective," in D. Della Porta and H. Reiter (eds.), *Policing Protest*, Minneapolis: University of Minnesota Press.

Wakefield, A. (2003). *Selling Security: The Private Policing of Private Space*, Cullompton: Willan.

Williams, R. and Johnson, P. (2008). *Genetic Policing*, Cullompton: Willan.

Wilson, J.Q. and Kelling, G. (1982). "Broken windows," *The Atlantic Monthly* March: 29–38.

2

CRIME AND CRIMINALS

WESLEY SKOGAN

THIS Chapter takes as its organizing theme what we know—and do not know—about macro-social trends in crime. Following a brief description of crime trends in comparative perspective, the Chapter reviews research on the factors associated with its rise and decline. The discussion is organized into six categories: demography and economic conditions; policing and incarceration; drugs, guns, and gangs; community and environmental factors; lifestyle and culture; and crime reporting and recording. The goal of this review is to provide an entry point into the literature on crime trends, point out what is known and what needs to be known about why crime goes up and down, and highlight some of the issues facing those who take up the challenge. Reflecting the English-language literature, much of the following discussion is North American in orientation. However, the factors associated with trends in crime and the technical issues involved in addressing their impact are all of broad, cross-national significance, and could easily find application elsewhere.

I. Crime Trends Illustrated

Figure 1 depicts national trends in homicide and robbery recorded by police agencies in Japan, France, the United States, and England and Wales. The data come from a variety of official and research reports. Depending on the availability of the data, the trend lines start between 1946 (Japan) and 1974 (France). In every nation robbery is much more frequent than homicide, so their rates are illustrated using separate scale axes. The data illustrate a variety of ways in which officially recorded violent crime rose and fell over this period. In Japan, homicide rose during the late 1940s and early 1950s. It then dropped by two-thirds, before leveling off in the 1990s. Robbery also dropped, but after 1997 the rate proceeded to double; theft was up during this period as well. However, despite the most recent increase, in 2006 robbery stood at only 25% of its postwar high. In the UK, both homicide and robbery peaked in 2003 after rising steadily for more than 40 years. By that year homicide had risen by 30% over its 1958 low, and recorded robbery was up by a factor of 55. In France, homicide peaked in 1984, then declined thereafter—with an uptick in the mid-1900s. By 2006 it was down by 40% from its peak. Like Japan, French homicide figures include incidents classified by police as attempted murder, but in recent decades actual killings (which are also depicted in Figure 1) have been separately reported in France, and their trend closely parallels the broader number. In the United States, crime has waxed and waned fairly dramatically since the late 1950s, with police recording three new highs for homicide and robbery. What is distinctive about the most recent national peak in American homicide is not its height—there had been similar spikes in 1974, 1980, and earlier in the 1920s—but the extent to which the crime rate subsequently declined during the 1990s and then remained low in the 2000s. The national homicide trend depicted in Figure 1 did not descend quite to the lows registered during the postwar 1950s, but in late 1950s the nation recorded the lowest homicide rate since 1910, and 2007 came close to that figure.

Not surprisingly, such fluctuations are of perennial interest. Newly released crime figures are headline numbers virtually everywhere, and politicians and criminal justice officials have to be prepared to offer some explanation for their trend. They are quickest to step forward when the numbers are down. Social critics

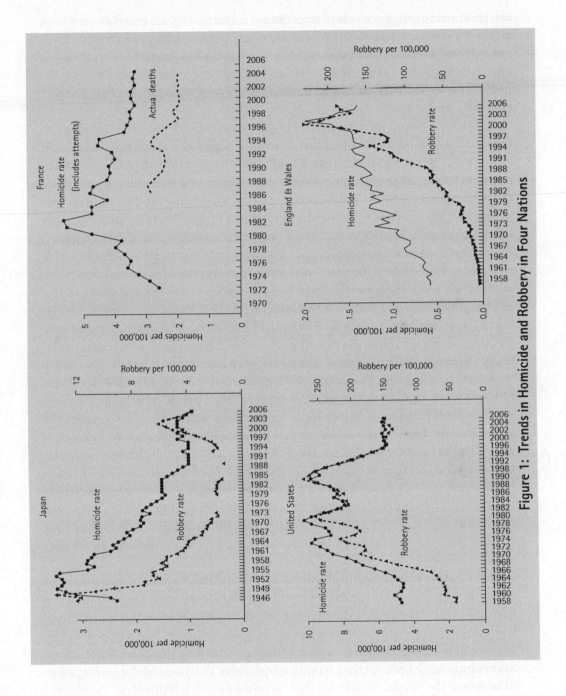

Figure 1: Trends in Homicide and Robbery in Four Nations

interpret rising crime as a reflection of deeper social tendencies that they view with alarm. Researchers have offered a variety of explanations for crime trends; these range from "a" (alcohol use, which is down in the United States) to "z" (zero tolerance policing, which is up). Researchers often conflict in their methods and differ in their views, but they are united in their concern for what the numbers actually measure.

Among the countries depicted in Figure 1, Japanese figures are interpreted as reflecting a distinct national culture, an aging population, a long period of economic success, and significant police-fiddling with criminal justice data. Recorded crime increases after 1990 appear to be due in part to a tightening-up of police recording practices by the National Police Agency following revelations of incompetence and nonfeasance (Leonardsen, 2006). In France, there are actually three official sources of homicide data. Only police statistics are presented in Figure 1; the others come from prosecutors and medical examiners, and they differ by a wide margin. About 60% of police-recorded homicides are actually *attempted* murders, and French researchers have pointed to police racism in the widespread practice of charging ethnic minorities with homicide in these cases. Econometric analyses of twentieth century data for England and Wales have found the long upward trend in predatory crime illustrated in Figure 1 to be driven by increasing affluence. However, the most recent British robbery numbers are widely discounted as reflecting changes in the way crimes are recorded in England and Wales. These changes were imposed on the police to ensure that all public complaints are taken seriously and are recorded more consistently across police forces. In contrast, the American data are locally collected and have avoided large-scale improvement efforts. It has been shown that trends in the data are, with careful controls, similar to those recorded in other systems, including the National Crime Victimization Survey and cause-of-death statistics gathered by public health officials. Differences in definitions and episodic changes in how crimes are recorded make comparing crime trends across nations even more perilous than examining them over time within nations, but even the latter requires extensive local knowledge of the data systems involved.

This Chapter reviews many of the research-based claims about why crime rises and falls within nations. The data behind these claims are more adequate for some than for others. Sometimes the data are not very good, or of only recent vintage, while other claims are based on relevant research which is handicapped by the absence of necessary data over time. It is important to note that there is not always a correspondence between the quantity or quality of the data and the potential significance of the claims. Sometimes there is no data at all, but this is not evidence of the unimportance of a particular claim. Rather, it is a consequence of what research has been funded and published, and whether or not some agency happened to begin collecting relevant data decades ago. In this Chapter, I discuss what I judge to be the serious claims.

II. DEMOGRAPHY AND ECONOMIC CONDITIONS

One of the most fundamental features of common crimes is that offending is disproportionally concentrated among the young. Youths are by far the most likely to be arrested and to admit high levels of involvement in crime when they are surveyed by researchers. In the UK, Field (1999) found a 1% change in theft and burglary for every 1% change in the number of males age 15–20. Roberts and LaFree (2004) report that the dramatic aging of the Japanese population, along with its economic strength in earlier decades, is among the most important predictors of declining violence. Because of the overall aging of the American population during the 1990s—a result of the graying of the large post-WWII baby-boom generation—many have speculated that the national post-1991 drop in crime was due to a decreasing proportion of youths in high-risk age categories. The two did drop in unison until the mid-1990s. However, toward the end of the twentieth century, the 15–24 age group began to grow again, as the grandchildren of the boomers (the so-called "second echo" of the original baby boom) aged into higher-risk categories. For example, the percentage of the U.S. population aged 18 (a prime age for homicide offending) hit bottom in 1995, and then rose again. The post-1995 growth of the 15–24 age cohort was touted by forecasters as putting new upward pressure on crime rates. But while the pressure was doubtless there, crime rates did not in fact rise as predicted.

It is more accurate to say that upward pressure on the crime rate has generally come from the number of young *males* in the population, for one of the most universal findings of social science is that they are by far more likely to get in trouble. Except for certain sex-related offenses, men are also more likely than women to be victims of violent crime. During the 1990s, victimization rates for men and women in the United States both dropped, with the gap between the sexes remaining virtually unchanged for many types of crime. However, the rate of female *commission* of violent crime rose a bit relative to that of males. The rate of male offending dropped more than the female rate during the 1990s, so the female percentage of violent crime rose (see Heimer and Lauritsen, 2008). By 2007, females accounted for 22% of arrests for violent crime in the US, and in that year they accounted for a majority of those arrested for simple theft.

Many have attributed the most recent decline in crime to the vigor of the American economy, which grew steadily between 1993 and 2001. During that period unemployment fell nationwide by almost a third, and real incomes rose for many groups. However, overall unemployment trends cannot explain much of the variation in national crime rates. Levitt's (2004) review yields an "elasticity" of 1.0 for unemployment. This means that, for every 1% change in the unemployment rate, crime shifts by 1%. However, national changes in unemployment are typically relatively small, just a few percentage points except in the hardest of times, and cannot account for much larger changes in crime rates. Rosenfeld and Fornango (2008) find that a national index of consumer confidence is the best representative of American economic conditions in models of robbery and property crime. There also may be an effect on crime of income *inequality*, but that moved in the opposite direction during the 1990s drop in American crime, toward an increase in wealth at the upper end of the economic spectrum.

However, criminologists know that it is more important to look at the economic condition of youths and poor people. Research indicates both wages and employment possibilities primarily have their effect on crime in these segments of the labor market. Most of the crimes considered here are committed by young men with little education, few skills, and a checkered job history. Grogger (1998) reports that a 10% increase in real wages in this group leads to a 10% decrease in economically motivated crime. One study concluded that changes in wages, an increase in the minimum wage, and improving employment prospects among young, low-income youths could explain almost one-third of the decline in crime in the U.S. during the 1990s (Gould et al., 2002). Staying in school is also important for this group. Compared to school leavers, students who remain in school get into much less trouble with the law, and they are much more likely to succeed in the job market as young adults.

Around the world, immigration was certainly a big story of the end of the twentieth century, and will be in the twenty-first century, and this too could influence crime. For example, in the early 2000s there were about 37 million foreign-born residents of the United States. About 11.5 million of them were citizens; another 40% were permanent resident aliens, officially admitted refugees, and students. It is estimated that in 2006, 12 million American residents were unauthorized migrants, or about one-third of the total foreign-born population. During the 2000s, the unauthorized population has been increasing by about 500,000 to 800,000 persons per year (Passel, 2006).

There are many reasons to fear that immigrants could contribute disproportionately to the crime rate. Much in their background suggests that immigrants should be very prone to getting into trouble. Compared to others, they typically are young, unmarried, and disproportionately male. Unauthorized immigrants, in particular, are likely to come with limited language abilities, few skills, and little in the way of formal education. They gravitate toward poor and disorganized immigrant neighborhoods where they can retain their anonymity. However, this crowds them into a context dominated by poverty and weak community ties, and it locks them out of the informal networks that frequently are required to get a good job. New immigrants may also not share the values of the dominant culture, which in any event is not much interested in theirs (Lee and Martinez, 2009). Based on all of this, presumptions about the criminality of immigrants have become entangled in larger national debates over immigration, both in the United States and elsewhere.

It is at least a theoretical surprise, therefore, that the American research literature overwhelmingly concludes that immigrants offend at *lower* rates than others, and their neighborhoods have unexpectedly low levels of crime. Further, their presence may help "inoculate" non-immigrants from crime. Evidence for those claims has been reported for immigrants of different national origins, and in multiple cities and neighborhoods. Sampson et al. (2005) set the pacifying effect of immigration at a 25% reduction when it comes to violent crime in Chicago. Detailed homicide studies indicate that immigrant immunity is strongest against acquaintance, domestic, and non-stranger murders. There is more uncertainty about the intergenerational transfer of this tendency toward immunity from crime. Most studies find that second and third generation immigrants are more involved in offending, but some report that the children of immigrants can show continued resistance to getting into trouble with the law.

This "immigrant paradox" extends beyond the domain of crime, into arenas such as health and educational attainment. It appears that many ethnic groups bring with them more "family values" and social structure than expected. By the end of the twentieth century there was much more back-and-forth communication and even travel to their countries of origin than for previous waves of migrants, reinforcing their traditions. Clustering together in their new communities may help preserve migrants' cultures and deter their children from easily adopting delinquent life-styles. In many American cities immigrants are the only part of the population that is growing, and—also strongly attached to the world of work—they have brought modest economic revitalization in their wake. Ironically, it appears that the culprit behind increasing criminality in future generations is assimilation, that long-sought goal of melting-pot theorists. The un-assimilated appear to fare better than those who succumb to the dominant culture.

III. Prisons and Policing

One of the liveliest debates in the crime policy community is over the impact of mounting national incarceration rates. In June 2007, 2.3 million people were locked up in the United States, two thirds of them in prisons and the remainder in city and county jails. Analysts differ in their methodologies, but they attribute a significant portion of the decline in crime in the U.S. during the 1990s to prisons alone. Levitt's (2004) estimate is one third of the total; Spelman (2000) used different methods and concluded it was 27%.

Prison influences crime rates through incapacitation, which is the reduction in crime that occurs because inmates cannot commit offenses while behind bars. The deterrent effect of fear of going to prison also keeps people from offending in the first place, or from re-offending in the future. However, separating out the impacts of incapacitation, general deterrence, and specific deterrence is a very difficult problem, and most research simply aggregates their total effect. Many studies report property crimes to be somewhat more responsive than violent crimes to changes in incarceration rates, and to shifts in levels of policing. In part this may be because rational calculations of the threat of punishment play a reduced role in offenses such as "crimes of passion," "going postal" (mass killings of co-workers), and violence fueled by alcohol. The consensus is that about 20% of the yearly change in U.S. prison populations is translated to subsequent changes in crime (Levitt, 2004; Donohue and Siegelman, 1998).

Very important recent research has documented that there are probably diminishing deterrent effects of prison as states push up their rates of incarceration (Liedka et al., 2006). This is probably due to lower payoffs from digging deeper into the pool of less chronic offenders and individuals caught up in simple drug possession cases, which many American states have done in order to continue to push up politically popular incarceration rates even though there has been a significant drop in serious violent and property crime. Averaging the overall deterrent effect of prison over a time series, which is the way that most research has been laid out, could disguise larger effects occurring at the beginning of a run-up in incarceration, when higher-rate offenders were more frequently the ones being targeted.

Growing jail populations could also account for a decline in crime. Research on crime reduction has focused on the impact of prisons, which house inmates who have been sentenced to long terms of punishment. However, many of those arrested by the police serve a short sentence or are released after being confined only briefly. In the American system, jails are places of short-term confinement either while awaiting trial or serving short terms (less than 12 months) of incarceration, and inmates come and go rapidly. A study of the Cook County jail in Chicago found that in a year it admits nine times the number of people it holds at any one time. Some admittees go on to prison. However, most are either quickly released on bail, diverted to electronic monitoring or day reporting programs, returned to community programs, or are fairly promptly sentenced to the time they have already served. There has been no applicable research on the preventive effects of jail on crime rates, which—because of short stays—would probably be due more to deterrence than incapacitation.

There are incapacitation issues that need to be monitored carefully, for they threaten to sustain rather than decrease crime. One is the adverse impact of the removal of large numbers of men from already fragile communities. While their disappearance may lend some degree of safety to the community, it is not without cost. Their stigma gets transferred to family, friends, and to the community as a whole. Breadwinners are lost, and many families have to reorganize and build new care networks if they are to survive. Children go fatherless, spousal relationships become unglued, and everyone may suffer a loss of self-worth. The return of large numbers of ex-offenders in turn further undermines the community, increasing the concentration of poverty, alienation from legal institutions, cynicism regarding conventional authority, and the stigma associated with "reentry recycling" (Clear et al., 2001). The fate of those who are released from prison is also a critical issue. Generally the fate of recently released inmates is strongly tied to the well-being of the communities to which they return, but this has disproportionally been to disadvantaged neighborhoods (Kubrin and Stewart, 2006). Often there are only limited programs for recent returnees, yet they have to succeed in the job market fairly quickly if they are to avoid getting into trouble again. However, their employment prospects are poor, and many do not succeed.

Increasing incarceration rates are not the only widely touted explanation for declining crime. Beginning in the 1990s, American police leaders joined politicians in stepping forward to claim a share of the credit. Many cities hired more police. This was facilitated by the Crime Act of 1994, which set aside federal funds to support police salaries. Police chiefs also claimed credit because, they argued, they were policing "smarter." They were focusing their efforts on crime hot spots, using computer technology to identify crime trends, and adopting community policing programs that brought them more cooperation from the neighborhoods they served.

A claim which has been evaluated is that increasing the *size* of American police forces helped account for declining crime during the 1990s and 2000s. The total did rise. In 1991 there were about 355,000 full-time officers serving in municipal police departments. By 2000 (when the decline in crime stalled) the total was 426,000, a 20% increase. That figure continued to increase, and by 2007 stood at 447,000. Nationally, there was a push to increase the number of uniformed officers assigned to community policing through federal police-hiring grants to cities.

How much of a decrease in crime could we expect from this quite sizeable increase in the number of police officers in the United States? There is not a clear consensus on the point, but the most prominently recommended estimates are that about half of the percentage increase or decrease in the number of police is translated into shifts in crime. Levitt (2004) concluded that between 1991 and 2001 the increasing number of police reduced crime by 5–6% across the board. Presumably, much of the deterrent effect of policing is through the experience—or fear—of being caught and possibly spending some time behind bars. However, there are no consensus estimates of how arrests independently affect the crime rate. Discussions of Japan's traditionally low crime rate usually allude to the extraordinarily high solution rates claimed by Japanese police. Roberts and LaFree (2004) found that the percentage of crimes that police claimed to solve, which began to deteriorate in the late 1990s, was among the strongest predictors of Japanese crime trends at the national and sub-national levels. However, crime solution or arrest rates are infrequently used in U.S. research. They are not reported by the FBI on a city-by-city basis, in order to avoid embarrassing apparently less effective police departments, and research indicates that there are vast differences in how agencies define and count these performance measures.

Like research on the link between crime and prisons, estimates of the impact of policing on crime are confounded by the reciprocal impact of crime (which creates a demand for greater security) on the size of police forces. To untangle this causal knot, analysts need to identify factors that independently influence the number of police officers and are not influenced by crime. In his statistical models, Levitt (2004) used police hiring increases leading up to local elections as a factor that independently affected police strength. Klick and Tabarrok (2005) used an even more powerful and focused event, the unexpected redeployment of police officers around Washington, DC, due to terrorism alerts. Interestingly, while their data showed that upsurges in police strength reduced property crime, its effect on violent crime was apparently zero.

Did crime go down because police are policing more *intelligently*? The world of policing was in ferment throughout the 1990s, in both the United States and other nations. It was a time during which both new policing strategies and refinements of tried-and-true tactics promised to increase their effectiveness. One of these refinements is focused "hot spot policing." Using computerized crime mapping and data mining techniques, police began pouring resources into the relatively small number of places that in any city account for a disproportionate number of emergency calls and recorded crimes. They became increasingly sophisticated about the timing and management of crackdowns on street drug markets. Focused patrols and traffic stops aimed specifically at reducing gun carrying became more prominent. Targeted "quality of life policing," which calls for aggressive arrest policies to counter seemingly minor crimes such as public drinking, graffiti writing, and panhandling, was credited by some as a theory-driven approach to reducing more serious crime (Kelling and Coles, 1996). Identifying and taking action at locations that are the source of repeat calls for police assistance became routine. Research indicates that one factor that makes neighborhoods high crime places is that an unusually large number of individuals and households there are repeatedly victimized. Targeting aid to first-time victims has been shown to reduce the extent of follow-on victimization, and thus area crime levels. During the 1990s a relatively new strategy, problem solving policing, became more popular, especially projects linking police with health, safety, housing, and other service and regulatory agencies, for this provided them with new tools for addressing chronic concentrations of crime. In addition, neighborhood-oriented community policing strategies were adopted on a large scale. This initiative called for community engagement and organizational decentralization, in addition to adopting a broad problem solving orientation.

Finally, in countries around the world, policing strategies of all kinds are increasingly guided by sophisticated police information systems that help managers discover and respond more nimbly to opportunities to prevent crime. Information technology is widely employed in managerial accountability systems (such as New York City's famous "CompStat" process) that put new pressure on police leaders to perform effectively. Collectively, these strategic initiatives could be characterized as the "smarter policing" of the 1990s and 2000s. Many attribute the drop in crime to increasing police effectiveness during this era.

The problem for this discussion is that there have been few evaluations of how well smarter and community-oriented policing work as city-wide initiatives, or how they influence the overall crime rate. Most of the research has been on the impact of experimental police teams in a few selected neighborhoods. Hot-spot policing, for example, has been evaluated by comparing before-and-after levels of crime in neighborhoods where police cooperated by trying out the program, with trends in a set of matched comparison neighborhoods where they did nothing new. Many neighborhood-oriented interventions, such as opening a storefront office, distributing newsletters, cleaning up neighborhoods, or instituting high-visibility foot patrol, have likewise been evaluated by trying them out in special test areas. However, the impact of the ensemble of the projects that make up a full-blown city program have not often been assessed, nor has the ability of the police actually to implement them on a city-wide basis. Further, the community policing movement has many important goals in addition to crime reduction, including reestablishing the legitimacy of the police in poor and minority communities, incorporating new immigrant communities into the body politic, improving the quality and civility of service (broadly defined) rendered by officers, and fostering civic involvement by residents. This greatly increases the range of outcome measures against which it needs to be evaluated.

A difficulty in evaluating claims that the diffusion of smarter policing or community policing around the country helped account for declining crime is finding ways to measure the breadth and depth of these diverse new policing strategies over the pre- and post-1990 era. An evaluation of community policing in Chicago found evidence that the introduction of the program in test districts reduced crime and fear, increased confidence in the police, and mobilized large numbers of residents around crime prevention projects (Skogan and Hartnett, 1997). Broadly focused national or multi-city studies do not even attempt to do this because there are no convenient over-time data on the quality, as opposed to quantity, of policing. A recent review of research on policing finds evidence supporting the effectiveness of many of the focused policing efforts described above, but those conclusions are based on the findings of city-by-city neighborhood evaluations (Skogan and Frydl, 2004). National-level and multi-city studies of the drop in crime focuses on the *number* of police, but it is surely what police *do*, rather than how many are on the payroll, that has an impact on the street. While their numbers went up, there is no reason to think what police *did* remained static during the 1990s, and the effects of adopting new tactics and technologies may by confounded with that of their increasing numbers.

IV. Drugs, Guns, and Gangs

This section examines the impact of three highly interrelated features of crime in America: drugs, guns, and gangs. There is good reason to consider them jointly, for together they lie at the core of big-city crime problems. A common narrative explaining the decline in crime which began in the early 1990s hinges on the rise and subsequent waning of interest in crack cocaine in American cities. It is argued that a crack epidemic during the late 1980s fueled an expansion of street drug markets and a broadening of the recruitment base for dealers and their assistants. This in turn precipitated wars among gangs over control of these markets, with the subsequent widespread diffusion of guns for both offensive and defensive purposes. Young African-American men in big cities were particularly drawn into the drugs-gangs-guns nexus. Killings by them (and of them) accounted for much of the upsurge in city violence that characterized the late 1980s. Then, it is argued, the crack market changed. What supposedly happened remains vague: crack markets are variously described as "maturing," "stabilizing," "waning," "ebbing," "becoming less lucrative," and facing "diminished demand."[1] This market shift presumably accounted for the sharp drop in homicides which followed.

The guns-gangs-drugs narrative described above is one plausible view of what happened. However, national or even multi-city studies typically do not have much independent information on drugs at all. Observers' conclusions appear to draw on the drop in crime and the changing profile of homicide victims and offenders—which is what they are explaining—rather than on systematic information about real changes in drug markets. Changes in drug markets may also affect crime through their impact on individual consumers. Drug abuse certainly remains at high levels among those arrested for violent and property crimes. Research on temporary police crackdowns on drug markets indicates one of their effects is to increase the frequency of robberies and burglaries nearby, presumably because a sharply constricted supply leads to upward spikes in drug prices (Sherman, 1990). Long-term studies have also documented that expanding heroin use leads to higher robbery rates through its criminogenic effect on consumers.

A difficulty with assessing the waning crack market argument is that the character and extent of drug markets are difficult to measure. Many studies primarily work with data on drug arrests. This is an enforcement measure, reflecting where and how police conduct their investigations, but there is evidence that the geographical distribution of drug arrests broadly mirrors the distribution of drug markets. The major alternative to police arrest reports is data on emergency room treatments and drug-related deaths.

---

[1] This story has been in many places; see Blumstein (2000), or Fagan and Wilkinson (1998). For a data-driven version of the story, see Grogger and Willis (2000).

What is certain is that there has been a tremendous increase in the number of drug-related *arrests* over this period. In Chicago, between 1991 and 1998, the number of drug arrests rose from 21,450 to 58,500, a 173% increase. After stabilizing, the drug arrest total rose a bit more, exceeding 59,000 by 2004. This growing number of arrests was particularly startling in light of the declining number of apprehensions in many other categories, reflecting the drop in crime. In 1991, drugs accounted for 9% of all the non-traffic arrests made by Chicago police; by 2004 drug offenses accounted for 30% of non-traffic arrests in Chicago. An important reason Illinois' prison population remained stable in the face of steadily declining violent and property crime during the 1990s was this new source of inmates. Another feature of this shift in crime control was that virtually all of these new arrests in Chicago targeted African Americans, and by 2004 they made up 79% of drug arrestees. When multiplied by the racially disproportionate prosecution, sentencing, and incarceration that takes place further downstream in the criminal justice system, this shifting enforcement pattern helped make Illinois one of the most racially disproportionate prison systems in the United States.

Gun availability and use also play an independent role in increasing the severity—and perhaps the rate—of violent crime. Zimring and Hawkins (1999) noted that American levels of non-gun violence do not particularly stand out in international league tables. Rather, it is what they describe as "the thin layer of *lethal* violence" that differentiates the United States from many other nations. A number of nations rank above the United States in terms of homicide rates, but none are in the same economic or political category. Why American homicide rates are so high has been widely discussed, with explanations ranging from racial divisions to its "cowboy culture." However, it is obvious that the widespread diffusion of firearms, coupled with a readiness by too many to actually use them, is a factor that differentiates the U.S. from otherwise comparable nations. Guns intensify the consequences of violent encounters because they increase the likelihood of death. They may also increase the overall frequency of crime somewhat, because some crimes—high-payoff commercial, cargo, and bank robberies come first to mind—simply are not practical to carry out without a gun. However, the statistical evidence is that it is the severity of injury and risk of death, not the general frequency of offenses, that is driven by the availability of firearms (Cook and Ludwig, 2000). Increasing use of semiautomatic handguns was the most important component driving overall homicide rates in the late 1980s and early 1990s, because of their lethality.

Local level data on the extent of gun availability is difficult to assemble. However, there are direct measures of the readiness of individuals to *carry* guns, such as the number of guns seized by police. Firearms are seized under a variety of circumstances that empower police to make lawful searches. These circumstances range from traffic and pedestrian stops to arrests for committing other crimes, so seizures reflect what police find in the segment of the population that comes under suspicion. A second measure of gun carrying is arrests for weapons violations when individuals are found in possession of a gun but other more significant criminal charges such as robbery or assault cannot be laid against them. As a practical matter, rates of gun carrying are certainly a more significant factor than rates of ownership, given that a majority of shootings now take place in public spaces and involve people who have brought a weapon to the scene. Police officials point to this fact to justify aggressive use of pedestrian stops and vehicle searches, and when they do not find many guns despite these efforts, they see it as evidence that potential shooters have been convinced to leave their hardware at home.

Gangs are certainly another important cause of crime in the United States. Americans used to call them "youth gangs," but they changed in character. During the 1980s, massive adult joblessness among African Americans extended the age profile of active gang members, because burgeoning drug markets provided them with a new way to make a living. Since then, members returning from prison have begun to rely on their old gangs for employment in the trade (Coughlin and Venkatesh, 2003). One of the functions of gangs is to recruit new members and steer them into the organization's many criminal enterprises. Depending on the city, gangs are typically implicated in drugs, gambling, extortion, theft, gun smuggling, reselling valuable parts from stolen cars, financing gypsy cabs, and selling "protection" from rival gangs. Another role of gangs is to recruit replacements for members who have been arrested and incarcerated. This contributes to a sad spiral of increasing overall criminality as a consequence of law enforcement efforts to counter the drug trade. Third, they cause crime to the extent to which they foster inter-gang violence and occasionally intra-gang violence when they end up making war on fellow gang members (Decker et al., 1998).

Gang homicide is different from other kinds of killings. While the many social and economic factors discussed here may have played a role in bringing about steadily declining levels of non-gang crime, a significant fraction of crimes in the United States are rooted specifically in the organizational dynamics and business environment of violent street gangs. In this world, disputes over honor and status can easily have violent outcomes. One attack leads to another. Killings lead to retaliatory killings, and violence ripples through the community, ricocheting among organizations, and sometimes catching bystanders in the line of fire. Between gangs, violence is a tool for settling disputes over drug markets and control of other illicit enterprises. Within organizations, violence is exercised in order to impose discipline, collect street taxes, and maintain the standing of power-holders (as when former kingpins return from prison demanding their share). In Chicago, the decline in homicide during the 1990s was driven by non-gang killings. Gang killings rose and fell, following their different logic. But because non-gang homicide fell precipitously, by 2005, gang killings comprised more than double the proportion of homicides they had a decade and a half earlier.

V. COMMUNITY AND ENVIRONMENTAL FACTORS

A significant fraction of all criminological research focuses on the role of community factors in controlling crime. These factors range from the strength of informal bonds of trust among neighbors to organized crime prevention efforts by community groups. Communities struggle to control crime on several different levels. At the most private level lies the strength of family values and the ability of parents to socialize and control their children. Neighborhoods vary in how well their families do this. At another level lies shared norms and trust among neighbors, and a willingness in the community to intervene when things go wrong. Together, widespread trust and willingness to intervene make up what is known as "collective efficacy," a community factor strongly linked to levels of crime (Morenoff et al., 2001). High-crime communities suffer from disrupted networks of friendship, kinship, and acquaintanceship, and this limits their capacity for mutual informal coordination and cooperation. Informal "pro-social" interventions and effective sanctioning behaviors are much weaker in these areas. Structural disadvantages, such as concentrated poverty and residential turnover, hurt communities in particular at the private and informal levels of cooperation. At a more overtly political level lie the groups and organizations that constitute civil society. There is some evidence that a strong infrastructure of organizations can sustain a community's capacity for self-healing social action. Controlling for other things, where organizations are strong, community residents are seen as more likely to take action and intervene, and this can compensate somewhat for weak informal ties among neighbors (Sampson, 2004).

Many decades of research have demonstrated that community factors are powerful determinants of levels of crime. However, little is known about whether community factors wax or wane over time. There has also been little research that actually addresses whether *changes* in community factors—as opposed to comparisons among communities that *vary* in those factors—are linked to changes in levels of officially recorded crime. In the main, collective efficacy is strongest in stable, white home-owning neighborhoods, so it could depend in part on whether such areas are growing or declining in number in a particular city (Sampson et al., 1997). Research on community factors typically stresses their complex and multifaceted character, and much of this research relies on specially collected local data. None of the prominent studies of crime trends in the United States have taken any notice at all of community factors. This void is certainly due in large measure to the absence of any relevant national, over-time data. For example, there is vigorous debate just over whether organizational involvement by Americans has gone up or down (Putnam, 1993; Paxton, 1999). Similarly, discussions of crime in Japan routinely point to the strength of informal social control as one explanation for the extraordinarily low levels of crime there. However, none actually advanced any measures of variations in social control across Japan, nor pointed to systematic evidence on whether or not informal control weakened as recorded crime (except for homicide) skyrocketed post-1995. Community has not figured in studies of trends in crime because the large body of richly theoretical research on this topic does not yield one or two index numbers which can be included in statistical models testing their role relative to other potentially important determinants of crime trends.

Another neighborhood factor could be the aggregate impact of housing and economic revitalization programs underway in many cities. These can be measured by such indicators as the number of building permits issued for residential and business projects, and the number of conventional residential mortgages registered each year. Housing and commercial investments are doubly important because they are cumulative, adding up over time. Trends in these indicators highlight the fact that many cities are far from moribund, and that new investments are being made in their future. What is unclear is whether this evident vitality is a cause of declining crime, or if it is a consequence of the drop in crime. Perhaps one reason for this quickening economic activity during the 1990s and early 2000s was the new sense of safety and security evident in neighborhoods in most of America's larger cities. Some of the best research on the relationship between crime and real estate activity has been done in New York City. It suggests that the decline in crime in that city sparked a real estate boom during the 1990s, and that crime decline accounted for about one-third of New York City's rise in real estate prices after 1994 (Schwartz et al., 2003).

Efforts in the United States to restore or demolish high-rise family public housing also began in earnest, toward the end of the 1990s. The Federal HOPE VI program in particular promised to replace these units with a mixture of public, subsidized, and private-market low-rise housing. Of course, the residents of the original apartment blocks did not go away; demolition just redistributed them somewhat. The limited research on the topic suggests their lives have taken a turn for the better. Residents leaving family high-rise projects with housing vouchers, or even unassisted, have mainly succeeded in moving to safer and substantially better-off areas with better-performing schools, and in surveys they report dramatically lower levels of concern about neighborhood drug markets, shootings, and other criminal activity. Relocatees who managed to move into private-market housing did better than did those who moved but remained in public housing (Popkin and Cove, 2007). There is broad agreement that the concentration of poverty created by massive public housing developments had bad consequences which were independent of the characteristics of the families living there. Gangs, drugs, and guns were an everyday feature of the lives of many residents, and there were few places to hide (Popkin et al., 2000). Now many of those developments are gone. In Chicago, crime in and around the sites of former high-rise developments is in rapid retreat, and there has been significant new construction and appreciating house prices in the neighborhoods of all of the major projects that were demolished. To date, research has appropriately focused on the former residents and their fate in the housing and job markets. We await follow-up work on the impact of demolition and relocation programs on crime prevention and displacement.

Finally, there may be some scope for environmental factors in causing crime and its trend over time. Crime is certainly highly *correlated* with pollution, measured (for example) by city levels of particulate matter in the air. This has long been used as an illustration of spurious correlation, because high crime and polluted air are often found together in declining rust-belt cities where the many causes of crime reviewed here abound. However, there are specific environmental factors that are known to have causal links to biological functioning, and through that to crime.

In particular, concentrations of lead in the human body have harmful effects on children's impulsivity, judgment, cognitive function, learning, and disciplinary behavior. Research has shown that the more lead there is in children's blood at a young age, the more likely they are to be arrested as an adult. The key point here is that the American states began requiring dramatically lower levels of lead in gasoline in the 1970s. They did so at different times and required these reductions at different rates, enabling researchers to examine with some confidence the lagged relationship between changes in lead exposure levels and subsequent declines in crime rates. Reyes (2007) reports that the reduction in childhood lead exposure in the late 1970s and early 1980s due to this policy was responsible for significant declines in violent crime in the 1990s, and may cause further declines in the future.

VI. Lifestyle and Culture

Lifestyle theories of victimization take note of the fact that crime has relational and situational features. Rather than just focusing on the supply of offenders, in this view crime occurs when motivated offenders come into contact with suitable targets in the absence of "capable guardians." Target suitability is flagged by affluence and other features that make for attractive opportunities for crime. The finding by Field (1999) and others that burglary and theft in England and Wales was driven *upward* over time by increasing consumer affluence during the 1950–1970 period is interpreted in this light—that a noticeably growing stock of consumer goods meant there was more around to steal. Guardianship may be exercised by bystanders, shopkeepers, or other persons whose presence deters on-the-spot offending, and by physical barriers such as locked doors or hardened automobile ignition systems. Research has established clear relationships between the extent of victimization and a broad range of indicators of target suitability and guardianship. Further, there is evidence of fairly dramatic changes in many of these indicators, shifts that portend changes in crime patterns.

Some lifestyle indicators can be found in how people live and how they organize their households. The industrial world has witnessed declining family size, fewer family households, more people living alone, higher rates of divorce, and a declining popularity of marriage: all factors that expose people to an increased risk of victimization. People are more at risk of personal crime when they are out, and of victimization of their homes when no one is at home. Pursuing more work and leisure away from home, and taking more vacations, has the same impact. A very significant fraction of the total victimization of adult women in the labor force takes place at work, or on the journey to and from work. On the other hand, declining rates of marriage, replaced by increases in cohabitation, seem to lie behind the precipitous decline in spousal and intimate partner violence registered in the U.S. during the 1990s. Domestic homicides in particular declined at a tremendous rate during that period. Rosenfeld (2000) documents that declining marriage rates explained 40–65% of declining spousal homicide rates among high-risk groups. In reference to a trend of "declining domesticity," he speculates that the ease with which failing relationships can come apart predicts the likelihood of one of the parties ending up divorced rather than dead.

Another lifestyle indicator, and one offering an intriguing explanation for declining crime, is alcohol consumption. In the United States, drinking has been on a nationwide decline on a per capita basis at the same time that violent crime has subsided. Research on alcohol use and its effects is very strong. The pharmacology of the product is well understood by criminologists. Physical testing of both offenders and victims documents that alcohol is frequently associated with violence. There have been many experiments and quasi-experiments gauging the impact of changes in alcohol distribution, at levels of analysis ranging from individuals to entire nations. This research finds the availability and volume of alcohol consumed is related to levels and trends in crime at the block, neighborhood, city, county, state, and national level. When it becomes harder for young people to acquire alcohol, youth violence (as well as traffic fatalities) subsides. A key point is that overall alcohol consumption has also been declining. Nationally, Americans' per capita beer consumption peaked in about 1976, and has since stayed about level. Consumption of spirits has plummeted since 1968, while wine consumption per capita has been fairly level since the mid-1980s. Parker and Cartmill (1998) find a two-year time lag in the relationship between declining levels of alcohol consumption and declining homicide rates.

Cultural explanations are frequently advanced to explain the relatively (and extraordinarily) low rates of crime in Japan. Japan is described as a homogeneous, group-based, other-directed, hierarchical society with a high consensus around conservative values that are reinforced by shaming practices which exact a high, if informal, price for non-conformity (Leonardsen, 2006). However, these features of Japanese life have proven difficult to capture statistically. They have been measured variously by divorce rates, female labor force participation, population mobility, and labor disputes. These are obviously very indirect indicators of what are reputedly very powerful social factors, so indirect that Roberts and LaFree (2004) describe most of them as measures of social disorganization rather than culture. It is also not clear if culture is changing, or why any such changes might currently dampen homicide rates but not other, rapidly increasing levels of crime in Japan.

Elsewhere, national culture is rarely invoked as an explanation for trends in crime. In the 1970s and 1980s, cultural shifts were identified by conservative critics as a cause of spiraling crime in the United States. They linked crime to the hedonism, self-indulgence, heedless consumerism, reckless individualism, unbridled self-expression, and standardless relativism that they claimed increasingly characterized a disintegrating liberal culture. However, I have no reason to believe that any such trends reversed their course dramatically following 1990, driving crime in the opposite direction. In any event, the drop in crime in the United States during the 1990s took place over such a short period of time that it would seem difficult to tie it to some cultural shift, because important values are unlikely to change so rapidly. Experienced urban ethnographers have reported that "the younger generation" (a group that grew more expansive with each passing year that crime declined) looked at the violence of the late 1980s, then decided in large numbers to turn away from a "culture of death" (Johnson et al., 2000). However, cultural claims about trends in crime will be particularly difficult to assess systematically.

It has also been claimed that changes in policy beginning in the 1970s reduced the number of "unwanted" children in succeeding generations, a reduction that is measured by state-level abortion rates. Donohue and Levitt (2001) argued that the remainder would be less likely to offend due to their more considered upbringing. Because they were "wanted," fewer in number than they otherwise would be, and less likely to be born to high-risk mothers, Donohue and Levitt thought that post-abortion-era children would receive more attentive care and control. Tracking arrests over time, they reported finding suddenly decreasing offending rates among youth cohorts of the appropriate age, using pooled state-level data. Further, this decline coincided to some extent with the crime decline of the 1990s. However, the implications of research on this topic grew murky with the discovery of serious computational errors in the study. Some statistical critics think the claim was wrong (Foote and Goetz, 2008), but others have gotten results approximating those of the original study. I never thought their argument squared with data on the generation entering the high-risk age category in the early 1990s, for it was in worse social and economic shape than previous cohorts and showed precious little evidence of the presumed benefits of having been "wanted."

There is also a view afoot that trends in crime are driven by "tipping points," and that they somehow naturally come back down when they hit some threshold. This is a "what goes up must come down" theory of crime that is no theory at all in the absence of explanatory variables that predict the turnarounds. Without them it is just a description of what happened. A related claim is that declines in crime from their highs represent "regression" (Fagan et al., 1988) or "mean reversion" (Harcourt and Ludwig, 2007). Declines (and, I presume, increases) apparently are to be expected when cities or police precincts have unusually high (or low) crime rates, as they revert to levels that Fagan et al. characterize as "historically normal." This view is a misreading of the well-known "regression artifact" issue in measurement theory. Regression artifacts threaten when researchers deliberately select a subset of cases that stand out based on their extreme scores and those scores include a significant random error term. On an ensuing measurement, scores for those extreme cases should indeed revert toward the middle of the distribution from which they were selected, to the extent to which the measures were dominated by random error. Credible statistical studies of crime decline are not seriously threatened by any of those factors. Unemployment does not come down because it went up without any intervening processes, and neither should we expect crime to follow that pattern for some artifactual reason.

More promising "turning point" concepts are "diffusion" and "contagion." I argued above that crime is contagious in the context of American gang violence. That is a world in which bands of young men are ensnared in networks of power, status, and business relationships which propel them into episodes of tit-for-tat violence of the worst kind. Arms races followed by wars that later subside due to the exhaustion of the combatants could look like tipping points, except they tip upward again when everyone recovers. A key point is that ups and downs in gang-related contagious violence have been largely unrelated to the general, unpunctuated decline in non-gang crime, which continued apace on a much more massive scale throughout the period considered here. Outside of the insular world of street gangs, the idea that marshaling the bravado to commit crimes can be affected by the perception that "everyone is doing it," and that there may be some "safety in numbers" when a lot of people are doing it, points toward a "critical mass" theory of crime causation. There is some evidence that crime diffuses like fads and fashions, fanning outward from big cities to the hinterlands. Police and journalists frequently refer to "copycatting," another process by which social contagion may increase the overall crime rate. But while all of this may be promising, there has been no clear explication of the factors that *dampen* group-think or discourage copycatting and bring offending down, but that was the predominant trend during the 1990s.

VII. CRIME REPORTING AND RECORDING

Perhaps increases or decreases in officially recorded crime reflect shifts in the willingness of victims to call the police, or variations in enthusiasm on the part of police to make an official record of crime reports that come their way. This could produce apparent shifts in the crime rate, not real ones. For example, there is speculation that negligence complaints against the Japanese police beginning in the late 1990s led them to record more completely reports of crimes that the public brought to police stations (which is how crime is reported in Japan), and that this increased attentiveness, plus more aggressive media coverage of crime encouraged more victims to step forward (Leonardsen, 2006). Likewise, in 1992 and 2002, changes were made to British crime recording practices which were intended to increase the fidelity with which public complaints—especially concerning common assault—were registered by police. However, in both cases it is clear from Figure 1 that robbery was increasing in both nations in advance of these shifts in record keeping, so they could be only part of the overall picture.

At least for the United States, recent evidence about trends in victim reporting of crime is to the contrary. The best over-time data is from the U.S. National Crime Victimization Survey, which interviews thousands of individuals each month. In the survey, victims are asked if their experiences came to the attention of the police. The NCVS finds that reporting of crime to the police actually went *up* during the 1990s, not down, as recorded crime dropped. Reporting of violent crimes rose by 6% during the period (Hart and Rennison, 2003). This put *upward* pressure on the official crime rate, leading it to perhaps understate the extent of crime decline. Likewise, there is speculation that community policing increases victim reporting, as public confidence in the police grows. However, little is known about the impact of changes in policing styles on crime reporting. A little research in the United States and abroad does suggest that effective neighborhood-oriented policing may encourage somewhat more crime reporting.

It is certainly plausible that immigrant communities may be particular reservoirs of unreported crime, and immigrant numbers are growing. When they are victimized, it is widely assumed that immigrants are less likely than others to report their experiences to the police. Refugees from many countries leave in part *because* of endemic corruption, violence, abuse, and incompetence among the police, whom they do not view as their friend. They may fear deportation if they are undocumented, and they may fear exposing family members and other undocumented people in their social network, even if they themselves are not. The problem is that police need the trust and cooperation of the community in order to respond effectively to crime. They rely on the willingness of victims and bystanders to cooperate with their investigations. To gain this cooperation, police need to remain in close and trusted contact with residents, and in many cities community policing units have taken on this responsibility (Skogan, 2009).

But there are counter trends. One is the new demands that are being placed on the police to become involved in enforcing immigration laws in the same communities where they are struggling to build trust in the immigrant community. Before 2002, it was a long-standing policy of the U.S. Department of Justice that local police should not be involved in enforcing immigration laws. State and local police were not empowered to arrest and detain violators; this was seen as the special responsibility of the (then) Immigration and Naturalization Service. Then, the Bush administration issued a memorandum announcing that local law enforcement officials have "inherent" authority to make arrests for civil immigration violations. They adopted a series of strategies aimed at expanding the role of local police in immigration enforcement (Skogan, 2009). In a study of Chicago, I found a dramatic difference in the rate at which English- and Spanish-speaking Latinos initiated encounters with the police and reported problems and concerns to them. Language and immigration factors played a very large role in shaping the relationship between the city's newcomers and institutions of government (Skogan, 2006). This also implies that official rates of crime—which depend upon ordinary citizens contacting the police to make official reports—may not adequately reflect the problems facing those living in heavily immigrant areas.

Police under-recording of the incidents reported to them may artifactually influence the crime rate as well. This has often been observed in individual American cities. For example, during the mid-1980s, Chicago police were "killing crime" by failing to write up official reports of huge numbers of offenses. An apparent run-up in crime in Chicago at the end of the 1980s was certainly due in substantial part to improvements in recording wrought by internal crime recording audits, which were instituted after the media became aware that detectives were cheating on their statistics. The breadth of this scandal makes it impossible to do meaningful statistical analyses of crime trends in Chicago that include the 1980s (Skogan, 2006). However, in my experience, outbreaks of recording malpractice are localized and scattered, and have become less common in recent decades. It is more likely that computerization, crime mapping, data-driven resource allocation, and the imposition of CompStat-like management accountability systems in police departments around the United States and elsewhere have *improved* the quality of crime data instead.

VIII. CONCLUSIONS

This Chapter has presented an item-by-item list of factors linked to macro-social trends in crime. However, the research on which it is based is multivariate, controlling for multiple factors in order to isolate the effects of particular variables of interest, and the list of significant coefficients is typically quite long. In my judgment, it is likely that the roots of the American drop in crime similarly lie in a *mix* of the factors described here, not just one, and this is likely true for significant, long-term shifts in rates of crime in any nation. Some or all of these social and economic trends and policies may be working in concert to reduce crime, each contributing to the end result.

A few of the factors discussed here could have pushed U.S. crime rates down through the entire period. Immigration proceeded at a (modern) record pace, and we have seen that this has paradoxically positive consequences for crime rates. Alcohol consumption dropped steadily as well, and that has long been known to be a feature of violence. The American economy was bad at the beginning of the drop, but improved a great deal later in the 1990s, including at the bottom end of the labor market. On the other hand, women became more criminally active. The proportion of young people in the population began to increase late in the 1990s, and the echo boom foretold increasing numbers of young men in the U.S. population from 1997 until about 2012. Causes may also simply run out of steam and no longer contribute to crime decline—witness the diminished effectiveness of incarceration as it reaches high levels relative to the pool of serious offenders.

Different kinds of crime can be sensitive to different factors. Property crime appears to be somewhat more "rational" than violence, in that it responds more directly to shifts in policing and incarceration. Upward and downward spirals of gang violence seem to occur in response to quite different forces than other kinds of violent crime, reflecting more the logic of arms races than social and economic trends. Interestingly, as gang killings have become a large percentage of the total homicide count in many places in the U.S., increasingly it is gang dynamics that drive the total. This disconnects overall homicide rates from the forces that previously drove them and the statistical models that apply to other types of crime. Likewise, over time, non-gun assault in the United States has dropped relative to gun violence, as domestic violence, fights in bars, and other kinds of relational and recreational violence subsided much more rapidly. As a result, in cities, aggravated assault figures increasingly measure shots that missed and are really indicators of poor marksmanship. In my own work I find that combining homicides (mostly shots that found their target) and gun assaults (a result of bad shooting) produces a "shootings" measure that is more robust than either component taken alone.

In this multi-causal view there is also room for programs and policies, as well as for demographics and economics. There is strong evidence that focused strategies like hot spot policing are effective, and surveys document that increasing proportions of police departments employ them. However, over time and aggregated or across-city measures of these developments have yet to be incorporated into influential models of crime rate trends. To argue that "the drop in crime began before they were introduced" is to reject the potential significance of programmatic innovations on an overly mono-causal basis. The crime drop of the 1990s in the United States continued to hold steady in the 2000s, and over an 18-year span it seems likely that combinations and reinforcing mixes of changing factors must have been at work.

I think the categories of factors considered here could describe research on crime trends in many nations. However, the specific indicators of (for example) the strength of communities would certainly vary with context. Demographic factors associated with crime will vary. For instance, what groups are socially and economically marginalized, and the nature of their condition, varies considerably from nation to nation. Lifestyle explanations of victimization point to factors such as housing patterns, family structure, and the role of women in the economy that can vary widely even among developed nations, creating an opportunity for comparative research on crime trends. Criminals also vary in their "modus operandi": gangs in the United States play an increasing role in determining the homicide trend, but Japan's gangs seem more focused on business affairs and play a much smaller role in large-scale trends in homicide. The importance of seemingly comparable causal factors could vary as well. For instance, it seems likely that crime will vary less with shifts in macro-economic conditions in societies with strong solidarity norms and social welfare policies that provide a true "safety net."

The discussion here did *not*, on the other hand, encompass the effects of ruptures in the social order, which are rare in industrial democracies. For example, it was feared that the joining of the two Germanys in 1990 might push the social order of the East to a precipice over which it could tumble, as existing economic, social, and lifestyle patterns were threatened with discontinuous change. It does not seem to have worked out that way. Germany's crime statistics have included the East since 1993, and since then there has been a very steady downturn in well-reported crimes such as auto theft, burglary, gun crimes, and homicide (Bundeskriminalamt, 2007). The physical destruction and administrative collapse of the city of New Orleans in the face of a 2005 hurricane presents another example of a rupture in the social order, the criminogenic effects of which have not yet been sorted out.

A limitation of this presentation is that it has neglected the contributions of survey studies of criminal victimization. All of the countries depicted in Figure 1, and a long list of others, have conducted victimization surveys, and they yield somewhat different pictures of crime. Survey data encourages victim-centric explanations of crime, including the impact of their lifestyles and routine activities, but add additional methodological problems that are not considered here at all. Except for the American crime survey, none have been frequent enough at this point to support the kind of time-series oriented, macro-social research reviewed here. This research model is fairly demanding in terms of its data requirements, requiring many decades of regularly spaced and uniformly gathered information.

Of the factors considered in this Chapter, data gathering is needed most in the community domain. Many decades of criminological research have established the importance of community factors in controlling crime. Strong families, deep informal bonds among neighbors, and a willingness of residents to intervene to maintain order are linked to lower levels of crime. Even in the face of concentrated poverty and residential turnover, there is some evidence that a strong infrastructure of organizations can help sustain a community's capacity for self-healing as well. But little is known about whether these factors strengthened or weakened during the 1990s and 2000s, nor how they might have been affected by community policing programs that emerged across the country. There is an absence of evidence concerning their role in explaining declining levels of crime, due in large measure to the absence of systematic, over-time data on community factors.

REFERENCES

Blumstein, A. (2000). "Disaggregating the Violence Trends," in A. Blumstein and J. Wallman (eds.), *The Crime Drop in America*, New York: Cambridge University Press.

Bundeskriminalamt (2007). *Police Crime Statistics 2006*, Wiesbaden: Bundeskriminalamt.

Clear, T., Rose, D., and Ryder, J. (2001). "Incarceration and the Community: The Problem of Removing and Returning Offenders," *Crime and Delinquency* 47: 335–51.

Cook, P. and Ludwig, J. (2000). *Gun Violence: The Real Costs*, New York: Oxford University Press.

Coughlin, B. and Venkatesh, S. (2003). "The Urban Street Gang After 1970," *Annual Review of Sociology* 29: 41–64.

Decker, S.H., Bynum, T., and Weisel, D. (1998). "A Tale of Two Cities: Gangs as Organized Crime Groups," *Justice Quarterly* 15: 395–425.

Donohue, J.J. and Siegelman, P. (1998). "Allocating Resources Among Prisons and Social Programs in the Battle Against Crime," *Journal of Legal Studies* 27: 1–43.

Donohue, J.J. and Levitt, S. (2001). "The Impact of Legalized Abortion on Crime," *Quarterly Journal of Economics* 66: 379–420.

Fagan, J., Zimring, F.E., and Kim, J. (1988). "Declining Homicide in New York City: A Tale of Two Trends," *Journal of Criminal Law and Criminology* 88: 1277–1324.

Fagan, J. and Wilkinson, D. (1998). "Guns, Youth Violence, and Social Identity in Inner Cities," in M. Tonry (ed.), *Crime and Justice: A Review of Research*, 24.

Field, S. (1999). *Crime Trends Revisited*, Home Office Research Study 195, London: Home Office.

Foote, C.L. and Goetz, C.F. (2008). "The Impact of Legalized Abortion on Crime: Comment," *Quarterly Journal of Economics* 123: 407–23.

Gould, E., Weinberg, A., and Mustard, D. (2002). "Crime Rates and Local Labor Market Opportunities in the United States: 1979–1997," *Review of Economics and Statistics* 84: 45–61.

Grogger, J. (1998). "Market Wages and Youth Crime," *Journal of Labor Economics* 16: 756–91.

Grogger, J. and Willis, M. (2000). "The Emergence of Crack Cocaine and the Rise in Urban Crime Rates," *Review of Economics and Statistics* 82: 519–29.

Harcourt, B.E. and Ludwig, J. (2007). "Reefer Madness: Broken Windows Policing and Misdemeanor Marijuana Arrests in New York City, 1989–2000," *Criminology and Public Policy* 6: 165–82.

Hart, T.C. and Rennison, C. (2003). *Reporting Crime to the Police, 1992–2000*, Washington, DC: Bureau of Justice Statistics.

Heimer, K. and Lauritsen, J.L. (2008). "Gender and Violence in the United States: Trends in Offending and Victimization," in National Research Council (ed.), *Understanding Crime Trends: Workshop Report*, Washington, DC: National Research Council.

Johnson, B., Golub, A., and Dunlap, E. (2000). "The Rise and Decline of Hard Drugs, Drug Markets, and Violence in Inner-city New York," in A. Blumstein and J. Wallman (eds.), *The Crime Drop in America*, New York: Cambridge University Press.

Kelling, G.L. and Coles, C.M. (1996). *Fixing Broken Windows*, New York: Touchstone.

Klick, J. and Tabarrok, A. (2005). "Using Terror Alerts to Estimate the Effect of Police on Crime," *Journal of Law and Economics* 42: 93–122.

Kubrin, C. and Stewart, E. (2006). "Predicting Who Re-offends: The Neglected Role of Neighborhood Context in Recidivism Studies," *Criminology* 44: 165–97.

Lee, M.T. and Martinez, R. (2009). "Immigration Reduces Crime: An Emerging Scholarly Consensus," in W. McDonald (ed.), *Sociology of Crime, Law and Deviance*, vol.16, New York: Emerald Publishing Company.

Leonardsen, D. (2006). "Crime in Japan: Paradise Lost?," *Journal of Scandinavian Studies in Criminology and Crime Prevention* 7: 185–210.

Levitt, S.D. (1996). "The Effect of Prison Population Size on Crime Rates: Evidence from Prison Overcrowding Litigation," *Quarterly Journal of Economics* 111: 319–51.

Levitt, S.D. (2002). "Using Electoral Cycles in Police Hiring to Estimate the Effects of Police on Crime: Reply," *American Economic Review* 92: 1244–50.

Levitt, S.D. (2004). "Understanding Why Crime Fell in the 1990s: Four Factors that Explain the Decline and Six That Do Not," *Journal of Economic Perspectives* 18: 163–90.

Liedka, R.V., Piehl, A.M., and Useem, B. (2006). "The Crime-Control Effects of Incarceration: Does Scale Matter?," *Criminology & Public Policy* 5: 245–76.

Morenoff , J., Sampson, R.J. and Raudenbush, S. (2001). "Neighborhood Inequality, Collective Efficacy, and the Spatial dynamics of Urban Violence," *Criminology* 40: 213–30.

Parker, R. and Cartmill, R. (1998). "Alcohol and Homicide in the United States 1934–1995—Or One Reason Why U.S. Rates of Violence May Be Going Down," *Journal of Criminal Law and Criminology* 88: 1369–98.

Passel, J. (2006). *The Size and Characteristics of the Unauthorized Migrant Population in the United States*, Washington, DC: Pew Hispanic Center.

Paxton, P. (1999). "Is Social Capital Declining in the United States? A Multiple Indicator Assessment," *American Journal of Sociology* 105: 88–127.

Popkin, S.J. and Cove, E. (2007). *Safety Is the Most Important Thing: How HOPE VI Helped Families*, Washington, DC: Urban Institute.

Popkin, S.J., Gwiasda, V.E., Buron, L., Olson, L.M., and Rosenbaum, D.P. (2000). *The Hidden War: Crime and the Tragedy of Public Housing in Chicago*, New Brunswick, NJ: Rutgers University Press.

Putnam, R.D. (1993). "The Prosperous Community: Social Capital and Community Life," *The American Prospect* 13: 35–42.

Reyes, J.A.W. (2007). "Environmental Policy as Social Policy? The Impact of Childhood Lead Exposure on Crime," *Berkeley Electronic Journal of Economic Analysis & Policy* 7: Article 51, available at <http://www.bepress.com/bejeap/vol7/iss1/art51>.

Roberts, A. and LaFree, G. (2004). "Explaining Japan's Postwar Violent Crime Trends," *Criminology* 42: 179–209.

Rosenfeld, R. (2000). "Patterns in Adult Homicide: 1980–1995," in A. Blumstein and J. Wallman (eds.), *The Crime Drop in America*, New York: Cambridge University Press.

Rosenfeld, R. and Fornango, R. (2008). "The Impact of Economic Conditions on Robbery and Property Crime: The Role of Consumer Sentiment," *Criminology*, 45: 735–69.

Sampson, R.J. (2004). "Neighbourhood and Community," *New Economy* 11: 106–13.

Sampson, R.J., Morenoff, J. D., and Raudenbush, S. (2005). "Social Anatomy of Racial and Ethnic Disparities in Violence," *American Journal of Public Health* 95: 224–32.

Sampson, R.J., Raudenbush, S.W., and Earls, F. (1997). "Neighborhoods and Violent Crime: A Multilevel Study of Collective Efficacy," *Science* 277: 918–24.

Schwartz, A., Susin, S., and Voicu, I. (2003). "Has Falling Crime Driven New York City's Real Estate Boom?," *Journal of Housing Research* 14: 101–35.

Sherman, L. (1990). "Police Crackdowns: Initial and Residual Deterrence," in M.H. Tonry and N. Morris (eds.), *Crime and Justice: A Review of Research*, 12, Chicago: University of Chicago Press.

Skogan, W.G. (2006). *Police and Community in Chicago: A Tale of Three Cities*, New York: Oxford University Press.

Skogan, W.G. (2009). "Policing Immigrant Communities," in W.F. McDonald (ed.), *Immigration, Crime and Justice,* London: Emerald Publishing.

Skogan, W. G. and Frydl, K. (eds.) (2004). *Fairness and Effectiveness in Policing*, Washington, DC: National Academies Press.

Skogan, W.G. and Hartnett, S.M. (1997). *Community Policing, Chicago Style*, New York: Oxford University Press.

Spelman, W. (2000). "The Limited Importance of Prison Expansion," in A. Blumstein and J. Wallman (eds.), *The Crime Drop in America*, New York: Cambridge University Press.

Zimring, F.E. and Hawkins, G. (1999). *Crime Is Not the Problem: Lethal Violence in America*, New York: Oxford University Press.

3

CRIMINAL PROCESS AND PROSECUTION

JACQUELINE HODGSON AND ANDREW ROBERTS

OVER the last few decades, legislative regimes regulating police and prosecutorial power have altered, prosecution priorities have changed, and the empirical research data available vary considerably across time and jurisdiction. However, a constant feature of the pre-trial criminal process in most countries is the exercise of discretion by police and prosecutors. How much discretion does the law allow? How is this controlled? Which factors influence the exercise of discretion, from "cop culture" to the politics of prosecution? Another feature across criminal justice is a general move away from courtroom disposition of cases, with a corresponding expansion in the role of the prosecutor, whether as a result of: the transfer of investigative power away from the investigating judge to the prosecutor in many European jurisdictions such as France and the Netherlands; conferral of new powers to charge and initiate alternative penalties in the UK; or the mandatory sentencing requirements in the U.S. that make the prosecutor effectively the sentencer. The powers of police, too, have increased, the liberty-versus-security rhetoric gaining momentum after the terrorist attacks in New York, London, and Madrid.

The criminal justice agenda has moved rapidly, and researchers are still playing catch-up. In England and Wales, major empirical studies have often followed a period of upheaval or reflection. For example, following the Report of the Royal Commission on Criminal Procedure in 1981 (established after police malpractice was revealed in the conduct of the investigation into the death of Maxwell Confait), two key statutes, the Police and Criminal Evidence Act 1984 (PACE) and the Prosecution of Offences Act 1985, were enacted, representing a major shift in the regulation of police powers and suspects' rights and establishing an independent Crown Prosecution Service (CPS). Researchers were quick to explore the nature and effectiveness of these new arrangements through major empirical studies examining the work of, and relationships among, police, prosecutors, and defense lawyers. In 1991, after a series of miscarriages of justice resulting from police and prosecution malpractice that shocked the public and undermined confidence in the criminal justice process, the Royal Commission on Criminal Justice (RCCJ) was established, reporting in 1993. This again provided a new opportunity for high quality research on key areas of the criminal process, funded by the Commission. The last ten years, however, have seen relatively little empirical work in the UK on criminal justice.

In the United States too, the 1960s through the 1980s saw the publication of important accounts of criminal justice practice, including ethnographic studies of policing and prosecution, and while these continue to serve as reference points for smaller projects, major contemporary studies are lacking. In much of continental Europe, socio-legal studies are a relatively new phenomenon, and critical empirical research is rare, even in the face of major crises or policy shifts. For example, in France, the "Outreau affair" concerned a suspected pedophile ring operating in the town of Outreau. After the case against most of the defendants collapsed in 2004, a Parliamentary inquiry into the investigation was established—the first time that such a step had been taken in France. Reporting in 2005, this produced interesting practitioner testimony that illuminated aspects of criminal justice practice, but crucially, no empirical research was commissioned or carried out. The Commissions, chaired by Mireille Delmas-Marty (1991), Pierre Truche (1997), and Philippe Léger (2009), made wide-ranging recommendations for restructuring aspects of the French criminal justice process, but these were based on the Commissions' own inquiries rather than any independently conducted empirical work. With the exception of organizations such as CESDIP (*Centre de Recherches Sociologiques sur le Droit et les Institutions Pénales*) and researchers based at the Max Planck Institute in Freiburg, there is no real culture of qualitative empirical legal research across most of continental Europe.

I. THE COMPLEX AND REFLEXIVE ENVIRONMENT OF DECISION-MAKING IN THE CRIMINAL PROCESS

The idea of a criminal justice *system* conjures up an image of "officials and institutions linked together for the pursuit of clear, harmonious, and common purposes" (Galligan, 1987). The reality, suggests Galligan, is a number of related processes in which decision-makers generally act independently and in ignorance of the actions of one another. The decisions made by officials will be influenced not only by abstract notions of crime control and the desire to ensure that the guilty are convicted and punished, but also by a range of structural, organizational, moral, and political factors. Hawkins (2003) has argued that if empirical research is to provide us with a satisfactory understanding of official decision-making in the criminal process, its focus ought to be broad. It should be concerned not only with "criteria" or "factors" that are immediately related to the particular decision, but with mapping the contours of the broader environment in which those decision-making processes are embedded. He suggests that decision-making processes have various dimensions and that we can make sense of their complexities by conceptualizing them in terms of *surround*, *field*, and *frame*.

The *surround* describes the social, political, and economic environment that provides the broad context for all forms of institutional and individual decisions relating to the criminal process. Public concern over various forms of antisocial behavior, the threat of terrorism, and perceptions as to the section of the community to which those likely to pose the threat will belong, and the publication of crime statistics, their reporting in the media, and their political implications are likely to have a pervasive influence on decision-making at all levels. The term *field* describes a narrower legal decision-making environment that is defined by political conceptions of the ends that are served by the law, by legal regulations designed to secure those ends, and by political perceptions of how those provisions ought to be used in order to further this objective. The idea of a *frame* provides a means of conceptualizing subjective aspects of decision-making. It describes the interpretative behavior of individual decision-makers faced with specific decisions and the means through which actors make sense of the matters with which they are expected to deal. Decision-making at this level proceeds through a process of categorization based on past experience and resorts to socially and institutionally conditioned stereotypes and to the use of informal working rules. The frame is determined, in part, by the decision-maker's own perception of the ends that are served by the decision-making process, and whether the legal standards that regulate that process are the most effective means of securing those ends.

Decision-making in the criminal process is the product of a complex and reflexive relationship between the broad socio-political landscape, the particular legal field, and the way in which decision-makers frame the circumstances that call for a decision to be made. For example, the factors that influence the prosecutor's exercise of her discretion range from the evidential strength of the case, local prosecution policies, personal relationships with lawyers and judges, changing legislative frameworks at state and federal level, and the career aspirations of the individual prosecutor.

The use of stop and search powers provides a good example of the complexities of these relationships. Among the values that ought to influence the content and form of criminal procedure in liberal democracies are respect for individual autonomy and equality of treatment. In the context of coercive and intrusive police powers, these have traditionally been manifested in a requirement that such powers be exercised on the basis of reasonable suspicion. However, reasonable suspicion is an inherently vague concept, and McConville et al. (1991) found that in the absence of a clear definition, police officers resort to informal working rules. Quinton and his colleagues (2000) found considerable variation in the level of suspicion that individual officers considered necessary before powers of stop and search could be used. Cases were found in which the grounds for searching suspects that were recorded by some police officers did not appear to reach the threshold of "reasonable suspicion," and overall, less than one third of police encounters were recorded.

Alongside a lack of clear legal grounds justifying stops on the street there appears to be a popular and enduring view that stop and search powers are used disproportionately against ethnic minorities, and official statistics year-on-year tend to support this. In England and Wales, black people are eight times more likely, and Asian people are two and a half times more likely, than whites to be stopped (Ministry of Justice, 2009: 28). Research (MVA and Miller, 2000) suggests that while ethnic minorities may not have been stopped disproportionately relative to the available population, the police did tend to target stopping activity in areas where ethnic minorities made up a large proportion of the available population. It was unclear whether the selection of these areas reflected local crime problems, or whether the police simply targeted "black areas" for stop and search. In the first study of its kind in France, researchers compared the race, sex, and appearance of those stopped in several busy areas of Paris, with the available population in the time-frame during which the person was stopped. Over 500 stops were observed at five locations at which there was a heavy police presence. The researchers (Jobard and Lévy, 2009) found that black people were overall six times more likely to be stopped than whites, and that those of North African appearance were 7.6 times more likely to be stopped than whites. A person's appearance was also a key variable. Although people wearing clothing typically associated with youth culture made up only 10% of the available population observed (and two thirds of these also belonged to ethnic minorities), these people constituted 47% of those stopped.

The influence of public perceptions of police racism on the exercise of these powers remains largely unexplored, although there does appear to be some correlation. In the year following publication of the Macpherson Report, which investigated the racially motivated murder in London of the black teenager Steven Lawrence, official figures suggested a dramatic decline in the use of stop and search powers against those from ethnic minority populations. In London the number of those searched who were from black and Asian communities declined by 35% and 42% respectively. It has been suggested that this can be attributed to greater circumspection on the part of the police in light of the findings of the Macpherson Report. Research conducted by Bland et al. (2000) touched briefly upon this issue, some police officers citing the "political climate" following publication of the Report as a factor affecting police decisions to stop and search those from ethnic minorities. Foster et al.'s large-scale study found that officers were more aware of the need for something "tangible" to justify a stop, rather than simply going on "fishing trips"; and where stops of ethnic minority people were made, the police felt under increased scrutiny to ensure that procedures were followed correctly. This highlights a wider issue: it seems that "the Inquiry brought into focus officers' uncertainty and confusion about the legitimate use of their powers" (Foster et al., 2005: 29–30). However, this effect upon police behavior has not lasted, and stops and searches of ethnic minority people are higher than ever. More sustained empirical analysis of this issue might have provided valuable insights into the complex nature of the environment in which decision-making occurs in the criminal justice system. Rarely will the apparent effect of changes in the broad socio-political environment on the practices of officials be so visible, and in view of this, there is a surprising paucity of longer-term research (which is also notably independent, i.e., not funded by the Home Office) exploring the influence of the Macpherson Report on police practice.

There are examples of research that acknowledge and explore the institutional and social influences on particular decision-making processes more generally, such as the study of police and prosecutorial decision-making in England and Wales conducted by McConville et al. (1991). Like many others, they acknowledged that positivist approaches to empirical research in the criminal justice system, in which legal standards are used as the criteria for evaluating the behavior of officials, will not lead to an adequate understanding of how decisions are made. The study illustrates that the manner in which the matters calling for a decision are framed can give rise to competing versions of "reality" within official decision-making. In the process of creating the "official reality," both the facts and the legal rules seem to be malleable. The prosecution's case does not consist of evidence "uncovered" during an objective inquiry into the truth of the matters being investigated. Rather, it is created by the way in which the police construe the alleged wrongdoing. The categorization of criminal conduct and the manner in which it is dealt with are contingent on wider considerations that are not evident in official records of the events. It was found generally that procedural rules and standards did not appear to be a significant consideration for most police officers when exercising their powers. This finding supports that of earlier studies, such as the research into police practice in London conducted by Smith and Gray, which found that "there may be sharp conflict between 'doing the job well'—that is, achieving objectives that are widely recognised inside and outside the [police] Force as being desirable—and sticking rigidly to the rules" (Smith and Gray, 1983: 170). It appears that although police officers may acknowledge legal rules, they are not always internalized and consequently do not guide police decision-making.

Hodgson's (2005) study of criminal investigation and prosecution in France demonstrates the ways in which legal concepts are widely subordinated to occupational cultures and individual interpretation, as well as practical considerations such as resources. The French code of criminal procedure presents a model in which prosecutors supervise criminal investigations through visits to the police station: by having suspects brought before them before extending the detention period and, if necessary, by conducting parts of the investigation in person. In practice, such an interventionist and surveillance-type model is never contemplated. While supervision exists in a minimalist sense, the prosecutor's dependence upon the police to conduct the investigations for which she is legally responsible means that such an approach would be counterproductive; trust is the key element, the glue that holds the relationship together and enables it to function. Police and prosecutor work as a team and come to share many of the same crime-control, conviction-oriented values; in most instances, the "truth" (the discovery of which justifies many coercive powers) was understood to be a confession. More comprehensive supervision was undertaken in cases likely to attract media attention or that would pass for further investigation to the investigating judge. Understanding the wider institutional functioning of supervision is an important part of understanding the choices made by the prosecutor, as well as the ways in which she comes to view her own role. In practice, prosecutorial supervision aspires to no more than ensuring the baseline legality of the process in which a properly conducted detention is understood to be one that *documents* procedural compliance. The prosecutor is unable and unwilling to extend her supervision into the *process* by which suspects are interrogated and evidence obtained.

McConville and colleagues found that compliance with legal rules was likely where there was a perception that any breach would lead to adverse consequences, e.g., formal disciplinary proceedings or other forms of censure by senior officers. The influence of the prospect of disciplinary proceedings (or in the case of the French prosecutor, media scrutiny) as a factor that might influence decision-making illustrates Hawkins' observation that decision-making surrounds, fields, and frames are not fixed over time, immutable, and independent of one another. Rather, they are shifting, contingent, and interrelated. Developments in the broad surrounding environment may lead to significant changes in the decision field: government guidance, legislative reform, etc. This may, in turn, lead to changes in the way that individual decision-makers perceive the environment in which they operate. A lack of public confidence in the institutional arrangements for dealing with complaints against police officers in England and Wales (Maguire and Corbett, 1990) led, in 2002, to the creation of an Independent Police Complaints Commission (IPCC). Its independence lies, partly, in its capacity to conduct investigations using its own investigators who are invested with various powers. Although the creation of the Commission constitutes a significant change in the field, the absence of relevant empirical research means that the extent of its influence on police culture and decision-making is unknown. Such changes in the broader context mean that the relevance and value of our stock of empirical knowledge relating to decision-making in the criminal process will diminish over time. The empirical research agenda needs to be sensitive and responsive to shifts in the broad social, legislative, and political environment, whether these are sudden and significant (as with responses to 9/11), or protracted and incremental (as with the continuing drive for improved case efficiency).

II. Broad Trends in Criminal Justice

In this section we will consider the pervasive influence of two broad issues—*efficiency* and *security*—on decision-making in criminal justice systems across various jurisdictions. While changes in the surround, and their effect on the fields in which decision-making occurs, can be readily identified, we suggest that the question of how these broad issues shape the way in which actors frame their decisions remains largely unexplored.

A. Efficiency

Efficiency is a rather nebulous concept. At a high level of generality, it forms part of the surround and will shape views on the appropriate form of the institutions of a criminal justice system. In Italy, for example, the requirement of the new accusatorial procedure that all evidence be presented at trial for verification was seen as very much less efficient than the earlier inquisitorial model which "solves the issue of guilt with a single investigative effort" (Illuminati, 2005: 578). However, Packer's Crime Control model of criminal justice remains a good starting point for considering what it means in the context of the operation of those institutions. Packer (1968) identified two abstract models of the criminal process distinguished by the way in which political objectives are prioritized. While avoiding miscarriages of justice and adherence to fundamental rights are central objectives of a due process model of criminal justice, repression of crime is the overriding concern of a crime control model. Instrumental to the repression of crime is a high conviction rate, which is achieved through efficiency and the processing of a high volume of offenders. There is a preference for swift disposal of cases, informal procedures, and discretionary official decision-making. These are characteristic features of many recent procedural developments.

While most criminal processes contemplate public trial as a key guarantee of the fair treatment of the accused (e.g., through Article 6 of the European Convention on Human Rights), in practice, it is seen as the exception rather than the rule. Growing caseloads and pressure on financial budgets have required criminal justice processes to adapt their procedures in order to process cases more efficiently. Plea bargaining, expedited procedures, mediation, and alternative penalties administered by the prosecutor exist in countries such as France, England and Wales, Germany, the Netherlands, and Italy, as well as the United States. In broad terms, this has meant a shift in power away from the judiciary to the prosecutor (and so an increase in prosecutorial discretion) and a tendency to dispose of cases without resort to trial. In England and Wales, more cases are now disposed of outside the courtroom than in it,[1] and more than half of all criminal cases in France are dealt with by mediation and restorative justice measures. In addition to impacting on court caseloads, these measures have adjusted the relative pre-trial roles of legal actors. For example, in administering these alternative penalties, the prosecutor takes on an almost judicial role, determining the outcome and the "sentence." In countries such as France, this also has significant implications for the defense role. Inquisitorial criminal procedure is dominated by the judiciary during the investigation, prosecution, and trial; the defense lawyer enjoys a relatively diminished role, often mediated through that of the judge. However, the successful operation of these new measures requires a greater pre-trial input from the defense lawyer (whose participation is written into the procedures) in order to

---

[1] According to Ministry of Justice statistics (see <http://www.justice.gov.uk/publications/docs/crim-stats-2007-tag.pdf>), around half of all "offences brought to justice" in 2007 (722,000 out of 1,456,000) are the result of a conviction; around one quarter (383,000) are the result of police cautions; the rest are offenses taken into consideration by the court (108,000), police penalty notices for disorder (144,000), and police formal warnings for cannabis possession (98,000).

demonstrate the protection of the accused. In the absence of research, it is unclear whether this will empower the defense or compromise its role by preventing it from acting as anything more than a rubber stamp, providing some legitimacy to the prosecutor's decision. There is, of course, also a concern that these new measures are experienced by the accused as coercive.

Space prevents fuller discussion, but we note in passing here that in contrast to other alternative case disposal measures, mediation and other forms of restorative justice have been driven as much by the desire that justice should meet better the needs of victims, as by efficiency or cost-saving. There is also evidence from a range of empirical studies in the UK and Australia that this form of "intervention," as it is often called, is more effective in reducing reoffending than traditional prosecution.[2] This poses new roles for the police whose involvement is an important factor in both victims and offenders regarding the process as successful.

Managerial efficiency is also a driver for various forms of performance indicators. In the 1980s, Smith and Gray (1983) concluded that attempts at internal performance management were generally ineffective, were perceived as such by officers engaged in operational duties, and consequently had little effect on how they performed. The advent of external scrutiny in the form of statutory performance indicators does, however, appear to have affected the manner in which police officers exercise their powers. Both empirical research (Halligan-Davis and Spicer, 2004) and official statistics suggest that cases of low-level offending that might have been disposed of informally prior to the introduction of external performance management (suspects being given "words of advice" or informal warnings), would now result in arrest and charge or the issuing of a fixed penalty notice. But while police-administered measures have increased, there has been no corresponding decrease in charges and prosecutions. The result is an overall net-widening, with behavior that was previously unsanctioned being punished through formal police summary measures. It has also been suggested that the failure to differentiate for the purposes of performance measurement between more and less serious offenses has incentivized the targeting of cases that will result in a charge or caution with little effort being given to the more complex and lengthy investigations. This is an important shift that requires careful monitoring in order to track the ongoing implications for the criminal process, notably the increased criminalization of behavior and the tendency toward police-led case disposal.

There are also success stories in more targeted and nuanced forms of performance review: Neyroud (2006) argues that police managers have a clearer idea of what is expected of them and how best they can achieve this. There is some research evidence to support this: in New South Wales, Chilvers and Weatherburn (2001) found that arrests increased and reported crime fell for those crimes targeted by

---

[2] See Robinson and Shapland (2008) for a review of three schemes.

"Operation and Crime Review Panels." And in the United States, the empirical work of Weisburd et al. (2006) in two major American cities tested whether geographical targeting can reduce crime or whether it simply displaces it elsewhere. Their findings suggest that police resources are most effectively utilized through targeting crime "hot spots," resulting in a reduction in crime in these target zones, without displacing it elsewhere.

B. Security

The discourse of security has manifested itself in criminal justice rhetoric in a number of ways. During the 1990s, the preoccupation was with the management of risk whether it be from knife crime, sex offenders, or simply recidivism. This century has been dominated by counter-terrorism measures couched in both a liberty-versus-security discourse and the language of war, with an emphasis on prevention and disruption of terrorist activity. Typically, new offenses have been created, police powers extended, due process rights attenuated, executive authority increased and, in some instances, administrative rather than criminal measures preferred. In England and Wales, for example, we have seen the police being given the power to stop and search without the need for reasonable suspicion; the creation of offenses aimed at preventing rather than punishing harm; the detention of terrorist suspects for up to 28 days; fewer rights for those detained on suspicion of having committed terrorist offenses; and the creation of quasi-criminal measures in the form of control orders to deal with those who cannot be prosecuted or deported, but who are considered a security risk. In the USA, the powers of the FBI were increased, as was the state's ability to use foreign intelligence, and it became easier to collect information on both U.S. and non-U.S. citizens—including through the entry and search of premises without notice. Although the stated aim has been to deal with terrorism through the ordinary criminal law, the range of new powers and offenses, together with the systematic invocation of the need for exceptional measures, makes the approach to counter-terrorism anything but ordinary.

The concern with exceptional measures is always that they will become commonplace and ultimately find their way into mainstream criminal justice. Across the globe, legislation has been enacted using emergency rapid procedures and creating what, in France, has been described as a subset of criminal law and procedure. As several commentators note, many of the legal measures enacted represent opportunistic changes that would not have been possible outside a period of crisis. We know that, historically, there is also a high risk that temporary, emergency legislation will become permanent. In the United States, six days after the 9/11 attacks, the Attorney General called on Congress to pass anti-terrorist legislation that suspended the writ of habeas corpus. The 2001 USA Patriot Act was passed in the House of Representatives on October 12, 2001. It amended 15 federal statutes, and those voting for it had no opportunity to read or debate the text, simply to give it a thumbs up or down. The sunset clause required renewal of the Act, but in fact, 14 of the 16 temporary powers were made permanent, and the 2006 USA Patriot Improvement Act expanded counter-terrorist powers and attached unrelated anti-drug measures (Donohue, 2008: 2). In addition, the definition of terrorism has expanded to include environmentalists, animal rights campaigners, and ill-defined groups such as anti-capitalists (what France has termed the anarcho-autonomist tendency). Does this fit with the public's perception of terrorism and the extreme legal measures needed to tackle it? Or do we risk criminalizing dissent?

While commentators warn of the loss of civil liberties and the disproportionate responses to the threat through both domestic and European legislation, there is little empirical data or research beyond the numbers of arrests and prosecutions. The assumption is that somehow more law will make it easier to fight terrorism and to prevent future terrorist attacks. Some commentators argue that the extreme legal measures implemented have had the reverse effect, alienating parts of the population and causing irreparable damage to our civil liberties. We simply do not know because we lack an empirical research base from which to measure the impact and effectiveness of legal measures.

There is much work to be done in understanding the ways these new offenses and powers are used and to what effect; how these have changed the decision frame, the way in which individual decision-makers perceive their roles, the purpose of the new offenses, and the powers that have been conferred. There is growing concern that the prevention and disruption agenda is spilling out into many aspects of policing and that the exercise of legitimate political and civil rights (such as that to protest peacefully or to attend public meetings) is seen as a legitimate focus of police surveillance. Images are recorded and individuals' details stored for later comparison, just in case the citizen seeking to be well informed through attendance at a public meeting becomes radicalized and turns into a domestic extremist. This level of surveillance (later to be turned into "intelligence") of ordinary citizens is chilling. We are becoming obsessed with the collection of information (despite data protection laws and a right to privacy)—whether through EU shared databases of evidence, fingerprints, and criminal records, airline passenger profiles, or requirements to provide intimate data simply in order to enter the country.

There have also been structural changes to the institutions of criminal justice, reflecting the emphasis on prevention and disruption and so earlier intervention. The growing use of intelligence within the criminal sphere is a key part of this. In the 1990s, French investigating judges began to work directly with the domestic intelligence agency, the *Direction de la Surveillance du Territoire*. This gives the specialist team of investigating judges direct access to intelligence, some of which will form part of the judicial file of evidence. More controversially, intelligence that will never make it into an official judicial dossier will nevertheless be taken into account by the judge in her legal decision-making, blurring the boundaries between intelligence and evidence in ways that have the potential to undermine the credibility of the case (Hodgson, 2006). The use of intelligence, and in particular telephone intercept material, has been problematic in prosecutions in England and Wales. France's procedure of judicial investigation enables material to be filtered pre-trial and transformed into "evidence" that can be used at trial, but the adversarial procedure in England and Wales requires a greater opportunity for evidential scrutiny by the parties and so does not sit comfortably with this (Hodgson, 2006). Britain has also seen a shift in the deployment of police, prosecutors, and intelligence agencies in order to be more effective in prevention and enforcement. The British Military Intelligence (MI5) has moved away from pure *intelligence* gathering toward gathering *evidence* that will be admissible in court. At the same time, the Anti-Terrorism branch of the Metropolitan Police works more closely, and at an earlier point in the investigation, with MI5, dispensing with the need for Special Branch to act as a kind of buffer between the two, instead, absorbing it within the police to create a Counter-Terrorist Command in London. The CPS has also adapted and has created a counter-terrorism division consisting of a dozen lawyers working with the police during the investigative phase. All of these initiatives are part of the "prevent" strategy, designed to ensure earlier and more effective intervention and prosecution of terrorist offenses, many of which criminalize activity at an early point. There is little information and no empirical research to evaluate the success of these initiatives and the shifting relationships between legal actors in the criminal process. And what of the wider implications of these changes, all of which center on obtaining admissible evidence as early as possible. Will this strengthen case building or lead to a premature narrowing of the case? Is it a pedagogic refinement to require intelligence services to gather *evidence* rather than *intelligence*, or does it change the brief of MI5 in significant ways that have implications for their accountability and the nature of the information that is gathered about individuals? These are potentially profound changes, the implications of which require exploration. Security is raised as something of a blanket alibi, but without systematic independent research data we cannot evaluate the real extent of these reforms and their likely impact across the wider criminal process.

III. CRIMINAL DEFENSE

The role of the criminal defense has become increasingly important in England and Wales, as the accused is co-opted to participate in the case investigation and trial, with penalties attached for failure to answer police questions, to provide details of the defense case, and to take the stand at trial. Research shows that admissions made during police interrogation are likely to be determinative of the case. Effective custodial legal advice on the nature of the evidence, possible charges, and defense strategy is more crucial than ever, given the evidential significance of what is said or not said in interrogation and the possibility that the case may be disposed of at the police station by, e.g., a caution. In more inquisitorially rooted procedures, too, such as that in France, the police–suspect encounter is key. Interrogations are not tape-recorded and are conducted without a lawyer present; and the suspect is not told of her right to silence. The principal safeguard is the supervision of the prosecutor who is responsible for the detention and interrogation of suspects, but across many different police stations. The small number of French studies on this topic have been sociological and have not explored the legal implications of observed practices. However, Hodgson's (2005) research is based on observational and interview data, and her legal analysis provides an insight into the nature of this pre-trial process and the extent to which it is able to protect the suspect. As described above, supervision does not entail visits to the station or presence in police interrogations; it takes place via the telephone and fax, and any personal visits to the station are rare and announced in advance. Although the prosecutor is responsible for the investigation and prosecution of crime, she is dependent upon the police to achieve this. As we have noted above, the core ingredient in this relationship is trust. As a result, supervision is largely bureaucratic and retrospective. Yet, the confession of a suspect in police interrogation will be regarded as the product of a judicially supervised inquiry and so be given considerable weight at court. Even where cases go on to be investigated by the *juge d'instruction*, an initial confession to the police can be difficult to displace. Other jurisdictions such as Germany and the Netherlands employ a similar procedure, and trust rather than surveillance is again the order of the day. The French are currently considering proposals to abolish the investigative role of the *juge d'instruction* and to make the prosecutor responsible for all criminal investigations. This will almost certainly have negative consequences for pre-trial defense rights and the accused's ability to receive a fair trial. Given the absence of a tradition of independent empirical research in France, this is unlikely to be monitored systematically; practitioners (notably prosecutors) are likely to be asked to report on the impact of any changes after a year or two of operation and any changes made accordingly.

In order to understand the position of the accused and the defense function more broadly, account must be taken of the police environment in which the early (and crucial) stages of the case are played out. Access to effective legal assistance is vital to the proper functioning of an adversarial model of procedure in which the court plays an adjudicative rather than investigative function. Yet, while the police and prosecution functions are seen as essential and in the interests of justice, the defense role somehow seems to lack the same legitimacy and is treated as something that can be diminished and re-crafted to suit wider system goals of efficiency. Perhaps unsurprisingly, the police see the defense function and, indeed, defense rights more generally, as antithetical to their role in investigation. The primary purpose of detention and interrogation is to obtain a confession. The presence of lawyers and the suspect's exercise of the right to silence appear to oppose this aim. Empirical studies in England and Wales found that working rules and police occupational culture are more significant than legal norms in governing the police–suspect encounter, just as they are in street stops: officers have sought to undermine the statutory right to legal advice by dissuading suspects from requesting a lawyer, insisting that it will only delay matters unnecessarily. This ploy appears to be effective: despite a universal right to legal assistance free at the point of delivery, 60 to 80% of suspects do not request legal advice even though half of these say they would have requested a lawyer if one had been present in the police station. Suspects continue not to request a lawyer where they believe this will result in further delay, but request rates are higher in newer stations where much of the custody role has been privatized, perhaps reflecting a greater willingness to wait where physical conditions are better (Skinns, 2009).

Despite the different legal framework of pre-trial supervision, Hodgson (2005) observed the same values and behavior patterns in French police stations. Officers were hostile to defense lawyers, attempted to persuade suspects that they did not need legal assistance, and sought to obtain a confession at all costs. The supervision of the prosecutor did not curtail this behavior but, rather, provided legally legitimized prolonged periods of interrogation through the extension of police detention. Although part of the judicial corps, the prosecutor shared many of the police's values and the prosecutor's ideology of the search for the truth translated in most instances into the desire for a confession. As EU countries increase their level of police and judicial cooperation through the European Arrest Warrant and the European Evidence Warrant, the right to custodial legal advice in all European jurisdictions has been proposed as a necessary safeguard. This has been resisted by many countries on the grounds that prosecutorial supervision provides adequate protection. There is a need for more independent empirical research data on the conduct of police detention and interrogation in order that this debate is informed by practice rather than aspirational ideal-types (Cape et al., 2007).

We know that the accused's position has become more vulnerable as pre-trial roles and procedures have changed, but have defense lawyers risen to this challenge? And what of the wider picture, the intersecting relationships of criminal justice actors (recall Blumberg's 1967 assertion that defense lawyers were more akin to double agents than advocates for their clients) and how these affect the defense function? The major ethnographic study carried out by McConville et al. (1994) demonstrated that it was not only the police who were required to undergo a legal cultural shift in the post-PACE era. Lawyers, too, had to engage with the new demands placed upon them by the statutory right to custodial legal advice. This large-scale study considered for the first time the organization, practices, and effectiveness of criminal defense lawyers in all aspects of their work in England and Wales. It found that the focus of solicitors' activity was the court, key case preparation being conducted, and client advice being given, by junior and often non-legally qualified (i.e., paraprofessional) staff, resulting in discontinuous representation and, in many instances, a poor level of service. This was especially true of the provision of legal assistance to suspects held at the police station for interrogation (McConville and Hodgson, 1993). Provision of custodial legal advice was routinely assigned to non-legally qualified and often inexperienced staff in order to maximize profit and to protect more senior lawyers from the inconvenience and unpredictability of 24-hour police station work.

The findings of these two studies and their negative implications for the proper functioning of the adversarial process dismayed the Royal Commission on Criminal Justice (1993). The Law Society and Legal Aid Board (now called the Legal Services Commission) responded rapidly with an accreditation scheme that ensured only properly trained and qualified individuals would be paid under the legal aid scheme for providing custodial legal advice. This scheme appears to have resulted in real improvements to the quality of advice provided to suspects (Bridges and Choongh, 1998). However, over the last decade, the financial landscape of criminal legal aid has changed, with franchising driving many small firms out of criminal work altogether, and a culture of audit and peer review replacing the assumption that as a profession, lawyers could be trusted to provide a quality service and represent the client's best interests. However, even those firms winning a franchise are not necessarily providing the best-quality service, and peer review is very light-touch (Bridges et al., 2000). The Public Defender Service was established in 2001, and while it exhibits many of the same problems as private practitioners (e.g., delegation of police station work to accredited representatives, a tendency to provide telephone advice rather than personal attendance when acting as duty solicitor), public defenders appeared more robust in their advice to suspects. They were more likely to advise silence, and their advice was generally of better quality (Bridges et al., 2007). These studies tell us that lawyers' behavior is influenced by many different factors and so can be addressed in different ways—through mandatory training linked to payment, for example. However, concern with the quality seems to have been overtaken by the audit/efficiency culture. Having recognized the need for quality defense provision, efforts are now centered on obtaining this as cheaply as possible. This creates a clear tension, and research in Scotland has demonstrated the negative impact this has on the quality of service received by accused persons: quite simply, the less you pay a lawyer, the less work they will do or are able to do (Tata et al., 2004). We appear to have come full circle. As fewer firms can afford to do criminal work with the very low rates of remuneration, access to justice is likely to decline and quality is likely to suffer.

The field in which the defense must operate continues to change in important ways. The curtailment of the right to silence occurred after McConville and Hodgson's study, but its impact on custodial legal advice has been tracked by others. Although the right to silence is rarely exercised (McConville and Hodgson, 1993) and silence is even more rarely sustained, it has taken on a symbolic importance. Silence has not been demonstrated to be a significant obstacle to conviction, but it symbolizes a challenge to the overarching police goal of obtaining a confession; and so its curtailment or abolition has been sought by the police. Following the recommendations of the RCCJ, the 1994 Criminal Justice and Public Order Act introduced the possibility of adverse inferences being drawn at court when a suspect remained silent under police interrogation.[3] In this way, evidential significance attaches to what the suspect says and what she does not say to the police during interrogation. This poses major challenges to those attempting to provide legal advice to suspects held for police questioning. Despite having little information on the police case against the suspect, the lawyer must try to assess what it would be reasonable to mention (in order to avoid adverse inferences at trial) in advising her client whether to remain silent. While the use of silence is reported to have declined since the 1994 reform, the rates of admissions and convictions remain unaffected. Bucke et al. (2000) report that just over half of suspects confess or make incriminating admissions—suggesting that silence was not such an obstacle to obtaining convictions as was often claimed.

More recently, statutory reform relating to the admissibility of evidence of an accused's bad character has changed the field in a way that may also have affected the manner in which interrogative interviews are conducted and, so, how legal advice should be framed. The "bad character" provisions of the Criminal Justice Act 2003 have relaxed the traditional common law prohibition on the admissibility of such evidence. Among the circumstances that might lead to the reception of evidence of previous convictions or of other facts that show the accused in a bad light is that she has made an attack on another person's character under police questioning. It applies irrespective of both the truth of the suspect's attack on the other person and whether the assertion is an integral part of the suspect's defense. Given the suspect's typical lack of information at the interrogation stage about the case against her, this is a potentially far-reaching reform which, like the silence provisions, restricts the conduct of the defense at almost the first stage of the investigation. Suspects with a chequered past who wish to challenge the evidence of a witness must tread a perilous path between risking the introduction of their previous convictions and failing to mention facts that they might later wish to rely on in their defense. The possible effect of these new provisions on the conduct of police interrogations, on the decision-making of defense solicitors providing custodial advice, and on suspects, is a matter worthy of further empirical investigation in order to explore whether this remains a marginal provision, or one which further challenges the extent to which an adversarial defense is permitted.

---

[3] The caution states: "You do not have to say anything, but it may harm your defence if you do not mention when questioned something which you may later rely on in court. Anything you do say may be given in evidence."

IV. PROSECUTION

A. The Role of the prosecutor

In all jurisdictions, the prosecutor is central to the functioning of the criminal process. Depending on how the field is shaped by the procedural tradition and legal culture of the system, the prosecutor might be an advocate, an investigative supervisor, a judge, a sentencer, a local policy-maker, a broker, and/or a gatekeeper. She is at the hub of the criminal justice machine and possesses broad discretion at various stages of the process. As with policing, it is the exercise of this discretion and the way in which decisions are framed that defines her role as much as the legal framework in which she operates. Unsurprisingly, therefore, the central concern of researchers is in understanding the discretion of the prosecutor—how much she possesses, whether it is sufficiently constrained, and how it is exercised and influenced. It is generally accepted that discretion is necessary for the efficient running of the system and to ensure that justice is done in individual cases—though uncertainty and wide inconsistency will tend to undermine the pursuit of justice. Across all jurisdictions, there is a clear trend toward expanding the role of the prosecutor as a primary measure to improve the efficient processing of cases and so reduce delays and caseloads. This may be through mediation and other methods of diversion away from prosecution and trial; prosecution powers to issue penalties; powers to expedite trial procedures; different forms of plea, charge, and sentence bargaining (or reduction as in the *correctionalisation* process in France).

In England and Wales, the field has changed significantly, the prosecutor's role having been expanded to encompass alternative modes of case disposal, such as the issuing of a conditional caution to individuals who have made clear admissions to the police. The original aim of this measure was to impose conditions requiring some form of reparation or to rehabilitate the offender, but explicitly punitive conditions, such as unpaid community work and financial penalties, may now be imposed. While earlier studies examined the impact of PACE and the relationship between the police and the newly formed CPS, there has as yet been no empirical examination of the impact of the initiatives described above and the major shift in the police-CPS relationship that they represent. Is the CPS maintaining a sufficient degree of independence? Are they performing a pedagogical role *vis-à-vis* the police, educating them as to the evidential requirements for charge, or is prosecutorial decision-making relating to case disposal being unduly influenced by police perspectives and value systems?

Such developments might lead us to question the nature of the prosecutorial function. The cumulative effect on the field in which the prosecutor operates might lead us to ask whether the prosecutor is a quasi-judicial figure committed to justice, or a partisan opponent of the accused. The professional ethics of the prosecutor's role will differ according to the answer. We might also ask how the changes in the field have affected prosecutors' perceptions of their own function and explore what effect that may have had on the way in which they frame decisions. In England and Wales, the DPP has recently introduced a Statement of Ethical Principles for Public Prosecutors, which emphasizes the values of fairness and impartiality and imposes a duty to ensure that all reasonable enquiries are made and the results disclosed— whether they point to innocence or guilt. The American Bar Association guidance makes clear that, although operating in an adversary system, the prosecutor's role is to protect the innocent as well as to convict the guilty, and to guard the rights of the accused as well as enforcing the rights of the public. In most European countries, the prosecutor enjoys a quasi-judicial status in overseeing the investigation and authorizing measures such as wiretaps; and her role is explicitly to investigate and to consider evidence that exculpates as well as evidence that inculpates the suspect. These accounts suggest a more neutral role for the prosecutor, which is surely right given the imbalance of power (and professional status in countries such as France) between prosecution and defense. Researchers have drawn on insights from psychology to consider the importance of role definition in carrying out the job of investigator (O'Brien, 2009; Simon et al., 2009). They found, unsurprisingly, that more partisan accounts were produced by those charged with investigating one side of a case in preparation for a prosecution than by those who were told that they were the sole investigator. This kind of research, exploring the manner in which individual's decision-making frames can be influenced by role definition, may provide a useful starting point for the design of prosecutorial institutions, policies, and procedures. Identification of the factors that tend to shape the decision frame in ways that produce undesirable consequences may lead to the adoption of more effective counterbalances within investigative and prosecutorial agencies, or through increased defense rights.

In the United States, attention has been paid to the shift in power toward the prosecutor as a result of being given wider scope to charge federal offenses carrying more severe federal penalties and of being able to exploit the more draconian measures under statutes such as RICO and other legislation purporting to target the war on crime, the war on drugs, etc., for the purpose of prosecuting other types of criminal activity, such as white-collar crime. Such legislation provides the prosecutor with greater bargaining power concerning charge, plea, and sentence.

The contours of the decision-making field are also being reshaped by developments in sentencing powers; mandatory sentencing of different kinds has shifted power away from the judge to the prosecutor, as the charge prosecuted determines the sentence that must be passed. Miller and Eisenstein (2005) conducted 39 interviews with lawyers, prosecutors, judges, and investigators to explore the implications for prosecutorial discretion of the increasing "federalization" of crime control. While numerically small, the prosecution of state-investigated cases in federal courts is becoming more common as a result of closer cooperative relationships, especially post 9/11. The researchers argue that as federal offenses carry longer sentences, prosecutors can effectively send a message to the judge and push up the "going rate" of sentence by using a federal prosecution. This increase shifts some power away from the judge to the prosecutor, as well as strengthening the prosecutor's position in plea bargaining with the defense. MVA and Miller (2004) argue that increased federal sentencing powers, together with an increase in the range of crimes that are the focus of federal attention, has resulted in a significant growth in the federal prison population. There are almost no trials taking place: guilty pleas in federal courts having risen from 87% to 97% between 1991 and 2003, with the result that the federal prosecutor has become, in effect, the federal sentencer. This is a concentration of power that invites abuse rather than a sharing of responsibility in line with U.S. constitutional principles. These accounts suggest that while the rhetoric of the prosecutorial function is one of objective detachment, in practice the prosecutor is adversarial in her approach, seeking always to maximize her chances of conviction.

In the United States, the fact that the state prosecutor is elected may be seen to inject some form of local accountability, as well as ensuring a prosecution policy that is adapted to local conditions. However, researchers have suggested that individuals cannot be held accountable for law enforcement decisions in this way because responsibility is spread across a range of individuals.

B. Prosecutorial independence

It seems that in most jurisdictions, the field in which prosecutors operate has been influenced by the principle that the prosecutor ought to be "independent." But what is understood by the notion of independence varies across jurisdictions. In some jurisdictions, concerns over independence are focused on the relationship between the police and the prosecutor. In others, the prosecutor's independence from the political institutions attracts greater attention.

1. *Prosecutorial independence from the police and other legal actors*

In England and Wales, it is the prosecution's independence from the police that is stressed. The removal of the prosecution function from the police constituted a significant change in the field which occurred only with the relatively recent establishment of a public prosecution service, the CPS, in 1986. A key aspect of the independence of the CPS was that it should have no involvement in the investigation, in order that the prosecution decision would be untainted and independent. Similar concerns have been expressed in New Zealand, where the prosecution of less serious cases remains the job of police prosecutors appointed from the ranks of sergeants. However, despite the opportunities that exist to compare the approach of police prosecutors with that of the "independent" Crown solicitors who conduct the prosecution of more serious offenses, there has been no systematic empirical research on prosecutorial decision-making in New Zealand (Stenning, 2008).

Research in the first years following the establishment of the CPS questioned the ability of the CPS to provide an independent review given that the decision to prosecute is based upon evidence provided by the police in the case file. Judicially ordered and directed acquittals remained high, suggesting that weak cases continued to be prosecuted. While still lacking any power to direct the police, the CPS now decides with which offense to charge a suspect, and the rates of overcharging and subsequent dropping of cases have both decreased. The 2007/08 CPS Annual Report attributes the falling discontinuance rate in the magistrates' courts (from 11.8% in 2005/06 to 9.9% in 2007/08) and the rising guilty plea rate (from 63.2% in 2005/06 to 67.5% in 2007/08) to the new charging procedures. However, this causal relationship is unclear: statistics show that discontinuances have been falling by at least a percentage point per year since 2000/01, five years before the new charging arrangements were put in place. Systematic research is needed to understand the factors driving change and to monitor the wider concern that in bringing the CPS closer to the investigation and being located on police territory, CPS staff will come to share the police outlook on cases and so be less independent; what effect, if any, will closer working relationships with the police and exposure to police institutional culture have on the subjective framing of prosecutorial decisions? Other changes have also brought the police and CPS closer together: in counter-terrorism investigations, the CPS works closely with counter-terrorist police during the pre-trial investigation. Again, we have no independent research on which to base any evaluation of the success of these initiatives.

In France and many other European countries, the field that provides the setting in which prosecutorial decision-making occurs differs significantly from that found in common law jurisdictions. The prosecutor enjoys a quasi-judicial status, and part of her role is to direct or oversee the police investigation. Indeed, the prosecutor possesses the same powers as the police and may conduct investigations personally, if she wishes, and determine which, if any, charges to bring. Thus, in contrast to the autonomy of the British police, officers in countries such as France and the Netherlands are accountable to the prosecutor for the conduct of a criminal investigation. In practice, this relationship is one of bureaucratic trust, and investigation and charge decisions are police-dominated. The prosecutor exercises little meaningful control in most instances, calling into question the wisdom of restricting pre-trial defense rights on the grounds of judicial supervision. The prosecutor's dependence upon the police to carry out her function means that police and prosecution come to see themselves as working toward the same outcome (Hodgson, 2005). It may be that the current arrangement in England and Wales allows the CPS to shape the investigation in part, without the negative consequences that "authority over" and "direction" might have on the working relationship. Inspectorates and Parliamentary Select Committees review aspects of the criminal process, but systematic empirical research is needed in order to evaluate the success of the changes that have taken place in England and Wales in terms of prosecutorial decision-making, the extent to which they require additional training and regulation to maintain clear boundaries between police and prosecution, and the impact of the changes on other pre-trial legal actors such as suspects and defense lawyers.

The prosecutor's relationships with other legal actors also determine the nature of her role; and these relationships are in turn structured by daily courtroom working groups. Utz (1979) describes the different ways in which prosecutorial discretion is influenced by other institutional actors in two U.S. court districts with, for example, strong defense lawyers serving to temper the prosecutor's tendency toward adversarialism and aggressive overcharging. Richman (2003) describes the changing relationships between U.S. federal prosecutors and law enforcement agents. For example, as agents focus more on prevention, they become less dependent on prosecutors. Enforcement and prosecution are not insulated from each other: their interactions affect their decisions and the allocation of resources. Even the prosecutor's career trajectory as a local player affects the exercise of her discretion. Lochner (2002) notes that assistant U.S. attorneys now stay in their positions longer, and so their priority need not be, as it may have been in the past, to take on high-profile and complex cases in order to build a profile for moving to the better paid private sector.

2. *Political independence*

In countries, including France and Australia, it is the prosecutor's independence from the executive that is emphasized. There is a tension, however, between independence and some form of democratic accountability. Italy perhaps represents one extreme, where researchers suggest that total independence from the executive has allowed prosecutors to act in arbitrary and political ways and has, ironically, compromised their independence. In France, at the other end of the spectrum, there is a clear hierarchical accountability to the Minister of Justice, a political appointee. Prosecution policy is filtered down through the hierarchy of senior- and area-level prosecutors to individual courts. There are also Ministry of Justice directives on specific issues and local court policy that will be determined by the local crime profile and resources. In England and Wales there is a hierarchical structure, with the CPS headed by the Director of Public Prosecutions, a political appointee. However, the wider legal and political cultures of the two countries are very different, leading Perrodet (2002: 422) to characterize the prosecution service in England and Wales as one of institutional dependence and functional autonomy, but that of France as one of institutional dependence and functional subordination. While they appear to be similar: "In practice, however, there is an enormous difference, because in France, unlike in England, the minister's legal right to control the prosecution system has not been tempered by a constitutional convention that it should be exercised very sparingly and not used to further the narrow political interests of the government and its supporters." The professional career structure of prosecutors may also compromise political independence. In France, while the political hierarchy of their profession may not impact on most prosecutors on a daily basis, ambitious prosecutors are unlikely to ignore the orders of those responsible for their career progression. The proposed abolition of the politically independent *juge d'instruction* will push the political independence of the French prosecutor yet further into the spotlight.

However we understand notions of independence, it might be said that the prosecutorial function is necessarily a political one in the sense that the prosecutor's exercise of discretion has the potential to create criminal justice policy. Provided with wide powers of prosecution and discretion in issues of seizure and sentence, the ways that prosecutors choose to exercise those powers can have a profound impact. Whether it is prosecuting or dismissing cases of domestic abuse or drug possession, prioritizing white-collar crime and corruption, or adopting a more punitive approach to African-American defendants, the prosecutor has the power to make a difference. The choice to prosecute one offense rather than another is one in which more than just evidence is taken into account. The politics of such decisions will change over time and place. For example, in an empirical study of cases between 1977 and 1981 in South Carolina, Paternoster (1984) found that the death penalty was sought more frequently where the victim was white and the assailant black. But in a study of cases in Tennessee between 1977 and 2006, Scheb et al. (2008) found that the race of neither the victim nor the defendant were significant predictors of the prosecution asking for the death penalty. Even in countries such as France, where discretion is said to be closely circumscribed by hierarchy, there is scope for personal preferences as well as local-level policy. More controversial can be the investigation and prosecution of political figures. In the United States, investigation of the Iran-Contra scandal and enquiries into President Clinton's financial and extramarital affairs were conducted by special prosecutors whose political independence has been questioned. In France, the *juges d'instruction* were accused of acting politically, rather than judicially, when investigating politicians and high-profile business people connected to government in the 1990s. Their response was that they were simply applying the law to individuals, albeit that the implications of the inquiry and the criminal behavior were inevitably political. The *juges*, on the other hand, accused the prosecutors of succumbing to political pressure to stymie these investigations. This might be done in a number of ways: the prosecutor may act politically in choosing the *juge d'instruction* for the case; the investigation might be delayed to keep it within the jurisdiction of the prosecutor supervising the police (thus delaying the involvement of the more politically independent *juge*); or the case may be divided into several related investigations, preventing the *juge d'instruction* from having overall control.

C. Prosecutorial autonomy: institutional policies and individual perceptions

There may be other factors influencing the individual prosecutor's exercise of discretion. As outlined above, the French prosecutor is responsible for the investigation as well as the prosecution of crime. Uniformity of decision-making and a public interest ideology are central to the hierarchical model of French prosecution, but there remains ample scope for the exercise of prosecutorial discretion at both the local and individual level (Hodgson, 2005: 79–85). Ministry of Justice circulars are framed in general terms, requiring prosecutors to pursue particular types of crime with more vigor. Some areas and individuals acted upon such directives, while others ignored them. O'Neill's (2004) study of the discretion exercised by U.S. federal prosecutors found that these kinds of national priorities were reflected in decision-making, but this was only one factor structuring the exercise of discretion. There were clear variations within these priority areas; for example, smaller frauds were more likely to be prosecuted than large ones, and possession of marijuana was more likely to be prosecuted than was possession of cocaine. Weak and legally insufficient evidence was the primary reason for discontinuance, suggesting (as in England and Wales) the need for better training and supervision of investigators and uniform prosecution guidelines.

The exercise of prosecutorial discretion is also affected by the prosecutor's perception of her role within the criminal process: part of what Hawkins terms the *frame*. Experimental research suggests that an admonishment to remain objective and detached has little effect on those who are presented with the task of preparing a case for trial. Participants' motivations and beliefs tended to be formed around the role they were assigned. Those asked to prepare a defense case demonstrated sympathy for the accused, while those asked to perform a prosecutorial role readily accepted the victim's account of events (O'Brien, 2009; Simon et al., 2009).

Although not typical, there is evidence of personal prejudice influencing the decisions of French prosecutors, including crude racial stereotyping (Hodgson, 2005: 232–36). In the Netherlands too, Weenink's (2009) study of prosecution decision-making in 409 juvenile cases demonstrates that ethnic minorities are summoned to court more frequently than "native Dutch" defendants, largely as a result of cultural stereotyping in the interpretation of observed and reported behavior and of what are regarded as "troublesome interactions" with judicial officials. Although the Netherlands is a jurisdiction in which the prosecutor is, in theory, more closely involved in the investigation phase, these decisions were based on information contained in the case file. This underlines the importance of understanding the nature of the police-prosecution relationship and the ways that it influences decision-making at different levels.

It might be argued that more generally, the fundamental process choices made by the prosecution also have a political dimension. In France, the prosecutor determines whether to keep the case under her supervision or that of the *juge d'instruction*, who is not hierarchically accountable to a government minister as the prosecutor is. She also determines the offense to be charged and prosecuted, recommends a sentence to the court, and decides whether to divert the case away from trial. While the power of the "civil party" (usually the victim) to initiate proceedings provides a potential check on the prosecutor's decision-making, this power is rarely used. The key decisions in processing a case through the criminal justice system are predominantly those of the prosecutor. The "public interest" is a fairly universal criterion for prosecution, but again, this is not value-free. Moody and Tombs' (1982) study of the decision-making of the prosecutor (the fiscal) in Scotland revealed the extent to which decisions taken in the public interest are shaped by the personal perceptions of the individual prosecutor, particularly those relating to public expectations, which form part of what Hawkins would describe as "the surround." Where the question was whether a trivial offense ought to be prosecuted, some fiscals took the view that proceeding with trivial offenses might have the effect of diluting the public opprobrium that serious crimes ought to attract. Others justified decisions not to proceed with prosecutions in relation to trivial matters on the grounds that this reflected the public's view that minor offenses, particularly road traffic offenses, should not be treated as "criminal" offenses.

In France, it is recognized that the prosecutor's discretion is an important part of adapting prosecution policy to local conditions and concerns—an example of the influence that certain social and systemic pressures in the broad surround can have on subjective decision-making. The aim may be to manage the flow of cases, charging some offenses at a lower level so that they remain in a mid-level court and are not subjected to the lengthy *instruction* procedure. (In some cases, however, such a decision may have wider political significance in that the *juge d'instruction* is not hierarchically accountable in the same way as the prosecutor.) Or the aim may be to respond to local mores and expectations. Possession of cannabis is regarded as trivial in Paris, but it may well be prosecuted in a small country town where such activity is considered more shocking. Prosecutors are also involved in making policy at the community level and within the local court. Interview data suggest that their discretion is closely circumscribed in this context (Bénec'h-Le Roux, 2007), but this suggestion needs to be tested more systematically through observations and case studies.

One of the more illuminating studies on variation in subjective framing of decisions is that conducted by Moody and Tombs, who found significant variation in the decision-making of individual prosecutors in cases involving violence between domestic partners or between neighbors. Some fiscals were reluctant to prosecute cases involving domestic violence. Various reasons were given for such decisions, including anticipated withdrawal of complaints by assaulted wives.

Some fiscals regarded domestic violence as a matter for which the criminal law was not suited and should not be invoked. Others attempted to act as mediators between husband and wife. However, many fiscals viewed such incidents as serious crimes that should always be prosecuted. Evaluation of a very recent initiative in England and Wales suggests that pre-trial interviews might have an influence on prosecutorial decision-making in domestic violence cases. This scheme involves cases in which the witness/complainant's credibility is central, there are gaps in testimony, and the commitment of the witness to trial is in question. Sexual offenses and domestic violence cases formed a significant proportion of those referred for interview in the pilot study. A small-scale evaluation of the scheme (based on 12 interviews with prosecutors and two group evaluation meetings) suggests that the procedure can strengthen prosecutorial decision-making, ensuring the early discontinuance of weak cases and clarifying issues in those cases taken to trial (Roberts and Saunders, 2007). More sustained analysis of a wider sample of data will tell us more about the prosecutor's approach to this new role in pre-trial witness interviewing and how it relates to the police investigation and the decision to prosecute. It will also help to build up a picture of the twenty-first century prosecutor, whose role has developed significantly since the origins of the CPS in 1985.

More specific measures have also been put in place to ensure that police and prosecutors take domestic violence seriously. A range of empirical studies have evaluated initiatives across the UK and contributed to the development of best practice. There are now specialist domestic violence courts; dedicated CPS coordinators; and arrest in domestic violence cases is a police performance indicator. For a long time, domestic violence was not taken seriously by the police, regarded as "just a domestic" and so a private matter. Edwards' (1989) research in London found an arrest rate of only 2%; and even after the pro-arrest policies of the 1990s, the arrest rate remained low, the victim's desire to take action being the determining factor. Mandatory arrest and prosecution policies have been adopted in some jurisdictions, but there is evidence that acting against the wishes of the victim may be counterproductive as well as disempowering. Coker (2001) reports that studies in the United States show that mandatory policies have only a short-lived deterrent effect, and in some groups (e.g., unemployed men), the risk of violence increases. The major problem in prosecuting domestic violence cases is the high rate of complainant withdrawal: Hoyle (1998) found that 42% of complainants withdrew their complaint after the arrest of the alleged perpetrator. The most effective strategy has been to provide support to victims, through specialized courts and victim advocacy, in bringing their cases to court, thus reducing the number of complaints withdrawn. The victim's ability to sustain her engagement (with a withdrawal rate of 11% compared to 50% nationally) has had a dramatic effect on prosecutions and the number of guilty pleas and has reduced incidents of repeat victimization (Hester and Westmarland, 2005).

D. Plea bargaining

An aspect of prosecutorial discretion that has attracted widespread concern is the practice of plea bargaining. This has been the focus of a significant body of research in the United States, probably because of the very high number of guilty pleas and the pervasiveness of plea bargaining, but also because of the concern that this appears to represent the antithesis to the common law ideal of a public hearing in which the case presented by the state is subject to testing by the defendant and is adjudicated on by a lay jury. Instead, plea bargaining makes the prosecutor, not the court, responsible for case disposition to a large extent. Understanding the motivation and drivers of plea bargaining is therefore central for researchers. What is the nature of the field and its relationship with surrounding political objectives and social concerns? Is the purpose of plea bargaining to reduce caseloads and increase system efficiency? Does it reflect a desire to ensure that the guilty are convicted and to eliminate the risk of acquittal? Are prosecution decisions based on evidence and a clear justice ethic? Or are they related to personal factors such as racism, political factors, or guidelines and directives from superiors at the local or national level? Or does plea bargaining reflect simply a reluctance to go to trial? Bibas (2004) argues that there are a range of factors that influence the conduct of plea bargains, ranging from lawyer competence and the extent of discovery available, to workloads, resources, and whether the defendant is in pre-trial detention. We know that plea bargaining does not simply take place in the shadow of expected trial outcomes; we do not know the extent to which other factors influence the bargain.

In many countries, including those with a more inquisitorial history, plea bargaining is seen as an extension of rapid trial procedures, a way of speeding things along. Across all procedural traditions, researchers have questioned the way that plea bargaining and related rapid or alternative procedures define the prosecutor's role. It gives her enormous power—to determine charge, to determine the offense for prosecution and the sentence recommendation. This power seems only to have increased. Whether phrased in terms of due process or fair trial, the concern is the same in both the adversarial and the inquisitorial tradition, namely that the prosecutor's role in case disposition undermines that of zthe court. Empirical research conducted in England and Wales in the 1970s revealed that while there was doctrinal resistance to the idea of plea bargaining, the practice appeared to be endemic. Indeed, so entrenched is the practice that the law has subsequently developed so as to accommodate it. It was legislatively acknowledged for the first time in the Criminal Justice and Public Order Act 1994, which required trial judges, when determining the sentence that ought to be passed, to take into account the stage in the proceedings at which the offender had "indicated his intention to plead guilty, and the circumstances in which that indication was given."[4] The guilty plea rates in the United States are astonishingly high, as are the penalties administered. As one U.S. commentator observed: "This system loves punishment... This system hates trials." (MVA and Miller, 2004: 1212). Much of the plea bargaining literature is critical of the practice on the ground that it provides a means of pressuring defendants to give up their trial rights in a way that offers them no real choice—and so is really no bargain at all. Routine overcharging means that the plea bargain simply brings the sentence down to a level that more accurately reflects the criminal behavior. In addition, victims complain that a guilty plea ensures that the facts of the case are denied a proper public airing.

Langer's (2006) analysis is that the plea proposal is coercive when the prosecutor becomes the sole adjudicator in the case, because the defendant's plea can be said to be involuntary. Coercion exists when the defendant is overcharged, faced with an excessive sentence following trial, or offered a plea in a weak case. Perhaps the ultimate pressure that might be brought to bear to secure a plea bargain is a threat of the death penalty. In Ehrhard's (2008) study of this, the accounts of the defense and prosecution lawyers interviewed were framed very differently. The defense lawyers thought the death penalty was used as a powerful lever, but the prosecutors denied this, though they thought other prosecutors elsewhere might indulge in the practice. Wright and Miller's (2003) empirical study presents a possible alternative to the coercive understanding of plea bargaining. They argue that prosecution screening may produce a more honest system, where charges and sentence match more closely the criminal behavior that is the subject of the charge. Their study looks at case screening as practiced in New Orleans, using a detailed database of cases dealt with over a ten-year period. Under this model, the prosecutor screens all cases to ensure there is sufficient evidence and to eliminate weak cases, thus ensuring that the charge that is brought is appropriate and can be proved in court. The result should be to severely restrict plea, and especially charge, bargaining. Supervisory personnel oversee the process to ensure its consistent and effective operation and in particular, that few changes are made after charges have been filed. Despite an under-funded indigent defense program, the process produced a trial rate of 14.4% compared with Louisiana's overall rate of only 2.2%.

Some commentators see plea bargaining as the ultimate expression of adversarialism, giving the parties maximum control over the case outcome. This would seem to ignore the vast inequalities between prosecution and defense and the fact that negotiations take place with little or no discovery or prosecution disclosure. It also highlights a tension in the prosecutor's role. She has no client as such, so in whose interests is she working? Under the broader heading of acting in the public

---

[4] Section 48 Criminal Justice and Public Order Act 1994, now replaced by section 144(1) Criminal Justice Act 2003. The practice has also been endorsed by the appellate courts, detailed judicial guidance on how trial judges ought to approach the issue of sentence discount having been promulgated in *R v. Goodyear* [2005] EWCA Crim. 888.

interest, she appears to have a quasi-judicial role in protecting the innocent and an advocate's role in pursuing convictions. Sigler's research (1979) suggests that American prosecutors are themselves similarly confused: of 36 prosecutors, 15 saw themselves as judicial officers and 14 as law enforcement officers. Melilli (1992) concludes that the adversary ethic is inappropriate for prosecutors, who must see their duty as being to prosecute only those who are, to their satisfaction, guilty beyond a reasonable doubt. Plea bargaining may be one way of achieving this, as is argued by those who believe that the desire to achieve convictions is motivated less by a concern for efficiency in the face of high caseloads and more by a concern to achieve justice in cases where the prosecutor believes the accused to be guilty. Mather's 1979 ethnographic study describes "the relative *un*importance of case pressure in explaining plea bargaining decisions," and reports instead that the strength of the prosecution's case and the seriousness of the offense (i.e., the likely sentence) were the key features (McDonald 1979, reports similar findings). However, Mather also concedes that assessment of legal guilt was tainted by the seriousness of the offense and the criminal history of the accused, neither of which should affect the assessment of the strength of the evidence. Her proposal was that sentencing, rather than plea bargaining itself, should be the focus of reform. Schulhofer (1984) also casts doubt on the case pressure theory, finding that many simple trials took little more time than a plea bargain. Others (e.g., Lynch, 1998) see plea bargaining as more akin to a form of administrative-inquisitorial justice, in which a state official adjudicates the case, with limited representation from the accused. A failure to acknowledge the reality of this role, argues Lynch (1998), perpetuates the prosecutor's erroneous view of herself as the partisan adversary of the defendant.

V. CONCLUSION

While it was not our intention to provide a comprehensive coverage of the literature, the preceding discussion has provided some indication of the breadth, quality, and value of the empirical research work that has been conducted in this area of the law. However, we hope that the preceding discussion has illustrated the contingent nature of the criminal process. The social and political issues, the institutions of the criminal justice system, legal doctrine, policies, and working practices are the product of complex reflexive relationships. The decision-making environment is constantly shifting, and one of the consequences of these changes is that the relevance and value of some research will diminish over time. This evolutionary process also presents new opportunities for empirical study. In recent years there have been significant changes in the landscape in which the criminal process is situated. But the empirical research agenda does not appear to have been shaped by broad and sometimes rather abstract concepts such as efficiency, risk, security, and rights which have informed these changes. We suggest that there is a pressing need for empirical research that reveals how policy and practice are influenced by these concepts.

REFERENCES

Bénec'h-Le Roux, P. (2007). "Chief Public Prosecutor: a Strengthened Professional Identity," *Penal Issues*, CESDIP (Nov).

Bibas, S. (2004). "Plea Bargaining Outside the Shadow of Trial," *Harvard Law Review* 117: 2463–547.

Bland, N., Miller, J., and Quinton, P. (2000). "Upping the PACE? An evaluation of the recommendations of the Stephen Lawrence enquiry," *Police Research Series Paper No. 128*, London: Home Office.

Bridges, L. and Choongh, S. (1998). *Improving Police Station Legal Advice: The Impact of the Accreditation Scheme for Police Station Legal Advisers*, London: The Law Society & The Legal Aid Board.

Bridges, L., Cape, E., Fenn, P., Mitchell, A., Moorhead, R., and Sherr, A. (2007). *Evaluation of the Public Defender Service in England and Wales*, London: Legal Services Commission, available at <http://www.legalservices.gov.uk/docs/pds/Public_Defenders_Report_PDFVersion6.pdf>.

Bucke, T., Street, R., and Brown, D. (2000). "The Right of Silence: The Impact of the CJPOA 1994," London: Home Office.

Cape, E., Hodgson, J., Prakken, T., and Spronken, T. (eds.) (2007). *Suspects in Europe: Procedural Rights at the Investigative Stage of the Criminal Process in the European Union, Ius Commune Europaeum*, Antwerp, Oxford: Intersentia.

Chilvers, M. and Weatherburn, D. (2001). "Do Targeted Arrests Reduce Crime?," New South Wales Bureau of Statistics and Research, Paper 63.

Coker, D. (2001). "Crime Control and Feminist Law Reform in Domestic Violence Law: A Critical Review," *Buffalo Criminal Law Review* 4: 801–60.

Donohue, L.K. (2008). *The Cost of Counterterrorism*, Cambridge: Cambridge University Press.

Edwards, S. (1989). *Policing Domestic Violence: Women, the Law and the State*, London: Sage.

Ehrhard, S. (2008). "Plea Bargaining and the Death Penalty: An Exploratory Study," *Justice System Journal* 29: 308.

Foster, J., Newburn, T., and Souhami, A. (2005). *Assessing the impact of the Stephen Lawrence Inquiry*, Home Office Research Study 294, London: Home Office.

Galligan, D. (1987). "Regulating Pre-trial Decisions," in I. Dennis (ed.), *Criminal Law and Justice*, London: Sweet & Maxwell.

Halligan-Davis, G. and Spicer, K. (2004). "Piloting "on the spot penalties" for disorder: final results from a one- year pilot," *Findings 257,* London: Home Office.

Hawkins, K. (2003). "Order, Rationality and Silence: Some Reflections on Criminal Justice Decision-making," in L. Gelsthorpe and N. Padfield (eds.), *Exercising Discretion: Decisionmaking in the Criminal Justice System and Beyond,* Cullompton: Willan.

Hester, M. and Westmarland, N. (2005). *Tackling Domestic Violence: Effective interventions and approaches,* Home Office Research Study 290, London: HMSO.

Hodgson, J. (2005). *French Criminal Justice: A Comparative Account of the Investigation and Prosecution of Crime in France,* Oxford: Hart Publishing.

Hodgson, J. (2006). *The Investigation and Prosecution of Terrorist Suspects in France,* Report for the Home Office, available at <http://papers.ssrn.com/sol3/papers.cfm?abstract_id=1321868>.

Hoyle, C. (1998). *Negotiating Domestic Violence: Police, Criminal Justice and Victims,* Oxford: Clarendon.

Hoyle, C. and Sanders, A. (2000). "Police Response to Domestic Violence: From victim choice to victim empowerment?," *British Journal of Criminology* 40: 14–36

Illuminati, G. (2005). "The Frustrated Turn to Adversarial Procedure in Italy," *Washington University Global Studies Law Review* 4(3): 567–81.

Jobard, F and Lévy, R. (2009). *Profiling Minorities: A Study of Stop- and- Search Practices in Paris,* Open Society Justice Initiative, available at <http://www.soros.org/initiatives/justice/focus/equality_citizenship/articles_publications/publications/search_20090630/search_20090630.Web.pdf>.

Langer, M. (2006). "Rethinking Plea Bargaining: The Practice and Reform of Prosecutorial Adjudication in American Criminal Procedure," *American Journal Criminal Law* 33: 223–99.

Lochner, T. (2002). "Strategic Behavior and Prosecutorial Agenda Setting in United States Attorneys' Offices," *Justice System Journal* 23: 271–94.

Lynch, G. E. (1998). "Our Administrative System of Criminal Justice," *Fordham Law Review* 66: 2117–51.

Maguire, M. and Corbett, C. (1990). *A Study of the Police Complaints System,* London: HMSO.

Mather, L.M. (1979). *Plea-Bargaining or Trial: The Process of Criminal-Case Disposition,* Lexington, Mass: Lexington Books.

McConville, M., Sanders, A., and Leng, R. (1991). *The Case for the Prosecution: Police Suspects and the Construction of Criminality,* London: Routledge.

McConville, M. and Hodgson, J. (1993). *Custodial Legal Advice and the Right to Silence,* London: HMSO.

McConville, M., Hodgson, J., Bridges, L., and Pavlovic, A. (1994). *Standing Accused: The Organisation and Practices of Criminal Defence Lawyers in Britain,* Oxford: Clarendon Press.

McDonald, W.F. (ed.) (1979). *The Prosecutor,* Beverley Hills: Sage Publishing.

Melilli, K.J. (1992). "Prosecutorial Discretion in an Adversary System," *Brigham Young University Law Review* 1992: 669–704.

Miller, J. (2000). *Profiling Populations Available for Stops and Searches,* Police Research Series Paper 131, London: Home Office.

Miller, L.L. and Eisenstein, J. (2005). "The Federal/State Criminal Prosecution Nexus: A Case Study in Cooperation and Discretion," *Law & Social Inquiry* 30: 239–68.

Ministry of Justice (2009). *Statistics on Race and the Criminal Justice System 2007/8*, London: Ministry of Justice.

Moody, S. and Tombs, J. (1982). *Prosecution in the Public Interest*, Edinburgh: Scottish Academic Press.

MVA and Miller, M.L. (2004). "Domination & Dissatisfaction: Prosecutors as Sentencers," *Stanford Law Review* 56: 1211–69.

Neyroud, P. (2006). "Ethics in Policing: Performance and the Personalisation of Accountability in British Policing and Criminal Justice," *Legal Ethics* 9 (1): 16–34.

O'Brien, B. (2009). "A Recipe for Bias: An Empirical Look at the Interplay Between Institutional Incentives and Bounded Rationality in Prosecutorial Decision Making," 74 *Missouri Law Review*: 999–105.

O'Neill, E. (2004). "Understanding Federal Prosecutorial Declinations: An Empirical Analysis of Predictive Factors," *American Criminal Law Review* 41: 1439–98.

Packer, H. (1968). *The Limits of the Criminal Sanction*, Stanford: Stanford University Press.

Paternoster, R. (1984). "Prosecutorial discretion in requesting the death penalty: a case of victim-based racial discrimination," *Law & Society Review* 18(3): 437–78

Perrodet, A. (2002). "The Public Prosecutor," in Delmas-Marty, M. and Spencer, J.R. (eds.), *European Criminal Procedures,* Cambridge: Cambridge University Press, 415–58.

Quinton, P., Bland, N. and Miller, J. (2000). *Police Stops, Decision-making and Practice*, Police Research Paper No. 130, London: Home Office.

Richman, D. (2003). "Prosecutors and Their Agents; Agents and Their Prosecutors," *Columbia Law Review* 103: 749–832.

Roberts, P. and Saunders, C. (2007). "Pre-trial witness interviews—Interviewing prosecution witnesses," *CPS Research, Monitoring and Evaluation Reports*, available at: <http://www.cps.gov.uk/publications/research/interviews_report.html>.

Robinson, G. and Shapland, J. (2008). "Reducing recidivism: a task for restorative justice?," *British Journal of Criminology* 48(3): 337–58.

Royal Commission on Criminal Justice (1933). *Report Cmnd 2263*, London: *HMSO*.

Scheb, J.M. II, Lyons, W., and Wagres, K.A. (2008). "Race, Prosecutors, and Juries: The Death Penalty in Tennessee," *Justice System Journal* 29: 338–47.

Schulhofer, S.J. (1984). "Is plea bargaining inevitable?," *Harvard Law Review* 97: 1037–107.

Sigler, J.A. (1979). "The Prosecutor: A Comparative Functional Analysis," in McDonald, W.F. (ed.), *The Prosecutor*, Beverly Hills: Sage Publishing, 53–74.

Simon, D., Stenstrom, D., and Read, J. (2009). "Adversarial and Non-Adversarial Investigations: An Experiment," available at <http://ssrn.com/abstract=1401723>.

Skinns, L. (2009). " 'I'm a detainee get me out of here' Predictors of Access to Custodial Legal Advice in Public and Privatized police Custody Areas in England and Wales," *British Journal of Criminology* 49: 399–417.

Smith, D. and Gray, J. (1983). *Police and People in London*, London: Policy Studies Institute.

Stenning, P. (2008). *The Modern Prosecution Process in New Zealand*, Wellington: Victoria University Press.

Tata, C., Goriely, T., McCrone, P., Duff, P., Knapp, M., Henry, A., Lancaster, B., and Sherr, A. (2004). "Does Mode of Delivery Make a Difference to Criminal Case Outcomes and Clients' Satisfaction? The Public Defence Service Experiment," *Criminal Law Review* 2004: 120–35.

Utz, P.J. (1979). "Two Models of Prosecutorial Professionalism," in McDonald, W.F. (ed.), *The Prosecutor,* Beverly Hills: Sage Publishing, 99–124.

Weenink, D. (2009). "Explaining ethnic inequality in the juvenile justice system," *British Journal of Criminology* 49: 220–42.

Weisburd, D., Wyckoff, L., Ready, J., Eck, J.E., Hinkle, J.C., and Gajewski, F. (2006). "Does Crime Just Move Around the Corner? A Controlled Study of Spatial Displacement and Diffusion of Crime Control Benefits," *Criminology,* 44(3): 549–91.

Wright, R. and Miller, M. (2003). "The Screening/Bargaining Tradeoff," *Stanford Law Review* 55: 29–118.

Young, R. (2008). "Street Policing After PACE: The Drift to Summary Justice," in E. Cape and R. Young (eds.), *Regulating Policing: The Police and Criminal Evidence Act 1984 Past, Present and Future,* Oxford: Hart Publishing, 149–89.

4

THE CRIME-
PREVENTIVE
IMPACT OF PENAL
SANCTIONS

ANTHONY BOTTOMS AND
ANDREW VON HIRSCH

I. Introduction

THE two-hundred year ethical debate between consequentialists and deontologists has been played out not only in the halls of academe, but also, so far as penal sanctions are concerned, in courts and parliaments. Consequentialists evaluate the appropriateness of penal sanctions by their results, particularly by the extent to which they reduce crime. Those in the deontological tradition, by contrast, place primary emphasis on punishment as censure for a wrongful act, and stress the need for the sanction to be proportionate to the seriousness of that act. Naturally, many intermediate positions are also possible.

In the present discussion, because our brief is to consider empirical research on the *impact* of penal sanctions, we shall be principally concerned with the consequentialist tradition. A *locus classicus* is therefore the work of Jeremy Bentham (1789/1982: 158), who, having stated that the "immediate principal end of punishment is to control action," went on to offer "a concise view" of the ways in which this might be achieved:

[The action to be controlled] is either that of the offender, or of others: that of the offender [punishment] controls by its influence, either on his will, in which case it is said to operate in the way of *reformation*; or on his physical power, in which case it is said to operate by way of *disablement*: that of others it can influence no otherwise than by its influence over their wills; in which case it is said to operate by way of *example* (emphasis in original).

These mechanisms remain the same today, and we shall accordingly structure this chapter around them, in a threefold division embracing (in modern language) *rehabilitation and special deterrence* (Bentham's "reformation"), *incapacitation* ("disablement"), and *general deterrence* ("example"—*pour encourager les autres*).

There are well-established empirical research literatures assessing issues of effectiveness in each of these fields. Within the space available, we will consider key features of these literatures, highlighting main results and relevant methodological and conceptual issues. As regards general deterrence and incapacitation, we shall also pay brief attention to the less well explored issue of the social dimensions of these penal aims.

Our discussion does not include the controversial question of the possible deterrent effect of the death penalty. There are two reasons for this. First, the available data and analyses do not "lead researchers with different prior beliefs to reach a [scientific] consensus" on this topic (McManus, 1985: 425), so whether the debate is truly empirical is doubtful. Second, there is merit in restricting the analysis of this Chapter to penal measures that are internationally considered to be morally acceptable punishments in at least some kinds of cases. Capital punishment fails this test; it has been abolished in most democracies, and its abolition has, on human rights grounds, been made a prerequisite for membership in the European Union.[1]

II. General Deterrence

A. The concept of general deterrence

There are three main kinds of empirical research into possible general deterrent effects—namely, association studies; quasi-experimental studies; and contextual and perceptual studies. We shall discuss the specifics of these methods shortly, but first we will analyze the concept of deterrence itself.

1. *Defining deterrence*

"Deterrence" may be defined as inducing avoidance of a given action through the threat of adverse consequences. The present discussion addresses *criminal* deterrence: namely, the prevention of criminal acts through the threat of legal punishment. Criminal deterrence is usually divided into special and general deterrence, with the former referring to discouraging already-identified offenders from reoffending, and the latter to discouraging members of the public generally from offending. The mechanism of successful deterrence is in both cases the same, but the audience is different. General deterrence (Bentham's "example") is the focus of the present discussion; as indicated previously, special deterrence is considered together with rehabilitation in the next section.

2. *Certainty vs. severity*

A recurring theme in discussions of deterrence is that the degree of "certainty" of punishment should be distinguished from the issue of "severity," although these terms have sometimes been confusingly employed. "Certainty" should be used to refer to the likelihood of being caught and convicted (or otherwise formally processed) by the criminal justice system. "Severity" should be used to refer to how stringently the offender is punished, once he has been caught and convicted. In the research literature, these are measured as *marginal* effects, comparing one level of certainty or severity with another, with other variables being held constant.

---

[1] For overviews of the research literature on the deterrent effect of capital punishment, with full citations, see Hood and Hoyle (2008: Ch. 9) and Tonry (2009). Both these sources favor the abolition of capital punishment, but the retentionist literature is fairly described.

3. *"Rational choice"*

Deterrence, although involving disincentives against offending, does not require that potential offenders act as fully rational, self-interested calculators. It suffices if they possess what the rational-choice literature terms "bounded rationality"—that is, they consider benefits and costs, to some degree, within parameters influenced by their attitudes, beliefs, and preferences, and by the information (however incomplete or inaccurate) available to them (see Gigerenzer and Selten, 2001).

It is also important to emphasize that "bounded rationality" does not assume that everyone shows the same degree and kind of rationality. Indeed, individuals appear to vary substantially in the degree to which they consider potential adverse consequences when acting. But the policy aim of general deterrence is to produce an *aggregate* crime-preventive effect. Thus a net general deterrent effect may be achievable even if only a portion of the intended audience alters its behavior through fear of the consequences—provided that the effect on this group suffices to reduce the overall offense rate.

4. *Deterrence and subjectivity*

Criminal deterrence is subjective in two senses. First, it depends not on what the certainty and the severity of punishment actually are, but on what potential offenders *believe* that they are. To the extent that changes in actual penal policies do not alter potential offenders' beliefs about the likelihood or severity of punishment, they cannot generate any marginal deterrence. This is what makes it so important, in research, to assess the link from actual policies to *perceived* risks of apprehension or punishment (see further below). Second, criminal deterrence depends not only on what potential offenders believe the sanction risks to be, but on how they evaluate those risks in terms of their subjective disutilities. For example, if penalties have increased and potential offenders know this, the change will still have no deterrent effect if those persons do not fear the increased penalties, or fear them but have overriding interests (e.g., financial ones) or inclinations (e.g., drug addiction) favoring offending. The subjective character of deterrence is one of its most important characteristics, but one that often is not recognized by policymakers when introducing policies intended to deter.

We have referred above to "potential offenders." This language also draws attention to a further important consequence of the subjective character of deterrence—namely, it can be effective only on those who might consider committing a given crime. As several writers have pointed out (e.g., Wikström, 2008), if burgling a house is an act that (for whatever reason) a person would not even consider, then variations in the probability of detection and conviction, or in the severity of the penalty, will necessarily be irrelevant for him; he is simply not a "potential offender" with respect to that crime.

B. Researching general deterrence

It should be clear from the foregoing that making valid inferences of deterrent effects is a complex undertaking. The methodological issues involved in deterrence research thus need to be carefully addressed. This will be done separately for the three main types of deterrence research, as previously described.

1. *Association studies*

Most modern deterrence research studies are association studies at the aggregate level. That is to say, they examine changes in law-enforcement or punishment levels in one jurisdiction at different times, or variations across different jurisdictions, or both of these together, and then assess how these differences correlate with variations in the crime rate.[2] If there is a negative correlation,[3] there is a possibility that this results from a deterrent effect. However, merely establishing a statistical association (a correlation) does not establish this, since of course a correlation does not imply causality. It is therefore worth outlining what further steps are needed to support an inference of deterrence. In outlining these steps, we hope also to make clear that it *is* possible to employ association studies as an appropriate tool of research for general deterrence. The study of deterrence, although difficult, is not impossible, and there are ways of inferring whether deterrent effects are at work.

i. Controlling for other influences. An adequate association study needs to consider other possible influences on crime rates. Thus the more sophisticated association studies attempt to control for at least some other variables that might have affected crime rates, such as demographic structures (age, gender, etc.), or unemployment rates among young males. The critical question is: *insofar as we know anything about the concomitants of crime, what factors (other than criminal justice policies) tend to be associated with changes in crime rates, and can they be adequately controlled for in the model?*

ii. The direction of causality. Suppose a researcher has identified a negative statistical correlation between crime rates and punishment levels (severity) in a given jurisdiction over time, even after controlling for other variables. If we are to draw an inference of a deterrent effect, we still need to be sure of the direction of

---

[2] Measuring "the crime rate" in a given country or area is not straightforward, but the complexities cannot be entered into here. The two main choices are (i) the "recorded crime rate," measuring crimes recorded by the police, and (ii) the "crime survey rate," based on victimization reports by representative samples of ordinary citizens. For a discussion of the strengths and limitations of these sources, see Maguire (2007).

[3] A "negative" correlation means that higher values on one variable are associated with lower values on the other. So a negative correlation between punishment severity and crime rates means that higher severity would be associated with a lower incidence of crime.

causality—that is, that a change in punishment levels has altered crime rates, and not vice versa. While "reverse causality" in this example might sound implausible, in fact it is not: for example, many jurisdictions have experienced overcrowded prisons because of increased crime, and have responded by sending fewer people to prison, or reducing durations of imprisonment, or both. This problem is known technically as the "simultaneity problem" (because causality can in principle operate in both directions simultaneously), and researchers have devised various methods to try to overcome it (see von Hirsch et al., 1999: 20, 30–1 for a summary).

iii. Subjective deterrence and its assessment. Even were the foregoing steps undertaken, one would still be left only with a statistical association: crime-rate changes that are negatively correlated with enforcement or penalty changes, in a context where we have reason to believe that the direction of causality is consistent with a deterrent effect. However, deterrence (as noted above) depends on *perceived* risks of being punished and on those perceived risks influencing behavior. These effects can be confirmed only by interview or questionnaire studies of persons' perceptions and attitudes—although too often association studies do not incorporate this type of research. In particular, two issues need to be explored: the "policy to perception" link and the "perception to action" link. These are most easily explained in the context of changes in certainty or severity over time in a given jurisdiction:

1. *Policy to perception*: To what extent are potential offenders aware of changes in the likelihood of conviction or in the severity of punishment? If people are ignorant of these changes, they cannot be deterred by them. Unfortunately, this question has been largely unexplored in existing deterrence research. The question is also more complicated than it seems, because what counts is (as we have noted) not so much the ordinary person's perceptions of certainty or severity, as the perceptions of potential offenders—of those more likely to consider committing the offense.

2. *Perception to action*: To what extent are altered perceptions of certainty or severity likely to affect the conduct of potential offenders? Even if one is aware of a change in certainty or severity, this may not affect actual behavior—for example, if one is drunk, or under the influence of drugs, or in an aroused emotional state, all of which conditions are frequently associated with criminal acts. There also is a further "subjectivity" problem, that of "thresholds." As Beyleveld (1979) pointed out, doubling a small fine (say, for a parking offense) will make no difference to those potential offenders who, while aware of the change, regard even the increased amount as too small to worry about. General deterrence only "works" if the altered risk of detection, or the altered level of the penalty, crosses the "threshold" where it will make a difference to the potential offender's choice. However, this problem of thresholds is exceptionally difficult to measure, not

least because thresholds, being subjective, may well differ in different groups of individuals.

2. *Quasi-experimental designs*

Quasi-experimental designs in deterrence research attempt to control for potentially confounding variables by the use of an analogue to an experimental research design. Such designs are constructed on a tailor-made basis for the particular enforcement or penal measure that it is proposed to study; the researcher will also attempt to identify in advance possible "threats to validity" arising from the particular design adopted and will seek to minimize their impact (see, generally, Shadish et al., 2002). In the field of deterrence, a few quasi-experimental designs have involved a researcher deliberately constructing a situation analogous to an experiment; but more usually researchers take an event, such as a change in penalty levels or in enforcement practice, and assess the "before and after" impact of this change (see e.g., Henstridge et al., 1997, on the effects of the introduction of random breath testing for drivers— intended to deter drunk driving—in four separate Australian states). To improve the validity of inferences of causality, such designs should ideally incorporate a control area where there has been no change, but this is not always feasible. In that event, a simple "one area before-and-after design" (technically known as an "interrupted time-series design") is often adopted.

The quasi-experimental approach, where feasible, has a number of advantages. First, the intervention can be well specified: it is ascertainable what new enforcement or sanctioning initiative is involved, when it was put into effect, and how thoroughly it was implemented. Second, short-term effects can be distinguished from long-term ones: if crime rates diminish immediately after (and apparently as a result of) the intervention, it can be examined how much these benefits "decay" over time. Finally, this technique can build into the design of the study itself controls for at least some other possible influences on crime rates. Limitations of the approach are that researchers often have to respond quickly to an initiative introduced by public authorities; also it works best when the effect of a discrete and identifiable initiative can be tested in a relatively narrow geographical area.

A recent Swiss "interrupted time-series" study of fare avoidance in Zurich's public transport system illustrates this type of methodology and also illustrates the issue of thresholds (Killias et al., 2009). From 1993, trains to and from Zurich's suburbs operated without attendants and with only sporadic ticket checks. Passengers found travelling without a valid ticket received an on-the-spot fine, and the rate of such defaulters among all ticket-checked passengers was stable at about 3.5%. From the beginning of 2003, concerns about safety on trains at night led to a large increase in the number of attendants after 9:00 p.m.: hours worked by train attendants rose more than tenfold in that year. Since all attendants were also expected to check tickets, this had the side effect of significantly increasing the probability of detection if one had no valid ticket. The violation rate decreased substantially (down to about 1%), which provides strong prima facie evidence of a deterrent effect from the increase in certainty, although the interviewing of passengers would have strengthened this inference. There was, however, no further decrease in this violation rate when attendants' working hours increased still more in 2006, suggesting that the thresholds of everyone who was deterrable had already been crossed by the earlier increase.

3. *Perceptual and contextual research*

There are two other types of research into deterrence (see von Hirsch et al., 1999: ch. 7). One is "contextual research," mainly consisting of studies into offender decision-making (see, for example, Wright and Decker's (1994) pioneering ethnographic research with burglars). The other is "perceptual research," using questionnaires or interviews. Methodologically, the strongest type of design for perceptual deterrence research is the so-called "scenario study," in which respondents are supplied with detailed vignettes of particular contexts in which offending behavior might take place, and are then asked about the sanction risks that they perceive in those situations, as well as their assessment of the likelihood of their committing an offense in the given circumstances. While valuable information has been gleaned from such studies, they are limited in that they do not directly measure individuals' actual behavior, and in practice they have usually been conducted with middle-class respondents. However, one important general conclusion has emerged from such studies; as Nagin (1998: 20) puts it, they have "consistently found that individuals who report higher stakes in conventionality are more deterred by perceived risk of exposure for law breaking." It seems clear that this is because, for such individuals, arrest (or other legal action) will bring the offense to the attention of people who matter to the respondent, and will therefore jeopardize valued social relationships and prestige. For example, in Klepper and Nagin's (1989) scenario-based research into possible tax evasion, "respondents *were* generally willing to consider tax noncompliance when only their money was at risk" (through possible civil enforcement actions by tax authorities, with no public disclosure); however, thoughts of non-compliance were immediately deterred by "a nonzero chance of criminal prosecution, ... putting reputation and community standing at risk" (Nagin 1998: 20–1, emphasis added). We will return to this issue shortly.

C. The results of general deterrence research

During the last forty years, there has been considerable research on general deterrence, particularly but not exclusively in the form of association studies; and in the last decade or so, several research overviews have been published. Most of these reviews have used the traditional "narrative-analytic" approach to the review process (e.g. Nagin, 1998; von Hirsch et al., 1999; Doob and Webster, 2003, with update in Doob et al., 2008: ch 9; Robinson and Darley, 2004); but recently, the first statistical meta-analysis of general deterrence research has been published (Pratt et al., 2006).[4] The results of this general body of research are fairly consistent, and, reassuringly, different types of methodology (see previous section) have tended to deliver similar conclusions. We will attempt to summarize these results succinctly.

(a) *The existence of deterrence.* In earlier decades, the existence of any criminal deterrent effect was a matter of some debate. The more recent research—particularly scenario-based perceptual studies and various quasi-experimental studies—dispel those doubts. The studies suggest that when potential offenders are made aware of substantial risks of being detected and punished, significant numbers of them may be induced to desist. Thus, it now seems clear that criminal punishment is capable, in practice, of having deterrent effects under appropriate circumstances.

(b) *Marginal deterrence: certainty effects.* Association studies do tend to show statistically significant correlations between certainty of punishment and crime rates. The leading association research studies of the 1990s, undertaken by David Farrington and his associates, show a significant statistical relation between the likelihood of arrest and conviction and the incidence of crime (see Farrington et al., 1994; Langan and Farrington, 1998). This comports with earlier research concerning the effects of certainty (for a summary, see Nagin, 1998). The findings are also supported by the recent meta-analysis of deterrence-study results (Pratt et al., 2006), which shows statistically significant negative correlations, albeit with modest effect sizes,[5] between punishment certainty and crime rates. Quasi-experimental studies, such as the Zurich study and the Australian random breath test studies mentioned earlier, further confirm the result.

(c) *Deterrence decay.* The phenomenon of "deterrence decay" has been shown to be important in relation to certainty effects. This has been shown, for example, in studies of police "crackdowns," but it is perhaps particularly clear in the case of random breath testing (RBT). The Henstridge et al. (1997) study of RBT in four Australian states highlighted strong initial deterrent effects, but this was followed by "the reality of constant decay in the deterrent effect of RBT, and the need to remedy this with continued high levels of visible...enforcement." The theoretical grounds

---

[4] A "meta-analysis" is a statistical procedure that pools the results of a number of separate research studies of a similar phenomenon, thereby creating a larger sample for analysis. It therefore differs markedly from narrative research reviews, which treat each research study separately and then attempt to make an overall inference about the net outcome of the research.

[5] An "effect size" is, as its name implies, a statistical tool used to measure the strength of an effect in a piece of evaluative research. By convention, an effect size of 0.10 is small, 0.30 is medium, and 0.50 is large. In the Pratt et al. (2006: 379) meta-analysis, the effect-size estimates for certainty, weighted for sample size, were -.334 for all studies taken together, and -.101 in studies using multivariate analysis.

for such results seem clear; deterrence relies for its effect on an *instrumental* decision; but if enforcement levels drop, then self-interested rational actors may notice this and cease to believe that they will be caught and processed. Thus, the certainty effect will probably need regular reinforcement (through high patrolling levels or other surveillance methods) if it is to continue being effective.

(d) *Marginal deterrence: severity effects.* The evidence concerning severity effects is less encouraging than that for certainty. The major association studies tend not to disclose statistically significant correlations between severity levels and crime rates. This was true of the Farrington studies of the 1990s, just cited, as well as research findings of earlier decades (see Nagin, 1998). The 2006 meta-analysis likewise fails to show statistically significant correlations in multivariate analyses (Pratt et al., 2006). Research into the deterrent effects of draconian "three strikes" laws in various American states also suggests that these measures have had little effect on the behavior of potential offenders (for a summary, see Doob and Webster, 2003). Such findings give scant support to claims that tougher penalties can demonstrably achieve greater success in deterring crime.

Indeed, so discouraging are these findings that Doob and Webster (2003) concluded it was time to accept "the null hypothesis": that variations in the severity of punishment have no effect on crime rates (see further Doob et al., 2008). We, however, are not sure that this suggestion is wise. Analytic considerations suggest that the degree of onerousness of potential penalties should matter, and that it will matter at least in certain limited conditions—that is, in situations where there are potential offenders who are sufficiently aware of those penalties, who believe they face a significant probability of being apprehended, and who have the requisite subjective utilities. The review by Robinson and Darley (2004) reaches similar conclusions and cites a limited number of studies where such conditions might apply.

1. *Why are severity effects apparently weak?*

The foregoing brief survey of the results of deterrence studies suggests two intuitively plausible results and a third result that seems counterintuitive. The two plausible results are that punishment can, in practice, have deterrent effects; and that the certainty of punishment will usually matter for deterrence, if enforcement levels are maintained. The puzzling result is the third: why does severity have such apparently weak effects? Although the issue remains under-researched, three reasons might help to account for this:

1. Information about changes in certainty of punishment often seems easier for potential offenders to obtain than information about changes in severity. If the police step up their presence in a neighborhood, or if tempting targets are visibly being surveyed by closed-circuit TV cameras, this may readily suggest that the risks of being caught have increased. The severity of punishments

which courts actually impose is a less visible phenomenon for many potential offenders.

2. Additions to the severity of punishment are contingent future events. Before higher sentence levels can apply to an offender, he must be caught and convicted. Detection rates, according to official criminal statistics, are low for many offenses, and they are much lower if one takes into account the many crimes that are never reported to the police. There is a general tendency for people to discount contingent future costs and much evidence that persistent offenders in particular are orientated toward immediate satisfactions (e.g., Wright and Decker, 1994). Given low detection rates and the fact that sentencing is very much a future event, it is perhaps not too surprising that sentence levels may often be discounted by potential offenders.

3. Threshold effects may also produce diminishing deterrent returns. As penalties rise, they may already have crossed the thresholds of the more deterrable potential offenders, leaving a residue of those increasingly less likely to be intimidated by increased threats.

D. General deterrence in social context

The subjectivity of deterrence gives rise to an important—though sometimes neglected—social consequence, namely that the same sanction can have different effects on persons differently placed within a given society. For example, the threat of exposure and punishment for a moderately serious offense might lead to a lawyer or business executive losing his/her job and suffering a severe reduction in the esteem in which he is held. By contrast, in some inner city areas in the United States, it is common for deprived young residents to have experienced imprisonment. Inevitably, these differing social contexts could significantly influence the subjective assessment of the potential threat to one's lifestyle posed by being caught and convicted—as is suggested by the results of the scenario research studies described above.

The strongest empirical confirmation of such effects is found in the meta-analysis by Pratt et al. (2006: 385) where "variables indicating the threat of non-legal sanctions were among the most robust of the deterrence theory predictors." These authors rightly emphasize, therefore, that "this pattern of findings illustrates the importance of linking the deterrence (or rational choice) perspective with theories that rely on other types of control mechanisms" in society (especially, normative attachments: see, further, Wikström, 2008; Tonry, 2009). Hence, it is now clear that the effectiveness of intended deterrent threats cannot be divorced from their social contexts—notwithstanding that social context has not been a major strand in the deterrence literature to date.

III. "Reductivism" (Rehabilitation and Special Deterrence)

Bentham (1789/1982: 158) spoke of the possibility that penal sanctions could influence the offender's will, "in which case [they are] said to operate in the way of reformation" (see I. above). In modern parlance, such influences embrace both "rehabilitation" and "special deterrence," each of which is intended to reduce the offender's inclination to offend (hence, the two together have sometimes been called "reductivism"). But there is, of course, an important intended difference between rehabilitation and special deterrence in the mechanisms through which the offender's (partial or complete) desistance from crime is sought. For this reason, we shall treat them largely separately.

The standard research method for evaluating the effectiveness of reductivist penal treatments is more straightforward than the techniques used to measure general deterrence, and is similar to that for social-science experimental studies generally. Some research subjects are selected for treatment in an "experimental" group; other subjects, matched as closely as possible with the experimental group by relevant characteristics, constitute the "control group" and do not receive the experimental treatment. If the experimentals subsequently reoffend significantly less often than the controls, the intervention is deemed to be a success. Obviously, a central concern in using this method is to ensure that the experimental and control groups really are comparable—for if they are not, then apparently "better" results for the experimental group might result, not from the treatment itself, but from the fact that these offenders had a lower risk of reoffending in the first place. The random allocation of subjects to treatment and control conditions is usually considered to be the best way of ensuring such comparability, as in trials of new drugs in medicine. However, ethical and practical considerations naturally limit the extent to which randomized designs can be used in the context of penal sanctions; additionally, such designs are not without their own methodological problems.[6] The alternative method, which in practice is much more frequently used, is either to try to match the characteristics of the experimental and control groups on an individual basis, or to control for aggregate differences by statistical techniques, using for these purposes characteristics that are known to be related to subsequent criminality (such as age and previous criminal record). In practice, non-randomized research designs vary considerably in quality, and it often requires skilled judgment to assess their adequacy.

[6] In particular, adoption of the so-called "double-blind" technique used in medical trials (whereby neither patients nor doctors know which patients are receiving the experimental treatment, and which the placebos) is normally not possible in penal contexts. If "double blind" is not available, subjects' different reactions to the experiment (depending on whether they are in the experimental or control group) can distort the experiment so that it measures not "Treatment A" vs. "Treatment B" but "Treatment A + reaction to experiment" vs. "Treatment B + reaction to experiment."

A. Rehabilitation

Rehabilitation, in a criminological context, consists of altering an offender's habits, reactions, outlook, or opportunities so as to make him or her less likely to commit crimes. Often, rehabilitation is said to involve "helping" the offender, but a benefit to him is not necessarily presupposed; those who benefit may chiefly be members of the public, whose risk of victimization is reduced.

1. *Penal welfarism and its decline*

Interest in the rehabilitation of offenders—especially young offenders—goes back to the nineteenth century. By the mid-twentieth century, the idea of rehabilitation had become institutionally embedded in parts of many Western penal systems, in practices that have been generically described as "penal welfarism." For example, in England in the 1960s, the standard medium-term custodial sentence for young adults was known as "Borstal Training," which by statute was set at a minimum of six months and a maximum of two years. The courts played no part in the determination of the actual period in custody, this being decided *entirely* by the Borstal authorities in the light of their perception of the individual's "progress in training" (and analogies to hospital discharges, made when the patient is "better," were frequently made).

Given this degree of official commitment to penal welfarism, it was something of a shock when, in the 1960s and 1970s, empirical research results began to appear, questioning whether rehabilitation was successful in preventing recidivism. The best-known publication in this vein is an article by Robert Martinson (1974), which prefigured the publication of Martinson and colleagues' major review of the research literature (Lipton et al., 1975). The Lipton et al. review did contain some positive findings, but what is now chiefly remembered is a single sentence in Martinson's (1974: 25) preview article: "*With few and isolated exceptions, the rehabilitative efforts that have been reported so far have had no appreciable effect on recidivism*" (emphasis in original). Despite the subsequent notoriety of Martinson's article, it is important to observe that other research reviews in the 1970s reached very similar conclusions—for example, a National Academy of Sciences report in the U.S. (Sechrest et al., 1979), and a Home Office research report in Britain (Brody, 1976). Indeed, the Home Office had recognized before Martinson that "the evidence ... suggested little if any difference in reconviction rates following different types of treatment," and had hypothesized that this might be because different kinds of treatment might have different effects on different kinds of offenders, with the "positive and negative results cancel[ling] each other out in any general comparisons" (Folkard et al., 1976: 1). Evaluation of a more differentiated approach was therefore attempted in a large-scale experimental study called IMPACT (Intensive

Matched Probation and After-Care Treatment), but the results continued to be disappointing (ibid).

Naturally, these reviews, taken together, dented confidence in the effectiveness of rehabilitation. With the benefit of hindsight, one can identify two major factors that helped to generate such disappointing results. First, some of the programs being evaluated were not very likely, even under optimum conditions, to produce positive results. In particular, what might be described as "general counseling" (often of a non-directive kind) was popular in this era, under the influence of the psychoanalytically based "casework model," but treatment of this kind has now been shown to be usually ineffective in preventing recidivism (see below). Secondly and more technically, many of the research projects on which the reviews were based were conducted with small samples, and that meant that modest differences in effectiveness were statistically nonsignificant, whereas had the samples been larger, a difference of similar proportions would have been significant.

2. "The new rehabilitation": meta-analyses and cognitive-behavioral approaches

To overcome the second of the difficulties just mentioned, researchers began from the mid-1980s to produce meta-analyses of treatment effects. This methodology (see note 4) reduces the possibility of overlooking positive or negative findings by aggregating the statistical results from many different studies of a similar type of treatment.[7] When this method was applied to the research literature on rehabilitation, some positive results began to appear, and these have been replicated in several meta-analyses that have been conducted since 1985. A representative overview of such research is that by Doris Layton Mackenzie in an influential volume, *Evidence-Based Crime Prevention* (2006). In her overview, Mackenzie (386) identifies a number of correctional treatments that the research shows to be ineffective in changing behavior, notably "rehabilitation programs that use vague, non-directive, unstructured counseling" (of the kind often used in the 1960s). More positively, Mackenzie (385) affirms that "there is now substantial evidence that rehabilitative programs work," and indeed that the best programs "reduce recidivism by as much as 10 to 20 per cent." Rehabilitative effectiveness, she concludes, is maximized where two conditions are fulfilled, namely: (i) that there is "substantial, meaningful contact between the treatment personnel and the participant"; and (ii) that the programs focus on "developing skills... and use behavioral (including cognitive-behavioral) methods."

---

[7] There is, however, an obvious pitfall, which meta-analytic researchers have to try to avoid. The pitfall is that one might inadvertently place together, in the same category of treatment, approaches that are in reality very different. If this occurs, the results from the meta-analysis will of necessity be flawed.

The "cognitive" and "behavioral" dimensions of successful treatments, referred to in this summary, merit brief elaboration. The cognitive dimension focuses on the offender's norms and on the reasoning processes he may deploy in potentially criminogenic situations; treatment agents attempt to change these as appropriate.

The behavioral dimension assumes that "criminal behavior, like almost all forms of social behavior, [is] largely learned, [and] is thereby modifiable through a schedule of ethically appropriate rewards and punishments" (Gendreau et al., 2006: 420). The focus is on *current and recent behavior,* rather than more distant antecedents. Those who lead treatment programs are accordingly encouraged (i) to promote and reinforce current "pro-social" behavior among participants (e.g., joining a karate club rather than hanging around on the streets with other delinquents); and also (ii) to engage participants in "concrete problem-solving" relating to their behavior (e.g., learning how to conduct oneself in arguments and disputes without resorting to violence—hence the focus on "developing skills" in Mackenzie's summary, above). Incentives, such as token economy systems, are used to assist the process of "behavior modification," with an emphasis on rewarding good behavior rather than punishing bad behavior, following research showing that the former is a more effective strategy. We are therefore here once again in the sphere of "bounded rationality"; behavior is to be altered largely by incentives and disincentives, especially the former.

It should be noted that the research results of the "new rehabilitation" literature (as reported especially in the meta-analyses) are not usually expressed in terms of types of court sanctions, but instead focus on the actual treatment modality that an offender undergoes while on probation, in prison, etc. If one considers the choice of sanction in itself, then the type of sentence alone is usually found to have little rehabilitative significance. For example, one English study examined reconviction rates for adults (age 17+) following four main types of sentence: prison; unpaid work; probation without special conditions; and probation with special conditions (Lloyd et al., 1994). There were large differences in the raw two-year reconviction rates between these four groups (from 49% to 68%), but the bulk of this variation was accounted for by offenders' background characteristics (e.g., differences in age, gender, offense type, and previous convictions). When these background variables were controlled for, the residual differences between sentence types were very small. A possible exception to this general picture is the suggestion in some (but not all) research that, by comparison with alternatives, short-term imprisonment is to an extent criminogenic, though this conclusion is "not sufficiently firm to guide policy" (Nagin et al., 2009; see also Cid, 2009).

3. *Too much, too soon*

The positive results of the meta-analyses led to an overturning of the pessimism that had been generated by the 1970s research reviews. The most widespread attempt to implement "the new rehabilitation" (based largely on cognitive-behavioral principles) has occurred in England and Wales, where a Home Office (2001) review of sentencing offered a very optimistic prospectus, stating as a "reasonable estimate" that "if the programmes are developed and applied as intended, to the maximum extent possible, [national] reconviction rates might be reduced by 5–15 percentage points."[8]

Large-scale delivery of "offending behavior programmes" was therefore implemented in England for adult offenders, both in prisons and in the community. However, the results proved, once again, disappointing (for a detailed summary, see Raynor and Robinson, 2009: Ch. 6). For example, in a pilot project on male prisoners serving sentences of two years or more, two cognitive-skills programs ("Reasoning and Rehabilitation" and "Enhanced Thinking Skills") produced better outcomes in the treatment group than in a matched comparison group. But after the same two programs had been "rolled out" much more widely across the prison system, evaluations showed no significant differences in outcome between program participants and comparison groups (for detailed references, see Bottoms, 2004: 77–8).

One interesting pattern of results that was repeated in several English studies at this time (e.g., Hollin et al., 2004) was that offenders who *completed* the prescribed treatment program were reconvicted less often than the control group, while program *non-completers* were reconvicted more often than the control group, thus canceling out the good results for the completers. This pattern of results suggests complex factors at work relating to offender motivation, but clear, empirically based explanations for the pattern are not yet available.

A principal lesson from the sobering English experience of the "national roll-out" of offending behavior programs is that effective implementation of such programs on a widespread scale is not a straightforward matter (see also Gendreau et al., 1999), and there are significant difficulties involved in moving from the "demonstration" to the "practical application" stage. (This issue had already been identified in Lipsey's (1999) meta-analysis,[9] but sadly its significance had not been recognized by those promoting policy developments in England in the early 2000s.) Raynor and Robinson's (2009: 135–6) conclusions about the "new rehabilitation" as applied in England are therefore a far cry from the high hopes of a few years ago:

The last ten years have seen a mixture of successes and failures, and an even larger volume of inconclusive outcomes: the process of judging what is working, what is promising and what would be better abandoned will continue for years, and conclusions drawn at this

---

[8] For a critique of this estimate, see Bottoms (2004: 62–3).

[9] In Lipsey's (1999) meta-analysis, the 205 "demonstration projects" reviewed were on average twice as effective as the 196 "practical programs."

point are necessarily provisional. However, our own provisional conclusion is that the ["new rehabilitation"] movement in Britain tried to move too fast, too soon.

4. *An alternative model: desistance-focused rehabilitation*

The cognitive-behavioral approach to rehabilitation has not been without its critics. One important critique has derived from research into desistance from crime. It is sometimes forgotten that most offenders, even persistent offenders, eventually desist, and there is a particularly rapid falling off in the frequency of offending in the decade from age 20 to 30. A recent empirical study confirmed and highlighted one recurring conclusion in desistance research, namely that there is "little evidence to suggest that interventions by [probation] officers [play] very much of a *direct* role in desistance" (Farrall, 2002: 175, emphasis in original). Instead, desistance, where it occurs, seems largely to be accomplished "by the probationers themselves ([through] their motivation), and from changes in the nature of the social context" in which they live (213). From a policy point of view, this is, of course, deeply ironic; it seems that rehabilitative success is often best achieved not through rehabilitative programs or skilled supervision (helpful though these might sometimes be), but through offender self-help. On current research evidence, successful elements in the development of self-generated desistance are, *first,* various "cognitive transformations" that offenders make (such as developing a new willingness to change following the onset of adulthood; or responding positively to "hooks for change," such as those offered by certain relationships) and, *second,* the positive subsequent impact of worthwhile social bonds such as romantic partnerships and employment opportunities (Giordano et al., 2002; Laub and Sampson, 2003).

Those interested in rehabilitation theory have pointed to two apparently successful features of these self-generated approaches. *First,* they tend to look *forward* to future goals, leaving offending behind; this offers a contrast with the cognitive-behavioral approach, in which past offending tends to be frequently revisited to assess how things could have been done differently. *Second,* they focus on the *strengths* that an individual can bring to thinking about and acting on his/her future, "rather than emphasizing and hence potentially exacerbating psychosocial deficits" (Ward and Maruna, 2007: 109). Using these and other insights, some criminologists have begun therefore to consider the development of "a desistance paradigm" of rehabilitation (McNeill, 2006), whereby probation officers and others would "stand alongside" offenders as they seek to change, helping them both practically and emotionally. More recently, this kind of approach has been more ambitiously developed into a so-called "good lives" model of rehabilitation (Ward and Maruna, 2007)—but this is still in its infancy, with limited empirical support, so potential future developments in this field are currently once again apparently in flux.[10]

---

[10] Restorative Justice (RJ) procedures have in recent years attracted growing support as a method of rehabilitation, and there is some empirical evidence for their rehabilitative effectiveness. However,

B. Special deterrence

Research on special deterrence has focused on two topics—fines and various other specially designed penalties, aimed at inducing convicted offenders to desist through "shock treatments."

Given the extensive use of fines in almost all jurisdictions, there is a surprising lack of research attempting to evaluate their effectiveness in preventing crimes. As a recent review concludes, such research as exists is, generally speaking, of mixed quality and is rather inconclusive—both as regards traditional ("fixed") fines and "day-fines" (i.e., fines based on the offender's daily income). Comparing research results for the two types of fine, the authors of the review cautiously conclude that "thus far, there is no indication that [day] fines are not equal to, or better than, fixed fines" (van Slyke et al., 2008: 115).

Over the last half-century, several jurisdictions have experimented with punishments that deliberately use "shock" or "fright" tactics in order to achieve a special-deterrent effect. Examples have been, in England, so-called "short sharp shock" detention centers; or, in the United States, programs such as "Scared Straight,"[11] "Shock Probation," and military-style "boot camps." Research, including meta-analysis, has now repeatedly demonstrated that such penalties are ineffective in reducing recidivism, and they are indeed consistently among the least successful programs that have been evaluated in reductivist research.

IV. Incapacitation

Incapacitation is the idea of simple restraint: rendering a convicted offender incapable, for a period of time, of offending again (Bentham's "disablement"). Whereas rehabilitation and special deterrence seek to affect offenders' choices so they refrain from committing crimes, incapacitation requires no such change. Instead, obstacles are interposed to impede the person from carrying out whatever criminal

---

RJ has usually been conceptualized as primarily reparative rather than rehabilitative in intent, and "certainly in some writing [RJ and rehabilitation] are contrasted, or viewed as oppositional terms" (Raynor and Robinson, 2009: 144). Given these complexities, the size of the RJ literature, and space constraints, it has not seemed appropriate to discuss RJ in this chapter. See more fully, Raynor and Robinson (2009: ch 7).

[11] In "Scared Straight" programs, young offenders are taken to a maximum security adult prison and required to listen to "horror stories" from the prisoners, detailing the deprivations of prison and explaining how they wished they had lived their lives differently.

inclinations he or she may have. Usually, the obstacles are prison walls, but other incapacitative techniques are possible—such as exile or house arrest.

There are two main types of incapacitation strategy: "selective" and "general" (or "collective"). Selective incapacitation aims to reduce crime by incapacitating "high-rate" (frequent) and/or "high-risk" (serious) potential offenders, relying on the well-established criminological finding that there is a marked skew in offending rates in the general population—with a smallish proportion of offenders committing over half of all crimes. General incapacitation aims, more straightforwardly, to reduce crime by increasing the use and/or length of prison sentences for crimes in general, or for specified crime categories. The strategy assumes that a significant number of those thus imprisoned would have offended and are prevented from doing so by being in custody.

Empirical research on incapacitation operates differently from research on deterrence or rehabilitation. As we have seen, research into these other penal aims centers around the question: "to what extent does the deterrent or rehabilitative measure, when it is applied, have the effect of diminishing the offender's (or someone else's) criminal activities?" In the case of incapacitation, the question is inverted. When the offender is incarcerated, this can be assumed to prevent him from committing crimes while he is inside. Instead, the critical issue becomes the counterfactual question of "how many more crimes would have occurred had the person not been incarcerated?"

A. Selective incapacitation

An initial research task for selective incapacitation policies concerns *prediction*, that is, identifying the indicia of potential recidivism. Various facts about offenders are collected: their age, previous arrests and convictions, social and employment history, and so forth; it is then statistically assessed which of these factors are most strongly associated with subsequent offending.

Prediction methods in criminology have a long history, going back to the 1920s. A contemporary example is the well-validated Offending Group Reconviction Scale (OGRS), which is routinely used by courts and penal agencies in England and Wales. The general OGRS scale provides an indication of the statistical probability of a given offender being reconvicted within a two-year period. However, like many other general prediction instruments, it does not distinguish between serious and less serious recidivism; both the offender who subsequently may commit a single minor offense and the individual who is apt to commit a significant number of serious new crimes are grouped together as "recidivists." This is of little value for the purposes of selective incapacitation, since on ethical grounds few would support a policy of extended imprisonment to prevent, say, petty thefts.

Nevertheless, the basic notion of prediction is apparently capable of adaptation to meet the needs of a selective incapacitation strategy. A major boost to such thinking was provided by a RAND Corporation study by Greenwood and Abrahamse (1982). These authors aimed to target *high-rate, high-risk (serious)* offenders—those likely to commit frequent acts of robbery or other violent crimes in the future. For that purpose, they took a group of incarcerated robbers, conducted a self-report survey asking them how frequently they had committed such serious crimes, and then identified the salient characteristics of those having the highest self-reported robbery rates. From this, they fashioned a seven-factor predictive index which identified the high-rate potential robbers on the basis of their self-reported previous crimes and histories of drug use and unemployment.

The authors also devised a novel method of estimating the aggregate crime reduction impact of this technique. On the basis of the offender self-reports, they estimated the average annual rate of offending of those robbers who, according to the prediction index, were identified as "high risk." They then calculated the number of robberies that would be prevented by incarcerating such individuals for given extended periods. They calculated that by increasing prison terms for the high-risk robbers while reducing the terms for the others, it would become possible to reduce the overall robbery rate by as much as 15 to 20%—without causing prison populations to rise significantly.

While this study initially attracted much interest, difficulties soon became apparent. A major problem lay in making such forecasts on the basis of official data of the kind that sentencing courts have available. The objective of selective incapacitation is to target potential high-rate serious offenders and distinguish them from recidivists who reoffend less frequently or less gravely. To make this distinction, the RAND studies, including Greenwood's, relied upon offender self-reports. But a sentencing court obviously cannot assume that defendants will be willing to supply detailed information about their criminal and social histories if this could result in their receiving longer prison terms. However, when Greenwood's data were reanalyzed to see how well the potential high-risk serious offenders could be identified from the information ordinarily available in court records, the results were disappointing. The officially recorded facts—arrests, convictions, and meager information about offenders' personal histories—did not permit the potential high-rate robbers to be distinguished from others.

Questions were raised, also, about the projections of aggregate crime-preventive impact. Greenwood had assumed that high-rate potential robbers would continue offending for long periods. When shorter (and more realistic) residual criminal careers were assumed instead, the estimated preventive effect diminished dramatically. These further doubts were confirmed by a subsequent report of the National Academy of Sciences' panel on criminal careers (Blumstein et al., 1986).

The Panel thus identified one of the most troublesome issues in this field: that of estimating the length of offenders' residual criminal careers. In order to be effective, selective incapacitation needs to identify not potential high-risk/high-rate offenders generally, but rather *those who would have been likely to continue with such offending for extended periods*. However, one of criminology's most universal and durable findings is that offenders, even recidivist offenders, tend to reduce their criminality with age. Moreover, recent research shows that offending levels among young offenders are not necessarily good predictors of later criminality—people change their apparent offending trajectories (Laub and Sampson, 2003).

A few studies have recently attempted to make estimates of the duration and intensity of offenders' residual criminal careers (see, e.g., Kazemian and Farrington, 2006). These studies confirm that residual career length and frequency of offending decline at a steady pace with age. Moreover, offenders' scores on risk-assessment indices—when based mainly on information included in official records—were significantly but only modestly associated with the extent of their remaining criminal careers. These results suggest that selective incapacitative benefits will be hard to achieve, and will decline significantly during a predictively based sentence.

Recently, the U.S. National Institute of Justice commissioned a fresh review of incapacitation strategies, both selective and general. Two papers from this review are of special interest in relation to selective incapacitation. Bushway and Smith (2007: 387) note that a considerable degree of incapacitation, based on risk assessment, already exists in everyday criminal justice practices in the United States (for example, in giving substantially longer sentences, or denying parole, to those with long criminal records), yet researchers have not adequately taken account of this point. But in another paper, Blokland and Nieuwbeerta (2007) report results from the Netherlands Criminal Career and Life-Course Study, the main data for which were collected at a time when the Dutch prison population was by international standards very low, thus minimizing the problem identified by Bushway and Smith. Blokland and Nieuwbeerta estimated the incapacitative effects of a variety of selective prison policies (explicitly disregarding possible deterrent effects), and they concluded that such policies would lead to a reduction in crime. However, the costs appeared to be disproportionate; for example, for this cohort, a 25% reduction in crime would have required a prison population 45 times the current national level in the Netherlands.

Where does this leave us? A limited capacity to forecast risk has long existed: persons with extensive criminal histories, drug habits, and no jobs tend to re-offend at a higher rate than other offenders. However, the limitations in that forecasting capacity must be recognized, especially as regards the difficult issue of estimating residual criminal careers. Research shows that the potential aggregate crime-prevention impact of selective incapacitation on crime rates is well below proponents' initial estimates. Following Bushway and Smith, we need also to recognize the degree to which existing criminal justice practices in many jurisdictions already incorporate risk-related strategies. Adopting fresh incapacitation policies that go beyond existing practice will also raise considerations of proportionality and the degree to which inequalities in sentence for comparably serious crimes may fairly be visited for the sake of restraining high-risk offenders, while limiting permissible inequalities on the grounds of fairness will, in turn, further restrict the technique's impact on crime. For these reasons, the attention of criminologists (although not always of policy-makers) has, in more recent years, often turned away from selective incapacitation.

B. General incapacitation

General (or "collective") incapacitation is a penal strategy that began to be discussed in the mid-1970s. It calls for prison sentences of increased duration to be imposed for specified crimes (mostly, crimes against the person), or sometimes for all more serious crimes, without attempts being made to identify which individual offenders constitute the higher risks. In principle, a general incapacitation strategy could also involve using imprisonment for some offenders currently receiving community penalties.

There is an obvious site for studying the possible effects of general incapacitation. The United States has, in the last 35 years, altered its incarceration practices in an extraordinary manner; the prison population has increased sevenfold, from 200,000 in 1973 to 1.5 million now. It is generally agreed that this increase has been principally driven not by population trends or crime-rate changes, but by "increased rates of sentencing to prison and increased lengths of stay" (Clear, 2009: 97). Not surprisingly, therefore, most research analyses of the effects of collective incapacitation have emanated from American researchers.

Two principal research strategies have been deployed in this field. Most analyses are based on what has been described as a "bottom-up" methodology similar to that applied to the study of selective incapacitation (IV.A, above). This involves projecting, from an analysis of individual criminal careers, an average annual rate of offenses prevented by incarcerating specific groups of offenders. The results of this type of research have recently been reviewed by Piquero and Blumstein (2007). One of their principal conclusions is that estimates of the amount of crime prevented by a given incapacitation policy often vary widely, even where researchers are using similar data sets; these variations arise from the particular assumptions used in the statistical model. Divergences arise especially in relation to: (i) how to calculate the average offending frequency (conventionally described as "lambda") of various groups of offenders, especially given evidence of considerable heterogeneity in offending rates by age and locality; (ii) issues of co-offending and of "offender replacement" (researchers might assume, for example, that incarcerating drug dealers for longer periods might have a limited incapacitative effect because others will have readily stepped in to fill their place in the market); and (iii) the likely length of criminal careers. Miles and Ludwig (2007: 301) identify a further measurement problem: estimates of lambda, if they are to include undetected crime (the majority of all crime), must depend on offender self-reports; but given the skews in the distribution of offending, estimates of the aggregate of crimes prevented are highly sensitive to the questionable validity of self-reports by a small number of high-rate offenders.[12] These various points illustrate how dependent this research method is on various assumptions in order to generate its estimates of crimes prevented. Despite the difficulties, however, Piquero and Blumstein believe that criminal-career research methodologies have made significant progress in the last twenty years and that future incapacitative research of the "bottom-up" variety can be improved by a systematic application of this knowledge.

The second method of studying general incapacitation is the so-called "top-down" approach, which uses an association-study methodology similar to that of the deterrence studies discussed previously. In the present context, studies of this kind treat the aggregate crime rate as the dependent variable (i.e., the variable to be statistically explained), and they then construct a model which seeks to account for variations in crime rates using data on age, gender, unemployment, and so forth. Among these "independent" (explanatory) variables is the size of the prison population; thus, estimates can be made of the extent to which changes in the prison population affect the crime rate. (For a fuller description of the methodology, see Spelman, 2000.) It is important to note that this methodology is unable to distinguish between the incapacitative and general-deterrent effects of incarceration levels; it simply estimates the *overall* crime-preventive effect of increased or reduced imprisonment. Some, however, view this as an advantage in policy terms (e.g., Miles and Ludwig, 2007); for such writers, it is more important to obtain an accurate estimate of the total crimes prevented by the imprisonment of particular categories of offenders than to worry about whether this effect has been caused by incapacitation or deterrence.

Studies using the "top-down" methodology are, like "bottom-up" studies, heavily dependent upon the assumptions incorporated in the model. Hence, once again, the projected incapacitative effects vary widely in different studies (see table in Stemen, 2007: 4).

A significant technical defect of most "top-down" research studies has recently been noted (Stemen, 2007; Blokland and Nieuwbeerta, 2007: 329): that is, only three studies to date have controlled for simultaneity effects (see section II.B(1) (ii) above). In these three studies, the estimated percentage reduction in crime rates arising from a 10% increase in incarceration varies between 2.6% and 4.4%. Spelman's (2005) study in Texas (using data for the decade 1990–2000) is the most recent of these three studies and is worth careful attention because it was also the first U.S. research to assess incapacitation at the local (county) level. (This level

---

[12] The estimates are questionable not only because of possible dissembling by interviewees, but also (and probably more importantly) because, for many such offenders, the number of their crimes is so large that they cannot recall their offending history with any accuracy.

of analysis was advantageous because the variance in crime rates among the 254 counties in Texas in the studied years was very large, and such variation assists statistical analysis.) Spelman's main conclusions were first, that "Texas' primary response to the crime problem—massive incarceration—worked. Crime went down and prisons are the biggest reason." But secondly, his analysis strongly suggested that "the costs of this apparently successful policy appear to be greater than the benefits" (p. 162).

It is clear from the above discussion that there are significant methodological problems with both the "bottom-up" and "top-down" methodologies. For this reason, Miles and Ludwig (2007) recommend the greater use in incapacitative research of quasi-experimental studies. As we have seen, such techniques have been deployed successfully in research on general deterrence, but they have rarely been used in incapacitative research.

From the existing research on general incapacitation, four main conclusions can perhaps be drawn. First, and unsurprisingly, prison expansion usually does have some incapacitative effect. Second, the extent of this effect is difficult to assess, because of the assumptions that it is necessary to make in order to build appropriate models (either bottom-up or top-down). Third, the fact that there is an incapacitative effect does not necessarily mean that there is a *cost-effective* incapacitative effect (see, e.g., the conclusions of Spelman's Texas study). Fourth, after a period of prison expansion (but exactly when is difficult to judge) substantially diminishing returns are likely to set in. As noted above, the offending population is highly skewed, with a limited number of offenders having disproportionately high offense rates. The evidence suggests that the most active offenders are often incarcerated early in any process of prison expansion, hence subsequently increasing the use and duration of incarceration will have a diminishing impact.

C. The social consequences of incarceration

We have seen that some researchers have used benefit-cost analysis to test the effectiveness of mass-incarceration strategies. The economists Miles and Ludwig (2007), discussing such analyses, interestingly argue that the "social costs" of the increased use of prison should be included in such analyses, although, as they rightly say, such costs "have been largely ignored in empirical research [on incapacitation] to date" (299).

Researchers have addressed the social costs of incarceration in two main ways: by considering its effects on offending among the children of imprisoned parents, and on the communities from which prisoners are drawn. There is a growing literature on prisoners' children, which has recently been reviewed by Murray and

Farrington (2009). They conclude that in multivariate analyses, "parental imprison-ment roughly trebles the risk for child antisocial behavior" and that it is also "a rela-tively strong predictor of multiple adverse outcomes," such as poor mental health and drug use (186–7). These are striking results; however, "very little is known about whether parental imprisonment *causes* these problems" (133, emphasis added), and if so how. But the risk analyses are clearly important for policy purposes, and the authors further note that "parental imprisonment differs from many classic risk fac-tors in criminology because it is determined not only by individuals' behavior but also, critically, by state actions" (187).

Turning to community effects, in most countries the imprisonment rate of resi-dents tends to be highest in the most socially deprived areas. Given the scale of imprisonment in the United States, this raises the possibility that, in such areas, the social effects of lifting (mostly) young males out of such communities in large numbers, and eventually coping with their return, may be substantial. In a recent review of the limited research evidence in this field, Todd Clear (2009: 122–3) con-cludes: "there is good evidence that high rates of incarceration destabilize fami-lies, increase rates of [juvenile] delinquency, increase rates of teenage births, foster alienation of youth from pro-social norms, and weaken labor markets." The evi-dence relating to the criminogenic consequences is more mixed, and this topic poses "considerable methodological challenges" (97). This is a topic requiring fur-ther research; but, as with deterrence, the work that has been done so far estab-lishes how important it is not to neglect the social dimensions of incapacitative policies.

V. Concluding Remarks

Given the complexity of the materials presented here, an attempted summary would be difficult and, perhaps, potentially misleading. Thus we restrict our concluding remarks to the following general points:

1. Improved methodologies for assessing the crime-preventive effects of some criminal justice policies have been developed in recent years. Examples of these are described throughout the text.
2. Intervention methods have also shown some successes, or potential successes. For example, progress has been made in the development of treatment meth-odologies, at least on a "demonstration project" basis (see III.A.(3)). Also, the greater likelihood of detection and apprehension of offenders is known to be significantly correlated with crime rates—providing hope that improved

policing strategies, or some of them, may yield enhanced general deterrence (see II.C).

3. In the sentencing context, however, crime-prevention strategies appear to hold less promise. In a series of reviews, and one meta-analysis, of deterrence studies over several decades, the severity of punishments appears to be only very weakly correlated with crime rates, suggesting that significant deterrent effects for increased punishment are not likely to be confirmed on any widespread basis. Selective incapacitative strategies (such as those involving extended imprisonment for selected "high-risk" offenders) are beset with considerable difficulties—including those related to estimating the duration and intensity of such offenders' residual criminal careers. Rehabilitative programs also continue to encounter problems at the "roll-out" stage when "demonstration" programs are implemented on a larger scale. "General" incapacitation strategies—simply increasing the use of imprisonment—initially reduce crime to some extent, but not always in a cost-effective manner, and such strategies are, in any case, subject to diminishing returns.

4. These last-noted results suggest that crime-preventive aims can justify sentencing policies only to a limited degree, at least for the foreseeable future. The hope of Bentham and his modern followers—that sentencing schemes can be developed systematically, through calculation of crime-preventive benefits and costs—is unlikely to be realized. Other concerns, such as those regarding desert and proportionality,[13] may need to be taken substantially into account. Researchers also need in the future to pursue more rigorously the important but relatively underdeveloped topic of the social effects of penal sanctions.

References

Bentham, J. (1789/1982). *An Introduction to the Principles of Morals and Legislation*, (J.H. Burns and H.L.A. Hart, eds.), London: Methuen.

Beyleveld, D. (1979). "Identifying, Explaining and Predicting Deterrence," *British Journal of Criminology* 19: 205–24.

Blokland, A.A.J. and Nieuwbeerta, P. (2007). "Selectively Incapacitating Frequent Offenders: Costs and Benefits of Various Penal Scenarios," *Journal of Quantitative Criminology* 23: 327–53.

---

[13] A number of contemporary penologists have maintained that considerations of proportionality and desert—related to the degree of blameworthiness of the criminal conduct, judged by the conduct's degree of harmfulness and the offender's culpability—should furnish the *prima facie* basis for sentencing. This, it is argued, would provide an ascertainable scale of penalties, ranked according to seriousness of offenses. Within such a desert-based structure, however, there may remain some scope for considering crime-prevention effects: for example, in choosing among noncustodial sentences. For a summary and analysis, see von Hirsch and Ashworth, 2005, Ch. 9.

Blumstein, A., Cohen, J., Roth, J., and Visher, C. (eds.) (1986). *Criminal Careers and "Career Criminals,"* Volume 1, Washington DC: National Academy Press.

Bottoms, A.E. (2004). "Empirical Research Relevant to Sentencing Frameworks," in A.E. Bottoms, S. Rex, and G. Robinson (eds.), *Alternatives to Prison: Options for an Insecure Society*, Cullompton, Devon: Willan Publishing.

Brody, S.R. (1976). *The Effectiveness of Sentencing*, Home Office Research Study No. 35, London: HMSO.

Bushway, S. and Smith, J. (2007). "Sentencing Using Statistical Treatment Rules: What We Don't Know Can Hurt Us," *Journal of Quantitative Criminology* 23: 377–87.

Cid, J. (2009). "Is Imprisonment Criminogenic? A Comparative Study of Recidivism Rates Between Prison and Suspended Prison Sanctions," *European Journal of Criminology* 6: 459–80.

Clear, T.R. (2009). "The Effects of High Imprisonment Rates on Communities," in M. Tonry (ed.), *Crime and Justice: A Review of Research* 37: 97–132, Chicago: University of Chicago Press.

Doob, A.N. and Webster, C. (2003). "Sentence Severity and Crime: Accepting the Null Hypothesis," in M. Tonry (ed.), *Crime and Justice: A Review of Research* 30: 143–95, Chicago: University of Chicago Press.

Doob, A.N., Sprott, J.B., and Webster, C. (2008). *Youth Crime: The Impact of Law Enforcement Approaches on the Incidence of Violent Crime Involving Youth: Matters Relating to Understanding the Implications of These Findings*, Report prepared for the Review of the Roots of Youth Violence, Toronto: Centre for Criminology, University of Toronto.

Farrall, S. (2002). *Rethinking What Works With Offenders: Probation, Social Context and Desistance From Crime*, Cullompton, Devon: Willan Publishing.

Farrington, D.P., Langan, P.A., and Wikström, P.-O. (1994). "Changes in Crime and Punishment in America, England and Sweden between the 1980s and 1990s," *Studies in Crime and Crime Prevention* 3: 104–31.

Folkard, M.S., Smith, D.E., and Smith, D.D. (1976). *IMPACT Volume II: The Results of the Experiment*, Home Office Research Study No 36, London: HMSO.

Gendreau, P., Goggin, C., and Smith, P. (1999). "The Forgotten Issue in Effective Correctional Treatment: Program Implementation," *International Journal of Offender Therapy and Comparative Criminology* 43: 180–7.

Gendreau, P., Smith, P., and French, S.A. (2006). "The Theory of Effective Correctional Intervention: Empirical Status and Future Directions," in F.T. Cullen, J.P. Wright, and K.R. Blevins (eds.), *Taking Stock: The Status of Criminological Theory*, New Brunswick, NJ: Transaction Publishers.

Gigerenzer, G. and Selten, R. (eds.) (2001). *Bounded Rationality: The Adaptive Toolbox*, Cambridge, Mass: MIT Press.

Giordano, P.C., Cernovich, S.A., and Rudolph, J.L. (2002). "Gender, Crime and Desistance: Toward a Theory of Cognitive Transformation," *American Journal of Sociology* 107: 990–1064.

Greenwood, P.W. and Abrahamse, A. (1982). *Selective Incapacitation*, Santa Monica, CA: RAND Corporation.

Henstridge, J., Homel, R., and Mackay, P. (1997). *The Long-Term Effects of Random Breath Testing in Four Australian States: A Time-Series Analysis*, Canberra: Commonwealth Department of Transport and Regional Development.

Hollin, C., Palmer, E., McGuire, J., Hounsome, J., Hatcher, R., Bilby, C., and Clark, C. (2004). *Pathfinder Programmes in the Probation Service: A Retrospective Analysis*, Home Office Online Report 66/04, London: Home Office.

Home Office (2001). Making Punishments Work: Report of a Review of the Sentencing Framework for England and Wales, London: HMSO.

Hood, R. and Hoyle, C. (2008). *The Death Penalty: A Worldwide Perspective*, Oxford: Oxford University Press.

Kazemian, L. and Farrington, D.P. (2006). "Exploring Residual Career Length and Residual Number of Offences for Two Generations of Repeat Offenders," *Journal of Research in Crime and Delinquency* 43: 89–131.

Killias, M., Scheidegger, D., and Nordenson, P. (2009). "The Effects of Increasing the Certainty of Punishment: A Field Experiment on Public Transportation," *European Journal of Criminology* 6: 387–400.

Klepper, S. and Nagin, D. (1989). "Tax Compliance and Perceptions of the Risks of Detection and Criminal Prosecution," *Law and Society Review* 23: 209–40.

Langan, P.A. and Farrington, D.P. (1998). *Crime and Justice in the United States and England and Wales, 1981–96*, Washington, DC: Bureau of Justice Statistics.

Laub, J.H. and Sampson, R.J. (2003). *Shared Beginnings, Divergent Lives*, Cambridge, MA: Harvard University Press.

Lipsey, M. (1999). "Can Rehabilitative Programs Reduce the Recidivism of Juvenile Offenders? An Inquiry into the Effectiveness of Practical Programmes," *Virginia Journal of Social Policy and the Law* 6: 611–41.

Lipton, D., Martinson, R., and Wilks, J. (1975). *The Effectiveness of Correctional Treatment*, New York: Praeger.

Lloyd, C., Muir, G., and Gough, M. (1994). *Explaining Reconviction Rates: A Critical Analysis*, Home Office Research Study No. 136, London: HMSO.

MacKenzie, D.L. (2006). "Reducing the Criminal Activities of Known Offenders and Delinquents: Crime Prevention in the Courts and Corrections," in L.W. Sherman, D.P. Farrington, B.C. Welsh, and D.L. MacKenzie (eds.), *Evidence-Based Crime Prevention* (revised edn.), London: Routledge.

Maguire, M. (2007). "Crime Data and Statistics," in M. Maguire, R. Morgan, and R. Reiner (eds), *Oxford Handbook of Criminology* (4th edn), Oxford: Oxford University Press, 241–301.

Martinson, R. (1974). "What Works? Questions and Answers About Prison Reform," *The Public Interest* 35: 22–54.

McManus, W.S. (1985). "Estimates of the Deterrent Effect of Capital Punishment: The Importance of the Researcher's Prior Beliefs," *Journal of Political Economy* 93: 417–25.

McNeill, F. (2006). "A Desistance Paradigm for Offender Management," *Criminology and Criminal Justice* 6: 39–62.

Miles, T.J. and Ludwig, J. (2007). "The Silence of the Lambdas: Deterring Incapacitation Research," *Journal of Quantitative Criminology* 21: 287–301.

Murray, J. and Farrington, D.P. (2009). "The Effects of Parental Imprisonment on Children," in M. Tonry (ed.), *Crime and Justice: A Review of Research*, 37: 133–206, Chicago: University of Chicago Press.

Nagin, D. (1998). "Criminal Deterrence Research at the Outset of the Twenty-first Century," in M. Tonry (ed.), *Crime and Justice: A Review of Research*, 23: 51–91, Chicago: University of Chicago Press.

Nagin, D.S., Cullen, F.T., and Jonson, C.L. (2009). "Imprisonment and Reoffending," in M. Tonry (ed.), *Crime and Justice: A Review of Research* 38: 115–200, Chicago: University of Chicago Press.

Piquero, A.R. and Blumstein, A. (2007). "Does Incapacitation Reduce Crime?," *Journal of Quantitative Criminology* 21: 267–85.

Pratt, T.C., Cullen, F.T., Blevins, K.R., Daigle, L.E., and Madensen, T.D. (2006). "The Empirical Status of Deterrence Theory: a Meta-analysis," in F.T. Cullen, J.P. Wright, and K.R. Blevins (eds.), *Taking Stock: The Status of Criminological Theory*, New Brunswick, NJ: Transaction Publishers.

Raynor, P. and Robinson, G. (2009). *Rehabilitation, Crime and Justice*, (revised edn.), Basingstoke: Palgrave Macmillan.

Robinson, P.H. and Darley, J.M. (2004). "Does Criminal Law Deter? A Behavioural Science Investigation," *Oxford Journal of Legal Studies*, 24: 173–205.

Sechrest, L., White, S.O., and Brown, E.D. (eds.) (1979). *The Rehabilitation of Criminal Offenders: Problems and Prospects*, Washington, DC: National Academy of Sciences.

Shadish, W.R., Cook, T.D., and Campbell, D.T. (2002). *Experimental and Quasi-Experimental Designs for General Causal Inference*, Boston: Houghton Mifflin.

Spelman, W. (2000). "What Recent Studies Do (and Don't) Tell Us About Imprisonment and Crime," in M. Tonry (ed.), *Crime and Justice: A Review of Research*, 29: 414–94, Chicago: University of Chicago Press.

Spelman, W. (2005). "Jobs or Jails? The Crime Drop in Texas," *Journal of Policy and Management* 24: 133–65.

Stemen, D. (2007). *Reconsidering Incarceration: New Directions for Reducing Crime*, New York: Vera Institute of Justice.

Tonry, M. (2009). "Learning From the Limitations of Deterrence Research," in M. Tonry (ed.), *Crime and Justice: A Review of Research* 37: 279–311. Chicago: University of Chicago Press.

van Slyke, S., Waldo, G.P., and Bales, W. (2008). "Hit 'Em Where It Hurts: Monetary and Nontraditional Punitive Sanctions," in S.G. Shoham, O. Beck, and M. Kett (eds.), *International Handbook of Penology and Criminal Justice*, Boca Raton, FL: CRC Press.

von Hirsch, A. and Ashworth, A. (2005). *Proportionate Sentencing: Exploring the Principles*, Oxford: Oxford University Press.

von Hirsch, A., Bottoms, A.E., Burney, E., and Wikström, P.-O. (1999). *Criminal Deterrence and Sentence Severity*, Oxford: Hart Publishing.

Ward, T. and Maruna, S. (2007). *Rehabilitation: Beyond the Risk Paradigm*, London: Routledge.

Wikström, P.-O. (2008). "Deterrence and Deterrence Experiences: Preventing Crime Through the Threat of Punishment," in S.G. Shoham, O. Beck, and M. Kett (eds.), *International Handbook of Penology and Criminal Justice*, Boca Raton, FL: CRC Press.

Wright, R. and Decker, S. (1994). *Burglars on the Job: Streetlife and Residential Break-ins*, Boston, MA: Northeastern University Press.

5

CONTRACTS AND CORPORATIONS

SALLY WHEELER

I. INTRODUCTION—THE GENERAL TERRAIN

As Stewart Macaulay, the father of empirical legal studies on contracting behavior, has pointed out, corporations and contracting practices among private individuals, corporate actors, and governments exist within the wider world drawn by law and society research. We have to see business practice as taking place in a world in which the use of law and lawyers is not free and may, even for parties to a business transaction, be prohibitively expensive. Resorting to formal legal dispute resolution methods in terms of court action or, as in the case of contract, to the pre-agreed sanctions in the parties' agreement, may not be appropriate for other strategic reasons that the parties have identified, such as reputation or the preservation of a continuing business relationship. Law matters as both an initial ordering mechanism and a resolution mechanism but not necessarily in the way that strictly legal or economic models might suggest (Macaulay, 2006).

The meticulous analyses provided by Bernstein in relation to dispute resolution in the cotton industry and the grain and feed industry (Bernstein, 1996, 2001) illustrate this. Bernstein's finding was that notwithstanding the presence of what doctrinal lawyers would consider a relationship involving a legally enforceable contract, business relationships were subject to two separate governance mechanisms—one formal, employing legal mechanisms, and one informal, based on social norms and relationships. Which governance mechanism prevailed depended on whether the business dealings between the parties were ongoing or not. If they were ongoing, then the parties employed strategies she called "relationship-preserving norms." It was important to the parties that they employed these norms and not a neutral third party, as would be the case in any litigation before a judge or arbitrator; and there was an explicit recognition that these norms, such as splitting the difference, would differ from the ones contained in the written form of any agreement. Only once the relationship between the parties has broken down do they resort to their legal rights under the contract and seek third-party enforcement of them. As Badawi demonstrates in his analysis of the terms of franchise agreements, the existence of relationship-preserving norms and more formal, legal governance mechanisms may not be complementary (Badawi, 2009). Franchise agreements require brand preservation at all costs, and the policing of these relationships may not be best achieved through the use of provisions to terminate the franchise. There are clearly relationship and industry-specific factors at play here.

A. First, second and third order studies

Empirical legal research on contracting behavior and the activities of corporations has expanded significantly in recent years as it both critiques more classical legal scholarship and seeks to create its own models of behavior. For the purposes of this essay, empirical studies of contracting behavior are divided into three categories: first, second, and third order studies. The categorization depends upon the theoretical position taken in the study in relation to the concept of contract as a legally enforceable obligation. First order studies seek to explain the "gap" between the "real deal" (the commercial relationship that exists between the parties) and the "paper deal" (the formal legal contract between the parties), as Macaulay so eloquently put it (Macaulay, 2003). The critique of first order studies (*inter alia* Macaulay, 1963; Beale and Dugdale, 1975; Lewis, 1982) is that by using categories of legal doctrine to construct the gap between what the parties in fact do and what they agreed in formal legal terms to do, the studies do not take forward an understanding of the alternative concepts and structures that their findings assert are more relevant to the parties than are the legally enforceable terms. This is because their analysis goes no further than observing that the formal contract doctrine and the structures that it recognizes are not relevant to actual contract practice (Cotterrell, 1992).

This concern can be rebutted by looking at the work of Ian Macneil and the empirical studies that have adopted his approach. Here the term "second order" is used in reference to empirical investigations of contract and contract practice which seek to use Macneil's contract norms as a way of creating categories or typologies of contracts. Acceptance of the findings of first order studies is implicit in Macneil's work. He begins from the point that an alternative philosophy of contract is consequently required. His philosophy is one that sees contract as social behavior rooted in cooperation, rather than the more adversarial paradigm which is favored by contract doctrine, the function of which is to plan exchange into the future (Macneil, 1980). Within this notion of cooperation, the parties retain their separate goals; the significance of this is that Macneil believes that cooperation is key not to the conclusion of the transaction but to the attainment of separate goals. Macneil's contract norms are grafted onto his first and second level relations, which he sees as necessary for exchange behavior to occur. At the first level there is the common bond of "society"— shared meanings, language, etc., and at the second level there are the political bonds of polite society which contain exchange behavior among utility maximizing individuals within the market place and prevent them from simply stealing from each other. At the third level come Macneil's external and internal norms. Macneil's concern is with moving legal analysis of exchange-based relationships beyond the idea of the simple regulated transaction toward identifying the norms that govern such transactions when they are viewed as continuing relationships between the parties. External norms are those restraints on behavior that result from legal strictures or trade association rules. Internal norms, of which Macneil identified ten, are linked to external norms and are the behaviors that underscore contract behavior by encouraging cooperative attitudes between the parties (Campbell, 2001). These norms are set out below in the section that deals specifically with second order studies.

Macneil's work has attracted the attention of those interested in contract from outside the law paradigm, based, for example, in management or economics schools. Oliver Williamson, building on the Coase Theorem, developed an analysis of the organization of transactions when transaction costs are not zero, as Coase's model supposed, but significant. What Williamson's analysis offers is an opportunity to examine facets of exchange behavior, such as planning or renegotiating, in different modes of governance such as arbitration, contract law, or market-specific practices (Williamson, 1979). There is an immediate interface here with Macneil's work. Williamson himself acknowledges this interface but somewhat surprisingly considers Macneil's framework, with its list of norms, to be too rich a classificatory apparatus, posing problems of recognition and application (Williamson, 1981). Instead, Williamson proposes that long-term contracts pose problems of uncertainty, bounded rationality, and a lack of competition at the point of relationship breakdown. In these circumstances, transaction costs will be incurred, and governance structures are required to rein in opportunistic behavior. Third order study is the term given here to studies which examine and/or test economic rather than legal (first order) or social (second order) concepts.

B. The role of law-and-economics

Discussion of the contribution of Williamson to studies of contracting behavior leads inexorably to a more general discussion of the role that law-and-economics plays in the context of the material covered in this Chapter. Law and Economics has a particular intellectual project, which is devoted to explaining how actors should behave rather than how they actually behave. It begins its analysis from the unit of the rational individual seeking to maximize their utility in any given transaction, the function of which is to achieve their preferences, which themselves remain stable over time. This it shares with Macneil's project. However, the law-and-economics approach takes the transaction as the unit of analysis and not the contractors, so it is concerned with finding the appropriate contractual form for each transaction. This creates an often-unacknowledged tension between the Macneil idea of contract and the law-and-economics approach to contractual analysis.

The law-and-economics approach is rather different from the trajectory of most other empirical legal studies, which begin by situating individuals and their behavior in a wider world of the social that sees behaviors and identities, including the economic, constructed by the individual in response to the rituals, norms, and institutions of society. In the context of commerce and contract, law-and-economics would seem to be an obvious methodology to employ as the questions that it sets itself are particularly relevant to the realm of private ordering and financial market interaction. If one were to study only the United States, this would largely be true. However, law-and-economics in its neo-classical incarnation has not had the same impact in either of these fields in the broader common law world as it has had in the U.S. There it has been used primarily as the research methodology for first order studies that support or reject the rules of formal legal doctrine (for example Posner and Rosenfield,

1977; Goetz and Scott, 1980; and McChesney, 1999). It has also enjoyed an influence in policy terms in the U.S. which it has never achieved in other jurisdictions, not least because the corpus of law-and-economics work outside the U.S. is simply insufficient to hold the attention of policy-makers. Within the U.S. it offers support to a particular and rather conservative legal and political agenda, as explained below.

In the common law world, the core assumptions of law-and-economics have been used as a starting point from which to model several alternative and entirely opposing approaches to those of law-and-economics—in essence, Macneil-inspired theories of contract behavior. This proposition is unpacked to a degree in the text which follows; but put succinctly here for the purposes of introduction—the assumptions of neo-classical law-and-economics are used as a straw target to produce either a feminist theory of contracting behavior, which then draws upon Macneil as a source of social norms to explain contracting behavior (Belcher, 2000), or a welfare/cooperation theory of contracting behavior, which then explains itself through the use of Macneil's relational contracting norms (Vincent-Jones, 2006). The apparent failure of law and economics to inspire empirical work in the common law world in anything other than a deconstructive sense can be seen in the rather cool reception given to empirical work that links Macneil not to Macaulay and the supposed non-use of contract but to Williamson and his claim that what determines the contractual arrangements that firms make are the key dimensions of the transaction (see Campbell and Harris, 1993; Lyons and Metha, 1997; Williamson, 1985). Williamson's contribution here is to see contracts as governance structures which can offer arrangements of differing flexibility and formality depending on the choices made by the parties. As I explain in the text that follows this introduction, the linking of Williamson and Macneil in this work goes a considerable way toward offering a more complete understanding of the empirical picture of contract. Unfortunately, the level of engagement with these contributions from those outside the immediate world of law-and-economics is no more than a vague nod to their existence and a small footnote to the idea that they might offer some unexplained insight into long-term business relationships. Nor has this work engaged an audience from within legal theory, where it might have added much to the discussions of concepts such as will and promise.

C. Corporations

At the same time as the idea of contract has been extended to encompass constitutional arrangements between citizen and state in the form of public, rather than private, ordering (Vincent-Jones, 2000), the corporation and the world of business have become the focus of increased scrutiny. For a considerable time, the corporation and the legal rules that surround it have been considered capable of explanation, in both an empirically grounded and a theoretically focused sense, through the metaphor of "nexus of contracts" (Fama, 1980; Fama and Jensen, 1983)—that is, private arrangements negotiated between actors, some of which take the form of recognizable legal contracts such as the contract of employment, others of which take the form of principal-and-agent contracts in the sense meant by neo-classical economics. In the world of the listed and publicly traded corporation (leaving aside market regulation, which has become a theoretical and empirical field of its own), commercial activity has moved to straddle the divide between public and private ordering through interest in areas such as corporate social responsibility and the interface between corporate activity on the one hand and state and supra-state level guarantees of human rights on the other hand. The world's largest corporations have turnovers (i.e., gross revenue) in excess of the GDP of many individual states, and many corporations have a transnational presence in the sense that their market listing is not confined to one nationally based stock exchange.

There is an argument to be made that corporations are no longer private actors. They are public actors in terms of power and influence in areas such as environmental impact, location and relocation decisions, and corporate social responsibility. The increasing availability and rapid transmission of information have been key in pushing forward these areas for critical examination. As I explain below, empirical legal research has had a significant impact in this emerging area in both definitional and exploratory ways; but there remain considerable opportunities for critical appraisal. The critique of non-governmental organizations (NGOs) that has emerged in the literature on political and social aspects of development has yet to be embraced by empirical legal studies. Access to multi-national corporations (MNCs) at the time at which corporate social responsibility policies are being created at the level of the board room rather than operationalized, has not yet been obtained. Few analyses have ventured beyond identifying the gaps between the aspirations of soft law, weak enforcement mechanisms, and the activities of wicked capitalists.

Corporate governance, once the lynchpin of the nexus-of-contracts analysis, has become a quasi-public site of inquiry in recent years. For the source of this interest it is necessary to look further back in time beyond the recent financial crisis of August 2008 to the high-profile corporate collapses of the 1980s onwards, the allegations of crony capitalism, the instances of overstated corporate earnings, and the financial remuneration and compensation packages paid to existing and departing executives that have scarred most major economies in the world at some point in the preceding half century. The result of these has been a loss of confidence by stakeholders, whether as investors, employees, governments, or those seeking corporate or domestic finance, in corporate governance provisions that rely upon notional contracts of agency between shareholders as providers of capital and managers as professional stewards of that capital. The marketization of pension provision for individuals through the use of 401(k) defined contribution plans,[1] the gradual decline of defined benefit pension plans, and growing realization that state welfare provision in retirement is unlikely to provide very much more than an extremely basic living allowance, have considerably increased the ranks of those interested in corporate governance. The idea, that the corporation is simply a legal construct invented to facilitate private ordering more efficiently than a series of market transactions would do (i.e., what an economist would describe as the traditional theory of the firm), is now under pressure.

Agency theory in general is interested in structures and in assessing the effectiveness or, in its own terms, the efficiency, or otherwise of those structures against its assumptions about what motivates opportunistic behavior (Davis and Greve, 1997) in its rather one dimensional picture of human nature (Daily et al., 2003). In the corporate governance setting, this means a focus on financial performance necessary for increased shareholder value and a limited model of accountability that supports this focus. Agency theory holds sway in law-and-economics analyses of the behavior of corporate executives in a way that fashion dictates it cannot in other areas. Empirical legal researchers have begun to ask much wider and more nuanced questions about the relationships between the corporation, the state, and the community, and about the nature of relationships within the corporation. Certainly, these inquiries are more interested in some nodes of the nexus of contracts than others; the relationship of the board of directors to shareholders and other constituencies is of primary interest, while other nodes fall within the areas of consumer protection and liability, labor law, and criminal law. This primary interest provides the central questions of corporate governance (an area governed by codes of self-regulation in the common law world and much of the civil law world but by hard law in the U.S.): in whose interests does the corporate entity operate, and how should these interests be protected? These questions appeal to a particular sort of political project in the same way that law-and-economics, by choosing to measure shareholder value, appeals to an antithetical political agenda (Campbell, 1997).

In some ways, law-and-economics scholarship has proved a disappointment in that the empirical studies it supports have not called for a reconfiguration of the relationship between social efficiency and the distribution of wealth. This is not to say that law-and-economics ignores altogether the question of social norms. Pressure from the inquiries pursued by more fashionable behavioral economics has forced engagement with the issue of socially constructed behaviors. In fact, law-and-economics sees the rationality of the individual in pursuing utility-maximization

---

[1] 401(k) retirement plans are a form of tax deferred retirement savings. A deduction is made from an employee's wages and, together with a contribution from the employer, this forms a retirement fund. The fund is invested on the employee's behalf in circumstances where the employee may be able to exercise a limited amount of choice over investment strategies. Income from the plan on retirement depends entirely on the investment performance of the fund, and there is no link to final salary.

as bounded by social norms. This applies to contract and business, where social norms are used to explain why non-legal self-governance works even in situations where contracts, in the principal-and-agent sense, are non-legal. Social norms can be broadly divided in into three categories: those that involve the quest for status by human agents; those that are internally enforced by feelings of guilt, for instance; and those that are externally enforced—for instance, by loss of reputation through breach of trust (Ellickson, 1998; Rock and Wachter, 2001). This is not an exhaustive list of norms. As the discussion of substantive studies below demonstrates, once the law-and-economics model has conceded the existence of behavioral or social norms, each study is likely to identify unique norms. This concession has the effect of shortening the distance that scholars might once have perceived between law-and-economics, empirical studies in the Macaulay model, and the work of Ian Macneil.

II. Contracting Behavior—First Order Studies

Macaulay's initial study is often cited, but his findings are too rarely discussed. Discussion of them is vital to understanding the nature of work that follows it. His 1963 study was situated in the machinery manufacturing industry of Wisconsin (Macaulay, 1963). The primary research question asked was when contract was used in this industry and when it was not. Macaulay used a snowball sample beginning with personal contacts. By the end of the project, 68 lawyers and business executives from 43 manufacturing firms and six law firms had been interviewed. As Macaulay himself points out, the study was never intended to produce a representative sample, something that he regards as impossible; but by being located in just one industry, the sample can be said to have kept inconsistency to a minimum (Macaulay, 2006). Macaulay was using a traditional legal definition of contract which sees contract not as a mechanism for achieving an efficient allocation of resources, as an economist would have it, but as the device that facilitates, and encapsulates the terms of, the exchange. To facilitate exchange, a contract must do two things: it must try to capture an element of rational planning by offering a risk-based solution for future contingencies and it must include legal sanctions to either induce performance or compensate for non-performance.

Macaulay's findings were that his sample of manufacturers only partially used contract law in setting up their exchanges and very rarely used contract law subsequently to adjust or enforce their exchanges. His interest in exchange planning was met by findings that machinery manufacturers did not completely plan their exchanges. Gaps were left to be filled in later during the performance of the exchange. The presence of "non-contractual relations" meant that disputes were avoided. These non-contractual relations were based around ideas of good faith in business, such as industry-wide customs, past dealings, and personal relations between actors in different organizations, and ideas of reputation, both personal and professional. The focus was on ensuring that business continued between the parties to the exchange. Macaulay explains that there was a view that the formalities of contract could get in the way of creating a good exchange relationship between business units. Contract was of more assistance in explaining detailed product specifications and requirements within the firm than in securing interfirm exchanges. Macaulay's account of business exchanges taking place in the world of manufacturing in Wisconsin takes us back to the pre-globalization era. The business world is a much bigger place than it was in 1963. There are likely to be far fewer "local" deals enhanced by personal relationships as production industries have gradually relocated to economies with low labor costs. As I explain below, globalized business practices have carved out a new role for supply contracts and sub-contracts.

Macaulay identifies two behavioral norms that are considered to be more important than the rational planning of an exchange: being seen as having and supporting a good product, and not "welching" on a deal. These are "ad personam" norms that tell us about the character of the individuals involved but convey little about the nature of the transactions they are undertaking or about the wider social norms that frame their interactions. This is the major difference between a Macaulay-inspired approach to empirical legal studies in contract and a Macneil-inspired approach, as will be clear from the discussion below. The question, of why some transactions are more formal than others in terms of the contract entered into, is not one that Macaulay seeks to answer. Macaulay is looking at categories of doctrinal contract law to see how far the "paper deal is the real deal." It is this concern with planning, understood in terms of the legal categories identified as relevant to contract formation and adjustment, that attracts my designation of first order studies. Other examples of this first order approach (aside from the ones mentioned above) would be Esser's replication of Macaulay's work (Esser, 1996): despite his engagement with the literature on transaction-cost economics and the sociology of institutionalization, and a nod to Macneil, Esser's primary reference point is classical contract law, and work by Marotta-Wurgler (2009) on software license agreements. Marotta-Wurgler's area of interest is the "pay now, see terms later" world of online and telephone ordering of goods. The work examines a sample of end-user license agreements collected from software sellers and codes them using a numerical indexing methodology to ascertain the correlation between contract bias toward seller or buyer and pre-purchase accessibility of terms to the buyer. Her theoretical frame of reference is taken from decided cases and jurisprudence surrounding rolling contracts. The findings are presented using statistical regression techniques, but this does not detract from the fact that it is a study about the presence or absence of particular contract terms as defined by classical contract law.

III. CONTRACTING BEHAVIOR—SECOND ORDER STUDIES

Macaulay himself has exhorted those who are thinking of undertaking empirical work on contract not to do so without first considering Macneil and his contribution to contract scholarship (Macaulay, 2000). Unlike contract doctrine, which requires the existence of certain formalities to convert an exchange into a contractual relationship, Macneil views all exchanges as contracts. This distinction is particularly important in the context of *umbrella contracts*. The idea of umbrella or framework agreements has recently become popular in management and economics literature and it is beginning to have resonance within legal research as well. As the name suggests, this is an arrangement where the parties recognize that they are engaged in a business relationship in which there are likely to be numerous individual exchanges over time between them. The umbrella or framework agreement does not exist to shape immediate decisions arising from the relationship but instead to set out jointly agreed principles which will provide flexibility in business dealings between the two in the future. In all likelihood, the parties to an umbrella agreement are basing their agreement on norms which either come from their own previous dealings or are known to be in common usage in their field of interest. The parties are planning how they will react to future changes of circumstances. The agreement may contain a myriad of options, many of which will not be drawn upon unless particular circumstances occur. An umbrella agreement does not contain fixed obligations but rather a series of agreed options and ideas which are used to underpin renegotiations and adjustments according to future circumstances. By using an umbrella agreement, the parties are indicating that they will not resort to litigation but will negotiate their way past obstacles and difficulties using the norms that they agreed upon at the outset. This is a typical site for a Macneil-inspired research but one which classic contract law would struggle to accept as coming within its definition of contract (Mouzas and Ford, 2006).

Macneil's analysis encourages the plotting of exchange relationships on a spectrum that runs from discrete or non-relational contracts (signifying thin contractual relations) to full relational exchanges where relationships are thicker. Macneil's internal contract norms will determine how an exchange works in practice. Their precise role and shape is determined by where on the discrete-relational spectrum an exchange sits. Macneil's contract norms are best expressed as a simple list:

1. Role integrity
2. Reciprocity
3. Planning
4. Effectuation of consent
5. Contractual solidarity
6. Linking norms: restitution, reliance, and expectation
7. Creation and restraint of power
8. Flexibility
9. Propriety of means
10. Harmonization of the social matrix

The discrete-relational spectrum is just that—a spectrum. A great number of both uses and analyses of Macneil's work erroneously posit it as a hard distinction, a line that can be drawn between different types of exchange relationships; but this is clearly not the case. Instead, what Macneil suggests is that some norms come to the fore when exchanges are closer to the discrete end of the spectrum, namely "implementation of planning" and "effectuation of consent"; while others, such as role integrity and solidarity, are more evident in exchanges that are further along the spectrum toward relational exchange. Nevertheless, all ten norms are present to some degree or another in each exchange. Of these ten norms, five hold special significance. These are *role integrity* and *propriety of means*, which come straight from the list of ten, and three others, which are a combination of the remaining eight. These three are *preservation of the relation* (an expansion of *contractual solidarity* and *flexibility*), *harmonization of relational conflict* (derived from *flexibility* and *harmonization of the social matrix*), and the *supra-contractual norm* (produced from the *harmonization of the social matrix*).

Macneil's norms and contextualization of exchange practices have been used to examine, *inter alia*, what underpins ideas of trust in contract relationships between business actors. A particularly interesting project which demonstrates this is that undertaken by a collaborative team of researchers from Parma, Cambridge, and Hamberg-Harburg Universities (Deakin et al., 1997; Arrighetti et al., 1997). Their inquiry spanned three countries—Britain, Italy, and Germany—and two industries selected for their different operating contexts in terms of competition within their respective sectors and their involvement with trade and other business associations—mining machinery manufacture and kitchen furniture manufacture. A very full account of the methodology employed is given in the published outputs. The point to note is that 62 firms across the three jurisdictions participated in interviews and released both qualitative and quantitative information about their business practices. Among the project's many findings, two are particularly interesting. Behavior around trust and cooperation is affected by the supporting institutional environment the parties find themselves in; the presence of relational factors, such as trade and business associations, codified contract conditions, and industrial standards, all assist in creating trust and cooperation. In contrast to Macaulay's findings, informal contract practices, such as the absence of a written agreement, were more likely to result in the parties using formal redress mechanisms. The presence of formalized contract relations (for example in Germany) was considerably less likely to result in court proceedings between the parties. Trust between the parties was built through the use of legal mechanisms rather than through the non-observance of legal mechanisms.

The once-natural division of arrangements into the public and the private has been increasingly challenged by the ordering and governing arrangements that many developed societies have adopted in recent years. Legal structures commonly used to order private relationships can be transplanted into the public sector, where they are used in quite a different way. The legacy of New Public Management is a series of arrangements, for a bewildering range of government-provided services and functions, and of services and functions that are provided by private sector actors on behalf of government, which use the language of contract to describe the relationship between the governor and the governed (Crawford, 2003) irrespective of whether the arrangements in question are legally enforceable as contracts. Macneil's emphasis on context is the key here to seeing these contractual relationships as forming a constitution in which procedures for monitoring service provision, incentivizing performance, and imposing administrative sanctions are laid out (Macneil, 1974, 1978, 1980, 1981, 1983; Whitford, 1985; Feinman, 2000).

The best study in terms of the breadth of material covered and the quality of analysis is that of Peter Vincent-Jones (2006). His work in this field began in the early 1990s with several empirically grounded projects on the use of compulsory competitive tendering in local government. Since then he has followed the use of contract by the state to achieve certain policy goals, such as increasing citizen choice or modifying citizen behavior, in areas as diverse as the behavior of school children and the delivery of welfare services. There is obviously a large hinterland of issues that are beyond the scope of empirical legal studies here, many of which this work addresses. For example, the policy choices themselves give rise to classic public law questions about the nature of citizen/state relationships; and beyond that, there are questions of applying market principles to areas of life that were once considered beyond the market.

Of interest to empirical legal studies is the way in which Vincent-Jones uses the Macneil model of exchange to define the three categories of contract into which he divides these relationships, eschewing the more familiar model of legally enforceable contracts on the one hand and non-enforceable contracts on the other. Without the encumbrance of using legal enforceability as the feature on which classification depends, he is able to employ a broad, threefold functional classification into administrative contracts, economic contracts, and social control contracts. His aim is to compare the norms of these arrangements with the norms identified by Macneil. Vincent-Jones observes that the idea of contract as a mutual arrangement which the parties can adjust in order to achieve wealth-maximization, is not applicable to public sector contracting, which is insufficiently flexible to adapt to changing circumstances. Reciprocity, which underpins trust, is not present because often the resources on the state side of the contract are insufficient to address the needs of the citizen. In many of the relationships, but particularly those involving social control contracts, the norm of consent is missing. In Vincent-Jones's view, it is because of the absence of so many of Macneil's norms that public sector contracting in its current forms fails to deliver on its policy objectives and fails the test of legitimacy. Vincent-Jones does suggest remedial steps that could be taken, but what is important here is the depth and richness of analysis he is able to achieve by using Macneil's contract norms in a setting which goes well beyond interactions between business actors into a world that classic contract law would not recognize as contractual.

IV. Contracting Behavior—Third Order Studies

The link between the neo-institutional or transactional-economics approach of Williamson and others and the relational model of Macneil was explained above. Third order studies empirically test ideas from law-and-economics about the role that investments specific to a particular transaction, frequency of transactions between the parties, and uncertainty of events both in the world and within the realm of the transaction, play in the different types of governance structures that are identified, *viz.* trilateral governance, bilateral governance, and unified governance. Unified governance, or "vertical integration" as it is often termed, holds the least interest for empirical legal scholars as study of transactions internal to the firm is unlikely to reveal much about formal contract doctrine or Macneil's social norms. Bilateral and trilateral governance, involving (as the labels suggest) the parties to the transaction or the parties and a third force such as arbitrator to deal with disputes, are of more interest. Obviously, it is impossible to undertake this sort of empirical inquiry without unearthing information about the sort of norms that underlie the transactions. Sometimes reference to Macneil and Macaulay is explicit but the purpose of the inquiry in these studies is not a direct engagement and testing of their approaches and findings, even though the studies may examine very similar material. Rather, the aim is to interrogate the transaction typology offered by law-and-economics. Anything that is discovered which sheds light on the use of formal contract doctrine or the existence of particular social norms is incidental to the main purpose of the study (for example Argyres et al., 2007; Zheng et al., 2008).

Joskow's study of coal supply contracts provides an example (Joskow, 1987). Joskow examined 272 coal supply contracts between coal producers and electric utilities. The purpose of his study was to test Williamson's hypothesis that the greater the relationship-specific or transaction-specific investment made by the parties, the longer in duration they would make their contract. Joskow found that the three aspects of relationship-specificity, namely site specificity, physical asset specificity, and dedicated assets, were indeed present to a greater degree in contracts of a longer duration and to a lesser degree or not at all in contracts of shorter duration. The nature of this inquiry reveals information about Macneil's norms and to a lesser extent about the circumstances in which formal legal contract is used as a governance mechanism, but this is very much secondary to the author's inquiry.

A rather different example is provided by Wilkinson-Ryan's study of the interaction between the concept of efficient breach and the presence of a liquidated damages clause in the contract agreed between the parties (Wilkinson-Ryan, 2010). The point of the research is to take a concept, efficient breach, which comes exclusively from law-and-economics, and test its relationship with the legal concept of liquidated damages and its intersection with shared community norms. The hostility of Macaulay to the possibility of efficient breach as a viable option in the world of the "real deal" should be noted (Macaulay, 2006). The methodology of the study is rather different from the other examples given in this Chapter. Instead of looking at actual contracts or contract practice within a particular community, it is based upon a series of experiments using model scenarios. The methodology is described in detail in the study. It is based upon a questionnaire distributed to 500 mainly U.S. respondents representative of the adult U.S. population in terms of age, income, and education. These respondents were asked their responses to a series of scenarios which involved the possibility of gaining an additional profit through the efficient breach of a contract and various different types of liquidated damage clauses. Wilkinson-Ryan's conclusion was that efficient breach was more likely to occur when a liquidated damages clause was present, suggesting that breach was considered to be a more acceptable and a less immoral action in these circumstances, and so reputational damage was less likely to result.

V. Corporate Behavior

This section is not intended to capture the complete picture of corporate behavior. It deals with activity within and between business units, but not with issues that fall more comfortably in the areas of consumer complaints, labor regulation, or environmental behavior (see Chapters 7, 13, and 19 in this volume for discussions related to these topics). Nor does it deal with interactions between the corporation and the state that are essentially regulatory; and so issues of tax compliance and corporate accounting, for instance, are not covered. Unfortunately, this excludes an extensive discussion of what is probably the most influential empirical work on business behavior in relation to regulation, namely that designed to test the creative compliance thesis of Doreen McBarnet (1992). McBarnet's original research was conducted with lawyers working on tax advice and has since been extended to look at both off-balance financing and corporate social responsibility. Her thesis is that there are two forms of compliance with regulatory instruments—creative compliance with the letter of the law and actual compliance with the spirit of the law. Corporations favor the former over the latter (McBarnet, 2006; McBarnet and Whelan, 1999). Structures established for state enforcement of directors' duties are not examined either, so interventions by the SEC and FSA are not included. Nevertheless, some of these topics will inevitably be touched upon because business activity cannot always be neatly categorized and boxed into a single subject heading.

Empirical studies that deal with the legal corporate behavior and corporate structures are not plentiful. The vast majority of empirical inquiry in this area falls within the provinces of economic sociology, political science, and management and economics. Even on a theoretical level, apart from a nodding acquaintance with the ideas of Berle and Means (1932), there was, until the 1970s, little engagement by the discipline of law with what others would have considered the key strategic political, social, and economic questions surrounding the corporate form and its legal institutions. Until comparatively recently, lawyers have paid little or no attention to areas, such as proxy voting and the conduct of shareholders' meetings, which it might have been thought would interest them empirically because these structures are central to the exercise of shareholder voice and control within the corporation; the link between executive pay and shareholder rewards through dividend; the role of activist shareholders; the dynamics of board membership and issues around majority and consensus governance; and the relationship between institutional investors and the board in terms of the flow of information between the two and communications outside the formal setting of shareholders' meetings.

Lawyers often accept the fruits of work produced within other disciplines and treat it as a given when formulating their own intellectual contributions. It is not unusual for transplants from other disciplines to retain their currency within legal discourse and legal argument when their stock is on the wane in their own discipline. For example, agency theory referred to above, which has had a very powerful influence on legal corporate-governance scholarship, has probably been replaced within its home discipline of economics by behavioral economics. We should, perhaps, not be surprised by the relative paucity of empirical research by lawyers in this area compared with the contributions of other disciplines, whose inquiries are of a different nature and are unlikely to require disclosure of market-sensitive information or to involve disclosure by the corporate subjects of the inquiry of illegal practices. Access to the corporate arena is more difficult to obtain if answers are required to questions of a legal nature. Within the confines of the Anglo-American law school, stress has been laid on corporate law in a doctrinal sense and on "what is needed in practice," often without very much first-hand knowledge of exactly what that is.

The most recent empirical import into legal thinking has come from finance theory. It is the "law matters" thesis, known more colloquially as the "LLSV thesis"—the acronym is made up of the first letter of the last names of the authors who proposed the thesis (La Porta et al., 1998) and developed and extended it in a series of papers in the years following 1998. Stripped to its essential terms, the LLSV thesis involves an attempt by finance theorists, using a sample of 49 developed market economies, to quantify the link between financial development and the type of legal system in which the economy is embedded. The precise results do not matter for the purposes of this essay; but in broad terms, the thesis is that common law systems are more conducive to financial development than civil law systems. Of note are two things: first, the methodology used involved straightforward numerical indexing that could be replicated easily; and second, while lawyers may disagree with the designation given to the various legal provisions that are scored, and even perhaps with the designation of particular legal systems as civil or common law, they cannot criticize the findings on the ground that legal provisions are not being engaged with on their own terms. While there has been comment on the LLSV thesis from legal scholars, it has yet to be subjected to any rigorous empirical testing by those scholars. This is an area where empirical research driven by the discipline of law should have something substantial to add in the future. Legal inquiry often limits itself to descriptions of normative provisions without more. This is particularly so in relation to corporate social responsibility, and corporate involvement in developing countries with issues such as human rights observance, and environmental protection.

VI. Corporations, Contracts, Environmental Standards, and Human Rights

Such empirical studies as there are raise a number of interesting questions both as to their findings and as to future research agendas. One such recent study is that of Vandenbergh (2007). The subject of his study is the use by corporations of provisions in supply chain contracts to place obligations on their suppliers located in developing countries to adopt environmental and employment practices that exceed those required by the suppliers' own governments. Having observed above that the largest corporations control more capital than many nation states, this use of contract has the potential to exert considerable influence. The more usual narrative in normative accounts is of the unwillingness of states, both developed and developing, to put in place anything that might restrict the flow of international capital and of the likely flight of the capital of multinational enterprise to jurisdictions with lower regulatory standards if such restrictions are imposed.

Vandenbergh's study looks at the contracts used in supply chains by 74 firms in eight different sectors ranging from industrial machinery and equipment manufacturing to discount and variety retailing. These sectors were chosen precisely because there was a high likelihood of supply chain use, with supply chains extending to developing countries. His finding was that firms in seven out of the eight sectors imposed environmental requirements in their supply chain contracts and that those firms which did so were the largest in their sector, thus indicating the potential of this practice to achieve change in circumstances where state intervention to achieve the same change was unlikely to occur. Drivers for corporations to impose these supply chain requirements were identified as the preferences of customers, shareholders, or employees, the desire to preempt possible future regulatory intervention, the need to reassure shareholders of the continuing availability of raw materials, and the desire to push up production costs in developing countries, thus forcing out rivals operating on lower cost margins or removing them from the market by using superior buying power to negotiate discounts. Contracts between corporations may have the effect, then, of driving up standards in some states not because corporate executives employed in other states think that raising environmental standards is a good and worthwhile idea in and of itself but because consumer power in the marketplace, often mediated through NGOs, indicates preferences for goods produced in a particular way that avoids particular consequences. These market preferences are changing the behavior of exporting firms in developing countries. There is, it seems, an implicit assumption that when standards of behavior migrate upwards this must be welcomed. However, the power that corporate contracting practices have in effecting change is not necessarily well informed and may not prioritize the most important and pressing issues because those are not the imperatives that drive such practices. Rather they are driven by the need to protect reputational capital, which may be threatened by the behavior of chain suppliers, and to manage the risk to such capital on behalf of its shareholders.

A similar study has been undertaken by McBarnet and Kurkchiyan (2007). Their findings focus more on emotive human issues such as child labor, living wages, and working hours, than on environmental standards. Their sample of corporations was taken from the FTSE 100 with the addition of five multi-national enterprises (MNEs) based outside the UK. The study involved documentary analysis of both internal and publicly available material coupled with follow-up interviews. As in the Vandenbergh study, suppliers at the bottom end of the supply chain were not interviewed, so once again the focus of the study is on the potential power of private contracting practices to achieve change where state intervention cannot. McBarnet and Kurkchiyan found a closer correspondence between contractual standards, international labor and UN standards and developing country laws in this area; and so corporate activity through contract was a matter of securing enforcement of local laws rather than increasing the protection offered by domestic legal systems. In terms of Macneil's discrete/relational spectrum, the supply contracts studied were situated at the relational end. For corporations at the top end of the supply chain, such contracts preserve flexibility and create a sense of partnership rather than domination and an adversarial relationship with suppliers at the bottom end of the chain.

The study demonstrates that simply adopting policies of corporate social responsibility is an insufficient safeguard for reputational capital. Corporations engage in both monitoring of implementation and educational programs for management and workers of supplier companies. Non-compliance with the demands of these programs was defined as an express unwillingness to comply; other failures were seen to present "learning opportunities" within the context of the partnership. As with Vandenbergh's study, this study found that end-consumer pressure was a key driver for supply-chain contractual monitoring: it was more likely to be found in cases involving well-known brand names. The issues most closely monitored are those considered to be most important to end consumers rather than ones selected by those whose employment circumstances are being monitored. The fact that monitoring of the selected issues leaves the workforce in a better position than it would be in without monitoring rather misses the point that the active participation of those whose lives are directly affected is a very important issue within the practice of development. As vehicles for raising standards, contractual supply chains have distinct limits, as McBarnet and Kurkchiyan point out. Some cultural issues, such as gender equality and ideas of childhood, can only be addressed at state level. Structures that remove local state responsibility for grappling with such issues are not necessarily desirable.

VII. Studies of Corporate Directors

The first empirical work to be done on corporate behavior within the discipline of law was that of Roman Tomasic in Australia. In the late 1980s and early 1990s, he conducted a number of studies funded by the Australian Research Council which looked at insider trading and litigation strategies in takeovers from the perspective of both the target and the raider. These studies are discussed and fully referenced in the first major legal empirical study of corporate behavior within the firm, which was also undertaken in Australia by Tomasic and his co-author, Stephen Bottomley in 1992–1993. Tomasic's background as a doctoral-level sociologist is evident in the careful methodology that he used to obtain a reliable sample. The study focused on the top 500 publicly listed companies in Australia. Company directors, 95 in number, were selected from a random sample of 20% of these companies, Within the sample (which for logistical reasons excluded companies located in New Zealand and outside the capitals for the six Australian mainland states), directors were selected for interview on the basis of their precise job within the governance framework in order to ensure as wide and as accurate a reflection of opinion as possible. Non-executive or independent directors were also included in the sample. A sample of 55 corporate advisors and regulators was also interviewed; "advisors" included lawyers, auditors, and liquidators.

The Tomasic and Bottomley study (1993) covers a large number of topics from the state enforcement of directors' regulatory obligations or the absence thereof, to directors' duties and the director/shareholder relationship. Corporate citizenship has become a very topical issue for corporations themselves; but Tomasic and Bottomley were questioning directors about this in the early 1990s and received responses that it was important for those firms that had a public profile, but that even then it was a label that could be dropped "in the bad times." Management by corporations of their ethical persona is clearly not a new issue. The findings that key executives were dominant in the context of board meetings and decision-making and that non-executive directors were unable to stem this dominance, are also echoed by Stapledon's study of institutional shareholder involvement in corporate affairs discussed below (Stapledon, 1996). Given that these studies were reported in the early to mid-1990s and that since then, regulatory interventions across the common law world in response to the corporate failures and excesses of the next 15 years or so increased the burden on non-executive and independent directors to act as the monitors of executive directors on behalf of shareholders (for example the 2003 Higgs Report in the UK), there would seem to be a case for a new investigation of the dynamics of board leadership, the position of non-executive directors, and their newly enhanced function. Tomasic and Bottomley found their sample of directors to be broadly aware of their legal duties as were their sample of advisors. More worryingly, the sample of advisors felt that directors' knowledge of, and concern to act within, the law decreased as company size decreased. Their findings in relation to ethical standards confirm what many commentators would anecdotally acknowledge as the case since Enron and subsequent corporate behavior scandals, namely that ethical behavior is not a black and white issue but a broad spectrum; and that it is quite possible to find so-called ethical breaches in the best-run corporations when the standard is generally pitched at a very high level. A more cynical way of expressing this would be to suggest that greed in particular and even, sometimes, commercial interest do not sit terribly well with the idea of ethical conduct.

Tomasic and Bottomley also asked questions of their director and corporate advisor sample about institutional shareholder involvement in corporate affairs. What emerged was a picture of two-way information flows, with corporations both volunteering information to institutional investors and the same investors seeking information. The relationship was seen as a mutually beneficial one which would forestall shocks. However, there was also a view that institutional shareholders could intervene very much more if they wished, but chose not to. This is interesting for several reasons. First, we know as a matter of fact that other types of shareholders, such as small individual shareholders and larger portfolio investors, engage in little or no private enforcement activity (Armour et al., 2009). The only candidates to be activist shareholders—if there are any in the context of monitoring—are institutional investors. Second, many of the corporate reforms of the 1990s onward (for example the 1992 Cadbury Report in the UK) place institutional shareholders in a privileged position *vis-à-vis* communication and the obtaining of information from the board of directors. Based upon the Australian evidence, relying on institutional investors to monitor performance for all shareholders would seem to be rather optimistic.

VIII. INSTITUTIONAL INVESTORS

The first detailed examination of the activities of institutional investors was undertaken by Geoff Stapledon (1996). He looked at the amount of direct and indirect monitoring of corporations that institutions undertook in a study which compared institutional investors in the UK and Australia. In his terms, direct monitoring occurs when institutional investors themselves are involved. Indirect monitoring describes instances where the parties involved are not the institutional investors themselves but, for instance, their trade association. Stapledon's study was based on semi-structured interviews in the autumn of 1993 with executives of 17 investment management firms in the UK, which together represented more than 25% of the value of the UK equity market. There is no information as to how these 17 firms or the Australian firms were selected. The Australian part of the study was conducted in February 1994 and comprised interviews with executives of 13 investment management firms. The 13 included seven of the eight largest firms managing Australian equity portfolios. Those who have not undertaken this type of project involving interviewing of elite finance professionals should not underestimate how difficult it is to gain access and obtain the amount of information that this study provides.

Stapledon produces a very interesting picture of the nature of institutional invest-ment, which is far more complex than might be imagined. His study highlights the different structures of share ownership in the UK and Australia. The UK is a classic outsider system of corporate control characterized by a large number of publicly quoted (i.e., publicly traded) corporations, a liquid capital market, and few cross-holdings. Australia, on the other hand, is a hybrid system that combines some of the characteristics of the UK with some elements of the insider systems that are found in France and Germany. Quoted companies do not form as large a part of the Australian economy as of the UK economy, and Australian quoted companies have a greater number of cross-holdings and a much higher proportion of closely held, "founder" shares. The Australian market is, therefore, much less liquid.

The principal findings from this study are that although there is considerable potential for involvement in both jurisdictions, actual serious intervention is rare (estimated by Stapledon at 18 serious interventions per annum in the UK between 1990 and 1993 and considerably fewer in Australia), Stapledon concludes that there are likely to be more poorly or very poorly managed companies than there are serious interventions. The reason for non-intervention he ascribes to disincentives within the corporate governance system, some of which are: the availability of share sale (which is a cheaper option in widely dispersed and liquid markets); a market which creates a huge free-rider problem; and, allied to this, assessment of the performance of fund managers in relative, not absolute, terms. Stapledon's study was carried out before the series of reforms which made institutional investors an object of com-munication and special interest for corporations; but nevertheless his description of corporate activities immediately prior to these reforms does encourage viewing them through a rather different lens.

IX. CORPORATE INTERACTION WITH THE MARKET

Rather oblique references are made above to changes in the structures of corporate governance across the developed world in response to the corporate collapses of the 1990s. The corporate collapses of the first decade of this millennium have made improvements and changes to these structures a continuing project. While many of these interventions are legislative in nature and so fall more properly under a discussion of regulatory compliance, the position in the UK and Australia is rather different. Both of those jurisdictions have a "comply or explain" system for corporate governance in public companies that is based upon a voluntary code. In the UK, the Code was produced not by the legislature but by selected corporate executives attempting to state current best practice. Revisions to the code have been produced in a similar way. In their annual reports, listed corporations, as a condition of their Exchange listing, must either state that they have complied with best practice in corporate governance as stated in the current version of the Code, or they must explain which parts they have not complied with. The Code is not legally enforceable so the market decides on the importance that should be attributed to particular failures to comply, expressing its disapproval of a particular instance of non-compliance by a drop in share price.

Two studies have looked at the degree of non-compliance with the Code, and the second of these studies also looks at the effect of compliance failure on share prices. The first of these studies, funded by the Economic and Social Research Council and undertaken by Alice Belcher (1996), examined the annual reports of 106 companies over three accounting periods—the period immediately preceding the publication of the Cadbury Code (the first iteration of the "comply or explain" formula in the UK chaired by Sir Adrian Cadbury), the period in which the Cadbury Code was published, and the period immediately after the Cadbury Code was published. The idea of the study was to look at how explanations of corporate governance practice changed with the promulgation of the Code. The study recorded not only whether or not compliance statements were made but also how informative these statements were. Belcher found a correlation between the size of the corporation and compliance statements. While 77% of the firms she looked at complied, the most common stated reason for non-compliance was the small size of the firm. In her conclusion she praises the degree of compliance in the period immediately after the Code was issued but injects a note of warning about the huge variation in the detail given both in statements of compliance and in statements of reasons for non-compliance.

The second study, undertaken by Macneil and Li (2006), concentrates on 17 FTSE100 corporations, all of which were serial non-compliers with the corporate governance Code. The nature of their non-compliance was examined over a four-year period from 2000 to 2005 in combination with fluctuations in their share price. Belcher's concern at the lack of detail available to investors in statements of non-compliance is echoed in this study. Non-compliance statements were found to record only the basic fact of non-compliance or to give such a brief explanation for non-compliance that current and future investors were left with no insight into whether non-compliance was justified or not. By looking at fluctuations in the share price of these 17 corporations, Macneil and Li concluded that in the absence of usable information from the corporation, investors constructed their own proxy measure of the importance of non-compliance, and that measure was financial performance. In their view, when financial performance was sufficiently strong, investors would overlook non-compliance and support the corporation's choice of governance structure;

but that choice was not tolerated if financial performance was poor. This would seem to indicate that investors only consider whether the corporation's governance structures are working and do not see the need to enter into a dialogue with corporate executives. This may be more efficient, but it is certainly not what the Code drafters intended. They clearly imagined an extensive dialogue between the two groups; but this empirical research would support both Tomasic and Stapledon's earlier findings that investors are generally non-interventionist unless financial performance is judged to be poor.

X. Conclusion

It would seem empirical legal research on the importance of contract law to business practice has failed to provide a clear picture of the importance of the linkage between law and practice. There would appear to be an irreconcilable difference of view concerning the relationship between the use of law, formalized contract relations, and the idea of trust between contracting parties. What is clear, however, is that there is a range of different research methodologies that are likely to produce different results. Contracts exist on a spectrum from discrete (contracts of short duration and relatively simple specification) to relational (contracts of longer duration, involving more extensive and involved dealings between the parties). Many of the norms referred to by Macneil have yet to be subjected to thorough empirical testing. Norms such as solidarity and role integrity are too often assumed by research rather than investigated. Macneil's norms could be extended to non-monetized relationships such as intimate relationships. There are also new arenas of contract practice to be examined such as Internet shopping and e-commerce more generally. With regard to empirical studies of business activities, it seems that we know almost nothing about what occurs in firms that are not listed on the stock market. That is not particularly surprising because one of the privileges of non-listing is the relative secrecy with which activities can be conducted. In relation to listed firms, we know that they are very powerful economic actors and that they can use this power to effect change by their use of contracts.

References

Argyres, N., Berkovitz, J., and Mayor, K. (2007). "Complementarity and Evolution of Contractual Provisions: An Empirical Study of IT Services Contracts," *Organization Science* 18: 3–19.

Armour, J., Black, B., Cheffins, B.R., and Nolan, R. (2009). "Private Enforcement of Corporate Law: An Empirical Comparison of the UK and the US," *Journal of Empirical Legal Studies* 6: 687–722.

Arrighetti, A., Bachmann, R., and Deakin, S. (1997). "Contract law, social norms and interfirm cooperation," *Cambridge Journal of Economics* 21: 171–95.

Badawi, A. (2009). "Relational Governance and Contract Damages: Evidence from Franchising," available at <http://ssrn.com/abstract=1443515>.

Beale, H. and Dugdale, T. (1975). "Contracts Between Businessmen: Planning and the Use of Contractual Remedies," *British Journal of Law and Society* 2: 45–60.

Belcher, A. (1996). "Compliance with the Cadbury Code and the reporting of corporate governance," *Company Lawyer* 17: 11–17.

Belcher, A. (2000). "A Feminist Perspective on Contract Theories from Law and Economics," *Feminist Legal Studies* 8: 29–46.

Berle, A. and Means, G. (1932). *The Modern Corporation and Private Property*, New York: Harcourt Brace and World, reprinted 1991, Transaction Publishers New Jersey.

Bernstein, L. (1996). "Merchant Law in a Merchant Court: Rethinking the Code's Search for Immanent Business Norms," *University of Pennsylvania Law Review* 144: 1765–822.

Bernstein, L. (2001). "Private Commercial Law in the Cotton Industry: Creating Cooperation Through Rules, Norms and Institutions," *Michigan Law Review* 99: 1724–90.

Campbell, D. (1996). "The Relational Constitution of the Discrete Contract," in D. Campbell and P. Vincent Jones (eds.), *Contract and Economic Organisation*, Aldershot: Dartmouth.

Campbell, D. (1997). "The Role of Monitoring and Morality in Company Law: A Criticism of the Direction of Present Regulation," *Australian Journal of Corporate Law* 17: 343–65.

Campbell, D. (2001). *The Relational Theory of Contract: Selected Works of Ian Macneil*, London: Sweet and Maxwell.

Campbell, D. and Harris, D. (1993). "Flexibility in Long-Term Contractual Relationships: The Role of Co-operation," *Journal of Law and Society* 20: 166–91.

Cotterrell, R. (1992). *The Sociology of Law*, London: Butterworths.

Crawford, A. (2003). " 'Contractual governance' of deviant behavior," *Journal of Law and Society* 30: 479–505.

Daily, C., Dalton, D.R., and Cannella, A.A. Jr. (2003). "Corporate Governance: Decades of Dialogue and Data," *Academy of Management Review* 28: 371–82.

Davis, G.F. and Greve, H.R. (1997). "Corporate Elite Networks and Governance Changes in the 1980s," *American Journal of Sociology* 103: 1–37.

Deakin, S., Lane, C., and Wilkinson, F. (1997). "Contract Law, Trust Relations and Incentives for Co-operation: A Comparative Study," in S. Deakin and J. Michie (eds.), *Contracts, Co-operation, and Competition*, Oxford: Oxford University Press.

Easterbrook, F. and Fischel, D. (1991). *The Economic Structure of Corporate Law*, Cambridge, MA: Harvard University Press.

Ellickson, R. (1998). "Law and Economics discovers Social Norms," *Journal of Legal Studies* 27: 537–52.

Esser, J. (1996). "Institutionalizing Industry: The Changing Forms of Contract," *Law & Social Inquiry* 21: 593–629.

Fama, E. (1980). "Agency Problems and the Theory of the Firm," *Journal of Political Economy* 88: 288–307.

Fama, E.F. and Jensen, M.C. (1983). "Separation of Ownership and Control," *Journal of Law and Economics* 26: 301–25.

Feinman, J. (2000). Relational Contract Theory in Context," *Northwestern University Law Review* 94: 737–48.

Goetz, C. and Scott, R. (1980). "Enforcing Promises: An Examination of the Basis of Contract," *Yale Law Journal* 89: 1261–322.

Joskow, P. (1987). "Contract Duration and Relationship-Specific Investments: Empirical Evidence from Coal Markets," *American Economic Review* 77: 168–85.

La Porta, R. et al. (1998). "Law and Finance," *Journal of Political Economy* 106: 1113–55.

Lewis, R. (1982). "Contracts Between Businessmen: Reform of the Law of Firm Offers and an Empirical Study of the Tendering Practices in the Building Industry," *Journal of Law and Society* 9: 153–75.

Lyons, B. and Metha, J (1997). "Private Sector Business Contracts: The Text Between the Lines," in S. Deakin and J. Michie (eds.), *Contracts, Cooperation, and Competition*, Oxford: Oxford University Press, 43.

Macaulay, S. (1963). "Non-contractual Relations in Business," *American Sociological Review* 28: 55–69.

Macaulay, S. (1985). "An Empirical View of Contract," *Wisconsin Law Review* 465–82.

Macaulay, S. (2000). "Relational Contracts Floating on a Sea of Custom? Thoughts about the Ideas of Ian Macneil and Lisa Bernstein," *Northwestern University Law Review* 94: 775–804.

Macaulay, S. (2003). "The Real and the Paper Deal: Empirical Pictures of Relationships, Complexity and the Urge for Transparent Simple Rules," *Modern Law Review* 66: 44–79.

Macaulay, S. (2006). "Contracts, New Legal Realism, and Improving the Navigation of *The Yellow Submarine*," *Tulane Law Review* 80: 1161–95.

Macneil, I. (1974). "The Many Futures of Contract," *University of Southern California Law Review* 47: 691–816.

Macneil, I. (1978). "Adjustments of Long-Term Economic Relations Under Classical, Neoclassical, and Relational Contract Law," *Northwestern University Law Review* 72: 854–905.

Macneil, I. (1980). *The New Social Contract*, New Haven: Yale University Press.

Macneil, I. (1981). "Economic Analysis of Contractual Relations: Its Shortfalls and the Need for a 'Rich Classificatory Apparatus'," *Northwestern University Law Review* 75: 1018–64.

Macneil, I. (1982). "Efficient Breach of Contract: Circles in the Sky," *Virginia Law Review* 68: 947–69.

Macneil, I. (1983). "Values in Contract: Internal and External," *Northwestern University Law Review* 78: 340–419.

Macneil, I. and Li, X. (2006). "'Comply or Explain': market discipline and non-compliance with the Combined Code," *Corporate Governance* 14: 486–96.

Marotta-Wurgler, F. (2009). "Are 'Pay Now, Terms Later' Contracts Worse for Buyers? Evidence from Software License Agreements," *Journal of Legal Studies* 38: 309–419.

McBarnet, D. (1992). "Legitimate rackets: Tax evasion, tax avoidance, and the boundaries of legality," *Critical Criminology* 3: 56–74.

McBarnet, D. (2006). "After Enron will 'Whiter than White Collar Crime' Still Wash?," *British Journal of Criminology* 46: 1091–109.

McBarnet, D. and Kurkchiyan, M. (2007). "Corporate Social Responsibility through contractual control? Global supply chains and 'other-regulation'," in D. McBarnet et al. (eds.), *The New Corporate Accountability*, Cambridge: Cambridge University Press, 59.

McBarnet, D. and Whelan, C. (1999). *Creative Accounting and the Cross-eyed Javelin Thrower*, London: Wiley.

McChesney, F (1999). "Tortious Interference with Contract versus Efficient Breach: Theory and Empirical Evidence," *Journal of Legal Studies* 28: 131–87.

Mouzas, S. and Ford, D. (2006). "Managing relationships in showery weather: The role of umbrella agreements," *Journal of Business Research* 59: 1248–56.

Posner, R. and Rosenfield, A. (1977). "Impossibility and Related Doctrines in Contract Law: An Economic Analysis," *Journal of Legal Studies* 6: 83–119

Rock, R. and Wachter, M. (2001). "Norms and Corporate Law," *University of Pennsylvania Law Review* 149: 1607–700.

Stapledon, G. (1996). *Institutional Shareholders and Corporate Governance*, Oxford: Oxford University Press.

Tomasic, R. and Bottomley, S. (1993). *Directing the Top 500*, St Leonards: Allen & Unwin.

Vandenbergh, M. (2007). "The New Wal-Mart Effect: The Role of Private Contracting in Global Governance," *University of California Law Review* 54: 3–52.

Vincent-Jones, P. (2000). "Contractual Governance: Institutional and Organizational Analysis," *Oxford Journal of Legal Studies* 20: 317–51.

Vincent-Jones, P. (2006). *The New Public Contracting*, Oxford: Oxford University Press.

Whitford, W. (1985). "Ian Macneil's Contribution to Contract Scholarship," *Wisconsin Law Review* 545–60.

Wilkinson-Ryan, T. (2010). "Do Liquidated Damages Encourage Efficient Breach? A Psychological Experiment," *Michigan Law Rev* 109 (forthcoming).

Williamson, O. (1979). "Transaction Cost Economics: The Governance of Contractual Relations," *Journal of Law and Economics* 22: 233–61.

Williamson, O. (1981). "Contract Analysis: The Transaction Cost Approach," in P. Burrows and C. Veljanovski (eds.), *The Economic Approach to Law*, London: Butterworths.

Williamson, O. (1985). *The Economic Institutions of Capitalism*, New York: The Free Press.

Zheng, J., Roehrich, J.K., and Lewis, M.A. (2008). "The dynamics of contractual and relational governance: Evidence from long-term public–private procurement arrangements," *Journal of Purchasing and Supply Chain Management* 14: 43–54.

6

FINANCIAL MARKETS

JULIA BLACK[1]

I. INTRODUCTION

THE task of this Chapter is to map the current state of empirical legal research in the law and regulation of financial markets. The conduct of empirical research in this area is not confined to lawyers, but extends to financial economists, sociologists, political

[1] I am grateful to Emilios Avgouleas, Michael Bridge, Hugh Collins, David Kershaw, Dimity Kingsford-Smith, and Niamh Moloney for valuable comments on an earlier draft of this paper.

scientists, and anthropologists. Lawyers are often users of this research, even if they are not its producers. Research by lawyers and others can either be explicitly normative, or ostensibly analytical, albeit often with an implicit normative agenda. Those analyzing financial markets also vary in the assumptions they make as to the nature of markets, the behavior of actors in the market, and the nature of law. Surveying all the empirical work done in those areas, even just as it pertains to law and regulation, would be a significant task. This Chapter accordingly aims to provide a brief survey of the main work done either by lawyers or by others but which is pertinent to the operation of law and regulation. It is deliberately descriptive and aimed at those who are new to empirical research in this area. It sets out briefly what has been done already, noting gaps and suggesting lines for possible future research.

II. Existing Empirical Legal Research into Financial Markets, Law, and Regulation

This Chapter focuses on six main areas of research and debate, clustering around either particular rules or particular debates on the operation and interaction of financial markets, law, and regulation. These are the debates on the efficient markets hypothesis and mandatory disclosure rules in securities regulation; studies on behavioralism and their impact on disclosure as a tool for protecting investors; studies on the impact of rules relating to market misconduct on market development; research into the relationship between legal rules and securities market development more broadly; evidence of the unintended impacts of regulation; and research into the dynamics of financial market regulatory regimes. For reasons of space, the Chapter does not cover research into financial fraud per se. As can be seen, the sites of empirical research are patchy, and research has focused primarily on securities markets and derivatives markets, rather than bond markets, insurance, or banking. The research which has been done varies both in its methodology, and in the level of its analysis. Some is quantitative and operates at the macro level; other work, mostly qualitative in approach, focuses on micro-level interactions. Researchers can also have quite different assumptions as to the nature of the markets and the nature of law. In economics-based research, markets are reified and seen as abstractions comprised of the interactions of rational buyers and sellers. In more sociologically or politically based research, markets are seen as socially constructed institutions developed to stabilize relations between actors, which are embedded in institutional structures that shape and are shaped by the behavior of market participants (e.g.,

Knorr-Cetina and Prada (eds.), 2004). It can thus be difficult to link the two sets of research, as they are in effect conducted in different languages and with different logics. However, to the extent that the existing bodies of empirical research focused on here are connected, it is by the common theme of inquiry, *viz.*, the nature of the interrelationship of markets, law, and regulation.

A. Studies on the efficient markets hypothesis and mandatory disclosure

One of the oldest lines of debate in securities markets regulation relates to the Securities and Exchange Commission's (SEC's) rules on mandatory disclosure by companies on offering their securities for sale. Dating from the 1930s, the debate has divided principally into two camps (see La Porta et al., 2006 for review). Supporters of mandatory disclosure argue that government regulation is required, as incentives for firms to disclose complete and verifiable information are too weak, and private law arrangements are too inefficient and expensive to use in practice. In turn, this group divides on whether government intervention should provide certain standard disclosure provisions and liability rules, so structuring the framework for private contracting, and rely principally on private enforcement, or whether the weaknesses of private enforcement in practice are such that in addition government should play an active role in enforcing securities laws.

Opponents argue that there is no need for securities laws as the market, supported by private law, will provide optimal disclosure, either through contracting arrangements, the use of third parties (such as auditors) to verify information, or the rules of private stock exchanges. Moreover, the prices of the securities would reflect all available information whether or not it was published. Thus an investor would not be prejudiced by not having the information themselves, as the price would be set by those who were informed.

As in many areas of empirical research with respect to financial markets, lawyers are keen debaters and users of empirical research produced by others, principally financial economists. Opponents of mandatory disclosure base their arguments in part on a particular economic theory of price formation in the securities markets, the efficient capital markets hypothesis (ECMH) (Fama, 1970). The strong form of the ECMH is that share prices reflect all information available or otherwise. The "semi-strong" form is that they reflect all available information; and the weak form is that they reflect the information provided by the historical sequence of prices (Fama, 1970). As a result, even sophisticated investors cannot systematically profit from newly available information as this will already be incorporated into the price. Moreover, as rational actors make decisions about the future in an unbiased manner, any price movement tomorrow will only reflect new information available today, and thus cannot be predicted. Stock market movements will thus exhibit a "random walk," with no predictable trends.

The theory has been modified over time, and Fama has accepted that prices do follow certain predictable patterns, but the central tenets of the theory are still strongly held (see, e.g., Malkiel, 2003 for review). Nevertheless, a line of research known as behavioral economics has been suggesting for some time that the model is flawed. Behavioral economists argued that if all traders were trading on the basis of information, and prices reflected all available information, few people would trade, and moreover there would be no markets for futures and options (Black, 1986). In practice, however, Black argued that people traded on the basis of expectations, which they may think is information, which Black termed "noise." The scale on which they trade may mean that rational traders may not want to trade against them, or at least not in significantly large positions, as this could expose the rational traders to risk in that the market may in fact move in the way that the noise traders expected. As a result, prices would reflect "noise" as well as information, but it would not be possible to tell in what proportions (Black, 1986). Prices may move closer to value over time, but ultimately "all estimates of value are noisy, and so we can never tell how far a price is away from value" (Black, 1986: 533).

The stock market crash of October 1987, the near collapse of the hedge fund Long Term Capital Management in 1999, the dot.com boom and bust the turn of the twenty-first century, and the recent financial crisis have provided a wealth of empirical data for behavioral financial analysts. Briefly, the most notable work is Robert Shiller's analysis of "herding" and "irrational exuberance" (see, e.g., Shiller, 2000). His empirical work demonstrated that not all information is accurately reflected in prices. Rather, markets exhibit significant price volatility and trading patterns which cannot be explained on the basis of company-specific information alone. Moreover, even when trading is mainly on the basis of available information, the inherent unpredictability of dividends and earnings for most companies means even "smart money" behavior is largely guesswork and intuition, and so unlikely to be a predictor of value even when all agree. Furthermore, he argued that decision-making by investors does not conform to the calculated rationality that economists assume, but exhibits many of the cognitive biases and heuristics discussed below. Moreover, most investors (not just retail investors) have limited capacity or inclination to make comparative investment decisions independently, and so rely on the views of peers to whom they are linked in communication networks and by whom they are heavily influenced in their trading decisions. As a result there is a group dynamic to the decision-making process of which the result is herd behavior, and trading on the basis of fashions and fads (Shiller, 2000). Moreover, decision-making is reflexive, and herd behavior creates endogenous risk: i.e., predictions about market movements become self-reinforcing and self-fulfilling as all act on them in the expectation that everyone else will too (see Callon, 1998).

The arguments of behavioral economists strike at the core of economic assumptions as to behavior of participants in financial markets. As is well known, in the classic economic model of behavior, actors act rationally to maximize their util-ity. They possess full information, and their preferences are stable, exogenously formed, and transitive (if they prefer apples to pears and pears to oranges, they will always prefer apples to oranges). Actors are also assumed to make unbiased forecasts about the future. In contrast, economic sociologists understand economic behavior to be strategic, but embedded in institutional structures (see, e.g., Knorr-Cetina and Prada (eds.), 2004). Rational maximizing is not an inherent human trait but a socially and culturally constructed strategy of action, enacted in the context of social relationships, cultural idioms, and institutions (Abolafia, 1997).

However, what has had a significant impact on (some) economists' understanding of their own assumptions are the insights not of sociology but of cognitive psychol-ogy and in particular Kahneman and Tversky's Prospect Theory (see Khaneman, Slovic, and Tversky (eds.), 1982 for an excellent collection of studies). Adherents to the dominant "rational actor" assumption resisted incorporating their insights, however, and it was only in the late 1980s and 1990s that behavioral finance became recognized as a key movement in economic analysis (e.g., Shiller, 1989). The financial crisis of 2007–2009 has given behavioral economics greater impetus.

Experimental and empirical work by cognitive psychologists, and increasingly by economists, demonstrates that people's preferences are far from stable and that preferences are shaped by the way in which information and options are presented. In particular, people's perception of the risk associated with different decisions can vary considerably depending on the way questions or options are framed (for review, see, e.g., Slovic, 2000). Moreover, people make decisions in accordance with certain heuristics or "rules of thumb." These heuristics are routinely made and are therefore predictable (one of the key requirements of economists for a theory of behavior because without predictability, modeling is far more open to error). They may be "rational" in the sense that they reduce the amount of time a person spends making a decision, but they may not result in the person maximiz-ing their utility.

Behavioralism is taking its hold in the legal academy, and although legal scholars are not producers of this research, they are becoming key users of it. Much of this work again has a normative agenda and is concerned with understanding what lessons behavioralism has for regulatory policy-making with respect to financial markets. However, whether or not the insights of behavioral economics should cause regulators to fundamentally rethink their policies depends not only on the validity of its arguments, but also on the extent to which financial regulation is indeed predicated on the assumptions of classical economists. A good example of research of this nature is Langevoort's analysis of the role of ECMH in U.S. securi-ties regulation. His research suggested that the theory was employed in regulatory and judicial decision-making, but mainly as a façade (Langevoort, 1992). His argu-ment suggests that widespread theoretical debates on the appropriateness of using neo-classical economic arguments as the basis for regulation may be interesting normatively, but may miss the point if regulation is not in fact premised on neo-classical economic theories, a question which itself merits empirical analysis.

B. Studies on behavioralism and its implications for investor protection regulation

Nevertheless, behavioralism can offer some key insights into market operation and thus can have normative implications for regulation. One of the key areas in which behavioral economics has attracted the attention of legal scholars is with respect to the role of disclosure requirements in regulation for investor protection. Behavioralism clearly calls into question the extent to which disclosure of information about products can lead investors, of varying degrees of sophistication, to make utility-maximizing, or even satisficing, investment decisions. Analyses of the use of disclosed financial information with respect to sub-prime mortgages and credit derivatives in the period leading up to the financial crisis demonstrate that both sophisticated and unsophisticated investors can fail to read the information they are given about complex products, to understand it if they do, and to act on the basis of it even if they have understood it (e.g., Schwarcz, 2009; see also Black and Nobles, 1998 for discussion with respect to pensions misselling in the UK).

These findings have led legal scholars to call both for simplified disclosure and for additional regulation such as product regulation for a wider range of complex financial products including derivatives, and extension of restrictions on which products investors can purchase (e.g., Schwarcz, 2009; Avgouleas, 2009a, 2009b). In many financial regulatory regimes, disclosure has never been the sole plank on which investor protection has rested. The regulatory regime in the UK and the EU, for example, contains product regulation for collective investment schemes and restrictions on the type of investments which can be marketed to retail consumers. In addition, it requires financial advisers to advise retail investors to purchase only products that are suitable or appropriate for them, based on their financial circumstances and their attitude to risk. There is also evidence that some financial regulators are beginning to invest more time and effort in investor education.

Nevertheless, greater empirical or experimental research on how investors make investment decisions, what information they use, and how they interpret it is badly needed. There are some examples of such work by legal scholars. Kingsford-Smith and Williamson (2004), for example, have conducted qualitative empirical research on the behavior of a sample of online investors in Australia, to understand how and where they obtained information about the securities in which they were investing. This work found that investors use a wide range of sources of information and confirmed the findings of behavioral economists that the views of peers are highly significant in motivating investment decisions. Moreover, investors' strategies varied from the "diligent" to the "dilettant," revealing patterns of behavior which demonstrated that some investors traded for the "play" of trading, treating online investing as a leisure activity akin to gambling. These investors, they argued, were far from the rational investors that regulation assumed, but instead were particularly vulnerable to the risks of online trading.

However, although there are some examples of empirical legal research in these areas, there is as yet no systematic empirical research conducted by lawyers looking at how market actors behave and what implications this has for their legal regulation, with the notable exception of work on legal deviance and white collar crime.

In the area of investor protection, regulators themselves are filling the gap that academic analysis has left. Regulators, particularly in the UK, Canada, and Australia, are beginning to learn more precisely how investors make investment decisions, how they perceive risk, and the degree to which they can understand information about the financial products in which they want to invest (for review, see Black, 2006). The British Columbia Securities Commission has even commissioned research into the victims of frauds to understand why they fell for fraudulent schemes (Black, 2006). Some regulators are also increasingly "road testing" with consumer focus groups the disclosure documents that they require firms to provide. The UK Financial Services Authority has been conducting this kind of research since 2000. In Canada, the Canadian Securities Association embarked on this kind of work in 2006–2007. In a welcome development, the EU has determined that it, too, will start testing consumers' understanding of proposed disclosure documents for authorized unit trusts. Greater empirical work in this area is needed if lawyers and regulators are to understand the operation of financial markets and the role of law within them.

C. Studies on market misconduct

A third line of empirical research focuses on the impact of particular trading rules on markets. In the legal literature on securities laws, by far the most debated rule or set of rules, aside from the mandatory disclosure rules noted above, is that relating to insider dealing. However, despite the huge volume of literature debating whether or not insider dealing should be allowed (for overview, see McVea, 1995), most of these debates are theoretical, and there has been little empirical work on the actual relationship between insider dealing regulation and market performance. Notable exceptions are the work of Bhattacharya and Daouk (2002) and Beny (2006). Separately conducted, their empirical research indicates that the mere presence of insider dealing prohibitions does not affect market operations. However, the public enforcement of insider dealing regulation does have a positive effect on price formation and liquidity. In other words, it is not law that matters so much as its enforcement (ibid). This research fits well with more recent work on the relevance of public enforcement to the efficient operation of markets, discussed further below.

There has been far more empirical work with respect to the impact of quite a different rule on markets: short selling. This research provides a good example of micro-level research by financial economists and law and economics scholars. The debate on short selling forms part of a wider debate on whether and how legal regulation can prevent market bubbles and market crashes (for discussion, see Gerding, 2007). Again, although legal scholars have not always been authors of the primary research, they have been its users, and there has been a long-standing debate particularly among U.S. legal scholars on the benefits or otherwise of regulation of short selling (see, e.g., Stout, 1999). A brief overview of recent research is thus included here for two reasons: first, because it has a bearing on the research questions that legal scholars in this area are usually interested in, *viz* the interaction of markets and law; and second, because it illustrates the very direct impact that this type of empirical research has on policy formation.

Short selling is the practice of selling securities, including derivatives, that the seller does not own. In order to be able to deliver the stocks, the seller enters into an arrangement to "borrow" those stocks from a third party, returning them at a specified date. In a falling market, the seller hopes to profit by selling the securities at a higher price than that for which she will have to buy them in the market at a later time when they are due to be returned to the lender. At the time of sale, the trader may or may not have put in place arrangements to ensure delivery (such as taking an option). In the latter case, the short selling is referred to as "naked," and is generally regarded with more opprobrium by opponents of short selling than other short selling practices.

Short selling has strong supporters and equally strong critics. Those in support of short selling argue that although as a trading strategy it can be used to profit from a declining market, it is also used to hedge risk, improve price discovery, provide liquidity, and, by market makers, to manage order flow (for review, see Curtis and Fargher, 2008). In contrast, critics argue that short selling itself increases volatility, is associated with manipulative practices, allows market participants to stimulate bear markets, and leads to market crashes.

Historically, regulators were, and to an extent still are, divided on whether and how to allow short selling, and legal rules varied around the world. In 1938 the SEC introduced a ban on short selling in securities whose prices were declining (the "uptick" rule, SEC rule 10a-1), only removing the ban in 2007 (SEC Reg. SHO). Outside the United States, other exchanges, including the Toronto Stock Exchange and the Australian Stock Exchange, restricted short selling, though many others, notably the London Stock Exchange and Tokyo Stock Exchange, did not (for a full survey, see Charoenrook and Daouk, 2008). Many other jurisdictions have recently relaxed their rules on short selling.

Short selling came under populist and political fire in the autumn of 2008, when in the wake of the collapse of the investment bank, Lehman Brothers, the prices of shares in financial institutions fell dramatically. Many policy-makers and commentators at the time blamed short sellers, and the academic debates moved directly into the policy arena (see Avgouleas, 2010 for discussion). Regulators introduced temporary restrictions on short selling in specified securities. Much to the irritation of market participants, these varied significantly in their details, timing, and scope, putting into sharp relief the contrast between the globalized equity markets and the national bases of their regulation, even across the EU.

Comparative research on the impacts of the restrictions on short selling, introduced in September–October 2008, gives no clear picture of whether or not short selling restrictions had adverse effects on the market (Curtis and Fargher, 2008). Although the predominant argument of financial economists is that short selling improves market quality, evidence on the effects of the temporary restrictions imposed in various countries in October 2008 is mixed. In addition, experimental research suggests that restricting short selling is unlikely to have an impact on preventing, bursting, or dampening bubbles (Gerding, 2007).

These findings suggest that other factors may affect the practice of short selling, such as transaction costs (Shiller, 2003) or the presence of other legal rules, such as those relating to disclosure (e.g., Beny, 2006). Further, although there may be correlations, albeit disputed, between short selling restrictions and market behavior, the findings of both empirical and experimental research suggest that the causal effects of the presence or absence of any single legal rule on market bubbles or crashes remain ill-understood (see, e.g., Gerding, 2007).

Although, as noted, legal scholars have been consumers rather than producers of empirical research in this area, it seems unnecessarily parochial to exclude consideration of this work, given the engagement of legal scholars with it, its direct relevance to the question of whether and how law affects markets, and indeed how market behavior affects regulatory policies. As such it has a clear connection with the work considered in the next section, although one which is rarely, if ever, noted. That research explores the relationship between law and the development of markets. The debate, as will be shown, is often conducted in terms of which came first, market development or the law. Research on the regulation of short selling suggests that the relationship is more reflexive than uni-directional. Law affects the performance of markets; but as the autumn of 2008 illustrated clearly, market behavior can prompt regulatory interventions to change the law in an attempt to affect that performance.

D. Law and market development

The key question that this line of research and policy development asks is: "Where well-developed legal systems exist, which laws in particular matter to the development of securities markets, and if so why, how, and to what extent?"

For the last decade or so, the agenda has been set in this area by the work of a group of financial economists, La Porta, Lopez-de-Silanes, Shleifer, and Vishny, and colleagues, whose work is referred to collectively as LLSV. Whether lawyers agree with it or not, their work is now the reference point in the field and has had a significant impact on the research questions that are now asked by legal scholars. Much of their work is focused on issues that lawyers traditionally define as relevant to corporate law, but it also has implications for scholars of financial markets.[2]

LLSV's work and the work it has prompted is a good example of the type of empirical work conducted both by financial economists and by law-and economics scholars into the impact of law on the operation of the markets. There is a standard overarching methodology, which is to correlate different indices of market performance with the presence or absence of particular legal rules. However, only some areas of financial markets lend themselves to this type of analysis, as it relies on the availability of significant amounts of data, for example, on prices and trading. The long history of organized securities markets and their disclosure requirements means that data on these markets is the most easily available; and therefore, the greatest concentration of this type of research concerns securities markets rather than the off-exchange (and so more opaque) bond and derivatives markets.

1. *LLSV—the main arguments*

The central question that La Porta and colleagues ask is why there are such different patterns of the use of debt and equity (shares) respectively to finance companies in different countries. They argue that the answer is to be found in the degree to which shareholders and creditors are protected by the legal system (La Porta et al., 1998, 1999, 2000, 2006).

Their starting point is to group all commercial legal systems into two "families": common law and civil law. Within civil law, they further distinguish three main camps: French, German, and Scandinavian. They argue that these systems of law have spread to other countries through processes of imperialism, conquest, borrowing, and imitation (La Porta et al., 1997, 1998, 2000). They developed an index of what they saw to be all the relevant rules of company law and insolvency law that protected investors from diversion of profits and assets of the firm by managers and

---

[2] There is a cross-over here between financial, or more particularly securities, law and corporate law. Securities law and corporate law are artificial boxes. Much of what—in the U.S.—is classified as securities law is classed in the UK as company law. This difference in classification has more to do with the allocation of legislative responsibility in the U.S. than with the presence of a "defining essence" of what constitutes securities law and what constitutes company law. In the United States, states are responsible for corporate law, but the federal regulator, the SEC, is responsible for securities law. Using securities law to make provisions relating to shareholder rights is thus a convenient way for the federal government to set the agenda to the exclusion of the individual states.

controlling shareholders for their own use, and scored them for degree of protection. They also looked at the quality of the legal system (in terms of efficiency of the judicial system, rule of law, corruption, and risk of appropriation of assets or repudiation of contracts by the government), as measured by credit rating agencies and the quality of accounting standards, as measured by separate comparative studies.

LLSV argue that this pattern of law, enforcement, and accounting standards has significant implications for corporate form and financial market development. The less investor rights are protected, on their index, and the less they are enforced, the higher the concentration of ownership, and vice versa (La Porta et al., 1997, 1998, 2000). Moreover, they argue that higher degrees of investor protection are associated with higher corporate valuations (La Porta et al., 2002). They have done more specific work on particular rules and argue, for example, that self-dealing by corporate insiders is best regulated by full disclosure and approval by disinterested shareholders, and that public enforcement matters little (La Porta et al., 2008). Overall, they argue that securities laws that are based on disclosure and private enforcement facilitate stock market development, whereas the amount of public enforcement of securities laws has little or no impact (La Porta et al., 2006).

Much of the work that has developed either directly or indirectly in response to LLSV's analysis focuses on the classic question in corporate law, which is how legal mechanisms can be used to address the principal-agent problem of enabling shareholders to control managers, expanded to include consideration of how smaller shareholders can control managers and dominant shareholders, and what impact corporate governance rules have on corporate value (see, e.g., Bebchuk et al., 2009). As such, it falls into the disciplinary "box" of corporate law and internal corporate governance.

Of more relevance to scholars of financial markets is how LLSV's work links with the work of law-and-economics scholars on the mandatory disclosure requirements applying to listings that were discussed above. The LLSV research clearly links with this work, in particular the debate on the best means of enforcing mandatory disclosure, or indeed any other securities or company laws. LLSV are in favor of mandatory requirements but, as noted, argue firmly that public enforcement has no effect on stock market development. Instead, they maintain that facilitating private enforcement through mandatory rules on disclosure, liability rules, and directors' self-dealing rules is the way to promote the development of securities markets. Their methodology and argument has been highly influential, and is now reflected in the work of key policy-makers, notably the World Bank, the IMF, and the European Central Bank (Jackson and Roe, 2009: 4).

Despite its influential following, their work has been criticized by legal scholars on a number of grounds. Criticisms have been directed first at the compilation of the indices and the scoring system used (Jackson and Roe, 2009; Spamann, 2008).

In particular, they have been criticized for ignoring functionally equivalent rules in different legal systems. As a result, countries may score lower than they should in the LLSV index (see, e.g., Coffee, 2001). In particular, Spamann has undertaken a systematic study of 46 of the countries in the original LLSV anti-director rights index to verify the index values used. Unlike the LLSV work, Spamann asked locally trained and qualified lawyers to perform the verification. With a more detailed knowledge of the relevant legal provisions, the re-valuation found errors in 33 of the 46 observations. Once revalued, the correlations found by LLSV with respect to common law and civil law countries, dispersed ownership, and stock market development are no longer found. This is clearly a significant finding, suggesting that the LLSV data and their conclusions are deeply flawed. These criticisms have led to further methodological refinements (e.g., Djankov et al., 2008). However, as their research sees only disclosure, liability, and anti-director rights as the relevant rules to measure, their work is criticized for pinning an analysis of financial market development on only a relatively few rules, and moreover those that do not address some of the main aspects of trading (Jackson and Roe, 2009).

Further, the research by financial economists is criticized by lawyers as being based on an overly formalistic conception of law, focusing only on formal rules and assuming that the mere presence (or absence) of a particular legal rule means that effective protection is (or is not) being provided (e.g., Coffee 2001). It is also criticized as being ahistorical. LLSV base their analysis only on the rules as they exist at a certain point in time. As such, critics argue, this leads them to mistake correlation with causation. LLSV argue that legal systems predate the development of securities markets and are therefore essential to them. By contrast, an empirical, historical analysis of the evolution of particular rules suggests that changes in the law followed changes in the markets, not the other way around (Armour et al., 2009).

Critics also argue that LLSV's classification of all legal systems into one of four legal "families" is too crude, masking significant heterogeneity within "families" and similarities between them. In particular, it takes no account of the impact of EU law on domestic legal structures of member states. UK securities law is now fundamentally shaped by EU law, which in turn is shaped by international codes and norms. Further, transnational harmonization of legal provisions in the area of securities law in particular makes it difficult to put the different regimes into the different "boxes" (Armour et al., 2009).

2. *The relative roles of public and private enforcement of law*

Much of the research that the LLSV work has prompted focuses on the extent to which different legal rules do or do not favor managers and/or majority shareholders. However, one area of the LLSV research that has attracted the particular attention of those interested in financial regulation concerns the relative roles public and private enforcement should and do play in ensuring vibrant securities markets. Recent work by Jackson and Roe calls into question La Porta et al.'s conclusion that public enforcement is irrelevant to stock market development. They have used La Porta et al.'s data on stock market development to compare their findings on the effects of private enforcement with public enforcement. Critically, however, to measure public enforcement, Jackson and Roe do not use the formal indicators of La Porta et al., but develop resource-based measures of enforcement intensity. In other words, they attempt to measure not law in the books, but law in action. Using securities' regulators resources as a proxy for enforcement intensity, they analyze the significance of public enforcement practice, as opposed to the presence of formal rules, on securities markets (Jackson and Roe, 2009).

Jackson and Roe systematically demonstrate that public enforcement is significantly correlated with financial market development and performance around the world[3] and is, moreover, as strongly correlated as the best performing index of private enforcement (disclosure rules) and substantially more strongly associated with robust capital markets than several other indices of private enforcement, including liability rules and anti-director rights (Jackson and Roe, 2009: 13; see also Jackson, 2007; Coffee, 2007). However, disclosure rules are more significant than public enforcement in determining ownership structures. Moreover, disclosure rules correlate more strongly with ease of market-access than public enforcement (though see Coffee, 2007). Finally, however, neither the private enforcement index nor the resource-based index of public enforcement correlates significantly with either market stability or efficiency.

Jackson and Roe also examined the correlation of the "families" of law (i.e., common law and civil law) with both enforcement intensity and stock market development. Controlling for real resources and private law indices, they found no correlation between stock market development and whether the legal system was common law or civil law; indeed, they found a negative correlation between the common law tradition and stock market development, contrary to the arguments of LLSV. Furthermore, they found, contrary to the widespread assumptions of financial economists and others, that civil law countries are associated with less enforcement rather than more enforcement (Jackson and Roe, 2009: 22–4). So, they conclude, rather than it being the traditional features of the common law that support robust securities markets, such as rules on fiduciary duties or judicial enforcement, it is regulatory institutions that matter (ibid: 23).

Their findings have significant policy implications, suggesting that countries that want to facilitate the development of stock markets are not handicapped from the start by their legal tradition, but rather need to put in place effective disclosure rules

---

[3] They measure market capitalization, trading volumes, the number of domestic firms, and the number of initial public offerings (Jackson and Roe, 2009).

and have well-resourced public enforcement regimes. They argue that this is directly contrary to the current policy recommendations of the key international financial institutions, suggesting that that policy is based on a fragile empirical base (ibid).

Their findings are also relevant to the question which animates much of the research in this area, *viz.* which comes first, stock markets, or legal institutions. Financial economists had assumed that because the common law supported financial markets, and because common law predated financial markets, it was legal institutions which structured the market, not the other way around. Moreover, financial economists have argued that common law systems support stock market development to a greater degree than civil law systems, as noted above (La Porta et al., 1998; Djankov et al., 2008). As they did not regard public regulation as relevant, they did not see any public regulation as being relevant to how the market developed, regardless of whether the regulation pre-dated or post-dated development of the market. As Jackson and Roe argue, their own findings put the question of causality firmly back into play (Jackson and Roe, 2009: 24), as indeed does the historical empirical analysis of Coffee and others (Coffee, 2001). Jackson and Roe conclude that the relationship between law, regulation, and markets is "bi-directional," though sociologists would prefer the term "reflexive."

E. Avoidance and unintended consequences of regulation

The question of whether law matters to the development of financial markets is clearly relevant to policy-making. As noted above, much empirical research has a normative orientation, which is often that law can either act as an obstacle to market development and so should be removed (a common prescription by financial economists), or that it can be used as an instrument directly to facilitate market development and behavior (a natural inclination of policy-makers).

Law has been a significant source of inspiration and innovation for the development of at least some new financial instruments. But although, in the following examples, law has prompted financial, and in turn legal, innovation, this innovation is of little comfort to instrumentalists. For innovation has not taken the form of a direct implementation of legal provisions. Quite the opposite is true: innovation is a manifestation of unintended consequences and avoidance strategies. Law and regulation have prompted innovation in financial instruments not because law itself has been innovative, though it often has been, but because markets have been innovative in avoiding legal restrictions.

There is little systematic empirical research on the incidence or dynamics of such "gaming" innovation. The examples that are documented usually appear in what would otherwise be considered "black letter" texts on financial law. But a brief review of some of the examples of such gaming innovation suggests that a broader empirical project could be fruitful in understanding both the relationship of law and the markets and how market actors respond to law. One of the chief characteristics of financial markets is that their products are legal creations; as such they can be easily manipulated to avoid legal requirements.

Avoidance strategies can lead to the development of particular financial instruments, and indeed to entire markets. For example, it is well documented that the Eurobond market[4] developed in London in the 1960s largely to avoid U.S. tax laws which imposed a tax penalty on U.S. investors buying foreign bonds, and restrictions on overseas direct investments by U.S. corporations (Wood, 1995: 10; Benjamin, 2008: 506). Several forms of financial derivatives also owe their origins to avoidance strategies. For example, swaps were originally developed from the back-to-back loans that were devised to avoid exchange controls in the 1970s (Wood, 1995).

Further, and notoriously, capital adequacy rules introduced in 1988 are widely credited as being responsible for the development of the asset-backed securities market. This dynamic of producing financial instruments to avoid regulatory requirements was observed by regulators as early as 1992, a fact which itself is a good illustration of "regulatory lag" (the time difference between regulators becoming aware of an issue and actually acting to address it). These securities could be developed and traded off-balance sheet, and so did not have to figure in the calculation of the amount of capital that a bank needed to set aside to offset its risks. Banks also set up separate corporate structures to house their derivative assets, ensuring that credit lines advanced to them fell short of the one-year rule that would have required their disclosure. Avoidance strategies can thus have significant negative impacts: it was the development, structure, and operation of these markets which led directly to the financial crisis of 2007–2009. So law clearly can affect markets, but not in the linear manner that instrumental policy-makers and "reform-through-law" scholars would find comforting.

F. The dynamics of financial regulatory regimes

The response of law reformists to avoidance strategies adopted by market practitioners is often to change the law. This brings us then to the question of the impact of the markets on law and regulation. As we have seen above, the argument that law is a key determining factor in the development of financial markets is being questioned. Many legal historians and commercial and financial law scholars argue that financial law and regulation are constituted and developed through market practices.

---

[4] Eurobonds are corporate bonds issued in the currency of a particular country (initially U.S. dollars) but which are traded outside that country.

Market developments can lead to changes in the regulatory provisions governing markets (see, e.g., Coffee, 2001). Indeed, as the short selling example above illustrated, the relationship of regulatory rules and market behavior is not one of linear causality in either direction, but is instead a complex dance in which market behavior and regulatory action shadow, anticipate, and react to each others' moves in turn.

The complex regulatory-market dance is one familiar to regulatory scholars. Where legal scholarship tends to bifurcate, however, is between that which focuses on private law and that which focuses on regulatory provisions. As indicated above, there is far more empirical research on the regulatory-market dance than there is in scholarship in private law of the interrelationship between market practices and the development of financial law by the courts. To the extent that observations are made by private law scholars on the relationship, this work tends to be micro-level, focusing on the development of particular legal rules as a result of particular market practices. As Cranston has observed, private lawyers rarely study markets; they study particular legal doctrines (Cranston, 2007). It is thus hard to make direct comparisons between the writings of private lawyers and the often macro-level and quantitative research of financial economists and legal scholars discussed above. The debates operate at different levels of abstraction and have quite different conceptions of law and of markets

Political scientists clearly have an interest in the dynamics of financial regulation, and international committees of financial regulators have attracted considerable academic attention. This work focuses on the political dynamics of the global system of financial services regulation, analyzing the principal actors, the coordination challenges, and the "democratic deficit" which exists in global financial regulation (e.g., Porter, 2001). These international committees of financial regulators are also regarded as prime examples of "governance" and regulation beyond the state, and have been studied by lawyers, sociologists and political scientists alike. Further, at the national level, both political scientists, and lawyers have analyzed the development of national regulatory systems and their changing character (e.g., Moran, 1986).

If we focus principally on empirical work by lawyers on the dynamics of regulation, or that by non-lawyers which appears in law journals, we find that it focuses in two main areas: regulatory competition and the dynamics of state and non-state regulatory regimes.

1. *Regulatory competition*

There is a significant literature on regulatory competition both by regulatory scholars and by corporate lawyers, though the two groups of researchers very rarely interact. In U.S. corporate law, the central preoccupation has been the competition among states for corporate charters and the "Delaware" effect: whether this leads to a race to the bottom and how the "bottom" is defined. Much of this work is theoretical, but there are also several empirical studies looking at the numbers and types of firms that choose to incorporate in Delaware and more recent qualitative work that looks at the reasons why they choose to do so (see Choi, 2001 for review).

With respect to financial markets, most recent analysis has focused on the implications of demutualization of stock exchanges and on competition between them for listings. This work is both national (within the United States) and cross-national, comparing IPOs and secondary listings between the UK and the U.S. markets in particular (Coffee, 2007; Jackson, 2007), and comparing listings to the regulatory regimes. This research suggests that exchanges whose regulators use formal enforcement action are less attractive to closely held corporations than those that use a more informal enforcement approach (Coffee, 2007).

2. *Regulatory practices*

There has been a range of work on the design and practice of different financial regulatory regimes. This work falls into two main areas: the dynamics of self-regulation and the dynamics of governmental regulation in the markets, including the dynamics of compliance within financial firms.

a. *Self-regulation and norm-production*

There is a tradition in many countries of self-regulation in financial markets, stemming largely from the history of the formation of organized securities and futures markets. Regarding financial markets, there has been a significant amount of research into the operation of the futures exchanges. Here, researchers differ as to the role that law has played in the development of markets. Some empirical research on the development of futures markets suggests that the primary reason for their emergence in the United States was legal recognition of futures contracts, which was essential for the liquidity of those contracts (Williams, 1986: 174).

In contrast, Collins argues that futures markets provide an excellent example of markets that exist without law. Futures markets are an example of what he terms "club markets" (Collins, 1999). Club markets are constituted by traders for their mutual protection and benefit. Membership confers a right to trade, and the markets are characterized by rules of trading with which members are required to comply. Ordering is achieved through mutuality, trust, and non-legal sanctions (see also Abolafia, 1997). Although contracts play a considerable role in that they are the vehicle for the club's rules, they are upheld informally. The thesis advanced is one of "markets in the absence of law." The use of social norms to enforce market arrangements is well illustrated in more recent times by the regulation of takeovers of public companies in the UK. For over 40 years, the Panel on Takeovers and Mergers, a non-statutory body, devised and implemented the rules for takeovers of public companies, entirely without legal underpinning, or as Donaldson MR notoriously put it "without visible means of legal support."[5]

However, in a detailed historical study of the development of futures markets in Liverpool and London in the nineteenth century, Cranston argues that although at least in the case of futures markets, the "markets in the absence of law" arguments have some validity, it is not the case that law was entirely irrelevant to their development. Although lawyers were largely absent from their development, law "entered in the way the markets were constituted and governed, the system of rules for transactions and how these were cleared and settled, the standard form contracts used for dealing, and the arbitration procedures used for dispute settlement" (Cranston, 2007: 34). Law enabled the markets by permitting unregulated association and freedom of contract. However, while law provided the framework, markets themselves did provide the detailed mechanics of their operation. Even if the courts were not always obliging, market practices provided a significant source of law, and common and statute law "provided a rare barrier to the pursuit of profit in their preferred way by the practical men working in the London and Liverpool commodity markets" (ibid: 35).

Cranston's work is notable for its detailed, historical empiricism. Although many commercial law scholars have noted the incorporation of market practices into law, and some, such as Benjamin, have drawn attention to the role of contemporary "law merchants" in producing new "legal" instruments (Benjamin, 2008), there is little sustained and systematic empirical analysis of how and where these norms are produced by the financial markets. There have been almost no detailed studies of micro-processes of the "bottom up" systems of norm production (excluding arbitration) or of the dynamics of the legal "shadow-land" of financial market practices, in which the "legal" instruments of private contracting are "legal" only because all who use them believe them to be so. There are scatterings of empirical research into how these norms develop. Flood and Skordaki, for example, have conducted an empirical analysis of how accountants and lawyers resolve conflicts between national rules in large cross-border insolvencies, where there are no legal solutions that can be applied to resolve the problems such insolvencies pose (Flood and Skordaki, 1997). Their study shows how solutions are crafted by a small but global community of professionals rather than through the application of established legal rules.

The dynamics of this legal shadow-land and of the extra-judicial development of the private "law" of financial markets have otherwise so far proved largely impervious to empirical legal analysis, by lawyers or non-lawyers. Perhaps this is because of an impoverished conception of law. Suggesting that private arrangements of contracts and associations can produce valid law without authorization and control of the state, even given the doctrine of freedom of contract, is an unsettling notion for

---

[5]   *R v. Panel on Takeovers and Mergers, ex p Datafin* (1987) QB 815.

lawyers trained in the traditions of positivism, and possibly a puzzling one for many outside the legal academy. The fact that it is so unsettling, or at least puzzling, should however make the dynamics of norm-production in the financial markets an even more fertile source of analysis by empiricists and theoreticians alike.

b. State based regulation and firms' responses to regulation

Moving to state regulation and "co-regulators," empirical work has focused here on the dynamics of rule making (Black, 1997); on the incidence and use of formal and informal enforcement techniques (Jackson, 2007); and on the practices of monitoring, particularly the growth of risk-based systems of monitoring and supervision in a number of different countries (Black, 2008). It has also looked at the reasons for regulatory failure, for example, with respect to misselling of financial products (Black and Nobles, 1998). The financial crisis led to further work on how and why regulators fail (e.g., Schwarcz, 2008) and should prompt much more.

Research by sociologists into market bubbles and crashes connects well with research by lawyers and political scientists into the dynamics of regulatory relationships. Abalofia and Kilduff, for example, analyzed the dynamics of the "bubble" in silver prices in the 1980s, arguing that the crisis was the outcome of a struggle between competing coalitions, each seeking to promote its own parochial interest, and was resolved by the carefully orchestrated actions of institutional actors, including regulators, concerned with preventing further damage to specific participants in this market and related markets (Abolafia and Kilduff, 1988).

Research into financial regulators has also focused on how they attempt to define their institutional position. This work shows how regulators are active in constructing their own perception of their role, and their appropriate institutional position *vis-à-vis* other actors in the regulatory system, not just firms, but other state and non-state regulators. Black and Gilad's work separately shows how, in an iterative process, they develop their own perceptions of their role and seek strategically to manage the competing role perceptions and demands for legitimacy that others make through this interpretation and articulation of their role and relative institutional position (Black, 1997; Gilad, 2008). Much of this work uses regulation of financial markets as a case study through which to explore dynamics of wider relevance to those interested in understanding the nature and complexity of regulatory processes in other domains.

Moving from regulators to firms, there has been some empirical work by legal scholars on compliance within firms. Again this work is of broader relevance to regulatory scholars as well as those interested in financial regulation. Weait's study of compliance officers in UK financial institutions found that to be effective, the compliance function had to have status within the organization and senior management support. It was perceived as standing in opposition to business; and in order to gain acceptance and to persuade employees to comply, it had to be shown how compliance could be "good for business" (Weait, 1994). This work is now quite dated, but the findings accord with those of others who have explored the role of compliance officers in the same or different areas.

There is recent empirical research into the dynamics and effectiveness of the imposition as a sanction, by a regulator or court, of a requirement that a firm undertake a compliance audit—also known as a monitorship—or a similar procedure. Ford and Hess recently conducted qualitative research into the role of the monitor in monitorships or audits imposed as sanctions on financial firms. They found that in practice there were a number of weaknesses, concluding that "monitorships that have the goal of reforming corporations are at a risk of falling short" (Ford and Hess, 2009: 728). This is because the incentives and motivations of the three main actors involved (regulator, firm, and monitor) can coalesce in a way that the monitorship process settles for considerably less in terms of operation and ambition than might be hoped. The corporation wants a monitorship report that is just rigorous enough to satisfy the regulator. The monitor wants to write a report that is just rigorous enough to maintain her professional credentials with both firms and the regulator without offending her client and threatening future business. And the regulator does not push the monitor to go beyond ensuring the stipulated requirements are met (at least on paper) as she needs to close the file and move on to the next case. The result can be "relatively conservative monitorships focused on technical compliance with policies and procedures" (ibid: 729).

Finally, there has been detailed, again qualitative analysis of financial firms' "legal consciousness" and their response to law. This work illustrates well the contrasting conceptions of law, markets, and behavior between sociological approaches and more economic and formalistic approaches, and their association with qualitative and quantitative methodologies respectively. Larson explored the extent to which securities brokers' behavior in Fiji and Ghana was structured by the legal and regulatory rules, or by norms within the social field, here the securities market itself. In both cases, the size and trading patterns of the markets were similar, as were the legal rules. In contrast to the quantitative nature of the LLSV studies examined above, the question was not "what is the impact of legal rules on markets," i.e., their liquidity, volatility, etc., but "what is the impact of legal rules on the *behavior* of actors within markets," i.e., how and to what extent do legal rules shape their conduct. He found that the nature of the day-to-day interaction of the regulator with market actors had a significant effect on the extent to which behavior was structured by formal legal rules or social norms. Where regulators were physically more present and more involved in the day-to-day operations of the market, legal rules dominated; where they were more distant and monitoring was based principally on annual audits, then the norms of the "social field," i.e., the trading floor, dominated (Larson, 2004). Linking with the discussion above on the relationship between law and markets, this work illustrates how markets may operate substantively in the absence of law, even where law is formally present.

III. Analysis and Conclusion

The empirical research is thus diverse, but the central question is often the same, even if only weakly articulated: what is the relationship between law and markets? Do markets shape law, or does law shape (indeed constitute) markets? The natural impetus of legal scholars, policy-makers, and to an extent of regulators, is to assume that "law matters": law shapes markets. Law is not simply a facilitator of personal transactions; it shapes and structures those transactions and moreover provides the essential framework for them to occur. In the extreme version of this thesis, markets could not happen without legal institutions to create and facilitate the exchange of property rights and interests and to provide a stable institutional environment in which those transactions can be honored. Consequently the markets can be "fixed" by changing the rules governing their structure and the conduct of those participating in them. On this view, the reformists' task in the wake of the financial crisis is relatively straightforward: find the right rules, ensure they are properly enforced, and the markets will alter accordingly. The alternative view is that "markets matter": law and regulation, rather than constituting and shaping markets, follows the path that they have set out and validates activities that already exist. It is markets that come first; law is simply an instrument, a gift (or irritation) of the state that market actors lobby for, deploy, avoid, or simply ignore in the pursuit of their own interests. Law may be used an in attempt to shape or change markets, but its success in doing so is by no means a foregone conclusion.

Existing research produces no clear answers. This is partly because there are notable gaps, some of which this Chapter has highlighted. There is very little empirical research on the dynamics of the "legal shadow-land"—for example, on how financial instruments are developed and traded in the absence either of organized exchanges or of legal confirmation. There is no systematic study of the unintended consequences of regulatory or legal interventions or of avoidance of legal rules through gaming. The most that can be credibly drawn from existing research is that markets and law are in a reflexive relationship in which each influences the other, often in uncertain and unpredictable ways driven by dynamics that are not yet fully understood.

More fundamentally, the reason there are no clear answers is that the methodological biases and cognitive assumptions of the researchers themselves are so diverse and conflicting that their findings are almost impossible to synthesize. The different strands of research use different languages and logics, reflecting the fundamental tensions in social science between different understandings of behavior, different conceptions of the market, different conceptions of law, and different empirical methodologies. The "box" of LLSV-related research, for example, which is predominantly quantitative and rooted in law-and-economics, rarely if ever interacts with the more micro-level, qualitative work which is rooted in, or at least more sympathetic to, the traditions of sociology or anthropology.

Lawyers are often too unquestioning of these different assumptions in their use of empirical and experimental research conducted by others. However, there are signs of an increasing skepticism and questioning by lawyers, notably with respect to the LLSV school of financial economics. Interestingly this questioning is in turn having an impact on the latter's methodology. That development leads to the questions: what is the role of lawyers in this cacophony of voices?; what particular contribution can they make? In a notoriously scathing review of Paul Craig's book, *Public Law and Political Theory* (1992), Brendan O'Leary, a political scientist, asked "what should public lawyers do?" (O'Leary, 1992). His answer was that they should not do political theory: that this was best left to the professionals. That sums up one view of interdisciplinary research: each discipline is probably best left to its own experts. How can (and why should) lawyers attempt to understand the construction of financial models, or how investors or traders behave, or how markets are constituted? Surely this is best left to financial economists or cognitive psychologists or sociologists. There is some force to that argument, but only some. Clearly there are issues of relative expertise, but research strategies, such as collaboration, enable those from various disciplines to bring their respective expertise to bear on common questions, as does the learning by each of different disciplinary skills, techniques, research, and arguments. Lawyers can engage with these questions, and moreover there are good reasons that they should. Understanding the general context in which law and regulation operate, and in particular the dynamics of the financial markets, deepens our understanding of the nature, potential, and limits of law and regulation themselves. Moreover, as has been seen above, to the extent that the observations of experts in other disciplines are based on an impoverished conception of law, lawyers may be able to offer them a far more nuanced and critical set of reflections than others often recognize and from which they can benefit.

References

Abolafia, M. (1997). *Making Markets*, Cambridge, MA: Harvard University Press.

Abolafia, M. and Kilduff, M. (1988). "Enacting Market Crisis: The Social Construction of a Speculative Bubble," *Administrative Science Quarterly* 33(2): 177–93.

Armour, J., Deakin, S., Lele, P., and Seims, M. (2009). "How Do Legal Rules Evolve? Evidence from a Cross-Country Comparison of Shareholder, Creditor, and Worker Protection," *American Journal of Comparative Law* 57(3): 579–629.

Avgouleas, E. (2009a). "The Global Financial Crisis and the Disclosure Paradigm in Financial Regulation: The Case for Reform," *European Company and Financial Law Review* 6(4): 440–75.

Avgouleas, E. (2009b). "The Global Credit Crisis, Behavioural Finance and Financial Regulation: In Search of a New Orthodoxy," *Journal of Corporate Law Studies* 9(1): 23–59.

Avgouleas, E. (2010). "A New Framework for the Global Regulation of Short Sales: Why Prohibition is Inefficient and Disclosure is Insufficient," *Stanford Journal of Law, Business and Finance*, forthcoming.

Bebchuk, L., Cohen, A., and Ferrell, A. (2009). "What Matters in Corporate Governance?," *Journal of Financial Studies* 22(2): 783–828.

Benjamin, J. (2008). *Financial Law*, Oxford: Oxford University Press.

Beny, L. (2006). "Insider Trading Laws and Stock Markets Around the World: An Empirical Contribution to the Theoretical Law and Economics Debate," *Journal of Corporation Law* 32: 237–300.

Bhattacharya, U. and Daouk, H. (2002). "The world price of insider trading," *Journal of Finance* 57: 75–108.

Black, F. (1986). "Noise," *Journal of Finance* 41: 529–43.

Black, J. (1997). *Rules and Regulators*, Oxford: Oxford University Press.

Black, J. (2006). *Involving Consumers in Financial Regulation: A Report for the Taskforce on Regulatory Reform*, Toronto: Ontario.

Black, J. (2008*). Risk-Based Regulation: Choices, Practices and Lessons Being Learned*, Paris: OECD, 2008 – SG/GRP (2008) 4.

Black, J. and Nobles, R. (1998). "Personal Pension Misselling: The Causes and Lessons of Regulatory Failure," *Modern Law Review* 61: 789–820.

Callon, M. (ed.) (1998). *The Laws of the Markets*, Oxford: Blackwell.

Cearns, K. and Ferran, E. (2008). "Non-enforcement-led Public Oversight of Financial and Corporate Governance Disclosures and of Auditors," *Journal of Corporate Law Studies* 2(2): 191–224.

Charoenrook, A. and Daouk, H. (2008). "A Study of Market-Wide Short-Selling Restrictions," *Journal of Banking and Finance* 32(7): 1255–68.

Choi, S. (2001). "Law, Finance, and Path Dependence: Developing Strong Securities Markets," *Texas Law Review* 80: 1657–727.

Coffee, J. (2001). "The Rise of Dispersed Ownership: The Roles of Law and the State in the Separation of Ownership Control," *Yale Law Review* 111: 1–82.

Coffee, J. (2007). "Law and the Market: The Impact of Enforcement," Centre for Law and Economic Studies, Columbia University School of Law, Working Paper No. 304.

Collins, H. (1999). *Regulating Contracts*, Oxford: Oxford University Press.

Craig, P. (1992). Public Law and Political Theory, Oxford: Oxford University Press.

Cranston, R. (2007). "Law Through Practice: London and Liverpool Commodity Markets c.1820–1975," London: LSE Law Department Working Paper, available at <http://papers.ssrn.com/sol3/papers.cfm?abstract_id=1021952>.

Curtis, A. and Fargher, N. (2008). "Does Short Selling Amplify Price Declines or Align Prices with their Fundamental Values?," available at <http://ssrn.com/abstract=817446>.

Djankov, S., La Porta, R., Lopez-de-Silanes, F., and Shleifer, A., (2008). "The law and Economics of Self-dealing," *Journal of Financial Economics* 88: 430–65.

Fama, E. (1970). "Efficient Capital Markets: A Review of Theory and Empirical Work," *Journal of Finance* 25(2): 383–417.

Flood, J. and Skordaki, E. (1997). "Normative Bricolage: Informal Rule Making by Accountants and Lawyers in Mega-Insolvencies," in G. Teubner (ed.), *Global Law without a State*, Aldershot: Dartmouth.

Ford, C. and Hess, D. (2009). "Can Corporate Monitorships Improve Corporate Compliance?," *Journal of Corporation Law* 34(3): 680–737.

Gerding, E. (2007). "Laws Against Bubbles: An Experimental Asset Market Approach to Analyzing Financial Regulation," *Wisconsin Law Review* 5: 977–1039.

Gilad, S. (2008). "Exchange without Capture: the UK Financial Ombudsman's Struggle for Accepted Domain," *Public Administration* 86(4): 907–24.

Jackson, H. (2007). "Variation in the Intensity of Financial Regulation: Preliminary Evidence and Potential Implications," *Yale Journal on Regulation* 24: 253–91.

Jackson, H. and Roe, M. (2009). "Public and Private Enforcement of Securities Laws: Resource-Based Evidence," Harvard University Law School, Public Law and Legal Theory Research Paper Series No 0-28 and John M. Olin Center for Law and Business Law & Economic Research Paper Series, Paper No. 638, available at <http://www.law.harvard.edu/programs/olin_center>.

Kahneman, D., Slovic, P., and Tversky, A. (eds) (1982). *Judgement Under Uncertainty: Heuristics and Biases*, Cambridge: Cambridge University Press.

Kingsford-Smith, D. and Williamson, K. (2004). "How Do Online Investors Seek Information, And What Does This Mean for Regulation?," *Journal of Information, Law and Technology* 2, available at <http://www2.warwick.ac.uk/fac/soc/law/elj/jilt/2004_2/kingsford-smithandwilliamson>.

Knorr-Cetina, K. and Prada, A. (2004). *The Sociology of Financial Markets*, Oxford: Oxford University Press.

La Porta, R., Lopez-de-Silanes, F., and Shleifer, A. (2006). "What Works in Securities Laws?," *Journal of Finance* LXI: 1–32.

La Porta, R., Lopez-de-Silanes, F., Shleifer, A. (2008). "The Economic Consequences of Legal Origins," *Journal of Economic Literature* 46(2): 285–332.

La Porta, R., Lopez-de-Silanes, F., Shleifer, A., and Vishny, R. (1997). "Legal Determinants of External Finance," *Journal of Finance* LII (3): 1131–50.

La Porta, R., Lopez-de-Silanes, F., Shleifer, A., and Vishny, R. (1998). "Law and Finance," *Journal of Political Economy* 106: 1113–55.

La Porta, R., Lopez-de-Silanes, F., Shleifer, A., and Vishny, R. (2000). "Investor Protection and Corporate Governance," *Journal of Financial Economics* 58: 3–27.

La Porta, R., Lopez-de-Silanes, F., Shleifer, A., and Vishny, R. (2002). "Investor Protection and Corporate Valuation," *Journal of Finance* LVII: 1147–70.

Langevoort, D. (1992). "Theories, Assumptions and Securities Regulation: Market Efficiency Revisited," *University of Pennsylvania Law Review* 140: 851–920.

Larson, E. (2004). "Institutionalizing Legal Consciousness: Regulation and the Embedding of Market Participants in the Securities Industry in Ghana and Fiji," *Law & Society Review* 38(4): 737–68

Mahoney, P.G. (1997). "The Exchange as Regulator," *Virginia Law Review* 83: 1453–1500.

Malkiel, B. (2003). "The Efficient Capital Markets Hypothesis and its Critics," *Journal of Economic Perspectives* 17(1): 59–82.

Marsh, I. and Neimer, N. (2008). "The Impact of Short Sales Restrictions," (London Investment Banking Association, 2008), available at <http://www.liba.org.uk/issues/2009/Feb/theimpactofshortsalesrestrictions.pdf>.

McVea, H. (1995). "What's Wrong with Insider Dealing," *Legal Studies* 15: 390–414.

Moran, M. (1986). *The Politics of Banking* (2nd edn.), London: Macmillan.

O'Leary, B. (1992). "What Should Public Lawyers Do?," *Oxford Journal of Legal Studies* 12(3): 404–18.

Porter, T. (2001). "The Democratic Deficit in Institutional Arrangements for Regulating Global Finance," *Global Governance* 7(4): 427–39.

Schwarcz, S. (2008). "Protecting Financial Markets: Lessons from the Subprime Mortgage Meltdown," *Minnesota Law Review* 93(2): 373–406.

Schwarcz, S. (2009). "Understanding the Subprime Financial Crisis," *South Carolina Law Review* 60(3): 549–72.

Shiller, R. (1989). *Market Volatility,* Cambridge, MA: MIT Press.

Shiller, R. (2000). *Irrational Exuberance,* Princeton: Princeton University Press.

Shleifer, A, (1999). *Inefficient Markets: An Introduction to Behavioral Finance,* Oxford: Oxford University Press.

Siems, M. (2005). "What Does Not Work in Comparing Securities Laws: A Critique on La Porta et al.'s Methodology," *International Company and Commercial Law Review* 16(7): 300–05.

Slovic, P. (2000). *The Perception of Risk,* London: Earthscan.

Spamann, H. (2008). "Law and Finance Revisited' Harvard Law School John M. Olin Centre Discussion Paper No. 12, available at <http://papers.ssrn.com/sol3/papers.cfm?abstract_id=1095526>.

Stout, L.A. (1999). "Why the Law Hates Speculators: Regulation and Private Ordering in the Market for OTC Derivatives," *Duke Law Journal* 48: 701–86.

Tett, G. (2009). *Fools Gold,* London.

Thaler, R (1999). "The End of Behavioural Finance," *Financial Analysts Journal* 55(6): 12–19.

Weait, M. (1994). "The Role of the Compliance Officer in Firms Carrying on Investment Business," *Butterworth's Journal of International Banking and Financial Law* 9(8): 381–3.

Williams, J. (1986). *The Economic Function of Futures Markets,* Cambridge: Cambridge University Press.

Wood, P. (1995). *International Loans, Bonds and Securities Regulation,* London: Sweet and Maxwell.

7

CONSUMER PROTECTION

STEPHEN MEILI[1]

[1] Many thanks to Mary Rumsey and Margaret Benz of the University of Minnesota Law School for their research and production assistance, respectively.

I. Introduction

Reviewing empirical studies of the interplay between consumer complaining behavior, dispute resolution mechanisms, and administrative enforcement of consumer laws illustrates the evolution of consumer protection over the past half century and its place within larger historical trends both in the developed and developing worlds during that same period. Not long after the proliferation of consumer protection legislation in the 1960s and 1970s in the United States and other parts of the West and North, empirical studies examining the effectiveness of those laws began dotting the scholarly and regulatory landscape. Some of the earliest studies covered the topic of consumer complaining behavior, which became more prevalent as consumers received more information about the products they purchased and services they received. As consumers learned more about what they were buying, they had a more extensive framework upon which to base complaints. This emphasis on information dissemination was the logical extension of the overall shift in consumer protection regulation from "let the buyer beware" to "let the seller disclose" (Meili, 2006). Other studies were designed to determine the effectiveness of new laws and regulations that, among other things, prohibited fraud and deceptive business practices, required disclosures on loan forms and other standard form contracts, and curtailed abusive debt collection practices.

Such a review also provides a logical framework within which to suggest areas for expanded empirical work in this area. For just as consumer protection has only fairly recently been recognized as a discrete area of the law, so too is the empirical analysis of various consumer protection laws and mechanisms relatively new. Thus, while many studies have been published, particularly in the developed world, much remains to be explored.

As the above discussion suggests, this Chapter is divided into two discrete parts. The first reviews empirical studies of consumer complaining behavior, consumer complaint-handling mechanisms, and the administrative enforcement of consumer protections laws in various parts of the world over the past several decades. The second part suggests areas where additional empirical research is needed.

II. Where We Have Been: Past Empirical Studies

Much of the empirical research into consumer complaints and how public and private institutions have addressed them has proceeded on parallel tracks that too infrequently coincide: consumer complaining behavior on the one hand, and the efficacy of mechanisms designed to resolve consumer disputes, on the other. And while both tracks have produced significant information about consumers and the means available to them for resolving disputes, future scholars would be well advised to consider utilizing both sets of findings in analyzing how third parties, both public and private, might better address the concerns of dissatisfied consumers.

Both tracks emerged out of the explosion in consumer goods and services (and readily available credit) that followed the post-World War II economic boom in the United States. Consumers, and their advocates in government and the public interest sectors, began to demand more detailed information about the products they were purchasing, as well as more stringent regulation of corporate conduct. More information and more laws led inexorably to more disputes between consumers and merchants, as well as outlets to air those disputes. Not long thereafter, empirical studies began to probe this new arena at the intersection of law and society.

A. Research on complaining behavior

In the broadest sense, studies on complaining behavior, primarily initiated in the United States, began with analyses of the various problems consumers encountered with the products they purchase (e.g., Mason and Himes, 1973). Several survey studies from the 1970s mapped the relative frequency of various consumer problems over issues such as price, misrepresentation, delays in delivery, and performance (e.g., Best and Andreasen, 1977). This research can be generally divided into two categories: marketing studies and socio-legal studies. The former were designed to understand the implications of consumer complaints on the marketing, development, sales, and service of consumer goods and services (see Kritzer et al., 1991). The latter were designed to understand the implications of consumer complaints on both formal and informal dispute resolution mechanisms. Both groups of studies provided important insights into factors affecting the degree of consumer perceptions of problems, most notably that such perceptions increase with a rise in socio-economic status, as well as interest in and awareness of consumer issues and law. They also found that most consumers are disinclined to be identified as the victim of consumer problems. These findings have persistent relevance to ongoing studies of consumer complaint-handling processes, particularly as to their effectiveness in protecting the interests of lower income consumers and others less inclined to perceive problems with the products they purchase or otherwise utilize.

A related set of early studies of consumer problems in the United States focused on several factors which contribute to a consumer's dissatisfaction with a particular product or service. These included knowledge of alternative products (complete knowledge of such alternatives, as well as how they compare to what was actually purchased, leads to less dissatisfaction); the ability to judge the alternatives (greater judging ability is likely to lead to more dissatisfaction); variability in the quality of alternatives (greater variability likely to lead to more dissatisfaction); and perceptions of importance of the product purchased (the more important the perceived purchase, the greater the likelihood of perceived problems) (e.g., Gronhaug and Arndt, 1980). Other studies examined the roles that warranties play in making a dispute between buyer and seller more likely (e.g., Palfrey and Romer, 1983). As with the studies linking socio-economic status to perceived problems with products, such empirical findings continue to have relevance for ongoing studies of the efficacy of consumer complaint-handling processes.

A third vital strand of the early empirical studies of consumer dissatisfaction in the United States and other countries linked perceptions of problems with the willingness to lodge complaints. While revealing a wide disparity in the propensity of dissatisfied consumers to complain, these studies demonstrated that, overall, only a fraction of disgruntled consumers lodge complaints, either directly to the seller of the product or through a more formal mechanism established by—and usually featuring—a third party, such as a governmental entity, professional association, or lawyer (e.g., Gronhaug and Arndt, 1980). This general reluctance to complain applies regardless of whether the dissatisfaction stemmed from a private purchase or receipt of a public service, such as education or public transportation. And of the small fraction of what might be called "dissatisfaction incidents" resulting in complaining behavior, an even smaller percentage result in complaints to third parties. Rather, the vast majority of complaints, at least in the context of private purchases, take one of three forms: either directly communicating with the seller, returning the defective product, or "exiting" (i.e., purchasing from a different seller in the future).

Analyzed collectively, the studies linking consumer dissatisfaction and complaining identify positive correlations between a variety of factors and a willingness to lodge complaints with third parties. Thus, for example, Kritzer et al. (1991) found that the most consistent factor in determining the likelihood of consumer complaints is problem context; their research revealed a descending order of complaint probability, beginning with non-professional services (the most likely source of complaints), followed by products and, lastly, professional services (the least likely source of complaints among the three categories) (Kritzer et. al., 1991). Other factors identified in various studies include the socio-economic status of the consumer, the significance and cost of the purchase (complaints are likelier with respect to more expensive products and those perceived by the consumer as more significant), the frequency with which the item is purchased (i.e., complaints are more likely to be lodged over a less regularly purchased item such as an automobile, rather than a consistently purchased household item like a cleaning product), the longevity of the prob-lem (complaints are more likely the longer a problem lingers), the simplicity (or perceived simplicity) of the complaint process (the simpler the process, the more likely the consumer is to utilize it), and whether the product was purchased on credit or with cash (credit users are more likely to lodge com-plaints) (e.g., Best and Andreasen, 1977). Given the credit explosion since the mid-1970s, this latter finding is particularly relevant for future empirical work on consumer complaint handling systems. These studies also shed light on the important question of whether complaining behavior is related to anticipation of a favorable response (ibid). And finally, just as with the studies on consumer dissatisfaction, most consumers are disinclined to see themselves as complain-ers (Andreasen, 1988).

In general, the extensive empirical research on complaining behavior has revealed that third-party dispute mechanisms are more likely to be utilized by consumers who are wealthier, white, better educated, better informed, younger, more inclined to view complaining in a favorable light, not fearful of antagonizing sellers or other providers of goods and services, more politically active, and more experienced in the particular purchasing category at issue. And perhaps not surprisingly, such mechanisms tend to disproportionally favor this very group of consumers, i.e., con-sumers who fit into one or more of these categories are more likely to prevail after complaining.

Socio-legal empirical research on complaining behavior reached its zenith in the late 1970s and early 1980s and had diminished significantly by the late 1980s (Andreasen, 1988). Marketing studies, on the other hand, have continued apace, as exemplified by the continuing vitality of the annual *Journal of Consumer Satisfaction, Dissatisfaction & Complaining Behavior* (see <http://lilt.ilstu.edu/staylor/csdcb/>), which, as the name suggests, includes empirical studies of con-sumer behavior. Such studies have analyzed detailed aspects of complaining behavior, including the sources, characteristics, and dynamics of post-purchase price complaints and the ways they differ from non-price complaints (Estelami, 2003). Some studies have analyzed consumer complaint behavior from the per-spective of a neoclassical economic model of the demand for consumer complaints (Kolodinsky, 1995). Others have developed increasingly sophisticated models for measuring the relative importance of a variety of factors in determining whether particular consumers are likely to lodge complaints, what types of complaining behavior they are likely to take, their perceptions of outcomes, and the effect that the process and outcomes have on future complainant behavior (e.g., Volkov, 2003; Singh and Widing, 1991; Blodgett and Granbois, 1992; Boote, 1998). Still others have analyzed complaint data over the course of many years and opined as to why, for example, the number of consumer complaints over automobile warran-ties declined markedly since its apex in the mid-1980s as compared to the first decade of the twenty-first century (Migliore, 2006). Another study examined the complaining behavior of consumers of sporting events (i.e., spectators) and how it contrasts with generally accepted notions of consumer complaint behaviors (Volkov et al., 2005). And while much of the early empirical research on consumer complaining behavior originated in the United States, the locus of this empirical research had expanded by the late 1980s to include numerous other countries, including Australia, Canada, China, Denmark, the Netherlands, Norway, Sweden, Turkey, Thailand, the United Kingdom, and the former West Germany (Andreasen, 1988).

One striking feature of the early empirical work on consumer behavior and information is how much of it was sponsored by governmental entities. Thus, for example, the U.S. Federal Trade Commission sponsored a conference in 1986 entitled "Empirical Approaches to Consumer Protection Economics" (U.S. Federal Trade Commission, 1986). The conference, which resulted in the publication of 13 papers, had the explicit purpose of encouraging empirical research regarding consumer information and how it relates to such consumer protection issues as minimum quality standards, advertising, deception and fraud, warranties, consumer shopping behavior, and dispute resolution (ibid). However, concomitant with the rise of deregulation through the late 1980s and 1990s, the U.S.'s role as a facilitator of empirical research into consumer affairs appears to have waned. This contrasts with other countries in the West and North, whose governments not only sponsor such empirical research, but frequently conduct it.

Another group of early studies in the United States explored the level of consumer satisfaction with third-party organizations or agencies to which consumers complained about a problem that was not resolved at the first level of complaint (e.g., King and McEvoy, 1976). Among other things, these early studies demonstrated that as to third parties (i.e., not the merchant, service provider, or manufacturer), governmental agencies, whether at the state or federal level, were less helpful in resolving consumer complaints than the Better Business Bureau or private attorneys (ibid). These studies also tracked consumer familiarity with federal and state consumer protection agencies. Mirroring many of the findings of early empirical research on consumer dissatisfaction and complaining behavior, these studies tended to show that familiarity with various consumer protection organizations is more common among consumers who are white, wealthier, and living on either coast of the U.S. (ibid).

As a result of this rich body of research, it is fair to conclude that we know significantly more about (1) why consumers are dissatisfied, (2) whether they are likely to complain about that dissatisfaction, and (3) how they are likely to complain, than we did 30 or 40 years ago. What is less clear is the extent to which the various consumer dispute resolution mechanisms that have sprung up over the past several decades have taken that knowledge into account in order to better serve the needs of *all* consumers who are dissatisfied, not merely those inclined to complain.

B. Research on complaint-handling mechanisms[2]

As studies of consumer dissatisfaction and complaining behavior began to ebb in the latter part of the twentieth century, the volume of research on the efficacy of consumer complaint-handling mechanisms in the U.S. and other parts of the West and North expanded. The earliest of these, mostly in the 1970s, were primarily concerned with the effectiveness of administrative agency consumer complaint apparatuses. In the United States, the most prominent among these were state-by-state analyses of the unfair and deceptive practice statutes that were promulgated by every state in the 1960s and 1970s. In one of these studies, published by the *Tulane Law Review* in 1984, the researchers examined a variety of factors within each of these statutes, including the availability of a private right of action, limitations on what kind of entities may be sued and other impediments to filing a claim, the types of damages permitted (e.g., actual, statutory, punitive, and attorneys' fees), as well as the degree to which the relevant administrative agency enforced the statute (e.g., number of injunctions obtained, the number of complaints received, and how many were resolved in favor of the consumer) (Dunbar, 1984: 438). The study acknowledged its own limitations, including the fact that the wide variation in record-keeping among states made accurate comparisons difficult. For example, as the report concedes, "one state's 'referral to another agency' is another state's 'resolution of a consumer complaint'" (ibid). Other problems with studies such as Dunbar's is that they take a descriptive rather than normative approach: they use the rather blunt instruments of hard data, such as numbers of complaints filed, to draw broad conclusions about which state agencies are doing a better job than others in protecting consumers (ibid). Aside from the fact that such generalizations are difficult to measure by any meaningful standard, they tell us nothing about whether a particular model for dispute resolution fully addresses the needs of those who complain, and are designed to meet the needs of those who, according to the abundant consumer complaining literature described above, are less likely to do so because of demographics or personality.

Outside the U.S., a similar volume of studies analyzed the effectiveness of various consumer complaint-handling mechanisms: e.g., Hodges and Tulibacka, 2009 (England and Wales); Ebers et al., 2009 (European Union); Viitanen, 2000 (Baltic Countries); Oliveira and Goldbaum, 2001–2002 (Brazil); Sourdin, 2007 (Australia). A significant subset of these studies examines the role of the ombudsman in various industries, sometimes as a means of comparison with how disputes in a similar industry are handled in the U.S.: e.g., Schwarcz, 2009 (reviewing empirical data on

---

[2] This Chapter does not address empirical studies of class actions (or other forms of large group litigation), which are frequently utilized by consumers with disputes against corporations and other entities. That subject is addressed in considerable depth in the Chapter authored by Christopher Hodges in this volume (see Chapter 29; see also Hensler, et al., 2009).

the British Financial Ombudsman Service); James and Seneviratne, 1996 (analyzing data about the Ombudsman for Corporate Estate Agents Schemes). Another study, published by the European Commission, examined the extent to which EU countries had implemented a 1993 EC Directive concerning the removal of unfair terms from consumer contracts (European Commission, 1999). And while this Chapter has focused primarily on empirical studies published in English, studies published in other languages have examined a similar range of issues: see, e.g., Gudde, 2004: (study on the handling of individual consumer complaints in Germany, where the results show that the state is much more likely to resort to courts in disputes with consumers, whereas consumers are more likely to seek redress through informal administrative complaints); and Kellner, 1972 (reporting on an empirical study in East Berlin showing a far higher number of consumer complaints against private companies than against consumer cooperatives, the latter of which handled about one-third of all consumer transactions at that time). These studies reveal that, in general, consumers and industries are both favorably disposed toward ombudsman services, and that such services are most valuable in facilitating communication (and accommodation) between parties in relatively minor disputes. Ombudsmen have less success when dealing with more complex (and expensive) problems encountered by consumers.

While some studies, both in the U.S. and elsewhere, focused on government-administered complaint handling mechanisms, the vast majority of empirical data over the past quarter century has examined a wide range of private alternative dispute resolution structures. (e.g., Ervine, 1993; Nordic Council of Ministers, 2002). These studies have compared various ADR procedures (i.e., informal negotiation, mediation, arbitration, small claims procedures, and more formal complaint mechanisms) and analyzed their effectiveness and the extent to which consumer protection authorities in various countries (particularly in the European Union) cooperate with private ADR systems so as to better educate consumers about the various dispute resolution options available to them. They also examine the effectiveness of online dispute resolution procedures ("ODR") (e.g., Hammond, 2003; Edwards and Wilson, 2007). In general, these studies conclude that while online dispute resolution systems are underutilized, they could become far more useful for consumers if designed to overcome various technological barriers, particularly those faced by less tech-savvy complainants. These studies also illustrate ODR's advantages over in-person dispute resolution mechanisms, including the absence of negative effects of face-to-face confrontations between disputants. As e-commerce becomes increasingly prevalent, the importance of empirical studies on the handling of disputes arising from that class of transactions will become increasingly vital.

Given the breadth and scope of these studies, as well as their different methodologies and the diverse legal structures they analyze, it is difficult (and dangerous) to draw general conclusions about what they have demonstrated. Perhaps the most that can be said in a summary fashion is that they conclude that a variety of factors influence the effectiveness of various ADR procedures, including the duration of the procedure, limitations on the kinds of disputes covered, the amount of money at stake in the dispute, the presence of lawyers in the process (i.e., as advocates for consumers), and the extent to which the recommendations of the decision-maker are enforceable. The findings as to these variables are sufficiently inconsistent as to prevent any sweeping generalizations.

Within the broad category of ADR, the area that seems to have received the most attention in recent years is arbitration, both voluntary and mandatory. Indeed, particularly in the United States, where mandatory, pre-dispute arbitration clauses in standard form consumer contracts have been the subject of much litigation, we have witnessed something of a cottage industry of empirical (and sometimes not particularly scholarly) studies of the pros and cons of arbitration, particularly in contrast to litigation. The United Kingdom, France, and New Zealand, on the other hand, have generally banned such clauses in consumer contracts, while the European Union has voiced its opposition to them. While some studies of mandatory arbitration clauses take a neutral approach (e.g., Demaine and Hensler, 2004), many others proceed from a more partisan perspective, as they tend to draw conclusions consistent with the groups and/or causes who support them, financially or otherwise. Many of these studies interpret statistics on outcomes (typically couched as "winning" and "losing") to demonstrate that mandatory arbitration is better—or worse—for consumers than going to court. Given the politically charged nature of the current arbitration debate, these studies do little to advance reasonable inquiry into the effectiveness of various consumer dispute resolution mechanisms.

Three substantive areas of consumer disputes have been particularly prevalent in the empirical literature on ADR over the past half century. In the 1970s and 1980s several studies examined the role of bar associations and other institutions in investigating and policing allegations of lawyer misconduct (e.g., Rhode, 1981). In the late 1980s and 1990s, most likely the result of the Clinton Administration's health care reform proposals and the insurance industry's effective publicity campaign against the so-called "litigation explosion" in the U.S., a host of empirical studies examined the issue of medical care (e.g., Saks, 1986). These studies addressed a variety of issues, including the factors leading patients to sue (or otherwise complain about) their doctors, patient success rates in various complaint-resolution mechanisms, and the ways that patient complaints are resolved. Very few of these studies focused on dispute-handling mechanisms for lower income consumers, e.g., those who are enrolled in Medicaid or other public assistance programs (but see Perkins et al., 1996). And most recently (i.e., in the first decade of the twenty-first century), we have seen a spate of empirical studies on securities arbitration (e.g., Gross and Black, 2008). These studies examined issues including investor success rates and perceptions of fairness. And, as is the case with many studies of arbitration more generally, some of the research was either funded or conducted by parties with an active stake in the debate over the issue.

Even a cursory review of the empirical studies on consumer complaint-handling mechanisms around the world reveals that most are centered in the Western and Northern Hemispheres. While this is certainly due in part to an imbalance in resources available for empirical research in various parts of the world, it is also the result of geopolitical factors. For example, in many Latin American countries, empirical work on the resolution of disputes has focused on users of courts (as opposed to, say, alternative dispute resolution mechanisms), given the emphasis on judicial reform in the wake of dictatorships and the long history of judicial non-independence throughout the region (e.g., World Bank, 2002). In many Latin American countries, ironically enough, the emphasis is on *encouraging* consumers and other individuals to use the judicial system (and feel comfortable with it), as opposed to many developed countries in the West and North, where the emphasis over the past few decades has been to develop mechanisms that seek to *discourage* people from going to court, as opposed to other forms of redress. This difference in emphasis is largely the result of the long-standing legal culture in many Latin American countries, where the judiciary has historically been seen as a force of oppression, serving as an adjunct of the military and/or a dominant executive, as opposed to the defender of individual rights.

C. Research on administrative agency enforcement of consumer protection laws

A final area of empirical study relevant to this Chapter is the efficacy of actual enforcement of consumer protections laws by regulatory agencies. Perhaps surprisingly, the number of studies in this area is rather limited. However, while the quantity is somewhat lacking, the quality is very thorough, informative, and, one hopes, helpful to such agencies as they seek to increase compliance with the law.

This empirical research is based on a combination of specific case studies of enforcement actions by governmental agencies, surveys of regulated businesses, and qualitative interview with regulatory staff, business executives, and private lawyers practicing in the relevant area. As a general matter, the goal is to determine what factors in the regulatory environment are more likely to enhance compliance by regulated businesses, particularly given the relatively modest budgets under which agencies are compelled to operate. Thus, for example, in a study of business compliance with Australia's competition law between 1997 and 2003, Parker concluded that the administrative process of investigating complaints, as well as publicity about those investigations, deterred legal violations more effectively than penalties (Parker, 2006). Her research also confirmed earlier scholarly findings that a mixture of regulatory practices and penalties is more effective than a single deterrent scheme (e.g., criminal penalties), given that budgetary considerations can make the latter difficult to consistently administer over time.

   In the United States, empirical studies of administrative enforcement have primarily focused on two areas: the Food and Drug Administration's enforcement of food safety standards, and state attorney general participation in multi-state lawsuits. Thus, for example, in a 2005 article that begins, appropriately enough, with the statement, "[e]conomists have devoted relatively little attention to analyzing how government officials actually enforce regulation," Law concludes that, given its limited deterrence capability, the FDA's enforcement of the Pure Food and Drugs Act between 1907 and 1938 was most effective when it was able to offer firms quality certification or direct assistance in improving food quality (Law, 2006). In a similar vein, based on a study of more contemporary food quality regulatory enforcement, Albertini et al. found that even though larger food processing plants are more likely to be subject to FDA inspection under its new Hazards Analysis and Critical Control Points regulations, those plants are actually more likely to be out of compliance with those regulations (Albertini et al., 2008). These researchers have developed vitally important information about what does and does not motivate compliance with consumer protection laws and regulations. The shame is that more studies have not shed this kind of extremely beneficial light on other industries and the agencies that regulate them.

   On a less industry-specific front, Provost has studied multi-state lawsuits filed by state attorneys general in the U.S. (e.g., Provost, 2006). His conclusion is that state citizen ideology, consumer group presence, median family income, and the elected or appointed status of the attorney general are the key factors in determining whether a given attorney general will join such a suit. According to Provost, "[e]ach state's political culture and attitude towards consumer protection strongly influences state attorneys general participation in multi-state consumer protection lawsuits" (ibid: 616). Sounding a familiar theme in this corner of the empirical studies universe, Provost notes that further research is necessary to better understand the various motivations behind these decisions, which can result in important consumer protections, as well as significant settlement proceeds, for a given state.

D. Summary: extant empirical research

As a general conclusion about the state of existing empirical research in this area, and at the risk of drawing overly broad conclusions based on sheer numbers of published studies, it nevertheless seems fair to conclude that over the past half century, scholars have provided us with rich empirical data about (1) whether and why consumers complain about the products and services they purchase or use, and (2) the various informal mechanisms that governmental bodies and private parties utilize in attempting to resolve those complaints. On the other hand, with a few notable exceptions such as those discussed in the preceding paragraphs, we know comparatively little about how well regulatory agencies enforce the vast number of laws and regulations they are charged with administering. This imbalance is both surprising and troubling, given that it is in the interests of all consumers, and society generally, for cash-strapped regulators to enforce the law as effectively and efficiently as possible.

III. Where We Need To Go: Ideas For Further Empirical Study

The empirical research on consumer complaints reviewed above suggests a number of avenues for future directions in this important area. Some of these suggestions would expand on research already conducted, while others would break new ground. Taken together, this kind of empirical work will provide policy-makers, corporations, and the general public with an increasingly sophisticated and informative analysis of whether a given complaint resolution mechanism is truly effective and worth replicating or expanding. Particularly during a time of economic crisis when funds for any initiative, public or private, are limited, such knowledge can go a long way in ensuring that whatever funds are expended for resolving disputes are well spent.

A. Research that combines prior work on consumer behavior, procedural fairness, and complaint mechanisms

As noted above, empirical research on consumer complaints has generally followed two parallel paths: the dynamics of consumer complaining behavior and the effectiveness of procedures designed to resolve consumer disputes, most typically measured through numerical analyses of "winning" and "losing." Research going forward should meld these two parallel strands. In other words, the research on consumer disputing behavior should inform research seeking to evaluate the efficacy of a given dispute resolution procedure. Given all we now know about (1) the kinds of problems consumers encounter with various products; (2) the factors that contribute to consumer dissatisfaction with those products; (3) the conditions—both internal and external to the consumer—that make it more or less likely that he or she will register a complaint; (4) the kinds of complaining behavior in which most consumers engage; and, perhaps most important, (5) the demographic characteristics that correlate with a propensity to lodge a complaint, researchers now have the ingredients for extremely rich and contextualized studies of dispute resolution mechanisms. Thus, for example, rather than simply looking at whether a consumer is more likely to "win" or "lose" if she engages with a particular mechanism, researchers should examine the design, marketing, and logistics of that mechanism in order to determine if it is likely to assist all consumers, rather than those with the greater propensity to complain in the first place.

Such studies should examine whether the mechanism is accessible to those individuals who, as earlier empirical studies suggest, are less likely to be aware of and utilize such mechanisms: e.g., consumers who are non-white, less well-educated, less well-informed and interested in consumer issues, older, less politically active, and more fearful of antagonizing sellers or other providers of goods and services. Factors such as how and where the mechanism is advertised, whether its sponsors reach out to local community groups to inform them of its existence, the ease of access and utilization, and stigmas likely to be attached to utilization should be probed. Indeed, while a few (though not many) of the studies reviewed for this Chapter examined complaint-handling procedures from the perspective of the complainant, these tended to analyze how the complainant viewed the process once she had opted into it; they did not analyze the extent to which the process was likely to attract complainants.

This form of research would assist policy-makers and those who administer dispute resolution mechanisms in bridging the well-documented gap between the number of dissatisfied consumers on the one hand, and those who bother to lodge a complaint, on the other. And given that most of the people who fall into that gap are less politically powerful and thus less likely to directly influence policy-making in this area (either by governments or corporations), this research can play a crucial role in assisting a group of consumers that might otherwise remain voiceless. Indeed, empirical studies of this sort would play a significant role in providing greater access to justice for many consumers.

In a related vein, future studies should also make use of the extensive empirical research on what has come to be known as "procedural fairness," a doctrine suggesting that disputants attach at least as much importance (and sometimes *more* importance) to the fairness of a given adjudicative procedure than to its outcome (which is often presented in monetary terms). The early work of Thibaut and Walker, as well as much that has followed, demonstrates that procedures matter profoundly to most participants because they believe that fair procedures produce fair outcomes (Thibaut and Walker, 1975). Similarly, in a recent study of participants in a mediation setting, Hollander-Blumoff and Tyler determined that there was "no relationship between the experienced fairness of the negotiation process and the numerical outcome" of the dispute. (Hollander-Blumoff and Tyler, 2008). In other words, participants in adjudicative processes (and in contexts beyond the judicial sphere) view the fairness of the process employed to resolve their dispute as "separate and apart from their interest in achieving a favorable outcome" (ibid). Similarly, Shestowsky has observed that "perceptions of how fair a procedure is tend to depend as much, if not more, on process characteristics than on whether particular disputants 'won' their case or were otherwise favored by the outcome" (Shestowsky, 2008).

This research has also suggested that a variety of factors influence a disputant's perception of whether a given process (as opposed to its outcome) is fair: e.g., was she provided with an opportunity to state her case? Was she treated with dignity and respect during the process? Was the decision-maker neutral and honest? Moreover, according to the "process control" theory developed by Thibault et al., disputants evaluate the fairness of a given procedure according to the distribution of control that it offers, and prefer those procedures that allow them (as opposed to third parties) to control the development and selection of information that will be used to resolve the dispute (Thibault et al., 1974).

With this extensive literature in mind (much of it based on empirical studies of disputants in various settings, including consumer protection scenarios), future empirical research into consumer complaint mechanisms should evaluate not only whether consumers were simply satisfied with the monetary result from a given complaint procedure, but whether they felt that the procedure was fair. Such perceptions of fairness would no doubt influence a participant's willingness to utilize (and encourage others to utilize) a given procedure in the future. And if part of the purpose in designing dispute-handling procedures is to ensure fairness to all parties, it would behoove the designers of such procedures to evaluate the extent to which the complainants themselves felt that it was fair. Researchers can provide significant value in this search for procedures that offer fairness, and not simply an opportunity for monetary reward, to consumers.

B. Comparative research on the effectiveness of various dispute resolution systems

Perhaps the most surprising aspect of a review of the extensive literature on the array of consumer complaint-handling and dispute resolutions mechanisms around the world is the dearth of research comparing the effectiveness of those mechanisms. As noted above, the range of dispute resolution options, both public and private, has increased dramatically over the past few decades to include such mechanisms as ombudsmen in a variety of industries (particularly in Europe), mediation, arbitration (both mandatory, pre-dispute arbitration, and non-mandatory, voluntary arbitration), and internal company grievance procedures. Many studies evaluate the effectiveness of these options in and of themselves (measured by factors such as success/failure rates, consumer satisfaction surveys, duration of procedure, etc.), but few compare the efficacy of different procedures. The major exception is the plethora of studies comparing arbitration to litigation. However, as noted above, the reliability of those studies is often compromised by the political and ideological agendas of their authors and/or financial underwriters. Thus, a much-needed direction for future scholarship in this area is comparative analyses of current and emerging forms of dispute resolution.

Of course, such analyses would introduce a host of complicating variables that do not encumber studies of single methods. However, any such potential obstacles are outweighed by the potential utility of such studies to consumers, policymakers, and businesses alike. Each of these parties is, presumably, interested in the design and implementation of dispute resolution mechanisms that maximize effectiveness and efficiency. Empirical research would assist in the realization of this worthy goal.

C. Research a more diverse group of disputes—and consumers

The United Nations Guidelines for Consumer Protection, passed by the General Assembly in 1985, advises that:

Governments should establish or maintain legal and/or administrative measures to enable consumers or, as appropriate, relevant organizations to obtain redress through formal or informal procedures that are expeditious, fair, inexpensive and accessible. *Such procedures should take particular account of the needs of low-income consumers*[3] (emphasis added).

Nearly 25 years later, we have little empirical data upon which to evaluate whether this directive has been followed. As noted above, there has been a plethora of empirical research, particularly in the United States, on dispute resolution—especially arbitration—in a few discreet issue areas, namely securities, private medical care, and legal services. Perhaps not surprisingly, these studies involve goods and services primarily available to wealthier consumers. Therefore, to the extent that empirical research results in improved procedures for consumers, these studies will mostly benefit those consumers who are already financially privileged and—as the consumer behavior research suggests—more likely to utilize dispute resolution mechanisms and favorably resolve their complaints. In order to obtain a more well-rounded analysis of the various dispute resolution procedures available, including those more widely used by a more economically and racially diverse segment of the public, research should focus on other types of consumer problems, including those stemming from what is often referred to as the "fringe-banking" arena (i.e.,

---

[3]   GA Res. 248, 39 UN GAOR (106th plen. Mtg), UN Doc A/Res/39/248 (1985).

payday loan and rent-to-own stores, pawn shops, check-cashing outlets, etc.[4]), sub-prime lending abuses, mortgage foreclosures, and low-income government assist-ance programs. Of course, there may not be much grist for the mill in such studies because there are few dispute mechanisms outside the court system for consumers to access when it comes to these problems. But studies revealing such a dearth of options for dissatisfied low-income and minority consumers would perhaps compel policy-makers to take corrective action. At the very least, they would demonstrate that the gap in dispute resolution resources devoted to wealthy and lower-income consumers is wide and ever-expanding.

Lower-income consumers are the most marginalized in the marketplace and the most alienated from the governmental systems which regulate it. They also tend to view the law as an arbitrary and capricious power (Ramsay, 2003). If individual states, and civil society more generally, wish to dispel this notion, and to encour-age a view of the law as a universal set of norms, it is in their interest to adopt pol-icies that provide access to justice, including dispute resolution mechanisms, that are equally welcoming and affordable to all consumers, regardless of income, race, and level of sophistication. Empirical research can be of great service in this regard, demonstrating which types of mechanisms encourage universal access to justice and widespread participation, and which are utilized primarily by those already in privileged positions.

D. Research on electronic transactions

The proliferation of consumer purchases over the Internet has created a need for empirical data concerning the type and efficacy of consumer complaint-handling mechanisms related to such transactions. A particular Internet-based company may or may not have an internal complaint mechanism, and even if it does, that mechanism may not be disclosed to consumers in a reasonably discernable man-ner. It may also be extremely cumbersome and confusing to navigate, particularly for less technologically savvy consumers. And to the extent that a consumer avails herself of any such mechanism, it is unclear to which state consumer protection agency (or state-based professional institution) she would turn if dissatisfied with the result. It is also unclear if the agencies (and the complaint-handling procedures they oversee) in the consumer's home state would have authority over a company whose only contact with the consumers in a given state is over the Internet. And, of

---

[4] These financial products target lower-income consumers and result in their paying more for goods, services, money, and credit than more well-off consumers. While a few individual states in the U.S. prohibit some of these products, most states merely license them, thus permitting them to operate relatively unfettered. While licensing allows state regulators to keep track of (and collect registration fees from) such businesses, it does not curtail their business model.

course, even if one could confidently assert such authority in theory, some Internet-based companies may be inclined to simply ignore requirements imposed on them by regulators and state legislators.

Thus, we need to know more about what kinds of internal complaint mechanisms Internet-based companies have established, the extent to which consumers are utilizing them, what happens when they do, and what recourse consumers have if they disagree with the result. One would hypothesize, for example, that the complaint rate over Internet-based transactions is far less than in the typical "bricks and mortar" scenario, and that whatever online complaint mechanisms exist are strongly skewed in favor of the merchant. We might also expect that the disproportionate use of online complaint mechanisms is even more pronounced in favor of white, better educated, better informed, and younger consumers than in the typical consumer complaint situation. But until we see the results of empirical research on these questions, we can only speculate.

E. Research on cross-border transactions

Another commercial phenomenon with which empirical research has only begun to grapple is the increasing number of consumer transactions that take place across national borders. This is of particular interest in the European Union, where, as a report published by the Study Centre for Consumer Law notes, some observers and officials are concerned that the "cocktail mix" of different ADR mechanisms in the various EU member states hinders cross-border trade (Stuyck, 2007). Similar studies in other regions of the world would shed light on this question, and help to determine if it is necessary for trading countries to adopt similar ADR mechanisms. Of course, one danger in such a "homogenization" approach is a "race to the bottom," as those countries with more stringent and consumer-friendly mechanisms might be tempted to relax their procedures in order to curry favor with their more laissez-faire trading partners.

Moreover, the opportunity to transact business across borders carries with it the temptation to commit fraud, as unscrupulous merchants assume that law enforcement authorities will stop at the national border. Just as we need research into the resolution of disputes against Internet-based companies, so too do we need empirical data on the extent to which individual states and other institutions have been able to resolve complaints alleging fraud by merchants operating in other, perhaps far distant, countries.

F. Research on regulatory enforcement

As the discussion earlier in this Chapter suggests, it is vitally important, from both a consumer protection and budgetary efficiency perspective, that empirical research explore more fully those factors that enhance administrative agency enforcement of applicable laws and regulations. Such research should expand to agencies beyond the few already studied (e.g., the FDA) and focus on why various businesses within the regulatory agency feel compelled (or not) to comply with the law. While the work in this area has set forth several important hypotheses, those theories need to be tested in other regulatory, commercial, and cultural contexts.

G. Additional research on arbitration

On the one hand, one is loathe to suggest that the world needs another study of arbitration procedures, given the glut of such research in the past few years. On the other hand, however, much of the research has been focused in the United States, suggesting that there is significant space available for studies about arbitration procedures elsewhere, particularly in countries that have prohibited mandatory, pre-dispute arbitration clauses. In addition, as the arbitration debate becomes increasingly heated, it will be necessary for unbiased research to counteract the studies funded by either side of that debate that produce more heat than light. That debate would be well served by studies comparing the effectiveness of, and participant perceptions of satisfaction with, mandatory and voluntary arbitration. Another subject that merits further research is the impact, if any, of mandatory arbitration clauses (which typically contain prohibitions against filing class actions and other group-based lawsuits) on the number of class actions filed in the United States.

H. Research on developing countries

As noted earlier in this Chapter, most of the empirical research on consumer complaint mechanisms has focused on institutions and legal systems in the developed world. However, over the past decade or two, many developing countries have established new consumer protection agencies or reinvigorated older ones, often as part of the overall democratization process following many years of military dictatorship and/or repression of individual rights and liberties. This is a particularly important time for analyses of these agencies and the ways that they deal with consumer complaints, given that the economic growth flowing from globalization has increased both possibilities and challenges for consumers throughout the developing world. As expanded consumer demand has made available all manner of new goods and services, it has also increased the likelihood that those same consumers will be defrauded. Empirical studies of consumer dispute mechanisms would help us to know whether the agencies and institutions recently established and/or authorized to combat fraud and other sharp practices in developing countries are responding adequately to consumer demands for justice. Such studies could also include comparisons between dispute resolution models in the developed and developing world, and whether one country (or set of countries) might learn from the experience of others.

I. Research on access to justice under new modes of consumer protection

Many of the suggestions for further research outlined above fall under the general rubric of the need to measure the degree of consumer access to justice under the new models of consumer protection that have emerged around the world in recent years (see Rickett and Telfer, 2003). Privatization and globalization have ushered in a host of new possibilities—and perils—for consumers around the world. While some governments have adapted to these and other changes with innovative mechanisms to resolve consumer disputes (ombudsmen, government-sponsored mediation, etc.), much of this function has been taken over by individual corporations, most notably those that offer alternate dispute resolution services or provide online dispute procedures for their Internet-based transactions. As such, in order to obtain a complete picture of how well civil society is affording its consumers proper access to justice, it is no longer enough—as it might have been 30 years ago—to simply measure the effectiveness of complaint-handling procedures set up by a particular governmental entity. Consumer protection, for better or worse, has become a matter of both public and private power. Penetrating the often obscure world of private dispute resolution systems to obtain the information necessary for solid empirical work is challenging. But it is the wave of the future in this area of scholarship.

REFERENCES

Albertini, A., Lichtenberg, E., Mancini, D., and Galinato, G. (2008). " 'Was It Something I Ate?' Implementation of the FDA Seafood HACCP Program," *American Journal of Agricultural Economics* 90: 28–41.

Andreasen, A.R. (1988). "Consumer Complaints and Redress: What We Know and What We Don't Know," in E.S. Maynes and ACCI Research Committee (eds.), *The Frontier of Research in the Consumer Interest*, Columbia, MO: American Council on Consumer Interests.

Best, A. and Andreasen, A.R. (1977). "Consumer Response to Unsatisfactory Purchases: A Survey of Perceiving Defects, Voicing Complaints, and Obtaining Redress," *Law & Society Review* 11: 701–42.

Blodgett, J.G. and. Granbois, D.H. (1992). "Toward an Integrated Conceptual Model of Consumer Complaining Behaviour," *Journal of Consumer Satisfaction, Dissatisfaction and Complaining Behaviour* 5: 93–103.

Boote, J. (1998). "Towards a Comprehensive Taxonomy and Model of Consumer Complaining Behaviour," *Journal of Consumer Satisfaction, Dissatisfaction and Complaining Behaviour* 11: 141–51.

Demaine, L.J. and Hensler, D.R. (2004). " 'Volunteering' To Arbitrate Through Predispute Arbitration Clauses: The Average Consumer's Experience," *Law and Contemporary Problems* 67: 55–74.

Dunbar, A.P. (1984). "Consumer Protection: The Practical Effectiveness of State Deceptive Trade Practices Legislation," *Tulane Law Review* 59: 427–71.

Ebers, M., Janssen, A., and Meyer, O. (2009). *European Perspectives on Producers' Liability*, Munich: Sellier.

Edwards, L. and Wilson, C. (2007). "Redress and Alternative Dispute Resolution in EU Cross-Border E-Commerce Transactions," *International Review of Law, Computers & Technology* 21: 315–33.

Ervine, C. (1993). Settling Consumer Disputes: A Review of Alternative Dispute Resolution: A Report, London: National Consumer Council.

Estelami, H. (2003). "Sources, Characteristics, and Dynamics of Postpurchase Price Complaints," *Journal of Business Research* 56: 411–19.

European Commission (1999). "The Integration of Directive 93/13 Into the National Legal Systems," presented at conference: 'The Directive on Unfair Terms, Five Years Later—Evaluation and Future Perspectives,' sponsored by the European Commission, available at <http://ec.europa.eu/consumers/cons_int/safe_shop/unf_cont_terms/event29_01.pdf>.

Gronhaug, K. and Arndt, J. (1980). "Consumer Dissatisfaction and Complaint Behavior as Feedback: A Comparative Analysis of Public and Private Delivery Systems," in J. Olsen (ed.), *Advances in Consumer Research*, Vol. VII, Urbana, IL: Association for Consumer Research.

Gross, J. and Black, B. (2008). "Perceptions of Fairness of Securities Arbitration: An Empirical Study," *University of Cincinnati Public Law Research Paper* No. 08–01, available at <http://papers.ssrn.com/sol3/papers.cfm?abstract_id=1090969>.

Gudde, T. (2004). "Onderzoek naar afhandeling van individuele consumentenklachten," quoted in Ministry of Economic Affairs, *Strategic Action Programme: Policy paper on consumer protection* (June 2004).

Hammond, A.G. (2003). "How Do You Write 'Yes'?: A Study on the Effectiveness of Online Dispute Resolution," *Conflict Resolution Quarterly* 20: 261–86.

Hensler, D., Hodges, C., and Tulibacka, M., (eds.) (2009). "The Globalization of Class Actions," *The Annals of the American Academy of Political and Social Science* 622: 7–349.

Hodges, C. and Tulibacka, M. (2009). "Civil Justice in England and Wales—Beyond the Courts," unpublished manuscript, European Civil Justice Systems Research Programme, Centre for Socio-Legal Studies, Oxford: University of Oxford.

Hollander-Blumoff, R. and Tyler, T. (2008). "Procedural Justice in Negotiation: Procedural Fairness, Outcome Acceptance, and Integrative Potential," *Law and Social Inquiry* 33: 473–500.

James, R. and Seneviratne, M. (1996). Offering Views in Both Directions: A Survey of Member Agencies and Complainants on Their Views of the Ombudsman for Corporate Estate Agents Schemes, Sheffield: Sheffield Hallam University.

Kellner, H. (1972). "Einordnung der gerichtlichen Tätigkeit in die Leitung und Gestaltung der Versorgungsverhältnisse," *Neue Justiz* 21: 61–3.

King, D.W. and McEvoy, K.A. (1976). A National Survey of the Complaint-Handling Procedures Used by Consumers, Rockville, MD: King Research.

Kolodinsky, J. (1995). "Usefulness of Economics in Explaining Consumer Complaints," *Journal of Consumer Affairs* 29: 29–54.

Kritzer, H.M., Vidmar, N., Bogart, W.A., and Zahorik, K. (1991). "Legal Mobilization in Canada and the United States: Consumer Problems in North America," paper presented at meetings of the Midwest Political Science Association, Chicago, April 18–20, 1991.

Law, M.T. (2006). "How Do Regulators Regulate? Enforcement of the Pure Food and Drugs Act, 1907–38," *Journal of Law, Economics, and Organization* 22: 459–89.

Mason, J.B. and Himes, S.H., Jr. (1973). "An Exploratory Behavior and Socio-Economic Profile of Consumer Action About Dissatisfaction With Selected Household Appliances," *Journal of Consumer Affairs* 7: 121–7.

McGonagle, J.J., Jr. (1972). "Arbitration of Consumer Disputes," *Arbitration Journal* 27: 65–84.

Meili, S. (2006). "Consumer Cause Lawyers in the United States: Lawyers for the Movement or a Movement unto Themselves?," in A. Sarat and S. Scheingold, (eds.), *Cause Lawyers and Social Movements*, Stanford: Stanford University Press.

Migliore, G. (2006). "Warranty Gripes Fall," *Automotive News* 80: 16–16 (reporting on a longer study by the Better Business Bureau. The study is reported by the BBB at <http://www.bbb.org/Alerts/article.asp?ID=671>, with 2005 data available at: <http://www.bbb.org/Alerts/2005data.pdf >).

Nordic Council of Ministers (2002). A study on Alternative Dispute Resolution and Cross-Border Complaints in Europe.

Oliveira, G. and Goldbaum, S. (2001–2002). "Relations Between Regulation, Competition Policy And Consumer Protection In Telecommunications, Electricity And Water Supply," *Brookings Journal of International Law* 27: 65–102.

Palfrey, T. and Romer, T. (1983). "Warranties, Performance, and the Resolution of Buyer-Seller Disputes," *Bell Journal of Economics* 14: 97–117.

Parker, C. (2006). "The 'Compliance' Trap: The Moral Message In Responsive Regulatory Enforcement," *Law and Society Review* 40: 591–622.

Perkins, J. et al. (1996). *Making the Consumers' Voice Heard in Medicaid Managed Care: Increasing Participation, Protection, and Satisfaction*, Chapel Hill, NC: National Health Law Program.

Provost, C. (2006). "The Politics of Consumer Protection: Explaining State Attorney General Participation in Multi-State Lawsuits," *Political Research Quarterly* 59: 609–18.

Ramsay, I. (2003). "Consumer Redress and Access to Justice," in C. Rickett and T. Telfer (eds.), *International Perspectives on Consumers' Access to Justice*, Cambridge: Cambridge University Press.

Rhode, D.L. (1981). "Policing the Professional Monopoly: A Constitutional and Empirical Analysis of Unauthorized Practice Prohibitions," *Stanford Law Review* 34: 1–112.

Rickett, C. and Telfer, T. (eds.) (2003), *International Perspectives on Consumers' Access to Justice*, Cambridge: Cambridge University Press.

Saks, M.J. (1986). "If There Be A Crisis, How Shall We Know It?," *Maryland Law Review* 46: 63–77.

Schwarcz, D. (2009). "Redesigning Consumer Dispute Resolution: A Case Study of the British and American Approaches to Insurance Claims Conflict," *Tulane Law Review* 83: 735–812.

Shestowsky, D. (2008). "Disputants' Preferences for Court-Connected Dispute Resolution Procedures: Why We Should Care and Why We Know So Little," *Ohio State Journal on Dispute Resolution* 23: 549–625.

Singh, J. and Widing, R.E. (1991). "What Occurs Once Consumers Complain: A Theoretical Model for Understanding Satisfaction/Dissatisfaction Outcomes of Complaint Responses," *European Journal of Marketing* 25: 30–46.

Sourdin, T. (2007). *Dispute Resolution Processes for Credit Consumers*, Melbourne: La Trobe University.

Stuyck, J. (2007). "An Analysis and Evaluation of Alternative Means of Consumer Redress other than Redress through Ordinary Judicial Proceedings," The Study Centre for Consumer Law– Centre for European Economic Law, Katholieke Universiteit Leuven, Belgium, available at <http://ec.europa.eu/consumers/redress/reports_studies/comparative_report_en.pdf>.

Thibaut, J. and Walker, L. (1975). *Procedural Justice*, Hillsdale, NJ: Erlbaum.

Thibault, J., Walker, L., LaTour, S., and Houlden, P. (1974). "Procedural Justice as Fairness," *Stanford Law Review* 26: 1271–89.

United States Federal Trade Commission (1986). "Empirical Approaches to Consumer Protection Economics: Proceedings of a Conference Sponsored by the Bureau of Economics, Federal Trade Commission, April 26–27, 1984," P.M. Ippolito and D.T. Scheffman (eds.), Washington, DC: U.S. Federal Trade Commission.

Viitanen, K. (2000). "The Baltic Model for the Settlement of Individual Consumer Disputes," *Journal of Consumer Policy* 23: 315–39.

Volkov, M. (2003). "Consumer Complaint Actions: A Conceptual Model Based on Complainants about Advertising in Australia," *Journal of New Business Ideas and Trends* 50: 50–60.

Volkov, M., Summers, J., and Morgan, M.J. (2005). "Consumer Complaint Behaviour in Sport Consumption: A Theoretical Model," Paper presented at the Australia and New Zealand Marketing Academy 2005 Sports Conference, Dunedin, New Zealand.

World Bank (2002). Report No. 22635-ME, "The *Juicio Ejecutivo Mercantil* in the Federal District Courts of Mexico: A Study of the Uses and Users of Justice and Their Implications for Judicial Reform."

8

BANKRUPTCY
AND INSOLVENCY

ROBERT M. LAWLESS AND
ELIZABETH WARREN

I. INTRODUCTION

IN a volume assessing the state of empirical legal research and chronicling the field's history, bankruptcy is appropriately the subject of its own Chapter. Bankruptcy law has a long history of empirical work, dating back to the 1930s and the studies of then-Yale law professor and later U.S. Supreme Court Justice William O. Douglas. Indeed, it may even be appropriate to claim bankruptcy law as one of the founts from which empirical legal studies grew, although as specialists in the field we will confess to possible bias on the topic.

Traditionally, the abundance of empirical legal research in bankruptcy has been primarily a U.S. phenomenon. Especially in the area of bankruptcies of individuals (that is, in bankruptcy parlance, the filings of live human beings rather than corporate entities), studies outside the U.S. have come principally from government agencies or, in fewer cases, from academics outside the legal discipline. One reason might be that bankruptcy filing rates historically were higher in the United States than elsewhere around the globe, and hence bankruptcy more readily suggested itself to legal scholars as a fertile field for empirical study. Indeed, many countries did not have a bankruptcy system for consumers until the global explosion of consumer credit made such a system necessary (Mann, 2009). As bankruptcy systems have been created and are beginning to mature around the world, empirical legal research in the area is not only spreading within different countries but also spreading across borders as international collaboration begins to occur (Niemi et al., 2009).

Because of bankruptcy's special relationship to empirical legal research, this Chapter seeks to accomplish three things. First, this introduction continues with a discussion of what might have attracted bankruptcy scholars to mine an empirical vein in their scholarly work. Second is a short chronicle of the development of empirical bankruptcy scholarship from Justice Douglas to the current generation. Because of the relative paucity of such scholarship outside the U.S., this chronicle inevitably focuses on that country. Also, it is divided into separate discussions of individual and corporate bankruptcy. Third, and perhaps most importantly, this Chapter will conclude with some thoughts regarding empirical questions on which bankruptcy scholars might profitably focus future attention.

Before turning to the historical narrative of how empirical bankruptcy scholarship has developed, it is important to reflect on why bankruptcy scholars have so long and so often used an empirical voice. First, the availability of bankruptcy data has had powerful effects. For more than 80 years, legal empiricists have exploited bankruptcy cases for the many quantifiable measures they produce. In a typical individual or business case in most any jurisdiction, the debtor must file detailed statements of assets and liabilities, listings of all creditors and amounts owed, and statements of income and expenses. The reorganization of a business might produce even further detail such as monthly operating statements and pre- and post-bankruptcy disclosures required under applicable securities laws. Moreover, in countries such as the United States, where a bankruptcy case is a judicial proceeding, these documents may be part of the public record, which allows scholars to easily turn bankruptcy case files into fairly detailed financial profiles of the individuals or businesses under consideration.

The financial data from bankruptcy case files come with a special bonus. Although the data are self-reported, the responses have indicia of reliability that a researcher can rarely claim for other types of personal financial information. A debtor's filings constitute part of the evidentiary record of the bankruptcy proceeding, and as such, any misreporting of data can subject the debtor to adverse outcomes, sanctions in the bankruptcy case, or even possible criminal prosecution for perjury or similar offenses for making false statements in a bankruptcy case. Thus, a debtor's statement of income is typically quite solid; in the United States it is accompanied by pay slips if the debtor is employed. Of course, financial data in a bankruptcy file contain a lot of estimates, but any individual-level financial data will involve estimates. In almost every country, the bankruptcy estimates, however, have been reviewed by professionals, such as accountants or lawyers, giving them an extra layer of reliability over survey-based estimates about an individual's financial status. This extra dose of reliability is especially important for the study of individual financial well-being, where self-reported data can be particularly susceptible to misreporting.

Bankruptcy systems are also prodigious producers of data because of the need to monitor actors in the bankruptcy system. The debtor's disclosures are the principal means by which creditors and the legal administrator can come to understand the debtor's financial state. The debtor's incentives, however, are rarely aligned with the creditors' interests, and the direction of the error will not always be self-evident, making it more difficult to detect possible cheating by the debtor. For example, in many cases, lower asset values can mean the debtor keeps property that otherwise might have to be distributed to creditors, but in other cases (and especially under U.S. law), a higher asset value might be more beneficial to the debtor to show that a creditor's position in collateral is secure and that the creditor should not be permitted to repossess the property. In some cases, declaring a lower income might result in lower payments to creditors, but in other cases, a debtor might want to project higher future incomes to demonstrate that a proposed repayment plan is realistic. Across jurisdictions, one nearly universal response to this misalignment of incentives is to require debtors to disclose reams of information about their financial status and to sanction misrepresentations.

Debtors are not the only players in the system who require some monitoring. The details differ from country to country, but many bankruptcy systems contemplate centralized collection of debtor payments by a bankruptcy trustee or administrator who then distributes payments to creditors. To guard against both malfeasance and mistake, any rational bankruptcy system will require the trustee to verify the claims against the estate and to keep records of the trustee's collections and payments. Scholars may have difficulties accessing detailed trustee reports, but where trustee data are available, they constitute an important—and largely untapped—resource. For example, the Australian Insolvency and Trustee Service makes available on the Internet its annual reports with aggregated data about the characteristics of bankruptcy filers (see Ramsay and Sim, 2009). Until 1957, the United States government compiled individualized trustee reports in voluminous government documents that were issued first by the attorney general and later by the court system (Attorney General of the United States, 1913–1942; Administrative Office of U.S. Courts, 1942–1957). For each U.S. federal judicial district, these reports detail the size of cases in terms of assets and liabilities, distributions to creditors, fees and expenses, property exempted, no-asset cases, and the number of cases in which the court waived the debtor's filing fees because of an inability to pay. Opportunities abound for scholars to explore these sorts of reports for projects ranging from social history to economic studies to descriptive work about the development of the bankruptcy system.

In addition to the availability of data, the nature of the disagreement among bankruptcy scholars also has led empiricism to play a pivotal role in bankruptcy scholarship. Although scholars vigorously contest the proper role for a bankruptcy system, the positions of the opposing schools of thought lead to readily testable empirical hypotheses. One school of thought sees the proper role of a bankruptcy system as limited primarily to ensuring that creditors do not destroy the value of the debtor's assets by acting precipitously in an uncoordinated, piecemeal fashion (often called the "common pool problem") (Baird, 1998; Jackson, 1986). The other school of thought sees other roles for bankruptcy such as debtor rehabilitation and the creation of a social safety net (Warren, 1987). Of course, the dichotomous presentation of these two ideas vastly oversimplifies the nuances of the competing positions and glosses over middle positions between the two extremes. Nonetheless, for purposes of this Chapter, these characterizations capture how the opposing schools of thought rest on unspoken factual premises that are subject to testing.

To be sure, the bankruptcy field—like virtually every other field of academic pursuit—is filled with legal scholars who prefer the clean world of abstract theoretical exploration to the unglamorous work of data-gathering. Nonetheless, the ability of theoreticians to ignore hard data that undermine their lovely paradigms has diminished. There is nothing quite like a well-placed fact or two to upset even the most carefully constructed hypothetical universe.

The questions suggested by the data are everywhere in the system. If a bankruptcy system's primary goal is creditor recovery, how much do creditors recover in bankruptcy cases? How much do bankruptcy cases cost to gain these recoveries? Debtor rehabilitation, in turn, suggests that debtors arrive in bankruptcy court in need of rehabilitation. Why do debtors—corporate or individual—find themselves in financial distress? Do debtors exit the bankruptcy system in better shape than they entered? The list could expand far beyond the pages allotted here, but these examples illustrate the point. None of this is to suggest that bankruptcy scholars more easily resolve debates than scholars in other fields of law. Rather, in explaining the substantial amount of empirical scholarship in bankruptcy as compared with other fields, the grounds on which academic debates play out offer significant explanatory factors.

II. Eighty Years of Empirical Bankruptcy Scholarship

With the rich history of empirical work in bankruptcy, any narrative must inevitably skip from highlight to highlight or be several book volumes in length. Necessarily, this section omits mention of many worthwhile works. Instead of focusing on the best and biggest studies, the following discussion is framed around works that particularly changed the then-current debates, whether for good or ill. Also, although scholars in fields such as sociology, economics, and finance have made important empirical contributions to our understanding of the bankruptcy system (e.g., Bhandari and Weiss, 1996; Carruthers and Halliday, 1998), this section focuses on studies that primarily had a legal focus and hence could be described as falling within the field of empirical legal research.

The two parts of this section recognize a dichotomy between individual and corporate bankruptcy, a dichotomy that exists both in the legal and academic world. Most countries have different legal regimes for corporate or individual bankruptcies. The U.S. bankruptcy system is a rare exception, but even there, some sections of its bankruptcy law, such as Chapter 13, are unavailable to corporations. To begin the review of empirical bankruptcy work, it is necessary to turn the clock back at least 80 years.

A. Individual bankruptcy

Eventually, William O. Douglas would become one of the first commissioners of the U.S. Securities and Exchange Commission and then serve a record 36 years as a pathbreaking justice of the U.S. Supreme Court. In 1929, however, he was a young professor at Yale Law School trying to figure out how to make the U.S. bankruptcy system work better for the debtors who needed to use it. The approach Douglas would adopt differed radically from that of many of his contemporaries who scoured dusty tomes to discern new legal principles:

That hundreds of businesses from corner cigar stores to large factories fail each year is common knowledge. That competition, fraud, the general state of business conditions, lack of business ability, low intelligence and sheer misfortune play significant parts is generally admitted. Most are content to leave the problem there. But those who are interested in social reform and those who are interested in problems of social causation want to go further. Here are current economic and social phenomena that have never been studied scientifically by analysing the factors involved, by tracing the social, economic and legal antecedents, and by estimating the causal processes. Yet such an analysis would lead to results of tremendous practical and scientific significance (Clark et al., 1930: 1013).

In voicing these thoughts, Douglas and his co-authors reflected the legal realist perspective of his time that was very skeptical that traditional doctrinal approaches to legal scholarship provided much guidance as to what actually drove legal decision-makers. If social or political concerns were actually what controlled legal outcomes, then empirical examination of the world held the key to productive legal change. All modern bankruptcy empiricists owe their intellectual origins to Douglas, and the methods he employed would be very familiar even today.

In 1929–1930, Douglas and sociologist Dorothy Thomas teamed up long before the term "interdisciplinary" had come into vogue. They gained the cooperation of a New Jersey judge who ordered all bankruptcy filers in his court to submit to a "clinic," which was essentially a face-to-face interview with the debtor lasting an hour or more (Clark et al., 1930: 1015–16). Later, the study was expanded to allow debtors to submit written answers to a survey asking the same questions through the mail and then expanded again geographically to include filers in Massachusetts (Douglas and Thomas, 1931; Douglas, 1932). Douglas and his colleagues would collect information on 1,500 debtors, capturing a wide array of data about the debtors themselves such as occupations, educational attainment, and financial record-keeping, as well as data about the bankruptcy proceeding itself such as its duration and the distributions to creditors.

Douglas's findings are scattered throughout several articles, but these findings clearly had an effect on later developments in U.S. bankruptcy law. For example, he found that fewer than one in four of the business owners in his study kept adequate records, a discovery that led to Douglas's recommendations that bankruptcy filings include a verified statement of assets and liabilities and for compulsory examination for every debtor (Douglas and Marshall, 1932: 59). Douglas also found a "large number and variety" of tort claims against the debtors in his study (Douglas, 1932: 337–40), a problem that has now largely been eliminated by the more widespread availability of insurance. Looking at the causes of individual bankruptcies, Douglas's findings fit consistently with the findings of later generations of empirical researchers:

Looking back on some bankruptcies it would be difficult to determine if at the time most of the claims were incurred the debtor was extravagant or without reasonable grounds of expectation of being able to pay. A subsequent event—illness, medical cost, a divorce, partial unemployment, reduction in salary, increase in cost of living, etc.—frequently occurs and changes and distorts the whole picture (Douglas, 1932: 348).

Although Douglas sought out business owners for his studies, he ended up with conclusions about why persons filed bankruptcy that went far beyond the stereotypes of why small business owners fail. The financial lives of both the person and the business were interdependent. When one failed, the other often failed as well. For business owners, this blurring of the line between their consumer and commercial lives continues today and challenges the usual divide of the world into consumer and business failures (Lawless and Warren, 2005).

Douglas's finding that exogenous shocks drove most individual bankruptcies has been continually reinforced in every generation of empirical bankruptcy scholarship. In his autobiography, Douglas discussed his bankruptcy studies in the same passage in which he mentioned his dissent in *United States v. Kras*, 409 U.S. 434 (1973), a case where the majority held the U.S. Constitution did not protect an indigent debtor who could not pay the court filing fee. Lessons he learned four decades previously as a bankruptcy scholar caused Douglas to use his autobiography as an occasion to repeat the dissent's lament: "Some of the poor are too poor even to go bankrupt" (Douglas, 1974: 175). He had not earlier persuaded his colleagues on the Court, but he fired the first shot in a debate that, in its latest incarnation, resulted in a 2005 amendment to the U.S. bankruptcy law to permit *in forma pauperis* petitions for those who could not pay the filing fee.

For the next several decades, empirical bankruptcy scholarship focused on discrete topics. Empirically driven, inductive reasoning would play a role in the 1938 revisions to the U.S. bankruptcy law, with congressional witnesses citing data regarding debtor characteristics and case outcomes as reasons to push the law in one direction or another. In the United States today, Chapter 13 of the bankruptcy law governs individual debt repayment plans, but the predecessor law, Chapter XIII, was especially influenced by data collected in one judicial district's pilot effort to find an alternative to straight liquidation bankruptcy. In the 1950s and 1960s, research papers or monographs appeared exploring some particular aspect of bankruptcy practice or delving into practices at a particular locale (e.g., Jacob, 1969). These studies supported a general feeling that the U.S. bankruptcy law, enacted in 1898, was outdated and especially that it failed to respond to the needs of individual debtors who found themselves overburdened from the debts of daily living expenses.

At the request of the judiciary, the Brookings Institution undertook a major empirical study of the condition of the U.S. bankruptcy system beginning in 1965. Published in 1971 and more commonly known to bankruptcy academics as "Stanley and Girth" in deference to its authors (public administration expert David T. Stanley and lawyer Marjorie Girth), the Brookings Report analyzed case files from eight judicial districts and interviewed 400 individual debtors from seven of those districts (Stanley and Girth, 1971). The Brookings Report found an inefficient and costly bankruptcy system, ill-suited to serve the needs of most business or individual debtors who found themselves in bankruptcy—usually due to circumstances beyond their control. In place of a court system, the report suggested an administrative agency as the best method to handle the many routine cases typical of a bankruptcy court docket. Only large corporations would continue to use the courts for their reorganizations. Although U.S. lawmakers heeded few of the Brookings Report's specific recommendations, the report nonetheless provided an empirically based narrative of a legal system sorely in need of change and defined the grounds for a seven-year debate that culminated in the 1978 overhaul of the U.S. bankruptcy laws. The Brookings Report remains an influential statistical portrait of the bankruptcy debtors it studied, and scholars continue to refer to its findings almost 40 years later.

The passage of the 1978 U.S. Bankruptcy Code opened a new era in empirical studies about individual debtors. At the time of Stanley and Girth, about one of every 1,000 U.S. adults filed bankruptcy each year. Within 15 years, that figure had more than doubled, and within 30 years, seven out of every 1,000 U.S. adults would file bankruptcy each year. More U.S. adults would file bankruptcy in a year than would graduate from college or be diagnosed with cancer (Warren, 2004a: 27–8). At the same time, personal debt also exploded due to coincidental regulatory developments. By 2004, U.S. households as an aggregate owed more than the total annual national personal income. Consumer debt became big business and a major part of the U.S. economy. Empirical bankruptcy scholarship became just as likely to find itself in the news as it was to lie unnoticed on the dusty shelves of a university library. As one of us observed about the 25 years after the passage of the Code:

Now bankruptcy is much more the province of interest groups that have spent millions to hire lobbyists, to launch a public relations campaign, and to make strategic campaign contributions. Why? Because legislation affects their profits. Change a few words in 11 U.S.C. § 524, for example, and the $140 million that retailer Sears was required to refund following a federal indictment for deliberate violation of the bankruptcy laws in trying to collect debts from its customers that were discharged is Sears's to keep—and to continue to collect on into the future.

The debates over policy have spilled into the public arena. No longer is bankruptcy a subject of interest to only a handful of people who have an intimate understanding of the structure of the system.... The public nature of the discussion has wrought another change: Empirical data have played a surprisingly important role in the ongoing effort to rewrite American bankruptcy laws (Warren, 2002: 5).

In fact, empirical work became so important to bankruptcy debates that academics were no longer the only ones providing the data.

In 1982, a group known as the Credit Research Center (CRC), funded by the credit industry and associated with Purdue University, self-published a two-volume study based on field interviews with consumer debtors (Credit Research Center, 1982). The study was never made available as a book or scholarly article. It was, however, distributed to members of Congress by a public relations agency (Sullivan et al., 1983: 1093). The CRC's study claimed to find evidence of significant abuse in the bankruptcy system, claiming over $1 billion in debt was discharged annually by individuals who could afford to repay. Despite concerns over the study's industry sponsorship and methods, it helped contribute to a significant shift in the political atmosphere centered on the notion that the 1978 changes had gone too far. In 1984, Congress passed the first in a string of measures that were progressively more restrictive on U.S. consumers.

The CRC study would find a new, albeit anonymous, life in 1998 with a major legislative push by the credit industry. Sixteen years after it had first appeared, the CRC study thus would play another role in legislative debates but this time as a mutated new narrative about the supposed burdens of bankruptcy on society at large. The congressman who introduced the new legislation proclaimed that the U.S. bankruptcy system was imposing a $400 "tax" on every citizen in the form of increased prices for goods and services. The apparent source for this statement was the CRC study, although the report had not made any statement that even approximated such an estimate (Warren, 2004b). The proposed legislation would be debated for seven years, with supporters of the legislation citing the $400 "bankruptcy tax" throughout.

The longest running and perhaps most well-known U.S. studies of individual bankruptcies began in 1981 when sociologist Teresa Sullivan teamed with law professors Jay Westbrook and Elizabeth Warren (one of this Chapter's authors) to start the Consumer Bankruptcy Project (CBP). To date, the CBP has had three more waves—in 1991, 2001, and 2007—making it the only repeating study of U.S. consumer bankruptcy filers.[1] Since 2001, the CBP team has expanded and now includes ten scholars at seven different major research universities. The CBP examines court records, collects responses to written surveys, and conducts extensive telephone interviews with consumer bankruptcy filers, and is itself a microcosm of changes in social science research. Because of fiscal and physical constraints, such as the transportation of photocopying machines to bankruptcy courthouses, the earliest waves were limited to five representative judicial districts. Technological advances permitted the most recent CBP wave to be a national random sample of more than 2,500 consumer bankruptcy filers with electronic download and storage of court records.

Scholars associated with the CBP have produced several books and numerous scholarly articles. The seminal work, *As We Forgive Our Debtors* (Sullivan et al., 1989), established some of the most important general themes that have emerged from the CBP's data. The authors found that bankruptcy was a phenomenon of the middle class, not the poor. The middle class file bankruptcy to protect income and assets that the poor lack. Moreover, bankruptcy filers are a cross-section of Middle America who find themselves in bankruptcy principally because of exogenous shocks—job loss, health problems, and divorce. The data belied the popular conception of bankruptcy filers as predominantly persons without resources who had simply lived beyond their means. Later works would confirm these findings from the 1991 and 2001 waves of filers (Sullivan et al., 2000; Warren and Tyagi, 2003).

During the policy debates that led up to the 2005 changes in U.S. bankruptcy law, researchers associated with the CBP published data showing a close connection between medical problems and bankruptcy. Almost half of all U.S. bankruptcy filers reported as a specific reason for filing bankruptcy an illness or injury, uncovered medical bills of at least $1,000, at least two weeks of work-related income loss because of illness or injury, or mortgaging their home to pay medical bills (Himmelstein et al., 2005). The research was criticized, especially by some in the health-care industry, for overstating the number of medical bankruptcies. Most notably, a study funded by health insurance companies was harshly critical; but applying even very conservative assumptions to

---

[1] As noted in the text, one of this Chapter's authors, Elizabeth Warren, founded the CBP and remains a principal investigator. The other Chapter author, Robert Lawless, has been a principal investigator on the 2001 and 2007 waves.

the same data, this industry-sponsored study still conceded that medical bills were a contributing factor in at least one in six bankruptcy filings. The CBP study permanently changed the policy debates about consumer financial distress, causing U.S. legislators, the president of the United States, and other government officials routinely to cite the high incidence of medical debt among bankruptcy filers as supporting initiatives in both health-care finance and changes to bankruptcy law.

In 2005, the United States enacted the most sweeping changes to the bankruptcy laws in almost 30 years. Despite a dearth of evidence suggesting widespread abuse of the U.S. bankruptcy system, the dominant narrative advanced by the credit industry was based on claims that debtors were abusing the system. The changes attempt to force debtors pay more to their creditors. After these changes, the CBP researchers found that debtors were postponing their decision to file bankruptcy and arriving at the courthouse in worse shape than previously (Lawless et al., 2009). The CBP is now moving toward web-based access to its previous data. The Bankruptcy Data Project at Harvard not only makes available bankruptcy filing statistics for all U.S. federal judicial districts but is also developing the site to allow qualified researchers access to scholarly bankruptcy databases such as those assembled by the CBP and others used in scholarly publications.

B. Corporate bankruptcy

Bankruptcy filings by individuals have not been the exclusive focus of U.S. academics. Beginning in the 1980s, corporate bankruptcy enjoyed a resurgence of attention in the business schools with a concomitant surge of empirical studies looking at corporate reorganization (e.g., Weiss, 1990; Franks and Torous, 1989). In the law schools, the pathbreaking set of papers that would establish a new standard for empirical study of corporate bankruptcy was published by Lynn LoPucki and William Whitford (1990, 1991, 1993a, 1993b). Examining all cases filed under the U.S. bankruptcy law that involved a corporation with more than $100 million of assets at filing, LoPucki and Whitford found that corporate shareholders had substantial bargaining power despite distribution rules that should have left them with little leverage. They also exposed stories of dominant control by creditors as overly simplistic. In some cases, creditors had control, but in others, shareholders or managers dominated. The negotiation dynamics were "complex" but often left companies unable to maximize value and returns to creditors. These studies also challenged the concept of corporate reorganization "success" and showed that corporate reorganizations often resulted in survival of valuable business assets regardless of the legal outcomes under the technicalities of the bankruptcy law.

The LoPucki and Whitford studies were influential, and their success would legitimate empirical studies of corporate bankruptcy as an area of scholarly inquiry in the legal academy. Later scholars (e.g., Lubben, 2008; Baird and Morrison, 2005; Ferris and Lawless, 2000; Ferris and Lawless, 1997) would expand LoPucki and Whitford's research questions to smaller businesses and bore into specific topics such as bankruptcy costs or the length of time in reorganization. Today LoPucki maintains a website with the data from his studies as well as from more recent corporate bankruptcies meeting the same size criteria of $100 million in assets as measured in 1980 dollars. Visitors to LoPucki's Bankruptcy Research Database (WebBRD) can compile their own, quick empirical studies of large corporate bankruptcies or, for certain purposes, make a request for the complete underlying database.

LoPucki and Whitford's most enduring finding was significant forum shopping by U.S. corporations in choosing where to file bankruptcy (LoPucki and Whitford, 1991). Because of lax venue rules, large U.S. corporations could pick almost any judicial district in which to file. LoPucki and Whitford found numerous large corporations that chose to file bankruptcy in New York City despite the absence of any substantial connection to the city. Over a decade later, LoPucki would follow up this study with more data and report that courts around the country were competing to attract corporate reorganization filings to their districts (LoPucki, 2005). LoPucki attributed the competition to judges who were attracted to the prestige such cases bring to the local courts where a large corporate bankruptcy is filed and to their desire to enhance their popularity (and odds of reappointment) by producing high-paying work for the local bar. Manhattan and Wilmington, Delaware, were the big winners in this competition, but LoPucki found that companies filing in these two jurisdictions had to refile bankruptcy at a much higher rate than companies that filed in other jurisdictions. LoPucki would famously and controversially label this competition a "corruption" of the U.S. bankruptcy court system. Despite the consistent findings of venue abuse by large corporations, legislative attempts to change the corporate bankruptcy venue rules have consistently failed. Nonetheless, LoPucki's work has kept the bankruptcy venue issue at the forefront of policy debates. As each high-profile Chapter 11 debtor—such as Enron, Chrysler, and General Motors—files away from their home jurisdiction, they attract the ire of local legislators who want the bankruptcy resolved on their "home field." LoPucki's research frames an issue in a way that may yet prompt a future Congress to change the law.

III. Looking to the Future

Bankruptcy empirical work has been notable for its successes. In a few cases, one can trace changes in statutory law directly to empirical work. More often, bankruptcy empirical work has been successful in establishing the narrative that is told about bankruptcy filers. Where profligate spending was once thought to drive most bankruptcy filings, it is now understood that exogenous shocks such as job loss, health problems, and divorce create the conditions in which most bankruptcy filings occur. Where bankruptcy was once dismissed as the province of marginal workers who lived in chronic poverty, it is now closely observed as a sign of the changing economic security of the middle class.

Because of its long history, there are numerous pieces of bankruptcy empirical work, and a newcomer might surmise that all of the big questions have been asked and answered. To distinguish their work and make their own mark on the field, more recent scholars have turned to narrower questions. For example, what factors help to determine how a court might rule on an exemption claim or what role does priority tax debt play in the bankruptcies of entrepreneurs (Efrat, 2009; Trujillo, 2006)?

These narrower questions are important, and many scholars will help fill in a more complete understanding of the bankruptcy system. Even so, much work remains to be done to understand core questions about how consumers and businesses come to find themselves in financial distress and how the consumer credit system—of which the bankruptcy courts are only a part—affects those who interact with it. In addition to the studies on specific topics, empirically minded scholars can turn back to these big picture questions. As time passes, of course, the characteristics of bankruptcy filers can change, and it is crucial that empirical researchers periodically return to the example of Stanley and Girth or the CBP to conduct macro-studies of the bankruptcy system as a whole. It is not simply a matter of updating past findings. As empirical research on bankruptcy moves forward, it also should move outward.

The first move should be to consider bankruptcy as part of a larger system. Individuals and corporations come to the bankruptcy system to solve a very simple problem: they have incurred obligations that at one time seemed manageable but changed circumstances have rendered impossible to fulfill. Scholars can back away from the bankruptcy system to consider many broader questions, including why debtors come to incur crushing obligations, what changed to cause the obligations to become unrealistic, and what are the collateral effects of having crushing debt.

Empirical scholars have explored the first two questions more than the third. For individual debtors, the immediate mechanisms of financial distress are somewhat understood. Beginning with Douglas's studies in the 1930s, continuing through Stanley and Girth's Brookings Report and onto the many papers and books of the CBP, scholars have continually found that the exogenous shocks of job loss, health problems, and divorce explain most consumer bankruptcy filings. Corporate bankruptcies more often seem to have endogenous explanations, such as poor managerial decisions or outdated business models, although exogenous causes like downturns in the economic cycle also play a role.

The next generation of studies might move from more proximate causes to more remote causes for both consumer and corporate debtors. For example, much has been written about the exogenous shocks that lead to individual bankruptcies. However, are particular individuals more susceptible to financial problems after an exogenous shock, or are these shocks dispersed randomly throughout the population? Does education help to insulate consumers from exogenous shocks by building human capital, or do educational debts make a consumer more susceptible to the exogenous shocks when they occur? For corporations, endogenous causes may explain financial distress for many, but are there individual managerial characteristics or corporate governance structures that make corporations more susceptible to making the sorts of decisions that foster these endogenous causes? Although the financial crisis of 2008–2009 led to many bankruptcies, in no industry did all firms go bankrupt. Thus, even after controlling for industry, there is cross-sectional variation that clever empirical researchers might exploit to better understand the causes of corporate bankruptcy.

A second broad theme of issues to which empirically minded bankruptcy scholars could turn relates closely to the idea of moving toward more remote causes of bankruptcy. Anecdotally, the collateral consequences of financial distress are severe. For individuals, financial distress is emotionally stressful and thereby thought to contribute to health problems. Domestic violence occurs at a higher rate in households experiencing financial distress. Children may be at risk. Although some useful studies on these topics have appeared, more needs to be done both to document the collateral consequences of financial distress and to map the effects. Work also must be done to understand the underlying causal mechanisms. To what extent does crushing household debt lead to stress and emotional problems? Or, do stress and emotional problems lead to income instability and financial distress? As part of this research, scholars might explore whether interventions are successful. For example, one recent study asked a question of U.S. bankruptcy filers that had surprisingly not been asked previously: are you better off than you were before you filed bankruptcy? One in three filers answered that they were not, raising serious questions about the role bankruptcy plays in the economic and emotional rehabilitation of families (Porter and Thorne, 2006). Scholars might also focus on whether pre- or post-bankruptcy credit counseling or financial education has any measurable impact. Most every country with a consumer bankruptcy system has such a requirement. But the premise behind the legal requirement is one of faith, not fact. In a world where most consumer filers find themselves in bankruptcy because of an exogenous shock, the effectiveness of financial education is worth questioning.

For corporations, legal doctrines in many countries try to shift the benchmarks managers should use when making decisions at or near the point of financial distress. Usually, legal institutions direct managers to make shareholder interests paramount, but financial distress can create perverse incentives for shareholders. For example, a particularly risky decision may make sense from the perspective of shareholders who have nothing left to lose but squander assets that otherwise would be available to pay creditors. This problem is known as "overinvestment" because, when considering the risk to all constituencies of the enterprise, the decision can actually have a net negative present value. Many legal systems employ diverse doctrines, such as director liability for trading while insolvent, director bans after an insolvency filing, or a shift in fiduciary duties from shareholder to creditors, to prevent overinvestment. There is little empirical evidence to show that corporate managers actually behave in this manner during times of financial distress, and this is another lacuna that empirical work could fill.

In corporate bankruptcy, researchers have had some success creating controls for a set of financially distressed firms by using a matched sample on parameters such as size and income. The matched firms are then compared to the financially distressed firms to learn more about the causes and outcomes of financial distress. Of course, this approach works best for the study of large, publicly traded companies with a multitude of readily available information than it does for small mom-and-pop businesses for which comparative financial data are not available.

Empirical work on individual bankruptcy generally has lacked an experimental control, which is considered a hallmark of social science research. Researchers can identify bankruptcy filers from court records, but it is difficult to identify financially distressed persons who do not file bankruptcy. In countries where consumers must enter credit counseling or attempt partial debt repayment before filing bankruptcy, researchers can turn to the agencies that provide these services (if access is made available), but that only moves the problem back a step, still omitting persons who are financially distressed but who do not use these agencies. Research designs that seek out financially distressed but non-bankrupt individuals will go a long way toward answering questions of causality and measuring the collateral effects of financial distress, although selection biases will remain a challenge. Archival sources such as the U.S.-based Survey of Consumer Finance or Panel Survey of Income Dynamics can provide data resources that include non-bankrupt households, but researchers should be aware that stigma often causes consumers to under-report bankruptcy filings in these general purpose surveys, thus sharply undercutting their usefulness (Sullivan et al., 2006.)

Another technique that would help tease out difficult causality issues is for empirical bankruptcy scholars to turn to cross-border studies. Looking simultaneously at consumers from several countries may help isolate the extent to which cultural attitudes, country-specific financial and legal institutions, or universal human behavior contribute to consumer financial distress. Professor Ronald Mann's comparative work on credit cards and bankruptcy offers one example (Mann, 2006). Of course, empirical work across borders presents special challenges. At the most obvious level, unless scholars cooperate and harmonize survey instruments, any results will reflect only the fact that the surveys asked different questions and thus lack generalizability across borders.

Because scholars working away from their home countries often lack institutional and cultural detail about the system in which they find themselves, the most promising efforts may be those of international groups of researchers. Collaboration across borders will help to ensure that studies are sensitive to institutional and cultural differences. For example, a study about the role health-care costs play in individual bankruptcies will raise very different issues for the United States, which has a largely private health-care system, than it will in parts of the world with strong public health-care systems. International efforts are in their nascent stage, with discussions beginning to occur at international conferences. As promising as cross-border efforts are, they will not happen until scholars have multiple occasions to interact. Organizations interested in consumer financial distress should look for opportunities to facilitate international scholarly conversations.

As it does elsewhere, technology will drive the future of empirical bankruptcy scholarship. In the United States, bankruptcy court records are available electronically through the federal system known as Public Access to Court Electronic Records (PACER). This technology has already changed the face of empirical research. Sullivan, Warren, and Westbrook wrote about buying a plane ticket for the very expensive, very heavy, and very fragile portable photocopier that they hauled to courthouses around the country for their first empirical study (1989: 350). Changes in online access may improve even more. Currently, U.S. bankruptcy attorneys must file their clients' petitions and schedules electronically, but the data are not marked with electronic tags identifying each piece of information. Once filing shifts to data-enabled forms, a research question that would require hundreds of research hours instead could be completed with a data query in a few mouse clicks. Although technologically possible today, opposition from the federal judiciary has combined with legitimate privacy concerns to prevent establishment of a universal requirement that attorneys use data-enabled forms when filing electronically. Over the long run, it is probable that the struggle against data-enabled forms will suffer the same negative fate that every struggle against technological progress eventually suffers.

Electronic filing is far from universal. Scholars around the world must often do what prior generations of U.S. bankruptcy scholars did and arrange for physical copies of the underlying records. But even now, copying has become quicker and cheaper, and data storage can be managed on a laptop computer instead of boxes of papers. Technology is clearly on the side of the empiricist.

This Chapter has reviewed both the past and present of bankruptcy empirical work. The area naturally lends itself to empirical studies, giving it a long and storied history of pathbreaking scholarship. Empirically oriented scholarship has changed perceptions of who suffers from financial distress and influenced both the shape of public discourse and the details of specific bankruptcy laws.

Many interesting questions remain unanswered. Indeed, despite its long history, empirical scholarship in the bankruptcy field seems to be enjoying a period of rapid growth, with senior scholars picking up new tools and younger scholars entering the fray armed with more questions and newer research techniques. The financial crisis of 2008–2009 has intensified interest in the related subjects of debt and bankruptcy most everywhere in the world. Financial distress is front-page news, and policy-makers clamor for information to solve the current crisis and prevent a future one. It is an exciting time to work in the field.

References

Administrative Office of US Courts (1942–1957) (separate volumes). *Annual Report of the Director of the Administrative Office of the United States Courts*, Washington, DC: U.S. Government Printing Office.

Attorney General of the United States (1913–1942) (separate volumes). *Annual Report of the Attorney General of the United States*, Washington, DC: U.S. Government Printing Office.

Baird, D. (1998). "Bankruptcy Uncontested Axioms," *Yale Law Journal* 108: 573–99.

Baird, D. and Morrison, E. (2005). "Serial Entrepreneurs and Small Business Bankruptcies," *Columbia Law Review* 105: 2310–68.

Bhandari, J. and Weiss, L. (1996). *Corporate Bankruptcy: Economic and Legal Perspectives*, Cambridge: Cambridge University Press.

Carruthers, B. and Halliday, T. (1998). *Rescuing Business: The Making of Corporate Bankruptcy Law in England and the United States*, New York: Oxford University Press.

Clark, W., Douglas, W., and Thomas, D. (1930). "The Business Failures Project—A Problem in Methodology," *Yale Law Journal* 39: 1013–24.

Credit Research Center (1982). *Consumer Bankruptcy Study, Volumes I and II*, West Lafayette, IN: Purdue University, Krannert School of Management.

Douglas, W. (1932). "Some Functional Aspects of Bankruptcy," *Yale Law Journal* 41: 329–64.

Douglas, W. (1974). *Go East Young Man, The Early Years: The Autobiography of William O. Douglas*, New York: Random House.

Douglas, W. and Marshall, J.H. (1932). "A Factual Study of Bankruptcy Administration and Some Suggestions," *Columbia Law Review* 32: 25–59.

Douglas, W. and Thomas, D. (1931). "The Business Failures Project—II. An Analysis of Methods of Investigation," *Yale Law Journal* 40: 1034–54.

Efrat, R. (2009). "The Tax Debts of Small Business Owners in Bankruptcy," *Akron Tax Journal* 24: 175–205.

Ferris, S. and Lawless, R. (1997). "Professional Fees and Other Direct Costs in Chapter 7 Business Liquidations," *Washington University Law Quarterly* 75: 1207–36.

Ferris, S. and Lawless, R. (2000). "The Expenses of Financial Distress: The Direct Costs of Chapter 11," *University of Pittsburgh Law Review* 61: 629–69.

Franks, J. and Torous, W. (1989). "An Empirical Examination of U.S. Firms in Reorganization," *Journal of Finance* 44:747–69.

Himmelstein, D., Warren, E., Thorne, D., and S. Woolhandler, S. (2005). "Marketwatch: Illness and Injury as Contributors to Bankruptcy," *Health Affairs* 24: 63–73.

Jackson, T. (1986). *The Logic and Limits of Bankruptcy Law*, Cambridge, MA: Harvard University Press.

Lawless, R. and Warren, E. (2005). "The Myth of the Disappearing Business Bankruptcy," *California Law Review* 93: 743–95.

Lawless, R., Littwin, A., Porter, K., Pottow, J. Thorne, D., and Warren, E. (2009). "Did Bankruptcy Reform Fail? An Empirical Study of Consumer Debtors," *American Bankruptcy Law Journal* 82: 349–406.

LoPucki, L. (2005). *Courting Failure: How Competition for Big Cases Is Corrupting the Bankruptcy Courts*, Ann Arbor, MI: University of Michigan Press.

LoPucki, L. and Whitford, W. (1990). "Bargaining over Equity's Share in the Bankruptcy Reorganization of Large Publicly Held Companies," *University of Pennsylvania Law Review* 139: 125–96.

LoPucki, L. and Whitford, W. (1991). "Venue Choice and Forum Shopping in the Bankruptcy Reorganization of Large, Publicly Held Companies," *Wisconsin Law Review* 1991: 11–58.

LoPucki, L. and Whitford, W. (1993a). "Corporate Governance in the Bankruptcy Reorganization of Large, Publicly Held Companies," *University of Pennsylvania Law Review* 141: 669–800.

LoPucki, L. and Whitford, W. (1993b). "Patterns in the Bankruptcy of Large, Publicly Held Companies," *Cornell Law Review* 78: 597–613.

Lubben, S. (2008). "Corporate Reorganization and Professional Fees," *American Bankruptcy Law Journal* 82: 77–132.

Mann, R. (2006). *Charging Ahead: The Growth and Regulation of Payment Card Markets*, Cambridge: Cambridge University Press.

Mann, R. (2009). "Making Sense of Nation-Level Bankruptcy Filing Rates," in J. Niemi, I. Ramsay, and W. Whitford (eds.), *Consumer Debt, Credit, and Bankruptcy*, Portland, OR: Hart Publishing.

Niemi, J., Ramsay, I., and Whitford, W. (eds.) (2009). *Consumer Debt, Credit, and Bankruptcy*, Portland, OR: Hart Publishing.

Porter, K. and Thorne, D. (2006). "The Failure of Bankruptcy's Fresh Start," *Cornell Law Review* 92: 67–128.

Ramsay, I. and Sim, C. (2009). "Trends in Personal Insolvency in Australia," University of Melbourne Centre for Corporate Law and Securities Regulation Research Report.

Stanley, D. and Girth, M. (1971). *Bankruptcy: Problem, Process, and Reform*, Washington, DC: Brookings Institution.

Sullivan, T., Westbrook, J., and Warren, E. (1983). "Limiting Access to Bankruptcy Discharge: An Analysis of the Creditors' Data," *Wisconsin Law Review* (1983): 1091–1146.

Sullivan, T., Westbrook, J., and Warren, E. (1989). *As We Forgive Our Debtors*, New York: Oxford University Press.

Sullivan, T., Westbrook, J., and Warren, E. (2000). *The Fragile Middle Class: Americans in Debt*, New Haven, CT: Yale University Press.

Sullivan, T., Westbrook, J., and Warren, E. (2006). "Less Stigma or More Financial Distress: An Empirical Analysis of the Extraordinary Increase in Bankruptcy Filings," *Stanford Law Review* 59: 213–256.

Trujillo, B. (2006). "Regulating Bankruptcy Abuse: An Empirical Study of Consumer Exemptions Cases," *Journal of Empirical Legal Studies* 3: 561–609.

Warren, E. (1987). "Bankruptcy Policy," *University of Chicago Law Review* 54: 775–814.

Warren, E. (2002). "The Market for Data: The Changing Role of the Social Sciences in Shaping Law," *Wisconsin Law Review* (2002): 1–43.

Warren, E. (2004a). "The New Economics of the American Family," *American Bankruptcy Institute Law Review* 12: 1–41.

Warren, E. (2004b). "The Phantom $400," *Journal of Bankruptcy Law and Practice* 13: 4–21.

Warren, E. and Tyagi, A. (2003). *The Two-Income Trap: Why Middle-Class Parents Are Going Broke*, New York: Basic Books.

Weiss, L. (1990). "Bankruptcy Resolution: Direct Costs and Violation of Priority of Claims," *Journal of Financial Economics* 27: 285–314.

9

REGULATING THE PROFESSIONS

LINDA HALLER

I. INTRODUCTION

THIS Chapter provides an overview of some of the key questions about the regulation of professions and examples of research done to assist in providing answers to those questions. As will be seen, two key issues demanding empirical answers have been the degree of tension between the interests of the profession and the public in regulation, and the most effective methods of regulating professions. Many of the studies described in this Chapter demonstrate well the important relationship between theory and practice: empirical studies have proved essential in testing theories critical of the public-regarding claims of professions themselves. Conversely, open-ended inquiries into actual influences in the day-to-day conduct of professionals have generated theories as to the importance of a broad and complementary range of regulatory strategies and sources of regulation and, perhaps ironically for empirical legal studies, the limited role that formal law often plays in the face of more informal norms.

Regulation generally is a burgeoning area for empirical legal research, largely due to higher rates of formal regulation in society through legislation, regulatory instruments, and codes of conduct but also to a greater appreciation of influences upon conduct that go beyond formal law. At its narrowest, regulation may refer only to the enforcement of legal rules by the state or other legally sanctioned formal bodies. But empirical studies have confirmed the importance of the much broader view taken in the discussion which follows: the regulatory mix to which professions are subject includes not only regulation applied through entry controls, certification, and licensing requirements, professional discipline, and civil and criminal liability, but also the influence exerted by professional indemnity insurers and "softer" informal forms of regulation (including those found in places of practice such as hospitals and law firms), and by individual colleagues and consumers of professional services.

In the next section we look at empirical studies that have sought to provide insight into the possible tension that might exist between the interests of the profession and the public in regulation before moving to the question of the most effective regulatory "mix" for professions.

II. In Whose Interest—the Profession or the Public?

Early empirical research into professions did not consider a possible tension between the interests of the professions and those of the public and often worked from an assumption that, provided a group of service providers could demonstrate all the traits of a profession, that group could be trusted to self-regulate with the best interests of the public in mind. This assumption largely reflected the work of those, such as Parsons (1954), who theorized about a profession that would fully subsume its self-interest in the public interest.

However, as critiques of professions and trait theory became more common, such research was considered to be of little social value, except to occupational groups wanting to legitimate claims to professionalism and prestige. One of the most influential critiques of the professions was by Larson (1977), who doubted the altruistic motives of professions. Instead, she thought they engaged in a professional project of market control and collective upward social mobility. This project was not static but engaged in "at different times by different groups of professional reformers, using the resources that were accessible in their specific environments" (ibid: 104) and according to particular pressures they experienced.

Theoretical work such as this created a need to test these competing claims empirically—did regulation work more to the benefit of members of the professions or to those they claimed to serve? A number of aspects of regulation might provide insight into this question. We consider some of them below: self-regulation; market closure; quality; front-end entry controls; public protection vs. public interest; and professional boundaries. Others might include restrictions on advertising and on business structures.

A. Self-regulation

The power to self-regulate is often seen as a key feature of professionalization, and empirical legal studies have taken a close interest in efforts and attitudes around obtaining or strengthening statutory self-regulatory powers, including the attitude of traditional professionals toward efforts by competing service providers themselves to become self-regulating (Kelner et al., 2004). The relationship between the state and professions here can be a complex one. The profession wants to be seen as fearlessly independent of the state but often requires the support and cooperation of the state to entrench and legitimate its monopoly of practice and power to self-regulate. In some cases it has been found that it is the state that initiates the granting of the monopoly to a profession in the state's interests (Dingwall, 2006: 137). The complexity of the relationship between the state and professions not only serves to warn us of the danger of considering only a dichotomy between professional *or* public interest—because the state itself has an interest—but also makes it a rich area for empirical investigation.

Empirical studies have also attempted to gauge how successfully professions have self-regulated in the public interest. This can be measured in many ways. For instance, quantitative studies have analyzed the number of complaints upheld after investigation by professional bodies, or the number of professionals formally and publicly disciplined by their peers. Qualitative, observational studies have provided valuable insights into phenomena not easily quantified, such as how professionals respond when they believe their own work or that of a colleague may have caused harm to a consumer.

Some studies into the efficacy of self-regulation have been criticized for too read-ily assuming causal relationships. For instance, quantitative studies that analyzed the number of disciplinary prosecutions by regulators and the outcomes of pros-ecutions as the basis for conclusions about the degree of self-interest were some-times criticized as overly simplistic. Halliday (1987: 350), in his empirical study of the Chicago Bar Association, sought a more nuanced approach than "vulgar monopo-listic theories" relating to self-regulation that discounted the possibility of multiple causes and motivations, complaining of the conclusions in some other studies that:

one consequence or even intent of professionalism becomes the *raison d'etre* of the entire professionalization enterprise. The part is taken for the whole. Latent consequences become explicit intents; accompanying motives become sole bases of action. Results of profession-alization are assumed to be the outcome of a professional "project." In a word, the entire interpretative model is overdetermined.

In a similar vein, Pue (1990: 405) notes that professional discipline is only one way in which a profession can control its members and is critical of the assumption made by some researchers that a lack of formal professional discipline necessarily assumes a failure to self-regulate and more particularly, a lack of *will* to self-regulate.

We will take up Pue's distinction between formal and informal regulation later in this Chapter, but his comment also reflects greater recognition that there is no simple or linear relationship between intentions and regulatory outcomes and further, that regulation might sometimes simultaneously serve the interest of both the profession and the public (Parker, 1999: 119). In recognition of this, qualitative studies that seek to explore the state of mind and aspirations of professionals have become more com-mon. Such studies have recognized that, despite the best intentions of professionals, structural impediments or a lack of resources or expertise may restrict their abil-ity to implement their public-regarding aspirations. Conversely, some studies have documented the frustrations felt by professionals who feel less able to provide opti-mal care to consumers in bureaucratic settings where self-regulation is weakened and that appear to the professional to prioritize managerialist concerns of cost and time efficiencies over expertise and optimal outcomes for individual consumers.

Self-regulation in the public interest assumes colleagues will take some action when they become concerned about the conduct of their colleagues. Numerous studies have found professionals reluctant to adversely comment or report on the work of their colleagues (e.g., Waring, 2005). Agreement on the reasons for this reluctance has proved more elusive. For those who believe self-regulation is part of a profession's self-serving project, this is taken as clear evidence that they cannot be trusted to self-regulate. Others argue that the reasons are many and more complex, and might include that colleagues consider quality difficult to measure, or that it is a breach of the autonomy of individual professionals for others to comment on their work. Nonetheless, empirical evidence of a disinclination to take action has obvious implications for claims to self-regulation.

B. Market closure

Another key feature of professions is that members have been given an exclusive right to provide certain services. In other words, there is market closure. The usual justification is that this is necessary in order to serve the public interest. Such claims spawn a number of empirical questions. These include: how such monopolies came about; how they have changed over time; what part the state, professions themselves, and interest groups have played in their creation and maintenance; and the degree to which such closure has enhanced or detracted from the best interests of the public.

Empirical studies might consider how market closure protects the public in an absolute sense. For instance, what evidence is there that services provided by professionals lead to fewer adverse events or are of generally higher quality than those provided by unqualified individuals? A distinction needs to be drawn between protecting the interests of current consumers of professional services ("absolute" protection) and protecting the wider public interest, including protecting members of the public seeking at least some level of service ("relative" protection). We will look at studies exploring a more "absolute" understanding of protection in more detail first before exploring the notion of public protection in a wider, more relative, sense.

C. Quality

One way to test the claim that monopoly is in the public interest is to consider how well non-professionals can provide a similar service. It will be difficult to get comparative empirical data if a profession's monopoly is strictly enforced; but as discussed more fully later, professionals have policed the boundaries of their monopolies with varying degrees of vigilance, and it is perhaps no coincidence that it is in less lucrative areas of practice, such as legal aid (Moorhead et al., 2003) and tribunal work (Kritzer, 1998) that researchers have found adequate numbers of non-professionals providing assistance to make comparison possible.

In the past it was generally agreed that it was difficult to assess the quality of the types of services traditionally supplied by professionals. Indeed, this was one justification for giving a monopoly over the supply and regulation of the service to professionals in the first place—only this highly educated and certified group had the necessary knowledge and insight to regulate the quality of services provided; and so they would need to be trusted to self-regulate in the public interest. Nevertheless, some (including Moorhead et al. in the United Kingdom (2003)) have attempted to study objectively the relative quality of services provided by, and the relative competence levels of professionals and unregulated non-professional providers of, legal services. Studies such as this, which aim to assess quality and competence against an objective standard, face methodological difficulties. Service recipients are the most available source of information, but may lack expertise or give only subjective accounts influenced by their satisfaction with the outcome or the professional's "bedside manner." If we accept that professional status is based at least partly on technical expertise, informational asymmetry, and professional mystique, reports from user groups may be useful for measuring consumer perceptions of professional competence, but are of much less value to the researcher seeking some objective measure of quality. Moorhead et al. overcame this difficulty by supplementing client surveys with covert observation and assessment by trained "dummy" clients and external peer review of files. Their study concluded that there was very little difference in the quality of the services provided by the professionals and the unregulated service providers respectively.

Given the difficulties of measuring quality directly, some studies have sought to use proxies for quality, such as the length of time a patient may need to wait for dental assistance. Not surprisingly, the value of proxies such as these has sometimes been questioned.

As we will see later, empirical work has alerted us to the significance of informal influences as well as formal mechanisms in regulating professional conduct. Of the formal influences, complaints and professional discipline have often been considered of central importance, and it is largely through complaints and discipline that professionals have traditionally exercised self-regulation. We have mentioned some of the shortcomings of complaints and disciplinary systems already, arising both from the reluctance of professionals to report their colleagues and the failure of clients, for various reasons, to detect and complain about sub-standard work. More fundamentally, some theorists attribute to complaints and disciplinary systems very little power to explain the professional project of self-regulation and the way self-regulation can be used to promote the interests of professions. For instance, Larson mentions professional discipline in her 244-page monograph only in a footnote (1977: 229). This may be because by the time a complaint is made, the professional in question has already been deemed fit and proper to join the ranks of the profession, and it might prove difficult now to successfully portray him or her as a "bad apple" and punish them or expel them from the profession. Instead, Larson gives much closer attention to "front-end" controls such as barriers to education and qualification, and enforcement of monopolies over areas of practice.

D. Front-end entry controls

Not surprisingly then, given their importance to such theoretical critiques of the professions, much empirical work has been done on entry controls and restricted practice. Comparisons of the cost of education or pass rates in entrance exams (Schenarts, 2008) with subsequent incomes, cost, supply, or quality in particular professions have led to conclusions that some professions were manipulating entry controls to maximize their own income and prestige with little eye to the best interests of the public. However, some such studies have been criticized as being simplistic and for failing to take account of the many possible factors at play in determining the cost, supply, and quality of professionals. These include innumerable factors beyond the cost of education, including some that may not spring immediately to mind, such as quality of life, tax rates, and mortality. For instance, while empirical studies might show that physicians earn 32.5% more than dentists and that only half of this can be accounted for by the higher education costs incurred by physicians, it would be wrong to conclude from this that physicians were benefiting from market imperfections if other evidence suggests that physicians work longer hours than dentists or experience higher levels of taxation or work-related mortality (Olsen, 2000: 1024). Rhode (1985) examined the way character requirements were applied by various states of the United States in individual applications for admission and concluded that there was great inconsistency among them. This, combined with other empirical and theoretical work suggesting the questionable predictive ability of character testing, led Rhode to argue that the front-end controls applied through admission procedures could not be justified and were more likely to be part of the legal profession's effort to restrict competition and enhance status.

E. "Relative" public protection

The research considered so far has been concerned primarily with a public interest in protecting the interest of consumers in the availability of high-quality professional services ("absolute" protection). However, there is also a broader public interest in maintaining the supply of an adequate range of professional services at an affordable cost ("relative" protection). Much empirical work has been done to test the degree to which professional monopolies and other regulatory controls might be adding unnecessarily to the cost of professional services or limiting their supply (Yang et al., 2008) or range.

For instance, Paterson et al. (2003, "IHS study") were asked by the European Commission to consider "the justification for and effects of restrictive rules and regulations in the professions" across Europe. The study compared the legislation, regulations, and codes of practice governing the legal, accountancy, architecture, and pharmacy professions in a number of member states of the European Union, and linked this with an assessment of the economic effects of different degrees of regulation to determine if various levels of regulation were "too high." The implicit bias in such an approach is toward deregulation and perhaps an assumption that preexisting levels of regulation have been primarily in the interests of the professions rather than the public. Indeed, the IHS study took it as a given that less regulation, greater competition, and lower fees were intrinsically good outcomes, and did not test or control for quality. The implied assumption that quality remains constant regardless of the intensity of regulation was the basis for much of the later criticism of this study (Henssler and Killian, 2003; Terry, 2009).

Professionals may face competition not only from foreigners seeking local rights of practice. The challenge may also come from within. For instance, alternative providers of health care, such as naturopaths and practitioners of traditional Chinese medicine, to name just two groups, have become increasingly popular with consumers seeking alternative forms of care. While the medical profession has often lobbied hard against the recognition of such alternative health services, Dingwall (2006: 136) has noted that this is not always the case: in some situations the medical profession has recognized that the existence of alternative health service-providers has in fact increased the consumption of health services rather than threatened the market and authority of the medical profession.

To close markets effectively, it would seem necessary to define the boundaries of that market. But as we will see below, more recent critical empirical studies have documented the poor track record of professions in being able to adequately define the boundaries of their area of monopoly, and their differing responses when it might seem that non-professionals or other professional groups were encroaching. This indeterminacy has provided some ammunition to those who argue that regulation is primarily for the benefit of the profession rather than the public.

F. Professional boundaries

It may seem curious to those who have not studied the regulation of professions closely that it has sometimes proved difficult to define the sort of work that comes within a particular profession's monopoly of practice. It would seem hard for any regulator to enforce an amorphous boundary. Fournier (2000: 71) describes studies that have tracked the way in which particular professional fields of knowledge such as medicine and accounting (Hopwood, 1987) have come into existence and continued to evolve.

Perhaps in recognition of the difficulty of defining an area of monopoly to a level that would satisfy courts in formal prosecutions of non-members for unauthorized practice in breach of the monopoly, professional groups have sometimes cooperated to carve out areas of monopoly for each other (American Bar Association, 1995: 23). While such agreements clearly benefit the professions involved, empirical studies have sometimes found it difficult to identify how they benefit the public: while they might save a regulator the expense of a prosecution, the nebulous boundary may suggest a prosecution would not have been warranted in any case.

If a profession itself appears at times ambivalent about enforcing boundaries, their public protective function might seem questionable. Particularly if professionals appear most active in policing the supply of services for which they are most handsomely rewarded, rather than those of most risk to consumers, the public-regarding nature of the professions must be questioned. As noted earlier in our discussion of testing the quality of professional services, it is perhaps not surprising that it was in the less lucrative areas of legal aid (Moorhead et al., 2003) and tribunal work (Kritzer, 1998) that researchers encountered a more lax enforcement of boundaries that made it possible to compare the quality of services provided by professionals and non-professionals. It is perhaps notable in this regard that some definitions of unauthorized practice include only the supply of services for reward—the professions appear to have made much less noise about services provided for free.

One often-cited example of an empirical study that casts professions in a more positive light than some of those mentioned previously is that of Halliday (1987), who took an optimistic view of the potential of professionalization to benefit the public. He sought to overcome what he saw as simplistic theories of professions that assumed a simple dichotomy between self- and public interest. Larson had theorized that the impetus for professional groups to seek greater market control and higher social status changed over place and time, depending on the state of knowledge, markets, and resources available to professional groups to mobilize (1977: 104). Halliday developed this historical imperative and applied it to the Chicago Bar Association. He conceded that the association pursued its own interests when establishing its professional legitimacy; but, once established, it became much more outward-looking, displayed much more altruism, and performed a greater civic role—in other words, went "beyond monopoly." Only in future periods of severe public scrutiny would it feel a need to refocus its energies on self-interest.

However, it would be wrong to use Halliday's work as affirmation that professions will regulate themselves primarily in the public interest. According to Halliday, one precondition of going "beyond monopoly" is that a profession's privileged monopoly position be entrenched; but regulation that truly pursues the public interest may weaken that monopoly. Second, while, as Halliday noted, the association continued to be interested in "soft" forms of regulation, such as continuing legal education, licensing of specialist practitioners, and office management, even when its monopoly was entrenched (ibid: 353), its interest in ethics and grievance committees and the "harder" end of regulation that could lead to professional discipline and expulsion from the profession in fact declined during these times of prosperity (ibid: 352). This fluctuating interest in discipline casts doubt on the degree to which the association could effectively and fully self-regulate in the public interest. It also highlights the important *symbolic* role that professional discipline plays in a profession's quest for legitimacy: discipline sends powerful messages about character and integrity in a way that more mundane activities such as continuing legal education and office management cannot.

A large proportion of empirical studies of regulation of the professions have been carried out in the United States, United Kingdom, Canada, and Australia, and have had a particular interest in various combinations of state, self-, and co-regulation and how these might enhance or detract from a profession's social power, status, and legitimacy. This is not surprising given that the traditional professions of law, medicine, and the clergy were more significant sources of social status in English-speaking countries than in Europe, where status was tied more to a person's place of education or employment: hence, Freidson's reference to the "Anglo-American disease of professionalism" (1983: 26). As we move outside Anglo-American jurisdictions to places where less social prestige is derived from professional status and self-regulation, it is not surprising to see less interest in empirical studies into professions and their regulation. Some have argued that "Europeanization"—the expectation that professions will be similarly regulated across the various countries of the European Union—will alter the preexisting regulatory balance between profession and state, and thereby diminish professional control and status; but Freidson's comment suggests that UK-based researchers will perhaps be more concerned about exploring this than academics in mainland Europe.

In summary, despite the empirical studies that have been undertaken, we still do not know much about the degree to which regulation has worked in the interests of professions and to the disadvantage of the public. Part of the difficulty has been in obtaining data—protected professions can be coy about disclosing their levels of income, adverse service outcomes, and other relevant information. But, as the preceding discussion has sought to demonstrate, much of the problem lies in the complexity of the phenomena being investigated and the need for caution before ascribing causal relationships.

Having looked at some of the empirical work exploring the degree to which regulation of the professions has or has not protected the public, we turn now to a second, important area of empirical research dealing with the optimal mix of various regulatory techniques and sources of regulation, both formal and informal.

III. Best Regulatory Mix

We looked at self-regulation earlier in the context of a profession's ability to regulate in the public interest. In this section we include the question of self-regulation but consider it in combination with other potential forms of regulation and with different questions in mind: what regulatory techniques are used by effective regulators; what sources of regulation exist and can be best utilized for optimal regulatory outcomes; and what other, less formal influences on the conduct of professionals exist. We will look first at the regulatory techniques used by regulators—whether professional bodies or external—before turning to the question of multiple sources of regulation and finally, informal influences on conduct.

A. Regulatory techniques—the regulatory pyramid

Until empirical work uncovered a much richer picture, it was generally assumed that regulation consisted primarily of top down "command and control" of those regulated: regulatory agencies charged with enforcement demanded compliance, and failures to comply were met with more punitive responses by regulators. However, innumerable studies, such as the examination by Braithwaite et al. of regulatory styles of the regulator and perceptions of those being regulated within nursing homes (1990), found a much more complex picture. They found that most regulatory activity occurs at the base of what later Braithwaite coined a regulatory "pyramid." Here at the base, regulators show respect for the autonomy of those they regulate and encourage personal monitoring. They engage in dialogue and employ incentives and encouragement to comply (in summary, they "speak softly"). However, effective regulators also ensure they carry a "big stick" while speaking softly and respond to failures to comply by escalating up the regulatory pyramid to more and more mandatory intervention and coercion by the regulator. At the apex of the pyramid is the regulator's "last resort" (Hawkins, 2002)—formal prosecution for regulatory breach. Empirical work continues to be done in exploring some of these theories in the context of professions and professional places of work, and Braithwaite (2009: 31) has emphasized how important these regulatory questions are in the context of hospitals today, with the sheer range of professions working together using complex technology on vulnerable patients.

Studies of regulatory styles have also emphasized the normative content of much decision-making by regulators at all levels of the pyramid, including a tendency for regulators to require moral blame before they externally report or prosecute conduct, regardless of whether the legislation they are charged with enforcing purports to impose strict liability offenses (Carson, 1970; Hawkins, 2002).

B. Regulatees

Similarly, just as empirical studies were important to test assumptions that command and control was the only style of regulation employed by regulators, they also provided important information about those subjected to regulation. The potentially corrupting influences on professional conduct were sometimes assumed to be the result of inherent character flaws—the "bad apple" who slipped through front-end professional admission controls. Qualitative, exploratory studies sought to find out from professionals themselves what they perceived to be the various influences over their conduct, both positive and negative, and their relative weight. Rather than assume that punitive, formal regulatory law was the primary source of influence, such studies have provided useful information as to the relative (and sometimes much greater) influence of factors such as client or employer support or pressure, a concern to please colleagues, reputational concerns, a desire to maximize income or prestige, workload, and training.

Empirical evidence such as this, which suggests that effective regulation requires regulators to use a mix of persuasion and command-and-control, and to acknowledge and harness the aspirational desires of those regulated, has also led to theoretical arguments about the futility of imposing legislative changes that move too far into risk-based, objective, and blame-free approaches: reporting of failure and risk often includes a normative element because it is reactive and arises out of dissatisfaction; and most would expect it to be part of a regulator's responsibility to allocate individual responsibility where necessary (e.g., Lloyd-Bostock and Hutter, 2008: 79). While Lloyd-Bostock and Hutter were referring to regulation of the medical profession, their warnings should also be heeded by those designing effective regulation for other professions, particularly in Anglo-American countries where professions have strong, traditional aspirations of self-regulation and individual responsibility (Dingwall, 2006: 139).

In addition to studies into what mix of regulatory strategies a single professional body or regulatory agency might use, others have attempted to identify and measure the regulatory impact of a much broader range of sources, including civil liability and insurers.

C. Multiple regulators

Past empirical studies into the professions can take some of the credit for revealing to us the pluralist nature of regulation. Unitary approaches were once assumed to be the only legitimate form of regulation, whether it was a professional body imposing its will on members or an external, independent statutory body responding to proven breaches of standards. Today it is accepted that a much broader range of sources of regulation exists beyond dedicated regulatory agencies and is desirable in the regulation of professions as in all regulatory contexts. The role of the empirical researcher then becomes to provide evidence as to what regulatory mix exists or is optimal in various circumstances and for various professions.

The theoretical work of Wilkins (1992) has had a lasting impact on thinking about the regulation of the legal profession because it took a broader view of regulation than simply licensing, complaints, and discipline, which had been the earlier focus. Wilkins proposed a four-celled typology of regulation comprising disciplinary, liability, institutional, and legislative controls. Wilkins was not seeking to explore the regulatory techniques used by a single agency, as discussed in the previous section. Instead, his focus was the multiple sources of potential regulation, and his work struck a chord when it was published in 1992 because it came at a time when many empirical studies had focused on complaints and disciplinary systems applicable to lawyers and there was less theoretical acknowledgement, let alone empirical work reflecting the regulatory potential, of other parts of Wilkins' framework, such as tort liability, controls applied by courts and other similar institutions, and legislative forms of control applied by state administrative bodies. Wilkins theorized that it was important to consider who had the greatest incentive to enforce high professional standards and argued that in some contexts, disciplinary and liability controls have a tendency to duplicate each other and have limited regulatory impact, given that they both only respond to small client, agency problems such as overcharging and neglect: large, powerful clients are unlikely to complain when lawyers engage in misconduct under pressure from the client.

We noted earlier the degree of informational asymmetry between professionals and consumers and the lack of transparency around professional conduct, making it difficult for unsophisticated consumers of professional services to identify poor-quality work—and how this fact was used as a justification for professional monopoly and self-regulation. It also has consequences for determining the most effective source of regulation. Even when clients do identify, and suffer as a result of, poor quality work, many factors determine whether or not they will go on to lodge a complaint. They may lack the resources or skill to complain. Where a third party, such as an insurer or a legal aid or sickness fund, has paid for the provision of services, it may be less likely that either the consumer or funder of the service has sufficient information or incentive to lodge a complaint, creating a moral hazard for enforcement.

Clients are not always a good source of control for other reasons. Clients will sometimes profit from the actions of their professional adviser, such as where an accountant or lawyer assists in a client's scheme of tax evasion, and clients will do all they can to hide the assistance provided by the professional. On the other hand, some consumers of professional services are so large and powerful that the professional may need protection—or at least guaranteed independence—from the client. The most dramatic and intractable example of this arises in the auditing profession where client and market controls are obviously inadequate when the legitimacy of the audit depends on the auditor's ability to demonstrate independence from the client. Empirical work has been done to find the effective form of regulation to protect auditor independence, although the results so far have proved inconclusive (Ramsay, 2001). While institutional controls, such as restraint proceedings in the courts, may effectively deal with externalities resulting from the provision of professional services, as when a lawyer assists a client whose activities cause harm to the community, Wilkins thought that such forms of control were vulnerable to misuse by large, powerful clients for tactical purposes against less well-resourced parties, thus reinforcing preexisting inequalities of access to the courts.

Empirical work in the United States has attempted to test some aspects of Wilkins' theory. A study by Joy in 2004 found that there was little duplication in the application of institutional (Rule 11) sanctions and professional discipline. Similarly, many of the studies of regulation of medical professions surveyed by Olsen (2000) looked at the interaction between medical malpractice and tort and licensing law. In the 1980s and 1990s, claims were made that the medical and legal professions were at least partly responsible for an explosion in the cost of tort claims, and that this justified the placing of further layers of regulation upon them. Empirical studies proved extremely useful in testing the veracity of such claims of a crisis and its potential culprits (Harvard, 1990). Work also continues to be done on the impact of the new sources of regulation—liability, insurance, and otherwise—on such factors as supply, cost, efficiency, defensive practice, and patient outcomes (e.g., Kessler and McClellan, 1996), although the results remain inconclusive and contested (Faure, 2009: 488).

We mentioned earlier that research hypotheses around the degree to which regulation promotes professional self-interest more than public interest may not strike a similar chord outside the United States and United Kingdom as they do in those countries. Equally, empirical findings on the existing and optimum regulatory "mix" may also be of doubtful relevance outside those same jurisdictions where there has traditionally been most interest in studying professions. However, the "policy pull" (Sarat and Silbey, 1988) on the empirical researcher to carry out comparative studies of regulatory mixes is becoming quite strong as a result, for instance, of the expectation that professions will be regulated across the European Union or, at least, that there will be greater harmonization of regulatory laws. This, of course, was the driver for the IHS study mentioned earlier (Paterson et al., 2003).

Comparative work on the regulatory mix is underway. Empirical studies have concluded that health professions in the United States are much more subject to regulation by the medical defense organizations and insurers that provide them with indemnity than by state management of markets—as occurs in the United Kingdom (Dingwall, 2006: 132). In Germany, sickness funds play a major role in regulation because of their strong economic interest in restricting the cost to them of financing health care, leading to less concern about regulating quality than in state-centered forms of regulation such as that in the United Kingdom (Kuhlmann, 2009).

Each source of regulation is likely to reflect its particular priorities and *raison d'être*: sickness funds in Germany focus primarily on reducing cost; internal ombudsman schemes try to settle consumer complaints as quickly and informally as possible, for instance by requiring the professional service-provider to apologize to the patient or client; a professional indemnity insurer will be concerned lest informal apologies or payments compromise its control over civil liability proceedings, but will still be pleased to see any civil claim resolved to the satisfaction of the individual plaintiff without the expense of court proceedings. A state-based regulatory body may be more concerned to uncover and respond to systemic failings in the provision of services by professionals. These various forms of regulation may be in tension with one another. For instance, the best way to "protect" a person already harmed by a professional may be to compensate that person for their losses; but if such compensation is provided on an informal, confidential basis without a public hearing into the harmful conduct in the form (for instance) of a civil trial for professional negligence or professional disciplinary proceedings, the result may be potential harm to the public more broadly and into the future as the professional remains in practice (Abel, 2003: 489).

D. Informal regulation

For many years, work has been done on the formal and informal ways in which the work of health professionals is controlled. Heimer (1999) spent a year in the field observing legal and other norms guiding interactions among doctors, nurses, and non-professionals in a neonatal ward. She observed daily routines and staff meetings of the neonatal intensive care unit, interviewed staff and parents, and reviewed medical records and the laws governing the practice of neonatal law, to provide a detailed assessment of the different impact that civil, criminal, and regulatory laws had on medical decision-making alongside the influences exerted by the norms of medical and familial institutions. She concluded from her observations that laws will vary in the degree to which they actually impact on actual behavior within organizations when competing against medical and family norms, depending on the degree to which the laws were insinuated into daily organizational demands. The higher-status health professionals, such as physicians, had a greater say in whether or not this occurred.

Heimer's study is an example of the many studies of informal regulation of the medical profession that occurs in hospital settings, which epitomize a group workplace and are likely to provide optimum opportunities for the operation of informal influences over conduct. By way of comparison, in 1975 Freidson published his seminal article about doctors practicing outside the hospital setting, *Doctoring*

Together, which recognized the informal controls operating between medical practitioners even when not working closely together on a daily basis. Nelson's *Partners with Power* (1988) was an early study of informal regulation within the legal profession, focusing on a large organization arguably analogous to a hospital—a big law firm. Mather et al.'s work (2001) on divorce lawyers was an important step forward because it recognized that even sole-practitioner lawyers operated within various communities of practice. While not necessarily within their immediate place of work, Mather et al. found that solo lawyers still drew understandings of norms and expectations from numerous other communities of practice, such as the profession within their state, colleagues from other firms with whom they interacted, and the courts and other forums within which they practiced.

While it is useful to acknowledge the ways in which formal and informal forms of regulation can complement each other, it should also be acknowledged that they can be in tension. For instance, while there are perhaps advantages for consumers, colleagues, and institutions in encouraging private apologies and settlements, these may compromise more formal action against the same individual in relation to the conduct for which the apology was received.

E. Comparing the regulatory mix across borders

Studies comparing the regulatory mix applying to professions in different jurisdictions have become more common in recent times. Such studies may be driven by the need for regulation and regulators to respond to the globalization of professional practice, which creates at least the perception of a need to establish trans-national regulatory frameworks or, alternatively, at least to adapt existing regulatory norms to achieve greater harmony among states. For example, Kuhlmann (2009) compared the dynamics of the regulation of medical professions in the UK and Germany to identify diverse drivers of change and to explain why the state plays a more influential role in the United Kingdom. She also found that state support through legislation for self-regulation by nurses and suppliers of alternative and complementary medicine was much less advanced in Germany than in the United Kingdom. She argued that one result of this relatively weak state regulation in Germany has been greater "bottom-up" informal regulation, such as through voluntary quality-support networks (ibid: 523). Also relevant to the issue of the effective "mix" of regulatory mechanisms across traditional borders are studies into the effectiveness of legal transplants, such as that by Dezalay and Garth (2002): they can tell us about the potential for "softer" regulation through professional culture and norms across state borders. However, this is not an area for the fainthearted empirical researcher. There is much complexity and the danger of ethno-centric understandings of central concepts, such as "self-regulation" and "self-administration," which can have fundamentally different meanings in different jurisdictions even among the countries of Europe (Henssler and Kilian, 2003: 13).

IV. Conclusion

What have we learned from empirical studies into the regulation of the professions? How successful have they been in testing theories about professions? The answers to these questions depend on a number of factors. Certainly, more narrowly framed investigations into regulation have sometimes tended to confirm theories that argue that regulation often speaks to the interests of the professions themselves rather than the public. However, as commentators such as Lewis, Pue, and Halliday have rightly pointed out, narrowly framed research questions, for instance ones that focus only on formal professional discipline, sometimes make overly wide claims about the failure of self-regulation. The empirical studies undertaken to date have alerted us to the great complexity of regulation of the professions. Causal relationships and intended consequences cannot be assumed. Regulators and those regulated sometimes aspire to high standards in discharging their roles, but are hampered by a lack of resources. Regulation might take many forms, and one of the most important revelations from empirical studies done to date has been the importance of recognizing and embracing a plurality of regulatory forms and the danger of assuming the central importance of law in regulation. We have discovered that often much more informal norms most influence the way professionals conduct themselves. The ongoing challenge for empirical studies is to find ways to adequately investigate and uncover the inter-relationship between various forms of regulation, both formal and informal.

References

Abel, R. (2003). *English Lawyers between Market and State*, Oxford: Oxford University Press.

American Bar Association Commission on NonLawyer Practice (1995). *NonLawyer Activity in Law Related Situations: A Report with Recommendations*, Chicago: American Bar Association.

Ayres, I. and Braithwaite, J. (1992). *Responsive Regulation: Transcending the Deregulation Debate*, New York: Oxford University Press.

Braithwaite, J. (2009). "Leading from Behind with Plural Regulation," in J. Healy, and P. Dugdale, *Patient Safety First: Responsive Regulation in Health Care*, Sydney: Allen and Unwin.

Braithwaite, J., Makkai, T., Braithwaite, V., Gibson, D., and Ermann, D. (1990). The Contribution of the Standards Monitoring Process to the Quality of Nursing Home Life: A Preliminary Report, Canberra: Department of Community Services and Health.

Carson, W. (1970). "Some Sociological Aspects of Strict Liability and the Enforcement of Factory Legislation," *Modern Law Review* 33: 396–412.

Carson, W. (1982). *The Other Price of Britain's Oil: Safety and Control in the North Sea*, New Brunswick: Rutgers University Press.

Dezalay, Y. and Garth, B. (2002). *The Internationalization of Palace Wars: Lawyers, Economists, and the Contest to Transform Latin American States*, Chicago: University of Chicago Press.

Dingwall, R. (2006). "Is 'Professional Dominance' an Obsolete Concept?," *Knowledge, Work and Society* 4: 77–98, republished in R. Dingwall (2008). *Essays on Professions*, Aldershot: Ashgate Publishing Ltd.

Faure, M. (2009). *Tort Law and Economics*, Cheltenham: Edward Elgar.

Fournier, V. (2000). "Boundary Work and the (Un)making of a Profession," in N. Malin, (ed.), *Professionalism, Boundaries and the Workplace*, London: Routledge.

Freidson, E. (1975). *Doctoring Together: A Study of Professional Social Control*, Amsterdam: Elsevier Scientific Publishing.

Freidson, E. (1983). "The Theory of Professions: State of the Art," in R. Dingwall and P. Lewis (eds.), *The Sociology of the Professions: Lawyers, Doctors and Others*, Oxford: Oxford Socio-Legal Studies.

Halliday, T. (1987). *Beyond Monopoly: Lawyers, State Crises and Professional Empowerment*, Chicago: University of Chicago Press.

Harvard Medical Practice Study (1990). "Patients, Doctors, and Lawyers: Medical Injury, Malpractice Litigation, and Patient Compensation in New York," *A Report by the Harvard Medical Practice Study to the State of New York*.

Hawkins, K. (2002). *Law as Last Resort*, Oxford: Oxford University Press.

Heimer, C. (1999). "Competing Institutions: Law, Medicine and Family in Neonatal Intensive Care," *Law and Society Review* 33: 17–66.

Henssler, M. and Kilian, M. (2003). "Position Paper on the Study Carried out by the Institute for Advanced Studies, Vienna: Economic Impact of Regulation in the Field of Liberal Professions in Different Member States," available at <http://anwaltverein.de/downloads/praxis/Positionspapier-Henssler-Kilian-Englisch-Endversion.pdf>.

Hopwood, A. (1987). "The Archaeology of Accounting Systems," *Accounting, Organizations and Society* 12: 207–34.

Joy, P. (2004). "The Relationship between Civil Rule 11 and Lawyer Discipline: an Empirical Analysis suggesting Institutional Choices in the Regulation of Lawyers," *Loyola of Los Angeles Law Review* 37: 765–818.

Kelner, M., Wellman, B., Boon, H., and Welsh, S., (2004). "Responses of Established Healthcare to the Professionalization of Complementary and Alternative Medicine in Ontario," *Social Science and Medicine* 59: 915–30.

Kessler, D. and McClellan, M. (1996). "Do Doctors Practise Defensive Medicine?," *The Quarterly Journal of Economics* 111: 353–90.

Kritzer, H. (1998). *Legal Advocacy: Lawyers and Nonlawyers at Work*, Ann Arbor: University of Michigan Press.

Kuhlmann, E., Allsop, J., and Saks, M. (2009). "Professional Governance and Public Control: A Comparison of Healthcare in the United Kingdom and Germany," *Current Sociology* 57: 511–28.

Larson, M. (1977). *The Rise of Professionalism: A Sociological Analysis*, Berkeley: University of California Press.

Lewis, P. (1989). "Comparison and Change in the Study of Legal Professions," in R. Abel and P. Lewis (eds.), *Lawyers in Society, vol 3: Comparative Theories*, Berkeley: University of California Press.

Lloyd-Bostock, S. and Hutter, B. (2008). "Reforming Regulation of the Medical Profession: The risk of risk- based approaches," *Health, Risk & Society* 10: 69–83.

Mather, L., McEwen C., and Maiman, R. (2001). *Divorce Lawyers at Work*, New York: Oxford University Press.

Moorhead, R., Paterson A., and Sherr A. (2003). "Contesting Professionalism: Legal Aid and Non Lawyers in England and Wales," *Law & Society Review* 37: 765–808.

Nelson, R.L. (1988). *Partners with Power: Social Transformation of the Large Law Firm*, Berkeley: University of California Press.

Olsen, R. (2000). "The Regulation of Medical Professions' in B. Bouckaert and G. De Geest (eds.), *Encyclopedia of Law and Economics*, Cheltenham: Edward Elgar Publishing.

Parker, C. (1999). *Just Lawyers*, Oxford: Oxford University Press.

Parsons, T. (1954). "A Sociologist Looks at the Legal Profession," in T. Parsons, *Essays in Sociological Theory*, New York: Free Press.

Paterson I., Marcel Fink, M., and Ogus, A. (2003). Economic Impact of Regulation in the Field of Liberal Professions in Different Member States: Regulation of Professional Services, Study for the European Commission, DG Competition ('IHS study'), available at <http://ec.europa.eu/competition/sectors/professional_services/studies/studies.html>.

Pue, W. (1990). "Trajectories of Professionalism: Legal Professionalism after Abel," *Manitoba Law Journal* 19: 384–418.

Ramsay, I. (2001). Independence of Australian Company Auditors: Review of Current Australian Requirements and Proposals for Reform, Report to the Minister for Financial Services and Regulation, available at <http://papers.ssrn.com/sol3/papers.cfm?abstract_id=298122>.

Rhode, D.L. (1985). "Moral Character as a Professional Credential," *Yale Law Journal* 94: 491–603.

Sarat, A. and Silbey, S. (1988). "The Pull of the Policy Audience," *Law and Policy* 10: 97–166.

Schenarts, P.J., MD, Love, K.J., MD, Agle, S.C., MD, and Haisch, C.E., MD (2008). "Comparison of Surgical Residency Applicants from U.S. Medical Schools with U.S.-Born and Foreign-Born International Medical School Graduates," *Journal of Surgical Education* 65: 406–12.

Terry, L. (2009). "The European Commission Project Regarding Competition in Professional Services," *Northwestern Journal of International Law and Business* 29: 1–118.

Waring, J. (2005). "Beyond Blame: Cultural Barriers to Medical Incident Reporting," *Social Science & Medicine* 60: 1927–35.

Wenger, E. (1998). *Communities of Practice: Learning, Meaning and Identity*, Cambridge: Cambridge University Press.

Wilkins, D. (1992). "Who Should Regulate Lawyers?," *Harvard Law Review* 105: 801–87.

Yang, Y.T., Studdert, D., Subramanian, S., and Mello, M. (2008). "A Longitudinal Analysis of the Impact of Liability Pressure on the Supply of Obstetrician-Gynecologists," *Journal of Empirical Legal Studies* 5: 21–53.

1 0

PERSONAL INJURY LITIGATION

PAUL FENN AND
NEIL RICKMAN

I. INTRODUCTION

WHEN one party (the prospective defendant) allegedly harms another (the prospective plaintiff), there is potential for legal action. This creates fascinating interactions between a variety of individuals (from litigants, to lawyers, to employers, and so on), as well as having potentially important consequences for those involved. Inevitably, this has resulted in litigation attracting the attentions of many disciplines and academics. Significant and relevant research has been undertaken by psychologists (e.g., Neil Vidmar), anthropologists (e.g., David Engel), insurance scholars (e.g., Joan Schmit), sociologists (e.g., Hazel Genn), and political scientists (e.g., Herbert Kritzer), to list but a few. In fact, legal action can perform valuable economic functions, such as the provision of deterrence and compensation, but at the expense of using valuable resources. As a result, economists also have a long-standing research interest in legal disputes and, in particular, the incentives provided by the legal system to those involved in them, and it is part of their work that we concentrate on in this Chapter.

Economic analysis of civil disputes can be traced to initial work by Posner (1973) and Gould (1973). This work, and much that has followed, employs economic theory to derive predictions about the role of legal rules in legal dispute resolution and to evaluate their welfare effects in terms of the efficient use and distribution of resources. The subsequent growth of competing hypotheses and relevant data sets has encouraged empirical analyses.

The aim of this paper is to survey the empirical work by economists and others in the area of personal injury litigation. It is immediate from this that important examples of litigation are beyond our scope, product liability and contract disputes being two that have received empirical scrutiny.[1] We should also point out that the paper ignores empirical research on many aspects of civil procedure, which is covered elsewhere in this book. Another dimension of scope relates to the methodologies we cover: we restrict attention to econometric and experimental analyses. While this certainly reflects a bias toward the techniques most frequently used by economists, we appreciate that it ignores much excellent work that uses other methods. Our logic is simply one of tractability and comparative advantage.

The survey is structured as follows. In the next section, we briefly describe the way that economists have tended to think about the "litigation process." We then turn attention to a number of areas of empirical work. We begin with case outcomes (how and when does a case end?) before looking at the ways in which the legal system itself can influence matters—in particular, through the encouragement of information transfer and the rules used for allocating legal costs. Next, we consider the role of lawyers by looking at the effects of different legal fee arrangements on case outcomes. The following two sections ask whether the liability-based legal system that is studied in the previous sections produces the deterrence benefits often claimed for it in conceptual work and, if not, how no-fault alternatives to compensation appear to operate. A final section draws some conclusions. In particular, we note that results

---

[1] Of course, it is difficult to apply these distinctions strictly. For example, some papers use data drawn from several areas of law.

in this area are only as good (and as useful) as the data and techniques available to analyze them. For example, gaps in our ability to conduct research into policy initiatives and comparative issues can both be traced to data inadequacies.

II. The Litigation Process

It is often helpful to think about litigation in terms of a "litigation process." This characterizes legal disputes as a series of sequential decisions that may, ultimately, see two parties facing each other at trial. Broadly, we can think of a legal dispute as involving

1. initial decisions by individuals about the care they will take in their activities;
2. decisions about seeking legal advice where others' care decisions might be felt to have caused harm;
3. decisions about hiring a lawyer and filing a claim;
4. decisions about whether to drop or settle the claim or pursue it to trial as information becomes available while the case proceeds.

Each of these stages takes place one after another, possibly over a long time; and, of course, they are connected. Therefore, rules and behavior need to be evaluated not only at the stage of the litigation process where they operate but also in terms of the effects they may have on other parts of the process. A particular example of this, which is often overlooked but is important for policy, concerns the potential effects of stages (2), (3), and (4) on (1): the so-called deterrence effect of litigation.

From the earliest economic models of litigation (e.g., Friedman (1969), Posner (1973), Shavell (1982)), a number of factors that should affect these decisions have been apparent. When deciding whether to settle (or drop) the case, the parties consider the costs and benefits of doing so. These, of course, relate to the expected net returns they will receive from continuing (as opposed to ending) the litigation, so that the anticipated damages and costs, and the probabilities of winning and losing might all be expected to influence case outcomes. As these considerations determine the "threat points" of the parties during bargaining (i.e., the maximum/minimum that defendant/plaintiff are prepared to settle for) it follows that they should also affect settlement offers and demands. In addition, by affecting drop/settle strategies at any given moment, these variables will also influence the *timing* of such outcomes.

Of course, a number of other factors may come into play to influence case outcomes. The parties' attitudes toward risk will influence their threat points, so that the different risk-sharing implications of fee arrangements may be important, as may various procedural and institutional variables—such as the way that costs are shifted or interest is calculated, or the details of pre-trial discovery rules. Economists (as well as other legal scholars and social scientists) have examined the effects of each of these, as we shall see below.

III. CASE OUTCOMES

A central focus of empirical work on litigation has been whether cases are dropped, settled or go to trial and the determinants of any settlement amount.[2] Given the foregoing discussion, it will not be a surprise to find that a number of statistical studies have attempted to link these outcomes to costs, damages, beliefs about case strength, and so on. In the context of personal injury litigation, a number of studies (especially) in this section use data drawn from medical malpractice litigation.[3] To some extent, this reflects the considerable interest in medical malpractice reform in the United States. Nonetheless, many of the other studies cited in this Chapter draw on other kinds of personal injury litigation and a number of these produce results that are consistent with those reported in this section—and this is also true of studies that look at other kinds of litigation (such as product liability studies).[4] Often, these studies draw on data sets that cover a wide variety of types of claims that involve monetary compensation (for example the U.S. federal court data used by Fournier and Zuehlke, 1989, 1996). Although there are important respects in which medical malpractice claims differ from other types of personal injury litigation, a degree of congruence between results from medical malpractice and other personal injury litigation contexts is to be expected. From an economic perspective, a number of the key influences on the decisions to drop, settle or try cases of different types are likely to be similar; in particular, a number of the factors that affect the parties' expected costs and benefits of pursuing various strategies in litigation. This is not to underestimate the importance of non-financial factors in personal injury litigation (which may be especially relevant in medical malpractice[5]), but to suggest that the

---

[2] We ignore the important issue of how to define settlement (and other outcomes). See Eisenberg and Lanvers (2009) for a detailed discussion of this issue.

[3] This is true, for example, of Danzon and Lillard (1983), Sloan and Hoerger (1989), Farber and White (1991, 1994), Hughes and Snyder (1989), Snyder and Hughes (1990), and Fenn and Rickman (1999).

[4] Several of the studies in this section make use of data from personal injury litigation other than medical malpractice: e.g., Fournier and Zuehlke (1989, 1996), Kessler (1996), Fenn and Rickman (2001)—indeed, of the papers cited elsewhere in this Chapter by Fenn et al., only Fenn, Gray and Rickman (2004) focuses exclusively on medical malpractice.

[5] Hospitals' reputations and plaintiffs' needs for explanations and apologies spring to mind here.

average medical malpractice claim will bear resemblance to other types of personal litigation in terms of the types of calculation and thinking undertaken by the parties involved.

A. The probability of dropping a case

Danzon and Lillard's (1983) U.S. study of medical malpractice claims finds that the higher the damages claimed by the plaintiff the less likely the claim will be dropped. One interpretation of this result is that the plaintiff is better able to meet the costs of litigation if the expected rewards are large. Of course, under a contingent fee regime the plaintiff is, to some extent, insulated from financial costs, and so an alternative interpretation is that the plaintiff is more willing to incur the non-pecuniary costs of litigation when stakes are high. Sloan and Hoerger (1989) find no significant effect of economic loss on the probability of dropping the case. They argue that this is because they have controlled for the plaintiff's estimate of defendant liability: if the defendant can be predicted to be liable, the plaintiff will proceed with the case. This is borne out by their finding that defendants with higher probabilities of being found liable face a lower drop probability (a finding confirmed by Farber and White, 1991; 1994).

These papers do not directly observe litigants' costs, so they employ proxies to capture the effect of this important variable. Danzon and Lillard, for example, adopt as a proxy for plaintiffs' costs the degree of court congestion (on the grounds that delay is costly to plaintiffs in terms of their prospects of proving their case). They find that higher costs raise the plaintiff's probability of dropping the case.

B. The probability of settlement

If the case is not dropped it may settle. The probability of settlement depends, of course, on the behavior of both parties. As a result, it is rare for a consensus to exist among various theoretical models about the effects of different variables on the settlement probability.

Fournier and Zuehlke (1989) find that damages and their variance both increase the probability of settlement (the latter reflecting some measure of the risk faced by the parties). As a proxy for private litigation costs they use public expenditure on the legal system in each jurisdiction in their sample; the implicit, and perhaps suspect, assumption being that higher public expenditure implies higher cost and, therefore, higher private expenditure on any given case. They find that higher costs lower the settlement probability. Initially, this may seem surprising (and it is at variance with a number of models of settlement timing—see below) but it is not necessarily unreasonable. For example, Nalebuff (1987) argues that, as costs for the plaintiff rise, trial becomes more unprofitable. This has the effect of weakening the plaintiff's bargaining credibility, which he restores by making a high settlement offer and reducing the settlement probability.

The complexity of the case, as signified by the severity of the injuries and the degree of uncertainty over liability, can also play a role in the settlement outcome. In fact though, none of Sloan and Hoerger's liability variables are significant here, possibly because their sample contains too few tried cases to provide accurate results. Indeed, the only significant variable in their settlement equation relates to medical treatment resulting in the death of a newborn child, for which damage caps exist: this increases the probability of settlement, presumably because of the implied limit on the stakes.

An important technical issue surrounds the estimates reported above. These estimate the probability of a case settling conditional on its not having been dropped. As Hughes and Snyder (1989) argue, this may not be appropriate for two reasons. First, the drop and settle decisions are likely to be linked because the former determines the pool of cases from which settlements are drawn. The above estimates are potentially inaccurate if these decisions are interdependent. Second, from a policy perspective it is the unconditional probabilities of settlement and going to trial that can be important: policy-makers might want to know the probability of a case reaching trial given that it was filed, not given that it was not dropped. Overcoming these problems requires the joint estimation of drop and settlement equations. Danzon and Lillard (1983) were the first to do this, but others such as Hughes and Snyder and Farber and White also use joint estimation techniques. Danzon and Lillard's study confirms those above concerning the role of damages (and, therefore, potential trial verdict).

C. Settlement timing and case duration

The above studies all ask "what is the probability of a case being settled?" An alternative approach asks, "what is the probability of a case being settled at a given point in time?"—i.e. what determines case duration? Studying this requires information on individual cases as they proceed; such information is reasonably rare.

Fournier and Zuehlke (1996) studied 18,498 U.S. cases (7,159 settled; 11,339 tried—an unusually high ratio of tried cases).[6] There are some case-level data (which measure the initial expectation of damages by the plaintiff) but the authors also use

---

[6] The data are interesting because they include a binary observation on whether the case was operated under the U.S. cost rule or fee shifting (see n 7), though note that these come from areas beyond the scope of this paper: copyright, marine tort, and Alaska diversity of citizenship cases.

estimates of state-level (i.e. public) expenditure on various types of litigation taken from RAND studies as a proxy for private litigation costs.

The authors find that the conditional probability of settlement rises (i.e. settlement becomes more likely) over time. Making the loser pay the winner's costs[7] increases settlement delay, but this effect diminishes over time. Higher litigation costs (proxied as described above) tend to increase the conditional probability of settlement while, generally, higher stakes and more uncertainty surrounding them tend to lower this probability. Interestingly, the effects of uncertainty diminish over time, no doubt as the parties' information is refined by settlement negotiations. Finally, Fournier and Zuelhke find that congestion in trial courts speeds settlement.

Fenn and Rickman (1999) use British data drawn from a number of English NHS Trusts relating to 734 medical negligence claims that were settled or abandoned during the period 1990 to 1995. A rich variety of information is recorded for each claim, including the dates of the initiation, settlement, or abandonment of the claim; and the defense costs incurred and damages paid (if any). In addition, and importantly, also recorded are the claims managers' estimates of likely value of the claim and the likelihood that the plaintiff would prevail in court.

Fenn and Rickman's results support those of Fournier and Zuelhke in several respects. Higher cost is associated with early settlement and high-severity cases take longer to settle (though this effect diminishes over time). Defendants who think themselves more likely to be held liable look to settle the case sooner. These results are also borne out by Fenn and Rickman's (2001) study of UK motor insurance claims.

Kessler (1996) focuses on the effects of several institutional arrangements on the timing of settlement. In particular, he is interested in comparing U.S. states which do and do not impose prejudgment interest on settlements. The reason for this lies in the received wisdom that such policies penalize delay and, therefore, encourage settlement.[8] The data used to estimate the conditional probability of settlement are from the American Insurance Research Council. The data set consists of 12,228 closed automobile insurance personal-injury claims from 34 insurers with variables including claimant characteristics, time from filing to closure, severity of injury, place of injury, and three types of legal environment: claims resolved in states employing prejudgment interest, claims resolved in states with comparative negligence rules, and states where the backlog of cases was large. Both of the latter control for factors which might reasonably be expected to affect settlement timing: in particular, Kessler (1996) indicates that comparative negligence increases the complexity of claims.

---

[7] This is the so-called "UK rule." Typically, in U.S. cases, both sides pay their own costs regardless of case outcome but there have been exceptions over time. Section IV.C discusses this in more detail.

[8] As Kessler notes, however, there is no clear theoretical support for this view.

In contrast to the findings of Fournier and Zuehlke (1996) and Fenn and Rickman (1999), the conditional probability of settlement generally declined over the first 30 months of the settlement process, and by this time 96% of claims had been settled. Thus, this probability falls over time. The factors contributing to this difference are not clear: it is possible that most insurance claims settle quickly and that this drives the result (though not in Fenn and Rickman's 2001 study of UK motor insurance data). Kessler finds that claims from urban areas take longer to settle than claims from rural ones, and more complicated/serious claims take longer to settle. Factors relating to the legal system itself, such as prejudgment interest, court backlogs and comparative negligence rules, each slow settlement. The effect of prejudgment interest is of interest because it may be counter-intuitive: a policy designed to speed up the settlement process actually leads to increases in the settlement delay. It is also notable that, in contrast to the finding in Fournier and Zuelhke's study, Kessler's finding suggests that court congestion works its way back into the settlement process.

D. Settlement amounts

What factors influence the settlement amount? There is unanimous agreement across Danzon and Lillard (1983), Fournier and Zuehlke (1989), Fenn and Vlachonikolis (1990), Sloan and Hoerger (1989), Farber and White (1991), and Farber and White (1994) that increases in economic loss (and hence, expected trial award) raise the settlement amount. In all the papers, however, the responsiveness here is less than one-to-one (generally located between 0.4 and 0.7). Sloan and Hoerger report that the sensitivity of settlements to economic loss also depends on the defendant's apparent liability: when this is uncertain, settlement sums are less sensitive to economic loss—the system appears to make adjustments for the quality of a claim. The authors estimate that settlements are 74% of the expected trial award. Danzon and Lillard (1983) infer even higher plaintiff bargaining power, with settlement levels estimated to be 87% of the defendant's maximum offers.

Costs seem to work in the expected direction, with both Fournier and Zuehlke's and Danzon and Lillard's proxies for plaintiff's costs lowering settlement amounts as the costs rise and raising them as defendant's costs rise (e.g., Danzon and Lillard estimate that greater court congestion lowers the settlement amount by 0.15% for every 1% increase in congestion). Finally, Danzon and Lillard also estimate that legal representation increases settlement amounts by 28%. Sloan and Hoerger find that *specialist* legal representation raises the settlement amount and they question why only 25% of their sample retained a specialist (something Williams and

Williams, 1994, also ponder).[9] Fenn and Vlachonikolis (1990) find that additional time between event and first offer increases the offer and that settlement offers rise over time.

E. Tort reform and the "freeway principle"

In Section II, we noted the linkages that may exist between different stages of the litigation process and the possibility that behavior at one stage may affect behavior at other stages. The "freeway principle" is the term coined by Danzon and Lillard (1983) to describe this.

Danzon and Lillard consider the effects of reducing plaintiff's and defendant's costs on a representative case by 30% (they interpret this as, perhaps, simulating the effects of switching to arbitration). Results are purely illustrative but they indicate that a reduction in costs of this scale would reduce overall expenditure on litigation by only 3%. The "freeway principle" explains the result: "adding more lanes does not simply move the current flow of traffic faster, because when the cost per trip falls more traffic enters the system" (p. 374). Effectively, lower costs reduce the probability of dropping the case (from 0.421 to 0.401), increase the probability of settlement (from 0.523 to 0.530) and increase the probability of trial (from 0.056 to 0.069).

IV. THE ROLE OF THE LEGAL SYSTEM

Having looked at the basic outcomes of litigation, we now consider several ways in which the legal system might help to shape these. In particular, we look at the role it has in providing information to help the parties reach a decision, how it selects cases for trial, and the role of the allocation of costs in determining outcomes.[10]

---

[9] Both conclude that the problem lies in the market for legal services, where clients do not have sufficient comprehensible information on the supply of specialists. Thomason (1991) reports a negative return to legal representation—see the discussion in Section V.

[10] A related empirical literature seeks to adjudicate between two views of litigation that are common in economic models: "divergent expectations" (where trials can emerge via genuine differences in litigants' interpretation of evidence) and "asymmetric information" (where trials can emerge because the parties hold private information and use it strategically). See Waldfogel (1998) and Osborne (1999) for specific attempts to compare these models, and Fournier and Zuehlke (1996), Fenn and Rickman (1999), and Sieg (2000) for attempts to estimate equations based on an asymmetric model of litigation.

A. Information transfer and informal dispute resolution

Several of the papers discussed in this section attempt to model the extent to which information flows between the litigants during negotiations. Fenn and Vlachonikolis (1990) and Sloan and Hoerger (1989) do this by choosing an interview sample that provides them with data on the settlement process itself. Farber and White (1991; 1994) do it by analyzing claims data on suing and settling.

Farber and White use data on a U.S. hospital's use of informal dispute resolution (IDR) processes, which they interpret as a mechanism for information transfer. In particular, the hospital can use IDR to transfer information to the claimant when it (the hospital) has a strong case. Alternatively, when the hospital has a weak case, it can use IDR to screen plaintiffs in terms of their "litigiousness." Thus IDR can reduce the hospital's exposure to legal claims in two ways: by enabling it to defeat claims speedily when it has a strong answer, and by forcing claimants to make a commitment (by filing a suit) when the hospital's position is weak (the hospital can then settle these quickly). Farber and White's results are consistent with this interpretation. In general, cases with lower reported care quality, or ones with more severe damages, are more likely to end in a lawsuit being filed. Among cases that are filed, lower care quality and more severe damages also generate higher settlement amounts. Interestingly, the (small) number of claims reaching trial are indistinguishable from those being dropped or dismissed, and Farber and White note that that is consistent with the conjecture that claims go to trial as a result of "mistakes" made by plaintiffs.[11]

Fenn and Vlachonikolis (1990) analyze British data from interviews with people who made claims for personal injury damages, most of which would be defended by an insurer. The picture that emerged from their econometric analysis is of settlement negotiations taking place in an environment where parties have information that their opponents do not and, implicitly, may behave strategically. Specifically, the plaintiff begins with private information about the harm she has suffered and the defendant seeks to elicit this through settlement offers. When offers are rejected, the defendant either revises the offer (upwards) or chooses not to make a fresh one. Higher offers are made in more severe cases but there is also a higher probability in such cases that no offer will be made or, if an offer is made, that it will be rejected (because the plaintiff's private information on damages is appreciably different than the defendant's expectations).[12]

---

[11] Farber and White (1991) also produce *tentative* estimates for the savings to the hospital from operating IDR. These amount to $2.5 million over the 597 cases in their sample. If plaintiffs also save this, total savings per case are $8,500.

[12] Kritzer (1990) also presents some interesting evidence for the existence, and effectiveness, of strategic bargaining by litigants' lawyers. He analyzes data from the U.S. Civil Litigation Research Project (a major study of U.S. civil litigation commissioned by the U.S. Justice Department in 1979), which spans five federal judicial districts and contains case-level information on approximately 1,500

Negotiations play a role in producing information, but certain procedures are also designed to achieve this. In particular, discovery rules aim to force cards onto the table and reduce incentives for strategic concealment of information. From one point of view, discovery rules are benign and constructive features of the legal process. However, from another perspective they allow parties to make expensive demands of the opposition, thereby driving up costs and deterring potentially legitimate claims. These are plainly legitimate issues for empirical research though, arguably, the literature has not taken them head on. Two partial exceptions are Shephard (1999) and Huang (2009). The former's U.S. study suggests that plaintiffs' use of discovery is driven by their opinion about the case's requirements while their opponent's appears to copy the plaintiff's. A change occurs if there is a possibility that the opponent's use of discovery is "excessive"[13]: plaintiffs seem to reduce discovery requests when there is a chance that the defendant's use is "excessive," while the defendant responds aggressively to "excessive" requests by plaintiffs. Rather than study the use made of discovery, Huang (2009) uses data from Taiwan to look at its effects, particularly on the likelihood of settlement. Huang argues that movement to an open discovery system in 2000 stopped litigants from holding back information until case meetings and, instead, encouraged the introduction of limited discovery. Huang's results suggest that this reform promoted settlement.

B. The selection of cases for trial

An extensive literature has developed to test a hypothesis originally proposed by Priest and Klein (1984).[14] The "selection hypothesis" argues that the cases which reach trial will not be a random draw from the population of cases but, instead, will be "selected out" by the legal system.[15] In particular, Priest and Klein argue that trials are most likely when the parties differ in their expectations over the likely trial verdict; in turn, this implies that there is a degree of uncertainty surrounding the quality of the plaintiff's case. The limiting case of the selection effect occurs when the parties have identical stakes at trial (i.e. they agree on the size of the verdict) and identical information sets (i.e., they agree about the issues at trial). In this

cases, supplemented by interviews with over 1,300 of the lawyers involved and several hundred of the litigants. Measuring the degree of strategic bargaining by the difference between initial demands and the plaintiff's (private) estimates of the stakes, he finds that strategic bargaining has a highly significant, positive, influence on plaintiff recoveries.

[13] "Excessive" use of discovery is obviously hard to measure since it relates to an unobservable optimum.

[14] For a different approach to selection effects in litigation, see Eisenberg and Farber (1997).

[15] Wittman (1985) and Priest (1985) debate the validity of Priest and Klein's hypothesis.

case, they can only disagree about the probability that the plaintiff will win and, as a result, only cases with the maximum degree of uncertainty—a 50% chance of victory for the plaintiff—go to trial. As a result, it is expected that the plaintiff will win 50% of trials. The selection hypothesis is important because it emphasizes the problems of extrapolating from research based on trial cases to the population of all cases. Both Kessler et al. (1996) and, more recently, Hylton and Lin (2009) provide good surveys of the literature here, so we simply indicate some of the results.

A number of papers confirm the existence of a selection effect on cases appearing at trial, although several (e.g., Eisenberg, 1990) reject the 50% prediction.[16] Hylton and Lin (2009) argue that some rejections are in areas of law (such as medical negligence) where information asymmetries favor the defendant; and so these results are consistent with amended versions of the selection hypothesis. Of course, they may also be associated with asymmetric stakes to the extent that the defendant has interests that are likely to stretch beyond the case at hand (e.g., hospital physicians may wish to avoid a high-profile court case).[17]

C. Cost rules

As pointed out earlier, costs can affect outcomes of litigation. Crucial here is the way these costs are allocated between the parties. Under the so-called "UK rule" the loser pays the winner's costs (in other words, it "shifts" the costs), while under the so-called "U.S. rule" each party bears its own costs. Comparison of the effects of these rules requires a situation where both have existed within sufficiently close jurisdictions or time periods to permit a controlled experiment (which is rare) or the design of experiments to simulate such situations (see Stanley and Coursey, 1988).

Two papers (Snyder and Hughes, 1990; Hughes and Snyder, 1995) analyze a sample of 10,325 medical negligence cases from the state of Florida, dating from the late 1970s to the middle of the 1980s. Of the cases in the sample, 58% were litigated under the UK rule (which operated for a time in such cases in Florida) and the rest were litigated under the U.S. rule. Because they have information on whether cases were dropped, settled, or tried, the authors are able to assess the impact of the costs rules

---

[16]   Other studies of note are Siegelman and Donohue III (1995), Waldfogel (1995), Kessler et al. (1996); Eisenberg and Heise (2009) examine the selection hypothesis in appellate cases. Further, Stanley and Coursey (1988) and Thomas (1995) provide experimental evidence for the selection effect. Finally, Elder (1989) applies the effect to criminal cases: the plea bargaining process is shown to select cases for trial on the basis of prosecution and defense views of case strength.

[17]   It is also interesting that Farber and White (1991; 1994) describe the cases that reach trial in their papers as being mistakes on the plaintiff's part: large defendants with a good deal at stake in a given case are likely to have settled cases which they might lose at trial well before this stage.

on these decisions by comparing the sub-samples of cases litigated under the U.S. and UK rules respectively.[18]

To begin with, Snyder and Hughes (1990) present evidence consistent with the hypothesis that the UK rule encourages plaintiffs to file (because it allows cost-shifting) but, as time passes, leads them to reassess and drop claims at a higher rate than occurs under the U.S.—possibly because the UK rule causes them to focus on the downside risks in the case as trial approaches.

Of course, these two results—on filing and dropping—work in opposite directions: an increased propensity to file a case raises the volume of litigation while a higher propensity to drop claims once filed lowers it. We therefore need some way of combining these in order to see the overall effect of cost rules on the number of cases being dropped, settled, and tried. To do this, Snyder and Hughes use their findings to predict how a hypothetical sample of cases would be treated under the UK and U.S. rules respectively. They find that, if 1,000 cases were filed under the two rules then over 100 more would be dropped under the UK rule than the U.S. one. Further, a smaller number of the cases (roughly half as many) would go to trial under the UK rule. Therefore, although the UK rule makes trial more likely for a given case if it is not dropped, the fact that this rule also leads to more cases being dropped means that, overall, it causes fewer cases to reach trial. Thus, it appears that the UK rule causes a more careful evaluation of the case's strengths to take place once it has been filed. The presence of conflicting linkages across the stages of litigation is another example of the "freeway principle" identified earlier.

Economic theory predicts parties' expenditures will be higher under the UK rule than its U.S. counterpart: effectively, the UK rule creates an "arms race" as the parties seek to shift litigation costs. Snyder and Hughes support this prediction, for both settled and tried cases. Also, the margins concerned appear to be quite large.

The results from this paper help illuminate the quantitative effects of UK and U.S. costs rules. Of particular interest is the empirical support they lend to the proposition that one should look at the whole litigation process before judging the overall effects of reform of costs rules (or any others). It is only when Snyder and Hughes combine the overall effects of the UK rule on cases dropped and settled that they are able to conclude that this rule will lead to fewer trials than its U.S. counterpart.

Hughes and Snyder (1995) estimate the effects in their sample of the UK rule on plaintiffs' rates of winning at trial, the size of trial judgments and settlement amounts. They find that the UK rule increases the probability of a plaintiff's success at trial by 8.2%. Trial judgments were 240% higher under the UK rule. The distribution of

---

[18] They are not, however, able to say anything about how the rules affect the number of accidents and, therefore, the overall volume of litigation.

judgments indicates that the UK rule induces relatively more high-value cases to go to trial. Finally, on settlement sizes, the authors again find that settlements in cases brought under the UK rule are generally higher by 30%—except for cases valued below $10,000.

The results from these papers raise an important question: does the UK rule have the effect of "taxing" litigants and therefore possibly damaging the prospects of small, reasonably meritorious claims? Or, does it instead act as a screening device for ensuring that cases proceeding through the litigation system are of high merit? The distributional consequences of this question are important, as are the efficiency implications. Arguably, before such a question can be addressed, more attention needs to be paid to the role of risk aversion in negotiating under different cost rules.

V. FEES AND LITIGATION

Significant debate surrounds the effects of different fee arrangements on the way in which lawyers handle litigation and the case outcomes achieved for clients.[19] Obviously, testing for such effects requires data with fee variation, and developments in a number of jurisdictions have made such work feasible in recent years. For example, variations in contingent fee regulations across American states, and changes in these regulations over time, have encouraged fee research in the United States. In England and Wales, the growth of conditional fee agreements and after-the-event insurance products, which has followed the removal of legal aid for most personal injury litigation, has created opportunities for comparative fee research. We summarize several papers here.[20]

In a series of research reports written for the UK's Ministry of Justice, Fenn, Gray, and Rickman examine the effects of developments in funding arrangements in England and Wales.[21] The demise of legal aid in 1999 followed the introduction of conditional fee arrangements in 1995. These made the lawyer's (hourly) fee contingent upon winning the case and, to compensate for this risk, allowed the lawyer to claim a pre-specified percentage mark-up on hourly fees in the event of a win. Under the UK cost rule, this still left the plaintiff liable for adverse costs if the case was lost, so "after-the-event" (ATE) insurance policies appeared to cover

---

[19] The economic issues are surveyed in Rickman (1994).
[20] See Fenn and Rickman (2009) for a more thorough survey.
[21] The studies were actually written for previous incarnations of the Ministry: the Lord Chancellor's Department and, then, the Department of Constitutional Affairs.

these. The combined package of conditional fee arrangements plus ATE policy is called a conditional fee agreement (CFA). Overall, the switch from legal aid toward CFAs exposed lawyers to new income risk, and the authors suggest that this may influence the types of case lawyers accept (stronger ones becoming preferable), litigation strategies (such as settling earlier to avoid risk), and the payoffs received by the plaintiff (e.g., via having to hand an element of winnings to the lawyer and insurer).[22] Interestingly, these themes mirror the complementary research on contingency fees from the US.

Fenn, Gray, and Rickman's studies span the removal of legal aid and development of CFAs. The first (Fenn et al., 1999) collected data from closed insurance claim files and clinical negligence claims. From a fees perspective, the former data set is more interesting because of a lack of variation in the funding of clinical negligence cases (where legal aid was still allowed for this higher-cost, riskier, class of claims). Importantly (both here and in their other studies), the authors collected data on the lawyer's private estimate of the probability of winning—the case merits. They find that legally aided cases appear to be screened only on the basis of injury-severity whereas cases taken under a CFA were also screened on their merits. There is also evidence of client "self-screening" in the sense that client-funded hourly-fee cases generally received the highest merits assessments from their lawyers. The authors also found that legally aided cases settled sooner than CFAs (see also Fenn and Rickman, 1999; 2001).

A follow-up study (Fenn et al., 2002) collected data from closed claim files held by lawyers. Again, the data concentrate on CFAs, hourly fees, and the remaining legally aided claims. Once more, plaintiffs bearing the most risk (self-funded under hourly fees arrangements) pursued cases with the best prospects, while estimated liability was similar across CFAs and legal aid. The authors were also able to comment on the return for risk-bearing required by lawyers; as would be expected, the percentage mark-up specified by lawyers in CFAs was negatively correlated with estimates of the defendant's liability. Looking at payoffs, CFA lawyers appeared to achieve higher gross settlements for plaintiffs, but these were reduced by subtraction of success fees and ATE premiums,[23] leaving a net payoff below those in legally aided and hourly-fee claims.[24]

---

[22] In fact, the success fee and ATE premium were made recoverable from losing defendants in 2000. In itself, this raised interesting problems beyond the scope of this paper (see Fenn and Rickman, 2003).

[23] Later reform made these recoverable from the losing defendant but, for the period covered by Fenn et al. (2002), the plaintiff was responsible for paying these.

[24] The results suggest support for both sides of the access-to-justice debate surrounding the regulation of no-win-no-fee-style arrangements. On the one hand, fee regulation may limit compensation for risk-taking so that cases with the highest risk profiles may not be accepted at the margin. On the other hand, they are also consistent with worries about the effects of lower net payoffs on access to justice, despite the fact that lawyers may partially offset this by pushing for higher gross payoffs.

By the time of Fenn et al.'s most recent study (2006), it was clear that funders such as legal expenses insurers offering "before-the-event" policies[25] and trade unions, as well as privately funded clients, were using CFAs. Thus, the role of funders needed to be controlled for. The study collected data from closed files held by defendants' and plaintiffs' insurers and found that the estimated probability that the defendant was liable was likely to be higher in CFA cases funded by third parties than in CFA cases funded by the plaintiff, and that cases of the former type were likely to settle sooner than cases in the latter category. This raises the possibility that the incentive to maintain a flow of cases from bulk purchasers, such as trade unions, may influence case screening and handling by lawyers—a possibility needing more research. The authors also collect data from clinical negligence claims where it is interesting to see a gentle rise in the use of CFAs relative to legal aid, perhaps suggesting that ATE insurers were becoming better at evaluating the costs and risks of these often more-heterogeneous claims. Nonetheless, CFAs still accounted for higher value, lower risk claims, as would be expected.

Turning to U.S. studies, which are based more heavily on contingency fees, Kritzer (1990) tests for what he calls a "structuring effect" (on how lawyers working under contingent and hourly fees handle their cases) and a "magnitude effect" (on how many hours they put into a case).[26] The motivation for such studies is that several economic models suggest that lawyers working under a contingent fee system will seek to settle a case quickly in order to maximize their surplus before costs wipe out the contingent percentage. In contrast, an hourly fee lawyer is paid to cover all costs, so this effect should not appear and the lawyer may spend more time on the case and perform more services in the course of pursuing it. These effects were tested using a sample of 273 contingent fee cases and 374 hourly fee ones.

The results indicate that "fee arrangement has a substantial impact on the process by which lawyers allocate time to cases" (p. 117), i.e., it has a structuring effect. In particular, contingent-fee lawyers are more heavily influenced by what Kritzer terms "productivity" variables and less by "craft-oriented" ones. Thus, these lawyers spend half as much time responding to opposing party briefs than hourly-fee lawyers, but offer relatively more hours when the stakes (and hence, the potential fee) are large. Further, the effect of the ability of the client to control or monitor the lawyer is to lower the time an hourly-fee lawyer spends on the case but to increase that spent by a contingent fee lawyer (though, in the case of contingency fees, the effect is statistically insignificant).

---

[25] I.e. policies purchased in advance of any potential accident (as opposed to after the accident—as with "after-the-event" policies).

[26] Kritzer has done other important work on the effects of contingency fees. These are well summarized in Kritzer (2004).

Turning to whether there is a magnitude effect, Kritzer's answer is "Maybe, but it depends" (p. 118). By varying the stakes in the case between $0 and $100,000, he finds that hourly-fee lawyers put in more hours in cases up to $30,000 while contingent-fee lawyers put more effort into cases with higher stakes. However, only at stakes below $6,000 are the differences statistically significant and the implied difference in hours (seven) "is not large" (p. 120). The results suggest little difference between the two fee schemes once other variables have been controlled for.

Thomason (1991) employs a different approach to finding variation in payoffs under fee types. He does not compare contingent and hourly-fee outcomes but employs data from workers' compensation claims in New York for the period (1971–1977) when a mixture of fee regimes were in operation: in particular, cases attracting lump-sum payments involved a flat fee (typically 10% of the award), while other claims involved a contingent percentage depending on the compensation recovered and stage reached. In addition, of course, workers' compensation claims are often made by litigants in person (and without legal fees)—another source of variation. Thomason's results suggest that contingency-fee cases tend to settle earlier and for less than their counterparts under other fee regimes. In a result that echoes Fenn et al. (2006), he also finds that that the removal of the contingent percentage leaves the return attributable to legal representation *negative*. Helland and Tabarrok (2003) note, however, that self-selection could play a role here, with weaker cases being taken to lawyers—i.e., a measure of underlying case quality is required in the data to take account of this. They also note that it is impossible to distinguish the effect of representation from that of fees in the results. Thus, although Thomason's evidence points to some areas of potential conflict between lawyer and client, the results may not be robust enough to indicate its extent and significance.

Helland and Taborrok (2003) extend Danzon and Lillard's (1983) earlier analysis by looking at different types of claim in different states. They examine determinants of "case quality" and the timing of settlement. The probability of the case being dropped is used as a proxy for the former: it is argued that more drops means poorer case screening at the beginning, making this a proxy for lawyer-monitoring strength. Of course, more drops could equally imply that lawyers take their monitoring role seriously once the case is in motion and information is produced.

The authors estimate the probability that a case is dropped, and the time to settle those that remain—they do this across, and across time in one state (Florida) either side of a change in contingency fee regulations. Taking drops first, the evidence from state courts suggests a statistically insignificant 7–13 percentage point increase in drops between the most loosely and the most tightly regulated states. The Florida data indicate a 15% increase in the drop rate immediately after the introduction of contingency fee limits. Moving to duration, the authors' estimates show a 21%

increase in time taken to settle when fee limits are present. The Florida data exhibited an 11.1% increase in time to settlement in the 13 months following the fee change, when compared with the ten months before it.

Helland and Tabarrok interpret their findings as being consistent with a hypothesis that contingency fee limits reduce the lawyers' incentives to monitor cases carefully: weaker cases are started and those that do not drop take longer to settle. Apparently, regulations designed to protect clients may have had unintended consequences. It is notable that the results on drops run counter to those in Danzon and Lillard's earlier study (which is consistent with the alternative interpretation of drops sketched above).[27] Other authors have suggested that contingency fees encourage lawyers to perform a gate-keeping role (e.g., see Kritzer, 2004: 67–88). and neither of the above papers is inconsistent with this because they do not benchmark against non-contingency fee regimes. Nonetheless, the conflicting results suggest that detecting this gate-keeping role may be a little more complicated than it initially appears.

VI. Deterrence

It was pointed out earlier that two key functions of a liability-based litigation system are to compensate injury victims and to deter future accidents (by making those who are liable bear the costs). Our remaining sections examine these issues by asking whether litigation achieves deterrence and how well alternative compensation systems operate. Space constraints permit only brief indicators of some of the issues. We begin with deterrence.

The deterrence properties of liability schemes are well known from seminal works such as Shavell (1987). These make clear that the conditions for liability schemes to provide "optimal" deterrence (where the marginal costs of care equal their marginal benefits) are demanding. This raises a question mark over whether sufficient deterrence can be achieved, but it does not necessarily follow that there will be no deterrence. Most empirical research has looked for evidence of some measure of deterrence rather than attempting to consider whether an optimal amount has been achieved.

Two sorts of relevant evidence are available. The first is provided by simulations that examine how different liability rules might affect behavior under plausible

---

[27] We have mentioned that a benefit of the data in Fenn, Gray, and Rickman's studies is the presence of estimated liability. This prevents the need to make inferences about case strength from observed actions.

circumstances (Danzon, 1994). The second is provided by looking at situations where liability and non-liability based schemes (so-called "no fault" schemes) operate in parallel; this permits comparison of the two schemes. Cummins et al. (2001) undertake an analysis of the latter type based on motor accident claims in the United States where some states operate a negligence-based liability scheme and others operate no fault schemes. They find that fatal accidents are 5–9% more likely under a no fault regime. Other research has found similar results in Australasia and Quebec. Other research suggests that liability-based schemes have no significant deterrent effect.

If liability systems do deter, can we gauge whether they do so to excess—i.e., do they generate defensive care levels? This question is difficult to answer because there is no clear way to assess the optimal level of care. A number of studies have sought to examine levels of care in more or less risky situations and to infer "defensiveness" from this. Results are mixed. For example, in early work, Localio et al. (1993) found statistically significant links between several obstetric procedures and previous claims experience (in New York State). However, Baldwin et al. (1995) could not confirm this result. Kessler and McClellan (1996) find a negative relationship between tort reform (i.e., reductions in liability) and the costs of a compensation system; and they interpret this as evidence of defensive medicine (see also Kessler and McClellan, 2002). The empirical ambiguities here are perhaps inevitable given the measurement difficulties involved. Resolving these is an important challenge for future research.

VII. Alternative Means of Compensation

We end this Chapter with a brief discussion of other means of compensating personal injuries, most notably "no fault" schemes. Under such schemes, compensation is paid regardless of any fault on the part of the injurer—or, at least, that is the starting point: in practice, a number of issues have affected the operation of no fault schemes, and these have met with different responses across different countries and settings. A natural way to assess different compensation arrangements is to compare their operation across different countries. This is difficult because assembling reliable comparable data is not straightforward.[28]

While "no fault" schemes do not apply an explicit negligence standard, they nonetheless operate eligibility criteria for payouts; otherwise they would face heavy

---

[28] Fenn et al. (2004) discuss comparisons in more detail.

claim volumes. Such criteria may take a variety of forms, including thresholds for minimum compensable injury and requirements to identify "error" as the source of the injury suffered. Studdert et al. (1997) model the application of a minimum four-week-off-work injury threshold and a cap on compensation for pain and suffering and find that it reduces claims from 132 per 100,000 population to 66. Thus, expenditure control is achieved at the expense of smaller-value claims, which tend to form the bulk of claims. The use of "error"-based compensation criteria has become common: in the medical injury compensation schemes in Sweden, New Zealand, Colorado, and Utah, no fault schemes have all used this. Taking Sweden as an example, a claim is compensable if (1) it occurred with "substantial probability" as a direct consequence of clinical error and (2) either the treatment was not clinically justified or the injury could have been avoided by offering different treatment. It therefore appears hard to define a basis for compensation that does not recognize clinical error.

Another important issue for no fault schemes is whether they allow victims a "parallel tort" claim. This can be quite important, as Florida's 20% tort "leakage rates" suggest (Sloan et al., 1997). Interestingly, Swedish claimants also have recourse to tort but are far less frequent litigators. One important reason is that the relatively generous social security provision available there significantly reduces tort awards, making litigation "uncompetitive."

One of the justifications for a no fault scheme is the saving in administrative costs that follows from not having to prove liability in a complex legal case. Studdert et al. (1997) suggest administrative costs of 30% per claim dollar under no fault (compared to 55% under tort in these states). Estimates for Florida in Bovbjerg et al. (1997) suggest that no fault administrative costs resemble fixed costs so that the cost/damages ratio falls as case value rises. As with liability schemes, an important question is whether these savings come at the cost of deterrence, which no fault decouples from the question of compensation. Deterrence may be pursued via some form of monitoring and reporting system (whose costs often do not appear in the estimates of administrative costs). It is hard to assess the performance of such arrangements, but question marks have been raised. For example, in Sweden a Medical Responsibility Board has monitored claims against clinicians and imposes penalties as required, but there are suggestions that it has not consistently been notified when a claim is brought against a clinician. Bovbjerg et al. (1997) raise a similar concern about monitoring and reporting arrangements in Florida. In New Zealand, by contrast, it was intended to levy experience-rated premiums on clinicians, but according to Paterson (2001) this has never happened. Studdert and Brennan (2001) are more sanguine about the prospects for experience-rating and enterprise liability in Utah and Colorado. Overall, while the deterrence effects of any scheme (fault or no fault) are hard to measure, there is some evidence that the costs of making alternative deterrence arrangements alongside no fault schemes should not be overlooked.

VIII. CONCLUSIONS

It is difficult (and dangerous) to draw firm conclusions from a wide-ranging survey such as this, particularly when studies relate to different jurisdictions. In such circumstances it is perhaps prudent to emphasize the results that appear regularly, thereby relying on the "weight of numbers" to give some strength to the conclusions. In this respect, several broad conclusions might be drawn.

First, there appears to be consistent evidence that economic variables, and the incentives they provide to litigants, do influence decisions taken during litigation. Thus, litigation costs, expected damages (and their variance), expectations about defendant liability, and the role of negotiations in transferring information all affect litigants' behavior in ways which are consistent with economic models of litigation. In particular, high expected damages tend to make cases more likely to be brought but have an ambiguous influence on settlement probability while increasing settlement amounts. There is evidence of risk aversion affecting these decisions, despite the fact that some plaintiffs can shift some risk to their lawyer under contingent fees, or CFAs with after-the-event insurance. High litigation costs (as measured by various proxies) generally make cases easier to settle, although there is some evidence that this may not be so when the strength of the plaintiff's case can be questioned. Defendants who think themselves liable seek to settle cases quickly, unless they have a mechanism to screen out some plaintiffs (such as an informal dispute resolution mechanism).

Second, it is important to be aware of the possibility that reforms at one stage of the litigation process may have offsetting effects elsewhere, thereby reducing (or negating) the effects of the reforms: the "freeway principle." This does not mean that successful reform is impossible but that research may improve the chance of success.

Third, there is good evidence that the selection of cases appearing at any stage of the litigation process is biased by what happened at earlier stages. It is important to be aware of this when drawing conclusions from a subset of claims. Such bias may particularly affect the category of tried cases since these typically represent a very small sample of all cases and have been through the most stages of litigation.

Fourth, empirical analysis is often particularly helpful for clarifying or assessing frequently stated opinions about aspects of litigation. A good example of this relates to contingency fees which, in a number of jurisdictions, have remained illegal on the basis of concerns about the outcomes they achieve for plaintiffs. It is not clear what the empirical basis is for such concerns.

Despite these observations, it is important to emphasize how much more there is to discover and test about personal injury litigation: a combination of theory and empirical work can play a central role here. As testable hypotheses and econometric techniques—as well as policy initiatives—are all developed, the crucial "missing link" is often data. Improvements in the collection and availability of internationally consistent data, particularly before policy initiatives are in place, would aid benchmarking comparison, and would be likely to pay for themselves in terms of better policy and understanding. Of course, multidisciplinary research must also play a role here. By indicating how economics can contribute, the current Chapter might also encourage fruitful collaborations with other disciplines in this area.

REFERENCES

Baldwin, L.M., Hart, L.G., Lloyd, M., Fordyce, M., and Rosenblatt, R.A. (1995). "Defensive medicine and obstetrics," *Journal of the American Medical Association* 274(20): 1606–10.

Bovbjerg, R.R., Sloan, F.A., and Rankin, P.J. (1997). "Administrative performance of 'no-fault' compensation for medical injury," *Law and Contemporary Problems* 60(2): 71–115.

Cummins, J.D., Weiss, M.A., and Phillips, R.D. (2001). "The incentive effects of no-fault automobile insurance," *Journal of Law and Economics* 44(2): 427–64.

Danzon, P.M. (1994). "The Swedish patient compensation system: Myths and realities," *International Review of Law and Economics* 14(4): 453–66.

Danzon, P.M. and Lillard, L.A. (1983). "Settlement out of court: The disposition of medical malpractice claims," *Journal of Legal Studies* 12(2): 345–77.

Eisenberg, T. (1990). "Testing the selection effect: A new theoretical framework with empirical tests," *Journal of Legal Studies* 19(2): 337–58.

Eisenberg, T. and Farber, H. (1997). "The litigious plaintiff hypothesis: Case selection and resolution," *RAND Journal of Economics* 28: S92–S112.

Eisenberg, T. and Heise, M. (2009). "Plaintiphobia in State Courts? An empirical study of State Court trials on Appeal," *Journal of Legal Studies* 38(1): 121–55.

Eisenberg, T. and Lanvers, C. (2009). "What is the settlement rate and why should we care?," *Journal of Empirical Legal Studies* 6(1): 111–46.

Elder, H.W. (1989). "Trials and settlements in the criminal courts: An empirical analysis of dispositions and sentencing," *Journal of Legal Studies* 18(1): 191–208.

Farber, H. and White, M. (1991). "Medical malpractice: An empirical examination of the litigation process," *RAND Journal of Economics* 22(2): 199–217.

Farber, H. and White, M. (1994). "A comparison of formal and informal dispute resolution in medical malpractice," *Journal of Legal Studies* 23(2): 777–806.

Fenn, P. and Rickman, N. (1999). "Delay and settlement in litigation," *Economic Journal* 109(457): 476–91.

Fenn, P. and Rickman, N. (2001). "Asymmetric information and the settlement of insurance claims: Theory and evidence," *Journal of Risk and Insurance* 68(4): 615–30.

Fenn, P. and Rickman, N. (2003). *Costs of low value RTA claims 1997–2002: A report prepared for the Civil Justice Council, UK.*

Fenn, P. and Rickman, N. (2009). "The empirical analysis of litigation funding," Conference paper, Mimeo, Nottingham University Business School and Department of Economics, University of Surrey," forthcoming in M. Tuil and L. Visscher (eds), *New Trends in Financing Civil Litigation in Europe: A Legal, Empirical, and Economic Analysis* (2010), Cheltenham: Edward Elgar Publishing.

Fenn, P. and Vlachonikolis, I. (1990). "Bargaining behaviour by defendant insurers: An economic model," *Geneva Papers on Risk and Assurance* 14(54): 41–52.

Fenn, P., Gray, A., and Rickman, N. (1999). *The impact of plaintiff finance on litigants' behaviour: An empirical analysis.* Lord Chancellor's Department Research Report, 5/99, London.

Fenn, P., Gray, A., and Rickman, N. (2004). "The economics of clinical negligence reform in England," *Economic Journal* 114, F272–F292.

Fenn, P., Gray, A., Rickman, N., and Carrier, H. (2002). *The impact of conditional fees on the selection, handling and outcomes of personal injury cases.* Lord Chancellor's Department Research Report, 7/2002, London.

Fenn, P., Gray, A., Rickman, N., and Mansur, Y. (2006). The funding of personal injury litigation: Comparisons over time and across jurisdictions. Department of Constitutional Affairs Research Report, 2/2006, London.

Fournier, G.M. and Zuehlke, T.W. (1989). "Litigation and settlement: An empirical approach," *Review of Economics and Statistics* 71(2): 189–95.

Fournier, G.M. and Zuehlke, T. (1996). "The timing of out–of–court settlement," *RAND Journal of Economics* 27(2): 310–21.

Friedman, A.E. (1969). "An analysis of settlement," *Stanford Law Review* 22: 67–100.

Gould, J.P. (1973). "The economics of legal conflicts," *Journal of Legal Studies* 2(2): 279–300.

Helland, E. and Tabarrok, A. (2003). "Contingency fees, settlement delay and low-quality litigation: Empirical evidence from two datasets," *Journal of Law, Economics, and Organisation* 19(2): 517–42.

Huang, K.-C. (2009). "Does discovery promote settlement? An empirical answer," *Journal of Empirical Legal Studies* 6(2): 241–78.

Hughes, J.W. and Snyder, E.A. (1989). "Policy analysis of medical malpractice reforms: What can we learn from claims data?," *Journal of Business and Economic Statistics* 7(4): 423–31.

Hughes, J.W. and Snyder, E.A. (1995). "Litigation and settlement under the English and American rules: Theory and evidence," *Journal of Law and Economics* 38(1): 225–50.

Hylton, K.N. and Lin, H. (2009). Trial selection theory and evidence: A review. Working Paper, School of Law, Boston University.

Kessler, D. (1996). "Institutional causes of delay in the settlement of legal disputes," *Journal of Law, Economics, and Organisation* 12(2): 432–60.

Kessler, D. and McClellan, M. (1996). "Do doctors practice defensive medicine?," *Quarterly Journal of Economics* 111(2): 353–90.

Kessler, D. and McClellan, M. (2002). "Medical liability, managed care, and defensive medicine," *Journal of Public Economics* 84(2): 175–97.

Kessler, D., Meites, T., and Miller, G. (1996). "Explaining deviations from the fifty-percent rule: A multimodal approach to the selection of cases for litigation," *Journal of Legal Studies* 25(1): 233–59.

Kritzer, H.M. (1990). *The Justice Broker: Lawyers and Ordinary Litigation,* Oxford University Press, Oxford.

Kritzer, H.M. (2004). *Risks, Reputations and Rewards: Contingency Fee Practice in the United States,* Stanford University Press, Stanford CA.

Localio, A.R., Lawthers, A., Bengtson, J.M., Hebert, L.E., Weaver, S.L., Brennan, T.A., and Landis, J.R. (1993). "Relationship between malpractice claims and cesarean delivery," *Journal of the American Medical Association* 269(3): 366–73.

Nalebuff, B. (1987). "Credible pretrial negotiation," *RAND Journal of Economics* 18(2): 198–210.

Osborne, E. (1999). "Who should be worried about asymmetric information in litigation?," *International Review of Law and Economics* 19(3): 399–409.

Posner, R.S. (1973). "An economic approach to legal procedure and judicial administration," *Journal of Legal Studies* 2(2): 399–458.

Priest, G.L. (1985). "Reexamining the selection hypothesis: Learning from Wittman's mistakes," *Journal of Legal Studies* 14(1): 215–43.

Priest, G.L. and Klein, B. (1984). "The selection of disputes for litigation," *Journal of Legal Studies* 13(1): 1–55.

Rickman, N. (1994). "The economics of contingency fees in personal injury litigation," *Oxford Review of Economic Policy* 10(1): 34–50.

Shavell, S. (1982). "Suit, settlement, and trial: A theoretical analysis under alternative methods for the allocation of legal costs," *Journal of Legal Studies* 11(1): 55–82.

Shavell, S. (1987). *Economic Analysis of Accident Law.* Cambridge, MA: Harvard University Press.

Shephard, G.B. (1999). "An empirical study of the economics of pretrial discovery," *International Review of Law and Economics* 19: 245–63.

Sieg, H. (2000). "Estimating a bargaining model with asymmetric information: Evidence from medical malpractice disputes," *Journal of Political Economy* 108(5): 1006–21.

Siegelman, P. and Donohue, J.J. III (1995). "The selection of employment discrimination disputes for litigation: Using business cycle effects to test the Priest-Klein hypothesis," *Journal of Legal Studies* 24(2): 427–62.

Sloan, F.A. and Hoerger, T.J. (1989). "Uncertainty, information and resolution of medical malpractice disputes," *Journal of Risk and Uncertainty* 4(4): 403–23.

Sloan, F.A., Whetten-Goldstein, K., Entman, S.S., Kulas, E.D., and Stout, E.M. (1997). "The road from medical injury to claims resolution: How no–fault and tort differ," *Law and Contemporary Problems* 60(2), 35–70.

Snyder, E.A. and Hughes, J.W. (1990). "The English rule for allocating legal costs: Evidence confronts theory," *Journal of Law, Economics, and Organisation* 6(2): 345–80.

Stanley, L.R. and Coursey, D.L. (1988). "Pretrial bargaining behavior within the shadow of the law: Theory and experimental evidence," *International Review of Law and Economics* 8: 161–79.

Studdert, D.M. and Brennan, T.A. (2001). "No-fault compensation for medical injuries: The prospect for error prevention," *Journal of the American Medical Association* 286(2): 217–23.

Studdert, D.M., Thomas, E.J., Zbar, B.I.W., Newhouse, J.P., Weiler, P.C., Bayuk, J., and Brennan, T.A. (1997). "Can the United States afford a 'no-fault' system of compensation for medical injury?," *Law and Contemporary Problems* 60(2): 1–34.

Thomas, R.E. (1995). "The trial selection hypothesis without the 50 percent rule: Some experimental evidence," *Journal of Legal Studies* 24(1): 209–28.

Thomason, T. (1991). "Are attorneys paid what they're worth? Contingent fees and the settlement process," *Journal of Legal Studies* 20(1): 187–223.

Waldfogel, J. (1995). "The selection hypothesis and the relationship between trial and plaintiff victory," *Journal of Political Economy* 103(2): 229–60.

Waldfogel, J. (1998). "Reconciling asymmetric information and divergent expectations theories of litigation," *Journal of Law and Economics* 41(2): 451–76.

Williams, P.L. and Williams, R.A. (1994). "The cost of civil litigation: An empirical study," *International Review of Law and Economics* 14: 73–86.

Wittman, D. (1985). "Is the selection of cases for trial biased?," *Journal of Legal Studies* 14(1): 185–213.

11

CLAIMING BEHAVIOR AS LEGAL MOBILIZATION

HERBERT M. KRITZER[1]

[1] This Chapter was much improved due to the comments of Peter Cane and Masayuki Murayama. Any errors are of course my responsibility.

I. INTRODUCTION

LAW provides a set of norms to govern behavior and a set of procedures to resolve problems and disputes that arise within the context of those norms. This Chapter focuses on the earliest stages of what in empirical legal research is called legal mobilization: using law and legal institutions to seek redress for "justiciable" problems—problems for which a remedy can potentially be obtained through legal processes (Genn, 1999: 12). The literature on legal mobilization is broad, encompassing individualized claiming by persons and organizations, group actions for aggregated claims, rights-claiming by groups as a political strategy, and the initiation of formal legal proceedings whether in courts, administrative tribunals, or private dispute-resolution organizations (Zemans, 1983). For reasons of space, I have chosen to focus primarily on the first of these: the seeking of redress for individualized justiciable problems, which I will refer to as "claiming." More specifically, I define claiming as the communication, directly or indirectly, explicitly or implicitly, of a desire for redress to whomever is deemed "responsible" for a justiciable problem.[2]

The seminal work that identified the complexities in understanding the process by which individuals seek redress describes a series of stages: naming, blaming, and claiming (Felstiner et al., 1980–81). The impetus for this work was to understand the nature of disputes that are the precursor of litigation. According to this model, disputes come into being through a process in which, first, some "injurious experience" is recognized by the injured party or her agent ("naming") and hence becomes a "perceived injurious experience" (a PIE). The injured party then attributes responsibility to another party ("blaming") thus producing a grievance. Once responsibility has been externalized and a potentially responsible party identified, the injured party may either choose to "lump it" (i.e., do nothing—see Felstiner, 1974) or approach the other party (directly or through an agent) and communicate a claim ("claiming"). One insight from this framework is that many claims never mature into disputes because the recipient of the claim may immediately provide satisfactory redress; a dispute results only if redress is not immediately forthcoming, and that dispute may eventually lead to formal legal action (a lawsuit, an arbitration proceeding, an administrative dispute resolution process, or something else). Equally important, many claims that do mature into disputes do not move on to formal proceedings either because some resolution is achieved short of beginning a formal process or because the person asserting the claim chooses not to pursue the claim for one reason or another.

---

[2] There are many problems about which claims might be made for which there is no *legal* recourse. While I recognize that the line between justiciable and non-justiciable problems is often fluid, this Chapter focuses specifically on justiticable problems.

It is important to emphasize that while "naming, blaming, claiming" suggests a particular sequence, it is only a model, and the real world does not always or precisely fit that model. For example, Lloyd-Bostock (1984) points out that blaming may be a consequence of a decision to seek compensation rather than an antecedent. Or, more simply, in some situations, the recognition of an injury (naming) may be essentially indistinguishable from "blaming" as, for example, when a pedestrian is struck by a car when crossing a street where motor vehicles are clearly obligated to stop (e.g., by a "walk" signal or in a "Zebra crossing" in England). While these complexities and ambiguities are important to recognize, "naming, blaming, claiming" nonetheless provides a useful framework to think about how to analyze claiming behavior.

The primary focus in the discussion that follows is on claiming as defined above: a claim may be directed to an individual, a business, a governmental body, or some other entity, and the request for redress may be in the form of an explicit claim demanding specific actions or an implicit claim in which the desired action is either implicit or undefined. While the bulk of the discussion below is on claiming itself (because that is where most of the research has been), this Chapter also considers the closely related issue of blaming, and to a lesser extent the issue of problem recognition (what Felstiner et al. labeled "naming").

The central argument of this Chapter is that there is now a fairly extensive body of research with a set of consistent findings about claiming itself. Even with those consistent findings, there are significant gaps. We know much less about naming and blaming. Moreover, it is probably the case that for most types of injurious experiences, the amount we can learn about naming—the recognition of an injurious experience—is severely limited.

This Chapter will proceed as follows. In the next section I discuss the idea of a "dispute pyramid," a metaphor that has been widely used in the literature. Following that, I will describe the broad methodological approaches that have been applied in empirical research regarding claiming. I then examine the explanations that have been advanced for variations in claiming patterns, both at the individual and the aggregate levels; in this section I will identify points of general agreement and issues where agreement is lacking. Finally, I propose an agenda for future research related to claiming.

II. THE DISPUTE PYRAMID

The study of behavior related to claiming in the context of justiciable problems has its roots in three closely related research themes: access to justice (Cappelletti and

Garth, 1978), legal needs (Abel-Smith et al., 1973; Curran, 1977),[3] and litigation rates (Blankenburg, 1992; Galanter, 1983; Grossman and Sarat, 1975; Wollschläger, 1998). The first focuses on whether individuals were able to obtain redress for their justiciable problems; the second focuses on whether individuals were able to obtain the assistance of a qualified legal professional to deal with legal problems they experienced (including non-contentious matters such as property transactions and drafting of wills);[4] and the third focuses on actual case-filings in courts or other formal dispute-resolution fora. None of these themes specifically focused on claiming and its antecedents; they focused more on access, either to legal assistance or to legal institutions. Claiming came to prominence in research focused on dispute processing (Bogart and Vidmar, 1990; FitzGerald, 1983; Miller and Sarat, 1980–81),[5] compensation for injury (Harris et al., 1984; Hensler et al., 1991), and a body of work relying explicitly on the concept of justiciable problems, which I will refer to as "justiciable problem studies" (Genn, 1999; 2009: 70–2). These are a cross between legal needs studies (focusing on access to assistance) and dispute processing studies (limited to contentious matters).[6]

It was the dispute-processing approach, when it was employed in a major study of civil litigation in the United States, that placed legal mobilization into the naming, blaming, and claiming framework. That framework was developed to gain insights into why PIEs did or did not mature into lawsuits. While students of the legal system have long known that only a small fraction of lawsuits lead to actual trials, the fact that most types of justiciable problems seldom mature into lawsuits was less well known. As this latter fact came to be recognized, researchers hit upon the metaphor of a pyramid (Engel and Steele, 1979: 300, 317–18) to capture the idea that fewer and fewer cases remained as one went from problems to claims to disputes to lawsuits. The pyramid metaphor is far from perfect because the patterns, as shown in Figure 1, lack the regularity of an actual pyramid. Still, the idea of a pyramid works better as a metaphor than does a possible alternative, the funnel, because the image of *climbing* the pyramid implies effort (e.g., cost) which seems to fit the facts better than the image of sliding down the funnel while being pulled by gravity.

The base of the dispute pyramid consists in principle of all injurious experiences;[7] the succeeding levels represent PIEs, then grievances, then disputes, then litigation (broadly

[3] Citations to a number of state-level legal needs studies conducted in the U.S. can be found in Kritzer (2008: 905–6); the article also has references to other national level U. S. legal needs studies as well as studies carried out in Australia, New Zealand, Germany, and Canada.

[4] The terms "legal needs" and "legal problems" tend to be used interchangeably, and are taken to include both contentious and non-contentious matters where legal assistance could be helpful.

[5] One area where one finds a long-standing interest in complaining and claiming is consumer behavior, and there is a specialized journal on this specific topic, *Journal of Consumer Satisfaction, Dissatisfaction & Complaining Behavior*, published now on an annual basis.

[6] A number of justiciable problem studies can be found listed in Genn (2010: 72).

[7] Alternatively, one could conceptualize the base of the pyramid as the population at risk for a particular type of injurious experience; for example, only those who are either tenants or landlords are at risk for a landlord/tenant problem.

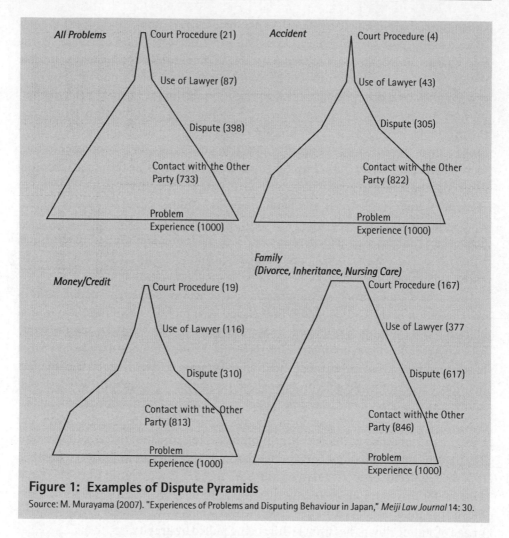

Figure 1: Examples of Dispute Pyramids

Source: M. Murayama (2007). "Experiences of Problems and Disputing Behaviour in Japan," *Meiji Law Journal* 14: 30.

defined to include any formalized, authoritative dispute-resolution activity), and then appeals. In some presentations, such as the examples shown in Figure 1, assistance-seeking such as consulting or hiring a lawyer appears as a level in the pyramid. Actual representations of dispute pyramids (the first of these can be found in Miller and Sarat, 1980–81, 544–6) start with either PIEs or with grievances, either of which may be referred to as "problems." As I will discuss below, one of the central findings of the research on claiming is that the shape of the dispute pyramid varies by type of problem. Figure 1 provides an example of several dispute pyramids from a study done in Japan (Murayama, 2007).

Empirical research on claiming behavior tends to focus on one of two broad questions: what is the shape of the dispute pyramid and what factors explain variations in claiming behavior at the individual and/or aggregate level? Central to the analyses dealing with the first question is how dispute pyramids vary by type of problem and by country (or possibly sub-regions of countries). With regard to the second question, analyses focus specifically on the issue of claiming assuming that blaming has occurred. Little empirical research has been done on attribution of blame, or on the recognition of an injurious experience (naming), a point that will be discussed in more detail below. As will be discussed in a later section, analyses have considered individual as well as institutional factors that might explain variations in claiming behavior.

III. RESEARCH METHODOLOGIES

A wide range of methodologies have been employed in the study of claiming behavior and its antecedents: structured surveys, institutional records, ethnography, and semi-structured, individual, and group interviews (the latter sometimes being referred to as "focus groups"). Most widely used is the random population survey (Curran, 1977; Miller and Sarat, 1980–81; Genn, 1999; Murayama, 2007), sometimes restricted to a particular segment of the population (e.g., those below some income threshold) or stratified to insure that certain groups (those on low incomes, minorities, etc.) are sufficiently represented to permit valid statistical analyses. Some such surveys involve a two-step process: first a large-scale screening survey to locate respondents with the types of problems of interest (defined by seriousness, timing, particular kind, etc.) followed by a more detailed interview focusing on one or more of the problems identified in the screening survey. In some cases, the two stages are combined into a single interview with some procedure whereby the interviewer selects specific problems for detailed, follow-up questions. While most surveys have been done in person or over the telephone, at least one recent study (from the Netherlands) has relied on a survey conducted via the Internet.

Institutional records are the basis of litigation-rate studies. Institutional records have also been used in some studies to identify persons who experienced particular kinds of problems and who can then be interviewed about their experience and decision-making process. One problem with this approach is that by definition, all of those who sought redress through the institution have claimed, and so there is no comparison group of people who had not sought redress. Institutional records have been used in a unique way in studies of medical negligence claims. Hospital records have been used to identify patients who experienced an injury in the course of medical treatment that could be attributable to negligence; researchers then seek to determine whether those who were injured made claims.

The community-study approach grew out of anthropological research on dispute-handling in African and other less developed settings. This approach involves intensive interaction with a specific community, whether defined geographically (Engel, 1984; Merry, 1990; Yngvesson, 1993) or in some other way (e.g., a "church community," Greenhouse, 1986). In these studies the researcher spends substantial time in the community being studied engaging in a combination of observation and interviews. In some cases the researchers also look at court records to document patterns in court use. However, the primary data gathered for analysis takes the form of detailed field notes and transcripts of interviews.

The last method, semi-structured interviewing, is used either in combination with surveys or ethnography or on a stand-alone basis. When used in combination with surveys, semi-structured interviews are an invaluable method both as an exploratory tool in the course of developing the survey instrument and also to "get behind" the patterns revealed in the survey data (e.g., Blackstone et al., 2009; Bumiller, 1988). Semi-structured interviews can also be used on their own to explore how a sample of potential respondents, who can be identified as having experienced a specific type of problem, dealt with the problem by, for instance, claiming or complaining (e.g., May and Stengel, 1990; Marshall, 2005). Semi-structured interviews may include some structured questions that facilitate certain types of comparisons (see Ewick and Silbey, 1998).

A. The problem of estimating problem incidence

If one works from the dispute pyramid metaphor, one would like to be able to say something about the number of problems that form the very bottom, or base, of the pyramid including those that are perceived by potential claimants and those that are not perceived (sometimes called "unPIEs," or "unperceived injurious experiences"). This presents two analytic problems: what should count as a problem and how can you measure problems that are not perceived? Possible answers to both of these questions are highly dependent on the nature of the problem potentially involved. In some settings the answers are fairly straightforward; in others, there may be no workable answers. Several examples can illustrate these issues.

Medical negligence is a hotly debated issue in a number of countries. If one were to construct a dispute pyramid specifically for this area, one would probably define the base as "iatrogenic injuries," meaning those injuries that result from medical treatment. One could divide this base into two parts: injuries that are due to negligence (and hence constitute justiciable problems) and those not due to negligence. In fact, as mentioned previously, methods of assessing the number of injuries of both types have been developed (at least for those injuries occurring in a hospital setting) involving review of hospital records to determine if an injury occurred and whether an injury that had occurred was likely to have been the result of negligence. More problematic, at least in relation to research done to date, is determining whether an injury was perceived; of those that are perceived, we have some data on the likelihood that a claim will be made, although there is ambiguity as to whether initial inquiries constitute claims or simply are part of an investigation to determine if the injury was due to negligence. A central finding of the research in this area (for a good summary, see Baker, 2005) is that a strikingly large percentage of hospitalizations lead to iatrogenic injuries, a significant subset of which are attributable to negligence, but that very few result in claims or compensation.

A second illustration of the challenges of looking at the base of the pyramid can be found in the burgeoning literature on sexual harassment. Is there an objective way to determine whether a comment on a person's appearance represents a compliment or a form of sexual harassment? Exactly the same behavior may be perceived by one person as of no importance, but as harassment by another person; for one person the telling of off-color jokes may be perceived as harassment while the same behavior is accepted (and participated in) by another person (see Marshall, 2005: 101)—in fact, what one person perceives as off-color may not be so perceived by another. Much of the recent research on the response to sexual harassment (e.g., Marshall, 2005; Blackstone et al., 2009) has been framed in terms of legal consciousness (Ewick and Silbey, 1998), in part reflecting the centrality of the social construction of behavior in this context. Blackstone et al. (2009) distinguish between "objective harassment" and "perceived harassment," asking respondents both whether they perceived themselves as having been subject to harassment and, separately, if they had experienced specific behaviors (offensive joking, personal questions, invasion of space, unwanted touching, being shown offensive materials, and physical assault). While having experienced one or more of the behaviors was associated with perceiving oneself as having been subject to sexual harassment, the relationship was very far from determinative. Whether this is because some (perhaps many) respondents failed to perceive the objective behaviors as constituting harassment, or because they preferred not to see themselves as victims of harassment, is not clear. Nonetheless, this example demonstrates the complexity of measuring the base of the dispute pyramid.

IV. Explaining Variations in Claiming Behavior

A. The incidence of grievances

A first question one might want to ask about the incidence of grievances that could lead to claims is how it might vary across countries. These comparisons are difficult to make given that the designs of specific studies tends vary in terms of (1) the time-frame respondents are asked about (ranging from one to five years), (2) whether questions are asked about individuals or households, (3) the list of specific problems asked about, and (4) the seriousness-threshold used for inclusion. Occasional studies do undertake such comparisons. For example, using the dispute processing approach, FitzGerald (1983: 24–6) compared the incidence of grievances in Australia and the United States circa 1980, finding that Australians were more likely to report tort, consumer, and government-related grievances than were residents of the United

States but less likely to report discrimination problems (there was essentially no difference in reporting of property, landlord, or post-divorce problems). Genn and Paterson (2001: 37) compare England and Scotland, finding only relatively minor differences, some of which are probably attributable to differences in how problem categories were defined; where the problem categories are directly comparable, the frequency of problems for the two countries is "relatively similar."

One theme in the legal needs studies and the later justiciable problems studies is how the incidence of problems varies by demographic factors. Curran (1977: 99–134) provides an extensive analysis along these lines showing that the number of legal needs (some of which involved non-contentious matters—i.e., transactional matters such as drafting wills, buying and selling property, adoption, name changes, etc.) varies by age, income, gender, and race. She finds that the overall frequency of problems has a curvilinear relationship with age, peaking for those in the 35–55 age range. This pattern, which is reported in other studies as well, is not surprising given that those in this age range will be dealing more with children, home ownership, and other issues than those both older and younger. She finds that the number of legal needs tends to increase with income, although it is not clear whether this would be true if the focus was limited to contentious matters given that matters such as drafting wills, buying and selling property, and the like, tend to be more common as income rises. Curran also provides a series of separate analyses for broad types of needs (real property, employment, consumer matters, marital matters, torts, government issues, etc.). Generally, after controlling for the type of need, Curran mostly found very modest relationships between having specific needs and demographic factors; perhaps surprisingly, this was even true for "infringement of constitutional rights" (pp. 120–2).

The first of the studies done in the dispute-processing tradition (Miller and Sarat, 1980–81: 547–51) also examined the relationship between various demographic factors (income, education, age, gender, ethnicity, family size), as well as specific risk factors (home-ownership and the like) and prior use of a lawyer. Their conclusion was that "[o]verall, the independent variables do not account for much of the variation in grievance experiences." They did find that certain factors correlated with certain types of grievances (race with discrimination problems, home ownership with property problems), but even these relationships were not particularly strong.

In her study of justiciable problems in England, Genn compared key demographic characteristics of those who experienced various types of problems to the demographic characteristics of the population as a whole (1999: 59–65) and found some differences. For example, people with higher incomes were more likely to report consumer problems than those with lower incomes; similarly, those with consumer problems were more likely to be home owners and to have higher educational qualifications. She reports various differences for other types of problems. However, none of the differences she describes suggests that there are strong relationships between demographic variables and the experiencing of problems, and many of the differences seem unsurprising: for instance, that those with higher incomes experience more consumer problems because they can afford to purchase more consumer goods, which in turn increases their exposure to potential problems with consumer purchases.

Perhaps the most interesting finding with regard to the incidence of problems concerns what Pleasence et al. (2004) describe as problem "clusters." By this they mean that certain types of problems often cluster so that if a person or household experiences one type of problem in the cluster they are more likely to experience others. A simple example would be that someone who experiences a significant injury might be unable to work, which in turn creates money problems and possibly puts significant pressure on family relationships. Drawing on data collected from households surveyed as part of the Legal Services Research Centre's English and Welsh Civil and Social Justice Survey (a study series modeled after Genn's 1999 study), Pleasence and his colleagues conducted a hierarchical-cluster analysis of over 4,000 problems reported by survey participants classified into 21 categories by type. They found that 17% had experienced two or more types of problems (something under half of those who experienced at least one problem). The analysis identified distinct clusters of problems around family issues, homelessness (which includes problems with the police), medical negligence combined with mental health problems, and a core cluster involving consumer issues, money and debt, employment, and neighbors. Of those with multiple problems, 73% experienced problems that fell within one or more of the problem clusters with the remainder experiencing a "random set of problems." Pleasence et al. then identified those respondents who experienced each cluster, and performed statistical analyses to see what factors were associated with experiencing each of the clusters respectively. This analysis revealed that respondents aged over 60 were less likely to have problems in the family cluster, economically "inactive" respondents were more likely to have problems associated with homelessness, and those with long-term illness or disability were more likely to have problems in the medical negligence/mental illness cluster. Thus, in the words of Pleasence et al., "justiciable problems do not necessarily occur in isolation."

B. Why people say they take no action

Overall, those who have justiciable problems are quite likely to claim or take some action such as seeking advice or assistance, For example, Curran (1977: 136) reports that, for 16 of 22 broad types of legal needs, 80% or more of those encountering the problem took some action to solve it, and only for eviction and job discrimination did fewer than 50% report taking action. Miller and Sarat find that with the exception of one type of problem, 70% or more of grievances lead to claims (for most categories examined, 85% or more result in a claim; see 1980–81: 537), which leads them to observe that "most, but by no means all, grievances result in a claim for redress" (p. 551). Genn (1999: 69) reports that "only a very small proportion failed to take any kind of action to deal with their justiciable problems (one in twenty)."

Before turning to the statistical analyses of claiming behavior in the following section, one might ask how the respondents themselves explain why they took no action to obtain redress. Many of the studies asked open-ended questions along the lines of "why did you not complain?" (the exact form of the question varies from study to study), and then grouped or coded the responses on the basis of a set of themes (see Bogart and Vidmar, 1990: 30; Bumiller, 1988: 27; Genn 1999: 106–35; Harris et al., 1984: 70–6; Hensler et al., 1991: 169–70). Common responses to this question include:

- Taking action would make no difference ("nothing could be done").
- To avoid the hassle of dealing with the problem.
- Because the respondent had removed himself or herself from the context where the problem occurred (left the job, moved, changed service providers, and so on).
- The problem had sorted itself out in some way.
- Reluctance to disrupt valued relationships (with a neighbor, for instance).
- Concern about the cost of obtaining necessary legal assistance.
- Fear of potential negative consequences of complaining.
- Not knowing who to complain to.

Vidmar (1988) relates the decision not to complain to Hirschman's ideas of "exit, voice, and loyalty"; some of the above explanations relate to the ability to exit and some to what might be labeled loyalty (e.g., to friends and neighbors). It is likely that the distribution of these explanations varies by problem type (some of the studies provide at least some indication of this), but the analyses tend to be too brief to allow strong conclusions on this point regarding such variation or why respondents gave a particular explanation for inaction.

C. Contextual characteristics—type of problem

I now turn to the question of what factors best account for decisions to claim in connection with justiciable problems. Across a range of studies applying various survey approaches and undertaken in various countries there is a consensus that the single most important factor influencing decisions to seek redress for legal problems is type of problem:

- "The results of the multivariate analysis confirm that problem type tends to swamp other considerations…" (Genn, 1999: 141).
- "The extent to which persons consulted lawyers about their problems or sought alternative sources of advice or help varied widely by the type of problem involved" (Curran, 1977: 138; see particularly Curran's Figure 4.29, p. 143).
- "Levels of claiming vary substantially with the type of problem" (Bogart and Vidmar, 1990: 48).

- "The [results] indicate very strongly that by far the most powerful explanatory factor for the various aspects of disputing behavior is the actual type of grievance involved (e.g., tort, consumer, post-divorce)" (FitzGerald, 1983: 39).

While Miller and Sarat (1980–81: 561) observe that "with the exception of discrimination and tort problems, claiming and disputing rates are relatively similar among different types of problems," their statistical analysis of claiming behavior shows that demographic and resource variables have about a tenth of the predictive power as does problem type.

FitzGerald (1983: 39) compared the rate of claiming in the United States (as reflected in a study of five federal judicial districts around the country) and the Australian state of Victoria for seven problem types; only in the case of discrimination problems was there a sharp difference, and for four of the problem types there was little difference at all. Figure 2 extends FitzGerald's comparison to four countries, showing a comparison of disputing behavior for six problem types in the United States (Miller and Sarat, 1980–81), Canada (Bogart and Vidmar, 1990), Australia (FitzGerald, 1983), and Japan (Murayama, 2007). As the figure shows, there are striking similarities in cross-national patterns by problem types.

Most of the studies of claiming behavior group problems into broad categories such as those shown in Figure 2. The significance of problem type as a predictor of the response to the problem is shown to be even stronger by studies that break down the problem-types further and examine differences in behavior in relation to the sub-types.[8] These studies show that within broad problem-types, the problem sub-type is the major predictor of claiming behavior. For example, in looking at injury problems, the distinction among road traffic accidents, workplace accidents, and other accidents is by far the best predictor of claiming behavior (see also Hensler et al., 1991: 123; Kritzer et al., 1991a). In relation to discrimination problems, the best predictor is the context in which the discrimination took place—job, education, or housing (Kritzer et al., 1991b).[9]

What accounts for the variation across problem-types and the relative similarity within problem-types cross-nationally? In their study of the use of lawyers, Mayhew and Reiss (1969: 312) speak in terms of "the social organization of the institutional arena subject to legal regulation." While they relate this to the nature of legal practice (not surprisingly since they specifically focus on contacting lawyers in connection with legal problems), the broader implication is that differences among problems are significant. Perhaps the best way to think about this is to recognize that a claim

---

[8] Some studies have examined other characteristics of the problems, such as the amount at stake and the nature of the opposing party (i.e., individual vs. organization), and found that they have some association with disputing behavior (see FitzGerald, 1983: 39).

[9] An unpublished analysis that examined consumer problems as a subtype found that the best predictor was whether the problem was a major purchase, a non-professional service, or a professional service.

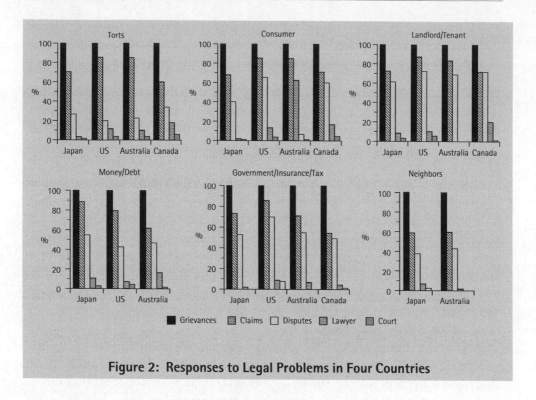

Figure 2: Responses to Legal Problems in Four Countries

creates a social relationship, and that social relationship takes on different character-istics depending on the context in which the relationship is formed, the value placed on the relationship, whether the relationship is pre-existing, and whether one or both parties to the relationship desire to continue it. Perhaps the best evidence in support of the role of the social context of the disputing relationship is the analysis of prob-lem sub-types discussed above. The significance of the social context is clearest in the analysis of discrimination problems that compares claiming behavior in the United States, Canada, and Australia. In all three countries, claiming is least likely in relation to issues of housing discrimination (i.e., discrimination in the rental or sale of housing), an area where exit (i.e., going elsewhere) may be easy and there is unlikely to be an exist-ing relationship to maintain. Claiming is most likely in relation to education discrimina-tion. Discrimination related to employment falls in between. For Canada and Australia, employment-related discrimination is further broken down into denial or loss of a job, conditions of employment (including salary), and other types of employment discrimi-nation. Claiming is most likely when the issue is salary or conditions of employment, and considerably less likely for other types of employment-related discrimination.[10]

While most research considers the context of the problem simply in terms of the type of problem involved, one study of responses to sexual harassment in the workplace

---

[10] Further analyses of the data discussed "teased out few relationships between individual level factors and complaining/claiming behavior."

examined context in more detail. Blackstone et al. (2009) include information on the type of industry (restaurant, sales, other), work hours, whether the respondent had friends at work, the nature of training related to harassment at work, and two variables related to supervision. Two of these, friends at work and restaurant setting, both related to taking action. Having friends at work increased the likelihood of action and occurrence of the problem in a restaurant setting decreased it. The latter finding reflected the fact that the most likely source of sexual harassment of restaurant workers was customers against whom there was no good avenue for legal redress.

One caveat worth noting here is that within a given problem-type, from the potential claimant's perspective some grievances may be more important than others. Consider, for example, the significance of the injury in a tort-type case. Hensler et al. (1991: 165–6) report that "[t]hose who feel their injury was extremely serious are ... six times as likely to take some action as those who feel their injury was not at all serious. Those who feel their injury had a very important effect on their household are [also] six times as likely to take some action as those who say the injury had little or no effect on their household."

D. Individual characteristics

Whenever one focuses on the behavior of individuals the question of the impact of individual characteristics inevitably arises. These individual characteristics can include various demographic characteristics (income, education, age, race, gender), prior experiences and other kinds of resources (e.g., personal contacts), and psychological factors. The research on claiming behavior has extensively explored the relationships of that behavior to demographic and various resource variables. Very little work has been done examining the more psychological or attitudinal factors.

Many, but by no means all, analyses report at least some relationship between one or more of the personal variables and taking action in response to legal problems. For example, while Genn reports that "the results of the multivariate analysis confirm that problem type tends to swamp other considerations" she goes on to say that "some personal factors, such as level of education, are [also] important" (Genn, 1999: 141). Miller and Sarat (1980–81: 553) report multivariate analyses within problem types and find certain individual characteristics important for certain problems, but no clear pattern.[11] A study of legal mobilization in the context of sexual harassment problems found that a measure of religiosity was related to taking

---

[11] Murayama and his colleagues have reported on additional results (not yet published in English) from the study summarized in Murayama (2007); these results show that most socio-economic variables do not predict claiming behavior; social capital and legal experience variables do seem to have some relationship but those relationships are fairly weak.

action: those who scored higher on the religiosity scale were *less* likely to take some action for redress (Blackstone et al., 2009: 653).

Analyses also examine personal resources such as experience and contacts. Again, with one notable exception, while specific relationships are uncovered here and there (e.g., those with a prior dispute experience or who have previously used a lawyer may be more likely to claim for some types of problems; see, for example, Blackstone et al., 2009: 647–55), no clear pattern is evident in the various studies. The notable exception is Michelson's finding in his study, conducted in 37 villages across six provinces of China, that families with strong political connections were more likely to pursue grievances than were families without such connections (Michelson, 2007).

Only a few studies have examined the potential effect of psychological variables on claiming behavior. For example, in their study of responses to sexual harassment, Blackstone et al. (2009) included a measure for personal efficacy (a person's belief about his or her own ability to obtain a desired result), but found that it had no relationship with seeking redress. Probably the most extensive such effort was made by Vidmar and Schuller (1987) who report a series of four studies examining "claim propensity," which they measured as a combination of six components: aggressiveness, competitiveness, assertiveness, perceptions of control, preference for risk, and preference for winning over compromise. The four studies involved both surveys and an experiment using university students. From these studies they found that differences in the proclivity to report problems and to engage in claiming behavior were positively associated with their measure of claim propensity. One study compared individuals who had taken a case to small claims court with those who had not, and found that the former scored higher on the propensity to claim measure (consisting of the six factors noted above) than the latter. Because for those who had taken a case to court, the data were collected *after* the court experience, there is no way to know whether the higher propensity score existed before going to court, and hence it is unclear whether the higher score should be viewed as a cause or effect of the court experience.

E. Institutional factors

To what degree do institutional factors affect legal mobilization through claiming? The kinds of institutional factors that might be important include:

- The potential size of recoveries. Factors influencing potential recoveries include the role of juries and legal limits on liability or damages, whether imposed by case law or statute.
- Costs of claiming, both pecuniary (e.g., court fees) and non-pecuniary (e.g., time required).
- The availability of legal representation (legal aid, legal expense insurance, no-win, no-pay fee systems).

- The nature of risks associated with claiming (loser-pays fee systems, availability of insurance to cover potential costs).
- Limits on claiming imposed by no-fault accident compensation systems.
- The impact of rules—governing "joint and several liability," contributory negligence, and the like—on the amount of compensation.
- Alternative sources of compensation and support such as social security benefits and publicly provided medical services.

Some of these operate directly on the actions of potential claimants (e.g., the risks of having to pay the other side's costs if a claim is unsuccessful) and others function by limiting access to legal assistance needed to bring claims (the absence of no-win, no-pay fees, or legal aid). There has been a lot of speculation about the influence of such factors, but empirical analyses are often difficult to conduct because of confounding factors.

Empirical research on these types of questions is generally done in one of three ways: cross-national comparisons, comparisons across the American states, or comparisons over time when institutional factors change. The results of this body of research—almost all of which has been done in the United States—are mixed, some showing that the institutional differences affect claiming behavior and others showing no such effects.

Some institutional factors clearly matter. Formal limits on the types of claims that can be filed affect claiming. For example Abrahamse and Carroll (1999: 138) show that there tend to be many fewer road traffic accident tort claims in American states that place limits on such claims as part of a no-fault insurance system, and fewest where the limits are the most stringent. For the effects of other kinds of limits, the evidence is more mixed (at least with regard to claiming). For example, Donohue and Ho (2007) find that statutory limits on damages in malpractice cases have no impact on claims filing; in contrast, data from Harris County, Texas, show that a sharp drop (approaching 50%) in filing of medical malpractice lawsuits occurred in the wake of the passage in Texas of a limit on non-economic damages in such cases (Daniels and Martin, 2009).[12]

While there is some quite convincing evidence regarding the impact of limits on damages, the evidence regarding other institutional factors does not always demonstrate the effects that one might expect. A good example comes from England. As reflected in Atiyah's writing (Atiyah, 1987), there is a perception that tort claims for personal injury are less likely to be made in England than in the United States. One possible explanation is the manner of funding of legal representation. Prior to 1995 such representation was not available (at least in theory) on a no-win, no-pay basis

---

[12] Using lawsuit filings as a proxy for claiming is tricky because large numbers of claims are resolved without filing. Medical malpractice is one area where the filing of lawsuits is probably a reasonably good proxy for claim filing because the overwhelming majority of such claims result in a filing if they survive initial screening by a lawyer.

although a significant portion of the English population was able to obtain third-party funding of representation through legal aid, legal expenses insurance, or as a union benefit; moreover, those who did not have access to third-party funding also had to be concerned about having to pay the defendant's costs should a claim go to litigation and prove unsuccessful. This situation changed in 1995, and then changed further in 1999. The key changes were (1) allowing solicitors to charge on a no-win, no-pay basis (through what is called a "conditional fee" arrangement, which allows the solicitor to charge an additional "success fee" if some recovery is obtained), (2) the marketing of "after-the-event" insurance that protects the claimant from having to pay the defendant's costs in an unsuccessful action, and (3) allowing a successful claimant to recover the success fee and the premium for the after-the-event insurance from the defendant. One result of these changes has been to greatly reduce for many plaintiffs the financial risks and costs of litigating. Another result was the rapid development of a "claims-management" industry of aggressively competitive companies whose business was to identify potential claimants and broker legal services for them; claims management companies engaged in extensive advertising to attract potential claimants as clients.

Such developments led to expressions of concern that England was developing a "compensation culture" marked by sharp increases in the likelihood that claims would be filed (and implicitly that many of the resulting claims had little merit). The perception that a "compensation culture" had developed was fanned by the popular media. The relevant question here is whether the frequency of claiming did in fact increase in the wake of the changes that reduced the financial risks associated with seeking compensation? The best evidence on this (Morris, 2007) is that there was no clear pattern of increase in the number of claims between 2000 (when the last set of changes went into effect) and 2006; some types of claims increased while others decreased. Thus, the evidence does not support the view that the changes starting in 1995 had a significant impact on claiming behavior, although the data cannot rule out the possibility that many more people approached claims handlers (solicitors and others[13]), resulting in sharp increases in the number of potential clients turned away.

Most of the work that has been done on the impact of institutional factors on claiming behavior has focused on tort claims. This probably reflects two issues. First, tort claims have been a major political issue in the United States for some time and have become somewhat more politically salient in England since the mid-1990s in the wake of changes described in the previous paragraph. Second, because of the ubiquity of insurance against tort liability, data on the frequency of claims, as distinct from the filing of law suits, are potentially available (and in some settings are routinely gathered). Outside of that area, obtaining information on claiming patterns requires data collection efforts that are often expensive and cumbersome. The

---

[13] Solicitors do not have a monopoly on representation in compensation claims; only once a claim becomes a formal court action are non-lawyers barred from representing claimants.

result is that we know relatively little about the impact of institutional factors (such as fee shifting, the availability of legal expense insurance, etc.) beyond the arena of tort claims for personal injury.

The best summary of our current understanding of how institutional factors affect claiming behavior is that some of these factors clearly do have an effect, particularly those that directly limit what claims can be filed. For example, in the United States claims related to job dismissal, for reasons other than violation of an explicit employment contract or discrimination on the basis of a protected category, are rare for the simple reason that, in contrast to the law in England and many other countries, U.S. law does not provide for such claims because it embodies the "employment at will" doctrine to the effect that in the absence of specific limitations, employers are free to hire and fire at will. However, the impact of institutional factors that work indirectly by controlling the incentives to claim is less clear. Some research shows such effects, some does not, and we lack an understanding of what might condition whether or not such effects occur.

F. Cultural differences

How do cultural factors impact claiming behavior? Here I use "culture" to refer to norms and expectations concerning what constitutes appropriate behavior. At a crude level, some might characterize a lower likelihood of claiming in England as compared to the United States (discussed below) as reflecting English stoicism, the stereotype of the "stiff upper lip." Sorting out what effects might be labeled "cultural" is challenging because research that focuses on cultural factors is seldom designed in a way that permits strong inferences. Still, there is some research suggestive of cultural effects.

One analysis that could be seen as providing support for a cultural explanation of claiming differences between England and the United States considered how blaming might affect the decision to claim (Kritzer, 1991). That study used several extant data sets to divide potential claimants into three groups: those who did not blame someone else for their injury, those who unambiguously blamed someone else for their injury, and those who were unsure whether someone else was to blame for their injury. There was relatively little difference between the two countries in the claiming behavior of the first two groups, but there was a sharp difference in relation to the third group. Americans who were unsure whether someone else should be blamed were much more likely to claim than English people who were similarly unsure about blaming. Conceivably the differences might reflect the greater risk associated (at the time of the research) with an unsuccessful claim in England, but the pattern does seem consistent with a cultural explanation.

There is a perception, and at least some evidence, that claiming is higher in urban environments than in rural settings (Daniels, 1982; Patel et al., 2008). An anthropological study by David Engel in a non-urban community he called "Saunders County" provides insights into the cultural factors that might explain this (Engel, 1984). Engel found local norms against seeking compensation for routine injuries even if someone else was arguably to blame. The local ethic was that one took care of oneself, and that one should not try to foist that responsibility on to others. According to Engel, this set of norms reflected rural living, and the inherent dangers associated with work common in settings such as farming. Importantly, Engel did not find a generalized norm against claiming, but one that was specific to the personal injury area. There did not appear to be norms against claiming when the matter arose from someone's failure to live up to a contract; in those circumstances claiming was accepted because people were expected to abide by their promises and a contract was considered a promise. While the patterns Engel reports are explainable in terms of local norms of the type one might expect in a rural community in the United States, ultimately Engel's analysis can only suggest why claiming may be less common in rural areas. As with all single site ethnographic studies, one is left with the question of whether the patterns found in "Saunders County" can be generalized to other non-urban communities, and even if they can be so generalized, one might also ask whether a similar study conducted in an urban area would find similar or different norms. Nonetheless, in the context of the literature on claiming behavior, Engel's study is important because of the explanation it suggests.

One study (Greenhouse, 1986) suggests that the norms created within a community defined by affiliation with a particular religious congregation might impact claiming behavior, suppressing claiming in the case of the community studied. This makes sense if one's religious beliefs say that events are predetermined or reflect God's will; such beliefs could lead adherents to view unfortunate events as something to be accepted and coped with as part of one's faith. Alternatively, religious beliefs might lead to the de-emphasis of conflict which in turn could reduce claiming behavior. In contrast, religious beliefs might view debate and conflict as natural and positive, and communities of adherents to such beliefs might create their own mechanisms for dispute resolution.

Comparisons of claiming behavior across countries often refer to cultural differences (e.g., Markesinis, 1990). Most prominently, Americans are seen as prone to seek redress for the slightest reason while in contrast, residents of other countries such as Japan, for example, are seen as likely to avoid conflict and disputes (but see Ginsburg and Hoetker, 2006; Kawashima, 1973; Miyazawa, 1987). The contrast between Japan and the United States appears very sharp, and the differences are often attributed to culture; however, procedure (see Tanase, 1990), availability of legal assistance, or factors such as the amounts of potential compensation, may adequately explain any differences between the two countries. As is true in other areas of research that compare behavior across countries, culture often seems to be a residual explanation: when other factors fail to account for differences in behavior, attribute behavioral patterns to culture. The yet-unsolved challenge is how to study culture directly using empirical methods.

V. FUTURE RESEARCH

Compared to other issues considered by those engaged in empirical legal research, at least some aspects of the work on legal mobilization, as reflected in claiming in response to justiciable problems, can be described as relatively mature. A number of findings have been consistently reported, both within and across countries. Most particularly, we know that individual characteristics (demographics, resources, experience, attitudes) are relatively weak predictors of individual claiming behavior (where they predict at all). Most, if not all, studies that have examined multiple problem types show that the dominant factor in explaining claiming behavior is the type of issue in dispute. Few other areas of empirical legal research can be described as producing such strong, consistent findings.

Given this, what are the fertile areas for future research on claiming behavior as a form of legal mobilization? An obvious first step is to better understand why problem-type is so powerful an explanation of claiming behavior. Does it reflect the relative ease of simply removing oneself from the situation (Hirschman's "exit")? How important is the need or desire to maintain a relationship (what might be thought of as a form of Hirschman's "loyalty")? Do the differences reflect specific norms and expectations within problem-types (as described by Engel in his study of "Saunders County")? The best ways to answer to these kinds of questions are likely to be methods that allow for in-depth exploration of cases and experiences: creating "life histories" of disputes, conducting group interviews where people can interact over their views, and undertaking ethnographic research. Crucial in any such research is to build in elements such as multiple cases or research sites that allow effective comparisons to be made so that we can have some confidence that the patterns uncovered are not specific to a particular group or setting and that any findings can be generalized to some extent.

A second issue that requires much more work is the role of attribution—an issue about which there is a substantial psychological literature (see Coates and Penrod, 1980–81)—in the claiming process. We use different terms in talking about attribution: blaming, responsibility, fault, and the like; each word has different connotations. What difference does it make how people are asked about the attribution process? Are there any factors influencing how people come to make attributions that do not depend on the specific terminology used to inquire about attribution? While (what might be labeled) the "standard" "naming, blaming, and claiming" model (Felstiner et al., 1980–81) suggests that attribution precedes claiming, is that always the case? When does attribution lead to claiming and when is attribution a rationalization for claiming (see Lloyd-Bostock, 1984)? One area where claims may frequently be filed (at least in the United States) in the absence of clear attribution is medical negligence; the explanation is that attribution requires good information, and potential medical negligence claimants often have to initiate a claim in order to obtain the information necessary to determine if someone is responsible for an injury. To what degree is this true in other areas such as discrimination?

In Chapter 29, Christopher Hodges considers a range of research related to procedures for collective redress, typically involving what are called "class actions" in the United States, but which can involve other forms of aggregation (e.g., the American multi-district litigation—MDL—procedure often used in mass torts, "group litigation orders" in England, and the like). Interestingly, there is virtually no research on claiming behavior in the context of such aggregated litigation. While many studies of class actions and mass torts report the number of claims that have been made, efforts to estimate *claiming rates* are much less common (but see Hensler et al., 1999: 549; Kritzer, 1988–89: 225). While, as Hodges notes, the amount of compensation to be paid is likely to influence actual claiming behavior, there is in fact no systematic research assessing the nature of this probable relationship (e.g., is there a monotonic relationship between claiming and amount to be paid, or is there some amount below which claiming is unlikely?). There are a variety of other factors that could influence claiming: the nature of the injuries involved (physical or purely financial), the seriousness of the injuries, the complexity of the claim-filing process, the nature of any formal notification process, the incentives of third parties to assist in the claiming process, and so on.[14] This is an area deserving significant attention by empirically oriented researchers interested in claiming behavior.

A final area that is clearly understudied is claiming by organizations, whether government, business, or other types of entities. Macaulay's seminal study of contract problems (Macaulay, 1963) suggests that businesses with ongoing relationships may tend to avoid legal claiming, and treat problems as simply part of day-to-day business to be dealt with in ways that preserve the relationship. While there is some research on litigation between businesses, there is virtually no research (beyond Macaulay) on how businesses initially respond when they have a problem with another business. Business claiming is by no means limited to problems with other businesses or with government; claims can be brought against individuals (or very small businesses). Leaving aside routine debt collection, when do businesses (or government or other organizations) bring claims against individuals? When is this type of claiming routinized and when is it done to create precedents and reputation (as in the case of copyright infringement actions brought by recording companies against individuals who have shared or downloaded music in violation of

[14] The potential role of third parties is best illustrated with an example. Imagine a claim where some or all of the compensation is to pay for medical monitoring. In such a case, if the third party providing the monitoring can bill a claim fund directly, that third party will have a strong incentive to encourage people to obtain the monitoring services. If the third party is the regular medical provider for the claimant, and hence sees the claimant periodically for other reasons, the third party can seek to have the claimant avail him or herself of the monitoring on other visits to the provider.

copyright laws)? How are decisions reached about bringing such claims? Which individuals in the organization are the major actors in this decision-making process? Organizational claiming is a potentially fruitful area of inquiry, although it will require creative methods by those undertaking such research in order to find sources within organizations that can provide information, or even to understand how organizations come to define something as a problem that might require action.

VI. Conclusion

This Chapter has focused on claiming and its antecedents as a form of legal mobilization. I have not sought to make the Chapter a comprehensive discussion of legal mobilization. The most prominent missing element is legal mobilization as a political strategy or a strategy for social change. My focus has been on legal mobilization to deal with specific justiciable problems, primarily the kinds of problems that people encounter in their day-to-day lives. As argued above, research on claiming behavior has produced some very consistent results: the centrality of context and the marginal role of individual characteristics.

Arguably the central findings that are now well established constitute the low-hanging fruit of inquiry in this area. They are the kinds of findings obtainable from research that is relatively easy to conduct (albeit by no means inexpensive of time or resources). The research to push beyond these findings will be more difficult to design. Moreover, given the importance of context revealed in extant research, studies focusing on a broad range of justiciable problems are not likely to advance our understanding of legal mobilization behaviors. Rather, it will be necessary to design research projects focused on specific problem contexts and problem types. Good examples of such projects can be found in the areas of responding to sexual harassment (e.g., Marshall, 2005; Blackstone et al., 2009), discrimination (Bumiller, 1988), medical negligence (May and Stengel, 1990), and the terrorist attacks of September 2001 (Hadfield, 2008). What this means is that our understanding of legal mobilization is likely to advance fairly slowly, and to be specific to particular problems rather than general to a wide range of issues. Still, there may be some countries (e.g., China: see Michelson, 2007) or other types of general settings where the consistent patterns reported in extant research do not hold, which means that there will be a continued role for the types of studies of broad legal needs, dispute processing, and justiciable problems that have been most prominent in this area.

REFERENCES

Abel-Smith, B., Zander, M., and Brooke, R. (1973). *Legal Problems and the Citizen: A Study in Three London Boroughs*, London: Heinemann.

Abrahamse, A.F. and Carroll, S.J. (1999). "The Frequency of Excess Claims for Automobile Personal Injuries," in G. Dionne and C. Laberge-Nadeau (eds.), *Automobile Insurance: Road Safety, New Drivers, Risks, Insurance Fraud and Regulation*, Norwell, MA: Kluwer Academic Publishers.

Atiyah, P.S. (1987). "Tort Law and the Alternatives: Some Anglo-American Comparisons," *Duke Law Journal* 1987: 1002–44.

Baker, T. (2005). *The Medical Malpractice Myth*, Chicago: University of Chicago Press.

Blackstone, A., Uggen, C., and McLaughlin, H. (2009). "Legal Consciousness and Responses to Sexual Harassment," *Law & Society Review* 43: 631–68.

Blankenburg, E. (1992). "A Flood of Litigation? Legal Cultures and Litigation Flows Before European Courts in Historical and Comparative Perspective," *Justice System Journal* 16: 101–10.

Bogart, W.A. and Vidmar, N. (1990). "Problems and Experiences with the Ontario Civil Justice System: An Empirical Assessment," in A.C. Hutchinson (ed.), *Access to Civil Justice*, Toronto: Carswell.

Bumiller, K. (1988). *Civil Rights Society: The Social Construction of Victims*, Baltimore: The Johns Hopkins University Press.

Cappelletti, M. and Garth, B. (1978). *Access to Justice: The Worldwide Movement to Make Rights Effective: A General Report*, Milan: Dott. A. Guiffre Editore.

Coates, D. and Penrod, S. (1980–81). "Social Psychology and the Emergence of Disputes," *Law & Society Review* 15: 655–80.

Curran, B.A. (1977). *The Legal Needs of the Public: The Final Report of a National Survey*, Chicago: American Bar Foundation.

Daniels, S. (1982). "Civil Litigation in Illinois Trial Courts: An Exploration of Rural-Urban Differences," *Law & Politics Quarterly* 4: 190–214.

Daniels, S. and Martin, J. (2009). "'It is No Longer Viable from a Practical and Business Standpoint:' Damage Caps, 'Hidden Victims,' and the Declining Interest in Medical Malpractice Cases," *International Journal of the Legal Profession* 16: 187–210.

Donohue, J.J. and Ho, D.E. (2007). "The Impact of Damage Caps on Malpractice Claims: Randomization Inference with Difference-in-Differences," *Journal of Empirical Legal Studies* 4: 69–102.

Engel, D.M. (1984). "The Oven Bird's Song: Insiders, Outsiders, and Personal Injuries in an American Community," *Law & Society Review* 18: 551–82.

Engel, D.M. and Steele, E.H. (1979). "Civil Cases in Society: Legal Process, Social Order, and the Civil Justice System," *American Bar Foundation Research Journal* 2: 295–346.

Ewick, P. and Silbey, S.S. (1998). *The Common Place of Law: Stories from Everyday Life*, Chicago: University of Chicago Press.

Felstiner, W.L.F. (1974). "Influences of Social Organizations on Dispute Processing," *Law & Society Review* 9: 63–94.

Felstiner, W.L.F., Abel, R.L., and Sarat, A. (1980–81). "The Emergence and Transformation of Disputes: Naming, Blaming, Claiming," *Law & Society Review* 15: 631–54.

FitzGerald, J.M. (1983). "Grievances, Disputes and Outcomes: Patterns of 'Middle Range' Disputing in Australia and the United States," *Law in Context* 1: 15–45.

Galanter, M. (1983). "Reading the Landscape of Disputes: What We Know and Don't Know (and Think We Know) about Our Allegedly Contentious and Litigious Society," *UCLA Law Review* 31: 4–71.

Genn, H. (1999). *Paths to Justice: What People Do and Think About Going to Law*, Oxford: Hart Publishing.

Genn, H. (2009). *Judging Civil Justice*, Cambridge: Cambridge University Press.

Genn, H. and Paterson, A. (2001). *Paths to Justice, Scotland: What People in Scotland Do and Think About Going to Law*, Oxford: Hart Publishing Co.

Ginsburg, T. and Hoetker, G. (2006). "The Unreluctant Litigant? An Empirical Analysis of Japan's Turn to Litigation," *Journal of Legal Studies* 35: 31–60.

Greenhouse, C. (1986). *Praying for Justice: Faith, Order, and Community in an American Town*, Ithaca, NY: Cornell University Press.

Grossman, J. and Sarat, A. (1975). "Litigation in the Federal Courts: A Comparative Perspective," *Law & Society Review* 9: 321–46.

Hadfield, G.K. (2008). "Framing the Choice Between Cash and the Courthouse: Experiences With the 9/11 Victim Compensation Fund," *Law & Society Review* 42: 645–82.

Harris, D., Maclean, M., Genn, H., Lloyd-Bostock, S., Fenn, P., Corfield, P., and Brittan, Y. (1984). *Compensation and Support for Illness and Injury*, Oxford: Oxford University Press.

Hensler, D.R., Dombey-Moore, B., Giddens, B., Gross, J., Moller, E.K., and Pace, N.M. (1999). *Class Action Dilemmas: Pursuing Public Goals for Private Gain*, Santa Monica, CA: RAND Institute for Civil Justice.

Hensler, D.R., Marquis, M.S., Abrahamse, A.F., Berry, S.H., Ebener, P.A., Lewis, E., Lind, E.A., MacCoun, R.J., Manning, W.G., Rogowski, J.A., and Vaiana, M.E. (1991). *Compensation for Accidental Injuries in the United States*, Santa Monica, CA: The RAND Corporation.

Kawashima, T. (1973). "Dispute Resolution in Contemporary Japan," in A. von Mehren (ed.), *Law in Japan*, Cambridge, MA: Harvard University Press.

Kritzer, H.M. (1988–1989). "Public Notification Campaigns in Mass Litigation: The Dalkon Shield Case," *Justice System Journal* 13: 220–39.

Kritzer, H.M. (1991). "Propensity to Sue in England and the United States: Blaming and Claiming in Tort Cases," *Journal of Law and Society* 18: 400–27.

Kritzer, H.M. (2008). "To Lawyer, or Not to Lawyer: Is That the Question?," *Journal of Empirical Legal Studies* 5: 875–906.

Kritzer, H.M., Bogart, W.A., and Vidmar, N. (1991a). "The Aftermath of Injury: Cultural Factors in Compensation Seeking in Canada and the United States," *Law & Society Review* 25: 499–543.

Kritzer, H.M., Vidmar, N., and Bogart, W.A. (1991b). "To Confront or Not to Confront: Measuring Claiming Rates in Discrimination Grievances," *Law & Society Review* 25: 875–87.

Lloyd-Bostock, S. (1984). "Fault and Liability for Accidents: The Accident Victim's Perspective," in D. Harris, M. Maclean, H. Genn, P. Fenn, S. Lloyd-Bostock, P. Corfield, and Y. Brittan, *Compensation and Support for Illness and Injury*, Oxford: Oxford University Press.

Macaulay, S. (1963). "Non-Contractual Relations in Business: A Preliminary Study," *American Sociological Review* 28: 59–76.

Markesinis, B.S. (1990). "Litigation-Mania in England, Germany and the USA: Are We So Very Different?," *Studi Senesi* 102: 372–433.

Marshall, A.-M. (2005). "Idle Rights: Employees' Rights Consciousness and the Construction of Sexual Harassment Policies," *Law & Society Review* 39: 83–124.

May, M.L. and Stengel, D.B. (1990). "Who Sues Their Doctors? How Patients Handle Medical Grievances," *Law & Society Review* 24: 105–20.

Mayhew, L.H. and Reiss, A.J., Jr. (1969). "The Social Organization of Legal Contacts," *American Sociological Review* 34: 309–18.

Merry, S.E. (1990). *Getting Justice and Getting Even*, Chicago: University of Chicago Press.

Michelson, E. (2007). "Climbing the Dispute Pagoda: Grievances and Appeals to the Official Justice System in Rural China," *American Sociological Review* 72: 459–85.

Miller, R.E. and Sarat, A. (1980–81). "Grievances, Claims, and Disputes: Assessing the Adversary Culture," *Law & Society Review* 15: 525–65.

Miyazawa, S. (1987). "Taking Kawashima Seriously: A Review of Japanese Research on Japanese Legal Consciousness and Disputing Behavior," *Law & Society Review* 21: 219–41.

Morris, A. (2007). "Spiralling or Stabilising? The Compensation Culture and Our Propensity to Claim Damages for Personal Injury," *Modern Law Review* 70: 349–78.

Murayama, M. (2007). "Experiences of Problems and Disputing Behaviour in Japan," *Meiji Law Journal* 14: 1–59.

Patel, A., Balmer, N.J., and Pleasance, P. (2008). "Geography of Advice Seeking," *Geoforum* 39: 2084–96.

Pleasence, P., Balmer, N.J., Buck, A., O'Grady, A., and Genn, H. (2004). "Multiple Justiciable Problems: Common Clusters and Their Social and Demographic Indicators," *Journal of Empirical Legal Studies* 1: 301–29.

Tanase, T. (1990). "The Management of Automobile Accident Compensation in Japan," *Law & Society Review* 24: 651–92.

Vidmar, N. (1988). "Seeking Justice: An Empirical Map of Consumer Problems and Consumer Responses in Canada," *Osgoode Hall Law Journal* 26: 757–96.

Vidmar, N. and Schuller, R.A. (1987). "Individual Differences and the Pursuit of Legal Rights," *Law and Human Behavior* 11: 299–317.

Wollschläger, C. (1998). "Exploring Global Landscapes of Litigation Rates," in J. Brand and D. Strempel (eds.), *Soziologie des Rechts: Festschrift für Erhard Blankenburg zum 60 Geburtstag*, Baden Baden: Nomos.

Yngvesson, B. (1993). *Virtuous Citizens, Disruptive Subjects: Order and Complaint in a New England Court*, New York: Routledge.

Zemans, F.K. (1983). "Legal Mobilization: The Neglected Role of the Law in the Political System," *American Political Science Review* 77: 690–703.

1 2

FAMILIES

MAVIS MACLEAN

I. Introduction

As Ira Ellman said in his inaugural lecture (Ellman, 2003), family law is hard. It is hard because, unlike other aspects of law, it is concerned with intimate relationships, individual beliefs, and social values, and these not only reflect the diversity of a society but continually change over time. Set within this varied and unstable landscape, family law is required to make decisions about what has happened in the past, and also face the challenge of planning for the future. The relationship between the family and the state where standards of individual behavior are unacceptable to the wider society must be regulated, as in cases of child protection or domestic violence. But the justice system is also available to those seeking help with managing relationships between family members at every stage in the life cycle where these have become complex and uncertain or conflicted, as in the case of separation and divorce, or disputed inheritance. The role of the law is not only to codify the social norms and expectations surrounding personal obligations in such a way as to provide guidance in accordance with the values of the society with a degree of certainty, but also to provide those experiencing conflict with a mechanism for at best conflict resolution and at worst ongoing conflict management. The justice system aims to make things better for individuals whose personal affairs have become so distressing and painful that they have become unable to manage them in any other way, and in particular to protect the vulnerable. In the traditional family this has led to a focus on children, those caring for them (still largely their mothers), and the elderly and infirm. But as we have moved away from traditional definitions of what constitutes a family and new forms of family organization have emerged, such as cohabitation, same sex partnership, and parenting apart from partnering, it becomes increasingly difficult to speak of family law. Instead, as John Eekelaar (2005) has advocated, we are beginning to use the term "the law of personal obligations." The roles and tasks facing family law have become so complex that not only the work but even the traditional name is in question.

However, there are ways of dealing with the "hard" nature of family law. A key weapon in the armory is empirical research, in so far as all the factors which are problematic for family law can be looked at to advantage through the lens of social enquiry. If we accept the words of the great anthropologist of law, Clifford Geertz (1977), "the law is as much a part of the culture of a society as its poetry or its music," then we can turn with enthusiasm to the contribution of social science to the understanding and development of law in general and family law in particular. In family law we have drawn on a wide range of empirical legal studies, from background data defining the demographic, social, and economic context for family matters, to detailed studies of child development and family functioning, and studies of policy development and implementation, including access to law and evaluation of change initiatives. The contribution of empirical work across many jurisdictions to family law has been outstanding, and is well equipped to address the key questions posed in this volume:

- What are the key issues in the development and implementation of family law, which cross jurisdictional boundaries? How has empirical work helped to clarify and respond to these issues in family law worldwide?
- In addition to these well-documented concerns, what are the newly emerging issues of local and international concern, and are these being addressed through

empirical study? Is our research agenda fit for purpose? Where are the knowledge gaps?

- Finally, what theoretical directions are indicated by the empirical research agenda?

This Chapter will begin by looking to three central concerns of empirical work from the 1960s to date, identifying three strands of work; the first two arise from demographic change reflected in marriage breakdown and its consequences for finance and parenting. The third strand sits closer to criminal law, and is concerned with the protection of children from abuse and neglect. We will then turn to the family law issues which are newly emerging and require research input as family structures change, particularly the emergence of cohabitation, the separation of parenting from partnering, and the development of same sex unions. Before closing we review the gaps in current empirical work with particular attention to the delivery of family justice through both traditional mechanisms and alternative methods of dispute resolution. Finally we offer reflections on the implications of the body of empirical work for the development of a theoretical framework for family justice.

The focus of the Chapter emphasizes the contribution of research to policy development and evaluation. This relationship is by no means straightforward. It is sometimes said that government has three possible approaches to research: it is valued when it supports a policy choice already made, or when it provides an excuse for delay in making a difficult decision. Only rarely do research findings directly affect the content and timing of a policy decision. But although there are clearly many motivations for carrying out empirical research from the purely academic to the availability of funding, nevertheless it has been a continuing feature of family law research that it is both policy aware and policy relevant.

II. Defining and Responding to Key Issues in Family Law: the Role of Empirical Research over the Last Fifty Years

A. The divorce epidemic

From the late 1950s onwards family law throughout the Western world was characterized by the rolling back of the state from policing spousal and parental roles, as the balance shifted between state interest and individual choice, between family diversity and homogeneity. The growing commitment to individual choice and private ordering was exemplified by the introduction of no-fault divorce reform in California in 1969, and this was rapidly followed by similar developments in other jurisdictions, leading to what is often termed the divorce epidemic of the 1970s. Public concerns about the collapse of family life became widespread, and the role of social science in legal policy-making accelerated (Grossberg, 2000).

In the United States studies of the economic implications of divorce led by Lenore Weitzman (1985; modified by Sorensen, 1992) highlighted the economic penalties for women and the advantages enjoyed by divorced men. When divorce reached the research agenda in the UK in the early 1980s the key issue also appeared to be the financial consequences; however, the findings of disadvantage were expressed not directly in terms of gender, but in terms of parenthood, related to the presence of children and those with primary responsibility for their care (Eekelaar and Maclean, 1986). The steep rise in the divorce rate was widely discussed in the media also as a symptom of the collapse of society in the UK. Plans for legislative reform were underway to try to accommodate the need for divorced men and women to move on with their lives, and for men to be free of permanent responsibility for their ex-wives and better able to support their new families. The research community attempted to provide the necessary background data, and these concerns were shared with American and European colleagues. At the same time, researchers from the University of Warsaw presented an entirely different picture. Their concern was the failure of the divorce rate to rise. In Poland, a Catholic country where religion was intertwined with the national concern to oppose Communist rule, divorce was unacceptable to the Church. The researchers found (Fuszara, 1997) that couples in conflict troubled by alcohol abuse and domestic violence were unable to separate when, especially from the woman's perspective, it was necessary to do so, because of the shortage of alternative accommodation.

This research demonstrates how empirical work can challenge an assumption, in this case that rising divorce rates were the key problem. Stepping back from a local version of the issue (a damaging divorce epidemic) made it possible to see the underlying question, which is whether the law is providing an appropriate framework for regulating change of civil status for those wishing to leave a marriage.

In both the United States and the UK, and in other jurisdictions where similar issues were under discussion, the research agenda was being driven by interest in the impact of changing family structures on the arguments for legal change (see Weitzman and Maclean, 1992, particularly chapters by Weitzman, Bastard and Voneche, and Funder). But the form taken by the change was shown by sociologists to depend on the cultural and political context. William J. Goode in the United States described access to no-fault divorce as a consumer good, suggesting that rates would rise with increasing affluence. He took the view that as women were now more present in the labor market, and had greater opportunities to make choices, so expectations about what marriage should provide were also increasing. Men and women were seeking divorce as part of their search for a better quality of life (Goode, 1956; see also Weitzman and Maclean, 1992). What was less visible at the time was the move toward setting aside marriage in some societies and the increasing number of less formal relationships. These came to include both opposite sex and same sex cohabitation (see Thery and Biet, 1989; Kiernan, 2001) and also couples who are described as emotionally close but do not share a household, i.e., they are Living Apart Togethers or LATS (Lewis and Haskey, 2006). These developments will be addressed later in this Chapter.

In appreciating the role of research in the development of family law, it is important to recognize that researchers do not work in isolation. In this instance, the academic community was able through the International Society for Family Law (ISFL), the Research Committee of the Sociology of Law (RCSL) of the International Sociological Association (ISA), and the Law and Society Association (LSA) to meet regularly and exchange information and ideas. Through these formal channels, and the informal links which they generate, a body of internationally informed scholarship developed. Researchers were able to bring together their local concerns and build a world picture of the drivers for change, the knowledge base required to inform change, and the kinds of policy developments which might have the desired outcomes in the differing contexts.

In the case of divorce research, a group drawn from the RCSL, the LSA, and the ISFL came together at the Rockefeller Centre in Bellagio, Italy, and their discussions were published as *The Economic Consequences of Divorce* (Weitzman and Maclean, 1992). This book brought together the available research, and from this knowledge base discussed the policy options available in the different jurisdictions. The impact of this kind of work is not only scholarly in helping us to refine our thoughts, but also practical in that as law reform becomes a possibility, the advice which scholars can give to their own governments is immeasurably strengthened by the background knowledge of what is happening in other jurisdictions. For example, in the case of divorce, we were told how the French government, in a predominantly Catholic country which had concerns about divorce, promoted law reform which binds the couple together as parents in perpetuity through shared parental responsibility, thus almost negating the separation of the marital couple (Voneche and Bastard, 2005). This approach is in marked contrast to the American concern with the freedom and rights of the adults involved to get on with their new lives, but paradoxically remaining the country where marriage appears to be standing up to the competition from cohabitation. The UK approach lies midway between the two with a powerful element of looking to the future through the use of the Children Act 1989 in the making of financial arrangements by parents on divorce. For example, the Act requires the court to give paramount consideration to the welfare of the child in any matter before it pertaining to the child. This enables a judge to give a house owned by the husband/father to his former wife if it would be in the best interests of the child to do so.

The practical local issues of how to allocate property in a particular jurisdiction, with a particular housing market, and particular female labor-force participation and child care arrangements, lie within the worldwide context of changing family structures. The comparative studies helped to reveal what exactly was being defined as the problem in the different settings. Was the divorce rate too high or too low? Was divorce seen as a private matter to be arranged by the parties, or is there is a need for state prescription? Finally, is divorce the end of a relationship, or a turning point at which a couple cease to be partners but continue to be joint parents? How can financial stability be provided for any children involved? What is expected of women in the labor market?

The epidemic of divorce studies associated with the divorce epidemic was followed by a series of studies of the consequences of divorce.

B. Post divorce and separation: the issue of Child Support

In both common law and civil law jurisdictions, the concerns of policy-makers and researchers about the divorce rate and the divorce process were swiftly followed in the late 1980s by a focus on the financial support of children who no longer (or never had) shared a household with both biological parents. As parenting became separated from partnering, how were their needs to be met? The process of problem definition and strategy development in the UK, the United States, and Australia was strongly and visibly influenced by empirical legal studies. Multi-disciplinary research programs, including distinct contributions from demographers, family sociologists, social policy experts, economists and lawyers, developed as did inter-disciplinary projects where the focus was "socio-legal," combining the various base disciplines in a more integrated way, as for example at the Centre for Socio Legal Studies established in Oxford 1974 (see Oldham and Melli, 2000).

The social context varied from country to country, but the central issue remained that second families are formed after separation or divorce, and a man on a low or average income will find it difficult to maintain two households. A child is supported to various degrees by the parents, by the market and by the state. In the UK, for example, women with school-age children are expected to work, but studies have shown that in the UK mothers tend to work part-time and in low-paid jobs. In other jurisdictions, such as the United States, part-time work for women is less common, and in parts of Europe (Germany and the Netherlands for example) mothers return to paid work later, when children reach secondary school aged 11. In many Arab countries, the child is the responsibility of the mother as a small child but is expected to return to the father at the age of seven.

In common law countries, there had traditionally been reliance on court orders for child maintenance made around the time of divorce, but these had often been set at low levels and had rarely been complied with in full (Bradshaw and Miller, 1990). In the UK, as in other jurisdictions, the rise in the numbers of lone parents and their increasing demands on the state for welfare support were a source of irritation to a government which was seeking to trim public expenditure during a period of economic difficulty.

The research contribution began with studies by demographers of the incidence of lone parenthood and of re-partnering (reviewed by Kiernan, 2001), by economists of the actual costs of raising a child (Espenshade, 1984; Garfinkel and McLanahan, 1986) and by socio-legal scholars of the efficacy of current forms of legal intervention (Eekelaar et al., 2000). The incidence of lone parenthood was high and increasing (though there were debates about definition and duration of the status, with five years being thought to be the maximum). But costs were higher than had been thought, especially if defined as including the impact on the earning capacity of the chief carer (Funder, 1992); and child support levels set by courts were generally low and compliance poor. These kinds of messages in the United States had led to concerns about the numbers of unsupported children in inner cities becoming part of the underclass, and policy-makers were turning their attention to more effective collection of child support payments through setting up a Federal Child Support Agency.

At the same time research was contributing to ideas about how a child support payment should be assessed and calculated, and what kind of guidelines for this could be introduced. The most powerful formulation came from University of Wisconsin Professor Irv Garfinkel, who argued that parents should be held to have an obligation to share their resources with their children in the same way after separation as they had done while sharing a common household (Garfinkel, 1982). His background in research and practice, as both social worker and economist, gave his approach a unique combination of sensitivity and practical economics. His ideas were taken up in Australia, where an administrative system bypassing the courts in setting and collecting child maintenance was in the process of being set up, and shortly afterwards exported to the UK (Fehlberg and Maclean, 2009).

As the policy process developed, new issues were emerging which attracted the attention of researchers. For example, in the UK, though poor compliance with support orders was well documented, there had been no consideration of the conflict faced by fathers when required to send money back to a first family while they tried to meet the immediate needs of their second family. Empirical work published as *The Parental Obligation* in 1997 (Maclean and Eekelaar, 1997) found very different attitudes expressed by men and women toward the relative financial responsibilities of resident and non-resident parents to their children. Fathers were far more sympathetic to the needs of second families than of mothers, perhaps because they are more likely to have direct experience of these needs.

However, in the midst of this debate about how much should be paid by fathers, and through what mechanism, the research community was again indebted to Central European research colleagues. This time, drawing on experience of studying life outside the rule of law during the communist period, they raised the issue of the implication of taking a matter out of the jurisdiction of the courts and putting it into the hands of an administrative authority, in this case the Child Support Agencies of Australia and the UK (Maclean and Kurczewski, 1994). These arguments carried little weight at the time, but with hindsight have considerable force in the light of the failure of the Child Support Agencies in both jurisdictions. In the UK the administrative Child Support Agency tried to deal with a matter in dispute between the parents as if it were an application to the state for a benefit, and sought detailed information on his circumstances from the father. In practice these facts were frequently disputed by the mother, and the agency could only make a bureaucratic decision, as it was not able to test evidence and reach a more transparent conclusion. The resulting challenges led to delays and loss of confidence in the schemes in both Australia and the UK, which have since been radically overhauled. Both sets of changes are currently under evaluation by large-scale empirical state-funded research (see Fehlberg and Maclean, 2009).

C. Child protection

The third area of ongoing concern in family law where we will describe key issues in research is the protection of children at risk of harm or neglect. Concern for children's safety and well-being is one of the clearest examples of an issue of universal concern. But there has been a sharp division of opinion between those who see a need for the state to be more proactive in seeking out and helping children at risk, and those who value the autonomy and diversity of the family unit and are more hesitant about intervention by the state. Empirical legal scholars have made important contributions to this debate.

In policy terms, attempts to improve prevention and step up intervention have been associated with high-profile tragic events, followed by retreat when intervention is thought to have become excessive. The high-profile cases are the subject of essentially anecdotal media accounts of events, and are accompanied by moral outrage. It is left to the empirical researchers to try to ascertain the incidence and prevalence of such tragic events, and to contribute to informed debate about the implications for policy and practice. For example, in the UK in the 1980s public inquiries were held into the deaths of two children, Jasmine Beckford and Kimberley Carlisle, who had slipped through the net of the responsible agencies and lost their lives at the hands of those caring for them. Allegations about networks of child abuse in the Cleveland area in the north of England and ritual Satanic abuse in the north of Scotland followed, but were found on investigation to be unfounded (see Cretney, 2003).

The complex web of legal responsibility was becoming unmanageable, and an uncomfortable debate about the conflict between family privacy and state intervention was developing. Government was advised by the Law Commission to make a thorough examination of the need for reform, and brought forward the Children Act 1989 (England and Wales) which codified the law relating to children and established the principle of welfare paramountcy. In any decision relating to the care or upbringing of a child the court must give paramount consideration to the welfare of that child. This balanced and constructive outcome after a period of some hysteria owes a great deal to the influential program of high-quality research leading up to the legislation. In particular, Dingwall and colleagues (Dingwall et al., 1995) for the first time observed the work of hospital and local authority staff in cases of suspected abuse. They formed the view that there was little danger of excessive state intervention but rather the opposite. Welfare agencies were so short of resources that they had practical reasons to hold back. Furthermore, professionals were operating under what they called the Golden Rule of Optimism, i.e., a belief that parents love and care for their children.

These circumstances were specific to the UK context. But the debate runs wider. In Spain, for example, the concern about child abuse hidden within a strong culture of the primacy and privacy of the family, led to legislation which enabled local authorities to take a child into care, if they were concerned for its safety and well-being, without any reference to the courts (Piconto Novales, 2007). In the U.S. on the other hand, the debate is more focused on theoretical concerns about autonomy, and how the law should divide control over children's development between parent, child and state (Buss, 2004). Buss argues that deferring to the parents' rights furthers the political aim of preserving a pluralistic society, but offers less discussion of the best interests of the child. The concept of "welfare" or "best interests" is itself complex, but has recently been shown by a small qualitative study to be more robust in its interpretation across European jurisdictions than might have been expected given the difference in approaches of the justice system in, for example, France with its inquiring magistrates, and England and Wales where the system is formally adversarial (George, 2007).

Removing a child from parental care is a major step in any society and the proportion of children taken into public care varies widely from country to country. Empirical work, such as that from the Thomas Coram Research Unit, University of London, is beginning to clarify exactly what being in care entails in the different jurisdictions. If we take foster care, in Germany fostering is a voluntary activity for women giving deprived children a pleasant experience, while in France foster carers are trained and licensed by the state and regarded as professional pedagogues.

The continuing visibility of child protection is driven by demographic factors, in particular the changes in family structures and the separation of parenting from partnering. But it is also associated with the increasing ghettoization of the urban poor, and the incidence of mental illness and drug use. Local context affects the way in which the issue is presented, but the underlying concern remains the nature of the relationship between individual, family, and state. Few would argue with the need to protect children from criminal or mentally unfit parents. But few would agree on what constitutes the best interests of a particular child, and even fewer would agree on how these interests should be pursued and protected. Is the family justice system, the criminal justice system, the health care system, or the local welfare or children's services the appropriate agent of the state in these circumstances? Or should the extended family network play a larger part as, for example, in the New Zealand family conferencing model? Empirical legal research has made a powerful contribution to family law at many levels, including philosophical debates about family autonomy and state intervention in the search for what helps children (Buss and Maclean, 2009).

There are two other ongoing issues where the contribution of empirical legal studies will not be discussed in this Chapter. The first is domestic violence between adults, for although there is an extensive body of research, it is important that this matter is seen as essentially a part of criminal law. The second area is that of the law relating to the elderly, where the legal issues related to discrimination have received little attention to date from empirical researchers though hopefully this area will develop further (there are honorable exceptions: for example van Houtte and Breda, 2005). The next task for this Chapter is to consider how empirical research is responding to newly emerging issues in the relationship between individual, family, and state.

III. The Role of Empirical Research in Meeting the Emerging Challenges of Changing Family Forms

A. Cohabitation

Empirical research data are particularly important in supporting the legal response to new forms of family organization, which tend to give rise to anxiety based largely on anecdotal evidence as they enter public debate. In this context family law has benefited greatly from research grounded in social demography and family economics. As previously noted, rising divorce rates and the economic consequences of these changes particularly for women and children were a key area in the development of the evidence base for family law. Following the increase in cohabitation in the UK, Europe, Australia, and Canada, though perhaps to a lesser extent in the United States, demographers have played a central role (Kiernan, 2001; Ermisch, 2003; Blumstein and Schwartz, 1983). Traditionally, couples have lived together as a precursor to marriage. Now demographic analysis reveals rather different patterns emerging. As social constraints on sexual relationships outside a formal union have relaxed, young people have formed live-in relationships, without necessarily a view to marriage. There is also the emergence of an older group of cohabitants who have been married previously but have divorced, and in their new relationships do not seek a formal change of civil status. And there are those whose lifestyle is less organized and whose relationships and parenthood have simply happened without any legal formalities. Setting aside religious concerns about the nature of marriage, there are practical implications of these informal unions for the parties themselves and for third parties, particularly any dependents and also the taxpayer. The issues arise not on the formation of these unions but on their dissolution. Where children are born to a cohabiting couple, in most jurisdictions they tend to be outside the protection offered by family law to children of a marriage after separation or the death of parents (Kiernan, 2004; Bjornberg, 2006; Clarke and Wright, 1997).

To give an example of the impact of empirical legal research in the UK, the Law Commission, the independent body charged with considering issues requiring legal reform, recently published a paper arguing that the economic consequences of cohabitants separating require regulation, particularly where there are children of the relationship (Law Commission, 2007). Concerns had arisen about the inequality of the outcomes of parental separation for children according to whether their parents had been married or not (see Hale, 2004). The debate was stimulated by accounts of the decline in marriage, the increase in cohabitation and the apparently higher degree of instability of these relationships compared with marriage, and the growing number of young children being affected by separation who were economically outside the protection of the divorce law. In addition, there had been empirical research on the women's understanding of their legal position as cohabitants, which demonstrated that many women were ignorant of their vulnerability (Barlow et al., 2005). Reliable information about cohabitation is notoriously difficult to obtain as the status is hard to define, except by duration or the presence of children because no officially visible event occurs which is recorded by standard data collection.

The Law Commission obtained additional analysis of Census data on household composition to give a fuller description of the cohabiting population. This enabled the Government to consider the costs of making cohabitants and married people equally eligible for benefits and pensions. These data were collated and analyzed by the Law Commission, which produced a powerful report arguing that their survey of public opinion supported treating separating parents equally before the law, whether or not they had made a legal marriage. The demographic analysis made it clear that the cohabiting population, though still tending to belong to a lower socio-economic group than the married and to have less stable unions, were gradually becoming more like the married population. Demographic data, attitudinal data for the general population, and legal analysis all pointed in the same direction.

At the same time, qualitative research seeking to understand why some couples marry and others cohabit found an unexpected variety of reasons (Maclean and Eekelaar, 2004). The level of commitment to the relationship among the cohabiting population did not differ from that described by the married group, which seems to support the case for legal reform. Some couples chose marriage for instrumental reasons, as they needed the legal recognition of their relationships in order to apply for immigration to countries such as Australia. Others saw marriage as a celebration and recognition of their established relationship and were planning a ceremony to celebrate the birth of a child or make public their enduring commitment. Others saw marriage as part of their religious or cultural heritage, and could not envisage cohabitation outside marriage. This latter group included Catholics, Muslims, and Sikhs. There are, however, an increasing number of Muslim religious marriages which, if not registered, have the legal status of cohabitation, an issue about which the government in the UK has expressed interest but has not yet committed itself to action. The contribution of empirical research to forming a rational and constructive debate rather than a media-driven anecdotal storm of stories has been substantial and of great value.

B. Shared parenting

The first example presented above of the challenge of emerging family forms gave evidence of convergence in the behavior and socio-economic characteristics of men and women in different legal forms of partner relationship, marriage, and cohabitation, accompanied by increasing debate about the continuing relevance of legal distinctions between the two forms of civil status. Similarly, convergence can be seen in the parenting roles performed by men and women, being accompanied by increasing demands from fathers for a change in the law to recognize this change, and have their rights to a full share in the upbringing of their children after separation or divorce legally recognized. The traditionally dominant role of women in childcare is being questioned by "new fathers," who see themselves as having an equal part to play in their child's life, even after separation from the mother. The demand by fathers' groups for shared parenting after divorce or separation has been a powerful movement throughout Europe, Australia, Canada, and the United States.

Research evidence from psychologists and therapists specializing in child development has been used to argue for and against the need for children to have frequent and substantial time with both parents despite the inevitable disruption caused by frequent moves (Lamb and Kelly, 2001; Lamb 1999; Warshak, 2000). The protagonists claim that as women's participation in the labor market and men's participation in the domestic sphere have increased, parenting has become a joint activity and children should spend time with both parents equally in the event of separation (Collier and Sheldon, 2008). Empirical research into time budgets and the composition of the labor market, however, suggest that both changes, though detectable, are limited in extent (Dex and Ward, 2007).

Fathers' movements became active worldwide, and ranged from constructive support groups studying cooking for the under fives to extremist groups, such as the Black Shirts in Australia, who picketed the homes of women thought to be obstructing contact with the father, and the Fathers for Justice in the UK, who publicized their position by climbing the walls of Buckingham Palace and planning to kidnap the youngest child of the then Prime Minister Tony Blair. In the face of strong media sympathy for the fathers, governments in Australia and Canada responded by setting up committees and commissions to investigate, and the preparation of primary legislation on contact began in London.

The research evidence, however, told a different story. Studies showed a clear picture of the limited extent of contact problems and the positive ways in which the justice system was responding. In the UK less than 10% of families were seeking the help of the courts, the rest making private arrangements (Hunt and Roberts, 2004). In New Zealand a retrospective study of persistent, highly conflicted contact disputes before the courts revealed a high incidence of mental health issues among the litigants, and a lack of good quality legal representation and advice (Barwick et al., 2003). Trinder and her colleagues explored the nature of those conflicts and found serious welfare issues in cases going to the English courts; in particular, there was a high incidence of maternal anxiety about paternal alcohol or substance abuse, and domestic violence (Trinder et al., 2006). Hunt's recent study of 300 English contact applications (Hunt and Macleod, 2008) found that in the majority of cases fathers succeeded in their applications, though sometimes with variation in the detail, and that most cases had proceeded by negotiation ending with court orders made by consent. There simply was no large-scale problem, but rather a small number of angry and distressed individuals unable to come to an agreed arrangement. The courts were encouraging contact, but putting some safeguards about supervision or support in place where necessary.

In Australia the report "Every picture tells a story" held to the view that there should be no formulaic approach to child contact, but that each case should be looked at individually. The report stated clearly that the right decision for each child should be based on the needs of that child. Despite this finding, the parliamentary commission responsible for policy in this area produced the Shared Parental Responsibility Act 2006, which provided for a more equal sharing of time between parents. In February 2008, however, an evaluation of the new regime was published showing how stressful shared parenting had been for many children (McIntosh and Long, 2008).

In the UK, initial government sympathy for the men's groups' demands for a statutory right to contact was modified in the light of research findings, effectively disseminated in a Briefing Paper from Oxford (Hunt and Roberts, 2004), which presented the available data in a short accessible format freely available online. The resulting legislation, the Children and Adoption Act 2006, reflects evidence-based policy. The new statute upholds the two key tenets of the Children Act 1989 (England and Wales): that the welfare of the child is the paramount consideration of the court, and that parents with parental responsibility do not lose that status on divorce or separation. The new legislation then provides for support in the form of parenting education programs to facilitate contact, and new remedies to deal with non-compliance with an order. Both provisions reflect best practice as evidenced by social and socio-legal research. There is no question but that empirical work was central to the outcome of a highly visible public debate in the UK over what constituted the best interests of children involved in family dissolution and that it is playing a major part in the critical evaluation of the recent reforms in Australia.

C. Same-sex unions

Our final example of a new family structure where empirical legal research is needed to develop an effective legal framework to bring together both new forms of partnership and new forms of parenting, is the same-sex partnership. As we have observed in the previous section, where good research is available and effectively communicated, the impact can be substantial. Difficulties arise when the research questions being addressed by the academic community have not caught up with the pressures arising from changing family forms, and when the findings are complex and raise questions rather than providing answers.

The debates regarding same-sex unions in the United States, including the 2008 reversal of moves toward liberalization in California, have been acrimonious perhaps because of the framing of the issue in terms of same-sex marriage rather than same-sex partnership. This is understandable in view of the centrality of marriage to U.S. family formation, and also reflects the hostility toward homosexuality among parts of the U.S. population. The contribution of legal analysis has been more "black-letter" than socio-legal (see Barron, 2000). In the UK change happened more quietly, perhaps because of a greater prevalence of heterosexual cohabitation and the framing of the debate in terms of same-sex partnership rather than marriage.

In England the Civil Partnership Act passed quietly through both Houses of Parliament and aroused remarkably little public debate. Perhaps this was because the bill was extremely long and tedious as it replicated every piece of existing legislation which referred to marriage, making all applicable to same-sex unions. But in the UK also there was an almost total absence of empirical research about the potential population of civil partners in preparation for the change. Given the focus of family law on sorting out problems at the end of a relationship rather than regulating what happens during the union, it would have been difficult for a research program to identify the issues in advance. But now that the first civil partnership dissolutions are beginning to reach the courts there is a growing need for empirical data. For example, the financial provisions which parallel those for divorce are largely based on the expectation of the presence of children and that one party is likely to have suffered financial detriment as a result of parental duties. This may be less frequent the case in same-sex unions, but there is no robust evidence whether this is in fact the case. A stronger empirical base is necessary for understanding how often a same-sex union includes children from a former heterosexual relationship (for example in the case of women seeking same-sex partnerships after a failed marriage) and how often a same-sex relationship produces children by assisted means of reproduction, through fostering, or by adoption.

We tend to assume that, without childcare responsibilities, there would be economic parity between the partners, but we may also see an age disparity resulting in different contributions to the partnership, or one party being expected to stay at home and give up paid work in order to carry out domestic duties. A recent case, which settled out of court, involved two men with a long relationship of 15 years, who had recently entered a formal civil partnership, where one had been the major earner and the other had stayed at home. It became clear that a court would order a 50-50 division of assets, to which the parties agreed without a trial. But is this what society expects where there are no children? How does this sit with a law on separating cohabitants that takes little account of children and basically expects parties to walk away with whatever they brought to the relationship? We might seek to achieve congruence in the legal approach to determining post-separation responsibilities of adults to each other as applied to those who marry and to those who enter a civil partnership. Or should the family justice system take the pragmatic approach of meeting the needs of the vulnerable? There are serious issues to consider, and the discussion would benefit from better information. Those charged with the responsibility for law reform can make well argued decisions based on legal theory taking in account factors such as equality, and human rights. But the legislative process can be greatly enriched by empirical underpinning.

D. Delivering family justice: a gap in the research agenda?

On turning from the social context and legal issues in family law to the process as it directly affects men, women and children, that is, the delivery of justice through the courts, unfortunately the role of empirical legal research appears to be less well developed. There is a great deal of information about what individuals expect and experience when undergoing family change and conflict, and how these social norms sit alongside the legal framework. But there are far less data on how the family justice system is currently serving those whose difficulties require this form of intervention. Recent policy initiatives in many jurisdictions (Australia, United States, Canada, UK, France, Germany, Japan) have focused on alternative dispute resolution (ADR) and the research agenda has followed the policy agenda, leaving us with information about these alternatives (e.g. Greatbatch and Dingwall, 1999; Pearson, 2000; Murayama, 2007; Bastard and Voneche, 1995) but a rather limited understanding of what these interventions are alternatives to, i.e. the work of the courts and the legal profession.

If we consider divorce and separation, men and women experiencing family difficulty of this kind follow a pathway through informal advice and support from family and friends through to professional intervention, with a tiny minority finding their way to the judges and lawyers at the heart of the justice system (Genn, 1999). In court they will find information, advice, support and guidance, a framework for negotiation, and then usually an agreed or more rarely an adjudicated management of the matters at issue, plus the mechanism to enforce what has been agreed or adjudicated. The emergence of mediation as an alternative to the traditional mode of dispute resolution has been the main family law story of the past decade. In the UK, for example, in 1993 the Government published a policy paper (Green Paper) entitled *Looking to the Future: Mediation and the Ground for Divorce* (Cm 2424), as the first stage in the development of the Family Law Act of 1996, which firmly established in statute the policy of placing mediation center stage. It was hoped that this change would perform the function of "enabling the couple to take responsibility for the breakdown of their marriage" and "providing an alternative to negotiating matters at arms length through two separate lawyers and to litigating through the courts." Yet despite the introduction of a required initial mediation appointment for applicants for public help with their legal costs, demand for the service remains below 15% of those seeking divorce. But while demand for mediation remains limited, the demand for legal advice remains high. The most robust empirical evidence at the time (Genn, 1999) showed that 85% of those divorcing in a large general population sample used lawyers for early pre-court information and advice and found them helpful.

The search for better ways of helping those with family problems continues, with attempts to find less adversarial approaches (see McIntosh and Long, 2008), particularly where children are concerned. In conflicted contact cases there have been many attempts to discover an alternative to a court hearing, but the innovative programs have rarely been subject to robust evaluation (Trinder et al., 2006; Hunt and Roberts, 2005). Many of the ADR approaches have been developed by gifted and charismatic individuals, who achieve local success. However, to take the example of Judge Lederman, who developed the Early Intervention Project in Florida for conflicted contact cases, when asked about evaluation by Joan Hunt, he answered that there had been no assessment because everyone could see that the scheme was a success. The search for a "silver bullet" to resolve these distressing cases is understandable and laudable, given that they reflect conflict embedded in a relationship for many years where black-letter law can offer little guidance. But though there are some pointers toward what might be developed (e.g., teaching communication skills and conflict management) there is little independent research evidence to substantiate the claims of current success.

Data and empirical analyses related to the work of the courts are even more limited in scope and quality than the far-from-comprehensive empirical work on ADR. There are assumptions about the aggressive behavior of advocates and the quality of adjudication, but these are rarely evidence-based. There has been some development in understanding the work of lawyers in family cases, particularly at the pre-court stage, following on from the ideas developed by Robert Mnookin and Lewis Kornhauser (1979) on bargaining in the shadow of the law and by Richard Abel and Philip Lewis (1995) describing the role of the legal professions. There are a number of studies (see Sarat and Felstiner, 1995; Mather et al., 2001; Eekelaar et al., 2000; Maclean and Eekelaar, 2009) which indicate a strong settlement culture in the United States and the UK, and the reluctance of lawyers to have to go to trial. Indeed, there is little financial incentive to do so as profits come from case volume rather than fighting a particular case all the way to court. The studies referred to agree that the skill of the lawyer lies in convincing the client to accept a position which lies within the range of outcomes a court would accept. If both sides go through this process they should find themselves taking positions which are close enough for agreement to be reached without trial.

We still know little about what happens when a matter reaches the court. In England and Wales judges are being asked to take on new roles as case managers, and it is important to gather data on how they do this, and who benefits. Standard data-collection procedures have their origins in measurement of court activity, and are essentially a management business tool for measuring whether court staff are busy and productive. These systems aim to measure units of work done, and are hard to modify into tools for evaluation of the activity. For example, in England information about child protection hearings is collected on each event, and on the work done for each party, making it difficult to piece together an account of the case of a particular family where a number of adults and children are involved, even more so if there are criminal justice issues (e.g., domestic violence) involved. In Scotland we have some information on the Children's Panels which deal with child protection and juvenile crime (Griffiths and Kandel, 2000), indicating that the aims of involving the young person more directly have not been successful, although some progress is being made.

The kind of empirical work which is of great interest but sadly rarely undertaken is that which cuts across the traditional division between looking at the business activity of the courts, the aims of the legal intervention, and the outcomes for parents and children. For example the evaluation of procedure known as "in court concilia-tion" carried out by Liz Trinder and colleagues for the Department of Constitutional Affairs (Trinder et al., 2006) measured not only the rate of agreement reached in contact cases, but also looked at how these agreements stood the test of time and whether there was any impact on the well-being of the adults and children involved. The study found that, although the adults reported reduced stress by being freed from the pressure of court proceedings, there was no discernible improvement in the well-being of the children.

IV. CONCLUDING OBSERVATIONS: THE IMPLICATIONS FOR THEORETICAL DEVELOPMENT

This Chapter has noted the wealth of empirical data, which aids understanding of the incidence, prevalence, and nature of the kinds of family difficulties which result in legal intervention as family structures change and become more flexible and diverse. These data are widely available internationally and well used. But there is also a comparative lack of data on the delivery of family justice, a knowledge gap which requires attention if there is to be an evidence-based family justice system.

Whether we are looking to the social context, the development of law or the day-to-day administration of the family justice system, there are bigger issues which empirical legal researchers might address. Starting from the social context, we need to think harder about what we mean by personal obligations, not only about the rela-tionships between family members but also about other relationships based in work or neighborhood or friendship (Fuszara and Kurczewski, 2005). We need to look beyond definitions of family life based on biological and legal ties to the network of obligations which arises from the full range of personal relationships as opposed to market-based or power-based relationships. What are the links between these dif-ferent kinds of relationships? As Carol Smart reminds us in her book, *Personal Life* (2007), the greatest compliment that can be paid to a family member is: "she's not just my sister, she's my best friend" and, conversely: "she's such a good friend she is really family." Eekelaar and Maclean carried out a small study of 35 men and women to ask about key stages in their lives: leaving home, partnering, having a child, taking responsibility for children as they get older, and for elder parents in turn. We asked about the personal obligations these men and women recognized and why, whether they spoke about rights or responsibilities, about obligations based on duty or status, and whether they used the language of feelings and emotion (a brief account is given in Eekelaar, 2005).

Given the complexity and speed with which social norms are changing, how are the legislators responding? In the UK, for example, the direction of law reform swung from liberalization of divorce law and more generous benefits to lone parents during the 1970s to a conservative counter-movement in the 1980s based on the view that family values were being debased, calling for the enforcement of the financial responsibilities of absent parents. Is there a move toward rights and individualism? Or are new forms of obligations and social cohesion emerging? How do we respond to the complex messages from an increasingly diverse society where the norms, values, and behavior of minority groups within society are at odds with the legal framework? Recent debates about the role of religious systems of law in secular states, for example Sharia law, are in urgent need of empirical background information.

In this changing social context the next "big" research question, on which we have little empirical background knowledge as yet, is what we want and expect from a family justice system. If we can clarify what we want from a justice system we will be better able to evaluate what we have. We have touched briefly on the question of moving away from an adversarial system. However, if we are to get to grips with the essential question of what a court does and why, we need to go further and might benefit from using the model-building tools of policy analysis:

- Do we want our courts to intervene only when the state has an interest in protecting the individual, what we might term a residual social control model?

 If so, we would be looking only at state-initiated action to protect children from abuse or neglect and adults from domestic violence or abuse, and to enforce the decisions of the court.

- Or do we want the justice system to be more proactive and to intervene in disputes between individuals in private law matters, which we might term a welfare model?

 If so, access becomes an issue. Should the courts be easily accessible to all individuals with a dispute, or only to those who are so distressed and angry that they are unable to deal with their problems in any other way? Should the courts refer people on to other sources of help such as mediation, counseling, or parenting classes, and, if so, with what degree of persuasion or compulsion? Or do we want courts to facilitate conflict-management by the individuals themselves, by providing a safe place with expert advice available where individuals can be helped to resolve their own issues, confident of support in putting the decision into effect?

- Or, finally, if we see the aim of family law as protecting the vulnerable, do we want to contemplate a third model for family justice which aims to provide information and advice for all with family issues, with the aim of preventing the escalation of problems and promoting early resolution? This would be an investment model, attractive but also costly

The research agenda for the coming decade might benefit from a consideration of these kinds of issues, so that the development of family justice systems can be informed by analysis of what kinds of personal obligations are perceived in the community, which of these the government has a legitimate interest in regulating, and how far it should intervene to protect the vulnerable, to support those with private quarrels, or to invest in educating the public in conflict management and resolution so that the role of courts can be restricted to that of a service of last resort.

REFERENCES

Abel, R. and Lewis, P. (eds.) (1995). *Lawyers in Society: An Overview*, Los Angeles: University of California Press.

Barlow, A., Duncan, S., James, G., and Park, A. (2005). *Cohabitation, Marriage and the Law*, Oxford: Hart.

Barron, J.A. (2000). "The Constitutionalisation of the American Family Law: the Case of the Right to Marry," in S.N. Katz, J.M. Eekelaar, and M. Maclean (eds), *Cross Currents; Family Law and Policy in the US and England*, Oxford: Oxford University Press.

Barwick, H., Gray, A., and Macky, R. (2003). Characteristics associated with the very early identification of complex Family Court cases, Department for Courts, Wellington New Zealand.

Bastard, B. and Voneche, L.C. (1995). "Interprofessional tensions in the divorce process in France," *International Journal of Law and Family* 9: 275–85.

Bjornberg, U. (2006). "Cohabitation and marriage in Sweden...does family form matter?," in J. Lewis (ed.), *Children, Changing Families and Welfare State*, Cheltenham, UK: Edward Elgar.

Blumstein, P. and Schwartz, P. (1983). *American Couples: Money, Work, Sex*, Northampton, MA: William Morrow and Company.

Bradshaw, J. and Miller, J. (1990). Lone Parents: Report to the Department of Social Security, London: HMSO.

Buss, E. (2004). "Constitutional Fidelity through Children's Rights," *Supreme Court Review* 355–89.

Buss, E. and Maclean, M. (eds.) (2009). *The Law and Child Development*, UK: Ashgate

Clarke, L. and Wright, J. (1997). *Cohabitation: the demographic aspects of cohabitation*, London: Family Policy Studies Centre.

Collier, R. and Sheldon, S. (2008). *Fragmenting Fatherhood*, Oxford: Hart.

Cretney, S. (2003). *Family Laws in the Twentieth Century*, Oxford: Oxford University Press.

Dex, S. and Ward, K. (2007). Parental care and employment in early childhood. Analysis of the Millennium Cohort Study, Sweeps 1 and 2, Institute of Education, London.

Dingwall, R., Eekelaar, J., and Murray, T. (1995). *The Protection of Children*, Aldershot: Avebury.

Eekelaar, J. (2005). "Personal Obligations," in M. Maclean (ed.), *Family Law and Family Values*, Oxford: Hart.

Eekelaar, J. and Maclean, M. (1986). *Maintenance after Divorce*, Oxford: Oxford University Press.

Eekelaar, J., Maclean, M., and Beinart, S. (2000). *Family Lawyers; The Divorce Work of Solicitors*, Oxford: Hart.

Ellman, I. (2003). "Why Making Family Law is Hard," *Arizona State Law Journal* 35: 269–74.

Ermisch, J. (2003). *An Economic Analysis of the Family*, Princeton: Princeton University Press.

Espenshade, T. (1984). *Investing in Children*, Washington DC: Urban Institute Press.

Fehlberg, B. and Maclean, M. (2009). "Child Support Policy in Australia and the UK; changing priorities but a similar tough deal for children?," *International Journal of Law, Policy and Family* 23: 1–24.

Fineman, M. and Opie, A., (1987). "The uses of social science in legal policy making," *Wisconsin Law Review* 107–17.

Funder, K. (1992). "Australia: A Proposal for Reform," in L. Weitzman and M. Maclean (eds.), *Economic Consequences of Divorce*, Oxford: Oxford University Press.

Fuszara, M. (1997). "Divorce in Poland," in J. Kurczewski and M. Maclean (eds.), *Family Law and Family Policy in the New Europe*, Aldershot: Dartmouth Onati Series.

Fuszara, M. and Kurczewski, J. (2005). "Family Values, Friendship Values: Opposition or Continuity," in M. Maclean (ed.), *Family Law and Family Values*, Oxford: Hart.

Garfinkel, I. and Melli, M. (1982). *Child Support: Weaknesses of the Old Features of a Proposed New System*, Institute for Research on Poverty, Report 32A, Madison: University of Wisconsin.

Garfinkel, I. and McLanahan, S. (1986). *Single Mothers and their Children: A New American Dilemma*, Washington, DC: Urban Institute Press.

Geertz, C. (1977). *The Interpretation of Cultures*, NY: Basic Books Classics.

Genn, H. (1999). *Paths to Justice: What People Do and Think About Going to Law*, Oxford: Hart.

George, R. (2007). "Practitioners Approaches to Child Welfare after Parental Separation: an Anglo-French Comparison," *Child Family Law Quarterly* 19: 337–56.

Goode, W.J. (1956). *After Divorce*, New York: Free Press.

Greatbatch, D. and Dingwall, R. (1999). "The Marginalisation of Domestic Violence in Divorce Mediation," *International Journal of Law Policy and Family* 13: 174–93.

Griffiths, A. and Kandel, R. (2000). "Legislating for the Child's voice: Perspectives from the ethnography of Proceedings involving Children," in M. Maclean (ed.), *Making Law for Families*, Oxford: Hart.

Grossberg, M (2000). "How to give the Present as Past: Family Law in the US 1950–2000," in S. Katz, J. Eekelaar, and M. Maclean (eds.), *Cross Currents*, Oxford: Hart.

Hale, B. (2004). "Unmarried couples," *Family Law* 14: 419–26.

Hunt, J. and Roberts, C. (2004). *Child contact with non resident parents*, Family Policy Briefing 3, Oxford: University of Oxford Department of Social Policy and Social Work.

Hunt, J. and Roberts, C. (2005). *Intervening in Litigated Contact: Ideas From Other Jurisdictions*, Family Policy Briefing 4, Oxford: University of Oxford Department of Social Policy and Social Work.

Hunt, J. and Macleod, A. (2008*). Outcomes of applications to court for contact orders after parental separation or divorce*, Family Law and Justice Division, London: Ministry of Justice.

Kiernan, K. (2001). "The rise of cohabitation and child bearing outside marriage in Western Europe," *International Journal of Law, Policy and Family* 15: 1–21.

Kiernan, K. (2004). "Unmarried Cohabitation and Parenthood in Britain and Europe," *Law & Policy* 26: 33–55.

Lamb, M.E. (1999). "Non custodial fathers and their impact on the children of divorce," in R.A. Thompson and P.R. Amato (eds.), *The Post Divorce Family Research and Policy Issues*, Thousand Oaks, CA: Sage, 105–25.

Lamb, M.E. and Kelly, J. (2001). "Using the empirical literature to guide the development of parenting plans for young children: a rejoinder to Solomon and Biriingen," *Family Courts Review* 39: 365–71.

Law Commission in England and Wales (2007). *Cohabitation: the Financial Consequences of Relationship Breakdown*, Law Commission Report no 307, London: The Stationery Office.

Lewis, J. and Haskey, J. (2006). "Living-apart-together in Britain," *International Journal of Law in Context* 2: 37–48.

Maclean, M. and Eekelaar, J. (1997). *The Parental Obligation*, Oxford: Hart.

Maclean, M. and Eekelaar, J. (2004). "The obligations and expectations of couples within families," *Journal of Social Welfare and Family Law* 26: 117–30.

Maclean, M. and Eekelaar, J. (2009). *Family Law Advocacy*, Oxford: Hart.

Maclean, M. and Kurczewski, J. (1994). *Families, Politics and the Law*, Oxford: Oxford University Press.

Mather, L. McEwan, C., and Maiman, R. (2001). *Divorce Lawyers at Work: Varieties of Professionalism in Practice*, Oxford: Oxford University Press.

McIntosh, J. and Long, C. (2008). *The Child Responsive Program, operating within the Less Adversarial Trial. A follow up study of parents and child outcomes*. Report to the Family Court of Australia, July 2007, available at <http://familycourt.gov.au/wps.wcm/resources/file/ebc70245d525f/CRP_Follow_up_Report_2007.pdf>.

Mnookin, R. and Kornhauser, L. (1979). "Bargaining in the shadow of the law," *Yale Law Journal* 85: 950–7.

Murayama, M. (2007). Experiences of Problems and Disputing Behaviour in Japan," *Meiji Law Journal* 14: 1–59.

Oldham, T. and Melli, M. (2000). *Child Support: the next frontier*, Ann Arbor: University of Michigan Press.

Pearson, J. (2000). "A Forum for Every Fuss: the growth of court services and ADR treatments for Family Law cases in the United States," in S. Katz, J. Eeklaar and M. Maclean (eds.), *Cross Currents*, Oxford: Oxford University Press.

Piconto Novales, T. (2007). The consolidation of the Spanish Child Welfare System, paper to the EC's 6th Framework Programme "The Well being of children" coordinated by Professor Lluis Flaquer at the Institute d'Infancia I Mon Urba, Barcelona.

Popenoe, D. (1998). "A demographic picture of the American family and what it means," in C. Wolfe (ed.), *The Family, Civil Society and the State*, Oxford: Rowman & Littlefield.

Sarat, A. and Felstiner, W. (1995). *Divorce Lawyers and their Clients*, Oxford: Oxford University Press.

Smart, C. (2007). *Personal Life*, Cambridge: Polity Press.

Sorensen, A. (1992). "Estimating the Economic Consequences of Separation and Divorce: a cautionary tale," in L. Weitzman and M. Maclean (eds.), *Economic Consequences of Divorce*, Oxford: Oxford University Press.

Thery, I. and Biet, C. (eds.) (1989). *La famille, la loi et l'Etat*, Paris: Imprimerie Nationale, Centre Georges Pompidou.

Trinder, L., Connolly, J., Kellert, J., Notley, C., and Swift, L. (2006). *Making contact happen or making contact work*, London: Department for Constitutional Affairs.

van Houtte, J. and Breda, J. (2005). "Maintenance of the Aged by their Adult Children," in M. Maclean (ed.), *Family Law and Family Values*, Oxford: Hart.

Voneche, L.C. and Bastard, B. (2005). "Can co-parenting be enforced? Family Law Reform and Family Life in France," in M. Maclean (ed.), *Family Law and Family Values*, Oxford: Hart.

Warshak, R.A. (2000). "Blanket restrictions: Overnight contact between parents and young children," *Family and Conciliation Courts Review* 38: 422–45.

Weitzman, L. (1985). *The Divorce Revolution*, New York: Free Press.

Weitzman, L. and Maclean, M. (eds.) (1992). *Economic Consequences of Divorce*, Oxford: Clarendon Press.

13

LABOR AND EMPLOYMENT LAWS

SIMON DEAKIN

I. INTRODUCTION

THERE is a large empirical literature on labor law which is nevertheless somewhat problematic from a methodological point of view. Dickens and Hall, reviewing empirical research on the impact of the post-1997 program of labor law reform in Britain, identified over 50 relevant studies for this period alone, covering a single national system. However, they also reported "only a relatively limited amount of interdisciplinary/multi-disciplinary research bringing together academic lawyers and those trained in social science" (Dickens and Hall, 2005: 33). Frazer (2009: 54) suggests that academic labor lawyers are principally interested in doctrinal exposition and policy evaluation, or in "critical" analysis undertaken without direct reference to empirical methods. Perhaps more surprising is the tendency of industrial relations scholars to study "labor markets and workplace relations focusing on areas where legal regulation is intended, or could be expected, to play a role (for example employers' labor use strategies; worker representation) without actively exploring or commenting on" the role of the law (Dickens and Hall, 2005: 33). A widely held view among labor sociologists that law is a peripheral force in industrial relations partly accounts for this. In economics, conversely, there has been a tendency to ascribe social and economic effects to labor law rules as if they were self-enforcing, without regard to the degree to which they are mediated or supplemented by workplace-level norms and practices. As a research field, labor law is contested terrain, with a multiplicity of approaches making it hard to assess empirical claims concerning the effects, or non-effects, of legal measures. Yet there is a continuous flow of new labor legislation, and a widespread belief that policy should be "evidence-based."

The demand for empirical analysis is driven in part by the transformation that virtually all national labor law systems have undergone over the past 25 years. The postwar consensus in favor of collective bargaining based on stable union-management relations at workplace and industry level has largely disappeared. The change is often associated with "deregulation" but this term is something of a misnomer. Attempts to "individualize" employment relations and to make labor markets more "flexible" have been accompanied by the enactment of ever more voluminous and complex legislation. As trade union influence has declined, more disputes are being settled through specialized labor courts or tribunals. Minimum wage laws and employment protection legislation have filled part of the gap left by collective bargaining, while often being applied on a selective basis which adds to the law's complexity.

These changes are reflected in the issues addressed by researchers and in the methods they have been using. Labor law reforms are increasingly judged, from a policy perspective, by how far they fulfill certain economic goals, in particular increasing employment and productivity. The impact of changes in the law on firm-level practice has accordingly become a major focus of case studies and survey-based research. In addition, a sizeable quantitative literature has grown up looking at the impact of labor regulation in a comparative perspective, using measures of the extent of cross-national variation in the strength of worker protection provided by law. Section II below looks at the emergence of new data sources and methods and considers the role of theory in shaping the empirical research agenda. Section III then reviews the state of the art on a number of substantive issues: the law governing collective labor relations; minimum wage laws; employment protection legislation; the operation of labor courts and alternative dispute resolution mechanisms; and the relationship between labor law and corporate governance systems. Section IV provides an overview and conclusion.

II. Theory, Methods, and Data

Theory has played a major role in framing the questions addressed by empirical work on labor law and the types of methods used. In the predominant sociological tradition of the immediate post-war decades, the industrial relations system was seen as stable and self-adjusting. The role of labor legislation was to provide a framework within which collective bargaining could be established and maintained, but not to shape outcomes directly. This was in part a normative position, based on the perceived political importance of industrial self-regulation and autonomy from direct state control. It was also derived from a view that the socially embedded nature of workplace norms made them resistant to legal intervention. As Kahn-Freund put it (1977: 2), law "is a secondary force in human affairs, and especially in labor relations." Empirical research in this period tended to look at industrial relations phenomena through field work and case study methods which assumed the existence of a supportive legal framework as a background condition, rather than treating the law as a variable of interest in its own right. In the British context this approach was understandable given the largely facilitative role played by labor legislation. In the United States the more interventionist legal regime of the National Labor Relations Act ("NLRA") imposed a duty to bargain in workplaces where the union could show majority support, as well as controlling union organization to a greater extent than in the UK. When elements of the U.S. model were transplanted to the UK in the early 1970s only to meet with a mixture of union resistance and employer indifference, empirical research seemed to confirm the hypothesis, at least for the British case, of the "limits of the law" (Weekes et al., 1975).

This view became harder to maintain when, from the early 1980s onwards, collective bargaining systems began to fragment in all systems; but, as we shall see in more detail below (section III.A), there is no consensus among researchers on whether this was the result of more restrictive labor legislation or of factors beyond the law including high unemployment, the decline of traditional industries, and the opening-up of product markets and of the public sector to increased domestic and global competition. The perception that workplace relations were undergoing significant structural change gave rise to a new research focus on employers' labor-management strategies and an associated demand for more comprehensive data on workplace practices. The first national-level survey of workplace-level industrial relations in Britain was completed in 1984, and went on to provide a model for subsequent surveys in Britain (the most recent one, the Workplace Employment Relations Survey or "WERS," was in 2004) and in several other countries including Australia and France. Surveys based on the WERS model have provided a new data source allowing for systematic statistical analysis at a time when the field was in any case moving in the direction of more quantitative research methods. WERS mostly provides cross-sectional data on a range of aspects of workplace relations, with a subset of the main question-naire being used to construct a panel dataset based on repeated surveys of the same firms. Although it can be used to chart changes in management practice and union activity which might, in principle, be affected by changes in the law, it provides little information on how particular legal rules are being interpreted or applied in prac-tice, limiting its value as an indicator of the impact of legal change. By contrast, the more recently developed Australia at Work Survey contains questions specifically addressed to managers' and workers' perceptions of how particular legal regulations are operating at workplace level, thereby providing evidence of the extent to which laws are working as intended (van Wanrooy et al., 2007).

The shift toward more quantitative research methods has taken place alongside the growing influence of economic approaches to the study both of industrial rela-tions and of labor law. The neoclassical economic model takes the labor market as the focus of analysis and sees it, in a striking but apparently unconscious parallel with the traditional sociological approach, as essentially self-equilibrating. Legal rules are accordingly characterized as external or "exogenous" interferences with the otherwise smooth operation of supply and demand (Stigler, 1946). The norma-tive implications of the economic approach are, of course, very different from those of the post-war industrial relations school, since collective bargaining and labor leg-islation alike are now seen as distortions of the market. While it is recognized that protective legislation may sometimes have a role to play in reducing transaction costs and correcting for negative externalities, the default position is that regulation induces inefficiency in resource allocation (Posner, 1984).

From an empirical point of view, the critical question is how far the state of the law in a given country, treated for this purpose as the independent or explanatory variable, can be shown to be linked to dependent or outcome variables in the econ-omy, such as labor productivity, employment growth, unionization rates, and earn-ings inequality. From the late 1980s onwards the OECD developed indicators of the strictness of employment protection legislation which attempted to quantify these differences, and its employment protection index ("EPI") has since become the most widely-used measure of this kind (OECD, 2004). The World Bank's *Doing Business* Reports, dating from the early 2000s, provide an alternative index which measures the costs to employers of labor law regulations relating to, among other things, the hiring process, working time controls and dismissal protection (World Bank, vari-ous years).

The World Bank indices developed out of the legal-origins hypothesis, which has been steadily reshaping empirical analysis in the law and economics field for the past decade or so, and which has implications for both theory and methods. In this approach, legal institutions, defined broadly to refer to the mechanisms for adjudication and law-making in a given country, are seen as having a long-run influence on the content of the law and hence on patterns of economic development and growth. The content of legal rules in such areas as corporate law and labor law is said to be shaped by the prevailing "regulatory styles" of the common law and civil law. The common law approach to rule-making by judges, it is claimed, tends to result in legal support for contract and property rights, whereas the civil law, with its emphasis on codes and legislation, tends to produce solutions based on the regulation of market relations (La Porta et al., 2008). The empirical basis for this claim consists of econometric analyses of indices which purport to capture the extent of cross-national diversity in the legal regulation of business firms. With regard to labor law, these studies show that countries with a civil law origin (those influenced by the French and German civil codes) provide, on average, a higher degree of protection for workers in respect of labor standards, termination of employment, worker representation, and the right to strike, than those with a common law origin. The same work also shows that these differences in legal regulation are reflected in higher unemployment rates and a larger informal economy in civil law countries (Botero et al., 2004).

Thus legal-origins theory arrives at the same conclusion as the neoclassical model: labor law regulation generally has negative economic effects. However, in contrast to the neoclassical model, the legal-origins approach does not see the labor market as self-equilibrating. On the contrary, markets are constituted and molded by legal institutions. Even if, as some argue, the legal-origins approach relies on over-stylized accounts of the differences between common law and civil law approaches to rule making (see Ahlering and Deakin, 2007), it has posed an important theoretical challenge to the view that the law is a marginal force in economic relations, or is simply an expression of underlying economic forces. This in turn has given rise to a growing interest in finding ways to capture the social and economic effects of legal diversity and of changes in the law over time.

Methodologically, the quantitative techniques used in the legal-origins literature mark a significant step forward, making it possible to analyze cross-national differences in business law regimes in a systematic way. The legal datasets developed by legal-origins scholars, which cover not just labor law but also aspects of corporate and insolvency law and civil procedure, have been very widely used in the comparative economics and management literature over the past decade (see La Porta et al., 2008 for a review). Critiques center on the extent to which the relevant indicators capture real or assumed costs of legal regulation, whether the coding protocols used to create the indices exhibit biases of various kinds, and how far the resulting values should be adjusted or "weighted" to reflect likely country-level variations in the relative importance of given laws and in approaches to enforcement. These arguments can be taken as implying not that the quantitative approach to legal analysis is fundamentally misconceived, but that more work needs to go into the construction of legal indices if they are to be accepted as a reliable measure of cross-national diversity in regulation (see Deakin and Sarkar, 2008).

The most significant limitation on the use of quantitative measures to generate findings concerning the economic impact of legal rules, in labor law as elsewhere, has been the lack of longitudinal data on legal change. Botero et al.'s study (2004) of labor regulation examined over 80 countries using an index consisting of 60 indicators, but only coded for the law as it stood in the early 2000s. A dataset such as this cannot straightforwardly be used to generate a relationship of causation between legal and economic variables. If, theoretically, it is just as plausible to believe that legal rules are shaped by national economic conditions as it is to believe that they are determining them, correlation cannot be equated with causation. This is a general problem in the econometric (and other statistical) analysis of legal and other institutions. One way to get round it is to conduct before-and-after studies of the impact of legal change, which compare the experience of the jurisdiction undergoing reform with that of another which is not, but which is otherwise comparable. This "natural experiment" technique was used to good effect in influential studies of minimum wage legislation in the mid-1990s (Card and Krueger, 1995; see section III.B., below).

Techniques for analyzing time series data have also developed to the point where inferences of causation can be made by comparing the impact of past ("lagged") values of the explanatory and outcome variables on their current values. Long-time series covering several decades of data, of the kind which have recently been developed for corporate, insolvency, and labor law (Armour et al., 2009), open up new possibilities for analyzing the impact of changes in the law over time, but they also pose particular methodological problems. Time series such as these often display the statistical property known as "non-stationarity," or the tendency for the series to display irregular movements over time, without returning to a stable, long-term trend. Where this is the case, false correlations can be obtained. Statistical techniques associated with the idea of "co-integration" offer ways of identifying when two non-stationary time series are linked by a common, stationary trend in such a way as to avoid spurious results, and for specifying the direction of causation from one variable to the other (Engle and Granger, 1987). These techniques are increasingly being used in empirical legal analysis (see, e.g., Deakin and Sarkar, 2008).

The growing popularity of quantitative methods, whether based on survey data or national level indicators of the state of the law, should not obscure the continuing need for qualitative work. Dickens and Hall (2005) give several reasons for thinking that case studies can provide important insights. Surveys which report evidence of employer use of a particular procedure, or which consist of the textual analysis of contracts or agreements, may not capture the extent to which given mechanisms are used in practice, or the way in which their use may be mediated by factors operating at firm level such as management style, union presence and the market environment. Qualitative work is also needed to test inferences of causation drawn from surveys of employer practice. Employers may already have been compliant with the standards set by legislation, or may have been driven to comply by extra-legal factors. Legislative change may have made the difference to the emergence of a given employer practice, or may have shaped a pre-existing trend. Assessment of legislative impact, they suggest, "calls for more in-depth, qualitative work," but such research "is time consuming, often dependent on access in areas where this may be difficult to secure, and is open to charges of being unrepresentative (not least where resource considerations constrain the scale of the research)" (Dickens and Hall, 2005: 35). Quantitative and qualitative methods should, ideally, complement each other, but relatively few studies achieve this—a consequence, perhaps, of increasing specialization in industrial relations research and the resulting segmentation of the field.

III. The State of the Art on Particular Issues: Collective Labor Relations, Minimum Wages, Employment Protection Legislation, and Labor Courts

A. Collective labor relations

The relationship between unionization and economic outcomes including productivity and employment, on the one hand, and the legal framework for collective labor relations, on the other, has been intensively studied over the past 25 years. Freeman and Medoff's seminal analysis (1984) developed a model in which unions display a "negative" wage-monopoly side and a "positive" worker-voice side. The positive aspects of collective voice, which include increased commitment and willingness on the part of workers to invest in firm-specific human capital, were thought by Freeman and Medoff to outweigh the market distortions brought about by wage monopolization. The Freeman-Medoff model, while highly influential, is rooted in analysis of the U.S. environment, in which unions represent a small and diminishing segment of the working population (around 8% of the private-sector labor force as of 2009) and where bargaining has long been decentralized to firm or workplace level. The legal framework of the NLRA, which dates back to the New Deal of the 1930s, grants unions rights to engage in collective bargaining with employers if they can acquire certified bargaining agent status. This depends on the union gaining a significant level of worker support within the relevant bargaining unit, which will normally be at firm or workplace level. In part because of a tendency toward rigid judicial interpretation of the NLRA, its preemptive effect (ruling out state-level initiatives), and a long-running political logjam over the issue of the Act's reform, alternative forms of worker representation have failed to emerge (Estlund, 2002). The resulting contrast between a highly organized and legally protected unionized sector, and an unorganized sector from which unions are by-and-large excluded and in which there is no role for codetermination-style mechanisms, has shaped the empirical literature on the US case. The questions addressed by Freeman and Medoff, in focusing on the contrast between unionized and non-unionized workplaces, have less relevance in contexts where unions, either through collective bargaining or through their involvement in co-determination mechanisms such as works councils, have legally or constitutionally guaranteed representation rights across a wider range of workplaces, and where sector-level collective bargaining ensures parity of labor costs for firms in the same industry regardless of whether they bargain with unions at workplace level, as is the case in many continental European jurisdictions.

Freeman and Medoff (1984) coupled their analysis with a call for the revision of the NLRA to support unionization. No such revision has materialized, and the remarkable stasis of U.S. labor legislation over most of the post-war period makes it an unsuitable case study for an examination of the impact on unionization, and related outcome variables, of legal change. The UK, by contrast, has seen extreme policy shifts since the late 1970s, with a pro-union legal framework, providing support for the closed shop, collective industrial action, and sector-level collective bargaining, giving way to a more hostile environment for unions from the early 1980s onwards. Because union density and strike activity fell over the same period, it might be assumed that these trends were driven by the changes in the law, but this is not clear. Union membership levels fell in all developed countries during the 1980s, and the decline in the UK was far from being the largest. Freeman and Pelletier (1990) were among the first to develop an index of legal change over time, and their analysis, by comparing the UK with the closely comparable jurisdiction of Ireland, claimed to identify a negative impact on unionization levels of the British legislation. However, increased product-market competition, low inflation, and high unemployment are plausible factors in explaining not just union decline but also changes in the laws themselves, which are to some degree a function of union strength. Some econometric studies suggest that unionization is a consequence of the macroeconomic cycle rather than a major influence upon it (Disney, 1990).

Evidence on the interaction between legal change, declining union influence, and employers' labor-use strategies can be found in the qualitative study carried out by Brown et al. (1998). They conducted 32 case studies in UK-based companies across 11 industrial sectors at a time (1996–97) when the legal environment was at its most hostile to trade unions. Statutory "props" to sector-level collective bargaining had been removed and restrictions on solidarity strike action imposed in the 1980s, as well as a series of court rulings in the early 1990s, opened the way to employers to differentiate, from the point of view of pay and conditions, between workers covered by collective bargaining arrangements and those accepting "individualized" (that is to say, non-collectively bargained) employment contracts. Following these judgments, employers in industries with a tradition of union militancy, such as the docks and printing, withdrew from collective bargaining (union "de-recognition"), as they were entitled to do in the absence of a legal duty to bargain of the kind provided in the U.S. context by the NLRA.

The research undertaken by Brown et al. was concerned with examining employers' motives for de-recognition, the effects of de-recognition on terms and conditions of employment, and the role of unions in the resulting arrangements. They found that de-recognition was driven by growing product-market competition and shareholder pressure for financial returns, and, in the public sector, by privatization and contracting out. Case law, which opened the way to rewarding employees who gave up the protection of collective bargaining arrangements, had been a catalyst for de-recognition but was not, in employers' eyes, the main driving force. De-recognition was accompanied by the greater use of performance-related pay and by a widening of pay differentials; however, there was no evidence of individual bargaining over terms and conditions, as employers' standard form contracts simply replaced terms previously incorporated from collective agreements. These standard terms introduced flexibility into the definition of pay and hours and reserved powers to employers to change employment conditions unilaterally. There was similar evidence of the effects of "individualization" in empirical studies from Australia (Fetter and Mitchell, 2004) and the United States (Dau-Schmidt and Haley, 2007), which, however, suggest that benefits to employers of increased flexibility may be offset by increased transactions costs and legal complexity.

It is far from clear that a strategy of union exclusion was capable of delivering competitive advantage to firms. Brown et al. (1998) carried out case studies in comparable firms which had retained collective bargaining. Most of these had also introduced flexible working arrangements. Where formal recognition rights were retained, it was on the basis that unions were expected to cooperate with management in raising productivity and otherwise maintaining the competitiveness of firms. Their study reported no evidence that firms which had withdrawn from collective bargaining had achieved greater flexibility over costs than their unionized counterparts, or had otherwise gained a superior competitive position.

The Brown et al. study was commissioned by a government department; it was begun while a Conservative government was in office but was completed and published after the election of a Labour government, which was committed to restoring some, but by no means all, of the legal rights which had been eroded in the course of the 1980s and 1990s. The *Fairness at Work* White Paper of 1998 and the Employment Relations Act 1999 put in place the new government's agenda for promoting "partnership" between unions and employers. This included legislation providing for a statutory right to recognition for representative trade unions, modeled loosely on

U.S. and Canadian practice, but it stopped short of restoring the right to take solidarity strike action, and nothing was done to revive or shore up sector-level collective bargaining. The implications of the Brown et al. study for policy were ambiguous. It could have been read as arguing for an extension of union recognition, on the ground that union involvement in the issue of work organization had positive impacts on firm-level competitiveness, as well as wider benefits. Quantitative research by some of the same authors, based on analysis of the WERS survey, showed that a strong union presence at workplace level was associated with more effective enforcement of statutory employment rights and with provision of occupational benefits by employers above legislative minima (Brown et al., 2000). On the other hand, the study was open to being interpreted as demonstrating that employers could realize the advantages of enhanced organizational flexibility whether they recognized unions or not. A new recognition law would not represent a "burden" to employers, but it was neither necessary nor desirable for public policy to push for the wider re-unionization of the British economy through the revival of sector-level bargaining or changes to strike law. There is evidence that this second interpretation was the one adopted by policy-makers. A review of the policy impact of social science research carried out by the UK Economic and Social Research Council found that the Brown et al. study had confirmed to civil servants and politicians that the 1999 Act could be adopted without bringing about "an increase in union militancy," with the result that the research "confirmed a policy decision" that was taken independently (ESRC, 2007).

B. Minimum wages

At the start of the 1980s there was a broad consensus among economists to the effect that minimum wage legislation had the effect of causing higher unemployment, particularly among younger workers. The literature focused on the U.S. case, which had (and has) some unusual features. Federal minimum wage legislation, which dates from the 1930s, contains no automatic indexing mechanism, with the result that new legislation is required to raise the basic rate. Because of the difficulty of getting political consensus about the level of the federal rate, there have been lengthy periods when the minimum wage stagnated or fell in value in real terms, and the proportion of the workforce directly receiving the minimum rate is now very low by international standards, around 2%. By contrast, the French minimum wage, which is revised annually according to a formula that takes both wage and price inflation into account, currently covers 16% of the workforce. The U.S. literature focuses on the issue of teenage unemployment, as it was mostly teenage workers who were affected by the minimum wage in that country. Data availability has also shaped the literature; the U.S. Current Population Survey supplied a lengthy time series of data on teenage unemployment. Analysis of this source confirmed the theoretical prediction that raising the minimum rate would have negative employment effects (Brown et al., 1982).

As already noted, the revisionist analysis of Card and Krueger (1995) was based on the opportunity for comparative case studies which was provided by variations in the rates set by individual states, which have the power to legislate minimum wages above the federal level. They carried out a study of the increase in the minimum wage in New Jersey using Pennsylvania, a neighboring state in which the minimum wage had not been increased, as a control. Their analysis showed that, after taking into account the effects of the national recession which affected both states, the implementation of the higher minimum rate in New Jersey was associated with an increase in full-time employment in the fast food restaurant sector there, by comparison to Pennsylvania. The result was theoretically plausible because of assumed monopsony effects. In other words, before the minimum wage was raised, employers had used their superior bargaining power and access to information to depress wages below the competitive rate; the increase in wages triggered by the New Jersey law had increased the supply of labor into fast food employment without depressing underlying demand. In addition, a study of California found that teenage employment and earnings both rose following an increase in the minimum wage, despite high coverage and evidence of compliance by employers. Survey evidence suggested that employers in the fast food sector were unlikely to respond to increases by dismissing workers or cutting fringe benefits, supporting the idea that employers acted as monopsonists in low-wage labor markets.

These studies generated a huge literature response. The main lines of criticism were that the survey data on which they were (in part) based were not entirely reliable; that the periods over which the effects of rate increases were studied were too short; and that the control groups used in the comparative state-level case studies were not appropriate. Long-run panel data studies have tended to find negative employment effects, leading a recent overview to conclude that around two thirds of the relevant studies "give a relatively consistent (although not always statistically significant) indication of negative employment effects of minimum wages" (Neumark and Wascher, 2006: 121).

The U.S. case, in its emphasis on the impact of minimum wage regulation on a very small segment of the working population, is not typical. The British case offers an alternative perspective. For most of the twentieth century there was no general legal minimum wage; instead, legal minimum rates could be set by statutory wage-fixing bodies (trade boards and, later, wages councils) in industries characterized by very low pay and the absence of voluntary collective bargaining. In 1986 the powers of the wages councils were cut back and in 1993 they were abolished altogether (leaving agriculture as the only sector with statutory wage fixing). Prior to the 1986 Act, it was "confidently postulated" by a leading economic critic of labor legislation that abolition would "serve to expand employment [and] offer competitive wages for the socially disadvantaged" (Minford, 1985: 122). However, econometric research carried out in the early 1990s found that as the wage-setting powers of the wages councils were reduced, employment in the low-paying sectors directly affected by this legal change fell, suggesting that in the absence of regulation employers were able to exercise monopsony power (Dickens et al., 1993).

In 1998 a new British national minimum wage was enacted, which was to apply to all sectors of the economy. A tripartite Low Pay Commission ("LPC") was given the task of recommending a minimum rate to the government. The LPC's first recommendation was for a minimum adult rate of £3.60 an hour from April 1999, a figure which represented 45% of median earnings and was estimated to affect 11% of the labor force, mostly in the cleaning, catering, and security industries, with women workers benefiting proportionately more than men. A series of special youth rates was also set. As in the United States there is no automatic indexing mechanism, but the government has accepted a series of LPC recommendations which have had the effect of raising the inflation-adjusted value of the minimum rate over time.

The LPC commissioned numerous pieces of research into the operation of the new legislation and several of its members have been economists who, along with industry representatives, have taken part in the deliberations which resulted in the setting of the recommended rate. One of the original commissioners, Metcalf, has recently reviewed the empirical evidence on the operation of the legislation (Metcalf, 2007). He found that there had been a positive impact on earnings, with the rate of increase in the real value of the minimum wage accelerating after 2002. The fall in the earnings of the lowest quartile which took place in the period without statutory regulation between 1993 and 1998 had been reversed, and there had been a narrowing in the gender pay gap which was attributable to the minimum wage. Wage inequality fell after 1998, having risen consistently since 1978. There was no evidence of negative employment effects in the majority of the sectors most affected (retail, hospitality, social care, cleaning, agriculture, security, clothing and footwear, and hairdressing; textiles, an industry in long-term decline, was an exception). There was no evidence of disemployment effects on particular groups including those most affected by periodic increases in rates. Metcalf's study considers reasons for the absence of negative impacts. He found evidence of redistribution (the profitability of firms most affected by the legislation declined) and of monopsony on the part of employers (survey evidence suggested that firms had discretion to set wages independently of supply and demand). Metcalf (2007: 53) concludes that "the LPC, via its evidence-based approach...has raised the real and relative wage of low-paid workers without adverse employment consequences."

The variety of forms of minimum-wage regulation makes generalization difficult. Some systems, like France, have extensive statutory wage floors set at a high level in relation to median wages, while other systems rely on a mixture of voluntary collective bargaining and legislation extending the terms of collective agreements to non-federated employers. In developing countries, the coverage of minimum wage laws is often higher than in developed ones, in part because collective bargaining mechanisms are either weak or missing. Comparative studies, such as the recent analysis of the United States and Turkey by Koçer and Visser (2009), suggest that minimum-wage forms are most likely to be related to country-level conditions, including the make-up of political coalitions, the stage of economic development, and the presence or otherwise of complementary forms of regulation. A perspective of this kind suggests a need for a more nuanced and context-sensitive approach to the study of the effects of statutory wage fixing than we have seen in most empirical studies to date.

C. Employment protection legislation

Employment protection legislation ("EPL") is, by origin, a continental European mode of labor law regulation, and the marked difference in levels of dismissal protection, for example, between the United States and Europe has been the focus of a numerous studies. U.S. unemployment, which was higher than that in Europe in the 1960s, began to decline in the mid-1980s and carried on falling at the same time as employment growth accelerated; in Europe in the same period, unemployment remained high after the shock of the late 1970s and early 1980s, and employment growth was sluggish. Because there have been relatively few changes to the legal and institutional framework in the United States across the period from the 1960s to the present day, it is not obvious, at first sight, that regulatory factors contributed to the United States' employment performance over this period. However, because the stringency of controls over dismissal in Europe was increased (from an already high base of regulation) in the early 1980s (see Deakin et al., 2007), it is possible to attribute part of the failure of the European economies to match US employment growth after that point to this factor, as suggested by the OECD's influential *Jobs Study* (OECD, 1994).

However, there is theoretical indeterminacy over the effects of employment protection laws. On the one hand, stricter EPL could lead to higher unemployment as firms are deterred from hiring and there is a reduction in productivity brought about by the slowing down of flows of labor from less productive to more productive firms. On the other hand, stricter EPL could reduce unemployment levels by making it more costly for firms to dismiss workers in a downturn, while at the same time providing incentives for retraining as an alternative to redundancy, thereby improving productivity. Studies which look at the interaction of EPL with other institutional factors find that it is, at best, a weak predictor of levels of employment and unemployment (Bertola, 2009).

Progress is being made by studies which take into account the extent to which employment protection laws are both endogenous to particular sectoral contexts and complementary to other institutions in labor, product, and capital markets, both factors which may be expected to mediate their economic impact. EPL can plausibly be said to put into legal form a model which originated in the practice of

industries with stable, bureaucratically organized employment. As a form of regulation, it is therefore likely to have more impact in industries which are characterized
by the opposite types of practices, such as those with a high level of labor turnover.
Recognizing this, Bassanini and Venn (2007) carried out an analysis of the impact
of EPL in what they call "EPL-binding" industries, which they define as those with a
higher propensity to dismiss workers in a downturn, and which they contrast with
"non-binding" industries. They reported a negative impact of EPL on productivity.
However, using the same approach, they found a positive impact of minimum wage
legislation on productivity in low-paying sectors, and a similarly positive impact of
parental leave laws in female-dominated industries.

A growing body of literature, using national-level data, is looking at possible
complementarities between EPL and related institutional variables such as product-
market regulation and corporate governance structures. Amable, Demmou, and Gatti
(2007) report evidence to the effect that, in OECD countries, product-market deregulation produces higher growth only in conjunction with the preservation of a high level
of EPL. This suggests that product-market regulation, rather than high EPL, may have
been a cause of slow employment growth in Europe compared with the United States.
Gatti (2008) finds that high levels of EPL are complementary to concentrated corporate ownership, with this conjunction leading to higher rates of growth; dispersed
ownership and more liquid capital markets are positively correlated with growth in
systems with low levels of EPL. The existence of links between corporate ownership
structures and modes of financing, on the one hand, and employers' labor-use strategies on the other, is also suggested by case-study research (Marshall et al., 2008).

Analysis of the longitudinal labor-regulation index developed at the Cambridge
Centre for Business Research (CBR) also finds evidence of complementarities in the
operation of employment protection laws (Deakin et al., 2007; Armour et al., 2009).
This index is constructed in such a way as to capture a wider range of information than
the OECD and World Bank indices. Information from collective agreements and other
self-regulatory mechanisms, which operate as the functional equivalents to formal
laws in some systems, is included. In another departure from earlier indices, the coding protocols also allow for the individual country scores to reflect the extent to which
labor laws take the form of default rules, applying unless the parties agree otherwise,
as opposed to being either completely mandatory or non-applicable. Explanations for
codings, providing the primary legal source in each case, are provided (this is not the
case with the World Bank index and is only partially achieved in the OECD index).

The CBR index is in the form of an annual time series, going back to the early
1970s. It is currently available for five countries (France, Germany, India, the UK,
and the U.S.) and covers the whole labor law field, which is broken down into five
sub-indices (form of the employment contract, working time, dismissal, employee
representation, and industrial action).

The picture of the law provided by the CBR index is not dissimilar to that given by the
analysis of Botero et al. (2004), in that civil law systems appear to have a significantly

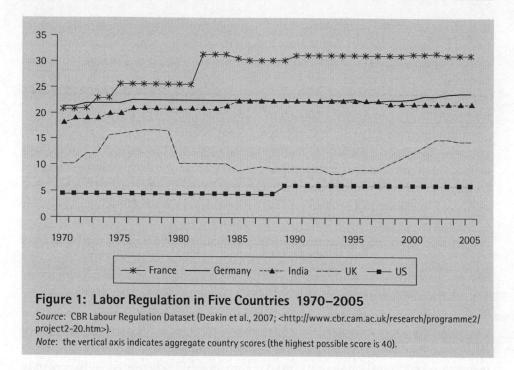

Figure 1: Labor Regulation in Five Countries 1970–2005

Source: CBR Labour Regulation Dataset (Deakin et al., 2007; <http://www.cbr.cam.ac.uk/research/programme2/project2-20.htm>).

Note: the vertical axis indicates aggregate country scores (the highest possible score is 40).

higher degree of regulation than common law ones (see Figure 1). However, the case of India is an exception here. Its labor laws are broadly comparable to those of Germany rather than to its "parent" system, the UK. The time series dimension of the CBR index is also revealing. It suggests that there has been considerable change over time in the content of labor laws, particularly in relation to the treatment of flexible forms of work and to working time controls. It appears that shifts in the political and macroeconomic environment are capable of bringing about significant changes to the substance of labor law, casting doubt on the idea of stable cross-country differences derived from legal origin, and emphasizing the endogeneity of the law to local political and economic contexts (Deakin et al., 2007; Deakin and Sarkar, 2008).

Deakin and Sarkar (2008) carried out a time series analysis of relationships in France, Germany, the UK, and the U.S. between the different components of the CBR index and employment and productivity growth, after controlling for growth of GDP. They found no evidence that the deregulatory labor market reforms carried out in the UK from the late 1970s onwards had had either a positive or negative long-run effect upon employment and productivity growth. By contrast, they found evidence of a positive impact of working time controls and dismissal protection on productivity in Germany, and a positive relationship between working time legislation and employment growth in France. The results for the United States indicate that a strengthening of dismissal laws there in the late 1980s (in the form of the federal-level Worker Advance Notification and Retraining Act (WARN) of 1988, which required employers to give notice of dismissal and make severance payments when downsizing their workforces) was associated with productivity gains, but at the expense of employment growth. A separate study using the CBR index by Acharya et al. (2009) finds evidence of a positive relationship between dismissal protection in the countries contained in the CBR dataset and innovation rates as measured by patent applications, suggesting a further channel by which EPL may be linked to productivity growth.

The WARN law does not impose legal constraints on the substance of the right to dismiss, it merely postpones the effect of dismissal and/or provides for compensation for lack of notification. There is no federal-level unfair dismissal legislation in the United States, but from the early 1980s up to the mid-1990s exceptions to the common law "employment at will" rule (by virtue of which the employer may terminate the employment relationship without just cause or even, in some instances, the giving of notice, mirroring a similar right to quit on the part of the employee) began to emerge in the case law of several states. There is some evidence that the "implied contract" exception to employment at will was associated, in this period, with higher unemployment without any countervailing productivity improvements (Autor et al., 2004) but this result is contingent on the way in which judicial rulings were coded for the purposes of legal index construction. An alternative coding, based on rulings which marked a shift in doctrine at the level of the appellate courts as opposed to the earliest instance of a pro-worker ruling, found no disemployment effect (Walsh and Schwarz, 1996). While there is a case for saying that employers may have begun to adjust their behavior at the point when adverse rulings were first announced as opposed to the later date at which a more definitive judgment was handed down, the sensitivity of the result to the coding method used is an indication of the methodological difficulties inherent in this type of work.

D. Labor courts and alternative dispute resolution mechanisms

While it is widely acknowledged that an understanding of modes of enforcement is critical to an assessment of the social and economic effects of labor legislation, and there is a substantial literature examining the operation of labor courts and other aspects of the machinery of labor law in particular countries, there are very few comparative studies. One of the most illuminating is by Blankenburg and Rogowski (1986), who examined the labor court systems of Britain and West Germany in the mid-1980s. Both countries have specialized courts or tribunals to deal with labor law issues, mostly individual disputes, with legally trained judges sitting with lay representatives from labor and management. When Blankenburg and Rogowski conducted their research, there were around 387,000 labor court filings each year in West Germany but only 47,000 equivalent applications in Britain. The West German courts had jurisdiction over a wider number of issues at that point, but not markedly so. Taking into account differences in overall employment levels and in the numbers of dismissals, litigation rates were six times higher in West Germany. The West German courts had seen an increase of over 40% of their caseload in the preceding decade while litigation rates in Britain had been more or less static (with even a small decline between 1981 and 1986). In Britain around two thirds of applications were settled or withdrawn before the hearing stage (the proportion is about the same today), while in West Germany fully 90% were. Of those cases that went to adjudication, employees had a 50% success rate in West Germany, and a 27% success rate in Britain.

The differences between the two countries, in terms of the importance accorded to judicial process within the industrial relations system as a whole and in the effectiveness of court mechanisms for dispute resolution, are historically rooted. The German labor court system dates back to the 1920s and developed from the outset with the active encouragement and involvement of the trade unions, and, in the post-war period, with a high degree of employer acceptance. By contrast, British employment tribunals were introduced in the mid-1960s and acquired jurisdiction over unfair dismissals only in 1971. Unions regarded them as a second-best alternative to collective bargaining and workplace- or industry-level dispute resolution, while employers tended to see them simply as a source of extra costs. The German courts are staffed by career judges with a specialized labor law training, many of whom are left-leaning or otherwise sympathetic to the overall goals of the labor law system (as indicated by high levels of membership of public-service trade unions). British tribunal chairs, on the other hand, are senior barristers or solicitors who, in the period of the Blankenburg-Rogowski study, had little or no special expertise in labor law. This has changed in the interim, as an experienced cadre of employment judges (as tribunal chairs are now called) has grown up over time. However, court procedure remains a significant point of difference. In the inquisitorial tradition of the civil law, German labor court judges have the power to intervene to direct arguments and shape the hearing to a much greater extent than their British counterparts. Under German legislation, the power to arrange conciliation is given to the labor-court judge rather than to a separate process administered by a government agency prior to the tribunal hearing, as in Britain. As a result, "the inquisitorial discretion that [the German judge] enjoys allows him to shift back and forth between mediation, arbitration and adjudication, using the letter of the law to encourage parties to settle" (Blankenburg and Rogowski, 1986: 83). The procedures of British employment tribunals, although intended to be relatively flexible, are, by the standards of the German labor courts, highly formal and adversarial.

The workload of British employment tribunals doubled in the early 1990s to reach over 70,000 applications by 1993–4, and the late 2000s also saw another very rapid increase, so that by 2007–8 the number of filings had reached nearly 200,000, in part because of a surge in discrimination claims. The overall number of filings is still well below the equivalent German figure of nearly 600,000, in both absolute and proportionate terms, but British policy has been focused for around a decade now on the goal of reducing the number of tribunal hearings on the dual grounds of the cost to government of running the tribunal system and the "burden" to employers of litigation. A study carried out for the UK government in the early 2000s (Burgess et al., 2001) suggested that the rise in tribunal hearings was linked, among other things, to union decline. There was a higher number of claims from workers in smaller businesses, which did not have internal procedures or an active union presence of the kind which tended to reduce the incidence of disputes. Union involvement in dispute resolution also helped to bring about pre-hearing settlements. Union influence in workplace industrial relations continued to erode after the publication of this study, and policy-makers sought other mechanisms for reducing tribunal workload. These included the introduction of a scheme for binding arbitration at the pre-hearing stage, an extension of tribunal powers to award costs against applicants in the case of unfounded claims (the normal rule is that no costs are awarded, regardless of outcome) and, from 2004, the exclusion of claims which were not first submitted to an internal grievance or disciplinary procedure. However, the new costs rules appear to have had a minimal impact on the volume of claims and only a tiny number of cases have been resolved through binding arbitration. The procedural reforms were found to have added a new layer of cost and complexity to workplace-level procedures, and were repealed in 2008. If recent attempts to streamline the tribunal system have generally proved a failure, reliance on labor legislation in place of collective bargaining has been no more successful in delivering effective protection to applicants who do not have union support. Access to tribunals is costly for the non-unionized workforce which now represents around 70% of the total, and the availability of legal or union-based representation is an important factor in the successful resolution of claims (Pollert, 2005).

In the course of the past four decades or so, the British system has undergone a transition from a largely voluntary and collectively oriented system of dispute resolution to one that is more individualized and legally-structured. As early as the 1970s commentators were identifying a high level of regulatory intervention and litigation in the American system, a pattern which has persisted as part of the "legal adversarialism" which characterizes American regulatory culture (Kagan and Axelrad, 1997: 150). The NLRB's highly judicialized approach to resolving claims concerning union organization and bargaining rights has been one of the factors contributing to the rigidity or "ossification" of U.S. labor law (Estlund, 2002). There is no specialized labor court system for individual disputes as there is in most western European countries, and there is a growing trend for legal claims to be resolved through employer-based arbitration systems, which can be made mandatory by agreement between employer and employee. There is a large literature on the detail of the operation of U.S. employment arbitration, which looks, among other things, at the impact on success rates of legal representation and the degree of specialization among lawyer and non-lawyer advocates (see Kritzer, 1998: 154-5). There is some empirical research to suggest that arbitration does not result in reduced success rates or in lower levels of awards for higher-paid employees by comparison to court-based dispute resolution, and may help to ameliorate problems of access to courts for lower-paid employees (Eisenberg and Hill, 2004), although there is evidence that employers introduce arbitration not just in order to reduce litigation costs but as part of union-avoidance strategies (Colvin, 2003).

There is a small but growing literature looking at the judicial resolution of labor law disputes from a behavioral perspective. Sunstein et al. (2006) find that the political composition of NRLB panels affects voting outcomes. There is some evidence that labor courts in Italy and Germany take a more restrictive view of the lawfulness of dismissals during times of high unemployment, and that regional labor market factors and the political basis of judicial appointments also influence the strictness with which labor laws are applied by courts (Ichino et al., 2003; Berger and Neugart, 2006).

IV. Conclusions: the Prospects for Evidence-based Labor Law

This Chapter has reviewed recent developments in the empirical study of labor and employment laws. A growing interest in cross-national, comparative analysis has prompted the emergence of new data sources, in the form of indices of labor regulation, and the utilization of statistical methods which can throw light on the nature of causal influences running from the law to the economy and vice versa. Through work of this kind, a more complete account of the economic effects of labor laws is being established. The conventional view, influenced by the belief that unregulated markets were, on the whole, competitive, maintained that labor regulation was an exogenous source of inefficiencies, leading to unemployment and slowing down growth. Revisionist accounts see labor laws as having a number of complex and potentially offsetting effects. For example, minimum wage laws, if set at the appropriate level, can be used to improve the position of low-income households and reduce earnings inequality. Employment protection legislation may have positive impacts on productivity by enhancing worker commitment and innovation at firm level. The new literature stresses that the effects of labor laws cannot be predicted in an a priori way, through the use of models with universal application, but depend on the interaction of legal rules with a number of national, regional and industry-specific conditions and with complementary institutions in capital markets and product markets. This implies a need for better and more reliable data on the content of the law, on modes of operation, and on the context in which legal rules are applied. It also suggests a continuing role for case study work in examining the operation of laws at workplace level and assessing claims for causal inference drawn from the quantitative literature.

Is the upshot of this likely to be the greater use of evidence from empirical studies in the policy-making process? The prospects for evidence-based policy are, in practice, uncertain. One reason for this is that the status of the knowledge produced by empirical research remains, to some degree, contingent. Many of the questions to which policy-makers would like to have answers are not susceptible to empirical research given the current state of data resources. As we have seen, it is only recently that data have become available on legal systems in a form which can be used in cross-national comparisons. In addition, statistical analyses involve limitations and trade-offs which may (or should) qualify any policy recommendations.

There are, however, wider constraints on evidence-based policy. Theory plays a highly significant role in shaping the policy-making process, and frames empirical research. In the immediate post-war decades the view that the industrial relations systems was largely stable, with law operating as a secondary force, limited research into the social and economic impact of legal rules. More recently, as part of a wider "deregulatory agenda," neoclassical economic models have tended to characterize labor law rules as "distortions" in the otherwise smooth operation of markets. Only recently has there been a growth of interest in legal rules and mechanisms as a variable of interest in their own right, with the capacity to shape economic outcomes, and this has been associated with a set of theoretical claims based around the legal-origins hypothesis, which makes strong a priori assumptions about the nature of different legal systems, assumptions which lack a strong empirical grounding.

At the level of the political process, the theory of competitive labor markets informs an ideological commitment to labor market flexibility and deregulation which, while weakening, continues to influence policy-makers. As we have seen, the empirical basis for the deregulatory approach is not very strong. It is perhaps surprising then to find the international financial institutions continuing to advise national governments that, as the World Bank *Doing Business* report for 2008 puts it, "laws created to protect workers often hurt them" (World Bank, 2008: 19). But this simply reflects the somewhat marginal role that empirical analysis plays in policy formation.

Instances of the use of evidence to set policy remain exceptional. The recent experience of Britain's Low Pay Commission (see section III.B., above) suggests that when empirical evidence feeds into the policy-making process, it does so only within tightly set parameters. The Labour government which was elected in 1997 had made a political commitment to the enactment of a national minimum wage. The issue which the LPC had to decide was what level to recommend. Empirical research was used to inform the deliberations of the Commission, but it did not determine the prior and far more momentous decision to introduce the national minimum wage in the first place. Similarly, research on union de-recognition carried out shortly before Labour returned to office was used to justify a cautious approach to the reform of collective labor relations law, when a more extensive restoration of union rights could equally well have been justified. To take the converse type of case, the analyses contained in the *Doing Business* reports have been framed by the World Bank's prior commitment to the Washington consensus formula of the minimalist state, property rights and trade liberalization as the basis for growth. However, as the Washington consensus fades, we are beginning to see the methodology of the *Doing Business* reports being increasingly questioned (Lee et al., 2008). This is a sign that a major policy shift is taking place which may help to open up new opportunities for empirical inquiry, and ultimately for a reformulation of theory.

References

Acharya, V., Baghai-Wadji, R., and Subramanian, K. (2009). "Labor Laws and Innovation," CEPR Discussion Paper No. DP7171.

Ahlering, B. and Deakin, S. (2007). "Labour Regulation, Corporate Governance and Legal Origin: A Case of Institutional Complementarity?," *Law and Society Review* 41: 865–98.

Amable, B., Demmou, L., and Gatti, D. (2007). "Employment Performance and Institutions: New Answers to an Old Question," IZA Discussion Paper No. 2731.

Armour, J., Deakin, S., Lele, P., and Siems, M. (2009). "How Legal Rules Evolve: Evidence From a Cross-Country Comparison of Shareholder, Creditor and Worker Protection," *American Journal of Comparative Law* 57: 579–630.

Autor, D., Donohue, J., and Schwab, S. (2004). "The Employment Consequences of Wrongful Discharge Law: Large, Small or None at All?," *American Economic Review Papers and Proceedings* 93: 440–6.

Bassanini, A. and Venn, D. (2007). "Assessing the Impact of Labour Market Policies on Productivity: A Difference-in-Differences Approach," OECD Social, Employment and Migration Paper No. 54, Paris.

Berger, H. and Neugart, M. (2006). "Labour Courts, Nomination Bias and Unemployment in Germany," CESIfo Working Paper No. 1752, Munich.

Bertola, G. (2009). "Labour Market Regulation: Motives, Measures, Effects," ILO Conditions of Employment and Work Research Series No. 21, Geneva: International Labour Office.

Blankenburg, E. and Rogowski, R. (1986). "German Labour Courts and the British Industrial Tribunal System: a Socio-legal Comparison of Degrees of Judicialisation," *Journal of Law and Society* 13: 67–92.

Botero J., Djankov, S., La Porta, R., Lopez-de-Silanes, F., and Shleifer, A. (2004). "The Regulation of Labor," *Quarterly Journal of Economics* 119: 1340–82.

Brown, C., Gilroy, C., and Kohen, A. (1982). "The Effect of the Minimum Wage on Employment and Unemployment," *Journal of Economic Literature* 20: 487–528.

Brown, W., Deakin, S., Hudson, M., Pratten, C., and Ryan, P. (1998). *The Individualisation of Employment Contracts in Britain*, Employment Relations Research Series No. 4, London: Department of Trade and Industry.

Brown, W., Deakin, S., Nash, D., and Oxenbridge, S. (2000). "The Employment Contract: From Collective Procedures to Individual Rights," *British Journal of Industrial Relations* 38: 611–29

Burgess, S., Propper, C., and Wilson, D. (2001). *Explaining the Growth in the Number of Applications to Industrial Tribunals, 1972–1997*, Employment Relations Research Series No. 10, London: Department of Trade and Industry.

Card, D. and Krueger, B. (1995). *Myth and Measurement—The New Economics of the Minimum Wage*, Princeton: Princeton University Press.

Colvin, A. (2003). "Institutional Pressures, Human Resource Strategies and the Rise of Nonunion Dispute Resolution Procedures," *Industrial and Labor Relations Review* 56: 375–92.

Dau-Schmidt, K. and Haley, T. (2007). "Governance of the Workplace: The Contemporary Regime of Individual Contract," *Comparative Labor Law and Policy Journal* 28: 313–49.

Deakin, S., Lele, P., and Siems, M. (2007). "The Evolution of Labour Law: Calibrating and Comparing Regulatory Regimes," *International Labour Review* 146: 133–62.

Deakin, S. and Sarkar, P. (2008). "Assessing the Long-run Economic Impact of Labour Law Systems: A Theoretical Reappraisal and Analysis of New Time Series Data," *Industrial Relations Journal* 39: 453–87.

Dickens, L. and Hall, M. (2005). "The Impact of Employment Legislation: Reviewing the Research," in L. Dickens, M. Hall, and S. Wood, *Review of Research into the Impact of Employment Relations Legislation*, Employment Relations Research Series No. 45, London: DTI.

Dickens, R., Gregg, P., Machin, S., Manning, A., and Wadsworth, J. (1993). "Wages Councils—Was There a Case for Abolition?," *British Journal of Industrial Relations* 31: 515–29.

Disney, R. (1990). "Explanations of the Decline in Trade Union Density in Britain: An Appraisal," *British Journal of Industrial Relations* 28: 165–77.

Eisenberg, T. and Hill, E. (2004). "Arbitration and Litigation of Employment Claims: An Empirical Comparison," *Dispute Resolution Journal* 58: 44–55.

Engle, R. and Granger, C. (1987). "Cointegration and Error Correction: Representation, Estimation, and Testing," *Econometrica* 55: 251–76.

ESRC (2007). *An Influential Business: The Impact of the ESRC Centre for Business Research*, ESRC Impact Case Study, Swindon: Economic and Social Research Council.

Estlund, C. (2002). "The Ossification of American Labor Law," *Columbia Law Review* 102: 1527–612.

Fetter, J. and Mitchell, R. (2004). "The Legal Complexity of Workplace Regulation and its Impact on Functional Flexibility in Australian Workplaces," *Australian Journal of Labour Law* 17: 276–305.

Frazer, A. (2009). "Industrial Relations and the Sociological Study of Labour Law," *Labour and Industry* 19: 73–96.

Freeman, R. and Medoff, J. (1984). *What Do Unions Do?*, New York: Basic Books.

Freeman, R. and Pelletier, J. (1990). "The Impact of Industrial Relations Legislation on British Trade Union Density," *British Journal of Industrial Relations* 28: 141–64.

Gatti, D. (2008). "Macroeconomic Effects of Ownership Structure in OECD Countries," IZA Discussion Paper No. 3415.

Ichino, A., Polo, M., and Rettore, E. (2003). "Are Judges Biased by Labour Market Conditions?," *European Economic Review* 47: 913–44.

Kagan, R. and Axelrad, L. (1997). "Adversarial Legalism: An International Perspective," in P. Nivola (ed.), *Comparative Disadvantages: Social Regulations and the Global Economy*, Washington, DC: Brookings Institution.

Kahn-Freund, O. (1977). *Labour and the Law* (2nd. edn.), London: Stevens.

Koçer, R. and Visser, J. (2009). "The Role of the State in Balancing the Minimum Wage in Turkey and the USA," *British Journal of Industrial Relations* 47: 349–70.

Kritzer, H. (1998). *Legal Advocacy: Lawyers and Nonlawyers at Work*, Ann Arbor: University of Michigan Press.

La Porta R., Lopez-de-Silanes, F., and Shleifer, A. (2008). "The Economic Consequences of Legal Origins," *Journal of Economic Literature* 46: 285–332.

Lee, S., McCann, D., and Torm, N. (2008). "The World Bank's 'Employing Workers' Index: Findings and Critiques: A Review of Recent Evidence," *International Labour Review* 148: 416–32.

Marshall, S., Mitchell, R., and Ramsay, I. (eds.) (2008). *Varieties of Capitalism, Corporate Governance and Employees*, Melbourne: Melbourne University Press.

Metcalf, D. (2007). "Why Has the British National Minimum Wage had Little or No Impact on Employment?," CEP Discussion Paper No. 781, LSE.

Minford, P. (1985). *Unemployment: Cause and Cure*, (2nd edn), Oxford: Basil Blackwell.

Neumark, D. and Wascher, W. (2006). "Minimum Wages and Employment: a Review of Evidence from the New Minimum Wage Research," NBER Working Paper No. 12663.

OECD (1994). *OECD Jobs Study, Evidence and Explanations, Part I: Labour Market Trends and Underlying Forces of Change*, Paris: Organization for Economic Cooperation and Development.

OECD (2004). *OECD Employment Outlook*, Paris: Organization for Economic Cooperation and Development.

Pollert, A. (2005). "The Unorganized Worker: The Decline in Collectivism and the New Hurdles to Individual Employment Rights," *Industrial Law Journal* 34: 217–38.

Posner, R. (1984). "Some Economics of Labor Law," *University of Chicago Law Review* 51: 988–1004.

Stigler, G. (1946). "The Economics of Minimum Wage Legislation," *American Economic Review* 36: 358–65.

Sunstein, C., Schkade, D., Ellmann, L., and Sawicki, A. (2006). *Are Judges Political? An Empirical Analysis of the Federal Judiciary*, Washington, DC: Brookings Institution.

van Wanrooy, B., Oxenbridge, S., Buchanan, J., and Jakbauskas, M. (2007). *Australia at Work: The Benchmark Report*, Sydney: Workplace Research Centre, University of Sydney.

Walsh, D. and Schwarz, J. (1996). "State Common Law Wrongful-Discharge Doctrines: Up-Date, Refinement and Rationales," *American Business Law Journal* 33: 645–89.

Weekes, B., Hart, M., Dickens, L., and Jones, M. (1975). *Industrial Relations and the Limits of Law: The Industrial Effects of the Industrial Relations Act*, Oxford: Blackwell.

World Bank (2008 and various years). *Doing Business Reports*, Washington, DC: International Bank for Reconstruction and Development.

1 4

···

HOUSING AND
PROPERTY

···

DAVID COWAN

THIS Chapter is concerned with empirical studies of property with a particular focus on residential occupation. The Chapter ranges widely, but has two central themes. First, property law is better conceived as a destination subject, through which contemporary understandings of social and crime control are mediated. In particular, attention is drawn to studies which intersect law with geography, possibly the most exciting and intellectually challenging development at the cutting edge of research into property law. Hence, some of the empirical research drawn upon in this Chapter is not necessarily about "law" as narrowly conceived, but provides a different way of seeing law.

Second, and related to that first theme, this Chapter takes advantage of the opportunity offered by Ewick and Silbey's observation that much of the focus in socio-legal studies has shifted from law *and* society to law *in* society (1998: 35). The concerns in this Chapter, then, are about the ways in which law and legality are interpreted and invoked in social life, focused specifically on their role in the commonplace construction of home, tenure, exclusion, and jurisdiction (ibid: 20). This Chapter considers how property is thought and talked about, for example through the use of metaphor to construct an ideal of belonging and identity (see, for example, Nedelsky, 1990) or through the creation of a community. It is in this way that law and legality emerge, rather than being the object of study in their own right. Equally, as Nielson (2000: 1059) points out, it is just as important to consider "how people do not think about the law; that is to say, it is the body of assumptions people have about the law that are simply taken for granted."

The starting point is an analysis of the relationship between the meanings of home and their relationship with housing tenure (broadly conceived as ownership and renting). It draws on interdisciplinary studies of housing, in which law is not the focus, to develop the proposition that the reception of tenure, particularly by home owners, offers a rich resource for the analysis of property law. One particular arena—home ownership at the margins, especially of affordability—is suggested as being particularly ripe for further empirical research which, to my knowledge, is as yet underdeveloped. The following section identifies defense and exclusion as particular aspects of the property relation, and draws on research into gated communities as a particular example of that relation. The Chapter then moves on to link this notion of exclusion with broader studies into mapping and jurisdiction. The particular focus of this section is on the formal and informal mechanisms through which the notions of home and tenure are thought and talked about. The final section draws on the law-geography interface as an example of research which has the potential to extend the boundaries of our appreciation of property in law.

I. Home and Tenure

Empirical studies of housing have developed a complex, nuanced understanding of home which demonstrate the porousness of the idea of home. Such studies may not be explicitly legal, although they implicitly speak about legal cultures and identities, most commonly through the notion of tenure. They form the backdrop to the complex constructions of property law in society. The experiences of property surveyed here concern the relation among different forms of tenure, the current insecurity in home ownership, as well as the regulation of the tenant's home. The range of constructions illustrates the diversity of settings of legality, from formal institutional regulation (through, for example, rent control) to informal appreciations of the difference that the form of tenure makes (particularly through the commonplace opposition of ownership with renting).

A. Home ownership

We tend to elide home with ownership, sometimes referring to it without a space as homeownership (e.g., Ellickson, 2008: 90–1). Home ownership is said to be what most people want and is said to provide ontological security (e.g., Saunders, 1990). It is the predominant tenure in much of the Western world, although this state of affairs only came about during the twentieth century. Surveys consistently show that demand for home ownership remains fairly constant at around 90%. Yet, as Forrest and Murie (1991: 123) suggest, "tenure preferences are not formed in a vacuum but are heavily influenced by the pattern of subsidy, general housing policies and the individual judgments regarding financial expectations and changes in family circumstances." One key external consideration has been the promotion of taxation and other major financial advantages for home ownership, which differ across jurisdictions.

The ideological nature of home ownership is most clear when it is compared with the alternatives. The principal point of comparison is usually between ownership and renting, which are respectively and broadly equated to power and powerlessness or normal and abnormal. Saunders' much criticized, but often-cited, *A Nation of Home Owners* (1990) draws attention to a consumption cleavage between ownership and renting. Owners, it is said, benefit from capital gains and investment potential, which reinforce social divisions and contribute to the creation of both a personal and a common interest. Owners have independence and autonomy over their property (as opposed to being under the control and surveillance of landlords, particularly in the expanding social sector of public and other affordable housing providers), which adds to the sense of ontological security. Saunders' argument was based on household survey evidence from home owners and council tenants residing in three English towns. Saunders accepted that his data collection method could only give indicative results, but he has been criticized both for over-extending his conclusions (e.g., to regarding home owners as a class, notwithstanding differentiation and fragmentation among home owners) as well as for not considering alternative conclusions supported by his data. A further, equally substantial critique was that his methods were not likely to answer his research questions, which demanded a richer, qualitative method.

Indeed, other research has demonstrated how gender, sexuality, ethnicity, disability, and their intersections, for example, all impact the experience of ownership (e.g., Moran and Skeggs, 2001). Such studies commonly focus less on home ownership as a choice, and more on the balance between that exercise of choice and the constraints on its exercise. Constrained choice might arise from an inability to access other tenures because of one's exclusion, and, more broadly, what have been described as "ethnic penalties" (a phrase which can be adapted to each and all such groups) (Karn, 1997).

Two rather different studies, addressing a similar question to those asked by Saunders, are more robust in their findings than Saunders. Using comparative documentary evidence from Sweden, Australia, and Britain, Kemeny (1981) develops an argument about the situated nature of home ownership. His research question concerned the relationship between housing tenure and social structure. Why, he asks, is home ownership assumed to be superior in the English-speaking world? Kemeny's answer, in part, is that tenure must be considered within the whole structure of individual societies:

At the most general level, the difference between societies with high and low home-ownership rates is a question not simply of the extent of home-ownership, but of the nature of home-ownership as a form of tenure in particular societies, what alternative forms of tenure relate to one another, and the ways in which the whole tenure system relates to wider social, political and cultural factors. (at pp. 7–8)

Gurney (1999) develops this position further through a case study conducted in Bristol, England. His paper takes a social constructivist perspective, and interweaves documentary evidence from policy reports with data from in-depth interviews with 27 households. The interview schedule was devised in part to discover everyday understandings of home. He draws attention to the construction of tenure which came from these interviews through the use of well-known aphorisms and metaphors about home ownership, for example: "an Englishman's home is his castle"; "it's yours at the end of the day"; "renting's just money down the drain." These aphorisms and metaphors formed part of the everyday understandings of Gurney's interviewees and were value-laden expressions of "common-sense." His interviewees also constructed a morality about housing tenure through providing prejudicial accounts of renting and moral fables. Council housing was "a metaphor for a stereotypical feckless class" (p. 1716).

In a rather differently focused study—of the psychology of property rights in the context of the law concerning eminent domain—Nadler and Diamond (2008: 715) found that the "strength of the owner's ties to the property, that is, how long the property was in the owner's family, had strong effects on perceptions of the propriety of giving up the property, on willingness to sell and on willingness to sell at any price." This conclusion was based on preliminary experimental work in the psychology of property rights, which promises to add much to the literature. The experiments tested two hypotheses concerned with eminent domain: the attachment of people to property over and above its price, and the legitimacy of different public purposes for the taking. This work is in its infancy. One of the research findings—that the purpose of the taking was a significant factor in participants' responses—suggests an emotional connection between occupier and home. This latter point offers an interesting line of enquiry, and experimental work is often lacking in this field, but again there is a need to match it with qualitative data through which the notion of home can be explored further.

The relationship between home and tenure raises a problem at the margins of tenure itself in certain jurisdictions where condominium title is not possible for multi-occupation buildings. This is the case in the UK. The solution consistent with the law of property is that flat owners usually take under long tenancy agreements of say 99 or 999 years with mutual covenants. The problem arises because, while property lawyers might regard such occupiers as long leaseholders, the household-ers themselves more usually perceive themselves to be owners. Cole and Robinson (2000) pursued this issue through a large-scale, government-funded survey of lease-holders. They were initially faced with the lack of a sampling frame and dealt with this by obtaining their sample through indirect contact via a government-funded advisory service. Their methods were mixed, drawing on postal survey evidence from a sample of 870 inquirers, a follow-up survey two years later with a sub-sample of 250 participants who gave telephone interviews and a further sub-sample of 40 participants who gave in-depth qualitative interviews about their experiences dur-ing the process of enfranchisement (buying an extension to their lease). Cole and Robinson's findings demonstrated that the owner/tenant dichotomy is manifested often in a lack of control exercised by the tenant-owner over what they are able to do to their property, the inadequate management of common parts, and the payment of often-excessive sums for repairs to those parts.

Although many of these studies were not explicitly focused on law or were not conducted by lawyers (or both), they demonstrate the ways in which property law emerges in society through understandings about the interrelation between home and tenure. Kemeny, Gurney, Cole, and Robinson, who are housing-policy spe-cialists rather than socio-legal scholars, nevertheless produced classic, sensitive examinations of a specific, socio-legal issue.

B. Home ownership at the margins: the production of insecurity

The production of ownership societies would not have been possible without con-siderable advantages accruing to mortgage lenders and borrowers throughout the twentieth century. In the UK, home ownership boomed in the 1920s and 1930s as a result of a combination of fortuitous financial events—such as the increasing availability of credit and innovations in lending (e.g., mortgage lenders working in conjunction with developers)—together with a decline in the availability of private renting, as well as a more benign set of regulations facilitating development. In the post-war period in the UK, Australia, and the US, housing policy particularly facilitated the growth of home ownership through tax advantages and, for example in Australia and the United States, rewards for returning war service personnel.

The new metaphor resulting from the 1980s financial crisis, however, has been "sustainable home ownership," a phrase which has turned into a cruel joke in the aftermath of the global financial crisis that began in the fall of 2008. That financial crisis created insecurity in the underlying notion of home ownership. There was a period of a few months in 2009 when it seemed that every day a bank or lending institution was becoming insolvent and required state intervention. Behind that financial crisis was the development, and increasing sophistication of, securitization techniques, which dramatically collapsed when the basis for the underpinning risk assessments became falsified leading to systemic uncertainty.

Securitization was the mechanism through which lending institutions changed form and started lending to more risky households using "affordability products." The changing lending patterns reversed the discriminatory lending practices of the twentieth century for the promotion of capital, to put the point crudely; and lending practices were hollowed out reaching low and no income households, the so-called "sub-prime" consumers (those households which were more risky because of their past credit histories). Instead of discrimination on lines of race, predatory lending practices emerged which resulted in higher interest rates for those in higher risk categories.

Wyly et al. (2006) focus on predatory lending, combining quantitative analysis of the sub-prime market with an examination of texts, such as industry documents and legal cases. The purpose of their study was to demonstrate how racially marginalized individuals and places are disproportionately targeted in the sub-prime market, focusing on mortgage lending patterns in Baltimore between 1998 and 2002. Their hypothesis derives from Harvey's classic work from the 1970s, which combines class, the force of law and access to financial institutions. The hypothesis tested was that sub-prime lending combined the generation of an expansion in aggregate consumer demand and an increase in the rate of profit through the segmentation of individuals and places. If redlining is discriminatory, then it might be argued that the sub-prime market, in opening up lending practices, must be anti-discriminatory. In a damning set of conclusions, Wyly et al. come to the opposite conclusion. They note, for example, that "econometric models of subprime segmentation reveal persistent racial targeting and disparate impact, even after controlling for applicant income and underwriters' evaluation of borrower risks" (p.126). In other words, the discrimination has changed its pattern so that previously marginalized groups have been targeted for more expensive loans.

There are a series of research questions about the repossessions process which empirical researchers focusing on property law might address in the future. The most basic question, as yet largely unanswered, concerns the repossession and foreclosure practices of mortgage lenders. We are regularly told (at least in the UK) that repossession or foreclosure is a last resort and that a range of other possibilities (such as restructuring the debt) are employed by mortgage lenders. There may be internal corporate rules and practices, but there is likely to be considerable discretion in those practices as to the meaning of "last resort." We might ask, for example, how that discretion works "on the ground" and the extent to which it works against already-marginalized groups so that there is an intersection of disadvantages. A further issue concerns the relationship between the corporate profit-maximization ethic and a particular version of corporate social responsibility, which recognizes a hypothetical financial and policy interest of the state in avoiding home loss.

There is some (although surprisingly limited) evidence in the UK of borrowers' behaviors when in arrears and, in particular, their interactions with courts and their processes (Ford et al., 2001: Chs 6–7; I know of no similar work in the U.S.). One issue which is regularly raised by borrowers is that they lack control in a process which is done and dusted in a few minutes. Such comments reflect on experiences of the final court hearing only; but we need to recognize that these are interactive processes which take place sometimes over considerable periods of time so that there is scope for studies of such extended processes as opposed merely to a court hearing and its aftermath. Further, the effectiveness of repossession amelioration strategies, whether formal or informal, could also form the subject of research.

Some formal rules require the borrower to take the stage as a victim. So, for example, in her study of the "victims" of repossession cases involving cohabiting partners acting as guarantors, or sureties, of mortgages, Fehlberg (1997) notes that the law "requires a surety to fit herself within a stereotype of the down-trodden and uninformed housewife" in order to place herself in the relevant legal category (of a person subject to undue influence from their partner in procuring their signature). Fehlberg's study begins by isolating differences between public judicial approaches and the cohabitants' private experiences regarding money and marriage as a means to identify the circumstances under which sureties should be entitled to escape liability to lenders as a result of the undue influence of their cohabiting partner. Her empirical research was, however, hampered by the lack of a sampling reference frame because no statistics on sureties were maintained by lenders. In any event, her research questions about the surety's lived experience essentially required a qualitative method. She therefore conducted a small number of interviews with sureties (n = 22) and others (debtors, lenders, and lawyers). Access to the sureties, which might ordinarily have proved problematic, was facilitated through an organization campaigning on a wide range of banking issues, including suretyship, and part of her sample was patiently gained through snowballing (that is, using the contacts of initial participants to generate a further sample of participants) and other methods such as newspaper reports about the research.

C. The tenant's home

The relation between landlord and tenant has proved a fruitful site for empirical legal research, whether about the nature of the contract itself or the legislative structures supporting that contract. In a study of practices of harassment and unlawful eviction of occupiers, I was struck by the (gendered) comment of a landlord who said that he would leave a bunch of flowers for a female or a bottle of wine for a male when they arrived as a new tenant because this was a far more effective practice than a written tenancy agreement. It demonstrated that he (the landlord) cared about the occupiers, and cared about the property. While there is considerable empirical legal scholarship on the end point of the relationship, there is less (to my knowledge) on the connections between the formal and informal orderings of the relationship (e.g., whether or not the parties knew each other prior to the relationship, or are related). Ellickson (2008: 125) suggests that the reputation of landlords and tenants in rural areas and small cities contributes to good relations, but that proposition has yet to be empirically tested. On the other hand, Nelken's classic study (1983) of landlords and the production of unlawful eviction and harassment laws in the UK suggested that one cause of problems was the landlord's belief that the property remained the landlord's home (which our own study, 20 years later, also highlighted).

A particular focus of empirical legal scholarship has been on the impact of legislative interventions restricting rents. Market economists rail against such interventions (for example, the collection published in IEA, 1972), suggesting among other ills that they result in disincentives to investment and encourage withdrawal from the sector by landlords contributing to under-supply, as well as lack of tenant mobility. So ingrained is this view now that such interventions are routinely used as examples when first year economics students are taught the consequences of price control.

Turner and Malpezzi (2003) provide a literature review and an associated bibliography of over 500 rent control studies (with a preponderance of U.S. studies, although, of course, rent control and regulation are global phenomena). They seek to test the bases of opposition to rent control among economists that has become more muted and qualified (at least compared with those found in studies conducted prior to the 1970s) plus the proposition that "a well-designed rent control program can be beneficial" because the losses which it inflicts can be offset by the security of tenure for the occupiers. Their literature review leads them to the conclusion that: "If there is a consistent finding from these studies of disparate regulations [beyond rent control and including, for example, zoning and land use regulation], it is this: regulation per se is neither good nor bad. What matters are the costs and benefits of specific regulations under specific market conditions" (p. 15).

In short, despite the enormous range of work in this field, there is more to be done. In particular, Turner and Malpezzi identify certain under-researched assumptions underpinning much of the economic work such as the competitiveness of the housing market. This picks up the argument made by Radin (1986) against treating housing as an ordinary market commodity. From the individual tenant's perspective, "The intuitive general rule is that preservation of one's home is a stronger claim than preservation of one's business, or that non-commercial personal use of an apartment as a home is morally entitled to more weight than purely commercial landlording" (at p. 360). The idea of home in this context ("a paradigm case of personal property") is suggestive and worth pursuing at an empirical level, perhaps comparing different types of rent-restriction regimes with non-restricted regimes including situations where the landlord also resides in the property. That idea of the tenant's home also offers a potential counterbalance to the studies discussed above in which home-owners regard their homes and habits as somehow better than those of tenants.

II. Defense and Exclusion

Defense and exclusion provide a good example of the correlation between the principles of property law and its reception. The question considered in this section concerns the extent of that correlation in the case of exclusion, commonly regarded as underpinning property law, and the conceptualization of exclusion as defense. The most vivid examples of the relationship between exclusion and defense appear in the media responses when householders are prosecuted for using allegedly disproportionate force against intruders. Often, such media responses offer a view of legality which is rather different from that which appears at the interface of property and criminal law.

The link between defense and exclusion leads to discussion of another particular set of relations when communities divide themselves off from others, either literally or metaphorically. Internally, the relationship between members of the community may be regulated by formal legal rules, to which the members have signed up, but without necessarily being aware of the extent of their obligations. The relationship between members and outsiders seems a good focus for empirical research into the correlation between formal rules and their mediation through the members' everyday lives. Although not conceptualized through a legal consciousness lens, the research considered in this section could be reinterpreted in this way. The section is concluded by using a corrective—a study in which the home was regarded (by homeless women) as something not to be defended, but as a site of oppression and abuse.

Atkinson and Blandy (2007: 444) develop the concept of "defensive homeownership," arguing that the insecurity of everyday life "has generated an imperative for the control and handling of domestic territory that seeks autonomy and refuge from dangers, as well as connecting to prevailing ideologies that celebrate personal autonomy and control." This notion of defensive homeownership has at its foundation the link, between property and crime-control strategies, which has formed the subject of numerous criminological and architectural theses (for example, Newman, 1972). Manifestations of this security are all around us (such as CCTV, lighting, etc.) but these techniques also enjoin us to police our own space.

The "gated community" is a particularly valuable example of the link between the understandings at the root of property law and our everyday lives. The gate—both literal and metaphoric—operates as a defensive mechanism against the savage and barbarous exterior, creating a kind of safe haven and excluding the other (Blakely and Snyder, 1987). McKenzie (2005) links the rise of gated communities to the actions and interests of developers, local government and middle and upper-class consumers. Although the definition of a "gated community" is contested, one thread common to all versions is that of interlocking legal rights and obligations, often through the use of covenants, to enforce community norms.

As such, gated communities represent the apotheosis of the logic of property law—a community, divided off from the outside by its own relational "local law" and norms, in which everything from security to refuse collection is privatized. Blandy and Lister (2005), in a pilot study for a larger project, demonstrated how little attention is given to the understanding of this local law. They conducted research using a questionnaire distributed by the developer to new residents (with a response rate of 38%) and semi-structured interviews with a small sub-sample (n = 10) of residents. The questionnaire element drew on community psychology literature to determine the importance of community to those residents. The majority of the interview sample had not previously understood that they would be called on to take part in the management of the community—a result which replicated larger American studies and reflected "the sheer complexity of the...legal documents, which include a 23-page lease with seven schedules as well as the management company documents" (p. 295). One is not concerned here with legal aptitude but the production of legality outside the formal legal documents.

But there are limits to the defensive home-ownership idea. For example, what has proved of considerable interest to empirical researchers is not just the symbolism of gated and similar communities but the ways in which homeowner associations within such intentional communities seek to control and manage what happens on the inside and, more particularly, internal conflicts between members and management

(McKenzie, 2005). A further example lies in the boundary between defending one's property and committing a criminal act (Atkinson and Blandy, 2007: 448–50).

Nevertheless, the notion of home as a safe space which must be defended is challenged by other experiences and the fact that most violence takes place within the home. Rather than a place of defense the home may be a site of oppression or abuse. Tomas and Dittmar's research with homeless women is notable in this context because of their novel method (certainly in terms of the literature surveyed here), which involved a narrative housing-history approach based on unstructured interviews with a small number of homeless women (n = 12), during which that history was plotted on a chart. The findings suggest that, for their sample, residential instability was in fact a *solution* to the problem of insecurity arising from the lack of safety in the home (Tomas and Dittmar, 1995: 510). Housing history (or pathways) methods have, subsequently, become prominent in housing policy studies, but less so in empirical legal studies, which might well benefit from their use (for example, in studies of the eviction process).

III. Going Outside, (Not) Going to Court

So far, the focus of this Chapter has been on the home as inside space, which for some is capable of being controlled. In this section, this theme of control is developed by extending it to outside space. The particular concerns of this section lie in the relation between formal and informal orderings through which home and tenure are performed. The section begins with a discussion of the significance of mapping as the basis for understanding the relationship between individuals and land, leading into a discussion of formal tenure as the basis for economic improvement. The discussion then moves on to the ways in which the home is ordered, using the garden as an example, and then to more traditional socio-legal territory with a consideration of studies about disputing regarding the home. The final part draws on studies of zoning and planning to demonstrate the importance of the link between the production and consumption of housing.

A. Mapping home

Nikolas Rose (1999: 36) writes of a "telling picture" in the Australian National Art Gallery: "It shows traces of hills, rivers, trails, borders, overlaid by a vast eye. It is entitled 'The Governor loves to go mapping'." The map was a crucial technique of governing the home as well as colonial sites. The production of the map enabled land to be carved up and sold as free space, or *terra nullius*, through the doctrine of discovery. That is to say, the indigenous inhabitants were regarded as non-subjects and mapped out. In Palestine, according to Home (2003: 298), "The mosaic of land parcels was plotted, a cadastral survey plan superseded verbal descriptions and the authoritative definition of land parcels, and new survey points were physically fixed on the ground."

In a study based on 30 semi-structured interviews and six participant observations in Israel and the occupied West Bank, Braverman (2008) offers a sophisticated analysis of the role of pine and olive trees as identifying respectively the cultivation and non-cultivation of land. Cultivation forms the basis for the contestation of ownership because Article 78 of the Ottoman Land Code enables long-time cultivators of land (ten years and more) to claim title through adverse possession. Cultivation of olive trees enables such a claim to be made by Palestinians because those trees are regarded as fruit trees; land on which pine trees are grown can be regarded as non-cultivated and, thus, state land because such trees were, until recently at least, not considered fruit trees. The Jewish National Fund has planted 240 million pine trees since 1901.

As Braverman (2008: 450) puts it, an examination of the genealogy of trees as totemic displacements in the occupied West Bank "demonstrates how the Israeli/Palestinian war is deflected onto the landscape and how this deflection erodes the boundary between law and war." Braverman goes on to demonstrate how the trees become a "legible" marker (that is, a legally recognized marker of property rights: p. 460–5) because they are static and their presence can be documented, for example, through aerial photographs whereas that of mobile animals and humans cannot. (The interview, excerpted at 466–9, with the aerial photo expert offers revealing insights into the law-expertise relation). The tree, however, is also regarded as an "enemy soldier," once planted, then ripped up and an alternative then planted (462–4). Braverman also demonstrates the re-readings and contestations over this legibility, so that new Israeli settlers plant olive trees, and contest the interpretation of pine trees as "non-fruit" trees. Braverman's article represents the type of work which is both rich in doctrinal technicality as well as identifying the significance of scale and jurisdiction (see Valverde, 2009).

Current claims of indigenous and First Peoples to property have been the subject of important critical legal scholarship but empirical legal scholarship appears to be lacking. My sense, though, is that there is considerable scope for empirical legal scholarship, which might concern the concept of belonging and the interaction between rights and obligations, on the one hand, and the land itself, on the other. Mawani (2005) has noted how Aboriginal peoples are required to demonstrate an "authentic difference" as a precondition to obtain reparative legislative rights, but that sets the bar at too high a level because of the circumscribed definition of Aboriginality.

A different but related approach can be gleaned from a modern feature of colonialism—the uses of security of tenure. This approach takes as its starting point the influential work of de Soto (2000) who argued, as have others before him, that the formalization of legal-tenure security within state property-law systems can unlock capital and investment, thereby creating potential for trading. The Market-Led Agrarian Reform (MLAR) program, which takes this line as its basis and requires mapping as the foundation for rights, has not produced the desired effects across different states. A number of empirical legal studies speak to the reasons for this failure. Van Gelder (2009) draws on responses to a questionnaire from 174 occupiers who had lived in a Buenos Aires *loteo* (a low-income, low-value area with poor infrastructure and no significant industry) for between 5 and 25 years. He powerfully argues that the binaries "formal-informal" and "legal-illegal" are fuzzier than accepted by the proponents of MLAR. That argument is developed through empirical data on two issues surrounding eviction—perceived security of tenure and the more affective fear of eviction—as predictors of housing improvement; and developed the proposition that there were varying degrees of legality, a proposition which offered a more fluid approach to formal legal tenure security.

In an important intervention, Musembi (2007) provides a critique of MLAR and the de Soto thesis by drawing on a range of sources, including the author's own in-depth, semi-structured interviews in an Eastern Kenyan district with 111 interviewees including disputants and officials, combined with observation of dispute resolution practices. In relation to boundary disputes in Eastern Kenya, formal dispute settlement approaches were unused in relation to formal titles; rather, dispute settlement was conducted by the chief or assistant chief (Musembi, 2007: 1461). As Musembi argues (ibid.):

Much as the legal-centric view would like to present property rights as simply "juridical constructs enforced by the centralized state," the legitimacy of property rights ultimately rests on social recognition and acceptance. Social institutions such as family networks and locally based dispute resolution processes play a much more central and immediate role in day-to-day interaction.

B. Ordering home

Blomley's study (2005) of the garden and acts of gardening illustrates the ways in which privacy and propriety (that is, social responsibility and civic obligation) operate as "entangled enactments" (p. 651) rather than antithetically. Gardening can be both private and public, and there are interesting observations of the research participants particularly about distinctions between front and back gardens, as well as the appraisal of others' gardens. The data developed in this study are both rich and varied, drawing on the author's own personal experience of living in the locality (Strathcona, Vancouver) and on 36 semi-structured interviews with participants selected on the basis of personal contacts of the author and research assistants, together with some other participants identified through a snowball sampling method. The research participants were not selected to be representative of the area, but in order to construct a diverse group of respondents based on ethnicity, gender, and sexuality. Interviewees were not simply asked questions in the usual semi-structured questionnaire routine; they were also asked for their responses to the author's photographs of boundary spaces and gardens. Blomley's conclusions from these data are expansive but, as regards the binary between public and private, he argues that rather than collapse private into public, "we remain alive to the entangled tensions..." between them (at 653). The study demonstrates, in one sense, the despotism of property, the public scrutiny of the exercise of the gardener's husbandry—a phenomenon reinforced by gardening competitions between tenants of social-housing estates designed to encourage such tenants to maintain their gardens, but always with the threat of eviction if gardens are neglected (Saugeres, 2000). A failure to garden, then, constitutes not just a breach of tenancy conditions but nuisance (or anti-social) behavior, which can be punished.

One of the insights from Blomley's paper, as from other empirical scholarship, concerns the multiple legal settings of property. Property is a "way of being in the world" entailing "at the very least, a set of beliefs, dispositions, and taken-for-granted norms, as well as embodied practices that relate to the world of things" (p. 649). Cooper (2007) extends this observation further in her study of Summerhill school as well as, for example, in her studies of a Jewish eruv (a boundary within which certain activities, prohibited on the Sabbath, can take place) and foxhunting (1998). In these studies, Cooper is arguing (in part) for property as a sense of belonging, both in terms of subject-object relations (a traditional property perspective) and as a constitutive relationship between part and whole (Cooper, 2007: 629–30). She demonstrates the interweaving of the different practices of property. Cooper's research method usually involves an element of observation combined with interviews and other documentary texts. Her theme in *Governing out of Order* (1998) concerned the governance of excess. This theme has been under-used in subsequent property studies but offers a promising method of illuminating practices of control (in relation, for instance, to planning, zoning and the sex industry, discussed below).

Similarly, albeit from a different perspective, Ellickson's classic study of disputes between ranchers in Shasta County, California, demonstrates the ways in which law was interwoven within the understandings of the ranchers and ranchettes about property. What is taken for law in this study is often rather different from formal law, and Ellickson questions why this should be so. In part, his reason for doing so depended on his starting point in Coase's theorem; but we might see this study as a relatively early attempt at understanding the legal consciousness of the research participants albeit in the form of traditional empirical legal research, concerned with the gap between law and social reality. As regards disputes over trespass by cattle,

Ellickson noted that "most rural residents are consciously committed to an over-arching norm of cooperation among neighbors" (p. 53). Whatever the formal legal entitlements, this norm operated because "most cattlemen believe that a rancher should keep his animals from eating a neighbor's grass…" (ibid.). Failure to do so did not result in court proceedings, but was mostly dealt with through self-help remedies such as negative gossip or threatening to kill the neighbor's animal. When disputes concerning highway collisions with livestock reached the courts, which invoked law's rules that were different from the cattlemen's understandings, "the cattlemen continue to assert that the legal specialists who reach these results incorrectly interpret formal law" (p. 103). They

resist absorbing information that is inconsistent with their folklore.…The cattlemen treat the receipt of these reports not as occasions for updating their beliefs but rather as occasions for railing about the incompetence of courts and insurance companies (p. 115)

For the ranchers, going outside might have referred to going to court over boundary infractions. By contrast, in a well-known early study of legal consciousness, Merry (1990) noted that people went to court over neighborhood problems when they were seeking to sever themselves from an existing relationship: "The intervention of the court is part of the process of separation" (p. 40). Separation was required because, most often in that study, claims were based only superficially on neighbor disputes and more deeply on ethnic, racial, and class issues (p. 39). Neighborhood problems were not necessarily property-related but impacted the consumption of property through noise, dog mess, children or car parking.

Genn's study of non-trivial justiciable problems in England and Wales (1999) sits somewhere between these studies. It is notable because of its large-scale multi-method approach, which extends the legal needs surveys of the 1970s to a focus on non-trivial justiciable problems. After pilot work, Genn and her research team conducted 4,125 screening interviews to estimate the incidence of such problems in the previous five years. They then conducted follow-up interviews with a sub-sample of 1,134 adults who had experienced such a problem (most of which were not property related), and, finally, 40 qualitative interviews to trace the processes through which disputes were handled. Although clearly extending beyond property, Genn's findings regarding property itself are interesting and could be further explored. She noted the way housing problems tended to cluster around other problems (money and employment), and that around 90% of her sample with ownership and renting problems actively attempted to deal with those problems (that is, they were not "lumpers"—see Chapter 11 on claiming in this volume). Neighbor problems were among the commonest experienced by property owners, and a considerable proportion sought to deal with their problem after obtaining advice. What these studies further reinforce is that the lived experience of property is that it is a "destination subject"—a sponge for a range of other considerations cluster, particularly social and crime control, and which affect its use.

Sometimes, of course, court proceedings cannot be avoided. Studies of court proceedings of evictions of tenants by social and public landlords have developed interesting and useful propositions for administrative justice. The most notable was a study by Lempert (1990) of the Hawaii public housing eviction board. This longitudinal research was conducted in two phases in 1969 and 1987, involving the examination of court records from the board's inception in 1957. These records were not just the transcripts of hearings, but also internal memoranda, training materials, correspondence, and inspections. They were combined with observations of court hearings in 1969 and 1987 and interviews with board members (which also helped identify certain relevant documents). Lempert is exemplary in detailing the weaknesses as well as the strengths of the data (particularly as regards explanatory variables) and the method of data analysis; such matters are sometimes edited out of studies (e.g., for reasons of space). A snapshot method applied to a period of 20 years might miss certain external contextual changes if outcomes remain constant, but here Lempert used his qualitative interviews to develop an understanding of local knowledge. In a memorable turn of phrase, Lempert (1992: 208) says that "familiarity…breeds precedent, and a precedent for interpreting facts may be every bit as powerful as precedential pronouncements of law." But he also observed changes in approach over time from an emphasis on non-eviction, or deferral, to an eviction-first approach. Lempert suggests a number of reasons for each approach, as well as the seismic shift. One such reason, to which too little attention has been given in other empirical legal studies, was the computerization of rental payments, which created a more efficient rent-collection system and allowed housing deviants (i.e. non-payers) to be quickly identified.

For Lempert, outcomes were only partially related to different models of the welfare relationship. Cowan et al. (2006), in a study in England and Wales of low-level judicial decision-making involving a combination of observation of 890 rent-possession cases and interviews with 26 first-tier judges, identified certain types of judicial approaches to non-rental payment cases. At the core of these types lay an instinctive identification of social housing, counter-posed against a legal contractual model, which facilitated routines of simplification. Some judges "tended to emphasize the role social housing plays in society and were concerned perhaps about rent levels as well as shifts towards management styles which focus on 'income maximization'" (Cowan et al., 2006: 556). Others identified the status of the contract as being of a higher order over and above the social relation. The authors develop their argument about the judges' instincts by reference to legal consciousness studies, demonstrating the interdependence, complexity and, indeed, contradictory effects of different versions of legality, including resistance to law. The further insight from Cowan et al.'s data was of the emotional dimension of judging possession cases based on rent arrears for some of their sample. This dimension led some judges to "work against the law *openly* in possession proceedings and regularly. Indeed, it was that very openness which was so striking" (p. 568).

C. The consumption-production relation

We have so far examined those studies concerned with the home and property rights which are essentially concerned with the consumption of property. This was the focus of many studies of housing and property, and seems to have remained so despite attempts at reorienting empirical studies towards an examination of the production-consumption relation. Studies of the production of housing demonstrate how owner-occupation became the predominant, favored tenure.

The history of zoning and planning policies and practices fits into this literature, demonstrating the interdependence of production and consumption. Fischel (2004), for example, provides an historical analysis of the development of zoning in the US, identifying how single-family units of accommodation became the protected form of production after the arrival of buses and trucks in the 1910s. Fischel (2004: 321) develops a thesis that trucks and buses (rather than the motor car) "undermined the security of suburban, single-family residences." Zoning provided a protective cloak which, unlike other devices such as covenants, offered a potent method of controlling development and which, after the civil rights movement, shifted towards general exclusion. Rothwell and Massey (2009) use sophisticated quantitative modeling techniques to demonstrate that density zoning strongly affected patterns and processes of racial segregation in post-civil-rights cities. Fischel's argument is well-developed and historically rigorous, no doubt, but it offers a meso-level analysis, which does not account for structural shifts (for example, in the planning and public health professions) and developments (the prior mapping out of cities for public health purposes).

More recently, zoning and planning instruments have been used to plan out or plan in sex-industry premises. Studies of New York zoning under Mayor Giuliani and of Sydney planning decisions demonstrate the way in which zoning and planning laws, rather than criminal and obscenity laws, have been used to manage sex-industry establishments (Valverde, 2003). For Valverde (2003: 48–53), the interest in such decisions lies in the deployment of knowledge and administrative, on-the-job expertise as well as in making the owners of such premises responsible for their own regulation. That knowledge is of the secondary effects and cumulative impacts of sex businesses, but it is not a scientifically-based knowledge; rather, it is made true by repetition (Papayanis, 2000: 346).

Prior's study of the zoning-in of gay bathhouses in Sydney demonstrates the role planning plays in governing the presence of sexuality. Drawing on a small number of semi-structured interviews with bathhouse proprietors, councilors, and council officers, together with documentary analysis of planning applications made in respect of two bathhouses as well as subsequent court cases, this study shows how, in the Darlington area of Sydney, discretionary concepts such as "amenity" are used negatively and positively as a result of the decriminalization of homosexuality and the introduction of anti-discrimination laws (Prior, 2008). Thus, the gay bath-house was transformed from being a dangerous place to being planned into the neighborhood.

IV. Boundary Crossing

Boundaries are not just physical but also metaphysical and disciplinary divisions. One of the key characteristics of much of the best empirical legal scholarship around property has been its disciplinary boundary crossing. Law schools neatly separate property law as a technical thing, most often (as I have done in this Chapter) relating it to land. But property law is all over the curriculum, and the most exciting branch of empirical legal scholarship in this field spatializes law. Blomley (2003: 30) has a neat way of expressing this when he "literally run[s] the words together, and refer[s] to the conjunction [space and law] as a *'splice'*" (original emphasis). Delaney (2004: 851) takes this one stage further when he describes the "nomosphere," by which he refers "to the cultural-material environs that are constituted by the reciprocal materialization of the legal and legal signification of the sociospatial."

Delaney offers practical empirical locations of the professionals and para-professionals who seek to interpret legislation creatively in the context of evictions. He uses the example of the U.S. Department of Housing and Urban Development regulation, which governs not only the conduct of residents in, and visitors to, their homes but also the conduct of any member of their household, guest or other person "on or off such premises while the tenant is a tenant in public housing." Further, it provides that "such criminal activity shall be cause for termination of tenancy." So, for example, tenants may be evicted where their co-occupiers or visitors commit drug offences, of which the tenant is unaware, some distance away from the property. That regulation was upheld in its fullest sense by the Supreme Court (*Department of Housing and Urban Development v. Rucker*, 535 U.S. 125 (2002)), despite the intense activity of those professionals, para-professionals and others.

A further example of this splicing and resplicing—without using this terminology—can be found in the exploration by Cowan and Carr (2008) of a legal challenge to similar, if less far-reaching, regulations in Northern Ireland, which required private landlords to control their tenants not just in their homes but also outside. Cowan and Carr demonstrate how territorial regulations relating solely to Northern Ireland came to be seen as a threat to English landlords, and how the claims of the landlords were translated (as it happened successfully) both by them and their lawyers into human rights claims.

V. Conclusion

The empirical research in property law discussed in this Chapter draws on a variety of fairly standard qualitative and quantitative techniques. It demonstrates, challenges, and goes beyond the more conceptual work of contemporary scholarship about the meanings of property. The recent development of interdisciplinary law-geography studies offers considerable promise in linking property law studies to cutting edge theoretical approaches, which will also influence the methods to be adopted. Certain research questions and methods have been identified as particularly worthy of further development around property, most particularly narrative housing history (or pathways) approaches through which one might develop a rich appreciation of the imbrication of property and its spaces in everyday life.

I have also sought to develop and maintain a potentially valuable dialogue between the empirical legal studies and housing studies traditions as these traditions run in parallel but have potential for cross-boundary working. The best way in which the latter studies might be used is through re-reading them as highlighting versions of truth about property law in society. Like Ewick and Silbey's example of an old chair left in recently cleared snow as a symbol of ownership of a parking spot on a New Jersey street (1998: 21), these studies provide versions of legality constructed extra-legally about, for example, home and tenure or defense. And when formal legal tenure is hierarchically imposed on populations, it is ignored or sidestepped. Between a continuum of the importance of the extra-legal and the unimportance of the legal lie a variety of diverse, complex, and contradictory appreciations of property.

There has also been a sense of frustration running through this Chapter. The way we teach property law and the way in which empirical legal scholarship is developing are, or seem to be, at odds with each other. One reason for this, at least in my jurisdiction, is the dominance of the professions in regulating the delivery of property law as a core subject within the law curriculum. However, what empirical scholarship about property is increasingly telling us is that property has no more core than any other subject and, indeed, may have rather less than we credit. Property is a sponge soaking up the diversity of other influences on its reception in society. At least some of the empirical scholarship considered in this Chapter could and should be incorporated within property law curricula both as a challenge to traditional understandings as well as to facilitate an appreciation of property law in society.

REFERENCES

Atkinson, R. and Blandy, S. (2007). "Panic Rooms: The Rise of Defensive Homeownership," *Housing Studies* 22: 443–58.

Blakely, E. and Snyder, M. (1987). *Fortress America: Gated Communities in the United States*, Washington: Brookings Institution Press.

Blandy, S. and Lister, D. (2005). "Gated Communities: (Ne)Gating Community Development?," *Housing Studies* 20: 287–302.

Blomley, N. (2003). "From 'What' to 'So What'? Law and Geography in Retrospect," in J. Holder and C. Harrison (eds.), *Law and Geography*, Oxford: Oxford University Press.

Blomley, N. (2005). "The Borrowed View: Privacy, Propriety and the Entanglements of Property," *Law and Social Inquiry* 30: 617–62.

Braverman, I. (2008). "'The Tree is the Enemy Soldier': A Sociolegal Making of War Landscapes in the Occupied West Bank," *Law and Society Review* 42: 449–82.

Cole, I. and Robinson, D. (2000). "Owners, yet Tenants: The Position of Leaseholders in Flats in England and Wales," *Housing Studies* 15: 595–612.

Cooper, D. (1998). *Governing Out of Order: Space, Law and the Politics of Belonging*, London: Rivers Oram.

Cooper, D. (2007). "Opening Up Ownership: Community Belonging, Belongings, and the Productive Life of Property," *Law and Social Inquiry* 32: 625–64.

Cowan, D., Blandy, S., Hunter, C., Nixon, J. Hitchings, E., and Parr, S. (2006). "District Judges and Possession Proceedings," *Journal of Law and Society* 33: 547–71.

Cowan, D. and Carr, H. (2008). "Actor-Network Theory, Implementation and the Private Landlord," *Journal of Law and Society* (Special Research Issue) 35: 149–66.

Delaney, D. (2004). "Tracing Displacement: or Evictions in the Nomosphere," *Environment and Planning D: Society and Space* 22: 847–60.

de Soto, H. (2000). *The Mystery of Capital: Why Capitalism Triumphs in the West and Fails Everywhere Else*, New York: Basic Books.

Ellickson, R. (1990). *Order without Law: How Neighbors Settle Disputes*, Cambridge: Harvard University Press.

Ellickson, R. (2008). *The Household: Informal Order around the Hearth*, Princeton: Princeton University Press.

Ewick, P. and Silbey, S. (1998). *The Common Place of Law: Stories from Everyday Life*, Chicago: University of Chicago Press.

Fehlberg, B. (1997). *Sexually Transmitted Debt: Surety Experience and English Law*, Oxford: Oxford University Press.

Fischel, W. (2004). "An Economic History of Zoning and a Cure for its Exclusionary Effects," *Urban Studies* 21: 317–40.

Ford, J., Burrows, R., and Nettleton, S. (2001). *Home Ownership in a Risk Society*, Bristol: Policy Press.

Forrest, R. and Murie, A. (1991). *Selling the Welfare State: The Privatization of Public Housing*, London: Routledge.

Genn, H. (1999). *Paths to Justice: What People Do and Think about Going to Law*, Oxford: Hart.

Gurney, C. (1999). "Lowering the Drawbridge: A Case Study of Analogy and Metaphor in the Social Construction of Home–Ownership," *Urban Studies* 36: 1705–22.

Home, R. (2003). "An 'Irreversible Conquest'? Colonial and Postcolonial Land Law in Israel/Palestine," *Social and Legal Studies* 12: 291–300.

Institute for Economic Affairs (IEA) (1972). *Verdict on Rent Control*, London: IEA.

Karn, V. (1997). "'Ethnic Penalties' and Racial Discrimination in Education, Employment and Housing: Conclusions and Policy Implications," in V. Karn (ed.), *Ethnicity in the 1991 Census, Volume 4*, London: HMSO.

Kemeny, J. (1981). *The Myth of Home Ownership: Private versus Public Choices in Housing Tenure*, London: Routledge and Kegan Paul.

Lempert, R. (1990). "Docket Data and 'Local Knowledge': Studying the Court and Society Link over Time," *Law & Society Review* 23: 347–98.

Lempert, R. (1992). "Discretion in a Behavioural Perspective: The Case of a Public Housing Eviction Board," in K. Hawkins (ed), *The Uses of Discretion*, Oxford: Oxford University Press.

Mawani, R. (2005). "Genealogies of the Land: Aboriginality, Law, and Territory in Vancouver's Stanley Park," *Social and Legal Studies* 14: 315–39.

McKenzie, E. (2005). "Constructing the *Pomerium* in Las Vegas: A Case Study of Emerging Trends in American Gated Communities," *Housing Studies* 20: 187–204.

Merry, S. (1990). *Getting Justice and Getting Even: Legal Consciousness among Working-Class Americans*, Chicago: Chicago University Press.

Moran, L. and Skeggs, B. (2001). "The Property of Safety," *Journal of Social Welfare and Family Law* 23: 379–94.

Musembi, C. (2007). "De Soto and Land Relations in Rural Africa: Breathing Life into Dead Theories about Property Rights," *Third World Quarterly* 28: 1457–78.

Nadler, J. and Diamond, S. (2008). "Eminent Domain and the Psychology of Property Rights: Proposed Use, Subjective Attachment, and Taker Identity," *Journal of Empirical Legal Studies* 5: 713–49.

Nedelsky, J. (1990). "Law, Boundaries, and the Bounded Self," *Representations* 30: 162–89.

Nelken, D. (1983). *The Limits of the Legal Process: A Study of Landlords, Law and Crime*, London: Academic Press.

Newman, O. (1972). *Defensible Space: People and Design in the Violent City*, London: Architectural Press

Nielsen, L. (2000). "Situating Legal Consciousness: Experiences and Attitudes of Ordinary Citizens about Law and Street Harassment," *Law & Society Review* 34: 1055–90.

Papayanis, M. (2000). "Sex and the Revanchist City: Zoning out Pornography in New York," *Environment and Planning D: Society and Space* 18: 341–53.

Prior, J. (2008). "Planning for Sex in the City: Urban Governance, Planning and the Placement of Sex Industry Premises in Inner Sydney," *Australian Geographer* 39: 339–52.

Radin, M. (1986). "Residential Rent Control," *Philosophy & Public Affairs*, 15: 350–80.

Rose, N. (1999). *Powers of Freedom: Reframing Political Thought*, Cambridge: Cambridge University Press.

Rothwell, J. and Massey, D. (2009). "The Effect of Density Zoning on Racial Segregation in U.S. Urban Areas," *Urban Affairs Review* 44: 779–806.

Saugeres, L. (2000). "Of Tidy Gardens and Clean Houses: Housing Officers as Agents of Social Control," *Geoforum* 31: 587–99.

Saunders, P. (1990). *A Nation of Home Owners*, London: Allen and Unwin.

Tomas, A. and Dittmar, H. (1995). "The Experience of Homeless Women: An Exploration of Housing Histories and the Meaning of Home," *Housing Studies* 10: 493–517.

Turner, B. and Malpezzi, S. (2003). "A Review of Empirical Evidence on the Costs and Benefits of Rent Control," *Swedish Economic Policy Review,* 10: 11–56

Valverde, M. (2003). *Law's Dream of a Common Knowledge*, Princeton: Princeton University Press.

Valverde, M. (2009). "Jurisdiction and Scale: Legal 'Technicalities' as Resources for Theory," *Social and Legal Studies* 18: 139–58.

Van Gelder, J.-L. (2009). "Legal Tenure Security, Perceived Tenure Security and Housing Improvement in Buenos Aires: An Attempt Towards Integration," *International Journal of Urban and Regional Research* 3: 126–46.

Wyly, E., Atia, M., Foxcroft, H., Hammel, D., and Phillips-Watts, K., (2006). "American Home: Predatory Mortgage Capital and Neighborhood Spaces of Race and Class Exploitation in the United States," *Geografiska Annaler* 88b: 105–3.

15

HUMAN RIGHTS INSTRUMENTS

LINDA CAMP KEITH

I. INTRODUCTION

AT the turn of the new century formal commitment to international human rights norms approaches near universality as each of the core conventions composing the international human rights regime has seen state parties reach 75 to 99%: 173 states are parties to the International Convention on the Elimination of All Forms of Racial Discrimination (CERD) (89%); 164 states have ratified or acceded to the International Covenant on Civil and Political Rights (ICCPR) (84%); 160 states are parties to the International Covenant on Economic, Social and Cultural Rights (ICESCR) (83%); 186 states have ratified or acceded to the Convention on the Elimination of All Forms of Discrimination against Women (CEDAW) (96%); 146 states are parties to the Convention against Torture and Other Cruel, Inhuman or Degrading Treatment or Punishment (CAT) (75%); and 193 states are parties to the Convention on the Rights of the Child (CRC) (99%), making it the most universally accepted of these core human rights instruments (UN Treaty Collection, 2009). While the progress toward universal formal adherence to international human rights norms is remarkable, the substantive meaning of this progress is much less clear. Does the high level of formal acceptance indicate that the states have internalized these delineated norms? Is the high level of formal commitment merely a symbolic gesture by states acquiescing to the global script of modernity? Is the commitment mere "cheap talk" engaged in to gain the rewards associated with membership or to avoid the costs associated with continued failure to participate in the international human rights regime? Will states adhere to the norm of *pacta sunt servanda* once committed and bring their human rights practices into alignment with their legal agreements?

An increasing number of social scientists and law professors, employing numerous and sometimes conflicting theoretical approaches, have begun to address these questions, and have created a growing and substantial body of rigorously systematic empirical analyses. These analyses have tended to focus on one of two underlying questions: why do states commit (or not commit) to international human rights treaties and why do states comply (or not comply) once they have made such a commitment?[1] Most empirical studies on commitment have largely conceptualized commitment as a dichotomous choice; however, a few studies have expanded their examination to include state practices of attaching reservations and declarations or signing bilateral agreements that limit or even negate their commitment. Almost all empirical studies on compliance with human rights treaties look for evidence of a treaty's effect on the human rights practices of the signatory state; however, a small number of empirical studies examine other dimensions of compliance such as whether domestic laws and policies (and even local conditions) have been changed to accommodate the commitment under international law.

Two broad sets of theoretical perspectives have tended to dominate the empirical examination of both the issues of commitment and compliance: one based

---

[1] As the body of research has evolved, some scholars have begun to conceptualize the decisions of whether to commit and to comply as a joint process (Landman, 2005; Powell and Staton, 2009).

on rational actor assumptions and the other largely focused on socialization and the diffusion of norms. In the sections that follow I will discuss more fully the general substantive expectations of each of the theoretical perspectives and then discuss the evidence and insights generated by the body of empirical analysis, first in regard to state commitment to human rights agreements and then in regard to compliance with these formal commitments. Finally, I will discuss the limitations that have constrained this body of research and what they suggest for future research.

II. Key Theoretical Debates

A. Rational actor theories

Realists and rational functionalists perceive states as unitary rational actors that primarily behave on the basis of self-interest, and thus they argue that decisions by the state, whether to join or comply with an international treaty, are largely a function of the state's calculation of the benefits and costs of joining the regime or complying with it. Realists in international relations (Morgenthau, 1948; Hoffman, 1956; Waltz, 1979; Gilpin, 1981) emphasize the dominance of power and the norm of sovereignty in a weak and decentralized international legal system in which legal authority is unlikely to constrain the behavior of states. They posit that any observed compliance simply reflects a convergence of interests that will dissipate once a state's material interests conflict with its normative commitments (Hoffman, 1956; Waltz, 1979; Mearsheimer, 1994). Realists ultimately remain skeptical about the development of international law beyond serving the interests of the most powerful states, which typically do not have sufficient self-interest to impose sanctions for violations of international human rights law (Krasner, 1993; Donnelly, 1998). Both realists and rational functionalists note that the formal mechanisms for monitoring and enforcing human rights commitments are deliberately weak. In addition, human rights treaties lack the potential effects of market forces, reciprocal benefits, or potential retaliation from other state parties that typically motivate compliance with international financial agreements (Neumayer, 2005). Rational functionalists also perceive state behavior as being interest-driven and recognize the dominant value of state sovereignty; however, they argue that international agreements provide a means through which states can cooperate to solve problems that they cannot handle unilaterally, and thus states are willing to sacrifice some measure of sovereignty for this benefit (Bilder, 1989). While the mutual benefits of interstate cooperation through trade and monetary agreements readily come to mind, it is much more difficult to identify the mutual benefit of agreements that regulate activities that are purely *internal* to the state and do not involve interactions among states (Moravcsik, 2000). However, it is possible that a state may acquire indirect benefits, such as bilateral or multilateral aid, through participation in the international human rights regimes. In addition, they may avoid reputational costs, particularly identification as a "pariah state" for failure to participate in the regime. While rational functionalism has tended to focus on the question of commitment, the theory is increasingly applied to the question of compliance as well, with the expectation that, given the weak enforcement mechanisms of the agreements and the low probability of sanctions, compliance will most likely be driven by calculations related to reputation (Simmons, 2000; Hathaway, 2005).

A third stream within the rational actor perspective dismisses the assumption of a unitary state actor and instead recognizes the role of numerous domestic actors and institutions within the state (particularly in democratic regimes) which may affect the regime's calculation of costs related to commitment and (non)compliance. Democratic electoral processes and legal institutions are seen as providing the public and other political actors with the tools and venues through which they can hold the regime accountable should it fail to keep its international commitments (Keith, 2002; Neumayer, 2005; Hathaway, 2007; Powell and Staton, 2009). From a broader perspective, democratic affinity for the rule of law and respect for constitutional constraints and judicial processes in the domestic context arguably carry over to the international context and increase the likelihood that democratic regimes will honor their international legal commitments (Simmons, 2000). While this logic leads us to expect strong compliance from democratic regimes, the same logic may also predict that democratic regimes, under particular circumstances, will be *less* likely to commit to the treaties in the first place. Moravcsik (2000) argues that newly established or unstable democratic regimes will create or join international human rights regimes to lock-in "democratic rule through the enforcement of human rights" and to "establish reliable judicial constraints on future non-democratic governments or democratically elected governments that may seek...to subvert democracy from within" (228). On the other hand, established democracies are less likely to legally bind themselves when costs of reduced sovereignty outweigh the benefits, which are virtually nil as human rights are already respected; and "authoritarian governments will not support human rights regimes for the obvious reason that they are the states most likely to violate these norms" (Goodliffe and Hawkins, 2006: 362). However, Vreeland (2008) argues that the domestic political institutions of authoritarian regimes are not monolithic, and that while all dictatorial regimes are arguably pro-torture regimes with "no interest in even making a symbolic gesture of signing the CAT," an authoritarian regime that faces multiple legal political parties may nevertheless have an incentive to concede to the party's pressure to make a small concession and commit to the CAT (p. 69).

The common thread that binds these three perspectives is the assumption that state behavior is rational and that the state acts to maximize its own interests, and thus that the decision whether to be bound by a human rights agreement and the concomitant decision whether to comply with the agreement are based on a calculation of costs and benefits to the state. Therefore much of the empirical literature attempts to identify and measure the perceived costs and benefits to the state's interest or to identify surrogate indicators of these considerations.

B. Theories related to international norms and socialization

The second set of theoretical approaches generally focuses on transnational or international socialization because this, rather than rationalist calculation, is believed to drive the creation of and commitment to international human rights treaties. These perspectives emphasize the transformative power of international normative discourse on human rights and the role of activism by transnational actors (international organizations and non-governmental actors) who support local efforts to press for human rights commitment and who also, through repeated interactions with state actors, socialize states to accept new norms. The transnational advocacy networks perspective (Keck and Sikkink, 1998; Risse et al., 1999) posits that international human rights norms are diffused through networks of transnational and domestic actors who "bring pressure 'from above' and 'from below' to accomplish human rights change" (Risse and Sikkink, 1999: 18). Risse et al. (1999) present a five-phase spiral model that assumes that: 1) repression triggers activation of the transnational network, which invokes human rights norms and applies pressure on the repressive state to make concessions; 2) the repressive state denies the validity of the human rights norms as a subject for international jurisdiction and asserts instead the norm of non-intervention; 3) the regime eventually makes some tactical concessions to the transnational network; 4) the regime becomes trapped in its own rhetoric and concessions, which can lead to either the opposition bringing about a regime change or a process of gradual liberalization; 5) the regime accepts international norms (ratifies treaties and institutionalizes norms domestically); and thus ultimately we see rule-consistent behavior due to regime's acceptance of the validity of the human rights and the increased scrutiny under the monitoring and reporting mechanism of the treaties.

Another perspective, the transnational legal process approach, specifically addresses the process through which state actors internalize norms codified in international treaties. Koh (1996) argues that states engage in repeated interactions, with other governmental and non-governmental actors in the international system, through which "they create patterns of behavior and generate norms of external conduct," such as international human rights treaties, which they in turn internalize "by incorporating [them] into their domestic legal and political structures." Eventually, through a "repeated process of interaction and internalization" international law acquires its "stickiness" and nations come to define promoting the rule of international law as part of their national identity and self-interest (Koh, 1996: 198).

A third perspective, the world society approach (e.g., Meyer et al., 1997) perceives states to be embedded in an integrated cultural system that "promulgates cognitive frames and normative prescriptions that constitute the legitimate identities, structures, and purposes of modern nation-states" (Cole, 2005: 477). Thus, with the proliferation of human rights treaties codifying human rights norms, states' legitimacy or "good nation" identity is increasingly linked to the formal acknowledgment of these norms (Cole, 2005; Wotipka and Ramirez, 2007). However, as Cole notes, many states join the traditionally weak human rights regime, "not out of deep commitment, but because it signals their probity to the international community" and thus "a decoupling is endemic to the human rights regime" (p. 477). This perspective posits three mechanisms through which states are influenced by the world polity: the degree of participation in global civil society, particularly membership in international governmental organizations (IGOs) and international non-governmental organizations (INGOs) (Boli and Thomas, 1997); participation in international human rights conferences (Goodman and Jinks, 2004); and normative band-wagoning (Finnemore and Sikkink, 1998).

III. Empirical Evidence: State Commitment to Human Rights Agreements

A growing body of empirical studies has examined the willingness of states to become signatories and to ratify or accede to one or more of the treaties that compose the international human rights regime. Most of these studies have simultaneously examined three categories of factors that represent the dominant theoretical perspectives: 1) state interests, 2) domestic politics or institutions, and 3) the diffusion of international norms and the embeddedness of states into global society. As a whole the empirical evidence suggests that our theoretical understanding of state commitment and compliance is incomplete because it does not account simultaneously for these three sets of factors.

A. State interests (costs-benefits)

Most empirical studies of commitment consider at least implicitly the reciprocal relationship between compliance and decisions to commit to a treaty, and thus assume that decisions to commit are linked to calculations of the likely costs and benefits of compliance. As noted above, human rights treaties provide no direct reciprocal benefits and pose no threat of the tit-for-tat retaliation associated with other international agreements; however, scholars have identified and attempted to measure a range of indirect costs while identifying relatively few indirect benefits that would influence state commitments. Empirical evidence is rather mixed. Scholars generally argue that the eventual costs of compliance will be less for states whose human rights practices are already in alignment with treaty expectations, and thus that rights-protecting states, and perhaps democratic states, would be more likely to join than repressive autocratic regimes. Early evidence demonstrates that congruent human rights practice does not influence commitment to the ICESCR (Cole, 2005), the ICCPR (Cole, 2005; Hathaway, 2007), CEDAW (Hathaway, 2007), or the CAT (Goodliffe and Hawkins, 2006), but rather influences only commitment to the Optional Protocol to the ICCPR (Cole, 2005). However, democratic states were found to be more likely to commit to CAT (Hathaway, 2003; Goodliffe and Hawkins, 2006) and to the ICCPR or ICESCR (Cole, 2005); and the democratic effect seems to be conditional upon congruent human rights practices within the democratic regime, which supports the theory that the accountability mechanisms of a democratic system make the anticipated costs for non-complying democratic regimes significantly greater. For example, democratic states with poor torture records were found to be *less* likely to commit to CAT and more highly democratized states with a poor history of providing civil freedoms and women's rights were found to be less likely to commit to the ICCPR and CEDAW, respectively; whereas, at lower levels of democratization, human rights practices had no effect on commitment on these treaties (Hathaway, 2003, 2007).

Cole (2005) argues that costs vary by the strength of the treaty's mechanisms for monitoring and enforcement, and he expects that democratic countries and rights-abiding regimes will be more likely to join strongly enforced treaties than will be repressive autocratic regimes. The ICESCR, with its limited commitment to "take steps...to the maximum of its available resources" is arguably the weakest treaty in terms of commitment and monitoring, and the First Optional Protocol to ICCPR provides the strongest enforcement mechanism, allowing individuals to file complaints—which, as Cole notes, provides a more "genuine, if limited, instance of international monitoring" (p. 475). While approximately equal numbers of states have joined the ICCPR and the ICESCR, of those states that joined the ICCPR, only 68.3% have ratified the First Optional Protocol. A state's human rights practices were associated only with commitment to the more stringent Protocol. In addition, Hathaway (2007) found that the conditional impact of human rights practices on democratic regimes' willingness to commit was even greater in regard to the Optional Protocol of the ICCPR and also in regard to state acceptance of Articles 21 and 22 of the CAT, which impose much stronger enforcement mechanisms. Thus we see some indirect evidence that suggests states may consider the costs associated with particular mechanisms.

Goodliffe and Hawkins (2006) identify and examine two additional sets of potential costs that may affect state commitment to the CAT: limitations on policy flexibility and unintended or unanticipated consequences. They argue that the CAT is potentially costly because it forecloses the regime's policy options; in particular, for regimes facing serious security threats, torture is likely to be considered a valuable tool of repression or information-gathering. Thus they attempt to test the effect of international and domestic threats to the regime, and while they do find that militarized disputes decrease the likelihood of ratification or accession, they do not find evidence that domestic threats influence commitment. The latter result, though, should be viewed with some caution as they do not measure internal threats such as armed domestic opposition, insurgencies, or civil war, but rather use poverty as a surrogate measure (and even then only use per capita GDP). They also argue that the likelihood of unintended consequences from commitment to the CAT is lower for powerful states which have considerable resources that can be brought to bear—for example to help their citizens escape the universal jurisdiction of the CAT. In fact they find that states with greater GDP are more likely to ratify or accede to the CAT. They also argue that common law judicial systems expose a regime to the possibility that the judiciary will apply international law in unintended ways, and thus will be less likely to commit to international treaties. Again they find evidence to support their expectation. This evidence fits with the broader literature on domestic institutions, which is discussed in the next section.

Finally, economic aid, which represents the clearest material interest at stake, surprisingly has received much less empirical attention than has other costs. Hathaway (2007) argues that new regimes are more likely to join the ICCPR, CAT, and CEDAW to attract aid, and she does find evidence that new regimes (under ten years old) are more likely to become parties to these treaties, although she does not specifically test the aid link itself. Wotipka and Ramirez (2007) argue that states that are economically dependent upon powerful actors that favor CEDAW will be more likely to join the treaty because of the possible cost of losing bilateral aid; however, they find only weak and inconsistent empirical support. Kelley's (2007) study of U.S.-coerced bilateral agreements concerning surrender of U.S. citizens to the International Criminal Court demonstrates that loss of U.S. bilateral aid was less important than affinity for the court and the state's commitment to keep its international agreements.

As a whole the evidence concerning the influence of state interests is somewhat weak, given that most of the measures that were found to be statistically significant are only indirect indicators of costs. Moreover, even when more direct measures of costs, such as bilateral aid, are employed the results are still inconsistent. Even so, we are left with the sense that any understanding of state commitment must include some calculation of state interest.

B. Domestic politics and institutions

Most explorations of domestic institutions have focused on majoritarian components of democratic institutions such as elections or party competition. As discussed above, consistent evidence demonstrates that democracies are more likely to commit to human rights treaties (Hathaway, 2003; Cole, 2005; Goodliffe and Hawkins, 2006; Powell and Staton, 2009) but are less likely to commit if their current human rights practices are not consistent with treaty obligations (Hathaway, 2003; Hathaway, 2007). The association appears to be more nuanced, though. While Landman (2005) found that democracies joined the international human rights regime at rates higher than non-democracies, he also found evidence that newer democracies had a strong tendency to ratify more treaties and to ratify them with fewer reservations than did older democracies. He argues that this tendency reflects the theory that newer democracies need to constrain or "lock in" future generations of political actors and limit their ability to undermine or overthrow democratic institutions.[2] Goodliffe and Hawkins's (2006) examination of the lock-in hypothesis in regard to the CAT is the most rigorous test thus far, as it examines separately three institutional contexts that condition the regime's willingness to commit: where the state is a new democracy and where it is one of two types of unstable democracies—unstable in that it had previously achieved democracy and regressed or unstable in the sense that politics in the country are volatile and the government changes frequently. Despite the rigor of their conceptualization, they find almost no support for lock-in theory in regard to commitment to the CAT, with the exception of very marginal evidence that being a new democracy increases the probability the state will ratify the CAT. Under lock-in theory authoritarian regimes are not expected to support human rights regimes; however, Vreeland (2008) finds that authoritarian regimes *do* join the CAT under certain domestic institutional conditions, specifically when there are multiple legal political parties which may be able to exert some political pressure on the regime to make the minor concession of joining the CAT (with little anticipated cost to the regime). As Powell and Staton (2009) point out, most empirical models that examine the effect of democratic institutions tend to focus on elements that reflect or promote majoritarian rule and tend to ignore the domestic judiciary, which in democratic systems is expected to act as a constraint upon the state, especially when rights are protected

---

[2] However, we will see below Landman finds that they have the worst compliance record of all democracies.

through bills of rights and similar protocols.[3] They examine the extent to which an effective domestic judiciary influences ratification, and they find almost no statistical effect across a variety of measures: three measures of judicial independence and a law-and-order measure, none of which demonstrates an effect, and a surrogate measure of property rights which does have a statistically significant effect. More importantly, they examine commitment and compliance as a joint process, which is a major contribution of their work, and they do find evidence that the joint probability of ratifying the CAT and torturing decreases when the regime faces an effective judiciary.[4] As noted above, Goodliffe and Hawkins (2006) found that states with common law systems were less likely join the CAT, presumably because it opened the state to possible unintended consequences through inappropriate, or overly broad and precedent-setting, judicial application of international law.

Thus far, the empirical evidence does not consistently support lock-in theory; however, as a whole, the evidence, though somewhat mixed, does suggest that democratic institutions influence commitment. More importantly, our understanding of the particular mechanisms at work remains rather limited.

C. Norm diffusion and state linkage to global society

The norms-based perspectives share a common problem in that norms are impossible to observe directly and it is quite difficult to measure their influence without creating a serious circularity problem. Thus, empirical studies have typically relied on indirect surrogates, which have included cumulative participation in human rights treaties (as an indicator of diffusion of the international norms), and linkage with international governmental or non-governmental organizations and human rights conferences (as indicators of global socialization and civil society pressure). Most studies examine the global community of states and/or regional communities of states as potential venues of norm diffusion. Overall, empirical evidence has demonstrated that the higher the rate of global and regional participation in a specific human rights treaty or the broader the human rights regime the greater the chance of fellow states' participation; however, the influence of cumulative ratification on subsequent ratification by remaining states falls away rather quickly for the ICCPR and ICESCR (Cole, 2005). In the case of the more stringent Optional Protocol to the

---

[3] It should be noted however that the Polity measure of democracy does include a dimension that captures executive constraints, and which has been shown to effect state repression when Polity is disaggregated into its core individual components (Keith, 2002; Bueno de Mesquita et al., 2005). As far as I can ascertain, no study of commitment or compliance has yet disaggregated these dimensions.

[4] The supportive evidence they do find is in relation to their surrogate measure of property rights which is "a ratio of non-currency money to the total money supply" (p. 159).

ICCPR the cumulative rate of global ratification actually *decreased* the odds of subsequent ratification, which Cole believes "implies the existence of a relatively fixed number of countries willing to ratify the protocol, and also suggests that countries are impervious to normative influences when treaties with relatively strong enforcement mechanisms are considered" (p. 485). Subsequent analysis supports his assessment; when he examines another indicator of higher level of state commitment—ratification *without reservations*—he finds that the level of global participation only influences the ICESCR, presumably because it has the weakest mechanisms of the two covenants. In contrast, the influence of global and regional participation in CEDAW on subsequent participation in the women's convention was quite consistent (Wotipka and Ramirez, 2007). It is in relation to the CAT that diffusion effects have received the greatest level of empirical attention, and while the results largely suggest a positive influence on the odds of subsequent ratification, here again we find significant inconsistencies. Goodliffe and Hawkins (2006) find strong support for both regional and global effects; however, Powell and Staton's (2009) examination produces mixed results that vary according to which measure of judicial effectiveness they employ in their analyses. When Vreeland (2008) replicated Goodliffe and Hawkins's analysis in the limited context of authoritarian regimes, he found that regional and global participation had no effect on ratification by authoritarian regimes. Hathaway's (2007) analysis at first glance seems to demonstrate overwhelmingly the positive influence of regional participation across a variety of treaties; however, the author urges caution in assuming normative diffusion from these findings as they disappear when she adds controls for region. She notes that rather than capturing the influence of neighbor states' ratification on other states, these measures may "also capture the influence of a common history and culture or even economic and political similarities" (p. 612). This important caveat is a reminder of the inelegant nature of current measures of norm diffusion.

Even though the measures of organizational embeddedness and civil society pressure (generally the number of organizations in which the state has membership) are less blunt indicators than those for norm diffusion, the evidence of their influence is also rather inconsistent and mixed. Most studies have focused on membership in INGOs and NGOs, but at least two empirical studies have examined membership in IGOs. While participation in IGOs is expected to increase state "exposure to value transfers and demonstration effects," Landman (2005) finds quite mixed results in that membership only positively affects CERD and CEDAW ratification, and actually has a negative influence on the ICCPR's two protocols, the CAT and CRC (p. 29). In fact when he controls for reservations placed on ratification, all significant effects are negative. Cole (2005) finds participation in IGOs to be too highly correlated with INGO memberships, and thus uses an aggregate measure of the two. Similarly to Landman, he finds no effect on participation in the ICCPR and ICESCR and also finds that INGO/IGO participation *decreases* the likelihood of participation in the ICCPR's first optional protocol. He posits three *ad hoc* explanations that deserve future attention. First, participation in INGOs increases the probability that human rights abuses will be exposed; second, participation in INGOs increases individual awareness of their rights and their likelihood of using the grievance procedure established by the protocol—thus participation in INGOs increases the likely cost of commitment; and third, participation in IGOs increases the state's adeptness at "navigating international politics generally" (p. 485), and presumably its awareness of the potentially greater costs of ratifying the optional protocol.

The observed effects of INGOs have been more consistent than those of IGOs. Landman (2005) found that INGOs consistently and positively influence state ratification of the various components of the international human rights regime, and he found that the effects were even stronger when controlling for reservations. Hathaway (2007) improves on other measures in that she specifically focuses on the effect of *human rights* NGOs rather than all NGOs. While she also finds a positive effect on CAT ratification, Powell and Staton (2009) find that INGO membership negatively affects CAT ratification; however, as they note, their model discounts ratification with reservations while Hathaway does not make such a distinction. Hathaway, like Cole, finds no influence on ICCPR ratification. Consistently with Cole she finds that NGO participation decreases ratification of the ICCPR Protocol. Hathaway finds no influence on CEDAW ratification; however, Wotipka and Ramirez (2007) find consistent positive influence from INGO membership (membership generally, as well as membership in human rights INGOs and women's rights INGOs specifically). The hypothesized socialization effects of human rights conferences receive consistent support in empirical studies; however, the measures are rather blunt dummy variables that delineate the presence of a conference in any given year rather than the actual level of participation by state government or non-governmental actors in the conferences (Cole, 2005; Wotipka and Ramirez, 2007).

As a whole the most promising empirical result is evidence of the role of non-governmental organizations in increasing participation in the human rights regime. Unfortunately, the current empirical literature does not provide an examination of the mechanisms through which these organizations work; clearly this is one of the most important directions for future work. The findings in regard to the effect of norm diffusion, as measured by cumulative participation in the regime, do not engender as much confidence, especially given that participation in most treaties is reaching universality. The near-universality of ratification increases the importance of understanding the role of reservations placed on treaty commitment, as do the mixed empirical findings above, which stem in part from differences in the way scholars conceptualize reservations and commitment to the human rights regime. Thus, empirical studies concerning reservations deserve at least brief attention here.

D. Reservations to human rights treaties

The Vienna Convention on the Law of Treaties specifically defines a reservation as "a unilateral statement…made by the State, when signing, ratifying, accepting, approving, or acceding to treaty, whereby it purports to exclude or modify the legal effect of certain provisions of the treaty in their application to that State." Reservations may affect state ratification decisions. On one hand, they may be "legitimate, perhaps even desirable, means of accounting for cultural, religious, or political value diversity across nations" (Neumayer, 2007: 398) or they may provide a mechanism for liberal democratic regimes, who take their legal commitments seriously, to avoid interpretations that might unduly restrict their sovereignty or that specifically conflict with domestic law (Cole, 2005, Neumayer, 2007). On the other hand, they may enable repressive states to "join treaties by eviscerating a treaty's effectiveness and enforceability" (Cole, 2005: 486). Several of the studies above attempt to deal with the potential confounding influence of these reservations through a variety of methods. Powell and Staton consider only ratification without reservation to the CAT, which seems to account for some differences between their results and Goodliffe and Hawkins' analysis. Cole (2005) and Wotipka and Ramirez (2007) deal with the issue of reservations by conducting parallel analyses of ratification with and ratification without reservations, but overall, they find generally the same factors influence commitment. Landman's (2005) nuanced weighting of the legal effect of reservations on each treaty's obligations provides the most rigorous control for reservation effects; even here we see that the factors associated with state ratification are largely the same, but with significant improvements in statistical significance and size of the effects. Neumayer (2007) specifically seeks to test the hypothesis that liberal democratic regimes are more likely to place reservations on their commitments to the core human rights treaties, and does find consistent evidence that these regimes have a greater propensity for placing more reservations than other regimes, suggesting they may indeed take their legal commitments more seriously. Overall, the evidence argues for more rigorous future work that specifically conceptualizes and models the role of reservations on commitment and compliance.

IV. Empirical Evidence: State Compliance with Human Rights Agreements

Most empirical studies of state compliance with international human rights treaty obligations focus on the state's provision or protection of the guaranteed rights embedded in the document; however, there are notable exceptions such as Heyns and Viljoen (2001), who examine the broader impact of the human rights regime on a wide range of state and non-state behavior, including legislative reform, judicial decisions, the use of a treaty by NGOs, references to the treaty in academic publications, and so forth. Their analysis suggests that in most states treaties have made an impact on at least some types of behavior, but while their analysis is very rich, it is limited to a qualitative analysis of a sample of 20 countries. Avdeyeva (2007) provides another notable exception in that she examines a broad range of measures taken by states to comply with CEDAW's provision for the protection of women against violence, including the creation of government shelters, police and judicial training programs, public awareness campaigns, and government support of related NGOs. Her qualitative analysis, while limited to post-communist countries of Central and Eastern Europe, significantly broadens the conceptualization of compliance, and should inform future large-n empirical studies. The bulk of the empirical compliance literature, while grounded in rich theoretical debate concerning the influence of human rights treaties, has largely been limited to tests of whether being a state party produces a positive or negative effect, controlling for a variety of factors. It does not enable us to determine which of the mechanisms that are hypothesized to be at work are actually operative. Realist theory views treaty commitments as cheap talk and therefore predicts no effect or perhaps even a negative effect. Rationalist theory does not provide as clear an expectation, but because of the lack of direct benefits of compliance and the weak enforcement mechanisms which make non-compliance relatively costless (except, possibly, in terms of reputation), treaties would be expected to have a weak effect at best. The decoupling effect posited by the world-society approach would predict that we would observe no direct effect and a negative effect over time. Thus, three theories predict little or no effect, or even a negative effect. The expectations of the domestic-institutions approach would be conditional, expecting better human rights, but only in democratic regimes or regimes with effective legal institutions. The normative perspectives, however, would predict compliance due to norm diffusion and the effect of transnational human rights networks, but perhaps would make the expectations contingent upon the strength of the networks (Neumayer, 2005).

A. Realist and rationalist assumptions

Extant empirical evidence has demonstrated consistently that being a state party to an international human rights treaty either produces no effect, or a negative rather than a positive effect. For example, Keith (1999) finds no effect from the ICCPR on personal integrity rights or civil rights and liberties, unless controlling for state derogations. Hathaway (2002) finds that most treaties within the human rights regime do not significantly affect human rights behavior, and that participation in some of the treaties, such as the Genocide Convention and the CAT produce negative effects, a result which is confirmed by Hafner-Burton and Tsutsui (2005) in regard to a wide range of treaties. In most empirical studies of compliance, the theoretical mechanisms (e.g., cost/benefit calculations and power relationships) are merely assumed rather than directly tested in the models. Kelley's (2007) work on bilateral non-surrender agreements represents a significant exception and takes advantage of a unique opportunity to test particular costs that a state could not have anticipated when it became a party to the Rome Statute. Contrary to realist expectations, she finds that approximately half of the countries pressured by the US went against their own self-interest and resisted the pressure, incurring diplomatic and sometimes economic costs. She does find some evidence to support realist assumptions in that states that have GSP status with the United States,[5] poor states, and members of the "Iraq coalition of the willing" were more likely to sign non-surrender agreements. We find another notable exception within the asylum literature. A growing body of research has examined the United States' obligations under the Geneva Convention relating to the Status of Refugees and under the CAT to respect the norm of *nonrefoulement*. Most of these empirical studies have demonstrated that US foreign policy interests (security and trade relationships) and domestic policy interests (economic and national security concerns) influence decisions on who receives a grant of asylum in the United States (Rosenblum and Salehyan, 2004; Salehyan and Rosenblum, 2008; Rottman et al. 2009; and Keith and Holmes, 2009). Overall, the general failure to find an association of better human rights with treaty commitment supports realist expectations. However, most of these studies do not specifically operationalize and test the underlying assumptions that would predict no effect; thus our confidence in this conclusion is rather weak. Moreover, Kelley's findings and those in the asylum literature, which more directly account for realist and rationalist assumptions, suggest that interests may not matter as much as the realists think; and, indeed, their analyses demonstrate that norms and domestic political contexts also matter, as we will see below.

B. Domestic political institutions

Assumptions of the domestic-institutions approach have received much more specific empirical attention than those of realist and rationalist theory, presumably

---

[5] Generalized System of Preferences is "a program designed to promote economic growth in the developing world by providing preferential duty-free entry for about 4,800 products from 131 designated beneficiary countries and territories" (Office of the United States Trade Representative, 2009).

because scholars can more readily observe and measure domestic institutional contexts than cost/benefit calculations or the diffusion of norms. Several studies have examined the conditional or interactive effect of democratic regimes on treaty compliance. When Hathaway (2002) limited her analysis to democratic regimes she continued to find no effect of the ICCPR and negative effects of the CAT on human rights behavior; but she does find that participation in the Genocide Convention, CEDAW, and the ICCPR's Optional Protocol produces a significant positive effect on related human rights. Neumayer (2005) examines whether the impact of ratification is conditional upon regime type, and finds that in pure autocracies, ratification of the CAT and the ICCPR is associated with worse human rights practices, but that ratification has a "more and more beneficial effect" as democracy strengthens.[6] Landman (2005) conceptualizes and models ratification as a function of the underlying processes of democratization, economic development, and global interdependence, which he finds influence human rights somewhat moderately but consistently across the various treaties that comprise the international human rights regime. It is difficult to separate out the influence of democratic institutions in his human rights analysis, although we do know that the relative weight of democratization is likely rather small because its effect on ratification was minor relative to that of other factors. As reported above, Powell and Staton's (2009) study of the CAT makes a significant contribution by moving our attention to the domestic legal system. They find that as the effectiveness of the judiciary increases, the joint probability of ratifying the CAT in full and then violating the treaty decreases; however, they find only mixed evidence that the joint probability of not ratifying and torturing increases with an effective judiciary in place. Kelley (2007) also demonstrates that states with stronger domestic commitment to the rule of law were less likely to violate their treaty commitment by signing a non-surrender agreement. Finally, if we broaden the scope of compliance to include the asylum literature, Salehyan and Rosenblum (2008) make a significant contribution, demonstrating that public and media attention to immigration and asylum issues increased the impact of humanitarian concerns in U.S. asylum outcomes. However, their findings in regard to congressional influence on human rights concerns in asylum outcomes are less encouraging as the effect is contingent upon partisan politics and whether congressional hearings are framed in terms of immigration enforcement, which reduces the humanitarian dimension of the outcomes, or in terms of refugee and asylum issues, which increases the importance of the humanitarian dimension. Overall, the literature clearly demonstrates that domestic institutions and politics influence states' compliance with their treaty obligations, and that the influence of

---

[6] He finds similar results in regard to Article 21 and 22 of the CAT and in regard to the Optional Protocol, although he notes that beneficial effect of ratification tapers off the more democratic the state becomes.

democratic institutions extends beyond the traditional electoral components to the judiciary and the rule of law.

C. Norms and socialization

Measuring norms is probably the most difficult task that empiricists face in testing normative approaches, and thus most empirical studies of compliance have examined surrogate indicators. Powell and Staton (2009) test regional and global norms, as indicated by past rates of torture, in their CAT models; however they find little evidence that norms influence state torture practices. Kelley's (2007) study of bilateral non-surrender agreements provides the best opportunity to examine the influence of norms or state values. She finds that even while controlling for a significant number of realist assumptions, states that had demonstrated a prior normative affinity for the ICC were less likely to sign non-surrender agreements; however she did not find human rights norms to influence signing the non-surrender agreements. Even though the asylum literature has consistently demonstrated that security and material interests strongly influence U.S. asylum decisions, these studies have also consistently demonstrated that humanitarian norms (especially human rights conditions) do influence U.S. compliance with its commitments under international law (Rosenblum and Salehyan, 2004; Salehyan and Rosenblum 2008; Rottman et al., 2009; and Keith and Holmes, 2009). The presence of transnational networks or civil society pressure (typically measured as the number of international NGOs in which citizens have membership) is much easier to measure than the presence of norms; however, the direct link between treaty ratification and civil society pressure is not typically tested in human rights models. Both Hafner-Burton and Tsutsui (2005) and Powell and Staton (2009) find that as the number of INGOs to which citizens belong increases, the level of protection of human rights increases. Neumayer (2005) provides the most rigorous analysis, examining specifically the effect of treaty commitment on human rights behavior, conditioned upon the strength of civil society organizations. His results are rather mixed: he does find that the stronger the state's participation in INGOs the greater the beneficial effect of ratification of the CAT on human rights behavior; however, the results do not hold for ICCPR ratification. He also finds mixed results in regard to regional treaties. For example, while the benefit of ratification of the Inter-American torture convention increases as INGO participation increases, the effect does not hold for the European torture convention.

Overall, the observable effect of norm diffusion is rather weak and inconsistent at best. The evidence of a strong positive influence by non-governmental organizations on states' human rights practices is more convincing; however, we must keep in mind that the civil society linkage through treaty ratification is not directly demonstrated except in Neumayer's work.

D. Bills of rights

One of the current limitations of this body of research is the lack of attention to domestic protection of human rights, particularly through constitutional provisions. Granted, realists and other skeptics would likely dismiss bills of rights as mere window dressing, at least for some regimes (e.g., Howard, 1991; Ludwikowski, 1996; Epp, 1998). From a rationalist perspective, however, collections of rights formally embedded in fundamental domestic law may provide concrete standards against which the regime's behavior can be assessed not only by itself, but also by the public and the world community (see Sartori, 1962; Murphy, 1993); and this would likely affect the regime's calculation of costs associated with non-compliance to the document. The provisions also provide a potential tool for the courts to constrain state actors from abusing human rights; however, their effectiveness would most likely be dependent upon the level of independence of the judiciary, the degree to which judges on the bench are rights-oriented, and the degree to which the courts are accessible to the general public. Similarly, from a domestic-institutions perspective, bills of rights are an integral part of the global model of democratization that provides constraints upon the power of government. But from a world-society approach, we would expect to find a significant degree of decoupling of practice from promise, at least over time because, as Ginsburg (2003) notes, a bill of fundamental rights, protected by an independent judiciary, especially one empowered to review legislation, has come to be seen, like presidencies and legislatures, as part of the global script of modernity. Thus regimes that lack real commitment to human rights may promulgate bills of rights to signal their legitimacy in the global society of states. From a norms perspective, constitutional provisions for human rights may articulate ideals and norms to which the regime aspires (Murphy, 1993; Finer et al., 1995), and they may "powerfully shape popular culture" (Epp, 1998: 13). In this sense bills of rights in particular, may serve as a socializing tool that conditions the expectations of the public, promoting the development of a rights consciousness among the mass public (see Epp, 1998; Murphy, 1993).

   A growing body of empirical studies has examined the effect of bills of rights on actual state protection or provision of the promised human rights; and overall, the findings of these analyses have tended to parallel those of studies of international human rights agreements: they largely report no effect, or a harmful association with state human rights practices, suggesting that indeed there is a decoupling effect in regard to domestic agreements as well. The earliest empirical analyses (Boli-Bennett, 1976; Pritchard, 1986) found evidence that would support the realists' assumptions, as well as those of the world-society model, in that not only were constitutional provisions not associated with improved rights behavior, they were associated with worse human rights behavior. It is tempting to dismiss these early findings due to the low-level bivariate analyses employed and the limited single-year focus; however, as subsequent analyses grew in rigor and sophistication, the evidence continued to document the failure of these formal promises to deliver rights, with only a few exceptions. Davenport (1996) examined the impact of 14 constitutional provisions on state repression and found that only the protection of freedom of press or the presence of a state-of-emergency clause reduced negative sanctions. Like Bennett and Pritchard, Keith (2002) and Keith et al., (2009) found consistent evidence that a substantial number of constitutional provisions for traditional rights and freedoms were associated with worse rights protection rather than improved behavior, with the exception of the guarantee of a fair trial and a public trial. In addition, they found that some dimensions of state-of-emergency provisions, that were intended to protect rights during such crises, were actually associated with worse human rights abuses. Two provisions—the provision of a list of non-derogable rights and provision for a time-limit for renewal of the declaration of emergency—appear to give regimes a cloak of legitimacy under which they may repress citizens during the emergency period and beyond. While domestic law, especially constitutional law, would seem to be a significant link between international human rights commitment and state human rights behavior, it remains unexamined in either of these literatures.

V. Limitations and Future Research

The empirical studies reviewed here form a relatively new field of inquiry that has quickly evolved, drawing upon several academic disciplines with increasing theoretical sophistication, as well as methodological innovation and rigor. As with most empirical endeavors, scholars face restrictions that are inherent in all behavioral studies, as well as those that are particular to the behavior they seek to understand. Thus, these studies face the same measurement problems that most human rights scholars do: scarce sources of uniform information and reliable data across the global set of states. Typically, scholars must choose between rather thin measures of human rights, usually limited to individual rights and freedoms, or richer qualitative measures that do not allow as much empirical rigor. Measures of economic rights or quality of life are much harder to construct, as are measures of cultural and social rights. Thus, compliance with many of the core human rights treaties, such as the ICESCR, CERD, and CRC (and many components of CEDAW) is largely ignored in empirical studies or examined using inappropriate measures of human rights (typically the readily available personal integrity rights measures). As a result, our empirical understanding of human rights treaties tends to be limited to those encompassing the more Western-oriented individual rights. Of equal importance, many of the core theoretical assumptions and mechanisms are difficult, if not impossible, to observe directly, and empirical studies have tended to study indirect effects, to assume the presence of mechanisms and calculations without specifically measuring and testing them, or to rely upon rather blunt surrogates. Moreover, most compliance studies (and human rights studies in general) tend to assume a unitary state actor in their measurements of human rights practices, even if their theory does not make such an assumption. Even though the domestic-institutions perspective represents a significant departure from this assumption, most studies still tend to rely on aggregate measures of the level of political democracy, without examining the effect of specific institutions and with little attention to a broader range of domestic institutions beyond electoral ones. Future research should build upon the work that Powell and Staton (2009) have begun in regard to domestic legal systems.

Conceptualization and measurement of compliance in this body of research has tended to focus rather narrowly on the current level of state human rights practices without considering the broader range of relevant behavior, such as implementation of domestic policies and programs, which may need to be implemented prior to full realization of the promised rights, and which in the meantime may represent only good faith efforts at compliance. Future research should build upon the work that Avdeyeva (2007) and Merry (2006) have begun which examines the translation of international law commitments into domestic and local realities, not just through changes in domestic statutory and constitutional law, but also through training programs for judges and police officers, public awareness campaigns, and state support of NGOs. The role of NGOs and INGOs seems to offer a tremendous opportunity for future study, but researchers will need to reach beyond simple counts of organizational memberships to examine empirically the processes and contexts through which these organizations influence compliance. It might be especially fruitful to examine the possibility that NGOs form "judicial support networks" that facilitate rights litigation and some level of judicial independence, even in authoritarian regimes (Moustafa, 2007; Moustafa and Ginsburg, 2008). The issue of reservations is a particularly problematic dimension for both studies of commitment and compliance. The lack of attention to reservations in most studies, coupled with the lack of uniform conceptualization and measurement in those studies that do pay attention to them, reduces the generalizability of, and ultimately our confidence in, the conclusions produced in this body of research. While reaching a consensus on the treatment of reservations may not be likely, or even desirable, clearly they merit specific theoretical and conceptual treatment in any future studies of compliance or commitment. Finally, researchers need to address more fully the impact of domestic threats and states of emergency, and the legal and institutional constraints that may check the tendency toward rights abuse under these circumstances. Special attention should be given to the issue of derogations allowed from some of the treaties, as well as the role of constitutional provisions for states of emergency, which may have the unintended consequence of providing repressive regimes with a cloak of legitimacy.

References

Avdeyna, O. (2007). "When Do States Comply with International Treaties? Policies on Violence against Women in Post-Communist Countries," *International Studies Quarterly* 51: 877–900.

Bilder, R.B. (1989). "International Third Party Dispute Settlement," *Denver Journal of International Law and Policy* 17(3): 471–503.

Boli, J. and Thomas, G.M. (1997). "World Culture in a World Polity: A Century of Non-Governmental Organization," *American Sociological Review* 62: 171–90.

Boli-Bennett, J. (1976). *The Expansion of National States. 1870–1970*, Ph.D. dissertation, Palo Alto, CA: Stanford University.

Bueno de Mesquita, B., Downs, G.M., Smith, A., and Cherif, F.M. (2005). "Thinking Inside the Box: A Closer Look at Democracy and Human Rights," *International Studies Quarterly* 49(3): 439–57.

Cole, W.M. (2005). "Sovereignty Relinquished? Explaining Commitment to the International Human Rights Covenants, 1966–1999," *American Sociological Review* 70(3): 472–95.

Davenport, C. (1996). " 'Constitutional Promises' and Repressive Reality: A Cross-National Time-Series Investigation of Why Political and Civil Liberties are Suppressed," *Journal of Politics* 58: 627–54.

Donnelly, J. (1998). *International Human Rights*, Boulder: Westview.

Epp, C.R. (1998). *The Rights Revolution: Lawyers, Activists and Supreme Courts in Comparative Perspective*, Chicago: University of Chicago Press.

Finer, S.E., Bogdanor, V., and Rudden, B. (1995). *Comparing Constitutions,* Oxford: Oxford University Press.

Finnemore, M. and Sikkink, K. (1998). "International Norm Dynamics and Political Change," *International Organization* 52(4): 887–917.

Gilpin, R. (1981). *War and Change in World Politics,* New York: Cambridge University Press.

Ginsburg, T. (2003). *Judicial Review in New Democracies: Constitutional Courts in Asian Cases,* Cambridge: Cambridge University Press.

Goodliffe, J. and Hawkins, D.G. (2006). "Explaining Commitment: States and the Convention Against Torture," *The Journal of Politics* 68(2): 358–71.

Goodman, R. and Jinks, D. (2004). "How to Influence States: Socialization and International Human Rights Law," *Duke Law Review* 54(3): 621–703.

Hafner-Burton, E. and Tsutsui, K. (2005). "Human Rights in a Globalizing World: The Paradox of Empty Promises," *The American Journal of Sociology* 110(5): 1373–411.

Hathaway, O.A. (2002). "Do Human Rights Treaties Make a Difference?," *Yale Law Journal* 111(8): 1935–2042.

Hathaway, O.A. (2003). "The Cost of Commitment," *Stanford Law Review* 55(5): 1821–62.

Hathaway, O.A. (2005). "Between Power and Principle: An Integrated Theory of International Law," *The University of Chicago Law Review* 72(2): 469–536.

Hathaway, O.A. (2007). "Why Do Countries Commit to Human Rights Treaties?," *Journal of Conflict Resolution* 8(51): 588–621.

Heyns, C. and Viljoen, F. (2001). "The impact of the United Nations human rights treaties on the domestic level," *Human Rights Quarterly* 23: 483–535.

Hoffmann, S. (1956). "The Role of International Organizations: Limits and Possibilities," *International Organization* 10(3): 357–72.

Howard, A.E.D. (1991). "The Essence of Constitutionalism," in K.W. Thompson and R.T. Ludwikowski (eds.), *Constitutionalism and Human Rights: America, Poland, and France*. New York: Lanham.

Keck, M. and Sikkink, K. (1998). *Activists beyond Borders. Transnational Advocacy Networks in International Politics*, Ithaca, New York: Cornell University Press.

Keith, L.C. (1999). "The United Nations International Covenant on Civil and Political Rights: Does It Make a Difference in Human Rights Behavior?," *Journal of Peace Research* 36(1): 95–118.

Keith, L.C. (2002). "Constitutional Provisions for Individual Human Rights (1976–1996): Are They More than Mere 'Window Dressing'?," *Political Research Quarterly* 55: 111–43.

Keith, L.C., and Holmes, J.S. (2009). "Determinants of Asylum Grants: A Rare Examination of Factors Typically Unobservable in US Asylum Decisions," *Journal of Refugee Studies* 22: 224–41.

Keith, L.C., Tate, C.N. and Poe, S.C. (2009). "Is the Law a Mere Parchment Barrier to Human Rights Abuse?," *Journal of Politics* 71(2): 644–60.

Kelley, J. (2007). "Who Keeps International Commitments and Why? The International Criminal Court and Bilateral Nonsurrender Agreements," *American Political Science Review* 1901(3): 573–89.

Koh, H.H. (1996). "The 1994 Roscoe Pound Lecture: Transnational Legal Process," *Nebraska Law Review* 75: 181–98.

Krasner, S.D. (1993). "Sovereignty, Regimes, and Human Rights," in *Regime Theory and International Relations*, V. Rittberger and P. Mayer (eds.), Oxford: Oxford University Press.

Landman, T. (2005). *Protecting Human Rights: A Comparative Study*, Washington, DC: Georgetown University Press.

Ludwikowski, R.R. (1996). *Constitutionmaking in the Region of Former Soviet Dominance*, Durham: Duke University Press.

Mearsheimer, J.J. (1994). "The False Promise of International Institutions," *International Security* 19 (Winter): 5–26.

Merry, S.E. (2006). *Human Rights and Gender Violence: Translating International Law into Local Justice*, Chicago: University of Chicago Press.

Meyer, J.W., Boli, J., Thomas, G.M. and Ramirez, F.O. (1997). "World Society and the Nation-State," *American Journal of Sociology* 103: 144–81.

Moravcsik, A. (2000). "The Origins of Human Rights Regimes: Democratic Delegations in Postwar Europe," *International Organization* 54(2): 217–52.

Morgenthau, H.J. (1948). *Politics among Nations*, New York: Knopf.

Moustafa, T. (2007). *The Struggle for Constitutional Power: Law, Politics, and Economic Reform in Egypt*, New York: Cambridge University Press.

Moustafa, T. and Ginsburg, T. (2008). "Introduction: The Function of Courts in Authoritarian Politics," in T. Ginsburg and T. Moustafa (eds.), *Rule by Law: The Politics of Courts in Authoritarian Regimes*, New York: Cambridge University Press.

Murphy, W.E. (1993). "Constitutions, Constitutionalism, and Democracy," in D. Greenberg et al., (eds.), *Constitutionalism and Democracy: Transition in the Contemporary World*, New York: Oxford University Press.

Neumayer, E. (2005). "Do International Human Rights Treaties Improve Respect for Human Rights?," *Journal of Conflict Resolution* 49(6): 925–53.

Neumayer, E. (2007). "Qualified Ratification: Explaining Reservations to International Human Rights Treaties," *Journal of Legal Analysis* 36: 397–429.

Office of the United States Trade Representative (2009). "Generalized System of Preference (GSP)," available at < http://www.ustr.gov/trade-topics/trade-development/preference-programs/generalized-system-preference-gsp>.

Powell, E.J. and Staton, J.K. (2009). "Domestic Judicial Institutions and Human Rights Treaty Violation," *International Studies Quarterly* 53: 149–74.

Pritchard, K. (1986). "Comparative Human Rights: An Integrative Explanation," *Policy Studies Journal* 15(1): 110–28.

Risse, T., Ropp, S.C., and Sikkink, K. (1999). *The Power of Human Rights: International Norms and Domestic Change*, New York: Cambridge University Press.

Risse, T. and Sikkink, K. (1999). "The Socialization of International Human Rights Norms into Domestic Practices: Introduction," in Risse, Ropp, and Sikkink (eds.), *The Power of Human Rights: International Norms and Domestic Change*, New York: Cambridge University Press.

Rosenblum, M.R. and Salehyan, I. (2004). "Norms and Interests in US Asylum Enforcement," *Journal of Peace Research* 41(6): 677–97.

Rottman, A.J., Fariss, C.J., and Poe, S.C. (2009). "The Path to Asylum in the US and the Determinants for Who Gets in and Why," *International Migration Review* 43(1): 3–34.

Salehyan, I. and Rosenblum, M.R. (2008). "International Relations, Domestic Politics, and Asylum Admissions in the United States," *Political Research Quarterly* 61(1): 104–21.

Sartori, G. (1962). "Constitutionalism: A Preliminary Discussion," *American Political Science Review* 56(8): 53–64.

Simmons, B.A. (2000). "Compliance with International Agreements," *Annual Review of Political Science* 1: 75–93.

UN Treaty Collection (2009). available at <http://treaties.un.org/pages/ParticipationStatus.aspx>.

Vreeland, J.R. (2008). "Political Institutions and Human Rights: Why Dictatorships Enter Into the United Nations Convention Against Torture," *International Organization* 62(1): 65–101.

Waltz, K. (1979). *Theory of International Politics*, Reading, Massachusetts: Addison–Wesley.

Wotipka, C.M. and Ramirez, F.O. (2007). "World Society and Human Rights: An Event History Analysis of the Convention on the Elimination of All Forms of Discrimination against Women," in B.A. Simmons, G. Garrett, and F. Dobbin (eds.), *The Global Diffusion of Markets and Democracy*, Cambridge: Cambridge University Press.

16

CONSTITUTIONS

DAVID S. LAW[1]

I. Two Types of Constitution; Two Strains of Research

ALTHOUGH constitutional scholarship has long been predominantly normative in character, that has certainly not been for a lack of interesting empirical questions. To name but a few: Why do some countries adopt entrenched formal constitutions while others do not? What are the practical consequences of adopting a formal constitution, or of choosing one set of political institutions over another? Is there a magic combination of adoption procedures and substantive provisions that renders formal constitution-making an effective instrument for achieving social, political,

[1] The author is grateful to the editors of this volume, and to Josh Fischman, Paul Gribble, Ran Hirschl, Anne Law, Miguel Schor, and Mila Versteeg, for suggestions that have improved this Chapter in a myriad of ways.

and economic goals? What influences the evolution of a country's de jure or de facto constitution? Do constitutions exhibit recurring patterns over space and time, and if so, what explains those patterns? Yet before these topics can even be broached, there are two broad and recurring questions with which those interested in the empirical study of constitutions must grapple. The first might initially appear to be definitional but in fact concerns the appropriate scope and content of the research agenda: what exactly are we studying when we study constitutions? The second is methodological: what methods are appropriate and feasible when it comes to the empirical study of constitutions?

Empirical research on constitutions addresses two different phenomena that both go by the name of "constitution." The distinction at issue has been expressed in a variety of ways, each of which has its own shadings and nuances, but the underlying divide is between de jure, written, codified, or formal constitutions ("large-c" constitutions), on the one hand, and de facto, unwritten, uncodified, or informal constitutions ("small-c" constitutions), on the other. A large-c constitution is a legal document, or set of legal documents, that (1) proclaims its own status as supreme or fundamental law, (2) purports to dictate the structure, contours, and powers of the state, and (3) may also be formally entrenched, in the sense of being harder to amend or repeal than other laws.

A small-c constitution, by contrast, consists of the body of rules, practices, and understandings, written or unwritten, that *actually* determines who holds what kind of power, under what conditions, and subject to what limits. Long before the first large-c constitutions came into being in the late eighteenth century, Aristotle used the term "constitution" in this small-c sense to describe the actual organization of a city-state. Small-c constitutions can include not only treaties and statutes that lack formal constitutional status, but also unwritten conventions that lack formal legal status of any kind (Dicey, 1915; Palmer, 2006). A small-c constitution is likely to depart from, and indeed may even contradict, its large-c counterpart in at least some respects. To use an extreme example, although Thailand's large-c constitution purports to specify the conditions under which the government can be removed from power or the constitution itself can be altered, it is tantamount to a small-c constitutional rule that both the government and the large-c constitution may be swept aside via a coup d'état, provided that the coup leaders obtain the blessing of the monarchy, refrain from harming civilians, and hold elections thereafter (Elkins et al., 2009: 190–1).

It is common for scholars to refer to "constitutions" without specifying which of the two phenomena they have in mind. This terminological confusion reflects not only a lack of conceptual clarity, but also a disciplinary divide. On the whole, social scientists have generally been more interested in actual as opposed to formal arrangements and thus have tended to focus on small-c constitutions, whereas legal scholars have been more inclined to equate the idea of a constitution with a formal legal document, and to pay greater heed to such documents. Failure to distinguish between the two types of constitution, however, begs analytical confusion. Because a jurisdiction's small-c and large-c constitutions are unlikely to coincide perfectly, they cannot be discussed interchangeably.

The literature on small-c constitutions is immense. This is because much of the literature in the fields of comparative politics and political economy can be characterized as empirical research on small-c constitutions, whether or not it explicitly labels itself as such. Common themes of this literature include the causes and consequences of different forms and structures of government, such as democracy as opposed to dictatorship, presidential as opposed to parliamentary regimes, and proportional as opposed to majoritarian electoral systems. Scholars have asked, for example, whether democracies are more likely to prosper (e.g., Przeworski and Limongi, 1993) or wage war (e.g., Reiter and Stam, 2002) than autocracies, and which type of democracy—presidential or parliamentary—is likely to last longer (e.g., Shugart and Carey, 1992) or lead to lower levels of government spending (e.g., Persson and Tabellini, 2005). Reflecting the fact that it is produced mostly by social scientists, this body of work frequently involves quantitative and statistical analysis.

The empirical literature on large-c constitutions, by contrast, is not nearly as extensive. To say that our knowledge does not match our aspirations in this domain would be an understatement. Large-c constitutionalism was born of the Enlightenment belief that the act of making reasoned, explicit commitments in written form would enable societies to establish better forms of government. Large-c constitutions have since become ubiquitous instruments of modern government: 90% of countries possess some document or collection of documents that advertises its own status as higher ("constitutional," or "fundamental," or "basic") law (Elkins et al., 2009: 49). In that same spirit of improving the technology of governance, scholars have sought to understand whether and how large-c constitutions can be designed and employed to achieve such fundamental and challenging goals as economic prosperity (e.g., Voigt, 1997), political stability (e.g., Lutz, 2006), respect for rights (e.g., Cross, 1999; Davenport, 1996; Keith, 2002; Lutz, 2006), lasting democracy (e.g., Elster, 1991), and peaceful coexistence among potentially warring factions of society (e.g., Choudhry, 2008; Horowitz, 2008; Lijphart, 2008). Efforts to devise large-c constitutional solutions to such challenges have focused on identifying, on the basis of a combination of theory and experience, the best answers to the interrelated questions of process and content: what should the content of the constitution be, and what is the process by which the content of the constitution should be determined?

For a variety of reasons, however, relatively little is known with confidence about how large-c constitutions can most effectively be used to achieve these goals or, indeed, whether they are effective at all. Much of the empirical work that does exist consists of case studies or small-n comparisons which, although valuable, have their limitations. Even at a purely descriptive level, surprisingly little was known until recently about the characteristics of the existing universe of large-c constitutions. There has been no convenient way of answering such basic questions as what proportion of the world's constitutions contain a right to education or executive term limits. The emergence of new data sets on the adoption and content of the world's written constitutions, at least some of which may be made available to the rest of the scholarly community in the near future, is now enabling quantitative researchers to tackle the full panoply of such questions (e.g., Elkins et al., 2009; Widner, 2008; Goderis and Versteeg, 2009). We now know, for example, what the average lifespan of a large-c constitution is (19 years), and what factors predict greater constitutional longevity (for example, the inclusion of a broad range of relevant actors in the constitution-making process, a relatively high degree of substantive specificity in the constitutional document itself, and amendment mechanisms that are neither too difficult nor too easy to invoke) (Elkins et al., 2009). An important next step will be the collection of thorough cross-national time-series data on how courts interpret large-c constitutions. Creation of a data set of such scope is a formidable undertaking but will make it possible to accurately describe and analyze the substance and development of constitutional law at a global level.

The growth of quantitative empiricism in the field of large-c constitutional scholarship comes not a moment too soon. Witness the question posed—and the answers offered—by a recently published symposium: "What, If Anything, Do We Know about Constitutional Design?" The answer appears to be, for the time being, not much (Levinson, 2009: 1265, 1271). The field remains a young one: as recently as 1995, it was ruefully observed that there existed "no body of literature that deals with the constitution-making process in a positive, explanatory perspective," and not "a single book or even article that considers the process of constitution-making...as a distinct object of positive analysis" (Elster, 1995: 364). With respect to the specific problem of constitution-making for divided societies, there remains no "definitive or uniformly accepted answer" to the question of either process or content: we know neither what process of constitution-making is "most apt to produce the best configuration of institutions," nor what the "best configuration of institutions" happens to be (Horowitz, 2008: 1213). Likewise, although the judicial use of foreign and international legal materials in constitutional cases has prompted a good deal of qualitative empirical discussion (e.g., Choudhry, 2008; Law, 2005a), an accurate global picture of the scope and degree of large-c constitutional "borrowing," "migration," and "diffusion" awaits comprehensive quantitative analysis of a type that is only beginning to occur (Elkins et al., 2009: 24–6). What Ginsburg et al. (2009) say about the state of the empirical literature on constitution-making in particular might well be said of the empirical literature on large-c constitutions as a whole: "In general, scholars have been far better at generating hypotheses...than at testing them. Individual case studies have provided some insights, but large-n work has been hindered by a lack of data and by a need for conceptual refinement" (p. 219).

II. Do Constitutions Matter?

Certain empirical questions about large-c constitutions have profound implications for much of the normative literature. First, to what extent and why do large-c and small-c constitutions diverge from one another? Second, what impact, if any, does a large-c constitution have on its small-c counterpart? There are many reasons why the two types of constitution may diverge. A large-c constitution may be partly or wholly an aspirational or expressive document, in which case we would expect at least some gap to exist between text and reality. It may be insincere, as in the case of an authoritarian regime that adopts an expansive bill of rights for ulterior motives that have more to do with, say, securing the acceptance of the international community (Meyer et al., 1997) or attracting foreign capital and skilled workers (Law, 2008) than protecting the freedom of its citizens. Or it may simply be ineffective: a constitution framed with sincere intentions and high hopes may fail to have much impact on actual practice.

The possibility that large-c constitutions may lack practical impact strikes at the heart of the literature on constitution-making and constitutional design. What is the point of debating, for example, what rights to include in a constitution if the inclusion of those rights has no practical consequence? Of what value is it to know that an authoritarian regime promises in a written constitutional document to respect judicial independence or personal freedom? How can it be meaningful to discuss how best to write a constitution that mitigates conflict in divided societies, if constitutions have no effect? Why is it helpful to know the factors that predict the endurance of large-c constitutions if large-c constitutions neither reflect nor shape actual practice?

Scholarship aimed at identifying the best ways to devise or write a large-c constitution embodies the assumption that *constitutions matter*: that is, large-c constitutions are not merely shaped by, but also shape, political, economic, and social life. If one assumes that large-c constitutions do in fact affect the prospects of achieving such mammoth and elusive goals as peace and prosperity, then the stakes involved in the empirical study of large-c constitutions are exceedingly high. It has been asserted, for example, that a "majority" of the world's constitutions not only purport to limit government power, but are also "reasonably or fully operative" in practice (Breslin, 2009: 27). Upon critical reflection, however, it may seem like something of a lawyer's dream to suppose that the mere drafting and adoption of a legal document that typically lacks any plausible prospect of third-party enforcement can nevertheless define the machinery of government and shape the welfare of a nation.

The evidence that large-c constitutionalism promotes human flourishing, for example, is hardly conclusive. As Hirschl observes, if one uses common measures of democracy and human development as the yardstick, the world's most successful nations do not appear to be characterized or distinguished by the presence of robust, "American-style written constitutionalism, active judicial review, or culturally engrained constitutional sanctity" (2009: 1357). The drivers of success would appear instead to include a combination of exogenous resource constraints (such as population size) and small-c constitutional factors (such as stable electoral processes, the existence of a large middle class, a healthy civil society, and a developed market economy characterized by high levels of public investment in science, education, and health care). By contrast, the impact of large-c constitutional variance would appear to be "[q]uite negligible" (p. 1360).

The empirical literature on the large-c constitutional protection of individual rights, in particular, is not very encouraging. A scholarly preoccupation with rights has defined the agenda of comparative constitutional law and spawned a vast literature on what rights large-c constitutions should contain and how they ought to be enforced (Choudhry, 2008). Much of this literature is normative in character and proceeds on the assumption that the inclusion of particular rights in large-c constitutions has an impact on actual government behavior. Considerably less attention has been given, however, to the question of whether this assumption is empirically justified. The existence of large-c constitutional rights is obviously neither a necessary nor sufficient condition for the observance of such rights in practice; compare, for example, the United Kingdom, which has long respected a variety of rights in the absence of a large-c constitution, with the former Soviet Union, which guaranteed a variety of rights that were routinely abused. Even the architects of the world's most enduring and best-known bill of rights appear to have held out only modest hope for such "parchment barriers" (Madison, 1789); the framers of the United States Constitution allowed merely that that the inclusion of specific rights provisions would not be "altogether useless" (Hamilton, 1789).

Scholars have struggled mightily, but with decidedly mixed results, to conclude that the existence of written rights guarantees leads to greater respect for rights in practice. The quantitative literature that does exist paints, on the whole, a discouraging picture of the efficacy of such provisions (e.g., Blasi and Cingranelli, 1996; Cross, 1999; Davenport, 1996; Hirschl, 2008; Keith, 2002; Keith et al., 2009; Pritchard, 1986).[2] Davenport (1996), for example, reports that the existence of constitutional provisions governing freedom of the press, martial law, and the declaration of states of emergency is associated with lower levels of political repression, but guarantees of freedom of speech (as opposed to freedom of the press) and of the freedom to unionize and strike lack such impact. Nevertheless, he arrives at the conclusion that "constitutions do matter" (p. 648). Likewise, a study by Cross

---

[2] A parallel debate over the actual impact of written rights guarantees can be found in the literature on human rights treaties (e.g., Hafner-Burton and Tsutsui, 2007; Simmons, 2009).

(1999) of the determinants of government behavior in the specific area of search and seizure finds that, by itself, the presence of an express constitutional prohibition against unreasonable search and seizure has no significant impact on actual practice.[3] Neither, for that matter, do such "institutional variables" as federalism and separation of powers. Yet he emphasizes in conclusion that "certain legal variables are important determinants of human rights protection" (p. 97).

Indeed, a number of studies have found a negative relationship between formal rights protection and actual rights observance (Boli-Bennett, 1976; Keith, 2002; Pritchard, 1986). For example, Keith (2002) evaluates the impact of various formal constitutional provisions on the incidence of severe rights violations such as torture, political imprisonment, kidnapping, and murder. Controlling for such variables as the extent to which the country in question is democratic, she finds that formal constitutional guarantees of freedom of speech, religion, association, and assembly are not significant predictors of respect for rights. Rather, constitutional guarantees of freedom of the press and habeas corpus are actually correlated to a statistically significant degree with a *higher* incidence of severe rights abuse. And in an especially ironic twist, constitutional bans on torture are associated with a higher incidence of torture. The only provisions that her analysis suggests are associated in a statistically significant way with increased respect for rights are due process guarantees of a fair and public trial (2002: 128). Although Keith rejects her own findings as to the negative impact of certain constitutional guarantees on actual respect for rights on the grounds that they point in the "wrong direction" and lack "theoretical justification" (pp. 127, 134), a subsequent analysis by Keith et al. (2009) incorporating a host of additional variables merely confirms these supposedly implausible results.[4]

Does this sort of evidence regarding the impact of written rights guarantees warrant skepticism about the efficacy of large-c constitutions more generally? It might be argued that rights guarantees are more prone to failure than other types of large-c constitutional provisions. The success of such guarantees might be dependent upon somewhat demanding institutional and environmental conditions, such

---

[3] Cross's findings suggest that the presence of an express constitutional prohibition against unreasonable search and seizure may have an impact on actual practice, but only in countries characterized by a lack of judicial independence: he notes that higher levels of judicial independence are associated with greater levels of actual freedom from unreasonable search and seizure, but this relationship emerges only in the absence of a constitutional provision.

[4] As the authors of the 2009 study acknowledge, their decision to use one-tailed statistical tests—which embody the assumption that written constitutional protections can only have the effect of *decreasing* rights abuse—ensured, as a mathematical matter, that any findings contrary to this assumption would not be statistically significant (p. 657). Had they used substantively agnostic two-tailed tests, as Keith (2002) did, they might have reported precisely the same result as the earlier study—namely, that constitutional provisions on torture, habeas corpus, and freedom of speech have a negative *and* statistically significant impact on respect for rights.

as the existence of judicial review by independent courts (Goderis and Versteeg, 2009; La Porta et al., 2004) and a legal profession organized in a manner that encourages and sustains rights advocacy (Epp, 1998). Another problem is that such guarantees are not always sincere. For various reasons, it has become de rigueur for even the most tyrannical of regimes to recite in their large-c constitutions a litany of constitutional rights sufficient to please the most ardent idealist (Alston, 1999).

By contrast, government actors may have both less incentive and less ability to ignore constitutional provisions pertaining to institutional design than individual rights. A would-be dictator may stand to gain much more by violating the rights of political dissidents, for example, than by converting a presidential system into a parliamentary one, or vice versa. He or she may also find it much easier to persecute dissidents than to abolish a rival government institution, such as the legislature, that is likely to possess greater ability to fend for itself than a handful of malcontents. There are also many reasons, however, why actual institutional arrangements might not correspond with formal constitutional provisions. To name just a few, the resources to create the constitutionally ordained institutions may be lacking, or the officials responsible for implementing them may lack the desire to do so (Blasi and Cingranelli, 1996: 228), or the arrangement may prove so unpopular that it persists only in form and not in practice (such as the legislative override provision of the Canadian Charter of Rights and Freedoms, or the U.S. Constitution's allocation of responsibility for selecting the President to the Electoral College).

It is not possible to draw any firm conclusions from the scant existing literature about the relative efficacy of other types of large-c constitutional provisions. Elkins et al. (2009) suggest that, as a general matter, "the functioning of important political institutions is described fairly accurately in constitutions, but the extent to which rights provisions are implemented in practice varies dramatically across countries, with some countries promising more than they deliver and others delivering more than they promise" (p. 55). In support of this assessment, they cite statistical evidence showing the existence of a much closer relationship between constitutional text and actual practice when it comes to the scope of legislative power than when individual rights are at stake. In a similar vein, Blasi and Cingranelli (1996) find that constitutional guarantees of federalism correlate strongly with actual government decentralization. Even the relatively modest claim that large-c constitutions tend to reflect the actual operation of a country's political institutions, however, may still be too broad. Consider, for example, the power and independence of the judiciary. Two-thirds of the world's large-c constitutions contain some form of explicit protection for judicial independence, and that proportion has only been rising over time (Constitutional Design Group, 2008). Yet the existence of formal constitutional guarantees of judicial independence appears to be poorly correlated with actual respect for judicial independence in practice: once one controls for such factors as wealth and education, de jure judicial independence ceases to be a meaningful predictor of de facto judicial independence (Feld and Voigt, 2006: 267).[5]

None of this is to suggest that large-c constitutions never succeed. The problem is, rather, that that we know little about the conditions under which large-c constitutionalism succeeds, in the sense of either defining actual practice or improving social welfare. It is not simply the case, for example, that the success of large-c constitutionalism is limited to long-established democracies or to certain geographic regions, as we know from countries such as South Africa and Taiwan. The most that can be said with confidence is that there is a continuing need for a "complete evaluation of the relationship between formal constitutional provisions and constitutional practice" (Elkins et al., 2009: 55). The challenge is to identify which factors determine large-c constitutional success, to what extent, and in what combination—and, ultimately, to do so in a way that holds true not simply for a handful of countries that have received close scrutiny, but on a global basis as well.

III. JUDICIALIZATION AND CONSTITUTIONALIZATION

There is one area in which scholars have made significant progress at understanding and explaining how and why large-c constitutions become effective. The growing body of work on the judicialization and constitutionalization of politics is a highlight of the empirical literature on constitutions more generally. Although the uses and definitions of the terms "judicialization" and "constitutionalization" sometimes overlap, "judicialization" has mainly been used to refer to (1) the expansion of the policy-making role of courts, at the expense of other actors and institutions; and (2) "the spread of judicial decision-making methods outside the judicial province proper," such as the use of adjudication as a policy-making mechanism and the deployment of legal concepts and arguments by non-judicial actors (Vallinder, 1995: 13). "Constitutionalization," in turn, refers to the process by which a body of formal law becomes an effective source of limits on state power and government actors. The legal regime at issue need not be, and often is not, explicitly or formally constitutional in character: one can speak, for example, of

---

[5] An earlier study by Blasi and Cingranelli (1996) of a smaller cross-section of countries over a single year found a positive correlation between de jure and de facto judicial independence but did not control for any other variables.

the constitutionalization of international law (Dunoff and Trachtman, 2009) or the European Union treaty regime (Stone Sweet, 2004), even in the absence of any legal instrument that is formally denominated as constitutional.[6] Where a large-c constitution does exist, however, the term can logically be used to describe the process by which the large-c constitution becomes effective as a practical matter or, in other words, becomes the small-c constitution.

Judicialization and constitutionalization are heavily symbiotic. In order for judges to decide a policy question, that question must be characterized as a legal question. But if judicial decision-making is to trump or displace policy-making by other actors, it helps if the question to be decided is not merely legal, but constitutional in character. Perhaps the most obvious and important way in which courts claim and exercise exclusive authority over policy questions is by acquiring and exercising the power of judicial review. As Stone Sweet puts it, "the judiciary's share of total governmental authority and influence varies with the degree to which it possesses and exercises the power to review the lawfulness of activity, public and private" (1999: 163). Large-c constitutional enforcement is the primary vehicle for the expansion of judicial power, but the expansion of judicial power, in turn, makes the large-c constitution more efficacious. That is, judicialization and constitutionalization form a virtuous circle: by enforcing constitutions, judges acquire power; by exercising their power, judges give effect to constitutions. To understand how and why judicialization occurs, therefore, is also to understand one way in which large-c constitutions become effective.

On the subject of judicialization, there is widespread agreement on two points. The first point is that judicialization is occurring around the world with increasing frequency and intensity, which bodes well for the ability of large-c constitutions to gain traction (e.g., Hirschl, 2004; Shapiro and Stone Sweet, 2002). The second point, which commands even stronger agreement, is that judicialization often occurs with the acquiescence or encouragement of powerful political actors, who frequently have self-serving reasons to refrain from making policy themselves, to empower courts to make policy instead, and to avail themselves of judicial fora (e.g., Ginsburg, 2003; Graber, 1993; Hirschl, 2004; Stone Sweet, 1999, 2004; Whittington, 2007). The "mantra" of this literature, as Graber puts it, is that "judicial review is politically constructed": "Elected officials provide vital political foundations for judicial power by creating constitutional courts, vesting those courts with jurisdiction over constitutional questions, staffing those courts with judges prone to

---

[6] A proposed "Constitutional Treaty" would have explicitly repackaged and redenominated the EU's treaty structure as "constitutional" in name as well as substance. The rejection of that treaty by French and Dutch voters did little to halt the constitutionalization of EU law, however, as the vast majority of its contents were simply transferred over to a more innocuous-sounding "Reform Treaty," better known as the Treaty of Lisbon, which did secure ratification. The result is a body of law that operates increasingly as a de facto or small-c European constitution but may owe its growing reach in part to the fact that it disclaims any large-c constitutional status.

exercising judicial power, assisting or initiating litigation aimed at having those courts declare laws unconstitutional, and passing legislation that encourages justices to make public policy in the guise of statutory or constitutional interpretation" (Graber, 2005: 427–8, 446).

This insight has profound implications that normative constitutional theory has yet to fully absorb. Combined with a substantial body of research documenting a relatively close relationship between public opinion and judicial behavior (e.g., Peretti, 2005), it is part of a multipronged empirical assault on the core premise of normative constitutional theory that judicial review of the constitutionality of the acts of elected officials poses a "counter-majoritarian dilemma" (Bickel, 1986). Constitutional theorists have sought for decades to reconcile the supposedly counter-majoritarian nature of judicial review with the idea of democracy by prescribing conditions for the legitimate exercise of judicial review. It becomes harder to argue, however, that judicial review lacks majoritarian legitimacy, or that restrictions upon the policy-making domain of the courts can solve the counter-majoritarian dilemma, if the elected officials who supposedly represent the will of the majority are the ones responsible for empowering the supposedly counter-majoritarian courts.

Scholars have identified a variety of reasons for which other political actors might permit or even encourage courts to give effect to large-c constitutional rules. Elected officials may be anxious to "defer" to the judiciary on controversial issues that have the potential to split existing political coalitions, and to "avoid responsibility" for "tough decisions" that are likely to expose them to substantial criticism, no matter what position they take: on this view, the U.S. Supreme Court's constitutional decisions on such politically sensitive topics as slavery and abortion are more accurately characterized as "non-majoritarian" than "counter-majoritarian" (Graber, 1993: 37). Stalemate among other political actors can create both an opportunity and a need for courts to fill what might otherwise become a policy vacuum (e.g., Ginsburg, 2010). A governing party or set of elites that fears or anticipates that it may soon lose power may seek to blunt the impact of a change in control and protect itself from radical changes by an opposition government by entrenching certain policies in constitutional form and empowering the courts to enforce them (Ginsburg, 2003; Hirschl, 2004). Judicial enforcement of constitutional rules can help governments to achieve certain otherwise elusive goals by making credible commitments: effective constitutional protection against uncompensated takings, for example, may enhance the credibility of a government's promises to repay its debts and thereby lower the cost of sovereign borrowing (North and Weingast, 1989; Law, 2005b). The ability of courts to successfully generate constitutionalization is likely also to depend upon institutional features of the judicial and legal system, such as a docket that affords courts adequate opportunity to make policy, "a minimally robust conception of precedent" (Keller and Stone Sweet, 2008: 8; Stone Sweet, 2004: 35), and a "support structure" consisting of the human and financial resources necessary for sustained constitutional litigation (Epp, 1998: 3, 5).

IV. METHODOLOGICAL CHALLENGES

The methodological challenges that characterize the study of constitutions are endemic to social science as a whole, but some happen to be especially pronounced in this context. The two overarching obstacles to empirical research on constitutions in general, and to reliable causal inference in particular, are inadequate data and causal complexity.

(1) *Data inadequacy.* Empirical data on constitutions are prone to inadequacy in both quantity and quality. With respect to quantity, the number of cases available for meaningful comparison and analysis may be quite low depending upon the research question. Many of the phenomena that interest scholars, such as constitution-making, are relatively rare events. There are fewer than 200 countries currently in existence, and the total number of large-c constitutions that have ever existed—the vast majority of which are no longer in effect—falls shy of 1,000 (Ginsburg et al., 2009: 6, 226). Thus, even if one wishes to focus upon a relatively broad phenomenon, such as constitution-making in new democracies over the last century, the slice of data available for analysis may not be especially large. Even less data will be available on more specific phenomena, such as constitution-making in the United States at the federal level (one observation) or amendment of the Japanese constitution (zero observations). The quality of the data that scholars can hope to employ, meanwhile, is constrained by the sheer difficulty of measuring constitutional phenomena. Many of the phenomena that are of greatest interest, such as judicial independence (Feld and Voigt, 2006; La Porta et al., 2004) or respect for human rights (Hafner-Burton and Ron, 2009), also happen to be multifaceted, ill-defined, hard to quantify, or costly to measure.

(2) *Causal complexity.* Constitutions are complex phenomena with a host of potential causes and effects that can interact or conflict with one another and evolve over time in ways that are difficult to predict. It is a daunting task to identify all of the variables that are relevant to, say, respect for human rights, much less to determine what importance to assign to each of them. The underlying causal mechanisms and chains of causation are also difficult to parse: even if a correlation between two variables reflects a causal relationship, that relationship itself may be attenuated or conditional upon other factors that may be difficult to identify without in-depth examination. And as scholars have long recognized, the problems of causal

complexity and inadequate data merely aggravate one another. Even if one some-how manages to identify and parse all relevant casual factors, a lack of data makes it difficult to isolate the impact of any particular factor: one cannot control for an abundance of factors when there are only a few cases to analyze—or, in the context of qualitative research, perhaps just a single case.

Path dependence also poses complications for empirical scholars interested in questions of causation. Certain phenomena, such as those surrounding the develop-ment of political institutions, can in a sense be described as causing themselves: they involve self-reinforcing dynamics and generate positive feedback loops (Pierson, 2004). Path dependence may help to explain why, for example, one of the best predic-tors of future constitutional longevity is past constitutional longevity: controlling for a host of other variables, Elkins et al. (2009) find that the longer a constitution has already lasted, the longer it is likely to endure into the future. It is not easy, however, to model such processes and dynamics using traditional statistical tools.

Another vexing problem for quantitative researchers in particular is that of bidirectional causation, or endogeneity, wherein the independent variable is both a cause and a consequence of the dependent variable. Large-c constitutions may be intended to structure political, social, and economic arrangements, but they are also the products of the very arrangements that they are supposed to shape. Even if they shape their environment, the environment is likely also to shape them, with the result that it becomes very difficult to say which is influencing which, or to what extent. Endogeneity is of particular concern for quantitative scholarship because the regression models on which such work generally relies assume unidi-rectional causation. Although techniques for dealing with endogeneity do exist, those techniques are not always feasible and can require considerable ingenuity to execute.[7]

To illustrate some of the challenges surrounding causal inference in the face of complexity, consider the finding of Keith et al. (2009) that the existence of consti-tutional guarantees of a fair and public trial is correlated with a lower incidence of repression. As the authors observe, it is effectively impossible to know what causal inference to draw from such a finding: "We cannot infer for certain that it is the adoption of the constitutional provisions that causes the reduction in repression. Perhaps governments adopt constitutional protections when they are already pre-disposed to enforce them and not to abuse personal integrity. Since we (and every-one else, so far as we are aware) lack indicators of governmental predispositions, we are not, ultimately, in a position to resolve this causal conundrum" (p. 646). Likewise, even if we know that the existence of a formal right to a fair and public trial causes less repression, it would remain necessary to explain why the existence of

---

[7] One such technique is to identify a source of variation in the explanatory variable that is unaf-fected by the dependent variable, and to substitute this instrumental variable for the original explana-tory variable (King et al., 1994: 187–95).

such a guarantee has such an effect, and to identify what conditions must be satisfied in order for the effect to occur. It might be that the effect of the right is conditional upon the existence of a competent criminal defense bar or the capacity of ordinary courts to exercise jurisdiction over politically sensitive cases, to name just a couple of possibilities.

Neither qualitative nor quantitative research, by itself, is likely to meet all of these challenges. The debate among methodologists over the relative merits of qualitative and quantitative approaches is a lively one (e.g., George and Bennett, 2005; King et al., 1994). It seems safe to say, however, that a combination of approaches—quantitative and qualitative, established and innovative—will be necessary if scholars are to gain traction on the many difficult empirical questions surrounding constitutions (large-c and small-c alike), constitutionalization, and constitutionalism. Qualitative methods, such as the case study approach (wherein the researcher explores a single instance of a phenomenon in depth or compares a small number of such instances), are widely thought to possess advantages when it comes to building theories and developing explanations of empirical relationships, whereas quantitative methods, such as regression models, excel at identifying and verifying the existence of empirical relationships, and at assigning the appropriate weight or significance to different factors. Understood in this way, the two approaches are clearly complementary rather than substitutes for one another.

Given the nature and severity of the methodological challenges that characterize the study of constitutions—not to mention the paucity of quantitative skills among constitutional law scholars—it is perhaps not surprising that case studies have thus far dominated the fields of comparative constitutional law and politics. This state of the literature, however, is not entirely healthy. First, whatever the full potential of the case study method may be, that potential remains largely unrealized by legal scholars. Although there are, of course, examples of highly systematic work in this vein,[8] the manner in which comparative constitutional scholars have tended to conduct case studies has been faulted for its inattention to "basic methodological principles of controlled comparison, research design, and case selection" that would permit meaningful causal inference (Hirschl, 2008: 39).

Second, other types of empirical scholarship are needed to compensate for the inherent limitations of small-n qualitative research. Even if one selects cases, constructs theories, and devises empirically testable hypotheses with the utmost care and ingenuity, it remains intrinsically difficult to draw reliable causal inferences solely on the basis of qualitative research involving a small number of cases (King et al., 1994). Thus, absent the development of a more extensive body of quantitative

---

[8] A conspicuous example is the collection of "structured-focused comparisons" edited by Keller and Stone Sweet (2008) on the subject of the constitutionalization of the European Convention of Human Rights: the volume consists of a series of comparisons of different pairs of European countries, wherein each comparison is "structured" and "focused" in such a way that it can itself be compared with the other comparisons in the volume.

research, empirical constitutional scholars are likely to continue to prove "better at generating hypotheses...than at testing them" (Ginsburg et al., 2009: 219). There is also some risk that overreliance on qualitative research can yield a systematically biased understanding of the world. Hafner-Burton and Ron (2009) note, for example, that case studies have generally painted a rosier picture of the efficacy of international human rights instruments than statistical studies. It is not difficult to see how case studies conducted by constitutional scholars regarding, say, the impact of large-c constitutions or written rights guarantees might exhibit a similar tendency. Qualitative methods entail a plethora of subjective judgments that lack transparency and "are inherently imprecise and subject to unconscious biases" (King et al., 1994: 152), and if there is any unconscious bias that constitutional scholars might be expected to share, it is that constitutions matter. This is not to say that legal scholars ought to forsake qualitative methods. The point is, rather, that the cause of empirical constitutional scholarship is better served by methodological pluralism than by disproportionate reliance upon a specific methodology.

V. Methodological Possibilities: Can Constitutions Be Computer-Simulated?

Tackling the problems of data inadequacy and causal complexity calls for scholars not only to combine familiar techniques, but also to pursue creative, unorthodox new approaches. There are two approaches in particular that are widely employed in other contexts and hold considerable promise in theory but have thus far seen little actual use in the literature on constitutions. The first is to conduct experiments. Not only do experiments generate original data, but the resulting data and findings are of a quality that one rarely encounters in social science research; the random assignment of subjects to control and experimental groups, in particular, ensures that any systematic differences in outcomes between the two groups of subjects are the result of the experimental treatment and not of other confounding variables. In some cases, it may be possible to substitute laboratory experiments for real-world experiments: one could, for example, observe the types of constitutional arrangements that human subjects in a laboratory setting actually reach under different procedural rules (Voigt, 1997: 20–2). Unfortunately, the prospects for genuine constitutional experimentation on a random sample of actual countries are effectively non-existent.

The second approach is to employ simulations. Improvements in computing power have expanded both the range of what can be accomplished using simulation-based techniques and the availability of such techniques to the research community. For example, Bayesian Markov Chain Monte Carlo methods that use simulation have become an accepted part of the social science toolkit for analyzing data that is too porous for conventional regression analysis (Jackman, 2000). It is neither possible nor necessary to explain these highly technical methods here. Suffice it to say, instead, that computer simulation techniques are already more ubiquitous in empirical scholarship than may generally be realized, and that software advances render it increasingly unnecessary to possess a technical understanding of such methods in order to make use of them.

A more ambitious form of simulation that may hold particular promise for the study of constitutional phenomena is agent-based modeling (ABM). An agent-based model consists of a simulated environment in which virtual actors, or "agents," are programmed to interact with and respond to one another. The fruits of their inter-action are cumulative: the results of one round of interaction become the point of departure for the next round. Computational simulation of these interactions enables the modeler to observe not only the eventual outcome after many iterations, but also the dynamics that produce the outcome.

The strengths of ABM align nicely with a number of the challenges involved in studying constitutions. Constitutions are challenging phenomena to model because, inter alia, they generate, and are generated by, complex and recurring interactions among large numbers of actors who do not necessarily make fully rational decisions, and whose choices both reflect and generate path dependence. One advantage of ABM is that it can cope with a much greater degree of complexity than the usual tools of formal modeling: whereas the outcome of a game with a large number of players can be prohibitively difficult to deduce mathematically, ABM employs raw computing power to simulate the entire game. Another advantage is that, unlike a typical game-theoretic model, an agent-based model need not assume that actors make decisions in a highly rational manner by assigning payoffs and probabilities to possible outcomes, then engaging in backwards induction so as to maximize the expected payoff. Instead, agents can be programmed to react to one another in ways that reflect limited cognitive capacity and carry the potential for unwanted conse-quences (De Marchi and Page, 2008). Finally, ABM is especially well suited to mod-eling systems that exhibit path dependence and other "emergent properties, that is, properties arising from the interactions of the agents that cannot be deduced simply by aggregating the properties of the agents. When the interaction of the agents is contingent on past experience, and especially when the agents continually adapt to that experience,... ABM might be the only practical method of analysis" (Axelrod and Tesfatsion, 2006: 1649).

Consider two relatively simple examples of how ABM might be used to shed light on questions of interest to constitutional scholars. One such question is that of con-stitutional convergence: are countries adopting increasingly similar rules and prac-tices in the area of constitutional rights? If the focus is on small-c constitutions, an obvious approach would be to compile quantitative measures of actual rights observance across countries and determine whether there is an aggregate trend or the variance between countries is decreasing over time (Law, 2008). If the focus is instead on large-c constitutions, a conventional quantitative approach might be to compute a measure of textual similarity among constitutions over time (Elkins et al., 2009: 24–5). But one might also use ABM to explore the conditions under which convergence occurs.

Axelrod's (1997) agent-based model of *cultural* convergence, for example, could be treated as a template for modeling *constitutional* convergence. The premise of the model is simple: the more similar that two countries already happen to be, the more likely that they will interact with and thus influence one another. The model takes the form of a virtual world of countries that are evenly distributed over a square grid. Each country's culture/constitution comprises five attributes, each of which can assume up to ten different values, with the result that a culture/constitution "can be described as a list of five digits, such as 8, 7, 2, 5, and 4" (p. 208). At the outset, each country's culture/constitution is a series of random digits. The simulation begins with the random selection of a country and one of its neighbors for "interaction." The likelihood that one country will influence the other depends upon how "compatible" their cultures/constitutions already happen to be. To be specific, the probability of influence is equal to the proportion of attributes that they already share in common: for example, a country with a culture/constitution of (8, 2, 2, 2, 2) has a 20% chance of influencing a neighbor that possesses a culture/constitution of (8, 3, 3, 3, 3) because the two countries already share 20% of their attributes in common. If influence occurs, then one of the second country's remaining unique attributes changes to match that of the first country: in this case, the second agent's culture/constitution (8, 3, 3, 3, 3) might become (8, 3, 3, 3, 2).

If this two-step process is allowed to repeat itself, the eventual result is a very high degree of convergence. Assuming an initial population of 100 unique cultures/constitutions, each of which can vary 10,000 ways, the model tends to stabilize at a total of three cultural/constitutional paradigms, one of which dwarfs the others. Indeed, 14% of the time that the simulation was conducted, a single paradigm ultimately dominated the entire world, whereas only 10% of the time did the simulation produce six or more stable paradigms. Meanwhile, the few paradigms that do survive are completely polarized, in the sense that they share nothing in common: convergence ceases to occur because the simulation reaches a point at which "every pair of neighboring sites has cultures [or constitutions] that are either identical or completely different" (p. 211).

This model, which is simple even by the standards of ABM, does not purport to offer a highly accurate depiction of actual interaction among countries. It does, however, illustrate the characteristics and potential of ABM as a tool for studying constitutional phenomena. Like formal modeling, ABM is used to model interaction among competing actors, and to test in rigorous and unambiguous terms the logical consequences of a certain set of assumptions about how those actors behave. By capturing the effects of path dependence, however, even the simplest of models can shed new light on how the operation of a single dynamic can, over time, generate non-intuitive outcomes. In this case, an elementary model of convergence illustrates (1) how little influence countries need have over one another in order for a high degree of convergence to occur, (2) how fragile diversity can be in the face of even mild tendencies toward convergence, and (3) how convergence can culminate in extreme polarization with potentially grim practical implications, as in the form of a conflict between, say, a secular liberal democratic bloc and a religious fundamentalist bloc that share no common ground.

In a more elaborate example of ABM, Kollman et al. (1997) tackle a pair of questions that ought to be of considerable interest to constitutional design scholars: what type of democratic institution encourages the adoption of welfare-maximizing government policies, and what is the impact of federalism on the capacity of different types of institutions to maximize citizen welfare? The agents in this model are citizens and governments. The model assumes that citizens have randomly assigned preferences over a particular set of policies and can move freely between jurisdictions, and that each jurisdiction has a particular institutional mechanism for aggregating citizen preferences and turning them into policy. Once policies in a jurisdiction are adjusted to reflect the preferences of its current residents, everyone is once again given a chance to move to a new jurisdiction. These interactions are then simulated repeatedly in order to evaluate the ability of three types of institutions to maximize utility per capita: "democratic referenda," meaning simple majority rule on an issue-by-issue basis; "direct competition," meaning "winner-take-all plurality voting among parties advocating different platforms"; and proportional representation, under which parties receive legislative seats in proportion to their share of their popular vote (pp. 980–1). The authors find that the ideal choice of institution depends upon, inter alia, the ability of citizens to move between jurisdictions offering different policies. In a world where citizens cannot move, government by referendum maximizes aggregate utility, followed by two-party electoral competition (either in the form of a winner-take-all or proportional representation system) and, lastly, proportional representation systems with more than two parties. If preferences are heterogeneous and citizens can move, however, the ranking of the various institutions is entirely reversed: proportional representation is best, whereas rule by referendum is worst. This reversal occurs because policy-making in jurisdictions with proportional representation is highly responsive to minor shifts in the preferences of the citizenry, which occur frequently when migration is possible.

As intriguing as computer simulation and laboratory experimentation may be, such approaches beg the question of whether one can generalize from findings generated in a simplified, hypothetical world to the vastly more complex operation of the real world. It may seem highly unrealistic that the workings of a country or constitution could ever be simulated with sufficient accuracy, either on a computer or in a laboratory setting, to permit any confidence in the results. Yet it would be a mistake not to pursue such approaches. First, a simulation need not capture the entirety of a phenomenon with complete accuracy in order to be of value to researchers. Much can be learned by devising and testing deliberately simplified models that yield clear predictions about the impact of specific dynamics. It may also be possible to break down complex phenomena into component parts that can individually be modeled with greater accuracy.

Second, the relevance and utility of computer simulations are certain only to improve with time. As computing power continues to advance, the accuracy and sophistication of agent-based models and substantive other forms of simulation will increasingly be limited only by the creativity and expertise of those who design them. Of ABM in particular, it might be doubted whether pre-programmed agents can adequately simulate actual human decision-making. Yet there is an obvious solution—namely, to combine the best aspects of computer simulation and live experimentation by incorporating actual human decision-makers into the simulations. Scholars in other fields, such as experimental economics, are already evaluating the use of social and economic behavior in virtual reality environments as a research proxy for real-world behavior (e.g., Friedman et al., 2007). The existence of virtual reality environments and video games in which people can lead entire lives through alter egos ("Second Life," "The Sims") and govern major cities ("SimCity") suggests that plausible simulations of constitution-making and constitutional politics are within reach. And the popularity of such programs demonstrates that human subjects would gladly volunteer, if not pay, to play assigned roles in a "SimGovernment" or "SimConstitution" simulation against one another online. If multiplayer computer tournaments can be used to test strategies for playing the Prisoner's Dilemma (Axelrod, 1984), surely they can also be used to evaluate, for example, the consequences of different strategies for making constitutions.

Third, and perhaps most importantly, it makes little sense to rule out novel approaches in the absence of any demonstrably superior alternative. Skeptics might fairly question whether the design of political and legal institutions and, by extension, the fate of entire nations should be entrusted to emerging technologies that resemble outsized video games. Yet the reality is that we already entrust matters of life and death to virtual reality. Scholars with an interest in constitutions are by no means the only ones who must study rare events of enormous consequence that are too costly or unthinkable to rehearse in real life. When it comes to evaluating the battlefield use of tactical nuclear weapons, for example, or the mid-air disintegration of fully loaded passenger jets, computer simulations are not so much a matter of choice as of necessity. It is unclear why the same tools cannot or should not be applied to the machinery of government. To reject computer simulation or laboratory experimentation on the ground that they may not solve every methodological challenge at one stroke or improve in every respect on existing tools is to allow the perfect to become the enemy of the good.

REFERENCES

Alston, P. (1999). "A Framework for the Comparative Analysis of Bills of Rights," in P. Alston (ed.), *Promoting Human Rights Through Bills of Rights: Comparative Perspectives*, Oxford: Oxford University Press, 1–14.

Axelrod, R. (1984). *The Evolution of Cooperation*, New York: Basic Books.

Axelrod, R. (1997). "The Dissemination of Culture: A Model with Local Convergence and Global Polarization," *Journal of Conflict Resolution* 41(2): 203–26, reprinted in R. Axelrod (1997). *The Complexity of Cooperation*, Princeton University Press: Princeton.

Axelrod, R. and Tesfatsion, L. (2006). "A Guide for Newcomers to Agent-Based Modeling in the Social Sciences," in L. Tesfatsion and K. Judd (eds.), *Handbook of Computational Economics: Agent-Based Computational Economics*, Amsterdam: North-Holland, vol. 2, 1647–59.

Bickel, A. (1986). *The Least Dangerous Branch: The Supreme Court at the Bar of Politics* (2nd edn.), New Haven: Yale University Press.

Blasi, G.J. and Cingranelli, D.L. (1996). "Do Constitutions and Institutions Help Protect Human Rights?," in D.L. Cingranelli (ed.), *Human Rights and Developing Countries*, Greenwich: JAI Press, 223–37.

Boli-Bennett, J. (1976). "The Expansion of Nation-States, 1870–1970," Ph.D. dissertation, Stanford University.

Breslin, B. (2009). *From Words to Worlds: Exploring Constitutional Functionality*, Baltimore: Johns Hopkins University Press.

Choudhry, S. (ed.) (2007). *The Migration of Constitutional Ideas*, Cambridge: Cambridge University Press.

Choudhry, S. (2008). "Bridging comparative politics and comparative constitutional law: Constitutional design in divided societies," in S. Choudhry (ed.), *Constitutional Design for Divided Societies: Integration or Accommodation?*, Oxford: Oxford University Press, 3–40.

Constitutional Design Group (2008). "Judicial Independence," available at <http://constitutionmaking.org/files/judicial_independence.pdf>.

Cross, F.B. (1999). "The Relevance of Law in Human Rights Protection," *International Review of Law and Economics* 19(1): 87–98.

Davenport, C.A. (1996). "'Constitutional Promises' and Repressive Reality: A Cross-National Time-Series Investigation of Why Political and Civil Liberties are Suppressed," *Journal of Politics* 58(3): 627–54.

De Marchi, S. and Page, S.E. (2008). "Agent-Based Modeling," in J.M. Box-Steffensmeier, Henry E. Brady, and D. Collier (eds.), *The Oxford Handbook of Political Methodology*, Oxford University Press, 71–94.

Dicey, A.V. (1915). *Introduction to the Study of the Law of the Constitution*, (8th edn.), London: Macmillan.

Dunoff, J.L. and Trachtman, J.P. (2009). "A Functional Approach to Global Constitutionalism," in J.L. Dunoff and J.P. Trachtman (eds.), *Ruling the World?: Constitutionalism, International Law, and Global Governance*, New York: Cambridge University Press, 3–35.

Elkins, Z., Ginsburg, T., and Melton, J. (2009). *The Endurance of National Constitutions*, New York: Cambridge University Press.

Elster, J. (1991). "Constitutionalism in Eastern Europe: An Introduction," *University of Chicago Law Review* 58: 447–82.

Elster, J. (1995). "Forces and Mechanisms in the Constitution-Making Process," *Duke Law Journal* 45: 364–96.

Epp, C.R. (1998). *The Rights Revolution: Lawyers, Activists, and Supreme Courts in Comparative Perspective*, Chicago: University of Chicago Press.

Feld, L.P. and Voigt, S. (2006). "Judicial Independence and Economic Growth: Some Proposals Regarding the Judiciary," in R.D. Congleton and B. Swedenborg (eds.), *Democratic Constitutional Design and Public Policy*, Cambridge, MA: MIT Press, 251–88.

Friedman, D., Steed, A., and Slater, M. (2007). "Spatial Social Behavior in Second Life," in Jonathan Gratch et al. (eds.), *Intelligent Virtual Agents*, New York: Springer-Verlag, 252–63.

George, A.L. and Bennett, A. (2005). *Case Studies and Theory Development in the Social Sciences*, Belfer Center Studies in International Security, Cambridge, MA: MIT Press.

Ginsburg, T. (2003). *Judicial Review in New Democracies: Constitutional Courts in Asian Cases*, New York: Cambridge University Press.

Ginsburg, T. (2010). "The Constitutional Court and the Judicialization of Korean Politics," in A. Harding, and P. Nicholson (eds.), *New Courts in Asia*, Abingdon: Routledge, 145–57.

Ginsburg, T., Elkins, Z., and Blount, J. (2009). "Does the Process of Constitution-Making Matter?," *Annual Review of Law and Social Science* 5: 201–23.

Goderis, B. and Versteeg, M. (2009). "Human Rights Violations after 9/11 and the Role of Constitutional Constraints," *Fourth Annual Conference on Empirical Legal Studies*, University of Southern California, Los Angeles, November 2009, <http://ssrn.com/abstract=1374376>.

Graber, M.A. (1993). "The Nonmajoritarian Difficulty: Legislative Deference to the Judiciary," *Studies in American Political Development* 7: 35–73.

Graber, M.A. (2005). "Constructing Judicial Review," *Annual Review of Political Science* 8: 425–51.

Hafner-Burton, E.M. and Ron, J. (2009). "Seeing Double: Human Rights Impact Through Qualitative and Quantitative Eyes," *World Politics* 61(2): 360–401.

Hafner-Burton, E.M. and Tsutsui, K. (2007). "Justice Lost! The Failure of International Human Rights Law To Matter Where Needed Most," *Journal of Peace Research* 44: 407–25.

Hamilton, A. (1789). "Federalist No. 83," in A. Hamilton, J. Madison, and J. Jay, *The Federalist Papers*, C. Rossiter (ed.) (1961 edn.), Harmondsworth: Penguin.

Hirschl, R. (2004). *Towards Juristocracy: The Origins and Consequences of the New Constitutionalism*, Cambridge: Harvard University Press.

Hirschl, R. (2008). "On the blurred methodological matrix of comparative constitutional law," in S. Choudhry (ed.), *Constitutional Design for Divided Societies: Integration or Accommodation?*, Oxford: Oxford University Press, 39–66.

Hirschl, R. (2009). "The 'Design Sciences' and Constitutional 'Success'," *Texas Law Review* 87: 1339–74.

Horowitz, D.L. (2008). "Conciliatory Institutions and Constitutional Processes in Post-Conflict States," *William & Mary Law Review* 49: 1213–48.

Jackman, S. (2000). "Estimation and Inference via Bayesian Simulation: An Introduction to Markov Chain Monte Carlo," *American Journal of Political Science* 44: 375–404.

Keith, L.C. (2002). "Constitutional Provisions for Individual Human Rights (1977–1996): Are They More Than Mere 'Window Dressing'?," *Political Research Quarterly* 55(1): 111.

Keith, L.C., Tate, C.N., and Poe, S.C. (2009). "Is the Law a Mere Parchment Barrier to Human Rights Abuse?," Journal of Politics 71(2): 644–60.

Keller, H. and Stone Sweet, A. (eds.) (2008). *A Europe of Rights: The Impact of the ECHR on National Legal Systems*, Oxford: Oxford University Press.

King, G., Keohane, R.O., and Verba, S. (1994). *Designing Social Inquiry: Scientific Inference in Qualitative Research*, Princeton: Princeton University Press.

Kollman, K., Miller, J.H., and Page, S.E. (1997). "Political Institutions and Sorting in a Tiebout Model," *American Economic Review* 87(5): 977–92.

La Porta, R. et al. (2004). "Judicial Checks and Balances," *Journal of Political Economy* 112(2): 445–70.

Law, D.S. (2005a). "Generic Constitutional Law," *Minnesota Law Review* 89: 652–742.

Law, D.S. (2005b). "The Paradox of Omnipotence: Courts, Constitutions, and Commitments," *Georgia Law Review* 40(2): 407–68.

Law, D.S. (2008). "Globalization and the Future of Constitutional Rights," *Northwestern University Law Review* 102: 1277–1349.

Levinson, S. (2009). "Foreword: 'I Read the News Today, Oh Boy': The Increasing Centrality of Constitutional Design," *Texas Law Review* 87(7): 1265–72.

Lijphart, A. (2008). *Thinking About Democracy: Power Sharing and Majority Rule in Theory and Practice*, Abingdon: Routledge.

Lutz, D.S. (2006). *Principles of Constitutional Design*, New York: Cambridge University Press.

Madison, J. (1789). "Federalist No. 48," in A. Hamilton, J. Madison, and J. Jay, *The Federalist Papers*, C. Rossiter (ed.) (1961 edn.), Harmondsworth: Penguin.

Meyer, J.W. et al. (1997). "World Society and the Nation-State," *American Journal of Sociology* 103(1): 144–81.

North, D.C. and Weingast, B.R. (1989). "Constitutions and Commitment: The Evolution of Institutions Governing Public Choice in Seventeenth-Century England," *Journal of Economic History* 49(4): 803–32.

Palmer, M.S.R. (2006). "Using Constitutional Realism to Identify the *Complete* Constitution: Lessons From an Unwritten Constitution," *American Journal of Comparative Law* 54(3): 587–636.

Peretti, T. (2005). "An Empirical Analysis of Alexander Bickel's The Least Dangerous Branch," in K.D. Ward, and C.R. Castillo (eds.), *The Judiciary and American Democracy: Alexander Bickel, The Countermajoritarian Difficulty, and Contemporary Constitutional Theory*, Albany: State University of New York Press, 123–45.

Persson, T. and Tabellini, G. (2005), *The Economic Effects of Constitutions* (new edn.), Cambridge: MIT Press.

Pierson, P. (2004). *Politics in Time: History, Institutions, and Social Analysis*, Princeton: Princeton University Press.

Pritchard, K. (1986). "Comparative Human Rights: An Integrative Explanation," *Policy Studies Journal* 15: 110–22.

Przeworski, A. and Limongi, F. (1993). "Political Regimes and Economic Growth," *Journal of Economic Perspectives* 7(3): 51–69.

Reiter, D. and Stam, A.C. (2002). *Democracies at War*, Princeton: Princeton University Press.

Shapiro, M. and Stone Sweet, A. (2002). *On Law, Politics, and Judicialization*, Oxford: Oxford University Press.

Shugart, M.S. and Carey, J.M. (1992). *Presidents and Assemblies: Constitutional Design and Electoral Dynamics*, New York: Cambridge University Press.

Simmons, B. A. (2009). *Mobilizing for Human Rights: International Law in Domestic Politics*, New York: Cambridge University Press.

Stone Sweet, A. (1999). "Judicialization and the Construction of Governance," *Comparative Political Studies* 32(2): 147–84.

Stone Sweet, A. (2004), *The Judicial Construction of Europe*, Oxford: Oxford University Press.

Vallinder, T. (1995). "When the Courts Go Marching In," in C. Tate, C. Neal, and T. Vallinder (eds.), *The Global Expansion of Judicial Power*, New York: New York University Press, 13–26.

Voigt, S. (1997). "Positive Constitutional Economics: A Survey," *Public Choice* 90: 11–53.

Whittington, K.E. (2007). *Political Foundations of Judicial Supremacy: The Presidency, the Supreme Court, and Constitutional Leadership in U.S. History*, Princeton: Princeton University Press.

Widner, J. (2008). "Constitution Writing in Post-Conflict Settings: An Overview," *William & Mary Law Review* 49: 1513–41.

17

SOCIAL SECURITY AND SOCIAL WELFARE

MICHAEL ADLER

I. INTRODUCTION

THE argument advanced in this Chapter is that, although there are undoubtedly some very good examples of empirical research on social security and social welfare law, in the U.S. as well as the UK, they are rather thin on the ground. This is due to the fact that there are too few empirical researchers with an interest in this area of law to produce a really sustained research effort. The Chapter reviews the empirical research on social security and social welfare law that has been carried out, identifies what needs to be done to promote empirical research in this area of law, and outlines an empirical research agenda of topics that should be given priority.

A. Definitions

Because there is considerable disagreement about the meaning and scope of the terms "social security" and "social welfare," it is appropriate at the outset to clarify how they are used in the Chapter. Social security, broadly defined, comprises the five schemes referred to below and this is the sense in which it is most frequently used in the UK:

1. *Social insurance (or contributory) benefits*, funded by contributions from employees, employers, and the government, which are paid to everyone who satisfies the contribution conditions. They are intended to cover loss or interruption of earnings for specified reasons, e.g., unemployment, sickness, retirement, and widowhood.

2. *Categorical (or universal) benefits*, funded out of general taxation, are paid to those who fit the designated category, e.g., households with children or people with disabilities.

3. *Tax-based benefits*, which use the tax system, rather than the social security system, to make payments (known as tax credits) to those with incomes below the tax threshold.

4. *Occupational benefits*, paid for by employers (and sometimes by employees) but regulated by the government. They include occupational pensions, statutory sick pay and statutory maternity pay.

5. *Social assistance (or means-tested) benefits*, funded out of general taxation, which are paid to people with low incomes relative to their household circumstances. They include benefits for people with no other sources of income as well as people whose incomes, from other benefits or from earnings, are insufficient for them to meet their general needs.

In the U.S., the term "social security" refers to the federal Old Age, Survivors and Disability Insurance (OASDI) program, which provides benefits for retirement, disability, survivorship, and death but does not include unemployment insurance, or means-tested social assistance benefits. Along with programs providing means-tested assistance in kind (e.g., food stamps) and means-tested services for the poor (e.g., Medicaid and public housing), this set of programs is referred to as "welfare" or "social welfare."

In this Chapter, the composite term "social security and social welfare" is used to refer to the five schemes listed above but is restricted to income maintenance schemes. It therefore excludes other programs that are provided on a means-tested basis, e.g., food stamps, Medicaid, public housing, or legal aid.

B. Background

Twenty-five years ago, Adler and Ewing (1983) carried out a review of social security teaching in law and social science courses in UK universities. Two versions of a questionnaire—one for law courses and one for social science courses—were sent out to universities and polytechnics in the UK. Most of the teaching was at a general, introductory level but significant numbers of institutions—particularly in their law degrees—offered courses "wholly or largely devoted to social security." This suggests that social security teaching was quite well established in undergraduate curricula, particularly in the law curriculum. Comparable data are not available today but a cursory review of university websites suggests that the position of social security in social science and, in particular, law curricula has not been maintained. Fewer courses on social security law mean fewer teachers and a substantially reduced capacity for research of any kind, and thus for empirical research.

In their article on "Empirical Research in Law" in the *Oxford Handbook on Legal Studies*, Baldwin and Davis (2003: 882) pointed out that "some legal disciplines have been transformed" by empirical legal research and cite "criminal law and criminal justice, family law and parts of regulatory or public law" as examples. Unlike most countries in Continental Europe, where social security law (often known as "social law") is closely allied to labor law, social security law in the UK, and likewise the U.S., is usually regarded as a (small) branch of public law. As such, we might expect that it would have been transformed by empirical legal research. However, the small number of specialists in social security law in British and American law schools suggests that this is not the case.

In 2006, the Nuffield Foundation published *Law in the Real World: Improving our Understanding of How Law Works*, the final report of its enquiry into the UK's capacity to conduct empirical legal research (Genn et al., 2006). The report concluded that there was clear evidence of a developing "crisis" in the capacity of UK universities to undertake empirical legal research, which was being made worse by the ageing of a cohort of experienced empirical legal researchers and the failure to attract new researchers to replace them. This conclusion applies with particular intensity to social security law because of its precarious position in UK law schools. Empirical research on social security may still be buoyant in the UK, mainly because of the role played by the Department for Work and Pensions (DWP) in conducting and commissioning empirical research on social security, and the existence of a number of university-based research centers that specialize in this area, but, within this body of research, the amount of empirical research on aspects of social security law is very limited. The position in the United States is very similar.

In his article on "The Welfare State" in the *Oxford Handbook on Legal Studies*, Wikeley (2003) refers to two British journals that are concerned with the legal aspects of the welfare state, namely the *Journal of Social Welfare and Family Law* (JSWFL) and the *Journal of Social Security Law* (JSSL). JSWFL specializes in articles on children (and has carried numerous articles on children's rights, child abuse, child protection and child welfare), family law, domestic violence, mental health and mental incapacity, and social housing, and has carried only three articles on social security in the last ten years. One reason for this is that JSSL has established itself as *the* specialist journal on social security law in the UK. However, very few of the articles it publishes are based on empirical research. A review of articles published in the last ten years reveals that the journal published only four articles on social security that could be described as empirical.

A survey of articles published in the last ten years in the *Journal of Law and Society* (published in the UK), the *Law and Society Review, Law and Social Issues*, and the *Journal of Empirical Legal Studies* (all published in the U.S.) tells a similar story. Moreover, the dearth of articles on social security and social welfare law in the leading socio-legal journals is reflected in the absence of papers on these topics at the annual conferences of the Socio-Legal Studies Association (in the UK) and the Law and Society Association (in the U.S.). There is, fortunately, one "saving grace." Although both of the authors of the standard textbook on social security law in the UK (Wikeley and Ogus, 2002) have very distinguished records as empirical legal researchers, the book adopts a doctrinal approach. However, a rival book, *Social Security Law in Context* (Harris et al., 2000), adopts a contextual approach and the individual chapters draw extensively on empirical research. This compensates for the fact that, although the first edition of the most comprehensive textbook on social security in the UK (Millar, 2003) contains chapters on the street-level implementation of unemployment policy (Wright, 2003) and social security fraud (Sainsbury, 2003), these topics were not included in the second edition (Millar, 2009), and neither edition contains any contribution from a lawyer.

The remainder of the Chapter reviews the corpus of empirical research on social security and social welfare law, broken down into research on first-instance decision-making (section II); on appellate decision-making (section III); on the impact of appeals on first instance decision-making (section IV); on administrative reviews as an alternative to appeals (section V), and on fraud and sanctions (section VI). The concluding section (section VII) emphasizes the need to find structural solutions for the weakness of empirical research in this area of law and identifies some priorities for future research. The primary focus of the Chapter is on the UK but there are many references to research in the U.S. and elsewhere.

II. First-Instance Decision-Making

A number of studies of first-instance decision-making in the UK have been inspired by *Bureaucratic Justice*, Jerry Mashaw's pioneering study of the Disability Insurance (DI) scheme in the U.S. Mashaw (1983) detected three broad strands of criticism leveled against the DI scheme: the first indicted it for lacking adequate management controls and producing inconsistent decisions, the second for not providing a good service and for failing to rehabilitate those who were dependent on it, and the third for not paying enough attention to "due process" and for failing to respect and uphold the rights of those dependent on it. Mashaw claimed that each strand of criticism reflected a different normative conception of the DI scheme, i.e. a different model of what the scheme could and should be like. The three models were respectively identified with *bureaucratic rationality, professional treatment*, and *moral judgment*.

Mashaw defined "administrative justice" (i.e. the justice inherent in routine day-to-day administration) in terms of "those qualities of a decision process that provide arguments for the acceptability of its decisions" (ibid: 24). From this it follows that each of the three models he described is associated with a different conception of administrative justice. According to Mashaw, each of these models is associated with a different set of *legitimating values*, different *primary goals*, a different *organizational structure*, and different *cognitive techniques*. Mashaw's analytic framework is set out in the Table 1 below.

Mashaw claimed that each of the models is coherent, plausible and attractive and that the three models are *competitive* rather than *mutually exclusive* (ibid: 23). Thus, they can and do coexist with each other. However, other things being equal, the more there is of one, the less there will be of the other two. His insight enables us to see both what trade-offs are made between the three models in particular cases and what different sets of trade-offs might be more desirable. Mashaw's approach is a *pluralistic*

Table 1: Models of Administrative Justice – Mashaw's analytic framework

Model	Legitimating values	Primary goal	Structure or organization	Cognitive technique
Bureaucratic rationality	accuracy and efficiency	program implementation	hierarchical	information processing
Professional treatment	service	client satisfaction	interpersonal	clinical application of knowledge
Moral judgment	fairness	conflict resolution	independent	contextual interpretation

one, which recognizes a plurality of normative positions and acknowledges that situations which are attractive for some people may be unattractive for others.

The trade-offs that are made, and likewise those that could be made, reflect the concerns and the bargaining strengths of the institutional actors who have an interest in promoting each of the models, typically civil servants and officials in the case of the first model; professionals and "street level bureaucrats" (Lipsky, 1980) in the case of the second model; and advisers, representatives, tribunal and court personnel in the case of the third model. In the case of the DI scheme, Mashaw concluded that the bureaucratic model, which he described (ibid: 172) as "an accuracy orientated, investigatorially-active, hierarchichally organised, and complexly engineered system of adjudication" was not only dominant but, in modern parlance, "fit for purpose."

In my view, *Bureaucratic Justice* succeeds in its aim of "integrating the normative concerns of administrative law with the positive concerns of organisational theory" by subjecting normative concerns to empirical study. Somewhat unexpectedly, it inspired a number of studies of first-instance decision-making in social security in the UK. First off the mark was Roy Sainsbury, who examined the ways in which decisions about entitlement to two disability benefits[1] were made. In a series of articles (e.g., Sainsbury, 2008), he took issue with Mashaw's approach to administrative justice. Accepting Mashaw's definition of administrative justice, he argued that "efficiency," which Mashaw regarded as one of the legitimating values of "bureaucratic rationality," has nothing to do with justice, and that "organisational structure" and "cognitive techniques" were not, as Mashaw contended, components or dimensions of administrative justice. Sainsbury (ibid: 52–61) claimed that there are only two (invariant) qualities that a decision process ought to exhibit. These are accuracy and fairness, the latter comprising promptness, impartiality, participation, and accountability. Sainsbury's is clearly a less *pluralistic* conception of administrative justice than Mashaw's since it follows from it that administrative arrangements can be evaluated in terms of these criteria and reformed in such a way as to maximize their achievement.

Another important study was *Judging Social Security* (Baldwin et al., 1992). Using Mashaw's terminology, Baldwin, Wikeley, and Young characterized the role of adjudication officers—officials who performed statutory functions in deciding claims for social security benefits but were required to do so independently of the Minister[2]—in the late 1980s in terms of "bureaucratic rationality"; and that of social security appeal tribunals, which heard appeals against the decisions of first-instance decision-makers, in terms of "moral judgement" (ibid: 17). In a subsequent article, Wikeley (2000b: 499) claimed that, as a result of recent

---

[1] Industrial Injuries Disablement Benefit and Mobility Allowance.
[2] They were abolished under the Social Security Act 1998.

Table 2: Models of Administrative Justice – Adler's revised and extended analytic framework

Model	Legitimating goal	Mode of accountability	Mode of redress
Bureaucratic	accuracy	hierarchical	administrative review
Professional	public service	interpersonal	second opinion or complaint to a professional body
Legal	legality	independent	appeal to a court or tribunal (public law)
Managerial	improved performance	performance indicators and audit	none, other than adverse publicity
Consumerist	consumer satisfaction	consumer charters	"voice" and/or compensation through consumer charters
Market	economic efficiency	to owners or shareholders (profits)	"exit" and/or court action (private law)

legislation,[3] the bureaucratic model had achieved "*complete hegemony* at the first-tier level" [my italics] and that the judicialization of tribunals "served as a cover for the triumph of the bureaucratic model at the appeals stage as much as with first-tier decision making." However, this claim is exaggerated—Mashaw made it clear that his three models of administrative justice were competitive rather than mutually exclusive and that, although one model tends to be dominant and "to drive the characteristics of the others from the field as it works itself out" (Mashaw, 1983: 23), it can (and does) co-exist with them. That is what being competitive rather than mutually exclusive entails. This is the case both with first-instance decision-makers and with appeal tribunals and, in both cases, while one model may be dominant, the others are also present. There were elements of both the "bureaucratic" and the "legal" models of administrative justice in decision-making by adjudication officers and appeal tribunals at that time, although the "bureaucratic" model was dominant in the former and the "legal" model in the latter.

Although Mashaw's approach was clearly a seminal one, his claim that the three models he identified, and only these three models, are always present in welfare administration, has been disputed on the grounds that, in many countries, they have been challenged by other models of administrative justice, in particular, by a *managerial* model associated with the rise of new public management, a

---

[3] He was referring to the Social Security Act 1998.

consumerist model, which focuses on the increased participation of consumers in decision-making, and a *market* model which emphasizes consumer choice.[4] In light of this criticism, Adler (2003, 2006) has characterized the different models of administrative justice identified by Mashaw somewhat differently and added three more. His revised and extended analytic framework is set out in Table 2 above.

In a study funded by IBM (UK), Adler and Henman (2008) applied this extended analytic framework of administrative justice to a comparative study of the impact of computer technology on social security in 13 OECD countries (10 Western European countries, Australia, Canada, and the United States). Data were provided by two expert informants in each country. The findings suggest, first, that bureaucracy, followed by managerialism and legality are the most important determinants of administrative justice in social security while the market followed by professionalism and consumerism are the least important; and, second, that the effect of computerization has been to further entrench the bureaucratic and managerial models and to undermine the professional model.

The final example of first-instance decision-making in the UK reviewed here (Wright, 2003) was inspired by another influential American study, Michael Lipsky's book on *Street Level Bureaucracy*. Lipsky (1980: 3) defines "street-level bureaucrats" as "public service workers who interact directly with citizens in the course of their jobs, and who exercise discretion in the course of their work." According to Lipsky (ibid: 83), street-level bureaucrats develop mechanisms for coping with uncertainty by limiting the demand for their services, maximizing the use of available resources, and securing client compliance. Thus, in order to make their jobs manageable they develop their own "routines and simplifications."

Wright (2003) applied Lipsky's insights to a study of employment officers in the UK, who were faced with the task of implementing active labor market policy. She found, inter alia, that staff were faced with the dual task of "helping" and "policing" the unemployed and described how policy was accomplished at the local level by Jobcentre staff, who routinely placed clients into a number of administrative and moral categories that influenced how they were treated and shaped the opportunities that were offered to them. The administrative categories were based on "objective" characteristics, such as previous or current occupation, but the moral categories were based on subjective judgments of the "attributes, behaviours and attitudes" of clients that distinguished between "good clients," who were offered help and support, and "bad clients," who were, at best, ignored and, at worst, punished through the application of sanctions.

---

[4] Other criticisms are that, in assessing the relative influence of the three models, Mashaw ignored their absolute strengths, and that Mashaw took the policy context for granted.

Although there do not appear to have been any published studies of first-instance decision-making in the U.S. in recent years, a comparative study has recently been published. *Agents of the Welfare State* (Jewell, 2007) is an important and innovative book that uses the approach associated with studies of street-level bureaucracy (see above) to describe how caseworkers in three countries assess eligibility for social assistance benefits and provide employment related services (activation measures) to those who are out of work. It analyses how front-line staff "trade off" consistency with responsiveness in the implementation of welfare-to-work programs in California (U.S.), Bremen (Germany), and Malmö (Sweden). The advantage of a research design that involves a comparison of local offices in the United States, Germany, and Sweden, representing different types of "welfare state regime," is that such a design makes it possible to explore a wider range of variation in program characteristics and decision-making practices than is found in a single country.

The observations and interviews with decision-makers and service providers are used to generate accounts of the ways in which "eligibility technicians" in the U.S., "entitlement scholars" in Germany, "social workers" in Sweden, and "welfare to work caseworkers" in all three countries perform their tasks. By assessing the responsiveness of decision-makers and service providers in terms of their *legal authority* (i.e., the range of options that are available to them) and their *organizational capacity* (i.e., the opportunity they have to develop rapport with their clients), this study generates an interesting set of ideal types, which are used to distinguish the roles of decision-makers and service providers in the three countries. Although these findings are very imaginative and quite plausible, there is, unfortunately, no way of knowing whether they are correct, and this study could usefully be followed up with further research in which its findings are tested. However, it provides ample support for the conclusion that, although welfare-to-work programs in all three countries seek to promote "client sufficiency through labor market integration," the routes into work that the programs in the different countries provide and the roles that caseworkers play vary considerably and are best explained, in each case, by a combination of past political choices and current institutional structures and processes.

Johansson and Hvinden (2007) analyze recent legal and policy reforms relating to the activation of unemployed citizens, in particular those claiming social assistance, in Denmark, Finland, Norway, and Sweden. Drawing on the results of a comparative study of the four Nordic countries, the authors identify two different means of regulating activation policy, one involving central regulation and the other involving local discretion. In all four countries, reforms have strengthened the legal duties on unemployed recipients to participate in activation measures and the application of sanctions to those who do not do so. In Norway and Sweden, activation is a duty not a right. In Denmark and Finland, by contrast, unemployed recipients have obtained stronger legal rights to activation. This is because the regulation of activation in Denmark and Finland is based on more legalistic standards, central directives, and detailed regulations while, in Norway and Sweden, it rests on stronger local and professional discretion, with a lesser degree of legal regulation. However, the reality as experienced by unemployed citizens claiming social assistance is much the same, a rather different conclusion from the one reached by Jewell (see above).

Research in the U.S. has addressed a different set of questions. In two contrasting studies, Joe Soss has examined the politics of social security and social welfare. In the first of these, *Unwanted Claims: The Politics of Participation in the U.S. Welfare System*, Soss (2002) uses qualitative methods to explore clients' experiences of participation in two federal programs: Social Security Disability Insurance (SSDI), a social insurance program for those who are unable to work by reason of disability, and Aid to Families with Dependent Children (AFDC), a social assistance program for the poor.[5] Based on in-depth interviews with 25 SSDI recipients and 25 AFDC clients, Soss found that, at every stage, SSDI recipients have an easier time and that, throughout the claiming process, it is easier for them to establish their eligibility, make a claim and get a response to any (reasonable) demands they make. He concluded that these contrasting experiences point to a hierarchy of social citizenship in which participants in social assistance programs are more likely to feel degraded while participants in social insurance programs are given more opportunities to express their needs in their own terms.

In the second study, Soss and Keiser (2006) used multivariate statistical methods to analyze variations in the demand for SSDI and Supplemental Security Income (SSI), both of which provide benefits for people with disabilities, over a three-year period (1991–1993). Since potential applicants for social security programs have to determine their own eligibility and take whatever steps are required to exercise their rights, demands on these programs, even when they are federally administered and when uniform eligibility rules apply across the country, vary a good deal between states. Soss and Keiser's findings show that, in addition to the need for benefits, "the density of civil society organisations, the political ideology of state officials and the generosity of state-run public assistance programs" all shape the aggregate level of demand for these benefits. This enables them to develop a model of claiming benefits that sees it as analogous to other forms of political demand-making.

---

[5]   AFDC was created by the *Social Security Act* of 1935 as part of the *New Deal*. In 1996, President Bill Clinton negotiated with Congress "to end welfare as we know it" and Congress passed the Personal Responsibility and Work Opportunity Act, which imposed a lifetime limit of five years on the receipt of benefits and introduced a replacement program called Temporary Assistance for Needy Families (TANF).

III. Appellate Decision-making

The Effectiveness of Representation in Tribunals (Genn and Genn, 1989) is a landmark study of representation in tribunals,[6] which hear appeals from first-instance decision-making in the UK, and which was carried out for the Lord Chancellor's Department.[7] The study compared Social Security Appeal Tribunals (SSATs)[8] with tribunals that dealt with mental health and immigration appeals, and employment disputes—almost 4,000 completed case files were analyzed, some 500 hearings were observed and 600 interviews were carried out. Although there were significant geographical variations in the extent to which appellants obtained pre-hearing advice and large differences in the rates at which appellants were represented at the tribunal hearing, being represented increased the probability of a successful outcome at all four tribunals, in the case of Social Security Appeal Tribunals, from 20% to 38%. Across the board, the "premiums" associated with representation were 15–18%.

A more recent study, *Tribunals for Diverse Users* (Genn et al., 2006), which was carried out for the Department for Constitutional Affairs, was designed to compare the experiences of white, black, and minority ethnic tribunal users in order to establish not only how different groups perceive and are treated by tribunals but also whether there was any evidence of direct or indirect discrimination against ethnic minorities in the tribunal system. The study was based on an investigation of access to and expectations, experiences, and outcomes of tribunal hearings from the perspective of tribunal users in three tribunals: The Appeals Service (TAS), the successor to Social Security Appeal Tribunals (see above), was compared with appeal tribunals dealing with criminal injuries compensation and special educational needs. The research comprised focus group discussions with 115 members of the general public, face-to-face interviews with 529 tribunal users before their hearing, observation of 391 hearings, face-to-face interviews with 295 users after their hearing, a statistical modeling exercise using 3,058 decisions, and telephone interviews with 63 members of the tribunal judiciary. Most appellants made generally positive assessments of their treatment at the hearing and their ability to participate but minority ethnic appellants were consistently more negative than white appellants in their assessments of hearings and more likely to perceive unfairness, especially if all the members of the tribunal were white. But, in TAS tribunals

---

[6] Their functions are similar to those of administrative hearings, i.e., hearings in front of Administrative Law Judges, in the United States.

[7] Replaced first, in 2003, by the Department for Constitutional Affairs (DCA), and then, in 2007, by the Ministry of Justice (MoJ).

[8] The predecessor of, first, the Independent Tribunal Service, second, The Appeals Service, and, following the establishment of the Tribunals Service in 2006, Social Security and Child Support Appeal Tribunals.

minority ethnic appellants were slightly less likely to be successful than their white counterparts.

Overall, 73% of represented appellants were successful compared with 61% of unrepresented appellants. However, the benefits of representation were far from uniform across tribunals. In the tribunals dealing with criminal injuries compensation and special educational needs appeals, the premiums associated with representation were 4% and 7% and only in the case of TAS, where it was 14%, was it comparable with those found by Genn and Genn in their earlier study. When case types were controlled for statistically, the difference in success rates between represented and unrepresented appellants in the comparator tribunals disappeared but, in the case of TAS, the difference in the success rates of represented and unrepresented appellants was statistically significant (Genn et al., 2006: 273).

Before the results of *Tribunals for Diverse Users* were published, Adler embarked on some further research on representation in tribunals. His decision was provoked by the publication in 2001 of the Leggatt Review (Leggatt, 2001), which recommended tribunal reform, and by the publication three years later of a White Paper (Department for Constitutional Affairs, 2004), in which the UK Government set out its proposals for reforming tribunals. Although the Leggatt Report and the White Paper both accepted that, because of learning difficulties, physical disability, or language problems, some people would always need representation, it aimed to create a situation where individuals who are in dispute with the state would be able to present their case without the help of a representative. In contrast to this view, Adler felt that, since it was unlikely that such a state of affairs could be achieved in the short or medium term, representation will still be required in the foreseeable future.

Adler selected tribunals in which there was an approximation to a "50:50 split" between represented and unrepresented litigants and compared the experiences of three groups—those who handled their application (in employment cases) or their appeal (in other cases) without any help, those who obtained pre-hearing advice but were not represented at the tribunal hearing, and those who were represented (by various types of representative). These tribunals comprised four *citizen vs. state* tribunals—including Social Security and Child Support Tribunals—and one *party vs. party* tribunal—Employment Tribunals. The research involved a telephone survey of 870 tribunal applicants/appellants; observation of 64 tribunal hearings; post-hearing interviews with applicants/appellants, and interviews with tribunal chairmen and members and with the President and Chief Executive of the five tribunals in the study.

Using data from the telephone survey, the effect of representation on outcomes was calculated. A comparison with earlier research indicates, first, that overall "success rates" were considerably higher than they were 20 years ago, and, secondly, that the representation premiums were considerably lower. For the sample as a whole, it was only 5%. In Social Security and Child Support Tribunals, the "representation premium" was 6% and, in only one comparator tribunal, where it was 15%, was it comparable with the "going rate" 20 years ago.

An attempt was also made to distinguish the "success rates" of unrepresented appellants/applicants who received pre-hearing advice from those who did not. For the sample as a whole, the premium associated with representation was 4% over unrepresented appellants/applicants who had received pre-hearing advice and 7% over those who had not. Thus, pre-hearing advice reduced the "representation premium" by almost 50%.[9] In the case of Social Security and Child Support Tribunals, unrepresented appellants who had received pre-hearing advice actually had marginally higher success rates than those who were represented (74% vs. 73%), while unrepresented appellants who did not receive any pre-hearing advice had significantly lower success rates (63%).

These findings suggest that Adler's initial assumptions were not only wrong but quite spectacularly wrong. The challenge was to explain how these unexpected results could have arisen and, in particular, why the premiums on representation appeared to be much smaller than they were 20 years ago and why the "success rates" for those who represented themselves, particularly if they had received pre-hearing advice, compared favorably with those who were represented at their hearing. Data from the observations of tribunal hearings, were used to characterize tribunal procedures and analyze what actually goes on in tribunal hearings.

First, an *activism indicator*, based on the assessed activism of the tribunal chair and members, was calculated. Then, an *interventionism measure*, based on whether members of the tribunal cross-questioned the appellant/applicant or their representative during the hearing, was recorded. Hearings were classified as *inquisitorial* if they were both "active" and "interventionist." The fact that most tribunals used inquisitorial methods does not imply that they did not also use *adversarial* techniques, which were most apparent in those cases where the "other side" was present and/or represented. In these cases, when the appellant was unrepresented and appeared on his/her own, the tribunal usually helped him/her to question the "other side" and explained what was going on. An *enabling score* was calculated from eight indicators of whether or not tribunal chairs adopted an enabling approach in the observed hearings.

Adler concluded from this that the main reasons why the premiums on representation are so much smaller today than they were 20 years ago and why the "success rates" for those who represented themselves, particularly if they had received pre-hearing advice, compared so favorably with those who were represented at their hearing, were:

1. the *active*, *interventionist*, and *enabling* ways in which tribunals deal with the generality of cases that come before them; and

---

[9] This may be due, in part, to the fact that pre-hearing advice screens out those with weak cases by persuading them not to proceed with their appeal.

2. tribunals' use of *inquisitorial* methods and the assistance in using *adversarial* methods that they give to unrepresented parties.

However, it does seem to be the case that, in order to take advantage of the tribunals' facilitating approach, unrepresented appellants need to have been prepared and briefed before the hearing, and those who were not were much less likely to be successful.

As far as Social Security and Child Support Tribunals are concerned, the small representation premium (6%) is due, in part, to the fact that it was quite unusual for the Department of Work and Pensions (DWP) to be represented at tribunal hearings and to the *active, interventionist* and *enabling* procedures that most tribunals adopted and the *inquisitorial* methods they used. This is in spite of the fact that unrepresented appellants frequently had no educational qualifications and had relatively low levels of literacy, oral skills and administrative competence.

Those whose appeal to a first-tier tribunal is unsuccessful can appeal again, on a point of law, to a second-tier tribunal, formerly the Social Security and Child Support Commissioners but, since 2008, the Administrative Appeals Chamber of the Upper Tribunal in the new Tribunals Service. A comprehensive assessment of the work of the Commissioners was recently undertaken. The study (Buck, Bonner, and Sainsbury, 2005) drew on in-depth interviews with all 23 Commissioners in the UK and examined their contribution to the "making" of social security law, discussed the implications of its findings for the tribunal reform program, and explored the wider implications of the Commissioners' role from an administrative law perspective. It not only gives a full account of what the Commissioners did and how they operated but also, because they constituted a well-established second-tier tribunal, informed public debate on how the appellate tier of the new Tribunals Service might be organized.

The series of studies (reviewed above) that have attempted to study the effects of representation on the outcomes of appeal tribunal hearings in the UK did have some parallels in the U.S. Popkin (1977) studied the effects of representation on outcomes in three disability programs[10] that resolve disputes using "non-adversary procedures." This study, based on statistical data provided by the agencies concerned, indicated that, those who were represented did significantly better than those who were not, notwithstanding the agencies' willingness to help. A later study (Kritzer, 1998) set out to examine what difference a lawyer makes in four different settings, two of which (unemployment compensation appeals and social security disability

---

[10] These programs were administered under the Federal Employees Compensation Act (FECA), with appeals heard by the Employees' Compensation Appeals Board; by the Bureau of Disability Insurance in the Social Security Administration (SSA), with appeals heard by the Appeals Council Bureau of Hearings and Appeals; and under the Veterans Disability Program, with appeals heard by the Board of Veterans Appeals.

appeals) are relevant to the concerns of this Chapter.[11] In each case, he observed hearings and, based on his observations, drew some tentative conclusions about the effectiveness of lawyers and non-lawyers that he subsequently "tested" using statistical data on the relationship between representation and outcomes. Kritzer identified three dimensions of influence (the nature of the representative's expertise, the relationship between the representative and the client, and issues of accountability and control), and divided each of them into three sub-dimensions. He concluded (ibid: 201) that expertise is central to effective advocacy and that, although legal representatives frequently achieved higher success rates than non-legal representatives, formal legal training is less important than expertise in the settling of the dispute. The other dimensions serve, at most, to modify the effects of expertise.

In the U.S., administrative hearings (or "fair hearings") have been required before benefit could be terminated since Aid to Families with Dependent Children (AFDC) was introduced in 1935, and they have become even more important since the replacement of AFDC by Temporary Assistance for Needy Families (TANF) in 1996.[12] However, until recently, all the research on administrative hearings, including Sarat's (1990) study of welfare recipients who sought legal help with their welfare problems,[13] had been conducted prior to 1996 and little was known about the circumstances in which welfare recipients currently exercise their right to a TANF hearing or how these hearings work. In an important series of publications, Vicki Lens has focused on these questions. In an inter-state comparison of appeal rates and outcomes, she found that appeal rates ranged from a low of 0.29% of the caseload in Texas to a high of 6.8% in New York City (Lens and Vorsanger, 2005). Using in-depth interviews with those in receipt of TANF who had been sanctioned for violating the work rules, she explored why some recipients appealed while others did not (Lens, 2007a). Her research indicated that nearly all the recipients felt they had been wrongly sanctioned and were aware of their right to appeal. However, for those who did not appeal, hearings were indistinguishable from the rest of the agency, which they viewed as inflexible and intractable. In contrast, those who appealed viewed fair hearings more favorably and social networks played a key role in encouraging them to appeal. In another paper, Lens (2007b) describes how those who appealed were as concerned with being heard

[11] The other two (tax appeals and labor grievance arbitration) are not.

[12] The 1996 Act ended welfare as an entitlement; imposed time limits, work requirements, and other punitive measures; and eventually resulted in a massive decline in the number of recipients, which fell from 13.24 million in 1995 to 5.33 million in 2002, a decline of nearly 60%.

[13] On the basis of interviews with welfare recipients and observations of meetings between them and legal services lawyers in two cities, Sarat (1990: 344) concluded that the legal consciousness of the welfare poor is substantively different from that of other groups in society. For them, "law is all over" because a significant part of their lives is "organized by a regime of legal rules invoked by officials to claim jurisdiction over choices and decisions which those not on welfare would regard as personal and private." Law is experienced as "power and domination" but also, in some cases, as "resistance."

by the agency as they were with the outcome of their case and were attempting to find a forum in which they could obtain recompense and respect. She also points out that the legalistic and rule-bound nature of the hearings made it difficult for them to present their claims. To obtain a more complete picture of administrative hearings, Lens (2009) observed 70 hearings and carried out in-depth interviews with the administrative law judges and appellants whose hearings she observed. On the basis of these interviews, she distinguished "moralist judges," who focus on the appellant's compliance with procedural rules and often fail to scrutinize the agency, from "reformer judges," who closely scrutinize the agency's actions and use the hearing as a means for resolving disputes, and showed how these different styles of judging have important implications for the processing of disputes and for appellants' perceptions of fairness.

IV. The Impact of Appeals on First-Instance Decision-Making

The number of administrative decisions that are appealed to tribunals in the UK is substantial. In 2007–2008, 670,781 cases were decided by a tribunal, of which the second largest number (165,264) was concerned with social security and child support (Administrative Justice and Tribunals Council, 2008: 66).[14] Although UK tribunals cannot, in general, question the merits of an administrative decision where this involves the correct application of law, they can question the facts on which the decision was based and make a new decision based on facts that the initial decision-maker may not have been aware of. However, on the basis of her research on tribunals, Genn (1994) concluded that there are considerable limits to their effectiveness as a check on administrative decision-making. According to her (ibid: 284), this is due the mismatch between the claim that tribunals are relatively informal and free from technicality and the reality that they have to make decisions in accordance with complicated regulations, statute and case law; the low levels of representation in many tribunals; and the fact that unrepresented parties in tribunal proceedings are much less likely to be successful.[15]

---

[14] The largest number (181,346) dealt with asylum and immigration. In addition, 6,258 cases were decided by the Social Security and Child Support Commissioners.

[15] Although that may have been true in the recent past, Genn's conclusions may need to be revised in light of Adler's research indicating that tribunals have become more "active," "interventionist," and "enabling," and that unrepresented appellants are much less disadvantaged than was previously the case. See Adler (2009).

Although tribunal decisions can, and do, benefit individual appellants, they have a rather limited impact on first instance decision-makers. In a study of decision-making in social security (Baldwin et al., 1992: 85), 53% of the adjudication officers who were interviewed claimed that, in making decisions, they were "not at all influenced" by a tribunal's likely response to an appeal. This compares to 25% of officers who claimed that tribunals had a procedural effect in that the prospect of an appeal led them to be more thorough and document their decisions more fully.[16] However, it should be noted that the tribunals referred to here were all first-tier tribunals and that second-tier tribunals probably have a greater impact on first-instance decision-makers. Nevertheless, as a means of enhancing the quality of first-instance decision-making, these findings indicate that tribunals are not particularly effective.

The most recent assessment of judicial review in "routine" social security cases in the UK (Robson, 1998) was carried out before the passage of the Human Rights Act 1998 and the incorporation of the European Convention on Human Rights (ECHR). Robson noted that, in spite of the fact that social security tribunals have been overwhelmed with cases and the Social Security Commissioners have been kept busy, "a mere handful" of social security cases has been subject to judicial review in the courts. His explanation for this paradox emphasizes the importance of accessible appeal rights: in social security, it does not cost anything to appeal to a first-tier (or second-tier) tribunal and most tribunal representation is carried out, without charge, by lay representatives; making an appeal to a tribunal a much more attractive option than a challenge in the courts. Robson concluded that, in spite of the fact that judicial review is seldom used, it has a "distinct function" in social security in that, in a small number of high profile cases, it can be used to stop the government in its tracks.

V. Administrative Reviews as an Alternative to Appeals

The Social Fund, which was established in the UK in 1988, provides a range of grants and loans, which may be paid to meet needs over and on top of normal

---

[16] Is it important to note that Baldwin, Wikeley, and Young's findings refer to what adjudication officers said they did rather than to what they did. As far as I am aware, there is no systematic empirical research on how decision-makers at all levels of the bureaucracy actually react to the decisions and activities of courts and tribunals.

weekly requirements for those on means-tested benefits. There is a structural division between the regulated and the discretionary part of the Social Fund. The former covers maternity, funeral, and cold weather payments, which are entitlements paid in accordance with regulations, and in relation to which claimants have a right of appeal to a tribunal. However, payments from the discretionary part of the fund, such as community care grants and crisis loans, are made at the discretion of officials constrained by local office cash limits, and are subject to internal review within the local office and external review by the Independent Review Service (IRS).

The establishment of the Social Fund was controversial largely because of the use of loans, rather than grants, to support vulnerable members of society; the exercise of discretion in decision-making; the imposition of cash limits (which can reduce the extent to which the fund can meet demonstrable need); the abolition of the right of appeal and its replacement by administrative review. When the scheme was introduced, it was closely monitored (by Government and by independent researchers) but, in recent years, the volume of research has declined. Research on the Social Fund, which has focused on the discretionary part of the scheme, has recently been comprehensively reviewed by Trevor Buck. Buck (2009: Ch 5) points out that research has investigated who successfully applies to the discretionary Social Fund; their awareness and understanding of the Social Fund; the needs met by the Social Fund; take-up; the process of application; administrative aspects of the Social Fund including discretionary decision-making, and the repayment of loans, redress and review.

Much of the research highlights how local budgets influence decision-making by Social Fund Officers (SFOs), and variations between offices serving similar areas have given rise to the notion of the discretionary Social Fund as a lottery (Craig, 2003). A claimant seeking redress can request an internal review, which takes place in the local office. If an applicant disputes the resulting decision, he/she can request an independent review, which is carried out by a Social Fund Inspector (SFI) employed by the Independent Review Service (IRS). A Social Fund Inspector's review of a decision is conducted in two stages. At the first stage, the SFI considers whether the Social Fund Officer interpreted and applied the law correctly, including whether he/she had regard to all the relevant considerations and excluded irrelevant considerations, exercised his/her discretion reasonably, and observed the principles of natural justice. If the decision was reached correctly, then the SFI conducts the second stage of the review during which he/she considers the merits of the case and decides whether the decision was the right one in the circumstances, taking account of any relevant changes in circumstances and new evidence. The SFI has the power to confirm the decision, refer the application back to the SFO to make a fresh decision, or make any decision that the SFO could have made. It is clear, therefore, that reviews, unlike appeals, can consider the merits as well as the legality of decisions.

Most claimants do not challenge or question the outcome of their application, in part because few of them are aware of the review process. But those who do ask for a review stand a very good chance of having the decision overturned.[17] However, it does not follow that an error was made since there may have been a change of circumstances or new evidence may have been presented.

Although the review procedure lacks the statutory guarantees of independence that courts and tribunals have, and does not use oral hearings, the IRS does operate independently, its decisions are binding on officials in local offices, and it has acquired a reputation for impartial decision-making. Its methods and procedures, which more closely resemble those of ombudsmen than those of courts or tribunals, are not as controversial today as they were when the scheme was introduced.

The effect of judicial review on the IRS has been the subject of research by Pick and Sunkin (2001), who analyzed documentary materials, including manuals, reviews and court cases, and interviewed IRS staff. They showed that the influence of judicial review on IRS staff has declined over time. Initially, there was a flurry of applications, which helped to clarify the role of the IRS and the independence of SFIs at a time when the Social Fund was controversial but, over time, the number of applications has declined to a trickle.

VI. Fraud and Sanctions

Sainsbury (2003) has published a comprehensive overview of the problem of social security fraud and the UK government's obsession with it. He provides a definition of fraud, distinguishes it from non-fraudulent errors made by claimants or officials, and lists the most common benefit frauds. He also reviews available evidence about the extent of fraud, concluding that it is only recently that any reliable estimates of its extent have been available, and demonstrates that, due to a significant increase in counter-fraud activity, the overall levels of fraud and error have declined. Sainsbury also points out that relatively little is known about why claimants commit fraud and refers, at some length, to the work of Dean and Melrose (1996, 1997).

In their study of fraudulent claimants, Dean and Melrose analyzed people's accounts and explanations of their behavior in terms of two dimensions, which they called *reflexivity* and *anxiety*. Reflexivity refers to the extent to which people who commit fraud think or reflect about their actions while anxiety refers to the extent

---

[17] According to Buck (2009: 280), 48% of decisions that were subject to internal review in 2005–2006 were changed and 51% of the 20,000 decisions reviewed by the Independent Review Service in that year contained a "fundamental error."

to which they experience feelings of guilt or insecurity about their actions and their possible consequences. By combining combinations of "high" and "low" reflexivity and anxiety, they produced a fourfold typology of fraudsters. *Subversive* claimants often used a discourse of justified disobedience and were able to offer quite complex explanations for their behavior but were comfortable with what they had done in the context of a mean and punitive social security system. *Desperate* claimants could also explain their actions but were more likely to refer to economic necessity and to be worried that they would be found out. *Fatalistic* claimants tended to be impulsive and opportunistic about which they worried afterwards. *Unprincipled* claimants tended not to justify their actions at all, or feel the need to do so, and, for them, social security was often just one of several sources of illicit income. Dean and Melrose suggest that distinctive policy responses may be needed for each of these four types of fraudster.

A recently published literature review on the behavior and motivations behind social security fraud (Mitton, 2009), which was commissioned by the Department for Work and Pensions, makes similar recommendations. It concludes that, although hardship and opportunity are crucial factors, the motivations for benefit fraud are complex and that fraud takes many forms and is committed by people with diverse motivations. It therefore suggests that improved compliance calls for an approach that recognizes the multitude of factors that can result in fraudulent behaviour.

Rich Law, Poor Law (Cook, 1989) compares the differential responses to two ways of defrauding the public purse—by engaging in tax and social security fraud—the former committed by "the rich" and the latter by "the poor." Although tax fraud frequently involves much larger sums than social security fraud, far more resources have been directed to investigating the latter than the former. Likewise, the enforcement strategies are stricter and the penalties awarded greater for social security fraud. Very few cases of tax fraud ever reach the courts since most cases are settled after negotiation between the parties, while prosecutions for social security fraud are commonplace and those who are found guilty are routinely fined and ordered to pay costs. Cook explains these paradoxes in terms of three interrelated considerations: the historical and ideological construction of taxpayers as "givers" to the state and welfare claimants as "takers" from it; the belief that taxpayers are seen as economic "successes" while claimants are seen as economic "failures"; and the fact that taxpayers embody the virtues of the "enterprise culture" while claimants embody the evils of the "benefits culture." Although *Rich Law, Poor Law* was published 20 years ago, there is no reason to doubt that its conclusions are still valid today. Soss's (2002) conclusion that, in the U.S., there is a hierarchy of social citizenship in which those in receipt of entitlement-based social insurance are less likely to feel degraded than those in receipt of needs-based social assistance, supports this view.

In the UK, sanctions for misconduct, voluntarily leaving work without just cause and refusal or failure to apply for or accept a job have always played a role in the administration of social security. The duration of these "variable-length" sanctions is a discretionary matter and, in recent years, the maximum period of disqualification has been increased from 6 weeks to 26 weeks (Wikeley and Ogus, 2002: 373,

n. 324). In addition, new "fixed-length" sanctions have been introduced. Moreover, since the introduction of the various New Deals—the "flagship" programs through which the Labour Government that was returned in 1997 sought to implement its "welfare to work" agenda—the sanctions that formerly applied only to work have been extended to cover prescribed training schemes and employment programs.[18]

In 2005, the DWP commissioned a review of the JSA Sanctions Regime, which included an account of its impact on claimants (Peters and Joyce, 2006). This was based on 3,017 15-minute telephone interviews with a range of "customer types" (including those not referred for a sanction, those referred but not sanctioned, and those who were sanctioned) and 70 in-depth interviews with a mix of unemployed "customers" who had received a sanction. Although most referrals from advisers to decision-makers did not result in the imposition of sanctions, sanctions have become rather commonplace events. 936,029 sanctions were imposed in the period April 2000–August 2005, 77% of which were variable-length sanctions while 23% were fixed-term sanctions. Claimants who disagree with the imposition of a sanction can ask for the decision to be reconsidered or can appeal against it. Internal evidence (ibid: 36) indicates that, between April 2000 and August 2005, 10–15% of decisions to impose a sanction were reconsidered in this way. Unfortunately, no data on the number of appeals against the imposition of sanctions or the outcome of these appeals is available, although anecdotal evidence suggests that appeals against sanctions are rather infrequent.

In a further attempt to apply the extended analytic framework of administrative justice (see Table 2 above) to recent policy developments in social security, Adler (2008) has argued that the emergence of the personal adviser, who manages a caseload of jobseekers, has considerable discretion in carrying out this task and is the key decision-maker in "active" welfare to work programs, and the corresponding demise of the adjudication officer, reflect a shift away from a situation in which bureaucratic and legal modes of decision-making were dominant, to one in which professional and managerial modes of decision-making have greatly increased in importance, and that this has made it extremely difficult for anyone who is required to take part in any of the New Deal programs to challenge the advice and help they are given, or about any sanctions that may be imposed on them. As Wright (2003, see above) has demonstrated, in research carried out before the merger of Jobcentres with Benefit Offices in 2002, personal advisers have in common with other semi-professionals and "street-level bureaucrats" the fact that they wield a great deal of power. However, it is no longer always clear which of their actions actually constitutes a "decision." That notwithstanding, many personal advisers undoubtedly do their jobs very well and assessed levels of user satisfaction are high.[19]

[18] These sanctions are non-discretionary. Claimants are disqualified for two weeks for a first breach, for four weeks for a second breach within 12 months and for 26 weeks for another breach within 12 months of the second breach. The latter penalty is particularly draconian. For a detailed account of the sanctions themselves, see Wikeley and Ogus (2002: 375–6).

[19] According to the National Audit Office (2006: paras. 21 and 31), Jobcentre Plus's customer survey shows that 77% of jobseekers and 90% of employers are satisfied with its performance.

Welfare sanctions in the United States have recently been the focus of Sanford Schram's research. Prior to 1996, they were used infrequently and were applied only to the head of the household, not to the entire family; but under the TANF program, they have become the primary disciplinary tool against recipients who fail to complete the required number of hours participating in work-related activities, such as job-search, job-readiness classes, vocational education, training, community work, and paid employment. Thus, according to Schram et al. (2009), they have played a key role in transforming welfare from a system focused on providing cash benefits to one focused on enforcing work. Schram et al. (ibid) presented two vignettes portraying hypothetical TANF participants who had fallen out of compliance with program requirements to 144 Florida-based case managers who had sanctioning authority. The results showed that black women with previous records were most likely to be sanctioned. These findings were then triangulated against administrative data. The authors conclude that, although welfare sanctions should be imposed as responses to client behavior, they are also imposed in response to client characteristics, and that, "under cover of a policy that is officially race-neutral, welfare systems [in the U.S.] reflect racial classifications [and] reproduce racial inequities" (ibid: 416).

VII. Conclusions

Although there are, undoubtedly, some very good examples of empirical research on social security and social welfare law, in the U.S. as well as the UK, they are sparse and episodic. With a few notable exceptions, they are not of great theoretical significance. This is attributable to the fact that there are too few empirical researchers with an interest in this area of law to produce a really sustained research effort. The general weakness of empirical research on law, combined with the marginal position of social security and social welfare law in law schools, militates against the emergence of a "critical mass" of theoretically informed empirical research in this area. This is highly regrettable because successful research is cumulative, with one piece of research building upon another, and competitive, with different research agendas competing with each other for ascendancy.

Since the weakness of empirical research on social security and social welfare law is structural in origin, the remedies must be structural ones too. They call for strengthening the capacity for empirical research on law, building up the position of social security and social welfare law in law schools and increasing the attention given to the study of law and legal institutions in schools of social policy and social work. It is not so much that there are "gaps" in an otherwise complete research profile, it is, rather, that the overall profile is weak. To remedy this situation most effectively, existing research resources need to be deployed strategically. Different commentators would, no doubt, have different priorities but, in my opinion, we need, first and foremost, more theoretically-informed empirical research that uses social security and social welfare as a context for testing and developing "middle-range" theory. We also need more empirical research in four areas of social security and social welfare law that have great contemporary significance for policy: the effects of new modes of delivery, in particular new public management (NPM) and computerization, on first-instance administrative decision-making, in particular on the implications of managerialism and IT for legality; the effects of appellate decision-making, at all levels, on first-instance decision-making; the relationship between the need for representation and the use of different modes of dispute resolution; and the legal aspects of activation policies, in particular their implications for rights, responsibilities, accountability and the use of sanctions. Unfortunately, although there is nothing to prevent the first of these priorities (the need for more empirical research that uses social security and social welfare as a context for testing and developing "middle-range" theories) from being addressed, until and unless a solution to the structural problems discussed above is found, it is unlikely that the volume of research in those areas of social security and social welfare law identified above will increase significantly.

REFERENCES

Adler, M. (2003). "A Socio-Legal Approach to Administrative Justice," *Law and Policy* 25(4): 323–52.

Adler, M. (2006). "Fairness in Context," *Journal of Law and Society* 33(4): 615–38.

Adler, M. (2008). "The Justice Implications of 'Activation Policies' in the UK," in T. Erhag, S. Stendahl, and S. Devetzi (eds.), *A European Work-First Welfare State*, Göteborg: University of Göteborg: Centre for European Research, pp. 95–131.

Adler, M. (2009). "Tribunals ain't what they used to be," *Adjust Newsletter* (March), available at <http://www.ajtc.gov.uk/adjust/09_03.htm>.

Adler, M. and Ewing, K. (1983). "Social Security Teaching in the United Kingdom," in *The Teaching of Social Security* (Studies and Research No. 20), Geneva: International Social Security Association, 74–97.

Adler, M. and Henman, P. (2008). "Justice beyond the Courts: The Implications of Computerisation for Administrative Justice in Social Security," in A. Cerillo and P. Fabra (eds.) *E-Justice: Information and Communication Technologies in the Court System*, Herschey, PA: IGI Global Ltd., 65–86.

Administrative Justice and Tribunals Council (2008) *Annual Report 2007/2008*, London: The Stationery Office.

Baldwin, J., Wikeley N., and Young, R. (1992). *Judging Social Security Claims: The Adjudication of Claims for Benefit in Britain*, Oxford: Clarendon Press.

Baldwin, J. and Davis, G. (2003). "Empirical Research in Law," in P. Cane and M. Tushnet (eds.), *The Oxford Handbook of Legal Studies*, Oxford: Oxford University Press, 881–900.

Bonner, D., Buck, T., and Sainsbury, R. (2001). "Researching the role and work of the Social Security and Child Support Commissioners," *Journal of Social Security Law* 8(1): 9–34.

Buck, T. (2005). "Evaluating the Commissioners," *Journal of Social Security Law* 12(3): 156–175.

Buck, T. (2009). *The Social Fund: Law and Practice* (3rd edn.), London: Sweet and Maxwell.

Buck, T., Bonner, D., and Sainsbury, R. (2005). *Making Social Security Law: The Role and Work of the Social Security and Child Support Commissioners*, Farnham: Ashgate.

Cook, D. (1989). *Rich Law, Poor Law: Different Responses to Tax and Supplementary Benefit Fraud*, Milton Keynes: Open University Press.

Craig, G. (2003). "Balancing the Books: The Social Fund in Action," in T. Buck and R. Smith (eds.) *Poor Relief or Poor Deal? The Social Fund, Safety Nets and Social Security*, Farnham: Ashgate, 40–56.

Dean, H. and Melrose, M. (1996). "Unravelling Citizenship: The Significance of Social Security Fraud," *Critical Social Policy*, 16(3): 3–31.

Dean, H. and Melrose, M. (1997). "Manageable Discord: Fraud and Resistance in the Social Security System," *Social Policy and Administration* 31(2): 103–18.

Department for Constitutional Affairs (2004) *Transforming Public Services: Complaints, Redress and Tribunals*, Cm. 6243, Norwich: The Stationery Office.

Genn, H. (1994). "Tribunal Review of Administrative Decision Making," in G. Richardson and H. Genn (eds.), *Administrative Law and Government Action*, Oxford: Clarendon Press, 249–86.

Genn, H. and Genn, Y. (1989). *The Effects of Representation in Tribunals*, London: Lord Chancellor's Department.

Genn, H., Lever, B., and Gray, L., with Balmer N. and National Centre for Social Research (2006). *Tribunals for Diverse Users* (DCA Research Series 1/06), London: Department for Constitutional Affairs.

Genn, H., Partington, M., and Wheeler, S. (2006). *Law in the Real World: Improving our Understanding of How Law Works*, London: Nuffield Foundation.

Harris, N. with Douglas, G., Hervey, T., Jones, S., Rahilly, S., Sainsbury, R., and Wikeley, N. (2000). *Social Security Law in Context*, Oxford: Oxford University Press.

Hvinden, B. and Johansson, H. (eds.) (2007). *Citizenship in Nordic Welfare States: Dynamics of choice, duties and participation in a changing Europe*, London: Routledge.

Jewell, C. (2007). *Agents of the Welfare State: How Caseworkers Respond to Need in the United States, Germany and Sweden*, Basingstoke: Palgrave Macmillan.

Johansson, H. and Hvinden, B. (2007). "Extending the Gap between Legal Regulation and Local practice? Legal and Institutional reforms in the Field of Activation in the Nordic Countries," *Journal of Social Security Law* 14(3): 131–149.

Kritzer, H.M. (1998). "Social Security Disability Appeals," in *Legal Advocacy*, Ann Arbor: University of Michigan Press, 111–49.

Leggatt, Sir A. (2001). *Tribunals for Users—One System, One Service*, Norwich: The Stationery Office.

Lens, V. (2007a). "Administrative Justice in Public Welfare Bureaucracies: When Citizens (Don't) Complain," *Administration and Society* 39(3): 382–408.

Lens, V. (2007b). "In the Fair Hearing Room: Resistance and Confrontation in the Welfare Bureaucracy," *Law and Social Inquiry* 32(2): 309–32.

Lens, V. (2009). "Confronting Government after Welfare Reform: Moralists, reformers and narratives of (ir)responsibility at administrative fair hearings," *Law and Society Review* 43(3): 563–92.

Lens, V. and Vorsanger, S. (2005). "Complaining after Claiming: Fair Hearings after Welfare Reform," *Social Service Review* 79(3): 430–53.

Lipsky, M. (1980). *Street Level Bureaucracy: Dilemmas of the Individual in Public Services*, New York: Russell Sage Foundation.

Mashaw, J.L. (1983). *Bureaucratic Justice: Managing Social Security Disability Claims*, New Haven: Yale University Press.

Millar, J. (ed.) (2003). *Understanding Social Security* (1st edn.), Bristol: Policy Press.

Millar, J. (ed.). (2009). *Understanding Social Security* (2nd edn.), Bristol: Policy Press.

Mitton, L. (2009). *Factors affecting compliance with rules: Understanding the behaviour and motivations behind customer fraud* (DWP Working Paper No 67), London: Department for Work and Pensions, available at <http://research.dwp.gov.uk/asd/asd5/WP67.pdf>.

National Audit Office (2006). *Jobcentre Plus: Delivering effective services through Personal Advisers*, HC 24 Session 2006–2007, London: The Stationery Office, available at <http://www.nao.org.uk/publications/0607/jobcentre_plus.aspx>.

Peters, M. and Joyce, L. (2006). *A Review of the JSA Sanctions Regime: Summary Research Findings* (DWP Research Report 313), London: Department for Work and Pensions, available at <http://research.dwp.gov.uk/asd/asd5/rports2005-2006/rrep313.pdf>.

Pick, K. and Sunkin, M. (2001) 'The Changing Impact of Judicial Review: The Independent Review Service of the Social Fund," *Public Law* 736–62.

Popkin, W.D. (1977). "The Effect of Representation in Non-Adversary Proceedings – A study of three disability programs," *Cornell Law Review* 62(6): 989–1048.

Robson P. (1998). "Judicial Review and Social Security," in T. Buck (ed.), *Judicial Review and Social Welfare*, London: Pinter, 90–113.

Sainsbury, R. (2003). "Understanding Social Security Fraud," in J. Millar (ed.), *Understanding Social Security: Issues for Policy and Practice* (1st edn.), Policy Press, Bristol, 277–95.

Sainsbury, R. (2008). "Administrative Justice, Discretion and the 'Welfare to Work' Project," *Journal of Social Welfare and Family Law* 30(4) 323–38.

Sarat, A. (1990). " 'The Law is All Over': Power, Resistance and the Legal Consciousness of the Welfare Poor," *Yale Journal of Law and the Humanities* 2: 343–79.

Schram, S., Soss, J., Fording, R.C., and Houser, L. (2009). "Deciding to Discipline: Race, Choice and Punishment at the Frontlines of Welfare Reform," *American Sociological Review* 74: 398–422.

Soss, J. (2002). *Unwanted Claims: The Politics of Participation in the US Welfare System*, Ann Arbor: University of Michigan Press.

Soss, J. and Keiser, L.R. (2006). "The Political Roots of Disability Claims: How State Environments and Policies Shape Citizen Demands," *Political Research Quarterly* 59(1): 133–48.

Wikeley, N. (2000a). "Two's Company, Three's a Crowd: Chairmen's views on the Composition of Appeal Tribunals," *Journal of Social Security Law* 7(2): 88–116.

Wikeley, N. (2000b). "Burying Bell: Managing the Judicialisation of Social Security Tribunals," *Modern Law Review* 63(4): 475–501.

Wikeley, N. (2003). "The Welfare State," in P. Cane and M. Tushnet (eds.), *The Oxford Handbook of Legal Studies*, Oxford: Oxford University Press, 397–412.

Wikeley, N. and Ogus, A. (2002). *The Law of Social Security* (5th edn.), London: Butterworths.

Wright, S. (2003) 'The Street-Level Implementation of Unemployment Policy," in J. Millar (ed.), *Understanding Social Security: Issues for Policy and Practice* (1st edn.), Policy Press, Bristol, 277–95.

1 8

OCCUPATIONAL SAFETY AND HEALTH

BRIDGET M. HUTTER

SINCE the late 1970s occupational safety and health (OSH) legislation has generated ever-increasing interest among academic researchers and has become the subject of a large number of empirical studies. Much of this work takes OSH legislation as an exemplar of regulatory law so these studies are very much bound up with the development of regulation as a discrete area of academic research and teaching. The major focus has been on OECD countries and has particularly concentrated on Australia, Europe (especially the UK) and North America. It is important to stress the inter-disciplinary nature of work in this area. While it is the case that many researchers are from law, there are many other disciplines involved in empirically investigating law, for instance, economics, history, management, political science and sociology. OSH laws have therefore been considered from a variety of multi-disciplinary and theoretical perspectives, each of which has its own distinctive methodologies. This Chapter will consider the main themes and findings of this body of research. It will highlight areas which remain relatively uncharted and those which warrant more research.[1]

I. THE FRAMING AND OBJECTIVES OF EMPIRICAL STUDIES OF LAW

Much of the early empirical work on OSH legislation emerged out of socio-legal studies[2] and consequently focused on understanding not only the social, economic and political processes that bring law about and shape its form, but also its enforcement and impact at the micro, everyday level, including how the broader structures incorporated in law influence the everyday actions of legal actors. Of course, empirical studies are always theoretically informed[3] and, in the case of empirical studies of OSH law, emerge from and contribute to a variety of theories about law, the nature of social control, theories of risk, and theories of work and employment.

In discussing empirical studies of OSH the reader should be mindful of the theoretical questions and assumptions informing the collection and analysis of empirical data. For example, OSH research is framed and interpreted according to the author's theoretical perspectives and assumptions about the nature of power in society. Some authors start from the premise of public interest theory, which regards regulation as a corrective to the operation of the market and as pursuing collective goals. The activities of relatively powerful groups are thus regulated in favor of a less powerful majority. An alternative perspective is offered by conflict or private interest theories, which argue that regulatory laws and policies do nothing to curb significantly the activities of business and industry. This perspective views business and industry as major players in the shaping of regulatory policies and as the players whose interests tend to be favored in the implementation process. These private

---

[1] It will not consider papers which are not based on empirical work, or those which debate policy options and do not report on original empirical findings.

[2] This section draws on Hutter and Lloyd-Bostock, 1997.

[3] It is important to emphasize this point as in the early days of socio-legal studies the term "empirical legal studies" aroused a certain amount of controversy when some authors criticized the attempts of lawyers to engage in empirical work, arguing that it was atheoretical and technical. It is, however, important to underline that theory and empirical work are inextricably related to each other and key to understanding the literature.

interest groups are seen as securing regulatory benefits for themselves through their use of the political and legal systems. Tensions between the public interest and conflict perspectives on regulation run through the OSH literature. These tensions can lead to some fairly unproductive discussions when unsubstantiated by empirical data. But, as we will see, these different perspectives can also affect the interpretation of empirical data.

OSH legislation focuses on stark and very often tangible risks, namely the risk of injury to life and limb in the work setting that can result in personal injury, fatalities and poor health. Quite understandably this leads to highly charged discussions most especially about the costs and benefits of regulation and in some settings, the criminality of conduct. The subject of corporate manslaughter has aroused a great deal of debate in the UK, although very few empirical studies.[4]

In addition to their role in theoretically driven socio-legal studies, empirical studies of OSH law contribute to policy discussions. This leads to the need to understand the limits of the law, raising questions about the efficacy of the criminal law as a regulatory tool and particularly the social, political, economic, legal, and organizational parameters of regulation. The area of OSH raises a familiar question about how useful the law can be as a regulatory tool, particularly when it is attempting to control activities which may be regarded as central to the economy. The crucial underlying question here concerns whether or not OSH laws make a difference to worker safety and health.

The bulk of this Chapter will be structured around a "natural history" approach to understanding law. This approach regards law as a process which starts with the recognition of a problem demanding legal intervention and the subsequent enactment of legislation. Important considerations here are the drafting of the law and the provisions made for its implementation. The ways in which those charged with enforcement interpret and employ the law then become important, followed in turn by the actual impact of the law (as interpreted and enforced) upon those it seeks to control and protect. This approach problematizes the very decision to enact legislation to protect OSH, recognizing that the debates and issues raised at this stage can influence the drafting of laws and their subsequent implementation and impact on safety and health in the workplace. This will be followed by discussion of OSH research on workforce representation, a topic which has attracted the interest of regulation and workplace relations scholars alike. The discussion focuses on efforts to legislate for worker participation in OSH in the workplace and the impact of these laws on workplace safety and health. The final section of the Chapter will consider future research agendas.

---

[4] Paul Almond's (2007) work is a notable exception. He considered the views of OSH inspectors about the then-draft bill on corporate killing. Almond's interview data found strong support for the bill among these inspectors and concluded that the new offense might lead to greater use of prosecution and more effective implementation.

II. Emergence of OSH Laws

The emergence of OSH legislation in nineteenth century Britain has attracted a number of historical studies which are clearly important empirical studies of OSH law involving the meticulous and systematic use of historical data. A prominent example of this is Carson's work[5] which is based on historical records from the Factory Inspectorate, records which he observes had hitherto remained "almost totally uninvestigated." His paper on the Factory Acts (1980) traces how OSH legislation first emerged in 1802 with the identification of child apprentices as a social problem. This was extended in 1819 and 1833 to working ages, hours and conditions in some factories, and in 1844 the working hours of women became the focus of concern. Bartrip and Fenn (1983), an historian and an economist, use agency records, in particular prosecution records, to develop the analysis further. They explain that during the course of the nineteenth century the concern of the legislation expanded to incorporate the whole workplace in manufacturing industry and to cover a wide range of aspects of work. The scope of this early legislation attracts critical analysis and there is particularly strong criticism of failures in its enforcement. In fact, a key theme running through historical studies of OSH laws is that the existence of a proper enforcement mechanism is crucial to the legislation's success in achieving improved safety and health among the workforce (it was not until the 1833 Act that any effective steps were taken to enforce the protective legislation enacted by Parliament).

Studies of other OSH regimes follow a similar pattern, arguing that early legislation was not very effective in protecting safety and health. Lewis-Beck and Alford (1980) come to this conclusion about early federal legislation relating to U.S. coal mines. Their data sets are quantitative, focusing on fatality statistics and using multiple interrupted time-series analysis. They view the first Federal Mines Inspection Act in 1941 as successful largely because it put the issue of mine safety on the map as a federal issue. The 1952 Federal Coal Mine Health and Safety Act they deem unsuccessful for reasons of limited scope (80% of mines were not covered by the legislation), limited enforcement powers, and lack of operator and union commitment. The 1969 Federal Coal Mine Health and Safety Act they see more positively, partly because it expanded both enforcement powers and regulatory budgets and was more comprehensive in its provisions.

Much attention has been directed to the role of OSH legislation in encouraging the development of specific forms of enforcement strategy, strategies which may well

---

[5] W.G. Carson wrote some of early papers on the history of the factory inspectorate and also one of the earliest studies of contemporary factory inspectors' enforcement practices. His critical work on the political economy of OSH law and its enforcement has been influential in the UK and most especially in Australia where he moved to and continued empirical work on OSH.

have longevity. Bartrip and Fenn (1983) describe Britain's Factory Inspectorate in the nineteenth century as divided on enforcement approach. They explain how during the period 1859–78 different views about enforcement practice came into conflict under the two joint Chief Inspectors. One, Alexander Redgrave, regarded prosecution as a last resort while the other, Robert Baker, "almost gloried in it" (Bartrip and Fenn, 1983: 215). The strategy which eventually came to dominate was that of Redgrave, and his evidential requirements meant that he only prosecuted when there was a high chance of conviction.

Authors place very different interpretations upon the emergence, framing, and enforcement of OSH legislation. Accommodative theorists portray this legislation as the result of a consensus between interest groups. They adhere to a pluralist model of society and argue that the legislation is neither as interventionist as the reformers would want it to be nor as lax as business would prefer. Conflict theorists regard economic interests as paramount. They argue that the dominant class has ensured that their interests are not seriously affected by regulation. Carson (1980), for example, firmly believes that powerful employer interests limited the scope and impact of the early Factory Acts in the UK and institutionalized ambiguity about the status of the legislation as criminal. These debates are well rehearsed in studies of railway workers (Hutter, 2001). In the nineteenth century safety referred very much to the safety of the travelling public rather than to the safety of railway workers. Parliament was very slow to act on behalf of railway employees. Indeed, Bartrip and Burman (1983), using historical records, and in particular worker compensation records, contrast the treatment of railway employees to the much greater protection offered to employees in the mines and factories. They argue that the issue of passenger safety overshadowed the railway debate and had crucial implications for the reform of worker safety. Explanations of why railway workers were ignored and subject to markedly less intervention than other workers center on the power of the railway interest: the railway companies were politically astute, well organized, and, according to some authors, ruthless in pursuit of their own interest (Bartrip and Burman, 1983).

The historical explanations of the emergence, framing and changes to OSH legislation overlap with implementation studies to the extent that decisions made at the law-making stage set the parameters of how the law is enforced.

III. Implementation

As noted above, historical studies of OSH law clearly identify the presence of an enforcement apparatus to implement the law as crucial to its impact. While studies of early OSH laws identify small, temporary, and poorly resourced enforcement inspectorates as major obstacles to implementing OSH laws, the twentieth century has witnessed the growth of these early inspectorates into large regulatory bureaucracies. Modern day inspectors are very different from their predecessors; yet many of the difficulties they face are much the same: how to resolve the tension between risk and cost, and how best to organize the enforcement apparatus to make a real difference to OSH.

Implementation embraces two main aspects, policy-making and enforcement. Policy-making is typically undertaken at the center of a regulatory bureaucracy and involves standard setting and organizational interpretations of the law (often in the form of regulations). In the context of OSH the focus of empirical research has been almost exclusively on the enforcement aspects of implementation. There have been relatively few studies of OSH policy-making by agencies charged with implementation and enforcement of OSH legislation.

IV. Policy-Making

The policy-making aspects of OSH have attracted rather more theoretical and speculative comment than solid empirical research. Practically and methodologically this is partly explained by the unwillingness of OSH inspectorates to give researchers access to themselves as opposed to their staff. Accordingly ethnographies, such as Heclo and Wildavsky's (1974) study of the UK Treasury, are sadly lacking. Much of the empirical work that does exist is based on documentary survey and interview data. An excellent example is Hawkins' study of the UK Health and Safety Executive's (HSE) policy-making about prosecution and legal decision-making throughout the organization. His 15-year study included a survey of documents including files, correspondence, memoranda, and interviews across the organization. Hawkins (2002) explains that HSE policy-making about prosecution involves organizational interpretations of the legislative mandate and takes the form of bureaucratic rules, statements, and practices. He finds that policy is not "clear and settled" partly because enforcement policy in HSE affords field level inspectors great autonomy, so policy is very reliant on how discretion is employed by inspectors. In other words, rather than policy determining what the enforcers do, enforcers' decisions are paramount. Hawkins sees the "real power" as lying with lower level officials "who exert power over their organizational superiors, who are left to legitimate field-level practices and decisions" (ibid: 203).

Different traditions in implementation appear to be significant in explaining policy-making in different countries. Various studies relate these differences to political factors. Wilson (1986) contrasts the consensual, persuasive approach adopted by UK OSH laws and institutions with OSH laws in the U.S., where a more conflictual and coercive approach emerged. He uses accident data from the U.S. and UK, supplemented by an analysis of the legislative process and enforcement strategies in both countries. This leads him to conclude that the differences between the two countries with regard to regulatory approach are not the result of cultural differences, for example, in attitudes to governmental intervention, but rather of the different strengths and relationships of the interest groups involved in legal implementation: in the UK the unions and employers cooperated with government whereas in the US these groups were competitive and fragmented. Kelman (1981), who compared standard setting in the United States and Sweden, found that the role of the unions in the process was significant in explaining differences. He used extensive interviews and documentary surveys and found that in the United States standard setting was relatively open and public compared to Sweden, where there was greater reliance on experts and negotiations between union organizations and the regulators. The U.S. system emerged as adversarial and the Swedish system accommodative; yet, argues Kelman, similar standards were set, except for a greater inclination of the Swedish standards to reflect worker participation.

The role of experts has become an important topic, especially in understanding decisions about the level of risk that should be accepted in regulatory policy-making. We know that this may not be straightforward as there may be a lack of adequate information or conflicting interpretation. Political decisions also need to be considered. Various interest groups may be prepared to tolerate different levels of risk. Administrative considerations are also important, especially in a system where standard setting is an agency rather than legislative task. There are few studies of this with respect to OSH, an important exception being Jasanoff's (1991) study of the role of science in regulatory decision-making in the U.S.. She takes the example of the regulation of chemical carcinogens during the period 1974–1986 by the Occupational Health and Safety Administration (OSHA) and the Environmental Protection Agency (EPA). Both agencies had to accommodate competing notions of science and rationality in setting policy within the same adversarial legal setting. OSHA took the advice of the scientific experts and then drew up explicit legalistic rules to cover all cases. EPA opted for flexible risk-assessment guidelines which acknowledged that carcinogen regulation might need case by case negotiation between scientists and policy-makers. The role of the scientific advisors was therefore very different depending upon the interactions between scientific, political, cultural, and administrative influences on various issues.

There have been attempts to standardize regulatory policy-making based on cost-benefit analyses (CBA). One argument is that it is essential to the pursuit of so-called "better regulation" or deregulation agendas, while the counter argument is that it is a misleading diversion of the debate about regulation. The advocates of CBA maintain that it is neutral, objective, and transparent to the extent that it clearly lays out what is at stake in the decision to regulate. Its critics question the techniques used to assess costs and benefits in CBA. For example, it is argued that the benefits are difficult to assess, many are non-monetary and others, such as the prevention of non-fatal diseases, are non-quantifiable. Doubters of the value of CBA argue that the benefits taken into account are often very restrictively defined: so, for example, non-economic social benefits may not be considered. At the same time the costs may be systematically over estimated, especially by employers. In short, some fear that these methods are biased toward certain interest groups, most particularly employers. Another argument, which has been put forward by Cass Sunstein (2007), is that CBA methods are not ideal but they are "better than nothing." Debates about the costs and benefits of regulation are technical and moral, and they go to the heart of what regulation is and should be. One of the most damning critiques of CBA focuses on its economistic frame which, some argue, denies social values and moral input and, in the view of some observers, is unethical. Once again these arguments are acute in the OSH domain as real lives and peoples' health are being discussed and quantified; and the very real dilemmas of risk regulation are revealed in these debates. Despite the centrality of this debate, there are surprisingly few empirical studies of the relationship between CBA and governmental policies aimed at either better regulation or deregulation. A particular gap is research how CBA-driven, macro-level "better" regulation policies impact on OSH inspectorates, and how these agencies adapt to broader policies in order to reduce their burden on employers while protecting the workforce.

V. Enforcement

Many early studies of regulatory enforcement followed in the interpretive tradition of sociological studies of policing, focusing on field-level inspectors as gatekeepers to the regulatory process. The interpretive practices of these inspectors were regarded as key to understanding the "law in action" and were seen as the bridge between legislation, both primary and secondary, and the impact of regulation. The appropriate method for research seeking to understand the inspectors' world-view was ethnographic, typically combining observational techniques with other forms of data collection. An example is Hutter's (1997) work with UK HSE inspectors, which was comprised of two stages of fieldwork: the first was ethnographic and involved accompanying 33 inspectors during the course of their normal working day. Documentary evidence associated with the visits was also examined; this evidence included communications to the business concerned, notices (where appropriate), and the file reports resulting from each visit. During the second stage of fieldwork some areas were revisited and a number of the cases observed during the first stage were followed up to see what had happened since. This provided a longitudinal view of the enforcement process. Data were carefully analyzed for patterns of enforcement and explanatory variables. This study, in common with studies in other regulatory domains, found a regulatory style of enforcement which is cooperative and conciliatory, the aim of which is to secure compliance through remedying existing problems and, most importantly, preventing future problems. The use of formal legal methods of enforcement, notably prosecution, is regarded as a last resort, something to be avoided unless all else fails to secure compliance. This style of enforcement allows for compliance over a period of time: instant remedy is not necessarily sought or considered feasible. This approach contrasts with the deterrence or sanctioning model, in which a penal style of enforcement accords prosecution an important role. The objective of this model is to prohibit certain activities. It is also accusatory and geared to catching out those who break the law.

The compliance approach to OSH enforcement has been identified in a variety of different countries with evidence that regulatory officials in Australia, Britain, Canada, the Netherlands, Sweden, and the United States favor compliance-based methods in some areas of occupational safety and health.[6] The first studies to document any significant deviation from this pattern were of American regulatory agencies in the 1970s. Kelman's (1981) study of OSHA and Shover et al.'s (1986) study of the Office of Surface Mining both describe regulatory agencies which adopted enforcement strategies closely approximating the sanctioning style. Studies such as these led to the gradual refinement of the early binary model of compliance and sanctioning approaches. For example, Braithwaite, Walker, and Grabosky surveyed 96 regulatory organizations in Australia, including OSH agencies, and collected data on 127 variables for each including structure, policy, behavior, statutory provisions and attitudinal variables. A number of different sources were used—documentary evidence, written answers to queries, written questionnaires and telephone calls. All compliance strategies of importance to these agencies were coded and analyzed by calculating correlation coefficients between agencies, followed by a principal-components factor analysis and hierarchical cluster analysis. These multivariate techniques resulted in a typology of regulatory agencies which refined the early binary models. Likewise, Shover et al. determined the major variables influencing different enforcement activities through data collected over a 30-month period spent with the U.S. Office of Surface Mining Reclamation and Enforcement. They interviewed 43 inspectors

---

[6] Australia: see the work of Braithwaite et al., 1987; Grabosky; Gunningham, 2007; Johnstone, 2003; and Quinlan, 2007. Britain: see the work of Dawson et al., 1988; Hawkins, 2002; Hutter, 2001; and Lloyd-Bostock, 1988. Canada: see Brown, 1994. Netherlands: see for example Wilthagen, 1993. Sweden: see Kelman, 1981; and the United States: see, for example, Rees, 1988.

about field-level enforcement and they sent a postal questionnaire to the entire inspectorate of 158 inspectors. In addition they sampled agency statistical data about inspection and enforcement operations with respect to a sample of 83 firms over a period of two years.

The most fruitful lines of analysis have focused on the variations which exist in regulatory enforcement. Research has identified intra-agency variations (Hutter, 1997), inter-agency variations (Braithwaite et al., 1987), and cultural variations between and within countries (Kelman, 1981; Shover et al., 1986). Also important is the recognition through this body of research that all enforcement officials use both accommodative and sanctioning techniques albeit to different extents. Searching for explanations of how these variations in enforcement approach come about helps us understand better how the law is enforced in practice. This highlights the importance of comparative research—in different regions of the same jurisdiction, between different types of agency and between different countries.

Explanations for variations in OSH enforcement styles center on two main areas: features of the law and legal system and features associated with the nature of the work being regulated and the social environment within which this work occurs. Issues of legal design emerge as important in explaining the practice of OSH enforcement. Hawkins's prosecution study (2002) included content analysis of the files for all prosecution cases over a six-month period in four regional offices, supplemented by interviews with personnel in those offices. He found that administrative discretion takes on central importance where OSH legislation consists of broad standards rather than precise commands. Field-level inspectors are especially important as they are vested with the discretion to decide what constitutes an offence or problem and whether to refer a case upwards for further attention. Broad standards thus have potential implications for prosecution rates. Meeting the evidential requirements of broad standards may be more difficult than meeting those of precisely framed rules. Lloyd-Bostock's (1988) analysis of accident and enforcement data—collected through a combination of agency documents, statistics, and interviews—found that the framing of the rules partly explained why many UK OSH prosecutions follow accidents. In some cases the clear evidence of non-compliance provided by an accident is perceived to increase the certainty of a successful prosecution and hence to justify the expenditure of resources and effort needed to assemble a case. As this indicates, organizational parameters are important in the decision to prosecute. These include considerations about the likelihood of success or the possibility of an appeal. There is a fear that if the regulator were to lose an appeal this would touch upon the credibility of the organization and could lead to a higher level of legal challenges to regulators' decisions. A key finding of Hawkins's work is that legal action is regarded as a very public and symbolic act which necessitates assessing the risks to the agency

The costs of legal action can be high—putting together a legal case demands a great deal of inspectorate time and may require the additional cost of obtaining a legal opinion. Inspectorate resources are limited and time spent on a legal case is time lost to other activities. Again, the costs and benefits of legal action have to be weighed at a case level as well as at the macro, legislative, and policy-making levels. Arguably, one of the risks, and hence potential costs, of legal action is that a precedent will be set that could limit future flexibility. Inspectors are particularly concerned that the courts might accept a standard lower than that they feel able to achieve through less formal means. Of course, arguments such as these may be differentially interpreted. They may be taken at face value as an explanation of choice of enforcement approach or they may be regarded as a sign of weakness and unwillingness to sanction business. Broadly, accommodative theorists tend to adopt the former position and conflict theorists the latter. Such analyses can also be extended to other features of OSH law. For example, low sanctions have been identified as an explanation for compliance-oriented OSH enforcement, but there is controversy over their effects. Some argue that low sanctions are ineffective and do not deter. Others can find no evidence that higher penalties provide more deterrence than lower penalties. Gray and Scholz (1991) considered the experience of 6,842 U.S. firms over a six-year period. They used injury data and OSHA enforcement records to evaluate the effect on OSHA enforcement of the nature of the firm, the intensity of inspection, and the size of the penalty. Their quantitative analysis led them to conclude that any penalty acts as a deterrent and also serves to attract broader managerial attention to OSH issues. The ease with which penalties can be imposed is undoubtedly relevant in this study. In the United States, inspectors are empowered to impose penalties and required to do so upon detecting violations of rules during inspections, whereas the UK system requires that penalties be imposed by the courts, requiring a case to be prepared and presented.

Studies of how the courts handle OSH cases are sadly lacking and this represents one of the gaps in empirical studies of OSH law. The dearth of studies may reflect the very few prosecutions which are taken to the courts. But arguably there are sufficient numbers across jurisdictions to make for a fascinating research topic. This would enable one to assess the evidence for claims that the courts do not take OSH cases as seriously as they might and also claims about sanctioning practices.

The second set of factors explanatory of varying enforcement styles focuses on the nature of the work subject to regulation and the social environment within which it takes place. Variations in enforcement have been found according to the type of industry involved. Because, in some industries such as chemical, petroleum, and nuclear works, attention to the workers' safety and health may have been imperative to the safety and viability of the whole site, there is a self-interest in compliance (Genn, 1993; Rees, 1988). In contrast, there are other industries, for example the building industry, where heavy, manual work is undertaken, the workforce is unskilled, and accident rates often exceed those in manufacturing industries. Hutter's (1997) ethnographic work details how such characteristics are important in determining the enforcement approach taken by inspectors. It also details how inspectors' enforcement decisions regarding individual sites are structured by such features as track record, commitment to OSH, quality of management, and capacity to comply.

The social environment of enforcement is particularly important in settings where inspectors develop a social relationship with those they regulate in which trust can emerge over repeated interactions. Various studies, both qualitative (Hutter, 1997) and quantitative (Braithwaite et al., 1987), have found a correlation between the tendency to use formal sanctions and the relational distance between the regulator and regulated. This is consistent with work on other regulatory sectors, such as that of Hawkins (2002) and Gunningham and Kagan's (2005) work on environmental regulation. The precise nature of regulatory relations is not simply worked out at the level of everyday interactions between inspectors and those they regulate but is a product of broader structural features of regulatory work. There is evidence that the macro environment influences micro-level activities such as the routine enforcement of the law by OSH inspectors and also agency policies. For example, whether or not the political climate is pro-regulatory or deregulatory may be influential; public concerns are taken seriously particularly when mediated through a politician; and the economic climate can also influence inspectorate demands. Another key finding is that inspectors are influenced in their decision-making by notions of moral blameworthiness. Carson (1980) found this was important in his early study of the enforcement of the Factories Acts. It has also emerged as significant in more recent studies of prosecution (Hawkins, 2002).

In many respects, there is extraordinary concurrence of empirical findings across a variety of studies of OSH, irrespective of the method used to collect data. Yet different theoretical perspectives give varying interpretations to these findings. Accommodative theorists regard low levels of prosecution as a rational response to limited agency resources, ambiguous legislation, and weak sanctions. Conflict theorists, however, cite a reluctance to prosecute as evidence of ineffective legislation, the "capture" of the regulatory agency by business, and the power of business to challenge regulatory demands. Certainly there are aspects of both perspectives which merit consideration but there are some dangers in considering just the issue of "effectiveness," since other social values must be taken into consideration. Ayres and Braithwaite (1992: 20 ff) refer to "a long history of barren disputation" between "staunch advocates of deterrence and defenders of the compliance model." Rather more interesting are the wider implications of the empirical findings of research on OSH law enforcement. For instance, the results of these studies have challenged our understanding of the meaning and definition of enforcement, particularly the view that enforcement refers simply to legal action. Rather, law enforcement encompasses a wide array of informal techniques such as persuasion, education, advice, and negotiation. These studies thus emphasized the negotiated nature of much law.

The studies of OSH enforcement have also led to policy discussions. For example, many authors have argued for responsive, flexible, or "smart" regulation which can accommodate different styles and techniques. These calls are premised on the finding that persuasion and prosecution are both needed; indeed, it is important to recognize that persuasion is more possible in some situations than others and that persuasion does not necessarily mean failure. Enforcement is a complex and complicated matter. It is too simplistic to adopt uniformly one approach or the other, or to criticize uniformly one method or another.

VI. Impact

A central socio-legal concern is how influential the law is in social and economic life. Distinguishing between the impact of "the law" and its enforcement is very difficult and the general message of empirical studies of OSH law, which has been repeated throughout this Chapter, is that the mere enactment of law is insufficient to effect change. It is crucial that the law be enforced. How to assess the impact of enforcement is riddled with difficulties as empirical studies of OSH law exemplify. For example, there is no clear-cut method for isolating and measuring the improvements which may have been effected by the law and its enforcement from the complex of other factors which may have been involved. Nevertheless governments have increasingly demanded measures of "performance." Some OSH inspectorates have tried to use legal action as a performance indicator; but the difficulties in using the number of prosecutions initiated or notices served as indicators of "effectiveness" is well illustrated in the earlier discussion of enforcement, which shows how these figures actually tell us very little about compliance and non-compliance with OSH laws.

One method of assessing the impact of legislation and its enforcement focuses on outcomes. Given that a central objective of occupational safety and health legislation is to prevent accidents and ill-health at work, the most obvious indicator in the area of occupational safety and health is improvement in accident and industrial injuries statistics. However, while these statistics do give us a crude measure of workplace safety and health, they are a problematic measure of the impact of the law. Specifically, there are problems with the available statistics (e.g., their accuracy), and there are even greater difficulties in causally relating a change in injury figures to the law. For instance it is impossible to isolate the effects of the law from the impact of other factors such as changes in technology and labor market factors. These difficulties are in many respects reflected in quantitative studies which evaluate the impact of OSHA in the United States. For many of these studies the key indicator of OSHA success is improvements in workplace injury rates. We should be mindful that these studies were undertaken in different time periods but nevertheless mixed messages emerge from these studies.

In the 1970s Smith (1979) found that the effectiveness of OSHA inspections varied. This quantitative analysis focused on the manufacturing sector and considered the number of employees, type of industry, and plant location for the years 1972, 1973, and 1974. It compared the lost-workday injury rate for inspected and non-inspected plants. The effectiveness of OSHA inspections was estimated by comparing the injury experience of plants inspected early in the year with that of plants inspected very late in the year. Using 1972 as the base year, the results showed a statistically significant injury-rate decrease associated with 1973 inspections, but an insignificant decline associated with 1974. Viscusi (1979) uses a different measure of impact, namely actual or planned investments in occupational safety and health. He analyzed pooled time series and cross-section data on industry safety and health investments, injury rates, and data on OSHA inspections, citations and penalties for the period 1972–1975. He found a weak relationship and thus concludes that no significant effect of OSHA was found from 1972–1975 on safety and health investment, planned safety and health investments, and worker injuries. He argues that this is explained by the probability of inspection being very low and the penalties for violation so weak that there was no financial incentive to change actions.

Quantitative studies in the 1980s are also skeptical about the impact of OSHA. Studies have found little or no impact of OSHA standards on injury frequency but enforcement does have some impact. Bartel and Thomas (1985) argue that it is important to distinguish between the direct and indirect effects of OSH regulation. They propose a three-equation model of workplace injuries, industrial non-compliance with OSHA safety standards, and OSHA enforcement. They focused on firms in the 22 states where OSHA directly enforced safety regulations (rather than the regulations being enforced by the state) during the period 1972–1979. Using data on safety inspections, violations of safety standards, and occupational injuries they found that enforcement has no direct effect on accidents but operates via its impact on non-compliance. Inspection is important, but more important, argue Bartel and Thomas (1985), is the penalty structure for violations, which gives firms an incentive to adjust their compliance levels in response to OSHA enforcement efforts, and this in turn affects workplace safety. This finding is supported by Gray and Scholz (1993) who find that OSHA inspections resulting in a penalty have significant effects on the frequency and severity of injury rates, which continue up to three years after the inspection, with particularly strong effects in years one to two. The authors regard the penalty as especially important as it triggers greater managerial attention (see also Mendeloff and Gray, 2005). While these studies differ in their assessment of the amount of impact OSHA has, all are in broad agreement that it only has an impact where there is enforcement activity, particularly if those enforcement activities result in the imposition of penalties. These findings led to major concerns about OSHA proposals to move to voluntary approaches and to limit enforcement activities.

The U.S. OSH system is more legalistic than that of the UK; but studies in the UK also identify inspections by OSH officials as important. Vickers et al. (2005) argue for a multidimensional approach to encouraging compliance—one that emphasizes more direct OSH contact and enforcement, which they regard as important because they found that the majority of their sample of small businesses had poor knowledge of regulation but responded to regulation when asked to by inspectors. Indeed Baldock et al. (2006), using a telephone survey of 1,087 British small enterprises, find that inspections are the most important influence on compliance in small businesses. Also relevant is membership of trade associations and features more associated with the internal workings of a business, such as management training and experience.

Features relating to the internal working of the regulated organizations have been addressed by a variety of studies, many of which are more qualitative in their methods and approach. Many of these focus on the impact of legal regulation on organizations. Typically, the influence of occupational safety and health law is mediated through workplace organizations. Understanding the complexity of organizations is important for exploring the impact of the constitutive effects of OSH laws and also for understanding the ability of organizations to self-regulate. This ability is of course a key policy question given the growing popularity of moves to incorporate some degree of self-regulation into OSH regulation. At the institutional level assessing the impact of law involves an examination of how legal demands might influence institutional structures, systems, policies, and procedures (Dawson et al., 1988; Gunningham and Johnstone, 1999; Rees, 1988).

Within firms, researchers have examined how much those subject to regulatory laws and policies know and understand about their provisions and about the regulatory apparatus in place for their implementation. Another important consideration is the extent to which the law might cause individuals and institutions to change their behavior and practices. Document surveys and interviews have been central methods of data collection for these purposes. Genn (1993), for example, interviewed 40 managers of industrial and agricultural sites in England and Wales about their knowledge of regulatory law, regulatory systems and regulatory practice. The sample of sites she selected varied in the size of the workforce, the degree of unionization, and the types of hazards likely to exist. Nelkin and Brown (1984) likewise interviewed workers about their understanding of risks in the workplace. More recently, Baril-Gingras et al. (2006), Corneliussen (2005), and Hutter (2001) have focused, largely through interviews, on business perspectives on regulation. Hutter, for example, conducted 134 in-depth interviews with a cross-section of staff working in one company, British Railways; the staff came from different regions, different departments, and different levels of the company's hierarchy. The interviews were designed to encourage open-ended discussions with the objective, shared with other qualitative work in this area, of discerning how respondents interpreted regulatory issues and perceived OSH.

The findings of these studies underline some of the real complexities and contradictions in considering the impact of OSH law and its enforcement. For instance, the research which has been done suggests that explanations of compliance and non-compliance involve a complex of factors which vary across time and geography.[7] Much neo-classical economic theory assumes that businesses are primarily motivated by profit, and that this inevitably inclines them to resist regulation. The research evidence is contradictory and reveals these assertions to be simplistic. For example, businesses vary widely in their knowledge and ability to comply, some having great capacity to comply. Genn (1993) found a clear distinction between employers who are highly motivated to maintain good OSH standards and those whose motivation is low. She took indicators of motivation to be self-education, a proactive approach to OSH, monitoring of accidents, and a willingness to ask for advice from inspectors. Highly motivated companies had a proactive approach to OSH which was often promoted by means of activities involving the workforce. Companies with low motivation tended to be small in size, have no obvious major hazard or well-recognized risk, and lack any safety personnel; for these companies OSH is subordinated to the time and financial pressures of production. Genn argues that in businesses with low OSH motivation, compliance strategies are largely reactive, limited to the action demanded by inspectors.

Understanding compliance and non-compliance at the individual level is also important and here research findings mirror those of studies of organizational compliance. Self-interest at an individual level very much depends upon competing objectives, including formal structural pressures and individual risk aversion to injury and to legal sanctions. Ignorance of the law and of risks is associated with non-compliance, and this appears to be a particularly likely explanation of small business non-compliance. But knowledge of the law and risks, even quite serious personal risks, may provide insufficient motivation to comply. For example, Hutter (2001) found that while her respondents could cite crossing the railways tracks in unauthorized places as a major risk to their OSH, they also readily cited it as an example of their own non-compliance.

Intra-organizational pressures are important in explaining compliance issues in a number of respects. Corporate culture plays an important role in inclination to compliance/non-compliance. Similarly worker morale has been found to influence OSH, with low levels of morale contributing to higher levels of injury and stress. Organizational pressures to prioritize production may also have very adverse effects on compliance. Early studies in the UK identified the motivation of managers and owners as important to understanding compliance. Dawson et al. (1988) used discourse analysis, analysis of law, case studies from differing industries and interviews in their study of compliance with the self-regulatory demands of UK OSH

---

[7] See Amodu (2008) for an excellent summary of research on compliance and OSH law.

legislation. They found managerial motivation and an organizational willingness and capacity to comply to be important.

Researchers in the U.S., Australia, and the UK have all noted the importance of the size of a business in relation to regulatory enforcement. They note a tendency for formal legal enforcement action to figure less prominently in regulatory officials' dealings with larger and more powerful organizations than in their dealings with smaller organizations. Researchers have reported a tendency for regulatory officials to believe that big business is more law-abiding than small business. Dawson et al. (1988: 261) found that the gap between standards of safety and health in large and small firms was considerable. A union report (GMB, 1986) into occupational safety and health regulation in Britain notes that small companies find compliance problematic and often do not comply. A variety of qualitative studies using interview data have reported similar findings (see Fairman and Yapp, 2005; Genn, 1993; Vickers et al., 2005; and Wilthagen, 1993). Arguably, this pattern is partly related to the perceived capacity of organizations to comply and their greater capacity to challenge how deviance is defined. One study suggests some caution in explaining this pattern. Drawing on semi-structured interviews with founders, managers, and senior scientists in seven Scottish and seven Norwegian start-up biotech firms, Corneliussen (2005) found that her respondents had good understanding of the law and were highly motivated to comply, partly because of professional norms and partly because of a concern to maintain public confidence. Other studies also warn against sweeping statements based on the size of the regulated business. For example, larger firms may be so differentiated within their organizations that non-compliance becomes a greater possibility (see discussion in Hutter, 2001). Indeed large firms remain susceptible to production pressures which may incline staff to "cut safety and health corners" and take risks (Genn, 1993; Hutter, 2001; Nelkin and Brown, 1984).

VII. WORKFORCE REPRESENTATION

An important feature of OSH law is that in many jurisdictions the workers are not simply afforded protection in the workplace but are actively encouraged and empowered to participate in enforcing OSH regulation. This may be through rights of access to information, and rights to be consulted and represented. These topics have attracted a broader range of scholars than other empirical studies of OSH law as those whose research focuses broadly on workplace relations have also contributed to research on these OSH topics. Generally, worker rights and representation are found to increase the impact of OSH law but only when these rights are enshrined in law (Baril-Gingras et al., 2006).

Research from the UK and Canada suggests that trade union presence does impact on workplace OSH but that the nature of this impact is mixed and complex. U.S. data suggest that the effects of unionization varies among establishments. For example, Bartel and Thomas's study of firms across 22 U.S. states (1985, see above) did not find that unionization increased the impact of the law, whereas Weil (1992) did find that OSH laws were more stringently enforced at unionized construction workplaces than at comparable non-union workplaces. There may also be national differences, with a number of Canadian and UK studies finding an association between trade union presence and a higher level of legal knowledge. For example, Walters and Haines (1988) found that worker knowledge of OSH law and company OSH arrangements increased with union membership in Canada. In 1984–1985 they undertook a questionnaire survey of 492 workers at eight workplaces in Ontario, including unionized and non-unionized, large and small, public and private sector. Respondents displayed a strong consciousness of ways in which work might damage health. They found that knowledge of the law and of company OSH representatives increased with union membership. The unions also provide crucial information and training in the UK (see Walters et al., 1993).

A number of studies have been based on the 1998 UK Workplace Employee Relations Survey, a nationally representative sample of workplaces in Britain with 10+ employees. Robinson and Smallman (2006) used the survey, focusing on structured interviews with managers from 2,191 workplaces in the service sector; the interviews included questions on the number of reported injuries and illness, OHS management practices, and the broader workplace and employment environment. The analysis found an association between trade union presence and higher levels of reported injury and illness; the researchers argue that this is because employees are encouraged to report accidents and need not fear retaliation because they have trade union protection. Fenn and Ashby (2004), using the same 1998 survey for all sectors, confirm the findings that workplaces with a higher proportion of unionized employees, and with safety and health committees, were associated with a greater number of reported injuries or illnesses. They speculate that this may indicate a greater willingness to report injuries and illness that might lead to compensation claims. The variations in reporting patterns are consistent with significant under-reporting of workplace injuries and, most especially, illness, which in turn means that caution needs to be exercised in interpreting official OSH data.

It is generally agreed that while legal provision for worker safety and health is important, legal provision alone is insufficient to reduce workplace risks. The laws need to translate into substantive action in order to have any legitimacy and impact. UK research, for example, has revealed scepticism about joint union-management safety committees with workers suggesting that these committees were just "a talking shop" and were perceived to be without authority (see Dawson et al., 1988; Hutter, 2001). Rees (1988: 138) observes that the few empirical studies of safety committees that do exist agree that the mere existence of safety committees makes little difference. He comments that these committees must be seen to effect a demonstrable improvement in occupational safety and health; communication is vital in order that workers feel that they are directly represented; and workers must have confidence in the committee and be willing to take complaints to it. Perhaps most important is his finding that the creation of the committee is, at best, just a first step, and that to have an impact workers need to continue to be involved in the committee's activities and be rewarded for their contributions (Rees, 1988: 144). Walters and Gourlay (1990: 121) further show that to be effective, committees need to be compact, meet regularly, be well organized, be regularly attended, and have good communication with workers. Research on joint manager-worker inspections of the workplace also find their success in improving worker safety and health to be related to demonstrable follow-up action (Gunningham, 2007; Hutter, 2001; Walters et al., 1993: 63).

Hall et al.'s (2006) research of worker representatives in small and medium-sized enterprises in Canada suggests that OSH law can be a useful resource which worker representatives can mobilize tactically in negotiations with employers. Generally, however, the effectiveness of safety representatives appears to be related to their working in a culture which is supportive of their goal. This includes the support of the unions, other employees, and management. Safety representatives need to maintain strong links with their constituencies and feel needed and valued by the workforce. And while management commitment is vital with respect to including safety representatives in decision-making, consulting with them, and responding to their concerns, there is no evidence that this support is forthcoming (see, for example, Walters and Gourlay, 1990).

A broader concern is structural change in the labor market, which may diminish workers' rights, representation, and protection. Quinlan (2007) uses the term "precarious employment" to identify some of the changes which may affect regulation and the impact of worker input concerning OSH issues. Precarious employment includes part-time and temporary work. It also includes subcontracting, which Mayhew and Quinlan (1997) studied in Australia and in the UK residential building industry. They conclude that OSH in the subcontracting and self-employed sectors is poorly regulated partly because regulation is not modified to accommodate differences in labor structuring; small businesses are exempted from legal requirements in some jurisdictions, and even where they are included inspectorates tend to focus on larger workplaces. Moreover, in some industries, such as the construction industry, there is fierce competition for building contracts which can lead to OSH being overlooked. Outsourcing has also been found to reduce employer responsibility for and attention to OSH.

A general observation throughout the literature is that safety concerns are generally privileged over health. Robinson and Smallman (2006) found that the legislative framework in the UK focuses more on accidents than illness. Studies in the UK and elsewhere have found that inspectors and enforcement officials tend to focus more factors that are likely to cause accidents than on factors likely to cause illness as the former are easier to detect than the latter. Moreover, it is easier to demonstrate a causal relationship in the case of injuries than in health-related cases. The visibility and tangibility of the various problems OSH inspectors encounter can influence perceptions of risk. Safety matters, for example, are often more visible and more tangible than those concerning health While it may be fairly easy to understand and explain that an unguarded machine could lead to a finger being chopped off, it may be more difficult to prove that sustained exposure to high levels of noise could, over a period of time, cause deafness. Likewise, asbestos fibers, rubber fumes, mercury, and microbiological hazards could all be difficult to "observe" and to relate causally to particular examples of ill-health. These factors especially manifest themselves in the likelihood of legal action because of the greater difficulty in establishing evidence to support a health claim, which may arise over a longer time scale and be subject to more questions of causation than an injury claim (Hawkins, 2002; Lloyd-Bostock, 1988). More empirical studies of OSH law as it relates to health issues are needed in order to better understand the differences that arise in dealing with accidental injury versus work-related illness.

VIII. Future Research Agendas

OSH law will inevitably continue to be a central area of empirical legal research. There is overwhelming evidence that the law does play a crucial role in promoting workplace occupational safety and health, particularly the former, and in guaranteeing representation of workers on these issues. But enforcement emerges as key to explaining the impact of OSH law and there is some evidence that the possibility of sanctions is integral to this impact.

This Chapter has only been able to touch on a fraction of the very fine work in this area, but it still is clear that there are some major gaps in our knowledge. The emergence of OSH laws remains an area for further study. There are many jurisdictions where historical work could usefully contribute to our understanding of the emergence and formation of OSH legal regimes. There is also space for a broader examination of the emergence of OSH laws across different areas of employment and in different countries.

The implementation of OSH laws has received substantial attention, at least from an enforcement perspective, but the policy-making work of OSH regulators is seriously under-researched. There is real scope for some high quality ethnographic study of OSH policy-making. The possibilities for this may be enhanced by the value that empirical studies of OSH law can provide for policy-makers. They provide an evidential basis from which regulators and governments can learn. This is especially so in an environment where "better regulation" is a major policy initiative of governments.

Another area of OSH which remains relatively under-researched is the handling of OSH cases by the courts and also by tribunals. Again, this can be a difficult area to research for methodological reasons such as the scarcity of cases reaching the courts. But it is nevertheless the case that arguments about the treatment of OSH cases by the courts and the sanctions they may impose continue to be marshalled as "evidence" in debates about the impact of law and enforcement. As noted previously, we need more research on how OSH law and its enforcement affect the incidence of occupationally related illness. Here, as in other areas, cross-national studies would give us a deeper understanding of the ways in which OSH laws might be framed to best serve their objectives.

Different patterns of OSH law-making and enforcement have been discerned between countries, notably between the United States and many other jurisdictions in Australia and Europe. There is no agreement on how to account for these differences. The vast majority of the extant research has focused on North America, Europe, and Australia. The few existing studies of Eastern Europe focus on Russia and suggest that OSH is a very real problem with very high levels of workplace accidents and fatalities, and a weak and poorly legitimated legal system (Petrick and Rinefort, 1999). Generally, however, there is a relative dearth of information about OSH laws in post-Soviet Eastern Europe, in particular empirical studies of these laws. There is also very little on rapidly developing economies such as China or countries in South America. One important research area is how Asian countries have responded to the risks of rapid economic change. There is evidence that the new risks facing Asian societies have produced some regulatory responses. For instance, one product of the rapidly developing Chinese economy has been the development of a legal framework covering a broad range of domains including OSH. Examination of these responses, and their enforcement and impact, should be prioritized moving forward. Another key area which urgently demands more research is the role of supranational institutions involved with OSH, such as the International Labour Organization (ILO), OECD, and European Union (EU). EU regulations are now the impetus for much of the OSH legislation emanating from EU states, and how these regulations are agreed upon and implemented in member countries, and then impact on national regimes is a rich area for further research on all aspects of OSH law, from its emergence, through policy-making and enforcement, to impact.

There are clear transnational aspects to OSH laws which touch on broader international agendas, particularly those involving trade agreements and fair-trade issues. The extent to which these matters are the subject of agreements rather than law is a subject for research. But most important is their impact about which, based on the existing evidence, there is no cause for optimism because of what some describe as "regulatory shopping." However, the evidence here is limited and more empirical investigation would be extremely valuable. International-relations and global-governance scholars could usefully be involved in researching OSH laws in these areas. The relationship between OSH and trade will undoubtedly remain in tension and is a subject which touches on the major themes of empirical studies of OSH law.

It is vital that empirical study of OSH law—and indeed other laws—remains interdisciplinary. Multidisciplinary approaches bring a broad range of perspectives and theories to our understanding. They also provide methodological variety which is extremely valuable. Triangulating empirical work derived from different theoretical traditions and employing varying research methods is important in developing our understanding of the social, economic, political, and legal worlds we inhabit.

REFERENCES

Almond, P. (2007). "Regulation Crisis: Evaluating the Potential Legitimising Effects of 'Corporate Manslaughter' Cases," *Law and Policy* 29(3): 285–310.

Amodu, T. (2008). *The Determinants of Compliance with Laws and Regulations with Special Reference to Health and Safety*, London: HSE Books.

Ayres, I. and Braithwaite, J. (1992). *Responsive Regulation: Transcending the Deregulation Debate*, New York: Oxford University Press.

Baldock, R., James, P., Smallbone, D., and I. Vickers (2006). "Influences on Small-firm Compliance-related Behaviour: the Case of Workplace Health and Safety," *Environment and Planning C: Government and Policy* 24(6): 827–46.

Baldwin, R. (1995). *Rules and Government*, Oxford: Clarendon Press.

Baril-Gingras, G., Bellemare, M., and Brun, J.P. (2006). "External Interventions in Occupational Health and Safety: the Influence of the Workplace Context on the Implementation of Preventive Measures," *Relations Industrielles* 61(1): 9–43.

Bartel, A.P. and Thomas, L.G. (1985). "Direct and Indirect Effects of Regulation: a New Look at OSHA's Impact," *Journal of Law and Economics* 28(1): 1–24.

Bartrip, P.W.J. and Burman, S. (1983). *The Wounded Soldiers of Industry*, Oxford: Clarendon Press.

Bartrip, P.W.J. and Fenn, P.T. (1983). "The Evolution of Regulatory Style in the Nineteenth-Century British Factory Inspectorate," *Journal of Law and Society* 10(2): 201–22.

Braithwaite, J., Walker, J., and Grabosky, P. (1987). "An Enforcement Taxonomy of Regulatory Agencies," *Law & Policy* 9(3): 323–51.

Brown, R. (1994). "Theory and Practice of Regulatory Enforcement: Occupational Health and Safety Regulation in British Columbia," *Law & Policy* 16(1): 63–91.

Carson, W.G. (1980). "The Institutionalization of Ambiguity: Early British Factory Acts," in G. Geis and E. Stotland (eds.), *White-Collar Crime: Theory and Research*, Beverly Hills: Sage.

Clark, L. (1999). "The Politics of Regulation: a Comparative-historical Study of Occupational Health and Safety Regulation in Australia and the United States," *Australian Journal of Public Administration* 58(2): 94–104.

Corneliussen, F. (2005). "The Impact of Regulations on Firms: A Case Study of the Biotech Industry," *Law & Policy* 27(3): 429–49.

Dawson, S., Willman, P., Clinton, A., and Bamford, M. (1988). *Safety at Work: the Limits of Self-regulation*, Cambridge: Cambridge University Press.

Fairman, R. and Yapp, C. (2005). *Making an Impact on SME Compliance Behaviour: an Evaluation on the Effect of Interventions upon Compliance to Health and Safety Legislation in Small and Medium-sized Enterprises*, Contract Research Report No. 336, London: HSE.

Fenn, P. and Ashby, S. (2004). "Workplace Risk, Establishment Size and Union Density," *British Journal of Industrial Relations* 42(3): 461–80.

Genn, H. (1993). "Business Responses to the Regulation of Health and Safety in England," *Law & Policy* 15(3): 219–34.

GMB [General, Municipal, Boilermakers and Allied Trade Union] (1986). "The Freedom to Kill?," GMB Health & Safety Policy Paper.

Gray, W.B. and Scholz, J.T. (1991). "Analyzing the Equity and Efficiency of OSHA Enforcement," *Law & Policy* 13(3): 185–214.

Gunningham, N. (2007). *Mine Safety: Law Regulation Policy*, Annandale: The Federation Press.

Gunningham, N. and Johnstone, R. (1999). *Regulating Workplace Safety: System and Sanctions*, Oxford: Clarendon Press.

Gunningham, N. and Kagan, R.A. (2005). "Regulation and Business Behaviour," *Law & Policy* 27(2): 213–18.

Hall, A., Forrest, A., Sears, A., and Carlan, N. (2006). "Making a Difference: Knowledge Activism and Worker Representation in Joint OHS Committees," *Relations Industrielles* 61(3): 408–36.

Hawkins, K. (2002). *Law as Last Resort: Prosecution Decision-making in a Regulatory Agency*, Oxford: Oxford University Press.

Heclo, H and Wildavsky, A. (1974). *The Private Government of Public Money*, London: MacMillan.

Hutter, B.M. (1997). *Compliance: Regulation and Environment*, Oxford: Clarendon Press.

Hutter, B.M. (2001). *Regulation and Risk: Occupational Health and Safety on the Railways*, Oxford: Oxford University Press.

Hutter, B.M. and Lloyd-Bostock, S. (1997). "Law's Relationship with Social Science: the Interdependence of Theory, Empirical Work, and Social Relevance in Socio-Legal Studies," in K. Hawkins (ed.), *The Human Face of the Law*, Oxford: Clarendon Press.

Jasanoff , S. (1991). "Cross-National Differences in Policy Implementation," *Evaluation Review* 15(1): 103–19.

Johnstone, R. (2003). *Occupational Health and Safety, Courts and Crime: the Legal Construction of Occupational Health and Safety Offences in Victoria*, Annandale: The Federation Press.

Kagan, R.A. (1994). "Regulatory Enforcement," in D.H. Rosenbloom and R.D. Schwartz (eds.), *Handbook of Regulation and Administrative Law*, New York: Marcel Dekker.

Kagan, R.A. and Axelrad, L. (2000). *Regulatory Encounters: Multinational Corporations and Adversarial Legalism*, Berkeley, Los Angeles and London: University of California Press.

Kelman, S. (1981). *Regulating America, Regulating Sweden: A Comparative Study of Occupational Safety and Health Policy*, Cambridge, MA: MIT Press.

Kolko, G. (1965). *Railroads and Regulations 1877–1916*, Princeton: Princeton University Press.

Lewis-Beck, M.S. and Alford, J.R. (1980). "Can Government Regulate Safety: The Coal Mine Example," *The American Political Science Review* 74(3): 745–56.

Lloyd-Bostock, S. (1988). Legalism *and Discretion: a Study of Responses to Accidents and Accident Information Systems in the Occupational Safety and Health Administration, USA*, Oxford: Centre for Socio-Legal Studies.

Mayhew, C. and Quinlan, M. (1997). "Subcontracting and Occupational Health and Safety in the Residential Building Industry," *Industrial Relations Journal* 28(3): 192–205.

Mendeloff, J. and Gray, W.B. (2005). "Inside the Black Box: How do OSHA Inspections Lead to Reductions in Workplace Injuries?," *Law & Policy* 27(2): 219–37.

Nelkin, D. and Brown, M.S. (1984). *Workers at Risk: Voices from the Workplace*, Chicago: University of Chicago Press.

Petrick, J.A. and Rinefort, F.C. (1999). "Occupational Health and Safety in Russia and the Commonwealth of Independent States," *Business and Society Review* 104(4): 417–38.

Quinlan, M. (2007). "Organisational restructuring/downsizing, OHS regulation and worker health and wellbeing," *International Journal of Law and Psychiatry* 30(4–5): 385–99.

Rees, J. (1988). *Reforming the Workplace: a Study of Self-Regulation in Occupational Safety*, Philadelphia: University of Pennsylvania Press.

Robens Report (1972). *Safety and Health at Work—Report of the Committee 1970–72*, A. Robens (Chairman), London: HMSO.

Robinson, A. and Smallman, C. (2006). "The Contemporary British Workplace: a Safer and Healthier Place?," *Work, Employment and Society* 20(1): 87–108.

Shover, N., Clelland, D.A., and Lynxwiler, J. (1986). *Enforcement or Negotiation: Constructing a Regulatory Bureaucracy*, Albany: State University of New York Press.

Smith, R.S. (1979). "The Impact of OSHA Inspections on Manufacturing Injury Rates," *Journal of Human Resources* 14(2): 145–70.

Sunstein, C.R. (2007). "Cost-Benefit Analysis Without Analyzing Costs or Benefits: Reasonable Accommodation, Balancing, and Stigmatic Harms," *University Chicago Law Review* 74: 1895–909.

Vickers, I., James, P., Smallbone, D., and Baldock, R. (2005). "Understanding Small Firm Responses to Regulation: the Case of Workplace Health and Safety," *Policy Studies* 26(2): 149–69.

Viscusi, W.K. (1979). "The Impact of Occupational Safety and Health Regulation," *The Bell Journal of Economics* 10(1): 117–40.

Walters, D. and Gourlay, S. (1990). *Statutory Employee Involvement in Health and Safety at the Workplace: a Report of the Implementation and Effectiveness of the Safety Representatives and Safety Committees Regulations 1977*, London: HSE.

Walters, D., Dalton, A., and Gee, D. (1993). *Worker Representation on Health and Safety in Europe*, Brussels: European Trade Union Technical Bureau for Health and Safety.

Walters, V. and Haines, T. (1988). "Workers' Perceptions, Knowledge and Responses Regarding Occupational Health and Safety—a Report on a Canadian Study," *Social Science & Medicine* 27(11): 1189–96.

Weil, D. (1992). "Building Safety: the Role of Construction Unions in the Enforcement of OSHA," *Journal of Labor Research* 13(1): 121–32.

Wilson, G.K. (1986). "Legislating on Occupational Safety and Health: a Comparison of the British and American Experience," *European Journal of Political Research*, 14(3): 289–303.

Wilthagen, T. (1993). "Reflexive Rationality in the Regulation of Occupational Health and Safety," in R. Rogowski and T. Wilthagen (eds.), *Reflexive Labour Law*, Boston: Kluwer-Nijhoff.

ENVIRONMENTAL
REGULATION

CARY COGLIANESE AND
CATHERINE COURCY

ENVIRONMENTAL regulation has grown vast in detail and scope over the past 30 years, addressing today a broad range of business operations and even certain household and individual behavior. Such rules vary widely in their pedigree, having been adopted by institutions at all levels of governance: international, national, sub-national, and even non-governmental. They have also grown highly varied in their form, ranging from technology to performance standards, and from market-based instruments to information disclosure requirements. The vast and varied collection of regulation aimed at reducing environmental harm and protecting public health has given empirical researchers excellent opportunities to study the relationship between law and society.

Environmental law's implications for both public health and the economy certainly make it substantively an important area for empirical scholarship. But even for researchers not particularly interested in the environment, the empirical study of environmental law provides a window into the role of law more generally in contemporary society. How do myriad social and political forces affect environmental law's design and implementation? How does environmental law in turn affect social behavior and conditions? At their core, the questions that have occupied the empirical study of environmental law are the same questions that motivate most empirical research on law. The emergence of the environment as a major object of government regulation in the 1960s and 1970s, and this field of regulation's extensive growth over the subsequent three decades, has established environmental law as a major area of research for anyone interested in understanding law and legal systems.

Empirical research on environmental law tracks four facets of the relationship between law and society. The first is the creation of new law, today a process involving primarily legislatures and regulatory agencies. An important goal of the empirical study of environmental law has been to explain how the creation of new law by these governmental bodies is affected by various interests, institutions, and procedural arrangements. Once laws are created, the second step is to enforce them. Empirical researchers have therefore extensively studied the behavior of regulatory enforcers, identifying key factors affecting their practices. The creation of law and its subsequent enforcement both aim, in the third step, to induce behavioral change in the businesses and individuals targeted by environmental regulation. Researchers have assessed the responses of regulated industry to environmental law and its enforcement, identifying variables that explain businesses' choices to comply with the law—and even sometimes to take responsive actions that go beyond what is required by law. Finally, any changes in business behavior lead, if all goes according to the regulator's plan, to the fourth step: improvements in environmental and other conditions of the world. Researchers have therefore sought to evaluate empirically the impacts of environmental law and its enforcement on the environment and the economy.

The aim of this Chapter is to make the central themes and findings from the empirical study of environmental law more accessible to legal scholars and social scientists across all fields. The empirical study of environmental law reveals a complex and reciprocal interaction between law and the larger society within which it operates. Environmental law has not emerged from a vacuum, but instead reflects political struggles between competing interests and ideas. Its enforcement is also hardly automatic or uniform, but instead is affected by a variety of social factors. As with the creation and enforcement of law, the impact of environmental law on behavior, and ultimately both its intended and unintended impacts on the environment and the economy, can be quite complex. Environmental law and its enforcement can be significant factors affecting the behavior of the businesses and individuals it targets, but other factors matter as much as, if not sometimes more than, law itself. Environmental law, like most if not all law, exhibits a semi-autonomous character (Moore, 1973), not truly independent of society nor a force rigidly or exclusively controlling behavior. At the same time, as law is deployed to shape society and improve the environment, it is also shaped by, and at times limited by, other compelling forces within society.

I. The Making and Design of Environmental Law

The interactive relationship between law and society reveals itself first in the making of environmental law. Although a few laws affecting natural resources and the environment can be traced back centuries, the bulk of what constitutes environmental regulation in the developed world emerged only as recently as the 1960s and 1970s, around the time when a post-materialist public began to place special value on environmental protection and when the environment took its place alongside social movements for consumer protection and civil rights (Coglianese, 2001). Many environmental laws emerged as a direct response to public demand in the wake of media coverage of major, visible environmental catastrophes, such as rivers catching on fire, oil spills near scenic beaches, and the surfacing and leaking of hazardous waste drums in citizens' backyards (Coglianese, 2001).

The environmental movement's growth in the 1960s corresponded roughly with the emergence of scholarly interest in the role of regulated industry in policy-making. Rather than viewing environmental law and other forms of government regulation as merely a public-interested response to overall societal needs, scholars increasingly viewed the making of regulatory policy as a political choice affected by interest groups. In particular, political scientists and administrative law scholars have since that time tended to focus on the extent to which industry has influenced—or captured—the policy-making process in such a way that legislators and regulators, often acting in concert, do more to serve business interests than advance overall social objectives. The design of environmental laws, like other laws, does certainly reflect the outcome of struggle between affected and organized interests (Ackerman and Hassler, 1981). The prevalence of so-called vintage-differentiated regulations, for example, under which new pollution sources must generally meet more stringent environmental standards than existing sources, can be explained by the superior influence that existing businesses have in the policy process over new sources, which are often unknown at the time of a law's passage (Stavins, 2006). Such a "new source bias" in many environmental laws also reflects the interests existing businesses have to try to impose additional costs on new competitors.

Although business interests are well-represented in policy-making, and some features of environmental regulation reflect those interests, industry capture cannot entirely explain environmental law-making. The expansive scope and cost of environmental regulation that has arisen in the last half of the twentieth century clearly indicates that industry is not the only force affecting the development and shape of environmental law (Kamieniecki, 2006). Over the last several decades, the environmental movement has become institutionalized within the policy process, as well-organized environmental groups have gained political influence over the direction of environmental law (Coglianese, 2001). Although environmental groups are outnumbered, and usually outspent, by industry groups, one study of a sample of environmental rules promulgated by the Environmental Protection Agency, Forest Service, and the Fish and Wildlife Service in the United States found that final regulations neither frequently nor substantially reflected industry influence (Kamieniecki, 2006).

Other factors, in addition to environmental and industry group pressures, can affect the shape or stringency of environmental law. For instance, cultural differences may explain variation in environmental law across jurisdictions such as the United States and European countries. According to the conventional view, the U.S. was in the forefront in environmental regulation in the 1970s, with Europeans taking a much more precautionary approach to environmental risk in the 1980s and 1990s (Vogel, 2003). Today, both the United States and Europe adopt precautionary approaches to risk; however, the risks they focus on are decidedly different (Hammitt et al., 2005). For example, the United States tends to be more cautious in regulating the use of tobacco and alcohol than Europe, whereas Europe tends to have more precautionary regulations on food and agriculture than the U.S. (Hammit et al., 2005). These variations may simply reflect underlying differences in the cultures of risk in the U.S. and Europe (Jasanoff, 1986).

Variation in environmental law may also be explained by differences in the institutional structures of government. One such structure is federalism, or the division of responsibility and authority between a central law maker and subsidiary governmental units. For example, although the national government has adopted most of the major environmental statutes in the U.S., much responsibility for implementing these laws rests with the states. In some areas of environmental law, states even retain the authority to adopt standards that differ from those adopted by the federal government. The discretion and responsibility afforded to states has provided scholars an opportunity to investigate the effects of inter-jurisdictional competition on environmental law.

The race-to-the-bottom theory predicts that inter-jurisdictional competition for business will lead to lenient environmental standards, as each state tries to lower costs for industrial operations so as to entice businesses to locate in their particular jurisdiction. It is not difficult to find examples of such race-to-the-bottom effects in environmental law. Strikingly, though, empirical research has shown that states do not always compete by lowering the stringency of their environmental standards. A study of state implementation of the Clean Air Act (CAA) in the United States indicated that a significant number of states (29%) had set stricter ambient air quality standards than the U.S. Environmental Protection Agency (EPA) required, and 68% of states had ambient air quality monitoring programs somewhat more extensive than the EPA required (Potoski and Woods, 2001). A contrasting phenomenon—what some have even considered a "race to the top"—has been identified as sometimes occurring on a global scale, with some countries leading others in terms of the stringency of their environmental regulations (Vogel, 1995). It would appear that public demand for environmental protection—that is, "green politics"—helps explain why some states have chosen to enact tighter standards, even though the pressures of regulatory competition also exist and can affect environmental law.

Different patterns of business-government relations that exist across jurisdictions might also affect the shape and stringency of environmental law. For example, researchers have considered whether more pluralist policy-making—such as the open, adversarial process characteristic of policy-making in the U.S.—leads to systematically different outcomes compared to corporatist policy-making—such as the formal, cooperative involvement of business organizations characteristic of policy-making in some European countries. Scruggs (2001) analyzed variation across OECD nations and suggested that the more corporatist the structure of policy-making, the more stringent were the resulting environmental laws, at least as measured by the proxy of pollution emissions. On the other hand, a more recent and rigorous econometric analysis of pollution levels across the same jurisdictions has shown that the presence of green and left-wing political parties has the most significant impact on environmental performance across jurisdictions, not the corporatist structure of policy-making (Neumayer, 2003).

In addition to broad-scale structural and political variations across jurisdictions, differences in more discrete procedures may affect environmental law, such as procedures authorizing courts to review new rules or requiring economic analysis of new regulations (Morgenstern, 1997). More recent experiments with consensus-based procedures, such as negotiated rule-making, have been suggested as a means of circumventing the adversarialism thought to afflict contemporary environmental policy-making, especially in the U.S. However, empirical research shows these alternative consensual procedures fail to meet their designers' objectives for more timely and less conflictual decision-making (Coglianese, 1997).

In recent decades, political economists have called attention to the ways in which legislators and presidents can impose procedures on regulatory agencies in a strategic attempt to influence their policies (McCubbins et al., 1987). Procedural requirements that agencies provide notice and an opportunity for interest groups to participate in the development of new regulations by filing comments can help interest groups mobilize to bring pressure on regulators. Requirements for cost-benefit and other types of analysis seek to shape agency decisions by taking certain values into account. Of course, it is also possible that agencies themselves may use procedures strategically. For example, the U.S. EPA's history of regulating diesel engine emissions suggests that the agency has used different types of procedures—traditional rule-making, negotiated rule-making, and litigation—to help the agency advance its own policy positions and avoid certain pressures from Congress or the president (Morriss et al., 2005).

Going forward, a central research challenge will be to understand better the relative impact of pressures from legislators, presidents, interest groups, and the public on the making of environmental law. This challenge is difficult in part because of the complex interaction of pressures and procedures that can potentially come into play in shaping legal decision-making. To gain traction, researchers have often needed to simplify the range of factors considered, and as a result there have been (understandably) too few studies that have assessed the full, integrated suite of pressures that confront government agency and other policy institutions.

Another way researchers have tried to gain traction has been to simplify the dependent variable—policy decisions—by deploying proxies or indices for just the *stringency* of environmental laws. Of course, environmental laws can vary in ways other than their stringency; they can also vary in terms of their design, for example. In principle, different kinds of environmental policies can be equally "stringent" in the sense that they would result in the same level of pollution reduction, but they still vary in that some set emissions limits, others mandate the adoption of specific control technologies, and still others deploy systems of tradable emissions permits.

In recent decades, environmental policy-makers (as well as empirical researchers) have taken a considerable interest in such differences in regulatory design. Much attention has been paid to alternatives to so-called command-and-control measures; some of these innovative alternatives are market-based instruments (emissions trading or taxes) (Stavins, 1998), environmental management systems (EMSs) (Bennear, 2007), voluntary environmental programs (VEPs) (Borck and Coglianese, 2009), and information disclosure requirements such as those required under the U.S. Toxics Release Inventory (TRI) program (Hamilton, 2005). However, this research has largely addressed the policy impacts these different tools have, rather than examining what factors might explain the initial regulatory tool choice.

Economists have long urged the adoption of market-based environmental regulation for its flexibility and efficiency, but policy-makers have generally been resistant to such a regulatory approach. What explains policy-makers' choice of regulatory instrument type? With respect to market-based regulation, factors other than just overall social welfare would appear to matter. For example, environmental groups have typically opposed market-based regulation, both out of concern that it may be harder to enforce and that it allegedly allows firms to sell "rights to pollute" (Keohane et al., 1998). Although businesses might be expected to favor market-based regulation's greater flexibility and cost reduction, they have actually been rather lukewarm. Market-based regulation generally requires firms to pay for all the pollution they emit, whereas conventional emissions limits allow firms to pollute for free below the limit. In addition, some firms worry that flexible forms of regulation will comparatively advantage competitors. For their part, legislators have been sensitive to regional disparities in the distribution of the costs and benefits of flexible regulation, leading to political opposition in regions likely to fare badly. For these reasons, the political forces that shape the design of environmental law still tend to support more conventional forms of regulation (Keohane et al., 1998). Beyond market-based regulatory instruments, though, the challenge remains to explain better what accounts not only for the stringency of environmental law but also its design elements, whether in the form of traditional regulatory tools or other innovative alternatives.

II. ENVIRONMENTAL LAW ENFORCEMENT

No matter what form environmental law takes, its impact will depend in no small part on how it is enforced. Research on the behavior of the agencies and individuals who enforce environmental laws has traditionally contrasted two types of enforcement strategies: legalistic (sanctioning or punitive) versus cooperative (compliance assistance) (Hawkins, 1984). Under legalistic enforcement, violations of the law deserve punishment, either for their own sake or as a means of deterring future violations either by the non-complying entity or other entities. By contrast, cooperative enforcement emphasizes supportive interaction between regulators and regulated entities that seeks to prevent and remediate harms. If the legalistic enforcer is punitive, the cooperative enforcer is educative and assistive in problem-solving.

Actual environmental enforcement behavior tends to fall along a spectrum between these two poles. The main challenge for empirical research on environmental enforcement has been to explain why certain regulators tend toward one end of the spectrum rather than the other. Regulators in the U.S., for example, have generally been regarded as more frequently using legalistic enforcement when compared with regulators in other economically advanced countries (Verweij, 2000). Even within individual countries, though, enforcement style may vary, both across different enforcement agencies and even between individual inspectors in the same agencies (May and Winter, 1999).

As with empirical research on the making of environmental law, social scientists have studied various political and structural factors to explain variation in enforcement strategies. For example, where political culture is characterized as more mistrustful of government, as in the U.S., legalistic enforcement may emerge as political overseers attempt to control the discretion of enforcement agencies. In such a political climate, regulators may seek to insulate themselves from criticism by generating records of frequent citations and fines.

Political ideology may also affect enforcement styles. In the U.S., EPA enforcement under the Clean Water Act (CWA) from 1974–1987 varied according to which political party controlled the agency, with industry-friendly administrations not surprisingly engaging in lower levels of enforcement activity (Ringquist, 1995). At the state level, there is also some indication that enforcement stringency correlates with partisan control of government (Atlas, 2007). Pressure from legislatures can also influence enforcement outcomes through appropriations and oversight (Wood and Waterman, 1991). This is not to say, of course, that agencies' enforcement efforts are completely subject to the control of the legislature or elected executives, but such overseers' influence can be significant.

The federal structure of environmental law in the United States, where enforcement responsibilities are shared by both states and the national government, has enabled researchers to study variation in agency enforcement style across jurisdictions. Some evidence suggests that environmental enforcement is subject to race-to-the-bottom effects. In at least one study, enforcement of hazardous waste regulations by states resulted in substantially lower administrative penalties, *ceteris* paribus, than did enforcement by the federal EPA (Atlas, 2007). On the other hand, in a study of enforcement stringency under three environmental statutes, Konisky (2007) finds that states strategically respond to the enforcement behavior of the states with whom they are in economic competition, adjusting enforcement efforts in response to other states' changes in enforcement actions. However, this strategic behavior does not align with the simplistic race-to-the-bottom hypothesis. Rather, states' enforcement behaviors are associated with multiple patterns, including sometimes a race-to-the-top as states attempt to meet a political demand for environmental quality.

Regulators may also choose an enforcement style based on the individualized characteristics of the entity they are inspecting or targeting. Larger firms with professional compliance staffs may induce a more cooperative approach from regulators; on the other hand, a more legalistic approach may be taken with smaller firms due to their lower visibility (Shover et al., 1984). This variation reflects the theory that a cooperative approach is more warranted when dealing with firms that have the capacity to comply with environmental laws and that face other social pressures to comply (Ayres and Braithwaite, 1992). Smaller, less visible firms that face little to no risk of public condemnation for non-compliance may require stronger, more legalistic enforcement responses by government.

Firms that show a willingness to cooperate or even a tendency to exceed the requirements of the law, such as by participating in voluntary environmental programs, have been shown to attract more relaxed enforcement (Sam and Innes, 2008). In some industries, firms that have established a strong environmental compliance record or report lower emissions in accordance with self-reporting requirements tend to receive less enforcement attention (Decker, 2005). This may reflect a tendency by regulators to address the largest-risk polluters (that is, those with the most potential for creating environmental or public health harm), rather than the most likely polluters (that is, those firms most likely to emit any pollution, regardless of potential harm) (ibid).

In addition to political factors and firm-specific characteristics, a variety of other factors may influence enforcement stringency and style. As noted, political culture in some countries may engender a more cooperative style of enforcement from the regulators (May and Winter, 1999). Likewise, environmental values within a regulatory agency can play a role in determining the kind and level of enforcement (Ringquist, 1995). Some studies suggest that agency sensitivity to surrounding economic and employment conditions may impact enforcement activity (Decker, 2005), although other research indicates that local economies have no impact on agency enforcement discretion (Atlas, 2007). It is possible, too, that enforcement officials can become "captured" by industries, whether through repeated interaction or economic incentives offered by industry, and in some cases such capture may explain more cooperative enforcement (May and Winter, 1999).

The variety of influences on enforcement decisions suggests a complex model for regulator choice. Rather than assuming that simply passing an environmental law will ensure its robust implementation, empirical studies of environmental enforcement demonstrate that environmental law, in practice, is also a function of the stringency and style of enforcement behavior. This behavior may respond to pressures from the entities involved in making the environmental law in the first place, but as these overseers change, so too can enforcement change. Environmental law in action can be a function of the larger political culture and the ideology of agency heads and their overseers, as well as characteristics and behavior of the regulated firms themselves.

Some prescriptive theorists view the empirical evidence of varied enforcement styles as justification for adopting flexible and dynamic enforcement strategies. They suggest that enforcement officials should try cooperative techniques first, but back up such techniques with the occasional use of more legalistic measures to provide greater deterrent incentives (Ayres and Braithwaite, 1992). Any prescriptions for what enforcement approach to employ—legalistic, cooperative, or some hybrid—ultimately depend for their success on an understanding of the interaction between enforcement behavior and the behavior of the targets of regulation.

III. Compliance and Beyond-Compliance Behavior

Environmental law responds to individual and organizational behavior that results in harm to other people or the environment—that is, to the creation of spillover

effects, or what economists call negative externalities. In the absence of environmental law, the costs of these harms are not imposed on those who create them, so
polluters have little incentive to incur the additional costs required to prevent or
control their pollution. Environmental law seeks to create such incentives—usually
in the form of the threat of a sanction—so that it is in polluters' interests to incur
the costs of pollution reduction. Organizations or individuals will incur these costs
when they confront even greater expected penalties for not incurring them. The
expected penalties for not complying with environmental laws are the product of
the probability of getting caught and the amount of the penalties that would be
imposed.

This rational model of deterrence provides the traditional theoretical basis for
regulatory enforcement. By inspecting and sanctioning firms, regulators seek to
deter future violations. Such deterrence can be specific to the individuals or businesses found to be in violation, but it can also be general when other individuals or
businesses perceive a credible enforcement threat, even if no specific enforcement
action is taken against them. Increased enforcement may not only encourage compliance with the law but also may induce businesses to take environmentally responsible actions that are not even required by the law, such as implementing internal
environmental management systems (Gunningham et al., 2003).

Yet enforcement activity by regulators is not the only factor affecting compliance with environmental standards. The characteristics of businesses themselves
can affect their compliance and environmental performance. For example, the size
and age of a facility might well correlate with compliance. Interestingly, although
older facilities have less advanced pollution technology, they do not appear systematically to exhibit worse environmental performance (measured by emissions)
than newer plants (Shadbegian and Gray, 2006). In some industries the amount
of resources spent on pollution abatement-technology actually correlates negatively with environmental performance, though this may simply be because facilities that pollute more to begin with need to spend more on pollution abatement
(ibid).

The values held by a company's managers seem to affect their facilities' compliance. What Gunningham et al. (2003) call a company's "environmental management
style" has been found to correlate with compliance and environmental performance. Firms' management styles can range, on one end, from that of "environmental
laggards," which are the least committed to environmental compliance, to "true
believers" on the other end, which are committed both to regulatory compliance
and to meeting the beyond-compliance demands of environmental activists and
regulators. Managers' commitment to the environment surely helps explain firms'
behavior, and when firms act on that commitment by adopting environmental management systems, this too correlates with at least modest improvements in regulatory compliance (Prakash and Potoski, 2006).

Regulatory compliance and environmental performance have also been linked with social pressures. Businesses face a "social license"—that is, social and political pressure both locally and on a larger scale—that motivates firms to comply with, or even exceed, environmental standards (Gunningham et al., 2003). For example, despite fewer inspections and less legalistic enforcement, Japanese companies exhibit better compliance with waste disposal regulations than do U.S. companies, arguably due to greater social pressures (Aoki and Cioffi, 1999).

Increasingly, researchers and regulators have taken great interest in why some firms do more than merely comply with regulations and take positive environmental steps on a "voluntary" basis. Of course, such beyond-compliance behavior may simply reflect a desire to ensure full compliance with the sometimes-complex standards imposed by law. Firms that want to protect themselves from regulatory sanctions may go beyond compliance to create a margin of safety to assure good compliance. They may also take actions, such as implementing an environmental management systems, that both help ensure compliance and yield additional environmental dividends (Johnstone and Labonne, 2009). Thus, merely wanting to comply well with existing regulations may induce firms to adopt beyond-compliance behavior.

Community and other social pressures also encourage some companies to go beyond compliance. A company's "social license" can be enforced by community and environmental groups, who wield not only social pressure backed up by potential economic threats, such as boycotts, but also legal pressure though citizen suits, for instance (Gunningham et al., 2003). Not surprisingly, the most visible polluters (the largest and worst) have responded with the most positive environmental improvements (Cohen and Konar, 2000). Of course, sometimes firms might attempt to appeal to, and appease, social pressures by participating in voluntary environmental programs or engaging in environmental advertising without actually making any improvements in their environmental performance or compliance. For example, evidence of such "greenwashing" was suggested in electric utilities' participation in a U.S. Department of Energy voluntary greenhouse gas registry, which allowed utilities to tout environmental success but not disclose their overall environmental performance, which apparently did not change at all (Lyon and Kim, 2006).

Although companies face social pressures to go beyond compliance with environmental standards, they also face economic pressures that constrain the extent to which they will invest in voluntary environmental action (Gunningham et al., 2003). Firms with more limited financial capacity to pay for improved environmental performance simply are less able to reduce their emissions as much as firms with higher cash flows (Cohen and Konar, 2000).

It is clear that multiple factors explain business behavior. Environmental regulations and their enforcement are among these factors. But social and economic

pressures also affect business behavior. Although empirical research has so far succeeded in identifying these varied pressures that bear on compliance and beyond-
compliance behavior, the challenge in the future will be to explain better how these
multiple factors interact with each other. Building improved models that take all
these factors into account will be needed in particular to understand better the precise role that law plays in affecting environmental behavior.

Researchers also know relatively little about how the design of environmental
law affects behavior: whether, for instance, market-based instruments induce better
compliance than more traditional regulatory tools. The growing complexity of environmental regulation needs more empirical attention as well. The law's complexity sometimes reflects a desire by regulators to shape behavior more precisely, but
ultimately that complexity may dampen the behavioral impact of law, if it grows ever
harder for individuals within companies and environmental agencies to understand
what the law requires.

IV. The Impact of Environmental Law

The behavioral impact of environmental law can be studied both for its own sake
as well as for insight into the general relationship between law and behavior. But
any behavioral change induced by environmental law also has implications for
environmental and economic conditions in the world at large. Empirical research
has therefore examined the causal connection between environmental law and
changes in environmental outcomes and economic costs. Ultimately, this connection should matter greatly to anyone interested in improving the design of environmental law and its enforcement.

As already suggested in the previous section, environmental law can affect
the behavior and performance of individual business operations (Gunningham
et al., 2003; Cohen and Konar, 2000). Do these individual effects result in aggregate improvements in overall environmental conditions? Although it is sometimes
assumed that environmental law must have had significant aggregate effects because
environmental conditions have generally improved dramatically in developed
countries following the introduction of extensive environmental laws (Davies and
Mazurek, 1998), such an overarching conclusion can only be tentative until alternative explanations are ruled out. If the passage of environmental laws stems from
broad changes in social expectations in developed countries, perhaps such changed
social norms—filtered through to the professionals who manage businesses—are
also a root cause of some or all of the observed improvements in the environment.

It is also plausible that declining pollution levels in developed countries stem from other factors, such as a shift in some countries' economies toward services, and away from inherently greater-polluting manufacturing due to the substantially lower costs of manufacturing labor in overseas countries.

Mindful of these kinds of empirical possibilities, researchers have attempted to assess the effects of environmental laws on the environment. To do so, they have sought to estimate the counterfactual—that is, what pollution levels or other environmental outcomes would have existed in the absence of environmental law—by analyzing either cross-sectional or longitudinal variation in measurable environmental conditions. Cross-sectional variation can be exploited when jurisdictions have different levels of regulatory stringency but are otherwise similar, or when other differences can be controlled for statistically. If jurisdictions with greater legal stringency experience lower levels of pollution, then all other things being equal it is likely the law explains the difference. When such cross-jurisdictional variation is absent, longitudinal variation can be used to draw inferences about the effects of environmental law by comparing outcomes before and after the implementation of a new environmental law. Of course, one problem with longitudinal analysis is that other factors occurring around the same time may potentially account for any observed changes. A better approach is to combine both cross-sectional and longitudinal variation through differences-in-differences estimation strategies which allow the researcher to compare, systematically, trends in environmental performance across different jurisdictions (Coglianese and Bennear, 2005).

When researchers have confronted the empirical challenges of evaluating environmental law's impact, their results have created a somewhat mixed picture. To be sure, law can foster improvements in environmental conditions, but not as often or dramatically as some might expect. Nor do these environmental improvements necessarily always correspond with tangible improvements in public health, which are frequently the underlying justifications for environmental regulation. For example, the U.S. Clean Air Act's core regulations imposed on local counties having the dirtiest air ("non-attainment" regions) have been found to be associated with a decline in total suspended particles but not with any corresponding reduction in adult or elderly mortality (Chay et al., 2003). Although sulfur dioxide air pollution has declined 80% in the U.S. over the past 30 years, the Clean Air Act's non-attainment regulations have apparently played only a minor role in that reduction (Greenstone, 2004). On the other hand, simulation results have suggested that the 1970 Clean Air Act reduced overall levels of certain types of air pollutants by 46% compared to what they would have been in the absence of the law, in large part because the law spurred long-term innovations in abatement technology (McKitrick, 2007).

Much less research exists on the impact of different enforcement styles on environmental conditions. A study comparing industrial emissions into the Rhine River in Germany and the Great Lakes basin in the United States suggests that German officials' more cooperative enforcement style resulted in greater reductions of toxic discharges than did the more stringent enforcement applied in the Great Lakes region (Verweij, 2000). Apparently, the cooperative enforcement style in the Rhine region helped foster a series of key voluntary agreements that have helped protect water quality. On the other hand, another study examining water quality improvements on Boston's Charles River in the wake of a cooperative management strategy by the regional office of the U.S. EPA suggests the opposite conclusion: namely that legalistic enforcement actions—and not cooperative efforts—were largely responsible for dramatic improvements to water quality (Ray and Segerson, 2006).

Beyond traditional forms of environmental regulation and legalistic modes of its enforcement, social scientists have investigated the effectiveness of newer, alternative regulatory tools. As with their more conventional counterparts, these new tools show some signs of being able to produce changes in environmental conditions—but at times their effects have been only modest. In the few cases when they have been used, such as the phasing out of lead in gasoline and the reduction of sulfur dioxide emissions from coal-powered utility plants, market-based instruments have successfully contributed to meeting pollution-reduction targets (Stavins, 1998; Hahn and Hester, 1989). State regulations mandating that companies develop pollution prevention plans have been associated with a 30% decline in toxic emissions, but such declines only appear to last for a limited period after the adoption of new regulations (Bennear, 2007). The information disclosure requirements of the U.S. Toxics Release Inventory have been hailed as remarkably effective alternatives to traditional regulation because a substantial decline in reported toxic emissions has followed their adoption (Fung and O'Rourke, 2000); however, because of measurement issues and possible alternative explanations (such as a general shift in the industrial base of the economy), it is far from clear how much (if any) of the reported decline in toxics can be said to have been caused by information disclosure regulation (Bennear, 2008; Hamilton, 2005). Similarly, voluntary environmental programs that seek to recognize and reward companies that undertake environmentally responsible actions have sometimes showed signs of improving environmental outcomes—but even in the best cases the effects have been quite small in substantive terms: reductions in the order of only a few percentage points (Borck and Coglianese, 2009).

The full impact of environmental law—whether traditional or innovative—encompasses more than just its effect on the environment. Its effect on the economy has also been a perennial concern. In the United States, for example, the costs of complying with environmental regulations quadrupled in the first two decades of the modern environmental era, to a point where the total compliance costs of U.S. environmental regulations exceed $100 billion per year (Jaffe et al., 1995). These costs have motivated interest in market-based and other innovative forms of regulation, as some of these alternatives have been shown to meet environmental goals at lower cost (Stavins, 1998). In addition, a considerable amount of research effort has been devoted to the effects of environmental regulation on economic competitiveness and jobs. The conventional view has been that the costs associated with environmental regulation harm industrial competitiveness, causing manufacturing operations—and their corresponding jobs—to flee to jurisdictions with less stringent environmental regulation. An alternative theory holds precisely the opposite, namely that environmental regulation is "win-win" in that stringent environmental regulation actually induces firms to become more efficient and innovative, and hence more competitive (Porter and Van der Linde, 1995).

The actual impact of environmental law appears to be somewhere between these two extreme views. Much of the cost of environmental regulation is real, in the sense that firms do not reap sufficient private gains to make them justified, in the absence of legal or social pressures (Palmer et al., 1995). But although in the aggregate these costs seem large, they do not appear to be as significant for the competitiveness of individual firms as do other factors of production, such as labor costs or other, non-environmental capital expenses. As a result, the effects of environmental law on competitiveness seem to be remarkably muted. To be sure, some research does show some effect on jobs. The designation of a U.S. county as in non-attainment of Clean Air Act standards does correspond with lost jobs, industrial flight, and diminished tax revenues (Greenstone, 2002), but an analysis of the impacts of environmental regulation in the UK finds no trade-off between jobs and the environment (Cole and Elliott, 2007). Overall, the weight of the evidence appears to be that environmental regulations have at most a small effect on economic competitiveness (Jaffe et al., 1995). Environmental law has almost certainly not been a major factor in explaining the shift of manufacturing jobs to the developing world, as the regulatory costs of operating in the developed world, however substantial, presumably pale in comparison with labor costs.

There remains much to be learned about the effects of environmental law. Empirical legal studies have so far subjected these ultimate effects to less extensive scrutiny than the making and enforcement of environmental law. For one thing, despite the prevalence of environmental regulation, there is comparatively little *ex post* assessment of the impacts of these rules. Admittedly, the research challenges can be daunting, as regulations are seldom established with empirical evaluation in mind, and the possibilities for confounding effects are great. Still, without more empirical research, future policy-making will remain a product of trial and error, with little systematic learning from policy choices made in the past.

More research is needed that specifically compares the environmental and economic impacts of different policy choices. Researchers have tended to view different types of regulatory instruments or enforcement strategies in isolation from each other. Remarkably little work exists that systematically compares the outcomes of conventional forms of regulation with those of more innovative forms, or the outcomes of legalistic enforcement with those of cooperative enforcement, controling for other variables affecting outcomes. In addition, much too little research has addressed the connection between compliance behavior and environmental performance—often the two are treated as synonymous, with performance measures treated as proxies for compliance, or compliance treated as a proxy for performance. It is important to distinguish the two concepts. After all, many environmental requirements simply mandate various reporting and administrative actions, and it is far from clear that being in violation of these requirements would *necessarily* represent poor environmental performance. Yet researchers have sometimes touted the environmental benefits of initiatives that may well simply induce greater "paperwork" compliance than substantive environmental improvements.

Likewise, not all substantive improvements in environmental performance are equally valuable. Much research investigating the effects of environmental law has relied on data on emissions, particularly toxic emissions reported under the U.S. Toxics Release Inventory (TRI). Yet not all TRI chemicals pose the same level of risk. If environmental law is supposed to improve public health, then social science researchers would do well to use performance measures that take differences in health risks into account. Although occasional studies have weighted emissions by their risk, the development of more meaningful measures of environmental performance remains a challenge to overcome in seeking to advance our understanding of the impact of environmental law.

V. Conclusion

Empirical analysis of environmental law promises to help decision-makers identify ways to improve regulation, so as to better align laws with their stated goals, but it can also help advance scientific understanding of law's role in society more generally. Empirical research on environmental regulation teaches that law operates in complex, and at times counterintuitive, ways within contemporary society. Although regulation had at one time been thought to be the handmaiden of industry, empirical study teaches that the era of regulatory capture is over—or at least that the phenomenon is much more complicated than once thought. The vast expansion of environmental law over the past 30 years, with its corresponding imposition of economic costs, has occurred even in the face of steady, organized industry objection, undoubtedly because of larger changes in society such as shifting norms, changing public demand, and an increasingly institutionalized environmental movement.

The enforcement of environmental regulations can be framed as a choice between cooperation and legalism, though enforcement practice usually lies between these two extremes. At the same time as enforcement personnel are seeking to change society by implementing environmental laws, their practices are themselves responsive to social and political pressures. Businesses' responses to regulation are also affected by a myriad of factors beyond law, including social and economic pressures as well as firms' own management styles. What emerges from empirical research is a push-pull relationship between environmental law and social realities, a relationship that seems consistent with what we know about the overall effects of environmental law. Regulations certainly have induced real changes in the environment and in business operations, but law has also not explained nearly as much of the positive and negative outcomes often attributed to it. Environmental law has not been as essential to achieving pollution reductions as its proponents would suggest, nor have its significant costs doomed industry nearly as much as its opponents have portended.

Untangling more clearly the push and pull of environmental law in society will require more research. We have noted ways that, going forward, researchers could better illuminate how choices in making and enforcing environmental law affect both business behavior and ultimately environmental and economic conditions. In an admirable effort to gain empirical leverage and isolate causal effects, scholars have targeted different stages in the relationship between environmental regulation—its making, enforcement, and compliance—and environmental and social outcomes. We know much less about how these different stages interact. For example, can a cooperatively enforced "command and control" regime be as cost-effective as a legalistically enforced market-based regulatory regime? Do firms comply better with information disclosure regulations than with performance standards, assuming one can control for all other factors affecting compliance? If firms face both legal and social pressures to act responsibly, how does the existence of the law influence the genesis, longevity, and force of the social pressures?

Empirical researchers have yet to give serious attention to such integrative questions. Existing research does show, though, that these are important questions to consider. Just as the environment itself is a complicated web of natural relationships, environmental law and society are themselves interwoven in a complex dynamic. To advance the understanding of law in society, as well as to inform improvements in legal design and practice, empirical analysts in the future should strive to piece together the various stages of environmental law, discovering more about how law and other factors in society interact along the way.

REFERENCES

Ackerman, B. and Hassler, W.T. (1981). *Clean Coal/Dirty Air: Or How the Clean Air Act Became a Multibillion-Dollar Bail-Out for High-Sulfur Coal Producers and What Should be Done About It*, New Haven: Yale University Press.

Aoki, K. and Cioffi, J. (1999). "Poles Apart: Industrial Waste Management Regulation and Enforcement in the United States and Japan," *Law and Policy* 21: 213–45.

Atlas, M. (2007). "Enforcement Principles and Environmental Agencies: Principal-Agent Relationships in a Delegated Environmental Program," *Law and Society Review* 41: 939–80.

Ayres, I. and Braithwaite, J. (1992). *Responsive Regulation*, New York: Oxford University Press.

Bennear, L. (2007). "Are Management-Based Regulations Effective? Evidence from State Pollution Prevention Programs," *Journal of Policy Analysis and Management* 26: 327–48.

Bennear, L. (2008). "What Do We Really Know: The Effect of Reporting Thresholds on Inference Using Environmental Right-to-Know Data," *Regulation & Governance* 2: 293–315.

Borck, J. and Coglianese, C. (2009). "Voluntary Environmental Programs: Assessing their Effectiveness," *Annual Review of Political Science* 34: 14.1–14.20.

Chay, K., Dobkin, C., and Greenstone, M. (2003). "The Clean Air Act of 1970 and Adult Mortality," *Journal of Risk and Uncertainty* 27: 279–300.

Coglianese, C. (1997). "Assessing Consensus: The Promise and Performance of Negotiated Rulemaking," *Duke Law Journal* 46: 1255–349.

Coglianese, C. (2001). "Social Movements, Law, and Society: The Institutionalization of the Environmental Movement," *University of Pennsylvania Law Review* 150: 85–118.

Coglianese, C. and Bennear, L.S. (2005). "Program Evaluation of Environmental Policies: Toward Evidence-Based Decision Making," in National Research Council, *Social and Behavioral Science Research Priorities for Environmental Decision Making*, Washington, DC: National Academies Press.

Cohen, M. and Konar, S. (2000). "Why Do Firms Pollute (and Reduce) Toxic Emissions?," available at <http://ssrn.com/abstract=922491>.

Cole, M. and Elliott, R. (2007). "Do Environmental Regulations Cost Jobs? An Industry-Level Analysis of the UK," *The B.E. Journal of Economic Analysis and Policy* 7: 1–25.

Davies, J. and Mazurek, J. (1998). *Pollution Control in the United States: Evaluating the System*, Washington, DC: Resources for the Future.

Decker, C. (2005). "Do Regulators Respond to Voluntary Pollution Control Efforts? A Count Data Analysis," *Contemporary Economic Policy* 23: 180–94.

Fung, A. and O'Rourke, D. (2000). "Reinventing Environmental Regulation from the Grassroots Up: Explaining and Expanding the Success of the Toxics Release Inventory," *Environmental Management* 25: 115–27.

Greenstone, M. (2002). "The Impacts of Environmental Regulation on Industrial Activity: Evidence from the 1970 and 1977 Clean Air Act Amendments and the Census of Manufacturers," *Journal of Political Economy* 110: 1175–219.

Greenstone, M. (2004). "Did the Clean Air Act Amendments Cause the Remarkable Decline in Sulfur Dioxide Concentrations?," *Journal of Environmental Economics and Management* 47: 585–611.

Gunningham, N., Kagan, R., and Thornton, D. (2003). *Shades of Green: Business, Regulation, and Environment*, Palo Alto, CA: Stanford University Press.

Hahn, R.W. and Hester, G.L. (1989). "Marketable Permits: Lessons for Theory and Practice," *Ecology Law Quarterly* 16: 361–406.

Hamilton, J. (2005). *Regulation Through Revelation: The Origin and Impacts of the Toxics Release Inventory Program*, New York: Cambridge University Press.

Hammitt, J., Wiener, J., Swedlow, B., Kall, D., and Zhou, Z. (2005). "Precautionary Regulation in Europe and the United States: A Quantitative Comparison," *Risk Analysis* 25: 1215–28.

Hawkins, K. (1984). *Environment and Enforcement: Regulation and the Social Definition of Pollution*, Oxford: Clarendon Press.

Jaffe, A.B., Peterson, S.R., Portney, P.R., and Stavins, R.N. (1995). "Environmental Regulation and the Competitiveness of U.S. Manufacturing: What Does the Evidence Tell Us?," *Journal of Economic Literature* 33: 132–63.

Jasanoff, S. (1986). *Risk Management and Political Culture: A Comparative Analysis of Science*, New York: Russell Sage Foundation.

Johnstone, N. and Labonne, J. (2009). "Why Do Manufacturing Facilities Introduce Environmental Management Systems? Improving and/or Signaling Performance," *Ecological Economics* 68: 719–30.

Kamieniecki, S. (2006). *Corporate America and Environmental Policy: How Often Does Business Get Its Way?*, Palo Alto, CA: Stanford University Press.

Keohane, N.O., Revesz, R.L., and Stavins, R.N. (1998). "The Choice of Regulatory Instruments in Environmental Policy," *Harvard Environmental Law Review* 22: 313.

Konisky, D. (2007). "Regulatory Competition and Environmental Enforcement: Is There a Race to the Bottom?," *American Journal of Political Science* 51: 853–72.

Lyon, T.P. and Kim, E.-H. (2006). "Greenhouse Gas Reductions or Greenwash?: The DOE's 1605b Program," (November), available at <http://ssrn.com/abstract=981730>.

May, P. and Winter, S. (1999). "Regulatory Enforcement and Compliance: Examining Danish Agro-Environmental Policy," *Journal of Policy Analysis and Management* 18: 625–51.

McCubbins, M.D., Noll, R.G., and Weingast, B.R. (1987). "Administrative Procedures as Instruments of Political Control," *Journal of Law, Economics and Organization* 3: 243–77.

McKitrick, R. (2007). "Why Did US Air Pollution Decline After 1970?," *Empirical Economics* 33: 491–513.

Moore, S.F. (1973). "Law and Social Change: The Semi-Autonomous Social Field as an Appropriate Subject of Study," *Law & Society Review* 7: 719–46.

Morgenstern, R. (ed.) (1997). *Economic Analyses at EPA: Assessing Regulatory Impact*, Washington, DC: Resources for the Future Press.

Morriss, A., Yandle, B., and Dorchak, A. (2005). "Choosing how to Regulate," *Harvard Environmental Law Review* 29: 179–250.

Neumayer, E. (2003). "Are Left-Wing Party Strength and Corporatism Good for the Environment? Evidence from Panel Analysis of Air Pollution in OECD Countries," *Ecological Economics* 45: 203–20.

Palmer, K., Oates, W., and Portney, P. (1995). "Tightening of Environmental Standards: The Benefit-Cost or the No-Cost Paradigm?," *Journal of Economic Perspectives* 9: 119–32.

Porter, M.E. and Van der Linde, C. (1995). "Green and Competitive: Ending the Stalemate," *Harvard Business Review* (September–October): 120–34.

Potoski, M. and Woods, N. (2001). "Designing State Clean Air Agencies: Administrative Procedures and Bureaucratic Autonomy," *Journal of Public Administration Research and Theory* 11: 203–22.

Prakash, A. and Potoski, M. (2006). *The Voluntary Environmentalists: Green Clubs, ISO 14001, and Voluntary Environmental Regulation*, Cambridge: Cambridge University Press.

Ray, T.K. and Segerson, K. (2006). "Clean Charles 2005 Initiative: Why the 'Success'?," in C. Coglianese and J. Nash (eds.), *Leveraging the Private Sector: Management-Based Strategies for Improving Environmental Performance*, Washington, DC: Resources for the Future Press.

Ringquist, E. (1995). "Political Control and Policy Impact in EPA's Office of Water Quality," *American Journal of Political Science* 39: 336–63.

Sam, A. and Innes, R. (2008). "Voluntary Pollution Reductions and the Enforcement of Environmental Law: An Empirical Study of the 33/50 Program," *Journal of Law and Economics* 51: 271–96.

Scruggs, L. (2001). "Is There Really a Link Between Neo-Corporatism and Environmental Performance? Updated Evidence and New Data for the 1980s and 1990s," *British Journal of Political Science* 31: 686–92.

Shadbegian, R. and Gray, W. (2006). "Assessing multi-dimensional performance: environmental and economic outcomes," *Journal of Productivity Analysis* 26: 213–34.

Shover, N., Lynxwiler, J., Groce, S., and Clelland, D. (1984). "Regional Variation in Regulatory Law Enforcement: The Surface Mining Control and Reclamation Act," in K. Hawkins and J.T. Thomas (eds), *Enforcing Regulation*, Boston, MA: Kluwer-Nijhoff.

Stavins, R.N. (1998). "What Can We Learn from the Grand Policy Experiment? Positive and Normative Lessons from SO2 Allowance Trading," *Journal of Economic Perspectives* 12: 69–88.

Stavins, R. (2006). "Vintage-Differentiated Environmental Regulation," *Stanford Environmental Law Journal* 25: 29–63.

Verweij, M. (2000). "Why is the River Rhine Cleaner than the Great Lakes (Despite Looser Regulation)," *Law and Society Review* 34: 1007–54.

Vogel, D. (1995). *Trading Up: Consumer and Environmental Regulation in a Global Economy*, Cambridge, MA: Harvard University Press.

Vogel, D. (2003). "The Hare and the Tortoise Revisited: The New Politics of Consumer and Environmental Regulation in Europe," *British Journal of Political Science* 33: 557–80.

Wood, D. and Waterman, R. (1991). "The Dynamics of Political Control of the Bureaucracy," *American Political Science Review* 85: 801.

20

ADMINISTRATIVE JUSTICE

SIMON HALLIDAY AND COLIN SCOTT[1]

I. INTRODUCTION

A key aspect of modern government is the delegation to ministers and agencies of power to make subordinate legal rules combined with the widespread conferment

[1] This Chapter draws in part on research funded by the Nuffield Foundation (Grant AJU:34879 – "A Conceptual Analysis of Administrative Justice and Feedback Mechanisms").

on ministers and public officials of discretionary powers to apply both primary and secondary legal rules. Administrative justice may be conceived as comprising the norms, processes, and institutions governing the exercise of such administrative powers. In many jurisdictions the norms are found in codifying instruments of one kind or another, though the common law principles of administrative law remain important in some jurisdictions. The processes range from rule-making and primary decision-making through to appeal against and review of decisions under a variety of institutional models.

The concept of administrative justice receives such varying emphasis in different jurisdictions that its value in underpinning comparative doctrinal inquiry has been questioned (Nehl, 2006: 24). For example, in the United States administrative justice is chiefly associated with the structuring of rule-making activities of regulatory agencies.[2] In Commonwealth countries, however, administrative justice is more frequently understood as relating to decision-making processes by the executive applying legal rules as part of delivery of services such as welfare. Civilian systems also tend to place greater emphasis in their administrative law on decisions affecting individuals than on more generalized rule-making. These differences in emphasis may partly be explained by explicit or implicit assumptions about the legitimacy of administrative discretion. In the United States anxieties about discretionary decision-making by unelected officials underpin a twofold response under which rules are favored over discretionary decision-making and the making of rules is constrained by extensive procedural requirements (Asimow, 1983).

Most legal systems have some mechanism for the judicial review[3] of administrative actions and, to some extent, the making of secondary legislation such as regulations.[4] However, a proliferation of alternative mechanisms of grievance-handling in many countries has generated a distinction between judicial review and these alternative mechanisms of administrative justice such as complaint to ombudsman offices and other grievance-handling agencies. Equally, a distinction can helpfully be drawn between decision processes ("decision-making"), whether rule-making or application of rules and discretion, on the one hand, and processes of grievance-handling, appeal, and review ("review"), on the other. Taken together these distinctions suggest two principal forms of decision-making involving the making and application of rules, and two principal forms of review: judicial and non-judicial.

---

[2] Somewhat by way of contrast, Nonet's study, *Administrative Justice* (1969), tracks the evolution of California's Industrial Accident Commission from an administrative agency with broad discretion to supervise the welfare of injured workers to a more passive tribunal adjudicating disputes between employers and employees.

[3] Statutory appeals to courts is included within our use of "judicial review."

[4] We do not refer here to the judicial review of primary legislation.

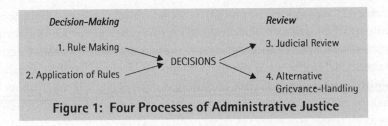

Figure 1: Four Processes of Administrative Justice

This division between decision-making and review is, of course, somewhat artificial, both ultimately being concerned with the exercise of administrative powers.[5] However, the division is useful as an initial way of organizing and mapping out the range of empirical research which falls under the banner of "administrative justice." More significantly, it helps us understand two discrete ways in which the notion of "administrative justice" is employed within the broad field. Empirical work which focuses on the application of law and policy in agencies interprets "administrative justice" as referring to the justice of the primary administrative process: what model(s) of justice is (are) implicit in agencies' administrative and rule-making operations? In contrast, empirical research which focuses on the machinery of redress and grievance-handling interprets "administrative justice" as referring to a subsystem of dispute resolution within the overall architecture of the legal system—on a parallel with criminal justice, or employment justice or family justice. In this work, the focus is on citizens seeking justice, after the event, for their plight as the subjects of the administrative process.

A. The Chapter's framework

Having made these initial clarifications and introductory points, we may now proceed to review the body of empirical legal research regarding administrative justice, offering a critique of existing work and suggesting some future directions for the field. The remainder of the Chapter is split into two main sections. In the first section, we explore empirical legal studies which fall on either side of the decision-making-and-review dividing line, before examining an example of scholarship which has attempted to link the two: research on the impact of dispute resolution and on-going administrative practices. We also highlight some limitations in existing impact research, focusing on the tendency to examine single dispute resolution mechanisms in isolation from others and the failure to examine the significance of oversight through regulation (as opposed to review) for administrative practices. In the second section, we suggest some future directions for empirical administrative

---

[5] Research that examines the "impact" of review mechanisms on ongoing decision-making straddles the divide rather well, for example.

justice research. We explore the potential of legal consciousness research for empirical administrative justice scholarship, and suggest new "territories" for administrative justice researchers: criminal justice processes and administrative activities of private agencies. Finally, we argue that a mapping of administrative justice institutions—both historically and cross-jurisdictionally—can tell us much about how the relationships between citizens and administrative agencies may shift across time and space.

II. Overview of Existing Administrative Justice Research

A. Administrative justice research on decision-making

Perhaps surprisingly, relative to empirical work falling within the "review" category, there has probably been less administrative justice research devoted to examining how decision-making takes place in government departments and administrative agencies and assessing the justice of these processes. This is surprising because administrative law is an important normative system focused, in part at least, on the justice of primary decision-making. One explanation for this omission is that legal researchers may find dispute resolution procedures more familiar, while researchers with the expertise to investigate behavior within agencies are likely to be less well equipped to identify and assess the role of administrative law in shaping processes. In this section we discuss research on rule-making before considering work on the application of rules and discretion.

1. *Making rules*

Though the detailed processes vary greatly, most legal systems make extensive provision for the delegation of secondary rule-making to government ministers and agencies. The United States is relatively unusual in the extent of delegation to agencies which originated in the evolution of the Interstate Commerce Commission (established in 1888) from an adjudicatory body to a monitor and enforcer of rules and then a maker of rules. The extent of delegation to independent agencies was greatly increased during the New Deal period, raising serious concerns about the legitimacy of the rule-making process. One response was the establishment of uniform procedural rules in the Administrative Procedure Act 1948. Research on rule-making in the United States has tended to focus on the application of these procedures in independent agencies, frequently focusing on judicial supervision of the procedures rather than the processes themselves (Williams, 1974). A more recent emphasis has been on other normative requirements overlaid on administrative procedures, notably requirements to engage in cost-benefit analysis of new rules introduced by the Reagan administration in 1981 (Hahn et al., 1999). The primary focus of such research has been on economic efficiency rather than administrative justice.

The extent of delegation to non-departmental agencies within parliamentary systems of government has tended to be more limited than in the United States. The primary focus of delegated rule-making within these systems tends to reside with ministers and its exercise typically involves use of parliamentary procedures (Asimow, 1983). The involvement of elected politicians in such delegated rule-making in the UK, with the potential for parliamentary oversight, has muted legitimacy concerns around the practices notwithstanding the growth in importance of the 3,000, or so, statutory instruments made each year in key areas of policy-making. The only major empirical study of ministerial rule-making in the UK found that the processes were substantially detached from the general run of democratic politics and frequently involved civil servants using their dominant role in mediating "privatized conflicts" between narrowly drawn interest groups (Page, 2001). It is telling that Page's study is one of policy-making rather than administrative law, there being few justiciable rights to participate in the process.

The assignment of powers to independent regulatory agencies, which occurred in many European countries and elsewhere toward the end of the twentieth century, was shaped by a widespread preference for rule-making by legislatures and ministers with the result that most of these agencies acquired only limited rule-making powers, if any. Decision-making by administrative authorities, both ministers and agencies, is characterized by a greater degree of discretion and less formal adjudication and rule-making than in the United States (Asimow, 1983: 271). A major study of the limited agency powers over rule-making in the UK financial services sector focuses more on the meanings and instrumental properties of rule-making than on the administrative justice dimension (Black, 1997). In the absence of traditions of judicial supervision, studies of supranational regulatory rule-making at EU (e.g., Pollack, 2003) and international (e.g., Braithwaite and Drahos, 2000) levels have focused on the legitimacy of rule-making procedure from the perspective either of outcomes or political acceptability, rather than on the justice or justiciability of rule-making.

It is hardly surprising, then, that the bulk of empirical research on agency rule-making focuses on the United States. Key concerns of empirical research on rule-making have been to understand the effects of procedures on the effectiveness and legitimacy of the rules amidst concerns that the legalization of the process has ossified agency policy-making (Coglianese, 2002: 1113, 1125). Such concerns have informed the search for alternative and non-adversarial means of making administrative rules, such as the negotiated rule-making procedures developed in the 1980s (crystallized in the Negotiated Rulemaking Act 1990). Studies of the effects of these innovations have been criticized on methodological grounds concerning case selection and observer bias (Coglianese, 2002: 1133). Coglianese's investigations of negotiated rule-making in the EPA concluded that there was no evidence that the new processes were either quicker or less prone to litigation than the formalized rule-making processes which they supplemented (Coglianese, 2002: 1134–6). Furthermore, empirical research on the process undertaken by Langbein (2002) suggests that the less formal procedures facilitated a greater responsiveness in rule-making overall but favored participants with greater resources, resulting in greater inequalities than occur under the traditional process.

2. *Applying rules and discretion*

As noted above, there is considerable variation in the scope and nature of power to make decisions delegated to officials within ministries and agencies. While analysis of such decision-making often assumes that the subject of the decision is an individual, such as a welfare claimant, there is also a vast literature on tax and regulatory enforcement affecting businesses. This research is frequently concerned with efficiency in promoting compliance, but empirical research has shown that administrative justice requirements, for example fairness and avoidance of bias, have to be addressed in achieving legitimate outcomes (Parker, 2004).

A central issue in the literature is the nature and extent of discretion granted to officials and how that discretion is exercised. One empirically informed perspective suggests that discretion is endemic to decision-making, including the application of rules, and that any proper concept of administrative justice must treat all decision-making on this basis (Sainsbury, 1992: 296). If discretion is ubiquitous within public administration, this begs the question of what shapes the decision-making of public officials. Considerable emphasis in the empirical research has been placed on the way that organizational factors shape the cognitive dimension of decision-making—what is knowable and doable by front-line administrators. Some decision-makers work within heavily legalized environments in which reference to legal rules and principles might be routine, whereas others work from short-hand scripts, some explicit and others implicit, which embody a variety of ideas about how the administrators are to carry out their tasks. In a study of immigration officers, for example, Gilboy (1991) found that, although it is a regime of individuated decision-making, a range of explicit or implicit categorizations (high and low risk travelers, high risk nationalities, "dirty flights") were used to screen passengers for secondary inspections. Such routines may be considered operationally necessary in administrative settings characterized by high workloads and low resources, but clearly have the potential to breach certain legal principles of procedural fairness in individuated decision-making (Hertogh, 2010).

Such insights can be formalized in considering different models of administrative justice that are deployed within particular regimes and bureaucracies. Such was the focus of Mashaw's pathbreaking study of the public administration of disability benefits in the United States. Mashaw moved away from a conception of administrative justice based in legal concepts to define it as "the qualities of a decision process that provide arguments for the acceptability of its decisions" (1983: 24). Such a definition embraces the justiciable norms of fairness, impartiality, and legality, but could also include other values such as courtesy and promptness (lack of the latter frequently being capable of investigation by an ombudsman, but not by a court: see Adler, 2006). One of the key features of Mashaw's work, then, is a pluralistic understanding of what administrative justice, so defined, entails. Mashaw constructed a threefold typology of administrative justice by reviewing the body of literature which criticized the process for administering disability benefits. Each model of justice, he suggested, was attractive in its own right and could be reflected in real-life administrative practices. He termed his first model of administrative justice "professional treatment," which has at its heart the service of the client. The goal of the system is to meet the needs of the individual claimant. It is about matching available resources to claimants' needs through the medium of professional and clinical judgment. The second model was that of "moral judgment." This model connects with traditional notions of court-centered adjudication. Of course, the basic element of adversarial court proceedings, where two parties are pitched against each other, is not usually replicated in the context of administrative adjudication. However, the logic of this model of administrative justice is that, in certain respects, the claimant is nevertheless treated *as if* s/he is in dispute over a rights claim.[6] The administrative system views the claimant as someone who has come to claim a right, and revolves around giving the claimant a fair opportunity to participate fully in the process of adjudicating whether the right exists or is to be denied. The third model Mashaw termed "bureaucratic rationality" which is focused on efficiency—the values of accuracy (targeting benefits to those eligible under the program) and cost-effectiveness.

Mashaw's research has proved influential and has inspired subsequent empirical and theoretical work. In particular, Adler (2006) has built on Mashaw's analytical framework by suggesting additional models of justice[7] to reflect the overlaying of New Public Management doctrines on traditional public administration: "manage

[6] A nice illustration of this is offered in Popkin's discussion of decision-making in three U.S. disability programs (Popkin, 1977: 991), where a hearing examiner is quoted as saying that he wears three "hats"—one representing the claimant, one representing the agency, and the third hat being that of the decision-maker. By way of contrast, Sainsbury's (2008) interpretation of the "moral judgment" model is that it only applies to administrative settings where a public agency has to decide between competing claims of two or more citizens, such as planning decisions.

[7] Adler uses the language of "ideal types" in preference to "models."

rialism," "consumerism," and "the market."[8] Although we have merely touched on the theoretical dimension of this research, it is important to recognize that this is integral to empirical enquiry. Such typological frameworks generally offer a starting point for empirical research—a set of analytical tools which can be put to use in the exploration of empirical questions. Notably, Adler has applied his framework to the empirical study of a wide range of social policy sectors such as social security, special education, and prison management.[9] The development of the typology permits him, for example, to explore the impact of information technology (Adler and Henman, 2001) on administrative justice practices in ten jurisdictions.[10] Similarly, Mashaw's work has been applied by Sunkin and Pick (2001) to track shifts over time in the model of administrative justice being practiced by the UK's Independent Review Service of the Social Fund; by Jewell (2007)[11] to compare street-level welfare administration in the United States, Germany, and Sweden; and by Sainsbury to examine how the model of administrative justice at play in UK social welfare administration has been altered by the introduction of welfare to work policies (Sainsbury, 2008).

B. Administrative justice research focusing on review

Empirical legal scholarship has contributed much to our understanding of the various redress and grievance-handling mechanisms available to citizens, both individual and corporate, within the architecture of an overall administrative justice "system." This body of research is very extensive indeed, not least because much of it has been commissioned by public bodies and is directly policy-driven. Accordingly, the eclecticism of the settings and issues researched reflects something of the range of administrative justice institutions in operation. The work cannot adequately be summarized here. Some useful literature reviews, however, exist (e.g., Adler and Gulland, 2003; Partington et al., 2007),[12] and while this body of work is both vast and fragmented, it is possible to detect three broad concerns which have animated the empirical work.

1. Decisions about whether to use administrative justice mechanisms

First, researchers have examined citizens' decisions about whether to engage with the mechanisms of an administrative justice system. The barriers which stand in the

---

[8] For a critique of Mashaw and Adler, see Halliday and Scott (2010).

[9] This body of work is summarized in Adler (2006).

[10] Australia, Belgium, Canada, Denmark, Finland, France, Ireland, Netherlands, Norway, and the UK.

[11] Mashaw is one of a number of scholars applied by Jewell in quite a sophisticated comparative analysis.   [12] These reviews focus mainly, though not exclusively, on UK research.

way of citizens using mechanisms of redress have been explored (e.g., Genn, 1994), as have the various motivations of those who do in fact use them (e.g., Berthoud and Bryson, 1997). A number of studies have examined both issues within single projects. Miewald and Comer (1986) have done so in relation to the use of public ombudsmen in the U.S. Cowan and Halliday's study of the administration of homelessness law in the UK (2003) focused on the use and non-use (despite a continuing sense of grievance) of internal administrative review processes. Cowan (2004) has also fruitfully applied a legal consciousness framework (to be discussed further below) to the same dataset, focusing in particular on the notion of dignity. More recently, Lens (2007a) has examined why public welfare recipients appealed or failed to appeal against work sanctions through the fair hearings system in the U.S.

In terms of the barriers to the use of administrative justice mechanisms, we might separate "practical" barriers such as cost, procedural complexity, ignorance, and physical accessibility (Adler and Gulland, 2003) from "attitudinal" barriers such as skepticism, fatigue, faith in the rectitude of rules, and satisfaction (Cowan and Halliday, 2003). The extent to which public administration itself contributes to such attitudinal barriers has also been considered (Cowan and Halliday, 2003). In relation to citizens' motivations in using administrative justice mechanisms, two broad models can be suggested. Lloyd-Bostock and Mulcahy (1994) develop an "account model" of complaints against public hospitals in contrast to the highly influential naming-blaming-claiming model developed by Felstiner, Abel, and Sarat, (1980–1981) in relation to disputing more generally. Lloyd-Bostock and Mulcahy's argument is that not all disputes are instrumentally targeted at seeking redress (compensation, restitution, or some other substantive benefit). Citizens may equally use grievance mechanisms such as complaints systems to call the public agency to account for its failure to meet their expectations.

2. Users' experiences and perceptions of administrative justice mechanisms

Second, research has examined users' perceptions and experiences of administrative justice mechanisms. Some of this research has explored quite specific questions such as how users respond to delays, formality of process and self-representation (e.g., Baldwin et al., 1992). Other research has been more open-ended. Lens (2007b), for example, used in-depth interviews to explore welfare applicants' experiences of the fair hearing system in the U.S. She argues that applicants value fair hearings as a vehicle (albeit an imperfect one) for self-assertion and resistance against bureaucratic domination. Like Cowan (2004), she uses a legal consciousness framework to observe that administrative law operates both as a means of oppression *and* as a means to resist oppression. Administrative justice mechanisms offer the opportunity to users to reclaim the dignity perceived as having been lost in the primary administrative process—the chance to "re-insert the self," as Cowan puts it.

Larger datasets have been collected to permit comparison of perceptions and experiences of various groups of users. Genn et al. (2006), for example, examined users' perceptions of three different public law tribunals[13] in the UK specifically with a view to comparing the experiences of white, black and minority ethnic citizens. Among a broad range of findings, they note that South Asian and some other non-European users were consistently more negative than other ethnic groups in the assessments of tribunal hearings, but are less likely to be so if the tribunal panel is ethnically diverse.

Genn et al.'s research is one of the few studies which has collected large datasets in order to test within the context of administrative justice some of the findings of a rich body of social psychological research on procedural justice and perceptions of fairness in relation to courts and police. This work, associated in particular with Tom Tyler (e.g., Tyler, 1988; Tyler and Huo, 2002), has argued that citizens' perceptions of procedural fairness have an effect, on their overall assessments of their encounters with legal authorities, that is independent of outcomes. Tyler's insights have influenced administrative justice scholars (e.g., Lens, 2007a; Adler, 2010). It is surprising, then, that his work has not been more widely tested in relation to public administration and review mechanisms. Further work like Genn et al.'s (2006) would benefit the field.

3. *Dynamics and operations of administrative justice mechanisms*

Third, empirical legal studies have examined the dynamics and operations of administrative justice mechanisms in action. Once again, this work is fairly eclectic in both methodological approach and subject matter. A much-visited research question, explored mainly through quantitative methods, has been the effect of citizens' legal representation on decision outcomes. Although Monsma and Lempert (1992) rightly warn that the nature of the representation effects will depend on a range of factors, including the style of decision-making and the nature of the issues involved, most studies, across a range of policy sectors, conclude that representation significantly improves the plight of citizens before decision-making bodies (e.g., Walker et al., 1977; Genn, 1994; Partington et al., 2007), including in non-adversarial settings (Popkin, 1977).

Although it is sometimes more difficult for researchers to gain access to administrative justice institutions to conduct qualitative and ethnographic work, some interesting work has been carried out. For example, Baldwin et al. (1992), through a combination of observations of tribunal hearings and qualitative interviews with tribunal panel members, were able to discern shifts in the extent to which inquisitorial methods were used

---

[13] "Public law tribunals" consider and review administrative decisions made in many public agencies in a number of commonwealth jurisdictions, including the UK and Australia. A roughly equivalent function in the United States would be performed by administrative judges.

by the panels and explain this in terms of whether or not claimants were represented. More recently, Gilad (2008) was also able to use observational methods within the UK's Financial Services Ombudsman to reveal an overlooked feature of complaints-handling: that complaints-handlers perform the role of managing what, from a professional point of view, are complainants' excessive expectations for redress.

C. Linking "decision" and "review" research: the impact of review on primary decision-making

One of the challenges for administrative justice research, we suggest, is to link decision and review research. In addition to Cowan's (2004) and Lens' (2007b) work noted above, a good example of work which has moved in this direction is research examining the "impact" of dispute resolution mechanisms in terms of their influence on continuing decision-making within public agencies. Much of this has related to judicial review[14] (e.g., O'Leary, 1989; Richardson, 2004; Creyke and MacMillan, 2004), though ombudsmen have been compared with administrative courts (Hertogh, 2001), and public law tribunals have been examined in their own right (e.g., Baldwin, et al., 1992). Halliday (2004) has proposed a framework for assessing the extent to which judicial review will influence administrative decision-making, which may be applied to dispute resolution mechanisms more generally. Influence, he suggests, is determined by the extent to which:

1. decision-makers learn about the decisions of external review/appeal mechanisms;
2. decision-makers are conscientious about complying with the rules/principles/law expounded by the mechanism in question;
3. decision-makers are competent in translating such knowledge into bureaucratic action;
4. the organizational environment privileges compliance with the particular rules/principles/law over other demands;
5. the rules/principles/law is/are clear and consistent.

Although this sub-field has shown promise, it still has some way to go in terms of understanding the full significance of dispute resolution mechanisms for administrative decision-making. The range of potential empirical questions is considerable, particularly when compared with the volume of existing empirical work. Below we set out some suggestions about how this body of work may be developed and about how existing limitations may be remedied.

[14] The pioneering statistical research of Schuck and Elliott (1990) examined the impact of a controversial higher court decision on lower courts and hypothesized that this would *indirectly* affect agency behavior.

1. *Cultural theory and cultural bias*

First, grid-group cultural theory, which Halliday and Scott (2010) have used to develop a new typology of administrative justice, may contribute to our understanding of the extent to which agencies identify data from dispute resolution experiences as being relevant to the improvement of their on-going administrative practices. The notion of "cultural bias" has significance for exploring the extent to which officials learn and care about the decisions of dispute resolution mechanisms. A cultural bias is a way of seeing the world, a set of mutually supportive assumptions and values that make up a coherent approach to life. The claim is that cultural biases may color everything from the social construction of nature, to perceptions of risk and blame, to normative views about political culture. "Cultural bias," we suggest, may also play a role in influencing whether and to what extent agencies focus on particular kinds of dispute resolution data in their attempts to monitor the quality of their performance. An agency's sense of what administrative justice entails—the goals and values it sees as being most important—will influence what kind of dispute resolution data it pays most attention to. For example, two of the leading grid-group cultural theorists, Thompson and Wildavsky, have noted in relation to information bias within organizations that:

[h]ierarchies collect vast amount of pre-audit and post-audit data on the legality of expenditures. Data on the results of the activities involved would be strictly secondary…Members of market cultures, by contrast, could not care less about proper procedures. All they care about…is the bottom line: profit or cost effectiveness or popularity…. Just the opposite view is held by [egalitarians]; they want to equalize differences both in regard to the organization in which they are part and to its clients…. [I]nformation opposed to central authority and against inequality is the focus of their attention (1986: 283).

We might apply these arguments to administrative justice and the role of dispute resolution data in educating agencies about their performance. So where, for example, an organization has a predominantly "hierarchist" vision of administrative justice, it is likely that it will be less concerned about customer satisfaction *per se* than it is with feedback about the application of rules or expert judgment, particularly from hierarchical authorities. Similarly, where an agency embraces an "egalitarian" model of administrative justice, it may be more concerned with the "voice" of stakeholders and consultative groups (through, for example, complaints systems), and less concerned with feedback from hierarchical authorities, such as courts or regulators. Or where an agency adheres to an "individualist" or market-oriented vision of administrative justice, feedback about the application of rules or the quality of expertise may be less important than the "exit" numbers of its "citizen-consumers."

Although they did not use the lens of cultural theory, the research of Sunkin and Pick (2001) provides an illustration of the above point. They traced the history of the UK's Independent Review Service of the Social Fund, focusing in particular on the impact of judicial review on its decision-making. Their historical method enabled them to detect an organizational shift in focus away from a concern with judicial review to a "customer focus":

The focus has...turned from the judges to the more immediate constituencies served by the organisation, namely the applicants and the other interested parties to the review process (2001: 751).

What this demonstrates is that a shift in an organization's vision of administrative justice can affect the value they place on particular kinds of dispute resolution data:

[t]he general shift in the concerns of the organisation, and in particular the shift from an early concern to establish its legitimacy to the more recent emphasis on service delivery...affected the emphasis placed on compliance with the predictable requirements of the courts and legal form more generally (2001: 760).

2. *Focus on redress/grievance mechanisms in isolation*

Second, research on the impact of various review mechanisms has generally suffered from the tendency to focus on individual mechanisms of review or redress in isolation. This individuated focus is best understood, perhaps, within the context of the long shadow cast by the courts over traditional administrative law scholarship. Judicial review is understood, explicitly or implicitly, as being the paradigm example of a mechanism for the delivery and/or expression of administrative justice. For example, most traditional texts on administrative law, at least in Commonwealth jurisdictions, focus predominantly on the judicial review of administrative action, supplemented by relatively small sections on ombudsmen, tribunals and inquiries—no doubt because of their perceived status as alternatives to the courts. Other review and redress mechanisms are often not discussed at all in such works. Internal processes such as complaints systems or internal review, for example, are rarely given any treatment. While some empirical research, as we have seen, has adopted the dominant focus on the courts by examining the impact of judicial review, other empirical work has responded by plugging the above gaps by looking beyond the courts to alternative avenues of redress and counterbalancing the weight of judicial review. Further, some of the focus on non-court redress mechanisms can be framed in terms of how non-court mechanisms might remedy the limitations of the courts. So, even though some of the empirical legal work on administrative justice can be understood as an act of frustration with the centrality of courts to traditional discussions of administrative law, the courts generally remain an important navigational reference point for such work, albeit indirectly.

Nonetheless, the individuated focus which has ensued has imposed a cap on the promise of this sub-field: such research has generally failed to examine the *relative* influence of various redress/grievance mechanisms on primary administration.[15] This is a significant omission because public agencies are subject to a range of accountability regimes, not all of which pull in the same direction (Adler, 2006). Agencies are often in the unfortunate position of having to "rob Peter to pay Paul." When, how, and why they do so are significant empirical questions for the field. A better understanding of the significance of accountability regimes for administrative agencies will be achieved by exploring how they respond to the full range of accountability demands which are made of them and how interventions through one regime affect their accountability overall. Our ability to answer such questions has been hampered by the tendency hitherto to focus fairly narrowly on the "impact" of particular dispute resolution mechanisms in isolation from the others.

3. *Insufficient focus on public sector regulation*

Third, following on directly from the above discussion, the existing "impact" research has suffered from a tendency to confine itself to considering the "regulatory effects" (Halliday, 2004) of dispute resolution mechanisms to the exclusion of clearer (and perhaps less contentious) examples of public sector regulation. Impact research, particularly ethnographic work, often begins with an exploration of the routine realities of policy administration and then seeks to isolate the significance to it of review mechanisms (such as judicial review or ombudsman decisions). However, in limiting the research focus to the impact of review mechanisms, such research runs the risk of paying insufficient attention to additional drivers of administrative behavior. In other words, the rich complexity of the influences upon administrative behavior may not be adequately captured by approaching policy administration with such a narrow question. While not denying that "bottom-up" pressures through review mechanisms may have "regulatory effects" (in an expansive interpretation of that term), it constitutes, at best, only one half of the picture. The scale of "top-down" regulation inside government is vast (Hood et al., 1999). Further, compared with review mechanisms, regulation is more systemic in focus in that it attempts, in part at least, to improve the quality of administration in the first place. Empirical research about what drives decision-making practices, then, may sensibly begin with the hypothesis that regulatory mechanisms have greater impact than dispute resolution mechanisms. Indeed, Hood et al. (1999) found that the impact of dispute resolution mechanisms on the administration was capable of being magnified through the issuing of guidance on how to respond to risks created by ombudsman schemes, judicial review, and other grievance-handling mechanisms. Thus grievance-handling acquires more regulatory significance. Administrative justice research should widen its focus to include regulatory institutions. Our point above about the importance of understanding the relative significance of various dispute resolution mechanisms extends beyond

---

[15] A notable exception is Hertogh (2001).

redress and grievance-handling to the world of auditors, inspectorates, league tables, and other familiar aspects of public sector regulation.

4. *The limits of dispute resolution as feedback to agencies*

A final limitation of existing research relates to a potential pitfall in the use of impact research to develop policy. Implicit in impact research is the notion that dispute resolution experiences can have educational value for public agencies in monitoring their own performance. However, at a policy level it is unclear whether agencies or their overseers *should* draw on dispute resolution "data" for quality-monitoring purposes. There are significant limits to the capacity of feedback obtained from dispute resolution mechanisms to provide accurate information about the performance of systems. The pursuit of grievances and formal redress by citizens is by far the exception rather than the rule. Only a tiny proportion of citizens pursue grievances despite a continuing sense of upset (Genn, 1994) and among those who do pursue redress, there is a significant drop-out rate at each subsequent stage of the overall review or redress process (Cowan and Halliday, 2003). Also, the notions of "complaint" or "review request" are open to varying organizational interpretation. What one organization may regard and record as a "complaint," for example, may be classified differently by another. In this way, "feedback data" may be skewed, or at least vary in its volume from agency to agency. Finally, the common organizational practice of filtering grievances at an early stage and managing them informally means that it may be very difficult to assess the representativeness of "formal" feedback data. In other words, such data are likely to offer, at best, only a partial picture of organizational performance and, at worst, a seriously unrepresentative one. Empirical research, and policy which may flow from it, needs to take account of these quality issues when considering dispute resolution mechanisms as educational-feedback resources. Indeed, the issues of data quality suggest that data are best used only as an adjunct to other systematic attempts at monitoring organizational performance. This links us back, of course, to the argument above about the importance of widening our focus to include regulatory institutions.

III. Future Directions for
Administrative Justice Research

In this section we discuss some new directions for empirical administrative justice research. These relate to (1) the study of the legal consciousness and its relation to administrative justice practices, (2) new areas of administrative activity whose empirical exploration will benefit the field, as well as (3) new research questions about the development of administrative justice institutions.

A. Legal consciousness

The study of legal consciousness has emerged as a significant area of enquiry within the field of "Law and Society." The work of Ewick and Silbey (1998), in particular, has become prominent as a theoretically sophisticated analysis of how "legality" is socially constructed for ordinary people in their everyday lives, thereby offering a sociological analysis of law which is grounded in cultural practices. They propose three forms of legal consciousness ("before the law," "with the law," and "against the law"), and various dimensions of legal consciousness (normativity, constraint, capacity, and time/space) which cut across the forms. This approach to the study of law helps us understand the various ways in which people relate to each other and their environments, and how they respond to problems and grievances. As an empirical approach to understanding law in society, we suggest it has significant promise for the understanding of administrative law and administrative justice.

We saw above through the work of Cowan (2004) and Lens (2007b) that legal consciousness scholarship may be applied to questions about why people do or do not use administrative justice mechanisms. It may also, we suggest, usefully be applied to the study of the implementation of law by administrative officials.[16] In particular, it would considerably deepen Halliday's (2004) notion of "legal conscientiousness"—the extent to which administrative officials have an internal commitment to complying with law. Whereas Halliday frames legal conscientiousness as a single sliding scale, a legal consciousness framework promises a more nuanced analysis of how various orientations toward legality might affect the administration of law and policy. A recent study in this vein has been made by Hertogh (2010) where he combines the legal consciousness framework with the notion of "legal alienation," producing a typology of administrators' orientations toward law: administrators as "legalists," "loyalists," "cynics," and "outsiders." Hertogh's research represents an important move in a productive direction. Further work in this vein will benefit the field.

B. New territories for administrative justice research

There are large areas of administrative activity which have to date been under-explored empirically. We would suggest that two main issues arise regarding

---

[16] Cooper (1995) is an early example of the application of legal consciousness to the study of administrative behavior, though she did not apply Ewick and Silbey's analytical schema, nor focus on the impact of dispute resolution mechanisms.

definition of the territory of administrative justice; that is, where the landscape of administrative justice ends.

1. Civil and criminal justice

The first issue is particularly pertinent for legal researchers and concerns the potentially distorting effects of a legal conception of administrative justice. Doctrinal approaches to the study of administrative law may impose some territorial limits on the scope of administrative justice which, in turn, may impoverish its empirical analysis. Within the binaries of doctrinal categorization, administrative law sits within the civil, as opposed to criminal, area of the legal system and the legal curriculum. This has led to a tendency to overlook the administrative justice aspects of the criminal justice system. However, if one conceives of administrative justice, as many scholars do, as comprising a "normative theory of the relationship between individual citizens and the administrative agencies of the state" (Sainsbury, 1992: 296), then there is no good analytical reason for bracketing off the organs of the state which deal with criminal justice, particularly when violation of administrative regulations can lead to criminal prosecution (often involving referral by an administrative agency to prosecution authorities). The distinction between criminal and civil justice is one which may be important for legal practice and process, or for some aspects of policy, but it breaks down if we concern ourselves with the justice inherent in the relationship between citizens and agencies that administer law and policy in relation to those citizens. Indeed, some of the most intense relationships between citizens and agencies occur within the criminal justice field. Consider, for example, the plight of criminal suspects or of prisoners. Further, given the use of detention in the area of immigration law, the divide between criminal and civil justice seems increasingly problematic from an administrative justice perspective. Some notable empirical work on administrative justice has concerned criminal justice (e.g., Adler and Longhurst, 1994), but it remains an under-explored area of administrative practices.

2. Public and private agencies

The second territorial question also relates to the nature of the agencies whose operations may fall under the gaze of administrative justice researchers. Traditionally, as the quotation from Sainsbury above suggests, empirical work has revolved around the administration of law and policy in public or state agencies. In terms of charting the landscape of administrative justice, however, this is not without its difficulties. The line between what is "public" and "private" in terms of state provision has been blurred by New Public Management trends. Does it make sense to ignore what happens inside privatized agencies or private organizations, such as airlines in the case of the immigration control (Gilboy, 1997), which are contracted or required to provide public services? Perhaps more contentiously, if an ombudsman oversees the activities of large, powerful but private organizations such as banks and financial institutions, could we and should we examine that oversight through the lens of administrative justice?

Our approach here has been to focus in the main (though not exclusively) on empirical work about public agency decision-making, which constitutes the bulk of research which has defined itself as being concerned with "administrative justice." However, we would suggest that there is no theoretical reason to restrict the province of administrative justice in this way. Indeed, it would enrich the study of administrative justice to move beyond the public-private distinction. If one is willing, as many empirical scholars are, to examine non-judicial review of administrative decisions (by ombudsmen or complaints handlers, for example), or to contemplate normative arguments about the acceptability of primary decision processes from sources beyond legal doctrine (from new public management or wider cultural theory), then the lens of administrative justice may be used to examine the procedural legitimacy of decisions by non-state organizations such as firms and NGOs.

The fragility of the public-private divide is demonstrated strongly within research on trends toward supranational administrative activities. A recent scoping paper identified five different types of global administration, involving inter-governmental organizations, networks of national administrators (e.g., regulatory agencies), distribution of administrative tasks to national agencies under supranational rules (as, for example, in the case of EC competition law), hybrid intergovernmental-private regimes, and wholly private regulatory regimes, such as the Forest Stewardship Council and the Fair Trade Foundation (Kingsbury et al., 2005: 20). The authors of this study detect the emergence of administrative justice procedures attaching to the supranational administration of a wide variety of tasks. Further research is required to assess the extent of such proceduralization and their impact on the legitimacy and effectiveness of particular regimes. Such issues have particular value in the supranational context given the distance of most of these activities from national democratic governance.

C. Charting the development of administrative justice institutions

The dominant focus of administrative justice research hitherto on qualitative aspects of agency decision-making and dispute resolution in particular sites or policy domains (whether in national or comparative context) has left the broad trends in administrative justice developments relatively under-explored in empirical terms. In the study of regulation, by way of contrast, perceptions of a growing significance of delegation of powers to regulatory institutions have been followed up with quantitative analyses of trends in "the rise of the regulatory state." Research has attempted to explain the trends and to assess the extent of variation in such matters as independence and accountability of regulatory agencies (e.g., Levi-Faur, 2005). However, there has been no equivalent investigation of the "rise of the adjudicatory state." Although there have been attempts to assess the growth of particular administrative justice mechanisms, both within particular jurisdictions (e.g., judicial review in Russia: Solomon, 2004) and cross-nationally (e.g., Children's Ombudsmen: Gran and Aliberti, 2003), the broader map of administrative justice's institutional evolution remains uncharted. This may be the result of an evident caution on the part of political scientists and public management specialists, especially outside the United States, about investigating aspects of legal systems, particularly processes of adjudication and grievance-handling. The time is ripe for such an endeavor by legal scholars in relation to administrative justice.

The research agenda here would begin with the task of charting—on both historical and comparative dimensions—the extent to which we can observe a growth in administrative justice adjudicatory mechanisms. From this general starting point, key issues which may ensue could include what we might call the "anatomy" of the evolving adjudicative state. A historical and comparative snapshot of adjudicatory mechanisms would be welcome. What might be described as "fads" in institutional developments may be observed. For example, the recent growth in ombudsmen in the UK has followed an earlier explosion in the volume of administrative tribunals. Mapping out the administrative justice landscape in this way would be a revealing exercise.

Following directly on from the above, we might also explore the "physiology" of the adjudicatory state by examining the jurisdiction of the various adjudicative bodies which make up the system as a whole. For example, the establishment of specialized appeals tribunals has led to growth of grievances against regulatory bodies. Thus, the rise of the regulatory state, and in particular of punitive regulation (Baldwin, 2004), is directly linked to at least one aspect of the growth and differentiation of the adjudicatory functions of the state. Equally, however, one might explore the remit or jurisdiction of new specialized adjudicatory bodies in relation to new claims against state bodies, whether justiciable (for example, relating to freedom of information) or non-justiciable (for example, relating to maladministration).

A third key issue concerns the extent to which the growth of non-court grievance-handling has channeled disputes away from the courts (for example judicial review; see Resnik, 2006). The deployment of non-court adjudication may be a response to perceptions of overloading in the court system and a targeting of weaknesses in internal review processes. A diversion of dispute handling away from courts, should this be the case, begs the question of the quality of justice delivered through proliferating non-court adjudicatory bodies. Statistical analysis of the overall success rates of claims made within non-court adjudicatory systems as compared with judicial review and statutory appeals might be supplemented with survey data concerned with the degree of satisfaction experienced by those with grievances (Tyler, 1988). Such analyses would enable an evaluation within the sphere of administrative justice of more general claims that alternative dispute resolution provides second class justice when compared with the decisions of the courts. Such an evaluation would not only support an understanding of non-court adjudication processes, but would also provide empirical evidence to underpin future reforms in the balance between different institutional approaches to administrative justice.

Finally, returning to our earlier focus on processes of privatization and contracting out, it is a fair question to ask whether private bodies performing public, or formerly public, functions act like public bodies in the way they handle grievances. Do they provide opportunities for complaints to be made to external grievance handlers (as do contracted-out prisons, for example)? Or do they behave more like market actors in recognizing only a contractual basis to complaints (as do utilities providers, for example)? And this raises the possible irony that a substantial expansion of administrative justice institutions in many countries may have been accompanied by a substantial reduction in their jurisdictions through the shrinking of state activities.

IV. Conclusions

By their nature, Chapters in a handbook such as this must cover considerable ground. We have offered a scheme for capturing the principal themes and concerns of the field, a set of critical reflections about the state of existing research, as well as some specific suggestions for new research directions. In overview, however, we would suggest that this Chapter poses two principal challenges for empirical research in the field of administrative justice. The first is to follow changes in public management over the public-private divide to secure a better understanding of the extent to which public and private administration, as they affect those who are subject to decisions, are alike or different in respect both of *ex ante* control over the justice of decision-making (noting that private rule-making at national and international level is emerging as a key theme of contemporary regulatory scholarship) and *ex post* dispute resolution mechanisms. Given the importance of private-sector ombudsman regimes in many countries this is not such a radical move. Investigation of primary decision-making may require some methodological re-tooling and perhaps the enrolment of organizational research specialists with an interest in decision-making processes. Nevertheless, although not particularly radical, it is still an important move for the field and one, we would suggest, which could be productively taken by empirical legal scholars.

The second challenge points in another direction in attempting to secure a more systemic understanding of administrative justice in jurisdictions that have

exhibited rather different patterns of growth of the institutional structures for grievance handling. In many common-law jurisdictions the understanding of trends in
administrative justice has focused largely on the growth of judicial review and the
emergence of ombudsman schemes. In Australia, however, administrative justice
is designed and understood as a system, with a particular focus on administrative
tribunals. To what extent could such a systemic approach to the investigation of
administrative justice institutions and processes underpin a stronger understanding of the impact of recent trends in terms of the quality of justice and the efficiency
of administrative justice overall?

REFERENCES

Adler, M. (2006). "Fairness in Context," *Journal of Law and Society* 33: 615–38.

Adler, M. (2010). "Understanding and Analysing Administrative Justice," in M. Adler (ed.),
Administrative Justice in Context, Oxford: Hart Publishing.

Adler, M. and Gulland, J. (2003). *Tribunal Users' Experiences, Perceptions and Expectations:
A Literature Review*, London: Council of Tribunals.

Adler, M. and Henman, P. (2001). "e-Justice: A Comparative Study of Computerisation
and Procedural Justice in Social Security," *International Review of Law, Computers and
Technology* 15: 195–212.

Adler, M. and Longhurst, B. (1994). *Discourse, Power and Justice: Towards a New Sociology of
Imprisonment*, London: Routledge.

Asimow, M. (1983). "Delegated Legislation: United States and United Kingdom," *Oxford
Journal of Legal Studies* 3: 253–76.

Baldwin, J., Wikeley, N., and Young, R. (1992). *Judging Social Security*, Oxford: Oxford
University Press.

Baldwin, R. (2004). "The New Punitive Regulation," *Modern Law Review* 67: 351–83.

Berthoud, R. and Bryson, A. (1997). "Social security appeals: what do the claimants want?,"
Journal of Social Security Law 4: 17–41.

Black, J. (1997). *Rules and Regulators*, Oxford: Oxford University Press.

Braithwaite, J. and Drahos, P. (2000). *Global Business Regulation*, Cambridge: Cambridge
University Press.

Coglianese, C. (2002). "Empirical Analysis and Administrative Law," *University of Illinois
Law Review* 1111–38.

Cooper, D. (1995). "Local Government and Legal Consciousness in the Shadow of
Juridification," *Journal of Law and Society* 22: 506–26.

Cowan, D. (2004). "Legal Consciousness: Some Observations," *Modern Law Review* 67:
928–58.

Cowan, D. and Halliday, S. (2003). *The Appeal of Internal Review: Law, Administrative Justice
and the (Non-)Emergence of Disputes*, Oxford: Hart Publishing.

Creyke, R. and McMillan, J. (2004). "The Operation of Judicial Review in Australia," in
M. Hertogh and S. Halliday (eds.), *Judicial Review and Bureaucratic Impact: International
and Interdisciplinary Perspectives*, Cambridge: Cambridge University Press.

Ewick, P. and Silbey, S. (1998). *The Common Place of Law: stories from everyday life*, Chicago: University of Chicago Press.

Felstiner, W., Abel, R., and Sarat, A. (1980–1981). "The emergence and transformation of disputes: Naming, blaming, claiming...," *Law and Society Review* 15: 631–54.

Genn, H. (1994). "Tribunal Review of Administrative Decision-Making," in G. Richardson and H. Genn (eds.), *Administrative Law and Government Action*, Oxford: Oxford University Press.

Genn, H., Lever, B. and Gray, L. (2006). *Tribunals for Diverse Users*, London: Department for Constitutional Affairs.

Gilad, S. (2008). "Accountability of Expectations Management? The Role of the Ombudsman in Financial Management," *Law & Policy* 30: 227–53.

Gilboy, J. A. (1991). "Deciding Who Gets In: Decision-making by Immigration Inspectors," *Law & Society Review* 25: 571–99.

Gilboy, J. (1997). "Implications of 'Third Party' Involvement in Enforcement: The INS, Illegal Travellers, and International Airlines," *Law & Society Review* 31: 505–30.

Gran, B. and Aliberti, D. (2003). "The Office of the Children's Ombudsperson: Children's Rights and Social-Policy Innovation," *International Journal of the Sociology of Law* 31: 89–106.

Hahn, R.W., Burnett, J.K., Yee-Ho, I.C., Mader, E.A., and Moyle, P.R. (1999). "Assessing Regulatory Impact Analyses: The Failure of Agencies to Comply with Executive Order 12,866," *Harvard Journal of Law & Public Policy* 23: 859–85.

Halliday, S. (2004). *Judicial Review and Compliance with Administrative Law*, Oxford: Hart Publishing.

Halliday, S. and Scott, C. (2010). "A Cultural Analysis of Administrative Justice," in M. Adler (ed.), *Administrative Justice in Context*, Oxford: Hart Publishing.

Hertogh, M. (2001). "Coercion, Cooperation, and Control: Understanding the Policy Impact of Administrative Courts and the Ombudsman in the Netherlands," *Law & Policy* 23: 47–67.

Hertogh, M. (2010). "Through the Eyes of Bureaucrats: How Front-Line Officials Understand Administrative Justice," in M. Adler (ed.), *Administrative Justice in Context*, Oxford: Hart Publishing.

Hood, C., Scott, C., James, O., Jones, G., and Travers, A. (1999). *Regulation Inside Government: Waste-Watchers, Quality Police and Sleaze-Busters*, Oxford: Oxford University Press.

Jewell, C. (2007). *Agents of the Welfare State: How Caseworkers Respond to Need in the United States, Germany and Sweden*, New York: Palgrave MacMillan.

Kingsbury, B., Krisch, N., and Stewart, R. (2005). "The Emergence of Global Administrative Law," *Law & Contemporary Problems* 68: 15–61.

Langbein, L. (2002). "Responsive Bureaus, Equity, and Regulatory Negotiation: An Empirical View," *Journal of Policy Analysis and Management* 21: 449–564.

Lens, V. (2007a). "Administrative Justice in Public Welfare Bureaucracies," *Administration and Society* 39(3): 382–408.

Lens, V. (2007b). "In the Fair Hearing Room: Resistance and Confrontation in the Welfare Bureaucracy," *Law & Social Inquiry* 32: 309–32.

Levi-Faur, D. (2005). "The Global Diffusion of Regulatory Capitalism," *The Annals of the American Academy of Political and Social Science* 598: 12–32.

Lloyd-Bostock, S. and Mulcahy, L. (1994). "The Social Psychology of Making and Responding to Hospital Complaints: An Account Model of Complaint Processes," *Law and Policy* 16: 123–47.

Mashaw, J. (1983). *Bureaucratic Justice: Managing Social Security Disability Claims*, New Haven: Yale University Press.

Miewald, R. and Comer J. (1986). "Complaining as Participation," *Administration and Society* 17(4): 481–99.

Monsma, K. and Lempert, R. (1992). "The Value of Counsel: 20 Years of Representation before a Public Housing Eviction Board," *Law & Society Review* 26: 627–67.

Nehl, H.P. (2006). "Administrative Law," in J. M. Smits (ed.), *Elgar Encyclopedia of Comparative Law*, Cheltenham: Edward Elgar.

Nonet, P. (1969). *Administrative Justice: Advocacy and Change in Government Agencies*, New York: Russell Sage Foundation.

O'Leary, R. (1989). "The Impact of Federal Court Decisions on the Policies and Administration of the U.S. Environmental Protection Agency," *Administrative Law Review* 41: 549–74.

Page, E.C. (2001). *Governing by Numbers: Delegated Legislation and Everyday Policy-Making*, Oxford: Hart Publishing.

Parker, C. (2004). "Restorative Justice in Business Regulation? The Australian Competition and Consumer Commission's Use of Enforceable Undertakings," *Modern Law Review* 67: 209–46.

Partington, M., Kirton-Darling, E., and McClenaghan, F. (2007). *Empirical Research on Tribunals: An Annotated Review of Research Published between 1992 and 2007*, Administrative Justice and Tribunals Council, available at <http://www.ajtc.gov.uk/publications/179.htm>.

Pollack, M. (2003). "Control Mechanism Or Deliberative Democracy?: Two Images of Comitology," *Comparative Political Studies* 36: 125–55.

Popkin, W. (1977). "The Effect of Representation in Nonadversary Proceedings—A Study of Three Disability Programs," *Cornell Law Review* 60: 989–1048.

Resnik, J. (2006). "Whither and whether adjudication?," *Boston University Law Review* 86: 1101–40.

Richardson, G. (2004). "Impact studies in the UK," in M. Hertogh and S. Halliday (eds.), *Judicial Review and Bureaucratic Impact: International and Interdisciplinary Perspectives*, Cambridge: Cambridge University Press.

Sainsbury, R. (1992). "Administrative Justice: Discretion and Procedures in Social Security Decision-Making," in K. Hawkins (ed.), *The Uses of Discretion*, Oxford: Oxford University Press.

Sainsbury, R. (2008). "Administrative Justice, Discretion and the 'Welfare to Work' Project," *Journal of Social Welfare and Family Law* 30: 323–38.

Schuck, P. and Elliott, E.D. (1990). "To the *Chevron* Station: An Empirical Study of Federal Administrative Law," *Duke Law Journal* 984–1077.

Solomon, P. (2004). "Judicial Power in Russia: Through the Prism of Administrative Justice," *Law and Society Review* 38: 549–81.

Sunkin, M. and Pick, K. (2001). "The Changing Impact of Judicial Review: the Independent Review Service of the Social Fund," *Public Law* 736–62.

Thompson, M. and Wildavsky, A. (1986). "A Cultural Theory of Information Bias in Organizations," *Journal of Management Studies* 23: 273–86.

Tyler, T. (1988). "What is Procedural Justice?: Criteria Used by Citizens to Assess the Fairness of Legal Procedures," *Law & Society Review* 22: 103–106.

Tyler, T. and Huo, Y. (2002). *Trust in the Law: Encouraging Public Cooperation with the Police and Courts*, New York: Russell Sage Foundation.

Walker, T., Blumenthal, M., and Reese, J. (1977). "An Empirical Examination of Citizen Representation in Contested Matters Before State Administrative Agencies: the Colorado Experience," *Administrative Law Review* 29: 321–66.

Williams, S.F. (1974). "'Hybrid Rulemaking' under the Administrative Procedure Act: A Legal and Empirical Analysis," *University of Chicago Law Review* 43: 401–56.

2 1

ACCESS TO CIVIL JUSTICE

RODERICK A. MACDONALD[1]

[1] I should like to thank my research assistant, Tom McMorrow (D.C.L. candidate 2010, McGill University) for his assistance in compiling and organizing the data discussed here and for his careful critique of various earlier versions of this essay. I am also grateful to Scott Scambler (B.C.L./LL.B. 2010) for comments on the penultimate draft of this essay. Peter Cane and Herb Kritzer generously provided a detailed critique of the essay, enabling me to focus on contemporary achievements and challenges of access to justice empirical scholarship. Finally, my colleagues Kim Brooks, Hoi Kong, and Robert Leckey rescued the final version of the text from numerous infelicities and errors. Of course, none of the above should be held accountable for anything said here.

I. Introduction: Defining the Question

THE promise of justice through law resonates with populations around the world; hence, preoccupation with the Rule of Law. Whether the Rule of Law is understood in its Anglo-American, its continental, its African, or its East Asian variants, the fundamental elements are similar. The imposition of constraints upon the will or actions of others is only legitimate if authorized by law.

As concerns relationships among non-state actors the root idea is as follows. No citizen may exercise physical coercion against another person (e.g., a family member, a neighbor, an employee, a tenant) in order to bend that person to its will. Nor should any citizen be able to coerce performance of an obligation or assert property rights without the authorization of the state legal order, and its dispute-resolution institutions. These impartial and independent institutions also should be broadly available to citizens to settle their conflicts where they cannot do so amicably.

After the mid-twentieth century, these foundational principles of the Rule of Law for the civil justice system came under intense scrutiny. Many lawyers and scholars took issue with the substance of private law doctrine, especially in fields of family, consumer, landlord-tenant, employment, and social welfare law. Even more disparaged procedural aspects of the regime of civil litigation. Lawsuits were costly and judgments rarely obtained expeditiously. Almost all decried the judicial justice system for its failure to provide adequate resources for litigants to vindicate rights before state-provided civil-disputing institutions.

Together these considerations led policy-makers and commentators to pay critical, rather than merely doctrinal, attention to the work of lawyers, judges, courts, and, later on, other court-like adjudicators. Research shifted away from structural elements of the criminal and civil justice systems (their substantive aspirations, their institutions and their processes), and toward inputs and outputs (the recourses and remedies available to litigants and their success in invoking the judicial process to obtain redress). By the late 1970s, a new orienting slogan had emerged to capture this preoccupation: access to justice (Cappelletti and Garth, 1978).

At the same time, this shift in analytical focus was accompanied by a shift in methodology. Inventorying institutions and glossing legal rules proved an inadequate metric for investigating access to justice: empirical studies of citizen needs and system responses became a privileged research vehicle (Messier, 1975; Cass and Sackville, 1975; Curran, 1977).

Scholarly associations (e.g., the Law and Society Association, the Socio-Legal Studies Association, the Canadian Law and Society Association, the Research Committee for the Sociology of Law), journals (e.g., the Law and Society Review, Law and Social Inquiry, Journal of Law and Society, the Windsor Yearbook of Access to Justice, and Droit et société), and research programs and institutes (e.g., the Rand Institute for Civil Justice, the Oxford Centre for Socio-Legal Studies, or the Civil Justice Forum) devoted to access to justice and empirical research proliferated between the mid-1960s and the mid-1980s. Yet, even though empirical research continues to flourish with new scholarly associations (the Society for Empirical Legal Studies), transnational research groups (the Tilburg Microjustice Initiative), and journals (the Journal of Empirical Legal Studies) being established during the past decade, and even though access to justice has been a rallying cry for almost half a century, there is still much scholarly uncertainty both about what the expression means and about the research endeavors it calls forth (Bass et al., 2005).

In part this uncertainty has a sociological origin: on-the-ground problems of access to justice have themselves changed over the years. Finding an adequate response to a more socio-demographically diverse population of rights-claimants, to different citizen expectations of law, to the challenges of globalization, and to newly emerging or newly recognized patterns of affect in personal relationships taxes the imagination of governments, lawyers, and scholars. Lack of agreement can also be traced to an evolution in thinking about what access to justice in a liberal democracy actually requires. Today, many question whether more official law and more lawyers are the remedy for a lack of access to justice—however the notion is defined. For this reason, an initial step in assessing the current state of empirical research into access to justice is to frame the question of scope.

An adequate empirical study of access to justice must rest on a normatively defensible account of justice. Any such account takes seriously the conceptions of justice that citizens themselves hold. This essay takes an expansive view of access to justice, pushing reflection beyond concern with official dispute-resolution processes and institutions. Part II is essentially descriptive of extant material. It provides an overview of the main international and national generators of data about access to justice, noting that these studies tend to be focused on the priorities of actors invested in the state legal system. Part III addresses institutional questions. Using the metaphor of "waves of access to justice" it reviews how well empirical research has kept up with the evolution of the idea of access to justice over the last half-century. Part IV expands upon the metaphor "barriers to access" to elaborate a citizen-centered conception of access to justice. This metaphor is then used to assess how well ongoing empirical research acknowledges and accounts for the different forms of inaccessibility experienced by different categories of justice-seekers.

II. Empirical Research on Access to Justice—from Data Collection to Analysis

Research into access to justice can be understood as a focused way of asking the fundamental governance questions of modern times: how do (and how should) legislatures, public officials, the legal profession, and civic-minded NGOs respond to a given policy issue? Here, the goal is to find ways to render civil justice to citizens on a fair and equitable basis. Empirical, as opposed to doctrinal, research into access to justice poses additional challenges. Many relate to design, administration, and analysis conundrums consequent upon decisions about the research questions to be explored. These research questions—for example, how do citizens view their basic legal needs and how are these needs reflected in their use of official institutions and procedures—define what data should be collected, from whom, what hypotheses are worth testing, and what analyses of the data will shed light on the question being explored.

A. Generating and accessing data and data sets

Reliable, non-anecdotal data is a foundational requirement for instrumentally useful empirical research into access to justice. Moreover, since access to justice also calls forth "systemic" inquiry, commensurable data and longitudinally or laterally replicable data sets are essential. In brief, the construction and interpretation of all data depends on a prior theorization of the relevance of information to be generated, collected or found; and the compilation of these data in systemic sets is particularly challenging in the field of access to justice (Pleasance et al., 2004).

Today, some of the most informative data sets are collected for other purposes. For example, statistics compiled by liability insurers about workplace injuries, automobile accidents, and household hazards or by life insurers and public health authorities can provide valuable clues about the accessibility of the justice system. Similarly, empirical data (whether collected in support of doctrinal studies or normative research by critical scholars) from any substantive legal field—for example, family law, torts, contracts, successions—can be mined as part of an inquiry into access to justice. Often, neither scholars nor policy-makers perceive the relevance of these data sets to access to justice issues (Dauer, 1991; Muno-Perez, 1993).

This said, in many countries there are substantial banks of original data collected through research projects that self-consciously describe themselves as focused on access to justice. These data sets are easier to track down and access than other sources mentioned. They are often available through well-indexed data archives, and are referenced in publications devoted to law and society research, empirical research or access-to-justice studies, or in reports of commissions and research groups with specific access-to-justice mandates (ABA, 1994; Woolf, 1996; Rush Social Research, 1999; Stein, 2001; Bass et al., 2005; CEPEJ, 2006). They do not, however, always tell the whole story. Because self-described empirical studies of access to justice are often designed and executed by organized interests such as Bar Associations, public interest groups and court administration services, the resulting data sets may occasionally (Baxi, 2007), although not inevitably (NSW, 2000; Genn et al., 2006; Ontario Legal Aid Review, 1997, updated 2008; Uzelac and Van Rhee, 2009) be skewed toward the institutional and financial interests of those undertaking or sponsoring the research.

A focus on applying social science methodology to topics that have a recognizably legal label tends to encourage the collection of quantitative data pertaining to familiar sites of law and qualitative data pertaining to familiar legal actors. This is notably true of government statistical compilations about the use of courts, the availability of legal services, the ability to obtain redress either from or against the state, public servants and administrative agencies and levels of satisfaction of court users (Ontario Law Reform Commission, 1966; BJS, 2001). While some legal scholars adopt non-institutional research perspectives, in general social scientists have shown greater inclination to undertake research that attempts to measure access to justice using non-recognizably legal labels in less familiar sites of dispute resolution—e.g., consensual arbitration, religious tribunals, recourse to elders—or where less familiar modes of justice achievement are deployed— e.g., talking circles, peer mediation, or even ad hoc processes (Silbey and Ewick, 1993; Noreau, 1993; Merry, 1995). In many states, public organizations that are well placed to support empirical research and to finance the collection of longitudinal data sets do not do so, focusing rather on policy research. Exceptionally, some of these organizations have devoted major resources to developing and deploying sophisticated longitudinal measurement instruments (Pleasance et al., 2004; Genn et al., 2006).

Though the overall record is disappointing, the prognosis is not bleak. About the time that the slogan "access to justice" entered the legal lexicon, a number of national studies of legal exclusion were published. Since then, the endeavor has been repeated on a sporadic basis, typically as a result of some crisis (real or perceived) in the official civil disputing system of a particular western state (Hutchinson, 1990; ABA, 1994; Access to Justice Advisory Committee, 1994; Pleasance et al., 2004; CEPEJ, 2006). Given the recurring claim by scholars about the importance of generating data sets that can be mined for analysis of access to justice it is appropriate to begin with a review of contemporary large-scale empirical projects at the international and national levels.

B. International projects

Three international initiatives illustrate how the concept of access to justice is reflected in large-scale civil justice research projects. These projects, along with cross-jurisdictional scholarly endeavors (e.g. Kritzer and Silbey, 2003) are the most important multi-national initiatives since the pioneering work of Cappelletti and Garth (1978). Sometimes they focus on the generation of new data, but just as often sponsor analysis of existing statistics available through state agency records—not just in law, but in disciplines as diverse as economics, political science, anthropology, sociology, and public administration. Moreover, these endeavors typically focus equally on criminal and civil access to justice, and often track citizen recourse to both official and unofficial legal institutions.

1. The World Bank's Justice for the Poor (J4P) Program

The most extensive attempt to map the transnational terrain of access to justice arises from the J4P collaborative effort among various units of the World Bank (World Bank, 2009). The overarching goal of the program is to promote justice-sector reform in a number of countries in Africa and East Asia. Recent studies and working papers address specific challenges in countries such as Cambodia, Indonesia, Kenya, Sierra Leone, Timor-Leste, Vanuatu, and the Solomon Islands. The J4P program adopts a more expansive view of access to justice than is commonly found in single-state civil-disputing projects, examining not just poverty-related exclusions, but also the situation of other marginalized groups: women, youth and ethnic minorities. Moreover, these studies confirm the interconnection between exclusion, poverty and a lack of access, drawing a close link between the success of initiatives to promote democratic development and the effectiveness of those to enhance access to justice. For example, in Indonesia, an empirical study examined how non-state law could be conscripted to promote reforms enhancing the accessibility of the state justice system; in Kenya, a qualitative study explored how the exclusion of women from social power structures was closely linked to their lack of access to justice (World Bank, 2009).

2. *UNDP Commission on Legal Empowerment of the Poor*

The United Nations Development Programme Commission on Legal Empowerment of the Poor (UNDP, 2009) is a second global access-to-justice initiative. The animating principle is the concept of legal empowerment—"the process through which the poor become protected and are enabled to use the law to advance their rights and their interests, *vis-à-vis* the state and in the market." Here also the research shows a connection between economic development more broadly, and access to justice. Projects involve both data collection and policy recommendations for legal reform in a wide range of legal domains, drawing empirical research into the contribution of effective and affordable court systems, to stronger legal aid programs, expanded legal service cadres with paralegals and law students, the simplification and standardization of contractual forms, and fair and expeditious modes of alternative dispute resolution to achieving more accessible justice.

A particularly interesting feature of the Commission's work is its assertion, paradoxically not buttressed by reported field studies, that the terrain of legal empowerment has to be elaborated primarily by those who are excluded. The goal of the project is to enable poor people to give voice to their legal needs, based on information and education on the one hand, and organization and representation on the other.

3. *The Tilburg Microjustice Initiative*

Complementing these macro-projects of international organizations, is a recent researcher-driven access-to-justice initiative established by Tilburg University and International Legal Alliances aimed at developing affordable and sustainable solutions to access-to-justice problems for those living at the "base of the pyramid" (Microjustice, 2009). The project is meant to stimulate local studies of justice enhancement and the bottom-up sharing of experience. As with the World Bank and United Nations projects, the Microjustice initiative takes an expansive view of access to justice that embraces both civil disputing as classically understood and other incidents of legal empowerment. While a medium-term goal is to develop commensurable multinational empirical studies about informal as well as formal processes to enhance the achievement of justice, for the moment the project is targeting problem definition and the elaboration of assessment criteria for Microjustice initiatives.

C. National surveys

The most comprehensive empirical projects on access to justice are those sponsored at the national or sub-national level by Ministries of Justice and governmental research organizations such as law reform commissions, civil justice institutes, and census bureaus. The primary non-governmental drivers of broad-based data collection are other legal actors such as bar associations, law foundations, law faculties, and research centers, legal aid commissions and judicial councils. State-funded research councils, independent think tanks, private foundations, and research corporations also sponsor or conduct data collection and analysis on specific topics. The scale and scope of research is highly variable. Today, most studies originate in common law countries. Nonetheless, modest national efforts exist in European civil law states, and the European Commission for the Efficiency of Justice does publish comparative empirical studies of member states' judicial systems (CEPEJ, 2006). First-level data about civil justice may also be found in India, China, Korea, and Japan, although given cultural differences around litigation in the latter three states it is difficult to assess the importance of these data as a marker of access to justice. The following are examples of empirical research in states that generate most data of this type.

1. *Australia*

Today, the key sponsoring institutions in Australia are law reform commissions and legal aid commissions, although the initial study (Cass and Sackville, 1975) was undertaken at the behest of the Commonwealth government. As in many other states, the recession of the early 1990s saw renewed interest in civil disputing and access to justice (Access to Justice Advisory Committee, 1994). These latter studies led to a major project conducted between 1996 and 1999 (Rush Social Research, 1999). Phase I surveyed the expressed needs of citizens as a vehicle for allocating legal aid funds to states and territories. Phase II attempted to discern the legal services that would enable citizens to adequately vindicate their rights. This work was complemented by an Australian Law Reform Commission study of the federal civil justice system, major parts of which were directed to access to justice questions (ALRC, 2000). More recently, the Law and Justice Foundation of New South Wales (Coumarelos et al., 2006), and the Council of Social Service of NSW (NSW, 2000) have sponsored major empirical projects on access to justice needs, and the impact of cuts to legal aid.

2. *Canada*

As in Australia official interest in empirical studies of access to justice began in the 1970s (Messier, 1975) and flourished in the 1990s (Hutchinson, 1990; Ontario Law Reform Commission, 1996). The most important stimuli of survey research have been provincial bar associations seeking enhanced financing for legal aid, courts dealing with unrepresented litigants, and anti-poverty and equality-seeking coalitions wanting funding for clinics and constitutional challenges (Bass et al., 2005; Ontario Legal Aid Review, 1997, updated 2008). Today, the primary generators of longitudinal data are governmental—the Canadian Centre for Justice Statistics, the Department of Justice—and quasi-governmental agencies, such as the Civil Justice

Forum in Alberta. Occasionally special projects and conferences lead to the generation of data about access to courts, but most empirical work today is not aggregated,
emanating instead from specific studies undertaken by scholars pursuing their own
civil-disputing research projects.

3. *France, Germany, Italy, the Netherlands*

Most European states collect civil justice statistics, including data on litigation rates,
the availability of legal aid and the use of other mechanisms for financing legal services. In France both governmental and academic studies (Muno-Perez, 1993; Breen,
2002) have examined these components of access to justice, but there is little else of
an empirical nature on the topic. A similar situation prevails in Germany (Killian,
2003), the Netherlands, and Italy (Varano and De Luca, 2007), where the central
preoccupations continue to be access to the courts and to lawyers (Uzelac and Van
Rhee, 2009).

4. *United Kingdom*

In the United Kingdom, one finds a plethora of empirical research over the past two
decades (Legal Action Group, 1996; Woolf, 1996). The Research, Development and
Statistics Directorate within the Home Office conducts its own studies and also provides funding for empirical research. In addition, the Legal Services Research Centre
(Pleasance et al., 2004), research councils (Economic and Social Research Council
(ESRC); Arts and Humanities Research Council (AHRC)), charitable foundations
such as Rowntree and Nuffield (Genn et al., 2006), the Vera Institute of Justice, and
university based socio-legal studies institutes (Oxford, Cardiff, Warwick, London
School of Economics (LSE), University College, London (UCL)), generate substantial empirical data. The most extensive set of access to justice studies is produced
through the Legal Services Research Centre, on topics as various as the accessibility
of legal aid, community legal clinics and advice centers, youth courts, the elderly,
and public legal education. The Centre also conducts a general civil and social justice
survey. Empirical research for the most part tracks existing doctrine and concepts
of substantive law or procedure, although the LSRC also undertakes studies that
frame research questions either functionally, or by reference to the conceptual tools
of such disciplines as psychology, sociology, anthropology, or criminology (Genn
and Beinart, 1999).

5. *United States of America*

By far the most voluminous, the most comprehensive and the most far reaching
data sets on access to justice are generated in the United States. Two are stagger-
ing in scope and scale (Curran, 1977; ABA, 1994). In addition, there have been a
number of state-level studies of the legal needs of the low- and moderate-income

public. The Rand Institute has produced numerous studies of civil disputing, both within and outside the formal justice system (Rand Institute for Civil Justice, 2009). The American Bar Foundation, the Russell Sage Foundation, and university-based research centers (e.g. Denver, Wisconsin) have also sponsored research projects on access-to-justice issues. The Bureau of Justice Statistics has also sponsored a massive Survey of Civil Appeals (BJS, 2001) which has been mined by researchers (Kritzer et al., 2007). A recurring focus of these studies is the impact of legal representation on litigation rates and judicial outcomes. In 2004, a new journal (the Journal of Empirical Legal Studies) began to publish empirical research into all aspects of the civil justice system. Finally, there is effort in specific substantive areas—consumer bankruptcies, tort law, and family law—to measure the impact on outcomes of different steps to enhance the accessibility of the official system. A significant feature of these data sets is their focus on litigants' perceptions of justice and the lessons about institutional design that can be learned from this (Galanter, 1989; Tyler, 1997).

6. *Other countries*

In addition to the countries listed above, national studies of access to courts and lawyers have been undertaken in Hong Kong (Meggitt, 2008), India (Baxi, 2007), Israel (Dotan, 2003), Russia (Hendley et al., 2003), and other countries (Kritzer and Silbey, 2003), as well as New Zealand, Bulgaria and Slovakia (Hadfield, 2006). In addition, the World Bank has sponsored national surveys in Cambodia, Indonesia, Kenya, Sierra Leone, and, Vietnam (World Bank, 2009), which have been complemented by numerous multi-state studies of developing countries or of regional best practices (World Bank, 2009).

D. Evaluation of international and national data collection projects

All empirical legal research rests on assumptions about what law is and the relationship of formal legal artefacts to social facts. Unpacking these assumptions and their impact on research design is especially important in projects that collect aggregate data about access to justice, where causation is a primary issue in data interpretation. First are questions of social structure: is lack of access a cause of injustice (an independent variable) or a symptom of more general social disempowerment (a dependent variable)? Second, there is the question of motivation: does the measured lack of access to state institutions flow from a litigant's inability to achieve official vindication of a wrong that has been suffered, or might it simply evidence that absent users have consciously chosen not to engage with the formal system (Paquin, 2001)? In brief, aggregate data about court usage alone do not reveal whether professional and scholarly understandings of the legal needs of the public actually track how those needs are felt by these publics. Scholars might imagine representation as the root need of a tenant evicted from slum housing, but tenants might perceive a fairer distribution of rights and obligations between landlords and tenants as primary. For these reasons, specific research with a significant qualitative dimension flowing from interviews and detailed, but open-ended questionnaires are necessary complements to studies of aggregated data sets (Silbey and Ewick, 1993). Recently, there has been an attempt to quantify the level of access to justice by creating an index of needs (Carfield, 2005).

Whether international or national in scope the major data collection initiatives of past decades have focused on identifying either "the legal needs of the public" (the demand side of access to justice) or "the use of the formal institutions of dispute resolution" (the supply side of the access to justice equation).

Most supply side research is sponsored by institutional players and tends to have an institutional focus (Messier, 1975; Curran, 1977; Cass and Sackville, 1975; Genn et al., 2006; Ontario Legal Aid Review, 1997, updated 2008). This research is generally conducted on the assumption that the existing constellation of justiciable rights defines the scope of supply: the empirical question concerns the extent to which the public is able to secure the benefit of these rights. In these studies other modes and sites of inequality and legal exclusion (e.g., the possible access-to-justice consequences of substantive rules in housing, employment, consumer, and credit-financing law) are usually not explored. Likewise, the sufficiency of supply is often assessed solely by reference to official institutions and actors: notably, courts and the legal professions. Few statistical surveys track access to ADR decision-making by administrative tribunals, private and consensual dispute-settlement institutions, or religious tribunals; even fewer explore access to legal services provided by paralegals, elders, shop-stewards, and so on. By contrast, there is an enormous literature on access to institutions of law-creation and law-administration, although empirical studies on the participation of citizens as police, public servants, lawyers, judges, and parliamentarians, are typically not indexed under the access to justice rubric. The next section (Part III) will focus on how well empirical research has kept up with changes in perception about the supply side of access to justice.

Demand-side statistical research into the needs of the public also typically rests on relatively narrow criteria of both need and the causes of inaccessibility. Lack of access is often theorized as correlated to poverty, and poverty is adopted as a primary metric of analysis. Nonetheless, some research conceives inaccessibility as grounded in social exclusion, focusing on data-collection about women, racial, religious, linguistic or ethnic minorities, the elderly, youth, and sexual minorities. In addition, a number of research studies suggest that demand for legal services correlates less with socio-demographic factors than with the type of issue or claim being made. Finally, many studies of legal exclusion define need formally and measure access only to existing institutions like legal clinics, courts, and administrative tribunals. This said, there is significant empirical research reporting what litigants want (Galanter, 1989; Ontario Law Reform Commission, 1996; Tyler, 1997; Genn and Beinert, 1999) although just a few such studies investigate how marginalized publics themselves both define their lack of access and what they imagine as optimal for overcoming it (World Bank, 2009; UNDP, 2009). The last section (Part IV) will explore how well empirical research acknowledges and accounts for changes in demand-side perception of inaccessibility.

III. DELIMITING THE RESEARCH TERRAIN: WAVES IN ACCESS TO JUSTICE THINKING

Delimiting the appropriate research terrain for supply-side access to justice studies immediately begs inquiry into what institutions should be the focus of empirical research. Here scholars confront the vexing question of means and ends: should the end in view (access to justice) define the means (the scope of empirical research), or should the available means (available empirical research tools) define the ends (the scope of access to justice)?

Consider the following research hypothesis: do small claims courts enhance access to justice? One might begin by comparing the socio-demography of non-corporate plaintiffs in the court with the socio-demography of non-corporate plaintiffs in the next level of civil courts, and with the socio-demography of the population in the court's catchment. Were the third to differ significantly from the first and second across a range of traits—ethnicity, age, gender, education, income, language, etc.—and were the persons of socially less-empowered demographics more present as plaintiffs in small claims courts than other courts, one might be able to develop hypotheses about the contribution of such courts to enhancing access to justice. But even if the socio-demography were very similar in all three data sets, it would not follow that less-empowered populations have no access to justice for small claims. To reach this conclusion it would be necessary to collect data about potential plaintiffs who were absent from the court. This would require surveying representative samples of absentees to determine if they otherwise obtained what they considered justice in resolving paradigmatic, small claims—whether through self-help, negotiation, mediation, arbitration by a religious tribunal, or some other means (Moorhead and Pleasance, 2003; Genn et al., 2006).

Yet the difficulty of obtaining and organizing such data led to the abandonment of one major six-year empirical study of small-claims-court disputing. Far from the end (did such populations actually benefit from accessible justice outcomes?) driving the means (what is the total set of institutions and processes by which justice is achieved and how effective are they in rendering justice?), the means controlled the end. In addition, the study concluded that the small claims court made a slight difference to the participation rates of under-empowered socio-demographic groups, but that the fine-grained data collected actually said very little about how accessible civil justice was for different members of the court's catchment (McGuire and Macdonald, 1996, 1998). Other researchers have also noted this tendency to make data collection too elaborate both in scope and in variables to produce statistically significant results (Pleasance et al., 2004).

To assess the state of supply-side research, data reported here will be organized around themes that have come to the fore as the notion of access to justice has evolved over the past 50 years. In what is now seen as the classical presentation, Cappelletti and Garth proposed three "waves" in access to justice thinking (Cappelletti and Garth, 1978). To bring this idea up to date, a slightly different, five-fold schema, periodized by decade—1960–70; 1970–80; 1980–90; 1990–2000; and 2000 onward—will be adopted here (Bass et al., 2005). Of course, the periodization of these five waves varies considerably among countries, and not all waves have yet broken on the shores of every state. Moreover, the schema is meant to highlight themes, not dates: while a different theme may dominate the policy agenda in each of these decades, the type of empirical research being undertaken is cumulative, and largely independent of policy priorities. For example, today one sees empirical studies investigating themes related to all five waves (and even predominantly to the first two waves) of the access to justice research agenda.

A. Wave 1: Accessing the official system —lawyers and courts

Access to civil justice was initially the slogan of jurists who sought to reform the institutions and processes of private law. Often working in store-front clinics, and generally "practicing law for poor people," these lawyers targeted obstacles to the effective vindication of welfare, housing, employment, family, and consumer rights. The key goals were to: (1) reduce the cost, delay, and complexity of litigation; and (2) ensure legal representation in pursuing or defending civil actions and making claims before administrative officials (Hutchinson, 1990). Over time, the concern expanded to embrace access to justice for the middle class as well. Today some of the best empirical studies focus on redress available from the official system and the availability (and impact) of legal representation, whether through legal aid programs, *pro bono* systems, community clinics, public defender offices, or paralegals (Stein, 2001; Kritzer and Silbey, 2003; Ontario Legal Aid Review, 1997, updated 2008).

Governments in many countries now gather comprehensive statistics about court usage and judicial performance: caseload, hours spent in the courtroom, number of judgments delivered, the nature and amount of the claims made, the socio-demography of litigants, and so on. While collected primarily for management purposes, these aggregate data have been used by access-to-justice scholars to understand, for example, the causes and meaning of apparently declining litigation rates (Galanter, 2004). The traditional conception of access to justice also generates research that seeks to correlate recourse to courts and judicial outcomes with party-specific, case-specific and institution-specific factors (Varano and De Luca, 2007; Kritzer and Silbey, 2003; Silbey and Ewick, 1993). For example, certain studies show that representation by lawyers and paralegals significantly affects outcomes for low-income tenants in housing courts. But this effect seems to be culturally specific in that little difference is noted in some non-western states (Meggitt, 2008).

B. Wave 2: Improving the official system—redesigning state institutions

With empirical studies of disputing behavior, the effectiveness of legal aid delivery, and the actual performance of courts, by the 1970s scholars came to perceive inadequacies in the original approach to access. In a second wave of access to justice thinking, the idea was to expand the range of official institutions for handling citizens' justice concerns, to simplify processes of recovery, to streamline the public bureaucracy, and to consider the impacts of the justice system on all citizens, regardless of socio-economic status. Initiatives included creating small claims courts, developing class actions, modifying discovery rules, permitting or liberalizing contingency fees, and changing costs rules. States also adopted procedures empowering judges to control the pace of litigation and to refer matters to pre-trial mediation. As a consequence, whole new areas for empirical research were opened up, with studies often being driven by hypotheses of scholars in fields such as law and economics, feminist theory, and critical theory (Hutchinson, 1990).

The goal was institutional redesign, which was meant to speed up lawsuits, reduce their cost and enhance their availability. Yet, over the years, the empirical research about the efficacy of these several adjustments is equivocal (Ontario Law Reform Commission, 1996; Uzelac and Van Rhee, 2009; Rand 2009). Some analyses indicate that access or lack of access to formal civil disputing institutions is more a product of perceptions of institutional receptivity than of structural or cost impediments (Galanter, 1989; Tyler, 1997). During this period, legislatures also established various non-judicial institutions—no-fault automobile compensation schemes, landlord-tenant tribunals, and consumer protection offices—to make civil disputing cheaper and more expeditious. The growth of mass adjudication agencies led, in turn, to the simplification of judicial and non-judicial recourse against state action though mechanisms such as Ombudsmen and Freedom of Information Offices. Since then, public law scholars have undertaken significant empirical research into the operation of these institutions, although this tends to focus more on accessibility understood in terms of the traditional judicial metric of procedural fairness, than on the systemic effect of their adoption on the justice system writ large (Noreau, 1993; Rush Social Research, 1999).

C. Wave 3: Demystifying official law—alternatives to state institutions

The 1980s saw the emergence of an understanding of access to justice as centrally a problem of citizen understanding—not just understanding of litigation, but understanding of civil disputing as a social process. As courts began to implement modern organizational thinking through notions such as "case management" and "streamlined procedures" for certain categories of cases, as well as through greater use of technology (e.g., computerized filing and video-conferencing) legislatures were also active, adopting a brace of alternative dispute resolution (ADR) mechanisms. Some were free-standing (neighborhood justice centers), while others were grafted onto the judicial process (court-annexed mediation, expert arbitration of damage awards, the use of referees in complex disputes and judicially mandated settlements, and mandatory arbitration). Each of these initiatives generated extensive empirical research involving both quantitative and qualitative studies (Coumarelos et al., 2006; Hutchinson, 1990).

A significant impact of empirical research into these developments was the recognition by policy-makers that everyday litigation could be complemented not only by state-managed ADR processes but also by non-state processes: consensual arbitration, industry ombudsmen, religious tribunals, and other means for de-judicializing civil justice. Yet studies showed mixed results. Citizens were often reluctant to use these alternatives unless pushed, and even then they frequently had difficulty navigating even informal, non-bureaucratic mechanisms, with the result that activists called for programs of public legal information and education. At the same time, scholars began to investigate whether the use of "plain language" in legislative and contractual drafting had any impact in demystifying law. Other initiatives to increase popular knowledge included the use of pictures, flow charts, FAQs, videos, and sample problems. While these efforts were accompanied, at least in North America, by a slowing of the growth in civil litigation, recent research does not seem to confirm either a causal relationship or that justice is increasingly accessible (Galanter, 2004). Some studies suggest that generalized citizen scepticism, changing perceptions of the judicial role, and doubts about the contribution of law, litigation, courts and lawyers to achieving social justice lie behind less recourse to courts (Ontario Law Reform Commission, 1996) while others argue that legislative propensity to enact justiciable rights is largely independent of the existence or success of de-judicializing initiatives (Burke, 2002). In some states, research into informal systems that were introduced under the auspices of a vindication of traditional practices suggests that access to justice may be primarily a rhetorical tool aimed at serving very different ends than the achievement of justice (Galanter and Krishnan, 2004; Baxi, 2007).

D. Wave 4: Preventative law—proactive access to justice

By the 1990s, scholars theorized that access to justice was not just about processes of redress: improving access to lawyers and courts, and pluralizing and streamlining alternative mechanisms of dispute settlement. Access to justice also required re-imagining the goals and values of the official civil-disputing system. The idea was to develop, in parallel with processes such as diversion and restorative justice in the criminal law, various strategies to help citizens avoid conflicts, or deal with them before they were perceived or crystallized as legal problems. Soon, a radically different view of ADR as preventative law was elaborated (Noreau, 1993). In pursuing the idea of preventative law, researchers also began to focus on the unofficial law made, administered and applied by non-public bodies: e.g. private standards organizations; shopping centers; condominium associations; gated communities; private police; industry ombudsmen; better business bureaus (Merry, 1995).

The correlation between citizen input into and the quality of outcomes produced by these unofficial bodies led scholars to undertake studies of proactive strategies to improve public engagement with all official institutions (Killian, 2003), a research topic first suggested at the outset of empirical inquiries into access to justice (Abel, 1982). Public policy consultations with funded NGO interveners, and processes to enhance citizen input into the administrative and legislative processes became the object of empirical studies into their impact on rule-making outcomes undertaken mostly by political scientists and public administration scholars. Indeed, the idea that access to justice means providing citizens with an equal right to participate in every institution where law is debated, created, administered, interpreted, and applied appears to be more accepted in empirical studies undertaken outside North America and Europe (World Bank, 2009; UNDP, 2009). One such study from South America suggests that the complex relationship between the aspirations of international legal institutions, multinational corporations, and indigenous peoples poses unique access-to-justice challenges in all these dimensions (Szablowski, 2007).

E. Wave 5: Making and administering law—holistic access to justice

The third millennium has seen the emergence of a fifth wave in access-to-justice empirical research. Acknowledging the manifold institutional and contextual facets of access to justice led policy-makers to explore disciplinary fields beyond law and the traditional social sciences. Whether reactive or proactive, whether official or unofficial, legal strategies alone were seen as insufficient to address the roots of the access-to-justice problems encountered by the poor and the disenfranchised. Some international studies focus on the perspectives of justice seekers, particularly the poor, and show how reform to enhance access to justice needs to commence with a detailed understanding of social, economic, and political disenfranchisement (World Bank, 2009). Moreover, empirical studies suggesting a correlation between health status, employment, victimization by violence on the one hand, and lack of access to justice on the other led to the establishment of community legal clinics with broad health and social service mandates (Stein, 2001; Pleasance et al., 2004; UNDP, 2009).

Under a holistic approach, access to justice is perceived as requiring equal opportunities for historically excluded population segments to gain access to positions of authority within the legal system. Multijurisdictional empirical research projects reveal significant differentials in access to the legal professions (Abel and Lewis, 1988, 1989), although the impact of these differentials on access to justice for socially subordinated groups and individuals has not been systematically measured and some studies suggest that better public legal education mitigates these differentials (Ontario Legal Aid Review, 1997, updated 2008). Many institutions such as law faculties, the judiciary, the public service (including the police) and law societies have undertaken significant quantitative and qualitative research into the socio-demography of their membership and the causes of differential access (Bass et al., 2005). Again, however, there is little empirical evidence about whether increasing the number of women, visible minorities, or the historically disadvantaged in legal education, the professions, and the judiciary will change the system enough to overcome the disempowerment felt by marginalized populations (NSW, 2000; Currie, 2006).

F. Where to next? Constraints on supply-side empirical research

The literature of the last half-century suggests a broadening inventory of concerns that fall under the access-to-justice research agenda. Yet both policy and empirical research continues to focus on the official civil dispute-resolution system. An accessible system is said to be one that produces: (1) just results, (2) and fair treat-ment, (3) at reasonable cost, (4) with reasonable speed; and that (5) is understandable to users, and (6) responsive to needs; that (7) provides certainty, and (8) is effec-tive, adequately resourced and well organized (Woolf, 1996; Rush Social Research, 1999). Notwithstanding increasingly sophisticated access to-justice theorizing, most empirical research remains oriented more to evaluating the attributes of an accessible official dispute-resolution system (courts and lawyers) than those of an accessible civil justice system more generally (Burke, 2002; Coumarelos et al., 2006; Uzelac and Van Rhee, 2009).

This preoccupation leads scholars to assess the institutions and processes of civil disputing without necessarily attending to the quality of outcomes they produce. There are numerous empirical studies of litigation outcomes, and the impact of institutional design, the presence of lawyers, the nature of the claim being advanced, and procedure on outcomes (Kritzer and Silbey, 2003), although measuring the quality of outcomes has proved challenging (Galanter, 1989). The focus is on litigant presence in, and the fair operation of, the court system. Equitable presence and fair operation no doubt enhance confidence in the official system (Tyler, 1997). But if the achievement of access to justice lies in the eyes of the beholder, empirical studies must attend to all the public and private institutions, processes and sites of norma-tive interaction where claims of justice are advanced and vindicated.

In view of this evolution in theorizing about access-to-justice, why has supply-side empirical research largely retained its relatively narrow compass? First, because of its high cost, most empirical research is funded by institutional play-ers such as governments, courts and bar associations that are principally inter-ested in framing questions and hypotheses relevant to them (Ontario Law Reform Commission, 1996; BJS, 2001). Second, state agencies are not pressured to collect even rudimentary data beyond aggregate litigation rates, time, cost, settlements, appeals, and other incidents of civil litigation, in part because till recently there was little demand for such data from university-based legal research establishments. Yet even with the expansion of inquiry in such surveys, data tends to focus on for-mal aspects of civil litigation. Third, it is much easier to identify sources of infor-mation, to decide what data to seek, to collect that data, to advance hypotheses, and to run multivariate regressions where the research target is an official institu-tion (McGuire and Macdonald, 1996, 1998; Kritzer et al., 2007). Finally, framing research to elicit people's conceptions of where and how justice may be achieved, and their success in the endeavor requires methodological sophistication beyond the capacity of most legal (although not social science) scholars and the reward structure for their undertaking it. Despite the prevalence of excellent studies by, for example, political scientists, sociologists, anthropologists, and economists, until there is a coincidence of theoretical comprehensiveness, funding, and scholarly capacity, supply-side access to justice research within law faculties will remain over-theorized but empirically under-developed.

IV. ORGANIZING INQUIRY: BARRIERS TO ACCESS AS FACTORS OF EXCLUSION

Historically, the privileged trope for assessing demand-side access-to-justice questions has been the metaphor of "barriers." Justice exists somewhere—in legal representation, in the court-house—and the goal is to identify and overcome obstacles to its delivery. The barriers idea is a reasonable conception for highlighting those problems of access that are either material or capable of "objective" measurement (Hutchinson, 1990). However, its usefulness as a frame for demand-side empirical research is limited in two ways. First, it does not capture lack of access resulting from "subjective barriers"—broader patterns of marginalization and social exclusion visited upon, for example, women, racial minorities, and the elderly. Of course, the impact of these socio-demographic factors on access is highly contextual: in Canada, for example, studies indicate significant effect of subjective barriers (McGuire and Macdonald, 1996); in the United States, by contrast, research does not do so (Kritzer and Silbey, 2003). Second, the barriers metaphor suggests that the solution for lack of access lies in fixing existing institutional frameworks. It does not contemplate that marginalized publics might themselves contribute to developing the types of responses they see as optimal for dealing with their lack of access. Interestingly, by contrast with most western scholarly approaches, almost all contemporary transnational access to justice projects for countries in course of development adopt a broad view of the terrain of inquiry (World Bank, 2009; UNDP, 2009), and aim at developing sustainable, bottom-up solutions to access to justice problems for those living at the "base of the pyramid" (Microjustice, 2009).

A. Physical, temporal, and material barriers

In the access-to-justice literature, the most elementary form of access to justice is material access to official institutions of civil disputing and to related legal services. Presumably, if any institution for administering and applying law is physically inaccessible, there is a barrier. Perhaps the most significant material barrier flows from the fact that the law requires citizens to come to it, not the reverse. Courts—even relatively low-value first-instance courts—are not always located in the most accessible buildings. Moreover, some studies (often undertaken by official institutions themselves) show that when courts, administrative points of service, and legal aid offices are open in the evening, client satisfaction increases; there does not, however, appear to be any empirical research indicating that actual utilization of these services increases (Coumarelos et al., 2006: Ontario Legal Aid Review, 1997, updated 2008).

A further type of material barrier relates to the ancillary services that are connected with the litigation process. Persons who have visual or auditory impairments, persons who do not speak a state's official language and persons who have diminished intellectual capacity all require significant assistance to understand what is going on in a court-room. Without the assistance of translators or services for the visually or hearing impaired, many justice seekers are simply passive participants in a complicated system that is intellectually inaccessible to them. Surprisingly, there is little empirical research about any of these material barriers, or the impact of enhanced access to legal representation on palliating them, other than that produced by lobbies or anti-discrimination agencies in the context of general studies of exclusion of the relevant group.

B. Objective barriers: cost, delays, and complexity

Where the research focus is on civil litigation processes, three so-called objective barriers to access are typically noted: cost, delays and complexity (Hutchinson, 1990). The first two are the most studied causes of a denial of access to justice, although depending on the configuration of legal aid programs in a state, cost can be primarily a concern of either the poor or the middle-class (Breen, 2002; Coumarelos et al., 2006; Currie, 2006). Some research indicates that delay constitutes a denial of access mostly for the poor or socially vulnerable; for middle-class litigants delay is perceived more as an annoyance. As for complex or arcane substantive legal rules, these typically are seen to produce longer and more costly trials, unless the matter is so complex that parties decide to settle.

Independently of the substantive complexity of a claim, the litigation process itself may be complicated or cumbersome to navigate—often, paradoxically, as a result of modifications to procedural rules—for example, contingency fees and cost-shifting rules — meant to ensure fairness between litigants. For represented litigants, complexity induces bafflement and worry about escalating costs. Where justice-seekers are self-represented, it often leads to frustration, desisting from litigation or the acceptance of a sub-optimal settlement offer (NSW, 2000). The most significant impact of complexity is that it produces major psychological barriers to engaging in civil litigation. Some people are more able than others to respond to the psychological demands that the legal system places on them when they seek to vindicate their rights (McGuire and Macdonald, 1996, 1998).

C. Process barriers: system design

Process barriers are often related to the psyche of the justice seeker. Uncertainty of outcome is a key psychological obstacle that the justice-seeker must overcome, whatever his or her socio-demographic status (Tyler, 1997; Stein, 2001). Uncertainty can also combine with costs, particularly within a fee-shifting regime, to make courts proceedings not seem worth it to prospective litigants (Kritzer, 1998). More than this, studies of disputing processes have suggested a number of other subjective factors that lead to inaccessibility. Some appear to indicate that an important reason for exclusion is that the judicial system and, more generally, western conceptions of law are rights-based and adversarial. They offer an advantage to those exhibiting certain types of aggressive behavior and to those who can frame their claims in certain ways (Paquin, 2001). Conversely, systems that emphasize reconciliation can provide advantages to those able to frame their claim non-aggressively or to apologize (Abel, 1982).

Not only do all systems favor certain types of agents, they also favor certain types of claims. Of course, this means that favored players will be different from state to state depending on system design. Some studies suggest that North American and European systems disproportionately favor one or more of: (1) the more-endowed party; (2) repeat players rather than one-shot litigants; (3) organized interests over unorganized interests; (4) social superiors over social inferiors; and (5) those who go to court to bring traditional rights-based claims rather than those who seek vindication (or an apology) as opposed to money (Black, 1991). The last point, that the character of the claim and the array of available remedies disserve litigants who seek a non-monetary outcome, suggests the need for more attention to the access consequences of choices about system design (Bass et al., 2005; Genn et al., 2006).

D. Socio-cultural barriers: immigrants and indigenous peoples

Social systems—including the civil justice system—are usually meant to meet the needs of the majority of users. So, for example, if the dominant socio-demographic is the white, male, middle-aged, middle-and-upper-class, English-speaking citizen, every step away from that socio-demographic is a step away from access: immigrants, women, the young, the old, the poor are less likely to be official justice seekers. This sometimes results from the nature of the putative claims these non-majority litigants are likely to have, but it also results from the sense of discomfort they may feel about the civil justice system. For example, in one jurisdiction, studies have shown that the socio-demographic group with the greatest access to justice (the greatest propensity to use disputing institutions—whether regular courts or small claims courts) is the group that has best internalized the social structures of that society (Ontario Law reform Commission, 1966).

There is some evidence of a general under-utilization of the formal civil justice system by women, especially single women raising families, but generally studies reporting under-utilization do not control for claim type. For example, a number of such studies rest on the simplifying assumption that legal conflict is evenly distributed across the population and that all litigants are likely to have the same legal problems. Without careful study of what types of problems are actually experienced by different socio-demographic groups it is difficult to attribute presence or absence from official institutions exclusively to differential utilization. Likewise, one generally also finds that people of color, racialized minorities, adolescents, the elderly, indigenous peoples, immigrants, refugees, those with physical or intellectual disabilities, or with a criminal record, and non-native speakers take less advantage of government programs meant to assist them and are less likely to seek legal assistance in making claims. Here again, however, without commensurable evidence as to prevalence or distribution of the types of disputes that ultimately come to litigation, it is impossible to tell whether the absence of such claimants is tied to the fact they do not experience such problems or whether it relates to their socio-demographic characteristics (Ontario Legal Aid Review, 1997, updated 2008). One recent multijurisdictional review of empirical data concludes that claim-type is more significant than income in the decision to "go to law" (Kritzer and Silbey, 2003).

Data from international empirical studies appear to confirm that the interrelationship between inaccessible justice and other social exclusions is hard to draw. They point to the need for demand-oriented, community-driven approaches to justice and governance reform. These studies substantiate the close link between the success of initiatives to promote democratic development and the effectiveness of those to enhance access to justice (World Bank, 2009). Likewise, empirical research sponsored by the UNDP Commission on Legal Empowerment for the Poor aims as much at exploring how political and governance structures affect access to justice as at conventionally understood cost barriers (UNDP, 2009).

E. Barriers linked to physical or mental health

It is common to consider persons with disabilities as another group for whom access to justice is a particular concern. More generally, full participation in society typically requires full capacities. Evidence from social service agencies indicates that those suffering from chronic sickness, or chronic workplace injury, or who are in poor health and in particular those whose poor health results from a socially stigmatized medical condition (such as being HIV positive), alcoholics, and people addicted to drugs (both medical and non-medical) are less likely to access social welfare and public health programs. Advocates for such people, as well as those who are institutionalized—whether incarcerated, or living in group homes, asylums, or treatment clinics—claim an equal exclusion from the civil justice system. There is, however, a dearth of large-scale empirical data supporting such assertions (Ontario Law reform Commission, 1966; Genn and Beinart, 1999; Bass et al., 2005), and most evidence is anecdotal or advanced in relation to a particular exclusion for the purpose of changing public policy.

Another type of exclusion more directly involves considerations of agency. Those with intellectual handicaps or mental health problems will always see their access to justice concerns mediated through litigation guardians or representative decision-makers. There are claims by interests groups that state curatorship systems under-protect the legal rights of such people although typically, no empirical evidence is adduced in support. There is, however, some data about the psychological reluctance to litigate of those who have experienced significant emotional trauma. Sometimes this occurs because of a particular act of violence committed against them (e.g., sexual, physical or emotional abuse; shunning by co-religionists; workplace harassment). In the above cases the effect of violence is said to destroy a person's capacity to act as an agent and, consequently to access legal redress for everyday civil-justice claims (Paquin, 2001; World Bank, 2009).

F. Poverty barriers and the middle class

One barrier that has attracted significant empirical research is economic disadvantage. In Canada, for example, there is evidence to the effect that the poor "are not just like those with money except that they don't have money" and that the access to justice problems they experience are correlated to their economic situation (Ontario Legal Aid Review, 1997, updated 2008). On the other hand, there are several studies in the U.S. suggesting that propensity to seek the assistance of a lawyer is only weakly (if at all) correlated to income (ABA, 1994). But the economics of litigation is not just an issue for the poor. There is evidence that frequency of civil disputing positively correlates with family income, and that the cost of justice imperils accessibility for the middle class (Currie, 2006). Mechanisms such as pre-paid or "before the event" legal insurance, class actions, contributory legal aid, and contingency fees are meant to attenuate the impact of these costs (Killian, 2003).

Again, however, the evidence is mixed as to whether any of these palliatives actually enhances access to lawyers and courts; likewise studies are equivocal as to whether deployment of lawyers by the poor to claim or defend lawsuits changes litigation outcomes (McGuire and Macdonald, 1996; Kritzer and Silbey, 2003). The primary research difficulty lies in trying to measure the impact of the channelling that begins at the point of perception (McGuire and Macdonald, 1998; Genn and

Beinart, 1999). Determining whether these subjective factors shape how a problem is perceived before it is named as a legal problem requires qualitative field research that translates category-based "needs assessments" into individual perceptions of available legal redress (Curran, 1977; Pleasance et al., 2004; Bass et al., 2005; Coumarelos et al., 2006). To date a suitable metric for generating quantitative data from this qualitative research has not been developed.

G. Users or justice seekers? Implications for demand-side empirical research

The review of demand-side access-to-justice research illustrates a macro-point: because not all citizens are similarly situated across a wide range of geographic, socio-demographic and economic variables, their legal needs can be quite different (Breen, 2002). Moreover, because courts and lawyers are not the only sites of inaccessibility, the type of broad-brush approach reflected in a preoccupation with the delivery of legal services by lawyers addresses only some of the causes of exclusion. For example, simply to assert that the recipe for accessible justice is to "make the forum fit the fuss" is to forget that "fusses" are not naturally occurring events: as with theorizing demand-side exclusions, so too with access-to-justice research. The research (and policy) problem is, however, complex. Measuring the impact of economic factors is essential, but it misses inaccessibility traceable to broader patterns of social marginalization (Ontario Legal Aid Review, 1997, updated 2008). Yet empirical evidence of demand-side inaccessibility does not itself answer the question whether absence results from exclusion or withdrawal, causes that would call forth radically different legislative responses.

A second implication is that the solution for a lack of access does not lie only in fixing institutional frameworks. These strategies presume that people have set justice preferences determined by the state and set preferences for vindicating these justice preferences (e.g., lawyer-assisted litigation) But some contemporary general studies suggest some population groups (especially marginalized populations) do not have fixed justice preferences (they define these preferences iteratively), and do not have fixed preferences about the optimal means (e.g., lawyers and courts) for negotiating these preferences. Once access to justice and its accessibility is seen this way, the frontier between official justice and the unofficial justice lived in everyday social interaction becomes porous (Abel, 1982; Merry, 1995). The challenge for empirical research into access to justice is to identify, measure, and assess the extent of access to justice in these informal sites of normative interaction and to correlate these data with comparable data derived from studies of the various components of the official justice system.

V. CONCLUSION: WHOSE ACCESS?
WHICH JUSTICE?

The above review counsels humility in assessing the terrain of empirical studies of access to justice. Despite an expansion in scope, the field remains ill-defined. Research objectives are often not well-grounded theoretically. While there is an extensive literature on procedural justice and public perceptions of lawyers and courts, apart from the general "legal needs of the public" inventories, few sector-specific studies explore access from the perspective of the justice-seeker. Most data flows from state agencies. The cost of legal services and litigation continues to be a research preoccupation. The glut of normative scholarship leads to much repetition and a lack of progress in determining what to measure and how to measure it.

At the international level, development studies provide the major impetus behind empirical research on access to justice. In many cases, however, development studies focus on official institutions that replicate those of the developed world and do not report data about informal access to justice (World Bank, 2009; UNDP, 2009). At the national level, ministries of justice, law reform agencies, law foundations, bar associations, not-for-profit research institutes, academic research groups, and NGOs are all key engines behind empirical research on access to justice (Rand Institute for Civil Justice, 2009; Genn et al., 2006; Bass et al., 2005; NSW, 2000).

The primary concerns driving quantitative empirical research are: the need to effectively record symptoms so as to be able to make well-informed diagnoses of social ills which manifest themselves as access-to-justice problems; and the need to test reform efforts so as to determine whether they have been effective, or whether palliative energies have been misdirected. Less frequently, although increasingly today given empirical research into ADR, public legal information and preventative law, scholars ask how to make access-to-justice research more inclusive, thereby aligning research methods with the overall objectives of an access-to-justice agenda. Doing so puts a premium on qualitative research into litigant expectations and experiences (Relis, 2009). While consumer satisfaction studies can assist in fine-tuning the official system to enhance access to justice, a complete picture also requires research into the expectations of those who currently do not use the formal justice system (Galanter, 1989; Merry, 1995; Tyler, 1997).

The relative absence of this last type of inquiry reflects the reality that the many groups collecting data do so for their own assessment and evaluation purposes, and not necessarily to serve better any particular needs of justice-seekers. Whether assembled by ministries of justice, legal aid corporations, bar associations or private actors such as legal-expenses insurers, the data usually does not address the functional core of access to justice beyond its institutional settings. In addition, these

types of study invariably aim at citizen access to justice problems and do not usually apply the survey metric to corporate and other institutional litigants (NGOs,
unions, voluntary associations).

In the pioneering surveys of the 1970s researchers observed that defining the
"legal needs of the public" even without attempting to assess how well they are
being met, is itself a difficult (and politically sensitive) task (Cass and Sackville, 1975;
Messier, 1975; Curran, 1977). Moreover, survey approaches that rely entirely on open-
ended questions and self-defining responses do not provide sufficient guidance to
enable citizens to provide researchers with data about which hypotheses may be
formulated or tested. This might explain why studies have found that much thinking and debate about access to justice is either conjectural or consciously polemical
repetition of cant (McGuire and Macdonald, 1996, 1998; Kritzer and Silbey, 2003). If
scholars don't really know the legal needs of the public, if they are unclear about how
they might conduct an agent-driven needs assessment, and if they lack comparative
baselines—either longitudinally, or laterally by engaging data from like empirical
surveys in other countries—demonstrable affirmations about the problem and its
solutions are impossible.

Merely gathering raw statistics about institutional usage is not enough. While
data about lawyers, courts, and public agencies increase the knowledge base, they
are often duplicative, only sporadically brought into the public domain, and rarely
collected in data sets that can be cross-referenced. With rare exceptions, what seems
to be missing is concerted action around a shared understanding of what kinds of
data should be aggregated and what vehicles are best for achieving that aggregation.
That is, good empirical scholarship on access to justice needs a theory of what the
statistics are meant to tell, how they can be interpreted, and where to find the "dogs
that are not barking."

I conclude with three recommendations for refocusing the targets and enhancing
the policy purchase of empirical research into how civil justice can be made more
accessible for the entire population.

First, the next generation of research should be framed on the hypothesis that
the civil justice system comprises the totality of modes and sites for discovering,
symbolizing and resolving human conflict. This means more than simply acknowledging that the state does not have a monopoly on elaborating the norms of justice
and that the courts are not the only dispute resolution vehicle. Most human conflict
finds expression in language that only remotely mirrors that of legislative and judicial processes. Empirical research must target the everyday law of social interaction where inaccessible justice is first perceived. That means examining how human
beings imagine and work through their conflicts even prior to the transformation of
those conflicts into formal, legal disputes; furthermore, it means exploring not only
the social functions of the official civil justice system, but those of other normative
systems, and seeing how they interact.

Second, the next generation of research should be framed on the hypothesis that a lack of access to justice cannot be remedied even principally by institutional redesign and reform of the formal justice system. No doubt, such reforms can enhance access to official redress mechanisms, but alone they do not enhance justice. Greater access to institutions that are the source of one's oppression is hardly a desirable outcome. Even though research into how legal expertise can be accessed and deployed and civil litigation undertaken without fear of reprisal remains important, it is no substitute for research into broad notions of a just social and political system. The key empirical research for the future must focus on the multiple ways in which citizens conceive justice and just institutions of civil disputing.

Third, the next generation of research should be framed to test the hypothesis that lack of access to justice is a symptom of a larger societal malaise. When lack of access is cast as a problem of disempowerment and disengagement, the remedy lies in re-building citizen commitment both to public and private institutions of civil justice. This calls for empirical research that focuses centrally on demand-side, rather than supply-side issues. Studies that enable policy-makers to understand the legal needs of the public, as expressed by citizens themselves—and not according to a matrix derived from the existing framework of substantive and procedural laws— are the optimal vehicles for ensuring that an accessible system of law is also an accessible system of justice.

References

ABA (1994). *Legal Needs and Civil Justice. Survey of Americans Major Findings from the Comprehensive Legal Needs Study*, Chicago: American Bar Association.

Abel, R. (ed.) (1982). *The Politics of Informal Justice*, 2 vols. New York: Academic Press.

Abel, R. and Lewis, P. (eds.) (1988–1989). *Lawyers in Society*, 3 vols. Berkeley: University of California.

Access to Justice Advisory Committee ALRC (1994). *Access to Justice: An Action Plan*, Canberra: Australian Public Publication Services.

ALRC [Australian Law Reform Commission] (2000). *Managing Justice*, Sydney: ALRC.

Bass, J., Zemans, F., and Bogart, W. (eds.) (2005). *Access to Justice for a New Century: the Way Forward*, Toronto: Law Society of Upper Canada.

Baxi, P. (2007). "Access to Justice and Rule-of-[Good] Law: The Cunning of Judicial Reform in Indian," working paper commissioned by the Institute of Human Development on the behalf of the UN Commission on the Legal Empowerment of the Poor, New Delhi. In *United Nations Development Programme*, available at <http://www.undp.org/legalempowerment/reports/National%20Consultation%20Reports/   Country%20Files/12_India/12_4_Access_to_Justice.pdf>.

BJS (2001). *US Department of Justice, Bureau of Justice Statistics. Supplemental Survey of Civil Appeals*, available at <http://www.icpsr.umich.edu/icpsrweb/ICPSR/studies/04539>.

Black, D. (1991). *Sociological Justice*, New York: Oxford University Press.

Breen, E. (ed.) (2002). *Évaluer la justice*, Paris: Presses Universitaires de France.

Burke, T. (2002). *Lawyers, Lawsuits and Legal Rights: Litigation in American Society*, Berkeley: University of California Press.

Cappelletti, M. and Garth, B. (1978). *Access to Justice: A World-wide Survey*, Milan: Sitjhof.

Carfield, M. (2005). "Enhancing poor people's capabilities through the rule of law: creating an access to justice index," *Washington University Law Quarterly* 83: 339–360.

Cass, M. and Sackville, R. (1975). *Legal needs of the poor*, Canberra: AGPS.

CEPEJ (2006). *European judicial systems. Facts and Figures*, Belgium: Counsel of Europe Publishing.

Coumarelos, Ch., Wei, Z., and Zhou, A. (2006). *Justice Made to Measure: NSW Legal Needs Survey in Disadvantaged Areas, Access to Justice and Legal Needs*, Sydney: Law and Justice Foundation of New South Wales.

Curran, B. (1977). *The Legal Needs of the Public: The Final Report of a National Survey*, Chicago: American Bar Foundation.

Currie, A. (2006). "A National Survey of the Civil Justice Problems of Low- and Moderate-income Canadians: Incidence and Patterns," *International Journal of the Legal Profession* 13(3): 217–42.

Dauer, E. (1991). "A Wider Notion of Unmet Legal Needs," in ABA (ed.), *Civil Justice: An Agenda for the 1990s*, Chicago: American Bar Association.

Dotan, Y. (2003). "Resource Inequalities in Ideological Courts: The Case of the Israeli High Court of Justice," in H. Kritzer and S. Silbey (eds.), *In Litigation: Do the "Haves" Still Come out Ahead?*, Stanford: Stanford Law and Politics.

Galanter, M. (1989). "Symposium: Assessing the Quality of Dispute Processing," *Denver University Law Review* 66: xi–xiv, 335–562.

Galanter, M. (2004). "The Vanishing Trial: An Examination of Trials and Related Matters in Federal and State Courts," *Journal of Empirical Legal Studies* 1(3): 459–570.

Galanter, M. and Krishna, J. (2004). "Bread for the Poor: Access to Justice and the Rights of the Needy in India," *Hastings Law Journal* 55: 789–834.

Genn, H. and Beinart, S. (eds.) (1999). *Paths to Justice: What People Do and Think About Going to Law*, Oxford: Hart.

Genn, H., Partington, M., and Wheeler, S. (2006). *Law in the Real World: Improving Our Understanding of How Law Works*, London: The Nuffield Foundation.

Hadfield, G. (2006). "Don't Forget the Lawyers: The Role of Lawyers in Promoting the Rule of Law in Emerging Market Democracies," *DePaul Law Review* 56: 401–22.

Hendley, K., Murrell, P., and Ryterman, R. (2003). "Do Repeat Players Behave Differently in Russia? Contractual and Litigation Behaviour of Russian Enterprises," in H. Kritzer and S. Silbey (eds.), *In Litigation: Do the "Haves" Still Come out Ahead?*, Stanford: Stanford Law and Politics.

Hutchinson, A. (ed.), (1990). *Access to Civil Justice*, Toronto: Carswell.

Killian, M. (2003). "Alternatives to Public Provision: the Role of Legal Expenses Insurance in Broadening Access to Justice: The German Experience," *Journal of Law and Society* 30: 31–48.

Kritzer, H. (1998). "Contingent-Fee Lawyers and Their Clients," *Law and Social Inquiry*, 23: 795–822.

Kritzer, H. and Silbey, S. (eds.) (2003) *In Litigation: Do the "Haves" Still Come out Ahead?*, Stanford: Stanford Law and Politics.

Kritzer, H., Brace, P., Gann Hall, M., and Boyea, B. (2007). "The Business of State Supreme Courts, Revisited," *Journal of Empirical Legal Studies* 4: 427–39.

Legal Action Group (1996). *Achieving Civil Justice*, London: Legal Action Group.

McGuire, S. and Macdonald, R.A. (1996). "Small Claims Courts Cant," *Osgoode Hall Law Journal* 34: 509–52.

McGuire, S. and Macdonald, R.A. (1998). "Tales of Wows and Woes from the Masters and the Muddled: Navigating Small Claims Court Narratives," *Windsor Yearbook of Access to Justice* 16: 48–89.

Meggitt, G. (2008). "Civil Justice Reform in Hong Kong—Its progress and its future," *Hong Kong Law Journal*, 38: 89–128.

Merry, S.E., (1995). "Sorting our Popular Justice," in Sally Engle Merry and Neal Milner (eds.), *The Possibility of Popular Justice: A Case Study of Community Mediation in the United States*, Ann Arbor: University of Michigan Press.

Messier, C. (1975). *Les mains de la loi*, Montreal: Commission des services juridiques.

Microjustice Initiative (2009), available at <http://www.microjustice.org/>.

Moorhead, R. and Pleasance, P. (eds.) (2003). *After Universalism: Reengineering Access to Justice*, London: Blackwell.

Muno-Perez, B. (1993). "Les statistiques judiciaires civiles, sous-produit du répertoire général des affaires civiles," *Droit et Société* 25: 351–60.

Noreau, P. (1993). *Droit préventive: le droit au delà de la loi*, Montreal: Themis.

NSW (2000). Council of Social Service of NSW and Law Foundation of NSW, *Going it Alone: A survey of the impacts of Commonwealth funding cuts to legal aid on community welfare agencies and legal practitioners and their clients*, Sydney: Law Foundation of New South Wales.

Ontario Law Reform Commission (1996). *Rethinking Civil Justice: Research Studies for the Civil Justice Review*, 2 vols, Toronto: Ontario Law Reform Commission.

Ontario Legal Aid Review (1997). *Report of the Ontario Legal Aid Review: A Blueprint for Publicly Funded Legal Services*, (Chair: J.D. McCamus) vol. 3, Toronto: Ontario Legal Aid Review; updated as Ontario Legal Aid Review. (2008). *Report of the Ontario Legal Aid Review*, (Chair: Michael J. Trebilcock), available at <http://www.attorneygeneral.jus.gov. on.ca/english/about/pubs/trebilcock/legal_aidreport_2008_EN.pdf >.

Paquin, J. (2001). "Avengers, Avoiders and Lumpers: The Incidence of Disputing Style on Litigiousness," *Windsor Yearbook of Access to Justice* 19: 3–38.

Pleasance, P., Buck, A., Balmer, N., O'Grady, A., Genn, H., and Smith, M. (2004). *Causes of Action: Civil Law and Social Justice. The Final Report of the First LSRC Survey of Justiciable Problems*. United Kingdom, Legal Services Commission, available at <http://www.lsrc. org.uk/publications/Causes%20of%20Action.pdf>.

Rand Institute for Civil Justice (2009). *Just, Speedy and Inexpensive? An Evaluation of Judicial Case Management under the CJRA*, available at <http://www.rand.org>.

Relis, T. (2009). *Perceptions in Litigation and Mediation: Lawyers, Defendants, Plaintiffs and Gendered Parties*, New York: Cambridge University Press.

Rush Social Research (1999). *Legal assistance needs project: phase one: Estimation of a Basic Needs-Based Planning Model*, Canberra: Commonwealth Attorney and Emancipation, General's Department.

Silbey, S. and Ewick, P. (1993). *Differential Use of Courts by Minority and Non-Minority Populations in New Jersey*, Trenton: New Jersey Supreme Court Task Force on Minority Concerns.

Stein, J.M. (2001). *The Future of Social Justice in Britain: A New Mission for the Community Legal Service*, London: Centre for the Analysis of Social Exclusion.

Szablowski, D. (2007). *Transnational Law and Local Struggles: Mining, Communities and the World Bank*, Oxford: Hart Publishing.

Tyler, T.R. (1997). "Citizen Discontent with Legal Procedures: A Social Science Perspective on Civil Procedure Reform," *American Journal of Comparative Law* 45: 871–904.

UNDP [United Nations Development Programme] (2009). *Commission on Legal Empowerment for the Poor*, available at <http://www.undp.org/legalempowerment/press/Interviews_Ebadi.html>.

Uzelac, A. and Van Rhee, C.H. (2009). *Access to Justice and the Judiciary: Towards New European Standards of Affordability, Quality and Efficiency of Civil Adjudication*, Oxford: Hart Publishing.

Varano, V. and De Luca, A. (2007). "Access to Justice in Italy," *Global Jurist* 7.1.6: 1–22, available at <http://www.bepress.com/gj/vol7/iss1/art6>.

Woolf, Rt. Hon Lord. (1996). *Access to Justice: Interim Report to the Lord Chancellor on the Civil Justice System in England and Wales*, London: HMSO.

World Bank (2009). *Justice for the Poor*, available at <http://go.worldbank.org/SMIKY7M6O0>, especially: "Forging the Middle Ground," "The Illusion of Inclusion," and "Breaking Legal Inequality Traps: New Approaches to Building Justice Systems for the Poor in Developing Countries," available at <http://go.worldbank.org/ZRKELPETD0>.

2 2

JUDICIAL RECRUITMENT, TRAINING, AND CAREERS

PETER H. RUSSELL

EMPIRICAL research on the personnel of the bench, as with many other fields of empirical legal studies, began in the United States and for many years was dominated by American scholars. The reason for this was the confluence of two factors: the emergence of legal realism early in the twentieth century as a major current of thought in American legal culture, and the prominent role of the judiciary in American politics from the very beginning of U.S. history. It is the confluence of these same two factors—legal realism and growing recognition of the political power of courts—that led to empirical study of the judiciary being taken up in other western countries later in the twentieth century.

The primary focus of empirical studies of judiciaries has been the recruitment of judges. Such studies are concerned with both the sectors of society from which judges are drawn and the processes through which they are selected and appointed. Much of the literature divides the judiciaries of the world into two different families: judiciaries that are recruited from the ranks of experienced lawyers and "career judiciaries" in which judges form a separate branch of the legal professions which legally qualified graduates enter soon after university graduation. Judiciaries of the first kind are associated with common law countries, and the second kind with civil law countries. Empirical research, however, shows that this sharp bifurcation of judiciaries can be misleading. In common law countries there is a possible career path for judges after their first appointment to the bench, and in many civil law countries lawyers frequently become judges after years of professional practice.

The other sharp distinction that is often made in the literature is between elected and appointed judiciaries. Though this distinction is clear enough, empirical research has shown that it is of peripheral importance. It is only in the United States that a significant number of judges are directly elected by the people. Indirect election of judges by legislative or political bodies is a practice followed in three U.S. states, in Germany and Switzerland for the judges of their highest courts, and at the UN for members of the International Court of Justice. Aside from this handful of exceptions, those who hold judicial office around the world are selected through a great variety of appointing systems. Research in the field of judicial recruitment has been mostly concerned with systems of appointing judges.

There has been little empirical research on judicial education. Livingston Armytage's *Educating Judges*, the only book-length study, covers developments in Australia, Canada, New Zealand, the UK, and the United States (Armytage, 1996). Armytage's empirical research focuses on judicial attitudes to the need for judicial education. Since the 1970s, governments in common law countries have funded educational programs proposed by the judiciary for newly appointed judges and continuing education programs for sitting judges. Concerns about judicial independence have been met by placing responsibility for these programs in the hands of judges and resisting any moves to make participation in them mandatory. The discussion below of judicial recruitment in civil law countries will touch on "judge-schools" and apprenticeship arrangements in these countries. But substantial comparative empirical research on judicial education in civil law countries remains to be done.

I. THE AMERICAN SCHOOL

In the United States "staffing the courts" has been a topic of political interest and discussion since the country's founding. There was no doubt in the minds of America's founding fathers that judges would wield political power in the new republic. Nor was there any doubt that the political views of judges would shape the way they interpreted the law. Hence the U.S. Constitution establishes a highly political process for appointing the justices of the Supreme Court and other federal courts: the President appoints the judges with the advice and consent of the Senate. That process has ensured that the appointment of federal judges, and especially the filling of vacancies on the Supreme Court, have been important aspects of national politics throughout the country's history. At the state level, Jacksonian democracy in the 1830s led many states to abandon the English system of executive appointment and adopt the practice of popular election of judges. By the early years of the twentieth century, the problematic aspects of recruiting judges through partisan elections were making judicial reform a major public issue. The American Judicature Society was founded in 1913 with the primary objective of removing partisan politics from judicial selection. The Society's journal, *Judicature*, has been an important source of information on judicial recruitment in the United States.

It was not until after World War II that scholarly research and writing on the judiciary emerged on a significant scale. This "American school" of judicial studies has been dominated by political scientists. Empirical research by political scientists has gone well beyond the legal formalities of appointment or election systems to identify societal and political factors which shape the pool of candidates for judicial office and influence success or failure in becoming a judge. Joel Grossman, an early leader of this school, showed that the professional politics of the bar can be just as important as party politics in influencing the process of judicial selection (Grossman, 1965). Grossman's major work showed how the American Bar Association, at the national and state levels, plays a major role both in defining judicial merit and in assessing candidates for judicial office.

Some American political scientists have taken a more sociological approach to the study of judicial recruitment. A leading example is John R. Schmidhauser's *Judges and Justices: The Federal Appellate Judiciary*. Schmidhauser's research produced a collective sociological portrait of the federal appellate judiciary. This kind of research by American scholars has focused much more on gender and race than on class. However, when U.S. social scientists look for connections between the backgrounds of federally appointed judges and their decision-making, it is the political affiliation of the President who appointed them that is consistently shown to be the strongest predictor of judicial behavior (Tate, 1981).

The appointment of justices of the U.S. Supreme Court has a huge literature of its own. In his book about appointing Supreme Court justices, Laurence Tribe, a leading American legal scholar, wrote that "[t]here are literally thousands of books, articles, and judicial decisions broadly relevant to this book's subject" (Tribe, 1985: 152). Because the filling of a Supreme Court vacancy is seen to have a significant bearing on critical issues in the interpretation of the U.S. Constitution, this literature is of interest to both political historians and constitutional lawyers. It is the exceptional scholar who draws out the broader implications of this distinctively American process. A leading example is Judith Resnik who has analyzed the highly political American system in the context of contemporary democratic theory (Resnik, 2005). Her work is important reading for scholars and practitioners in other countries who, in an age of increasing judicial power, are concerned with squaring the processes of judicial recruitment with the norms of democratic government.

State judiciaries in the United States have provided their own distinct field for empirical research. Widespread concerns in the legal profession about how the election of judges threatens judicial independence and prevents the recruitment of a well-qualified professional judiciary, led to reform of the elective system in many states. The most emulated approach to reform was the American Judicature Society's 1914 proposal for judicial nominating commissions. The commissions assess candidates for openings on the bench and submit one or more names, of the candidate(s) deemed to be best qualified, to the state Governor. The chosen candidate is appointed for a year, or in some states a somewhat longer term, and then stands unopposed in a "retention" (confirmation) election. Judges selected in this way have limited terms and must stand unopposed for re-election ("retention") at the end of their term. This system as implemented is referred to as either "merit selection" or the "Missouri Plan" (after the first state to adopt it). Close to 90% of state judges must stand for election to secure or retain their position on the bench. A burgeoning political science literature shows that judicial elections have become increasingly competitive. Even in so-called "nonpartisan" elections, there is evidence of partisan influences. As a result of a 2002 U.S. Supreme Court decision, states can no longer prevent candidates from announcing their position on controversial legal issues (Streb, 2007).

The co-existence of a variety of judicial recruitment systems among the 50 U.S. states creates exceptional opportunities for comparative empirical research. Daniel Pinello has developed a sophisticated methodology for testing the impact of different selection systems on judicial decision-making (Pinello, 1995). Pinello's study shows, among other things, that judges who face popular election (and this includes judges selected under the Missouri Plan who stand for re-election) tend, in criminal cases, to be much more favorable to the prosecution than those who are appointed by state governors or elected by legislatures. Other studies have shown the same trend: judges whose tenure depends on popular re-election are much more submissive to populist law-and-order sentiments and demands for harsher sentences.

The work of this American school of empirical judicial research resonates with the raw politics of U.S. methods of judicial recruitment. Recognition of the political character of adjudication is so ingrained in American political culture that the legitimacy of the judiciary seems to be unaffected by the openly political nature of judicial selection processes. But this work has not traveled well to other western democracies where, at least until recently, judiciaries have not been seen as sites of significant political activity in either the prevailing legal culture or the popular political culture. This does not mean that American scholarship in this field has been entirely insular. Quite to the contrary, American scholars have been instrumental in encouraging international empirical research on judiciaries.

II. The Emergence of Comparative Global Studies

Most of the earliest work comparing judiciaries across national boundaries was done by American researchers. John Dawson's 1967 Cooley Lectures at the University of Michigan Law School, presented the fullest account we have of the historical roots of the judiciaries of England, France, and Germany (Dawson, 1968). Dawson's study is one of the most important sources of information on the origins of different traditions of judicial recruitment and their jurisprudential consequences. Martin Shapiro's comparative account of courts in England, imperial China, the civil law countries of Europe and the Islamic world focused on the social backgrounds of judges and their political ties to the governing regimes in these vastly different judicial systems (Shapiro, 1981). Mary Volcansek, an American political scientist and Jacqueline Lefon, a French legal scholar, also employed an historical methodology in comparing the American and French judicial recruitment systems (Volcansek and Lafon, 1988). Their research demonstrated the strong path dependency of the two systems—the one producing a highly politicized judiciary and the other a highly bureaucratized judiciary.

The United States was the first country to offer entire university courses on the judiciary outside of law schools. Many of the texts used in these courses contained comparative material about the selection of judges in other legal systems. Henry Abraham's *The Judicial Process* is a good example (Abraham, 1980). Its section on "Staffing the Courts" has substantial coverage of the English and French systems of appointing judges. But American scholars like Abraham did not have access to empirical work on judicial selection that goes beyond the formal procedures of appointing systems. It was not until the late 1970s that researchers outside the United States were beginning to do that kind of empirical research.

The Research Committee on Comparative Judicial Studies established by members of the International Political Science Association (IPSA) in the 1980s has been an important vehicle for stimulating the empirical study of the judiciary internationally. American scholars, with their long-standing recognition of the political dimensions of the judicial process, were instrumental in establishing the IPSA committee. But the membership quickly expanded to include scholars from all around the world. Participants in the committee's meetings and publications have included legal academics and practicing jurists as well as political scientists. The Committee's meetings and conferences have produced several published collections of papers, three of which report on research related to judicial recruitment. Many of the contributions to *The Global Expansion of Judicial Power*, edited by Neal Tate and Torbjorn Vallinder (1995), discuss changes in judicial recruitment systems resulting from the recognition of judicial power in a number of countries. The volume on *Judicial Independence in the Age of Democracy* (2001), edited by Peter Russell and David O'Brien, examines the degrees of judicial independence enjoyed by judiciaries in 12 different political settings. Most recently, Kate Malleson and Peter Russell (2006) co-edited a volume reporting on developments in judicial appointing systems in 18 countries and for major international courts.

The Malleson/Russell volume is the most comprehensive and up-to-date compendium of information about judicial recruitment around the world. It shows that the career patterns of judges and the systems through which legally trained people acquire judicial office are deeply embedded in distinctive legal cultures and political systems. Unlike electoral systems, judicial appointments systems are not simple devices that can be easily changed or readily transplanted from one country to another. This comparative study generated two other broad generalizations about judicial recruitment in the contemporary world. The first is that every system of political selection and appointment has its own politics—although there are great differences in the degree to which the politics of judicial selection is publicly recognized. The second is that in virtually all countries where the judiciary has come to exercise significant power there are concerns that judicial appointing systems should become more transparent and accountable, and that the judiciaries they produce should become more reflective of a country's social and political diversities.

III. The Common Law World Outside the United States

Throughout the common law world, governments appoint judges—with one notable exception—from the ranks of experienced lawyers. It was not until the latter half of the twentieth century that there has been a significant amount of empirical research on this system of judicial recruitment. Much of the research interest has stemmed from exposure of the politics that underlie the appointing process and has been concerned with developing reforms to check what is seen to be the undue influence of partisan politics and social bias on the selection of judges.

A. The lay judiciary

The remarkable exception to the general pattern of common law judicial recruitment is the lay magistracy of England and Wales, and Scottish Justices of the Peace (JPs). While English settlers brought to various parts of the British Empire the practice of local notables sitting as magistrates to hear cases involving lesser criminal offenses, it is only in the UK that courts presided over by lay magistrates have continued to operate right up to this day. Morgan and Russell reported in 2000 that there were 28,029 lay magistrates in England and Wales, almost evenly divided between men and women (Morgan and Russell, 2000). In Scotland there are 4,000 JPs, many of whom function as full judges hearing cases. An impressive amount of empirical research has been done on Britain's lay magistracy. Studies published in 1979 (e.g., Burney, 1979) show how post-World War II reforms reduced the class and conservative political biases in recruiting persons to serve on the benches of lay magistrates that provide the first level of criminal and family court justice in communities outside of London and other metropolitan centers.

There are studies of lay judges in the United States and of lay justices of the peace in Canada, but these non-lawyer judicial officers play a much less prominent role in the judicial systems of these countries (Provine, 1986; Doob et al., 1991). In Canada, there is considerable interest in involving Aboriginal people as peacemakers and assessors in criminal and family justice (Seniuk and Borrows, 2007).

B. Appointing judges in England: politics and class

In 1977, J.A.G. Griffith said that "The most remarkable fact about the appointment of judges is that it is wholly in the hands of politicians" (Griffith, 1977: 17). Griffith was writing about the English judiciary, but what he said applies to the appointment of judges in most other common law countries. Nonetheless, there are notable differences in the ways in which common law systems select lawyers for judicial appointments. Yet very little comparative research of an empirical nature has been carried out on these differences. Notable exceptions are Professor Kate Malleson's chapter on appointments in her book, *The New Judiciary*, and a paper on "Comparative Perspectives on Judicial Selection Processes" written by Professor Carl Baar for a Canadian Law Reform Commission (Malleson, 1999; Baar, 1991).

Scholarly writing on the judiciary began earlier in England than in the other common law countries. A major contribution was the *Lives of the Lord Chancellors*, a series of biographical volumes on the heads of the English judiciary that began in 1848 and comes right up to the modern period (Heuston, 1987). These biographies of England's highest judges include illuminating accounts of the social and political circumstances that influenced their rise to the top of the judicial ladder. Harold Laski was the first British social scientist to examine the social and political backgrounds of English judges. An essay he published in 1932 showed that 80 of the 139 barristers appointed to the judiciary between 1832 and 1906 were MPs and that 63 of these belonged to the party in power at the time of their appointments. Laski also drew attention to the fact that members of the English judiciary were "from a class which, as a rule without being wealthy will at least be comfortable" and will "be pretty well committed to the philosophy of economic individualism" (Laski, 1932: 172–3).

Following World War II, the influence of partisan politics on judicial appointments diminished in the UK. Sir Robert Megarry and other observers see the Labour government's appointment of Conservatives to senior judicial positions in 1946 as marking the point where partisan politics ceased to play any real part in judicial appointments (Megarry, 1973; Malleson, 1999: 97). Research carried out by Neal Tate, an American political scientist, shows that between 1909 and 1972 there was a marked decline in the influence of party affiliation on judicial selection (Tate, 1975). The work of Burton Atkins, another empirically trained American researcher, demonstrates that removing party politics from judicial recruitment does not mean that the political views of those appointed to the judiciary cease to matter. Atkins's comparative research shows that there is as much diversity of opinion among British appellate judges as there is among the federal appellate judges in the United States (Atkins, 1988–1989). With the passage of the Human Rights Act, apprehension that attitudes to social and political values would become a significant factor in judicial selection was an important part of the rationale for the 2005 reforms that removed the unfettered discretion of the Lord Chancellor and Prime Minister in the selection of judges.

C. The politics of appointing judges in the older Commonwealth countries

In other common law countries, the "selectorates" (to use Burton Atkins's term for the persons or groups who select judges) tend to be more political than in the UK. In the older Commonwealth countries Attorneys General and Ministers of Justice are the cabinet ministers who take the lead in identifying candidates for judicial office. These judicial recruiters lack the judicial aura of the Lord Chancellor's office and may be pressured to select political friends of Cabinet colleagues. In several countries, notably Canada and Australia, Prime Ministers play a decisive role in filling positions on the highest court and are vulnerable to being influenced by candidates' political connections to the governing party or the government's views on how judges should interpret and apply the law particularly with respect to constitutional interpretation.

Empirical research has shown that in Canada politics continues to be a major influence on the selection and promotion of judges by the federal government. Canada, like India, is a federation in which the judicial appointing power is highly centralized. The federal government in Canada appoints not only the justices of the Supreme Court and the Federal Court but also the judges of the provincial courts of appeal and superior courts. Provincial governments appoint judges to the lower criminal courts and family courts. While most provinces by the 1980s had reformed their system of appointing judges by introducing non-partisan nominating committees, a study conducted by the Canadian Bar Association reported that political favoritism continued to have an "undue influence" on the appointment of judges at the federal level (Canadian Bar Association, 1985). A research project conducted by Peter Russell and Jacob Ziegel five years later showed that 47.5% of the 228 judgeships filled by the Mulroney Conservative government in its first term of office had known political associations with the Conservative Party (Russell and Ziegel, 1991). More recent research indicates that political patronage continues to be an important influence on federal judicial selection in Canada—one study reported that 30% of the judges appointed by the federal government from 1989 to 2003 had donated money to the party that appointed them (Hausegger et al., 2008: 162).

There has been no systematic empirical research on judicial recruitment in the two other older Commonwealth common law countries, Australia and New Zealand. The political prominence of Australia's High Court in constitutional interpretation and responding to Aboriginal rights claims has meant that appointments to it attract a good deal of political attention. What has been written about High Court appointments indicates that judicial selection is more like the Canadian federal process than the reformed UK model discussed below. In 1999, David Solomon wrote that "about half of the Chief Justices and Justices" appointed to the High Court over its history had been active in politics at some time in their careers, mostly on the conservative side (Solomon, 1999: 220). Since the controversial appointment in 1975 of Lionel Murphy, who at the time of his appointment was the Labor Government's Attorney General, High Court appointees have not come directly from politics. However, the Prime Minister and Cabinet continue to be involved in considering the names of candidates put before them by the Attorney General, and their assessment will certainly be influenced by political and policy considerations (Evans, 2001).

Judicial recruitment in New Zealand comes closest to the unreformed UK model. The Attorney General narrows the list of leading barristers primarily by consulting with the Solicitor General and senior judges (McGrath, 1998). Partisan politics do not appear to play a role in the process. This was evident in 2002 when New Zealand finally abolished appeals from its highest court to a committee of British Law Lords called the Judicial Committee of the Privy Council. Positions on the country's new Supreme Court, although entirely at the discretion of Labour Prime Minister Helen Clark, were filled simply by elevating the most senior members of the Court of Appeal (Allan, 2006).

D. Differences in the recruitment pool

Among the countries with judiciaries recruited from the ranks of experienced practicing lawyers, the UK is exceptional in having a relatively small pool of candidates available for judicial office. Until 1990, only the 10% of the legal profession who are barristers were eligible for appointment to the higher courts. The 1990 reform has scarcely dented barristers' monopoly of senior judicial positions. Moreover, only a small elite group of barristers who have become Queen's Counsel are considered for appointment to the superior trial courts and appellate courts. Burton Atkins estimated that the recruitment pool to these higher courts numbered about 500, and when barristers not interested or unavailable for judicial service are eliminated, the effective pool "narrowed, to literally, a handful of barristers..." (Atkins, 1988–1989: 593). Indeed the pool was so small that Robert Stevens quotes Lord Coldstream, a former Permanent Secretary to the Lord Chancellor, saying that "the judges select themselves" (Stevens, 2002). Kate Malleson's more recent research reports that the number of appointments to English courts increased from between 60 and 80 in 1978 to over 600 in 1997 (Malleson, 1999). This suggests that the judicial recruitment pool must have grown considerably since Atkins did his research.

Nonetheless, the judicial recruitment pool in England (and in Britain generally) is very much smaller than in countries such as Canada and the United States where the barrister/solicitor distinction was long ago abolished and lawyers are just lawyers. Atkins estimates that this makes the American judicial recruitment pool over a hundred times larger than in England. To a somewhat lesser extent the same point applies to Canada with its large unified legal profession, and in Australian states which have done away with the barrister/solicitor distinction, although in both countries lawyers who practice solely as advocates have a better chance of a judgeship than others. Significantly larger judicial recruitment pools increase the possibility for taking account of considerations other than recognized excellence at the bar.

E. Judicial diversity

Social diversity is an aspect of judicial recruitment that in recent years has become a matter of concern in virtually all common law countries. As societies became more egalitarian the monopolization of senior judicial positions by older white men was bound to become an issue. Male domination of the judiciary is a lesser issue in civil law countries where judicial service is entered after university graduation and judges do not enjoy the high social status of, or salaries as high as, judges in most common law countries. Empirical research has certainly exposed the lack of social diversity of common law judiciaries. Burton Atkins's 1988–1989 paper showed that up until the appointment of Elizabeth Butler-Sloss in 1988, white males had a 100% monopoly of positions on England's appellate courts. This monopoly was only slightly less complete in the United States where 92% of judges serving on federal appellate courts were white males (Atkins, 1988–1989: 595). Kate Malleson reported in 1999 that less than 2% of the English judiciary (above the magistracy level) were non-white and only 9% were women (Malleson, 1999: 104). The lack of diversity extends beyond gender and race. Burton shows that through the course of the twentieth century there was little change in the educational background of the English judiciary: most were educated at elite "public schools" and at Oxbridge.

Concerns about social diversity have generated debate about the kinds and degrees of diversity that judiciaries ought to have. A strong consensus has developed among both academics and political leaders that, while judiciaries cannot be expected to reflect the full diversity of the general population, there are good reasons for making common law judiciaries more inclusive than they have been in the past. These reasons include the need to ensure that outstanding candidates for appointment are not excluded from consideration by systemic bias in the recruitment system, the value of broadening the range of life experiences that are brought to bear on judicial decision-making and the need for the judiciary, in the words of Dame Brenda Hale, "to have the confidence of society as a whole and in particular those who use the courts" (Paterson, 2006: 29). The ideal of a judiciary reflecting juridically relevant dimensions of a society's diversity has broadened the understanding of "merit" in judicial appointments systems that aim at "merit selection." The work of Erika Rackley points to a jurisprudential benefit of judicial diversity.

Rackley argues that by paying careful attention to the considerations women judges bring to bear on adjudication we can transcend the suffocating notion of the neutral judge (Rackley, 2007).

F. Researching reforms of common law appointing systems

In recent years much of the work of empirically oriented judicial researchers has focused on reforming traditional ways of recruiting and appointing judges. Some of this reform interest has been driven by empirical research showing the undue influence of partisan politics and the white male legal establishment on judicial recruitment. It also reflects popular concerns generated by the expansion of judicial power. When democracies adopt constitutional or semi-constitutional bills of rights there is a concern that the judiciaries who interpret and apply these instruments are appointed through an open and transparent process that is not controlled or dominated by any political party or sector of society.

The approach to reforming judicial appointment systems which has been most widely adopted is the introduction of judicial nominating committees. Here we can see the influence of comparative judicial studies. Judicial nominating committees have a long lineage going back to their introduction as reform mechanisms by a number of U.S. states beginning with Missouri in 1940. President Jimmy Carter introduced them at the federal level in the United States in 1976 primarily to promote the appointment of more women and more African Americans to positions on the lower federal courts (Goldman, 1997: 238). Following the Carter reforms, comparative judicial researchers began to argue for a similar reform in other common law countries (Russell, 1987). In the late 1970s, a number of Canadian provinces began using judicial councils or advisory committees to play the lead role in selecting judges for the provincial courts by advertising positions, interviewing candidates and passing on short lists of highly recommended candidates to the provincial minister of justice (Hausegger et al., 2008). The Canadian nominating committees, like their counterparts in the U.S. states, include a mix of lawyers, judges, and non-lawyers.

In selecting the judiciaries of the highest courts which have a politically salient role in interpreting the constitution there is apt to be as much interest in political diversity as social diversity. This has certainly been the case among Canadian judicial reformers (Ziegel, 2002). And there has been some response to this concern. In 2005, the federal government, in filling a vacancy on the Supreme Court of Canada, used an ad hoc advisory committee to provide the Prime Minister with a short list of three candidates. Reflecting the high political salience of Supreme Court appointments, representatives of the four parliamentary parties were added to the mix of lawyers, judges, and lay people on the committee, and the nominee chosen by the Prime Minister was interviewed by a committee of MPs on national television (Russell et al., 2009: 14–16). In Israel, even though its constitution does not contain a bill of rights, the judicial appointments commission that selects judges for its Supreme Court includes two members of the Knesset. By tradition, one is from the government party and the other from the opposition (Salzberger, 2006).

Many of the newer members of the Commonwealth established judicial service commissions in their Constitutions. These commissions, in effect perform the function of nominating committees. The Constitutions of Jamaica, Nigeria, and Namibia, for example, all give Judicial Service Commissions responsibility for selecting candidates and recommending appointments to the President. Typically, such Judicial Service Commissions are chaired by the country's chief justice and include judges, representatives of the legal profession, and in some instances non-lawyers—but not politicians (Corder, 1992). However, in post-apartheid South Africa, where the role of the judiciary in advancing justice and protecting rights is widely recognized, politicians are prominent in the Judicial Services Commission (JSC). Under South Africa's new Constitution the JSC is responsible for recommending to the President the appointment of judges to all courts above the magistrates level. The JSC is chaired by the Chief Justice of the Constitutional Court and includes two other judges, five members of the legal profession (one of whom is a law professor), the minister of justice and ten other politicians chosen by the two houses of Parliament, three of whom must be from the opposition, and four other persons selected by the President through a political process (du Bois, 2006). South Africa's JSC functions in a very open manner, advertising vacancies, publishing lists of candidates, conducting open interviews, and inviting comments. The new South African process of judicial recruitment has made significant progress in developing a more representative judiciary for that country: a higher court judiciary whose 166 judges in 1994 included only three (male) black judges and two (white) women judges by 2003 was 36% black and 12% female (du Bois, 2006: 287).

In adopting judicial appointments commissions and boards to perform the primary functions of judicial recruitment, the UK was catching up with developments elsewhere in the common law world. The UK's adaptations of the nominating commission device have their distinctive features. Both the small commission that makes recommendations for Supreme Court appointments and the large commission that makes recommendations for the 900 judgeships in England and Wales, give only one name to the Lord Chancellor for each appointment. If the Lord Chancellor rejects the name, he or she must give reasons. The UK has thus gone further than any other common law jurisdiction in reducing the discretion of politicians in the selection of judges. The UK commissions are remarkably apolitical in that there are no politicians on any of them. The UK commissions also give non-lawyers a prominent role in judicial recruitment. Scotland's Judicial Appointment Board has a majority of lay people and is chaired by a lay person (Paterson, 2006). The UK judicial appointment commission has a majority of non-judges and is chaired by a lay person (Malleson, 2006).

Australia and New Zealand remain the outliers in the old Commonwealth, eschewing nominating commissions and leaving judicial recruitment under the control of politicians, with senior judges and leaders of the bar playing a major role as consultants (Allan, 2006; Handsley, 2006). In the newer Commonwealth, India, Pakistan, and Malaysia are countries in which there has been little effort to reform the process of judicial recruitment (Corder, 1992)

Thus far research on reforming systems of judicial recruitment in the common law world has concentrated on the politics of reform and the resulting institutional changes. It remains for future empirical research to track and assess the results of these reforms.

G. Career ladders

Before moving to the "career judiciaries" of civil law countries, something needs to be said about judicial careers in common law jurisdictions. In all common law court systems there are steps in a ladder by which a judge may ascend to higher positions in the court hierarchy. The introduction of a number of part-time and apprentice-type judicial positions in England has created mini-ladders that can lead from Assistant Recorder to Recorder, and from District Court Judge and Recorder to Circuit Judge, and from Circuit Judge to High Court Judge (Malleson, 1999: 80–1). While the first two kinds of promotion are frequent, "elevation" to the High Court is rare. This renders nearly meaningless the 1990 reform that made solicitors eligible for appointment to the senior bench, as solicitors are almost always appointed to the junior levels and rarely make it to the High Court (Malleson and Russell, 2006: 117–8).

In the UK, as in other common law countries, the politically most significant judicial promotions are to chief justiceships and to positions on the country's highest court. Typically, the latter are from courts of appeal one level below the highest court, and occasionally from superior trial courts. Leaving such promotions to the untrammeled discretion of ministers raises serious concerns about judicial independence. In a country such as Canada, where the decisions of federal and provincial appeal courts and of the Supreme Court of Canada have significant bearing on the powers of governments and the rights of citizens, there is a concern that ambitious judges will shy away from making decisions that are at odds with government policy (Ziegel, 2010). Empirical research on the extent to which political considerations affect judicial "elevations" in the common law world is very much needed.

IV. CIVIL LAW COUNTRIES

When civil law countries are said to have "career judiciaries" this connotes that most judges are men and women, educated in law, who belong to a single cadre of public servants which they join soon after university graduation. Whereas in common law countries most judges have had careers practicing law before they accept a judicial appointment, being a judge in a civil law country is typically a full career from graduation to retirement. In civil law countries there are a number of different legal professions, one of which is the judiciary. While this contrast between civil law and common law judiciaries generally holds true, there has been a good deal of convergence in recent decades. In many civil law countries there is now a considerable amount of lateral entry into the judiciary by members of other legal professionals in mid-career. Appointments to constitutional courts in civil law countries are recognized as having great political significance and are made through a much more political process. The same is true for judges on the highest court of appeal. As judicial realism challenges the myth of the judge as simply a technician applying the law, there are increasing concerns over the politics of judicial recruitment in civil law countries parallel to those that animate discussion and reform in common law countries.

The civil law conception of the judge as a technical public official applying the law in a logical and non-creative manner did not encourage social science study of civil law judiciaries. Consequently empirical judicial research was much slower to develop in civil law countries than in common law countries. The interaction of European scholars and empirically oriented scholars from the common law world in the activities of the IPSA Committee on Comparative Judicial Studies generated a considerable amount of comparative work accessible in English.

Such work shows that there are significant variations among civil law judiciaries beginning with points of entry to a judicial career. The best known model is that of France, which in 1958 established the *Centre nationale d'études judiciaries*, since 1970 called the *Ecole nationale de la Magistrature* (*ENM*) (Volcansek and Lafon, 1988). Law graduates are admitted to the *ENM* through competitive examinations (*concours*). John Bell reports that of the 220 who entered the French judiciary at this point of entry, 82% were women (Bell, 2006: 52). The 31-month program at the *ENM* combines courses taught mostly by judges, with practical apprenticeship in courts, and concludes with exit examinations, performance in which influences the kind of courts in which graduates will have their first posting. By holding *concours* for legally educated civil servants and lawyers with professional experience, France has broadened the recruitment pool for the *ENM* and developed a richer mix of experience in its judiciary. A 2002 profile of the French judiciary shows that only 72% embarked on a judicial career immediately following university graduation (Bell, 2006: 53).

Judicial recruitment in Spain and Portugal is based on the French model. Both countries have established judicial schools which students enter on the basis of competitive examinations written after university graduation (Guarnieri, 2001). In Portugal, on entering the school judicial trainees decide whether to become a judge or a prosecutor. Although enrollment in the judicial school is the principal point of entry to the judicial profession, as in France, practicing lawyers have opportunities for lateral entry on the basis of merit. However, improvements in the remuneration and status of practicing lawyers in Spain are making it more difficult to recruit successful *abogados* to the judiciary (Bell, 2006: 191). In both Spain and Portugal, the judiciary is proving to be a relatively high-status profession and a popular career for women; although research indicates that, as in France, the participation of women in the judicial profession is concentrated in lower echelons of the system.

Among the Latin countries of Europe, Italy is the outlier. Competitive national examinations following university graduation are the only way to enter the judicial corps. Instead of recruits attending a judicial school, they go through a 15-month apprenticeship with sitting magistrates (Volcansek, 2006). This system of recruitment produces a judiciary that is highly insulated from the rest of government and society. Until quite recently, magistrates and prosecutors were in the same professional stream and the magistracy has played a prominent political role in prosecuting elected politicians (Guarnieri, 2001). The Italian judiciary, like the judiciaries of the other Latin countries, is unionized; however, the Italian magistrates' unions are more competitive and partisan. This has produced strong resistance to political influence on judicial careers, with the result that promotions are based entirely on seniority.

The civil law countries of northern Europe have a somewhat different model of judicial recruitment. Graduates of university law programs apply to justice ministries for judicial appointments. Judges in these countries have high social status and are well remunerated so that competition for judicial positions is very competitive and, at the entry level, based largely on academic merit. Successful applicants undergo apprenticeship-type training, rather than attending judge schools. Opportunities for lateral entry to judicial positions exist in all of these countries.

Each of the northern European countries has its own distinctive entry qualifications and career structure. In Germany, for instance, there is one nationally regulated law program for all universities which is "designed to produce standardized jurists" (Kommers, 2001: 143), even though only 5% of qualified lawyers end up being judges (Bell, 2006: 113). This helps to maintain national standards in a federation where most judges are appointed by the *Länder* (i.c., the provinces). In the Netherlands, a recruitment policy aimed at reducing the bureaucratic character of the judiciary has resulted in increasing participation of so-called outsiders in the judiciary from 55% in 1986 to 72% in 2000 (de Groot-van Leeuwen, 2006). The judicial system of Sweden, like that of the Netherlands, is marked by historical continuity. Besides the university-educated judges, recruited through highly competitive examinations and forming a small, elite, professional judiciary, a Nordic tradition of local community justice maintains a cadre of lay magistrates who sit with judges at both the trial and appellate levels (Bell, 2006: 284–5).

As the political systems of civil law countries became more liberal and democratic, institutional arrangements were developed to temper government control of the judicial appointment process. The Superior Council of the Magistrature established in Italy's postwar Constitution provided a model for the Latin countries of Europe. Although the President is designated head of the Council, this is just a formality. Judges elected by their peers make up two-thirds of the Council. The other third are lawyers or law professors named by Parliament and apportioned among the political parties. The Minister of Justice is also an active member of the Council. The Council is responsible for managing judicial recruitment, promotion, education, and discipline. Judicial councils with slightly different compositions perform similar functions in France, Portugal, and Spain (Guarnieri, 2001: 119). While recruitment in these countries is based strictly on academic merit, they do not follow Italy in making seniority the only basis for career advancement. Thus there are opportunities for political considerations to influence career advancement. In the northern European countries similar advisory committees or councils of jurists play the key role in judicial selection. In Germany, the committees that advise Ministers of Justice of the *Länder* are made up entirely of judges, whereas in the Netherlands the large 71-person judicial selection committee is dominated by lawyers. In Sweden, an executive board that includes judges, politicians, and lawyers is responsible for most aspects of court staffing, but judicial self-government is promoted by giving a committee of judges control over the first level of promotions (Bell, 2006).

The Japanese system shows that judicial autonomy in selecting and promoting judges entails another kind of threat to the independence of the individual judge. Japan's senior judges control the recruitment, education, and advancement of judges. Though this means that the judiciary collectively enjoys total independence of the government, empirical research has shown that there is great pressure within the judiciary to conform to the jurisprudential views of the senior judiciary (O'Brien and Ohkoshi, 2001).

V. TRANSITIONAL REGIMES

In countries with authoritarian regimes, where the rule of law as a check on government has no real meaning, empirical judicial studies focus on how judiciaries are developed to serve as instruments for enforcing the regime's policies. Over the last three decades, there have been efforts in many of these countries to make more use of law and adjudication as a means of regulating public administration and relationships within civil society. These efforts aim at enhancing a regime's legitimacy both with its own citizens and with the international community, especially foreign investors. There is a growing literature on the judiciaries of countries at various stages of this transition. As regimes become more committed to giving reality to the rule of law, they find it necessary to reform their judicial systems so that courts are seen to have a modicum of legal competence, independence, and integrity. The empirical study of judiciaries in these transitional regimes tracks progress toward judiciaries that exercise real power and possess some credibility as impartial adjudicators.

Considerable progress in judicial reform has been made in Russia and the former countries of Eastern Europe. The relative speed of judicial reform in these countries reflects the existence of well-developed judiciaries in the pre-Communist era. Lustration policies aimed at removing judges tainted with complicity in the Communist regime understandably gave a political coloring to judicial recruitment in many of these countries (Beers, 2008). In addition to pressure to purge ideologically suspect jurists from the judiciary, post-Communist regimes have not been able to refrain from meddling in the staffing of courts as they take on significant governmental powers. Alexei Trochev's penetrating study of the transformation of the judiciary in post-Communist Russia traces the zig-zag course of judicial reform under Yeltsin and Putin (Trochev, 2008). Despite the centralization of political influence on judicial recruitment that has occurred in the Putin era, judicial qualification committees have become well entrenched at the regional level and have been instrumental in raising the professional caliber of the Russian judiciary. The participation of representatives of the public in these commissions has provided some protection against judicial corporatism. A number of east European countries have established judicial councils modeled on those of western Europe to manage judicial recruitment and career advancement. While these councils provide some protection against political interference, a well-established judicial culture may be more important than institutional reforms. Survey research by Daniel Beers shows that in Romania, which has a self-governing Superior Council of Magistrates, judges have a greater tolerance of corruption than in the Czech Republic, which has an executive-dominated system of recruitment and promotion but a strong pre-Communist judicial culture (Beers, 2008).

Relatively little empirical research has been done on the judiciaries of states at the other end of the transition to democracy. The illiberal nature of these regimes makes independent empirical research very difficult. The empirical research that has been done, such as Colin Hawes's work on China and Mahmoud Hamad's on Egypt, reports some progress in raising the professional legal competence of the judiciary but very little in securing judicial independence or reducing corruption (Hawes, 2006; Hamad, 2006). Colin Hawes has been able to learn much about the Chinese judiciary by combining a practitioner's experience with scholarly study. He shows how reforms since the mid-1990s have been gradually producing a much larger and more professional judiciary. In stark contrast to the days of the cultural revolution, China today has more judges per capita than many western countries, and most judges have a modicum of legal education. While this is giving some reality to the Chinese government's aspiration to be a "rule of law society," Hawes reports that there continues to be evidence of the judiciary at the local level being led by older judges who have close associations with the local party leadership.

VI. Staffing International Courts

The emergence of more than 30 international courts and tribunals over the last two decades has opened up a new frontier for empirical judicial studies. British scholars Ruth Mackenzie and Phillipe Sands are leaders in this field (Mackenzie and Sands, 2006). Their contribution to the Malleson/Russell volume shows how political pressures and diplomatic bartering can affect judicial nominating systems which on their face appear to be entirely merit-based. Kate Malleson has joined Mackenzie and Sands to carry out an empirical study of the appointment of judges to the International Court of Justice and the International Criminal Court. The final report of their study, *Selecting International Judges*, provides a penetrating analysis of the actual processes through which judges on the International Court of Justice are nominated and elected.

VII. Conclusion

Empirical research on judicial recruitment, careers, and education has been driven by legal realism and concerns for judicial reform. This is certainly true of the United States where systematic empirical research of judiciaries began and where, up to the present day, more empirical research on judiciaries is undertaken than anywhere else in the world. The United States is also the cradle of comparative research on judiciaries both internationally and among the U.S. states. American scholars have also done the pioneering work in using quantitative social science methods to study the background characteristics of judges and their impact on judicial decision-making.

Empirical judicial research outside the United States, up to now, has been mostly descriptive and institutional. Much of it in the older common law countries has been concerned with institutional reforms of judicial appointment systems. This is also true of the first major study of appointments to international courts. Empirical research on judicial recruitment, careers, and education in civil law countries and transitional democracies has been highly descriptive. Still, this research is showing the variations among career judiciaries and their convergence with common law models of the judicial career.

It is to be hoped that the next wave of empirical research on judiciaries will be comparative and aimed at showing how differences in recruitment systems, career patterns, and judicial education influence judicial decision-making.

REFERENCES

Abraham, H.J. (1980). *The Judicial Process: An Introductory Analysis of the Courts of the United States, England and France*, (4th edn.), New York, Oxford: Oxford University Press.

Allan, J. (2006). "Judicial Appointments in New Zealand," in K. Malleson and P.H. Russell (eds.), *Appointing Judges in an Age of Judicial Power: Critical Perspectives from Around the World*, Toronto: University of Toronto Press.

Armytage, L. (1996). *Educating Judges: Towards a New Model of Continuing Judicial Learning*, The Hague: Kluwer Law International.

Ashman, A. and Alfini, J.J. (1974). *The Key to Judicial Merit Selection: The Nominating Process*, Chicago: The American Judicature Society.

Atkins, B. (1988–1989). "Judicial Selection in Context: The American and English Experience," *Kentucky Law Journal* 77: 577–617.

Baar, C. (1991). "Comparative Perspectives on Judicial Selection Processes," in Ontario Law Reform Commission, *Appointing Judges: Philosophy, Politics and Practice*, Toronto: Ontario Law Reform Commission.

Beers, D.J. (2008). *Culture in the Courts: Formal Rules, Informal Practices, and the Politics of Postcommunist Judicial Reform*, PhD dissertation, University of Indiana.

Bell, J. (2006). *Judiciaries within Europe: A Comparative Review*, Cambridge: Cambridge University Press.

Burney, E. (1979). *J.P.: Magistrate Courts & Community*, London: Hutchinson.

Canadian Bar Association (1985). *The Appointment of Judges in Canada*, Ottawa: Canadian Bar Foundation.

Corder, H. (1992). "The Appointment of Judges: Some Comparative Ideas," *Stellenbosch Law Review* 3: 207–30.

Dawson, J.P. (1968). *The Oracles of the Law*, Ann Arbor: The University of Michigan Law School.

de Groot-Van Leeuwen, L.E. (2006). "Merit Selection and Diversity in the Dutch Judiciary," in K. Malleson and P.H. Russell (eds.), *Appointing Judges in an Age of Judicial Power: Critical Perspectives from Around the World*, Toronto: University of Toronto Press.

Doig, J.W. (2010). "Judicial Independence in the United States," in A. Dodek and L. Sossin, (eds.), *The Future of Judicial Independence*, Toronto: Irwin Law (forthcoming).

Doob, A., Baranek, P.M., and Addario, S.M. (1991). *Understanding Justices: A Study of Canadian Justices of the Peace*, Toronto: University of Toronto Centre of Criminology.

du Bois, F. (2006). "Judicial Selection in Post-Apartheid South Africa," in K. Malleson and P.H. Russell (eds.), *Appointing Judges in an Age of Judicial Power: Critical Perspectives from Around the World*, Toronto: University of Toronto Press.

Evans, S. (2001). "Appointment of Justices," in T. Blackshield, M. Coper, and G. Williams (eds.), *The Oxford Companion to the High Court of Australia*, Melbourne: Oxford University Press.

Goldman, S. (1997). *Picking Federal Judges: Lower Court Selection from Roosevelt through Reagan*, New Haven: Yale University Press.

Griffith, J.A.G. (1977). *The Politics of the Judiciary*, Manchester: Manchester University Press.

Grossman, J.B. (1965). *Lawyers and Judges: The ABA and the Politics of Judicial Selection*, New York: John Wiley.

Guarnieri, C. (2001). "Judicial Independence in Latin Countries of Western Europe," in P.H. Russell and D.M. O'Brien (eds.), *Judicial Independence in The Age of Democracy: Critical Perspectives from Around the World*, Charlottesville and London: The University Press of Virginia.

Hamad, M.M. (2006). "The Politics of Judicial Selection in Egypt," in K. Malleson and P.H. Russell (eds.), *Appointing Judges in an Age of Judicial Power: Critical Perspectives from Around the World*, Toronto: University of Toronto Press.

Handsley, E. (2006). "The Judicial Whisper Goes Round: Appointment of Judicial Officers in Australia," in K. Malleson and P.H. Russell (eds.), *Appointing Judges in An Age of Judicial Power: Critical Perspectives from Around the World*, Toronto: University of Toronto Press.

Hausegger, L., Hennigar, M., and Riddell, T. (2008). *Canadian Courts: Law, Politics and Process*, Toronto: Oxford University Press.

Hawes, C. (2006). "Improving the Quality of the Judiciary in China: Recent Reforms to Procedures for Appointing Judges," in K. Malleson and P.H. Russell (eds.), *Appointing Judges in an Age of Judicial Power: Critical Perspectives from Around the World*, Toronto: University of Toronto Press.

Heuston, R.F.V. (1987). *Lives of the Lord Chancellors 1940–1970*. Oxford: Clarendon Press.

Kommers, D.P. (2001). "Autonomy versus Accountability: The German Judiciary," in P.H. Russell and D.M. O'Brien (eds.), *Judicial Independence in the Age of Judicial Power: Critical Perspectives from Around the World*, Charlottesville: University Press of Virginia.

Laski, H.J. (1932). *Studies in Law and Politics*, New Haven: Yale University Press.

Mackenzie, R. and Sands, P. (2006). "Judicial Selection for International Courts: Towards Common Principles and Practices," in K. Malleson and P.H. Russell (eds.), *Appointing Judges in an Age of Judicial Power: Critical Perspectives from Around the World*, Toronto: University of Toronto Press.

Mackenzie, R., Malleson, K., Martin, P., and Sands, P. (2010). *Selecting International Judges: Principle, Process, and Politics*, Oxford: Oxford University Press.

Malleson, K. (1999). *The New Judiciary: The Effects of Expansion and Activism*, Aldershot: Ashgate.

Malleson, K. and Russell, P.H. (eds.) (2006). *Appointing Judges in an Age of Judicial Power: Critical Perspectives From Around the World*, Toronto: University of Toronto Press.

McGrath, J. (1998). "Appointing the Judiciary," *New Zealand Law Journal* 314–18.

Megarry, Sir R. (1973). "A Symposium on Appointment, Discipline and Removal of Judges," *Alberta Law Review* 11: 279–309.

Morgan, R. and Russell, D. (2000). *The Judiciary in the Magistrates' Courts*, London: Home Office, RDS Occasional Paper No. 66.

O'Brien, D.M. and Ohkoshi, Y. (2001). "Stifling Judicial Independence from Within: The Japanese Judiciary," in P.H. Russell and D.M. O'Brien (eds.), *Judicial Independence in the Age of Democracy: Critical Perspectives from Around the World*, Charlottesville and London: University Press of Virginia.

Paterson, A. (2006). "The Scottish Judicial Appointments Board: New Wine in Old Bottles?," in K. Malleson and P.H. Russell, *Appointing Judges in an Age of Judicial Power: Critical Perspectives from Around the World*, Toronto: University of Toronto Press.

Pinello, D.R. (1995). *The Impact of Judicial-Selection Method on State-Supreme-Court Policy*, Westport, CT: Greenwood.

Provine, D.M. (1986). *Judging Credentials: Non-lawyer Judges and the Politics of Professionalism*, Chicago: University of Chicago Press.

Rackley, E. (2007). "Judicial diversity, the woman judge and fairy tale endings," *Legal Studies* 27: 4–94.

Resnik, J. (2005). "Judicial Selection and Democratic Theory: Demand, Supply, and Life Tenure," *Cardozo Law Review* 26: 579–658.

Russell, P.H. (1987). *The Judiciary in Canada: The Third Branch of Government*, Toronto: McGraw Hill/Ryerson.

Russell, P.H. and Ziegel, J.S. (1991). "Federal Judicial Appointments: An Appraisal of the First Mulroney Government's Appointments and the New Judicial Advisory Committees," *University of Toronto Law Journal* 41: 4–37.

Russell, P.H. and O'Brien, D.M. (eds.) (2001). *Judicial Independence in the Age of Democracy: Comparative Perspectives from Around the World*, Toronto: University of Toronto Press.

Russell, P.H., Knopff, R., Bateman, T.M.J., and Hiebert, J.L. (eds.), (2009). *The Court and the Constitution*, Toronto: Emond Montgomery Publications Ltd.

Salzberger, E.M. (2006). "Judicial Appointments and Promotions in Israel: Constitution, Law, and Politics," in K. Malleson and P.H. Russell (eds.), *Appointing Judges in an Age of Judicial Power: Critical Perspectives from Around the World*, Toronto: University of Toronto Press.

Schmidhauser, J.R. (1979). *Judges and Justices: The Federal Appellate Judiciary*, Boston: Little Brown.

Seniuk, G.T.G. and Borrows, J. (2007). "The House of Justice: A Single Trial Court," in P.H. Russell (ed.), *Canada's Trial Courts: Two Tiers or One?*, Toronto: University of Toronto Press.

Shapiro, M. (1981). *Courts: A Comparative and Political Analysis*, Chicago: University of Chicago Press.

Shetreet, S. (1976). *Judges on Trial: A Study of the Appointment and Accountability of the English Judiciary*, Amsterdam: North-Holland.

Solomon, D. (1999). *The Political High Court*, Sydney: Allen & Unwin.

Stevens, R. (2002). *The English Judges: Their Role in the Changing Constitution*, Oxford: Hart.

Streb, M.J. (ed.). (2007). *Running for Judge: The Rising Political, Financial and Legal Stakes of Judicial Elections*, New York: New York University Press.

Tate, C.N. (1975). "Paths to the Bench in Britain: A Quasi-Experimental Study of the Recruitment of a Judicial Elite," *Western Political Quarterly* 28: 108–29.

Tate, C.N. (1981). "Personal Attribute Models of Voting Behavior of U.S. Supreme Court Justices: Liberalism in Civil Liberties and Economic Decisions, 1946–1976," *The American Political Science Review* 75: 355–67.

Tate, C.N. and Vallinder, T. (eds.), (1995). *The Global Expansion of Global Power*, New York: New York University Press.

Tribe, L.H. (1985). *God Save This Honourable Court: How the Choice of Supreme Court Justices Shapes Our History*, New York: Random House.

Trochev, A. (2008). *Judging Russia: Constitutional Court in Russian Politics, 1990–2006*, Cambridge: Cambridge University Press.

Volcansek, M.L. (2006). "Judicial Selection in Italy: A Civil Service Model with Partisan Results," in K. Malleson and P.H. Russell, *Appointing Judges in an Age of Judicial Power: Critical Perspectives from Around the World*, Toronto: University of Toronto Press.

Volcansek, M.L. and Lafon, J.L. (1988). *Judicial Selection: The Cross-Evolution of French and American Practices*, Westport, CT: Greenwood.

Ziegel, J. (2002). "Merit Selection and Democratization of Appointments to the Supreme Court of Canada," in F.L. Morton (ed.), *Law, Politics and the Judicial Process in Canada*, Calgary: University of Calgary Press.

Ziegel, J. (2010). "Promotions of Federally Appointed Judges and Appointment of Chief Justices: The Unfinished Agenda," in A. Dodek and L. Sossin (eds.), *The Future of Judicial Independence*, Toronto: University of Toronto Press (forthcoming).

2 3

TRIAL
COURTS AND
ADJUDICATION

SHARYN ROACH ANLEU AND
KATHY MACK[1]

[1] Thanks to Carolyn Corkindale, Lilian Jacobs, Leigh Kennedy, Rose Williams, Rae Wood, and the librarians at the International Institute for the Sociology of Law, Oñati, Spain for research and administrative assistance. We also appreciate suggestions from Pim Albers, Andrew Cannon, and Anne Wallace. Assistance for this Chapter has been facilitated by an Australian Research Council Discovery Project Grant (DP0665198).

I. INTRODUCTION

MUCH empirical legal research into courts and adjudication starts, either implicitly or explicitly, with a formal model of trial courts and the nature of adjudication: a party-controlled adversarial process before a judge leading to an adjudicated outcome in common law jurisdictions; a more judge-led or inquisitorial process in civil law countries. This stream of empirical legal research then demonstrates ways in which the activities of trial courts and the nature of adjudication depart from this paradigm.

The most robust findings of the empirical legal study of trial courts and adjudication are that these courts conduct very few trials and much adjudication occurs outside of trials (Baldwin and McConville, 1977; Mack and Roach Anleu, 1995; Maynard, 1988; Mileski, 1971). These findings emerge across the full range of research studies using a wide variety of methods, from large scale analyses of criminal and civil filings, to micro analyses of decision-making and ethnomethodological case studies. The dynamics and dilemmas of trial courts in action is also a theme in research on civil law systems, especially in Western Europe (Blankenburg, 1997; Komter, 1998).[2]

While trial courts rarely hear trials, their adjudication activities can be broad. Trial courts make many decisions and orders in advance of a trial (e.g., admissibility of evidence, summary judgment, discovery, injunctions, and referral to ADR) which will impact on the outcome of the case or whether it goes to trial. Courts also make decisions after the core questions of guilt/innocence or liable/not liable are resolved, whether by trial or other means (such as sentencing, enforcing settlement, or deciding quantum of damages).

Defining trial courts simply as courts that conduct trials does not narrow the field. Some courts that conduct trials also have appellate or other special jurisdiction (e.g., problem-oriented courts, such as drug courts do not conduct trials, but typically exercise special adjudicatory and sentencing functions after a defendant pleads guilty). Some trial courts utilize juries, others do not. Much dispute resolution leading to legally enforceable decisions now takes place largely or entirely outside public trial courts, for example commercial arbitration or specialist administrative tribunals.

This Chapter organizes the discussion of empirical legal research on trial courts and adjudication into three dimensions of analysis:

1. Macro: institutional,
2. Meso: organizational,
3. Micro: individual.

---

[2] The diversity among civil law judicial systems makes comparability and broad generalization especially tenuous (see European Commission for the Efficiency of Justice [CEPEJ] 2008, available at <http://www.coe.int/cepej/>).

Macro analyses tend to focus on types of courts and their outputs or decisions over a period of time or across jurisdictions. Researchers discuss court activity and trends, for example litigation rates or sentencing patterns, at a fairly high level of generality. Meso, or middle range, approaches examine the courts as an organization constituted by various occupational groups which are inter-dependent and intersect with the community. Researchers investigate how the structure and organization of a court and the day-to-day practices, usually in just one or a few settings, affect the legal process and the administration of justice. The micro dimension includes empirical research that focuses on the judicial officer and investigates trial judges' perceptions of their roles and activities, attitudes to their work, and approaches to adjudication. Given these different levels or dimensions of trial courts and adjudication, questions of sampling become paramount. Empirical legal research undertaken on a limited number of sites, or from a particular sample of participants affects the generalizability of the findings.

Connective mechanisms between the macro, meso, and micro dimensions need analysis, as well. For example, when looking at individual judges, it is important to take account of organizational or institutional factors to understand judicial decision-making. There is also the risk of the ecological fallacy, which is moving inappropriately from one level of analysis to another, for example using large data sets on court files and outcomes to draw unwarranted inferences about an individual judge's decision-making. Sometimes the organization of the court is equated with the activities of the judge (Seron, 1990: 452). This can be a problem with studies that look at disparity in outcomes as a way of explaining judicial discretion in sentencing.

The kinds of research on trial courts and adjudication that fall within the empirical band is very wide. The motivations for conducting empirical research on trial courts and adjudication and the research methods used are diverse and not mutually exclusive. Multiple approaches and methods may be combined in a single study. Often empirical research into trial courts focuses primarily on criminal courts. Empirical research may be:

- *theoretically* driven, for example to test general theories of change, administration, or decision-making in judicial settings;
- *pragmatic*, seeking to fill gaps in research findings, for example findings in relation to higher, superior courts and judges may lead to parallel research projects in lower courts, and vice versa; and/or
- *policy-oriented* or problem-based, including explicitly evaluation research which usually results in recommendations for reform or solutions to problems identified by governments or research organizations, both public and private.

Empirical legal studies into trial courts and adjudication often combine quantitative and qualitative methodologies using various combinations of interviews, surveys, court observations, court documents, and/or officially collected court data, including crime statistics. The reasons for research designs of mixed methodologies vary: sometimes there is a desire to look at a problem or issue from different vantage points; some methods are more appropriate for particular kinds of research question; and sometimes choice of method is pragmatic: certain data is available and accessible and can be supplemented with additional data collection. Resource constraints, especially time, funding, and access also affect decisions about research design. While these are general problems attached to any empirical research, they are often magnified in studies of courts, judicial officers, and legal personnel.

The vast range of motives, frameworks, and research designs means that empirical legal research on trial courts and adjudication is undertaken by various kinds of researchers and at research sites of various kinds, ranging from individual universities to large-scale research centers both within and outside the academy. Products of this research can be found in diverse outlets, including conventional refereed publications and books, often in multidisciplinary journals, law reviews, and in so-called grey literature, such as commissioned research reports or government materials which are publicly available but not necessarily published commercially (Genn et al., 2006).

This Chapter uses the micro, meso, and macro distinctions to frame the discussion of empirical legal studies into courts and adjudication, the various methods researchers use, and some of the more significant findings. These distinctions are analytic and conceptual, and the overview of research studies is necessarily selective. The studies chosen provide important examples of a particular research design, are significant pieces of empirical research, and/or have become benchmarks for subsequent research and conceptual development of trial courts and adjudication. Particular details of the research designs are included to illustrate the enormous breadth and depth of empirical investigation in this field.

II. Institutional/Macro Level

Studies at this broad level tend to focus on trends in the activities or outputs of large numbers of trial courts aggregated together. There is considerable empirical legal research on litigation rates, especially for the U.S. federal district courts and U.S. state courts of general jurisdiction which are the primary trial courts of their respective judicial systems (Galanter, 2004; Ostrom et al., 2004). Statistics produced by courts and reported by court administration agencies provide an important source of data. These statistics are in the public domain and can be found in annual reports and commissioned research reports and are often located in data archives.[3] Secondary data (which are already collected) bring several advantages to the researcher, especially accessibility and availability, but such data are inevitably limited by the definitions, coding practices (that often change), and accuracy in reporting of the court administration that produced them (Hadfield, 2004).

These empirical studies of courts and adjudication tend to be quantitative and include variables relating to the number and type of cases filed, adjudicated, settled, or otherwise terminated. These studies are usually comparative over time (longitudinal) and/or across jurisdictions or nations (cross-sectional). Sometimes the research addresses a problem such as how to make trial courts more efficient, or how to reduce the number of trials, or how to reduce the cost of litigation, and has explicit policy recommendations or relevance. Part of the trend of vanishing trials and the shift to ADR is the conscious decision by courts to move matters, especially civil, out of the trial docket and to adopt more vigorous case-flow management practices (Kakalik et al., 1996; Chapter 21 in this collection). Another substantial area of macro empirical legal research relates to court administration and case-weighting systems, especially in the United States and Europe. Its aim is to develop common measures for case assignment to judges and the evaluation of judicial systems in different countries (see Douglas, 2007; Langbroek and Fabri, 2004). A third type of inquiry relies on litigation rates to identify different legal cultures, especially national variations (Blankenburg, 1997).

A. Data issues

Publicly available court statistics are important for deciphering broad trends, but this data often erases any heterogeneity in terms of region, state, or local differences and often contains few independent variables such as number of lawyers, economic conditions, political circumstances or events, all of which can affect litigation patterns. Much care should be taken in interpreting findings based on such data. According to Jacob (1984: 9), published statistical reports "are like the apple in the Garden of Eden: tempting but full of danger."

---

[3] See, for example, the U.S. Bureau of Justice Statistics (<http://www.ojp.usdoj.gov/bjs/>), the UK Department of Justice (<http://www.justice.gov.uk/publications/statistics.htm>), the Canadian Justice Department (<http://www.justice.gc.ca/eng/pi/rs/index.html>) and Statistics Canada (<http://www.statcan.gc.ca/>), the Australian Bureau of Statistics (<http://www.abs.gov.au>), and Statistics New Zealand (<http://www.stats.govt.nz/>). An important data archive is the Inter-University Consortium for Policy and Social Research held at the University of Michigan (<http://www.icpsr.umich.edu/icpsrweb/ICPSR/>). Also see links to databases at the Society for Empirical Legal Studies website (<http://www.elsblog.org>).

Relying on data from the Annual Reports of the Administrative Office of the U.S. Courts from 1962–2002, Galanter demonstrates that the drop in civil trials in the United States (by bench or jury) has been recent and steep—an increase in trials peaked in 1985 after which the absolute number of trials in federal courts decreased by more than 60% (Galanter, 2004: 461). Within this overall decline, the mix between bench and jury trials shifted, with more trials before juries and fewer bench trials (ibid: 465), and a change from the predominance of tort cases to a pre-dominance of civil rights cases. He also maps a parallel decline in criminal trials (ibid: 465).

This research reflects some limitations of official records. Galanter relies on the Administrative Office's definition of trial as "a contested proceeding at which evi-dence is introduced" (ibid: 461). The measure, then, is the number of cases in which a trial event commenced, including the classic trial and other proceedings. This is an indicator of trial activity, but not a measure of completed trials in which a judg-ment was given. It includes cases that settle after evidence is introduced, as well as those that reach final determination. Care in definitions or identification of scope of data is important to ensure that the same phenomena are being counted, measured, and compared. It is also essential for monitoring the kinds of inferences the data supports.

Quality of data is better for some courts than others, making comparability across different types of courts treacherous, and this is magnified in cross-national comparisons (Ietswaart, 1990). One of the challenges of comparing litigation across jurisdictions (states, nations) is incompatibility between definitions and recording practices. This can also be a problem in longitudinal studies as a result of chang-ing definitions or changes in recording periods. Reliance on carefully constructed archival data is also essential for research which seeks to track litigation rates over longer historical periods.

Basic data limitations have impeded the ability to determine national trends regarding the work of the U.S. state courts, where the vast majority of litigation occurs. While more data are available at higher levels of aggregation, with few crime or civil subcategories, the way cases are classified and counted and the commit-ment to data compilation can vary among states. Notably, the definition of what constitutes a trial is not consistent. In some states a jury trial is counted at jury selec-tion, while in others a jury trial is counted only following a verdict (Hadfield, 2004; Ostrom et al., 2004).

The State Court Disposition Trends database is a major initiative at the National Center for State Courts, covering data from nearly half the states over the period 1976–2002 (see <http://www.ncsc.org>). Generating this database required careful examination of archival material and explicit documentation of the many issues related to data accuracy and comparability (Ostrom et al., 2004). Having this data set enables comparisons of trial courts in state and fed-eral jurisdictions.

B. Interpreting trial court trends

A major challenge is to decipher the meaning of observed trends in civil and criminal trials. Research finding that cases are departing the court at an earlier stage is taken to indicate changing strategies by plaintiffs and defendants (Galanter, 2004: 487), though research which directly asks litigants or their lawyers about their decisions is rare. Another explanation for the trend is that courts are more involved in the early resolution of cases than previously. Alternatively, trends might result from other factors unrelated to court users' behavior, such as legislative changes. Despite the falling number of trials, judicial involvement in, or supervisory oversight of, pre-trial and non-trial decisions is increasing (Galanter, 2004: 529–30). There seems to be a diffusion and displacement of trial-like events into other settings, including administrative boards, tribunals, and ADR forums. Analyzing dispositions in federal courts from 1970–2000, Hadfield found that what increased as bench trials (but not jury trials) disappeared were non-trial legal decisions, not private settlement (Hadfield, 2004). However, following a very thorough investigation of the coding of "disposition," and discovery of significant error[4] she cautions that conclusions about such trends must be "tentative only" (ibid: 733).

There are studies in other countries, including several commissioned inquiries into civil justice, which entail some empirical, often comparative, investigation of trial trends. An examination of publicly available data on litigation rates measured by annual filings (cases commenced) provided by New South Wales's (Australia) courts of civil jurisdiction (excluding family) concludes that "the belief that litigation is increasing cannot be sustained, and in fact the very opposite may be true" (Wright and Melville, 2004: 97). They explain fluctuations in filing rates over comparatively short periods of time as stemming from a range of micro processes including jurisdictional changes and other factors affecting choice of court; changes creating, abolishing, or affecting legal rights, and litigant behavior; as well as the way court administrators collect data and decide what to include. Similarly, Kritzer (2004: 738) uses the annual statistical reports for England and Wales detailing cases disposed of during or after trial between 1958 and 2002. While noting the absence of data for some years, he maps an overall downward trend, with some fluctuations, in the numbers of civil trials. He attributes at least some of this pattern to major court and civil justice reforms, and associated shifts in jurisdictional boundaries and procedural rules, though this data set contains no variables that would allow direct testing of the effect of the reforms on litigation patterns.

---

[4] Note use of the term "error" here does not denote that the agency collecting or recoding data made errors in that process; rather, it refers to the error that researchers will make if they incorrectly assume that categories have the same meaning and contain the same types of data over time or in different jurisdictions (Hadfield, 2004: 723).

A significant portion of all dispute-resolution takes place not in the courts but in various administrative tribunals and other forums, especially commercial arbitration. Some of these "alternative" sectors are becoming more like trial courts. Several prominent forms of arbitration have acquired features associated with traditional court trials, such as published decisions and the availability of punitive damages. Rather than viewing declining trial rates as indicative of the disappearing trial, it may be more meaningful to interpret these trends as the relocation of adversarial processes and binding decision-making outside public courts, especially as these new fora establish processes similar to conventional trials.

This trend is also occurring at the international level. Following almost 300 interviews in 11 countries with participants in the field of international commercial arbitration, Dezalay and Garth conclude that international commercial arbitration has evolved into a relatively adversarial, formalized and legalized variety of offshore litigation (1996). Litigators in large U.S. law firms servicing the corporate elite insisted that arbitrators adopt more adjudicative behavior. In this way, arbitration in the context of transnational business disputes has become a forum for litigation.

C. Conceptually/theoretically driven research

Some macro level empirical research on trial courts engages more fully with theoretical concerns rather than policy objectives and consequently incorporates data on independent variables. An example of this is Heydebrand and Seron's (1990) longitudinal study of the U.S. federal district courts. The authors rely on the concept of rationalization to describe and analyze changes in the demands on U.S. district courts from 1904 to 1985, especially after 1950. Specifically, the "rationalization of justice ... [refers to] the decline of the adversary system of formal justice and the rise of informal and alternative forms of dispute resolution and case disposition" (ibid: 13). They provide a descriptive overview of the total volume of cases filed in federal district (trial) courts per capita and document an overall shift from criminal cases to larger and more complex civil matters with an increasing proportion of routine or administrative cases involving the federal government as plaintiff or defendant.

Heydebrand and Seron's central hypothesis is that the environmental profile (measured by government and economic activity and demographic patterns) of a particular court will shape the court's workload (ibid: 59–80). They examined the effect of these factors on three indicators of the structure of the court's task—total demand, total filings, and civil filings—at three points in time: 1950, 1960 and 1973. They found that the rising demand for court services results from changing environmental complexities, particularly the internal relations between the government and the economy, and to a lesser extent population increases.

This research differs from many of the "litigation rate" studies. Its theoretical approach is structural not behaviorist. It goes beyond publicly available court data to generate a parallel data set containing independent variables obtained from other public statistical sources, for example numbers and types of government employees as a measure of government size and activity. This allows the research to move beyond descriptions of rates and does not rely on the behavior of legal actors as explanatory; rather, it identifies institutional or social factors to explain changes in the courts.

Researchers, especially in political science, often use quantitative data about published decisions, including final case rulings, to draw conclusions about judicial behavior. Data about judges' gender, the gender composition of the court and other biographical information reported by the Federal Judicial Center (<http://www.fjc.gov/public/home.nsf.hisj>) are publicly available and subject to multivariate analyses and model building. The rationale is to assess the impact of gender, race, political affiliation, or judicial philosophy on judicial decision-making. In this kind of research, behavior is extrapolated from outcome data, rather than directly asking judges how they decide actual cases, or how they approach adjudicative tasks. In this sense, this research is non-reactive, that is the data is not affected by judge's perceptions, assessments, or justification of decision-making.

Findings from this body of research are mixed, in part due to the wide range of factors that might affect decision-making, and to measurement difficulty. Political affiliation, usually as a proxy for judicial ideology, has strong correlation with outcomes, at least in some kinds of cases in the United States (Sisk and Heise, 2005). Some studies do identify gender and race differences in decision-making and adjudication, for example showing that women judges exhibit more liberal voting patterns than men judges, especially in criminal cases (see discussion and references in McCall, 2008). However, uncovering systematic differences has proved elusive and observed differences are usually context-specific.

The behavior of judges in trial courts facing particular challenges, for example judiciaries in transitional societies, has also been approached in this way. A study of trial courts in Estonia tests two assumptions: whether service under the former Soviet regime biases judges in their subsequent decision-making and whether the new courts can be fair to people of the ethnic group that oppressed them under the previous regime (Annus and Tavits, 2004: 712). Examining all decisions of trial-level judges that deal with embezzlement during 1996–2001, and controlling for characteristics of the defendant and the offence, this research found no evidence for the two assumptions. Their findings support the importance of impartiality to judicial decision-making and they conclude that dismissing all existing judges as a new democratic regime is implemented is not necessary to ensure impartiality (ibid: 730).

D. Official crime statistics

Crime data collected by administrative agencies can provide important, relatively accessible resources for empirical legal research. However, using official crime statistics to measure crime and sentencing trends raises methodological issues, especially regarding the ways in which offenses and offenders are classified and counted in different jurisdictions. Albonetti used data on 2,158 felony cases processed in the Superior Court of Washington, DC during 1974 to examine the way in which judges use defendant characteristics, circumstances of the crime, and case processing outcomes, to assess the defendant's disposition toward future criminal activity (1991: 250). She confronted problems of missing data and needed to go back to court records to ascertain whether the missing data was random or, by contrast, systematic, thus biasing the sample. Relying on such data typically means that the coding of the variables is limited by the official definitions. For example, in this data set race was recorded as black/white, prior record as yes/no, and type of offense was divided into seven categories, providing limited detail.

Albonetti finds a strong and statistically significant effect of prior record, race, weapon use and the pre-trial release outcome on sentence severity (Albonetti, 1991: 261). She uses this finding to understand decision-making by sentencing judges and discusses a complex relationship between uncertainty avoidance, racial stereotypes and levels of punishment. The link between sentencing outcomes and judicial discretion is theoretically specified; she did not collect data directly from judges themselves, but concludes: "When judges attribute stable, enduring causes of crime to black offenders, the defendant's race affects the exercise of discretion" (Albonetti, 1991: 261). This kind of research goes beyond the data by attributing decision-making behavior to judges, and is not affected by judges' subjective interpretations, rationalizations, or reinterpretations of their decisions.

E. Sentencing

Sentencing studies often rely on official statistics to compare sentencing outcomes across different offence categories, while controlling for certain variables to discern sentencing disparity, particularly disparities attributed to race and gender discrimination. This is a very large literature.

Sentencing outcomes are combined with data on extra-legal variables, such as the race or gender of the sentencing judge, as well as variables relating to the offense and the offender, including race, gender, age, and socio-economic status to examine judicial discretion, decipher the effect of extra-legal variables on sentence severity and type, and identify disparities and judicial bias. The thrust of much of this literature is testing theories of discrimination and bias by identifying divergence between formal understandings of sentencing and outcomes, which suggests unacceptable biases and disparities (Snowball and Weatherburn, 2007). This research produces consistent findings of the effect of defendant's prior record of conviction on sentence severity but inconsistent findings on the effect of extra-legal variables. The effect of extra-legal variables can depend on certain legal factors, such as type of offense (Steffensmeier and Demuth, 2001).

Recent studies consider the effects of extra-legal defendant characteristics on sentence outcomes in the context of sentencing guidelines. Albonetti (1997) used the Monitoring of Federal Criminal Sentences 1991–92 data for over 14,000 convicted defendants to assess the effects of ethnicity, gender, education, and citizenship on sentence outcomes in drug offense cases under the federal sentencing guidelines. The multivariate analyses find that these defendant characteristics exert significant direct effects on sentence outcomes (Albonetti, 1997: 817). Moreover, "the federal sentencing guidelines have not eliminated sentence disparity linked to defendant characteristics for defendants convicted of drug offenses in 1991–92" (Albonetti, 1997: 818–19). Schanzenbach (2005) uses data collected by the U.S. Sentencing Commission on every individual sentenced under the sentencing guidelines to investigate the impact of the guidelines on sentences. Variables include prison sentence length; downward departure from the guideline sentence and reasons for the departure, the offender's criminal history; primary offence of sentencing; and demographic variables, such as age, race, educational attainment, number of dependants, and citizenship. In addition, he obtained data on the changing political composition of the district courts from the Federal Judicial Center's biographical data on federal judges (see <http://www.fjc.gov/public/home.nsf.hisj>). Controlling for offense and offender characteristics, this research concluded that in the period under review—1993–2001—prison sentences changed little over time. He suggests, in contrast with Albonetti's findings, that "the Guidelines are working largely as intended" (Schanzenbach, 2005: 39).

To sum up, while there are issues with data, including official crime statistics, trend research can effectively identify changes in the kinds and volumes of cases over time or across jurisdictions. Such trend data rarely provides insight into the situational factors that directly contribute to the observed patterns. The concept of judicial behavior as an aggregate is not a description of how any individual judge makes a decision, but, importantly, demonstrates the aggregate outputs of trial courts collectively. Sentencing research shows that defendants with certain characteristics not thought to be relevant to sentencing may experience unequal outcomes, suggesting institutional discrimination. However, the ways in which various situational characteristics interact to constitute a picture of the defendant is lost with multivariate analysis of the effects of race, sex, or other independent variables.

The next part of this Chapter looks more directly at elements that are not accessible in the large scale macro empirical research discussed above. Meso-dimension research investigates issues such as the mechanisms that lead to settlement and trial avoidance in civil and criminal matters, and the ways courts operate on a day-to-day basis.

III. Trial Courts as Organizations

A large body of research approaches the study of courts and adjudication from an organizational perspective, looking at court structures and how they affect daily operation. Local practices, interrelationships between regular, key participants—especially the judge, the prosecution, and the defense lawyer in criminal cases—which involve reciprocity and shared informal understandings of appropriate outcomes shape the work of trial courts and the adjudicative process. Some of this research explicitly compares different courts or courthouses; others focus in-depth on one courthouse or courtroom. These studies deploy a variety of research methods, including interviews, and observational research. While the bulk of the research is undertaken in common law countries, especially the United States and UK, some examples exist in civil law jurisdictions (e.g., Komter, 1998).

Obtaining information directly from trial court participants and/or spending time in the court setting to collect data raises questions of access and ethics. Often a high level of personal trust is essential. Research collaborations with courts or government agencies can facilitate access and enhance rapport between researchers and the researched. It is also important that the researcher is not "captured" by the trial court or judges (Lofland et al., 2006). As quasi-public, complex organizations, courts are frequented by regular and transient participants, and ensuring consent can be a challenge, especially in unanticipated situations where individuals not previously identified as research participants appear. Several researchers identify the value of learning about the trial court by just "hanging around" and "poking and soaking" (Carlen, 1976: ix; Flemming et al., 1992: 15), but this carries risks that not all participants will either be aware of the researcher's status or be able to consent to participate in advance of disclosing confidential information. When data collection efforts depend more on information provided by individual judicial officers, problems of access and response rates can intensify.

Eisenstein et al.'s (1988) large-scale, in-depth examination of trial courts in the early 1980s provides a good example of research that incorporates variation and a comparative perspective into the research design. It exemplifies the way in which practical constraints—location, time, budget—affect choices about which sites to study to gain an understanding of the everyday work of trial courts. For this reason, this research will be discussed in some detail.

Their comparative approach involved collecting data on the criminal work of nine trial courts in three U.S. states. They did not use a random sample of courts because practical constraints and ease of access led them to conduct research in their own home states. They chose three middle-sized courts in similar-sized counties in each of three states. Their research goal was "to develop an integrated approach by researching individual, organizational, and environmental factors in each of nine middle-sized jurisdictions and by comparing our findings across all nine" (Eisenstein et al., 1988: 9).

This research is pragmatic in that it sought to fill a gap in extant research which focused primarily on criminal courts in major metropolitan areas. It is also theoretically driven in choosing an organizational approach to guide the research method and analysis, with the goal of illuminating how courts work, more than explaining case outcomes or litigation patterns (Flemming et al., 1992: 15–17). They also used a variety of different methods, including collecting data from court records, interviews, and questionnaires. They gathered three types of information (Eisenstein et al., 1988: 19):

1. Court records containing information on each defendant (n = 7,400 defendants) in relation to the charges, outcomes, and the identity of the judge, prosecutor and defense attorney.
2. Interviews with approximately 300 judges, prosecutors, defense attorneys and other major participants. The semi-structured, open-ended, guided discussions followed a standard outline of topics and were nearly all tape-recorded and transcribed.
3. Interviewees also completed several questionnaires about prior career; political and community activities; attitudes regarding criminal justice; personality measures; and the legal ability and trustworthiness of other participants.

Consistent with much other research (Carlen, 1976; Mack and Roach Anleu, 1995; Mather, 1979; McCoy, 1993) guilty pleas dominated court proceedings in each of the nine jurisdictions (Flemming et al., 1992: 18). The metaphor of community, conceptualized as "common workplace and interdependence" (Eisenstein et al., 1988: 24) guides their portrayal of the ways in which the dynamics of the disposition process in criminal courts influence case outcomes and the trajectories of defendants. One of their key findings is that "[m]ost of the crucial decisions producing an outcome in a case result from joint interaction among the three members of the triad: the judge, prosecutor, and defense attorney handling a case" (Eisenstein et al., 1988: 37). The content and quality of interdependence varies and characterizes court communities.

A second metaphor is "craft," displayed, for instance, in the use of rough classifications of defendants in terms of their behavior and cases, and relatively simple decision rules, which in turn leads to patterned behaviors that resemble routines (Flemming et al., 1992: 4). The concept of craft has also been used more widely in analyses of trial courts and adjudication (Moorhead and Cowan, 2007).

To explain variation across courts, Flemming, Nardulli, and Eisenstein (1992) use the concept of county legal culture, that is "the values and perceptions of the principal members of the court community about how they ought to behave and their beliefs about how they actually do behave in performing their duties" (Flemming et al., 1992: 28). They indicate that the content of county legal culture significantly shapes both the behavior of court communities displayed in members' ways of dealing with each other, and the outcomes of cases. Emergent local legal work cultures may emphasize plea negotiation, regardless of whether defendants do or do not want a trial. An examination of local legal culture—defined as the practitioner norms governing case-handling and participant behavior in a criminal court—in four courts found that two emerged as plea-bargain oriented and two trial-oriented (Church, 1985: 506).

Interviews with participants provide data on their perceptions of what happens, though this is not necessarily the same as what actually happens. Especially where the interviewees are part of one ongoing work group, views may converge into accounts or rationalizations of what is happening, including justifications of their actions as ethical and appropriate. Tape or video recordings of trial-related activities can give insights into courtroom activities as they occur and clarify the interrelationships between key participants.

Maynard (1988) undertook a conversational analysis of audio-tape transcripts of pre-trial conferences in misdemeanor criminal cases recorded in a California municipal court, to examine the ways in which participants bring facts, biography, law, and other considerations into the decision-making process. Tape recordings of 52 cases were transcribed according to a conversation-analytic system designed to preserve and reproduce as much detail as possible from the actual conversations, which were thus more accurate than interviewees' later construction of events and decisions (Maynard, 1988: 452, n.4). The focus is on the talk, the conversation, and in particular on the ways in which person-descriptions are used by the different participants, whether prosecution, defense or judge. Understanding the actual processes of plea bargaining requires attention to the discourse of negotiation and the active involvement of participants. "Practitioners *construct* and *execute* a system of negotiation that works to bring about a preponderance of arranged dispositions rather than trials" (Maynard, 1988: 206, emphases in original).

Empirical research that documents a large amount of trial-connected activity occurring outside the courtroom may create the impression that the courtroom is marginal to the trial process. Observational studies of in-court processes and events reinforce the importance of viewing the courtroom as an organizational setting and directly recording the interrelations of and interaction among participants. Observation "allows the opportunity to investigate the situational factors that may be associated with various kinds of cases and their dispositions" (Mileski, 1971: 475), as well as uncovering patterns that may not be apparent to participants.

Observational research, such as Carlen (1976) and McBarnet (1981) can produce qualitative data about quasi-public settings, such as the courtroom; but observational data can also be quantified, as in Mack and Roach Anleu's (2010) observations in Australian magistrates courts. As observations rely on the observer's interpretations or assessments of events, they raise epistemological questions about whether they accord with those of the perceptions of the participants in the courtroom and whether, in such complex interactional settings constituted by formal and informal activities, any observations are inevitably partial.

An ethnographic style of observational research is exemplified by Carlen's (1976) observations in English magistrates courts, combined with some interviews. In addition to the more structured components of the research, Carlen talked informally with police, defendants, and solicitors waiting outside courtrooms in order to understand the ways social relationships produce justice. Her research documents the "converging imagery of court officials and defendants themselves to analyse how both abstract and situational rules can be systematically manipulated to facilitate an appearance of legitimated social control" (ibid: 128).

Mather's (1979) study of the disposition process for adult felony cases involved fieldwork in the downtown Superior Court of Los Angeles County, which included extensive observation, interviews, handwritten field notes, examination of case files, and the collection of some statistical information. She studied the network of people involved in the whole court process and spent time in many of the individual courtrooms. She identified two distinct "cultural scenes": one made up of the court regulars comprising the judges, district attorneys, public defenders, private defense lawyers, courts staff; and the other consisting of non-regulars, including some private attorneys, defendants, jurors, police officers, victims, and other witnesses (ibid: 9). Shared knowledge, informal working arrangements among courtroom regulars, language, and implicit rules shaped the ways participants organized and understood their work.

Other research designs that entail the researcher's immersion in and around the court setting demonstrate the way in which the trial and the possibility of a trial, even while plea discussions are occurring, is an essential component of participants' consciousness and decision-making. Emmelman's (1998) participant observation of court-appointed defense attorneys—in their offices, judges' chambers, and jails, as well as in 13 in-depth interviews—demonstrate how they assess information against the backdrop of the trial court. Defense attorneys routinely gauge the strength of evidence prior to plea bargaining through a largely elusive, taken-for-granted, unspoken process that emulates the trial (ibid: 928). Thus, legal norms may influence decisions to settle cases in ways imperceptible to outsiders. Similarly, Lynch's (1997) analysis of tape-recorded conversations between Crown and defense attorneys in Ontario indicate that "the projectable actions of a particular judge can become a contingency for a lawyer's presentation of the cases, even when the judge is not immediately present" (Lynch, 1997: 102).

One empirical study which combines trend data with attention to workplace dynamics is McCoy's (1993) investigation of how a 1982 California law restricting plea bargaining in serious felony cases in the Superior Court did not effectively reduce or limit bargaining but shifted it to the lower courts. She assembled quantitative, administrative data on court dispositions and sentencing outcomes and obtained qualitative data from observations in and out of court, as well as questionnaire and interview material (McCoy, 1993: 77–80). As almost every felony prosecution initially came before the Municipal Court, prosecution and defense were able to continue plea bargaining; and that court became the primary forum for plea bargaining in serious cases. The prosecution, the defense and the judge had to work together to implement this strategy to respond to the changed legislation. Paradoxically, the new law actually encouraged rather than eliminated plea bargaining (ibid: 37–8, 79–82). This study demonstrates the ways in which legislation aiming to alter sentencing patterns and reduce the amount of plea bargaining on a macro level had unanticipated effects on the work practices and organizational norms of court professionals.

Much of the research on the professional interrelationships, and the organization of courts and courtrooms as workplaces, relies on the experiences and viewpoints of regular participants. In the accounts of the court as organization, the defendant has been characterized as outside the court community (Eisenstein et al., 1988: 37) and as a temporary rather than a regular participant (Mather, 1979). On the other side, defendants' experiences and perceptions can be important sources of data not obtainable from interviews with regular participants or observations of the courtroom, though few studies use the defendant as a source of information about trials and adjudication.

Asking convicted defendants about their experiences can raise questions about reliability and credibility, about the defendant's insight into or knowledge of the criminal justice process, and about their capacity to exaggerate or minimize certain information. Yet questions about the motives or biases of professional participants, who also have much at stake and perhaps greater sophistication in rendering their standpoint credible, are rarely made. Whether use (or non-use) of defendant interviews obstructs research integrity depends on the purpose of the interview—are interviewees providing objective information about the offence or the criminal justice process? Or, are the defendants relating, in their own words, their experiences and perceptions of the process. If it is the latter, then researchers have little basis on which to assume that the interviewees are lying or fabricating stories, as that implies an objective truth that the researcher can, but the research participants cannot, ascertain. An important safeguard against bias in responses is random selection of a large number of interviewees, though this is not always practical. Nonetheless, the defendant's perspective is an important part of the trial court and adjudication story.

The first major empirical study of guilty-plea negotiations in the UK did incorporate defendants' perspectives. This issue emerged in the context of a case study of contested trials in the Birmingham Crown Court in the mid-1970s. The research aimed to identify in advance of trial those cases that would ultimately be tried by jury. However, the researchers found that many "folded" at the last minute which led to the new research question of why so many defendants changed their decision about plea so abruptly and so late (Baldwin and McConville, 1977: 4).

The researchers interviewed 121 defendants (81% of their late change of plea sample) at the serious end of the crime continuum. To minimize the potential for bias the interviewees were not given any prior warning, beyond a general introductory letter, of the purpose of the interview. (One wonders if this would be sufficient for ethics approval these days.) The researchers did not use the terms "bargain" or "negotiation" except in response to a defendant's use of them (Baldwin and McConville, 1977: 10). The interviewees were asked to tell their own story in response to simple and neutral questions dealing with defendants' own experiences and perceptions of events immediately preceding the court appearance and which resulted in their change of decision and guilty plea.

The research describes a variety of negotiations and discussions surrounding the plea and concludes that these defendants did participate in plea bargains, as they had agreed to plead guilty following negotiations between their barrister and the judge and/or the prosecution which reduced the charges. The researchers conclude that "[m]ost of the offers described by defendants were of such a nature that undue pressure [as defined by the researchers not the interviewees] was brought to bear" (Baldwin and McConville, 1977: 35). This research has significantly influenced the development of empirical research agendas on guilty pleas, especially in jurisdictions where the existence of "bargaining" or undue pressure is formally denied (e.g., Mack and Roach Anleu, 1995).

Another non-professional participant in the criminal court trial process is the victim of crime. Traditionally, the victim's role in the criminal justice process is minimal, limited to being called as witness if a matter goes to trial. If a defendant pleads guilty, victims may not have the opportunity to describe the facts and circumstances of the crime in their own words.

Many of the reforms designed to address concerns of victims—including restorative justice, conferencing, and victim impact statements—have been subject to explicit evaluation research. Findings are mixed and often location-specific. An early evaluation of a New Zealand restorative justice program finds that the goal of diverting young people from either prosecution or from custodial sentences has been achieved, and most juveniles agree to perform tasks that appear to make them accountable for their actions. In only around a half of the Family Group Conferences in the study were victims or victims' representatives present and around one-third of young offenders said that they felt worse as a result of their involvement. Victims felt inadequately prepared in terms of what to expect from the conferences (Morris and Maxwell, 1993: 84–9).

An Australian evaluation of a community conferencing program relied on official criminal histories and conferencing case files for all young people (n = 200) who had participated in statutory community conferences from 1997 to 1999.

These conferences aim to divert young people who admit their offenses from further processing in the juvenile justice system. A key finding is that when a conference rather than a court appearance or a police caution is the first intervention for the youngest offenders, the likelihood of recidivism is reduced, though the overall recidivism rate was still over half (56%) (Hayes and Daly, 2004: 187). Other evaluations report more chances of success. A study of three restorative justice schemes for adult offenders in England, some convicted of very serious offences, finds evidence that those offenders who participated in the scheme committed significantly fewer offences subsequently. Interestingly, demographic variables— age, ethnicity, gender—and offense type did not affect the findings (Shapland et al., 2008: iii). Where offenders perceived the conference as useful, realized the harm done to victims following their offending behavior, and were actively involved in the conference, the likelihood of reconviction decreased (Shapland et al., 2008: iv).

A large-scale evaluation of the role of victim impact statements in South Australia, using both quantitative and qualitative data, finds that the involvement of victims in the form of victim impact statements has not increased sentences (Erez and Rogers, 1999). Overall, the legal professionals involved consider that victim impact statements offer a voice to victims and symbolic recognition of their needs, and that victims view their involvement as relevant and essential for justice. Other research in the same jurisdiction, based on interviews with members of the legal profession, judges, prosecution, and defense counsel (n = 42) suggests regular courtroom processes and legal occupational culture tended to downplay the significance of victim impact statements (Erez and Rogers, 1999). Canadian research involving in-depth interviews, and small group discussions with victims shows that they are not necessarily opposed to community-based sentences but do experience the justice system as complex and confusing (Roberts and Roach, 2005).

In sum, studies of the courtroom in criminal cases as an organization demonstrate the ways in which the decisions, practices, and interrelations between the regular, professional participants all point to the guilty plea as the normal way of managing cases. Organizational dynamics and values can thwart criminal justice reforms initiated by the legislature, including laws to reduce plea bargaining (McCoy, 1993), or to give victims a greater role (Erez and Rogers, 1999). While these studies show that case outcomes are the collective product of several participants and their decisions, the trial-court judicial officer remains paramount and retains adjudicative authority. Studies of civil law cases, especially divorce and family law, suggest that the settlement process is far more private with less court interaction (Conley and O'Barr, 2005).

Small claims courts are less formal and less adversarial than conventional trial courts. These courts encourage litigants to argue their own cases using everyday language and discourage (or even prohibit), the use of legal representatives. Judges are allowed to intervene proactively in the proceedings (Baldwin, 1997). Despite these differences, judges retain an apparently neutral impartial stance listening to both sides without simply agreeing with a claimant's view of events (Conley and O'Barr, 2005: 94–5). Following an analysis of court files, observations, and interviews with UK judges, Baldwin (1997: 46–8) identifies a particular institutional dilemma in small claims courts: pressure to make determinations strictly according to law, in contrast to exercising more flexible judgment to reach outcomes that might accommodate a wider concept of justice.

A third strand of empirical legal research into trial courts and adjudication focuses on the ways in which trial court judges approach their role and make decisions, and identifies important sources of influence.

IV. INDIVIDUAL JUDGES

Empirical legal studies and popular consciousness usually cast the trial judge as the figure most closely and routinely associated with courts and adjudication. However, macro level studies demonstrate that most cases are concluded without trial. Organizational and courthouse studies show how the resolution of most civil and criminal matters is the product of work-group interrelations which may receive little direct judicial input (Roach Anleu and Mack, 2009). Much trial court activity involves ratifying outcomes produced without trial, or making decisions following those resolutions, for example about sentencing. This raises questions about trial judges' perceptions of their role, attitudes toward their work, and approaches to adjudication and decision-making more broadly. These practical, everyday activities of trial court judges are one dimension of the organizational dynamics of the courthouse, which in turn are constitutive of trial rates and trends.

One very extensive study of the "nature and patterns of judicial work in the trial courts" (Ryan et al., 1980: 9) examines influences such as personal background and experiences, on-the-job learning and adaptation (socialization), and perceptions of the work environment (morale) (ibid: 10). This research also takes account of organizational influences. Gaining a very high degree of access, the researchers, who described their status as the "the judge's shadow," observed some 40 judges in 15 courts across eight U.S. states for between three to five days each (ibid: 11). They observed the judges "under virtually all work conditions—on the bench, in chambers (though not all judges allowed this) during meetings, inside and outside the courthouse, and at lunch" (ibid: 249). Their sampling was purposive in order to include courts that varied in terms of jurisdiction, number of judges, state political culture, type of case assignment system, as well as size and type of community. The researchers also obtained statistics, work records, docket books and introductions to other judges and court staff.

The observational component led to the mail questionnaire with a 63% response rate (n = 3,032) which sought judges' views and experiences of the performance of their everyday work (ibid: 1980). A central finding was that the image of trial courts as plea-bargaining courts, while true, "conceals or distorts the nature of most of the work performed by judges" (ibid: 43). Documenting the variety, volume, and nature of the tasks judges confront, including administrative and routine activities as well as jury and non-jury trials, gives a more in-depth picture of the judicial role, which is necessarily obscured in aggregated court statistics. Other interview and survey research describes some of the particular, situational challenges for trial judges, especially in the lower courts, including the need to engage in emotion management (Roach Anleu and Mack, 2005) and to navigate the challenges that unrepresented litigants present.

Some studies seek to detail judges' approaches, orientations, and attitudes, both personal and work-related. These individual level qualities are assumed to affect adjudication, though demonstrating precise links between individual judges' approaches and outcomes is often difficult because of the large number of institutional, organizational and individual factors that affect decision-making. Farole (2009) studied judges' practices and attitudes to problem-solving justice through a nation-wide survey of a representative sample of just over 1,000 U.S. trial court judges, drawn from the 2007 edition of *The American Bench*. The survey generated a 50% response rate and indicated broad support for problem-solving methods by trial court judges throughout the country. Other mail surveys sent to trial court judges report high levels of job satisfaction and agreement regarding the important skills for judicial work (Mack and Roach Anleu, 2008).

Examining trial court judges' approaches to their work, including adjudication, using survey research has also been undertaken in non-English speaking jurisdictions. A representative sample of the Bolivian judiciary was interviewed to assess the effects of career ambitions and subjective expectations, such as fear of reversal, on judicial decisions. The research concluded that strategic considerations, especially fear of reversal, did affect decision-making orientations among these judges. Questions of this type cannot track what judges do when confronted with actual cases but they enable the measurement of general orientations (Pérez-Liñán et al., 2006).

Some research directly examines the ways trial judges approach decision-making and describes different styles of judging through observations in court, often combined with interviews and other types of data. Mileski (1971) conducted one of the early observational studies of daily trial court behavior. She observed a total of 417 cases over a three-month period in a criminal court of first instance in a middle-sized U.S. city. She undertook the observations in one of the two courtrooms which disposed of most of the city's minor cases, a high volume court with only two judges.

Only arraignments and final dispositions were studied; continuances (also known as adjournments), which accounted for under half of the cases observed, were not analyzed (Mileski, 1971: 475). Mileski found that: "The lower court is largely a sentencing court, rarely a trial court–more a sanctioning than a truth-seeking system" (ibid: 491). In particular, she identified the importance of judicial demeanor and the use of "situational sanctions." She observed that the judge used firm or harsh demeanors more often in less serious cases, especially when the accused received what might be regarded as a lighter penalty, but that harsh demeanor was more likely to be used when the defendant had breached courtroom standards than in relation to the criminal offences, even when serious. Her research design has influenced several subsequent court observation studies and elaborations of the concept of judicial demeanor (Mack and Roach Anleu, 2010).

Other research combines court observations with interviews to understand judges' orientation to their work in court. A study of the exercise of judicial discretion in rent cases (non-criminal) finds that judges recognize a diverse range of factors as influencing their exercise of discretion. The question for the judge in these cases is whether to evict a tenant of a social landlord (i.e. a local authority or housing association), from their home for rent arrears (Cowan and Hitchings, 2007). The research involved observations of 894 housing possession cases at four courts and interviews with 26 District Judges drawn from the geographical area of the observational research. From this empirical material the authors describe three different judicial styles—"liberal," "patrician," and "formalist"—which might influence the outcome of particular cases and the courtroom experience. However, the research design did not enable the researchers to demonstrate empirically the actual impact of the different judicial styles on adjudicated outcomes. Indeed this would be very difficult given the very large range of factors—on macro, meso, and micro dimensions—that affect trial court adjudication.

One of the important tasks for judges in trial courts in criminal matters is sentencing, whether conviction comes after trial or a guilty plea. A number of studies investigate the process of sentencing and decision-making from the point of view of the judicial officer and thus represent a break from empirical scholarship that looks at sentencing patterns. One author concludes: "What judges *think* about sentencing and how they *approach* this task are largely missing links in sentencing research" (Mackenzie, 2005: 2, emphases added). Following interviews with 31 judges in Queensland (Australia) Mackenzie concludes that judges view the "sentencing task in fairly practical and procedural terms, as opposed to a process based more on theoretical rationales or justifications for punishment" (ibid: 20). Judges tend to see sentencing as a process which entails the balancing of competing considerations and one in which they are the key players. Many of the judges also experience sentencing as a difficult and stressful decision, one of the hardest things judicial work involves (ibid: 39). A national mail survey sent to all judges and magistrates in Australia found a variety of views about the stressfulness of decision-making and about half of respondents reported their experience of work as emotionally draining at least sometimes (Mack and Roach Anleu, 2008: 19). There is also a large amount of psychological research on decision-making that is used to understand possible influences on judicial decisions, especially sentencing.

Another aspect of the sentencing decision is the role of information especially that contained in pre-sentence reports (PSRs). Judicial decision-making is not an entirely individualistic enterprise and relies on inputs from a variety of courtroom participants. In a number of jurisdictions, empirical research indicates a high level of congruity between the PSR's recommendations and the sentencing decision (Deane, 2000). Does this correlation mean that judges rubber stamp recommendations the PSR writers make, thus shifting the penalty decision away from the judge, or does it mean that PSR writers anticipate the appropriate legal sentence, and correctly predict the decision of the court, and thus shape reports accordingly?

In examining the connections between report writers' recommendations and judicial decision-making, Tata et al. (2008) adopted an innovative research design that contained four complementary components: an ethnographic study of criminal justice social workers, including observations and preparation of shadow reports; observation of and interviews with Sheriff Court (first instance) judges, and interviews with defense solicitors and prosecutors before and after sentencing hearings; focus group discussions with sheriffs throughout Scotland; and a series of simulated sentencing diets (courts) based on cases from two sites. With few exceptions, most sheriffs disliked the idea of report writers proposing a sentence or indeed appearing to be directive or explicitly judgmental. Sheriffs generally considered that the sections of reports dealing with personal and social circumstances were much less significant than sections on the offence in question and the individual's pattern of offending behavior (Tata et al., 2008: 839–43).

Information obtained directly from judges provides important insights into the perceptions, experiences and approaches of the judicial officer, who remains the central participant in the trial court. Examining the trial court and adjudication from the vantage point of the judge enables identification of the variety of factors—organizational, professional, legal, and individual—that can affect the process of adjudication and decision-making.

V. CONCLUSION

Empirical legal research into trial courts and adjudication has confirmed a number of key themes. First, the rate of both civil and criminal trials is declining, although a substantial amount of adjudication occurs within trial courts. This trend is most visible in common law countries with more mixed patterns in civil law justice systems (Lande, 2006). Second, attention to organizational processes and workplace culture is essential for understanding the operation of law and the fate of cases in trial courts. Third, there is no single model of judging/adjudication in practice.

There is often a disjunction between these empirical findings and public or popular consciousness. One study of print news and interviews with journalists and reformers concludes that academic studies of litigation are: "by standards of ordinary discourse, unfamiliar and difficult, and, by standards of opinion leaders, esoteric and tedious. Such sophisticated forms of knowledge simply do not translate into modern mass communication" (Haltom and McCann, 2004: 109). There is a similar disjunction in relation to criminal trial courts where a growing body of empirical research shows low levels of public confidence in the courts, especially displayed in public views about sentencing. Criminologists have also noted the way in which policy-makers and politicians frequently ignore empirical research findings in favor of populist approaches.

Empirical legal study of trial courts and adjudication can be found in policy-oriented and evaluation research which aims to assist reform of the administration of courts. Other research, perhaps more academic or theoretically motivated, seeks to understand the work of courts and judicial officers as social and political processes. Given the variety of styles and aims of empirical research in this field, the need for appropriate training of future researchers and cross-disciplinary exchange is paramount (Genn et al., 2006).

Trial courts are multidimensional and changing institutions, and adjudication is a complex process. Understanding their roles and significance requires many different kinds of ongoing empirical legal study. While the three levels—micro, meso, and macro—are constructed for the purpose of analysis, they indicate the importance of research design that is appropriate to the level of study. For example, court statistics provide overall patterns that do not directly measure individual participants' perceptions or experience. Equally, it is important to recognize the interconnectedness of the different levels. The approach of trial court judges to their work, including adjudication, forms an integral part of the organizational structure of the courthouse. Research obtaining information from participants—organizational work groups and individuals—details the complex everyday workings of trial courts and adjudication which contribute to courtroom outputs. When these outputs are aggregated across a large number of courts, they constitute data on which litigation patterns and trend data are constructed. This review of selected research emphasizes the breadth of empirical legal research. Each type of research design has specific strengths and advantages, as well as limitations, but each contributes, in different ways, to advancing knowledge about the nature, role, and reality of trial courts and adjudication.

References

Albonetti, C.A. (1991). "An Integration of Theories to Explain Judicial Discretion," *Social Problems* 38(2): 247–65.

Albonetti, C.A. (1997). "Sentencing under the Federal Sentencing Guidelines: Effects of Defendant Characteristics, Guilty Pleas, and Departures on Sentence Outcomes for Drug Offenses, 1991–1992," *Law & Society Review* 31(4): 789–822.

Annus, T. and Tavits, M. (2004). "Judicial Behaviour after a Change of Regime: The Effects of Judge and Defendant Characteristics," *Law & Society Review* 38 (4): 711–36.

Baldwin, J. (1997). *Small Claims in the County Courts in England and Wales: The Bargain Basement of Civil Justice?*, Oxford: Clarendon Press.

Baldwin, J. and McConville, M. (1977). *Negotiated Justice: Pressures to Plead Guilty*, London: Martin Robertson.

Blankenburg, E. (1997). "Civil Litigations Rates as Indicators for Legal Cultures," in D. Nelken (ed.), *Comparing Legal Cultures*, Aldershot: Dartmouth.

Carlen, P. (1976). *Magistrates' Justice*, C.M. Campbell and P.N.P. Wiles (eds.), Law in Society Series, London: Martin Robertson.

Church, T.W. (1985). "Examining Local Legal Culture," *American Bar Foundation Research Journal* (Summer): 449–518.

Conley, J.M. and O'Barr, W.M. (2005). *Just Words: Law, Language and Power* (2nd edn.), Chicago and London: University of Chicago Press.

Cowan, D. and Hitchings, E. (2007). "'Pretty Boring Stuff': District Judges and Housing Possession Proceedings," *Social & Legal Studies* 16 (3): 363–82.

Deane, H. (2000). "The Influence of Pre–Sentence Reports on Sentencing in a District Court in New Zealand," *Australian & New Zealand Journal of Criminology* 33: 91–106.

Dezalay, Y. and Garth, B.G (1996). *Dealing in Virtue: International Commercial Arbitration and the Construction of a Transnational Legal Order*, Chicago: University of Chicago Press.

Douglas, J.W. (2007). *Examination of NCSC Workload Assessment Projects and Methodology*, Institute for Court Management Court Executive Development Program 2006–2007. Phase III Project, Washington, DC: National Center for State Courts.

Eisenstein, J., Flemming, R.B., and Nardulli, P.F. (1988). *The Contours of Justice: Communities and Their Courts*, Boston: Little, Brown and Company.

Emmelman, D.S. (1998). "Gauging the Strength of Evidence Prior to Plea Bargaining: The Interpretive Procedures of Court-Appointed Defense Attorneys," *Law and Social Inquiry* 22: 927–55.

Erez, E. and Rogers, L. (1999). "Victim Impact Statements and Sentencing Outcomes and Processes," *British Journal of Criminology* 39(2): 216–39.

European Commission for the Efficiency of Justice (CEPEJ) (2008). *European Judicial Systems Edition 2008 (Data 2006): Efficiency and Quality of Justice*: Council of Europe.

Farole Jr, D.J. (2009). "Problem Solving and the American Bench: A National Survey of Trial Court Judges," *The Justice System Journal* 30(1): 50–69.

Flemming, R.B., Nardulli, P.F., and Eisenstein, J. (1992). *The Craft of Justice: Politics and Work in Criminal Court Communities*, Philadelphia: University of Pennsylvania Press.

Galanter, M. (2004). "The Vanishing Trial: An Examination of Trials and Related Matters in Federal and State Courts," *Journal of Empirical Legal Studies* 1(3): 459–570.

Genn, H., Partington, M., and Wheeler, S. (2006). *Law in the Real World: Improving Our Understanding of How Law Works (Final Report and Recommendations)*, The Nuffield Inquiry on Empirical Legal Research, London: Nuffield Foundation.

Hadfield, G.K. (2004). "Where Have All the Trials Gone? Settlements, Nontrial Adjudications, and Statistical Artifacts in the Changing Disposition of Federal Civil Cases," *Journal of Empirical Legal Studies* 1(3): 705–34.

Haltom, W. and McCann, M.J. (2004). *Distorting the Law: Politics, Media, and the Litigation Crisis*, Chicago: University of Chicago Press.

Hayes, H. and Daly, K. (2004). "Conferencing and Re-Offending in Queensland," *Australian & New Zealand Journal of Criminology* 37: 167–91.

Heydebrand, W. and Seron, C. (1990). *Rationalizing Justice: The Political Economy of Federal District Courts*, Albany: State University of New York.

Ietswaart, H.F.P. (1990). "The International Comparison of Court Caseloads: The Experience of the European Working Group," *Law & Society Review* 24(2): 571–93.

Jacob, H. (1984). *Using Published Data: Errors and Remedies*, Beverly Hills, CA: Sage Publications.

Kakalik, J.S., Dunworth, T., Hill, L.A., McCaffrey, D., Oshiro, M., Pace, N. M., and Vaiana, M.E. (1996). *An Evaluation of Mediation and Early Neutral Evaluation under the Civil Justice Reform Act*, Santa Monica, CA: Rand.

Komter, M. L. (1998). *Dilemmas in the Courtroom: A Study of Trials of Violent Crime in the Netherlands*, Mahwah, NJ: Lawrence Erlbaum Associates.

Kritzer, H. M. (2004). "Disappearing Trials? A Comparative Perspective," *Journal of Empirical Legal Studies* 1(3): 735–54.

Lande, J. (2006). "Introduction to Vanishing Trial Symposium," *Journal of Dispute Resolution* 1: 1–5.

Langbroek, P.M. and Fabri, M. (2004). *Case Assignment to Courts and within Courts: A Comparative Study in Seven Countries*, Netherlands: Shaker Publishing.

Lofland, J., Snow, D., Anderson, L., and Lofland, L.H. (2006). *Analyzing Social Settings: A Guide to Qualitative Observation and Analysis*, Belmont: Thomson Wadsworth.

Lynch, M. (1997). "Preliminary Notes on Judges' Work: The Judge as a Constituent of Courtroom 'Hearings'," in M. Travers and J.F. Manzo (eds.), *Law in Action: Ethnomethodological and Conversation Analytic Approaches to Law*, Aldershot: Ashgate.

Mack, K. and Roach Anleu, S. (1995). *Pleading Guilty: Issues and Practices*, Melbourne: Australian Institute of Judicial Administration.

Mack, K. and Roach Anleu, S. (2008). "The National Survey of Australian Judges: An Overview of Findings," *Journal of Judicial Administration* 18: 5–21.

Mack, K. and Roach Anleu, S. (2010). "Performing Neutrality: Judicial Demeanour and Legitimacy," *Law & Social Inquiry* 35(1): 137–73.

Mackenzie, G. (2005). *How Judges Sentence*, Sydney: Federation Press.

Mather, L. M. (1979). *Plea Bargaining or Trial? The Process of Criminal-Case Disposition*, Lexington, MA: Lexington Books.

Maynard, D. W. (1988). "Narratives and Narrative Structure in Plea Bargaining," *Law & Society Review* 22: 449–79.

McBarnet, D. J. (1981). *Conviction: Law, the State and the Construction of Justice*, London and Basingstoke: Macmillan Press.

McCall, M. (2008). "Structuring Gender's Impact: Judicial Voting across Criminal Justice Cases," *American Politics Research* 36(2): 264–96.

McCoy, C. (1993). *Politics and Plea Bargaining: Victim's Rights in California*, Philadelphia: University of Pennsylvania Press.

Mileski, M. (1971). "Courtroom Encounters: An Observational Study of a Lower Criminal Court," *Law & Society Review* 5(4): 473–538.

Moorhead, R. and Cowan, D. (2007). "Judgecraft: An Introduction," *Social and Legal Studies* 16: 315–20.

Morris, A. and Maxwell, G. M. (1993). "Juvenile Justice in New Zealand: A New Paradigm," *Australian & New Zealand Journal of Criminology* 26: 72–90.

Ostrom, B.J., Strickland, S. M., and Hannaford-Agor, P. L. (2004). "Examining Trial Trends in State Courts: 1976–2002," *Journal of Empirical Legal Studies* 1(3): 755–82.

Pérez-Liñán, A., Ames, B., and Seligson, M. A. (2006). "Strategy, Careers, and Judicial Decision: Lessons from Bolivian Courts," *The Journal of Politics* 68(2): 284–95.

Roach Anleu, S. and Mack, K. (2005). "Magistrates' Everyday Work and Emotional Labour," *Journal of Law and Society* 32(4): 590–614.

Roach Anleu, S. and Mack, K. (2009). "Intersections between in-Court Procedures and the Production of Guilty Pleas," *Australian & New Zealand Journal of Criminology* 42(1): 1–23.

Roberts, J.V. and Roach, K. (2005). "Conditional Sentencing and the Perspectives of Crime Victims: A Socio–Legal Analysis," *Queen's Law Journal* 30: 560–600.

Ryan, J.P., Ashman, A., Sales, B.D., and Shane-DuBow, S. (1980). *American Trial Judges: Their Work Styles and Performance*, New York: Free Press.

Schanzenbach, M. (2005). "Have Federal Judges Changed Their Sentencing Practices? The Shaky Empirical Foundations of the Feeney Amendment," *Journal of Empirical Legal Studies* 2(1): 1–48.

Seron, C. (1990). "The Impact of Court Organization on Litigation," *Law & Society Review* 24(2): 451–65.

Shapland, J., Atkinson, A., Atkinson, H., Dignan, J., Edwards, L., Hibbert, J., Howes, M., Johnstone, J., Robinson, G., and Sorsby, A. (2008). *Does Restorative Justice Affect Reconviction? The Fourth Report from the Evaluation of Three Schemes*, Ministry of Justice Research Series 10/08, London: UK Ministry of Justice.

Sisk, G.C. and Heise, M. (2005). "Judges and Ideology: Public and Academic Debates About Statistical Measures," *Northwestern University Law Review* 99(2): 744–93.

Snowball, L. and Weatherburn, D. (2007). "Does Racial Bias in Sentencing Contribute to Indigenous Overrepresentation in Prison?," *Australian & New Zealand Journal of Criminology* 37(3): 272–90.

Steffensmeier, D. and Demuth, S. (2001). "Ethnicity and Judges' Sentencing Decisions: Hispanic-Black-White Comparisons," *Criminology* 39(1): 145–78.

Tata, C., Burns, N., Halliday, S., Hutton, N., and McNeill, F. (2008). "Assisting and Advising the Sentencing Decision Process: The Pursuit Of "Quality" In Pre-Sentence Reports," *British Journal of Criminology* 48: 835–55.

Wright, T. and Melville, A. (2004). " 'Hey, but Who's Counting': The Metrics and Politics of Trends in Civil Litigation," in W.R. Prest and S. Roach Anleu (eds.), *Litigation: Past and Present*, Sydney: University of New South Wales Press.

24

APPELLATE COURTS

DAVID ROBERTSON

....[the] result suggests that some alternative explanation exists for such voting behavior; we offer several possibilities—including the influence of legal considerations—in our conclusions (Edelman et al., 2008: 819–52).

We thought—incorrectly, as it turned out—that the trial courts would simply follow our opinion even if they disagreed with it. Stare decisis and all that stuff. But sometimes it seems as though we have to remind the lower court there is a judicial pecking order when it comes to the interpretation of statutes. *Gwartz v. Superior Court*, 71 Cal. App. 4th, April 16, 1999 (Cross, 2005: 369–405).

I. Prologemena

Academic work one could describe as in the "empirical legal research" domain is rich and multi-faceted even when restricted, as in this Chapter, just to the field of appellate courts. It should be noted that I am taking a historically "long view" of empirical legal research, and not restricting my coverage to the time when a self-consciously so-labeled movement developed. Rather than cover all aspects of this field in an inevitably shallow way, I have concentrated mainly on two problems. These are (1) how best to characterize and explain judicial decision-making and (2) what can we say about who, typically, wins on appeal. Of these, the former gets the greater space. Dozens of other questions have been addressed, all of them important and useful, and I try to say a little about some of them in the course of the Chapter. They are however secondary in urgency—and as a consequence, they have been less considered by researchers.[1]

Section II raises some general questions about the nature and coverage of empirical legal research on appellate courts, and discusses some very general methodological questions. The core of the Chapter is the following two sections. In section III I look at rival approaches to describing what judges do in making decisions, and what motivational assumptions are most commonly made. In section IV I pick up the question, simply put, of "who wins on appeal?" My final comments in very brief form indicate the broad outlines of how the field should develop, especially methodologically in the future.

II. General Considerations

The idea that "legal considerations" might possibly partly explain judicial voting in collegial appellate courts ought to be so obvious that it should, for legal scholars, be the first and primary explanation, not a partial alternative explanation. (By legal considerations I understand the sort of acceptance of norms and techniques

---

[1] Among the many issues I have to ignore are: when and why do litigants appeal at all? How do the relatively small number of cases actually chosen by upper courts from those seeking leave to appeal get selected? What dynamics of the courts determine the nature of judicial opinion-writing, which judges get to write them, with what consequence for judicial coalition-making? What role does oral argument play in different judicial cultures? How important are court staff such as the law clerk in the United States? How does the structure and professional formation of the bar affect appellate outcomes? What are the consequences of different judicial career ladders and promotion policies?

found among judges and lawyers with neither interest nor belief in sociological or economic modes of explanation for legal outcomes.) Or so it would have appeared before the birth of empirical work of the type that became known as Empirical Legal Studies (ELS), although legal realism and the slightly later judicial behaviorism prefigured current concerns. The second quotation at the beginning of the Chapter perhaps shows why this discipline has emerged, and why it is useful, even necessary—although it should immediately be said that Cross, whose article itself starts with the quotation from the Californian upper court, produces an answer to the question of why precedents are adhered to that is at odds with the thrust of much literature in the field. The fact that Cross is a lawyer may turn out to be relevant.

As soon as one starts reading in the field one thing is apparent: the vast bulk of empirical work on appeal courts is American. Most research is on American courts. Where courts of other countries are studied, they are mainly studied by American academics using the same theories and methods used to study American appellate courts. The few articles written on other countries and not by Americans nearly all import the assumptions and methodologies of Americans writing on American courts. So one question to be answered is how well understanding American appellate courts helps us to understand courts elsewhere. Because, as I try to show later, although certain key assumptions about judicial motivation and behavior may make more sense inside American political and judicial culture than in other countries, this unavoidable American emphasis in the literature may be problematic.

Naturally there are exceptions—although much of the earliest work which can be legitimately described as "empirical," such as Schubert and Danelski's pioneering comparative study, was American or American-influenced, not all was (Schubert and Danelski, 1969). A major study undertaken in England was Louis Blom-Cooper and Gavin Drewry's, *Final Appeal,* a massive and ground-breaking work on the House of Lords (Blom-Cooper and Drewry, 1972). This was followed by Paterson's study of the same court (Paterson, 1982). While these are different in tone, style, and methodology from recent work, for sheer factual information one would do much better to read *Final Appeal.* In fact the early authors, writing in a less methodologically sophisticated manner, were able to pose and answer questions—for example whether the UK needs a second appeal tier, or how law lords explain their own decisions—in a much more direct and less straight-jacketed way than authors writing in a more modern, social-science-influenced manner might be able to. Many now seem to feel a need to do Kuhnian "normal science" within a "paradigm." *Final Appeal* opened many eyes, forced lawyers and a handful of political scientists to consider Britain's highest court as an institution, and even set some, myself included, on a life-long research trajectory. It was, at the most basic, full of information, and it asked probing questions. By modern standards it does not look like a piece of social science research. The most sophisticated numerical analyses amounted to a few percentages, and there was no theory guiding which issues to select, what questions to pose, or the grounds for accepting or rejecting answers offered. Yet it clearly was neither normal legal research nor conventional history (like Robert Stevens's superb history of the development of the House of Lords, published only a few years after *Final Appeal* (Stevens, 1979)). There was a difference, though one hard at the time to see, between a social science approach to how a court behaved and interacted with its legal and political environment, and a legal historian's account. This was so even when the periods covered overlapped, the historian was as politically aware and nuanced as Stevens, and even though neither study could be described as "doctrinal."

This was a good beginning, but there was very little follow-up by American or British political scientists. This is shown dramatically by the publication in 2009 of what must be seen almost as a second edition, this time edited rather than written by Blom-Cooper and Drewry (now joined by Brice Dickson), and produced to mark the end of the judicial House of Lords as it morphed into Britain's Supreme Court (Blom-Cooper et al., 2009). This work is no more sophisticated, no more a product of empirical social-science research than its predecessor. But while no one can fault *Final Appeal* for not being ahead of its intellectual times, it is hard to understand how the new book can be justified in being no different. Many of its sections look frankly amateurish by modern social-science standards; and leaving aside the overtly doctrinal part, it does not even have that much raw information in it. Between these two publication dates political and other social sciences have created a huge, complex and demanding professional literature of empirical legal research on appellate courts.

A. Problems of restriction on coverage

The research literature is almost exclusively about the common law world, or near analogues such as the courts of South Africa. The main exception to this is that the European Court of Justice (ECJ) has received some attention; but the ECJ is not an appeal court. Continental European court systems below the constitutional court level have not really been researched; and stand-alone "Kelsen" courts cannot easily be treated as appellate courts. Kelsen's model from Austria, widely applied in post-war Europe, insisted that constitutional courts not hear appeals in any usual sense of that process. It is true, of course, that to some extent the very idea of an "appeal" court is a function of the common law approach—the idea of "appeal" used here has no direct equivalent in civil law systems. Indeed it has plausibly been argued that one cannot properly even translate into English terms that might seem to connote "appeal" in European languages (Geeroms, 2002). This geographical and national concentration in the discipline does matter, however, in quite fundamental ways. One way of seeing this quickly is to take up the question of why there are almost no "empirical" studies of courts of cassation.

Cassation involves a superior court deciding whether a decision from an inferior appellate court is compatible with the law. When a Cour de Cassation decides that an error in law has been made it remits the case for re-decision to another court of the same rank as the original. It does so with only the shortest summary opinion, containing nothing like a *ratio decidendi*. The cassation order does not determine the result of the reconsideration, nor is it a new precedent. Indeed the systems with cassation do not recognize precedent as such. (One classic study, Martin Shapiro's *Courts* (Shapiro, 1981), has something to say on this matter, but the emphasis in the empirical literature on the common law world is largely unchallenged.) This may be explained by the fact that it is extremely hard to characterize a cassation order as a policy-making statement. At the extreme it is as though court one asks court two, regarding a decision, "is this right?" and court two just says "No." Obviously legal policy is changed over time through the cassation process, though slowly and in terms of changing interpretations of a "Code." However, such change is largely based on inferences, and these are drawn primarily not from the cassation order, but from the writings of jurists. It must be remembered that such writers have, in the continental tradition, a much higher status with judges than do legal academics in the common law world. Given the shortness and frequent opacity of court rulings in the continental system, the jurist is much freer to decide what the law really is than his or her comparator in the UK or U.S.

Imagine trying to apply the techniques, theories and methods of much of the work done on American appellate courts if they gave only brief (and unanimous) "Yes" or "No" responses to decisions of lower courts and referred the case back for reconsideration. Imagine, further, that most of the work of interpreting what the "Yes" or "No" implied for the meaning of some federal statute was done in the pages of law journals.

Leaving aside constitutional tribunals, the missing policy-formulation aspect of cassation, at least in its official and purest mode, makes the sort of empirical study of appellate courts discussed in this Chapter largely irrelevant outside common law jurisdictions, not because it has not been done, but because it probably cannot be done (Lasser, 2004). There are formidable technical difficulties presented to empirical scholars dealing with most continental European appeal courts, the biggest being the one alluded to above—most do not allow public dissents. Without being able to see dissent, only Herculean assumptions let one even model what goes in the Black Box that the court presents (Hönnige, 2009). In fact the U.S. Supreme Court is one of the simplest courts to model or study empirically for many reasons, one being that it always sits *en banc*. By contrast, although the UK House of Lords, for example, allowed dissent, for several reasons constructing judge/judge agreement matrices was extremely difficult. First, it typically sat in five-judge panels chosen largely at random under the authority of the Senior Law Lord with a senior civil servant doing the actual choosing. Secondly, the case-load was comparatively low—about 50 cases a year. Thirdly, being appointed to the court late in their judicial careers and with a fixed retirement age, the Law Lords seldom served for very long (ten years on average). As a result, any given pair of Law Lords would be likely to have sat together on only a tiny number of cases divisive enough to generate dissents.[2]

B. What sorts of appeal courts?—Constitutional courts and policy-making

One problem arising from the dominance of American examples and methods is that the literature is overwhelmingly concentrated on courts with a constitutional review function. This problem is exacerbated by the fact that one of the few courts outside the United States to get much attention is the constitutionally and culturally similar Canadian Supreme Court, and although there are some studies of the Australian High Court and indeed of the Indian High Court, they have as yet had little impact on scholarship in this field (Bhattacharya and Smyth, 2001; Pierce, 2006).

The difficulty of exporting studies of U.S. courts, especially but not only at the Supreme Court or Court of Appeals level, is that most countries not only do not have so wide and common an application of constitutional law to ordinary life, but also limit what constitutional appeal there is to specialized courts. We badly need to know something, rather a lot in fact, about—for instance—the English Court of Appeal, the French Cour de Cassation, the South African Supreme Court, and the German *Bundesgerichtshof*; there are literally hundreds of "ordinary" appeal courts about which there has been absolutely no empirical research. For that matter, we need to know much more than we do about the "ordinary" law on appeal in the U.S., cases which do not involve constitutional issues. Yet so important is the "policy-making" aspect of U.S. constitutional law that the models developed, and the assumptions about judicial behavior expressed or implied, are not easily applicable outside the American scenario. The American literature, of course, is largely restricted to statutory interpretation and administrative law cases—very little unfortunately is written about the common law. There is a concentration on constitutional matters because of the importance of policy and the interest in studying political ideology, which is more important, or certainly more obvious, in such courts.

Of course an "ordinary law" judge can have policy preferences. Lord Denning, who, as Master of the Rolls, oversaw civil appeals in the English Court of Appeal for many years, was quite open about his policy preferences in the law of contract, for instance. Still, it is hard to distinguish a judge trying to solve a contract law issue as a natural result of his professional formation from one intent on deliberate

---

[2] In September 2009, the Judicial Committee of the House of Lords was abolished, and was replaced by a new Supreme Court. At this stage no changes in personnel or practice have occurred.

long-range change, and thus harder to equate the latter to policy in the sense of developing, for example, a constitutional rule about abortion. The policy concerns in ordinary judging are not as obviously political, although of course one certainly finds a good deal of interest by business interests in some aspects of common law, especially torts. A Law Lord once admitted to me that he always had an eye on the attractiveness of London as a litigation center in crafting certain types of decisions. It would be of real practical utility if ELS studies cast light on the extent to which such highly pragmatic motivations occur—but the studies required to do this might require a different methodology than that which is used for most research in the field, which often infers motivation from politically consistent patterns of decisions. Perhaps one can infer motivations from behavior but the philosophical basis for using ideas like "unconscious motivations" is complex and demanding. Judicial motivation—what aims, role beliefs, ambitions lie behind judicial decisions—is real but difficult to measure and understand. There have been some successful attempts to study judicial motivations, though they are often just assumed. Lawrence Baum has pioneered several approaches, including a particularly interesting one focusing on the "audiences" to which judges address themselves. Many of us who have interviewed judges have noticed the extent to which they read law review articles almost like actors reading their notices; but Baum has tried to systematize this. However, he does not break free from one crucial assumption: that judges can be divided into law pursuers and policy pursuers, even though he at least notes that the human drive for approval modifies the purity of these orientations (Baum, 2006). This law/policy distinction turns out to be vital in much of the research to be discussed here.

The literature, largely a journal article literature, is large, diverse, and growing. This diversity makes it difficult to gather research outputs into manageable fields for discussion. I choose therefore to concentrate on only a few research sub-fields in an attempt to draw out commonalities of approach. Inevitably this means much good work is ignored: there is, for example, no discussion in what follows of the influential early contributions by Martin Shapiro. Indeed many good works are ignored precisely because they are good, but, like Shapiro's seminal book, have not been much followed (Shapiro, 1981; Shapiro, 1964). Quite a few contributions are omitted from my discussion because though insightful, they have not had much impact on steering the research agenda. I give now, though, two examples of issues that indicate something of the range of the discipline.

C. A typical problem

At its simplest, empirical legal research on appellate courts asks questions which concentrate on patterns of case results. We can start with the brute fact that most appellants lose. The literature is studded with figures on the varying success rates of appellants and respondents in different sorts of courts. To take an example almost at random, between 1977 and 1987 the rate of reversal by U.S. Circuit Courts of Appeals of decisions of the federal district courts (and certain administrative agencies) varied between 13.5% and 17.7%. The English Court of Appeal was more appellant-friendly, but between 1952 and 1983 still only reversed the lower court on average 35% of the time (Atkins, 1990). Unfortunately there is a tendency to assume that a "fact," once established, is a permanent fact about a particular court. For instance, during this period overall the House of Lords reversed the Court of Appeal in only one third of cases, but in the last decade has done so in over 50% of cases. Why the change? We have no theory to explain that, and we should have. The lack of a theory comes from the way empirical legal research is somewhat divorced from mainstream social science. Very probably such changes in rates arise because the courts, in ways we do not understand, mirror deeper social change. However, without such a theory the precise question of why the reversal rate changes cannot even be formulated properly.

Such brute comparative facts are neither very interesting nor, taken statistically, very difficult to explain, and, once one has controlled for differences in rules of appeal entitlement and those governing appeal courts' rights to "intervene," may not even remain—which is roughly what Burton Atkins ought to have concluded given his own arguments in the piece referred to in the previous paragraph. But the mere fact that appeals do not often succeed does not address the more interesting question—is there any pattern regarding who typically wins at the appellate level? A good deal of the literature is taken up with this question, often under the label of "Party Capability Theory" (derived from Galanter, 1974). I discuss such studies at greater length later. The facts become even more interesting when one notes that it is not just that appellants do not do well, but that defendants, appellant or respondent, do not do as well as plaintiffs in U.S. Circuit Courts of Appeals (Eisenberg, 2004). Or do they? Because another study shows that defendants get reversals in 31% of appeals from civil jury trials, and plaintiffs succeed on appeal in only 13% of cases (Clermont and Eisenberg, 2000). Both studies were by the same author (in one case working with a co-author), and there is probably no inconsistency because the second study covered only one particular area of the law. This shows the need to read very carefully. Either way, there are possible asymmetries in appeal success, which may be of a systematic nature, and require empirical investigation.

D. Fundamental questions

The facts about appeal success raise another question in the literature the answer to which one might have thought, because one had not thought about it at all, was obvious: Why do we have appeal courts? This leads us to a particular form of empirical legal study of appeal courts where the word "empirical" has to be expanded rather widely, because much of the work is abstract modeling. The assumption made in the articles cited above is that appellate decisions correct mistakes by lower courts— indeed the "defendants do better" thesis is explained on the grounds that appeal courts think trial courts, and juries in particular (one must remember that most American civil cases are tried to juries), are too plaintiff-friendly. So is that what appeal courts are for, error correction? If so, they may not be the ideal mechanism to accomplish this. How might we examine the hypothesis that some other mechanism might serve the error correction function better than do appeal courts?

A good deal of effort has been put into deriving analytic models of various aspects of the court system, largely concentrating on appeal courts, and one of the questions raised has been whether they are error-correcting mechanisms or exist for some other reason. My hesitancy about the word "empirical" is that this part of the literature, though most certainly not traditional legal scholarship, and most certainly deserving of consideration, usually has no empirical content in the sense of data that have been collected and analyzed. Instead it uses relatively simple micro-economic modeling methods to analyze stylized interactions among judges, courts, and other legal actors under varying hypothetical rules. Though connected to the "Law and Economics" school, often by authors like Richard Posner, who has written on courts of appeal as well, the two research areas are different. The material relevant to appeal courts is often described as "positive political theory," or PPT for short. The best research does go on to offer genuinely empirical tests of the models, but even that which is entirely formal can make us look very carefully at our assumptions, or force us to ask questions normally ignored. For example, why do lower courts follow the precedents set by appeal courts? Or, an unusual question never raised by other forms of research—are the decisions of multi-member (collegial) appeal courts rational? If so, what makes them so? These are just a small sample of the issues studied by empirical legal researchers, all of which deserve more space were it available. I turn now to the most fundamental part of my discussion.

III. Policy, Precedent, and Strategy

Throughout the literature on appeal courts, whether it is positive political theory work, the study of the role of precedent, macro-pattern studies like those dealing with party capability theory, or even work on the nature and role of doctrine, one thing is common. Judges are assumed to be motivated, either entirely or to a very great degree, by a desire to achieve policy ends. Though this assumption can occur in all these approaches, and under a variety of methodologies, its origin lies in the early political science research on the U.S. Supreme Court, and before that in the general thrust of American Legal Realist perceptions of judicial behavior (Robertson, 1982). Sometimes these policy preferences are specified as political preferences, sometimes left undefined and not characterized in concrete terms. No one can doubt the conviction of most people working in the field that judges pursue these policy preferences whenever and wherever they can. The detailed theories are simply explications of how this judicial drive works out. As Cross notes, theorists will go to great lengths to maintain the purity of their conception of judges as simple political actors untouched by anything that might make a judge see the world differently from an elected politician or member of the executive.

PPT theoreticians seem extraordinarily determined to prove that lower court compliance results purely from political preference and not from any judicial preference for legal variables (Cross, 2005: 384).

Part of the reason so much reliance is placed on a judge's political policy preferences, as opposed to policy simply in the sense of desired outcome or set of outcomes, may be that we have a metric for this arising from the early dominance of the "attitudinal" model in American political science. Almost from the beginning in the political science study of judicial behavior, techniques were developed to translate a judge's voting in cases into "ideological" or "attitudinal" scores (the two terms being treated as synonyms). It was demonstrated, to the satisfaction of many, that one could "explain" judges' votes in cases by their position on a single and simple left/right or liberal/conservative dimension. In fact this was itself clearly a tautology because ideology was measured behaviorally, and then used to explain that behavior. Most recent studies have sought independent measures of the judge's ideological position, and arrayed the cases, by coding their import, on such a scale. So to take recent examples, the question of when courts will find for both appellant and respondent on different issues relied in part on the hypothesis that one group of judges will seek to attract the vote of another group, by allowing the second group's preferred side to win on at least some of the issues. Thus, cases with such outcomes are explained by the ideological diversity in the court. There was no problem in operationalizing these ideological positions and distances, and no need was felt to justify the approach because it became so routine in the literature (Lindquist et al., 2007). The sense that a judge's vote is predictable is shown by another example which powerfully demonstrates the scholarly consensus that judges are policy-maximizers whose preferences can be quite precisely measured and placed on a scale. The very title of the piece in question makes the point: "Measuring Deviations from Expected Voting Patterns on Collegial Courts." Not only does this rely on a strong measurement capability, but nowhere in the article is there any sense at all of its being remarkable to assert that one knows what to expect about a judge's vote choice (Edelman et al., 2008). It is worth noting that most measures of a judge's ideological position are highly inferential. Given the near impossibility of asking judges to fill out attitude questionnaires, the most common measurement approach is to equate a judge's ideological score to that of the politician most closely involved in his or her appointment, often the president in the case of federal judges (but see Brace et al., 2000, for an application at the state level).

The attitudinal model is well established, and in many ways has been shown to be a workable model of judicial behavior. Though perhaps only in a weak form, where attitudes are a partial rather than complete explanation, it commands extensive support. It is perhaps underspecified compared with the use of attitude measurement in political science, and even more in its discipline of origin, social psychology, where there is a mass of technical and theoretical work on attitudes. This may not matter at a practical level, but there is a sense that "attitude" is not fully explicated or explored. We could certainly do with knowing a good deal more about these attitudes—where do they come from, are they simply a projection onto the legal/constitutional sphere of more general social or psychological attitudes, how robust or flexible are they? It has been possible to make considerable progress without doing this where the attitudes in question relate to the relatively broad issue clusters of American constitutional jurisprudence. But if the model is to be developed to give us an understanding of a broad range of appeal courts doing other legal tasks, such questions have to be addressed. To take one simple example—how do judges' individual preferences regarding risk influence their decisions in areas such as bankruptcy appeals? One might hypothesize that judges who were highly risk-averse would be less friendly to debtors and more protective of those to whom some financial recompense can be guaranteed.

Those in the PPT and law-and-economics traditions who rely on the attitudinal model, and its core assumption that judges are policy driven, do so for a specific reason. All the models are based on *homo economicus,* the self-interested utility-maximizer, beholden to no other values, constrained only by the costs an action may incur if those costs would amount to more than the utility the action would bring. Some assumption about the utility stream to a judge from deciding appeals in particular ways is held to be the minimum a model must posit to treat judicial decisions as rational. Richard Posner, in an early effort to model judicial behavior says quite bluntly:

Are judges rational? Or have the elaborate efforts made to strip them of incentives placed their behavior beyond the reach of rational-choice models?

Posner is not a good support for the way the models are developed by others, because he specifically denies policy preference as a motivating factor—preferring, as the title of the article suggests, to treat judges as very much more like ordinary people who may want to maximize things like leisure, salary, esteem (Posner, 1993). Nonetheless, he is right that the models require an assumption of something other than normal job satisfaction as a motivation for judicial behavior. The "something else" is the satisfaction of having a policy preference written into the law by deciding a case in a specific way, though on lower courts, or courts with fixed term appointments, career advancement and security may play a part.

This assumption about judicial motivation is uniform throughout the field of empirical studies of appeal courts, even if more subtle writers will sometimes adduce other motivations running alongside policy preferences (Baum, 1997). The very language of some analyses reinforces this—the policy-preference point of a court is sometimes called its "Bliss Point." Not all authors treat policy preferences as entirely political rather than legal. So, for example, Bruno de Mesquita uses examples about desired levels of care in tort liability in his attempt to square the fact of precedents being followed with the assumption of pursuit of policy preferences by judges. Whether this extension to common law is important to the author is unclear, but it is certainly welcome (de Mesquita and Stephenson, 2002). Even this is an interesting choice of non-political policy preference, because it enables him to talk of judges having a preference point on a dimension, a device he uses to facilitate his model construction. It might be harder to use dimensional analysis on a problem of contract interpretation, where no obvious underlying scale is involved—though one might, for example, construct a scale where one end represented a highly formal strict-interpretation stand, and the other a desire to give effect to obvious intentions. Alternatively an underlying scale based on connections of equality might apply—powerful contracting parties losing out to weaker ones. The trouble is that no work has been done of this type. The essence of the modeling game is still there however. For de Mesquita, the disjunction between wanting to "make policy" and being "legalistic" is removed—judges follow precedents because they are policy-driven. Up to a point, precedent-following is, under certain conditions, a more efficient mechanism for ensuring that the courts below render judgments which maximize the appeal judge's policy utility, if only because it sets a norm throughout the judicial hierarchy of doing what the court above wants done.

The validity of these assumptions about motivations of appeal court judges is crucial if the American approach is to have meaningful application elsewhere. This raises at least two questions: is the policy-making assumption valid even for America? If it is, are there any good reasons for *not* applying the assumptions elsewhere?

We need really to start one step earlier—is the "policy" versus "law" distinction itself intelligible? It helps to remember what English courts understand by a "public policy decision"—essentially it refers to cases in which an applicable rule, which makes sense and is undisputedly part of the law, would require a result which seems inappropriate in the circumstances. The result that would be required by application of the rule might be disliked for practical reasons—the "floodgates argument," for example—or because it offends some more general moral principle embedded in the law. So a judge may be unwilling to extend a certain form of liability, even if the logic of the existing law would require such extension, because of the risk of precipitating a flood of claims. Or we refuse to follow the law of contract all the way to enforcing a gambling contract because of a general moral objection. Either way, the "policy" implies a rule in the first place, because policy means, among other things, a similar resolution to similar conflicts, and there has to be a general rule, even if somewhat latent, to identify such suitable resolutions (Bell, 1983).

This is not the sense of policy implied in treating judges as policy-maximizers, because the judges I refer to here are normally rule-followers rather than free agents solely concerned, if strategically, with maximizing their own policy preferences. Nonetheless, it seems improbable that free-agent judges simply decide cases on their merits according to non-legal values they hold. They might in fact do so, sometimes they surely must do so, though they can never admit to doing so. But it would be pointless to act like this as a general strategy, simply because it would achieve so little, given how few cases of the behavior they seek to change will ever come before them. Manifestly policy-oriented judges would have to act so as to create and sustain general rules designed to impose their ideological preferences in all relevant cases. Indeed, it is a recognition of this which produces the felt need to explain precedent-following in the positive political theory models.

We must remember also that, whether they are genuine or fake, arguments have to be adduced. Judges always have to provide reasoned arguments cast in largely non-policy terms, if only because the legal cultures adhere to a traditional conception of the law as "found" by judges, or because there is deep suspicion by elected politicians of judges as policy-makers. Thus we have the following problem: how would one distinguish between a judge, who sincerely felt that the logic of the law itself required a rule which, as it happens, produces result X, from a judge who strategically chose to craft or support the same rule, but only because he wanted result X replicated throughout society?

This is not nit-picking, and to some extent the American literature on appellate judicial behavior does try to provide at least an inferential answer. The conviction that judges decide on the basis of ideology or policy preference comes from the following, consistent empirical finding. One can array judges on an ideological dimension from left to right and show that cases, when independently scored on a similar dimension, are voted on such that groups of judges form on either side of the case's position on the ideological dimension. If an outcome-choice in a case scores toward one or other extremes of the dimension, it will probably fail because it will represent an ideological choice too extreme for a majority of judges. This is why Edelman, Klein, and Lindquist can talk of "deviations from expected votes" (Edelman et al., 2008). An early article by one of the leaders of this approach, Jeffrey Segal, demonstrated the power it can have in an analysis of Fourth Amendment search and seizure cases (Segal, 1984; Segal and Spaeth, 2002). What is interesting about this analysis is that it could, as Segal says, perfectly well stand as a proof of the much-criticized "legal model," if that model were at all sophisticated. Effectively the analysis demonstrates that the more egregious invasions of privacy will cause even the more conservative judges to vote against the police, while minor invasions will draw the wrath only of liberal justices. But is this evidence of policy preference, or just evidence that

Supreme Court Justices, like all judges, have coherent understandings of the law, in this case constitutional law, which may correlate with extra-legal ideology, and that in the day-to-day work of balancing arguments, fact situations will, predictably, strike judges in different ways? Some judges will give greater salience to one part of the factual description, others to another aspect. There was, indeed, during the early days of judicial realism, a whole approach called "fact skepticism," prominent in Jerome Franks' *Law and the Modern Mind*. It may be the very language of American constitutional argument that makes it look as though judges are fighting for policy preferences. Re-cast the search and seizure jurisprudence in Continental European public law terms of proportionality and one just gets the fact that different judges make different judgments about what is proportional, and these judgments may be correlated to other attitudes the judges have (Robertson, 2010). For example, a judge whose private ideology is generally more sympathetic to the police may see some breach of arrest protocol as entirely proportional to the need to get a suspect into custody, while another, from equally basic value orientations, may see it as quite outside acceptable proportionality margins.

The main question is not whether the attitudinal model explains the behavior of the U.S. Supreme Court. The question is whether or not the assumption, that judges are policy-driven and do not act with "legalistic" motives, is exportable—or, even, to what degree it is generalizable to a broad range of appellate court work within the United States itself. Even within the realm of U.S. constitutional cases it has been shown that the outcome of less salient, less politically charged cases does not seem well predicted by the attitudinal model (Unah and Hancock, 2006). It may very well be that one particular institution, the U.S. Supreme Court, historically has developed a role for which much of the "professional formation" of judges is irrelevant. The historic behavior of the U.S. Supreme Court may in part be a function of the difficulties of applying the U.S. Constitution, which is shorter and more abstract than most other such documents, either those of the individual American states or of countries around the world. Certainly, part of the explanation must be the more overtly political nature, in a partisan sense, of appointments. The history of that court, immersed as it is in a legal culture highly influenced by legal realism and operating against a wider culture which expects its Supreme Court Justices to be politically aware, may have produced an institution remarkably inapplicable as a model for describing the behavior of other courts. If this is so, the empirical legal study of appeal courts has to come to terms with this difficulty in applying the attitudinal model more widely both within the United States and beyond. The centrality of the attitudinal model to the whole field may need to be revised.

Even committed practitioners of the attitudinal school are concerned about its exportability. There are few studies which try to import an American approach to the UK, but even the earliest of these admit to doubts about whether the import can work given different judicial approaches and styles (Atkins, 1990; 1991). Two recent studies of the Canadian Supreme Court, certainly the court where the U.S.

model is most likely to apply if it applies anywhere abroad, show that though identifiable ideological dimensions exist in Canada, they are vastly more complex than the uni-dimensional model American theorists usually apply (Ostberg and Wetstein, 2007). Other studies cast serious doubt on the stability of Canadian judicial ideological positions, suggesting, *inter alia*, that a key aspect, appointments of ideologically sympathetic judges by politicians, may be missing from the system (Green and Alarie, 2009). Generally empirical legal studies of appellate courts may make little progress with the attitudinal model unless "policy" preferences can be brought more closely within the realm of specifically legal problems. It may be safe, perhaps, to posit that something like a "liberal" approach to finding liability in tort, or to expanding the fairness of contractual terms, might exist. Such policy spectra might even correlate with more general ideological attitudes—perhaps all those who would extend the range of the duty of care, or look favorably on third party rights to sue under a contract, are also "liberal" in general political ideology, but there is as yet no evidence for such propositions. The danger would be of slipping, from the suggestion that a judge's overall value-set will affect his evaluations of legal issues, to an application of a simple policy-preference model. The attitudinal model in itself is, in fact, just that, a model, perhaps merely a description, rather than a theory. It is deeply under-theorized and is compatible with, or useful to, a variety of theories.

Future research might well benefit from one or more current theories in political science. The theoretical approach which might be most useful is some form of "value" institutionalism as opposed to "rational choice" institutionalism. Both approaches are parts of the general thrust in the social sciences often called "The New Institutionalism." Rational choice approaches treat institutions, for example the U.S. Congress, essentially as arenas within which non-altruistic utility-maximization influences behavior both of individuals and in the aggregate. The rules that define the institution are rules of a game, zero or positive sum, and provide resources for the actors, while the social product the institution exists to provide determines, at least partially, what is fought over. One can see easily how existing assumptions about judicial behavior are quite similar to the assumptions of this approach. The alternative, often called "value institutionalism," takes the defining rules of the institution as creating roles, the incumbents of which strive to follow role expectations, and are governed by a "logic of appropriateness." The distinction between the two approaches can be put in terms of whether judges are selfish players in an institutional context or, by contrast, try to be good judges. The truth will inevitably be a mixture.

We really know very little about how appellate judges see their role, about what might enter their conception of the "logic of appropriateness." The defense against this criticism by Segal and Spaeth, for example, rests largely on the difficulties that would beset such studies (Segal and Spaeth, 2002). Instead of knowing how judges see their role, we have inferences by social scientists based on analysis of their decisions. This "New Institutionalism" approach in political science has slowly begun to appear in empirical legal research, either in its own right or as part of the growing field of "American Political Development (which focuses broadly on political change and institutional development in the U.S.)" as it bears on courts. Both rational choice and value institutionalism are represented. Further research, however difficult, on judges' understanding of their roles and the factors which influence this, is urgently needed. It may well lead to more precise work being done also on the idea of judicial or, more generally, legal culture. After all, few would deny that English judges do hold quite strongly to the value of deference to parliament but also that this is changing. Why is it changing and with what, if any, observable effects?

To anticipate slightly, the much-vexed question of whether judges vote their immediate preference, called a "sincere" vote, or vote "strategically" with an eye to long-term legal policy development, and to the welfare of the court itself, can be studied effectively from these institutionalist perspectives. So, for example, Gillman's major work on the Lochner era is very much an empirical, if not statistical, analysis of a court, and the fact that it takes judges to be doing what they perceive to be their constitutional duty rather than maximizing anything does not prevent it being a valid approach for empirical legal researchers (Gilman, 1995). One of the most powerful analyses of the problem of attributing "strategic" as opposed to "sincere" motivations comes from a work in the American Political Development field, aptly titled "Legal, Strategic, or Legal Strategy: Deciding to Decide During the Civil War and Reconstruction" (Graber, 2006). The point of this study is that multiple stories could be told to fit the same set of cases, producing different assessments of the role of strategic policy-making versus sincere, legally-driven court decisions.

The strategic theoretical interpretation of the attitudinal model is not always welcomed by the most adamant attitudinalists, even though consideration of the strategic situation is not incompatible with the core idea of ideological preferences as the initial judicial motivation. The strategic interpretation is a form of rational choice theory, whether in its economic or positive political theory mode. Strategic models of judicial behavior are sometimes presented as an alternative to the attitudinal model, but, as suggested above, there is no fundamental contradiction, at least with subtle models which do not require attitudes to be a complete model. At its narrowest, all the strategists do is to note that various factors may combine to make a judge's "sincere" vote (i.e., the straightforward vote for his preferred position) less in his long-term interest than voting otherwise in any particular case. The need to build coalitions, or the need to protect a "second best" precedent, one that will do less harm to the judge's preferences than would occur if he strove for the rule he actually preferred and lost, may lead a judge to vote for something other than for the decision he would get most utility from in the instant case. While this is a useful insight, it adds relatively little to the general thrust of the attitudinal model. In particular, it is unclear that such insights can be generalized enough to provide more than a post hoc explanation of a decision.

The basic idea is in fact compatible with almost any theory of judicial behavior on collective courts.

At their broadest strategic models of the courts do something quite different. They take the court as a unit, intent on maximizing its own power and standing in a system populated with potentially hostile, competing legislative and executive bodies. "Strategy" refers to the way the court may make decisions some distance from the judicial policy preferences. This is a strategic move in an ongoing competition, which often looks rather like an international relations balance-of-power game. This analytic approach has been used with some effect in relation to the European Court of Justice, which occupies an analogous role to that of the U.S. Supreme Court, though the actual nature of the political constraints is different. The analogy is that the ECJ also functions like a supreme court in a federal system. Two of the clearest exponents of a strategic approach to the latter court are economists Rafael Gely and Pablo Spiller who have demonstrated it in reference to a more-or-less ordinary example of statutory construction as well as to a major incident in constitutional law, the Roosevelt court-packing plan (Gely and Spiller, 1990, 1992). One of the cases they studied involved the interpretation of a federal agency's ruling on car safety; another interpreted federal legislation on gender equality in education. In both cases the authors depict Supreme Court decision-making as a matter of playing off other political actors—political parties in Congress, the president and the agencies. It is at least possible that this sort of approach can bring some enlightenment to problems ordinary appellate courts face when presented with interpretative issues where the government has a clear preference for one answer rather than another.

Why appellate courts follow precedent, or whether they do so or not, is a problem involving both attitudinal and strategic matters. Attitudes have to be brought in to show that the justices or the court have a reason *not* to follow the precedent. The idea, that a court which could get away with ignoring a precedent they disliked could still have a motive for following it, clearly requires something like a strategic analysis. A considerable amount of positive political theory modeling has been devoted to this issue, but it is useful to consider first the major piece on the U.S. Supreme Court which purports to demonstrate that the court does not, in fact, follow precedent. This again is by Segal and Spaeth and involves an interesting definition of what a fair test of precedent-following would involve. They argue that one can only be sure a judge is following a precedent because he believes he ought to when it can be definitely shown that he would rather not follow it. The research does not involve inferring a judge's preference from his general attitudes. They take cases where a judge voted against the decision that became the rule, and then look to see how he votes in what they call the progeny cases. If a judge who has shown he clearly disapproved of the rule-establishing decision then follows the rule in future cases, he must be following precedent for its own sake. However, the idea of "following a rule" is quite complicated. Apart from anything else, the issue in so-called progeny cases is seldom simply whether the rule should be followed or ignored.

Given their definition of adhering to precedent, Segal and Spaeth find that, for the sample of cases they study, precedent is ignored 90% of the time (Segal and Spaeth, 1996). There are many features of this research design which might be questioned, but it certainly establishes that there must be doubts about the reliability of precedent-following in certain circumstances.

It is important to note that Segal and Spaeth's analysis has been challenged by other attitudinalists who came to different conclusions. Brenner and Stier (1996) found that one group of judges followed precedents 47% rather than the 10% of the time reported by Segal and Spaeth. Some critics rejected Segal and Spaeth's entire measure; for example Epstein and Knight, who take on one of the variants of the "no one follows precedents" argument and proceed to dismiss it. Epstein and Knight (2000) provide a very good general discussion of the many ways strategic theory of court behavior can be developed in a later article—they are by no means opposed to the empirical study of courts, just because they accept that the following of precedent is a powerful judicial norm.

Despite the fact that precedent does seem to be more or less as important as "legalists" might believe, modelers in the rational choice fraternity continue to find it something requiring explanation. Admittedly, following a precedent cannot easily be modeled—it is a complicated activity, as is shown, for example, by the common situation where judges on both sides of an issue actually cite the same precedents in their otherwise conflicting arguments (Robertson, 1998). For some, there seems no reason for utility-maximizing rational judges to bother following precedents—indeed, several discussions show that the only obvious reason, fear of being overturned, simply cannot account for such behavior, given that the proportion of cases reviewed by a higher court is so small. This point is admirably demonstrated by one of the few scholars writing in the field who is both a lawyer and committed to a sophisticated version of both attitudinal and rational choice approaches. Frank Cross develops a model in which ideological preferences and a sincere belief in *stare decisis* combine to explain adherence to precedent by U.S. Circuit Courts. In so doing, Cross produces a detailed criticism of most of the alternative rational choice approaches which find precedent-following so problematic (Cross, 2005).

But if the assumption of precedent-following, so basic a part of our usual understanding of courts, is made problematic, it might be legitimate instead to suggest that the assumptions that make it so are simply not worth following. The whole approach to precedent is probably the weakest element in the empirical study of appellate courts. Models of precedent based on economic approaches are as inappropriate now as when Richard Posner first wrote about the issue before the modern ELS movement existed, using a clever analogy between the building up of a stock of precedents and capital formation in the economy (Posner, 1976).

IV. WHO WINS IN APPEAL COURTS? AND WHY DO WE HAVE THEM?

The second question in the sub-heading may be one that no one would ever have seriously addressed but for the Empirical Legal Studies movement. There are expectations about why appeal courts exist, and it is at least possible to test whether such courts fulfill any of these expectations. That there should be some sort of second chance just seems tied up with the idea of fairness. Yet what common law appellate courts do not do, anywhere, affects the ways our legal systems impact on most litigants, except, perhaps, in the small number of criminal law appeals. Appeals are infrequent, compared with the number of cases commenced and even with the number resolved by a formal decision after a contested hearing. Both the rules on who gets to grant second chances and on what criteria, and even more the sheer consequence of the cost of appealing, ensure that any increment of fairness is systemically slight, however crucial for the lucky litigant. Some studies do exist on the decision to appeal (Barclay, 1999). Also, as mentioned earlier, there is a part of the literature which provides analytic, micro-economically inspired models of court systems (Kornhauser, 1999). Though, in one sense, such studies sometimes seem to do no more than demonstrate the obvious, or to support common intuitions, from another perspective they clarify these common assumptions, and invite research.

This may well be true of the models which deal with court hierarchy. From the earliest example, such as Shavell's 1995 piece, the idea of appeal courts as error-correcting mechanisms has been modeled (Shavell, 1995). Shavell's conclusion is that we do need an appellate system to correct error, and that this is more efficient than, for example, just improving the first-instance courts by improving their resources and the number of judges. The invitation for research implied in this, however, comes from his assumptions, especially those which rely on the idea that the litigants themselves can recognize an "error" and will only appeal when there is an error. The reason an appellate system is efficient, if it is, lies in the way the model assumes the appeal court does not know, by itself, which cases to review, and thus the voluntary, litigant-initiated appeal system maximizes information in the system. The truth, though, is that we do not know anything systematic about why people appeal.

Examining the empirical plausibility of assumptions, even heroic assumptions, in the formal modeling literature would be a very useful first step toward improving our understanding of the entire appellate process. In his general discussion of the literature, Kornhauser divides models of the appellate process into two types, only one of which treats error-correction as fundamental. The second type focuses on law-creation. Though it is seldom spelled out, an open question is whether or not these two functions are entirely compatible. Or are they one function, in as much as the supervision of lower courts by developing doctrine both requires the idea of error in the courts below and is a method of dealing with it? How much of the time of appellate courts is spent on which function, and how do appeal court judges see these roles? Part of the reason we do not know the answers is that the very idea of "error" is opaque, including both obvious and simple error (resulting from use by the judge below of the wrong test) and "policy disobedience"—which refers to the judge below refusing to use a test the result of which he does not like. But most of all, we do not know the answer to these and most questions because we never ask the judges, the lawyers, or the litigants. The vast bulk of empirical legal studies on appellate courts, and not only those involving formal modeling, are highly inferential. Much of social science depends heavily on surveys or interviews. Some such work does happen, but it plays a smaller role in empirical legal research than in the social science studies of other institutions. Perhaps greater attention to judges' perceptions of what they do, or to litigants' own explanations of why and when they appeal, might help?

Studies that are somewhat less inferential attempt to give a partial answer to the question "Who Wins in Appeal Courts?" The literature on this issue has an unusually precise starting point, an article published in 1974 by Marc Galanter, "Why the 'Haves' Come Out Ahead: Speculations on the Limits of Legal Change" (Galanter, 1974). This article has inspired a mass of research, testing and teasing out the implications of Galanter's fundamental idea. Indeed it has been described as "the most visible, widely cited, and influential article ever published in the law and society field" (Grossman et al., 1999). The idea is, at one level, very simple and perhaps obvious, and is contained in the title: the big battalions win. What Galanter brings to this idea is a real insight into why the big battalions win, and this idea is contained in another simple but less obvious distinction he makes between "repeat players" and "one shot" appellants. Repeat players are either institutions, like government departments and local government, or large corporations, including (in some models) trade unions, that develop expertise, or have counsel possessing that expertise, in particular types of litigation. One-shotters, usually individuals but also small firms and the like, are in a weaker situation for many reasons. To start with, the value of the claim may be too large to ignore relative to the claimant's resources, but also too small compared with the cost of legal action that may or may not succeed; in contrast, repeat players risk less and can afford to fight more. Repeat players can also afford to settle, something not as easily accepted by a one-shotter. Repeat players, experienced in and anticipating more repeated litigation, not only have more experience but also the resources to pursue their long-term interests. A repeat-playing corporation may be able to construct legal plans and pre-prepare defenses. Above all they can litigate with a long-term aim which may involve losing cases in order to help the courts come up with a rule in their long-term interests— setting precedents even when losing. In the words of Grossman et al., they can "play for rules." Repeat players settle (often with low visibility) cases where they expect unfavorable verdicts or rule out-comes. They can trade symbolic defeats for tangible gains. One shotters, by definition, are necessarily more interested in immediate outcomes.

Is it true? Do the legal big battalions have an in-built advantage at the appellate level? One hypothesis developed from Galanter's work is often called "Party Capability Theory" (i.e., the more capable, better resourced party is advantaged), and when tested seem, more often than not, to be true. The work is especially true in the case when governments and their agencies are ranged against individuals. Indeed, it is inevitably true in criminal law, but seems largely to be true in civil and constitu-tional law as well. Studies in several countries other than the United States, includ-ing Canada, South Africa, and England, show at least limited support for the idea that the appeal system at large gives an advantage to the "big players" (see Atkins, 1991; McCormick, 1993; Haynie and Sill, 2007). Admittedly, some of the research treats any form of imbalance as fitting the model—Haynie and Sill's piece on South Africa might be thought to be saying little more than that experienced advocates do better than new ones (see also, Szmer et al., 2007; McGuire, 1995; McAtee and McGuire, 2007).

If there is a weakness in the study of the Party Capability thesis it is that it has not taken up the more detailed and interesting implications. Research has largely confirmed the basic fact that repeat players and other "haves" do better. What it has not done is to examine, for example, Galanter's ideas about such players being able to strategically "play for rules." Much more fundamentally, we know nothing about whether appellate courts are complicit in these results. Do judges themselves tend to favor the "haves"? Is there something about appellate procedures that helps the "haves"? It is perhaps more interesting to know, as has been shown, that docket space seems to be handled in a way that favors the "haves" rather than the "haves" just win-ning more often in the cases that do happen to come up (Brace and Hall, 2001).

V. FINAL COMMENTS

All this is to say that the empirical legal research on appellate courts, according to the Galanter thesis, suffers from the main weakness of the entire body of empirical research applied to appellate courts. The simple thing is studied—simple things are easily counted, simple things are easily modeled, simple things require little read-ing of cases. We urgently need a shift of focus to remind us that law is rich and diffi-cult, cases and judges are complex, and large-n studies, or elegant models will only get us some of the way. Deeper than this is a problem mentioned several times—the way the research agenda has been conditioned by the dichotomy between judges as seeking to make *either* law *or* policy. Of course this is simplistic and of course it can represent no more than a pair of ideal types—that much is inevitable in any research paradigm. But the dichotomy is far more injurious than that, because it is inadequately theorized. If the disjunction is going to work it must represent a real choice—there must be (many) situations where a judge's policy preference clashes with what he would accept was the correct "legal" answer. This relies on a curiously positivistic notion of law. To be forced into a choice a judge must feel that what he regards as morally correct would be inconsistent with existing law. Such a sense of law's values is unlikely to be common. Lord Atkin cannot be that unusual in his views, expressed in the great English negligence case, *Donoghue v. Stevenson*:

I do not think so ill of our jurisprudence as to suppose that its principles are so remote from the ordinary needs of civilized society and the ordinary claims it makes upon its members as to deny a legal remedy where there is so obviously a social wrong.

For Atkin, but surely for most of our leading judges, a legal answer that leads to seriously wrong policy ends would not be the correct legal answer. At the very least, empirical legal research on appellate courts needs to clarify the terms of its discourse. Why is there so very little theoretical work? It is not that work has not been done: There is a huge theoretical and legal literature on precedent, for instance, and on the concept and role of "policy" in judicial decision-making. The problem seems to be that not enough people in the empirical legal research community seem aware of it. Much the same could be said of the mass of theoretical work in other disciplines on the rational actor model. Why does the discipline seem to rest on a forced choice between rather elderly judicial realism or rather poor doctrinal study? A closer attention to the value-institutionalist approach would make us focus, first, on the idea of the "logic of appropriateness" as the motivating factor, and then on the real work of finding out what is seen as appropriate and why.

References

Atkins, B.M. (1990). "Interventions and Power in Judicial Hierarchies: Appellate Courts in England and the United States," *Law & Society Review* 24: 71–103.

Atkins, B.M. (1991). "Party Capability Theory as an Explanation for Intervention Behavior in the English Court of Appeal," *American Journal of Political Science* 35: 881–903.

Barclay, S. (1999). *An Appealing Act: Why People Appeal in Civil Cases*, Evanston, IL: Northwestern University Press.

Baum, L. (1997). *The Puzzle of Judicial Behavior*, Ann Arbor: University of Michigan Press.

Baum, L. (2006). *Judges and Their Audiences*, Princeton: Princeton University Press.

Bell, J. (1983). *Policy Arguments in Judicial Decisions*, Oxford: Clarendon Press.

Bhattacharya, M. and Smyth, R. (2001). "The Determinants of Judicial Prestige and Influence: Some Empirical Evidence from the High Court of Australia," *Journal of Legal Studies* 30: 223–52.

Blom-Cooper, L. and Drewry, G. (eds.). (1972). *Final Appeal: A Study of the House of Lords in its Judicial Capacity*, Oxford: Clarendon Press.

Blom-Cooper, L., Dickson, B., and Drewry, G. (eds.) (2009). *The Judicial House of Lords 1876–2009*, Oxford: Oxford University Press.

Brace, P., Langer, L., and Hall, M.G. (2000). "Measuring the Preferences of State Supreme Court Judges," *Journal of Politics* 62: 387–413.

Brace, P. and Hall, M.G. (2001). " 'Haves' and 'Have Nots' in State Supreme Courts: Allocating Docket Space and Wins in Power Asymmetric Cases," *Law & Society Review* 35: 393–417.

Brenner, S. and Stier, M. (1996). "Retesting Segal and Spaeth's *Stare Decisis* Model," *American Journal of Political Science* 40: 1036–48.

Clermont, K.M. and Eisenberg, T. (2000). "Anti-Plaintiff Bias in the federal appellate courts," *Judicature* 84: 128–34.

Cross. F. (2005). "Appellate Court Adherence to Precedent," *Journal of Empirical Legal Studies* 369–405.

de Mesquita, E.B. and Stephenson, M. (2002). "Informative Precedent and Intrajudicial Communication," *American Political Science Review* 96: 755–66.

Edelman, P.H., Klein, D.E. and Lindquist, S.A. (2008). "Measuring Deviations from Expected Voting Patterns on Collegial Courts," *Journal of Empirical Legal Studies* 4: 819–852.

Eisenberg, T. (2004). "Appeal Rates and Outcomes in Tried and Non-tried Cases: Further Exploration of Anti-Plaintiff Appellate Outcomes," *Journal of Empirical Legal Studies* 1: 659–88.

Epstein, L. and Knight, J. (2000). "Toward a Strategic Revolution in Judicial Politics: A Look Back, A Look Ahead," *Political Research Quarterly* 53: 625–61.

Galanter, M. (1974). "Why the 'Haves' Come Out Ahead: Speculations on the Limits of Legal Change," *Law & Society Review* 9: 95–160.

Geeroms, S.M.F. (2002). "Comparative Law and Legal Translation: Why the Terms Cassation, Revision and Appeal Should Not Be Translated," *American Journal of Comparative Law* 50: 201–28.

Gely, R. and Spiller, P.T. (1990). "A Rational Choice Theory of Supreme Court Statutory Decisions with Applications to the State Farm and Gove City Cases," *Journal of Law, Economics and Organization* 6: 266–300.

Gely, R. and Spiller, P.T. (1992). "The Political Economy of Supreme Court Constitutional Decisions: The Case of Roosevelt's Court-packing Plan," *International Review of Law and Economics* 45–67.

Gilman, H. (1995). *The Constitution Besieged: The Rise and Fall of Lochner Era Police Powers Jurisprudence*, Durham: Duke University Press.

Graber, M. (2006). "Legal, Strategic, or Legal Strategy: Deciding to Decide During the Civil War and Reconstruction," in R. Kahn and K.I. Kersch (eds.), *The Supreme Court and American Political Development*, Lawrence: University Press of Kansas.

Green, A.J. and Alarie, B. (2009). "Policy Preference Change and Appointments to the Supreme Court of Canada," *Osgoode Hall Law Journal* 47: 1–46.

Grossman, J., Macaulay, S., and Kritzer, H. (1999). "Do the 'Haves' still come out ahead?," *Law & Society Review* 33: 803–10.

Haynie, S.L. and Sill, K.L. (2007). "Experienced Advocates and Litigation Outcomes: Repeat Players in the South African Supreme Court," *Political Research Quarterly* 60: 443–53.

Honnige, C. (2009). "The Electoral Connection: How the Pivotal Judge Affects Oppositional Success at European Constitutional Courts," *West European Politics* 32: 963–84.

Kornhauser, L.A. (1999). "Appeal and Supreme Courts," in *The Encyclopedia of Law and Economics*, <http://encyclo.findlaw.com/7200book.pdf>.

Lasser, M.D.S.-O.-L.E. (2004). *Judicial Deliberations: A Comparative Analysis of Judicial Transparency and Legitimacy*, Oxford Studies in European Law, Oxford: Oxford University Press.

Lindquist, S., Martinek, W.L., and Hettinger, V.A. (2007). "Splitting the Differences: Modelling Appellate Court Decisions with Mixed Outcomes," *Law & Society Review* 41: 429–55.

McAtee, A. and McGuire, K.T. (2007). "Lawyers, Justices, and Issue Salience: When and How Do Legal Arguments Affect the U.S. Supreme Court?," *Law & Society Review* 41: 259–78.

McCormick, P. (1993). "Party Capability Theory and Appellate Success in the Supreme Court of Canada, 1949–1992," *Canadian Journal of Political Science* 26: 523–40.

McGuire, K.T. (1995). "Repeat Players in the Supreme Court: The Role of Experienced Lawyers in Litigation Success," *Journal of Politics* 57: 187–96.

Ostberg, C.L. and Wetstein, M.E. (2007). *Attitudinal Decision Making in the Supreme Court of Canada*, Vancouver: University of British Columbia Press.

Paterson, A. (1982). *The Law Lords*, London: Macmillan.

Pierce, J.L. (2006). *Inside the Mason Court Revolution: The High Court of Australia Transformed*, Durham: Carolina Academic Press.

Posner, R.A. (1976). "Legal Precedent: A Theoretical and Empirical Analysis," *Journal of Law and Economics* 19: 248–307.

Posner, R.A. (1993). "What Do Judges and Justices Maximize (The Same Thing Everybody Does)," *Supreme Court Economic Review* 3: 1–41.

Robertson, D. (1982). "Judicial Ideology in the House of Lords: A Jurimetric Analysis," *British Journal of Political Science* 12: 1–25.

Robertson, D. (1998). *Judicial Discretion in the House of Lords*, Oxford: Oxford University Press.

Robertson, D. (2010). *The Judge as Political Theorist: Contemporary Constitutional Review*, Princeton: Princeton University Press.

Schubert, G.A. and Danelski, D.J. (eds.) (1969). *Comparative Judicial Behavior: Cross-cultural Studies of Political Decision-making In the East and West*, New York: Oxford University Press.

Segal, J.A. (1984). "Predicting Supreme Court Cases Probabilistically: The Search and Seizure Cases 1962 -1981," *American Political Science Review* 78: 891–900.

Segal, J.A. and Spaeth, H.J. (1996). "The Influence of *Stare Decisis* on the Votes of United States Supreme Court Justices," *American Journal of Political Science* 40: 971–1003.

Segal, J.A. and Spaeth, H.J. (1996). "Norms, Dragons and *Stare Decisis*: A Response," *American Journal of Political Science* 40: 1064–82.

Segal, J.H. and Spaeth, H.J. (2002). *The Supreme Court and the Attitudinal Model Revisited*, Cambridge: Cambridge University Press.

Shapiro, M. (1964). *Law and Politics in the Supreme Court*, New York: The Free Press of Glencoe.

Shapiro, M. (1981). *Courts: A Comparative and Political Analysis*, Chicago: Chicago University Press.

Shavell, S. (1995). "The Appeals Process as a Means of Error Correction," *Journal of Legal Studies* 24: 379–426.

Stevens, R. (1979). *Law and Politics: The House of Lords as a Judicial Body, 1800 to 1976*, London: Weidenfeld and Nicolson.

Szmer, J., Johnson, S.W., and Sarver, T.A. (2007). "Does the Lawyer Matter? Influencing Outcomes on the Supreme Court of Canada," *Law & Society Review* 41: 279–304.

Unah, I. and Hancock, A.-M. (2006). "U.S. Supreme Court Decision Making, Case Salience and the Attitudinal Model," *Law and Policy* 28: 295–320.

25

<hr>

DISPUTE
RESOLUTION

<hr>

CARRIE J. MENKEL-MEADOW[1]

<hr>

<hr>

[1] Thanks to Katherine M. Hayes and Jonathan Kooker for excellent research and editorial assistance.

I. Introduction: What is ADR as Compared to What?

A. Normative and methodological issues: what is the "baseline" measure and comparison process in ADR research?

THE field of ADR (originally known as "alternative" dispute resolution in the United States) has more recently been called "appropriate" dispute resolution, or just dispute resolution. Although originally framed as both a social movement and a set of legal reforms designed to challenge various aspects of formal litigation (brittle, rigid, and binary outcomes, excessive cost and delay, limited bipartisan and bilateral participation, emphasis on the past and precedent rather than future and more creative outcomes and relationships), the field has become quite institutionalized and renamed "appropriate" dispute resolution to connote the importance of the availability of a variety of processes for "resolution" of legal, and more broadly, social, political, and interpersonal disputes and conflicts. The field has now been described, by this author, and others, as "process pluralism" (Menkel-Meadow, 2006: 554).

Though I will use the acronym ADR here (for me connoting the more recent understanding of "appropriate" dispute resolution), what is really at stake in the research reported in this Chapter are comparisons of various forms of dispute resolution (DR) with each other on a variety of dimensions (fairness, justice, cost and efficiency, party satisfaction, and systemic accountability), and evaluations and assessments of the efficacy of various practices, and alternative forms of dispute resolution. Thus, empirical research on ADR can be viewed as falling into two broad categories:

1. *Empirically descriptive work*, documenting the various processes and procedures used and the effects or outcomes of those processes. The processes include arbitration, mediation, consensus building and negotiated rule-making, and bilateral negotiation; outcomes include results achieved as well as the behaviors exhibited in the course of the processes. In the discussion below, I have labeled these studies "*descriptive process*" studies.

2. *Empirically comparative work*, purporting to compare, through data analysis, differences in process, outcome, and other operationalized measures of efficiency or fairness, of different forms of DR. For example, researchers have asked whether various forms of ADR (e.g., mediation or arbitration) are, in fact, cheaper and faster, or offer deeper and richer solutions than formal litigation or regulation (Coglianese, 1997; Freeman, 1997), and how various forms of ADR compare to each other on a variety of dimensions (e.g., facilitative vs. evaluative, or caucus vs. non-caucus models of mediation). I have labeled these studies "*comparative process*" studies.

This essay focuses on four important themes in assessing empirical studies of process: 1) difficulties in assuring conceptual and definitional clarity about what those processes actually consist of, reflecting the variations existing within, as well as between, different process categories; 2) difficulties in developing truly comparable cases that can be subjected to various treatments in order to accurately assess real differences in process or outcome measures; 3) the virtual impossibility of using true experimental techniques in real world settings to subject the same or matched disputes to different treatments to independently assess the influence of key factors such as case types, disputant and decision-maker types, etc.; and, finally, 4) the continually changing and open nature of the field itself reflecting ongoing innovations and hybridization, as well as significant differences in different legal systems and cultures where different practices exist. If various forms of ADR have developed to respond to various problems with litigation, litigation itself varies across legal systems and changes through time, just as does ADR.

From the beginning, ADR has had a highly contested and political quality about it—with proponents of various forms of ADR urging that particular processes are *better than* various other kinds of processes, most prominently litigation or formal administrative regulation. Proponents are often met by an equally assertive claim about the superiority of public, court-managed litigation or other public governmental processes. In recent years, even proponents of various forms of ADR have had significant differences with each other as, for example, in debates between facilitative and evaluative mediators, and the highly polarized debate in the United States about pre-dispute arbitration clauses in contracts for employment and consumer disputes (Menkel-Meadow, 1997).

Stark political, practical, and policy debates about the appropriate uses of various forms of "non-litigative," "non-adversarial," or "alternative-to-court" processes have led to heated debates about definitions, categorizations, methodologies, measurements, and conclusions from a wide range of studies attempting to "settle the scores" on practical issues of cost, fairness, efficiency, consumer satisfaction, and more jurisprudential issues such as voice, democracy, self-determination, rule of law, and the "justice" produced by the use of different processes. There are a variety of contested issues such as:

- whether there should be voluntary or mandatory assignment to a particular form of dispute resolution;
- whether the privacy of the parties is more important than or should be measured against the transparency to others of both processes and outcomes;
- whether vesting of power in privately paid professionals, rather than state officials, for dispute decisions is desirable;
- whether some forms of dispute resolution are more likely to serve the empowerment of parties, communities, and other non-elites, rather than those in the more expensive and elite controlled litigation systems;

- whether the resources invested in alternative systems are justified or improve compliance and enforcement of outcomes over commanded litigation results; and
- whether institutional design of alternative justice systems at very advanced stages of legal development can serve as a model in more newly created legal systems and political orders.

All of this has led to a serious "baseline" problem in empirical analysis of dispute resolution processes. With so many issues about how processes deliver fairness and justice being so hotly contested, it is difficult, if not impossible, to know what is being compared to what. Litigation varies as much in different venues (e.g., civil law versus common law, or federal versus state courts) as mediation does in private or court-annexed settings or, as arbitration does in domestic and international settings. Whenever I read any attempt to "compare" and "contrast" the efficacy or quality of different processes, I always ask, "compared to what?" Close scrutiny of virtually any comparison will dampen one's confidence in the conclusions reached. Put simply, truly experimental methods are virtually impossible in this field; one cannot submit the same actual dispute to two treatments.[2] At best, so-called "like" cases in one "treatment" are compared to "like (similar) cases" in another "treatment" and therein lies the problem.

In large aggregate studies, such as in the "Vanishing Trial" statistics demonstrating decreasing uses of full civil trials (Galanter, 2004), we can see general trends in processes used and in variations in gross outcomes (e.g., Eisenberg and Hill, 2003–2004). But when the focus is more on "internal" experiences of fairness of process and outcomes in particular cases, it is much harder to match totally homologous case types. Processes with the same name are practiced differently; different private ADR institutions and providers use different rules, standards, procedures, and definitions. Even in the public sector, when courts or administrative agencies use various forms of ADR, they do so with different intentions, different requirements, and different effects such as whether or not negotiated agreements can serve as public outcomes without formal governmental ratification.

Thus, while in this essay I review some of the recent studies on the uses of ADR, my theme is one of skepticism that we can ever truly determine with any degree of confidence whether one particular process is "better" or "worse" than another in a specific case.

This is related to another theme illustrated here. In some cases there are "communities" of interest in promoting particular forms of ADR. It is often argued that big business prefers the control and economic efficiency of arbitration against individual

---

[2] The closest to this is a study which attempted to "match" similar types of cases in the formal justice system which were then assigned to different "treatments"—arbitration, litigation, or some form of negotiation or mediation. See Lind et al., 1989.

employees, consumers, and investors, and that some courts prefer to deflect "smaller" cases to arbitration or mediation. Yet it is also often true that individual disputants might have very different motivations for seeking a particular kind of process. Thus, we have an additional measurement problem of aggregating individual preferences when those preferences may not be uniform, either for individuals or for organizations (Menkel-Meadow, 1995).

Those engaged in design of dispute-resolution institutions (whether in courts or private organizations) often ask instrumental questions, wanting to know what forms of process are "better" in terms of factors such as efficiency or fairness for a particular type of conflict. Existing studies seldom provide clear answers to such questions. In ADR some criteria of quality measurement for some factors, such as efficiency, can be quantitative, while other factors—fairness, availability of tailored and flexible solutions, and the degree of self-determination in such processes—resist quantitative measurement and must be assessed in a more qualitative fashion. Thus, the core question is not "which process is better?" but "which process is better for what and for whom?" Some form of "process pluralism" and choice is usually the answer.

To summarize, as we try to understand the meaning of many attempts to weigh and evaluate the successes and failures of ADR processes it is useful to always ask—*what is the baseline—compared to what*? In assessing what we know, don't know, and should know about ADR's actual empirical practices, it is important to recognize that ADR is itself variable, and it may be difficult, if not impossible, to specify with any degree of reliability what is going on inside particular processes and how particular processes can be compared to each other. But many have tried.

B. Definitional prerequisites for empirical salience

Dispute resolution processes differ in various respects. First, there is the *number of participants* in any dispute resolution process. Beginning with a number of one $(n = 1)$, we can treat any individual's personal and intra-psychic decision-making as a negotiation or conflict resolution with him/herself. This is usually considered in psychological studies of conflict resolution but it has implications for what we review here—how does an individual decide in which process of dispute resolution to engage? Next is negotiation in which two parties to a dispute or conflict $(n = 2)$ directly negotiate with each other or engage in some duel or other form of physical encounter. In legal disputes negotiation processes can often involve more than 2, as when parties are represented by lawyers or other agents $(n = 4)$ or when there are multiple parties to a legal dispute, whether in the large class action form or not—then we have multi-party negotiation $(n > 4)$. When we add a mediator (who facilitates negotiation but does not make any decisions for the parties) or an arbitrator who does decide, as would a judge, there are at least three (n = 3) parties to the dispute, two disputants, and a Third Party Neutral (TPN). Increasingly, mediators may work with represented parties so that n = 5 (at least, and more where there are many parties and legal representatives). In some court programs a TPN can be a Neutral Evaluator (as in the federal courts in Northern California's Early Neutral Evaluation Program) who gives advisory, non-binding opinions about the value of cases or helps the parties plan their discovery and litigation schedules. In the American federal court system, magistrate judges or formally appointed Special Masters may deal with motions, facilitate pre-trial settlement conferences, mediate and manage, or, with the parties' consent, decide cases of varying degrees of complexity.

In a range of newer, hybridized forms of dispute resolution the numbers of parties may expand exponentially. In facilitated negotiation or "negotiated rule-making" (reg-neg), which can involve hundreds of parties (n > x), one or more professional facilitators structure processes of consensual decision-making prior to formal administrative rule-making (Susskind et al., 1999). In both the private and public sectors such processes of "consensus building" can engage members of communities in land use, environmental, religious, public policy, economic development, and community disputes.

The effect of the number of participants on the processes used and the outcomes achieved is a relatively new, but essential, topic of further study, pioneered by mathematically trained game and decision theorists and related to empirical research about decision-making in groups, such as recent jury research that has investigated cognitive biases in group decision-making. As an illustration, concerns about how different numbers of participants affect the formation of coalitions and the stability of negotiation and mediation behavior are the motivation for intensive case studies now available in research about international dispute resolution (e.g., Sebenius, 1996).

A second major differentiating characteristic is whether *entry to or choice of process is voluntary or assigned*. In its purest form mediation is intended to be a totally voluntary process in which parties choose to negotiate with the facilitation of a TPN who has no decision-making power over the parties. Agreements, if they are made, may become formal contracts but only if the parties so desire. Arbitration also is considered a "voluntary" process, chosen, at the will of the parties, often in advance of any dispute in a contract for the sale of goods or services (known as *pre-dispute or contractual* arbitration). Here the third party makes an award and sometimes writes a full opinion. Increasingly, these "voluntary" forms of dispute resolution have become less than voluntary. Courts often order parties to attend court-annexed mediation or arbitration processes before permitting full trials, and increasingly, in the United States, parties to a range of consumer and employment contracts find they have agreed to a compulsory arbitration process in the event of

a contractual dispute, often having done so unknowingly. The compulsory assignment to pre-dispute arbitration or court-mandated mediation or arbitration has
been a hotly debated policy issue in the United States and this debate has spawned a
large number of empirical studies about the effects and differences between voluntary and compulsory assignment to dispute processes (see, e.g., Searle Civil Justice
Institute, 2009).

In many other countries, particularly in the European Union, pre-dispute contractually ordered arbitration is prohibited in consumer and employment settings.
In some countries (Israel and several South American countries), mediation agreements are now given the same legal status as arbitration awards, so that such an
agreement can be enforced (like an arbitration award) as equivalent to a court judgment. Thus, legal treatment of "alternatives" such as mediation and arbitration varies by legal system and jurisdiction. We have very few, if any, comparative empirical
studies of how these agreements, whether enforced by courts or not, vary across
different legal systems

A related third point of differentiation is whether the outcome is *consensual
or commanded*. Mediation and negotiation processes (and some hybrid forms
of dispute resolution such as mini-trials, summary jury trials, arb-med[3] and
consensus-building, facilitated multi-party decision-making processes, as well
as "non-binding" arbitration) are designed to produce agreements between the
parties, with party control over outcomes or, as mediation purists put it, "self-
determination." Formal adjudication-litigation (including pre-trial summary
dispositions on the law without a trial to resolve factual issues, and decisions by
administrative judges and tribunals), arbitration, and traditional administrative rule-making (notice and comment)—involves binding decisions by those
outside the dispute—judges, arbitrators, or executive-branch governmental
officials.

On a fourth dimension, dispute processes can be *public* or *private*, although this
variable has also recently been hybridized to some extent. International commercial arbitration, for example, is the leading form of dispute resolution for international commercial (non-state) issues under contractual arbitration clauses which
provide for private arbitration, usually utilizing one of the leading international
administering institutions, such as the International Chamber of Commerce (ICC
in Paris) or the London Court of International Arbitration (LCIA). Although private, these institutions rely on a public international treaty, the United Nations' New
York Convention for the Recognition and Enforcement of Foreign Arbitral Awards
(1958), for formal enforcement in a domestic court. Court adjudication is almost

---

[3] Med-arb is a hybrid process in which mediation is attempted first as a facilitated settlement process but when it doesn't succeed, the mediator makes a decision as an arbitrator. In some settings
the process may be reversed—one chosen to "decide" a matter as an arbitrator may try to facilitate a
settlement first, called arb-med.

always public and mediation is almost always private (with no reported decisions or public access to the process itself) and most arbitration is private (with increasing pressures for publication of awards and transparency in international, as well as domestic, settings). While there is great controversy as to whether the public has some right to know about the outcomes of private disputes (and the enforcement of laws and rules), especially when competing against claimed rights of parties for desired privacy and secrecy, it is a difficult issue to study empirically. By definition, private dispute processes are private and it has been virtually impossible to acquire data on the operation of such private processes, thus making comparison studies virtually impossible.

As the field of ADR has grown to include more kinds of disputes and a greater variety of processes, other structural and policy issues have been raised. Early on, one of the most important claims made against ADR was that compared with formal adjudication, it was likely to cause unfair or unequal outcomes for subordinated or disempowered parties (especially women, and various racial and ethnic minority groups). A variety of studies have been designed to test whether there are systematic biases and structural inequalities in how different parties and groups experience various dispute resolution processes (La Free and Rack, 1996), including arbitration, and mediation in court and in private settings.

Related to claims about the effects of differences in power or resources between the parties, debates in the ADR literature have focused on the "repeat player effect" (Menkel-Meadow, 1999; Bingham, 2003). The argument is that parties who participate often in the same process (e.g., company-controlled arbitration) or third-party neutrals (whether arbitrators or mediators) who work often for the same parties produce unfair or structurally biased outcomes. As I will discuss below, the many recent attempts to evaluate this assertion have produced decidedly mixed and contested results (Drahozal and Zyontz, 2009; Choi, Fisch, and Pritchard, 2009; Hadfield, 2004; Bingham, 1997).

In studies which attempt to evaluate ADR processes there is always the question of what the yardstick of "measurement" of fairness, justice, or efficiency should be, which has given rise to another important dispute: Should the outcomes of all dispute resolution conform to legal rules or precedents or are the parties free to resolve their disputes in creative, tailored ways that might provide fair or just outcomes for particular parties but might depart from formal legal rules or precedents (without themselves constituting unlawful outcomes). This important jurisprudential question is not easily studied in direct form but some surrogates of measurement, such as compliance with agreements as opposed to commanded or law-based rulings, are increasingly the subject of evaluation in some areas such as in environmental and land-use, divorce and family (e.g., Pearson and Thoennes, 1989), and labor and employment matters (Bingham, 2003).

II. Empirical Descriptions of Dispute Resolution Processes

A. Negotiation and settlement processes

A number of studies have documented and described patterns of uses of particular forms of dispute resolution. Many of these studies are designed to explore variations of behavior or outcomes within a particular process, such as what kind of "negotiation style" is employed by legal negotiators (Schneider, 2002; Genn, 1988; Kritzer, 1991); what impact factors, such as fees, or "endowment effects," have on negotiating behavior (Guthrie, 2003; Kritzer, 1991: 100–03); what interpersonal or demographic factors (e.g., gender or race, Ayres, 1991) affect negotiation behavior (Babcock and Laschever, 2003); and most recently, what kinds of "cognitive and social errors" adversely affect negotiation behaviors (e.g., Kiser et al., 2008).

Although these studies are designed to test variations within a process, there is often an implicit, if not explicit, comparison to other dispute resolution processes (this is more fully reviewed in Section III below). In the case of negotiation or settlement of legal cases, that implicit comparison is often to litigation and is based on assumptions about what might happen if a case were tried. This hypothetical approach itself is deeply flawed as various social scientists have established that although only about 2% of all civil cases filed (at least in the U.S. federal system) proceed to full trial, only about another 60–65% of them are settled through some kind of negotiation activity. Fully 30–35% of filed legal cases are, in fact, "disposed of" with some kind of summary judgment or other motion, and such outcomes are closer to non-consensual dispositions "on the legal merits" (Kritzer, 1986; Hadfield, 2004).

In a significant article questioning whether negotiated settlements, in some contexts, were contrary to important law enforcement goals, Janet Alexander (1991) found that securities class-action cases were most often settled, not litigated, and most often settled for transaction costs or "nuisance value," rather than for amounts reflecting assessments of the legal or economic "merits" or value of the case, a conclusion now contested in more recent research on securities class-action settlements (Cox et al., 2008). Alexander sparked a much larger debate about whether negotiated settlements or mediated outcomes should track legal outcomes. Claims about whether settlements are intended to satisfy goals other than following legal rules (such as granting parties not only money, but other forms of future-oriented relief which could not be ordered by courts) continue to be made, with little empirical assessment about either 1) how outcomes of negotiated settlements differ from results in litigated cases (the comparability issue), or 2) what parties actually want (assuming they could know enough about the different possibilities to accurately assess alternatives). What I have labeled "litigation romanticists" argue that in many contexts, including individual lawsuits, class actions, and cases with important policy implications, private settlements are anathema to justice concerns—transparency, developing precedent and rules for other parties and the larger system, and accountability, among other values. The issue of whether legal claims "belong" to the claimants (to resolve or deal with however they see fit) or to the larger society or justice system remains a philosophical and jurisprudential question unanswerable by empirical study or data.

When parties seek to negotiate in the legal context they may do so for several different purposes: creating new legal relationships (contracting, development of new organizations or legal entities), dispute resolution (before or following the filing of any formal legal claim), and law-making itself (constitution-formation, legislation, and regulatory activity). Much of the most interesting work on negotiation processes attempts to describe how people negotiate and what factors or variables affect their negotiation behavior and the outcomes they obtain. A major challenge for both theory development and empirical assessment remains whether there are any universal "principles" about negotiation behavior, or whether any and all findings about negotiation behavior are contextually based so as to depend on factors such as the number of parties; domain or subject matter of negotiation; numbers of issues; cultural, national, gender, race, or other differences among the negotiators; personality; and organizational or institutional locations (Menkel-Meadow, 2009). For example, in the U.S., settlement rates in litigated cases vary considerably by geographic region and case type.

Economic analysts of both litigation behavior and negotiation behavior, now joined by more "behavioral" economists and cognitive and social psychologists, seek to describe "general" human behavior, assuming "rational actor" models, but documenting common "cognitive errors" and departures from rational behaviors. Studies have shown the effects of "prospect theory," demonstrating, among other things, how the "endowment" or "status quo" effect influences sellers to ask for more than buyers are willing to pay. "Reactive devaluation" causes parties on opposite sides of an issue to discount accurate information from their counterparts; inaccurate risk and loss aversion assessments cause negotiators to both overvalue and undervalue what they bargain about; and "overconfidence" and the strategic aspects of the negotiation process itself ("winner's curse") cause distortions in negotiating processes that lead to less than "optimal" outcomes.

In contrast to this "universalizing" theoretical and empirical work, another body of empirical work on negotiation behaviors has exposed a variety of areas in which negotiation behavior is far from "universal." Ian Ayres's (1991) pathbreaking work on the negotiation of prices for both used and new cars has demonstrated a hierarchy of price outcomes, with white males achieving the lowest prices and black women and black men paying the most regardless of the race or gender of the salesperson. Race is also a factor in employment settings. In another striking set of studies, researchers have uncovered a variety of gender variations in negotiated processes and outcomes. Noting that her female business students were earning lower starting salaries than her male students, Linda Babcock systematically studied the negotiations of job seekers (Babcock and Laschever, 2003) and revealed that women are less likely to perceive certain events (e.g., a starting salary for a new job) as even negotiable and, thus, are less likely to "ask for," demand, or even contest, a first offer made by someone else. The debate on gender differences in negotiation behavior has provoked a legion of studies, with continuing variations in study findings. Other variables such as nationality, ethnicity, age, profession, class, and educational level are all factors now explored, mostly in laboratory settings, with little rigorous opportunity for study in real-world settings, raising more general questions about the usefulness of laboratory studies in assessing real-world negotiation and dispute-resolution behavior.

Perhaps somewhat surprisingly, not all negotiators "maximize individual gain." There is laboratory-based experimental evidence that most negotiators have some implicit sense of "fairness or justice" and will seek to achieve what they regard as "fair" outcomes, especially, but not exclusively, when they have some relationship with their negotiation counterpart (Bazerman and Neale, 1992).

Recent empirical work on negotiation in litigation contexts demonstrates that a variety of complex interactions of factors may influence settlement behavior and negotiation judgments. Randell Kiser, Martin Asher, and Blakely McShane (2008) rigorously studied the "error rates" in settlement negotiations when they systematically looked at trial outcomes following rejected settlement offers (in California, New York, and, more recently, with a wider data-set). They found high error rates for both plaintiff (higher error rates for plaintiffs' counsel than defense) and defense counsel, but found those error rates were differentiated and highly context-specific. For example, although plaintiffs' lawyers turned down settlement offers which were better than what they actually won at trial more often than defense counsel (an error rate of 61.2% as against 21.3%), defense counsel errors were of greater magnitudes. Having refused an offer to settle by a plaintiff, the mean cost of error for a defendant was $1,140,000 to a "mere" $43,100 cost of error for plaintiffs' counsel. Sadly, this study revealed, as well, that error rates appear to be increasing, both in number and in magnitude (chilling the spine of a civil procedure and negotiation teacher who sees young lawyers untutored in case evaluation in these numbers!).

But, of greatest interest to students of negotiation processes are the findings that contextual factors are most significant in predicting error rates—case type for example, was more salient for error in settlement judgment than actor characteristics. Plaintiff errors were higher in cases involving contingency fees (e.g., personal injury), while defense errors were more common where there was absence of insurance coverage (simple contract cases).

This study also found that where parties made offers pursuant to rules of procedure, offers did cause some case evaluation to occur, and one may infer that insurance cases also had lower error rates because of the "second look" or "second chair" phenomenon of more than one lawyer assessing the case. Forum also affected decision errors. Defendants were less likely to commit errors in jury settings than bench settings and for plaintiffs it was the opposite. Plaintiffs were considered to be overconfident in front of juries. Interestingly, for purposes of this essay, decision errors were lower for both plaintiffs and defendants in arbitration cases (perhaps due to greater predictability of decisions made by party-chosen decision-makers).

Cases in which punitive damages were at issue were most likely to cause defendants to make errors. Plaintiffs had lower error rates in punitive damages settings (more experience or more accurate demands?). Lawyers with mediation experience were less likely (on both plaintiff and defense side) to make decision errors in settling cases. Perhaps those with mediation experience have more case evaluation experience and are less likely to commit errors or be unaware of the variety of cognitive distortions that occur in negotiation settings.

Sophisticated studies have also revealed other variations in negotiated forms of dispute resolution. My early research suggesting that negotiation processes could be made more effective by responding to parties' underlying needs and, if possible, creating solutions that increased the size of the pie, rather than simply seeking monetary solutions as "proxies" for a whole range of human needs, or even by slavishly following the law, was challenged by Herbert Kritzer (1991: 101–03) who demonstrated, in a rigorous study of negotiations in civil justice contexts, that most negotiations were too "routinized" to provide the kind of "creative problem solving" necessary for individually crafted solutions. "Low intensity" (single offer-acceptance) negotiations, which were most common in state and many federal cases, were unlikely to produce careful and searching inquiry into what parties actually want. And, in cases where lawyers are paid by contingency fees, monetization of negotiated outcomes is the most likely result, precluding more creative "in-kind" or alternative non-monetary settlements. Thus, negotiation outcomes are often dependent on the locations and structures in which those negotiations take place. Routinized actors and repeat players, like insurance agents, are less likely to engage in complex, multi-issued, and time consuming, if more intensive, negotiations.

In what I regard as one of the best empirical studies of negotiation context ever conducted, Pamela Utz (1978) intensively studied differences in plea bargaining and sentencing in two different jurisdictions in California. One, in northern California, provided individualized sentencing and creative treatment programs, while the other, in southern California, provided harsher, if more consistent, conventional sentencing for similar (mostly drug) offenses. Judicial variation, prosecutorial negotiation styles, and court cultures accounted for differences, which, at least in the federal courts, can no longer vary responsively due to determinate sentencing,[4] raising the question of whether regulation to universalize or regularize dispute processes is necessarily desirable (or realizable).

One of the most hotly contested issues within the negotiation field is whether different orientations, approaches, or styles of negotiation affect negotiated outcomes. With an inability to observe actual negotiations experimentally or rigorously, a variety of researchers, including Gerald Williams (1983), Hazel Genn (1988), Herbert Kritzer (1991), Andrea Schneider (2002), and myself (1993), have attempted (through self-reports, reports of negotiation partners, interviews, and limited observations) to document variations in negotiation behavior from traditional competitive and adversarial models, to more creative, integrative, problem-solving models with variations in between a competitive-collaborative matrix. Despite continued exhortations to lawyers to "zealously advocate" for their clients, most of the extant studies provide a picture of either relatively passive negotiation behavior in routinized, low-intensity cases or a more conciliatory, cooperative style in which lawyers seem to know their reputation is their bond.

If the empirical picture of lawyer negotiation and dispute settlement remains somewhat obscured by the private settings (with lawyer-client privilege) in which it occurs, other forms of dispute resolution, with facilitators or other third party neutrals (mediators and arbitrators) are only slightly more visible. What goes on inside the "black box" of mediation and arbitration may be even more obscure, except that there may be more "witnesses" than in negotiation, especially when there is no "consent" to settle.

B. Mediation and other facilitated consensual processes

When direct efforts to negotiate a resolution of a dispute fail, parties and their lawyers increasingly turn to facilitated dispute resolution, asking a third party to assist them in their conflict-resolution efforts. Mediators do not make decisions for the parties but manage communication, help develop agendas and issues for discussion, and occasionally, and now quite controversially, "suggest" possible solutions and outcomes. Mediators are not arbitrators (see below) who decide matters between disputing parties, but in recent years the role of the mediator has become more complex as different models of mediation have emerged, including facilitative, evaluative, transformative, narrative, and "understanding" models

---

[4] A recent rigorous study of differential outcomes in an administrative-judicial setting, that of immigration, found great variations in grants and denials of asylum by gender of immigration judge, region of country, and country of origin of asylum applicant, see Ramji-Nogales, Schoenholtz, and Schrag (2009).

of mediation, each of which places different values on how active the mediator is in the substantive resolution of a dispute and how the mediator conducts the mediation session (e.g., whether by meeting with the parties separately in caucus sessions or not, whether by defining the issues broadly or narrowly, and whether by being passive or active with respect to specific solution proposals for the parties).

The early years of mediation emphasized consensus and party empowerment in the dispute resolution process. Consequently, early proponents were committed to such ideas as party self-determination and empowerment, open communication, relationship preservation, solutions tailored to parties' particular problems that were not overly legalistic, and a focus on future consequences of conflicts for relationships (Grillo, 1991). Mediation has now moved from such consensual and mostly "private" environments as divorce and (some) labor disputes, to more public institutional settings such as court-mandated mediation programs, facilitated governmental public policy and rule-making, and to "restorative justice," where criminal offenders and their victims meet and confer over apologies, restitution, and other forms of individualized outcomes beyond formal punishment and court sentences (see Menkel-Meadow, 2007). The move to more public contexts creates challenges for some of goals of the early proponents.

There have been many attempts to study a wide variety of important questions in the use of mediation. Researchers have attempted, as with all ADR processes, to document what actually happens in mediation—when do mediators caucus, when do they use more "coercive" techniques to get parties to agree, when do they facilitate, and when do they become more active with case evaluations or suggestions for concrete solutions? As in the efforts to categorize "types" of negotiators (e.g., competitors, integrators, problem-solvers: Schneider, 2002), students of mediation have attempted to classify mediators as instrumental problem-solvers or bargainers, or more emotionally affective, therapeutically oriented interveners (Silbey and Merry, 1986). Much ink has been spilled on the question of whether mediators broadly or narrowly define disputes and whether they evaluate and suggest solutions or, instead, encourage parties to communicate well and negotiate their own solutions.

As with negotiation, the study of mediation is quite problematic for empiricists because mediation usually begins with both contractual, and in some cases statutory, protections of confidentiality, for both the parties and the mediators, making direct observations of mediation processes very difficult unless all parties consent.[5] Nevertheless, through post-hoc interview studies, surveys of users and, in a few cases, direct observation of some mediations, we are beginning to get a picture of just how diverse mediation practice is (e.g., Kolb, 1994). With party agreement

---

[5] Needing to obtain consent to study such processes would likely present a selection bias problem and reduce the representativeness of any sample.

and court permission, some researchers have been able to transcribe actual mediation sessions for close linguistic analysis and have documented the uses, by at least some mediators, of more "manipulative" behaviors, as opposed to styles that serve to empower the parties (Greatbatch and Dingwall, 1989). And, in one of the leading U.S. studies, so far, of what actually happens in mediation that fails, James Coben and Peter Thompson (2006) analyzed the complete data set of all reported legal cases (state and federal) of challenges to mediated settlements between 1999 and 2003, finding many examples of coercive mediator behavior, breaches of confidentiality, lack of expertise, failure to document agreements, and a variety of other mediator "malpractice" including non-feasance, which can be as problematic as malfeasance.

Those studying one of the most contested policy questions in the use of mediation—whether it must be voluntary to lead to acceptable or legally legitimated solutions, or whether it can be mandated—have differed in their assessments. Following their empirical studies of court-mandated mediation in Minnesota and Pennsylvania, Bobbie McAdoo and Nancy Welsh (1997) have worried that institutionalization of mediation has rendered rigid and routine a process designed to be flexible and intended to empower parties. Based on her work in California courts with mandatory mediation programs, Trina Grillo (1991) has written forcefully and eloquently on how mediation's ideological focus on the future and forgiveness has excluded important narratives of blame and the need for a measure of retribution in some settings. Richard Delgado and his colleagues (1985) worried early that when courts privatize legal processes inequalities of the parties (including racial, ethnic, gender, and other forms of social "subordination") would prevent justice in the absence of the transparency and publicity of court hearings and the resulting potential for public scrutiny. This evocative piece has produced efforts to evaluate these claims, and in the Metro Court study, conducted in New Mexico (discussed more fully below), Michelle Hermann (1993), Gary LaFree and Christine Rack (1996) and their colleagues, found gender, race, and ethnic differences in both outcomes of and party satisfaction with mediated versus adjudicative processes. Process differences interact with other important variables in disputing—demographics of the parties, case-type, and demographics of the third party judges or neutrals (see also Relis, 2009).

Early studies of mediation have documented that mediation agreements are more likely to be adhered to by the parties than judgments of courts (see, e.g., McEwen and Maiman, 1981, in small claims matters, and Pearson and Thoennes, 1989, in divorce and family cases). After a series of violent employee episodes, the United States Postal Service implemented a "transformative" model of mediation that encourages direct communication within a structured mediation model. An evaluation of that mediation program reports that employee relations have greatly improved resulting in greatly reduced employment-related violence (Bingham, 2003).

In the early years, claims were made that "community board mediation" would transform communities by developing a more participatory form of local conflict resolution. Studies of the results of these programs were less than encouraging (see Merry and Milner, 1993), revealing that the mediators were more "transformed" than the community. However, in contrast to the many critiques of the use of mediation in mandatory settings, Roselle Wissler has found in a series of studies (e.g., 2002) that mandatory court mediation programs can have beneficial effects in educating lawyers and recalcitrant or reluctant parties about the advantages of the mediation process. She has found that lawyers who have been required to attend mandatory mediation programs are more likely to recommend mediation in subsequent cases and to be somewhat, if only instrumentally, "transformed" by the process.

The use of mediation to resolve a variety of legal disputes has also led to proposals for changes to legal rules and to law practice. With a focus on direct communication and taking of responsibility for causing conflicts, mediation has often resulted in parties apologizing to each other and offering some form of restitution or other relief. Based on some empirical evidence of the effects of apologies on settlement rates and satisfaction (e.g., Robbenholt, 2003), legal commentators and policy-makers have urged the changing of legal rules to allow admission into evidence of apologies made in some settings (medical malpractice, personal injury, and other claims) as a way to enhance voluntary dispute settlement, both for cost reduction and for realignment of incentives for changing behaviors.

In the criminal arena, an adaptation of mediation has produced "Victim-Offender Mediation" or "restorative justice," used in both minor cases to reduce caseloads and in quite serious cases to facilitate forgiveness and deeper healing processes for both victims and perpetrators. There have been many studies of whether restorative justice has decreased recidivism, particularly when used in juvenile matters, where it has been most successful. International data show that the technique has been successfully adapted in Australia, New Zealand, Canada, and the Netherlands in a variety of contexts including indigenous and juvenile justice systems, as well as formal state systems (Menkel-Meadow, 2007).

From its early use in two-party disputes, the techniques of third-party facilitated negotiation have moved into increasingly complex domains. In non-court settings mediation has been used to resolve community disputes, budget and resource allocations, public policy disputes, environmental issues, and even extreme social conflicts over issues such as abortion, gun control, animal rights, gay rights, and AIDS policies (see, e.g., Susskind et al., 1999). In government, facilitated multi-party consensus building procedures (a multi-party form of mediation) have been used to draft administrative rules, legislation, and other government policies, in efforts to "solve" problems before, not after, enactments, and thus, to decrease post-adoption litigation challenges and increase compliance (empirical assessments of these processes are explored below).

Mediation and "restorative justice" models of non-adjudicative dispute resolution have also expanded to help develop new justice institutions in post-conflict, post-military dictatorship, and transitional justice settings. In South Africa, Argentina, Bolivia, Chile, Guatemala, and now Liberia, among others, Truth and Reconciliation Commissions have drawn on strategies of narrative and confession, usually with promised amnesty from prosecution, to "move forward" in peace to new regimes, borrowing, at the nation-state level, from the two-party mediation process. In other settings, indigenous "mediation-like" processes, such as Rwanda's *gacaca,* combine confession, and public and group decision-making, with ritual and forgiveness to attempt to forge new relationships, sometimes while prosecutions for serious crimes occur in other national or international settings such as the International Criminal Tribunal for Rwanda and the hybrid tribunal currently operating in East Timor. Scholars of international law, human rights, and conflict resolution are currently engaged with each other as they study and debate the relative merits of these different approaches to conflict resolution in the most horrific situations of conflict and violence such as those involving genocide and systematic rapes. When is peace more important than "justice"? Can peace be achieved without justice?

C. Private adjudication-arbitration

Perhaps the oldest form of dispute resolution is arbitration where parties ask a third party to make a decision when they cannot arrive at a negotiated solution (recall King Solomon's biblical resolution of the case of the disputed baby). In its current usage for many contractual and other legal disputes, arbitration is usually a privately selected form of dispute resolution specified either before a dispute actually happens ("predispute contractual arbitration") or chosen after the dispute ripens ("post-hoc arbitration") involving the use of private decision-makers and private or institutionally developed rules of procedure. Arbitration results in awards and decisions, sometimes, but not always, accompanied by reasoned opinions. In many legal settings arbitration awards are enforceable as if they were court judgments. In essence, arbitration is a privatized justice system. Through contracts and other legal documents (such as personnel manuals) parties can determine what substantive rules to apply to their disputes, what procedural rules they want to use, and even who the decision-makers will be. Historically, arbitration has been most commonly used in commercial relations, among merchants and vendors, dating from their use by medieval guilds. Presently, the most controversial issue in the United States with respect to arbitration is the use of "mandatory, binding arbitration" contract clauses in everyday common consumer, commercial, and employment dealings (Sternlight, 2002).

In the international arena, arbitration is increasingly viewed as the most effective way to resolve conflicts between parties from different nations (avoiding jurisdictional and enforcement problems). Most of the Bretton Woods international organizations—(the United Nations, World Bank, International Centre for the Settlement of Investment Disputes (ICSID), International Monetary Fund, and now the World Trade Organization (WTO)—have established arbitral tribunals for conflicts and disputes arising out of international and state-to-private-investor disputes, providing for a form of consensual jurisdictional authority through treaties and membership, even if enforcement remains somewhat problematic. The disputes about arbitration in the employment and consumer settings described below are peculiarly American because many countries, such as most of the European Union, expressly prohibit the use of non-consensual (adhesion), pre-dispute contractual arbitration in consumer and employment matters.

In a series of important 1970s and 1980s cases, the U.S. Supreme Court upheld the use of contractual arbitration in cases involving statutory claims (under securities, antitrust, discrimination, conspiracy, and consumer laws) where before most legal commentators believed courts were required to resolve such claims. Increasingly, large companies began to place mandatory arbitration clauses in their employment and consumer contracts (e.g., sales of motor vehicles, banking services, computers, cell phones, and even medical services provided by hospitals and doctors). People who filed consumer or employment claims in courts were often referred back to arbitration, with specified rules and arbitrators, where they had no idea they had agreed to such processes in their purchase agreements or employment terms. For the last 20 years or so most legal challenges to these compulsory clauses have been rejected by the American courts. Although claimants have argued that forced arbitration is a violation of the Constitutional right to a trial by jury, most courts have found that the right is waived by signing a contract, even if the contract is not freely negotiated.

This legal and policy dispute has produced many lawsuits and now a large number of empirical studies that have sought to examine whether this form of dispute resolution is systematically unfair. All of these studies have been questioned methodologically because of the lack of transparency and secrecy surrounding most arbitral proceedings. In the employment context, Lisa Bingham (1997) has conducted a series of studies on American Arbitration Association employment disputes to document a "repeat player effect" in which employers are more likely to "win" or do better in arbitration proceedings than are employees (without any baseline comparison with litigation results in similar kinds of litigation). Subsequent studies have demonstrated some more subtle differences, such as that high-end professional employees who are represented in arbitration by counsel may not do as "badly" as lower-level or unrepresented employees.

Advocacy groups on both sides have commissioned studies to determine whether there are systematic biases or differences in arbitration outcomes (as contrasted to judicial or other processes); but once again, the comparisons are methodologically suspect because perfect experimental comparisons of like cases are virtually impossible. Business groups release studies arguing that consumer and employment arbitration is faster and cheaper; consumer and public interest groups release studies demonstrating "repeat player" bias, both in win rates and in amount of monetary awards (see, e.g., for a summary of studies, Searle Civil Justice Institute, 2009; Colvin, 2007).

It is probably fair to summarize this work by saying that there are no consistent patterns, although some evidence of "repeat player" effects does exist (Menkel-Meadow, 1999). One recent study of National Association of Securities Dealers securities disputes found that arbitrators in securities cases who, as lawyers, represented brokerage houses in other arbitrations, were much more likely to rule in favor of brokerage houses or award less in damages to investors in securities disputes. Arbitrators who represented both investors and brokerage houses were less likely to do so. Political party affiliation of the arbitrator and control of the "chair" of the panel also had an effect on award rates and amounts (Choi et al., 2009). A recent study of consumer arbitrations before the American Arbitration Association demonstrated that consumers bringing claims did win something in about 50% of the cases, but businesses that brought cases won something in more than 80% of the cases and generally won greater monetary amounts, lending credence to the claims that "repeat player" businesses do tend to do better in consumer-business disputes than the usually "one-off" consumer (Drahozal and Zyontz, 2009). Those studying employment arbitration have found some evidence of "repeat player" bias in favor of employers, but some of the variance is explained by lawyer representation and whether or not the employer has a sophisticated "internal" or organizational dispute resolution system (Edelman et al., 1993; Eisenberg and Hill, 2003–2004).

This essay is not intended to summarize and evaluate all of the competing data sets. In my view, whether arbitration is faster, better, or less fair and biased remains context-specific and impossible to universally assess—see below for comparisons with litigation; but there clearly is a strong need for rigorously designed studies of how arbitration is conducted and how it compares to other processes.

In the international arena, commercial arbitration is the norm for dispute resolution, usually provided for contractually and with the selection of one of the leading international institutional providers for administration, procedural rules, and some support of the process. An international arbitration process formally dominated by European "grand old men" and the civil law system is gradually being transformed by American and British lawyers into a more procedurally adversarial and common law system, a process well studied by sociologists of law and experienced by lawyers and parties in the system (Dezalay and Garth, 1996).

D. Other hybrid forms of ADR

The growth of private forms of alternative processes for dispute resolution in the 1980s and 1990s spawned a variety of innovative adaptations of those primary processes, such as mediation and arbitration, in both the private and public sectors. In the labor relations context, "med-arb" and "arb-med" begin with either facilitated negotiation of grievances or a conventional arbitration hearing and by reversing the processes, converting a decision-maker (arbitrator) into a facilitator (mediator) or vice versa. This kind of process has been used, controversially, in some family law courts. In some states in the United States, mediation or conciliation of child custody disputes is now often conducted by mediators who then, if the mediation fails, become, by court order, "probation officers" or other court officials making recommendations about outcomes (Grillo, 1991). This mixture of roles has been criticized by some as violating the "integrity" and purposes of particular processes whose structures and goals should not be mixed (Menkel-Meadow, 2006).

In the 1970s a group of innovative lawyers developed a private dispute resolution process, called a "mini-trial," which combined use of adversary presentation of evidence (witnesses and documents) to party decision-makers (CEOs in big cases), with use of negotiation and mediation conducted by parties and their lawyers, and deploying a third party neutral in a non-judgmental capacity to assist as a mediator if necessary. This confidential private process successfully resolved a variety of very large-scale corporate disputes. Following the success of the private "mini-trial," a group of U.S. federal judges adapted this procedure for court use (called a "summary jury trial"): actual jurors heard shortened evidentiary presentations, and then issued a non-binding "advisory" verdict to spur party negotiations. While both of these processes were popular in the 1980s and part of the 1990s particularly in high-value, confidential (utility rate-setting, civil rights, and contract) disputes and aggregate litigation such as asbestos and other mass torts, legal criticism (e.g., the use of jurors for non-statutory purposes), and a lack of empirical evidence of cost savings have diminished their use over time.

Although mini-trials and summary jury trials did not totally revolutionize litigated disputes, courts have increasingly brought various forms of ADR into the "public" sector. Mandatory mediation and mandatory arbitration for certain classes of low-value cases are now used routinely in both state and federal courts, with much criticism that this institutionalization of more flexible processes is distorting both public adjudication processes and the private, more flexible processes. Other hybrid processes, such as Early Neutral Evaluation, which involves case assessments by volunteer lawyers designed to spur negotiated settlements, have been adopted by a few courts but only sparsely evaluated and empirically assessed for their value in reducing case-processing time (see discussion of RAND studies below) or pleasing their users.

Just as new forms of dispute resolution have moved to the public courts (and some forms of administrative rule-making as well), adaptation of new forms of dispute resolution have also affected private-sector dispute resolution. In what is now called "internal" dispute resolution, organizations, including both private institutions and government agencies, provide private justice systems for employees, or consumers or users of products and services. Ombuds personnel, initially thought to be neutral advisors about governmental complaints, have now become counselors, mediators, and dispute system designers for large organizations in both public and private sectors. In the U.S. federal government, employees in one agency may mediate disputes in another agency as "collateral duty." The U.S. federal government offers awards for well-designed dispute programs. Although many in both the public and private sectors claim cost reduction and time savings from the various institutional innovations, we actually have little rigorous empirical evidence to support these claims.

In the international arena we also have little empirical data on the private commercial sector (Whytock, 2009). A little more exists for the World Bank's ICSID, investment treaty dispute resolution program (Franck, 2008), and the WTO's appellate body, which promote transparency by publishing arbitral awards; but in this context there really is little with which to compare the arbitral system, since transnational litigation is so problematic in terms of jurisdiction and enforcement, and because state-to-state disputes differ in structure and legal requirements from state-and-private-actor disputes.

Thus, as both primary and more hybrid dispute processes proliferate, the crucial questions are:

- How does X process compare to other processes that might be used?
- When are public or private processes respectively most effective?
- For whom are they effective (the parties or those outside of the dispute)?
- For what kinds of disputes are they effective?

III. EMPIRICAL COMPARISONS OF DISPUTE RESOLUTION PROCESSES

As the use of various forms of dispute resolution proliferated in the private sector and courts began to use various forms of ADR in the 1980s in the United States (and elsewhere) social scientists and court administrators were anxious to discern whether ADR actually delivered what it promised—processes that were faster, cheaper or "better" (more individually tailored, producing higher compliance rates, more satisfaction, more "justice"). In the mid-1990s the U.S. Congress authorized several major studies of the use of ADR and other "case management" tools in the federal courts. These studies, the "RAND" studies (Kakalik et al., 1996) and the Federal Judicial Center (FJC) studies (Stienstra et al., 1997) offered some different conclusions from studying different courts within the federal system (Menkel-Meadow, 1997: 1922–30).

There were attempts to "match" similar courts, with similar caseloads (e.g., the eastern district of Pennsylvania (Philadelphia) with the central district of California (Los Angeles)), but with different case management and ADR practices, in order to test hypotheses about relative case processing times etc. In general the RAND studies found that case processing time was not generally reduced by the use of mediation, arbitration, or such programs as Early Neutral Evaluation, but that it was sometimes positively affected by such devices as setting early trial dates—a result consistent with earlier studies of mandatory settlement conferences (Menkel-Meadow, 1985). The FJC studies revealed some decrease in case processing time and reduction of litigation costs. Both the FJC study and some of the data in the RAND studies supported claims that parties generally had high satisfaction rates in their use of "alternative" processes. Other studies suggested that mandatory arbitration programs were not popular (and were often considered to be a denial of due process rights to civil juries). Many studies documented that if ADR programs were "voluntary," rather than mandatory, they were not well utilized (Wissler, 2002, 1997; Kakalik et al., 1996).

More recent studies of state court programs also show "mixed results," including high satisfaction rates and subsequent recommendations of ADR when participation is mandated (Wissler, 2000), but low usage when not mandated. Low usage of voluntary mediation programs has been documented in the United Kingdom as well (Genn, 1999). Recent budgetary problems for both federal and state courts have ironically increased the pressure to use ADR as a docket-clearing or diversionary device at the same time that there are reduced funds available for rigorous court-based evaluation research. One recent study has documented cost and time savings in the use of ADR in federal government litigation (Bingham et al., 2009).

In a series of important and rigorous research studies, Theodore Eisenberg and his colleagues at Cornell Law School have used publicly available aggregate data from the FJC combined with data they collected on such issues as arbitration clauses in corporate contracts to test some of the most controversial claims about comparisons among various forms of adjudication and other forms of dispute resolution. Among their important findings are that employees fare no worse in arbitration settings than in litigation settings in outcomes and may, in fact, save money and time by resorting to arbitration (Eisenberg and Hill, 2003–2004); and that plaintiff "win" rates in adjudication may ultimately be worse in court than in other forms of dispute resolution because appellate courts may overturn even fact findings favoring plaintiffs (e.g., Clermont and Eisenberg, 2002). Perhaps somewhat ironically, Eisenberg and his colleagues have also noted that despite all of the controversies about the use of mandatory arbitration in contracts (especially in employment and consumer settings), there is little evidence of increased use of mandatory arbitration clauses in major corporations' contracts with one another (Eisenberg and Miller, 2007).[6]

[6] Especially in international contracts, a finding which challenges the assertions of many international business lawyers that arbitration remains the most common form of chosen dispute resolution (Whytock, 2009).

A variety of other controversial claims about the comparative value of different processes have also spawned inconclusive and contradictory studies. Cary Coglianese (1997) has long questioned whether the use of negotiated rule-making or public policy consensus-building processes has in fact decreased the cost of administrative rule-making or bolstered its "consensual" and non-contested quality, against continuing claims by its proponents that well managed multi-party negotiation processes can provide rule-making in administrative contexts that is less likely to be challenged in post-hoc litigation. Freeman (1997) has provided one of the most in-depth empirical case studies of several collaborative rule-making efforts, but her work is challenged by Coglianese who insists on the need for more aggregate data and for comparisons with more conventional rule-making administrative processes before drawing conclusions about relative costs, compliance, and other post-hoc effects. In my own view, attempts to study and compare these particular uses of ADR are even more problematic than attempts to match aggregate cases in traditional litigation settings. Rule-making proceedings in front of different U.S. federal agencies (Environmental Protection Agency, Federal Drug Administration, Departments of Labor, Interior, etc.) are so factually, scientifically, legally, and historically complex that comparisons across case types are quite resistant to rigorous comparisons.

In my view, one of the few rigorously successful studies of comparability of process is the Metro Court study (Hermann, 1993; LaFree and Rack, 1996) of outcomes and satisfaction rates among adjudication and mediation users in New Mexico state courts. In an attempt to test Delgado et al.'s (1985) thesis that private processes would be adversely experienced by minority litigants, Michelle Hermann and her colleagues found far more complex relationships in the mix of process used, demographics of litigants and third party neutrals, and case types. Some women, for example, fared "better" in mediation outcomes, but were more skeptical of that process, and somewhat distrusting of its informal quality (see Grillo, 1991). Hispanics and some Blacks preferred mediation, even when their outcomes were relatively inferior to what they might have achieved in litigation, demonstrating some distrust of formal justice systems (particularly among immigrants who carry memories of corrupt courts from their native lands). This study generally refuted Delgado's "informality" hypotheses by demonstrating that factors other than race, gender, and ethnicity such as case-type, repeat player effects, and whether parties had representatives or not, accounted for more of the differences in both outcomes and satisfaction rates. One important finding was that, in general, parties were more satisfied with processes in which the third party neutral, whether a judge or mediator, "matched" their own ethnicity.

This study had a unique "natural" control setting, with almost equal numbers of Anglo, Hispanic, and African-American judicial officers and mediators, and a relatively equal division by gender. The complexity of the findings of this study and efforts to explain its multivariate relationships are a model (yet to be replicated) of how rigorous comparative process research might be conducted. The access given to court and mediation proceedings in this study has not been replicated.

The study of comparative dispute processes continues in a variety of settings. In the U.S. researchers have attempted to evaluate the claim that "ADR" explains the phenomenon of the "vanishing trial" in the United States (Galanter, 2004; Hadfield, 2004), producing, in the view of some, an inadequate number of litigated cases for rule production. In the international arena, researchers have asked whether transnational disputes are similarly being handled "under the radar screen" in private settings (commercial arbitration) with little public or transparent rule development. One recent attempt to study this latter phenomenon reports that international arbitration in commercial settings, using the major institutional administrative agencies, is rapidly increasing while, at least in the United States, transnational litigation (use of federal courts in transnational disputes) may be decreasing (Whytock, 2009), even as empirical studies document that foreign litigants are faring relatively well in the federal courts (Clermont and Eisenberg, 2007). Yet the same study also reports on increasing judicial activity in vacating international arbitration awards, at least in American courts, suggesting that studying the interaction of private and public dispute processes is far more complicated than studying either separately.

If formal litigation and "law" is considered to cast a "shadow" on private dispute resolution endowments in negotiation (Mnookin and Kornhauser, 1979), private dispute processes also cast a "competitive" shadow on public processes. Several commentators, besides this author, have observed that formal litigation and various forms of ADR now compete with and affect each other. Competition means disputants and their representatives make choices on such dimensions as privacy, cost, timing, rule clarification, expert decision-makers, and rules of procedure based on concerns about both efficiency and justice (Priest, 1989).

IV. Implications for Future Empirical Study of ADR Processes

As the field of dispute resolution grows to describe and map the many new uses of and varieties of dispute processes it is instructive to return to the themes of this essay: 1) the need for clarity in describing processes that vary as much internally as they do across processes; 2) the great difficulty of developing accurate or truly "comparative" treatments of processes for handling similar disputes; 3) the virtual impossibility of using experimental models that subject the same dispute to several different treatments for comparison or for co-varying factors of influence (such as case types, gender of disputants, etc.); and 4) the open boundaries and dynamism of the field itself.

Recent extensions of ADR to "on-line dispute resolution," truth and reconciliation commissions, transactional mediation in contract formation, not to mention such conventional uses of various forms of dispute resolution in diplomacy, market transactions, family relations, and ordinary day-to-day disputes and conflicts, suggest that the domain of dispute-resolution research is far more capacious than assessing how disputes are managed in formal legal arenas such as lawsuits or courts. These new domains of dispute resolution suggest a number of new and interesting research questions, combined with the still unresolved "older" research questions explored in this essay—some descriptive, others comparative, still others relevant to normative or prescriptive issues:

1. Must dispute resolution be conducted face-to-face to be effective? What will the role of new technologies be in dispute resolution?
2. When can disputing "culture" be changed? Can people be taught to "collaborate" or is the assumption of scarcity and competition the human default? What difference would it make in lawyering behavior if legal rules allowed "apologies" to be admitted as evidence? Can publicity about alternative forms of dispute resolution (e.g., South Africa's Truth and Reconciliation Commission) change political or disputing cultures?
3. Do particular domains (e.g., transnational and inter-organizational) or subject matters (e.g., ongoing relationships) require particular forms of dispute processing? In other words, is "trans-substantive" process a misconceived or impossible notion?
4. What factors influence party choice in dispute processes?
5. Does any form of dispute resolution require particular expertise?
6. When should dispute processing be public and transparent and when should parties be permitted to resolve disputes privately? Does a legal system require totally public dispute processes for all of its conflicts?
7. Finally, as this essay began, can we ever fully study and know whether particular structural patterns of parties, case types, and processes are "better" for the parties or for outsiders than any other set of process structures or choices?

Clearly, this is one realm of "empirical legal study" that continues to suggest new questions, challenge methodological design, and affect a wide variety of policy choices.

References

Alexander, J.C. (1991). "Do the Merits Matter? A Study of Settlements in Securities Class Actions," *Stanford Law Review* 43: 497–598.

Ayres, I. (1991). "Fair Driving: Gender and Race Discrimination in Retail Car Negotiations," *Harvard Law Review* 104: 817–72

Babcock, L. and Laschever, S. (2003). *Women Don't Ask: Negotiation and the Gender Divide*, Princeton: Princeton University Press.

Bazerman, M.H. and Neale, M.A. (1992). *Negotiating Rationally*, New York: Free Press.

Bingham, L.B. (1997). "Employment Arbitration: The Repeat Player Effect," *Employment Rights and Employment Policy Journal* 1: 189–99.

Bingham, L.B. (2003). "Mediation at Work: Transforming Workplace Conflict at the United States Postal Service," Washington, DC: IBM Center for The Business of Government.

Bingham, L.B., Nabatchi, T., Senger, J., and Jackman, M.S. (2009). "Dispute Resolution and the Vanishing Trial; Comparing Federal Government Litigation and ADR Outcomes," SSRN, available at <http://ssrn.com/abstract=1127878>.

Choi, S., Fisch, J., and Pritchard, A. (2009). "Attorneys Arbitrators," University of Michigan John M. Olin Center for Law and Economics Working Paper # 94.

Clermont, K.M. and Eisenberg, T. (2002). "Plaintiphobia in the appellate courts: civil rights really do differ from negotiable instruments," *University of Illinois Law Review* 2002(4): 947–77.

Clermont, K.M and Eisenberg, T. (2007). "Xenophilia or Xenophobia in U.S. Courts? Before and After 9/11," *Journal of Empirical Legal Studies* 4(2): 441–64.

Coben, J. and Thompson, P. (2006). "Disputing Irony: A Systematic Look at Litigation About Mediation," *Harvard Negotiation Law Review* 11: 43–146.

Coglianese, C. (1997). "Assessing Consensus: The Promise and Performance of Negotiated Rulemaking," *Duke Law Journal* 46: 1255–1337.

Colvin, A.J.S. (2007). "Empirical Research on Employment Arbitration: Clarity Amidst the Sound and Fury?," *Employment Rights and Employment Policy Journal* 11: 405–47.

Cox, J.D., Thomas, R.S., and Bai, L. (2008). "There are Plaintiffs and…There are Plaintiffs: An Empirical Analysis of Securities Class Action Settlements," *Vanderbilt Law Review* 61: 355.

Delgado, R., Dunn, C., Brown, P., Lee, H., and Gubert, D. (1985). "Fairness and Formality: Minimizing the Risk of Prejudice in Alternative Dispute Resolution," *Wisconsin Law Review* 1985: 1359–1405.

Dezalay, Y. and Garth, B. (1996). *Dealing in Virtue: International Commercial Arbitration and the Construction of a Transnational Legal Order*, Chicago: University of Chicago Press.

Drahozal, C.R. and Zyontz, S. (2009). "An Empirical Study of AAA Consumer Arbitration," SSRN, available at <http://ssrn.com/abstract=1365435>.

Edelman, L., Erlanger, H., and Lande, J. (1993). "Internal Dispute Resolution: The Transformation of Civil Rights in the Workplace," *Law & Society Review*, 27: 497–534.

Eisenberg, T. and Hill, E. (2003–2004). "Arbitration and Litigation of Employment Claims: An Empirical Comparison," *Dispute Resolution Journal* 44–63.

Eisenberg. T. and Miller, G.P. (2007). "The Flight from Arbitration: An Empirical Study of Ex Ante Arbitration clauses in the Contracts of Publicly Held Companies," *DePaul Law Review* 56: 335.

Franck, S.D. (2008). "Empiricism and International Law: Insights for Investment Treaty Dispute Resolution," *Virginia Journal of International Law* 48(4): 767–815.

Freeman, J. (1997). "Collaborative Governance in the Administrative State," *UCLA Law Review* 45: 1–98.

Galanter, M. (2004). "The Vanishing Trial: An Examination of Trials and Related Matters in Federal and State Courts," *Journal of Empirical Legal Studies* 1: 459–570.

Genn, H. (1988). *Hard Bargaining: Out of Court Settlement In Personal Injury Actions*, Oxford: Oxford University Press.

Genn, H. (1999). *Mediation in Action*, London: Calouste Gulbenkian Foundation.

Greatbatch, D. and Dingwall, R. (1989). "Selective Facilitation: Some Preliminary Observations on a Strategy Used by Divorce Mediators," *Law and Society Review* 23: 613–39.

Grillo, T. (1991). "The Mediation Alternative: Process Dangers for Women," *Yale Law Journal* 100: 1545–610.

Guthrie, C. (2003). "Panacea or Pandora's Box? The Costs of Options In Negotiations," *Iowa Law Review* 88: 601–52.

Hadfield, G.K. (2004). "Where Have All the Trials Gone? Settlements, Non-Trial Adjudications and Statistical Artifacts in the Changing Disposition of Federal Cases," *Journal of Empirical Legal Studies* 1: 705–34.

Hensler, D. (2000). "In Search of Good Mediation: Rhetoric, Practice and Empiricism," in L. Sanders and V.L. Hamilton (eds.) *Handbook of Justice Research in Law*, New York: Kluwer Academic/Plenum Publishers.

Hermann, M. (1993). *The Metro Court Project Final Report*, Albuquerque: University of New Mexico Center for the Study and Resolution of Disputes.

Kakalik, J.S., Dunworth, T., Hill, L.A., McCaffrey, D., Oshiro, M., Pace, N.M., and Vaiana, M.E. (1996). *An Evaluation of Mediation and Early Neutral Evaluation Under the Civil Justice Reform Act*, Santa Monica, CA: RAND.

Kiser, R.L., Asher, M.A., and McShane, B.B. (2008). "Let's Not Make A Deal: An Empirical Study of Decision-making in Unsuccessful Settlement Negotiations," *Journal of Empirical Legal Studies* 3: 551–91.

Kolb, D. and Associates (eds.) (1994). *When Talk Works: Profiles of Mediators*, San Francisco: Jossey-Bass.

Kritzer, H. (1986). "Adjudication to Settlement: Shading in the Gray," *Judicature* 70 (October–November): 161–5.

Kritzer, H. (1991). *Let's Make a Deal: Negotiation and Settlement in Ordinary Litigation*, Madison: University of Wisconsin Press.

LaFree, G. and Rack, C. (1996). "The Effects of Participants' Ethnicity and Gender on Monetary Outcomes in Mediated and Adjudicated Civil Cases," *Law and Society Review* 30: 767–97.

Lind, E.A., MacCoun, R.J., Ebener, P.A., Felstiner, W.L.F., Hensler, D.R., Resnik, J., and Tyler, T. R. (1989). *The Perception of Justice: Tort Litigants' Views of Trial, Court-Annexed Arbitration and Judicial Settlement Conferences*, Santa Monica, CA: RAND.

McAdoo, B. and Welsh, N.A. (1997). "Does ADR Really Have a Place on the Lawyer's Philosophical Map?," *Hamline Journal of Public Law and Policy* 18: 376–93.

McEwen, C. and Maiman, R.J. (1981). "Small Claims Mediation in Maine: An Empirical Assessment," *Maine Law Review*, 33: 237–268.

Menkel-Meadow, C. (1985). "For and Against Settlement: Uses and Abuses of the Mandatory Settlement Conference," *UCLA Law Review* 33: 485–514.

Menkel-Meadow, C. (1993). "Lawyer Negotiations: Theories and Realities—What We Learn From Mediation," *Modern Law Review* 56: 361–79.

Menkel-Meadow, C. (1995). "Whose Dispute Is It Anyway? A Philosophical and Democratic Defense of Settlement (in some cases)," *Georgetown Law Journal* 83: 2663–96.

Menkel-Meadow, C. (1997). "When Dispute Resolution Begets Disputes Of Its Own: Conflicts Among Dispute Professionals," *UCLA Law Review* 44: 1871–1933.

Menkel-Meadow, C. (1999). "Do The Haves Come Out Ahead in Alternative Justice Systems? Repeat Players in ADR," *Ohio State Journal of Dispute Resolution* 15: 19–61.

Menkel-Meadow, C. (2006). "Peace and Justice: Notes on the Evolution and Purposes of Legal Processes," *Georgetown Law Journal* 94: 553–80.

Menkel-Meadow, C. (2007). "Restorative Justice: What Is It and Does It Work?," *Annual Review of Law and Social Science* 3: 10.1–10.27.

Menkel-Meadow, C. (2009). "The Complexification (and Usefulness) of Negotiation Theory and Practice," *Negotiation Journal* 25 (4): 415–28.

Merry, S.E. and Milner, N. (1993). *The Possibility of Popular Justice: A Case Study of Community Mediation in the United States*, San Francisco: Jossey-Bass Publishers.

Mnookin, R. and Kornhauser, L. (1979). "Bargaining in the Shadow of the Law: The Case of Divorce," *Yale Law Journal* 88: 950–97.

Pearson, J. and Thoennes, N. (1989). "Divorce Mediation: Reflections on A Decade of Research," in *Mediation Research: The Process and Effectiveness of Third-Party Intervention*, San Francisco: Jossey-Bass Publishers.

Priest, G. (1989). "Private Litigants and the Court Congestion Problem," *Boston University Law Review* 69: 527–59.

Ramji-Nogales, J., Schoenholtz, A.I., and Schrag, P.G. (2009). *Refugee Roulette: Disparities in Asylum Adjudication and Proposals for Reform*, New York: New York University Press.

Relis, T. (2009). *Perceptions in Litigation and Mediation: Lawyers, Defendants, Plaintiffs and Gendered Parties*, New York and Cambridge: Cambridge University Press.

Robbenholt, J.K. (2003). "Apologies and Legal Settlement: An Empirical Examination," *Michigan Law Review* 102: 460–516.

Schneider, A.K. (2002). "Shattering Negotiation Myths: Empirical Evidence on the Effectiveness of Negotiation Style," *Harvard Negotiation Law Review* 7: 143–233.

Searle Civil Justice Institute (2009). *Searle Center on Law, Regulation and Economic Growth. Consumer Arbitration Before the American Arbitration Association*, Chicago: Northwestern Law School.

Sebenius, J.K. (1996). "Sequencing to Build Coalitions: With Whom Should I Talk First?," in R. Zeckhauser, R.L. Keeney, and J.K. Sebenius (eds.), *Wise Choices: Decisions, Games and Negotiations*, Boston: Harvard Business School Press.

Silbey, S. and Merry, S. (1986). "Mediator Settlement Strategies," *Law & Policy Quarterly* 8: 7–32.

Sternlight, J. (2002). "Is the US Out on a Limb? Comparing the US Approach to Mandatory Consumer and Employment Arbitration to That of the Rest of the World," *University of Miami Law Review* 56: 831–64.

Stienstra, D., Johnson, M., Lombard, P., and Pecherski, M. (1997). *Report to the Judicial Conference Committee on Court Administration and Case Management: A Study of the First Demonstration Programs Established Under the Civil Justice Reform Act of 1990*, Washington, DC: Federal Judicial Center.

Sunstein, C. (2000). "Deliberative Trouble? Why Groups Go to Extremes," *Yale Law Journal* 110: 71–119.

Susskind, L., McKearnan, S., and Thomas-Larmer, J. (eds.) (1999). *The Consensus Building Handbook: A Comprehensive Guide to Reaching Agreement,* Thousand Oaks, CA: Sage Publications.

Utz, P.J. (1978). *Settling the Facts: Discretion and Negotiation in Criminal Court,* Lexington, MA: Lexington Books.

Williams, G. (1983). *Legal Negotiation and Settlement,* St. Paul, MN: West Publishing Co.

Wissler, R. (1997). "The Effects of Mandatory Mediation: Empirical Research on the Experience of Small Claims and Common Pleas Courts," *Willamette Law Review* 33: 565–604.

Wissler, R. (2000). "Attorneys' Use of ADR is Crucial to Their Willingness to Recommend It to Clients," *Dispute Resolution Magazine* 36.

Wissler, R. (2002). "The Effectiveness of Court-Connected Dispute Resolution in Civil Cases," *Conflict Resolution Quarterly* 22: 55–88.

Whytock, C.A. (2009). "The Arbitration-Litigation Relationship in Transnational Dispute Resolution: Empirical Results from the Federal Courts," *World Arbitration & Mediation Review* 2(3): 39–82.

2 6

LAY DECISION-MAKERS IN THE LEGAL PROCESS

NEIL VIDMAR[1]

[1] This research was supported by funds provided by Duke Law School. The author is indebted to Duke Law librarian Jennifer Behrens for important assistance.

I. INTRODUCTION

THE first thing that comes to mind involving "lay decision-makers" in the legal process is the common law jury and offshoots of that system that exist in Europe (see Vidmar, 2000) and, very recently, in South Korea (Lee, 2009). Research attention has also been directed toward mixed tribunals of laypersons and judges that are used in much of continental Europe (e.g., Jackson and Kovalev, 2006–2007; Sperlich, 2007) and the recent development of Saiban-in Seido in Japan (see Fukurai, 2007; Hans, 2008; Sasahara, 2009) Some countries around the world also use lay assessors who provide advice to the judge, but who do not have an official vote in the decision-making process (Vidmar, 2002). Grand juries in the United States and elsewhere determine whether the prosecution has sufficient evidence to bring a case to trial. Coroner's juries in England, Canada, and other common law countries decide causes of death and make recommendations bearing on safety.

Conceiving of the topic more broadly, however, we see that laypersons serve at many other critical junctures in the legal process. Thus, in England, the majority of lower-level criminal matters are decided by a panel of three volunteer layperson magistrates (Darbyshire, 1997). Provine (1981) drew attention to the fact that New York State, not unique among the 50 states in this regard, had more than 10,000 layperson justices of the peace who presided over trials of minor criminal and quasi-criminal offenses, such as traffic violations. In North Carolina lay magistrates have replaced justices of the peace and serve many criminal and civil functions, including approval of arrest warrants, bond hearings, and adjudication of civil claims involving less than $5,000 (North Carolina Magistrates Association, 2009). In Canada, Australia, New Zealand, and small island nations throughout the Pacific Ocean, aboriginal courts composed of laypersons decide punishments for lesser criminal offenses and serve other functions reserved for legal personnel elsewhere in the world (e.g., Blagg, 2008; Whonnock, 2008). Courts all over the world utilize laypersons as intermediaries between litigants and the courts (see, e.g., Mestitz and Ghetti, 2005; Wissler, 2002). In Ontario, Canada "independent paralegals" represent traffic violators in court and in immigration hearings (Ianni, 1990).

The above examples suggest a widespread use of laypersons in legal systems across the world. Many empirical questions arise about similarities and differences in the functions of laypersons and their performance, in absolute terms, in comparison to how legally-trained persons would perform these functions, and in comparison to differences across national and legal cultures.

This Chapter provides a limited overview of research about these layperson roles and draws attention to the research methodologies used in studying them. A substantial section of the Chapter will be devoted to the jury system because, in addition to the fact that this institution has attracted the greatest quantity of empirical research on lay participation in legal processes, the studies have also involved the greatest range of methodological approaches, thus allowing exploration of their various strengths and weaknesses. Research on mixed tribunals, lay magistrates, justices of the peace and other forms of lay participation are also discussed in the Chapter.

II. JURIES

The Anglo-American jury system and its accompanying adversarial mode of legal procedure is a unique institution. Between six and twelve persons are summoned from the general public to hear evidence that is controlled and presented by contending parties in serious criminal and civil disputes. Although guided by instructions from the presiding trial judge during the trial and before they begin to deliberate, these ordinary citizens deliberate alone about the evidence and render a verdict on who should prevail in the litigation. In cases involving capital punishment they may also decide if the defendant merits a death sentence.

Criminal juries are used in more than 50 countries whose legal systems are derived, in whole or in part, from English common law (Vidmar, 2000). These include not only Australia, Canada, New Zealand, Ireland, and Scotland but also Caribbean countries, such as Jamaica, Barbados, and Trinidad; and the Central and South American countries of Guyana, Belize, and Panama. Hong Kong, Sri Lanka, Tonga, and The Marshall Islands use juries and the African countries of Liberia, Ghana, and Malawi have provisions for the jury system. Belgium, Denmark, Norway, Brazil, Russia, and Spain, whose systems are not founded on common-law jurisprudence, use variations of the jury for serious criminal offenses. In some of these latter countries jurors deliberate with the judges on the matter of the sentence after they have found the accused guilty. Civil juries were once widespread, but with minor exceptions, such as trials involving defamation or slander, civil juries today exist primarily in the United States, the Canadian provinces of Ontario and British Columbia, and the Australian state of Victoria.

Jury trials account for a relatively small number of dispositions of criminal offenses, even in the United States, but, in every country that uses it, jury trial is an important democratic institution. Nevertheless, some critics within those countries assert that laypersons lack competence to decide complex matters or that juries idiosyncratically deviate from legal principles.

There are literally hundreds of empirical studies bearing on jury competence and behavior. Most have been concerned with United States criminal and civil juries (see

Vidmar and Hans, 2007). A primary handicap in undertaking jury research in other countries has been laws that proscribe jurors from disclosing anything about their deliberations. Nevertheless, very recently this rule has been suspended in a limited number of instances to allow researchers in Australia and New Zealand to pursue research bearing on important jury policy issues.

Methodologies for studying jury issues are quite varied. They include archival research; simulation research; comparison of jury decisions with decisions of legally-trained professionals or other experts; and post-trial interviews with jurors. Each methodology has strengths and weaknesses. The selective review of this extensive literature that follows calls attention to these differences.

A. The ecology of the jury trial

The jury's tasks must be seen in context to properly assess its behavior and per-formance. The jury pool, or venire, from which the jury is formed, is made by ran-dom selection from voter lists, sometimes supplemented by drivers' license lists. Traditionally, the jury was composed of twelve persons and that remains true for the most serious offenses; but in the United States juries of eight or six persons are sometimes used for lesser criminal charges and for civil disputes. In civil trials some jurisdictions have provisions accepting a super-majority of the jurors as sufficient to render a valid legal verdict. In the United States jurors are usually questioned by the judge, or the parties or both, about their impartiality in a process called the *voir dire*. With certain exceptions in Canada, all other countries take the first twelve persons, although each side usually has a small number of "peremptory challenges" which they can use to reject a juror they feel may not be impartial. After the jury is chosen, the formal trial begins with preliminary comments by the judge. The open-ing statements by counsel typically involve an outline of the basic contested issues in the case and a foreshadowing of the evidence to be called. In the United States, both prosecution and defense usually make opening statements, but in many other countries the defense does not speak to the jury until the prosecution has presented its case. (In civil trials, the procedure is roughly the same with the plaintiff going first and the defense second.)

After direct testimony each witness is subject to cross-examination by the oppos-ing lawyer. At the end of the evidence phase each side makes closing arguments. In most countries, the United States being an exception, the judge then reviews the evidence for the jury in a "summing up." Finally, the judge instructs the jurors on the law and sends them out to deliberate. Though the traditional decision rule required the verdict to be unanimous for a finding of criminal guilt, in 1967 England modi-fied the rule to permit ten of twelve votes for a valid verdict of guilt. (The states of Oregon and Louisiana also allow super majority verdicts, except for the most serious criminal offenses.) Scotland is an anomaly in that the jury is composed of 15 persons and a majority of eight is sufficient for a verdict of guilty, but jurors have a third option of returning a verdict of "not proven."

In reality, the jury trial is not as tidy as the above summary suggests. Trials are about historical events and the jury's task is to determine what happened. In the adversary procedural system in which jury trials are embedded the evidence is not necessarily presented in chronological order. Each side is free to call evidence in any sequence they choose. Moreover, after the prosecution's case is presented, the defense presents a counter version of the events that led to the trial. The jurors have to sort out the conflicting versions of events, develop a chronology that they believe is most logical, and reconcile their different views during deliberations. In many trials experts are called to testify about evidence pertaining to the dispute, and sometimes the testimony involves arcane fields of science, medicine, or complicated financial transactions. The complexity of some trials has led to the criticism that layperson juries are not competent to render reasonable verdicts in such cases.

Before turning to the issues of jury performance, it is important to consider research on how juries go about their assigned tasks.

B. Creating narratives from conflicting stories

Pennington and Hastie (1991) conducted a series of experiments involving a murder trial that assessed how jurors integrated conflicting trial evidence. The trial was a simulation in that it was artificial and the participating persons knew they were part of an experiment. Applying lessons from a body of social psychological research on the effects of schemas and scripts on human decision-making, Pennington and Hastie proposed that jurors impose a narrative story structure on the trial evidence. They listen to the conflicting versions of the evidence at trial and then use their knowledge about analogous information and events, as well as generic expectations about what makes a complete story—e.g., that human actions are usually driven by goal-directed motives—to construct plausible, more or less coherent narratives explaining what occurred. When factual gaps occur in the evidence jurors fill in those gaps by surmising the facts necessary to develop a complete narrative. Combining their various findings, Pennington and Hastie developed what they called the "story model." In their model, juror decision-making consists of three stages: developing stories from the trial evidence, considering the verdict alternatives from the legal instructions provided by the judge (such as murder, manslaughter, or self-defense), and matching the various stories to these verdict categories. The verdict, according to the model, is derived from the best fit between the narrative and the verdict category. Subsequent research by many other researchers has supported the story model and demonstrated how jurors reconcile differing narratives during their deliberations.

Vidmar and Hans (2007) provided a number of examples of the unique insights derived from the Arizona Jury Project that videotaped the discussions of 50 actual civil juries during recesses in the trials and during their final deliberations on the verdict. The following excerpt shows the story building and evaluation process at work:

Juror 1: He [plaintiff] said he [the defendant] sped up when he saw the yellow light and then it was red. I didn't get that straight—was it a yellow or a red light [the plaintiff] saw [the defendant] going through?

Juror 7: It was red and he had to go because he was stuck in the middle.

Juror 1: But another time he [the plaintiff] said he saw the other person see the light changing so he [the defendant] sped up, or maybe that is what the [other witness] told him. There was no left turn arrow.

Juror 7: Cause if you see someone speeding up, what do you do? I sit there.

Juror 1: Yeah.

Juror 6: That's why we have to wait for the judge to talk. What are the laws in this state?

Juror 1: Yeah, you are not supposed to be in the intersection....

Juror 6: Well, there was no turn signal, right? No arrow, what was he doing in the intersection?

Juror 7: We need witnesses to tell us if he ran the light....

In this example, the jurors focused on conflicting testimony from witnesses and applied their own experience about whether the driver should have been in the intersection. In doing so, they saw that, at this point in the trial, there was missing evidence that they needed in order to make a complete narrative bearing on whether the defendant ran the light. The example is typical of the way that jurors evaluate the evidence as they develop narratives and respond to the complex and conflicting evidence that they hear and see in the courtroom.

Other research has shown how jurors incorporate normative values in evaluating evidence. Sundby (1998), for example, conducted detailed interviews with jurors who decided death penalty cases. Frequently, defense lawyers instruct their client, often poorly educated and from a very different socio-economic background than many of the jurors, to sit quietly in court and not react to testimony even if they disagree with it. Yet, this tactic seemed to backfire in many cases because the jurors concluded that the defendant expressed no remorse. Some examples are as follows:

It was just like, "I'll get off." I mean really it was stone face. There was no emotion.

I felt sick thinking how anyone could do such a thing and sit there and act like nothing is going on.

He appeared relaxed, just like another day, and of course, no remorse, because he didn't do it, so why should he be sorry?

Many other examples of juror reasoning processes during deliberations are contained in Vidmar and Hans (2007). But now let us turn to a central question, namely how well do jurors perform when judged against various criteria.

C. Juries' decisions compared to judge decisions

Kalven and Zeisel (1966) conducted what is considered to be the classic study of jury decision-making by comparing jury verdicts in 3,576 criminal trials and over 4,000 civil trials with the verdicts the presiding trial judge, who saw and heard the same evidence as the jury, would have rendered. Over 500 judges participated in the research. While the jury was deliberating, the trial judge filled out a questionnaire indicating how he would have decided the case and answered a number of other questions, including the degree to which the judge believed evidence was difficult and the degree to which the weight of the evidence was sufficiently close to the required standard of proof. In both criminal and civil trials the agreement between judge and jury was about 78%. However, in 19% of criminal trials the judge would have convicted when the jury acquitted, and in 3% the judge would have acquitted but the jury convicted. In civil cases the judge-jury agreement rate was similar to that in criminal cases, but when they disagreed, half the time the jury sided with the plaintiff when the judge would have ruled for the defendant and vice versa.

An immediate hypothesis from the above findings is that the 22% of cases in which judge and jury disagreed were cases in which the evidence was difficult for laypersons to understand. However, the clever design of Kalven and Zeisel's research allowed testing of this hypothesis. It received no support: there was no relation between evidence difficulty and disagreement, strongly indicating some other factors were at play. Kalven and Zeisel used additional data to infer that the jury was just applying a different set of values to the evidence than the judge applied. And Kalven and Zeisel were also quick to point out that the judges' values were not necessarily the correct values. After all, the point of using of lay decision-makers is precisely to add community perspectives and values that are potentially different than those of legally-trained judges. Regardless, the high agreement rate strongly suggested that juries applied principles roughly similar to those the judges used. The basic methodology used by Kalven and Zeisel has been replicated in a number of subsequent studies and has produced roughly similar rates of judge-jury agreement (see Vidmar and Hans, 2007). Devine et al. (2009), for example, used post-trial questionnaires given to judges, lawyers and jurors in a sample of 179 criminal jury trials. The data indicated that the jury verdicts were positively and strongly associated with the strength of the evidence, once again supporting Kalven and Zeisel's basic findings.

Taking a different methodological approach, Robbennolt (2002) conducted an experiment in which 87 federal and state trial judges responded to several variations of a claim for punitive damages. She then compared the results to responses made by 140 jury-eligible citizens. She found the decision-making of judges and the lay-persons in awarding punitive damages was quite similar. Vidmar (1995) conducted comparable experiments involving medical malpractice lawsuits and he too found that in general laypersons and legally trained individuals decided cases in roughly similar ways.

D. Other comparisons of jury performance

Taragin et al. (1992) conducted a study of 8,231 insurance claims made on a major New Jersey doctors' liability insurance company. Each time a malpractice claim was made against a doctor, the insurance company had its own independent experts review the medical records to assess whether the doctor had been negligent. The purpose of the review was to aid the insurer in deciding whether to contest the claim or try to settle it before trial. For claims that went to trial, the jury verdict was compared to the opinions of the medical experts. Cases in which the jury's verdict favored the doctor tended to be those in which the claim had been classified as "defensible" by the independent experts, and cases in which the verdict favored the plaintiff tended to be those in which the claim had been classified as "indefensible" or "unclear." In addition, Taragin et al. found that the jury outcome was not related to severity of the patient's injury, strongly suggesting that sympathy for the plaintiff was not a factor in the juries' decisions. Other research consistent with these findings is reported in Vidmar (1995) and Vidmar and Hans (2007).

E. Juries and experts

Modern trials regularly include expert evidence about many subjects. In criminal and civil trials, experts are called to provide testimony involving science- or engineering-based technologies regarding such matters as police procedures, accident reconstruction, fire and arson analysis, handwriting, blood spatter patterns, DNA matches, and fiber composition. Pathologists and other medical experts are called, as are psychiatrists, psychologists, and social workers. Chemists, accountants, lawyers, and financial securities experts also provide expert testimony. As noted earlier, jury critics frequently argue that a jury composed of laypersons is not up to the task of evaluating the competence of the experts or the complex testimony that they give in court. Doctors have long held that juries should not decide medical malpractice cases because of the arcane issues involved in the practice of medicine. In England serious attempts, so far unsuccessful, have been made to abolish trial by jury in complex financial fraud cases.

Kutnjak Ivkovic, and Hans (2003) conducted tape-recorded interviews with 55 jurors who served in trials involving disputes about medical malpractice, work-place injuries, product liability, asbestos injuries, and motor vehicle accidents. On average, each trial had slightly over four testifying experts. Those authors found that rather than uncritically accepting expert opinion at face value, the jurors recognized that the experts were selected within an adversary process and from the outset regarded them with a critical eye. The jurors assessed the completeness and consistency of the testimony and evaluated it against their knowledge of related factors.

Fordham (2006) sat as an observer in a sample of Australian criminal trials. After the verdict, she conducted detailed interviews with the jurors, specifically focusing on how they understood the expert evidence. The interviews revealed that the jurors were very aware of potential biases of experts. They appreciated experts who were willing to alter their opinions in the face of new information presented during the trial; and they compared the congruence of the expert's opinion with other trial evidence. Fordham concluded that, generally speaking, jurors usually have a sophisticated view of the trial proceedings.

The Arizona Jury Project (see Vidmar and Hans, 2007), mentioned above, also collected written questions that civil jurors submitted to experts immediately at the conclusion of their testimony. In one case, the plaintiff claimed he had severe back and leg pain resulting from an automobile accident. As is not so infrequent in such claims that go to trial, this plaintiff had preexisting injuries and health problems. The treating physician and another physician testified for him regarding tests they performed and the prescribed treatments. Here are questions the jurors asked one of the medical experts:

Why [are there] no medical records beyond the two years prior to the accident? What tests or determination besides subjective patient's say-so determined [your diagnosis of] a migraine? What exact symptoms did he have regarding a migraine? Why no other tests to rule out other neurological problems? Is there a measurement for the amount of serotonin in his brain? What causes serotonin not to work properly? Is surgery a last resort? What is indothomiacin? Can it cause problems if you have prostate problems?

In another automobile injury case, questions to the plaintiff's accident reconstruction expert included the following:

Not knowing how she was sitting or her weight, how can you be sure she hit her knee? Would these factors change your estimate of 15 ft./sec. travel speed? If a body in motion stays in motion, and she was continuing motion from prior to the impact, how did this motion begin and what do you base this on? How tall is the person who sat in your exemplar car to reconstruct the accident and how heavy was he? What is the error in your 10mph estimate? Is the time of 50–70 milliseconds based on an estimate of the size of the dent? Do you conclude that the Olds was slowed and pushed to the left by the Lincoln and [if so] how would the plaintiff move to the right and forward?

The above examples support other findings indicating that jurors follow the evidence and are attentive to gaps in it.

Nevertheless, various studies confirm that many people have trouble with employing concepts of statistical probability that may form the basis of an expert's opinion (see Vidmar and Hans, 2007). DNA evidence, for example, depends on the statistical probability of a match with the defendant's DNA. Some simulation experiments have found that mock jurors tended to give inappropriate weight to such evidence, sometimes overvaluing it and sometimes undervaluing it.

A realistic jury simulation study conducted by Kaye et al. (2007) assessed jury comprehension of mitochondrial DNA evidence. Conducted over a period of several months and involving almost 500 persons called for jury duty, the subjects in the experiment viewed a videotape of a mock trial based on a bank robbery in which the defendant was linked to the crime through two human hairs found on a sweatshirt. Among other evidence, an FBI expert presented basic information about mitochondrial DNA. Jurors then heard conflicting expert opinions by an FBI analyst for the prosecution and a geneticist for the defense regarding the significance of DNA analysis of the two hairs. The FBI analyst estimated that only six men in the local geographical area of about 40,000 people could have the relevant DNA profile, whereas the defense expert estimated as many as 57 local men could have that DNA pattern. The jury deliberations were videotaped for subsequent analysis and the jurors also filled out questionnaires about their understanding of the issues. While some of the individual jurors showed susceptibility to fallacies in reasoning about probabilities, the results showed that overall the simulated juries demonstrated basic comprehension of the expert evidence. Many jurors could explain the technical terms and their relevance to the contested issues. As a group, the jurors did not appear to be overwhelmed by the prosecution evidence. Deliberations improved juror comprehension of the scientific issues.

F. Other complex trials

Statistics are not the only possible source of complexity in trials. Richard Lempert (1993) systematically examined details of twelve complex trials. The trials included corporate law violations, toxic torts involving injuries to many persons, conspiracies, stock manipulations, sexual harassment allegations, claims under antitrust laws, breaches of contract, and matters relating to the disclosure of trade secrets. In two cases, one involving highly technical evidence about patents and trade secrets and the other involving both epidemiological and hydrogeological testimony, the expert evidence was so complex and arcane, Lempert concluded, that it is likely that neither judges nor juries would have been able to properly understand it. However, in the remaining ten cases, Lempert decided that the evidence was not so esoteric that jurors would be confused by it and that there was no clear evidence that the jurors were confused in reaching their verdicts.

Another complexity problem involves what is called joinder. In some cases, a defendant is charged with multiple crimes and the issue is whether the defendant can obtain a fair trial if all charges are considered in a single trial rather than in separate trials of the individual charges. A number of simulation experiments, varying in verisimilitude to real trials, examined the effects of joinder (see Bordens and Horowitz, 1985). The basic research paradigm in the experiments was to compare the likely verdict when the defendant was tried alone on a single charge as opposed to being (a) tried on multiple charges or (b) tried with other defendants. The results across experiments showed rather consistently that joinder was prejudicial to the defendant. There are a number of possible explanations of the effect: jurors may be confused about which evidence relates to which charge or defendant; they may treat evidence relating to one specific charge or defendant as also being relevant to other charges or defendants; multiple charges may lead jurors to infer that a defendant has a disposition to crime. Additional research on issues of joinder is warranted. It should be noted that roughly similar issues arise in civil trials involving multiple plaintiffs or multiple defendants. There is also some relevant research on this subject (see Vidmar and Hans, 2007).

Dating back to the 1980s, certain long and complex fraud trials in England have caused critics to argue that jury trial should be abolished in favor of trial by judge alone. In 2006 a bill introduced into Parliament to do just that was defeated, but the topic remains controversial in England and Wales. Honess, Levi, and Charman (1998) conducted important simulation research bearing on jury competence in the highly publicized British "Maxwell fraud trial" that involved charges resulting from the loss of millions of pounds from company-run retirement funds. The four defendants were accused of conspiring to defraud the beneficiaries of the retirement funds. Despite enormous amounts of negative publicity about the defendants, they were acquitted after a lengthy trial. Many members of the public were dissatisfied with the verdict and felt the jury had gone astray.

Honess and his colleagues conducted their study some time after the Maxwell trial had taken place. Jury-eligible participants were interviewed to determine their recall of the case and then asked to participate in an experiment involving a six-hour video simulation of the trial. Actors portrayed the trial participants using verbatim transcripts and documents from the actual trial. The simulating jurors were interviewed at four points throughout the trial presentation. Honess et al. found that the degree of participants' factual recall of details of the Maxwell case had minimal influence on their judgments about the trial evidence as represented in the video re-enactment. In contrast, negative attitudes associated with the case did have an effect, but in a complicated and unexpected way. At the first interview point the judgments of participants with greater degrees of negative affect toward the Maxwell case were not significantly different than those of participants who held lesser negative affect. However, those with greater negative affective responses began to express reasoning favoring guilt at the end of the prosecution's case. This reasoning about guilt was maintained during and after the defense presentation. Honess et al. hypothesized that these jurors had withheld judgment at the early stages of evidence presentation because they were waiting for more evidence before reaching a decision, suggesting that the jurors were not preemptively deciding guilt but rather that the negative attitudes had led them to interpret the evidence using a prosecutorial mental framework.

Another English fraud trial, the 2003 so-called "Jubilee Line Case," involved charges of fraudulent undertakings given in relation to the construction of an extension to the London underground. The prosecution of the case before a jury involved six defendants, took almost two years, cost the British public over £25 million, and was terminated without a verdict after the prosecution announced that it would not contest a defense motion to discharge the jury. The main reason given for the termination was that the evidence had become too complex for a jury to comprehend.

Ordinarily, interviews with English jurors are legally proscribed, but because the trial was terminated without a verdict, Lloyd-Bostock (2007) was allowed to conduct extensive interviews with the dismissed jurors, both in a group session and then individually. Although the interviews took place approximately five months after the trial ended, the jurors exhibited considerable understanding of the evidence, especially when they were considered as a group. The jurors exhibited "impressive familiarity with the charges, issues and evidence." Some jurors reported that they took copious notes during the trial, submitted notes to the judge during the trial seeking clarification of testimony, and asserted that they did not have difficulty with technical language. The process of understanding was probably aided by the fact that the jurors were allowed to discuss the evidence with the other jurors during the trial, a conclusion similar to the Arizona Jury Project's finding that discussions between jurors during trial recesses aided understanding in more complex trials (Diamond et al., 2003).

In short, many studies using different methodologies have addressed the question of jury competence. Generally, the jury system has fared well in the research findings. One exception involves United States death penalty juries, but concerns about their fairness and competence have been ascribed in large part to the "death qualification" process by which otherwise qualified jurors are eliminated from jury service because they have serious reservations about the death penalty (see Vidmar and Hans, 2007, for a review of some of the extensive literature).

G. Methodological issues in jury research

As already mentioned, there have literally been hundreds of simulation experiments attempting to understand jury behavior. The important set of simulation studies by Pennington and Hastie (1991), discussed earlier, was used to develop the widely accepted "story model" of jury decision-making. In another example of useful simulation research, Elwork et al. (1982) obtained a videotape of an actual trial, and, after editing it for experimental purposes, those authors compared jurors' comprehension of the original jury instructions with instructions that were rewritten to increase layperson comprehension. The rewritten instructions improved comprehension. Other simulation studies, such as the one by Kaye et al. (2007) assessing responses to DNA evidence, have shed light on issues that could not otherwise be investigated.

Yet, the relevance of many simulation experiments to legal policy is problematic. The vast majority of studies in the literature involve college students, minimal trial information, and individual rather than group decision-making. These are serious problems if the goal of the study is to make meaningful statements bearing on legal policy. In thinking about the relevance of simulation research to legal policy it is useful to consider three types of validity (see Vidmar, 2008). *Internal validity* is the extent to which a study controls for extraneous variables that could confound assumptions about causal relationships between variables. Experimental simulation studies are specifically designed to do just that. *External validity* is the extent to which the results of studies can be generalized across settings and subject populations and times. Repeated replications of studies that differ in those variables are the way researchers reach conclusions about the robustness of experimental findings. *Ecological validity* is the degree to which experiments create conditions as they actually occur in the real world. Bornstein (1999) and Devine et al. (2001) reviewed decades of research in order to assess concerns about validity regarding matters such as the composition of mock juries (students versus non-student adults), the research setting (laboratory versus courtroom), the trial medium (written summaries versus more realistic trial materials), the trial elements (e.g., presence or absence of deliberation), dependent variables (dichotomous versus probability judgments), and the consequentiality of the task (e.g., making a hypothetical versus a real decision). Their reviews revealed that most published studies involved college students and minimal stimulus materials. Furthermore, relatively few of the experiments engaged the subjects in deliberation, instead examining their individual responses. These review articles highlight the obvious questions about the relevance of many simulation experiments to real world policy questions.

A series of experiments by Sunstein et al. (2002) designed to assess how civil juries decide punitive damage claims helps put the problems in stark relief. Those authors conducted experiments ultimately involving hundreds of non-student mock jurors; some studies involved individual decisions, but others involved deliberating groups. There was considerable similarity of results across the experiments, a finding consistent with external validity. Drawing on their aggregate results the authors concluded that juries are erratic and unreliable in awarding punitive damages and suggested that legal policy should be changed. Two high-profile decisions of lower courts approvingly cited the research.

However, a close examination of the findings revealed that that there were very major problems with the research (see Vidmar, 2004, for a detailed discussion). In many of the experiments the materials did not present a balanced picture of the evidence, creating problems of internal validity. At least equally important were the problems of ecological validity. Many of the stimulus materials used in the experiments to represent "trial evidence" consisted of as few as 13 sentences bearing on the amount to be awarded for punitive damages. Compare such materials to real trials in which jurors sit through days or weeks of evidence, first decide liability and compensatory damages, and then hear arguments from legal counsel from both sides, not to mention judicial instructions on the burden of proof, assessment of credibility and other evidence bearing on the reprehensibility of the defendant's conduct.

In short, despite the fact that the Sunstein et al. mock jury experiments demonstrated external validity in that they involved non-student adults and were replicated over similar artificial settings, the conditions under which they were conducted bore little resemblance to the conditions faced by actual jurors. For this reason, the studies had extremely poor ecological validity. Finally, the authors of the research ignored substantial bodies of archival data involving actual jury verdicts that were inconsistent with their findings. While the Sunstein et al.'s simulations are an extreme example, the "trial evidence" in many jury simulation experiments in the literature consists of no more than one or two pages of written materials. Under these conditions the fact that student samples and non-student samples produce similar results tells us very little about how laypersons make decisions in real legal settings.

Researchers have frequently noted the hypothetical nature of simulation decisions, but dismiss the problem as not researchable. However, Breau et al. (2007) carried out a preliminary experiment to examine issues of ecological validity. Law students were recruited to serve on panels to consider testimony that another student had violated the law school's examination honor code. Two of the panels were led to believe that they were part of a real jury deciding a real honor code case and two were told that they were participating in a mock jury experiment. With such a small sample the results could not be tested for statistical significance and so must be treated very cautiously; but they are, nevertheless, suggestive. The two "juries" that believed they were deciding a real case deliberated for 40 and 85 minutes, respectively, compared to the hypothetical juries that deliberated for 30 and 25 minutes. One "real" jury voted "not guilty" and the other "real" jury hung, whereas the two hypothetical juries voted "guilty." The "real" jury that voted "not guilty" recommended that the offending student should write a new memo on a different topic that would be graded by a different instructor and one of the hypothetical juries made a similar recommendation. However, one member of the other hypothetical jury recommended suspension for one semester, three members recommended the harshest sanction short of suspension, and one was undecided.

The Breau et al. study thus raises serious questions about many highly artificial simulation experiments.

In summary, simulation studies can be highly useful for developing theory, but caution flags need to be raised when the research lacks verisimilitude or is used as the basis for policy recommendations. Researchers need to consider whether their findings comport with other data such as archival material or interviews with actual jurors. More ecologically valid research is to be encouraged (see also Rozin, 2009). Additionally, researchers might better devote their efforts to qualitative studies involving observation of trials and subsequent systematic interview of jurors. The most extensive literature, involving interviews with hundreds of jurors over two decades, has been focused on death penalty juries as part of the Capital Punishment Project: in addition to the Sundby (1998) research, discussed above, see Bowers et al. (1998) and Fleury-Steiner (2004). Despite this precedent, relatively few attempts have been made to systematically interview jurors in non-capital trials. There are major legal obstacles to such interview research outside the United States, but in addition to the Fordham study discussed above, some jury interview research involving the possible effects of pre-trial publicity has been undertaken by Chesterman in Australia and by Cameron, Potter, and Young in New Zealand (chapters reporting some of their findings are contained in Vidmar, 2000). In contrast, the recently established jury system in Korea has been the subject not only of a number of simulation studies, but preliminary attempts are being made to compare the verdicts of the juries with the decisions of the trial judges and the outcomes of appellate reviews of the verdicts (see Lee, 2009).

H. The jury as a democratic institution

There is a good deal of writing about the jury as a democratic political institution (see Abramson, 1994; Vidmar and Hans, 2007). Yet, compared to the many studies devoted to investigating jury competence, empirical research on their political functions is sparse. Yet, several studies illustrate important aspects of these political functions.

MacCoun and Tyler (1988) assessed perceptions of the criminal jury. In a first study a telephone survey found that 97% of citizens supported the jury system and that juries were preferred to judges for making decisions of guilt or innocence. In a follow-up experiment students were asked to place themselves in the role of either the defendant or the victim in a case involving a crime that resulted in a mild or serious outcome. The experiment also involved variations of jury characteristics such as the voting rule (unanimity or majority) and the size of the jury (six or twelve persons). The study suggested trade-offs between procedural costs and crime seriousness. Specifically, when the crime resulted in a more serious outcome the respondents showed a preference for the thoroughness of deliberation provided by larger juries operating under a unanimity decision rule.

Kahan, Hoffman, and Braman (2009) conducted a study based upon the U.S. Supreme Court ruling in *Scott v. Harris*, 550 U.S. 372 (2007). In that case, a young driver, Harris, engaged police in a high-speed chase. A policeman, Scott, who subsequently argued that Harris was endangering lives of the public, rammed his police cruiser into Harris's car, causing it flip over an embankment. As a result of the crash Harris was rendered a quadriplegic. Harris sued Scott on the ground that the use of such deadly force was unreasonable. In overturning a lower court ruling that Harris was entitled to a jury trial on the issue of whether Scott acted reasonably in using deadly force to stop Harris, the Supreme Court took the unusual step of viewing *de novo* the police car videotapes of the chase (Scott was driving 73 miles per hour in a 55 mile-per-hour speed zone). All but one of the nine Justices concluded that it was "obvious" that Harris was posing an extreme danger to the public.

Kahan et al. (2009) put the Supreme Court's hypothesis about the "obviousness" of the danger to a test. They presented the video to a diverse sample of 1,350 citizens and asked a series of questions about their perceptions of the chase. Although a majority of the respondents in the study assessed the chase in a manner similar to the Supreme Court Justices, a significant minority assessed the police chase as not worth the risk to the public. Strikingly, the dissent of this minority of viewers was not random, but was associated with cultural, political, and other ideological variables. Persons who tended to see society as organized around hierarchical and individualistic values agreed with the Supreme Court majority, but persons whose values tended to be egalitarian and communitarian saw in the evidence a smaller risk to the public. While previous research has found differences between lay and judicial judgments about the reasonable person and other matters, these findings raise important issues about not only the relative virtues of juries versus judges in deciding such matters, but also about the need to have representative juries. Juries composed of persons with diverse values and perspectives are possibly more likely to have robust deliberations and more successfully fulfill the ideal of a democratically representative jury.

In his classic study, *Democracy in America*, published in 1835, Alexis De Tocqueville argued that the jury had a secondary effect of inculcating the jurors with understanding of laws and democratic values. As part of a broader project investigating deliberation and public participation, Gastil, Deess, and Weiser (2002) studied the effect of jury service on subsequent civic participation. They sampled 794 persons who had served as jurors in 110 criminal trials. Using public data, they gathered information about the jurors' voting history in prior general elections, a presidential primary election, and a special election about a new stadium. Controlling for voting behavior prior to jury service, Gastil et al. found that persons who had served on juries in more complex cases and on juries that engaged in more lengthy deliberations and reached verdicts were more inclined to engage in voting.

In a rare cross-cultural study of the effects of layperson participation on democratic attitudes, Fukurai (2007) surveyed a sample of Japanese citizens who served on its recently instituted Prosecutorial Review Commission, roughly equivalent to a common law grand jury. Fukurai further divided the Japanese sample into those whose service required deliberations versus those who did not require deliberations. He then compared the Japanese layperson responses with those of American citizens who had served on juries. The Japanese laypersons who had had deliberative experience were similar to their American jurors in reporting positive democratic views about their experiences. Fukurai concluded that such participation has the potential to increase public confidence in the criminal justice system. Thus, both Gastil et al. and Fukurai have produced findings supportive of De Toqueville's thesis about the effects of jury service on democratic institutions.

III. Mixed Tribunals

Mixed tribunals must be viewed in the context of legal procedure because an appreciation of the procedural context is critical in assessing the performance of mixed tribunals. Mixed tribunals are associated with what is commonly called inquisitorial procedure, as opposed to adversarial procedure, that is prevalent in common law systems (see Damaska, 1986). In adversarial procedure responsibility for developing evidence and arguments rests on the two contesting parties in the litigation with the judge acting as a neutral referee. Adversarial procedure is largely oral with the evidence being presented to the adjudicators by witnesses at trial. In contrast, inquisitorial procedure vests the major responsibility for investigation and development of evidence with trial judges; proceedings may be conducted primarily through written documents rather than oral testimony. Whereas common law jurors are conscripted from the general citizenry, lay participants in mixed tribunals are typically volunteers appointed by legal officials.

Books by Kutnjak Ivkovic (1999) and Sperlich (2007) provide details about these procedural differences. McKillop (1997) provides a fine case study of a mixed tribunal in a French murder case that illustrates in detail procedural differences between inquisitorial and adversary systems.

Jackson and Kovalev (2006–2007) surveyed lay adjudication in the 46 countries belonging to the Council of Europe and found variations in inquisitorial procedures from country to country. The authors presented a detailed questionnaire to legal experts within each country and assessed how specific issues were treated within each procedural model. The research carefully delineated the various histories and subsequent forms of lay participation. The authors found that twelve countries did not have any form of lay participation in their criminal justice systems.

In the remaining countries Jackson and Kovalev uncovered five models of lay adjudication. The continental jury model, which is derived from the Napoleonic Code, involves a modification of the English jury and is found in Austria, Belgium, Denmark, Malta, Norway, Russia, Spain, Sweden, and some Swiss cantons. Typically, these forums are reserved only for the most serious crimes. In the continental jury model the jurors render their decisions about guilt independently of the trial judges. The French collaborative court model involves a modification of the jury into a tribunal of three judges and nine laypersons who deliberate together. The German collaborative court (or "*schoeffen*" court) model is found in Austria, Bulgaria, Croatia, Czech Republic, Denmark, Estonia, Finland, Germany, Hungary, Latvia, Macedonia, Norway, Poland, Serbia and Montenegro, Slovakia, Slovenia, Sweden, Switzerland, and Ukraine. The German collaborative court model varies somewhat from country to country, but the main common characteristic is that the number of laypersons exceeds the number of professionals by only one. The expert assessor collaborative court model is found in Croatia, France, Germany, Iceland, and Norway. The assessors are not lawyers but specialists in some other area, such as pedagogy, medicine or engineering. In the pure lay judge (or "magistrate") model a panel of laypersons sitting alone decides the case. This model is reserved for less serious criminal offenses and is used in England, Wales, and Scotland, as well as in Italy, Northern Ireland, Russia, and France. In the United States, as mentioned previously, layperson magistrates also adjudicate minor law violations. The magistrate model will be considered separately below.

While the Jackson and Kovalev survey shows the scope of mixed tribunals, research on how they function in practice is sparse. The classic study of mixed tribunals was conducted by Casper and Zeisel (1972). Using methodology similar to that used in Kalven and Zeisel's study of American juries discussed previously, the authors persuaded judges in three German courts to provide details about 570 cases. The details included the nature and amount of information uncovered in the pre-trial inquisitorial proceedings, the extent to which the lay judges participated in questioning witnesses, and the tribunal's deliberations about both guilt and sentencing. Among other findings, Casper and Zeisel found that lay judges asked questions of witnesses in almost one half of the trials. The research also documented any disagreement between lay and professional judges at the beginning of deliberation and how such disagreement was resolved. The data indicated that the lay and professional judges often agreed on the issue of guilt at the outset, but that in instances of disagreement the view of the professional judges prevailed. When the lay judges disagreed with the professional judges on punishment the laypersons influenced the sentence in about 32% of cases. Casper and Zeisel concluded that, overall, the lay judges had only a small effect on the verdicts of the German courts.

Kami and Hamalainen (1992) conducted a study of lay judges in Finland and Sweden and reviewed other research on lay tribunals in Europe, including a subsequent study by Casper and Zeisel that included data on mixed tribunals in Poland and Austria. Their research included non-random surveys of lay and professional judges in order to assess differences in perceptions of law and facts. The research also included simulation experiments in which hypothetical cases were presented to professional judges, lay judges and students in order to further explore differences in approaches to law and facts. Additionally, Kami and Hamalainen seized upon changes in Swedish law that allowed the lay judges to outvote the professional judge. Using data on appealed cases they found that the agreement rate between the lay and professional judges was 95%.

As part of a study of Croation mixed tribunals Kutnjak Ivkovich (1999: 165–202) reviewed research literature bearing on 13 countries in Europe. The studies involved surveys and interviews. Kutnjak Ivkovich summarized the main conclusion to be drawn from these studies as follows:

> Previous studies consistently reported the low frequency of lay judges' participation and the small impact their participation had on the final product, the verdict. As may be expected, lay judges tended to be more active during deliberations than during trial. They were more likely to voice their opinion (to the point of disagreeing with the professional judge) when the discussion focused on the sentencing issues than when the discussion targeted the defendant's guilt (p. 200).

Kutnjak Ivkovich's very systematic research on Croatian mixed tribunals yielded a detailed description of the functioning of the tribunals. Croatia's Criminal Procedures Law provides for different sizes and composition of the tribunal depending on the seriousness of the offense. Lay judges also serve in civil trials. All Croatian citizens over 18 years of age are eligible to serve and they are elected by legislatures based on recommendations by the Minister of Justice. The lay judges serve only a few days per year and receive compensation; many have had past experience serving on the tribunals.

Kutnjak Ivkovich asked a large sample of professional judges, layperson judges, and lawyers to fill out questionnaires about the processes of decision-making in the mixed tribunals. Both professional and lay judges indicated that lay judges rarely disagreed with the professional judges. However, while the lay judges reported that they were active during deliberations, the professional judges reported that the lay judges played a lesser role and viewed them as contributing little during either the trial or the subsequent deliberations. Both professional judges and lawyers were skeptical of lay judges' ability to understand law but the lay judges reported that they did understand the evidence.

Machura (2007) conducted similar research with German mixed tribunals involving both civil and criminal matters. Administrative courts in Germany deal with public law matters, such as disputes over where a house can be built, public concern about night-time flights at an airport, or appeals by asylum seekers. Machura sent questionnaires to lay judges in a number of administrative courts in both West Germany and the former East Germany in order to assess differences, especially any arising from social-cultural factors from the socialist regime that had previously existed in East Germany. The questionnaire asked about participation rates during deliberations and included a number of procedural justice items. Machura found differences between East and West Germany and that when the lay judges perceived that the professional judges were prejudiced against them, they viewed the process as less fair. From his findings Machura concluded that when there were major power differences between the professional judges and the lay judges the intended democratic functioning of the tribunal was undermined.

A. Methodological issues

Simulation research such as that undertaken by Kami and Hamalainen may yield modest insights into lay tribunals, but there is a much greater need to undertake research similar to that of Casper and Zeisel's study in order to understand how lay judges perform their roles. That is, researchers should find ways to obtain data bearing on specific cases rather than surveys of the opinions of professional and lay judges about the general operation of the system. To be sure, Casper and Zeisel did not obtain data directly from the lay judges, but they did use indirect methods and case studies to form opinions about how laypersons performed. Questionnaires asking general questions seldom yield as much rich information as qualitative interviews or actual observation. Assuming no proscriptions against post-trial interviews, systematic qualitative research involving lay and professional judges about their interactions in specific cases could yield much greater insight about the functioning of mixed tribunals. Additional studies on how accused persons and the general citizenry see the role of lay judges as fitting into democratic justice would also be beneficial. Fukurai's (2007) study of Japanese laypersons serving on the Prosecutorial Review Commission, discussed earlier, though not without limitations, suggests a way to study this issue.

IV. Lay Magistrates

England and Wales have long depended on magistrates courts in which typical trials are presided over by three unpaid lay magistrates assisted by a law-trained clerk. The magistrates hear evidence, deliberate, and render decisions on guilt and punishment. Although their verdicts are potentially subject to review by higher courts, magistrates' decisions are similar to juries in terms of their autonomy of deliberation and decision-making. However, like judges, magistrates have the added duty of imposing criminal sentences.

Darbyshire (1997) drew attention to the fact that in England and Wales during 1995 proceedings were commenced in magistrates courts against roughly 1.93 million defendants, compared to 89,000 defendants in the Crown Courts, of whom approximately 20,700 were tried by jury. In short, approximately 95% of criminal proceedings were commenced in magistrates courts, and while many defendants eventually pleaded guilty, a defendant was approximately four times more likely to be tried by magistrates than by a jury. She further noted that changes in the law over recent years meant that some grave offenses that had previously been the preserve of Crown Courts were now tried in magistrates courts.

In an earlier study, McBarnet (1981) reported qualitative data on exchanges between the lay judges and accused persons, prosecutors and policemen in magistrates court proceedings. Her data indicated an often-informal process that violated legal norms of procedure during trials. Magistrates exhibited sarcasm or hostility toward the accused, took over cross-examination of witnesses, and made assumptions inconsistent with a presumption of innocence. She also noted that since no formal record of the proceedings was made, appeals against a magistrates court verdict were dependent on the magistrate stating the facts of the case to the higher court. McBarnet concluded that:

The law has created two tiers of justice, one which is geared in its ideology and generality at least to the structures of legality, and one which, quite simply and explicitly is not (p. 140).

Diamond (1990) undertook a study of magistrates courts in London. She used multiple methodologies to examine the sentencing decisions of magistrates: simulated cases, interviews, archival analyses, and systematic observations of trials. She found that magistrates were primarily middle, and upper class in background and predominantly middle-aged males who had political connections (perhaps this has changed in recent years). In a series of simulation experiments, the sentencing decisions of lay magistrates were compared to those of salaried, law-trained ("stipendiary") magistrates. The sentences rendered by the lay magistrates were generally somewhat more lenient. The simulation study results were supported by the archival analyses and by observations of sentencing hearings.

Lloyd-Bostock (2006) assessed the potential effects of changes made by the Criminal Justice Act 2003. That Act provided that both juries and magistrates could, in certain circumstances, hear evidence about a defendant's prior convictions. In a study of how jurors might respond to these changes, Lloyd-Bostock found that jurors were influenced by the conviction evidence. In most instances it increased jurors' perceptions of guilt. However, in some limited circumstances, such as when jurors learned of a dissimilar prior conviction, the evidence decreased assessments of the likelihood of guilt. Lay magistrates, some professionals argued, might not be as susceptible as jurors because, like judges, lay magistrates have experience with many cases and thus make decisions in a routine way.

To test this hypothesis, Lloyd-Bostock conducted a study in which magistrates were shown two sets of videos of criminal evidence, one relating to a case of handling stolen goods and the other to a case of indecent assault by a man on a woman. There were 16 versions of the two scenarios with various manipulations of the evidence. One version had no mention of a previous conviction and another mentioned good character. Other versions involved a previous conviction for an offense that was similar or dissimilar to the charge at trial and was either a recent or an old conviction. Among magistrates as well as jurors, a very small amount of information about a single past conviction was sufficient to evoke a "quite rich and potentially damaging stereotype" about defendants' fixed patterns of behavior. Old convictions had a greater influence on magistrates than on jurors, suggesting that magistrates tended to be inclined to see behavior patterns as fixed. Other data indicated that the judgments of magistrates as well as jurors treated the evidence as bearing on propensity, not credibility of the evidence. Lloyd-Bostock's findings appear similar to findings that American trial judges are just as susceptible as laypersons and other professionals to cognitive biases in a wide variety of decision-making settings (see, e.g., Wistrich et al., 2005).

Given the importance of magistrates courts to the system of criminal justice in England and Wales, more research on this institution is warranted. The same can be said of magistrates courts in Scotland and other countries. McBarnet's qualitative research in particular raises serious issues involving procedural and substantive justice that deserve further study.

V. JUSTICES OF THE PEACE

A study of Canadian justices of the peace by Doob, Baranek, and Addario (1991) found that in the various provinces of Canada, justices of the peace "can be seen to fill a bewildering variety of roles: buffering the public from the excesses of the state; keeping the bureaucracy of the criminal justice system moving; diverting routine or minor matters away from judges; serving as a resource to police agencies; and serving as a convenient stand-in for judges in remote communities" (p. 84).

These functions include filling out subpoenas; accepting guilty pleas in minor criminal offenses; swearing out an information; approving bail applications;

presiding at hearings in offenses not covered in the Criminal Code; and filling out arrest warrants and search warrants. A survey questionnaire involving justices of the peace throughout Canada documented perceptions of inadequate training, inadequate workplaces, lack of respect from others in the criminal justice system and attempts by police to intimidate them.

Provine (1981) researched non-lawyer judges in the United States. She pointed out that non-lawyers served in settings in district, town, village, county, city, municipal traffic, police, alderman's, mayors, magistrates, common pleas, surrogate orphan's probate, and justice courts, depending on the particular state. At the time of the research, there was a trend for members of the legal profession to assert non-lawyers in these positions were not competent to deal with legal questions that arose in their work. Nevertheless, a Google search shows that in 2009 substantial numbers of justices of the peace were fulfilling these judicial roles in Texas and a number of other states.

The studies of justices of the peace, such as that of Provine, have been largely descriptive. Research on how they actually function in practice, such as McBarnet's (1981), study of magistrates described above, would provide a good starting point.

VI. Laypersons in Other Legal Settings

In England, Scotland, and Wales laypersons serve on appeals tribunals involving various types of disputes, including those involving social security benefits. Baldwin, Wikeley, and Young (1992) visited 11 social security offices throughout the United Kingdom and interviewed both "adjudication officers," who made initial determinations of claims, and the layperson members of the tribunals that decided appeals from those initial determinations. They also observed appeal hearings and interviewed appellants. A principal finding was that rigid legal rules constrained the tribunals to being little more than rubber stamps for the decisions of the adjudication officers. Observations confirmed that layperson members were marginalized in other ways, particularly because the legally qualified chairmen frequently dominated the questioning of appellants and did not bother to allow the layperson members to ask supplementary questions during the hearings.

Meridith (2001) compared the relative performance of non-lawyers with lawyers who served on workers compensation boards in South Australia. Her criteria were the rates and success of appeals from their decisions. She concluded that non-lawyer decision-makers did as well as those with legal qualifications. However, her overall sample was small (n = 15), and no statistics were used.

Throughout the United States and Canada, laypersons serve as mediators of civil disputes that are filed in small claims courts. There is an extensive literature on these mediators that was reviewed by McEwen and Wissler (2002). Wissler (2002) systematically studied mediations in nine Ohio courts by means of questionnaires completed by mediators, litigating parties, and lawyers. Her research examined how the mediators functioned and the effectiveness of their efforts regarding the time and costs of resolution.

VII. Conclusion

This brief overview has centered on a number of settings in which laypersons participate as decision-makers in legal systems. In most of the areas, juries excepted, the corpus of research is undeveloped, especially with regard to evaluations of lay person performance. The review is limited to works published in English. Research published in other languages, to the degree that it exists (see, e.g., Kutnjak Ivkovich, 1999, for references), can certainly add to insights. More systematic research simply surveying the extent of layperson roles in different cultures and countries is needed, but studies of how laypersons actually perform in these roles are crucial. The different methodologies illustrated in this Chapter can be used to empirically assess that performance. With important exceptions one of the weaknesses in much of the research is that investigators have tended to rely on a single methodology when in fact multiple methodologies, including systematic qualitative research, would have added much greater insight to the subject under study. Multi-method studies should be strongly encouraged.

References

Abramson, J. (1994). *We the Jury: The Jury System and the Ideal of Democracy*, New York: Basic Books.

Baldwin, J., Wikeley, N., and Young, R. (1992). *Judging Social Security: The Adjudication of Claims for Benefit in Britain*, Oxford: Clarendon Press.

Blagg, H. (2008). *Crime Aboriginality and the Decolonization of Justice*, Annandale, New South Wales: Hawkins Press.

Bordens, K.S. and Horowitz, I.A. (1985). "Joinder of Criminal Offenses: A Review of the Legal and Psychological Literature," *Law and Human Behavior* 9(4): 339–53.

Bornstein, B.H. (1999). "The ecological validity of jury simulation research: is the jury still out?," *Law and Human Behavior* 23(1): 75–91.

Bowers, W.J., Sandys, M., and Steiner, D. (1998). "Foreclosed impartiality in capital sentencing; jurors' predispositions, attitudes and premature decision-making," *Cornell Law Review* 83: 1476–547.

Breau, D., Brook, B., and Alencar, A. (2007). " 'Mock' Mock Juries: A Field Experiment on the Ecological Validity of Jury Simulations," *Law and Psychology Review* 31: 77–92.

Casper, G. and Zeisel, H. (1972). "Lay Judges in the German Criminal Courts," *The Journal of Legal Studies* 1: 135–91.

Damaska, M.R. (1986). *The Faces of Justice and State Authority: A Comparative Approach to the Legal Process*, New Haven: Yale University Press.

Darbyshire, P. (1997). "An Essay on the Importance and Neglect of the Magistry," *The Criminal Law Review* 32(2): 627–43.

Devine, D.J., Clayton, L.D., Dunford, B.B., Seying, R., and Pryce, J. (2001). "Jury Decision Making: 45 Years of Empirical Research on Deliberating Groups," *Psychology, Public Policy, and Law* 7: 622–727.

Devine, D.J., Buddenbaum, J., Houp, S., Studebaker, N., and Stolle, D. (2009). "Strength of Evidence, Extraevidentiary Influence and the Liberation Hypothesis: Data from the Field," *Law and Human Behavior* 33: 136–48.

Diamond, S.S. (1990). "Revising Images of Public Punitiveness: Sentencing by Law and Professional English Magistrates," *Law and Social Inquiry* 15: 191–221.

Diamond, S.S., Vidmar, N., Rose, M., Ellis, L., and Murphy, B. (2003). "Juror Discussions During Trials: Studying an Arizona Innovation," *Arizona Law Review* 45: 1–81.

Doob, A.N., Baranek, P., and Addario, S. (1991). *Understanding Justice: A Study of Canadian Justices of the Peace*, Toronto: Center of Criminology.

Elwork, A., Sales, B., and Alfini, J. (1982). *Making Jury Instructions Understandable*, Charlottesville, VA: Michie Co.

Fleury-Steiner, B. (2004). *Jurors' Stories of Death: How America's Death Penalty Invests in Inequality*, Ann Arbor: University of Michigan Press.

Fordham, J. (2006). "Illuminating or Blurring the Truth: Jurors, Juries, and Expert Evidence," in B. Brooks-Gordon and M. Freeman (eds.), *Law and Psychology*, New York: Oxford University Press.

Fukurai, H. (2007). "The rebirth of Japan's petit quasi-jury and grand jury systems: a cross-national analysis of legal consciousness and the lay participatory experience in Japan and the U.S.," *Cornell International Law Journal* 40: 315–54.

Gastil, J., Deess, E.P., and Weiser, P. (2002). "Civic Awakening in the Jury Room: A Test of the Connection Between Jury Deliberation and Political Participation," *Journal of Politics* 64: 585–95.

Hans, V.P. (2008). "Jury Systems Around the World," *Annual Review of Law and Social Science* 4: 275–97.

Honess, T.M., Levi, M., and Charman, E.A. (1998). "Juror Competence in Processing Complex Trial Information: Implications from a Simulation of the Maxwell Trial," *Criminal Law Review* 763–73.

Ianni, R. (1990). *Task Force on Paralegals*, Toronto: Ontario Ministry of the Attorney General.

Jackson, J.D. and Kovalev, N.P. (2006–2007). "Lay Adjudication and Human Rights in Europe," *Columbia Journal of European Law* 13: 83–123.

Kahan, D.M., Hoffman, D.A. and Braman, D. (2009). "Whose Eyes are You Going to Believe? Scott v. Harris and the Perils of Cognitive Illiberalism," *Harvard Law Review* 122: 837–906.

Kalven, H. Jr. and Zeisel, H. (1966). *The American Jury*, Boston: Little, Brown.

Kami, H. and Hamalainen, M. (1992). *Lawyers and Laymen on the Bench: A Study of Comparative Legal Sociology*, Helsinki: Suomalainen Tiedeakatemia.

Kaye, D.H., Hans, V.P., Dann, B.M., Farley, E., and Albertson, S. (2007). "Statistics in the Jury Box: How Juries Respond to Mitochondrial DNA Match Probabilities," *Journal of Empirical Legal Studies* 4: 797–834.

Kovalev, N.P. (2004). "Lay Adjudication Of Crimes in the Commonwealth of Independent States: An Independent and Impartial Jury or a 'Court of Nodders'?," *Journal of East European Law* 11: 123–57.

Kutnjak Ivkovich, S.K. (1999). *Lay Participation in Criminal Trials: The Case of Croatia*, Lanham, MD: Austin and Winfeld Publishers.

Kutjnak Ivkovich, S.K. and Hans, V.P. (2003). "Jurors' Evaluations of Expert Testimony: Judging the Messenger and the Message," *Law and Social Inquiry* 28: 441–82.

Lee, J. (2009). "Getting Citizens Involved: Civil Participation in Judicial Decision-Making in Korea," *East Asia Law Review* 4: 177–206.

Lempert, R.O. (1993). "Civil Juries and Complex Cases: Taking Stock after Twelve Years," in R. Litan (ed.), *Verdict: Assessing the Civil Jury System*, Washington, DC: Brookings Institute.

Lloyd-Bostock, S. (2006). "The Effects of Lay Magistrates of Hearing that the Defendant is of "Good Character", Being Left to Speculate, or Hearing that he has a Previous Conviction," *Criminal Law Review* 189–212.

Lloyd-Bostock, S. (2007). "The Jubilee Line Jurors: does their Experience Strengthen the Argument for Judge-Only Trial in Long and Complex Fraud Cases?," *Criminal Law Review* 255–73.

MacCoun, R.J. and Tyler, T.R. (1988). "The Basis of Citizens' Perceptions of the Criminal Jury: Procedural Fairness, Accuracy, and Efficiency," *Law and Human Behavior* 12: 333–52.

Machura, S. (2007). "Lay Assessors of German Administrative Courts: Fairness, Power–Distance Orientation, and Deliberation Activity," *Journal of Empirical Legal Studies* 4: 331–63.

McBarnet, D.J. (1981). *Conviction: Law, State and the Construction of Justice*, London: Macmillan Press Ltd.

McEwen, C. and Wissler, R. (2002). "Finding Out If It Is True: Comparing Mediation and Negotiation Through Research," *Ohio State Law Journal* 2002: 131–42.

McKillop B. (1997). "Anatomy of French Murder Case," *American Journal of Comparative Law* 45(3): 527–83.

Meredith, F. (2001). "How Would You Know, You're Not a lawyer: Decision-Making in a Merit Review Tribunal," Journal of Judicial Administration 10: 149–65.

Mestitz, A. and Ghetti, S. (2005). *Victim-Offender Mediation with Youth Offenders in Europe*, New York: Springer.

North Carolina Magistrates Association (2009). Available at <http://www.aoc.state.nc.us/magistrate/magistrate.htm>.

Pennington, N. and Hastie, R. (1991). "A Cognitive Theory of Juror Decision-Making: The Story Model," *Cardozo Law Review* 13: 519–56.

Provine, D.M. (1981). "Persistent Anomaly: The Lay Judge in the American Legal System," *Justice System Journal* 6: 28.

Robbennolt, J. (2002). "Determining Punitive Damages: Empirical Insights and Implications for Reform," *Buffalo Law Review* 50: 103–203, 158.

Rozin, P. (2009). "What Kind of Research Should we Publish, Fund and Reward? A Different Perspective," *Perspectives on Psychological Science* 4: 435–39.

Sasahara, K. (2009). "Juries return to Japanese justice in Katsuyoshi Fujii trial," *London Times* (Aug 4), available at <http://www.timesonline.co.uk/tol/news/world/asia/article6737305.ece>.

Sperlich, P. (2007). *The East German Social Courts: Law and Popular Justice in a Marxist-Leninist Society*, Westport, CT: Praeger Publishing.

Sundby, S. (1998). "The Capital Jury and Absolution: The Intersection of Trial Strategy, Remorse and the Death Penalty," *Cornell Law Review* 83: 1557–98.

Sunstein, C., Hastie, R., Payne, J., Schkade, D., and Viscus, K.W. (2002). *Punitive Damages: How Juries Decide*, Chicago: University of Chicago Press.

Taragin, M., Willett, L., Wilczek, A., Trout, R., and Carson, J. (1992). "The Influence of Standard of Care and Severity of Injury on the Resolution of Medical Malpractice Claims," *Annals of Internal Medicine* 117: 780–84.

Vidmar, N. (1995). *Medical Malpractice and the American Jury: Confronting the Myths About Jury Incompetence, Deep Pockets, and Outrageous Damage Awards*, Ann Arbor: University of Michigan Press.

Vidmar, N. (2000). *World Jury Systems*, Oxford: Oxford University Press.

Vidmar, N. (2002). "Juries and Lay Assessors in the Commonwealth: A Contemporary Survey," *Criminal Law Forum* 13: 385–407.

Vidmar, N. (2004). "Experimental Simulations and Tort Reform: Avoidance, Error and Overreaching," in Sunstein et al. "Punitive Damages," *Emory Law Journal* 53: 1359–403.

Vidmar, N. (2008). "Civil Juries in Ecological Context: Methodological Implications for Research," in B.H. Bornstein et al. (eds.), *Civil Juries and Civil Justice*, 35–65.

Vidmar, N. and Hans, V.P. (2007). *American Juries: The Verdict*, New York: Prometheus Books.

Whonnock, K. (2008). "Aboriginal courts in Canada," available at <http://www.scowinstitute.ca/library/documents/Aboriginal_Courts.pdf>.

Wistrich, A., Guthrie, C., and Rachlinski, J. (2005). "Can Judges Ignore Inadmissible Information? The Difficulty of Deliberately Disgregarding," *University of Pennsylvania Law Review* 153: 1251–341.

Wissler, R. (2002). "Court-contested Mediation in General Civil Cases," *Ohio State Law Journal* 17: 641.

27

EVIDENCE LAW

GARY EDMOND AND
DAVID HAMER

I. Introduction

"Evidence law," as a "subject suitable to be treated as a unified field of regulation and of study," is a product of the Anglo-American adversarial tradition (Damaška,

1997: 109). Continental civil law systems have fewer rules of evidence, and these tend to be associated with specific bodies of substantive law. While Anglo-American evidence law is broadly accepted as a relatively discrete domain, it is generally viewed as "labyrinthine" and "dishevelled," "largely ununified and scattered, existing for disparate and sometimes conflicting reasons...a mixture of astonishing judicial achievements and sterile, inconvenient disasters" (Damaška, 1997: 10–11; Heydon, 1984: 3).

There are many unanswered questions about evidence law, concerning its historical development, its various purposes, and the interrelation between its diverse components and other areas of legal and non-legal practice. Most, if not all, invite empirical inquiry. And yet, notwithstanding that evidence law is itself concerned with evidence and proof and is generally supposed to have developed in a "rationalist tradition" (Twining, 2006: 75), legal practice and evidence scholarship have been remarkably indifferent, and even hostile, to empirical study and evidence-based proposals for reform. Political expediency and the experience of legal practitioners, especially the judiciary, appear to be more important than scholarly attempts to understand evidence law in terms of its legal and social context(s).

Rather than providing a comprehensive account of empirical studies pertaining to evidence law, our goal here is to present a brief review and contemporary response to several contrasting strands of recent empirical work. We begin by setting the scene with an outline of the scope and rationale of evidence law.

II. Evidence Law in the "Rationalist Tradition"

A. Scope of evidence law

To varying degrees evidence law regulates the admissibility and presentation of evidence and fact-finding at trial. The trial is a highly formalized system of empirical enquiry, operating within a prescribed procedural framework. In a jury trial, the jury is responsible for fact-finding while the judge determines the applicable law. In the absence of a jury the judge is responsible for legal *and* factual decisions. Jury trials are becoming increasingly rare, though a notional bifurcation between the tribunal of law and tribunal of fact remains.

In the adversarial tradition the parties identify the areas of factual dispute, and decide what evidence to make available to the court. At trial the plaintiff or prosecutor presents her case first, and then, if there is a case to answer, the defendant makes his case. Most evidence takes the form of witness responses to questions directed by the parties, though the traditional preference for oral evidence is in decline, as documentary evidence and "paper trials" become more prevalent, most conspicuously in civil litigation without juries. Those few disputes which are not abandoned or negotiated are generally litigated through a single continuous trial. While jury decisions, incorporating factual reasoning and the application of law to facts, are left unexplained, in many jurisdictions judges provide reasons for interlocutory decisions and their verdicts.

The trial judge should only admit evidence that is relevant to a fact in issue and survives exclusionary rules, such as those pertaining to hearsay, opinion, bad character, propensity, and so on. Evidence that is otherwise admissible may nevertheless be excluded as a matter of judicial discretion, for example, due to the risk of unfair prejudice to the defendant, or the public policy against obtaining evidence in certain ways (such as through physical coercion). Litigants, witnesses, and interested parties may also be able to prevent the admission of evidence by the exercise of legal professional privilege, the privilege against self-incrimination, and public interest immunity.

Once all of the evidence has been tendered, the judge will instruct the jury as to how it can be used. In a judge-only trial interlocutory decisions and instructions often form part of the written judgment. While evidence law is concerned primarily with admissibility rather than weight, some types of evidence—such as eyewitness identification and the testimony of prison informants—give rise to special concerns and the fact-finder will be directed to exercise special caution. The trial judge also instructs the jury on the burden of proof. Generally, the state (or prosecution) must prove a defendant's guilt beyond reasonable doubt, and a civil plaintiff must prove liability on the balance of probabilities (or preponderance of evidence).

Appeals are frequently focused on the (mis)application of rules of evidence (and practice), usually the admission of inadmissible evidence and/or the exclusion of admissible evidence. Appeals on matters of fact are more restricted, though possible where the evidence does not support the verdict or some new (or "fresh") evidence emerges after the verdict or appeal.

B. Rationale of evidence law

Evidence law, as the foregoing discussion indicates, consists of a mass of rules and exceptions, many of which confer choices, discretions or require particular actions. Whether they can be coherently accommodated within a single theoretical framework is open to question. Most scholars have viewed evidence law as being concerned with "rational methods of determining questions of fact," in which a central goal is to "maximize accuracy in fact-determination" (Twining, 2006: 76). Jurists have debated how accuracy is best achieved, and the relative weight to be assigned to sometimes competing goals—such as efficiency, due process, and accuracy—though, these debates have been conducted almost entirely within this shared rationalist tradition.

One major ongoing debate concerns freedom of proof (Twining, 2006: 43–4; Stein, 2005: 107–16). Factual inquiries in other spheres of endeavor are not governed by formal rules, so why are legal disputes governed by rules of evidence? In the Anglo-American legal tradition evidence law (along with the choices and discretions it confers) now exerts far greater influence on practice than in most other legal traditions (Damaška 1997: 19–20; cf. Gluckman, 1955), routinely excluding evidence on various grounds. As early as the turn of the nineteenth century Jeremy Bentham (1843: VII, 24) forcefully opposed this approach: "Evidence is the basis of justice: to exclude evidence is to exclude justice."

Various justifications have been offered for Anglo-American exclusionary rules. One is provided by the "best evidence" rationale (e.g., Gilbert, and Nance)—encouraging the parties to uncover and provide stronger alternatives to the excluded evidence. Exceptions to exclusionary rules are frequently grounded in necessity—particularly the absence of alternative evidence. But this reveals a potential weakness with handing responsibility for gathering and presenting evidence to the parties. Understandably, parties consider utility as well as reliability. Why then are parties afforded so much control? This freedom reflects the Anglo-American perception of the trial, not only as a vehicle for the pursuit of truth and justice, but also as a means of socially legitimate conflict resolution (Damaška, 1997: 110–11; Tyler, 1990).

Another common explanation for exclusionary rules focuses on the position of the jury as fact-finder (e.g., Thayer, 1898 and Wigmore, 1940). Evidence is excluded because of the danger that the jury will *improperly* value it. This, of course, immediately raises supplementary concerns. If lay juries cannot be trusted with the evaluation of evidence, then why should they be used as fact-finders? Persistence with the jury might suggest it serves several functions, including a celebrated form of participatory democracy and a means to disseminate social norms (Damaška, 1997: 29). However, the jury's ability to handle complex evidence and the effects of popular beliefs and culture (exemplified in high-rating television shows such as "CSI: Crime Scene Investigation") remain controversial (Cole and Dioso-Villa, 2009).

Both the jury's role and the scope of exclusionary rules have tended to diminish over time. The general trend has been in the direction of free proof. However, in recent years several scholars have resisted this trend, either questioning the attribution of some putatively proper value to the evidence (e.g., Edmond) or seeking to demonstrate the importance of values other than accuracy (Ho, 2008; Stein, 2005: 133).

III. DIVERSE EMPIRICAL STUDIES

Empirical research is being undertaken in many areas of evidence law. Perhaps the most influential body of work has been directed toward eyewitness evidence (e.g., identification evidence), in part, perhaps, because it involves a neat factual issue with few normative complications (Park and Saks, 2006: 960, 973).

Experimental studies on eyewitness memory and testimony illustrate the potential value of empirical studies to the practice of investigations, prosecutions and appeals. Of scholarly interest for more than a century, from the 1970s psychologists, such as Elizabeth Loftus and Gary Wells, began to conduct systematic experiments on the ability of people to remember things, particularly past events and the identity of persons of interest. Subsequent research focused on how the conditions of observation and investigative processes might influence (and compromise) memory and on ways of improving investigative procedures so as to minimize risks of contamination, suggestion, and displacement.

This research has exerted a positive influence on the ways police, trial and appellate courts respond to identification evidence, although the substantial and convergent results of numerous experimental studies have not been fully implemented (Park and Saks, 2006: 960–4). Most jurisdictions routinely allow investigators and others to subvert protections designed to enhance the reliability of eyewitness testimony, and retain practices and directions that are antiquated in terms of empirical research and mainstream academic consensus (Wells and Quinlivan, 2009). Further, in many jurisdictions, psychologists are not permitted to explain to fact-finders the general problems with identification evidence or known problems with particular practices or specific circumstances. And yet research on wrongful convictions demonstrates that even in sexual assault cases, where the eyewitness often has a relatively good opportunity to observe the offender at close proximity, mistaken eyewitness identification is notorious (see Figure 3).

The reluctance to engage with empirical legal studies is an issue to which we will return. In the remainder of this section we report on research in three domains more fraught than eyewitness memory, namely hearsay, expert evidence, and probabilistic reasoning. The studies discussed below illustrate great diversity in empirical research styles, the types of scholars involved, the mix with theory and data, the socio-political implications, and the scope the research creates for intervention and change.

A. The exclusion and admission of hearsay

Ordinarily, witnesses give sworn testimony about their observations, and are available for cross-examination. The hearsay witness, however, testifies as to what

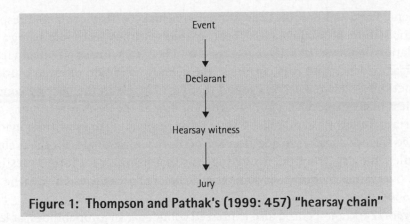

Figure 1: Thompson and Pathak's (1999: 457) "hearsay chain"

someone else (the "declarant") has said about her observations. Relative to ordinary evidence, hearsay evidence involves at least one additional step, making the fact-finder more remote from the event under consideration (Figure 1). The traditional bases for exclusion are that the declarant's out-of-court statement is not under oath and the declarant is unavailable for cross-examination.

Damaška (1997: 1), a comparativist, describes the hearsay rule as "so bizarre [as to] occupy one of the most forbidding corners of the entire Anglo-American legal structure." The stringency of the historical rule has been tempered by numerous exceptions, but these have added complexity to legal practice. The modern rule, as Rakos and Landsman (1992: 668) report, "remains an amalgam of concerns about juror competence, cross-examination, and fairness."

Most of the empirical work on hearsay has been carried out by psychologists. Following Hugo Munsterberg's, *On the Witness Stand* (1908), Hutchins and Slesinger (1928) drew upon the psychological literature to question the rule's scientific legitimacy. However, with few exceptions, only in the last two decades have experimental psychologists and lawyers approached hearsay rules and evidence in ways that transcend historical and doctrinal approaches or attempts to make extant psychological knowledge accessible to a legal audience (McGough, 1999: 487). Here, we review recent experimental research relating to mock juror assessment of hearsay evidence and related work focused on the hearsay evidence of children.

1. *Mock juror responses to hearsay evidence*

The first experimental studies endeavored to determine whether jurors overvalue hearsay evidence. In the early 1990s, Rakos and Landsman systematically manipulated the strength of hearsay testimony across versions of a trial transcript pertaining to a prosecution for theft and compared the mock juror responses. They concluded that the "mere introduction of hearsay testimony may not disproportionately influence juror decisions" (Rakos and Landsman, 1992: 664).

Miene, Park, and Borgida drew similar conclusions. They compared responses to combinations of circumstantial, hearsay and eyewitness testimony using a video simulation of a theft trial. The eyewitness and hearsay witness provided virtually identical evidence, and participants in the hearsay condition received cautionary instructions. These researchers found that participants in the hearsay condition were less likely to produce a guilty verdict and rated the hearsay testimony as less important, influential, and reliable than those responding to eyewitness evidence. This led the investigators to question one of the major rationales for the exclusionary rule: "the data from this study suggests that hearsay as a form of testimony is not overvalued by jurors, as some legal scholars have suggested" (Miene et al., 1992: 699).

Kovera, Park, and Penrod also expressed confidence in juror abilities, at least in relation to hearsay. Their mock jurors were "more sceptical of the value and reliability of hearsay testimony than of eyewitness testimony" and, further, gave more weight to hearsay testimony when there was a short delay (one day) as opposed to a longer delay (one week) (Kovera et al., 1992: 719). However, these mock jurors, also exposed to eyewitness identification evidence, were apparently insensitive to its limitations, particularly the corrosive effects of delay.

In contrast, Paglia and Schuller (1998) formed a less favorable view of juror reasoning. Participants in their experiments used hearsay evidence in ways that were inconsistent with judicial instructions included in the audio recording of a mock trial. Regardless of their form and timing, cautionary instructions about prosecution hearsay evidence exerted little discernible impact on the decisions. In an earlier study, focused on exculpatory hearsay provided through an expert witness, Schuller (1995: 359) found that the participants had difficulty ignoring hearsay evidence even when instructed to do so.

2. *Persuasiveness and reliability of children's statements*

A prominent strand of hearsay research focuses on out-of-court declarations by children. This type of hearsay, common where sexual assault is alleged, is of interest for a number of reasons. Early reports may be valuable as the memory of children is especially vulnerable to influence and degradation. Concerns also arise about child complainants being traumatized by testifying in court in the presence of the alleged perpetrator (Buck et al., 2004). More broadly, there is widespread social concern about pedophilia, but relatively low rates of complaint, prosecution, and conviction. In this environment, many jurisdictions have made special provision to admit the out-of-court statements of children, and researchers have sought to understand their potential effects (McGough, 1999).

Initially research focused on the believability of hearsay evidence and whether jurors might convict in cases of alleged sexual assault where the child complainant does not testify. In an experiment using a fictional summary of a child sexual assault trial, Golding, Sanchez, and Sego found that the child complainant's testimony was considered more believable than the child's complaint presented as hearsay. Nevertheless, the hearsay evidence seemed to influence "conviction" decisions and the authors concluded that "it may *not* be necessary for the alleged victim to testify on her own behalf for the defendant to be judged culpable" (Golding et al., 1997: 318).

Subsequent research considered the identity and status of the hearsay witness. Using a "highly realistic" video of a sexual assault trial, Ross, Lindsay, and Marsil concluded that the persuasiveness of child testimony in hearsay form depended upon the identity of the hearsay witness. Apart from one condition, where the hearsay witness was the mother of the complainant—embroiled in a "heated divorce" with the alleged perpetrator—the child's testimony was "significantly less likely to produce 'guilty votes'" than the evidence of the mother, the child's doctor and teacher (Ross et al., 1999: 450–1). Studying the effects of the ages of the complainant and the hearsay witness, Golding, Alexander, and Stewart (1999) found that mock jurors split along gender lines, with women generally more likely to accept the hearsay evidence of assault.

So far, the studies in this subsection have focused on the persuasiveness of hearsay evidence. Another strand is concerned with reliability and the competence of jurors. Pathak and Thompson (1999) sought to address a limitation with the studies by Rakos and Landsman (1992), Miene et al. (1992), and Kovera et al. (1992). These earlier studies had concluded that "hearsay is unlikely to be overvalued," yet they did not include an "objective or normative standard against which to compare [mock] jurors' evaluations." Pathak and Thompson sought to test "people's inferences about the reliability of hearsay evidence in circumstances that allowed the actual reliability of the evidence to be objectively verified" (1999: 373). They contrived a situation where they covertly controlled a (child) witness's experiences of a mock janitor's behavior and elicited an account through questioning.

Following a complaint, children are usually interviewed by social workers, police, or other professionals. Pathak and Thompson's experiments considered how hearsay is evaluated depending on whether the child is interviewed in a suggestive or neutral manner. They concluded that mock jurors failed to take sufficient account of suggestive questioning:

Although the videotaped "hearsay witnesses" commented on the suggestiveness of the interrogations with the child, the "jurors" did not realize that the suggestive interrogations had a greater influence on children's reports than the neutral interrogations (Pathak and Thompson, 1999: 381).

Where there is no video or audio recording, the hearsay testimony of the interviewer, along with any notes, may be the only "record" of such exchanges. As Warren and Woodall (1999: 356) explain, "to properly evaluate a child's statements presented through hearsay, jurors and fact finders need to hear not only what the child said (the gist of the interview), but how it was said (a verbatim account including spe-cific questions and answers)." They found that while interviewers recalled the gist of interviews accurately, they incorrectly recounted the use of open-ended questions even when they made extensive use of specific and leading questions. Further, "[e]ven immediately after an interview, important content was omitted from hearsay accounts, and the majority of the verbatim information (specific wording and content of questions and answers) was lost" (Warren and Woodall, 1999: 369). Their conclusion: "asking adults to recreate the structure of their conver-sations or interviews with children after the fact (i.e. during courtroom testimony) is risky" (ibid: 365).

These preliminary results prompted further investigation. Warren, Nunez, Keeney, Buck, and Smith compared the impact on mock jurors of: (1) a video of an interview with a child; (2) the interviewer providing a verbatim account of the inter-view; and (3) the interviewer providing the gist of the interaction. Participants rated the credibility of the adult gist witness "higher than that of the verbatim witness or child witness, and the verbatim witness was rated as significantly more credible than the child" (Warren et al., 2002: 852; cf. Golding et al., 1997). Gist evidence was perceived as less suggestive, more spontaneous and more open-ended. Counter-intuitively, the greater the displacement of the interview from the testimony, the more persuasive it seems to have been (Warren et al., 2002: 850–1). Results such as these led Buck, Warren, and Brigham to suggest that the use of video or a transcript would provide "a better compromise between protecting the child and the rights of the defendant than the use of testimony by a hearsay witness" (Buck et al., 2004: 618–20).

Finally, one of the most recent studies examined "the veracity of children's accu-rate, unintentionally false, or intentionally false eyewitness reports" (Goodman et al., 2006: 368). Like the study by Pathak and Thompson, it was undertaken in cir-cumstances where the child's experience it was controlled. Young children reported being touched on the stomach, nose, or neck by a "defendant." Some children who had not been touched during the play session were instructed to falsely claim that they had been. Comparisons were drawn between mock juror responses to live tes-timony, video of forensic interviews with a social worker, and the social worker tes-tifying about what the child had said during the interview.

The conclusions might be considered disconcerting:

First, this study demonstrates, quite provocatively, that children coached to lie can main-tain that lie in the face of repeated questions. In fact, children who were instructed to "fool" the interviewer (and the others in the mock trial) were often more consistent in their claims than children who really had been touched.... Second, our results indicate that adults, when faced with the task of determining whether unauthorized touching of a child occurred, were poor at distinguishing whether a particular child was lying or telling the truth. Furthermore, adults' abilities were neither helped nor hindered, for the most part, by seeing the child live or on videotape, or by hearing a social worker recount what the child said.... Third, [mock] jurors relied on predictable aspects of the children's accounts when making judgments about the veracity of the allegations...jurors tend to use witness consistency as an indicator of accurate statements. However, ...ironically it was the liars—not the truth-tellers—who were more consistent, particularly in the two hearsay conditions (Goodman et al., 2006: 390–1).

B. Expert opinion evidence

Opinion evidence is also subject to exclusion. As far as practically possible, witnesses should describe their sensory perceptions in concrete factual terms, without the overlay of interpretation or opinion. A very important exception to this exclusionary orientation is opinion evidence provided by experts. Where, by reason of "specialized knowledge," a witness can provide a relevant opinion that is beyond the ken of the average juror, that opinion may be admissible.

Until quite recently the most important empirical work on experts was primarily qualitative or historical (e.g., Jasanoff, Jones, and Golan). Case studies, and a few surveys, examined the roles of expert evidence in public inquiries (e.g., Wynne), litigation clusters (e.g., Schuck, Green, and Sanders); miscarriages of justice (e.g., Nobles and Schiff; Dwyer, Neufeld, and Scheck; and Gross); civil litigation (e.g., Shuman, Champagne, and Whittaker); and civil justice procedures such as court-appointed experts and concurrent evidence (e.g., Cecil and Willging, and Edmond). Scholars, such as Monahan and Walker, were influential in documenting the legal uses of social scientific evidence. Empirical research, particularly quantitative work, has increased in recent years as longstanding concerns about partisanship, expense, comprehension and reliability have become more prominent, particularly in response to social and legal developments in the United States.

1. *Admissibility decision-making in the United States*

One important strand of empirical research has focused on the impact of the U.S. Supreme Court's *Daubert v. Merrell Dow Pharmaceuticals, Inc.* (1993) decision. *Daubert* was an appeal over the admissibility standard for expert evidence under the Federal Rules of Evidence (1975). There, the Court explained that scientific evidence must be both "relevant and reliable" and emphasized the trial judge's gate keeping responsibility. The majority provided four criteria to help trial judges determine the *reliability* of scientific evidence. The criteria are whether the theory or technique: (1) has been tested (referring to Karl Popper's notion of "falsifiability"); (2) has been published and/or peer-reviewed; (3) has a known or potential rate of error; and (4) is "generally accepted" in the relevant specialist community. The last of these was drawn from *Frye v. United States* (1923).

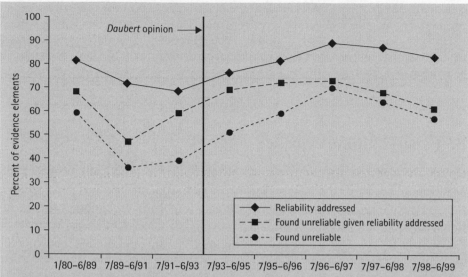

Figure 2 Frequency with which reliability was addressed and evidence was found unreliable.

Reprinted with permission from Dixon and Gill (2002: 273).

In the aftermath of *Daubert*, Dixon and Gill examined 399 decisions issued in civil proceedings between 1980 and 1999. Starting in the early 1990s the number of challenges to the reliability and admissibility of expert evidence began to rise (Figure 2). They concluded that the "standards for reliability have tightened" and judges "have become more watchful gatekeepers" against expert evidence proffered by plaintiffs.

The number of successful challenges began to decline after 1996–1997 which Dixon and Gill thought might be attributable to changes in the behavior of lawyers and parties as they gradually "tailored the evidence... to the new standards" (Dixon and Gill, 2002: 299).

These findings were generally consistent with the results of investigations by Krafka et al. (2002). These scholars surveyed federal district court judges in 1991 (responses = 335) and 1998 (responses = 303) about their most recent experience with expert evidence in a civil case. More judges excluded expert evidence in 1998 (41% of cases) than in 1991 (25%). There was also an increased use of pre-trial admissibility hearings (that became known as *Daubert* hearings). Just over half of the judges reported using pre-trial hearings in 1991 whereas more than three-quarters reported using *Daubert* hearings in 1998 (p. 327).

Interestingly, Krafka et al. found that the actual *Daubert* criteria did not seem to play an important role in these developments:

Judges who excluded testimony in the recent survey did so most often because it was not relevant, the witness was not qualified, or the testimony would not have assisted the trier of fact. These reasons are similar to the reasons most frequently cited by judges in 1991, and they do not reflect the factors cited in *Daubert* (Krafka et al., 2002: 330).

Further insights into the impact of *Daubert* were provided by Cheng and Yoon (2005). They examined the rate at which defendants removed cases from state to federal courts in tort and product liability suits—which are usually dependent on expert evidence. *Daubert* is binding on all federal courts, but only some state courts. A higher rate of removal from non-*Daubert* states (e.g., *Frye* jurisdictions) than from *Daubert* states would suggest that defendants thought they had a greater chance of excluding plaintiffs' expert evidence under *Daubert*. Cheng and Yoon (2005: 503) found that the difference was not statistically significant, and inferred that "debates about the practical merits and drawbacks of adopting a *Frye* versus a *Daubert* standard are largely superfluous." This was not to deny that *Daubert* had an impact, but its exclusionary influence seems to extend to non-*Daubert* jurisdictions: "[T]he power of the Supreme Court's decision was not so much in its formal doctrinal test, but rather in its ability to create greater awareness of the problems of junk science" (Cheng and Yoon, 2005: 503; Harris 2008).

2. *The forensic "sciences"*

Most of the admissibility studies have focused on civil litigation. However, a study of criminal appellate decisions between 1988 and 1998 suggests that *Daubert* may have exerted a more limited impact on criminal proceedings. Groscup et al. (2002) observed more "discussion" of expert evidence in judgments after *Daubert,* but no change in the proportion of evidence excluded in criminal proceedings. These researchers also noted the "mysterious . . . lack of discussion" of the *Daubert* criteria, particularly "falsifiability, peer review, and error rates" (p. 353).

The "exclusionary ethos" associated with civil proceedings does not seem to have been applied, and certainly not with the same level of rigor, to forensic science evidence produced and relied upon by the state. Studies of commonly admitted forensic science techniques—including fingerprint, voice, image, bite mark, hair, and footprint comparisons, document examination, blood spatter analysis and so on—reveal that: most have not been validated; error rates are often unknown; "expert" witnesses are often poorly educated (relative to research scientists); systemic bias and exaggeration are ubiquitous; and limitations and problems, even if known, are not always disclosed or explained during criminal proceedings (Saks and Koehler, 2005).

A recent review of institutionalized forensic sciences by the U.S. National Academy of Sciences (NAS) lamented that:

With the exception of nuclear DNA analysis . . . no forensic method has been rigorously shown to have the capacity to consistently, and with a high degree of certainty, demonstrate a connection between evidence and a specific individual or source (NAS, 2009: 5).

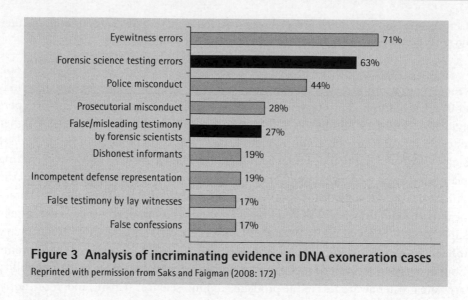

Figure 3 Analysis of incriminating evidence in DNA exoneration cases
Reprinted with permission from Saks and Faigman (2008: 172)

Reviews, such as those associated with Innocence Projects (Figure 3), suggest that mistaken or misleading forensic science evidence is a feature in many wrongful convictions (Garrett and Neufeld, 2009; Findley, 2008).

Several psychologists, lawyers, and scientists, responding to these disturbing revelations, have characterized the identification sciences as the "nonscience forensic sciences" (Saks and Faigman, 2008: 149).

3. *Surveys of judicial understanding of "science"*

The focus on admissibility standards in recent decades has also generated interest in judicial understanding of the *Daubert* criteria. One explanation for the ostensible lack of engagement is provided by Gatowski, Dobbin, and their colleagues.

Gatowski et al. (2001) surveyed hundreds of judges about the *Daubert* criteria. They asked questions designed to elicit information about judicial understanding of falsification ("Falsif."), error rates ("ER"), peer review and publication ("PR/Pub.") and general acceptance ("GA"). The results, presented in Figure 4, led them to conclude:

[M]ost judges have a questionable level of understanding with respect to the basic concepts of science, or of most *Daubert* guidelines and their underlying scientific meaning, with the concepts of falsifiability and error rate particularly problematic for many judges (Dobbin et al., 2007: 13).

Such results are often used to ground reforms, particularly proposals based on judicial re-education, although their implications for fact-finders are less clear.

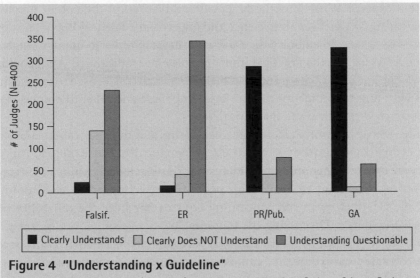

Figure 4 "Understanding x Guideline"

Reprinted from Gatowski et al. (2001: 445) with kind permission from Springer Science+Business Media.

4. (Reflexive) interventions in the "fingerprint wars"

One interesting aspect of the controversy over the forensic sciences (and judicial scientific literacy) emerged out of recent contributions from post-Kuhnian Science & Technology Studies (STS). STS scholars form part of a scholarly tradition that values qualitative empirical investigation of what scientists, doctors and engineers actually do. On the basis of laboratory (and other workplace and institutional) studies they have concluded that scientists do not adhere, in any simple way, to a prescriptive scientific method doctrine (such as falsification) and are not consistently constrained by universal norms (such as disinterestedness and skepticism).

STS has much to say about law-science interactions (e.g., Jasanoff, 2008). Simon Cole's work on fingerprints is of particular interest in the present context. Cole has produced impressive scholarly accounts of problems with individualization, validation, and the social organization of fingerprint examiners. He has also appeared as an expert witness, contesting the admissibility and probative value of fingerprint evidence. Through a commentary on his participation in a *Daubert* hearing, Cole and Michael Lynch explored some of the dilemmas encountered when an STS scholar is confronted with a challenge to the admissibility of his own expert evidence (Lynch and Cole, 2005).

In *People v. Hyatt* (2001) Cole had to carefully negotiate questions about his expertise and interventions. Did it matter, for example, that he was not a fingerprint examiner? Was he a scientist or something else (such as historian, sociologist, or meta-expert)? What were the practical and theoretical difficulties involved in demarcating between genuine science and fingerprint evidence? Was it appropriate for an STS scholar to embrace the *Daubert* criteria in order to impugn fingerprint evidence? What are the practical limits of epistemic radicalism? And, could tacit knowledge and experience (central to many STS analyses) be used to excuse limitations with fingerprint identification? Resolving these and other dilemmas raised a series of tricky practical and theoretical issues.

Cole, whose opinion evidence has been admitted in other cases, approached his performance as an expert witness pragmatically. Nevertheless, the judge in *Hyatt* excluded his opinion evidence as "junk science" while admitting the *impugned* fingerprint evidence. This pejorative rejection provided ammunition for Cole's detractors in the continuing controversy over the reliability of fingerprint evidence. Discussing his ongoing "participation" more recently, Cole (2009) questioned the generalizability of particular experiences in court, stressed the protracted nature of the "campaign" to improve fingerprint evidence and placed his activities in the context of broader criticisms of the forensic sciences. Reflexively, and defensively, Cole also explained that exclusion and not "winning" in a *Daubert* hearing (or trial) cannot simply be equated with "failure." The exclusion of his opinions in *Hyatt*, for example, may have actually discredited the judiciary and the institutionalized forensic sciences, thereby consolidating support and allies in the ongoing campaign (e.g., NAS, 2009). Cole's (2009: 135) work demonstrates the difficulty of intervening to effect legal change and confirms that judgments about interventions can be just as "difficult and ambiguous" as the interventions themselves.

C. Subjective probability and human inference

The studies discussed in sub-sections A and B concern the operation of exclusionary rules. However, once evidence is admitted, fact-finders are largely unconstrained as to how it is used. This raises empirical and normative questions about how human inference operates and its accuracy.

Considerable research has been undertaken in this area over the last few decades. In experiments conducted by Daniel Kahneman, Amos Tversky, and others (e.g., Gilovich et al., 2002) the probabilistic reasoning of participants was found to depart from that prescribed by Bayes's Theorem—a rule of probability theory which provides a means by which a prior probability assessment can be updated to take account of the impact of additional evidence. Investigators suggested that, rather than reasoning probabilistically, humans may employ a limited number of inference mechanisms or "heuristics," which sometimes produce a "bias." Gerd Gigerenzer and others responded to the negative implications of the "heuristics and biases" (H&B) studies by emphasizing the ecological rationality of heuristics. For Gigerenzer and his colleagues, heuristics operate effectively—often more effectively than the "normative" Bayesian methods of the H&B researchers—in the environments in which they are typically employed (Gigerenzer and Selten, 2001; for legal implications, see Saks and Kidd, 1980; Gigerenzer and Engel, 2006).

Another significant contribution is Pennington and Hastie's "story model" of juror decision-making (1992). This descriptive model encompasses the juror's various tasks at trial, from the hearing of evidence right through to the selection of a verdict. According to the fact-finding component of the model, the juror settles upon a version of facts by organizing the evidence into one or more stories. The acceptability of a particular story is governed by a set of certainty principles, such as coverage, coherence and uniqueness.

Here we focus upon a strand of research informed by the H&B endeavors and connected with the story model. This work, inaugurated by Gary Wells (1992), investigates the relationship between fact-finders' subjective probability assessments and liability verdicts.

Wells's experiments all took a similar form. In the first experiment, for example, participants were given the following information. A woman is suing the Blue Bus Company (BBC) for having caused the death of her dog. It was killed by the reckless driving of a bus driver. The woman is color blind. Only two bus companies use that road. BBC runs 80% of the buses on the road and the Grey Bus Company (GBC) runs the other 20%. Wells's second experiment contained the same basic information except that the volume-of-traffic data was replaced with the evidence of a weigh-station attendant. He logged a blue bus passing along the road just before the accident, but his log entries are only 80% accurate. In both the volume-of-traffic and weigh-station-attendant versions, most participants said there was an 80% probability that the dog was hit by a blue bus. This would appear to satisfy the civil standard of proof requiring a "preponderance of probabilities." However, whereas a clear majority of participants would hold BBC "liable" in the weigh-station-attendant version (67.1%), very few participants would on the basis of the volume-of-traffic data (8.2%).

Wells conducted further experiments with slight variations in order to understand why a high subjective probability was viewed as an insufficient basis for liability in certain situations. He tested the hypothesis that fact-finders have a preference for causally strong evidence by replacing volume-of-traffic data with accident statistics. The bus company that is involved in more accidents may, for example, have poorer drivers, which may be the explanation for the occurrence of this particular accident. However, with this evidence most participants were still not prepared to make a finding of liability. The hypothesis that jurors were concerned with distributional fairness was also rejected A verdict based upon the volume-of-traffic data would blame all the accidents on the company that happened to run the majority of buses along the route. Instead, the participants were given forensic evidence that tire tracks on the dog matched 8 out of 10 of BBC's buses, but only 2 out of 10 of GBC's buses. Utilizing this kind of evidence, a company's liability would tend to be in proportion with the company's involvement in accidents. Participants arrived at a "correct" probability assessment but remained reluctant to assign liability.

Wells's final experiment again involved matching tire tracks. On this occasion, the forensic witness testified that the technique is 80% reliable, and expressed his belief that the dog was run over by a BBC bus. In this tire-track-belief version most participants were prepared to attribute liability to BBC. Wells explained these results in terms of a preference for "bidirectional" evidence: "in order for evidence to have a significant impact on people's verdict preferences, one's hypothetical belief about the ultimate fact must affect one's belief about the evidence" (1992: 746). Only in the weigh-station-attendant and tire-track-belief variations would the fact that a GBC bus hit the dog invalidate the evidence. The evidence in the other variations, although making it more likely that a BBC bus hit the dog, is consistent with it having been a GBC bus.

Two groups of investigators subsequently confirmed the "Wells effect" but questioned Wells' fact-to-evidence hypothesis. Niedermeier et al. (1999: 534) suggested that it attributed to participants a "rather complex process" for dealing with the evidence. Sykes and Johnson (1999: 201) suggested that Wells's hypothesis "constitutes more of an analytical description of the phenomenon than a theoretical account of why it occurs." Both groups sought an alternative and simpler explanation for the "Wells effect." Experiments led to the rejection of an obvious possibility—that participants would prefer to base a finding of BBC's liability on the professed belief of a witness rather than statistical data (Sykes and Johnson, 1999: 204, 208; Niedermeier et al., 1999: 536).

Ultimately, both groups advanced similar explanations for the "Wells effect." Niedermeier et al. suggested that participants may be less prepared to hold BBC liable where they can "more easily think of or about an alternative scenario in which [BBC] is not liable" (1999: 537). Sykes and Johnson contended that participants would be less prepared to believe an event where it is "relatively easy . . . to imagine an alternative . . . and to regard this alternative as a plausible scenario" (Sykes and Johnson, 1999: 202). The evidence in all versions supports an 80% probability of BBC's liability but the evidence in the tire-track, accident-statistics, and volume-of-traffic versions expressly refers to the possibility of GBC liability, and therefore allows the creation of a scenario where a GBC bus hit the dog.

While the investigators identified a connection between their hypothesis and the "story model" of Pennington and Hastie, it should be noted that the present hypothesis is concerned with the ease or difficulty of imagining the "alternative scenario" or "counterfactual" rather than the liability scenario itself (Sykes and Johnson, 1999:

205; Niedermeier et al., 1999: 540 fn 5). For Sykes and Johnson, the decisive factor is "the difficulty of mutating [the liability scenario] into the alternative possibility involving the grey bus" (Sykes and Johnson, 1999: 210).

One additional point is worth mentioning. Wells suggested that his experiments revealed a situation where the participants' subjective probabilities were "statistically correct" (1992: 739), unlike those in the H&B research, but participants were reluctant to find liability on this basis. Sykes and Johnson questioned this interpretation, explaining that "there may be a difference between calculated probability estimations based on participants' understanding of the rules of probability, and measures affecting participants' 'gut feeling', or subjective sense of the likelihood of an event" (1999: 201). To test this, Sykes and Johnson asked participants to record both the "probability" that the bus was blue, and "how certain they felt... [based] on intuition or their 'gut feeling'" (p. 204). They found that, unlike "probability," "[s]ubjective certainty was... significantly affected by evidence form, and... was a significant mediator of liability" (p. 209). This suggests a stronger link with the H&B work: the divergence between the subjective certainty and statistical probability might be viewed as a "bias."

IV. Discussion

Having briefly reviewed several lines of empirical inquiry employing diverse methodologies—experiments, surveys, quantitative and qualitative approaches—we now discuss some of their limitations, and their implications and significance for the understanding and practice of law.

A. Abstraction from trial environment

Research on juror reasoning relied upon experiments that were, in various ways, abstracted from the trial environment, thereby raising issues of ecological validity. Do real jurors, for example, behave like the "mock jurors" of the experiments? And, do the experiments resemble real world trials. Much of the information in the hearsay and human inference studies was presented via written summaries, audio and video recordings or, at best, via live actors. (An exception is Goodman et al.'s (2006) experiments where, in one variation, children reported their actual experiences to mock jurors.) The presentation of evidence in such forms is questionable, and particularly problematic in relation to hearsay, because the rule is directed toward providing fact-finders with first-hand accounts. In some of the studies, the "non-hearsay evidence" was, strictly speaking, hearsay, while the "hearsay evidence" was actually hearsay upon hearsay.

A related problem is that the participants tended to be provided with a single piece of evidence in isolation. The subjective probability studies were, in part, concerned with the impact of *naked* statistical evidence on fact-finders. However, it is questionable whether any piece of evidence can be truly naked. As Sykes and Johnson observed, "our study does not assess whether the effects for our manipulation may be attenuated by other factors that exist in the information-rich forum of an actual trial" (1999: 211). And, here we should not overlook procedures and strategy as well as other evidence.

Many of the hearsay studies compared mock-juror responses to hearsay evidence with their responses to the observer/declarant's testimony with essentially the same content. But this misses another significant epistemic effect of the hearsay rule. By requiring the actual observer of the events to testify (rather than someone who merely heard about them), it may be possible to obtain further detail, particularly through cross-examination. This additional testimony may be relevant both to the events in issue and the declarant's credibility. As far as the comparison between hearsay evidence and declarant testimony is concerned, this additional testimony may confer a greater epistemic advantage to the fact-finder than the declarant's oath or demeanor.

B. Specificity of conditions, generalizability of conclusions

An empirical experiment inevitably involves a quite specific set of conditions raising a question as to the generalizability of any conclusions from that experiment. Of course, variations can be introduced through further experiments. Across the hearsay studies, for example, variations included: different ages of declarants and hearsay witnesses; different types of relationships between declarants and hearsay witnesses; differences in the status and experience of the hearsay witness; differences in whether mock jurors reached decisions individually or in groups; differences in the gender of mock jurors; differences in the nature of the experience leading to the declaration; different types of "crime"—whether theft, innocent touching, or sexual assault; differences in procedure—whether the hearsay witness (or declarant) was cross-examined; whether there was other evidence; and whether the evidence was presented by the state or the defense. However, it is not obvious that the experimental results are sufficiently consistent, coherent, or robust to provide a solid basis for drawing generalizations and conclusions justifying specific hearsay reforms with application to real world litigation.

Even where the studies do seem to identify potential problems with current rules and assumptions, as with the suggestibility of children or the recollection of interviewing techniques, questions remain about the precise implications for practice. Should we, for example, insist on recorded interviews with children at the earliest opportunity? If so, what happens when interviews are not recorded? Should we allow expert witnesses (e.g., the psychologists) to explain potential problems to fact-finders at trial? If so, should they be required to adhere strictly to the results of published studies or allowed to extrapolate? Should *Daubert* play a role? Would recourse to experimental psychologists as expert witnesses make any difference? And, how should the lengthening of trials, the added costs, and greater complexity in evidence (and judicial directions) be factored in?

Significantly, the "high degree of convergence" in empirical research as to the dangers of eyewitness testimony (Park and Saks, 2006: 960) may be exceptional, as may be the relative clarity of the procedural prescriptions flowing from this research. Empirical legal studies often present as many questions as answers. And, proposals for law reform—such as additional judicial education—are often simplistic or naïve in political, sociological, and institutional terms.

C. Factual uncertainty and the benchmark problem

Evidence law is an institutionalized (and socially contingent) response to the inherent difficulty of arriving at an accurate version of past events. It is rare that the factual accuracy of inferences can be assessed, let alone the extent to which accuracy is advanced by particular evidentiary principles. Not insignificantly, DNA profiling, particularly when it provides the basis for exonerations, has enabled some verdicts to be benchmarked against the accused's actual innocence. Regrettably, interventions by Innocence Projects give criminal justice systems few grounds for complacency. Many wrongful convictions had, prior to DNA-based exoneration, survived multiple appeals and re-trials.

The benchmarking issue also arises for empirical researchers seeking to assess the epistemic value of an evidentiary rule, type of evidence or verdict. A number of the studies sought to draw normative conclusions about the accuracy with which human fact-finders handled particular types of evidence. The earlier hearsay studies concluded that mock jurors appropriately discounted hearsay evidence. Yet, in most of the experiments the "accuracy" of the hearsay evidence was unknown and unknowable—there was no benchmark, as the ultimate factual question was fictitious. Some investigators sought to respond to this issue by basing their experiment on real events. One study, for example, began with the staging of the actual event—an adult touching (or not touching) a child (Goodman et al., 2006). For obvious reasons, there are limits to the degree of realism that can be introduced to such experiments.

Some of the accounts of human inference have looked to Bayesian probability theory rather than objective fact as a benchmark. The H&B researchers, in particular, labeled departure from the calculus of probability, and Bayes's Theorem in particular, as a "bias." Wells and others, in conducting their subjective probability experiments, were more concerned with developing a descriptive model. However, their work, revealing a similar departure, also implies that human reasoning in conditions of uncertainty is suboptimal. Perhaps there is a role for evidence law to intervene and address empirically-identified biases (Saks and Kidd, 1980).

An immediate difficulty with this proposal is that the Bayesian norm is highly contentious. Several legal commentators agree that "naked statistical evidence" provides an inadequate basis for liability. For them, a high probability figure must be supported by sufficient weight, detail and/or resilience (Stein, 2005: 120; Ho, 2008: 166). If a high base-rate probability is sufficient, what incentive is there to seek more specific evidence? And yet, subject to resource considerations, the enterprise of juridical proof is founded on the assumption that the more evidence the better. This preference underlies Benthamite criticisms of the exclusionary rules and, sometimes, their justifications. Recall that the hearsay rule can be rationalized on the basis that it increases the quality and quantity of evidence available to the fact-finder.

As noted in Section II, in recent decades Bentham's free-proof position has come to predominate, albeit indirectly. *Daubert's* tightening of admissibility requirements for expert evidence in civil proceedings represents something of an anomaly shaped by institutional pressures and socio-economic impressions and beliefs (more below).

D. Competing goals and values

A further issue arising from the empirical studies is the tendency to focus predominantly on the goal of factual accuracy. Prescriptions derived from the studies *may* provide benefits in this particular area, but these need to be weighed against potential costs elsewhere. Factual accuracy may be the primary goal of evidence law, but it is certainly not the only goal (e.g., Twining, 2006: 76; Ho, 2008: 339). Rules dealing with the dangers of eyewitness evidence may fall fairly squarely under the accuracy heading, but principle may implicate other goals. Depriving the fact-finder of probative evidence, via the hearsay rule may, on balance, be preferable to denying the opposing party the right to confront an accuser. The remoteness and lack of detail of hearsay or naked statistical evidence may make verdicts reliant upon them unfocused and impersonal, and hinder the effective expression of norms. A verdict based upon inaccessible or incomprehensible expert opinion may present similar problems.

It may be that the primacy of factual accuracy is such that many of these arguments can ultimately be dismissed. Our point, however, is that they cannot be ignored or disregarded altogether because concern about factual accuracy underpins only some of the goals, values and assumptions shaping rules of evidence and legal practice.

E. Bigger pictures

Empirical research and attendant legal reform should be sensitive to broader socio-political considerations and theory. STS perspectives, for example, may help to expand the focus from rules, processes and simplistic images of expertise to interests, institutions and social processes.

The majority in *Daubert,* for instance, supported its first criterion with reference to the work of Popper and Carl Hempel. The juxtaposition of these two irreconcilable philosophical accounts, and their eclectic combination with other, more sociological criteria (e.g., peer review and general acceptance), not only renders the Supreme Court's philosophical understanding open to doubt, but raises questions about the epistemological legitimacy of its admissibility jurisprudence (Haack, 2001). Yet, in their survey of judicial understanding of *Daubert,* Gatowski et al. based their assessments on folk versions of falsifiability and abstract questions rather than studying what judges *in situ* actually do. In Figure 4 the lines between understanding, misunderstanding and uncertainty are not merely blurred but conceptually suspect. Judicial responses to a survey instrument were assessed against idealized, and philosophically inflected, representations of science rather than empirical studies of actual scientific practice (see also Freckelton et al., 1999; cf. Edmond, 2005).

STS perspectives encourage us to ask: If *Daubert* does not represent a neutral vision of science, why were the particular criteria favored? And, are the criteria well suited to determining the admissibility of expert evidence in civil and criminal proceedings? Answers to such questions might help us to understand why *Daubert* and "gate-keeping" seem to have achieved such symbolic significance even though their conceptualizations of science and expertise appear simplistic, philosophically flawed and under-utilized.

One way to interpret the Supreme Court's admissibility jurisprudence is as a response to perceived problems with civil litigation, especially litigation "explosions," "junk science," excessive damages awards, and resulting deleterious economic effects (Haltom and McCann, 2004). Vigorous gate-keeping is a less overtly political intervention than changes to substantive tort or product liability laws and policies. *Daubert* provided judges with a means of regulating civil claims deemed "unworthy," ideologically as much as factually, while publicly affirming their commitment to factual accuracy, the Seventh Amendment and the rule of law (Finley, 1999).

This more speculative reading of *Daubert* also brings trends in the criminal sphere into sharper relief. Trial and appellate judges have been relatively unresponsive to defense attempts to impugn incriminating scientific evidence. Expert evidence favoring the compensation of plaintiffs has been held to higher standards than forensic science evidence implicating defendants in criminal activities. This seems to reflect, directly and/or indirectly, socio-economic, and ideological concerns about excessive litigation as well, as the perceived need for more severe crime control.

There is obvious value in trying to integrate quantitative studies, and even surveys, into a more hermeneutic synthesis. These kinds of meta-analyses, while tentative and controvertible, generate new understandings and testable theories as well as questions about current practice and reform. They suggest, for example, that improving judicial scientific literacy might not be particularly effective. Confronted with a civil justice system purportedly "in crisis," U.S. judges would probably have operationalized any admissibility standard more aggressively. If we reflect on admissibility trends (recall Figure 2) we find that in civil cases federal judges began to exclude expert evidence more pro-actively before *Daubert*, and practice in *Frye* jurisdictions was almost indistinguishable.

More critical approaches to expertise help to release scholars from slavish adherence to the descriptively dubious *Daubert* criteria, as well as polemical concepts like "junk science." STS-inflected approaches allow for admissibility criteria to be indexed to the kinds of principles, values, and outcomes to which particular institutions and societies aspire. If, for example, we claim to value the presumption of innocence, fairness, and factual accuracy, then we should be more interested in the reliability of forensic science techniques. Rather than disguising our policy-political preferences in terms of appeals to purportedly proper definitions of science, demonizing the evidence of opponents as "junk science" or invoking longstanding practice (as with fingerprint evidence), it might be preferable to formulate strategic models of science and expertise based on explicit policy preferences and principle.

V. Rationalist and Empiricist Legacies

Most of those operating in the rationalist tradition have invoked or exploited the experiential and pragmatic nature of evidence and evidence law, though without much engagement or interest in empirical study. This is almost as true of legal scholars as it is of legal practitioners and judges (Park, 2003). Years spent in legal practice (or scholarship), so it is thought, gives practitioners and judges privileged exposure to both the *real world* and *human nature*.

While it might be fair to say that many of the contributions from empirical legal studies are provisional and their precise value for practice is uncertain or ambiguous, it would be equally unfair to suggest that they did not raise important issues worthy of serious consideration (Park and Saks, 2006). Moreover, by identifying problems with eyewitness evidence and the limitations of many of the forensic sciences, and in many other ways, empirical and experimental studies have substantially outpaced and repeatedly embarrassed legal *experience*. Nevertheless, in most jurisdictions judges have responded even to mature research traditions at best superficially and, at worst, with disdain shored up by complacent reference to collective experience or legal exceptionalism.

The obdurate indifference of lawyers, judges and policy-makers to empirical research on evidence law seems misguided (Leiter and Allen, 2001). It is difficult to know how to promote more principled and empirically calibrated approaches to evidence and proof. One response might be to encourage the most attentive and influential legal practitioners to participate in qualitative and quantitative forms of inquiry. The complexity and diversity of legal practice, along with its relative inaccessibility, makes multi-disciplinary investigation with research teams composed of empirical scholars and theorists, as well as lawyers and judges, a potentially productive, if practically and methodologically awkward, means of facilitating relevant real world research with direct bearing on practice (Edmond et al., 2009). It might also serve to remind us that law reform and empirical research should be related and ongoing.

Sir Francis Bacon (1561–1626), an early proponent of experimental natural philosophy and sometime Lord Chancellor of England, reputedly died from pneumonia after endeavoring to preserve the flesh of fowls with snow. Most of those involved with evidence law, particularly our lawyers, judges, and evidence scholars, seem to have taken more from Bacon's empirically induced fate than from his experimentally oriented philosophy. Perhaps ironically, commitment to legal *experience* places modern Anglo-American judges in a position similar to the Aristotelian schoolmen Bacon railed against. Unabated, indifference to empirical legal study is likely to reduce the social legitimacy of our legal institutions and undermine the fairness and accuracy of their rules, processes, and results.

REFERENCES

Bentham, J. (1843). *The Works of Jeremy Bentham*, J. Bowring (ed.), 11 vols, Edinburgh: Simpkin, Marshall, & Co.

Buck, J., Warren, A., and Brigham, J. (2004). "When does quality count? Perceptions of Hearsay Testimony about Child Sexual Abuse Interviews," *Law & Human Behavior* 28: 599–621.

Cheng, E. and Yoon, A. (2005). "Does *Frye* or *Daubert* Matter? A Study of Scientific Admissibility Standards," *Virginia Law Review* 91: 471–513.

Cole, S. (2009). "A Cautionary Tale about Cautionary Tales about Intervention," *Organization* 16: 121–41.

Cole, S. and Dioso-Villa, R. (2009). "Investigating the 'CSI Effect': Media and Litigation Crisis in Criminal Law," *Stanford Law Review* 61: 1335–73.

Cranor, C. (2006). *Toxic torts: Science, law and the possibility of justice*, Cambridge: Cambridge University Press.

Damaška, M. (1997). *Evidence Law Adrift*, New Haven: Yale University Press.

Dixon, L. and Gill, B. (2002). "Changes in the Standards for Admitting Expert Evidence in Federal Civil Cases since the *Daubert* Decision," *Psychology, Public Policy & Law* 8: 251–308.

Dobbin, S., Gatowski, S., Eyre, R., Dahir, V., Merlino, M., and Richardson, J. (2007). "Federal and State Trial Judges on the Proffer and Presentation of Expert Evidence," *The Justice System Journal* 28: 1–15.

Edmond, G. (2005). "Judging Surveys: Experts, Empirical Evidence and Law Reform," *Federal Law Review* 33: 95–139.

Edmond, G., Biber, K., Kemp, R., and Porter, G. (2009). "Law's Looking Glass: Expert Identification Evidence Derived from Photographic and Video Images," *Current Issues in Criminal Justice* 20: 337–77.

Findley, K. (2008). "Innocents at Risk: Adversary Imbalance, Forensic Science, and the Search for Truth," *Seton Hall Law Review* 38: 893–973.

Finley, L. (1999). "Guarding the Gate to the Courthouse: How Trial Judges are Using their Evidentiary Screening Role to Remake Tort Causation Rules," *DePaul University Law Review* 49: 335–76.

Freckelton, I., Reddy, P., and Selby, H. (1999). *Australian Judicial Perspectives on Expert Evidence: An Empirical Study*, Carlton, VIC: AIJA.

Garrett, B. and Neufeld, P. (2009). "Invalid Forensic Science Testimony and Wrongful Convictions," *Virginia Law Review* 95: 1–97.

Gatowski, S., Dobbin, S., Richardson, J., Ginsburg, G., Merlino, M., and Dahir, V. (2001). "Asking the Gatekeepers: A National Survey of Judges on Judging Expert Evidence in a post-*Daubert* World," *Law & Human Behavior* 25: 433–58.

Gigerenzer, G. and Engel, C. (eds.) (2006). *Heuristics and the Law*, Cambridge, MA: MIT Press.

Gigerenzer, G. and Selten, R. (eds.) (2001). *Bounded Rationality: The Adaptive Toolbox*, Cambridge, MA: MIT Press.

Gilovich, T., Griffin, D., and Kahneman, D. (eds.) (2002). *Heuristics and Biases: The Psychology of Intuitive Judgment*, Cambridge: Cambridge University Press.

Gluckman, M. (1955). *The judicial process among the Barotse of Northern Rhodesia*, Manchester: University Press for the Rhodes Livingston Institute.

Golding, J., Alexander, M., and Stewart, T. (1999). "The Effect of Hearsay Witness Age in a Child Sexual Assault Trial," *Psychology, Public Policy & Law* 5: 420–38.

Golding, J., Sanchez, R., and Sego, S. (1997). "The Believability of Hearsay Testimony in a Child Sexual Assault Trial," *Law & Human Behavior* 21: 299–325.

Goodman, G., Myers, J., Qin, J., Quas, J., Castelli, P., Redlich, A., and Rogers, L. (2006). "Hearsay versus children's testimony: Effects of truthful and deceptive statements on juror's decisions," *Law & Human Behavior* 30: 363–401.

Groscup, J., Penrod, S., Studebaker, C., and Huss, M. (2002). "The Effects of *Daubert* on the admissibility of expert testimony in state and federal criminal cases," *Psychology, Public Policy & Law* 8: 339–72.

Haack, S. (2001). "An Epistemologist in the Bramble-Bush: At the Supreme Court with Mr. Joiner," *Journal of Health Politics, Policy & Law* 26: 217–48.

Haltom, W. and McCann, M.. (2004) *Distorting the law: Politics, Media and the litigation crisis*, Chicago: University of Chicago Press.

Harris, R.C. (2008). *Black Robes, White Coats: The Puzzle of Judicial Policymaking and Scientific Evidence*, New Jersey: Rutgers University Press.

Heydon, J.D. (1984). *Evidence: Cases and Materials*, (2nd edn.), London: Butterworths.

Ho, H.L. (2008). *A Philosophy of Evidence Law: Justice in the Search for Truth*, Oxford: Oxford University Press.

Hutchins, R. and Sleisinger, D. (1928). "Some observations on the law of evidence," *Columbia Law Review* 28: 432–40.

Jasanoff, S. (2008). "Making Order: Law and Science in Action," in E. Hackett et al (eds.), *The handbook of science and technology studies*, (3rd edn.), Cambridge MA: MIT Press, 761–86.

Johnson, M., Krafka, C., and Cecil, J. (2000). *Expert testimony in federal civil trials: A preliminary analysis*, Washington, DC: Federal Judicial Center.

Kahneman, D., Slovic, P., and Tversky, A. (eds.) (1982). *Judgment under uncertainty: Heuristics and biases*, Cambridge: Cambridge University Press.

Kovera, M., Park, R., and Penrod, S. (1992). "Jurors' Perceptions of Eyewitness and Hearsay Evidence," *Minnesota Law Review* 76: 702–22.

Krafka, C., Dunn, M., Johnson, M., Cecil, J., and Miletich, D. (2002). "Judge and Attorney Experiences, Practices, and Concerns Regarding Expert Testimony in Federal Civil Trials," *Psychology, Public Policy & Law* 8: 309–32.

Leiter, B. and Allen, R. (2001). "Naturalized Epistemology and the Law of Evidence," *Virginia Law Review* 87: 1491–550.

Lynch, M. and Cole, S. (2005). "Science and Technology Studies on Trial: Dilemmas of Expertise," *Social Studies of Science* 35: 269–311.

McGough, L. (1999). "Hearing and Believing Hearsay," *Psychology, Public Policy & Law* 5: 485–98.

Miene, P., Park, R., and Borgida, E. (1992). "Juror Decision Making and the Evaluation of Hearsay Evidence," *Minnesota Law Review* 76: 83–701.

Munsterberg, H. (1908). *On the Witness Stand. Essays on Psychology and Crime*, New York: Doubleday.

NAS (2009). *Strengthening the Forensic Sciences in the United States: A Path Forward*, Washington, DC: The National Academies Press.

Niedermeier, K.E., Kerr, N.L., and Messé, L.A., (1999). "Jurors' Use of Naked Statistical Evidence: Exploring Bases and Implications of the Wells Effect," *Journal of Personality and Social Psychology* 76: 533–42.

Paglia, A. and Schuller, R. (1998). "Jurors' Use of Hearsay Evidence: The Effects of Type and Timing of Instructions," *Law & Human Behavior* 22: 501–18.

Park, R. (2003). "Visions of Applying the Scientific Method to the Hearsay Rule," *Michigan State Law Review* 1149–74.

Park, R. and Saks, M. (2006). "Evidence Scholarship Reconsidered: Results of the Interdisciplinary Turn," *Boston College Law Review* 46: 949–1031.

Pathak, M., and Thompson, W. (1999). "From Child to Witness to Jury: Effects of Suggestion on the Transmission and Evaluation of Hearsay," *Psychology, Public Policy & Law* 5: 372–87.

Pennington, N. and Hastie, R. (1992). "Explaining the Evidence: Tests of the Story Model for Juror Decision Making," *Journal of Personality and Social Psychology* 62: 189–206.

Rakos, R. and Landsman, S. (1992). "Researching the Hearsay Rule: Emerging Findings, General Issues, and Future Directions," *Minnesota Law Review* 76: 655–82.

Ross, D., Lindsay, R., and Marsil, D. (1999). "The Impact of Hearsay Testimony on Conviction Rates in Trials of Child Sexual Abuse: Toward Balancing the Rights of Defendants and Child Witnesses," *Psychology, Public Policy & Law* 5: 439–55.

Saks, M. and Faigman, D. (2008). "Failed Forensics: how forensic science lost its way and how it might yet find it," *Annual Review of Law & Social Science* 4: 149–71.

Saks, M. and Kidd, R.F. (1980). "Human Information Processing and Adjudication: Trial by Heuristics," *Law and Society Review* 15: 123–60.

Saks, M. and Koehler, J. (2005). "The Coming Paradigm Shift in Forensic Identification Science," *Science* 309: 892–895.

Schuller, R. (1995). "Expert Evidence and Hearsay: The Influence of 'Secondhand' Information on Jurors' Decisions," *Law & Human Behavior* 19: 345–62.

Stein, A. (2005). *Foundations of Evidence Law*, Oxford: Oxford University Press.

Sykes, D.L. and Johnson, J.T. (1999). "Probabilistic Evidence Versus the Representation of an Event: The Curious Case of Mrs. Prob's Dog," *Basic and Applied Social Psychology* 21: 199–212.

Thayer, J.B. (1898). *A Preliminary Treatise on Evidence at Common Law*, Boston: Little Brown.

Thompson, W. and Pathak, M. (1999). "Empirical Study of Hearsay Rules: Bridging the Gap Between Psychology and Law," *Psychology, Public Policy & Law* 5: 456–72.

Twining, W. (2006). *Rethinking Evidence: Exploratory Essays*, (2nd edn.), Cambridge: Cambridge University Press.

Tyler, T.R. (1990). *Why people obey the law: Procedural Justice, Legitimacy, and Compliance*, New Haven: Yale University Press.

Warren, A., Nunez, N., Keeney, J., Buck, J., and Smith, B. (2002). "The Believability of Children and their Interviewers' Hearsay Testimony: When less is more," *Journal of Applied Psychology* 87: 846–57.

Warren, A.R. and Woodall, C.E. (1999). "The Reliability of Hearsay Testimony: How well do interviewers recall their interviews with children?," *Psychology, Public Policy, and Law* 5: 355–71.

Wells, G.L. (1992). "Naked Statistical Evidence of Liability," *Journal of Personality and Social Psychology* 62: 739–52.

Wells, G.L. and Quinlivan, D.S. (2009). "Suggestive Eyewitness Identification Procedures and the Supreme Court's Reliability Test in Light of Eyewitness Science: 30 years later," *Law and Human Behavior* 33: 1–24.

Wigmore, J.H. (1940). *A Treatise on the System of Evidence in Trials at Common Law* (3rd edn.), Boston: Little Brown.

28

CIVIL PROCEDURE AND COURTS

CARRIE J. MENKEL-MEADOW AND BRYANT G. GARTH

I. INTRODUCTION: EMPIRICAL STUDIES OF PROCEDURE IN SERVICE TO WHICH PROCEDURAL VALUES?

COURTS play a central role in both legal and political processes in many countries, especially in the common law world. Legal actors have a stake in making sure that legal processes and procedures are perceived as legitimate, both by the general population who might use the legal system and by the professionals who operate it. A relatively constant series of issues, about whether courts are fair, efficient, and provide justice, serve to structure a long-standing debate about how courts operate and the best rules of process to determine how disputes and substantive legal claims are resolved. Over time, the issues of whether there is too much cost and delay in litigation, too much litigation in general, or not enough access to courts, with overly complex rules for litigation and excessive costs of procedures, continue to be studied and contested decade after decade, with advocates using social science to promote rule change and reform over and over again as these debates repeat themselves in slightly different forms from generation to generation.

In the field of civil procedure, where there is a continuing demand for some procedural rule reform, empirical studies of how rules actually operate have, for the most part, been used in partisan ways to advocate for particular reforms in the interests of one or another legal or client constituency. Empirical studies have been commissioned by policy-makers and rule-drafters to learn how much litigation costs, how long it takes, whether other forms of dispute resolution should be employed instead of trials, how much discovery or information should be shared in each case, whether particular rules and practices (such as summary judgment rules, sanctions for inadequate verification, and taxed costs for failure to accept settlements) have their desired effects, what role judges should play in managing cases, and whether there are particular patterns of outcomes for particular classes of litigants. Only relatively rarely has empirical study of civil procedure been conducted by more disinterested or "neutral" social scientists and legal scholars: an example is Martin Shapiro's attempt to explain the "universal" in triadic structures of disputants and third party neutrals (1981).

Indeed, as this Chapter shows, many of those conducting or commissioning empirical studies of civil processes have been directly involved as advocates for particular procedural reforms. Examples are Charles Clark (law professor, Dean, then federal judge) in the United States, who took part in the development of the 1938 Rules of Civil Procedure and Lord Harry Woolf, architect (as a senior judge) of the 1998 Civil Procedure Rules in England and Wales. Thus, this essay reviews the political, personal, and policy issues that have marked empirical studies of civil procedure and justice.

Most studies of civil procedure recognize the inevitable tensions between values of *accuracy* (truth ascertainment), *efficiency* (time to disposition), *access* (costs of litigation, availability of representation, and relative transparency and simplicity of rules), achievement of *substantive justice*, and, more recently, *procedural justice* (or perceptions of or satisfaction with the process of dispute resolution itself (Zuckerman, 1999; Tyler, 1997)). To achieve true decisional accuracy (a factually correct result) or true substantive justice (the combination of accurate fact finding, law application, and considerations of equity) often involves long, costly, complex, labor-intensive, and intrusive actions on the part of litigants (parties), their representatives, judges and court personnel, and other adjuncts of the legal system. Evaluation and consideration of who is served by these competing values requires assessment of whether costs should be borne by parties (or their lawyers) or the system, and whether any procedural system benefits the parties alone (through dispute resolution) or the larger society (by generating law and precedents as well). Is the purpose of civil procedure and process to allow both private and public parties to peacefully resolve their disputes or are their disputes "public goods" generating law and normative orders for the rest of us (Menkel-Meadow, 1995)?

Can answers to these perhaps irresolvable questions be supplied by data and empirical study? Since so many countries have recently explored these issues in various efforts to reform civil procedure, we can here review the uses to which empirical studies have been put in debates about such concrete issues as pleading rules, discovery and information exchanges, verification (Rule 11, Fed. R. Civ. Pro. for Americans), summary judgments and proceedings, class actions, case management, and alternative dispute resolution. Looking at larger issues, social scientists have demonstrated that process, often without overt reference to outcomes, is integral to how disputants experience the fairness of the legal system (Lind et al., 1990). This Chapter will therefore present a body of empirical research about courts and procedural rules, and their role in different societies. Part of our task is to analyze that research and how it has been used in policy debates and reforms. We also discuss the question of the demand and supply for empirical research about rules of procedure and courts, and explore the difficulty of doing empirical research that goes beyond a focus on the institutional needs of the courts themselves and the reformers interested in their own court-reform agendas. Our challenge in this review is to tell a story that is simultaneously about the "progress" of empirical research and the accumulation of knowledge about process, but also about a systematic structural tilt toward political uses of that research, which works to deprive us of systematic social science research that can actually explain the changing position of courts, litigation, and law in the larger economy and state.

The questions that social science researchers and procedural reformers have asked about process, procedures, and rules are typically defined by the institutional needs of the courts. These questions include the following:

1. Is the process fair (as perceived by those within it, and those who are affected or governed by it) and accessible?
2. Is the process efficient? Is there a reasonable relation between costs of use, time of use, amount of use, and production of outcomes?
3. Is the amount of use of civil legal processes appropriate for societal needs, and how does that relate to arguments about the "litigation explosion" and alleged cultural and class differences in use of processes and outcomes delivered?

4. Do differences in process (relating, for instance, to fora, decision-makers, method of fact-finding (such as inquisitorial or adversarial)) make a difference to outcomes, user satisfaction, legitimacy of the process, or the larger legal and political system?

5. How can we usefully compare different processes to each other, where experimental conditions for real case analysis and comparison are virtually impossible to achieve?

6. How do claimants choose particular processes, such as settlement rather than trial (see Priest and Klein, 1984)?

7. How do the requirements and resources of different processes affect their use and outcomes (relevant factors include the respective roles of attorneys and non-attorney representatives in processes; amount and type of discovery and information exchange, economic and linguistic resources of parties and decision-makers (juries/judges))?

8. What effects do resource-allocation rules (dealing, for instance, with costs and penalties for not accepting settlements) have on the use and outcomes of processes?

9. How can the effects of choices among processes be measured? Relevant matters include the choice between quantitative and qualitative assessments of process differences; issues of methodology; and the problematics of operationalization of such variables as fairness, satisfaction, and justice. See Chapter 25 in this volume.

Our brief review of the history of empirical research in civil procedure will seek to reveal both the progress of this research and some of the limitations that are necessarily built into it. This Chapter concludes with a critical review of some of the current controversies in assessing the competing empirical analyses of rule and process reforms.

II. A Brief History of Empirical Research in Process and Procedure: Law Reform, Career Capital, or Academic Interest?

Civil procedure, in both common law and civilian legal systems, has been historically known for its complexity, technicalities, and esoteric requirements, with the result that litigants generally require professional assistance for the pursuit of a civil legal claim. The twentieth century produced a vast amount of procedural reform in many countries, all intended to simplify, streamline, and in some cases "unify" the rules of process so that the "merits" of the matter, and not some procedural technicality, would control the outcome and produce substantive justice for the parties. In some countries this meant the "merger" of law and equity, differentiations of court procedures and remedies that called for arcane and different procedures for different civil lawsuits; in other countries, this meant simplifying procedure generally in pleading rules and "rounds" of necessary responses. Beginning with reforms in the nineteenth century (the Field Code in 1848 in the United States and Benthamite reforms leading to the 1875 Judicature Acts in the UK), pleading rules were simplified and courts' powers somewhat unified (e.g., in merger of law and equity) and rationalized. Indeed, as a continuation of this project across national boundaries, most recently the American Law Institute and UNIDROIT (the International Institute for the Unification of Private Law) have joined in a project to draft streamlined procedural rules for "harmonization" in transnational civil litigation.

In the United States, federalism continued to produce different sets of rules for federal courts and state courts with different reformers taking on different levels of rule reform. Beginning with the famous speech by Roscoe Pound, in 1906, on "the Causes of Popular Dissatisfaction with Justice," movements to reform the rules of procedure grew in force (with strange exchanges and mutations of "political" views as conservatives and liberals eventually joined together) and eventually led, at the federal level, to the Rules Enabling Act and the 1938 Rules of Federal Procedure. Together, these reforms unified procedure in the federal court system, which merged actions at common law with those in equity, produced new rules on discovery and information exchange, and authorized summary proceedings and more liberalized rules for joinder of claims and parties, all done on a platform of both efficiency and "justice on the merits" for the parties. Over time, most, but not all, of the states adopted many of the federal procedural reforms.

As these reforms were being proposed in the 1930s, the Legal Realists, drawing on the new visibility of the social sciences, attacked procedural formalism by calling for empirical studies of how rules and laws actually worked (Garth, 1997). With the mechanistic study of formal legal rules increasingly discredited, understanding the behavior of lawyers and judges within legal institutions (called "the administration of justice") was considered necessary in order to perfect systems through law reform. As some of the Legal Realists sought to explore the social science side of the "science of law," not through deductive derivation of legal principles from reading cases, but through more inductive methods of data collection about what happened in courts (beyond the production and elaboration of legal rules), they developed at least two radical projects. One was to use different methods to study legal phenomena (a project which involved both scholarly and curricular challenges to legal knowledge). The other was to use social science instrumentally as a hopeful arrow in the quiver of social change. To the extent that debates about rules of procedure and the role of courts and judges have always been politically contentious, social science was early deployed (with all the militaristic connotations such a word invokes) both to "win" particular arguments about particular legal reforms and to claim a new form of argumentative high ground based on the "objectivity" of statistics. These themes in the early use of social science in relation to legal process continue today, as we will trace with some representative examples.

Charles Clark, in his empirical work on procedure, began his study of the operation of the Connecticut civil courts by stating that he was to study "the actual effect of procedural devices on the progress of litigation" (Clark and Schulman, 1937). Modeled somewhat on the early Pound-Frankfurter Cleveland Crime Survey, Clark's study was one of simple (not sampled) counting and classification of such items as the frequency of jury trials, use of motions, defaults, etc. What he found, as John Schlegel (1995) aptly puts it, is that with the high proportion of matters being uncontested and settled, state court civil litigation had already become largely "administrative" by 1925 in urban Connecticut. Clark was also among the first to study the new "small claims" court, designed to simplify procedures for ordinary people and allow lawsuits without representation, but in the beginning, as now, actually most often used by companies to collect debts from individuals.

The early Clark studies of court statistics illustrate several important aspects of empirical research on courts and procedure that persist to this day. First, they were highly dependent on particular people—their energy and ambitions, their funding, their research minions, and their political objectives. These early studies, like their later counterparts, could not be conducted by a single scholar as was the norm in the case of traditional legal scholarship (and even sociological scholarship). Second, even from the beginning, with the difficulty of finding large funding sources, governmental, political, and policy interests were behind the research, if not controlling it or desiring particular outcomes. Third, the results were often disappointing to the sponsors of the research for failing to completely prove that cumbersome rules or delay in the administration of justice were responsible for some legal or social problem. Fourth, Clark had used a set of completed cases and thus helped establish the methodological norm for future studies of courts (which differs from the assembly line or mortality research model of following a case from filing until it falls off the docket by some form of termination). Fifth, the work was time-consuming, expensive, and demoralizing when the years of work and collection of many cases failed to produce desired outcomes. Even before modern academic-productivity measurements were used, this was surely a disincentive to continue such large-scale, low-yield projects.

More modern readers of this early work have been able to mine it for other observations; for example, that the high incidence of plea bargaining (in the criminal arena) and settlement (in the civil arena) might indicate a very efficient system, with accurate charging and selective prosecution—a kind of rough efficient justice. Astute readers have suggested that formal court data might need to be supplemented with data from the period before cases are filed in order to determine how formal case filings do or do not reflect the total population of matters that could have entered the formal legal system (Clermont and Eisenberg, 1992). Critics at the American Law Institute at the time were reported to have asked for more "interpretation" and fewer facts (Schlegel, 1995: 96), suggesting that the tension between norm-oriented lawyers and number-crunching social scientists has been with us since the beginning.

Clark, as a law professor, Dean, and eventual Reporter and drafter of the Federal Rules of Civil Procedure, and then federal judge, was able to use his claim to social science expertise to build his career and to legitimate reform. Other Legal Realists engaged in early empirical projects about the law (e.g., William O. Douglas's work on failed businesses and bankruptcy), and they too gained stature and influence through these studies. However, as some of these early scholars took their place on the bench or in the New Deal alphabet agencies, their stance shifted from critics armed with social science to legal insiders operating mainly with the usual legal tools. In the Realist era, it is difficult to detect any major changes inspired by empirical research. The research established and built credentials in law for particular individuals, but law itself was not affected in any substantial way. The legal and policy battles that led to the resultant Federal Rules of Civil Procedure were more the product of bar and legal politics (conflict between big-firm lawyers and smaller, state-based practitioners, for instance) than of rigorous discussions about what the data demonstrated. This theme will be repeated often in our examination of modern procedural reform (Leubsdorf, 1999).

After the busy legal activity of academics in the New Deal and World War II legal agencies, there was little further investment in empirical projects on courts until the 1950s. The rising prominence of social science after the war led some important foundations, including the Ford Foundation, the Walter E. Meyer Research Institute, and the Russell Sage Foundation, to invest, at least temporarily, in blending law and social science. One of the most successful of the studies of courts and rules produced by this new burst of empirical energy was Maurice Rosenberg's study of pre-trial conference rules and practices in New Jersey (1964). Drawing on funds from the Meyer Institute and forming a partnership consistent with the spirit of collaboration of the day, Rosenberg, a civil procedure professor at Columbia, joined with the Columbia University Bureau of Applied Social Research. In what remains today one of the classic studies of courts, Rosenberg found that the pre-trial conference, which was often promoted as a delay-diminishing device, actually prevented judges from taking the bench and resolving cases through trial. With the cooperation and assistance of the Chief Justice of New Jersey, Rosenberg had cases assigned experimentally to mandatory pre-trial conference and non-mandatory (lawyer choice) treatment conditions. With the authority of this science, Rosenberg shifted the defense of pre-trial conferences away from the idea of saving time and expense. He suggested another defense for the process, namely "improving the litigation process." Although judges who did pre-trial conferences had less time to preside over trials and dispose of cases, the pre-trial conference did often turn out to be beneficial in clarifying issues both for trial simplification and for settlement purposes. Following this research, the New Jersey mandatory pre-conference rule was changed in accordance with the study's recommendations. Rosenberg's findings have been confirmed in a variety of replications (e.g., Kakalik et al., 1996a, 1996b; Menkel-Meadow, 1985).

Kalven and Zeisel's (1967) pathbreaking study of the American jury was another product of this era. In another collaboration of lawyer and social scientist, this research demonstrated that judges and juries had agreement rates of about 80%. At a time when the jury system was under attack, the research buttressed the system against charges that juries were poor decision-makers. Modern socio-legal scholars have replicated this study (overcoming problems of accessing actual juries for study purposes which has been almost impossible to gain) by using other research designs to study (from real cases, rather than simulated laboratory settings) decision-making by juries both in comparison with that by judges and as examples of group decision-making on such issues as liability and damage assessment (see Eisenberg et al., 2005; Diamond, 2006; and Chapter 26 on Lay Decision-Makers in the Legal Process, *infra*).

The era of interdisciplinary ferment also attracted psychologists who conducted a series of laboratory experiments about legal process that helped develop the field we now call the "social psychology of procedural justice." This new field can be traced especially to John Thibaut and Laurens Walker's studies of the differences that adversarial and inquisitorial processes make to perceptions of fairness and a series of "tests" of a variety of different rules and procedures of evidence. More recent work, following from this early work, but looking at actual court settings and other real legal procedures, has explored a greater variety of processes, ranging from full adjudication and arbitration to mediation and negotiated agreements (Lind et al., 1990). The procedural justice literature, in very much the same manner as the Rosenberg study, provided a scientific defense of procedural innovations as opposed to the presumption that the reforms saved time and expense. Court-annexed arbitration plans, in particular, gained legitimacy from the finding that litigants who were provided with an opportunity to tell their stories and receive an authoritative decision were more satisfied with the process than those who lacked such an opportunity, as a result, for instance, of their lawyers settling in private negotiations or at pre-trial settlement conferences without consulting them.

The growing social science interest in courts and procedures in the 1970s culminated in the Civil Litigation Research Project (CLRP), funded by the United States federal government and housed at the University of Wisconsin. CLRP collected extensive federal and state court data in five federal and state jurisdictions from interviews, surveys and other material made available by court officials, lawyers, and clients. The CLRP data set provided insights into a number of contested issues about the functioning of the legal system. Some of the remarkable findings were that most cases were handled with little involvement of lawyers and very few negotiation interactions (Kritzer, 1991); that there was little discovery in the average state and federal case (Trubek et al., 1983, consistent with several studies by the Federal Judicial Center: see, e.g., Connolly et al., 1978, and Willging et al., 1998);

and that the regime of lawyers' fees structured incentives for lawyer expenditure of activity. As in the case of other general studies of courts, the main finding was that the processes operate in a very mundane and unsurprising manner, and without major problems. Perhaps because the findings fit no group's political agenda, or perhaps because the Reagan administration was much more interested in economic than legal reform, there was, once again, a relatively long period without major new attention to empirical research on courts. At the time of the CLRP research project, there was hope of permanent funding for a research-oriented Institute of Justice in the U.S. Department of Justice (modeled on the National Institutes of Health for medical research) to systematically study justice issues, but such was not to be. (A small research division of the Federal Judicial Center does conduct some empirical research on procedural issues, as directed by Congress and the federal courts, when there are appropriate allocations of funds and statutory authorization for study of particular issues—see below.)

At the same time, however, certain academic initiatives were important in the development of social-scientific understandings of civil procedure. In particular, Professor Wayne Brazil conducted empirical studies of the behavior of lawyers and judges in discovery and settlement activity (1978, 1984). While he, too, found that discovery was mostly an ordinary and unproblematic process (despite complaints about its "abuse" in some cases, e.g., "big" antitrust and class actions), his studies provided important ammunition in a call for more judicial attention to the discovery process (and his own expertise moved him from academia to a position as a federal magistrate, which he held for several decades, becoming a judicial innovator and leader in the alternative dispute resolution movement).

The social reform agenda of the 1960s and 1970s also brought both theoretical and empirical studies relevant to procedural issues. Marc Galanter's classic article, "Why the 'Haves' Come Out Ahead," published in the *Law and Society Review* (1974), suggested a taxonomy of cases and classes of litigants—principally wealthier and more resource-rich and experienced corporate litigators—advantaged by their ability as "repeat players" to win cases and control procedural and court reform. At the same time, Galanter's diagnosis suggested that by changing the endowments of the players, using class actions (procedural reform) and legal services lawyers (access), the less well endowed could be made as "powerful" as repeat players too.

Demographic, economic, and other endowments make equal access to, and use of, rules and procedures virtually impossible. The research of the 1980s tended to demonstrate that rule reforms perpetuated the absolute power of those with economic, race, gender, or other legal super-endowments. Even processes, like the class action, that seemed to be intended to alter the balance of legal power to create new classes of repeat players, were derailed by others (including securities lawyers and mass tort defendants) who learned how to use the rules to benefit themselves (Coffee, 1995). Consistent with the Reagan-era emphasis on economic reform, promoting business growth, and shrinking the state, the holders of political power sought to discourage litigation as a tool to bring benefits to disadvantaged groups. Partly in response to the social reform literature about how the courts could be used for social change, conservatives promoted reform of procedural rules to curtail "frivolous" litigation (by changes (in Rule 11) to requirements for verification of facts and sanctions for failing to do so and by imposing cost sanctions for failure to accept settlements in Rule 68), and to divert cases out of the courts and into "alternative dispute resolution" fora. There were also procedural reforms by legislation limiting class actions in both securities and prisoner civil rights litigation (e.g., the Private Securities Litigation Reform Act of 1995 and the Prisoner Litigation Reform Act of 1996).

Empirical research has played an important role in the attack on these sets of politically inspired reforms. Indeed, these rule changes provoked a whole new group of empirical researchers from the traditional legal academy challenged by the new conservatives and forced to resort to empirical research because their political arguments no longer succeeded. Claims that rules were meant to be "neutral" but were believed to be having "disparate impacts" on classes of litigants spurred research on a variety of rule changes. Studies of Rule 11, Rule 68, and the new discovery disclosure rules (e.g, Mullenix, 1994) prompted both academic researchers (from within the legal academy) and policy researchers (at RAND and the Federal Judicial Center) to try to demonstrate the actual impact of the rules and whether the reforms "cured" the abuses they were ostensibly designed to remedy or produced other "unintended" effects and distortions. With the political stakes now recognized in debates about civil procedure, investment in social science research increased. Different sides recognized that their positions could be advanced to the extent that they could mobilize the authority of social science on their behalf.

Accordingly, a few distinguished researchers have begun to utilize large data sets to analyze the quantitative patterns revealed by court docket data, now more systematically collected by the Administrative Office of the Courts at the federal level and the National Center for State Courts at the state level in the United States. Among those researchers, Theodore Eisenberg (e.g., 1989, 1990, 1998), working with a number of collaborators in different substantive fields of law, has spent the last 20 years studying important empirical trends and patterns in civil rights, bankruptcy and civil actions. This work has demonstrated, for example, that the treatment of certain classes of cases varies before judges and juries respectively, that grant of summary judgment varies by case type, and that those who transfer or remove cases within the federal system do better after transfer from state courts. Further, this work has demonstrated that cases that go to trial and are recorded on docket entries may not be representative of the full universe of cases. Taken together, this body of research gets behind the ideal of "trans-substantive" rules of procedure toward an understanding of how the rules of procedure are used by particular groups at particular times and how even uniform procedural rules may have different effects in different substantive areas of law. Differences have been found, for instance, in the granting of summary judgment, the manipulation of class actions by both plaintiffs and defendants (Marcus, 2009) and the enforcement of pleading and other procedural rules, such as Rule 11 (Spiegel, 1999, dealing with civil rights cases).

Specifically commissioned research to look at the empirical data supporting rule change has been employed by other nations as well. Lord Harry Woolf's multi-year study and report on Access to Justice (1996) in England and Wales drew on the research of socio-legal researcher Hazel Genn (1999) on patterns of usage of English courts, on costs and timing of litigation, and on litigation practices in the United States (to support proposals for alternative dispute resolution and case management initiatives) and Germany (to support proposals for court-appointed experts and fixed fee schedules). Now that many procedural reforms have been enacted, researchers and a new generation of judges are busily studying the data on the effects of the "Woolf reforms" dealing with case tracking, judicial case management, recommendations to mediate, and other matters. The preliminary results are mixed. Court of Appeal Judge Rupert Jackson (2010) has reported the effects of increased judicial case-management in increasing and "front-loading" costs, while at the same time reducing the time taken to dispose of cases and increasing settlement rates. Hazel Genn (2009) has recently criticized the turn to mediation and settlement (though there is little empirical evidence in England of increased use of court recommended mediation) as a failure of the civil justice system to take its public role of dispute settlement and law-making more seriously. Other researchers in the UK are documenting and decrying the reduced allocation of public funds for legal aid, thus decreasing access to the courts at the same time as formal legal incentives are being provided to attempt out-of-court settlements. In a loser-pays regime, recent case law[1] has suggested that a party may not claim attorneys fees if it has refused to attempt mediation; and legal aid incentives (legal aid not paid unless settlement pursued) also push toward out-of-court resolution. New cost-shifting regimes, allowing some "contingent or conditional fees" in some areas, are also said to be affecting litigation patterns in England and Wales, with little systematic research as yet available. Research on the effectiveness of the Woolf reforms continues apace but is criticized, in part, because most of the funding for such research comes from the same source as the implementer of the reforms, the Ministry of Justice. To the north, Scotland (Scottish Consumer Council, 2005)

---

[1] See, e.g. *Cowl and Others v. Plymouth City Council* [2001] EWCA Civ 1935 (parties seeking public money must consider ADR), *Dunnett v. Railtrack plc* [2002] EWCA Civ 2003 (costs not granted to party who refused to mediate), *Hurst v. Leeming* [2001] EWHC 1051 Ch (up to the judge to decide if mediation is appropriate), and *Leicester Circuits ltd v. Coates Brothers plc* [2003] EWCA Civ 290 (withdrawal from mediation contrary to rules of procedure); but *cf. Halsey v. Milton Keynes General NHS Trust* [2004] EWCA Civ 576 (holding courts have no power to order mediation, which might arguably violate Article 6 of the Human Rights Act, guaranteeing rights of hearing).

commissioned its own separate assessment of whether civil justice reform and rule changes were, in fact, necessary and a Scottish version of the Woolf inquiry was underway as of 2010. (Scotland's legal system operates separately from England and Wales and is a hybrid of common law and some civil law traditions, though it relies more on common law procedural traditions in civil matters and some inquisitorial traditions in criminal process).

III. PROCEDURAL POLICY CONTROVERSIES AND DATA: A FEW EXAMPLES

A selected review of more current empirical studies of procedural rules and court practices illustrates how empirical work has recently been deployed in discussions of some highly contested policy issues—the "litigation explosion" controversy, its opposite and more recent cousin, "the vanishing trial" (research on which has included studies of the effects of rule and case law changes encouraging summary proceedings, verification requirements, and incentives or pressures to settle), the use and effectiveness of ADR, and the desirability and effects of discovery reform.

A. Cost and delay? How much litigation is optimal?

If there is one constant in the contests that have occurred around civil process and litigation (and slightly different versions of the same controversies in criminal law), it is the question of whether there is too much cost and delay and just too much litigation altogether. Note that these two concerns have a way of appearing to be inconsistent with each other. To the extent that there is too much cost and delay in the system, parties will undoubtedly give up and exit the system, using self-help or arranging private settlements, or will begin to use the myriad new ways of processing disputes by some form of public or private alternative dispute resolution. If there is too much litigation (meaning the queues to trial are too long), presumably fewer people will likely initiate litigation. In an important insight (as yet empirically untested, as far as we know), George Priest (1989) has suggested that litigation queues will find an equilibrium point (perhaps at one to two year waits for trial in most matters). If waits for trial are too long, parties will go elsewhere, using ADR or private settlement or dispute avoidance. If ADR, case management, and other efforts to reduce the wait for litigation are effective, then trials will be available more quickly, the "supply" of trials (courtrooms and judges) will increase and more cases will be attracted back into the system. Delay will again develop (unless more judges are appointed and courtrooms are built), and litigation filings will decline again or be redirected to ADR or private dispute resolution programs. Thus, according to Priest, litigation will find its equilibrium point. Others have suggested, however, that if the courts and their adjunct institutions appear to be providing efficient and high quality justice, perhaps through a variety of fora, then more satisfied users will be attracted to the system and total "access" to the civil justice system will be increased and one of our leading democratic institutions—the courts—will be deemed more responsive to the populace (Hornby, 1994).

Whether attraction of new and more cases (as a result of the creation of new statutory entitlements, as in the civil rights and consumer revolutions of the 1960s and 1970s) to civil court processing is a good thing or not evokes the "litigation explosion" controversy, which has raged in the United States for at least two decades. Responding to claims by Warren Burger, Chief Justice of the U.S. Supreme Court, and other academic commentators that the United States suffered from "*hyperlexia*" (Manning, 1977), several social scientists have attempted to measure and evaluate how much is too much and how different nations' "litigiousness" should be compared, either to some baseline within each nation (a "temporal" measure) or to a baseline based on the experience of some other nation(s). Meanwhile, academic researchers like Marc Galanter (1983) and a few others (e.g., Genn, 2009; Marvell and Daniels, 1986) have rigorously demonstrated that such questions about how much litigation is appropriate or "too much" or "too little" (Galanter, 2004: "the vanishing trial") cannot be answered without considering particular social and cultural contexts. In addition to differences between the wording of particular rules and the structures of particular rule regimes, there are larger cultural differences which remain "traces" in procedural rule reforms such as that between more adversarial and more inquisitorial systems (Menkel-Meadow, 2004). As scholars are now drawn to "the vanishing trial" debate it might surprise them to note that Clark and Shulman (1937) noted decreasing trial rates as early as the 1930s (less than 4% of civil cases filed were tried, a decrease from earlier decades), though we know those rates later increased again, suggesting that trial rates may be more variable over time than suggested by those current scholars who lament the current low trial rates (about 1% of civil cases filed in federal courts) (Galanter, 2004).

B. Increasingly adversarial procedure and practice?

Complaints about the conduct of litigation have suggested that lawyers, particularly in discovery, but also in trial and in other settings, have become nastier, more adversarial, and less "gentlemanly," and that they have abused the system of discovery, which was established in 1938 to counteract the "trial by surprise" regime of older, more conventional, and, certainly cheaper, litigation. While some lay the blame for bad behavior in psychological and cultural terms (a short-fuse, fast-paced, less mentored, more aggressive legal culture), others suggest that "scorched earth" and aggressive practices can be explained better by economics (successful class action plaintiffs' lawyers who finance big litigation by seeking "smoking gun" documents in one litigation to be used to finance another, e.g., asbestos to tobacco to guns) or defense lawyers who use scorched earth tactics to beat back litigation altogether with *in terrorem* attacks on plaintiffs of all kinds (Nelson, 1998). While socio-legal scholars can explore the dimensions of whether cultures (either professional or national) have changed or whether the business or economic interests of the profession have become more dominant, the response of legal rule-makers to undesirable "overzealous" advocacy has been to enact (partly in response to Wayne Brazil's (1978) excellent studies and articles documenting this behavior) new rules such as those in the United States imposing automatic disclosure requirements and increased sanctions for dilatory or unethical behavior, and those in England and Wales requiring pre-trial protocols (by case-type) and providing for disallowance of costs.

What a perfect project for socio-legal scholars concerned about process! Scholars (mostly people concerned with law and legal policy, not sociologists or psychologists) have jumped into the arena to debate the effectiveness of rulemaking as an agent of behavioral change and have, for the most part, found it wanting (Marcus, 1993). Researchers have documented the remarkable strength and resilience of the adversary system, the larger legal culture in which this activity is embedded, and the professional self-interest of the lawyers who feed it (Sorenson, 1995; Mullenix, 1994). There is no evidence, as of yet, that the allegorical beast of adversariness has been tamed by rule changes.

C. Discovery and disclosure—too much, not enough?

Scholars continue to point out, however, that the empirical world of discovery is varied and complex. Uniform rules may not be appropriate when there are different realities for the big cases, which involve a large amount of discovery and more potential for abuse, and for the more modal and smaller cases. In England, Lord Woolf's proposal, to send cases down different procedural "tracks" according to their size (e.g., numbers of parties, complexity of claims, and the amount in controversy) was an effort to provide procedural variation in the treatment to different kinds of cases (with perhaps an explicit acknowledgement that trans-substantive or uniform procedural rules will not suffice in this modern age; see Marcus, 2010).

D. Uniformity and neutrality or case type variations in rules?

As a result of two recent United States Supreme Court cases, which seem to require more specificity in pleading (thus reversing 50 years of "notice" pleading), there will undoubtedly be studies to see whether these "enhanced pleading" rules will have disparate impacts on particular categories of "disfavored" cases (e.g., antitrust and civil rights from which cases these rulings were derived).

Other scholars have explored whether, as in studies of verification and sanction under Rule 11, there are case type differentials in the granting of motions to dismiss or for summary judgment, or whether changes in case law, suggesting more permissive rules for granting summary judgments without trials, also are differently affecting different types of litigants, such as civil rights claimants, as opposed to corporate litigants (Kritzer, 1986; Schneider, 2007).

E. Case management, alternative dispute resolution, and litigation reform

Perhaps the most contentious use of social science in law in recent years has been the multi-million dollar effort to evaluate the effects of the Civil Justice Reform Act (CJRA) of 1990. Designed as a Congressional program to tame the perceived or alleged, ferocious "cost and delay" problem in the United States federal courts, the CJRA asked each federal district court to consider a number of case management devices, such as mandatory settlement conferences, firm trial dates, tracked litigation (requiring different handling for more complex cases) and some forms of ADR. The RAND Corporation was authorized by Congress to evaluate the effectiveness of these different devices and the Federal Judicial Center was given a small budget to examine a group of five demonstration courts that were working on particular projects or programs to be tested.

Several million dollars later, the RAND Report confirmed some of Maurice Rosenberg's early findings: of the various recipes that were tried, the most effective way to reduce time to trial was to set a firm trial date and to cut off discovery early. Intervention by judges in extensive case management was itself time-consuming and expensive (though some evidence suggested that costs of case management to the larger system were offset by savings to the litigants in earlier dispositions and more efficiently tried cases). Others have argued that with increased judicial attention, lawyers, feeling increased judicial scrutiny of their activities, will work harder and charge their clients more, thus increasing costs. Similar findings on the increased costs of "front-loading" case management and pre-trial procedures, even in a tracked system, are now being confirmed in England and Wales (Jackson, 2010;

Genn, 2009). Whether "case management" is effective, both from an efficiency perspective and a philosophical perspective of debated conceptions of "justice," has also become one of the most discussed issues in studies of comparative (particularly civil vs. common law) procedure (Shoenberger, 2009).

On the other hand, much to the chagrin of the proponents of ADR, the RAND Reports (Kakalik et al., 1996a, 1996b) failed to demonstrate any cost or time savings from the use of mediation, arbitration, or early neutral evaluation in a number of courts which had pioneered such alternative processes. The proponents were able to find some methodological problems with this evaluation study—the courts studied were moving targets, some having begun their experiments before the study began, others having instituted programs during the study period, and some courts having forms of ADR that the ADR community did not support (Menkel-Meadow, 1997; McEwen and Plapinger, 1997). The variations between these alternatives made comparison of time and costs quite difficult—e.g., some arbitrations were more likely to be completed as full hearings than trials, details of mediations are difficult, if not impossible, to ascertain with principles of confidentiality operating in mediation, and early neutral evaluation procedures varied as settlement conferences or discovery planning events—thus making comparisons of widely different forms of process difficult, if not impossible. Some critics suggested that the study itself asked the wrong questions and narrowly focused on the more measurable issues of cost and delay, rather than the more interesting and complex jurisprudential issues of what constitutes a fairer, more "just," and higher-quality result from the legal system. Others suggested arguments untested by the RAND study, for example, that ADR provides more party-tailored and Pareto-optimal solutions to problems, permits the kind of party participation that procedural justice scholars have told us is so important, and provides a variety of processes tailored to the different structures of different types of disputes studied by anthropologists and legal scholars (Fuller, 2001). What was striking, however, was the strength of the attack on this work by the ADR community, including the federal judges identified with ADR experiments.

As discussions about whether civil and common law systems are converging or diverging are explored at an ever-increasing number of academic venues (Marcus, 2009; Zuckerman, 1999), common trends and issues include case management and the use of ADR as explored above, whether different fees and costs structures (punitive damages, contingent and conditional fees) affect patterns of court usage, and whether litigation rates are decreasing. For example, the "vanishing trial" in the United States (Galanter, 2004) is alternatively attributed to ADR, formal and informal pressures to settle, and the growing criminal docket in a time of "three strikes and you're out" (mandatory lifetime incarceration after three convictions reduces plea bargains and increases court usage for criminal, not civil, trials). Studies of different deployment of "newer" processes include mapping the use of class actions in the United States and elsewhere, and creative uses of technology, both for discovery and for trials themselves. Whether rigorous empirical studies of comparative civil (and criminal) processes are possible in widely varying local, national, and legal cultures remains an open and often contested question, even as new justice systems seek guidance about dispute system design (for informal, formal, and, sometimes, transitional-justice institutions, see Menkel-Meadow, 2009).

IV. Toward a Socio-legal Jurisprudence of Process, Procedure, and Courts

Our review of the literature of social science and civil procedure suggests an increase over time in the importance of social science research to debates about civil procedure. The emerging empirical research has developed into a small industry oriented toward the Federal Rules of Civil Procedure in the United States and measurement and comparison of the efficiency of rules and processes outside of the United States. We have seen a move, from a time when Charles Clark used his authority as an empirical student of the courts to produce the Federal Rules of Civil Procedure, and Lord Woolf used similar authority, backed up by empirical study and comparative arguments, to produce major rule change in England and Wales, to a time where the rules are constantly being tested through empirical research.

Almost all of the research we have discussed can be characterized as legally driven. Researchers use empirical research to question or support the need for a particular procedural innovation, whether relating to discovery, case management, ADR, fees and costs, or the role of the jury. The leading empirical researchers, and even the judges who support and interpret the procedural research, gain stature as leading voices about the courts and dispute resolution.

Social science and social scientists matter increasingly in these policy debates as rule reforms are proposed. At the same time, however, it is useful to reflect more deeply on the process of studying court processes. First, while the value of the empirical research is clearly increasing, there are some timeless patterns in the conduct, engagement with, and use of this work, suggesting that even with more empirical research, there is little change in its absolute influence. The patterns include criticism of the courts for their failure to work effectively, suggesting that they are too expensive, too adversarial, or too slow. Typically the criticism is made on behalf of a group that thinks the courts should serve its needs better, but the criticism is expressed mainly in terms of cost and delay. Responding to the criticisms, reformers suggest changes in the rules that will make the system work better. Since the relevant actors know that any change will serve some groups—such as litigants, attorneys, and judges—better than others, the potential reforms must be cloaked in neutral language, such as efficiency. Then the policy reformers recognize that they can buy some time and potentially mobilize support for their position if they can call for systematic empirical research and hard data. The research, however, rarely provides definitive information in support of or against particular reforms. The courts and the lawyers who appear in those courts do not change very quickly, and one of the recurring findings is how ordinary most litigation is, even in the federal courts.

From Clark's Connecticut study to the Civil Litigation Research Project to the RAND study of the Civil Justice Reform Act (CJRA) and Genn's studies in the UK, for most litigation we find little evidence of any major procedural problems. We find relatively few "runaway" jury verdicts, relatively few examples of discovery abuse, and expenses that are not typically that high in relation to the amount in controversy, except perhaps, in some small-amount controversies that are, in fact, quite complex factually or legally, or in the outlier "mega-case." Nevertheless, the empirical studies can usually be used to support some change that is responsive to external criticisms. The external critics are to some extent mollified, and the system proceeds until new rounds of criticism emerge, often in reaction to the then successful rule reform (see, e.g., the Rule 11 controversies in the United States and related studies). Improvements in empirical research methods and increasing investment in empirical research help to tame this process. Radical criticisms are seen to be overstated and not all reforms gain support as in the retrenchment on Rule 11 and the addition of a "safe harbor" provision for corrections to pleadings, to avoid disparate and draconian sanctions.

There is a related process that complements the empirical research on cost and delay. Increasingly, it appears, the U.S. actors connected to both federal and state judiciaries (both judges and lawyers) compete for innovation and distinction in issues related to court reform, and they often use highly quantitative empirical research as one of their tools. This phenomenon is not new. The study by Maurice Rosenberg was used as a way to justify pre-trial hearings, and the pattern of the study is instructive. The evaluation, conducted in terms of cost and delay, revealed findings of no major impacts on cost or delay, and the "findings" were used to construct a different justification for the reform—improving the litigation process. Similarly, procedural justice research was used extensively to evaluate court-annexed arbitration in the 1980s. The evaluations were conducted in terms of cost and delay, often under the auspices of the RAND Institute for Civil Justice, but the theories of procedural justice and findings could be used to provide another justification for the innovations—namely that the parties would be more satisfied with the procedure because they would be permitted to tell their stories to a decision-maker.

Studies of mediation-based alternatives to trials can be seen to have a similar trajectory. Again, there is considerable innovation in rules and practices in many systems directing the parties towards mediation or other "alternative to trial" modes; these innovations are often followed by empirical studies that are inconclusive as to whether the innovations reduce cost and delay, but provide some evidence of user satisfaction. This leads the proponents of the innovations to attack the results of the study concerning cost and delay and to offer alternative justifications for mediation based on the data of "user satisfaction."

The cycle may be continuing. There are jury experiments in Arizona now subject to comprehensive experimental evaluations. While not bound in this instance by concerns of cost and delay, it will nevertheless be interesting to see how the innovators, suggesting new jury processes (such as jury note-taking and allowing jurors to talk during the trial), will deal with inconclusive data results (Diamond and Vidmar, 2001). If trials have not totally vanished, juries certainly have in most of the world. The United States and just a few provinces and states in Canada and Australia continue to use juries in civil cases (the UK and a few others still use them in criminal cases and in a very limited subset of civil cases such as those alleging slander or libel), though some nations (especially those with young legal systems or new constitutional orders) see experimentation with juries as a way of enhancing democratic participation in the polity. As Japan, for example, begins to use juries, the social scientists are ready to study group process, deference, and decision patterns in a society thought to be more homogeneous than many others. Questions of how participation in litigation systems affects democratic participation are important ones, but answering them is fraught with complex methodological, inferential, and evidentiary difficulties.

And, as we move from "litigation explosions" to "vanishing trials," different sets of reformers argue about how much litigation is optimal, both for the parties themselves and for the important public function of generating court decisions and legal precedents for the rest of us. Counting the number of trials does not directly respond to the question of "how much public or private justice is enough?"

What may be surprising is that there is very little attempt in law or in social science to get beneath the formal legal categories to try to understand changes in procedures and procedural reform in relation to the changing social role of the courts. If we ask only if mediation works better than litigation, for example, we neglect the way that both processes change over time—different kinds of cases, different kinds of lawyers, and, above all, different types of mediators. Scorched-earth litigation (pursuing every possible avenue of discovery, disclosure, and contention, regardless of cost of one side to drive up the costs for the other side) is called the "adversary system," when in fact it has almost no resemblance to the adversary system of a generation ago when there was little discovery at all and adversarial justice meant surprising your opponent with totally new information at trial. The problems of the courts are considered timeless, requiring solutions which are gradually being improved with new technologies such as ADR, case management, and now use of computers in courts. Can data help us answer the question of what kind of processes are optimal for what kinds of disputes?

If we go beneath these categories and the rituals of criticism and reform, we find a number of issues that are difficult to assimilate into those categories. For example, prior to the 1970s and 1980s, large-firm litigators were unlikely to appear in the federal courts except on the side of the defense. Big businesses did not sue other big businesses. Now they do. This phenomenon suggests the need for more attention to be paid to who uses the courts—not just litigants but lawyers. For most of English history only barristers had "rights of audience" in the higher courts; now some solicitors do, too. What difference might this make in case handling? Court usage and practice? Client choices? It may make a difference *who* handles particular cases. A leading trial lawyer is selected because he or she will most likely get a larger settlement offer. There are some law firms that are hired for "bet the company" (or high-risk) litigation, as in patent or trade secrets cases with winner-take-all results; and we can hypothesize that the tactics used in and the costs of such cases will be different from the tactics and costs associated with other cases that may, on the surface, seem the same. There are studies of how civil procedure reforms affect different types of litigants, but not how they may affect different kinds of lawyers and law firms. Will the use of solicitor advocates reduce costs with increased competition with barristers? Will solicitors have to learn and study more court procedure than before? Again this research is hard to do, since differences among types of lawyers, that are known to litigants and courts, are not necessarily readily apparent to researchers.

To return to historical issues that studies of cost and delay tend to miss, class actions enjoyed a period of ascendency in the 1970s before declining in the 1980s, and moving back up in the 1990s, but the nature of the class action changed dramatically from civil rights—with some antitrust—to tort and securities. Similarly, legal services (legal aid) and public interest lawyers dominated most of the show-case litigation of the 1970s and 1980s, while business lawyers and those who represent plaintiffs in securities and personal injury litigation have dominated in the last 15 years. We now routinely recognize that litigation is part of "business" used for strategic economic reasons, not simply a matter of a "dispute," as illustrated in the growth of intellectual property and trade secret litigation. Litigation may be an economic tool to put competitors at a disadvantage. The Justice Department lawsuit against Microsoft, for example, was recognized by many as a fight begun by Netscape, Sun, and the companies of the Silicon Valley. These changes over time are often hard to see in quantitative studies, since the categories that are available to sort the cases may not change even if what is meant by the category does, such as whether class action is chosen by a group of plaintiffs or defendants and whether trade secret and intellectual property litigation is pursued offensively or defensively. Judges, who used to make their careers through the quality and quantity of their published opinions, now tend to make their reputations by efficient case processing—and by innovations in case processing, such as mediative judges in the construction and commercial courts of England and elsewhere. On retirement, leading judges increasingly "go private" (not only in the United States but in England as well; see Genn, 2009), making much more money as private judges of business disputes than they made as public judges. Leading academics in the 1970s could assert that the U.S. federal courts only existed to protect constitutional values and to resolve the civil rights litigation that implemented them. Their approaches now seem almost anachronistic—as do the many studies of inequality in the resources of those who sought to enforce civil rights (Bumiller, 1988). The paradigmatic case in the minds of the rule reformers today is a business lawsuit, which may be wasting shareholder assets, rather than litigation involving public values. Procedural reformers of each decade seem disproportionately to come from particular segments of the bar.

What this suggests is that U.S. federal courts may be playing a very different role today than they were a generation ago, refereeing complex business disputes and managing routine matters, rather than enunciating great constitutional principles. It appears obvious also that the phenomena of scorched-earth litigation, discovery abuse, alternative dispute resolution, and even cost and delay are related to the "social" and "economic" changes that are external to the courts, but are experienced and problematized within the formal justice system. These changes, in who litigates and for what reasons, also affect quite dramatically the agenda for reform—the rise of in-house counsel, for example, is relevant to the increase in business litigation and then to new criticisms of the courts. The new agenda that responds to the criticisms gets translated into issues of cost and delay, but the agendas for reform are also ones that are designed to respond to the constituencies who are now most prominent in the minds of judges and some scholars—notably business litigants. When all is said and done, the new cycle of criticism and reform, aided by innovative judges, and social science that stays within the categories of cost and delay, allows the courts to remain relatively the same while repositioning themselves to be more responsive to business concerns. The repositioning moves, at the same time, away from responding mainly to the concerns that used to be identified with the activist state. Now only a few call for "more active" courts—promoting a social agenda (Genn, 2009; Galanter, 2004). Empirical research on civil procedure rules and practice, which began as a search for understanding justice and access to courts now often becomes a tool of argument for those who wish to use the courts for their own ends—business interests, as well as those who still hope to achieve social reform through litigation. Use of procedural empirical research, then, becomes tied to substantive, not "neutral" procedural, issues. There is very little that social science research and data can do to help resolve the fundamental questions about what purpose(s) courts serve and for whom (dispute resolution for the parties or public law generation for the larger society?). At best, social science research can help us to understand if particular rules are more or less likely to let in particular claims or particular claimants or whether particular procedural systems disproportionately serve particular kinds of cases or litigants.

We suggest some useful questions to look at in future research about courts and process by looking at who is doing and who is using that research. One issue to explore is to look at how the researchers who do empirical research on the courts are rewarded within legal fields, whether in practice or scholarly rewards, and whether the "price" for that reward (especially when courts themselves are sponsoring the research) is to abandon testing of the theories that come from the social science disciplines themselves (about "voice," democratic participation, trust in governmental institutions, and so on), in favor of addressing the problems that respond to the needs of the courts. Are researchers who adopt external perspectives able to do such research and gain recognition in their disciplines or in law? Second, what kinds of activities reward judges, both within the judicial sphere and, after retirement from the bench, in reinventing themselves as private judges, politicians, or corporate lawyers? Is it correct, as we have asserted here, that judges a generation ago made their careers much more through opinion writing and law generation than case management?

What civil procedure and the courts are today, and the role of the social science that attempts to study these issues, depend on the institutional incentives (human capital in promotions and recognition of innovations or reforms that serve the system or particular litigants, as well as potential future pecuniary or reputational gain) that surround those whose activities as judges, lawyers, rule reformers, and scholars focus on the courts and their procedures. It would certainly be useful to have more information on the players in the reform of civil procedure. What kinds of cases and clients, for example, do the lawyers and judges active in reform have? How did they get to be the spokespersons, committee members, and rule-drafters on the issues they take up? How do they compare with the spokespersons a generation ago? Whose issues and whose needs are represented in debates about court reform and who chooses the researchers to study them? These kinds of questions may be more "external" to particular rule-reform research in the sense that they derive from theories about institutions, institutional actors and the forces which produce institutional change. This type of research, which ranges from rational choice to more historical work, offers some potential to change our understanding of courts and procedures by placing them within an evolving social context. Such research could also challenge our notions of "pure" disinterested research, unaffected by funding source or policy pulls, our belief in the importance of tinkering with procedures in order to reduce cost and delay, and faith in research that "simply" counts cases or steps in litigation. If empirical researchers studying courts and civil procedure can be self-reflective and ask themselves why the research is being conducted and in whose interests, then perhaps such research can be more than a "pawn" in the ongoing and cyclical policy debates about rule reform. We could perhaps find out what people want of their justice system and how different processes might serve both different people and different causes differently.

References

Brazil, W. (1978). "The Adversary Character of Civil Discovery: a Critique and Proposals for Change," *Vanderbilt Law Review* 31: 1295–1361.

Brazil, W. (1984). "Settling Civil Cases: What Lawyers Want From Judges," *Judges' Journal* 23: 15–19.

Bumiller, K. (1988). *The Civil Rights Society: The Social Construction of Victims*, Baltimore: Johns Hopkins University Press.

Clark, C. and Shulman, H. (1937). *A Study of Law Administration in Connecticut: A Report of Investigation of the Articles of Certain Trial Courts of the State*, New Haven: Yale University Press.

Coffee, J. (1995). "Class Wars: The Dilemma of the Mass Tort Class Action," *Columbia Law Review* 95: 1343–1465.

Clermont, K. and Eisenberg, T. (1992). "Trial by Judge or Jury: Transcending Empiricism," *Cornell Law Review* 77: 1124–77.

Connolly, P.R., Holleman, E., and Kuklman, M.J. (1978). *Judicial Controls and the Civil Litigation Process: Discovery*, Washington, DC: Federal Judicial Center.

Diamond, S.S. (2006). "Beyond Fantasy and Nightmare: A Portrait of the Jury," 54 *Buffalo Law Review* 717–63.

Diamond, S.S. and Vidmar, J. (2001). "Jury Room Ruminations on Forbidden Topics," *Virginia Law Review* 87:1857–1915.

Eisenberg, T. (1989). "Litigation Models and Trial Outcomes in Civil Rights and Prisoner Cases," *Georgetown Law Journal* 77: 1567–602.

Eisenberg, T. (1990). "Testing the Selection Effect: A New Theoretical Framework with Empirical Tests," *Journal of Legal Studies* 19: 337–58.

Eisenberg, T. (1998). "Measuring the Deterrent Effect of Punitive Damages," *Georgetown Law Journal* 87: 347–57.

Eisenberg, T., Hannaford-Agor, P., Hans, V.P., Mott, N.L., Munsterman, G.T., Schwab, S.J., and Wells, M.T. (2005). "Judge-Jury Agreement in Criminal Cases: A Partial Replication of Kalven and Zeisel's *The American Jury*," *Journal of Empirical Legal Studies* 2: 171–206.

Fuller, L. (2001). *The Principles of Social Order: Selected Essays of Lon L. Fuller*, K. Winston, (ed.), Oxford and Portland, Oregon: Hart Publishing.

Galanter, M. (1974). "Why the 'Haves' Come Out Ahead: Speculations on the Limits of Legal Change," *Law and Society Review* 9: 95–160.

Galanter, M. (1983). "Reading the Landscape of Disputes: What We Know and Don't Know (and Think We Know) About Our Allegedly Contentious and Litigious Society," *UCLA Law Review* 31: 4–71.

Galanter, M. (2004). "The Vanishing Trial: An Examination of Trials and Related Matters in Federal and State Courts," *Journal of Empirical Legal Studies* 1: 459–570.

Garth, B. (1997) 'Observations On An Uncomfortable Relationship: Civil Procedure and Empirical Research," *Alabama Law Review* 49: 103–31.

Genn, H. (1999). *Paths to Justice: What People Do and Think About Going to Law,* Oxford and Portland, Oregon: Hart Publishing.

Genn, H. (2009). *Judging Civil Justice.* Cambridge: Cambridge University Press.

Hornby, B.D. (1994). "Federal Court Annexed ADR: After the Hoopla," *FJC Directions* 7: 26–9.

Jackson, R. (2010). *Review of Civil Litigation Costs: Final Report,* London: Royal Courts of Justice.

Kakalik, J.S., Dunworth, T., Hill, L.A., McCaffrey, D., Oshiro, M., Pace, N.M., and Vaiana, M.E. (1996a). *Just, Speedy and Inexpensive? An Evaluation of Judicial Case Management Under the Civil Justice Reform Act,* Santa Monica, CA: RAND.

Kakalik, J. S., Dunworth, T., Hill, L.A., McCaffrey, D., Oshiro, M., Pace, N.M., and Vaiana, M.E. (1996b). *An Evaluation of Mediation and Early Natural Evaluation Under the Civil Justice Reform Act,* Santa Monica, California: RAND.

Kalven, H. and Zeisel, H. (1967). *The American Jury,* Chicago: University of Chicago Press.

Kritzer, H.M. (1986). "Adjudication to Settlement: Shading in the Gray," *Judicature* 70: 161–5.

Kritzer, H.M. (1991). *Let's Make A Deal: Understanding the Negotiation Process in Ordinary Litigation,* Madison: University of Wisconsin Press.

Kritzer, H.M. (2009). "Fee Regimes and the Cost of Civil Justice," *Civil Justice Quarterly* 28: 344–66.

Leubsdorf, J. (1999). "The Myth of Civil Procedure Reform," in A.A.S. Zuckerman (ed.), *Civil Justice in Crisis: Comparative Perspectives of Civil Procedure,* Oxford: Oxford University Press.

Lind, E.A. and Tyler, T.R. (1988). *The Social Psychology of Procedural Justice,* New York: Plenum Press.

Lind, E.A., MacCoun R.J., Ebener, P.A., Felstiner, E.L.F., Hensler, D.R., Resnik J., and Tyler, T.R. (1990). "In the Eye of the Beholder: Tort Litigants' Evaluations of Their Experiences in the Civil Justice System," 24 *Law and Society Review* 24: 953–96.

Manning, B. (1977). "Hyperlexis: Our National Disease," *Northwestern University Law Review* 767–82.

Marcus, D. (2010). "The Past, Present and Future of Trans-Substantivity in Federal Civil Procedure," *DePaul Law Review* 59 [forthcoming].

Marcus, R. (1993). "Of Babies and Bathwater: The Prospects for Procedural Progress," *Brooklyn Law Review* 59: 761–825.

Marcus, R. (1999). "Malaise of the Litigation Superpower," in A.A.S. Zuckerman (ed.), *Civil Justice in Crisis: Comparative Perspectives of Civil Procedure,* Oxford: Oxford Press.

Marcus, R. (2009). "Modes of Procedural Reform," *Hastings International and Comparative Law Review* 31: 157–91.

Marvell, T. and Daniels, S. (1986). "Are Caseloads Really Increasing?," *Judges' Journal* 25: 34.

McEwen, C. and Plapinger, E. (1997). "RAND Report Points the Way to Next Generation of ADR Research," *Dispute Resolution Magazine* (Summer): 10.

Menkel-Meadow, C. (1985). "For and Against Settlement: The Uses and Abuses of the Mandatory Settlement Conference," *UCLA Law Review* 33: 485–514.

Menkel-Meadow, C. (1995). "Whose Dispute Is It Anyway? A Philosophical and Democratic Defense of Settlement (in some cases)," *Georgetown Law Journal* 83: 2663–96.

Menkel-Meadow, C. (1997). "When Dispute Resolution Begets Disputes Of Its Own: Conflicts Among Dispute Professionals," *UCLA Law Review* 44: 1871–1933.

Menkel-Meadow, C. (2004). "Is the Adversary System Dead? Dilemmas of Legal Ethics as Legal Institutions and Roles Evolve," in J. Holder, C. O'Cinneide, and M. Freeman (eds.), *Current Legal Problems,* Oxford: Oxford University Press.

Menkel-Meadow, C. (2009). "Are There Systemic Ethics Issues in Dispute System Design? And What We Should [Not] Do About It: Lessons from International and Domestic Fronts," *Harvard Negotiation Law Review* 14: 195–231.

Michalik, P. (1999). "Justice in Crisis: England and Wales," in A.A.S. Zuckerman (ed.), *Civil Justice in Crisis: Comparative Perspectives of Civil Procedure,* Oxford: Oxford University Press.

Mullenix, L. (1994). "Discovery in Disarray: The Pervasive Myth of Pervasive Discovery Abuse and the Consequences for Unfounded Rulemaking," *Stanford Law Review* 46: 1393–1445.

Nelson, R. (1998). "The Discovery Process as Circle of Blame: Institutional, Professional and Socio-Economic Factors That Contribute to Unreasonable, Inefficient and Amoral Behavior in Corporate Litigation," *Fordham Law Review* 67: 773–808.

Pound, R. (1906). *The Causes of Popular Dissatisfaction with the Administration of Justice,* Speech at the American Bar Association Annual Meeting, Aug. 29, 1906.

Priest, G. (1989). "Private Litigants and the Court Congestion Problem," *Boston University Law Review* 69: 527–59.

Priest, G. and Klein, B. (1984). "The Selection of Disputes for Litigation," *Journal of Legal Studies* 13: 1–55.

Rosenberg, M. (1964). *The Pre-Trial Conference and Effective Justice: A Controlled Test in Personal Injury Litigation,* New York: Columbia University Press.

Schlegel, J.H. (1995). *American Legal Realism and Empirical Social Science,* Chapel Hill, NC: University of North Carolina Press.

Schneider, E.M. (2007). "The Dangers of Summary Judgment: Gender and Federal Civil Litigation," *Rutgers Law Review* 59: 705–77.

Scottish Consumer Council (2005). *The Civil Justice System in Scotland—A case for Review?,* Glasgow: Scottish Consumer Council.

Shapiro, M. (1981). *Courts: A Comparative and Political Analysis,* Chicago: University of Chicago Press.

Shoenberger, A. (2009). "Change in European Civil Law Systems? Infiltration of the Anglo-American Case Law System of Precedent into Civil Law System," *Loyola Law Review* 55: 5–21.

Sorenson, C. (1995). "Disclosure Under Federal Rule of Civil Procedure 26(a)—Much Ado About Nothing," *Hastings Law Review* 46: 679–796.

Spiegel, M. (1999). "The Rule 11 Studies and Civil Rights Cases; An Inquiry into the Neutrality of Procedural Rules," *Connecticut Law Review* 32: 155–207.

Stewart, S. (2009). "Civil Court Case Management in England, Wales and Belgium: Philosophy and Efficiency," *Civil Justice Quarterly* 28: 206–17.

Thibaut J. and Walker, L. (1975). *Procedural Justice: A Psychological Analysis,* Hillsdale, NJ: L. Erlbaum Associates.

Trubek, D. et al. (1983). "The Costs of Ordinary Litigation," *UCLA Law Review* 31: 72–127.

Tyler, T.R. (1997). "Citizen Discontent with Legal Procedures: A Social Science Perspective on Civil Procedure Reform," *American Journal of Comparative Law* 45: 871–904.

Willging, T., Stienstra, D., Shapard, J., and Miletich, D. (1998). "An Empirical Study of Discovery and Disclosure Practices Under the 1993 Federal Rules Amendments," *Boston College Law Review* 39: 525–96.

Woolf, H. (1996). *Final Report to the Lord Chancellor: Access to Justice in the Civil Justice System in England and Wales*, London: HMSO.

Zuckerman, A.A.S. (1999). *Civil Justice in Crisis: Comparative Perspectives of Civil Procedure*, Oxford: Oxford University Press.

29

COLLECTIVE ACTIONS

CHRISTOPHER HODGES

THIS CHAPTER examines the powerful phenomenon of collective or aggregate civil litigation, manifested in different forms as a class action, representative action, group action or in some other form. The aggregative technique, in the form of a class action, has proved to be a powerful feature of the legal system in the United States of America since the 1960s, and spread to Australia and Canada during the 1990s, whereas different forms have so far colonized Europe and Latin America. However, no single procedural model or blueprint has emerged and, indeed, different countries have adopted sometimes bewilderingly different models, and variations are proliferating. This diversity presents a real challenge in drawing comparisons, and raises a particular need to study the different techniques involved, so as to determine which features are mechanistically useful or favorable in particular situations. As we shall see, there is so far limited data for anything approaching a comparison to be made on a global basis. We are only at the start of undertaking this comparative evaluation, and initial results are proving to be fascinating (Hensler and Hodges, 2009).

Even more fundamental reasons to evaluate differing techniques have recently emerged, particularly out of debate in Europe, and it is these issues that form the principal focus of this Chapter. There has been a realization by some policy-makers that desired objectives (discussed below) may be achieved by one or more of a number of different techniques, drawing on forms of public or private enforcement (Hodges, 2008) and that an empirical approach can significantly assist design choices. Hence, the need for empirical data arises from a need to compare and evaluate different procedures for aggregation that may be applied not just within civil procedure systems (as has frequently been the focus hitherto) but also within other public, or even private, enforcement systems. In other words, the goal is not just to compare a U.S.-style class action procedure with a European or Latin American style representative action procedure, or, at a technical level, to compare an opt-in technique with an opt-out approach, but to compare aggregation mechanisms that exist within litigation systems with those that can be found within regulatory or private sector enforcement systems. This approach involves a strong recognition of the importance of collective techniques, but also of a need to answer questions over which ones should be preferred, in which combinations, and in what circumstances.

Such a wider field of inquiry is new and daunting, but also exciting. One of the major challenges is to transcend traditional silos of expertise: those who are familiar with civil procedure may have little knowledge of regulation and its enforcement, or *vice versa*, and in any event there is a need to bring to bear the differing expertise and insights found in law, economics, and political science. While some data now exist on the internal operational features of class actions in the United States, and some are beginning to emerge from Canada, Australia, and England as collective procedures begin to build up sufficient track records in those jurisdictions, very little data collection has taken place or even been envisaged, on the wider issues that now arise in comparing liability and regulatory systems. Accordingly, rather than list the major studies that have so far emerged on particular procedures in particular countries, this Chapter will focus on identifying the major issues on which research is needed in order to be able to further the wider agenda referred to here, and indicating those parts of that agenda where some (usually limited) research has been done and those parts where there are gaps. The starting point is to identify the fundamental questions that arise on the wider viewpoint and that call for answers.

I. Fundamental Questions

Four broad categories of questions arise. Firstly, what are the goals of the collective procedure? Secondly, what level of need exists for such a procedure, so that resources can be prioritized? Thirdly, how do particular procedures and sub-techniques work, and in what circumstances? The fourth question is evaluative, and in two parts. Firstly, in relation to any given procedure, how well does it work (internally) in delivering the outcomes and goals that are desired, and with what level of cost or undesirable features? Secondly, how do all of the available procedures compare in delivering optimal outcomes and goals with lowest acceptable undesirable effects? Hence, which individual procedures are to be preferred, in what circumstances? Finally, and most difficult to decide, what combination of procedures should best apply, and when?

Before giving an overview of the major extant attempts to answer these questions, it is necessary to say something, first, about the different types of procedures that exist, since the great variety among procedures presents barriers to understanding and comparability and, secondly, about the availability and limitations of the research techniques in relation to what we want to know.

II. Terminology and Typology: Challenges of Comparisons

The first challenge is to understand the differences and similarities among the various models, in order to ensure that like is being compared with like. Adopting a technical perspective, the main models might be summarized as follows. In one model, a single claim is taken to represent all others in a defined class of similar claims so that not all who have such claims are required to sue, but the outcome of the representative claim will bind all the class members (unless they have opted out or opted in if the rule requires them to do that). This class action model is prevalent in the United States of America, Canada, Australia, and Sweden, but with significant technical differences in each case (a series of national reports covering some 30 jurisdictions is available online[1] and summarized in Hensler and Hodges, 2009).

---

[1] See <http://www.globalclassactions.stanford.edu>.

In a variant on that model, a collective claim is not advanced by a lead representative plaintiff but by a representative body, such as a consumer association or public authority, which may or may not itself have an individual right of action separate from its representative function. This approach has developed for consumer protection claims throughout European jurisdictions and is spreading in Latin American jurisdictions, to date primarily giving rise to injunctive relief rather than an award of damages.

A second model, illustrated by the Group Litigation Order of England and Wales[2] and the American multi-districting rule (MDL),[3] is pluralist, and gathers all individually issued proceedings on a particular subject together for management purposes, not necessarily resolving them by deciding a single representative case. A third model, found widely but not necessarily requiring a specific rule framework, is the individual test case. In this model, the resolution of a number of similar cases may occur following a decision in single illustrative case, without any formal aggregated procedure. The technique is effective for resolving points of law.

A further model is emerging, notably in Europe, which emphasizes negotiation and settlement through non-court alternative dispute resolution techniques sometimes supported or replaced by the public enforcement activities of authorities, with judicial collective procedures being relegated to last place in the sequence (Hodges, 2008). For example, in the Netherlands, settlements reached even before proceedings are issued can be made binding on those with similar claims unless they opt out of the agreement. In Nordic states and the United Kingdom, public regulators may have power to bring collective actions, or to encourage repayment in return for a lenient approach to enforcement.

This array of different techniques presents a series of challenges for both individual analysis and collective comparison. Further, the techniques exhibit a range of options in their involvement of public or private actors or functions. Collective disputes can also be resolved through a range of non-court avenues in the private sector or by public (or semi-public) officials to resolve collective disputes, such as involving ombudsmen, business codes of conduct, compensation schemes, or powers for officials to make or seek restitution or compensation orders, or to approve or support restorative schemes as part of enforcement activities.

A further complicating factor is that jurisdictions differ in the remedies that are permitted. Broadly speaking, all of the jurisdictions that have a recognizable judicial collective procedure (using that term as a generic term) permit claims for injunctive relief, but only a subset of jurisdictions provide for monetary damages (certainly available in class actions in the United States, Canada, and Australia, and under the GLO procedure in England and Wales). Whether such damages should be available is a matter of sometimes-heated consideration in other jurisdictions (Hensler and Hodges, 2009).

---

[2] Civil Procedure Rules, Part 19.III.   [3] 28 U.S.C. § 1407 (1997).

III. Techniques and Limitations on the Availability of Information

Where collective procedures exist, two basic factors have limited the ability to undertake research. These are, first, the lack of a sufficiently large number of cases, which is a function of the length of time for which the procedure has existed and the extent of use; and, second, the unavailability of data on such large and complex beasts. The second problem has been ameliorated by the development of some large and readily accessible databases.

Not surprisingly, therefore, the only jurisdiction to have produced a significant body of research on class actions is the United States of America, since class actions have been a notable feature there since 1966 and investment has been worthwhile by courts and others in creating computerized records of key features for managerial and financial monitoring purposes. Accordingly, the research and data quoted below almost all relate to the United States, save where otherwise stated. A summary of the empirical research on various aspects of class actions in the United States was made by Pace (2007). He also noted a number of reasons why a surprisingly small amount of data has been collected even in that jurisdiction, and the limitations of existing data.

While the quantity of empirical data almost everywhere other than the U.S. is miniscule, some studies are available from Canada (where Ontario was the first province to introduce a class action procedure in 1982, and other provinces have followed since then: Kalajdzic, 2009),[4] England and Wales (where the GLO rule was introduced in 1999: Hodges, 2001 and 2008; Mulheron, 2007), and Australia (where a class action rule was introduced at federal level in 1992 and in Victoria in 2000: Morabito, 2009). Little of the debate over collective actions in Canada, Latin America, Europe, and Australasia has been illuminated by empirical data. Even where there are a significant number of class actions, it clearly takes at least a decade for meaningful overviews to emerge that begin to give a picture of the many different aspects that are of interest. Investment in electronic data capture by official sources is strongly advisable.

There are some instances in which review of individual case files may be necessary in order to obtain particularly detailed information (such as on particular procedural events or ways of pleading cases), but availability in electronic form of claim dates, types, costs, outcomes and the like is hugely valuable in terms of enabling efficient, and therefore cost-effective, access to the data and the drawing of significant

---

[4] See the Canadian Bar Association's National Class Action Database for all class actions filed in Canadian provinces after January 1, 2007, <http://www.cba.org/ClassActions/main/gate/index/about.aspx>.

conclusions. The availability of large numbers from United States databases has produced studies with considerable statistical power. Leading examples of such studies include Willging et al. (1996) with data from four federal district courts; Eisenberg and Miller (2004, 2010) with two large data sets of class action settlements approved by courts in the period 1993–2002; Cox et al. (2006) examining publicly available electronic databases of court decisions between 1966 and 2004 (129 decisions), and also proprietary databases from securities claims administrators (355 class actions, and 35 settlements); Cox et al. (2008) on 733 securities class actions settled from 1993 through 2005, with sources including Pacer, SEC Enforcement Releases, Nexis electronic database, COMPUSTAT data on the size of corporations, and the Bankruptcy Research database of UCLA; Pritchard and Sarra (2010) examining a series of databases in the United States and Canada; and Fitzpatrick (2010) collating 668 federal class action settlements between 2006 and 2007. In reviewing these studies, the difficulties of comparing information from multiple databases should not be forgotten.

Where a database does not exist, or where it is desirable to study aspects that are not verifiable from a database, it is necessary to undertake laborious and costly analysis of court files (where access can be arranged) or to adopt traditional methods of structured interviews of the actors involved (judges, officials, lawyers, parties). Some instructive, sometimes heroic, attempts to produce such data have been made. Important examples of telephone interview studies are Bartsch et al. (1978), Olson (1988), and Meili (2009). Garth (1992), for example, interviewed 43 plaintiffs' lawyers and 26 class representatives and reviewed data assembled on 67 other cases, in order to provide an insight into the spread of case types. He found in that particular data set that employment discrimination cases predominated among a range of other case types. Interviews are essential in order to identify attitudes and qualitative opinions, such as on satisfaction with outcomes (Meili, 2009).

Some aspects of what we want to know can present considerable challenges to investigate. There are plenty of data on the duration and cost of class actions in the United States, and some on settlements as approved by courts, but less on ultimate outcomes. An obvious barrier may be that settlements were confidential (perhaps 95% of class actions, like other litigation claims, are settled, so public judgments will not be created and courts or parties may resist providing access to files, as has occurred in Australia and elsewhere, although if a class has been certified in the United States the settlement will be public since it is subject to court approval). It is also one thing to ascertain the size of a settlement fund created for distribution to class members, but another to discover how much money was actually received by how many people. A particular challenge—and gap in knowledge—is to determine to what extent judgments or settlements produced behavioral change by individual defendants or by other players within markets. If, as is claimed, issues of behavioral control and deterrence are important functions of collective private enforcement, these are important aspects to verify but, as will appear below, few have attempted to address this very difficult and multi-factored task.

IV. QUESTION 1: GOALS OF COLLECTIVE PROCEDURES

In order to be able to reach the ultimate goal of evaluation of one or more collective procedures, it is necessary to begin by stating what the objectives are of such procedures, which can then form the criteria against which the procedures can be evaluated. There is a considerable degree of consensus in the policy writings, court judgments and scholarly literature over the objectives of collective court procedures (Hensler et al., 2000; Hensler and Hodges, 2009). This review does not, however, purport to encompass an evaluation of the goals of the non-judicial techniques, such as regulatory oversight of collective redress, about which there has so far been little discussion (but see Ontario Law Reform Commission, 1982). The list of objectives given below is not intended to be complete, but indicative: there is a need for a wider debate on these issues.

The first objective is the pragmatic one of facilitating judicial economy in the managerial activity of processing multiple similar claims through the courts. It is more efficient to deal with multiple claims together than separately, provided they are sufficiently similar. A second objective is to provide a remedy, such as compensation for damage, where rights have been infringed. This objective recognizes the fact of cost-effectiveness, in that some claims are too small to be worth processing given the cost of using the court system. Hence a collective procedure serves a function of improving access to justice by aggregating such claims. A third objective is regulatory, whether supporting observance of the law in general, or increasing observance of specific provisions (such as anti-cartel rules), especially where the provisions are concerned with regulating the commercial markets. A fourth objective is to provide a mechanism for identifying social or political issues that call for reform, or indeed to provide such reform where other social or political pathways have not been able to deliver it. Collective procedures may, therefore, either provide an early warning signal of an issue that may need to be addressed, whether through the courts or other political or societal means, or, if alternative means of addressing an issue are not preferred or forthcoming, provide a solution to the issue.

The inter-relatedness of these objectives can be seen from a brief consideration of some leading examples of where class actions have been launched. Collective actions have raised and addressed serious issues of human rights, consumer protection, safety, market competition, investor protection, prisoners' rights, environmental protection, and genocide. As that incomplete list of issues shows, concerted action can raise important and contentious issues of public and private law and policy, encompassing aspects of regulation, behavior, the existence and vindication of rights, as well as compensation. Significant social and political issues, as well as legal issues, can be raised, and the legal solutions that are delivered by courts or the parties can have profound influences on behavior. Class litigation was, for example, instrumental in producing profound change in the access of people of certain races to education in the United States of America during the 1960s, which had a profound effect on social equality and opportunity (see Yeazell, 2004).

Raising issues through large actions frequently attracts significant publicity and can lead to the confronting of major political issues, which legislative or other political avenues have sometimes been unable to resolve, but for which the legal process has to provide solutions. There is huge potential for the outcomes of collective actions (and even apparently failures) to have strong influence on legal and public policy. The sheer complexity, size and importance of the various aspects of law and society that are dealt with in class actions are themselves intrinsically interesting and the power of collective procedures can be immense. Collective redress is a deeply political weapon and activity. Studies on these political aspects include Haltom and McCann (2004) and McIntosh and Cates (2009).

V. Question 2: Levels of Need

A threshold question is how many collective actions there are. Answers have proved illusive even in America. In Australia, Morabito has recently undertaken a laborious manual trawl through court records to identify 244 federal class actions between 1992 and 30 June 2009, an average of 12 a year. In Canada, the Bar's database records 142 actions in 2007 and 97 in 2008 (but see Kalajdzic, 2009). In England and Wales, multi-party litigation emerged in the 1980s, but there have still only been around 300 GLO cases since the rule was introduced in 1999.[5] Five years of experience of a modified class action rule in Sweden have produced only 12 cases between January 2003 and August 2009, mainly in consumer law (Lindblom, 2009). In the United States, Pace (2007) reports that there are no reliable numbers for total class action activity—but, as appears from data quoted below, it is clearly orders of magnitude higher than in the countries just mentioned.

It can be important to analyze different case types, since they may exhibit significantly different features and trends, and may provide opportunities for alternative non-court techniques to be applied. The RAND Institute for Civil Justice's (Hensler et al., 2000) survey of all federal and state class actions identifiable in

---

[5] Data from the English Legal Services Commission on the number and costs of GLOs were published by Hodges (2007) and Mulheron (2007).

1995–1996, suggested that social policy reform cases, despite their importance in the development of the 1996 amendments to Federal Rule 23, comprised only a minority of all class actions. The most frequent types of actions found were securities and financial injury matters, which then[6] exceeded mass tort cases, although the latter are the most discussed in academic literature. Claims against insurance companies have been shown to be significant (Pace et al., 2007), as are antitrust cases (DuVal, 1976). Employment and business torts were the largest types in Heiman's California study. At the federal level, securities and investor cases appear to form the largest single type, in which the majority of total monetary sanctions are delivered through private, rather than public, enforcement routes (Coffee, 2006).

Stanford Law School operates a Clearinghouse and index of filings for securities class actions.[7] Working with Cornerstone Research (2009), the Stanford project found that a total of 210 federal securities class actions were filed in 2008, a 19% increase over the 176 filings in 2007, and a 9% increase over the annual average of 192 filings observed between 1997 and 2007. Financial companies were defendants in 49% of those filings, and 91 of the filings related to the sub-prime liquidity crisis. NERA Economic Consulting publishes an annual survey of trends (that to November 2009 being Plancich and Starykh, 2009) which shows that federal securities class actions surged from 2007, after a marked decline in 2005–2006, driven by sub-prime lending cases and the credit crisis. The Plancich and Starykh data illustrate that one or two big cases must be considered to gain a true picture of general trends. The average 2002–2007 settlement value was $40.2 million including those nine "mega-settlements," each worth over $1 billion that occurred after 2005 (including Enron Corporation, settled for $7,231 billion in 2007 and WorldCom, Inc., settled for $6,156 billion in 2005), but $24.4 million excluding them. Based on the 2005 filing rate, Miller et al. (2006) found that over a five-year period the average public corporation faced a 10% probability that it would face at least one shareholder class action. The annual likelihood rose from 1.6% in 1995 to 1.9% in 2005. The rise in the probability of dismissal, being 40.3% in 2003–2005 and 19.4% in 1993–1995, was attributed to the introduction of the Private Securities Litigation Reform Act of 1995 (PSLRA). Fitzpatrick (2010) and Eisenberg and Miller (2010) found that securities cases comprised 39% of their cohorts.

The availability of records from a particular court provides consistency of local experience and should normally enable a comprehensive picture to emerge of changes over time and issues that are more or less important. Consideration can then be given to which individual issues deserve particular attention or tailored approaches. Examples include DuVal's (1976) study of antitrust class actions between 1966 and 1973 from the court records of the Northern District of Illinois,

---

[6] However, since Supreme Court decisions such as *Castano v. American Tobacco Company* 84 F. 3d 734 (5th Cir. 1996) and *In re: Rhone-Poulenc Rorer, Inc.*, 51 F. 3d 1293 (7th Cir. 1995) mass tort cases tend not to be certified as class actions but to appear as MDLs.   [7] See <http://securities.stanford.edu>.

Bernstein's (1978) comparison of class action cases in the Southern District of New York and the Eastern District of Pennsylvania, and Garth's (1992) examination of class actions in the Northern District of California 1979–1984. Many of the studies involve federal courts, but some studies of state courts produce the finding that local variations occur in trends and tendencies, such as case types, that do not stand out within a larger database. This was noted by Heiman's 2009 study of 3,711 class actions in California between 2000 and 2006, which produced the observations that class actions are a small subset of civil litigation (less than one-half of 1% in this cohort), and may not lend themselves to typical empirical analysis of trends, patterns, and long-term behavior, for reasons that include the fact that attorneys use class actions as immediate responses to events (such as construction defect cases after a housing boom, or business tort claims centered around a particular local concentration of an industrial sector), and the success of a particular tactic can quickly be adopted within a tight-knit exclusive grouping of players.

It is important to be able to provide continuity of data over sufficiently lengthy time periods. Repetition of individual studies provides reassessment of whether initial conclusions remain valid in the light of subsequent accumulation of evidence. It has also been possible to examine the effects of significant changes, particularly those changes in substantive law that were intended to reform practice and outcomes, to see whether the desired effects were in fact produced and whether any unexpected consequences occurred—even questioning whether reforms such as the PSLRA should be repealed (in the case of the PSLRA because claimants were worse off after it).

Thus, there is now good evidence of the levels of *use* of class actions in the United States but, as is suggested below, that evidence does not directly answer questions about underlying levels of need for, or the overall utility of, a particular procedure. Having taken note that some issues can affect many people, some governments have recently adopted an empirical approach to verifying what level of demand might exist for new procedures, before considering what particular techniques might best address a given problem. Sometimes, results create surprise by indicating that the level of need was lower than predicted. Studies for the European Commission have attempted to quantify levels of consumer detriment caused by infringements of consumer or competition law that could be addressed by collective redress mechanisms (GHK et al., 2008) but the studies' methods have been criticized (Micklitz, 2010). Mulheron (2007) summarized data on numbers of class actions and the types of legal claims involved in the United States, Canada, and Australia, but her conclusion that they showed a level of need in England and Wales was not convincing because she did not consider the availability of other types of dispute resolution and regulatory mechanisms.[8] This illustrates the

---

[8] UK Government's Response to the Civil Justice Council's Report: "Improving Access to Justice through Collective Actions," Ministry of Justice, July 2009, available at <http://www.justice.gov.uk/about/docs/government-response-cjc-collective-actions.pdf>.

dangers of assuming that a particular technique (e.g., a class action) is required (or is all that is required, because it is there) and working backwards in an attempt to justify its introduction.

VI. QUESTION 3: TECHNICAL MODES OF OPERATION

In studying collective procedures, we clearly need to start by answering a set of descriptive and analytical questions that are essentially simple but may be difficult to answer simply. What procedural regimes exist? What are their important design features and how do they work? What are the costs? What are the advantages and disadvantages of a given procedure?

We also need to ask why a procedure does or does not work. This requires understanding of the preconditions and parameters of a procedure, which may not be either stated or even obvious, and of the procedure's place within the overall architecture of its legal system. For example, a particular procedure might have a very limited function, and other procedures might apply to other situations or a decision might have been taken not to allow other approaches. There are several examples of these situations in European jurisdictions, such as the limitation of the collective procedure rule in Germany to investor suits, where the existence of a large number of particular investor claims needed to be processed in a new and more efficient way, but there was strong desire not to introduce a generic collective procedure. Given that collective actions can have a strong sectoral focus, such as in human rights, consumer, antitrust, or corporate investor areas, it is important to understand the legal architecture of a particular area (i.e., the range of rights, remedies, and dispute resolution pathways, whether public or private), to avoid misleading generalizations or false conclusions (Armour et al., 2009).

It can be illuminating to study individual large cases as a means of identifying important features that deserve attention in similar cases. Hence, the real value of retrospective histories of individual cases comes when such analyses can be combined to identify trends and to enable comparison of techniques, procedures and policies. It may be important to examine, for instance, the effectiveness of different modes of notification of consumers and the reasons why some methods of communication were or were not effective or cost-effective (Bartsch et al., 1978 on tetracycline antibiotics, involving some 889,000 consumers, telephone interviews of some 1,000 consumers; Kritzer, 1988 on the Dalkon Shield medical device, a telephone survey of roughly 1,000 individuals, repeated two years later; Green, 1996 on Bendectin;

and Hadfield, 2008 on 9/11 victims). The Kritzer study proved valuable in repeating telephone surveys at different times so as to measure any changes in important variables, such as awareness of how a particular health hazard was viewed in the context of health hazards generally and, therefore, how effective a notification campaign of the right to claim in a bankruptcy had been, and whether expenditure on it had been worthwhile. Few studies have evaluated the MDL procedure, as opposed to the class action procedure: see Olson (1988) and the Report by the Judicial Conference of the United States, Advisory Committee on Civil Rules (1999). An overview of the leading cases in England during the 1990s illustrates the development of the GLO-type procedure by the courts almost from thin air (Hodges, 2001); most of the cases involved pharmaceutical products but there were subsequently more cases concerning abuse in care homes.

The accumulation of a sufficient quantity of collective litigation in Canada has recently meant that cross-border comparative studies with the United States have become feasible. Pritchard and Sarra (2010) studied a cohort of 76 securities class actions in Canada between 1992 and 2006, and also the interesting phenomenon of individual class actions that were filed in both jurisdictions. This phenomenon has enabled some comparisons to be made between different technical procedural features, such as the existence of different defenses in the two jurisdictions, and the clear finding that overall litigation exposure for Canadian companies remains relatively low when compared to that of companies in the United States. The ability to look at class actions filed in both jurisdictions showed that Canadian companies that were listed on stock exchanges in the United States faced the greatest litigation exposure, and cases involving them were costly to resolve. The findings were supported by insurance company data on Directors and Officers liability policy premiums for the largest 250 firms listed on the Toronto Stock Exchange between 2004 and 2006, which illuminated issues such as risks of being a director and different approaches toward offsetting or not offsetting court costs and the cost of settlements.

Collective procedures, in particular class actions for damages, give rise to concerns over unintended and undesirable effects, such as ethical conflicts, high transaction costs, and "blackmail settlements" in which claims and the fees of intermediaries are paid without sufficient analysis of the underlying merits of a case (Hensler et al., 2000). Unquestionably, there are big effects at work here. Accordingly, this is an area where it is particularly important to know how the procedures work, and which techniques give rise to significant consequences, intentional and unintentional, so that approaches can be adopted that produce the former and avoid or reduce the latter. However, reliable data are scarce and difficult to verify, other than in relation to levels of attorney compensation, which is mentioned below. The most important issue, also mentioned below, is whether claims that are brought, and particularly settled, have sufficient merit, and on that there is little reliable evidence but much assertion. A further issue concerns how effective any anti-abuse mechanisms might be. This complex issue has only recently been recognized. Again, there is very little reliable understanding of how (and how well) different controls work.

Various studies have examined settlements. In five large case studies of settlements, Tidmarsh (1998) found that no two are alike. Several studies considered the issue of whether merits matter in settlements, or whether the private enforcement technique of a class action merely attracts attorneys to claim against companies over a threshold size with cases then being settled favorably to the claimants irrespective of the underlying merits (see Alexander, 1991 and Cox et al., 2008, both examining securities cases). Cox et al. (2008) found that since PSLRA was enacted, institutions are more likely to intervene in cases with larger estimated provable losses, and against firms with greater total assets, and where the SEC has previously taken enforcement action. They expressed disquiet at finding that 20.5% of the settlements in their cohort were below $2 million, and those cases involved shorter class action periods, significantly lower provable losses and quicker settlements than the norm, and yielded investors lower recovery on their provable losses than in larger settlements. Such cases indicated characteristics of "strike suits," i.e. opportunistic claims that raised concerns over merits.

VII. QUESTION 4: EVALUATION

Obvious parameters against which the internal efficiency of particular procedures can be evaluated include cost, speed, efficiency, the balance between costs and benefits, numbers of people who benefited and by how much, percentage of good or bad claims resolved, and prevention of abuse. It is striking, however, that even in those few jurisdictions that have managed to assemble a body of empirical data, there has been little discussion of what parameters or qualitative standards might be acceptable, and, hence, whether the given procedure or system is operating satisfactorily. For example, while there is a substantial body of American data on the number of class actions, their factual outcomes and the level of costs and sums paid, there remains a striking reluctance to make judgments about what costs are acceptable. Instead, reforms have been driven by politically inspired views over abuse or cost, without a consensus emerging over whether empirical evidence regarding prevailing practice satisfies some normative standard. In contrast, there has recently been some attempt in the European Union to establish criteria to assess procedures for consumer collective redress.[9]

---

[9] See Green Paper on Consumer Collective Redress, COM(2008) 794, 27.11.2008, <http://ec.europa.eu/consumers/redress_cons/collective_redress_en.htm>; Draft European Commission paper published at <http://ec.europa.eu/consumers/redress_cons/docs/consultation_paper2009.pdf>.

A series of studies has led to widespread criticism of the operation of the class action mechanism as a means of private enforcement in the United States in relation to securities, notwithstanding some improvements in practice produced by legislative changes (Alexander, 1991; Coffee, 2006; Cox et al., 2006, 2008). Research has been notably successful in illuminating whether, in securities cases, the procedure serves merely to transfer wealth among shareholders, or to diminish investments of small long-term investors while favoring large institutional funds, or to effectively deter firms from issuing shares or making forward predictions, or to encourage nuisance claims of certain types.

A. Costs

Funding and costs are crucial to understanding the viability, incidence, operation and outcomes of any system of aggregate litigation. They are also complex and extensive topics that deserve separate consideration in the wider context of civil justice systems as a whole. As far as class action practice in the United States is concerned, it needs to be understood that the general litigation rules differ from almost every other jurisdiction in the world, first, by having no general loser-pays rule (except in Alaska), but a number of specific statutes which provide for one-way fee-shifting (to plaintiffs); and, secondly, by permitting contingency fees in single claims and awards of attorneys' fees in class actions (Hodges et al., 2009). Detailed study of costs in class actions is comparatively recent, and confronts various methodological problems. Different jurisdictions have differing funding sources and costs rules, which makes it difficult to provide an overview. There is considerable scope for further research here.

For the United States, however, some depth of detail is now available, and this illustrates what might be achieved elsewhere. In their study of ten federal and state consumer and mass tort class actions, Hensler et al. (2000) found that class action attorneys received substantial fees in all successful suits. Awards to class action attorneys ranged from about half a million dollars to $75 million. Average hourly fees ranged from $320 to almost $2,000. In the nine cases where data were available, class counsel fee-and-expense awards ranged from 5% to about 50% of the total settlement value, which the researchers regarded as a modest share of the amounts negotiated, given the size of the settlements. In eight of the nine cases, class counsel received one-third or less of the total settlement value. In three of the mass tort cases, class counsel were awarded less than 10% of the actual settlement value, but the absolute dollar amount of fees was very large, because these settlements were huge. In three of ten cases studied in detail, class counsel received more than the total received by class members altogether.

In contrast, those researchers found that most consumer class members have only a small financial stake in the litigation. Few if any consumer class members actively monitored the class action attorney's behavior. Such "clientless" litigation held within itself the seeds of questionable practices. The powerful financial incentives that drive plaintiff attorneys to assume the risk of litigation intersect with powerful interests on the defense side in settling litigation as early and as cheaply as possible, with the least publicity. These incentives can produce settlements that are arrived at without adequate investigation of facts and law and that create little value for class members or society. For class counsel, the rewards and fees may be disproportionate to the effort they actually invest in the case. Kalajdzic (2009) raises similar issues for Canada.

Eisenberg and Miller's (2004) study of court-approved class actions between 1993 and 2002 found that a scaling effect existed, with the amount of client recovery overwhelmingly the most important determinant of the attorney fee award. While the absolute size of the fee increased as the size of the recovery increased, fees as apercentage of the recovery decreased. The mean fee award in common fund cases (i.e., where a common settlement fund was created) was 21.9% of the recovery across all cases. Higher fees were associated with higher risk, and low-risk cases generated lower fees. Class counsel dominated and controlled the litigation. In non-fee-shifting cases, very few awards exceeded 35% of client recovery. In fee-shifting cases, there was a much wider distribution of fee awards. Fitzpatrick (2010) also found a scaling effect, but only 13% of the total settlement amount was awarded as fees and expenses, with awards ranging from 3% to 47% of the settlement sums. He noted that only 350 cases appear to be responsible for transferring 10% of the entire American tort system's annual transfers and nearly $5 billion in fees and expenses (15% of the class action settlements in his cohort). However, Eisenberg and Miller's (2004) and Fitzpatrick's (2010) figures record fees awarded by courts against reported gross settlement amounts. Since Hensler et al. (2000) showed that sums actually paid out from the common fund can be lower, at least in some cases, the result in those cases would be that the ratios of attorneys' fees are correspondingly higher in those cases.

Pace et al. (2007) obtained information on awards to class counsel for fees and expenses in 48 insurance class actions. Those awards ranged from $50,000 to $50,000,000 with a median award of $554,000. They calculated an approximate fee and expense percentage for 27 cases, which ranged from 12 to 41% of the fund, with a mean of 29% and a median of 30%. However, the "effective" fee and expense percentages—in other words, those based on the fee and cost awards divided by the sum of the distributed benefits, attorneys' fees, and other costs—increased to a median average of 47% (based on 36 cases in which this information was available). In a quarter of these cases, the effective fee and cost percentages were 75 percent or higher and, in 14% (five cases), the effective percentages were over 90%.

As Hensler et al. (2000) point out, determination of whether the fees of attorneys or other service-providing intermediaries are reasonable is a political judgment, influenced by local social factors. She argues that the issue is not how class counsel fees compare to payments to individual class members, but rather how the fees compare to the "common benefit" produced by the class action attorneys' efforts. The American policy of favoring widespread and decentralized private enforcement over federal public enforcement requires intermediaries to be given positive incentives to institute and pursue litigation, and insulation of claimants from the cost consequences of such actions. Other jurisdictions have markedly different policies, and adhere widely to the "loser pays" rule and more modest levels of lawyer compensation (Hodges et al., 2009). Hence, direct comparisons of cost and funding outcomes among jurisdictions that have totally different legal architectures will be misleading. It is in this context that debates over the pros and cons of public or private enforcement are now emerging. It should also be remembered that in comparing the costs, benefits and outcomes in different jurisdictions, account needs to be taken of not only the costs of lawyers and discovery in a system that emphasizes private enforcement, but also the costs of public enforcement in a system that emphasizes that approach.

B. Outcomes

Research has illuminated some interesting and possibly unexpected outcomes of class actions in the United States. First, although it is clear that enormous amounts of money can be claimed, individual consumer claims typically involve low sums. Secondly, success rates of class actions may be lower than expected, at least for some types of claims. Thirdly, even though total notional settlement amounts may appear large, sums actually reaching individual claimants may be modest. These issues raise questions over the efficiency and effectiveness of the class action procedure that are unresolved. Various studies illustrate these points.

Illustration of the large size of aggregate outcomes in class actions can be seen from Eisenberg and Miller's (2004) finding that the average class action recovery in the cases studied was $138.6 million and aggregate class action recoveries averaged $5.13 billion per year, although these figures were amounts approved by courts, rather than actually paid. The gross recovery across Eisenberg and Miller's 370 cases (in 2002 $) had a mean of $100 million and median of $11.6 million. Although total sums can appear to be large, cases can in fact be large or small. This appeared in the RAND insurance study (Pace et al., 2007), where total funds offered by the defendants to pay benefits to class members and the fees and expenses of class counsel were reported in 32 cases and ranged from $150,000,000 to $360,000, with a median fund size of $2,600,000. The common fund was less than $5 million in 63% of the reported cases, a finding of interest in estimating the impact of the Class Action Fairness Act of 2005. In the 36 cases in which the respondent provided information on class size estimated at the time of settlement, the classes ranged from as large as 4,300,000 members to as small as 127 members, with a median of 28,000 members. However, the number of final recipients of funds appeared lower.

Several studies have found that individual consumer losses and recoveries are of modest size, and that sums paid may be lower than envisaged in settlements. Hensler et al. (2000) found that estimated losses in consumer suits ranged from an average of $3.83 to an average of $4,550; in five of the six cases the average was probably less than $1,000. They also found that negotiated compensation amounts varied dramatically: total compensation offered ranged from just under $1 million to over $800 million. Average payments to individual class members ranged from about $6 to $1,500 in consumer suits, compared with from about $6,400 to $100,000 in mass tort suits. In three cases, class members claimed one-third or less of the funds set aside. In the Willging et al. (1996) study, the largest median per-member award (not reduced for attorneys' fees) in the four districts studied was $528 and the maximum award was $5,331. In the RAND insurance study (Pace et al., 2007) a mean average total payout of $9.5 million was made in 39 cases (but including a single case in which $149 million was paid out). However, distributions were typically much smaller, with a median total payout of $500,000 and, in one case, the total was just $200. In some instances, the total payout represented a fraction of the net compensation fund. Although the mean number of recipients in 33 reported cases was 27,000 class members and the median size was 1,500 members.

Recognition of the facts that individual consumer claims typically involve low sums, and that many individuals may not claim sums available to them in settlements, gave rise to concern that plaintiff attorneys' remuneration was inappropriately based on total theoretical settlement amounts of unclaimed coupons. This led to various reforms in the Class Action Fairness Act of 2005 (CAFA). These findings are also of some significance in the debate in Europe and elsewhere over whether certification of a class should be on an opt-out or opt-in basis. The effectiveness of the former, in theoretically including more individuals than the latter, may be diminished where claimants who are notionally included in a certified opt-out class subsequently have to opt-in in order to claim from a common fund established by a settlement or judgment. Questions remain over which approach is more effective and economical, and in what circumstances.

Some studies have highlighted differences in success rates of class actions. In the antitrust area, DuVal's (1976) study of antitrust class actions in the Northern District of Illinois between 1966 and 1973 found that the results in class actions have been modest. Class members obtained relief in less than one-third of terminated class actions; one-third were dismissed without any settlement.

The RAND insurance study found that only 14% of the cases in its data set wound up with certified classes. The judges denied certification in 11% of the cases, and the remainder (about 75% of the total) never had a decision either way. There were striking differences in final outcomes depending on the status of the motion for certification. For all attempted class actions in the RAND study, a negotiated settlement that bound a certified class took place in only 12% of all closed cases. Settlements involving only the small number of plaintiffs specifically named in the original filings, and not a class, occurred in 20% of the cases. The judge ruled in favor of the defendant on some sort of dispositive pre-trial motion in 37% of the cases. In 27% of the cases, plaintiffs dismissed their complaints voluntarily, presumably without prejudice, which would have allowed them to re-file the same case later. For class actions in which the plaintiffs made a motion for certification, however, the distribution of outcomes changed considerably. Class settlement in those cases was much more likely, with a third of all cases resulting in a settlement for a certified class. The frequency with which plaintiffs voluntarily drop their cases is reduced, as are pre-trial dispositive rulings for the defense. When a class was, in fact, certified, the end result in nine of the ten cases in the RAND study was a class settlement.

Low success rates may be of limited concern where a legal system places reliance on class actions to regulate conduct, since deterrence may be enhanced irrespective of success or failure rates. An issue may still arise, however, over whether a mechanism is efficient. An illustration of this issue is the finding by Hensler et al. (2000) that class members collected amounts ranging from 20 cents per dollar paid in costs to about 90 cents. In three cases, class members collected substantially less than 50 cents on the dollar; in two cases, they collected about 50 cents; in five cases they collected 65 cents or more.

A key point is to be able to assess the merits of individual cases and thus conclude whether they are justified, or whether settlements have been reached at levels that were justifiable. However, Hensler et al.'s conclusion (2000) was that benefits and costs are very difficult to assess. They concluded that their enquiry into whether cases involved principled outcomes, in which individual compensation and deterrence were related to quantified approaches, proved inconclusive. Instead, they found that the process of reaching these outcomes suggests that class counsel were sometimes simply interested in finding a settlement price that the defendants would agree to, rather than in finding out what class members had lost, what defendants had gained, how likely it was that defendants would actually be held liable if the suit were to go to trial, and negotiating a fair settlement based on the answers to these questions. They commented that such instances undermine the social utility of class actions, which depends on how effectively the lawsuits compensate injured consumers and—many would argue—deter wrongful practices. Moreover, among the class actions studied, some settlements appeared at first reading to provide more for class members and consumers than they actually did, and class action attorneys' financial rewards sometimes were based on the settlements' nominal value rather than on the actual payout in the cases.[10] Such outcomes contribute to public cynicism about the actual goals of class actions for damages in contrast to the aspirations of class action advocates.

Hensler et al. (2000) also found that consumer litigation was associated with changes in practice although some of the changes may be explainable independently of the class action itself. In all six of the consumer cases studied in depth, the litigation was associated with changes in the defendants' business practices. In four of the six cases, the evidence strongly suggests that the litigation directly or indirectly produced the changes in practice. In the other two, the evidence was more ambiguous. Hensler et al. concluded that at the time of settlement, considerable uncertainty remained about the defendants' culpability and plaintiff class members' damages. So Garth's (1992) observation that there is no general agreement on what constitutes success or failure

---

[10] The position may subsequently have been affected by the Class Action Fairness Act of 2005.

in lawsuits that typically end in negotiated settlements was echoed in Hensler et al.'s conclusion that it remained unclear which cases "just ain't worth it" and which were.

Do class actions induce social change? A principal finding of Garth's (1992) study was that litigation tends to narrow the dispute that gives rise to it and that individual initiators take a more prominent role in certain types of cases than in others. Thus, Garth found, first, that securities and antitrust cases were brought predominantly by entrepreneurial plaintiffs' attorneys (Garth described securities cases as often involving small investors, but more recent cases have involved large corporate investors, as Coffee (2008) discusses). Secondly, welfare cases are frequently initiated by public organizations so as to raise topical welfare and political issues. Thirdly, individuals often initiate employment discrimination cases, in which a sense of grievance or public fairness is often a necessary motivator. The process can transform employment discrimination victims into activists, but they do not always personally benefit from the outcome in the way initially envisaged.

The issues of how collective processes transform both claimants and their lawyers are being taken further by Meili (2009). Among his emerging findings are the rare identification of deterrence as a motivating factor and differing attitudes of claimants and lawyers to objectives and success. From this study it appears that lead plaintiffs have broader views of success and often value an imagined positive impact that the lawsuit would have beyond the confines of the parties in the particular case.

It follows that an important area for future research would be to study the extent of the impact of individual or class litigation on corporate or governmental behavior, and to examine which motivational factors produce what effects. Particular variables, for example, might include not just the financial impact of any money paid in settlement or costs, but also mitigating effects of insurance and the ability to recycle costs across customers generally, the effect on brand reputation, and the incidence and effect of any internal sanctions (such as on bonuses, promotion, or pensions) and of public sanctions (such as prosecution of the company or of individuals, and particular penalties). In short, the research and doctrinal literature seems to have been notably one-sided in concentrating on enforcement effects and on procedures, without looking into the longer-term effects, such as to what extent deterrence or behavior modification is produced or whether undesirable gaps are left open.

C. Wider comparisons

What has emerged in global consideration of collective procedures is an unresolved debate over the balance to be struck within a legal system between public and private enforcement and redress mechanisms. For example, the American emphasis on private enforcement as a means of maximizing identification and pursuit of wrongdoing and providing deterrence as well as compensation as a means of influencing behavior, contrasts with the European model of keeping public and private enforcement as more separate functions and placing significant emphasis on public enforcement. It follows that private class actions in the United States of America perform a highly important function in law enforcement, and are positively encouraged by design choices on matters such as ease of initiation, no cost shifting, incentivization of intermediaries, and public sanctions (punitive damages), whereas the European approach places more emphasis simply on delivering compensation in private actions and seeks to impose behavioral control and sanctioning more through separate public enforcement mechanisms (Hodges, 2008). Thus, collective cases may now be brought in some jurisdictions by public or private representative bodies, such as consumer associations or trade associations. Recent debate in Europe has adopted the generic term "collective redress" (see Hodges, 2009) to encompass all varieties of mechanism, including public (especially regulatory and administrative) as well as self-regulatory or voluntary redress mechanisms. These fundamentally different architectural features constitute a major trap for the unwary who seek to compare or generalize about the collective procedures in different countries, since conclusions may simply be non-translatable between different legal systems.

Therefore, if we are to ask how different collective procedures compare, we need to have answers not only to many questions about how individual procedures work internally, but also about far more wide-ranging constitutional and enforcement policy issues concerning the place and function of particular procedures within the architecture of domestic legal systems. Much interesting work remains to be done here and comparative data is almost nonexistent. One question, for example, is whether strong reliance on private enforcement mechanisms in fact delivers more widespread enforcement than public enforcement alone. Helland and Klick (2007) found that litigation and regulation tend to piggy-back on each other in a cohort of 748 insurance class actions filed between 1992 and 2002, and no evidence to support the proposition that public regulation and private enforcement function as substitute channels to deter harmful behavior. Those findings raise important questions over whether American class actions, with their significant incentives, provide sufficient enforcement or value for money. If the functions of public sanctioning and of compensation are separated, is duplication of costs acceptable?

VIII. Conclusion: the Way Forward

The ultimate goal is to be able to compare different techniques and decide which ones might work best and in what circumstances or types of situation. This challenge has only recently been recognized as collective procedures have spread around the world. There is as yet insufficient data that provides meaningful comparisons between different techniques and procedures of court-based private law collective litigation (i.e. class actions, representative claims, and the like), and no attempt has been made to produce data comparing such private law, court-based systems and the expanding range of alternative solutions, especially public law techniques.

A concerted global plan of research is called for at this stage. It might look like this. First, there needs to be a reconsideration of the ultimate objectives of collective procedures—do they remain as they have hitherto been considered to be? Second, an effort should be undertaken to map the range of collective procedures that exist in different jurisdictions, whether public or private. This process can only be done on a country-by-country basis, since the particular mixture of public and private techniques that are available can vary considerably among jurisdictions. It also needs to identify qualitatively how the techniques in the particular mix inter-relate. Individual techniques can no longer be considered in isolation, but must be viewed within their political, legal, and cultural context as part of a national or regional matrix of different techniques. The architectural features are important. Different states may prefer to place more reliance on certain techniques, such as on either public or private enforcement, so it is unlikely that a global blueprint would be acceptable. Third, quantitative evidence should be collected on how, and how well, each technique and matrix of techniques works. Fourth, the techniques and matrices should be evaluated against the objectives established in stage one.

This pragmatic and functional approach should seem logical given the form that this Chapter has followed. We should not, of course, underestimate challenges in completing the task. Methodological difficulties will be obvious in collecting, for example, verifiable evidence on actual outcomes, such as the extent to which behavior has been modified and in identifying what the real causes of such changes are. Given vested interests and preferences for certain techniques, political difficulties can also be predicted, for instance from the intermediaries, whether public or private, who operate existing procedures. But it should be possible to bring about a situation in which policy-makers will be enabled to reach decisions on the important issues that arise in identifying and solving problems that affect many people based on far more substantiated grounds than have been available hitherto. There is certainly plenty of important research to be done in this field. Coordinated plans are being drawn up for taking matters forward on a global basis.

REFERENCES

Alexander, J.C. (1991). "Do the Merits Matter? A Study of Settlements in Securities Class Actions," *Stanford Law Review* 43(3): 497–598.

Armour, J., Black, B., Cheffins, B., and Nolan, R. (2009). "Private Enforcement of Corporate Law: An Empirical Comparison of the US and UK," *Journal of Empirical Legal Studies* 6: 637–86.

Bartsch, T.C., Boddy, F.M., King, B.F., and Thompson, P.N. (1978). *A Class-Action Suit That Worked. The Consumer Refund in the Antibiotic Antitrust Litigation*, Lexington, MA: D.C. Heath and Company.

Bernstein, R. (1978). "Judicial Economy and Class Actions," *Journal of Legal Studies* 7(2): 349–70.

Choi, S.J. (2004). "The Evidence on Securities Class Actions," *Vanderbilt Law Review* 57: 1465–525.

Coffee, J.C., Jr., (2006). "Reforming the Securities Class Action: An Essay on Deterrence and its Implementation," *Columbia Law Review* 106: 1534–86.

Coffee, J.C., Jr., (2008). "Accountability and Competition in Securities Class Actions: Why "Exit" Works Better Than 'Voice'," *Cardozo Law Review* 30: 407–44.

Cornerstone Research (2009). *Securities Class Action Filings. 2008: A Year in Review.*

Cox, J.D., Thomas, R.S., and Bai, L. (2008). "There Are Plaintiffs and . . . There Are Plaintiffs: An Empirical Analysis of Securities Class Action Settlements," *Vanderbilt Law Review* 61: 2:355–86.

Cox, J.D. and Thomas R.S., with Kiku, D. (2006). "Does the Plaintiff Really Matter? An Empirical Analysis of Lead Plaintiff s in Securities Class Actions," *Columbia Law Review* 106: 1587–940.

DuVal, B.S., Jr., (1976). "The Class Action as an Antitrust Enforcement Device: The Chicago Experience (II)," *American Bar Foundation Research Journal* 1(4): 1273–358

Eisenberg, T. and Miller, G.P. (2004). "Attorney Fees in Class Action Settlements: An Empirical Study," *Journal of Empirical Legal Studies* 1(1): 27–78.

Eisenberg, T. and Miller, G.P. (2010). "Attorneys Fees and Expenses in Class Action Settlements: 1993–2008," *Journal of Empirical Legal Studies* 7(1): 248–81.

Fitzpatrick, B.T. (2010). *An empirical study of class action settlements and their fee awards*, Vanderbilt University Law School, Public Law & Legal Theory Working Paper No 10-10, available at <http://papers.ssrn.com/sol3/papers.cfm?abstract_id=1442108>.

Garth, B.G. (1992). "Power and Legal Artifice: The Federal Class Action," *Law and Society Review* 26: 237–72.

GHK, Civic Consulting, and van Dijk (2008). *Study regarding the problems faced by consumers in obtaining redress for infringements of consumer protection legislation, and the economic consequences of such problems. Final Report*, at <http://ec.europa.eu/consumers/redress_cons/finalreport–problemstudypart1–final.pdf>.

Green, M. (1996). *Bendectin and Birth Defects: The Challenges of Mass Toxic Substances Litigation*, Philadelphia: University of Pennsylvania Press.

Hadfield, G.K. (2008). "Framing Choice between Cash and the Courthouse; Experiences with the 9/11 Victim Compensation Fund," *Law and Society Review* 42(3): 645–82.

Haltom, W. and McCann, M. (2004). *Distorting the Law: Politics, Media, and The Litigation Crisis*, Chicago: University of Chicago Press,.

Heiman, H. (2009). *Findings of the Study of California Class Action Litigation, 2000–2006*, Judicial Council of California, Administrative Office of the Courts.

Helland, E. and Klick J. (2007). "The Tradeoff s between Regulation and Litigation: Evidence from Insurance Class Actions," *Journal of Tort Law* 1(3): Art. 2.

Hensler, D.R., Dombey-Moore, B., Giddens, B., Gross, J., Moller, E.K., and Pace, N.M. (2000). *Class Action Dilemmas. Pursuing Public Goals for Private Gain*, Thousand Oaks, CA: RAND Institute for Civil Justice.

Hensler, D.R. and Hodges, C.J.S. (2009). *The Globalization of Class Actions*, Proceedings of the American Academy of Political and Social Sciences, Sage.

Hodges, C.J.S. (2001). *Multi-Party Actions*, Oxford: Oxford University Press.

Hodges, C.J.S. (2008). *The Reform of Class and Representative Actions in European Legal Systems: A New Framework for Collective Redress in Europe*, Oxford: Hart Publishing.

Hodges, C.J.S. (2009). "From Class Action to Collective Redress: A Revolution in Approach to Compensation," *Civil Justice Quarterly* 28: 41–66.

Hodges C.J.S. (2010). "Towards Parameters for EU Civil Justice Systems," in S. Vogenauer and C. Hodges (eds.), *Civil Justice Systems in Europe: Implications for Choice of Forum and Choice of Contract Law*, Oxford: Hart Publishing.

Hodges, C.J.S., Vogenauer, S., and Tulibacka, M. (2009). *Costs and Funding of Civil Litigation: a Comparative Study* at <http://papers.ssrn.com/sol3/papers.cfm?abstract_id=1511714##>.

Judicial Conference of the United States, Advisory Committee on Civil Rules (1999). *Report of the Advisory Committee on Civil Rules and the Working Group on Mass Torts to the Chief Justice of the United States and to the Judicial Conference of the United States*.

Kalajdzic, J. (2009). *Access to Justice for the Masses? A Critical Analysis of Class Actions in Ontario*, Master of Laws thesis, University of Toronto, available at <http://hdl.handle.net/1807/18780>.

Kritzer, H.M. (1988). "Public Notification Campaigns in Mass Litigation: The Dalkon Shield Case," *Justice System Journal* 13(2): 220–39.

Lindblom, P.H. (2009). *Class Actions in Sweden. National Report to the 18th International Congress on Comparative Law—Washington 2010*, available at <http://www.globalclassactions.stanford.edu>.

Logan, S.J., Moshman, J. and Moore, B.C. Jr. (2003). "Attorney Fee Awards in Common Fund Class Actions," *Class Action Reports* 24: 167–234.

McIntosh, W.V. and Cates, C.L. (2009). *Multi-Party Litigation: The Strategic Context*, Vancouver: UBC Press.

Meili, S. (2009). "Perceptions of Consumer Class Actions: The Views of Plaintiffs' Lawyers and their Clients," Paper at Law and Society Association Annual Meeting, Denver, Colorado, May 30, 2009.

Micklitz, H.-W. (2010). "Collective private enforcement in antitrust law—What is going wrong in the debate?," in L. Tichy and J. Terhechter (eds.), [Title to be Determined], Baden-Baden: Nomos Verlagsgesellschaft mbH and Co. KG (forthcoming).

Miller, R.I., Foster, T., and Buckberg, E. (2006). *Recent trends in Shareholder Class Action Litigation: Beyond Mega-Settlements, is Stabilization Ahead?*, NERA Economic Consulting.

Morabito, V. (2009). *An Empirical Study of Australia's Class Action Regimes. First Report. Class Action Facts and Figures*, Department of Business Law and Taxation, Melbourne: Monash University.

Mulheron, R. (2007). *Reform of Collective Redress in England and Wales: A Perspective of Need, A Research Paper for submission to the Civil Justice Council of England and Wales*, London: Civil Justice Council.

Olson, S.M. (1988). "Federal Multidistrict Litigation: Its Impact on Litigants," *Justice System Journal* 13(3): 341–64.

Ontario Law Reform Commission (1982). *Report on Class Actions*, 3 Volumes, Toronto: Ministry of Attorney-General.

Pace, N.M. (2007). *Class Actions in the United States of America: An Overview of the Process and the Empirical Literature*, Global Class Actions Project, at <http://www.globalclassactions.stanford.edu/>.

Pace, N.M., Carroll, S.J., Vogelsang, I., and Zakaras, L. (2007). *Insurance Class Actions in the United States*, Santa Monica, CA: RAND Institute for Civil Justice.

Plancich, S. and Starykh, S. (2009). *Trends in Securities Class Action Litigation: 2009 Year-End Update*, NERA, available at <http://www.nera.com/image/Recent_Trends_Report_1209.pdf>.

Pritchard, A.C. and Sarra, J.P. (2010). "Securities Class Actions Move North: A Doctrinal and Empirical Analysis of Securities Class Actions in Canada," *Alberta Law Review* 47(4): 881.

Tidmarsh, J. (1998). *Mass Tort Settlement Class Actions: Five Case Studies*, Washington, DC: Federal Judicial Center.

Willging, T.E., Hooper, L.L., and Niemic, R.J. (1996). *Empirical Study of Class Actions in Four Federal District Courts: Final Report to the Advisory Committee on Civil Rules*, Washington, DC: Federal Judicial Center.

Willging, T.E. and Lee III, E.G. (2007). *The Impact of the Class Action Fairness Act of 2005: Third Interim Report to the Judicial Conference Advisory Committee on Civil Rules*, Washington, DC: Federal Judicial Center.

Yeazell, S.C. (2004). "*Brown*, the Civil Rights Movement, and the Silent Litigation Revolution," *Vanderbilt Law Review* 57: 1975–2003.

3 0

LAW AND COURTS' IMPACT ON DEVELOPMENT AND DEMOCRATIZATION

CATALINA SMULOVITZ

I. INTRODUCTION

WHAT is the power of law and courts? Can they influence the emergence or quality of democracy? Can they redress an unequal distribution of social burdens? Academic debates about the connection of laws and courts to development and democracy are characterized by disagreements about the nature and direction of those causal links, the types of effects that do, or could, exist, how effects should be measured, and the intervening variables that affect connections that do exist.

In this Chapter, law is understood as a public, general, and binding command enforceable through state coercion. Even though laws may be perceived and used as aspirational goals, at the end of the day, their impact depends on the way courts enforce those commands. For this reason, the impact of law on democracy and development cannot be considered separately from the way courts interpret and enforce the law.

Laws can be found both in democratic and authoritarian systems. However, while democratic and authoritarian regimes can be *"ruled by law," "rule of law"* exists only in democratic regimes. *"Ruled by law"* regimes are characterized by the existence of public, relatively stable, and general rules but they do not include requirements regarding law-making procedures or the law-makers' subordination to their own rules. In contrast, *"rule of law"* regimes are characterized by the presence of law combined with limitations on the power of government and the discretion of public authorities (Barros, 2002).

Another term that requires clarification is economic growth. Economic growth is not equivalent to development. Economic growth, understood as the increase in the amount of the goods and services produced by an economy, can expand the liberties enjoyed by members of a society. However, as Sen (1999) noted, well-being also depends on the way those resources are distributed in the population. For this reason, definitions of development contemplate not only levels of economic growth but also the way benefits are distributed. (e.g., access to education and health).

With these definitional caveats in mind, we can now consider how law and courts relate to and impact democracy and development. Assessments of these relationships are inconsistent. While some authors suggest that courts and laws are increasingly being used for the promotion and realization of civil and social rights (Gauri and Brinks, 2008; Langford, 2008), others argue that impacts have been limited (Rosenberg, 1991). However, if effects have been disappointing, what explains the increasing role of law and courts around the world? Is it because they produce other effects? Is it because, even though measures of impact are still unsatisfactory, they do affect the distribution of wealth and burdens? This Chapter discusses three topics regarding the relationship between law, democracy and development. First, I will analyze the changing ways in which academic debates have studied the causal relationships. Second, I consider the effects laws can have as well as the difficulties involved in measuring those effects. Third, I examine the factors that condition those effects. In the final section, I conclude with some comments regarding the relation between law and governability.

II. FROM MACRO VARIABLES TO
MICRO FOUNDATIONS

Does economic growth and development depend on the existence of law, or does development produce a demand for law and institutions? Can law have an impact in authoritarian contexts or is democracy a precondition of such impact?

Study of the relationships among law, development, and democracy is characterized by controversies about the nature and causal direction of their connections. Variations in the character of these relationships are associated with changes in the understanding of their causal linkage, with changes in the definition of development, and with changes in the value ascribed to democracy and development as social goals. While, in certain periods, law has been considered a necessary condition for the achievement of economic growth, development, and democracy, in others, law was understood to be an obstacle to development. When development was defined restrictively as economic growth and was preferred over democracy, concerns about law and its benefits had a secondary character since it was believed that rule of law would follow eventually. On the other hand, when democracy was considered a necessary condition for economic growth and development, worries centered on the conditions that could make the rule of law flourish, on the extent of law's impact, and on the types of changes law can bring about. In recent times, questions have also been raised about the ability of legal mobilization to democratize authoritarian environments (Moustafa, 2007; Barros, 2002; El-Ghobashy, 2008; Diamant et al., 2005); and, in third-wave democracies, there have been debates about the ability of laws to enhance the quality of these democracies. Recent discussions have particularly focused on the capacity of law to increase equality, to modify the distribution of rights and social burdens, and on the impact transitional-justice[1] procedures have on the human-rights indicators of emerging democratic regimes (Sikkink and Walling, 2007; Gargarella et al., 2006).

Debates focus on the conceptual underpinnings of causal relations, of normative arguments, and on the interpretation of ambiguous empirical results. Discussions about the relationship between economic growth and democracy involve two different issues: the degree of association between these two variables and the causal mechanism that explains that association (Przeworski et al., 2000; Boix and Stokes, 2003). In regard to the causal connection, some authors argue that for the rule of law to flourish, economic growth has to come first; while others contend that law

---

[1] Transitional justice refers to the legal and non-legal responses used in recently established democracies to address systematic abuses of human rights committed by former dictatorial regimes (Elster, 2004: Sikkink and Walling, 2007).

is a necessary condition for the expansion of economic growth and development. Two justifications are cited for the first position. First, in order for economic growth to occur, "modernizing" elites need to carry out some unpalatable and unpopular measures that cannot be implemented if the rule of law limits the governing elite's use of power. Second, the extreme social and political inequalities associated with underdevelopment prevent the establishment of successful and sustainable legal restrictions capable of controlling powerful actors. Thus, unless "benevolent authoritarian" (sic) elites can carry out development programs in an unrestricted fashion, the expected social differentiation that modernization theory associates with economic growth will not take place, with the result that neither rule of law nor development will flourish.

This position is contested by authors who argue that underdevelopment is associated with "unrule" of law and that "unrule" of law reproduces underdevelopment. From this other perspective, lack of legal rules leads to underdevelopment because it prevents the existence of predictable and stable signals needed by economic agents in deciding whether to make investments. Thus, until those rules are established and consolidated, economic growth and development cannot take place. Stable legal systems are necessary for growth and development because they minimize transaction costs associated with arbitrary rule. Consequently, rule of law must come first and is a precondition for economic growth and for eventual changes in the distribution of social burdens.

Those who contend that the rule of law is not a precondition note that its absence did not prevent the economic modernization and development of China, the USSR, and the Southeastern Asian countries, or of Brazil before its democratic transition. On the other hand, those who contend that it is a precondition note that "per capita incomes grow faster in democracies," that "poor people are much more likely to be ruled by dictators," and that democracy does not reduce the rate of investment in poor countries (Przeworski et al., 2000).

Recent comparative empirical evidence shows that the linkage between rule of law and development is complex (Przeworski et al., 2000; Boix, 2003). Przeworski et al. argue, for example, that economic growth, development, and democracy are related to intervening variables, such as differentials in population growth between authoritarian and democratic regimes, rather than being explainable by a direct causal relationship between law and development. Boix, on the other hand, asserts that the connection between development and democracy is related to changes in tax structures and income distribution that result from development. Even though Przeworski et al. report that they "did not find a shred of evidence that democracy needs to be sacrificed on the altar of development," they also noted that "at least in regard to the growth of total economies, political regimes are not what matters." It is worthwhile asking then, whether rule of law, although not necessarily associated with economic growth, is related to improvement in human well-being (e.g., declining death rates and infant mortality, and increasing life expectancy and school enrollment)?

According to Macguire (1999) changes in well-being indicators are related to the distribution of the social and political actors' organizational capacities rather than to the nature of political regimes. He contends that since the ability to exert pressure is unequally distributed and depends on organizational capacities, only organized actors—trade unions, business associations or political parties—are able to enhance their material well-being. This means that regardless of the political regime, organized actors will do better than non-organized actors. However, it also follows that in democracies organized actors will do even better because democracies provide them with more favorable opportunities to demand and protect their rights.

These findings highlight that analysis of the impact of law and courts on democracy and development must consider the legal, political and social conditions that enable the production of effects. As classical legal sociologists were well aware, the impact of law cannot be understood independently of the social reality in which the law works. Although there is nothing radically new in this perspective, the renewed recognition of the social and political determinants reminds us that outcomes do not follow from the autonomous existence of laws but from conditioned social interactions. While actors' endowments (e.g., organization, money) condition their ability to use laws and courts as social tools, political, institutional and economic scenarios affect which actors have access to legal institutions, the way judiciaries decide as well as the implementation of those decisions.

These findings also show that to understand how laws and courts produce effects, research needs to move from macro relationships to the examination of micro or medium level factors. As I will discuss in section IV, contingent medium and micro level institutional and social conditions rather than macro causal relationships explain differences in the performance and outcomes of laws and courts. Thus, exactly what those conditions are, and why and how they produce effects is the central focus of the discussion that follows. This approach demystifies the ability of law to produce changes autonomously, but it also acknowledges its distinctiveness as a social institution characterized by mandatory, enforceable commands.

III. WHAT EFFECTS AND HOW TO MEASURE THEM?

What are the impacts of law and how can they be measured? Assessments of the effects of laws on democracy and development have usually focused on changes in specific social indicators such as poverty levels, distribution of rights, or of public goods such as health, education, or justice. In some studies, results did not show significant improvements, leading certain authors to dismiss the relevance of *litigation* as an instrument for social reform. For example, Rosenberg (1991) shows that ten years after *Brown v. Board of Education*, the percentage of black school children attending mixed schools in the Deep South states had not significantly increased; he attributed the changes that eventually came starting in the mid-1960s to a combination of increased political support for ending school segregation, penalties for non-compliance imposed by statutes, and the creation of the necessary administrative capacities for enforcement. In other words, while a narrow interpretation of his findings leads to the conclusion that judicial action is irrelevant as a vehicle of change, a broader interpretation concludes that the impact of such action depends on its relationship with the political and institutional environment. Other analysts, such as Galanter (1983), have warned that evaluations of impacts should consider not only the narrow and direct effects of laws and court decisions but also their radiating consequences: that is, how their workings diffuse into other issues and arenas and how they alter the resources available for negotiating other conflicts. The implication is that the study of impact should include not only an assessment of direct gains but also of the changes in the opportunity structure for claim-making, in the ways in which results diffuse into other types of issues, and in the ideological orientation of judicial responses to claims.

Studies of impact have also distinguished between the direct and indirect effects of law. Direct effects include the number of cases decided in favor of plaintiffs, the gains accrued by them or the percentage of the population affected by a legal decision. Indirect effects comprise, among other things, the establishment of precedents that spur claim-making regarding other issues, public scrutiny mechanisms for rights enforcement, and what might be labeled educational outcomes such as judicial and public awareness of rights. However, it is not always clear how to distinguish between direct and indirect effects: how to evaluate, for example, situations in which direct plaintiffs lose but those losses spur political reactions that lead to winning in other policy arenas? Furthermore, how does one evaluate these impacts when studies also show that losing in the short run can become a powerful strategic tool to activate involvement of other actors, which might lead to the achievement of direct gains in other arenas. In Latin America, for example, losing in human rights trials in domestic courts allowed plaintiffs to take their cases onto international courts where the cases received a more sympathetic reception. Similar trajectories were observed in the Mexican and Colombian mortgage crises where initial losses in the courts led, first, to political turmoil and then to legislative changes (Grammont, 2001; Uprimny Yepes, 2007). An ongoing study evaluating the effects of health-rights litigation highlights another problem related to the evaluation of impact: the unintended distributive consequences of litigation success (Wilson, 2009). The country studies in this project show that in spite of the positive direct effects, litigation success has led to reallocation of resources in inequitable and inefficient ways and reoriented policy goals in ways that undermine collective priorities (i.e. forcing concentration of health budgets on curative rather than preventive policies, on high-tech treatment rather than on basic assistance). These examples show that narrow evaluations of impact could result not only in incomplete but also in erroneous assessments of the outcomes achieved.

Discussions of law's effects become, then, a methodological debate about adequate indicators and places where law's workings can be observed. Given that laws can have immediate but also wider effects, indicators must be multiple and complex. Evaluation of immediate effects concentrates on tangible changes such as the modification of the ethnic composition of schools in a particular district, or in the number of individuals that receive a particular state-provided drug, or on the effects the provision of a drug has on the mortality rate of a certain population. Evaluation of the wider effects requires assessment of radiating consequences, such as changes in legislation, unintended changes in associated policies (COHRE, 2003) or modifications in the agenda. For example, when Colombian courts accepted that health demands could be understood as human rights claims, petitions requesting public funding for new drugs and treatments increased. The resulting expansion of health spending challenged the state's ability to fulfill other public obligations and a legislative reform regulating the provision of health services had to be approved (Yamin and Parra-Vera, 2009). Evaluations also need to consider that since outcomes of laws and court decisions take time to become evident or can be achieved "by losing," the adoption of a narrow perspective may result in inaccurate conclusions.

Another problem confronted in the evaluation of impact relates to the availability and reliability of judicial statistics. Galanter noted that until recently this was an important obstacle even in developed countries such as the United States where "what courts and litigants and lawyers were actually doing was only dimly known" (Galanter, 2006), and it continues to be so in underdeveloped countries. Lack of information has not only obvious consequences on the quality and specificity of judicial policy-making, it also prevents adequate evaluation of the consequences of laws and court decisions and conditions the type of research that can be done. Indeed, because in most Third World countries, comprehensive, disaggregated judicial statistics are generally unavailable, systematic empirical legal research about the impact of laws has mainly taken the form of case studies or has concentrated on major decisions by apex courts (COHRE 2003; Gargarella et al., 2006; Coomans, 2006; Langford, 2008). Lack of systematic, disaggregated, and reliable information about sentences, caseloads, and the implementation of judicial decisions, which has hindered quantitative research, has also limited the study of lower courts' behavior and comparisons within and across countries. In this regard, Linn Hammergren (2002) has shown that in Latin America inadequate and unreliable statistical information has produced not only erroneous evaluations of performance but also misguided policy recommendations. Due to poor record keeping in the courtroom and poorly maintained judicial archives, statistical information about the courts is inadequate, creating serious problems for designing samples that might produce better information. The information available has at best produced "partial snapshots" of national situations; it is inadequate for any type of more sophisticated or comparative studies. Data tend to be limited to a few years and a few jurisdictions, and do not cover the same indicators across countries or districts.

Such informational inadequacies have also impaired some recent attempts to measure impact using, for instance, the formula designed by Gauri and Brinks (2008: 327) to evaluate the effects of legalization. Their own description of the formula and of problems they faced in finding data raises doubts about the utility of the indicator. The weakness of the judicial statistics has led researchers interested in carrying out systematic empirical studies to laboriously build their own data bases (see Helmke, 2004; Gauri and Brinks, 2008; Uprimny Yepes, 2007). In spite of these commendable efforts, the nature of the data sets limits the ability to pursue comparative analysis across countries, issues, and times. However, as the next sections show, researchers building their own, specially designed data sets have produced some useful analyses of specific conditions that foster or hinder the impact of laws and courts. Although informational difficulties have limited the comparability and time frame of these studies, results have revealed the complex nature of the interactions that make laws and courts work.

IV. How Impact Comes About: Interactions and Contingent Outcomes

The impact of laws depends on political and social conditions and on the way laws are applied by the courts. But what are the contextual conditions that constitute the relevant intervening variables? How do they influence the emergence of claims, judicial decisions, enforcement, and in turn, the impact of law on development and democracy? This section examines the interaction of laws with three contextual variables: a) the structure and competitiveness of political systems, b) the structure and performance of the judiciary, and c) the organizational endowments of the social or political actors, such as social and labor movements, that use the law. This list could have included other contextual factors, such as colonial legacies or legal traditions. However, for reasons that I explain below, this Chapter does not analyze all of the possible factors. The goal of this section is multiple: to show how and why these selected conditions affect impact and to speculate, based on the findings of empirical research, about some additional developments that might follow from the relationships between law and these three variables.

A. Structure and competitiveness of political systems

The competitiveness and structure of political systems affect the ability to pursue legal actions, to adjust to legal changes, and to enforce judicial decisions. Studies have considered the impact of the following political factors: (i) the democratic or autocratic character of the political regime; (ii) the federal or centralized character of the political structure; (iii) the degree of political competitiveness; (iv) the state's administrative and fiscal capacities; and (v) the extent and type of constitutionalization of rights and international treaties.

(i) It is usually assumed that the impact of law is greater in democratic contexts than in autocratic ones. Democratic regimes limit authority's arbitrary actions, increase citizens' opportunities to organize and to pursue legal claims, create the conditions for independent judicial decisions, and give voters the opportunity to oversee enforcement of those decisions. However, studies have also shown that laws and courts can have an impact in authoritarian regimes. In authoritarian contexts, actors use the courts and the rhetoric of rights to expose the illegitimacy of authoritarian governments and decisions and use international courts to expand the scope of conflicts. Studies focused on Chile, Argentina, Egypt, and China have described the democratizing effects of these uses of laws and courts in authoritarian contexts (Barros, 2002; Ginsburg and Moustafa, 2008; El-Ghobashy, 2008; Acuña and Smulovitz, 1997; Groisman, 1983). Thus, although democracy is generally associated with the function of law as a protective or transformative tool, research has shown that such effects can also be found in autocratic systems.

(ii) The federal or unitary character of the political structure also produces ambiguous results. Research on federal countries indicates that the simultaneous existence of diverse and local judicial structures results in the uneven achievement and enforcement of legal outcomes. Since the production and enforcement of legal outcomes depend on the specific institutional, legal, and social endowments found in each district, legal outcomes end up being important in some districts but not in others. Federalism is associated with inconsistent results because the "translation" of federal laws into local norms varies but also because local, legal, and political conditions enable compliance in some districts and preclude them in others. Laws and courts can produce unequal effects in unitary political systems in so far as the distribution of state capacities, actors' resources and support structures also vary in this type of system. However, in federal countries variations tend to be more intense because the autonomy of provincial governments results in unequal "translations" of the normative contents of federal laws and in unequal mechanisms for their enforcement. Thus, differences among districts tend to be more significant than in unitary states because what can be claimed and what is enforced also differ. In a federal state such as Brazil, research has shown that the achievements of social-economic litigation and the interventions of the Ministerio Publico vary between Northeastern and Southern States (Hoffmann and Bentes, 2003; Arantes Bastos, 2003). Similar results are found in another federal country such as India, where public interest litigation (PIL) has led to different outcomes between Bimaru and other states (Gauri, 2009). Thus, although the federal or centralized character of a polity does not necessarily determine the likelihood of achieving results, federal countries show greater variation in the distribution of rights due to differences in the definition of the protected rights and in the enforcement policies among districts (Epp, 1990; Riddell, 2004; Smith, 2005).

(iii) Degree of political competitiveness is another factor that influences people's ability to pursue legal actions, the judiciary's decision-making process, and the enforcement of legal decisions. Analyses of the effects of political competitiveness also show contested results. Some authors note that since high competitiveness diminishes powerful actors' ability to control results, it ends up fostering judicial independence. These outcomes build confidence in the judiciary and encourage legal mobilization to redress the distribution of rights. In competitive scenarios nobody is certain who will win, leading all parties to be interested in preserving the impartiality of the arbiter and in preventing future encroachments on their rights. Rebecca Bill Chavez's research (2003) showed that differences in political competitiveness in two Argentinean provinces determined variations in judicial autonomy and in the achievement of outcomes. While in one province lack of political competition allowed the governor to subordinate the judiciary and to dismantle sources of countervailing power, in a neighbouring province, competition among three parties bolstered checks on executive power and created incentives for all parties to support a system of checks and balances. Perez Liñan and Castagnola (2008) found similar results regarding the impact of competitiveness on judicial appointments. Their study shows that when inter-party competition is high, executives develop a meaningful system of checks and balances including an independent judiciary, and that when one party controls the government for prolonged periods of time, executives control judicial appointments and removals in a way intended to preserve their own power.

In contrast, other authors report that lack of political competition can have a surprising effect: it can promote legal mobilization. They contend that when winning in the political arena is precluded, legal claims become the only political tool available. McIntosh (1983) highlighted this paradoxical effect of lack of competitiveness. He argues that when traditional political participation and competition are restricted, legal mobilization becomes *the* alternative form of political participation and courts an additional arena. Studies about the use of legal mobilization in authoritarian contexts seem to confirm his finding (Groisman, 1987; Barros, 2002; El-Ghobashy, 2008; Giles and Lancaster, 1989). It follows, then, that competitiveness levels may have multiple and distinct effects. While high competition may increase judicial independence and the ability of the courts to produce results, low political competition may increase the use of law as a political tool. The first argument highlights the effects of competition on the outcomes of law, and the second its impact on the propensity to use the law. Both results have consequences for democracy and development. High competition promotes the protection of rights and is likely to affect the distribution of social burdens, while low competition appears to expand legal mobilization by increasing the number of actors turning to the law.

(iv) The state's implementation capacities influence the impact of laws and courts on democracy and development because they determine whether and how legal decisions are enforced and thus affect the strategic use actors make of the law. State implementation capacities depend on the supply of bureaucratic resources such as the human capital of administrative agencies or the coercive capacities of police forces. State implementation capacities also depend on the availability of fiscal resources, on the number of agencies that intervene in enforcement, and on the centralized or decentralized character of state bureaucracies. Acknowledgment of the relevance of implementation capacities highlights the fact that impacts do not flow automatically from the content of laws or courts decisions. Without enforcement capacities, laws and judicial decisions can become irrelevant. Even if a judiciary considers claims and issues decisions about them, and even if the power configuration is favorable, enforcement will only follow if appropriate bureaucratic capacities and fiscal resources are available. Availability of administrative and fiscal resources can affect the likelihood of enforcement and influence the substantive content of the decisions. Knowledge about bureaucratic and fiscal capacities informs actors about the potential efficacy of their actions, and informs judges about the costs of making controversial decisions. When judges know their decisions will not be implemented because bureaucratic capacities are low, they also know that it is likely that the fiscal consequences of their decisions will be irrelevant. If that is the case, judges playing for popular support are prone to decide in favor of plaintiffs since they can anticipate that the cost of their decision will be immaterial. Similar developments can be expected, in hierarchically organized judiciaries, when judges know their decisions will be automatically appealed. In those situations lower court judges may feel free to advance controversial decisions because they can expect that appellate courts will block enforcement or because they may want to displace responsibility for unpopular decisions to higher courts.

The increasing number of proceedings seeking the enforcement of sentences achieved in public interest litigation (PIL) illustrates how weak state capacities and scarce fiscal resources can water down the impact of laws and court decisions. Weak state capacities have been critical in the Latin American case where, as Lynn Hammergren noted (2002; see also Gauri and Brinks, 2008), winning does little good because enforcement is problematic. Lack of fiscal resources has also effectively negated some well known and praised judicial decisions, and impaired the ability of law to affect the distribution of public goods. In 2000, for example, the South African Constitutional Court established that the government had not met its obligation to provide adequate housing for residents of the Grotboom informal settlement and held that it had to implement a program to provide housing for those living in intolerable situations. Analyses of the Grootboom case indicate that difficulties in coordination among different bureaucratic agencies, lack of human resources, and insufficient fiscal resources to ensure implementation at the local level have led to a lack of compliance with the decision (Wickeri, 2004; Pillay, 2002). In other words, if bureaucratic capacities and fiscal resources are weak, court decisions become irrelevant and lack impact. Thus, evaluations of impact need to include an appraisal of their availability.

Gauri and Brinks (2008) have additionally noted that knowledge about the availability of fiscal resources also influences the types of claims actors advance. Their study of social rights litigation shows that when actors know fiscal resources are insufficient, claims tend to target private actors or to request the regulation of public services. In contrast, when actors estimate that fiscal resources are available, claims concentrate on the state and demand for the direct provision of goods and services. Thus, availability of fiscal resources determines not only the state ability to enforce decisions but also the target and type of claims that actors advance. In turn, both the orientation of claims and the degree of compliance with decisions determine the type of influence laws and courts may have on development and democracy.

(v) The extent and type of constitutionalization of rights and international treaties also influence the effects of law and courts on democracy and development. After 1945, some constitutions expanded the charter of protected rights, others modified the number and standing of the actors authorized to advance claims related to rights, and still others gave constitutional status to international human rights treaties. These changes created opportunities for litigation on new matters and led to the juridification of conflicts previously solved through political processes. They placed the justice system within the reach of public interest advocacy organizations and expanded the types of rights enforceable through the courts. In addition, constitutionalization of international treaties expanded the types of actors that could oversee and demand enforcement of rights and gave international courts authority over certain domestic legal disputes.

The crisis of the welfare state and the resulting shrinkage in the provision of services has made evident the impact of constitutionalization of rights. Studies have shown the increased use of these new tools to confront unfavorable scenarios (Fix Fierro, 2004; Sousa Santos, 1996). In India, for example, the Constitution allowed the central and state governments to make special provision for the advancement of socially and educationally backward classes of citizens or for the Scheduled Castes and Scheduled Tribes. These constitutional reservations led to the creation of compensatory discrimination programs that included benefits, such as jobs and places in professional schools for members of these groups. Analysis of the Indian case demonstrated that, in spite of their shortcomings, constitutional reservations succeeded in getting members of the beneficiary groups into government employment and in increasing their presence in the legislature (Galanter, 1984). Important impacts have also been noted in Costa Rica, where the expansion of constitutionally protected rights and of the actors authorized to advance rights claims significantly increased the number of cases considered by the Constitutional Court. More specifically, a claim of rights was used to compel public health authorities to make AIDS treatment publicly available, resulting in an 80% reduction of AIDS mortality (Gauri and Brinks, 2008; Wilson and Rodríguez Cordero, 2006). Similar increases in rights claims have been reported in Colombia, South Africa, Brazil, Bangladesh, and Argentina; in all of these countries constitutionalization of social rights has led to increased litigation over provision of health-related services and to changes in policy orientations (Gargarella et al., 2006).

Finally, it is worth mentioning two other consequences of the recent constitutionalization of rights. Some authors argue that the constitutionalization of rights communicates to judges changes in prevailing political orientations and signals the policy areas where decisions will confront fewer obstacles and find greater political support. When judges know where and when jurisprudential innovations will be less costly, changes in the ideological orientation of their decisions become more likely (Gauri and Brinks, 2008). Other studies have shown that constitutionalization of international human rights treaties provides actors with an additional legal vehicle for claiming rights and increases the prospects for compliance. For example, claims made before the Inter-American Human Rights Court have led to the reopening of human rights trials that had been terminated by local amnesties and to decisions demanding the implementation of housing, health or education rights (Langford, 2008). Thus, while there are still debates regarding the extent of the impact of the constitutionalization of new rights, its relevance is not disputed.

B. The structure and performance of the judiciary

Those who assume that the impact of laws depends on their content, application or interpretation concentrate their research on the effects that the structure and performance of the judiciary has in producing rights-enforcing legal decisions. Since this perspective assumes laws and legal decisions are themselves sufficient to produce impacts, the main topics of the research agendas of people who make this assumption are how decisions are made and what factors affect those decisions. While I do not accept the assumption that laws and court decisions alone are sufficient to explain impact, I recognize that without laws and legal decisions the question of impact becomes irrelevant. Thus, how the structure of the judiciary affects actual decision-making and the content of the decision is an important topic for inquiry. Research on the legal decision-making process considers variables such as case-selection procedures, the role of precedent, ideological orientation of judges, selection procedures (and tenure) for judicial personnel, and judges' strategic calculations. Studies have also examined issues related to the accessibility of courts, such as the quantity and geographical distribution of court facilities and judges; the economic cost and timeliness of legal processes; the availability of free legal assistance for criminal, civil and commercial claims; the type of actors authorized to make legal claims or to demand constitutional review; and the existence of language requirements or legal representation requirements.

What have these studies shown? Let's consider some findings. Regarding precedents, studies have shown that when legal precedents are not binding, the outcomes of cases may be uncertain. Some judges will follow precedents, while others will disregard them. Since results will vary according to the judges' ideology, their strategic calculations or the plaintiffs' ability to engage in repeated litigation, impact of court decisions will be uneven. In some cases, uncertainty about the likely outcome of cases will be perceived as an opportunity while in others as an additional cost. It will be an opportunity if actors understand that lack of mandatory precedents does not close their prospects of getting more favorable decisions from another judge in a new claim. It will become an additional cost if actors hoping to get a more favorable decision do not have resources to engage in repeated litigation.

The absence of a norm of binding precedent has another consequence. When previous decisions do not determine future ones, actors have incentives to keep re-litigating the issue, which can lead to increased numbers of cases and judicial congestion. While court congestion is usually attributed to a lack of judicial resources, research has shown that it can also result from deliberate and coordinated action by social actors seeking to force the intervention of political authorities. Analyses of the "corralito case" in Argentina and of the "Barzon case" in Mexico demonstrate that actors deliberately used the weakness of precedents to "play the congestion card" in order to force the intervention of political authorities (Smulovitz, 2006; Grammont, 2001). Thus, although a system of binding precedent minimizes transaction costs and reduces uncertainty—two results usually associated with democracy and development—empirical research also shows that actors can take advantage of the lack of binding precedents to develop and sustain sophisticated strategies.

Studies about the consequences of judicial tenure and selection procedures on the content of judicial decisions have a long tradition. In recent years, Lisa Hilbink (2007), Gretchen Helmke (2004), and Santiago Basabe Serrano (2009) have analyzed the impact of these factors in several Latin American cases. Hilbink, for example, shows the relevance of such institutional factors to Chilean judges' decisions. She notes that procedures giving the Court almost complete control of the selection of its own membership enables the Court to discipline and ideologically control lower tribunals and their decisions. On the other hand, Helmke's analysis of the Argentinean Supreme Court illustrates that when judges' term in office is uncertain, strategic calculations affect the content of their decisions. She shows that in the absence of guaranteed tenure, and in order to avoid being ousted by a succeeding government, judges tend to be loyal to the current administration unless a change in power seems likely, in which case they may rule against the incumbent administration. Judges' strategic calculations about the strength of the government in office and about their chances of being ousted affect the pro- or anti-government content of their rulings. In her view, judges' strategic calculations rather than institutional factors have a greater effect in the content of decisions. Basabe Serrano's study of judges' behavior in Ecuador shows a different and surprising connection between tenure and the content of court decisions. According to this study, in highly unstable contexts the best strategy for judges is to vote according to their previous ideological preferences. Since judges know that they may be ousted anyway, ideological sincerity appears as the best strategy to maintain or improve their reputation, which can benefit them when they return to their former activities. These studies show that both institutional and strategic considerations can affect the content of judicial decisions. However, the conditions determining when each of these variables influences the content of judicial decisions remain to be established. From the perspective of potential litigants this information is relevant both for timing claims in order to maximize the chance of success and for deciding when to pay attention to the appointment process.

A court's ability to control its docket can also influence the content of legal decisions and thus potential litigants' ability to obtain desired results through legal action. Under a system of discretionary jurisdiction, the courts determine which disputes merit legal responses and when. Beyond its administrative benefits, docket control gives courts a powerful political instrument. It allows them to decide and signal which public policy issues will get legal attention and gives them an instrument they can strategically use in their relationship with the executive and (other) potential litigants. In unstable political systems docket control can also be used to show compliance or to threaten hostile executives with unfavorable decisions. When relationships between the executive and judicial branch are friendly, courts can decide to concentrate on those cases that do not threaten executive policies and leave conflicting issues for future treatment. On the other hand, when relationships are tense, courts can decide to pursue cases executives would have preferred to delay. The history of the legal conflict about savings deposits that took place in Argentina from 2001 to 2006 illustrates how the courts' management of the docket was used as a political tool in a power conflict between the courts and the executive (Herrero, 2007).

The accessibility of courts is also critical when evaluating the effects of laws and courts on democracy and development. The various access factors mentioned determine not only who but also what type of topics get to the courts. For example, when public interest organizations are not entitled to initiate claims on behalf of other actors, it is less likely that topics such as human rights, environmental protection, or lack of access to public services due to poverty discrimination[2] will become subjects of legal

---

[2] For example, ACIJ, an Argentinean public interest advocacy organization, advanced several claims based on inequalities in the provision of public services (education, transportation, and garbage collection) as between high and low income neighborhoods. They accused the Argentinean State of discriminating in the provision of these public services against lower income populations. The

disputes. Accessibility factors also affect enforcement of judicial decisions. They influence, for instance, whether it is easy to initiate proceedings seeking the enforcement of judgments. Studies about the implementation of court decisions indicate that public bureaucracies only start to comply with those rulings after proceedings to enforce judgments are initiated (Smulovitz, 2005). Thus, it follows that when barriers to initiating these types of proceedings are high, reluctant public bureaucracies can compromise the enforcement of legal decisions and thus neutralize their impact.

Discussions about the impact of accessibility factors are not new and their relevance is usually not contested. In recent times, research has also drawn attention to some lesser-known micro-level institutions that affect access. For example, a comparative analysis of the outcomes of human rights trials across the world suggests the significance that the existence of the "private prosecutor in criminal cases" (*querellante adhesivo o asociado*)[3] has in the prosecution of certain public criminal cases. The study shows that when this institution is in place, human rights trials are more common and last longer. Sikkink and Walling (2007). demonstrate that, when public prosecutors are reluctant to act, this micro-institution is particularly relevant. They show that when plaintiffs confront official resistance, this institution allows victims to initiate, sustain and oversee trials. We also know that the institution has another consequence: countries that held transitional justice trials for long periods of time, a development associated among other things with the existence of the "querellante adhesivo," had a higher improvement in their human rights conditions than countries that held them for shorter periods or that did not have them at all. These studies show, then, that in addition to the usual accessibility variables, research should also analyze the impact that these rarely observed micro-legal institutions have in the achievement of outcomes.

C. The socio-economic and organizational endowments of the actors

The social and organizational resources of the participating actors constitute a third set of variables affecting the ability to pursue legal claims, the content of the

courts favorably considered these claims and ordered the government to mend the identified asymmetries in future budget allocations.

[3] There is no adequate English translation for the phrase "querellante adhesivo o asociado." Some authors translate it as "auxiliary prosecutor" and others as "private prosecutor in criminal cases." The institution allows the victim the right to recourse before the courts as a party in the criminal proceedings, or as a participant in judicial investigation preparatory to pursuing penal sanctions. It allows, for example, victims of human rights violations to present a case even if the public prosecutor is not willing to pursue the case. "Private prosecution" enhances access because it is assumed that victims' direct participation increases the effective protection of their rights and diminishes the likelihood of reluctance—due to conflict of interests—on the part of public prosecutors in cases involving State crimes.

decisions, and the enforcement of those decisions. To influence outcomes, actors need certain basic endowments such as minimum levels of economic and educational resources. While basic material resources provide the wherewithal actors need to exercise choice, organizational resources and educational attainments provide technical and informational opportunities. However, these endowments do not ensure that actors will organize or that they will have resources to transform wants into entitlements. In addition, actors need to coordinate their actions (organizational resources) and need access to support structures. Especially for weak actors, support structures provide sophisticated knowledge of the law and legal processes plus access to specialists that can assist them in their claims. In other words, they need organizations dedicated to litigating rights claims, willing and competent lawyers, and the financial resources needed to pursue claims in courts. Favorable political conditions and low institutional thresholds for legal claiming can be irrelevant if weak actors lack the support structures needed to work within the judicial system. Epp's work (1998) showed how differences in the density of support structures in the United States, UK, Canada, and India explained variations in the pursuit of results through the courts (Epp, 1998). The recent growth of public interest litigation (PIL) in India and in Latin America has been facilitated by the development of local support structures and by increases in economic support from donors (USAID, Ford Foundation, Open Society, National Endowment for Democracy, British Council) to organizations pursuing this type of strategy (see McClymont and Golub, 2000; Sikkink and Keck, 1998)

Although the relevance of support structures for the likelihood of law's impact is not disputed, studies indicate that their specific consequences vary. For example, the relevance of support structures diminishes when courts do not have docket control, since less effort is needed to ensure the sustainability of claims or to call the court's attention to a specific claim. Support structures are also less relevant in countries where the private bar is well developed and individual claiming is more frequent. The significance of support structures is also related to the presence of legislation authorizing collective claims (Gauri and Brinks, 2008). Underprivileged individuals need organizations acting on their behalf in order to pursue collective claims, and where such claims are possible, support structures are more important. While geographic variables affect the distribution of claims and outcomes, sources of funding affects the litigation agenda and strategy. In 1983, for example, the Ford Foundation announced that future grants in the South American region were to be assigned to research centers, universities, and bar associations that promoted research, and actions on topics related to administration of justice and non-politically motivated rights violations such as police violence, denial of access to public information and of due process, and gender discrimination. Given this change in the donor's priorities some existing human rights organizations shifted their strategies while newly created groups adopted these issues as part of their own agenda. The use of laws and courts to address non-politically motivated rights violations became the prevalent activity of local advocacy organizations (Fruhling, 2000). Sources also note that the reorientation of financial support to associations promoting the use of public interest litigation was critical for the development of this legal strategy as a political tool (Sikkink and Keck, 1998). Thus, even though the relevance of support structures is not disputed, research shows that the scope and type of impact of their activities is, in turn, conditioned by the selection of their agenda and strategies.

The impact of law and courts on democracy and development is also conditioned by variables such as colonial legacies or legal traditions (civil or common law). Some have argued that colonial domination affects the type of development and degree of autonomy of courts, and that the independence of judiciaries and their ability to protect political freedom and property rights are related to the legal tradition inherited from a former colonial power (see La Porta et al., 1997). Research has shown, however, that the connection between these variables is complex. The impact of colonial rule varies because colonial legacy is not the same everywhere. It varies, for instance, according to the type of settlements colonizers established,[4] the alliances set up between colonial rulers and local populations, and the ways in which colonial linkages were broken. Thus, although it is possible to trace the specific impact of colonial rule on the legal system of a particular country, understanding its impact depends on the specific arrangement of colonial rule found in each case rather than on having been under "colonial rule" (Acemoglu et al., 2001; Mahoney et al., 2006; Coatsworth, 2008). Recent empirical research has also questioned the distinctive impact of legal traditions (civil law and common law). A study comparing courts in twelve countries concludes that legal tradition is not a good predictor of the willingness and ability of superior courts to exercise accountability functions; and it also reconfirms previous observations about the blurring of the distinctions between the two traditions (Gargarella, 2010). While analyses of each of these traditions show that achievements in each of them exhibit important internal variations, comparisons between the two indicate that their workings appear to be converging. These findings thus raise questions about the relevance of the common law/civil law distinction for explaining variation in development and democracy.

[4] Recent accounts of varying colonial experiences indicate that differences in local endowments at the time of colonization led to the establishment of different institutions that, in turn, had lingering effects in post-colonial times. Acemoglu et al. (2001) argue, for example, that when, due to population density or mortality risks, colonizers could not settle permanently, they set up extractive institutions. These institutions allowed them to manipulate local labor and resources from afar, but did not lead to the settlement of population in the colonies or to the creation of local institutions of government. The post-colonial results were unequal societies and less institutionalized political systems. On the other hand, when conditions allowed the creation of permanent settlements, colonizers shaped the local demographics and institutions. Settlers had an interest in establishing a system of rights to protect their lives and properties and this led to the establishment of production enhancing institutions that tended to persist in post-colonial times.

V. FINAL REMARKS

The main lesson of recent empirical research regarding the impact of laws and courts on economic and political development is that outcomes are contingent and depend on interactions with political and social conditions. Laws and court decisions are important catalysts for change but neither is a sufficient condition. Even though the general and mandatory character of law defines law's peculiar and unique features as a social institution, its impact depends on the conditions within which it operates. Analysis of the relationships between these conditions and the impact of law and courts shows that similar laws can have different impacts. These variations suggest that although the specific content of laws cannot be disregarded, impacts must be understood as contingent on historically and geographically contextualized variables. The inclusion of the sociological and political variables in the analysis reflects the reality that legal conflicts do not take place in the void. Moreover, understanding the workings of law and courts requires that we consider all stages of the legal process (initiating claims, adjudication of those claims, and enforcement of the decisions).

The definition and measurement of the impact of laws and courts continue to be the subject of disagreements and uncertainties. The main problem regarding the definition of impact relates to its reach. The distinction between direct and indirect impacts does not solve the problem since it does not provide clear lines of demarcation that differentiate among types of effects, and does not readily identify the set of possible indirect impacts that needs to be considered. These difficulties have led to ambiguous assessments about the actual scope of impacts. While studies using a narrow definition probably result in incomplete pictures of the effects, broader definitions make it difficult to establish whether impacts might have resulted from some other cause and thus raise questions about the relevance of laws and courts in the production of indirect impacts. Furthermore, if impacts radiate across institutions and policy areas, throughout time, and if they can be even achieved by losing, it is unclear how to establish when laws do *not* produce results.

In spite of these difficulties, research has shown that law and courts have had some positive results. The interaction of law with social, legal, and political conditions has modified the mortality rates of some populations (Gauri and Brinks, 2008), induced executive agencies to advance public policies that had been detected by the "judicial radar," altered the negotiating resources available to parties, and provided actors with additional legitimating arguments. Studies also indicate that countries that held human rights trials for longer periods show greater average improvement in their human rights indicators than those that held them for fewer years or that did not have them at all (Sikkink and Walling, 2007). Thus, the question for future studies is not whether laws and courts can have an impact but what combinations and interactions among variables lead to the production of results.

Another difficulty that hinders evaluation of impact is related to the availability of adequate and systematic judicial information. Some countries do not produce information to track the progress of legal processes, others only report highly aggregated results or do not produce specific information regarding lower court decisions and still others do not collect judicial statistics at all. Problems include not only the lack of systematic data regarding basic judicial indicators, but also confidentiality restrictions that prevent access to information. Informational deficits impose different types of restrictions. Lack of disaggregated databases has led to the concentration of studies on apex courts, has prevented the study of impact, and has made comparative studies difficult or impossible to execute. Although researchers have designed innovative strategies to cope with some of these difficulties, such solutions do not substitute for good state-produced statistics. At least in underdeveloped countries, advancing the research agenda on the impact of law and courts on economic and political development requires the improvement (if not the creation) of systems for compiling and disseminating judicial statistics. Without reliable and systematic information, basic facts such as the scope, nature, and types of cases, and hence the impacts of those cases, cannot be established, and comparative studies will continue to be limited. Given the increased use of legal instruments as political tools, accurate and informed knowledge about their effects has become even more necessary.

Research has also highlighted different impacts that laws and courts have on the governability of political systems. Some studies emphasize the non-democratic political effects that arise when judges have the power to nullify decisions reflecting the preferences of political majorities. Other studies stress the democratic implications of laws and courts since they increase the number of tools for democratic participation. And still other studies note that laws and courts allow actors to initiate collective claims without coordinating actions with others. Regarding the impact of law and courts on governability, two primary claims have been advanced. First, laws and courts have a virtuous effect because they imply the use of institutional, legal, and non-violent instruments to advance demands. Second, laws and courts have troubling consequences because they move to the unelected judiciary debates that should be taking place in legislative or executive arenas. The main concern raised by this latter claim is that the judicial framing of disputes transforms outcomes into "trumps," and undermines the legitimacy of the decisions made by democratically chosen representatives. These perils cannot be totally dismissed. Research shows that the impact of laws and courts on governability can lead either to social disorder and maintenance of the status quo, or to more equalitarian distribution of goods and rights. In the end, however, the relevance of laws and courts depend on the complex, often changing dynamics of the context in which they are used.

In addition to information needs, the preceding pages identified areas and questions where future research needs to concentrate. Some questions relate to the impact of laws and courts on the distribution of social burdens. What results do laws and courts actually produce? Do they lead to a more fair distribution of benefits or do they just increase the privileged access of organized actors? Other questions relate to the impact of litigation and laws on public policy. Does successful litigation reorient public policy in ways that leave the public's interests and the problems of unorganized actors unaddressed? Does successful litigation serve to reorient budget allocations in ways that endanger the provision of other public goods? In underdeveloped contexts, characterized by significant budget restrictions, how can public authorities deal with legal decisions that do not take into account economic or policy byproducts? Other areas of inquiry relate to the interactions between laws, courts, and the political structure. As was noted previously the effects of laws and courts show significant variations across and within countries. Are these variations the result of insufficient state capacities, differences in political competitiveness, the ideology of the judges, or what?

The research agenda is vast and the social and political consequences of the potential findings could be extremely important. However, both academic studies and policy recommendations confront a pragmatic limitation: inadequate comparable country-based information. Beyond the negative consequences of this deficit for academic research, poor empirical information has and will lead to faulty policy decisions. The wave of judicial reforms that recently took place in many underdeveloped countries shows some of the consequences of these deficits. Policy-makers, unable to evaluate the magnitude, relevance, and urgency of the problems they were confronting reached decisions in a fog. Lack of adequate information not only strengthened unsubstantiated public beliefs about the workings of laws but also led, in many cases, to faulty policies.

REFERENCES

Acemoglu, D., Johnson, S., and Robinson, J. (2001). "The Colonial Origins of Comparative Development: An Empirical Investigation," *American Economic Review* 91: 1369–401

Acuña, C. and Smulovitz, C. (1997). "Guarding the Guardians in Argentina. Some Lessons about the Risks and Benefits of Empowering the Courts," in J. McAdams (ed.), *Transitional Justice and the Rule of Law in New Democracies*, Notre Dame: University of Notre Dame Press.

Arantes Bastos, R. (1999). "Direito e Politica: O Ministerio Publico e A Defesa Dos Direitos Coletivos," *Rev. Brasilera Ciencias Sociais* 14(39): 83–102.

Arantes Bastos, R. (2003). "The Brazilian "Ministerio Publico" and political corruption in Brazil," University of Oxford: Centre for Brazilian Studies.

Barros, R. (2002). "Dictatorship and the Rule of Law: Rules and Military Power in Pinochet's Chile," in A. Przeworski and J.M. Maravall (eds.), *Democracy and the Rule of Law*, Cambridge: Cambridge University Press.

Basabe Serrano, S. (2009). *Jueces sin Toga: Políticas Judiciales, Preferencias Ideológicas y Proceso de Toma de Decisiones en el Tribunal Constitucional del Ecuador (1999–2007)*, PhD Dissertation, Buenos Aires: Universidad Nacional de San Martin.

Bill Chavez, R. (2003). "The Construction of the Rule of Law in Argentina: A Tale of Two Provinces," *Comparative Politics* 35(4): 417–37.

Boix, C. (2003). *Democracy and Redistribution*, New York: Cambridge University Press.

Boix, C. and Stokes, S. (2003). "Endogenous Democratization," *World Politics* 55(4).

Coatsworth, J. (2008). "Inequality, Institutions and Economic Growth in Latin America," *Journal of Latin American Studies* 40(3): 517–49.

COHRE (2003). *Litigating economic, social and cultural rights: Achievements, challenges and strategies*, Geneva: Center on Housing Rights and Evictions.

Coomans, F. (2006). "Justiciability of Economic and Social Rights: Experiences from Domestic Systems," Intersentia and Maastrict Centre for Human Rights.

Diamant, N., Lubman, S.B., and O'Brien, K.J. (eds.) (2005). *Engaging the Law in China: State, Society, and Possibilities for Justice*, Stanford: Stanford University Press.

El-Ghobashy, M. (2008). "Constitutionalist Contention in Contemporary Egypt," *American Behavioral Scientist* 51(11): 1590–1610.

Elster, Jon (2004). *Closing the Books: Transitional Justice in Historical Perspective*, Cambridge: Cambridge University Press.

Epp, C. (1990). "Connecting Litigation Levels and Legal Mobilization: Explaining Interstate Variation in Employment Civil Rights Litigation," *Law & Society Review* 24: 145–64.

Epp, C. (1998). *The Rights Revolution*, Chicago: The University of Chicago Press.

Fix Fierro, H. (2004). *Courts, Justice, and Efficiency. A Socio-legal Study of Economic Rationality in Adjudication*, Oxford: Hart Publishing.

Fruhling, H. (2000). "From Dictatorship to Democracy: Law and Social Change in the Andean Region and the Southern Cone of South America," in M. McClymont and S. Golub (eds.), (2000) *Many Roads To Justice: The Law-Related Work Of Ford Foundation Grantees Around The World*, New York: Ford Foundation.

Galanter, M. (1983). "The Radiating Effects of Courts," in K. Boyum and L. Mather (eds.), *Empirical Theories about Courts*, New York: Longmans.

Galanter, M. (1984). *Competing Equalities: Law and the Backward Classes in India*, Berkeley: University of California Press.

Galanter, M. (2006). "In the Winter of Our Discontent: Law, Anti-Law, and Social Science," *Annual Review of Law and Social Sciences* 2: 1–16.

Gargarella, R., Domingo, P., and Roux T. (eds.) (2006). *Courts and Social Transformation in New Democracies: An Institutional Voice for the Poor?*, Aldershot: Ashgate Publishing.

Gargarella, R., Gloppenn, S., et. al. (2010). *Courts and Political Power in Latin America and Africa*, Palgrave Macmillan.

Gauri, V. (2009). "Ten Questions (and a Few Answers) About Public Interest Litigation in India," New Delhi: Lassnet International Conference.

Gauri, V. and Brinks D.M. (eds.) (2008). *Courting Social Justice: Judicial Enforcement Of Social And Economic Rights In The Developing World*, Cambridge: Cambridge University Press.

Giles, M. and Lancaster, T. (1989). "Political Transition, Social Development, and Legal Mobilization in Spain," *American Political Science Review* 83(3): 817–34.

Ginsburg, T. and Moustafa, T. (eds.) (2008). *Rule By Law. The Politics of Courts in Authoritarian Regimes*, Cambridge: Cambridge University Press.

Grammont, H. (2001). "El barzon, un movimiento social inserto en la transicion hacia la democracia politica en Mexico," in N. Giarracca (ed.), *¿Una nueva ruralidad en América Latina?*, Buenos Aires: CLACSO.

Groisman, E. (1983). *Poder y derecho en el 'Proceso de Reorganización Nacional*, Buenos Aires: CISEA.

Groisman, E. (1987). *La Corte Suprema de Justicia durante la dictadura, 1976–1983*, Buenos Aires: CISEA.

Hammergren, L. (2002). "Uses Of Empirical Research In Refocusing Judicial Reforms: Lessons From Five Countries," Washington, DC: World Bank. Available at <http://www1.worldbank.org/publicsector/legal/UsesOfER.pdf>.

Helmke, G. (2004). *Courts Under Constraints: Judges, Generals, and Presidents in Argentina*, Cambridge: Cambridge University Press.

Herrero, A. (2007) *Court-Executive Relations in Unstable Democracies: Strategic Judicial Behaviour in Post-Authoritarian Argentina (1983–2005)*, PhD Dissertation, Oxford University.

Hilbink, L. (2007). *Judges Beyond Politics In Democracy And Dictatorship: Lessons From Chile*, Cambridge: Cambridge University Press.

Hoffmann, F. and Bentes, F. (2008). "Accountability for Social and Economic Rights in Brazil," in V. Gauri and D.M. Brinks (eds.) (2008). *Courting Social Justice: Judicial Enforcement Of Social And Economic Rights In The Developing World*, Cambridge: Cambridge University Press.

La Porta, R. et al. (1997). "Legal Determinants of External Finance," *Journal of Finance* 52(3): 1131–50.

Langford, M. (ed.) (2008). *Social rights jurisprudence: Emerging Trends in International and Comparative Law*, Cambridge: Cambridge University Press.

Macguire, J.W. (1999). "Labor Union Strength and Human Development in East Asia and Latin America," *Studies in Comparative International Development*.

Mahoney, J., Vom Hau, M., and Lange, M. (2006). "Colonialism and Development: A Comparative Analysis of Spanish and British Colonies," *American Journal of Sociology* 111: 1412–62.

McClymont, M. and Golub, S. (2000). *Many Roads to Justice. The Law-Related Work of Ford Foundations Grantees Around the World*, New York: The Ford Foundation.

McIntosh, W. (1983). "Private Use of a Public Forum. A Long Range View of the Dispute Processing Role of Courts," *American Political Science Review* 77(4).

Moustafa, T. (2007). *The Struggle for Constitutional Power: Law, Politics, and Economic Development in Egypt*, Cambridge: Cambridge University Press.

Perez Liñan, A. and Castagnola, A. (2008). "The Appointment and Removal Process for Judges in Argentina: The Role of Judicial Councils and Impeachment Juries in Promoting Judicial Independence," Berlin: Symposium New Frontiers on Institutional Research in Latin America.

Pillay, K. (2002). "Implementation of Grootboom: Implications for the enforcement of socio-economic rights," in *Law Democracy and Development*, available at <http://www.communitylawcentre.org.za/Socio-Economic-Rights/research-project/2002-vol-6-lawdemocracy-and-development/kameshni-pillay-12-march.pdf/>.

Przeworski, A. et al. (2000). *Democracy and Development: Political Regimes and Material Well-Being In The World, 1950–1990*, Cambridge: Cambridge University Press.

Riddell, T. (2004). "The Impact of Legal Mobilization and Judicial Decisions: The Case of Official Minority-Language," *Education Policy in Canada for Francophones Outside Quebec Law & Society Review* 38(3): 583–610.

Rosenberg, G.N. (1991). *The Hollow Hope: Can Courts Bring About Social Change?*, Chicago: University of Chicago Press.

Sen, A. (1999). *Development as Freedom*, Oxford: Oxford University Press.

Sikkink, K. and Keck, M. (1998). *Activist Beyond Borders*, Ithaca: Cornell University Press.

Sikkink, K. and Walling, C.B. (2007). "The Impact of Human Rights Trials in Latin America," *Journal of Peace Research* 44(4): 427–45.

Smith, M. (2005). "Social Movements and Judicial Empowerment: Courts, Public Policy and Lesbian and Gay Organizing in Canada," *Politics & Society* 33(2): 327–53.

Smulovitz, C. (2005). "Petitioning and Creating Rights. Judicialization in Argentina," in R. Sieder, A. Angell, and L. Schjolden (eds.), *The Judicialization of Politics in Latin America*, New York: Palgrave Macmillan.

Smulovitz, C. (2006). "Protest by other means. Legal mobilization in the Argentinean Crisis," in E. Peruzzotti and C. Smulovitz (eds.), *Enforcing the Rule of Law. Citizens and the Media in Latin America*, Pittsburgh: Pittsburgh University Press.

Sousa Santos, B. (1996). "Os tribunais nas sociedades conteporaneas," in *Revista Brasilera de Ciencias Sociais* 30: 29–62.

Uprimny Yepes, R. (2007). "Judicialization of Politics in Colombia: Cases, Merits and Risks," *Sur. Revista Internacional de Derecho Humanos* 6: 49–65.

Wickeri, E. (2004). *Grootboom's Legacy: Securing The Right To Access To Adequate Housing In South Africa?*, NYU School Of Law: Center For Human Rights And Global Justice. Working Paper, Economic, Social and Cultural Rights, Series Number 5.

Wilson, B.M. (2009). "Enforcing Rights and Employing an Accountability Function: Costa Rica's Constitutional Court," *Judicial Politics in Latin America Conference*, Mexico: CIDE.

Wilson, B.M. and Rodríguez Cordero, J.C. (2006). "Legal Opportunity Structures and Social Movements: The Effects of Institutional Change on Costa Rican Politics," *Comparative Political Studies* 39(3): 325–51.

Yamin, A. and Parra-Vera, O. (2009). "How do courts set health policy? The case of the Colombian Constitutional Court," in *PLoS Med* 6(2): e1000032. doi:10.1371/journal.pmed.1000032.

31

HOW DOES INTERNATIONAL LAW WORK?

TOM GINSBURG AND GREGORY SHAFFER[1]

[1] The authors thank Karen Alter, Daniel Bodansky, Elizabeth Boyle, Chad Bown, Marc Busch, Tim Büthe, Oona Hathaway, Mark Pollack, Arthur Stein, and Christopher Whytock for helpful comments, and Peter Cane, Mary Rumsey, Herbert M. Kritzer, and Ryan Griffin for excellent research assistance.

LIKE many other fields of legal scholarship, international law has seen an explosion in empirical work in recent years. On the one hand, this long-overdue change reflects developments in international relations (IR) theory, the sociology of law, and globalization, economics (with its institutional turn), and the increasing influence of social science in legal scholarship. On the other hand, it reflects the objective expansion in the importance and visibility of international law in the 1990s, and the increased role played by international institutions, which has spurred this empirical work. Although the empirical project is still in an early phase, it is expanding through the efforts of scholars in multiple disciplines.

The earlier dearth of empirical work on international law reflected, in particular, the enduring importance of the realist tradition in international relations scholarship. For classical realists, state power determined outcomes on the international stage, and international law was "epiphenomenal," without independent causal impact on outcomes. While realism is still an important paradigm and has been applied to international law, the mainstream of international relations scholarship now reflects the rational choice institutionalist tradition and (to a lesser extent) constructivist insights. For rational choice institutionalists, international institutions facilitate state cooperation by reducing the transaction costs of negotiating agreements with multiple parties, and by assuring states that compliance with them will be better monitored and enforced. For constructivists, international institutions exercise normative power, shaping states' perceptions of problems, available solutions, and their own state interests. Legal institutions, as embodiments of international cooperation, are central objects of study within these traditions, and so political science has contributed a good deal to the recent expansion of empirical work on international law. In addition, economists have increasingly turned to study the role of institutions at the international level, whether for the supply of global public goods or to facilitate the resolution of other cooperation and coordination challenges.

In parallel, there has been a rise in scholarship on law and globalization that comes out of or is heavily informed by sociology. Halliday and Osinsky (2006) categorize four such approaches: world systems theory (focused, like IR realism, on structural power, but also attending to the role of transnational capital, with law again being epiphenomenal); world polity theory (a constructivist theory in which international legal scripts are conveyors of globalized cultural norms); postcolonial theory (focusing on the interaction of global legal norms and domestic systems in developing countries); and law and development theory (addressing the impact of transnational legal transplants). Scholarship linked to these approaches has also empirically studied the actors, mechanisms, and arenas through which international and transnational law have effects within countries, as well as the limits of these impacts.

From the other end of the methodological spectrum, traditional international legal scholarship was mainly focused on doctrinal and normative concerns, and paid special attention to the International Court of Justice (ICJ), a relatively little-used tribunal. Such scholarship tended to *assume* rather than examine the efficacy of international law and cooperation, and was normative in character, bemoaning instances in which international legal institutions were unable to constrain power or affect domestic practice. In contrast, much of the new empirical scholarship, rooted in the various social science institutionalisms, takes the reach and efficacy of international law as empirical questions, to be neither assumed (as in traditional doctrinal scholarship) nor explained away as unimportant (as in the realist and world systems traditions). In tackling these questions of scope and efficacy, scholars are using a wide variety of methodologies, both qualitative and quantitative, and examining a diverse array of questions in various substantive areas of international law. A central question becomes the *conditions* under which international law is produced and has effects, as well as the *actors* and *mechanisms* involved. Both quantitative and qualitative methods are needed. Many discussions of "empirical legal studies" focus almost exclusively on quantitative work, and we thus complementarily stress the importance of qualitative research, particularly for uncovering the mechanisms and key actors involved. We point to leading examples of different empirical approaches suited for particular questions, as well as studies that use mixed methods.

This Chapter is organized around three overarching questions: (i) *why international law is produced and invoked* in particular situations—focusing on the role of law in facilitating international cooperation, the legitimating role of law as a reflection of hard or soft power, and the expressive aspects of law; (ii) *how international law is produced*, focusing on the actors, institutions, mechanisms, and processes involved in such production; and (iii) *how and under what conditions international law matters*, in terms of affecting domestic law, the behavior of states, and other relevant actors. These questions regarding different stages of the international law process are both interrelated and distinct. On the one hand, the questions are interrelated since, for example, the effectiveness of international law can be a function of how it is produced and invoked, and such effectiveness (or lack of effectiveness) recursively creates incentives (or disincentives) for the production of new international law. On the other hand, the questions are distinct since the answers to the questions why and how international law is produced do not necessarily tell us how international law has effects. The effects, for example, may be unintended. It is thus important to delink the questions and empirically investigate each stage of the international legal process (see, e.g., Simmons, 2009).[2]

For each of these organizing questions, we contend that future insights will require increased attention to the domestic bases of international law. Understanding state behavior requires "unpacking" the state and exploiting variation at the national and subnational level. This strategy applies to studying both the production of international law and its implementation, as well as to the dynamic interaction between

---

[2] We thank Karen Alter for her comments on this point.

these two processes. Understanding the interaction of international and domestic law, politics, and institutions also requires continued use of diverse mixed-method research strategies. The combined effect of relaxing the assumption of the state as a unitary actor, and the introduction of more complex research strategies, requires a definitive break from the realist tradition of international relations. International empirical legal scholarship must remain a distinct interdisciplinary field that takes both law and power seriously. Finally, we should assess variation between different areas of international law. Different actors and institutions are present, and distinct processes and mechanisms are used in areas ranging from international human rights and criminal law to international trade, investment, and regulatory law.

I. Why Produce and Invoke International Law?

International law can help resolve different types of common challenges that states and other actors face, ranging from collective action problems (such as addressing common environmental concerns) to coordination problems (such as harmonizing regulatory standards). International law, in addition, can serve to institutionalize and legitimize policy outcomes desired by particular states and other actors, advancing some positions over others. We can think of the former approach as focused on problems, and the latter on power as the primary explanatory factor in understanding international law. In many situations, problem-focused and power-based explanations both have purchase. Finally, in some areas, such as human rights law, international law serves primarily expressive functions.

The problem-focused approach conceptualizes the question of why states use international law as a function of different types of challenges that states face. Stein (1983) classifies the problems that states confront in international politics into two categories: "dilemmas of common interests" and "dilemmas of common aversions." Dilemmas of common interests arise when two or more states would benefit from cooperation but face incentives to renege on their agreements, as in prisoners' dilemma and collective action problems. The solution to these dilemmas is cooperation, in which states may create formal legal regimes to provide monitoring, clarification, and enforcement of international agreements, thus reducing the temptation to renege. Dilemmas of common aversion arise when states seek to avoid a particular outcome, and need to coordinate their behavior in order to do so. This situation often arises in international standard setting because states have reasons to agree on one standard, but may disagree on which standard to use. International agreements regarding air travel and telecommunications are examples where states agree on common international rules to coordinate behavior. Certain problems by their nature involve trans-border externalities and collective action and coordination challenges, and there are numerous case studies that use process-tracing methods to assess what gives rise to international cooperation.

Related problem-oriented approaches examine how state leaders and other actors invoke international law to respond to domestic political challenges. States may invoke international law to make credible commitments to domestic audiences. Similarly, interest groups and institutions within states may seek to lock in particular policies through international agreements. Helfer et al. (2009), for example, assess how "islands" of effective international adjudication arise in their study of the Andean Tribunal of Justice, which has issued over 1,400 decisions over a 25-year period, more than 90% of which concern intellectual property. Using a multi-method approach, they attribute the success of the international IP law "island" to demand from domestic institutions in the region.

State leaders may also invoke international law to provide themselves with domestic political cover in situations where there is domestic resistance to policy change. Allee and Huth (2006) examine 348 territorial disputes across all regions for the period 1919–1995, and assess whether decisions were made to resolve the dispute (politically) through bilateral negotiations or (legally) through a third party arbitrator or tribunal. Their statistical analysis supports the argument that leaders pursue international dispute settlement when they anticipate considerable domestic political opposition to the making of concessions regarding an international boundary dispute. The litigation outcome provides leaders with political cover when they eventually settle the dispute. Their work complements the findings of Ginsburg and McAdams (2004) whose empirical analysis of ICJ decision-making illustrates that international courts are most effective when they help facilitate coordination by disputants through creating a focal point for settlement, rather than imposing a solution. They show that the ICJ is relatively effective in helping states coordinate their behavior in areas such as border disputes, but less effective when conflict has already broken out.

Other scholars focus on power as a determining factor in the production of international law. They argue that where the selection of different terms in an international agreement has distributive implications, power is likely to be a central factor in shaping these terms. In the case of global communications, Krasner (1991) examines how powerful states can use their superior bargaining power to dictate the terms of cooperation to weaker states. A synthetic approach views international agreements as involving both negotiation over the terms of cooperation and the subsequent monitoring and enforcement of these terms, such that power-based mechanisms are always present in the production of international law.

A related empirical literature examines the extent to which power attributes affect law's invocation after states agree to an international treaty. This issue has been most thoroughly considered in the rich empirical literature assessing the patterns of invocation of the dispute settlement system of the World Trade Organization (WTO), and, in particular, whether the system's use reflects bias in favor of large and wealthy countries. Bown (2005) examines whether the legal system's operation is biased because of power-oriented factors, contending that the WTO's enforcement mechanism favors use of the legal system by powerful countries with large markets. He finds that, controlling for other factors, a country is less likely to initiate legal claims when it is poor or small, when it is particularly reliant on the respondent for bilateral assistance, and when it lacks the capacity to retaliate against the respondent by withdrawing trade concessions. Busch et al. (2009), in parallel, assess the impact of legal capacity in international dispute settlement. They conducted a survey of all WTO members to derive a new measure of WTO-related legal capacity based on survey responses. They find that WTO members who possess greater legal capacity are more likely to challenge domestic antidumping (AD) measures before the WTO, and less likely to be targeted by national AD measures. Their data indicate that legal capacity affects patterns of dispute initiation and underlying antidumping protection among WTO members at least as much as market power.

Where states choose to cooperate, they have choices over the form and legal nature of the instrument used. These instruments can assume a more or less binding nature, be more or less precise in their terms, and involve more or less delegation to third parties for the monitoring and enforcement of legal commitments (Abbott and Snidal, 2000). Quantitative empirical work which examines choices in the design of international law instruments is still in its infancy, but scholars are increasingly producing large-n databases regarding treaties. Koremenos (2005, 2007) uses a random sample of treaties to assess when and why states choose to delegate issues to international organizations. She shows (2005) that states are more likely to include dispute settlement provisions in treaties when they face complex cooperation problems characterized by uncertainty, incentives to defect, or time inconsistency. She also finds (2007) that states respond to uncertainty through limiting the duration of treaties and including escape clauses. Mitchell (2003) and Gamble et al. (2005) also have compiled databases which will facilitate future quantitative empirical research within and across issues. Mitchell comprehensively surveys international environmental agreements regarding their features and formation, while Gamble's Comprehensive Statistical Database of Multilateral Treaties focuses on multilateral treaties of all types over an extended time period. In comparison, there is significantly less quantitative work on state decisions to use customary international law or general principles of law. These sources of law have been subject to much speculation but need more empirical analysis.

These two approaches (problem-focused and power-based) are less helpful in explaining the production of human rights treaties that address the treatment of individuals within states. Both rationalists and constructivists have advanced and empirically tested expressive theories regarding why states ratify international human rights treaties. The world polity school (introduced above) contends that states enter into international human rights treaties to signal their adherence to global cultural norms, variably stylized as "universal," "modern," and "advanced"; these scholars maintain that treaties expressively reflect and convey a global acculturation process. Simmons (2009), working in the rationalist tradition, provides quantitative evidence in support of the claim that states indeed ratify international human rights treaties for expressive reasons, but they are more likely to do so if they believe in the norms and can comply with them at a reasonable cost.

Beyond examining the legitimating and expressive functions of international law in international and domestic politics, we have relatively little literature on the interaction of national characteristics (such as levels of democracy, type of legal system, trade integration, and internal heterogeneity) and the decision to invoke international legal institutions. Miles and Posner (2008) have created a dataset of over 50,000 treaties to examine which states enter into treaties and their reasons for doing so, finding that "older, less corrupt and larger states...enter into more bilateral treaties and 'closed multilateral treaties'" while small states are relatively more likely to join "universal multilateral treaties." In the rationalist tradition, they explain these findings based on differential benefits and costs, particularly transaction costs. Powell and Mitchell (2007) analyze the domestic legal system as a determinant of the propensity to accept and maintain the compulsory jurisdiction of the International Court of Justice. They find that civil law countries are more likely than common law or Islamic legal systems to accept compulsory jurisdiction, and that common law systems are more likely to include reservations when accepting compulsory jurisdiction. They show that states accepting compulsory jurisdiction are also more likely to include mandatory reference to the ICJ in compromissory clauses of treaties.[3]

In sum, empirical studies have assessed the reasons why international law is produced and invoked, including, in particular, functional problem-based, power-oriented, and expressive explanations. A key ongoing role for empirical work will be to document variation in the explanatory factors giving rise to international law in different domains, both generally and regarding the particular terms agreed. The literature's evolution suggests, in particular, the payoff from unpacking the state in the empirical assessment of why international law is produced and invoked. This approach opens up the black box of the state to examine how international law provides tools for a wide variety of actors on the domestic plane in different national contexts.

---

[3] A compromissory clause is a clause which provides for the submission of disputes to a specified forum, such as the ICJ.

II. How is International Law Produced?

The discussion of *why* international law is produced and invoked is closely related to the question of *how* international law is produced. Empirical work, and in particular resulting from qualitative research, depicts the range of actors engaged in international law's production and the key mechanisms and processes they use. This section continues to examine how empirical work has broken down the state in assessing the production of international law, looking at the role of state bureaucracies and private actors, together with the independent role of international institutions, and in particular international tribunals, in producing, consolidating, and clarifying international law. It concludes by examining the various mechanisms and processes used in producing international law in distinct domains. International law can be constituted from above by powerful states and international organizations, from below by sub-national public and private actors, and by a combination of forces working transversally across borders.

A. The role of states and state bureaucracies

The modern system of international law as usually understood emerges with the rise of the modern interstate system, canonically originating with the Peace of Westphalia. International law for its first centuries was interstate law, and hence states are the main object of analysis. This tradition continued with the rise of American political science and international relations theory, and states remain central actors in most empirical analyses of international law and politics. International law, it is often argued, develops as a function of state interest and state power, as discussed in Part I. States are traditionally modeled as having a unitary preference function on the international plane.

Focusing on states has certain methodological advantages. Because there is a discrete number of states in the international system, and because all states share certain characteristics, the state forms a workable unit of analysis in studying international phenomena. The range and variety among states, the concepts used for assessing variation among states in comparative politics, and the availability of state-level data on a wide range of variables, all serve to make state-centered research questions amenable to large-n statistical analysis.

Yet states are also *arenas* for the interaction of sub-state entities, non-governmental actors, and individuals. Analysis of how the interaction of sub-state forces produces a "preference" thus provides a useful supplement for many state-level studies. Such analysis leads us to consider, first, the role of state bureaucracies, which may be in competition with each other for policy leadership, and then the role of private actors, who may work with public actors or independently of them.

Particular state agencies often take the lead in representing the state in different functional domains of international law. State-level agencies realize the need to coordinate and cooperate with their counterparts in other countries to achieve domestic regulatory goals, spurring the production of international law in specific areas. They respond, in particular, to the mismatch between the spread of global markets and the limited reach of national law, which has permitted private actors to engage in jurisdictional arbitrage. Moreover, the externalities of foreign regulation (or the lack of regulation) on domestic constituencies mobilize these constituencies to press regulatory agencies to take action. These two phenomena have spurred agencies, particularly in larger states, to take the initiative in developing trans-governmental regulatory networks that operate under treaties or in less formal ways. These networks can, in turn, be in competition with each other where a particular problem falls within the jurisdiction of multiple agencies (such as the regulation of agricultural biotechnology, to give one example) (Pollack and Shaffer, 2009). Scholars have used case studies to assess how these trans-governmental regulatory networks operate in many different domains to produce international hard and soft law instruments, including for the regulation of finance, competition, and environmental and health and safety protection (Raustiala, 2002; Pollack and Shaffer, 2001). These attempts to unpack the state provide a richer account of state actors and their motivations, and are useful for understanding the micro-processes of international law production.

B. The role of private actors

Private actors such as corporations, non-governmental organizations (NGOs), and activist networks also play significant roles in producing international law and in creating international institutions to apply it. Sometimes these actors seek to work through national governments, while at other times they are direct participants in international law's construction. Empirical studies which examine the role of private actors "unpack" the state to understand how sub-national interest groups attempt to advance or entrench policy commitments through shaping international law.

Private actors often enroll states to act on their behalf in the production of international law. Braithwaite and Drahos (2000) interviewed over 500 individuals from international organizations, government, business, labor, and civil society associations to map the webs of influence that work to define regulatory principles and standards in 13 areas of global business regulation. They show how U.S. and European

businesses are often favored because of their ability to enroll the world's most powerful states to act on their behalf, working through public-private partnerships. Scholars
have studied how these strategies operate in WTO dispute settlement. Shaffer (2003)
has done extensive field work on the WTO to uncover how private businesses hire
lawyers to develop WTO claims and use the threat of bringing a complaint as leverage
in bargaining to settle international trade disputes. Judicialization of WTO dispute
settlement has unleashed competition for expertise in trade law, which in turn has
affected the dynamics of WTO litigation. In this bottom-up way, public-private actor
networks shape WTO jurisprudence over time.

Private actors, whether they are businesses, NGO activists, or knowledge-based
epistemic communities composed of scientists or members of professions, also act
independently of states in shaping perceptions of international problems and solutions. In indirect ways, they affect the development of international legal norms
and the institutions that enforce them. In international environmental and human
rights law, many studies have addressed the key role of NGOs in shaping outcomes
in various domains. For example, Meidinger (2006) shows how transnational civil
society networks have created new forest stewardship norms and institutions to
enforce them. He assesses the role of these networks in defining and implementing
soft law standards, including through labeling regimes that convey whether lum-
ber has been harvested in an environmentally sustainable manner. Civil society
programs frequently stimulate competition by business-based programs, spurring
dynamic processes of competitive standard setting.

Mattli and Büthe (2003) have taken the lead in empirical work on private standard setting, using an Internet-based survey to create a comprehensive data set on
international standardization. While realists in international relations theory
contend that state power explains the outcome of international standards negotiations (Krasner, 1991), Mattli and Büthe find this explanation to be insufficient. They
argue that domestic institutional arrangements also matter because they affect the
mobilization of domestic business interests. From their survey data, they find that
European firms are much more involved than U.S. firms in international standard-
setting institutions because the European Union domestic regulatory context
gives them an advantage compared to the more decentralized U.S. model in which
authority is frequently retained by sub-national units of government. The result is
that U.S. institutions are less conducive to U.S. business coordination for purposes
of international standard setting.

Some international law is privately produced, and private parties then invoke it
before domestic courts. Private actors directly produce international commercial
law. Levit (2008) has engaged in extensive field work and interviewing regarding
the creation and application of the law of documentary credits by the International
Chamber of Commerce (ICC) based in Paris, France. She shows how the ICC has
adopted a set of rules, known as the Uniform Customs and Practice for Documentary
Credits (UCP), which governs business practice. The ICC interprets its rules through

issuing hundreds of "advisory opinions" intended to clarify ambiguities. Most banks will not issue letters-of-credit unless they are subject to the UCP. When exporters and importers identify the UCP as their chosen law, these rules are applied by national courts and arbitral bodies that enforce them.

Because international commercial law is typically applied by national courts, private international law scholars stress the importance of analyzing how international law interfaces with domestic legal systems. Empirical studies of private transnational litigation show how international, and national law and institutions, interrelate. Whytock (2008) finds that while transnational arbitration rates in the United States are increasing and transnational litigation rates are declining, both arbitration and litigation remain important methods of transnational dispute resolution. He finds that there is considerable judicial involvement at the post-award stage of the transnational arbitration process, and thus contends that national courts remain very involved even when arbitration is used. International commercial law thus does not displace national law, but rather supplements it.

C. The role of international institutions: international tribunals

The rise of international organizations has forced scholars to consider them as independent actors worthy of analysis. International organizations are not only a product of interstate interaction, but are also forums for state negotiation, and themselves sources of international norms). Scholars have undertaken ethnographic work to understand how international organizations operate internally, affecting the role that they play in international policy formation and the production of international law (see, e.g., Merry, 2006). These organizations sometimes compete with each other for primacy in establishing international legal norms (Halliday and Carruthers, 2009). In this section, we focus on the role of international tribunals, an increasingly important international organizational form for the construction and clarification of international law.

Recent years have seen a proliferation of international tribunals exercising jurisdiction over trade, human rights, investment, criminal and other matters. While there were only a handful of standing international courts in the mid-1980s, the Project on International Courts and Tribunals (PICT) identifies 25 as of this writing. These tribunals include 12 international courts and arbitral bodies, nine regional bodies, and four hybrid criminal courts involving a mix of domestic and international judges. This development has generated some descriptive comment, analysis of judicial biography and much normative speculation as to whether or not the tribunals can be considered "independent" of the states that create them, and thus whether they exercise independent authority in the production, consolidation, and application of international law. Critics have argued that international tribunals are simply agents of states that create them, and are of minor importance. Others have responded that international courts do in fact play important roles, if not as central as the doctrinalists might wish. The key analytic question concerns whether the institutionalization of dispute settlement affects the production, consolidation, and application of international law, and, as a result, policy outcomes.

Much of this debate echoes an earlier one concerning the European Court of Justice (ECJ), whose critical role in the construction of the European Union is now uncontested. Virtually all agree that, by making European law directly effective and superior to national law, the ECJ spurred member states to closer cooperation. Scholars disagree, however, as to whether or not the ECJ should be understood as an agent of its member states (simply facilitating states' ability to accomplish their goals, and thus implying a lack of independence in some sense), or as an actor that, once established and institutionalized, exerts an independent influence on the production of European Community law and on downstream outcomes. Stone Sweet and Brunell (1998) developed a comprehensive data set of preliminary references to the Court. From their analysis of this data, they argue that the process of integration through ECJ case law was unanticipated by national governments and that private litigants as well as the ECJ played an active role. Alter explains how ECJ decisions mobilized domestic actors, including lower court national judges that helped to consolidate EU law (Alter, 2001). Nonetheless, Carruba et al. (2008), while they do not call into question the ECJ's significant role in European integration, present quantitative evidence that political constraints do affect ECJ resolution of particular legal issues within cases, whether out of judges' concern with potential legislative override or (especially) with non-compliance. The unit of analysis in their study is the within-case legal issue rather than the case outcome as pro-plaintiff or pro-defendant. Stone Sweet and Brunell (2010) vigorously contest their findings and, in our view, have the better argument.

Ultimately, the independence of international judges from the states that designate them (and thus judges' role in the production, consolidation, and application of international law) is an empirical question which a small but increasingly sophisticated literature has begun to address. In some ways, the independence of judges is easier to analyze at the international than at the national level because judges are typically appointed by states that are parties to international agreements. A relatively straightforward hypothesis is that judges will favor their own state when given a chance. This hypothesis is somewhat easier to test at the international level than the corresponding thesis at the national level: domestic analyses tend to use proxies (such as the party of the appointing president) for political preferences to explain variation in judicial voting, whereas the identity of the appointing state for international judges is easy to identify. The relative independence of individual judges from the states that appoint them does not in itself mean that international tribunals as a whole do (or do not play) an independent role in producing, consolidating, and applying international law. Yet everything else being equal, evidence that judges decide cases independently of the positions of their appointing state suggests that international tribunals are more likely to adopt independent roles based on their own policy preferences in interpreting and constructing the law's meaning over time.

Empirical research has reached conflicting results regarding the independence of judges from the states that appoint them, which could reflect differences in the jurisdiction of the courts studied. Analyzing the International Court of Justice, Posner and de Figuierdo (2005) use a multivariate analysis and find that judges rarely vote against their home state, and that they favor states whose wealth level is close to that of their own state. They also show weaker connections between voting patterns and political and cultural similarity of the states that are parties to a dispute, but find no evidence of regional bias (although they have little data regarding this last issue because of the lack of participation of two-thirds of the UN membership).

Voeten (2008) takes a similar approach in his comprehensive analysis of voting patterns on the European Court of Human Rights (ECtHR), the judicial body that oversees compliance, by the 47 states belonging to the Council of Europe, with the 1950 European Convention for the Protection of Human Rights and Fundamental Freedoms. Voeten concludes that the overall picture of the ECtHR is mostly favorable in terms of judicial independence. He finds that ECtHR judges frequently vote against their home state, although they are somewhat less likely to vote against this state than are the other judges on a panel. When the state in question loses the case, judges from the state vote against it 84.2% of the time, as opposed to the base rate of 92.3% for non-national judges. When the state in question wins, the judge from the state is likely to vote against it only 4.7% of the time, compared with the base rate of 19.4%. Thus, judges exhibit considerable independence, but cannot be considered fully impartial. Judges deciding cases in which their country is not a party are not more likely to vote in favor of the positions of countries with whom their own state trades or otherwise shares similar interests, compared to other countries (Voeten, 2008: 429). These findings contrast with those of Posner and de Figueirdo who find bias at the ICJ. This contrast could reflect the fact that the membership of the ECtHR, and thus the appointment of judges to it, is limited to European countries, which are relatively more homogeneous in their interests and views than is the overall body of UN members, as well as the fact that the ICJ is structured more like an arbitral body than a court (Ginsburg and McAdams, 2004), and so there is some expectation of loyalty on the part of national judges.

Voeten also finds considerable evidence that ECtHR judges exhibit policy preferences along a spectrum of activism and restraint. He finds, in particular, that judges from former socialist countries were more likely to be activists in rectifying human rights injustices. They were also less likely than judges from other European states to support their own government, or to support governments from other former socialist countries when their government was not a party. This latter finding is (nonetheless) consistent with arguments in the rationalist tradition regarding underlying state preferences. New democracies, it is argued, are using international legal devices as a pre-commitment mechanism, tying their own hands at the international level.

Given its status as the most mature and productive of the international criminal tribunals, and its role in producing and consolidating the field of international criminal law, it is natural that much attention has focused on the International Criminal Tribunal for the former Yugoslavia, commonly referred to as the ICTY (Hagan, 2003). Some of this literature has addressed whether the tribunal has been biased. Meernik and King (2003) found no evidence that Serbs were treated more harshly by the Tribunal, allaying concerns of "victor's justice." Meernik (2003) also finds that the presence on a panel of more judges from NATO countries is associated with higher rates of acquittal, and no higher levels of sentencing. From a constructivist perspective, such exercises of impartiality help to legitimize an international court, empowering it as an actor in constructing the emerging field of international criminal law.

In the field of international trade, studies have examined whether WTO jurisprudence has shaped the meaning of WTO law in ways not anticipated by states. These studies focus on the fact that complainants win far more frequently than respondents at the WTO (about a 90% complainant success rate for panel and Appellate Body decisions combined). This pattern raises the empirical question of whether international trade tribunals have been biased in favor of free trade outcomes. Maton and Maton (2007) use multivariate analysis to show that the complainant advantage in winning cases is not explained by such external factors as economic power, involvement of third parties, or status of the complainant as an experienced repeat player. Colares (2009) covers a broader set of cases, and adds additional control variables, such as case type and subject matter, party identity, and product type, but uses a bivariate approach. He finds that selection effects, asymmetric incentives, and "playing for rules" cannot explain the finding that complainants win some 90% of cases. Instead he contends that interpretation of the WTO agreements has favored a free-trade normative vision, indicating biased rule development, and providing some evidence of judicial law-making.

Colares, however, does not examine the possible explanation that respondents are systematically contesting low-quality cases for domestic political reasons, even though they know they will lose these cases. That is, respondents may be using WTO dispute settlement to provide political cover, attempting to show the affected domestic industry and its political supporters that the government is doing everything possible to uphold the trade-restrictive measure. The fact that the WTO system lacks retrospective remedies facilitates this political response because a member can effectively maintain an illegal trade measure for almost three years of litigation without being subject to any retrospective legal sanction. Complementary qualitative research would help to explain the quantitative findings.

Individuals and individual backgrounds can have an impact on the institutional development of courts, which, in turn, affects the construction and production of international law. Hagan (2003) examines how a charismatic chief prosecutor, Louise Arbour, strategically chose key cases and worked the media to establish the legitimacy of the ICTY and help build the evolving field of international criminal law. Dezalay and Garth (1996) assess the backgrounds of international arbitrators in the construction of the field of international arbitration. They find that Americans from elite law firms played a central role, transforming international arbitration to become more formalized and litigious, reflecting a more American litigation model and a less continental European one. More ethnographic work on international tribunals would help to round out the picture of judicial motivation in issuing decisions, shaping procedure, and generating jurisprudence. It would complement the better-developed quantitative research program on the independence of international judges from their appointing states.

In sum, international tribunals have become increasingly important players in producing, consolidating and applying international law. There remains disagreement as to whether they are facilitating states' abilities to advance interests, or whether they are acting independently of states' intentions. Regardless of the resolution of this debate, the bulk of evidence indicates that international tribunals do affect policy outcomes in a wide array of contexts, contrary to IR realist contentions.

D. Processes and mechanisms

Different processes and mechanisms give rise to international law in distinct contexts. The predominant mechanisms used are reciprocity, coercion, persuasion, and acculturation. Through the mechanism of reciprocity, states agree to coordinate policy around international law standards to advance mutual interests, sometimes involving exchanges of reciprocal concessions on different issues. States exercise coercion when they use systems of punishment and reward to get other states to agree to particular outcomes. Through the mechanisms of persuasion and acculturation, in contrast, states change their policies because they become convinced of the "correct" or "appropriate" policy, whether by observing and learning from each other's policies, or by becoming socialized over time (Goodman and Jinks, 2004). These mechanisms can, in turn, interact.

These mechanisms can be further broken down or consolidated. For example, Braithwaite and Drahos (2000) list the following seven mechanisms used in the area of global business regulation: military coercion, economic coercion, systems of reward, modeling, reciprocal adjustment, non-reciprocal coordination, and capacity-building. Halliday and Osinsky (2006) add persuasion as an eighth mechanism. We consolidate their more expansive lists. For us, both reciprocal adjustment and non-reciprocal coordination entail mechanisms of reciprocity, the former involving agreement around a single standard and the latter involving exchanges of concessions through issue linkage. Similarly, we see military coercion, economic coercion, and systems of reward as involving the exercise of power in that powerful states can use political and economic rewards and punishments to influence other state behavior. Likewise, we view modeling (which Braithwaite and Drahos define as "observational learning") and capacity-building as involving different forms of the mechanism of persuasion, but they operate in more or less direct ways. In contrast, Goodman and Jinks (2004) only refer to the three mechanisms of coercion, persuasion, and acculturation in the area of human rights, probably because they do not view the mechanism of reciprocity as operating in this area.

A number of empirical studies examine variation in the use of these mechanisms in different contexts, whether in distinct domains of international law (Braithwaite and Drahos, 2000; Simmons et al., 2006), or in relation to particular countries in a single area of law, reflecting variations in the power of the target state and its social context (Halliday and Carruthers, 2009), discussed further in Part III. Scholars often uncover the mechanisms at work through case studies using process-tracing methods.[4] A number of scholars have applied ethnographic tools to study how these processes operate in particular domains (Merry, 2006; Halliday and Carruthers, 2009). Other scholars test these findings more systematically (Simmons, 2009).

In the area of economic regulation, studies focus primarily (although not exclusively) on the role of state interest and power in determining outcomes. Studies that focus on power as the primary causal mechanism generally measure it in terms of a country's market power—that is, its ability to exercise leverage by threatening to curtail market access. Studies that examine how international economic law facilitates mutual gains tend to focus on the mechanism of reciprocity, which permits states to realize these gains. In international trade negotiations, for example, states obtain trade concessions of importance to them by offering reciprocal trade concessions in other sectors. In practice, the mechanisms of reciprocity and coercion through the exercise of market power can overlap in international trade negotiations in some cases, since states with small markets are unable to obtain concessions from other states, so that they have little power to shape the terms of international trade agreements. They are largely takers, and not makers of international trade law, joining the regime only because they would be worse off if they did not.

Market power is exercised to shape not only multilateral regimes, but also bilateral arrangements. Here the driving mechanism is competition among states.

---

[4] Researchers engaged in process-tracing attempt to trace the links between causes and outcomes in a case, identifying sequences and the relative importance of different variables.

Sometimes states compete for inbound investment from large, wealthy countries, and at other times for outbound access to these countries' markets. Powerful states enter serial bilateral treaties with weaker states in a particular area, which, in turn, can shape an area of law over time. Elkins et al. (2006), for example, examine the spread of bilateral investment treaties (BITs) and find evidence that developing countries compete against each other to conclude BITs with capital exporters. In the process, developing countries agree to terms in bilateral negotiations which conflict with the positions they advance in multilateral fora. We see a similar dynamic in bilateral free-trade agreements where developing countries commit to greater intellectual property protection.

Other studies complement market power-based explanations with domestic ones, showing how institutional developments affect a state's ability to exercise market power. Elliott Posner (2005), for example, finds that U.S. and EU bargaining power over financial services regulation is affected by each side's institutional characteristics. He observes that once the EU established and exercised regulatory competence over financial services regulation, U.S. firms pressed the U.S. Securities and Exchange Commission to work with EU authorities to accommodate and recognize EU standards in a number of areas, following an extended period of benign (or malign) U.S. neglect of European approaches. Changes in domestic and regional institutions thus enhance a state's ability to exercise market power to affect international harmonization processes (see also Mattli and Büthe, 2003).

Many empirical scholars nonetheless caution that the production of international law should not be reduced to power-based explanations. In their study of 13 areas of global business regulation, Braithwaite and Drahos (2000) find that powerful states and business actors indeed play leading roles, but that other mechanisms are more important than coercion (see also Simmons et al., 2006). They contend that the mechanism of "modeling" is "the most consistently important mechanism" used in the harmonization of business regulation. Modeling consists of observational learning through which one state's regulatory approach becomes a model for others, and may be harmonized through international soft-law guidelines, provisions of technical assistance, or hard-law instruments. They find that U.S. and European regulatory models are most frequently chosen as global templates, with the result that global legal norms actually reflect local ones, constituting a form of "globalized localisms." Yet these models are not chosen simply because the U.S. and EU exercise political and economic power. Rather, the depth of U.S. and European regulatory expertise and the detailed analytic reasoning that their agencies offer in relation to particular regulatory problems persuade other countries to adopt their models. These models are often conveyed through the intermediary of international institutions that operate as nodes for networks of public and private actors, including elite business, legal and government representatives. Braithwaite and Drahos (2000: 546–7) find that modeling has "a significance neglected in the regulatory and international relations literature."

Finally, scholars have assessed how international law can be produced through processes of persuasion and acculturation. Scholars refer to these processes in explaining, for example, the creation and ratification of international human rights treaties, where the mechanisms of reciprocity and coercion are less frequently used. Since states may not intend to change their human rights practices, scholars often find it a paradox that states sign and ratify these agreements. Most scholars contend that states do so largely for expressive reasons to obtain legitimacy, but scholars diverge regarding whether they do so rationally or through acculturation processes (Goodman and Jinks, 2004), and whether these expressions have any effect (Hathaway, 2002; Simmons, 2009). We address this latter question in the next section. We reiterate here, however, that the processes of international law production and international law implementation are not necessarily dichotomous, but are part of dynamic, recursive processes that affect the production of international law over time (Halliday and Carruthers, 2009). The domestic reception of international law can feed back into the understanding of existing international legal norms and the production of new ones.

In sum, an array of actors and mechanisms are involved in the production of international law. U.S. and European public and private actors have been the most influential. In economic and regulatory fields, this influence can often be traced to the power that the U.S. and the EU wield because of the size of their markets and the desire of other countries to gain access to them. However, mechanisms other than coercion are also critical for explaining how international law is produced, and in particular the mechanism of modeling, which can reflect processes of active persuasion and diffuse acculturation. We will see these mechanisms at play in the domestic reception of international law as well.

III. DOES INTERNATIONAL LAW MATTER?

Louis Henkin (1979) famously observed that almost all states observe almost all their obligations almost all of the time. Downs et al. (1996) have pointed out that this observation tells us little about the efficacy of international law because states may be selecting those obligations with which it is easy to comply. Generally, issues of selection effects, endogeneity, and reverse causation lie at the center of empirical debates over whether international law matters. Skeptics argue that international agreements can merely reflect state intentions, and do not change state behavior. For example, Von Stein (2005) shows how treaties can serve as a screening device that signals a signatory's future policy intentions. Thus, failing to control for the sources of selection can lead one to overstate considerably the effect of international treaty commitments on compliant behavior. States may begin their compliant behavior before signing a treaty because of the extensive requirements to become a member.

These contentions have driven empirical work regarding not only whether international law "matters," but also the conditions under which it matters, and the processes through which it has effects. We find that most empirical work indicates that international law indeed matters, but only under certain conditions. International law's impact varies in light of such factors as the situation of the state in question (including its regime type and level of wealth); the congruity of the issue with domestic political contests; and the role of intermediaries such as government elites or civil society in conveying international law norms into domestic systems. Often international law works in indirect ways, involving the local appropriation of international legal norms to advance positions in local political struggles. Scholars need to unpack the state to understand the mechanisms leading to the implementation of international law, including the ways in which international law can become embedded in domestic law and institutions. Trends in scholarship in this direction are welcome, especially because taking the state as the basic unit of analysis is more difficult to maintain when the state is itself transformed through international interactions (Shaffer, 2010). Since international law has impacts in varying ways in different domains, this section divides its coverage by functional domain, respectively examining international human rights law, criminal law, the law of war, trade law, investment law, and regulatory law.

A. International human rights law

What does it mean to say that law matters? Social science tends to look for associations between events, say the passage of the law and some outcome of interest, such as compliance or implementation. Thus a common research strategy is to ask whether the accession to a human rights treaty predicts subsequent improvement in human rights protection. An increasing number of large-n studies take this approach regarding the efficacy of the human rights instruments that emerged in the aftermath of World War II. Given the persistence of massive human rights violations, critics have suggested that these forms of international cooperation are mere "cheap talk" and have no independent effect on state behavior. Hathaway (2002) showed that states ratifying human rights agreements were, on average, actually *more* likely to violate the agreements than other states. Hathaway's claim has prompted numerous responses both theoretically and empirically (e.g., Simmons, 2009).

Answers to the key question of *whether* improvements are associated with international law are typically linked to the existence of certain conditions. One emerging theme in this literature is that effective human rights protection requires domestic institutions, so that accession is more likely to improve performance in democracies than in autocracies (Hathaway, 2002). The engagement of civil society, in particular, appears critical.

Because the nature of the state and institutions within it affects whether international law matters, one potential problem with empirical studies is the use of over-inclusive samples. In a subtle book-length treatment of international human rights law, Simmons (2009) takes the important methodological step of disaggregating the sample of countries so as to exclude both false positives (countries that ratify treaties without intending to comply) and false negatives (countries that credibly enforce human rights guarantees but do not ratify human rights treaties for domestic institutional reasons). She finds that for the middle group of countries (after excluding the outliers), ratification of human rights instruments is associated with positive improvements in rights protection. In her words, "[a]t least in the case of civil and political rights, a treaty's greatest impact is likely to be found not in the stable extremes of democracy and autocracy, but in the mass of nations with institutions in flux, where citizens potentially have both the motive and the means to succeed in demanding their rights" (Simmons, 2009: 155).

Empirical studies on international human rights consistently find that the effectiveness of international law is mediated by domestic institutions and domestic actors. Because international human rights law largely depends on mechanisms of norm diffusion, the effect of human rights treaties is typically indirect, depending on the domestic channels used in specific contexts. Simmons, for example, finds that international human rights treaties have effects on domestic policy and practice through shaping executive agendas, through supporting litigation of human rights issues before domestic courts, and through sparking domestic popular mobilization.

Most empirical studies stress the role of civil society mobilization in domestic settings where international human rights law is implemented effectively. Local actors, NGOs, cause lawyers and others interested in advancing particular claims use materials from the international plane when instrumentally valuable. The international, then, becomes not just an arena but also a repository of materials available for invocation in the domestic sphere. In an important ethnographic study, Merry (2006) investigates the links between the global production of human rights instruments and their local appropriation in five countries in the Asia-Pacific region, showing how international human rights law provides tools for domestic actors seeking to advance agendas and legitimize actions in domestic politics. She casts light, in particular, on "the role of activists who serve as intermediaries between different cultural understandings of gender, violence, and justice," and who appropriate international legal norms for local ends (Merry, 2006: 2). Her work indicates that international human rights law is more likely to matter where non-state actors operate effectively as intermediaries to convey and adapt international human rights norms to address particular domestic contexts. These

processes of local adaptation of international law constitute forms of indigenization, or "localized globalisms."

Kim and Sikkink (2010) reach similar conclusions regarding the role of NGOs
in their quantitative assessment of the impact of conflicting human rights and
neo-liberal development norms on education policy in low-income and middle-
income developing countries, although they focus on the issue of convergence
toward global norms (in the world polity tradition), as opposed to indigenization.
Hafner-Burton and Tsutsui (2005) also use quantitative methods to show that the
larger the number of international NGOs operating in a country, the higher the
protection of human rights in that country, holding other factors constant. These
findings regarding NGO-mobilization as a causal factor may be challenged since it
is possible that countries with relatively good or improving human rights records
are more likely to allow international NGOs to operate. That is, the causal mechanism may go in the opposite direction, although the authors try to address this
concern through the use of time lags. The presence of international NGOs and
human rights improvements, nonetheless, can also reciprocally play off each other,
with improved human rights facilitating greater international NGO access, and
with greater international NGO access facilitating the conveyance of international
human rights norms.

The questions of whether, when, and how international human rights law
makes a difference will remain important, and there is still a long way to go in this
area of research. We see three major next steps for this literature. First, there is a
continuing need to follow Simmons' approach of disaggregating large-n analysis,
discarding outliers that either sign international human rights agreements with
no intention of enforcing them (Zimbabwe), or comply with international human
rights provisions without any need for signing them (the United States). Second,
the literature desperately needs better measures for human rights outcomes (the
dependent variable in quantitative research). Much of the existing quantitative
work relies on subjective indicators of human rights violations. The U.S. State
Department Annual Reports, for example, are attractive because of their breadth
and longitudinal coverage, but are subject to some political biases. Indeed, a small
but important literature on the challenges of measuring human rights has arisen,
and is likely to produce incremental improvements in the indicators used in evaluating human rights performance (see, for example, Landman and Carvalho,
2010).[5] Producing new indicators is difficult, but all the standard indicators of
human rights abuses have their flaws. Finally, a combination of quantitative methods and case studies involving sustained field work would be helpful in assessing
patterns of variation regarding the conditions under which international human
rights law matters.

---

[5] Cingranelli and Richard, for example, have developed a database available at <http://ciri
.binghamton.edu/index.asp>.

B. International criminal law and the law of war

The explosive growth of international criminal law has without a doubt been one of the major developments of the past two decades. Nearly 50 years after Nuremberg, the international community created two major ad-hoc international criminal tribunals (the ICTR for Rwanda and the ICTY for the former Yugoslavia), followed by the standing International Criminal Court (which was created pursuant to the Rome Treaty in 2002), as well as further ad-hoc tribunals for the Lockerbie bombing, the assassination of former Lebanese Prime Minister Rafik al Hariri, and for war crimes committed in Sierra Leone, among others.

A growing body of theoretical and empirical literature addresses the effects of international criminal law in which individuals, as opposed to states, are held accountable for human rights violations. A central claim of the anti-impunity movement, from Nuremberg onward, has been that criminal prosecutions for grave violations of human rights will have a significant deterrent effect, will facilitate democratic transitions, and will help shape collective memories in ways more conducive to enduring peace. Others argue, however, that the prosecution of war crimes may spur leaders and insurgents to resist negotiations to cease combat because of fear of prosecution, perversely leading to exacerbated human rights abuses. Empirical work on the effects of such prosecutions has important implications in light of these divisions.

The empirical evidence to date suggests that the impact of international criminal law enforcement should be broken down in terms of long-term and short-term effects under different scope conditions.[6] Regarding long-term effects, evidence exists that Nuremberg had an important educative effect on reconstituting German national identity (Karstedt, 1998). International criminal tribunals can serve a long-term educative purpose, affecting national reconciliation efforts and, over time, collective memories of the past, implicating future interstate relations. Scholars have empirically shown that the development of domestic criminal law and legal institutions has significantly reduced violence within countries. Whether the recent rise of international criminal law and criminal law institutions under very different conditions of legitimacy will have long-term deterrent effects, especially in situations involving civil conflict, remains an important empirical question.

There is mixed evidence regarding the short- and medium-term impacts of international criminal tribunals, and further empirical work is needed. Impacts likely vary as a function of different scope conditions, such as the level and nature of the civil conflict, the timing of the trial in relation to the conflict, and whether a country is on the road to democratization. Scholars should also assess the impact of factors

---

[6] "Scope conditions" refers to the conditions under which a particular event or class of events is likely to occur.

such as the location of trials and the identity of those conducting them: that is, whether the trials are international, foreign, domestic, or hybrid. Some empirical work conducted by security-oriented scholars is skeptical of the role of international criminal trials, and suggests that amnesties are preferable to international criminal trials in resolving civil wars. Snyder and Vinjamuri (2003–2004) survey the claims of proponents of international prosecution and, in a study of 32 cases of civil war, find that prosecution according to universal standards is often not helpful in reducing violations. In contrast, they find that credible amnesties are generally associated with better outcomes. Similarly, Ku and Nzelibe (2007) find that coup-leaders in Africa are unlikely to be deterred by the threat of prosecution before an international criminal tribunal. However, a large number of other studies, both case-specific and general, suggest that the use of criminal trials for human rights abuses has had some positive effects.

The literature on international criminal law and criminal law trials overlaps with the broader literature on mechanisms of transitional justice following civil conflicts. The most prominent transitional justice mechanisms used are criminal trials, truth commissions, and the barring of individuals from future public employment. International institutions are often linked, directly or indirectly, with the use of these transitional justice mechanisms, and international criminal law developments can affect them. Much of the empirical work in this area is case-specific, which makes sense given the importance of contextual factors for the effective use of particular transitional justice mechanisms. Yet it is difficult to generalize from this work.

A number of scholars, however, have engaged in broader cross-national studies. The majority of studies find that the use of transitional justice mechanisms results in modest or limited improvements in human rights protection, though it is too early to reach definitive conclusions. Sikkink and Walling (2007) find a significant increase in truth commissions and criminal trials for human rights violations throughout the world from 1979 to 2004, representing a judicialization of politics. Their data counter the findings of skeptics such as Snyder and Vinjamuri that amnesties are preferable to criminal trials in resolving civil conflicts and that criminal trials will worsen human rights outcomes. Sikkink and Walling, moreover, find that amnesties and trials for human rights violations are typically used in combination over time, with earlier amnesties sometimes being eroded, so that it is wrong to contrast the use of amnesties and trials in a dichotomous manner. They stress the importance of diachronic studies.

In an important follow-up to this analysis, Kim and Sikkink (2010) conducted the first large-n analysis to assess whether domestic criminal trials for human rights abuses have reduced such violations. Similar to the approach of Simmons (2009) in studying the impact of human rights treaties, their data excludes fully democratic and authoritarian regimes because human rights trials are less likely to be a cause of change in human rights practices in those countries. Their data relate to domestic criminal trials for human rights abuses in 100 transitional countries during the period 1980–2004. They find that "countries with human rights trials after transition have better human rights practices than countries without trials." However, because they focus on the role of domestic institutions, in this case on domestic human rights trials, their findings do not speak directly to the debate on the impact of international prosecutions and trials.

Empirical research has also begun to address the related question of the effect of international treaties regarding the conduct of war, and the evidence is again mixed. Morrow (2007) analyzes when states follow the international laws of war, focusing on reciprocity as the primary mechanism which explains countries' compliance. He finds that ratification of treaties does not affect the behavior of non-democracies, but does affect that of democracies. This finding is consistent with work regarding the role of domestic institutions in explaining variation in compliance with human rights treaties, discussed above. However, Valentino, Huth, and Croco (2006), using statistical analysis of interstate wars from 1900 to 2003, find no evidence that signatories to the Hague Convention of 1907 or Geneva Conventions of 1949 killed fewer civilians than did non-signatories, nor that democratic signatories killed fewer than others. They find that strategic incentives overwhelmed any pressure to exercise restraint attributable to the treaties. Given the security threat to the state in war, it is not surprising that international law has less impact in this area.

Overall, given the conflicting claims regarding the impact of criminal-law enforcement for human rights abuses, and the impact of international humanitarian law, further empirical work will be required to assess the conditions under which they are more likely to have positive effects. The Kim and Sikkink (2010) study nonetheless represents an important step regarding the assessment of law's effectiveness in this area over time.

C. International trade law

The question of whether international trade law matters has also attracted considerable empirical attention, probably because this area of international law is particularly legalized and judicialized, and because economists have long been interested in international trade matters and have applied their methodological tools to studying them. The resulting empirical work examines both the impact of international trade law on trade commitments and trade flows, and the effect of the WTO dispute-settlement system on member compliance and member practice.

A number of studies assess the impact of international trade institutions and institutional design on trade commitments and trade flows. Empirical studies suggest that countries are more willing to make trade commitments where there are escape valves to deal with economic shocks or unanticipated political demands.

Kucik and Reinhardt (2008), for example, find that those states who take advantage of the WTO's flexibility provisions agree, on average, to more and deeper tariff commitments under WTO agreements and implement lower tariffs in practice than those states which do not use these provisions. They focus, in particular, on states taking advantage of antidumping provisions which permit them to raise tariffs on goods sold at "less than fair value."

Whether the WTO and its predecessor regime, the General Agreement on Tariffs and Trade (GATT), have affected actual trade flows is a separate question. In a controversial study, Rose (2004) finds that joining the GATT/WTO regime has not affected bilateral trade flows, calling into question the relevance of international trade institutions and law. Goldstein et al. (2007), however, challenge this finding on account of the study's measurement of trade effects. They conclude that the data show that the GATT/WTO regime has had a positive impact on trade flows once one includes its effects on colonies, newly independent states, and provisional applicants.

Many empirical studies have assessed the impact of the WTO/GATT regimes' renowned dispute-settlement system in terms of member-compliance and actual effectiveness. It is widely acknowledged that WTO members have largely complied with the dispute-settlement system's rulings. Hudec's (1993) comprehensive analysis of GATT dispute resolution shows that the system successfully resolved some 90% of legally valid claims. Busch and Reinhardt (2000) find similarly high success rates under the more judicialized WTO system. The WTO system now includes an appellate process, as well as separate proceedings regarding respondent compliance with rulings, and regarding the amount of trade concessions that the complainant may withdraw if the respondent has failed to comply. Compliance with a ruling, however, does not necessarily guarantee that a market has been liberalized because a respondent might substitute a new trade barrier for the existing one. Bown (2004), however, has assessed the trade impact of WTO rulings and found that the concessions made following a WTO judicial decision have mattered economically. He found that three years after the date of adoption of the WTO decision in favor of the complainant, imports of the complainant's goods that had been affected by the prior trade barrier increased substantially into the respondent member, controlling for other factors.

Actual litigation and formal rulings represent only the top of the pyramid of disputing. Dispute settlement systems are also important for their "shadow" effects on settlement negotiations. Scholars have empirically assessed the effect of WTO litigation on negotiations to settle disputes in the shadow of a potential litigation outcome. Busch and Reinhardt (2000) investigated the impact of the negotiating stage of WTO disputes after a WTO claim is filed and before a decision is rendered. They find that, on average, complainants fare best (in obtaining greater trade concessions) when they successfully settle a filed dispute before a final judgment is reached. They explain that full litigation indicates that a defendant may face severe domestic political constraints against modifying its trade-restrictive measures, and thus might refuse to comply with a ruling or comply with it only partially. Interestingly, they find that although developed and developing countries fare equally well in terms of their success as complainants in fully litigated cases, large developed countries fare better in obtaining advantageous concessions during the negotiating phase prior to a judicial decision being rendered. Thus, although the evidence suggests that the system is not biased from a formal perspective, there is evidence of some bias in the law-in-action as regards settlements, illustrating the continued relevance of different forms of power disparities among members.

D. International investment law

Another very rich debate concerns the question of whether bilateral investment treaties (BITs) actually result in increased investment flows between the contracting states.[7] A common hypothesis is that BITs provide "credible commitments" to foreign investors when investors have grounds to believe that a country's domestic legal system is inadequate and thus cannot be trusted to uphold a contractual bargain. Some studies find no positive relationship between BITs and investment flow (Yackee, 2008), while others show such a relationship (Büthe and Milner, 2009). Yackee (2008) examines approximately 1,000 BITs between developing and major capital-exporting countries, and divides them into two categories: "stronger" BITs that provide automatic access to arbitration, and "weaker" BITs that do not. He finds that the stronger BITs are not associated with increased investment, which he contends contradicts the "standard story" that BITs make contractual commitments more credible to investors and thus enhance foreign direct investment. Büthe and Milner (2009), in contrast, find empirical support for the credible commitments hypothesis. They survey existing empirical work on BITs, and argue that BITs help signal commitment to a whole range of liberal policies, and thus improve all investment flows, not simply the bilateral flows between the signatory countries. They also find that membership in multilateral and preferential trade agreements results in increased overall foreign direct investment flows into a country, and they contend that such membership provides information that helps to assure investors of domestic political stability.

Existing studies' conflicting findings are explained by their use of different measures of investment flows. Studies focusing on only bilateral investment flows between BIT signatories find that BITs have little impact, while studies focusing on overall investment flows into signatories of BITs find that they have positive effects.

---

[7] We lack, however, empirical work on the issue of compliance with international investor-state arbitration awards, probably on account of the relatively small number of awards and the lack of a clear data set.

The authors of the latter studies maintain that the signature of BITs creates signals for investors generally regarding a country's commitments to investor protection.

E. International regulatory law

The impact of international regulatory law within states has likewise been the object of sustained study, for the most part building from case studies. Scholars have closely assessed the variety of mechanisms that are used in light of such factors as the externalities of regulation (or the lack of regulation) in one jurisdiction on others, power asymmetries between a country and global actors, the role of modeling, learning, and persuasion, and the affinity of transnational prescriptions with the demands of domestic elites and other constituencies (see, e.g., Braithwaite and Drahos, 2000; Halliday and Carruthers, 2009; Shaffer, 2010). Due to space limitations, and since we have also addressed the use of these mechanisms at the end of Part II, in this section we discuss only one exemplary work which again demonstrates the need for unpacking the state to understand the processes through which international regulatory law is implemented and has effects. Although international regulatory law often acts as a catalyst for change within domestic legal systems, domestic factors condition both the extent and the type of effects. As in the field of international human rights, international regulatory law is translated and appropriated into domestic contexts.

In their path-breaking work on the implementation of global bankruptcy law norms within Asia, Halliday and Carruthers (2009) build from years of field work to show how processes of modeling, persuasion, and learning work through recursive processes involving both the production of international bankruptcy law norms and their reception in Asian states. Using multiple empirical methods, they examine the different mechanisms used to implement international bankruptcy law norms within three Asian states in light of three key factors: the extent of asymmetric power between the target state and global actors; congruencies with local social and cultural contexts; and the availability and role of intermediaries between the national and international levels. They find that coercive measures (such as IMF loan conditionality) were used to a greater extent toward Indonesia than toward Korea, which required more active persuasion to effect legal change. In China, in contrast, change occurred primarily through the mechanism of modeling: China modeled its national bankruptcy law reforms on global templates. Similarly, they find that where discursive frames and policy prescriptions resonate in domestic settings, domestic actors more easily harness the transnational legal norm to further their goals. For example, the gap between local and global corporate insolvency norms constituted a greater challenge in Indonesia and China than in Korea, which is an OECD member and which had more local intermediaries and practitioners educated abroad.

Their account emphasizes the limits of coercive mechanisms to achieve effective domestic implementation, and the role of recursive interaction between international law-making and domestic implementation. Halliday and Carruthers stress, in particular, the role of feedback loops between the international and domestic levels in the production and diffusion of international legal norms over time, and contend that scholars need to assess the production of international law diachronically in response to domestic implementation challenges.

IV. CONCLUSION

As recently as two decades ago, empirical work on international law was exceedingly rare. Scholarly discourse tended to focus on normative debates between proponents and opponents of international law, with lawyers focusing on cases, and international relations scholars focusing on international organizations. The end of the Cold War and intensified processes of economic and cultural globalization prompted extensive institutionalization on the international plane and enhanced international interaction. The growing number of international regimes and tribunals, combined with developments in the social sciences and legal scholarship, has spurred an increase in empirical scholarship on international law.

In contrast with the theoretical work on globalization and international relations, much of the empirical work on international law is focused on specific issues and areas, providing rich materials on which to build further theory. Yet coverage is uneven. Some questions, such as the efficacy of WTO dispute settlement or the effect of BITs on investment, have received a good deal of attention and are the subject of robust quantitative literatures. International criminal law has also been a popular topic, with in-depth sociological studies of the major tribunals and their functioning. Human rights law is the subject of a large and increasingly sophisticated literature that uses multiple methodologies, though lack of reliable dependent variables is a concern. Other issues, however, have been less well covered. The law of diplomatic protection and the law of the sea, for example, are considered areas of great success for international law, but have not been the subject of sustained empirical research. Private international law work has lagged behind, although there has been a burst of recent work to close the gap. There is much more to international law than human rights and trade, but the scholarly agenda seems dominated by those important areas, so that many lacunae remain to be addressed.

There is certainly more room for methodological pluralism. In particular, we have relatively few ethnographies of international law and organizations. The continued development of large-n data sets promises even more statistical work; hopefully this development will be accompanied by careful consideration of issues of conceptualization and measurement. To some degree, the state of the discipline in this regard reflects the great difficulties in gathering data and developing relevant concepts and measures. Other challenges result from the complexity of the topic. States are the primary actors on the international plane, but are themselves complex organizations with competing motivations. Identifying behavioral regularities is difficult enough, let alone attributing those behaviors to the effect of international law. Broadening out from states to examine international organizations, transnational corporations, and individuals as actors on the international plane creates additional challenges, but provides research payoffs as well.

Much of the work to date has focused on the three important overarching questions identified at the outset, namely why international law is produced and invoked, how international law is produced, and whether it is effective. We have relatively less empirical work on the first question, but a good amount on the second, using a wide range of methods. Study of the third question is plagued by problems of the counterfactual—namely that we do not know how a world without international law would look. The challenge posed by IR realists is to explain how international law induces states to behave differently than they otherwise would. The weight of studies reviewed here, including in areas such as human rights and criminal law, where the realist claims would seem to be particularly relevant, maintains that international law is effective under certain conditions. This process typically involves the mobilization of domestic interests and institutions which translate, appropriate, and embed international law into domestic contexts. This work suggests that further inquiry into the domestic bases of international law production and implementation will be central to the future of empirical research in this field.

REFERENCES

Abbott, K. and Snidal, D. (2000). "Hard and Soft Law in International Governance," *International Organization* 54: 421–56.

Allee, T. and Huth, P. (2006). "Legitimizing Dispute Settlement: International Legal Rulings as Domestic Political Cover," *American Political Science Review* 100(2): 219–34.

Alter, K. (2001). *Establishing the Supremacy of European Law: The Making of an International Rule of Law in Europe*, Oxford: Oxford University Press.

Bown, C. (2004). "On the Economic Success of GATT/WTO Dispute Settlement," *The Review of Economics and Statistics* 86: 811–23.

Bown, C. (2005). "Participation in WTO Dispute Settlement: Complainants, Interested Parties and Free Riders," *World Bank Economic Review* 19: 287–310.

Braithwaite, J. and Drahos, P. (2000). *Global Business Regulation*, Cambridge: Cambridge University Press.

Busch, M. and Reinhardt, E. (2000). "Bargaining in the Shadow of the Law: Early Settlement in GATT/WTO Disputes," *Fordham International Law Journal* 24: 158–72.

Busch, M., Reinhardt, E. and Shaffer, G. (2009). "Does Legal Capacity Matter? A Survey of WTO Members," *World Trade Review*.

Büthe, T. and Milner, H.V. (2009). "Bilateral Investment Treaties and Foreign Direct Investment: A Political Analysis," in K. Sauvant and L. Sachs (eds.), *The Effect of Treaties on Foreign Direct Investment: Bilateral Investment Treaties, Double Taxation Treaties, and Investment Flows*, Oxford: Oxford University Press.

Carruba, C., Gabel, M., and Hankla, C. (2008). "Judicial Behavior under Political Constraints: Evidence from the European Court of Justice," *American Political Science Review* 102: 435–52.

Colares, J.F. (2009). "A Theory of WTO Adjudication: From Empirical Analysis to Biased Rule Development," *Vanderbilt Journal of Transnational Law* 42: 383–439.

Dezalay, Y. and Garth, B.G. (1996). *Dealing in Virtue: International Commercial Arbitration and the Construction of a Transnational Legal Order*, Chicago: The University of Chicago Press.

Downs, G., Rocke, D. M., and Barsoom, P.N. (1996). "Is the Good News about Compliance Good News about Cooperation?," *International Organization* 50: 379–406.

Elkins, Z., Guzman, A. and Simmons, B. (2006). "Competing for Capital: The Diffusion of Bilateral Investment Treaties 1960–(2000)," *International Organization* 60: 811–46.

Gamble, J. K., Ku, C., and Strayer, C. (2005). "Human-Centric International Law: A Model And A Search For Empirical Indicators," *Tulane Journal of International & Comparative Law* 14: 61–80.

Ginsburg, T. and McAdams, R. (2004). "Adjudicating in Anarchy: An Expressive Theory of International Dispute Resolution," *William and Mary Law Review* 45: 1229.

Goldstein, J., Rivers, D., and Tomz, M. (2007). "Institutions in International Relations: Understanding the Effects of the GATT and the WTO on World Trade," *International Organization* 61: 37–68.

Goodman, R. and Jinks, D. (2004). "How to Influence States: Socialization and International Human Rights Law," *Duke Law Journal* 54: 621–703

Hafner-Burton, E.M. and Tsutsui, K. (2005). "Human Rights Practices in a Globalizing World: The Paradox of Empty Promises," *American Journal of Sociology* 110: 1373–411.

Hagan, J. (2003). *Justice in the Balkans*, Chicago: University of Chicago Press.

Halliday, T. and Carruthers, B. (2009). *Bankrupt: Global Lawmaking and Systemic Financial Crises*, Palo Alto: Stanford University Press.

Halliday, T. and Osinsky, P. (2006). "Globalization and Law," *Annual Review of Sociology* 32: 447–70.

Hathaway, O. (2002). "Do Human Rights Treaties Make a Difference?," *Yale Law Journal* 111: 1935–2042.

Helfer, L., Alter, K., and Guerzovich, M.F. (2009). "Islands of Effective International Adjudication: Constructing an Intellectual Property Rule of Law in the Andean Community," *American Journal of International Law* 103: 1–47.

Henkin, L. (1979). *How Nations Behave: Law and Foreign Policy*, New York: Columbia University Press.

Horn, H. and Mavroidis, P. (2007). *A Survey of the Literature on the WTO Dispute Settlement System*, CEPR Discussion Papers: 6020.

Hudec, R. (1993). *Enforcing International Trade Law: The Evolution of the Modern GATT Legal System*, Salem, NH: Butterworth Legal Publishers.

Karstedt, S. (1998). "Coming to Terms with the Past in Germany after 1945 and 1989: Public Judgments on Procedures and Justice," *Law & Policy* 20: 15–56.

Kim, H. and Sikkink, K. (2010). "Explaining the Deterrent Effect of Human Rights Prosecutions in Transitional Countries," *International Studies Quarterly* (forthcoming).

Koremenos, B. (2005). "Contracting Around International Uncertainty," *American Political Science Review* 99: 549–65.

Koremenos, B. (2007). "If Only Half of International Agreements Have Dispute Resolution Provisions, Which Half Needs Explaining?," *Journal of Legal Studies* 36: 189–212.

Krasner, S. (1991). "Global Communications and National Power: Life on the Pareto Frontier," *World Politics* 43 (3): 336–56.

Ku, J. and Nzelibe, J. (2007). "Do International Criminal Tribunals Deter or Exacerbate Humanitarian Atrocities?," *Washington University Law Quarterly* 84: 777–833.

Kucik, J. and Reinhardt, E. (2008). "Does Flexibility Promote Cooperation? An Application to the Global Trade Regime," *International Organization* 62: 477–505.

Landman, T. and Carvalho, E. (2010). *Measuring Human Rights*, New York: Routledge.

Levit, J. (2008). "Bottom-Up Lawmaking Through a Pluralist Lens: The ICC Banking Commission and the Transnational Regulation of Letters of Credit," *Emory Law Journal* 57: 1147–225.

Maton, J. and Maton, C. (2007). "Independence under Fire: Extra-Legal Pressures and Coalition Building in WTO Dispute Settlement," *Journal of International Economic Law* 10: 317–34.

Mattli, W. and Büthe, T. (2003). "Setting International Standards: Technological Rationality or Primacy of Power?," *World Politics* 56: 1–42.

Meernik, J. (2003). "Victor's Justice or the Law?: Judging and Punishing at the International Criminal Tribunal for the Former Yugoslavia," *The Journal of Conflict Resolution* 47: 140–62.

Meernik, J. and King, K.L. (2003). "The Sentencing Determinants of the International Criminal Tribunal for the Former Yugoslavia: An Empirical and Doctrinal Analysis," *Leiden Journal of International Law* 16: 717–50.

Meidinger, E. (2006). "The Administrative Law of Global Private-Public Regulation: the Case of Forestry," *European Journal of International Law* 17(1): 47–87.

Merry, S.E. (2006). *Human Rights and Gender Violence: Translating International Law into Local Justice*, Chicago: University of Chicago Press.

Miles, T. and Posner, E. (2008). *Which States Enter into Treaties, and Why?*, Chicago: University of Chicago Law School, Law and Economics Working Paper 420.

Mitchell, R. (2003). "International Environmental Agreements: A Survey of Their Features, Formation, and Effects," *Annual Review of Environment and Resources* 28: 429–61.

Morrow, J.D. (2007). "When Do States Follow the Laws of War?," *American Political Science Review* 101: 559–72.

Pollack, M.A. and Shaffer, G. (2001). *Transatlantic Governance in the Global Economy*, Lanham, MD: Rowman and Littlefield.

Pollack, M.A. and Shaffer, G. (2009). *When Cooperation Fails: The International Law and Politics of Genetically Modified Foods*, Oxford: Oxford University Press.

Posner, E. (2005). "Market Power Without a Single Market: The New Transatlantic Relations in Financial Services," in David Andrews, Mark Pollack, Gregory Shaffer, Helen Wallace (eds.), *The Future of Transatlantic Economic Relations: Continuity Amid Discord*, Florence: European University Institute.

Posner, E. and de Figuiredo, M. (2005). "Is the International Court of Justice Biased?," *Journal of Legal Studies* 34: 599–630.

Powell, E. and Mitchell, S. (2007). "The International Court of Justice and the World's Three Legal Systems," *Journal of Politics* 69: 397–415.

Raustiala, K. (2002). "The Architecture of International Cooperation: Transgovernmental Networks and the Future of International Law," *Virginia Journal of International Law* 43: 1–92.

Rose, A. (2004). "Do You Really Know that the WTO Increases Trade," *American Economic Review* 94: 98–114.

Shaffer, G. (2003). *Defending Interests: Public-Private Partnerships in WTO Litigation*, Washington, DC: Brookings Institution Press.

Shaffer, G. (2010). "Transnational legal process and state change: opportunities and constraints," available at <http://papers.ssrn.com/sol3/papers.cfm?abstract_id=1612401>.

Sikkink, K. and Walling, C. (2007). "The Impact of Human Rights Trials in Latin America," *Journal of Peace Research* 44, 427–45.

Simmons, B. (2009). *Mobilizing for Human Rights: International Law in Domestic Politics*, New York: Cambridge University Press.

Simmons, B., Dobbin, F., and Garrett, G. (2006). *The Global Diffusion of Markets and Democracy*, New York: Cambridge University Press.

Snyder, J. and Vinjamuri, L. (2003–2004). "Trials and Errors: Principles and Pragmatism in Strategies of International Justice," *International Security* 28: 5–44.

Stein, A.A. (1983). "Coordination and collaboration: Regimes in an Anarchic World' in S.D. Krasner (ed.), *International Regimes*, Ithaca: Cornell University Press.

Stone Sweet, A. and Brunell, T. (1998). "The European Court of Justice and the National Court: A Statistical Analysis of Preliminary References 1961–95," *Journal of European Public Policy* 5: 66–97.

Stone Sweet, A. and Brunell, T. (2010). "How the European Union's Legal System Works and Does Not Work: A Response to Carruba, Gabel, and Hankla," available at <http://papers.ssrn.com/sol3/papers.cfm?abstract_id=1569594>.

Valentino, B., Huth, P., and Croco, S. (2006). "Covenants without the Sword: International Law and the Protection of Civilians in Times of War," *World Politics* 58: 339–77.

Voeten, E. (2008). "The Impartiality of International Judges: Evidence from the European Court of Human Rights," *American Political Science Review* 102: 417–33.

Von Stein, J. (2005). "Do Treaties Screen or Constrain? Selection Bias and Treaty Compliance," *American Political Science Review* 91: 245–63.

Whytock, C.A. (2008). "The Litigation-Arbitration Relationship in Transnational Dispute Resolution: Empirical Insights from the U.S. Federal Courts," *World Arbitration & Mediation Review* 2: 39–82.

Yackee, J. (2008). "Bilateral Investment Treaties, Credible Commitment, and the Rule of (International) Law: Do BITs Promote Foreign Direct Investment?," *Law and Society Review* 42: 805–32.

3 2

LAWYERS AND OTHER LEGAL SERVICE PROVIDERS

RICHARD MOORHEAD

THE empirical literature on lawyers and other legal service providers contributes significantly to our knowledge of "who" the profession is, how it is organized, and how it operates and applies the law. To provide some framework to this Chapter, I have concentrated on a topic to which much of this literature speaks and one which is certainly of central interest to those interested in understanding the legal profession and how it should be regulated. That central question, faced directly or indirectly in most studies of the legal professions is, do the legal professions deserve their status as professions?

This Chapter looks at how the empirical literature addresses this issue in a number of ways. Most of the work concentrates on attorneys or solicitors in law firms. Advocates and barristers in particular have received less attention, as have civil law professions, at least in the English language. For reasons of space, this Chapter concentrates on lawyers working within law firms in common law systems. Work on professional regulation, including regulation of the legal profession, is dealt with in Chapter 12 of this volume. Section I considers literature which addresses the way the profession is structured. Here, in particular, the way that large, elite firms develop has been subject to critical scrutiny. It seeks to question whether growth serves client needs or professional needs and also whether the commercialization of practice drives a reduction in the ethical standards of the profession.

A discussion of the way the profession is structured, and the creation of elites within elites, has intersected with arguments about the demography of the profession. This brings us to the second stream of literature: a profession's legitimacy depends on entry to it being open and meritocratic. Work on gender and ethnicity suggests this is far from the case and that the profession is divided along class, gender and ethnic lines. Demographic divides mirror fault lines between work for commercial/wealthy clients and "ordinary" private client work (sometimes called personal plight work). This leads to the third section which looks beyond how the profession is structured to serve business and the wealthy, and takes a closer look at how lawyers serve ordinary clients. The essential thrust of this literature is that lawyers sell their (poor) clients short, providing sub-standard, sometimes even unethical, service to their clients. This contrasts with the discussion in the fourth section, which sees the commercial and reputational rewards of serving wealthier clients as suggesting that lawyers do too much "bad stuff" for their rich clients.

Having considered the debates in the polarized contexts of big business and personal plight clients, the Chapter moves on to consider the literature which looks more generally at quality of lawyering. As we will see, while the empirical literature has often focused on the dimension of lawyers' performance as one of deliberate agency (that is competent lawyers *deliberately* selling out the poor against the state or *deliberately* advancing the interests of commerce against the public interest), there is also a set of literature that sees this as an issue of competence: (some) lawyers aren't deliberately amoral or immoral, they're just not very good at their jobs. The literature on lawyer performance takes a subtler turn when it looks at interactional and contingent approaches to understanding lawyer-client relationships. Sometimes lawyers perform badly (be it incompetently or unethically) because of systems and incentives; and at other times clients may demand unethical behavior to promote their interests over the interests of justice. Sometimes they perform to high standards and with ethical or political courage, although empirical explanations for that are less apparent. A point true of most scholarship is we are more content to understand the bad than understand the good.

Just as much of this literature is concerned with legitimacy, another *leit motif* is how economic incentives influence lawyers. This is particularly apparent in work on lawyers and their fee arrangements and reflects a recurring concern about relationships between supply and demand in legal services. This raises tricky normative issues around what lawyers do and what they ought to do, that are discussed in section V.

The final challenge to the legitimacy of the profession comes from research on non-lawyers in section VI. The research compares how the quality of the work of non-lawyers compares with the work of formally qualified lawyers. It poses the question: if non-lawyers provide similar or better quality than qualified lawyers, what is the basis for the elite status and protections from competition afforded to the professionals?

Economic incentives are often seen as threatening professional ideals, but the Chapter ends by considering how economic incentives are a necessary part of any market-based service and suggests that we need a more nuanced understanding of professional competence and the contribution, such as it is, of professionalism to the quality of services. The application of professional knowledge is classically beset by problems of indeterminacy: in applying uncertain knowledge to complex problems the "right" answer is likely to be unknown. Evaluating the application of that knowledge is similarly fraught.

I. Structures and Splits

A key starting point in discussing the legal profession is to acknowledge that when one talks of lawyers or the legal profession, one is talking of a range of *different* occupations. Many common law jurisdictions have formal or informal splits between litigators and advocates (or trial lawyers). In continental systems there are splits between notaries and advocates. In England and Wales, as well as barristers and solicitors, there are a host of other relevant professions: patent agents; trademark attorneys; insolvency practitioners; and tax advisers, some of which blur the boundaries between accounting and law. These splits are often institutionalized in historical divisions of labor and are not well researched in spite of the anti-competitiveness inherent in such sub-divisions (although see, for example, Shaw, 2006).

A less formally institutionalized, but increasingly profound, split, is that between corporate lawyers (who represent large, powerful organizations) and those who practice in personal plight cases for ordinary individuals. Most famously Heinz and Laumann (1982) saw the practice of law for individual clients and for large organizations (mainly businesses) as two (relatively) distinct hemispheres. The distinctions were not simply in the organization of work: social origins (especially ethno-religious background), prestige, career histories, mobility, social and political values, and professional and personal networks were found to be distinctive for the two groups (ibid: 128).

The concern about the splitting of legal services into two spheres is, in part, distributional. In answering the question, who gets more legal services from the profession, the answer is unsurprisingly those who pay the most. Indeed, it is commonplace to advert to the ways in which legal resources are heavily biased toward the interests of the wealthy (Galanter, 1974). This is the first of many ways in which it is claimed the profession subverts its claimed role as guardian of the administration of justice to economic forces: it serves the rich and powerful not the weak and needy.

Heinz and Laumann go further than the distributional point. If a profession is supposed to be built around the refinement of specialist knowledge, then lawyers are a special case organized not around areas of knowledge but around groupings of clients: "We do not say that law lacks theory but rather that its theory does not appear to organize the profession" (ibid: 138). This is partly because clients' problems are embedded in the social: problems are ultimately defined in the clients' language and should be solved in their world. Clients may want the lawyers to speak their language and empathize (ibid: 138–9), but also need to integrate legal solutions into the social contexts from which the problems derived. More fundamentally, this emphasis on the social (clients as the organizing construct), over the professional (a neutral body of specialist knowledge) casts some doubt on the objective value of legal knowledge. Furthermore, Heinz and Laumann emphasize the ways in which the "elite" hemisphere invert conventional norms of professionalism. In particular, autonomy—ordinarily a *sine qua non* of professionalism—is surrendered. "[L]awyers doing high-prestige work are less likely to define their client's problems than are lawyers doing lower-status work" (ibid: 140). Big clients, by virtue of their purchasing power and repeat client status, may have more power and exercise more control over purse strings and tactics (ibid: 141). Indeed, on this analysis, autonomy becomes somewhat irrelevant: "what enhances the status of a lawyer is not autonomy as a professional but access to centers of influence and avoidance of service to the powerless and despised" (ibid: 158). If Heinz and Laumann are right, a lawyer's professional status is parasitic. It is not derived from autonomy or other virtues but from the status of their clients. The elite distances itself from the more autonomous but less prestigious lawyers who provide services to low-status clients of personal plight (criminal defendants; divorcing spouses; and those who have suffered personal injury) (ibid: 158–9, citing Auerbach, 1976 and Carlin, 1962). This is partly because of a socio-political distaste among wealthy clients for the personal plight work of the poor, but also because of (a related?) belief that such practitioners, concerned with the seedier problems of individuals, are ethically questionable as a result. This is a theme returned to below.

More recent work has emphasized the spectacular growth of larger law firms (Heinz et al., 2005). There has been a vigorous debate about what has driven the growth of such firms and in particular whether it is internally driven by the need to incentivize salaried lawyers to perform well through a "promotion" to partner tournament (Galanter and Palay, 1991). The central point of this work is that firms must offer their salaried lawyers reasonably stable prospects of promotion to partnership as a form of deferred salary for their efforts as employees to prevent them defecting to other firms or shirking their responsibilities. To offer this stability, firms have to grow and grow strongly, even exponentially. This theory of law firm growth suggests that such growth is determined by the internal dynamics of law firms. It follows that the provision of legal services is driven not by client needs but the narrower economic interests of firms. Unsurprisingly, this theory has been hotly contested with other scholars suggesting that firm growth is better explained by external economic factors than internal firm dynamics (Sander and Williams, 1989). Galanter has, with Henderson, softened his own line (Galanter and Henderson, 2008).

While the normative benefits provided by the legal profession, particularly the commercial sector, in promoting "justice" are frequently questioned, the economic benefits of lawyers to society are much less often considered (Gilson, 1984). This is remarkable for a number of reasons. Lawyers occupy a pivotal role in many commercial transactions, levying significant costs along the way. The growth in the legal profession has been extraordinary, outstripping growth in the economy, particularly in the commercial sector (Heinz et al., 2005) but sometimes beyond that (Moorhead, 2004). Growth in lawyer income and lawyer numbers may give cause to wonder: are they worth it? Similarly, and importantly, growth in costs in the commercial sector has distributional effects: the more expensive law becomes at the top end, the harder it is for ordinary mortals to get access to justice because commercial demand for services drives up costs (Hadfield, 2000).

There has been significant interest in why there are so many lawyers and why growth has been concentrated in large law firms. Sander and Williams (1989) consider whether growth in the legal profession is driven by demand for or supply of lawyers. They find that increase in both demand for lawyers, in terms of services purchased, and supply of lawyers (graduating from law schools) explains the increase in the overall size in the market and the absence of substantial reductions in price. While increases in demand could be attributed to external drivers of growth in the need for legal services (such as increases in legal rights and their complexity) there was also a "scenario for self-sustaining growth" (ibid: 473) whereby corporate law firms could develop high-cost strategies for dealing with problems which were then met with similarly expensive counter-strategies. For high-value transactions or disputes, Sander and Williams argue these strategies are economically rational. If the investment in high cost legal strategies makes the desired outcome more likely, then that investment is likely to be economically beneficial.

Of course, even sophisticated clients may struggle to judge the relationship between their investment in lawyers and any marginal gain: legal services, like many professional and other services, are credence goods. Yet it is elsewhere that the critique of self-sustaining growth has been most forceful: that is where the government pays for lawyers (through legal aid programs). Reframed in the idea that lawyers engage in "supplier-induced demand" Bevan (1996) has sought to demonstrate that lawyers encourage more cases to be funded and more work to be done than would be the case if a consumer was perfectly informed and paying themselves. Through relating billing data to proxies for legal need, Bevan makes a plausible case, and the idea of supplier-induced demand has been seized on by governments around the world keen to control the legal-aid budgets. However, other work has pointed to substantial causes of inflation in legal costs which are largely driven by the state: increases in the volume and complexity of legislation; prosecution policies; and increases in the volume of evidence resulting from use of new technology (CCTV for instance) (Cape and Moorhead, 2005).

II. A Meritocratic Profession?
Lawyers and Diversity

That the structuring of the profession is both economic and social, points powerfully to a social apartheid within the profession. It flags as an issue, the extent to which the profession lives up to a key promise: "As a 'learned profession' avowedly devoted to high ideals, the bar professes the principle that attainment within the profession should be determined by merit" (Heinz and Laumann, 1982: 136).

The evidence consistently suggests the legal profession may profess meritocracy but they also fall short. The best example is a cohort study which tracked a group of over 4,000 undergraduate students through and beyond graduation and qualification in the English and Welsh legal profession. Six surveys were conducted between 1991–99 (summarized in Shiner, 2000). By tracking students as they attempted to progress through the profession, the study is able to look more closely at social and educational differentiation among them. Shiner et al.[1] were able to examine whether particular groups were *disadvantaged* by particular socio-economic and educational backgrounds. The study provides powerful evidence of the difficulties particular social groups face in seeking entry into the legal professions. Crucially, through a cohort study tracking the same research subjects across a substantial

---

[1] Shiner et al. refer to the team of researchers working across the studies, which Shiner summarizes in the Chapter contained in the References section.

period of time, Shiner et al. are able to look more closely at issues of agency (e.g., do ethnic minorities or women choose to go into particular areas of the law) and structure (e.g., are their choices significantly affected by barriers the "system" throws up) as determinants of career trajectories for different groups.

Unsurprisingly, Shiner et al. found that law students are typically a privileged group. With parental education and occupation being predominantly in the upper strata, they also were more likely than other students to have hailed from independent (fee-paying) schools (Shiner, 2000: 92). Conversely, ethnic minority and female students were more strongly represented in the population of students than census comparisons would predict; a trend common to students generally but particularly marked in law (ibid: 92–3). Students coming through the conversion route (i.e., doing a degree other than law and "converting" with a one-year law course) were more privileged, male and white than law students more generally (ibid: 94). This last group is interesting because they are lauded by big firms as providing extra skills from their non-law background while the same firms criticize law students for not knowing enough law even though non-law graduates will only have had one year of undergraduate-equivalent legal training.

It is the evidence of disadvantage which is most compelling. Law firms would typically claim to make their decisions purely on the merits of the candidates. Analysis suggests this is not the case. The study looked in particular at the allocation of training contracts, the two-year period of on-the-job training essential to becoming a solicitor. Allocation of these places is controlled by individual firms, not by universities or the professional body. Once a training contract is secured, it is likely to be completed, allowing the trainee to qualify as a solicitor, with the probability of career in the profession if they want it.

While the analysis showed that improved academic qualifications significantly increased the chances of securing a training contract, multivariate analysis established that certain socio-economic characteristics had an independent impact on the likelihood of students securing a training contract. Those receiving early offers of a training contract were particularly fortunate. They were most likely to receive financial support to meet the considerable cost of the vocational training course that predates their training contract. They were also most likely to be destined for the larger "elite" firms. Shiner et al. found that gender (a slight bias against women), ethnicity, school type, parental education, type of university, legal work experience (itself more difficult access for lower socio-economic groups), and the existence of close relatives in the legal profession all had an independent impact on the likelihood of a student getting an early offer, with early offers being most likely to be made by elite firms. The likelihood of late offers, more widely spread across the profession and less likely to bring financial support, was also independently affected by ethnicity, parental education, type of university attended, and legal work experience (Shiner, 2000: 118 *et seq*). Shiner et al. were also able to provide evidence that differences in destination were not explained by different preferences as to career trajectory.

For instance, the level of women getting training outside of private practice was not explained by a greater desire to work outside private practice (ibid: 113).

Importantly, evidenced biases were also mutually reinforcing: individual candidates not uncommonly had the "wrong" gender, ethnicity, *and* educational background which confounded their attempts to enter the legal profession. Based on their statistical model, Shiner et al. estimate that the hypothetical elite student has a 70% chance of entering the profession compared to only an 11% chance for a black woman with the same level of formal qualification (Shiner, 2000: 109).

Such statistics make sobering reading for any profession claiming to be meritocratic. A critique of the research would suggest that relying on degree results as one indicator of education qualification (as any such research probably must) inevitably disguises real differences between the quality of degrees given by each institution. Nevertheless, the research rightly created a furore at the time and forced the solicitors' profession, which commissioned it, to take diversity more seriously.

In a similar vein, there is an extensive body of empirical work on how women in the profession are marginalized or paid less. Interview-based studies are common (Webley and Duff, 2007). There are also econometric studies of pay differentials which tend to show that gender effects are not fully explained by human capital claims (i.e., the suggestion that women are paid less than men because their parental "career breaks" diminish their human capital, does not explain all the gender difference between salaries; see Wass and McNabb, 2006). While many in the professions point to bottom line figures which show increasingly large proportions of women and ethnic minority students entering the profession, stratification and exclusion continue to occur but more subtly. The lesson appears to be that if entry into the profession is less of a problem than it was, progression within it is not. A factor common in many of these studies, in spite of the divergence between quantitative and qualitative methodologies, is the extent to which the processes of organizing and allocating work within firms continues to impact on those outside the socio-economic elite. So, for example, a recent, quantitative study in the U.S. demonstrates significant attrition of black lawyers recruited to large firms. The author associates this with career opportunities for black lawyers being perceived to be significantly worse than those for white lawyers (Sander, 2006).

III. Lawyers Sell Their (Poor) Clients Short

Internal stratification within the profession is one thing, but is quality of service to clients similarly stratified? A number of studies have tended to emphasize the ways in which clients are poorly served by their lawyers and that work has particularly emphasized service to poorer clients, especially criminal defendants. Blumberg's study of criminal courts is a classic example (Blumberg, 1967). His principal goal was to challenge the view that defense lawyers act as adversarial protagonists for their clients' rights, instead pointing to the lawyer's leading role in persuading clients of the merits of pleading guilty. They often did this in the absence of confession evidence. Large numbers of clients indicated in interviews, perhaps reluctant to confess to wrongdoing to a researcher, that they were innocent or had been manipulated into pleading guilty (ibid: 34). The mechanisms through which lawyers were alleged to achieve guilty pleas was abuse of information asymmetry (the fact that lawyers know more about the law and the professional actors and so can pull the wool over their clients' eyes) and institutional dependence (the fact that professional links with courts and other professionals are much stronger than their links with individual, even repeat, clients whose position in the system is transient and inexpert).

Blumberg's picture of criminal justice might be criticized for being overly simplistic. There are obvious reasons why interview evidence from defendants protesting their innocence might be treated with skepticism. Similarly, Blumberg's conclusions are based on participant observation which is reported without being tied back to the actual evidence base. Thus, Blumberg speaks from experience rather than showing the evidence base on which that experience is founded. Yet it is a powerful, and in many ways an apparently accurate picture of how criminal defense lawyers have practiced as subsequent, more refined research has shown.

McConville et al. (1994) in particular conducted an exceptional study of criminal defense practice in England and Wales. It similarly suggests that criminal defense lawyers prioritize the interests of the state and themselves over their clients' interests. The research was conducted through meticulous direct observation of 48 firms over about four years of research time, covering solicitors' interactions with clients, prosecution and magistrates/judges at court, in the police station, and in their offices with cross-reference to solicitors' files in order to overcome an experimenter effect (ibid: 13–18). One key way in which the lawyers neglect the clients' interests is by treating all cases alike and, in particular, by making guilty pleas routine. The lawyers justify this through working practices that regard the best interest of clients as being well served by routine guilty pleas because clients generally have no legal or factual arguments to counter an overwhelming prosecution case. McConville et al. insist that this justification is unfounded. They report evidence of the ways lawyers manipulate their clients using their professional knowledge and status to persuade clients of the "good sense" in pleading guilty.

Why would defense lawyers do this? McConville et al. reject a traditional justification that lawyers are dependent on the police for client referrals, and they are skeptical of the explanatory power of Blumberg's claim that courts exert peer pressure on lawyers to coerce their clients toward compliance. Similarly, they are unconvinced that lawyers undergo a process of adaptation as they enter practice coming to learn that defendants are factually guilty. They surmise that no such learning process takes place because lawyers' beliefs in their clients' guilt arise from assumptions of guilt and not from legal judgments:

[T]hese beliefs are *ideological* and not the result of a technical legal assessment of the evidence in the case.... They are founded in part on the material experiences that legal advisers have with clients, in part on beliefs about the legitimacy of the prosecution case and its inviolability to attack, and in part on the failure of clients, as the undeserving poor, to survive the advisers' moral screening. They do not, however, arise out of a rational, technical-legal assessment of the strengths and weaknesses of individual cases (McConville et al. 1994: 137).

Lawyers interview clients in a way likely to maximize the likelihood of the client admitting guilt and thus being susceptible to a guilty plea. In the examples given by McConville et al., clients are often not perturbed by the lawyer's approach and readily admit their guilt. The concern is not that clients are routinely innocent, but that the lawyers (or their paralegal clerks) do not interview clients with an eye to identifying a line of defense worth exploring; they do not in any meaningful sense evaluate the prosecution's evidence; and more generally, they are not as adversarial as the legal system seems to expect (although some legal ethicists debate whether they ought to be so adversarial even in criminal defense cases (Simon, 1998)). Sometimes, however, the lawyers were seen to be maneuvering resistant clients toward guilty pleas, when the evidence suggested those clients were innocent of the charges they faced.

To be sure, McConville et al. do not show that large numbers of innocent clients were convicted or that a more robustly adversarial approach to defense lawyering would have led to different outcomes. What their evidence does establish in a compelling and detailed way is how the organization of criminal defense firms and the detailed work practices of individuals in those firms fall well short of the general expectations of an adversarial legal system. Indeed, one of the reasons that McConville et al.'s study would never be able to show convincingly that innocent clients were routinely being convicted in large numbers is because the criminal defense system was operating without any significant evaluation *by those clients' own lawyers* of their clients' guilt on the evidence. The criticisms of McConville et al. have been echoed in other jurisdictions.

Further concerns about the quality of lawyers have been expressed in a number of studies (Moorhead, 2010). Some link concerns to the marginal nature of small practice (Carlin, 1962) see also (Seron, 1996). Personal injury has been an area of particular focus: methods have ranged across peer observation, interviewing, and assessment of outcomes (sometimes by peer review). Of particular concern have been weaknesses in bargaining strategies employed by lawyers and the impact of those strategies on outcomes (Genn, 1987; see also a small-scale but influential study suggesting that an approach to lawyer-client relations which is less patrician and more client-centered is likely to lead to better outcomes: Rosenthal, 1974).

These studies tend to have at their core concerns that lawyers, possessed of the professional power engendered by their knowledge and institutional role, exploit that knowledge to the detriment, or not sufficiently to the benefit of, their clients. Interestingly, another area where we might expect findings to be similar, given the existence of large numbers of lay clients in difficult circumstances, is family law. Relevant work suggests a much more contingent picture: a lawyer's performance is more intimately related to his client's expectations, the exigencies of the situation, and the professional style of individual lawyers. A particular theme has been to add complexity to the notion that professions are powerful and clients are weak: Sarat and Felstiner (1995), in particular, identified an interactionist approach—power shifts between lawyer and client more than mere simplistic notions of professional-lay client relationships suggest. Interestingly, the evidence base provided by research on family lawyers is also more sympathetic to the work of lawyers (Davis et al., 1998; Eekelar et al., 2000; Mather et al., 2001).

IV. LAWYERS DO TOO MUCH FOR THEIR RICH CLIENTS?

One, albeit partial, explanation for lawyers serving poor clients badly is that such lawyers are poorly paid. Mann's work on white collar crime shows clearly how lawyers representing well-resourced, "white collar" criminal defendants provide a classically adversarial service (Mann, 1985). The reversal of autonomy engendered by commercial practice, where rich/large organizational clients with in-house expertise appear more able to dictate the approach to their legal problems and can (and do) devote huge resources to legal issues, suggests the potential for wealthy and commercial clients to lead their lawyers astray.

The legal ethics literature is replete with concern about the way in which commercial pressures on and within large firms may diminish the ethical standards of practitioners within those firms. A priori, the resources that clients can expend and the pressure those clients can exert on practitioners, coupled with the potential of adversarial legal paradigms to lead to relativistic thinking about what is ethical under the guise of treating the client's interests as paramount, provide a powerful set of reasons for thinking that big law firms do too much for big clients. A series of financial and other scandals such as those surrounding the collapse of Enron, U.S. Savings and Loans, and BCCI and the role of lawyers in tobacco litigation, all raise ethical concerns about "elite" lawyers, yet empirical evidence on this crucial area is thin on the ground.

There are a number of reasons why this might be the case: ethical violations are shielded by confidentiality and the lack of public fora in which positions taken in transactional and advisory work can be tested; powerful interests are well protected; and any analysis demonstrating that such transactions are *in fact* handled below ethical standards is highly contestable. Another reason is that larger firms may individually have stronger commitments to professional ethics (see Shapiro, 2002, but contrast Griffiths-Baker, 2002). The empirical work that imputes a negative relationship between lawyers and business usually does so indirectly from the structural and economic characteristics of large law firms. Nelson (1985) starts from this position, looking at the extent to which individual lawyers concentrate on the work of one client (making them vulnerable to pressure), while also probing for the extent to which and the circumstances in which lawyers give non-legal advice. Nelson uses non-legal advice as a potential proxy for advice which may have an ethical, as opposed to legal, content, but finds that the reasons for non-legal advice are found to be largely pragmatic and business-related rather than responses to broader ethical concerns. He then looks at the extent to which lawyers in such firms have turned down assignments for reasons associated with their personal values; 16% had, half of whom cited a professional ethical reason for so doing (often associated with alleged criminal or dishonest conduct on the part of the client). The vast majority (92%) of those who had not turned down a case for such reasons said they had not handled a case which conflicted with their personal values. The lesson drawn is that lawyers in large firms do not have value conflicts with their clients and ethical conflicts do not therefore appear to arise. That, of course, leaves open the possibility that the corporate values of clients and their lawyers are aligned but unethical. Furthermore, ethicality is addressed indirectly and on the basis of self-reports.

Parker et al. (2009) challenge the simplicities of the professional paradigm (that lawyer professionals restrain misconduct by clients) and the skeptical paradigm (that clients co-opt their lawyers as agents of wrong-doing or are encouraged by lawyers' adversarial approach to play the system and employ tactics to avoid compliance obligations). They do so by looking at the ways in which lawyers influence the compliance of large corporations with competition regulation, sidestepping the problems of studies which rely on lawyer interviews and self-reporting by looking at what factors influence the *clients* in their choice of corporate lawyers. They conclude that some lawyers are gamesters (or resisters of compliance) whereas some lawyers encourage greater compliance because they are normatively committed to it. The same variability of predisposition is true of clients and one can influence the other. Whether a lawyer is a gamester/resister is not purely a reflection of their clients' inclinations: they are not always acting purely as agents and on occasion have noticeably less ethical approaches to compliance than their clients. In particular, in-house "lawyers are more likely to lead their organizations into a game-playing posture toward compliance when they are put in charge of compliance than business executives, company secretaries or compliance officers" (ibid: 49). Whether they are acting as agents or as leaders, they are likely to deny responsibility for increasing non-compliance with the law.

V. Quality, Cost, and the Indeterminacy Problem

Research which suggests that commercial legal services are too expensive, that commercial lawyers are too adversarial, or that personal plight lawyers are not adversarial enough, raises a set of tricky normative issues. The correct level of adversarialism is a key area of debate in the ethics literature. Work on the balance between supply and demand has been undertaken largely by economists who, like socio-legal empiricists have been reluctant to address normative issues directly. One reason may be that even a cursory understanding of the arguments readily supplies the answer that there is no clearly "correct" level of adversarialisms or right balance of supply and demand. More specifically, it is extremely difficult for empirical research to successfully disentangle issues of supply from issues of demand in a way that can plausibly determine optimal levels of cost and quality. In research comparing American and English fee-shifting rules, simply establishing whether those rules have an impact on incentives (to charge more) and on case selection (which cases are worth pursuing) is difficult enough, and dependent on natural experiments (Hughes and Snyder, 1995) or simulations (Coursey and Stanley, 1988). Interview-based work, triangulated with more objective data sets, has been used to counteract some of the more pervasive and misleading ideas about the ways lawyers do business using contingency fees (Kritzer, 2002; Moorhead and Cumming, 2008). Fenn et al. (2002) include a simple assessment of case merits within their model exploring the impact of conditional fees in England and Wales, and a quasi-experimental approach has been used to explore the interrelationships of quality and cost incentives utilizing a range of quantitative and qualitative methods (Moorhead et al., 2001). All of this work tends to demonstrate that economic incentives influence the ways in which lawyers work and the quality of that work but they do not answer the optimality question—what incentives work best?

Similarly there is no work which looks at the extent to which what lawyers do for their clients is "worth the money" in the commercial sphere. Here one might expect that question to be more capable of evaluation. Gilson's theoretical and experience-based articulation of the benefits of commercial lawyers tends to rest primarily on the assumption that if lawyers were not worth the money, commercial clients would not pay (Gilson, 1984) (itself a dubious proposition (Hadfield, 2000)), or that lawyers help save costs, or increase revenue through avoidance activity (McBarnet, 1994).

Similarly, while much of the evidence shows how lawyers respond to economic incentives, there is a struggle to evaluate the normative implications of such behavior. Two reasons for this normative difficulty can be emphasized. One is the inevitable need to trade off cost and quality: only naïve understandings of a professional duty to put the client first would fail to recognize that cost exerts some constraint on professional service. Secondly, ethical and economic understandings of professional service interact: there is what Tata calls "ethical indeterminacy." Using mixed-methods empirical work to show how lawyers respond to fixed fees (they do less work with uncertain impacts on quality and outcome), he claims that professional judgments are of their nature uncertain and permit a range of strategies which may appear to be in the client's interests. In such circumstances, he claims, it is understandable that lawyers favor the more self-interested strategy (Tata, 2007).

The interface between economic incentives and professional values is likely to become increasingly important. Globalization has been impacting on the business practices of international law firms and the delivery of law for some time (see, for example, Dezalay and Garth, 1996). Relationships within and across professional firms, including relationships with and across law and other professions, are becoming more fluid. Work is not simply structured within firms (with, for example, an increased use of paralegals as fee carners) but across them (sub-contracting of work to the Indian sub-continent for example). This raises questions about the identity and regulation of legal professions and about the structure and relevance of legal education and training and its transferability across jurisdictions (a particular issue in the EC but likely to become so elsewhere over time).

A not-unrelated phenomenon is a trend toward greater competition and deregulation. Multi-disciplinary practices are in place in some Australian states and are coming in England and Wales. There seems to be a general trend toward greater liberality in lawyer fee arrangements in countries where such arrangements have been tightly regulated or limited (see Jackson, 2009). Information technology and new forms of provision also blur the boundaries between professional and non-professional models of service as well as potentially transforming the very nature of that service (Susskind, 2009). These areas have not been much researched by empiricists to date.

VI. COMPARING LAWYERS WITH NON-LAWYERS

One of the concerns raised by an examination of the economics of legal services is that the legal professions' rules and working practices inhibit competition and enable them to extract market rents (increase their prices beyond levels which are justified). A key area here is the extent to which professional rules inhibit the practice of law by service providers who have not gone through the full professional training and accreditation mechanisms. There is relatively little empirical work on non-qualified providers of legal service. Rules forbidding unqualified practice of law in the United States, and the general restriction of work that non-lawyers can do to more marginal or the less socially controversial work, limit the occasions on which non-lawyers perform work that can be compared with that done by "real" lawyers. Several studies acknowledge the importance of paralegals within practice, but relatively few look at the differences between the quality of work that they do and the work that lawyers do. Significantly, where this has been done, it has generally been observed that specialization, not professional qualification, is the key determinant of quality (e.g., Genn and Genn, 1989). Moorhead (2010) identified the ways in which non-lawyer providers sought to distinguish their service from traditional "stuffy" professional paradigms. Case outcomes, client satisfaction ratings, and the judgments of (specialist lawyer) peer reviewers of the quality of work done on case-files, all pointed to non-lawyers being significantly better than lawyers at equivalent work. These differences have been replicated in several subsequent studies including one where researchers were trained to simulate clients and, unknown to the lawyers in question, approach them for advice; the level of incompetence by qualified, but non-specialist lawyers was of great concern (Moorhead and Sherr, 2003). Cumulatively, such work challenges the professional mandate claimed by lawyers but it is evidence confined to the areas where non-lawyers are permitted to practice. Professional monopolies are protected from empirical scrutiny in a way that more contested terrains are not.

VII. CONCLUSIONS AND BEYOND

This Chapter has only sketched some of the literature in what is a vast field. Significant volumes of work look at what goes on in big firms; and an area largely neglected here but not in the literature concerns in-house counsel and the increasing complexity of relationships within law firms and between law firms and other actors (Rosen, 2002). Some more novel research techniques have been employed such as network analysis (Lazega, 2001) and simulation (Gunz and Gunz, 2002; Levin, 1994). Certain ethnographic and interview-based approaches have tended to reveal a picture more sympathetic to the profession, particularly where the authors have selected radical lawyers as their focus (Sommerlad, 2001; Travers, 1994). Work on cause lawyering and lawyers' roles in the law and development field are also more suggestive of the transformative potential of lawyering (Sarat and Scheingold, 1997).

At the heart of many of the studies discussed in this Chapter are well-evidenced critiques of the legal profession, and at the heart of many of these critiques is money. That filthy lucre should shape the organization of lawyers and the ways they work is often treated as a perversion of the professional ideal; acid proof that lawyers come up short. After all, professionals are supposed to demonstrate a level of selflessness, a willingness to put their clients' interest before their own, particularly where their own economic interests conflict with their clients'.

One criticism of this is that it treats as critical what is in fact banal. Lawyers predominantly operate in market contexts, even where they are subsidised through legal aid programs. Quite simply, they cannot do what they do without getting paid. To a degree, they have to organize around what is profitable. If they do not, they will cease to exist. While one way of testing the idea of professionalism is to examine the extent to which its ideals are corrupted by the market, another approach is to investigate how ordinary market behavior is adapted by professionals. In some ways this may be a more mature approach. In comparing (legal) services provided in a purely economically rational manner with services provided in a professional manner, it might be possible to see the reverse of "market corruption of professionals." We might be able to see how "professionalization" modifies market behavior so that professional services are more genuinely provided in the public interest. Such an approach might not see professionalism as an ideal compromised but rather as a positive, somewhat gentle, modifier of market's red in tooth and claw.

Similar points may be made about structuring and segmentation of the profession. Critiques of the profession's diversity tend to recognize but downplay the extent to which class, gender, and ethnicity structure most "elite" institutions. That is not an argument for resisting greater diversity within the profession, but it is an important acknowledgement that larger forces shape the legal profession. On the other hand, there is the powerful argument that a profession so strongly associated with notions of equality and legality has to lead in areas of social justice. Too often the profession does not appear to be leading, with arguments that *the client wouldn't put up with it* being used to trump higher ideals.

Another approach to understanding the array of research findings is to emphasize the importance of the way in which research questions are contextualized and of the benchmarks against which lawyers are compared. Saying that professions are none too bad is not an instant way to academic fame, particularly when the case has to be put on the basis that the profession is a "gentle modifier" of markets rather than a paragon of virtue. Where such research has emerged it has generally been in a context where the professions have been under attack. For instance, work that defends the personal injury bar and the use of contingency fees in the United States relies on a combination of surveys, observations in practitioners' offices, and semi-structured interviews with additional practitioners to defend practitioners against charges that they commonly take on and charge for cases irresponsibly (Kritzer, 2002; Kritzer, 2004) developed in the context of a vigorous political battle over tort law (Daniels and Martins, 1999).

It is tempting to suggest that underlying the substantive position of much research on lawyers is a symptom of the underdog syndrome: when lawyers appear powerful or rich, relative to us or their clients, researchers criticize them; when they are under attack, researchers defend them. Similarly there is the journalistic reflex to contend with. Positive stories about lawyers rarely make good (attention-attracting) news. Empirical research in this, as in many areas, is very sensitive to policy agendas and perhaps to a preference for the good story. Such research needs to be read in context. Equally, something perhaps more profound is suggested about the struggle to find clear normative benchmarks for judging lawyers. Lawyers work at the heart of social and economic controversies. In evaluating what they do, researchers have to grapple with major instabilities in our understandings of law and justice. To assess whether lawyers do a good job at a fair price one has to make judgments about the extent to which they take on "good" cases; deal with them in "good" ways—ethically, efficiently and purposefully; and the extent to which they reach "good" outcomes. Many, but not all, of the constituents of what would constitute "good" are contested, particularly when two lawyers represent clients with opposing interests. Many of the solutions to these normative dilemmas are dealt with by the system, by lawyers, and often dyadically by the parties. Such resolution as occurs usually takes place away from the scrutiny of courts; and with only a shadowy influence accorded to rules. This emphasizes the socially constructed and unregulated nature of this normative universe. What lawyers do, and who they are, thus plainly matters but the complexities of understanding and evaluating them are enormous.

Ethical concerns are perhaps preeminent among legitimacy concerns because they represent the most unsettling critique of what lawyers do and the way in which the legal system is perceived to work. In particular, the idea that lawyers protect their clients' interests above those of society goes to the heart of popular and ethical debates about the legal profession. Empirical literature tends to reflect on the normative question of whose interests are preeminent differently depending on the context. The status and resources of clients are seen as critical in distinguishing commercial/rich client practice from personal plight/poor client practice. The literature also tends to invert popular preconceptions about lawyers (they are not routinely helping guilty clients "get off," quite the reverse) as well as theoretical preconceptions about what defines professionals (contrary to theoretical constructions of professionalism "elite" lawyers are not autonomous). That said, when research turns to evaluating lawyers normatively and on their own terms the results are troubling for the profession's claim to legitimacy. The profession is not open to all solely on merit; criminal lawyers are not found to be as adversarial as the system or professional rhetoric demands; and, where they are permitted to compete, qualified lawyers do not perform better than non-lawyers. Empirical scholarship may challenge some of the popular stereotypes of lawyers, but it does very little to establish the legitimacy of lawyers *as professionals*. Generally, it has challenged that legitimacy.

References

Auerbach, J.S. (1976). *Unequal justice: lawyers and social change in modern America*, New York: Oxford University Press.

Bevan, G. (1996). "Has There Been Supplier-Induced Demand for Legal Aid?," *Civil Justice Quarterly* 15: 98–114.

Blumberg, A.S. (1967). *Criminal Justice*, Chicago: Quadrangle Books.

Cape, E. and Moorhead, R. (2005). *Demand Induced Supply? Identifying Cost Drivers in Criminal Defence Work*, London: Legal Services Research Centre.

Carlin, J.E. (1962). *Lawyers on Their Own: A Study of Individual Practitioners in Chicago*, New Brunswick: Rutgers University Press.

Coursey, D. and Stanley, L. (1988). "Pre-trial Bargaining Behaviour Within the Shadow of the Law: Theory and Experimental Evidence," *International Review of Law & Economics* 8: 349–67.

Daniels, S. and Martins, J. (1999). "It's Darwinism—Survival of the Fittest: How Markets and Reputations Shape the Ways in Which Plaintiffs' Lawyers Obtain Clients," *Law & Policy* 21: 377–99.

Davis, G., MacLeod, A., and Murch, M. (1998). *Partisans and Mediators The Resolution of Divorce Disputes*, Oxford: Clarendon Press.

Dezalay, Y. and Garth, B. (1996). *Dealing in virtue: international commercial arbitration and the construction of a transnational legal order*, Chicago: University of Chicago Press.

Eekelaar, J., Maclean, M., and Beinart, S. (2000). *Family Lawyers: The Divorce Work of Solicitors*, Oxford Oregon: Hart.

Fenn, P., Gray, A., Rickman, N., and Carrier, H. (2002). *The Impact of Conditional Fees on the Selection, Handling and Outcomes of Personal Injury Litigation*, No. 6/02, London: Lord Chancellors Department.

Galanter, M. (1974). *Why the Haves Come Out Ahead: Speculations on the Limits of Legal Change*, Law and Society Review 9: 1.

Galanter, M. and Henderson, W. (2008). "The Elastic Tournament: a Second Transformation of the Big Law Firm," *Stanford Law Review* 60/6: 1867

Galanter, M. and Palay, T. (1991). *Tournament of Lawyers: The Transformation of the Big Law Firm*, Chicago: University of Chicago.

Genn, H. (1987). *Hard bargaining: out of court settlement in personal injury actions*, Oxford: Clarendon.

Genn, H. and Genn, Y. (1989). *The Effectiveness of Representation at Tribunals*, London: Lord Chancellor's Department.

Gilson, R.J. (1984). "Value Creation by Business Lawyers: Legal Skills and Asset Pricing," *Yale Law Journal* 94: 239–313.

Griffiths-Baker, J. (2002). *Serving Two Masters: Conflicts of Interest in the Modern Law Firm*, Oxford: Hart.

Gunz, H. and Gunz, S. (2002). "The Lawyer's Response to Organizational Professional Conflict: An Empirical Study of the Ethical Decision Making of In-House Counsel," *American Business Law Journal* 39: 241.

Hadfield, G. K. (2000). "The Price of Lawyers: How the Market for Lawyers Distorts the Justice System," *Michigan Law Review* 98: 953–1006.

Heinz, J. and Laumann, E. (1982). *Chicago Lawyers: The Social Structure of the Bar*, New York: Basic Books, 1982; Revised Edition, Northwestern University Press and American Bar Foundation, 1994.

Heinz, J.P., Nelson, R.L., Sandefur, R.L., and Laumann, E.O. (2005). *Urban Lawyers: The New Social Structure of the Bar*, Chicago and London: University of Chicago Press.

Hughes, J.W. and Snyder, E.A. (1995). "Litigation and Settlement under the English and American Rules: Theory and Evidence," *Journal of Law and Economics* 38: 225–50.

Jackson, R. Lord Justice (2009). *Review of Civil Litigation Costs: Preliminary Report*, London: Review of Civil Litigation Costs.

Kritzer, H.M. (2002). "Seven Dogged Myths Concerning Contingency Fees," *Washington University Law Quarterly* 80: 739–94.

Kritzer, H.M. (2004). *Risks, Reputations, and Rewards: Contingency Fee Legal Practice in the United States*, Stanford: Stanford University Press.

Lazega, E. (2001). *The Collegial Phenomenon; The Social Mechanisms of Cooperation among Peers in a Corporate Law Partnership*, Oxford: Oxford University Press.

Levin, L.C. (1994). "Testing the Radical Experiment: A Study of Lawyer Responses to Clients Who Intend to Harm Others," *Rutgers Law Review* 47: 81–164.

Mann, K. (1985). *Defending White Collar Crime: A Portrait of Attorneys at Work*, New Haven and London: Yale University Press.

Mather, L., McEwen, C.A., and Maiman, R.J. (2001). *Divorce Lawyers at Work: Varieties of Professionalism in Practice*, New York: Oxford University Press.

McBarnet, D. (1994). *Legal creativity: law, capital and legal avoidance in Lawyers in a Postmodern World—Translation and Transgression*, Buckingham: Open University Press.

McConville, M., Hodges, J., Bridges, L., and Pavlovic, A. (1994). *Standing Accused. The Organisation and practices of criminal defence lawyers in Britain*, Oxford: Clarendon.

Moorhead, R. (2004). "Legal aid and the decline of private practice: blue murder or toxic job?," *International Journal of the Legal Profession* 11: 159–90.

Moorhead, R. (2010). "Lawyer Specialisation—Managing the Professional Paradox," *Law and Policy* 32(2): 226–59.

Moorhead, R. and Cumming, R. (2008). *Damage-Based Contingency Fees in Employment Cases: A Survey of Practitioners*, Cardiff: Cardiff Law School Research Series.

Moorhead, R. and Sherr, A. (2003). An *Anatomy of Access: Evaluating Entry, Initial Advice and Signposting using Model Clients*, London: Legal Services Research Centre.

Moorhead, R., Sherr, A., and Paterson, A. (2003). "Contesting Professionalism: Legal Aid and Nonlawyers in England and Wales," *Law & Society Review* 37: 765–808.

Moorhead, R., Sherr, A., Webley, L., Rogers, S., Sherr, L., Paterson, A., and Domberger, S. (2001). *Quality and Cost: Final Report on the Contracting of Civil, Non-Family Advice and Assistance Pilot*, Norwich: Stationery Office.

Nelson, R.L. (1985). "Ideology, Practice, and Professional Autonomy: Social Values and Client Relationships in the Large Law Firm," *Stanford Law Review* 37: 503.

Parker, C.E., Rosen, R.E., and Nielsen, V.L. (2009). "The Two Faces of Lawyers: Professional Ethics and Business Compliance with Regulation," *Georgetown Journal of Legal Ethics* 22: 201–48.

Rosen, R.E. (2002). "We're All Consultants Now: How Change in Client Organizational Strategies Influences Change in the Organization of Corporate Legal Services," *Arizona Law Review* 44: 637.

Rosenthal, D.E. (1974). *Lawyer and Client: Who's in Charge?* New York: Russell Sage.

Sander, R.H. (2006). "The Racial Paradox of the Corporate Law Firm," *North Carolina Law Review* 84: 1755.

Sander, R.H. and Williams, E.D. (1989). "Why are There so Many Lawyers? Perspectives on a Turbulent Market," *Law and Social Inquiry* 14: 431–73.

Sarat, A. and Felstiner, W.L.F. (1995). *Divorce Lawyers and their Clients—Power and Meaning in the Legal Process*, New York: Oxford University Press.

Sarat, A. and Scheingold, S. (1997). *Cause Lawyering: Political Commitments and Professional Responsibilities*, Oxford: Oxford University Press.

Seron, C. (1996). *Business Of Practicing Law (Labor And Social Change): The Working Lives of Solo-and Small-firm Attorneys*, Philadelphia: Temple University Press.

Shapiro, S.P. (2002). *Tangled Loyalties: Conflict of Interest in Legal Practice*, Ann Arbor: University of Michigan Press.

Shaw, G. (2006). "Notaires in France—An Unassailable Profession. Or are they?," *International Journal of the Legal Profession* 13: 243–71.

Shiner, M. (2000). "Young, Gifted and Blacked! Entry to the Solicitors Profession," in P.A. Thomas (ed.), *Discriminating Lawyers*, London and Sydney: Cavendish.

Simon, W.H. (1998). *The Practice of Justice: A Theory of Legal Ethics*, Cambridge: Harvard University Press.

Sommerlad, H. (2001). "I've lost the plot: An Everyday Story of the Political Legal Aid Lawyer," *Journal of Law and Society* 28: 335.

Susskind, R. (2009). *The End of Lawyers? Rethinking the nature of legal services*, Oxford: Oxford University Press.

Tata, C. (2007). "In the Interests of Clients or Commerce? Legal Aid, Supply, Demand, and "Ethical Indeterminacy" in Criminal Defence Work," *Journal of Law and Society* 34: 489–519.

Travers, M. (1994). "The Phenomenon of the Radical Lawyer," *Sociology* 28: 245–58.

Wass, V. and McNabb, R. (2006). "Male-female earnings differentials among lawyers in Britain: a legacy of the law or a current practice?," *Labour Economics* 13: 219–35.

Webley, L. and Duff, E. (2007). "Women Solicitors as a Barometer for Problems within the Legal Profession—Time to Put Values before Profits?," *Journal of Law and Society* 34: 374–402.

33

LEGAL PLURALISM

MARGARET DAVIES

I. INTRODUCTION

"LEGAL pluralism" refers to the deceptively simple idea that in any one geographical space defined by the conventional boundaries of a nation state, there is more than one "law" or legal system. At the basic level, empirical accounts of legal pluralism consist of descriptive analyses of dual or multiple laws or legal systems in particular areas of the world. Legal pluralism has been identified and studied in relation to colonial and postcolonial societies where it is common for an imposed legal system to co-exist and interconnect with customary, indigenous and/or religious laws. Scholars have also extended the idea to states apparently governed by a single state-based legal system, where non-state normative systems often co-exist with state law, sometimes competing with it for authority over citizens. Legal pluralism is sometimes understood to depict relatively autonomous or discrete normative systems, but the trend in recent empirical research has been toward illustrating the dynamic interconnections between normative orders. This more fluid understanding of pluralism reflects disciplinary developments in anthropology, ethnography, and sociology as well as a greater sensitivity to globalization. It also poses a challenge to positivist conceptions of law which traditionally emphasize the practical or conceptual separation of state law from other normative contexts. This Chapter examines several aspects of legal pluralism focusing in particular on the relationship between the empirical "facts" of pluralism and its conceptual foundations. This analysis will, I hope, draw attention to a certain productive tension between legal philosophy and empirical studies of pluralism.

II. Producing the "Facts" of Pluralism

The plurality of legal or normative mechanisms in a social field is sometimes put forward as an empirical state of affairs, a set of facts, which is said to counteract the statist concept of law which some pluralist theorists regard as ideological, hypothetical, or simply presumed as a result of its hegemonic status. John Griffiths explicitly contrasted pluralist "fact" and monistic "myth" by claiming that "[l]egal pluralism is the fact. Legal centralism is a myth, an ideal, a claim, an illusion" (J. Griffiths, 1986: 4). Griffiths repeatedly calls legal centralism an "ideology." The distinction drawn by Griffiths is (in part) disciplinary: on the one hand, social science, dealing in observed facts, has demonstrated the plurality of law whereas legal thought, with its basis in an internal view of statist legal systems, has glossed over these facts in the interests of illustrating the singularity and coherence of law. The pioneering legal anthropologist Malinowski (1926) laid some of the groundwork for this factual social scientific analysis in his study of the Trobriand Islanders. In contrast to the anthropological orthodoxy of the time, Malinowski argued that those who followed "primitive" law were not merely driven by blind acquiescence to custom, by superstition, or by fear, but rather that their laws were enforced "by very complex psychological and social inducements" (ibid: 15). His work extended the definition of law to non-state forms of order. In the case of Trobriand society, this order was characterized as "a body of binding obligations" which Malinowski argued have the status of rights and correlative duties, with specific enforcement mechanisms entrenched in the social structure (ibid: 58).

Once law was more widely defined in such a way, it became possible to perceive non-state law in situations where there was no recognizable state but also in situations where in the same geographical space a state offered a different type of law. Early issues of the *Journal of Legal Pluralism and Unofficial Law*[1] are full of empirically based analysis of co-existing normative orders, at first in Africa, and subsequently throughout the world. Here one finds discussions that consider in detail the issues that arise in specific contexts when indigenous, customary, religious and state law overlap or are in conflict, and the mechanisms used by the state to resolve such conflicts. Crawford (1971), for instance, described the conflicts between (potentially and sometimes actually polygynous) indigenous marriage provisions and colonial state marriage laws in Ghana; Smart (1980) analyzed the operation of Islamic law in Sierra Leone in its relationship to general or state law; and Pospisil (1981) describes the transformation of traditional practices of authority, jurisdiction, procedure, and sanction under Dutch and Indonesian colonialism in West Papua. Pospisil's analysis of change evokes, though does not fully theorize, a now standard anthropological pluralist insight (see J. Griffith's critique of Pospisil: 1986, 16–17); that is, that the relationship between legal orders is dynamic rather than static, often resulting in hybrid or reconstructed systems developed in the shadow of state law. Sometimes unofficial law is directly controlled by the state, for instance under repugnancy provisions or provisions incorporating elements of traditional law into state law (Hooker, 1975). Sometimes, however, unofficial law remains within an area of self-determination which, nonetheless, may interact with state law.

Especially as it is understood by lawyers, "law" in the contemporary West very strongly evokes the singular system of law tied to a nation state. For this reason, the "fact" of pluralism in the West is more difficult to discern in the present tense than it is historically. For the thousand or so years between the crumbling of the Western Roman Empire in the fifth century and the rise of the nation state in the seventeenth, that is, prior to the consolidation of the state's law-making capacity, law in Western Europe was dispersed according to different centers of political power, different types of activity, and even different legal subjectivities. It was located in custom, feudal aristocracies, the church, guilds, municipalities, as well as monarchs and their councils (MacDonald, 1998: 74–5; Tamanaha, 2008: 377). The rise of the nation state and the positivist theory which later strengthened the state monopoly

---

[1] This journal started its life as the Journal of *African Law Studies* and changed its name in 1981 with a new editorial policy specifically focused upon legal pluralism as explained by the editor, John Griffiths, in Volumes 18 and 19.

on law removed the practice, the experience, and knowledge of the law from the people and their communities. As Tamanaha comments "[t]he fact that we have tended to view law as a monopoly of the state is a testimony to the success of the state-building project and the ideological views which supported it" (Tamanaha, 2008: 379; cf. Santos, 2002: 90). The monopoly is therefore based not only upon the process of centralizing previously dispersed laws. It is also a consequence of defining law in such a way that by the twentieth century it was understood to be necessarily centered on a state.

Tamanaha also argues that there has more recently been a change of perspective which has once again *produced* a pluralistic view of the legal world (2008: 389–90). He attributes the change to two factors: first, theorists are now taking the global, supra-national, and international scales seriously as a starting point of analysis. From this vantage point there are a multitude of overlapping and indeterminate types of law, regulation, and control, which might be contrasted to the more solid, bounded and determinate notion of law which results from starting with the nation state and national sovereignty. The global perspective brings to the forefront the decentered nature of global normative influences, whether these stem from "official" sources or from unofficial sources such as transnational corporations, NGOs, "private" regulatory codes (such as those promulgated by sporting bodies), shared legal cultures, transnational religious groups, and so forth (see, generally, Santos, 2002: 163–311). Second, Tamanaha says that pluralism is produced by a more expansive notion of "law" (therefore generating a multiplicity of legalities). If all of these heterogeneous normative influences are defined as "law," then of course the perception that pluralism is *legal*, becomes unavoidable.

There are in my view some other changes of perspective which "produce" legal pluralism for contemporary empirical scholars and legal theorists. A change in perspective away from the nation state has also occurred at the micro scale; that is, research has recently centered on the officials, citizens and subjects who have different experiences and perceptions of law. Roderick McDonald and David Sandomierski ask "How do *legal subjects* imagine, invent, and interpret legal rules? . . . How do the actions and practices of *legal subjects* instantiate the rules they conceive and perceive?" (2006: 614; see also Cover, 1983). In the ethnographic context, a significant strand of legal pluralist scholarship has moved away from trying to understand distinct bodies of "law" or normative orders, to a far more dynamic and sophisticated analysis of the ways in which local peoples engage with and construct various normative orders in specific contexts. Richard Wilson (2000), for example, has analyzed the affinities and discontinuities between the South African Truth and Reconciliation Commission with its human rights rhetoric and Christian ethos, and neighborhood courts with their more traditional patriarchal focus and unofficial status. Wilson's objective, and that of others who have undertaken similar work (notably Anne Griffiths, as I discuss below), is to bypass legal pluralism's traditional obsession with the law-society dichotomy and replace it with a critical account of the synergies and resistances between normative orders which create law-as-process (rather than law-as-object). Such an understanding of legal pluralism takes it well away from the identification of somewhat discrete objective systems toward a far more fluid account in keeping with current critical legal theory.

Finally, pluralism undoubtedly resonates quite strongly with the general trend in scholarship away from "grand narratives." Pluralism is not necessarily conceived in postmodern terms and indeed the empiricism of much pluralism is at odds with the postmodern emphasis on discursive constructions of objective reality (Davies, 2006: 581). A specifically postmodern angle on legal pluralism remains a minority position both within the broader domain of postmodern-inspired legal scholarship and within legal pluralist scholarship (but cf. Manderson, 1996). Despite this, there does seem to be a certain synergy or resonance, if not theoretical coherence, between the anti-statism of legal pluralism and the anti-grand-narrative stance of postmodernism.

In sum, a variety of factors produce the perception of legal pluralism which is reflected in intensified interest in the concept in contemporary scholarship. However, to say that pluralism is "produced" is no criticism of this scholarship since monistic statism may equally be regarded as the product of a narrow and ethnocentric concept of law. Thus, John Griffiths' claim that legal pluralism is "the fact" while centralism is "a myth" and "ideological," is contested by the theory-dependence of any claim to *either* singularism or monism. Either "law" is defined exclusively by the state or it is not, but there is no universally satisfactory definition of law which will solve the uncertainty. One kind of definition gives us monism as a fact, while the other gives us pluralism as a fact: confining "law" to the state seems too narrow as a definition of law, while allowing that "law" exists beyond the state can seem too inclusive and vague. I will come back to this central question of how law is defined for legal pluralism toward the end of this Chapter.

III. Disciplinary Contests: Sociology, Anthropology, and Legal Philosophy

In many ways the archetypal instance of the conflict between law as a state-based unity defined in conceptual terms and law as a socially based plurality which can be empirically understood occurred in the early twentieth century between Hans Kelsen and Eugen Ehrlich. Ehrlich postulated a distinction between official law and living law (Ehrlich, 1922; 1962).[2] He argued that law was not reducible to the state with its official, formal law, but was to be found in social practices. Formal law and its official "legal provisions" was merely one aspect of the social practice of law, and not necessarily the part with the greatest normative impact on people (cf. Ehrlich, 1922: 144). Most significantly, law's "center of gravity" for Ehrlich was society and its "living law," not state machinery (Ziegert, 1998: 115). In contrast to Ehrlich's broad understanding of the social locus of law, Kelsen proposed a conception of law which was rigorously singular, hierarchical, and centralist. Kelsen did recognize the plurality of norms which made up a legal system (it would be hard to do otherwise) but hypothesized that they were all constituted within a system defined by a basic norm (or *grundnorm*) which represented the "unity of a plurality of legal norms" (Kelsen, 1992: 55). Any norm which could not be traced back to the basic norm was not, in Kelsen's system, part of law, though of course it might be part of some other system of norms.

There is an evident political history to this intellectual contestation: Ehrlich's sociological stance challenged the movement toward codification in Europe which had reached its peak in the nineteenth century, while Kelsen's monism directly reinforced the trend toward state monopoly on law. For the duration of the twentieth century, the statist view was not only more popular among jurists and legal scholars than its alternative, it became the assumed point of departure for the definition of law. As Santos comments, "with the consolidation and expansion of the liberal constitutional state, and with the conversion of the legal positivist hypothesis into a hegemonic (i.e., commonsensical) thesis about law, state legal centralism, or exclusiveness disappeared as such and became law *tout court*" (Santos, 2002: 90). Arguably, what began as the *theory* of state-based legal positivism became by the middle of the century a self-fulfilling prophecy: the term "law" was by then so firmly connected to state institutions, that it was impossible to classify any other normative order as "law"—state law covered the field of law, and *legal* pluralism became a contradiction in terms. On this hegemonic concept of legal centralism, evidence of "other" normative orders, systems, or forms was not evidence of non-state *law* but, by definition, evidence of custom, superseded law, positive morality, or social practices.

The differences between Ehrlich and Kelsen are emblematic of a disciplinary and attitudinal divide between socio-legal thought and legal philosophy. The former takes an external and empirical approach to law, seeing it as simply part of a social complex, while the latter takes an internal and often conceptual approach to law, and therefore fails to theorize fully the inter-relationship between law and society (Cotterrell, 2002: 636). Kelsen went so far as to insist on the purity of his theory of law

---

[2] Ehrlich's distinction is different from the more commonly cited distinction made by Roscoe Pound between "law in the books" and "law in action" (Pound, 1910). As Nelken explains, whereas Pound was drawing a distinction between two modes or manifestations of state law, Ehrlich's distinction refers to two types of law—state and non-state law (Nelken, 1984).

by defining it negatively against any historical, sociological, or economic approach to law (Kelsen, 1967: 1).

Despite the centralism assumed by mainstream legal thought, sociologists, and anthropologists of law continued to present non-statist depictions of law and legal pluralism throughout the twentieth century. In 1988, after several decades of pluralist scholarship, Sally Engle Merry diagnosed two main strands—occurring first as a result of colonialism, and second as a result of ordinary normative pluralism in any complex society. A third category of pluralism arising from scholarship of the last two decades might also be added, with globalization as its central focal point in terms of subject-matter (Santos, 2002: 92). The landscape is further complicated by the fact that there are undoubtedly pluralist scholars whose work fits within one of these three categories (colonial, national, global) in terms of subject-matter, but who have moved beyond traditional social science methodology toward a more critical, sometimes postmodern, and reflective empiricism. This alternative methodological stream of pluralist scholarship therefore sometimes overlaps with and sometimes moves beyond the forms of pluralism identified by Merry (1988) and Santos (2002). Whether it has its own coherence as a social scientific approach to law is another matter, as I will explain shortly.

A. Pluralism in colonial and postcolonial contexts

In the first place, then, legal pluralism was studied in colonial and postcolonial contexts, where customary, indigenous, and religious laws often operated concurrently with the colonial state law, and were sometimes officially recognized and incorporated into the state law (Hooker, 1975). The preexisting law in colonized societies was itself often pluralistic, having undergone diverse influences of war, settlement, trade and religion (Merry, 1988: 870; Tamanaha, 2008: 381). Within this study of legal pluralism in postcolonial situations, much research has been undoubtedly technical and formalistic in that it focuses upon the doctrinal and procedural interaction between different areas of law: how are conflicts between bodies of law resolved? What law applies in what situation? Is a particular body of law officially recognized or not? Hooker's classic work, for instance, takes as its point of departure that the "form of political organization within which plural legal systems exist today is the nation state" (1975: 1). In Hooker's analysis, the colonial legal system is a "dominant" system, while the various indigenous or native laws are "servient," meaning that they can be abolished, reformed, or prevailed over by the national law. His work is, essentially, an exceptionally detailed account of how—in a number of different colonial situations—the various religious and indigenous laws interact with the national legal system. As Griffiths argues, such scholarship takes a legal point of view, and replicates the legal positivist perspective that "law" is a closed set of rules and institutions able to be described objectively at any particular point in time (J. Griffiths, 1986: 7). This is underlined by the fact that Hooker's source material about the relationship between state and non-state law consists basically of the legislation, regulations, cases, ordinances, and so forth which have been issued under colonial or state rule.

A much more imaginative ethnographic approach, but one still framed by the pluralist focus on colonial or postcolonial societies, considers the dynamic interaction between official or officially recognized institutions and codes, and the cultural norms and modes of power technically regarded as "outside" the law (Moore, 1993; A. Griffiths, 1998; cf. Merry, 1988: 880–1). For instance, throughout the 1980s and 1990s, Anne Griffiths conducted a study of marital disputes regarding family property in Botswana. Taking an approach that centered on the analysis of the disputes themselves rather than the legal rules which technically govern them, she found a high degree of "cross-fertilization" and "plasticity" in the law, meaning that different bodies of law in practice influence each other, rather than remaining in their own insular shell of legitimacy (ibid: 613). The analysis also brings to the foreground the ways in which cultural forms of power—in this case gender—are interwoven with legal interpretation, undermining any broader claim that positive state law operates autonomously from politics. Such work illustrates the fluidity of any mobilization of "law" in a normatively complex context: not only is a system of "law" *not* confined to its own internal logic or rule of recognition, but it overlaps in an operational sense with cultural norms regarded by traditional legal theory as outside the "core" definition of law.[3] Such conclusions support the work done in the 1980s and onwards by feminist and critical legal theorists. This work hypothesizes the embeddedness of law in forms of cultural power, and illustrates this internally by reference to legal doctrine and legal decision-making. The distinctive social-scientific contribution reinforces these conclusions with micro-level observation and analysis of complex everyday legal situations.

B. Pluralism in the national context

Secondly, the "new" legal pluralism discussed by Merry encompasses socio-legal research into the "unofficial" and non-state forms of ordering in *any* society, outside the context of colonialism. In contemporary Australia, New Zealand, Canada, and

---

[3] Of course, some mainstream legal theory has partially recognized the interconnection between community and law. Ronald Dworkin's *Law's Empire* (1986) is probably the most famous example. However, Dworkin's analysis is limited by two matters: first, he confines the influence of community values to hard cases and second, his picture of community is not characterized by diversity but rather singularity and idealism, as represented in the hypothetical judge Hercules.

the United States, there is an evident colonial context and a pluralism of laws which owe their "plurality" or differentiation to colonialism. Within colonizing nations such as Britain as well, migration from formerly colonized nations (and others) leads to a pluralistic normative context which may be addressed (or not) by a variety of legal methods (Shah, 2005; Yilmaz, 2001). Varying levels of assimilation, compromise, or recognition have taken place between the original and the colonial laws in each of these nations. However, leaving the colonial past and present aside, there are also pluralities of normative ordering in and around the state or official law and mainstream society. The classic analysis in this field came from Sally Falk Moore in the early 1970s. In this paper, Moore argued that there was value in returning "to the broad conceptions of Malinowski who set out to "analyse all the rules conceived and acted upon as binding obligations" (Moore, 1973: 720, quoting Malinowski, 1926: 23). In this instance, however, Moore applied the concept to a non-colonial situation, the clothing industry in New York. Moore identifies various normative patterns which order relationships between the designer/label ("jobber"), the contractors responsible for producing garments, the union, and various "officials" within each group. The normative patterns Moore analyzed at times interact with and unofficially alter legal obligations, for instance where they concern flexibility around contractual obligations. At other times, the normative patterns were completely extra-legal, such as when gifts and favors were provided to facilitate business relations. Moore juxtaposes this analysis of the clothing industry with her long-standing study of the Chagga people of Mount Kilimanjaro in Tanzania where state and non-state ordering also interact in specific ways. Both groups, the clothing industry and the Chagga, are, according to Moore, conditioned by interconnected "legal, illegal and non-legal norms" (ibid: 723), but are also to a significant degree self-governing in their normative patterns. To denote the existence of rule-generation and some method of enforcing compliance to these norms within a particular context, Moore coined the term "semi-autonomous social field." This is the "small field observable to an anthropologist" which can itself "generate rules and customs internally, but... is also vulnerable to rules and decisions and other forces emanating from the larger world by which it is surrounded" (Moore 1973: 720).

According to Moore, semi-autonomy is a normal attribute of a field of study bound together by some common purpose. She argues that it would be unusual for such a field to be completely autonomous from state law, because state law affects or shapes to some degree so much ordinary activity in contemporary society (ibid: 742). A complete lack of autonomy is equally hard to imagine because even highly law-governed sites of practice develop their own codes, cultures, and modes of behavior (ibid: 742–743). Parliament, the courts, and legal practice are, for instance, as close as any arenas of society to the state legal hierarchy, but their normative patterns are never completely determined by state law (Galanter and Roberts, 2008; Nelken, 2004). Nor can state law itself be so contained because its abstract principles are always grounded in some concrete context, and because interpretation of state law is always informed by wider socio-cultural values (see, e.g., Post, 2003; Cover, 1983).[4] As Tamanaha points out (2008: 394), Moore did not refer to the semi-autonomous social field as "law," preferring instead to maintain an analytical distinction between state law and other normative spheres. Her work was, nonetheless, immensely influential in the development of a sophisticated approach to normatively governed fields, and was taken as a framework for some forms of pluralist theory (e.g., J. Griffiths, 1986).

The notion of *semi*-autonomy is useful because it facilitates analysis of both interdependence with other systems and the self-identity of a particular system: the idea has proved to be enormously useful in the study of normative pluralism in non-colonial situations. As with studies in the colonial situation, since the 1980s such research has emphasized the dynamic inter-relationships between normative orders, rather than their autonomy. Merry summarized the situation in these terms:

> Research in the 1980s has increasingly emphasized the dialectic, mutually constitutive relation between state law and other normative orders. I think this reflects a new awareness of the interconnectedness of social orders, of our vulnerability to structures of domination far outside our immediate worlds, and of the ways implicit and unrecognized systems of control are embedded in our day-to-day social lives (Merry, 1988: 880).

There are many illustrations of this type of research (see, generally, Merry, 1988: 881–6). One of the best known is Boaventura de Sousa Santos's study of Pasagarda law in Brazil. As he explains, "Pasagarda is the fictitious name of a squatter settlement (or *favela*) in Rio de Janeiro" (Santos, 2002: 99). The residents in Pasagarda have their own system of law which has developed as an adaptive response to the inadequacy and inaccessibility of state law in dealing with issues surrounding (civil) order and rights. Santos describes the unofficial law as one mechanism in a class conflict: it provides a tool through which the urban poor can take control of their own communities and, to some degree, resist hegemonic structures (ibid: 156). At the same time, Santos does not see the relationship between state and unofficial law as purely oppositional: in some contexts the Brazilian state tolerates and uses the unofficial system, while in its turn Pasagarda law also draws upon state law where necessary.

C. Globalization and pluralism

Thirdly, over the past two decades, discussion of legal pluralism has been much more attentive to the interaction of local law with normative ordering emanating

---

[4] A more elaborate (though perhaps for that reason less flexible) approach to quasi-legality in social theory is to be found in Niklas Luhmann's work on social systems and autopoesis (Luhmann, 1993). Luhmann's work has been influential to some degree in legal pluralist scholarship (Teubner, 1992; 1997).

from processes of globalization. Clearly the increasing prominence of international law and human rights plays a significant role in creating a legally plural environment on the global scale—after all, the relationship between international and domestic law immediately creates (at least) a duality of law across the entire globe, while human rights is a global normative discourse which enters into local normative patterns in many distinct ways (see, e.g., Wilson, 2000; Santos, 2002: 270–2). However, globalization comprises a multitude of other equally significant forms of transnational normative orders beyond the state, such as religious groups, multinational corporations, trade regimes, non-government organizations, and so forth (Teubner, 1997). These interpenetrate both state law and the sub-state or informal normative systems operating within a state (Santos, 2002: 163). While in many cases persons residing in a particular area might be influenced by several of these overlapping normative orders, the subjects of plural global law are themselves also increasingly "mobile," as the content of a recent edited collection (*Mobile People, Mobile Law*) makes clear (von Benda Beckman et al., 2005). To take just one example from this work, Werner Zips considers the repatriation and self-determination claims of Rastafari on behalf of formerly enslaved African peoples. This struggle brings into play a variety of intersecting legalities and normativities within and across state boundaries:

[Transnational] Rastafari organizations seek links to the African heritage, interpret it by means of the religious law which they extract by their idiosyncratic interpretations and exegeses of the Bible, especially the Old Testament, and appropriate at the same time transnational law, if it applies to what they consider as their natural (human) rights (Zips, 2005: 71).

The image which emerges from analysis of such distinctive empirical situations is a highly dynamic normative terrain, with many forms of legality and many forms of unofficial or non-state law intersecting in particular contexts. The dominant narrative emerging from such empirical research is not one of increasing uniformity across the globe, but rather a proliferation of specific micro-contexts which are unique in some respects but which also have discursive and formal connections with broader national and global communities (see also Drummond, 2000).

D. Pluralism and legal theory

It can be seen from this brief overview that social scientific accounts of plural normative orders in a society challenge the legal and jurisprudential idea that state law is separate in some way from other social codes. State law may be "*semi*-autonomous" in the manner described by Moore, but it is hardly self-contained or even self-determining. If empirical legal pluralism simply analyzed the existence of relatively self-contained parallel systems of norms, some conventionally known as "law" and others not, then the pluralist challenge to state law could be seen as essentially practical (which systems of norms are the most authoritative, influential, and for what reasons?) and/or semantic (on what basis do we call something "law"?). However, the challenge to the centralist concept of law is deeper than this—empirical pluralism provides support to critical theories which have insisted on analyzing state law from positions other than that of the legal insider, and which critique isolationist tendencies in legal thought. Thus, as Roger Cotterrell says:

> [legal pluralism] enables us to look for phenomena sufficiently like state law in some respects to make comparison illuminating. It also highlights the possibility that some types of regulation whose formal origins or primary bases of practical authority do not lie in the state are becoming so important that to ignore their interpenetration with or consequences for state law is impermissible. Most importantly, a legal pluralist approach raises the question of where law's ultimate authority ultimately resides and whether simple positivist tests adequately explain legal validity (Cotterrell, 2002: 638).

One challenge for legal theory is to take up systematically this "interpenetration" of state law with non-state forms of normative ordering (which may or may not be termed "law"). Rather than critique the conventional boundaries of "law" legal theory has often presumed that non-state law is of relevance only at the edges of law, or where there is some gap or lack of clarity in state law. Critical legal theory has of course undermined this presumption, especially in relation to the ways in which constructed patterns of social normality (normative gender assumptions, heteronormativity, whiteness, and so forth) are both reflected in and constructed by law. But critical legal theory has done less to challenge seriously the image of law as essentially bound to a state. A second challenge for legal theory is to reconsider the idea of legal validity in light of the undoubted complexity of contemporary landscapes of law, quasi-legality, and normative diversity. Arguably, an adequate legal theory will theorize not only state law as such, but also the position of this form of law in a complex of plural normative orders.

IV. The Theory-Dependence of Legal Pluralism

As stated in the Introduction, legal pluralism is in many ways a deceptively simple idea; "deceptive" in its simplicity because, essentially (and as many others have noted), any straightforward claim that law "is" plural (or singular for that matter) begs the question of what *law* is. Legal philosophers are not agreed on this question, and social scientists have also come up with various definitions of "law." As the history of pluralist scholarship reveals, there is an uneasy relationship between empirical research concerning legal pluralism and its conceptual underpinnings. Two basic questions might be asked about the claim that a society is characterized by legal pluralism: is it really pluralist? And is it really law? When does observed normative diversity become "legal pluralism," a term which joins together the ideas of *plurality* and *legality*? These issues pretty much cover the field as far as conceptual complexity goes, and I will deal with each in turn.

A. Is it pluralist?

There are a multitude of particular things in the world, and many conflicting ways of classifying and understanding those things. In an obvious sense, each empirical datum is different from each other and, of course, all empirical "facts" require taxonomies—of language, scholarly disciplines, symbolic orders, or cultural norms—in order to be classified and understood. Whether two or more things are "plural" or essentially singular might ultimately depend on matters such as values, perspective, ideology, discourse, prevailing paradigms, and so forth.

Legal pluralism describes the situation where there is more than one form of law in any geo-political space. But, in the first instance, what does it mean to say that there is more than *one* law? Putting aside the matter of whether the object in question is "law," is it more than one thing? After all, ordinary state law has a plurality of elements, including individual norms which must number in the hundreds of thousands. Above the level of particular rules or principles, plurality is found in imperfectly individuated areas such as contracts, property, criminal law, constitutional law, and so forth. It is found in the different foundational concepts which inform these areas. The plural elements of state law can also appear in separately institutionalized layers, for instance the state/provincial and federal law of a federal system. But this is not what is ordinarily meant by "legal pluralism," because these "plural" areas or institutions are regarded simply as sub-sections of a single system. They are parts of a whole, "plural" if considered on their own terms outside the framework of the legal system (which in many cases would be implausible), but singular when considered in the context of the ordinary definition of state law. Conceptualizing this "unity of a plurality" was, as already indicated, Kelsen's purpose in hypothesizing the basic norm, to which all laws could be traced. The relationship between the different parts of law is managed and comprehended (albeit imperfectly) within a legal totality. To be meaningful then, "pluralism" must refer to some plurality outside the ordinary limitations of state law or, at least, which tests or stretches those limitations (cf. Davies, 2006: 586–9; A. Griffiths, 1998). Pluralism means, broadly speaking, that there is more than one classification, system, type, mode or form of law within a particular space.

Pluralism is normally defined in contrast to monism, centralism or statism in descriptions of law. In the 1980s John Griffiths made an important analytical contribution to the theory of legal pluralism, classifying legal pluralist approaches as either "weak" (juristic) or "strong" (social scientific). Weak or juristic pluralism describes a situation where there is some form of law originally different to state law (that is, defined by reference to "ethnicity, religion, nationality, or geography" (J. Griffiths, 1986: 5), but which is nonetheless recognized by state law—included within the same rule of recognition, validated by the one basic norm, commanded by a sovereign, and so forth. This form of legal pluralism is pluralistic in the sense that differences in legal heritage are reflected in "law" and it is juristic because it is a form of pluralism acknowledged by law and lawyers. It is internal to state law: in Kelsenian terms one might say that the reason for the validity of the indigenous law or religious law subsequently recognized by the state has shifted from its own basic norm to that of the state. However, according to Griffiths, juristic pluralism is not *ultimately* pluralistic, because law as a whole is still defined and constrained by the state, an entity defined by its monism. "It would be a complete confusion," he says, "to think of 'legal pluralism' in the weak sense as fundamentally inconsistent with the ideology of legal centralism" (J. Griffiths, 1986: 8). On the contrary, it is that very ideology which demands that any non-state law be appropriated and defined within the domain of state law—weak pluralism is a symptom of and reinforces state centralism, rather than existing in opposition to it. There remains one overarching system which contains all the law for that state.

Except for the different heritages, religions, or ethnicities which perhaps generate a qualitative difference in the values or styles of law, a situation of "weak" pluralism is arguably found in a federal system of law—several provincial laws contained and recognized within one federal law. This is not a very interesting form of pluralism for social scientists, though it undoubtedly poses very significant questions for lawyers and legal scholars about the relationships between self-contained but formally interconnected legal systems. However, the paradigmatic case of weak legal pluralism envisaged by Griffiths was quite different from simple federalism. It concerned the efforts of monistic legal systems to manage different forms of law for different peoples within the one national scheme. So, for instance, a colonial (or post-colonial) state might recognize all or part of an indigenous law, granting some degree of self-determination but maintaining ultimate control over what this law is and becomes, how it is administered, and the extent to which it can be called official "law." It is a "messy compromise" between the demands of legal statism, and the factual existence of and adherence to, an alternative law (J. Griffiths, 1986: 7).

A situation of strong or true legal pluralism, by contrast, is observed where there is no overarching rule, sovereign, state or system to manage parallel and conflicting legal orders. According to Griffiths, strong legal pluralism reflects the empirical incommensurability of normative orders. This might exist, for instance, when a colonial state fails to acknowledge a preexisting law which continues, nonetheless, to govern the lives of a community. Or, a case of strong legal pluralism might emerge in a non-colonial society when distinct systems of norm-production arise within various social groupings. Because the existing or unofficial law is not recognized or incorporated into the state law, it does not trouble a legalist monism, derived from the internal perspective of jurists. From the external perspective of social scientists, however, the empirical field encompasses incommensurable laws, where "law" is defined (after Sally Falk Moore) as "the self-regulation of a 'semi-autonomous social field'" (J. Griffiths, 1986: 38; Moore, 1973).

John Griffiths' analysis of pluralism raises many fascinating questions about the relationship between an empirical and a conceptual understanding of legal pluralism and, therefore, of law. It provokes examination of the different perceptions of the legally defined social field held by lawyers and social scientists; it raises the problem of what type of difference is truly "pluralist" (for instance, empirical specificity, conceptual incommensurability and so forth), and ultimately it raises the problem of the distinction between fact and concept. In Griffiths analysis the jurist's effort to manage pluralism through legal techniques and concepts lines up with an ideology of monism and state centralism, while the social scientific attention to the actual ways in which social groups order their affairs lines up with the strong empirical facts of legal pluralism. Ironically though, some recent theory has seen a reversal of this quite plausible diagnosis: it is the social scientists who are charged with a certain kind of monism (conceptual essentialism), while a more "pluralist pluralism" (Melissaris, 2004; Davies, 2006) is advocated which, among other things, demands a recognition of the diversity in possible concepts of law (see, e.g., Tamanaha, 2001; Melissaris, 2009).

The difference between weak and strong pluralism is a difference in *how* the social field is perceived—through the eyes of jurists trained in the presumptions of state-based law with their singular constructions of their subject, or through the eyes of social scientists with emphasis upon the "facts" of pluralism such as those described above. Yet since the same "object" may be perceived, and ultimately constructed, differently within different scholarly disciplines, there is no contradiction in saying that a juridical space can be characterized at once by weak and strong pluralism. As in many colonial and post-colonial nations, elements of Aboriginal law in Australia are recognized and given effect by the colonial legal system. Native title law asks courts to examine the claimants' customary relationship to a tract of land, for instance, an exercise which involves the acknowledgement of indigenous law as it operates in a particular area. In some criminal cases, indigenous law or the likelihood of a customary punishment being carried may be of relevance in sentencing. There is a "weak" legal pluralism in that elements of indigenous law are recognized by state law. At the same time, these partial forms of recognition account for very little indigenous law, which maintains its own existence independently from state law. Clearly, the enforcement of state law and its self-definition as *the* (only) law does not entail the factual extinguishment of indigenous laws. There is therefore a "weak" pluralism of partial recognition by state law and a strong pluralism of a multitude of co-existing legal systems.

B. Is it law?

The second conceptual issue which casts a shadow over all legal pluralist scholarship is whether it is really possible to talk of a plurality of "law" rather than a plurality of normative orders or customs. What is "law," for a start? Does it not simply confuse the issue to start calling all sorts of things "law," when this goes against conventional usage? As I have explained, the idea of legal pluralism has been extended well beyond the effects of colonialism on preexisting law to the normative diversity within everyday life. But on what basis can informal or alternative "legalities" be designated "law"? As Sally Engle Merry commented:

Why is it so difficult to find a word for nonstate law? It is clearly difficult to define and circumscribe these forms of ordering. Where do we stop speaking of law and find ourselves simply describing social life? Is it useful to call all these forms of ordering law? . . . The literature in this field has not yet clearly demarcated a boundary between normative orders that can and cannot be called law (Merry, 1988: 878–9).

The problem can be most straightforwardly summed up by reiterating two related questions which continue to trouble legal philosophy—what is law? And what is the relationship between law and non-legal normative principles which order a society? Whether legal pluralism is detected in a particular society depends very much upon the concept of law utilized by the would-be pluralist scholar. In the simplest terms, whether one *sees* pluralism or not in a society depends on how "law" is defined. After all, one plausible—though by no means universally accepted—understanding of law is that it is *uniquely* definitive of binding obligations within a society and therefore necessarily excludes any other "law." Such an understanding of law by definition precludes legal pluralism as a meaningful category.

Unavoidably then, the empirical aspect of specifically *legal* pluralism is always in danger of being undermined by the uncertainty surrounding the concept of law. Of course, it would always be possible to speak of a pluralism of normative systems, one of which is state-based law, or simply a pluralism of norms rather than a specifically *legal* pluralism, but the preference of the pluralist scholarship is for the latter. This is possibly because "law" implies a stronger obligation, a mandatory form of ordering, than what might otherwise be described as belief-systems, cultural norms, or social practices (see also von Benda-Beckman and von Benda Beckman, 2006: 14–17). There has therefore been some pressure on legal pluralists to provide an answer to the question of why non-state forms of ordering should be termed "law." Rather than answer the question, Santos turns it around:

It may be asked: Why should these competing or complementary forms of social order-ing...be designated as law and not rather as "rule systems," "private governments," and so on? Posed in these terms, this question can only be answered by another question: why not? To take the [example of medicine]...it is generally accepted that, side by side with the offi-cial, professionalized, pharmochemical, allopathic medicine, other forms of medicine cir-culate in society: traditional, herbal, community-based, magical, non-Western medicines. Why should the designation of medicine be restricted to the first type of medicine, the only one recognized as such by the national health system? Clearly, a politics of definition is at work here, and its working should be fully unveiled and dealt with in its own terms (Santos, 2002: 91).

Santos makes an important point here. By demanding justifications for classifying non-state norms as "law," we deflect attention from providing an adequate justifi-cation for the status of state law as "law." Arguably, any answer to the "why not?" question rests only on convention, hegemony, and power—that law is conventionally and discursively tied to a state—rather than on any philosophical necessity. It is a "politics of definition." In this context, we could recall the legal philosopher H.L.A. Hart's view that the rule of recognition providing law's ultimate identity and unity is something "recognized" by legal officials (Hart, 1994). Although Hart did not himself explore the full implications of this view, there can be no doubt that there is a political subtext at work here which cements the power of a conventional legal hierarchy.

Tamanaha, however, answers the question differently. In response to Santos's "why not?," he says, "The short answer is that to view law in this manner is con-fusing, counter-intuitive, and hinders a more acute analysis of the many different forms of social regulation involved" (Tamanaha, 2008: 394). Tamanaha's argument is equally important. Undoubtedly it *is* counter-intuitive to expand the idea of law beyond conventional usages of the term, in particular that which ties it to the state: the law-state framework is pervasive, hegemonic and—as I have said earlier—self-fulfilling. (This is also Santos's point.) It is a descriptively true framework for the contemporary understanding of law because it still dominates the discipline and practice of law.

The issue in this context is surely not just whether it is somehow legitimate (or productive) to call non-state normative processes "law" or whether it is illegitimate (and counter-productive) to confine the idea of law to a state. But several significant matters are revealed by this debate. First, socio-legal and anthropological scholars need to be able to analyze the empirical patterns of interconnection between, and dynamism of, normative systems without being distracted by debates over nomen-clature: up to a point, it really does not matter whether a particular set of norms is definitively termed "law" or not (cf. Tamanaha, 2008: 396). What matters is an under-standing of the group or field within which a normative code or pattern has arisen, its dynamic processes of self-replication and change, and its relationship with other normative systems, including state law (cf. Roberts, 1998: 101–2). A significant consequence of such analysis is that it also illustrates the conceptual permeability of state law: it shows, for instance, that state law is unavoidably inflected by ordinary social patterns and that it is, moreover, refracted into social life in diverse ways. As illustrated in the first two sections of this Chapter, theoretical insight about the fluidity and interconnectedness of different normative orders has been underpinned by extensive empirical research in (post) colonial, non-colonial, and global contexts.

Second, although "law" does have a conventional usage binding it to a state, it also has various usages which challenge this conventional concept of law. It is equally important that a pragmatic acceptance of a conventional notion or a conventional hierarchy of law does not thereby foreclose or downgrade the possibility of alternative concepts of law, and in particular non-state forms of law which are also conventionally known by that name, such as indigenous law. It might be confusing and counter-intuitive to call indigenous law "law," but to exclude it because it does not match conventional notions of law is simply to reinforce a theoretical ethnocentricity, the assumption that "law" must look a particular way. And third, however we determine the question, we must not lose sight of "the politics of definition" here (Santos, 2002: 91). By naming a particular object "law" we undoubtedly give it credibility as such and, correspondingly, downgrade the status of norms outside the domain of law. The resulting theoretical imperative is therefore not how we choose to deploy the term "law" but that we remain reflective about the political consequences of the choice (Kleinhans and Macdonald, 1997: 33, n. 21). It is, after all, normally possible to avoid confusion by speaking of "state," "official," or "centralized" law, in contrast to a more dispersed and less formal object.

V. Pluralist Pluralism

As indicated above, over the past two decades, there have been further developments beyond the two streams of pluralism identified by Merry in 1988. Some of these developments might be characterized as the evolution of these two strands in directions influenced by contemporary critical social theory. For instance the work of Anne Griffiths, mentioned above, emphasizes the complexity and dynamism of normative patterns in specific situations, illustrating the inadequacy of accounts of pluralism which visualize empirically and conceptually separate parallel normative orders. Work such as that of Griffiths challenges the idea that there is a single, essential, concept of law by illustrating the factual plasticity and multi-layering of normative engagement in a complex society. Yet other approaches take pluralism beyond national boundaries to the interconnections of legalities at local, national, and global scales (Santos, 2002; Teubner, 1997).

However, pluralism has also taken a conceptual turn and a turn inwards toward critical legal theory (see, generally, Melissaris, 2009: 33–42). "Critical," in this sense, refers to the Frankfurt school heritage and in particular its challenge to positivist social thought and objectivist epistemology (Horkheimer, 1972: 210–11). Critical legal theory has noted that the images of pluralism promoted by the positivist social scientific approach have themselves been essentialist reifications of "the legal" and "the social" which fail to acknowledge the agency of legal subjects in their complex environments (Kleinhans and Macdonald, 1997: 35; Manderson, 1996: 1060; Davies, 2006).[5] From this point of view, the "social field" itself cannot be described simply from the neutral observer's position as a matrix of objectively identifiable and overlapping normative patterns. Rather, what those normative patterns are, what they mean in different settings, and how they are interconnected with the processes by which people understand themselves and their environments, provides a highly mobile and dynamic account of legal pluralism.[6] Desmond Manderson, for instance, deploys the notion of misreading to illustrate that normative systems are not closed, are not even interpretively stable, and are constantly in flux:

The human dimension of misreading is necessary to any genuine pluralism, for it rejects the reification of "law," "system," "culture," or "community".... Law is not manufactured by "a multiplicity of closed discourses" precisely because it is only realized through the actions of particular human beings who exist in several discourses and who are, therefore, themselves plural. We must go beyond understanding law as a system (like positivism), a clash of systems (like pluralism), or even as the interaction of subsystems (like autopoesis) (Manderson, 1996: 1064).

The point is simple enough. All normativity is produced by interactions between human agents who are, however, not abstract individuals with unattached free wills, but rather already situated in diverse contexts of social meaning. Normativity (including anything termed "legal") is necessarily constructed and reconstructed across these discursive environments by virtue of the fact that agents circulate between them: norms and the "systems" attributed to them by theoretical reification are therefore not closed and stable but intrinsically open and contingent.

[5] Similarly, Tamanaha argued that social scientific legal pluralism was "essentialist" in the sense that it took a single definition of "law" and applied it to different normative fields. In response, he devised a "non-essentialist" notion of law: "Law is whatever people identify and treat through their social practices as "law""(Tamanaha, 2001: 194). Tamanaha's solution, however, does not really solve the problem of reification—although he sees that different types of normative modalities may be called "law," once determined, these systems appear to have a defined content, meaning that the interpretive dynamism of a pluralist pluralism is lost.

[6] Because of its strong association with positivist social science, the label "legal pluralism" is not necessarily adopted by critical legal theorists. The question whether legal pluralism can be reformulated as a critical approach to law, or whether it is too tainted by its dominant positivism is an interesting one, which I will leave to one side here.

The standard qualification should be made, however: a subject-centered concept of law does not imply that norms and laws can be made to mean anything at all, or that we are free to reconstruct them in whatever way we desire. Such an implication would ignore the many forms of institutional and social power (i.e. the empirical data) which constrain such innovation. Nor does it mean that we must abandon any engagement with state law conceived in the monist and positivist sense. Critical pluralism understands state law within a pluralist context and sees it as answerable to mobile and pluralistic conditions, rather than being built upon a certain and identifiable foundation. But the "systematic" and closed understanding of law persists, and in many contexts demands engagement (Davies, 2008). Nonetheless, critical or pluralist pluralism shifts the locus of norm-construction away from a reified system of norms, to the complex and dynamic relationships between human agents which necessarily exceed and thereby contest the boundaries of any limited system.

This critical view offers another perspective on the hybridity and plasticity of normative orders identified by empirical scholars, such as A. Griffiths, Wilson, and Zip (and even to a certain extent by earlier anthropologists, such as Pospisil and Moore). Normativity is *always* channeled through human subjects with their diverse interpretations and applied contexts: multiply situated subjects are responsible for reinterpreting and synthesizing norms and therefore for defining both law and legally pluralistic environments. While Manderson's is essentially a "theoretical" claim, social scientific research can be understood as illustrating the objective consequences of this process-oriented and intrinsically open account of law. Even more importantly, it is at this point that theoretical and empirical statements about law become indistinguishable: as a concept, "law" is created, interpreted, applied, and empirically observable in the one moment or process. If law is intrinsically a social phenomenon defined in specific ways in different social and cultural contexts, then legal theory inevitably exists in dialogue with (and must eventually comprehend) the empirical matter of law. What have often been seen as two distinct approaches to law—socio-legal and theoretical—are in fact interdependent. As I hope to have shown, this mutuality is illustrated in scholarship on legal pluralism, with its debates over the inclusiveness (or not) of the idea of law. However, it is a general point which can be made about all legal theory and all socio-legal scholarship.

VI. CONCLUSION

Legal philosophy and sociological approaches to law often still occupy quite separate scholarly terrains. Whereas legal philosophy is conceptual and analytical, and takes the perspective of the legal insider or expert, sociological approaches to law tend to be empirical and take the perspective of an observer of law. However, this disciplinary division is ultimately conventional, arbitrary, and contestable, based as it is upon the notion that law has clear conceptual and practical limits which a theorist can be "inside" or "outside." Because it is based on the perception that there are multiple, interacting, normative systems and (from the critical point of view) that law-creating subjects are embedded simultaneously in these multiple systems, legal pluralism has been identified as one fruitful area for constructive engagement between legal philosophy and the sociology of law (Cotterrell, 2002; Davies, 2006). The concept of law it supports is non-state-based, and non-singular, thus challenging some of the most significant and resistant philosophical paradigms of law. With the decline of nation states as the locus of political and legal power, it seems inevitable that traditional state-centered legal philosophy must give way to a different paradigm which recognizes the plurality of law.

REFERENCES

Cotterrell, R. (2002). "Subverting Orthodoxy, Making Law Central: A View of Sociolegal Studies," *Journal of Law and Society* 29: 632–44.

Cover, R.M. (1983). "Nomos and Narrative," *Harvard Law Review* 97: 4–68.

Crawford, T. (1971). "Ghana: Marriage and Divorce," *African Law Studies* 4: 27–46.

Dalberg-Larsen, J. (2000). *The Unity of Law: An Illusion? On Legal Pluralism in Theory and Practice*, Berlin: Galda & Wilch Verlag.

Davies, M. (2006). "Pluralism and Legal Philosophy," *Northern Ireland Legal Quarterly* 57: 577–96.

Davies, M. (2008). "Feminism and the Flat Law Theory," *Feminist Legal Studies* 16: 281–304.

Drummond, S. (2000). "The Process Geography of Law (As Approached Through Andalucian Gitano Family Law)," *Journal of Legal Pluralism* 45: 49–70.

Dworkin, R. (1986). *Law's Empire*, London: Fontana.

Ehrlich, E. (1922). "The Sociology of Law," *Harvard Law Review* 36: 130–45.

Ehrlich, E. (1962). *Fundamental Principles of the Sociology of Law*, W. Moll (trans.), New York: Russell and Russell.

Galanter, M. and Roberts, S. (2008). "From Kinship to Magic Circle: The London Commercial Law Firm in the Twentieth Century," *International Journal of the Legal Profession* 15: 143–78.

Griffiths, A. (1998). "Reconfiguring Law: An Ethnographic Perspective from Botswana," *Law and Social Inquiry* 23: 587–616

Griffiths, J. (1986). "What is Legal Pluralism?," *Journal of Legal Pluralism* 24: 1–55.

Hart, H.L.A. (1994). *The Concept of Law* (2nd ed.), Oxford: Clarendon Press.

Hooker, M.B. (1975). *Legal Pluralism: An Introduction to Colonial and Neo-Colonial Laws*, Oxford: Clarendon Press.

Horkheimer, M. (1972). *Critical Theory: Selected Essays*, New York: Continuum.

Kelsen, H. (1967). *Pure Theory of Law*, Berkeley: University of California Press.

Kelsen, H. (1992). *Introduction to the Problems of Legal Theory* 1st edn. of the *Reine Rechtslehre* [1934], Oxford: Clarendon Press.

Kleinhans, M.-M. and Macdonald, R. (1997). "What is a Critical Legal Pluralism?," *Canadian Journal of Law and Society* 12: 25.

Luhmann, N. (1993). "Operational Closure and Structural Coupling," *Cardozo Law Review* 13: 1419–41.

MacDonald, R. (1998). "Metaphors of Multiplicity: Civil Society, Regimes and Legal Pluralism," *Arizona Journal of International and Comparative Law* 15: 69–91

MacDonald, R. and Sandomierski, D. (2006). "Against Nomopolies," *Northern Ireland Legal Quarterly* 57: 610–33.

Malinowski, B. (1926). *Crime and Custom in Savage Society*, London: Routledge and Kegan Paul.

Manderson, D. (1996). "Beyond the Provincial: Space, Aesthetics, and Modernist Legal Theory," *Melbourne University Law Review* 20: 1048–71.

Melissaris, E. (2004). "The More the Merrier? A New Take on Legal Pluralism," *Social and Legal Studies* 13: 57–79.

Melissaris, E. (2009). *Ubiquitous Law: Legal Theory and the Space for Legal Pluralism*, Ashgate: Farnham.

Merry, S.E. (1988). "Legal Pluralism," *Law and Society Review* 22: 869–96.

Moore, E. (1993). "Gender, Power, Legal Pluralism: Rajasthan, India," *American Ethnologist* 20(3): 522–42.

Moore, S.F. (1973). "Law and Social Change: The Semi-Autonomous Social Field as an Appropriate Subject of Study," *Law and Society Review* 7: 719–746.

Nelken, D. (1984). "Law in Action or Living Law? Back to the Beginning in Sociology of Law," *Legal Studies* 4: 157–74.

Nelken, D. (2004). "Comparing Legal Culture," in A. Sarat (ed.), *The Blackwell Companion to Law and Society*, Oxford: Blackwell Publishing.

Pospisil, L. (1981). "Modern and Traditional Administration of Justice in New Guinea," *Journal of Legal Pluralism and Unofficial Law* 19: 93–116.

Post, R. (2003). "Fashioning the Legal Constitution: Culture, Courts, and Law," *Harvard Law Review* 117: 4–112.

Pound, R. (1910). "Law in Books and Law in Action," *American Law Review* 12: 12–36.

Roberts, S. (1998). "Against Legal Pluralism: Some Reflections on the Contemporary Enlargement of the Legal Domain," *Journal of Legal Pluralism and Unofficial Law* 42: 95–106.

Santos, B. de Sousa (2002). *Toward a New Legal Common Sense* (2nd ed.), London: Butterworths.

Shah, P. (2005). *Legal Pluralism in Context*, London: Glasshouse Press.

Smart, J. (1980). "The Place of Islamic Law within the Framework of the Sierra Leone Legal System," *African Law Studies* 18: 87–102.

Tamanaha, B.Z. (1993). "The Folly of the Social Scientific Concept of Legal Pluralism," *Journal of Law and Society* 20: 192–217.

Tamanaha, B.Z. (2001). *A General Jurisprudence of Law and Society*, Oxford: Oxford University Press.

Tamanaha, B.Z. (2008). "Understanding Legal Pluralism: Past to Present, Local to Global," *Sydney Law Review* 30: 375–411.

Teubner, G. (1992). "The Two Faces of Janus: Rethinking Legal Pluralism," *Cardozo Law Review* 13: 1443–62.

Teubner, G. (1997). " 'Global Bukowina': Legal Pluralism in the World Society," in G. Teubner (ed.), *Global Law Without a State*, Aldershot: Dartmouth, 3–28.

von Benda-Beckman, F., von Benda-Beckman, K., and Griffiths, A. (eds.) (2005). *Mobile People, Mobile Law: Expanding Legal Relations in a Contracting World*, Aldershot: Ashgate.

von Benda-Beckman, F. and von Benda-Beckman, K. (2006). "The Dynamics of Change and Continuity in Plural Legal Orders," *Journal of Legal Pluralism and Unofficial Law* 53–54: 1–44.

Wilson, R. (2000). "Reconciliation and Revenge in post-apartheid South Africa: Rethinking Legal Pluralism and Human Rights," *Current Anthropology* 41(1): 75–99.

Yilmaz, I. (2001). "Law as Chameleon: The Question of Incorporation of Muslim Personal Law into the English Law," *Journal of Muslim Minority Affairs* 21: 297–308.

Ziegert, K.A. (1998). "A Note on Eugen Ehrlich and the Production of Legal Knowledge," *Sydney Law Review* 20: 108–26.

Zips, W. (2005). " 'Global Fire': Repatriation and Reparations from a Rastafari (Re) Migrant's Perspective," in F. von Benda-Beckman, K. von Benda Beckman, and A. Griffiths (eds.), *Mobile People, Mobile Law: Expanding Legal Relations in a Contracting World*, Aldershot: Ashgate.

....

PUBLIC
IMAGES AND
UNDERSTANDINGS
OF COURTS

....

JAMES L. GIBSON[*]

IN recent times, political scientists, most especially in the United States, have devoted a great deal of research effort to studying the linkages between courts and their

  * This research has been supported by the Law and Social Sciences Program of the National Science Foundation (SES-0533156). Any opinions, findings, and conclusions or recommendations expressed in this material are those of the author and do not necessarily reflect the views of the National Science Foundation. I also greatly value the support provided for this research by Steven S. Smith and the Weidenbaum Center on the Economy, Government, and Public Policy at Washington University in St. Louis.

constituents. Indeed, it is not hyperbolic to assert that there has been an explosion of interest in understanding the interconnections of judges and public opinion. And "interconnections" is the correct word in the sense that some research posits that public preferences influence the behavior of judges and courts, while other studies test the hypothesis that courts shape public opinion. This new emphasis on the views of the mass public is common to those who study trial courts, state appellate courts, and federal courts at all three levels. Given this up-tick in scholarly productivity, taking stock of where the literature stands seems appropriate and timely.

The literature on courts and the public is as diverse as it is vast. Examples of this body of work include:

- Research on the legitimacy of courts among their constituents. Legitimacy in this approach is defined in terms of the attitudes of the mass public. Considerable work has been accomplished on this topic, ranging from studies of state courts to studies of the U.S. Supreme Court to studies of courts around the world.
- Research on the responsiveness of courts to public preferences. On this topic, scholars have become extremely interested and creative. Important work has been reported, on both trial and appellate courts, on the question of the degree to which judges respond to public preferences in their decisions on the bench.
- Research on state judicial elections in the United States. This work does not always focus on public opinion, although some does consider the attitudes and behaviors of the mass public.
- Research on public attitudes toward various legal issues, such as so-called tort reform and attitudes toward the rule of law.
- Research on public knowledge and understanding of courts. Commensurate with a broader re-thinking of the knowledge of the American mass public, scholars are showing that ordinary people are far more aware of and informed about the judiciary than heretofore thought. Indeed, revisionist findings on public knowledge of law and courts undergird much if not all of the revival of interest in the connections between judges and their constituents.

My purpose in this Chapter is not to address all of these topics—the literature is too vast and disparate. Instead, I focus specifically on contemporary work on public knowledge of, information about, and perceptions and judgments of law and courts. Thus, this Chapter begins with the assumption that the beliefs, values, attitudes, expectations, and behaviors of ordinary people influence, and are influenced by, the operation of legal systems. Because this assumption does not seem to be universally embraced, I begin this Chapter with a brief digression on the nature of the scholarship on public opinion and the operation of courts.

Throughout this Chapter, I postulate that courts are "political institutions." If politics is defined as the "authoritative allocation of values for society" (Easton, 1953: 129), then there can be no doubt that the term "political" applies to judicial institutions. Less abstractly, courts make public policy that extends beyond the instant dispute in a case; judges invariably have discretion in making decisions; and the decisions of judges can be enforced through the coercive actions of state institutions. In a similar but not necessarily identical vein, an influential set of legal scholars has recently asked: "Are Judges Political?" (Sunstein et al., 2006). The answer their empirical analysis provides to the question, at least with regard to federal judges in the United States, is an emphatic "yes." At least since about 1948, political scientists have rejected the view that ignoring the political aspects of judging is of some value.

I. Public Opinion, Politics, and Courts: An American Scholarly Enterprise

Although my intention in writing this Chapter is not to focus unduly on research conducted on the American legal system, in fact little research on public attitudes toward law and courts has been conducted outside the United States. There are no doubt many reasons for this, but one overriding explanation may be that American scholars are convinced that the mass public provides an important constraint on the actions of the legal system, while scholars outside the U.S. are not so convinced. As a simple illustration, American scholars must pay attention to the mass public because the vast majority of judges in the U.S. are required to face the electorate in one form or the other. The election of judges is exceptionally rare outside the U.S. (see Kritzer, 2007). More generally, American scholars seem willing to weigh the views and preferences of ordinary people when considering the nature of legal cultures, while other scholars tend to assign exclusive weight to the views and preferences of legal elites. Moreover, to the extent we know anything about the views of ordinary people toward law and courts outside the United States, it is largely (but, of course, not exclusively) owing to the efforts of American scholars, and therefore reflects American conceptualizations of the topic. The consequence of this dearth of research outside the United States is that this Chapter must rely heavily on analyses from a single country even if that necessarily constrains the generalizability of the conclusions I draw.

I begin this Chapter with the elemental empirical issue of how informed ordinary people are about things judicial (see Caldeira and McGuire, 2005, for an earlier review). But before addressing the empirical evidence, it is perhaps useful to indicate clearly why knowledge is important. To do so, a short detour into democratic theory is required.

II. How Much Do Ordinary People Know About the Judiciary?

Conventional wisdom holds that ordinary people are woefully ignorant about law and courts. A number of studies, typically not done by serious academics, poke fun at the ignorance of the people, as for instance in reporting that Americans are more likely to be able to name Snow White's seven dwarfs than they are to be able to name the Justices of the United States Supreme Court, or that while 54% of those surveyed could name the judge on the popular television show, The People's Court, only 29% could name even one member of the U.S. Supreme Court (Morin, 1989).

A number of important normative issues flow from these empirical findings. Some believe that, because ordinary people are so poorly informed, the role of the mass public in the judicial process should be minimized. This view is particularly dominant in Europe. Often undergirding this belief is the argument that public influence over the judiciary is fundamentally at odds with the rule of law. Ordinary people know little about law and courts, but when they become engaged with legal issues, they seek improper or even illegal outcomes because their preferences are driven by emotion, not reason. The imagery of the mob is apposite here; when the mass public gets involved in legal controversies, the rule of law is often the first victim, or so the argument goes.

In the U.S. case, this fear of the mass public played a significant role in the thinking of the founders of the American Republic. No better example of this sentiment can be found than in the insulation of the federal judiciary, by appointment for life, from any meaningful accountability for its decisions. Under this theory, judges are "free" to "do the right thing," to use the rule of law to arrive at decisions in lawsuits. Similarly, the fact that in nearly every corner of the globe judges are appointed, not elected, indicates that institutional designers have routinely sought to minimize the accountability of judges to the mass public, even in democratic regimes.

Of course, the U.S. federal system of minuscule accountability has rarely been replicated even in the American states. Upwards of 90% of state judges (and therefore most judges in America) are subject to some form of electoral accountability (Brandenburg and Schotland, 2008: 102). Dating from the Jacksonian era, the American people were deemed capable of judging their judges and holding them to account for their decisions. Nowhere else in the world do citizens have so much potential direct control over their judiciary (Kritzer, 2007); in most countries, judges are regarded as technocrats, not makers of public policy, and therefore electoral accountability is non-existent.

Legal reformers have long abhorred making judges accountable to the mass public and, consequently, many movements are currently afoot in the United States that would re-direct accountability from the people to legal and political elites. Inevitably, these arguments invoke popular ignorance about things judicial. Ordinary people (it is said) are incapable of understanding legal arguments, including legalese, and therefore judicial affairs cannot be entrusted to them. Thus, the simple empirical issue of how much ordinary people know and understand about law and courts is tremendously important for a panoply of normative issues affecting legal systems.

So how ignorant are ordinary people of the third branch of government, the judiciary? Table 1 reports levels of knowledge among the American people, based on the findings of Gibson and Caldeira (2009b) and my 2008 Freedom and Tolerance Survey. The assumption undergirding these questions is that democratic politics profit from citizens knowing basic facts about the institutions that govern them. For the Supreme Court, key structural attributes are that the justices are appointed, not elected, for a life, not fixed, term. Functionally, the Supreme Court has the power of constitutional review (which in the U.S. is referred to as "judicial review"), giving it the "last say" over the meaning of the constitution; in the words of Chief Justice Rehnquist (*United States v. Morrison* [2000]): "No doubt the political branches have a role in interpreting and applying the Constitution, but ever since *Marbury* this Court has remained the ultimate expositor of the constitutional text."

Table 1: Knowledge of the United States Supreme Court 2001, 2005, 2008

	Percentages (rows total to 100% except for rounding errors)		
	Correct answer	Incorrect answer	Don't know
Justices are appointed			
2001	73.9	10.4	15.7
2005	65.4	14.9	19.7
2008	63.7	13.8	22.4
Justices serve a life term			
2001	66.4	16.1	17.4
2005	60.5	19.5	20.0
2008	59.0	19.2	21.8
Court has "last say" on the Constitution			
2001	60.7	28.4	10.9
2005	56.8	27.7	16.0
2008	53.8	31.9	14.3

Note:

2001 N = 1,418
2005 N = 1,000
2008 N = 800
The questions read:
Some judges in the U.S. are elected; others are appointed to the bench. Do you happen to know if the justices of the U.S. Supreme Court are elected or appointed to the bench?
Some judges in the United States serve for a set number of years; others serve a life term. Do you happen to know whether   the justices of the U.S. Supreme Court serve for a set number of years or whether they serve a life term?
Do you happen to know who has the last say when there is a conflict over the meaning of the Constitution—the U.S. Supreme Court, the U.S. Congress, or the President?

In every instance, a majority of the American people is able to answer these questions correctly. The questions vary slightly in difficulty, with it being fairly easy to know that justices are appointed, and relatively more difficult to know that the Supreme Court has the last say over the meaning of the constitution. The responses also vary slightly over time, with the period of the controversy over the 2000 presidential election (*Bush v. Gore*) representing the apogee of public knowledge. In 2008, across all three of these measures, 38.8% gave correct answers to all; 21.7% gave incorrect (or don't know) replies. A majority of the respondents (59.4 %) got at least two of the three items correct. In 2008, we asked two additional questions: one about "how many decisions with opinions the Court issues per year" (correct answer: "less than one hundred decisions with opinions each year"), and the other about whether a Supreme Court "decision is final and cannot be further reviewed" (correct answer: yes). For the former, 36.2% of the respondents answered correctly; the latter question was easier, with 42.8% knowing that a Supreme Court decision is final. Thus, across the five-item set of knowledge measures used in 2008, the percentage giving correct answers ranges from 36.2% to 63.7%. Given the conventional expectations of low public knowledge of law and politics, the actual level of such knowledge is impressively high.

Other researchers have also reported evidence of the competence of the mass public. For instance, Kritzer (2001: 37) discovered that nearly 72% of the American people know that the Supreme Court has control over its own docket, and that almost 75% know that the Court does not use juries to make its decisions. It is also true, however, that only 20% could say who the Chief Justice was (at the time of his survey, William Rehnquist). Nonetheless, Kritzer concludes (2001: 37): "One striking feature of the data is the relatively high awareness of the public."

There are fragmentary data from research outside the United States. For instance, Caldeira and Gibson (1995) report evidence on the awareness of ordinary Europeans of the high court of the European Union (EU), the European Court of Justice (ECJ). They discovered that the ECJ is "remarkably well known" among the mass publics of the EU (ibid: 361). Indeed, in a handful of countries, the ECJ is more widely known than the European Parliament. Caldeira and Gibson speculate that knowledge of the ECJ is connected to salient rulings by the Court; if so, people are likely more informed about this important political institution today than they were in the 1990s (the time of the Caldeira/Gibson survey).

While survey data on detailed knowledge about courts outside the United States do not appear to be available, Caldeira and Gibson do report evidence on awareness of the national high courts of the member states of the EU. In general, Europeans are more aware of their national high court than they are of the ECJ, a finding that is not surprising. Their data also indicate considerable cross-national variability in awareness, ranging from a high of 78% among residents of the former East Germany (no doubt due to the importance of the Federal Constitutional Court (FCC) for many issues associated with the reunification of Germany—e.g., abortion) to a low of 34% among the residents of Luxembourg. This empirical evidence indicates that the courts of Europe are far from being invisible to ordinary people.

Social scientists debate endlessly the question of how much political knowledge is required in order for one to be a competent democratic citizen. For a long time, the dominant view has been that citizens ought to be walking political almanacs, able to reach up into their memories and recall significant—and numerous—political facts at a moment's notice during an interview for a public opinion survey. Much of this research has assigned primacy to being able to associate political personalities with the offices they hold. A skillful democratic citizen should be able to tell an interviewer the position Tony Blair or Gordon Brown holds, what job Dick Cheney used to hold, and who pays the salary of John Roberts. Rather than knowing that baseball is played for nine innings, is refereed by an impartial umpire, and with three strikes one is out, this approach asks "who's on first," who hits the most, and, more recently, who is currently accused of using performance-enhancing drugs.

To be fair, this approach assumes that if one knows that John Roberts is "Chief Justice of the United States" (his official title) then one probably knows something more about the structure and function of the Supreme Court. This may be true. But the opposite side of this coin is more dubious; when one cannot answer the question "What job does John Roberts now hold?" it is not necessarily clear that one is entirely bereft of other information about the Supreme Court—e.g., that its Justices are appointed for life and are therefore not accountable for their decisions, or even that the Court makes enormously important public policy decisions in the American context. I daresay that if asked: "has the U.S. Supreme Court established any important policies with regard to the availability of abortions, the rights of criminal suspects, the rights of political and racial minorities, the use of the death penalty, or even whether one's house can be taken under the power of eminent domain?" vast proportions of the American people would easily answer "yes." After all, it is difficult to envisage an actual political scenario in which it would be necessary for citizens to be able to recall a judge's name without any prompting. Imagine, for example, the following Rehnquist-era conversation among three voters:

Voter 1: The Supreme Court is out of control, what with its decision to give Bush the presidency, the threats to a woman's right to choose whether to have an abortion, etc.

Voter 2: Yes, I agree. I bet it has to do with the Chief Justice, who, I think, is a staunch Republican.

Voter 1: Yeah, I agree. What is his name? I can't remember.

Voter 2: Neither can I, but the guy ought to be impeached.

Voter 3: I think his name is Rehnquist, Ringgold, or something like that.

Voter1: Maybe. But whatever his name is, we need a new judge on the Supreme Court. I guess I'll have to vote for the Democrats next time so as to get a better Supreme Court.

It is difficult to see that this conversation would be any more politically meaningful were the discussants able to remember the name of the Chief Justice. And, after all, even Richard Nixon, as he was about to nominate him to the Supreme Court, had difficulty remembering the Assistant Attorney General's name, referring to him instead as "Renchburg," at least according to John Dean (2001)!

But there is even a more basic fallacy in contemporary approaches to measuring political knowledge and that is that citizens must hold information in their minds that is readily accessible in response to the questions asked in public opinion surveys. The American National Election Study (ANES) regularly measures political knowledge by asking people to identify the position held by various political leaders, national and international. The question stem reads as follows:

Now we have a set of questions concerning various public figures. We want to see how much information about them gets out to the public from television, newspapers and the like.

In the 2008 study, ANES asked about "Nancy Pelosi," "Dick Cheney," "Gordon Brown," and "John Roberts."

Imagine how difficult it is to be asked to identify the job of Pelosi, Cheney, and Brown, and then "John Roberts." The context established by the first three questions is explicitly political; then comes the curve-ball (at least for those respondents who do not readily associate the Supreme Court with ordinary politics): John Roberts. As it turns out, in contemporary times, the Chief Justice's name, John Roberts, is a relatively common name, easily confused, for instance, with John Roberts, the host of the CNN show "American Morning." Finally, it is not at all clear why being able to spontaneously name a Supreme Court Justice is a useful skill for citizens. As simply a stimulus to measure political knowledge, perhaps "John Roberts" is useful (although the utility most likely also varies over time); as a measure of public knowledge of the U.S. Supreme Court, this variable, especially as it has been coded in the past, is practically useless as an indicator of public knowledge of the U.S. Supreme Court.

There are at least two ways one can think about measuring political knowledge. The first assumes that the stimuli are largely irrelevant and that the measures need only include items of varying degrees of difficulty. In this approach, stimuli are interchangeable so long as they are of the same degree of difficulty. The second approach attributes substantive significance to the stimulus. For instance, knowledge of the position held by John Roberts is often used as an indicator of the degree of Americans' knowledge of the U.S. Supreme Court. There are many issues about the measurement of political knowledge (e.g., would the results be the same were the respondents asked about Felipe Calderón instead of Gordon Brown?), but consideration of such issues is beyond the scope of this Chapter (see Mondak, 2001 for an excellent analysis). My focus here is on knowledge of law and courts; political scientists and legal scholars routinely use the ANES question on the Chief Justice to indicate that the American people are woefully ignorant when it comes to law and courts. My argument here is simply that they are wrong to do so.

A different approach to political knowledge is one that requires people to perform political tasks, like *becoming* informed, in contrast to *being* informed. In this view, being able to identify Dick Cheney as vice president of the United States is perhaps less important than being able to find out the government's policy on due process and the Guantanamo detainees, and to use that information in decision-making on political matters.

Moreover, people forget. Ordinary people do not walk around with the names of politicians on the tips of their tongue. Especially since judicial politics is often seasonal (e.g., in the United States, the Supreme Court announces most of its important opinions in June and July of each year; elections for judges are held at particular times of the year), it seems likely (and reasonable) that people would learn and unlearn political information as it varies in salience and relevance. Political knowledge often goes into hibernation; for example, although I have lived in Missouri for ten years, I have not thought about the Missouri Supreme Court for quite some time. But when it becomes important for citizens to become informed, many can do so. Nearly all Americans, for instance, had an opinion about whether Clarence Thomas ought to have been confirmed as a justice on the U.S. Supreme Court, 95% according to one study (Gimpel and Wolpert, 1996). While the Samuel Alito nomination was not as controversial as the Thomas nomination, roughly two-thirds of the population was aware of that nomination (Gibson and Caldeira, 2009c). I do not know the name of my plumber. But when the plumbing gets stopped up, I know how to get a plumber to come out and repair my plumbing. I may not know at any given moment who is most responsible for the detention camp at Guantanamo Bay. But when I hear discussion of this issue during the election season, I likely learn who is responsible (even if I might soon forget); and, perhaps more important, I learn which political party, not individual actor, is responsible. This understanding of what it means to be knowledgeable certainly makes it more difficult to study political knowledge— the concept and its measures are transformed from being static to dynamic entities. But just because something is difficult to study when it is properly conceptualized should not be excuse for inappropriate, or not useful, conceptualizations.

As I have indicated, democratic theorists typically assert that citizens in a democracy ought to have some level of knowledge of politics. At least some evidence indicates that they do. In the judicial case, however, being informed about law and courts is also important because of the consequences of that knowledge for attitudes toward the third branch.

III. The Consequence of Judicial Knowledge: Loyalty toward the U.S. Supreme Court

Politicians and scholars worldwide have long been impressed with the fragility of judicial power. When it comes to securing compliance with their decisions, courts are said to have neither the power of the "purse"—the ability to raise and expropriate money to encourage compliance—nor the power of the "sword"—the ability to coerce compliance. In the absence of these tools, courts really have only a single form of political capital: legitimacy. Compliance with court decisions is contingent upon judicial institutions being considered legitimate. Legitimacy is a normative concept, basically meaning that an institution is acting appropriately and correctly within its mandate. Generally speaking, a great deal of social science research has shown that people obey law more out of a felt normative compunction deriving from legitimacy than from instrumental calculations of the costs and benefits of compliance (e.g., Tyler, 1990).

As a consequence, political scientists have paid considerable attention to the legitimacy of courts. The empirical analysis of legitimacy dates back to Easton's (1965) work on "systems theory", with Easton substituting the phrase "diffuse support" for judgments of legitimacy. Diffuse support is a fundamental commitment to an institution and a willingness to support the institution that extends beyond mere satisfaction with the performance of the institution at the moment ("specific support"). The idea here is that institutions—especially courts—must be free to make decisions in opposition to the preferences of the majority; indeed, it is specifically a function of courts (at least in the American and many European cases, where the judiciary is vested with the power of having the last say on the meaning of the constitution) to overturn the actions of the majority when those actions infringe upon the fundamental rights of minorities. Courts must on occasion make hard decisions that are greatly displeasing to the majority, as in freeing obvious criminals due to violations of due process, restraining the majority from imposing its religious beliefs on the entire society, and spying on dissenters and malcontents who threaten the political security of the majority. If democracy can be simply defined as "majority rule, with institutionalized respect for the rights of the minority, especially rights allowing the minority to compete for political power," then the judiciary clearly represents the "minority rights" half of the equation. If courts are dependent upon majority approval for their decisions to be accepted, then one of the most important political functions of courts is in jeopardy.

This approach to legitimacy led Easton to coin a telling phrase: institutions require a "reservoir of goodwill" in order to function effectively. Gibson and Caldeira (2009a) liken this reservoir to loyalty, even to the loyalty between two friends. One may disappoint a friend without necessarily destroying the friendship. Loyalty to another requires standing by that other even when one might disapprove of the other's actions. Indeed, it is easy to be loyal to another who acts in an approving fashion; the test of loyalty involves disapproval or discontent. In similar fashion, institutions do not require legitimacy when they are satisfying people with their policies. Legitimacy becomes crucial in the context of dissatisfaction; legitimacy requires an "objection precondition." Problems of compliance do not typically arise when court decisions align with preferences; when they do not align, legitimacy or institutional loyalty provides the rationale for accepting or acquiescing to the ruling of a court.

This concept of legitimacy is related to unwillingness to punish institutions for their actions, which is historically important in the American case (see Whittington, 2003; Geyh, 2006) and of considerable contemporary relevance in the European case (see Schwartz, 2000). The federal judiciary, including the U.S. Supreme Court, is not the subject of much discussion in the American constitution. Indeed, practically none of the important aspects of the structure and function of the judiciary is determined by the constitution, ranging from the jurisdiction of the courts, to the size of the courts and the remuneration of judges, to fundamental powers, such as judicial review. To take just the simplest structural factor, the size of the U.S. Supreme Court can be changed by ordinary legislation, and in fact it has been changed several times throughout American history.

Political elites who are dissatisfied with court opinions often seek to punish the institution through structural or functional "reform" (see Friedman, 2005, 314–15, for U.S. examples, and Schwartz, 2000, for European examples). The most common such ploy is to try to alter the jurisdiction of the federal courts; every year numerous bills are introduced in Congress to prohibit the federal judiciary from ruling on various hot-button issues. For instance, the "Safeguarding Our Religious Liberties Act," H.R. 4379 (introduced by Representative Ron Paul from Texas) had the purpose of eliminating federal court jurisdiction over state and local policies regarding the free exercise or establishment of religion, any privacy claim related to issues of sexual practices, orientation, or reproduction, and any equal protection claim based on the right to marry without regard to sex or sexual orientation. The "Congressional Accountability for Judicial Activism Act of 2004" (introduced by Representative Ron Lewis of Kentucky and 26 co-sponsors in the House of Representatives) would have empowered Congress to reverse by a two-thirds vote any judgment of the U.S. Supreme Court that concerned the constitutionality of an Act of Congress (H.R. 3920). Specific, high-stakes Court decisions have drawn vicious and legitimacy-challenging criticism—as in the direct attack by various law professors on the Court's legitimacy after its ruling in *Bush v. Gore* (the case that effectively decided the 2000 Presidential election). Serious proposals to change the structure of the judiciary have been floated—e.g., various plans to convert the life tenure of Supreme Court judges to a fixed term. For instance, Farnsworth (2004: 2) asserts: "In recent years at least ten distinguished scholars (as well as two distinguished judges and a distinguished journalist) have proposed abolishing life tenure for Supreme Court Justices and replacing it with fixed terms of years in office." While not all dissatisfaction with judges in the U.S. is focused on the Supreme Court, there can be little doubt that the Justices of the Court are correct to worry about the implications of the current political climate in the country for the legitimacy of law and courts in general and their court in particular. Finally, some longitudinal studies of trust in the United States Supreme Court argue that partisan polarization in attitudes toward the Court has risen significantly in recent times (e.g., Mate and Wright, 2006), although the evidence of such a trend depends upon which survey series one looks at (Kritzer, 2005: 173; see also Gibson, 2007). From Roosevelt's court-packing scheme during the New Deal (which would have allowed Roosevelt to shift the balance on the Supreme Court by immediately appointing six new Justices) to contemporary refusal to increase the pay of federal judges, the legislative and executive branches have tried to impress on judges their vulnerability to political displeasure.

Similar controversies have emerged with European high courts. For instance, in Bulgaria, the National Assembly, controlled by the Bulgarian Socialist Party (BSP), passed the Law on Judicial Power, which included new retroactive rules for the Supreme Judicial Council and judiciary, including new eligibility requirements and new grounds for dismissal. In the ensuing conflict, the BSP ended up "slashing the budget for the entire judicial system. Again their actions were blocked by the Court" (Schwartz, 2000: 175–7). The situation was ultimately resolved by the fall of the BSP-controlled government later that year.

A similar case occurred in Slovakia, when the Constitutional Court of the Slovak Republic ruled against movements in the National Council by members of the Movement for Democratic Slovakia (HZDS), the party of then Slovakian prime-minister Vladimir Meciar. The HZDS proposed that some opposition members of the Council were not eligible and that their seats "be divided among the remaining parties, giving the HZDS and its coalition parties the three-fifths necessary to change the Constitution." When the Constitutional court ruled against this petition, "Meciar's government . . . took away [Chairman Milan] Cic's car and his bodyguard as 'economy measures'" (Schwartz, 2000: 199–207). Conflicts between the various branches of government are common in newly democratizing systems, and courts without popular legitimacy are particularly vulnerable to being punished by governments. (Schwartz, (2000: 47) describes similar incidents in Bulgaria and Russia.)

Elite efforts to punish courts often fail owing to the fundamental legitimacy of the judiciary among the ordinary people. Institutions with a "reservoir of goodwill" can survive institutional attacks if elite schemes do not resonate with the mass public. From this perspective, it is not difficult to understand how institutional legitimacy is seen by many as a more powerful form of political capital than purses and swords.

Political scientists routinely measure the legitimacy of courts via public opinion polls. Implicit in this approach, of course, is the fundamental assumption that the views of ordinary people matter. Many judges, lawyers, and legal scholars believe that elite opinion should dominate and that ordinary people are insufficiently well informed to have meaningful opinions of courts and judges. As it turns out, the empirical evidence from the American case is that the American people do indeed have meaningful attitudes toward the U.S. Supreme Court (Caldeira and Gibson, 1992).

One of the questions routinely used to measure institutional support requires respondents to either agree or disagree with the following statement: "If the U.S. Supreme Court started making a lot of decisions that most people disagree with, it might be better to do away with the Supreme Court altogether." It is not difficult to see the logic connecting this statement with the reservoir of goodwill notion. In effect, the item can be understood to say: "if a court makes a lot of bad decisions, I still support the fundamental integrity of the institution because I am loyal toward that institution." This statement and a handful of others have been used in surveys of public opinion conducted over the past 25 years. Data from surveys conducted by Gibson and Caldeira are reported in Table 2.

Perhaps the most useful way to understand Table 2 is to focus on the column labeled "Percentage Supportive." This is the percentage of all respondents giving answers indicating institutional loyalty. So for instance, in 1987, 77.7% of the respondents polled said the U.S. Supreme Court should not be done away with, even if it made decisions displeasing to people. Although there is some variability in the responses to the various measures of institutional support (as there should be), a number of important conclusions can be drawn from examination of the replies to these questions.

The first conclusion supported by these data is that the U.S. Supreme Court enjoys a very high level of institutional support. Big majorities of the American people do not want to do away with their Supreme Court; roughly a majority wants to protect the Court's jurisdiction; and sizable majorities trust the Court. These data do not indicate unanimity; but they do indicate that the institution enjoys a significant bedrock of support among the American people.

The same cannot be said of all constitutional courts in the world. Figure 1, assembled from various studies conducted primarily by Gibson and Caldeira, shows the responses to the "do away with" questions for more than 20 courts. The high level of support for the U.S. Supreme Court stands out in this figure; just as impressive are the very low levels of support enjoyed by the Bulgarian and South African Constitutional Courts. In comparative perspective, the U.S. Supreme Court is among the most legitimate high courts in the world. Perhaps more interesting is the relatively low level of support enjoyed by many European high courts, including courts in Spain, Ireland, France, Belgium, and Portugal. One possible explanation for these findings is that not all high court judges view their role as including efforts to reach out to ordinary people to justify their decisions and enhance the institutional legitimacy of their courts. Without such efforts, courts remain invisible, and invisibility undermines legitimacy (see the discussion below).

A second important conclusion from the data in Table 2 is that there has been little diminution in support for the U.S. Supreme Court over the past 25 or so years; none of the sets of percentages indicates any clear upward or downward trend over time. As one would expect, to the extent that institutional support is not contingent upon performance satisfaction, we observe practically no short-term changes in loyalty. It

Table 2: Loyalty Toward the United States Supreme Court, 1987–2008

Level of Diffuse Support for the Supreme Court

Item Year	Percentage			Mean	Std. Dev.	N
	Not Supportive	Undecided	Supportive			
Do away with the Court						
1987	9.4	12.9	77.7	3.9	0.9	1218
1995	16.8	7.2	76.0	3.8	1.0	803
2001	12.9	4.4	82.7	4.2	1.2	1418
2005	18.2	12.9	68.9	3.7	1.0	995
2007	13.6	12.5	73.8	3.9	1.0	902
2008	15.9	13.2	70.8	3.8	1.1	800
Limit the Court's jurisdiction						
1987	28.4	24.4	47.2	3.3	1.0	1216
1995	35.5	11.7	52.8	3.2	1.1	803
2001	28.3	11.0	60.7	3.6	1.3	1418
2005	32.4	16.2	51.4	3.2	1.1	996
2007	31.1	24.1	44.7	3.2	1.1	899
2008	30.0	25.2	44.8	3.2	1.1	800
Court can be trusted						
1987	–	—	—	—	—	—
1995	25.1	9.6	65.3	3.4	1.0	804
2001	17.0	5.1	77.8	3.9	1.2	1418
2005	18.7	15.8	65.5	3.5	0.9	996
2007	22.2	17.8	60.0	3.4	1.0	902
2008	21.0	18.8	60.2	3.4	1.1	799

Source: 1995–Gibson, Caldeira, and Baird, 1998, 350–1, Table 4.

Note: The percentages are calculated on the basis of collapsing the five-point Likert response set (e.g., "agree strongly" and "agree" responses are combined). The means and standard deviations are calculated on the uncollapsed distributions. Higher mean scores indicate more institutional loyalty.

The propositions are:

Do away with the Court:

1987: If the Supreme Court continually makes decisions that the people disagree with, it might be better to do away with the Court altogether.

1995/2001/2005/2007/2008: If the U.S. Supreme Court started making a lot of decisions that most people disagree with, it might be better to do away with the Supreme Court altogether.

Limit the Court's jurisdiction:

1987: The right of the Supreme Court to decide certain types of controversial issues should be limited by the Congress.

1995/2001/2005/2007/2008: The right of the Supreme Court to decide certain types of controversial issues should be reduced.

Court can be trusted:

1995/2001/2005/2007/2008: The Supreme Court can usually be trusted to make decisions that are right for the country as a whole.

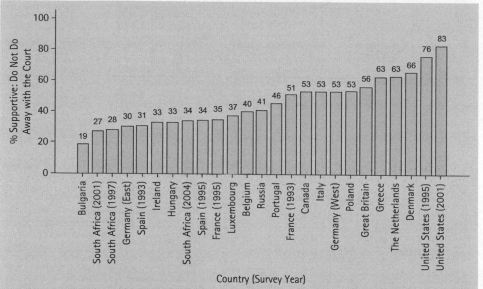

Figure 1. Cross-National Variability in Support for Constitutional Courts, Do Not Do Away with the Institution

Note: Most of these data are taken from Gibson, Caldeira, and Baird, 1998, Table 4, p. 340. When not otherwise indicated, the data are taken from surveys conducted in the period 1993–1995. For a few countries, more than a single survey is available; for these, the year of the survey is indicated in the country caption.

is important to note that the measure of institutional support used in Figure 1 is not a simple measure of the satisfaction with the specific decisions made by the Supreme Court. As reported by Gibson, Caldeira, and Spence (2003b), the correlation with performance satisfaction is only moderate, as it should be. The entire point of institutional loyalty is that support for the institution is not overly dependent upon short-term satisfaction with decisional outputs. The U.S. Supreme Court is generally judged to be doing a good job by a large proportion of the American people (e.g., Kritzer, 2005), but even when the Court makes unpopular decisions its legitimacy is not at risk.

One important exception to this conclusion must be noted: 2001, a time at which the U.S. Supreme Court seemed to enjoy a slight upward spike in its legitimacy. As it turns out, that particular survey, conducted around the time the U.S. Supreme Court decided the 2000 presidential election via its decision in *Bush v. Gore*, has been the object of considerable study and has generated some important conclusions about how support is formed and maintained.

Gibson, Caldeira, and Spence (2003a) discovered that the legitimacy of the U.S. Supreme Court was not harmed by its decision in *Bush v. Gore*. Indeed, while it is not surprising that support for the Court rose among Republicans—the winners in the decision—their findings indicate that support did not decline among Democrats.

Because of the reservoir of goodwill enjoyed by the Supreme Court, people were predisposed to view the decision as grounded in law, not politics, and they therefore accepted it. The 2000 presidential election controversy provides an outstanding example of the value of institutional legitimacy.

In-depth research on public attitudes toward courts other than the U.S. Supreme Court is sparse, but far from non-existent. In the American case, the theory of institutional legitimacy advanced by Gibson and Caldeira and others has been applied to lower federal courts (e.g., Benesh et al. 2009), state high courts (Gibson, 2008a), and to the American state courts (Benesh, 2006). Outside the United States, Gibson et al. (1998) reported an analysis of public support for the high courts of the EU member states in Europe, and Baird (2001) extended this research with a more detailed study of the legitimacy of the Federal Constitutional Court in Germany. In general, this research finds that older courts are more legitimate than younger courts, in part because courts are able to claim credit for "good decisions" but shirk blame for "bad decisions," that legitimacy is acquired in part from meeting the expectations of citizens (which themselves are not uniform), and that those more informed about courts tend to support them more. Their research also indicates a considerable degree of variability across countries in the legitimacy accorded to their national high courts.

The South African Constitutional Court is one court that has been the object of sustained research (e.g., Gibson and Caldeira, 2003; Gibson, 2004, 2008b), and the findings of that work support some interesting and perhaps more general theoretical conclusions. The researchers found that as a young court, the South African Constitutional Court enjoys little legitimacy. The court was created amidst partisan political controversy, and one of its earliest rulings, widely reported and condemned, invalidated the death penalty in South Africa. Unfortunately for the Court, the death penalty is much beloved by nearly all South Africans, of every race and class (Gibson, 2004; see also Spitz and Chaskalson, 2000). Finally, like many courts in the world, the South African Constitutional Court has made no concerted efforts to reach out to its constituents (the South African people),[1] and to try to take advantage of the enormously influential symbols of judicial power—the black robe, the honored form of address, etc. (see Gibson and Caldeira, 2009a). Legitimacy does not attach to courts automatically; unless an institution is mindful of the need to develop support among its constituents, support takes a long time to develop and can be relatively fragile.

Finally, I should note that some cross-national research exists on public trust in national judiciaries. For instance, Toharia (2003) reports survey data on trust in the judiciary, which he labels "social legitimacy," for the countries of the EU in

---

[1] This observation is based upon me living in South Africa for about one-third to one-half of the last decade and observing little outreach activity on the part of the Court, and on my discussions with two of the judges of the Constitutional Court. As a verifiable matter, the Constitutional Court, like many high courts in the world, resists televising its proceedings.

1999. By his measure (p. 29), trust is highest in Denmark (70%), lowest in Belgium (22%). Care must be taken with any measure of confidence or trust in institutions (or the leaders of the institutions); earlier research (Gibson et al., 2003b) has shown that confidence in an institution is more closely related to performance satisfaction (specific support) than to legitimacy (diffuse support). If so, then these measures tell us little about institutional legitimacy in that satisfaction with decisional outputs is both theoretically and empirically distinct from the sort of legitimacy considered in this Chapter. Nonetheless, this research is noteworthy in its attention to the preferences of the constituents of important judicial institutions.

A. Connecting knowledge to institutional support

Much of the literature on public knowledge begins with a vague model of what citizens must know about law and politics and why. As I have noted, being able to recall the name of a public official spontaneously, largely without context, is obviously thought by some scholars to be a mark of a good democratic citizen.

A more important consequence of political knowledge has been identified in the work of Gibson and Caldeira: those who are more knowledgeable about courts tend to extend more legitimacy to them (e.g., Gibson and Caldeira, 2009b). Indeed, this seems to be a tendency not at all limited to the United States (see Gibson et al., 1998 for cross-national evidence). Gibson and Caldeira posit that this "to know them is to love them" effect is largely a function of the knowledgeable being exposed to the

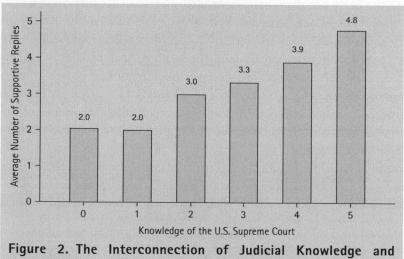

Figure 2. The Interconnection of Judicial Knowledge and Institutional Support

highly legitimizing symbols of judicial power: the black robe, the privileged form of address ("your honor"), the deference, even the temple-like building housing most courts.

To what degree is knowledge of courts associated with institutional support? Figure 2 reports the relationship between an index of court support and levels of political knowledge based on my 2008 Freedom and Tolerance Survey. The data clearly depict a strong relationship, with those who knew more about the Supreme Court tending to support the institution more strongly. Information per se is perhaps useful for citizens in a democracy. But in the case of courts, to know more is to have been exposed to the highly legitimating symbols of judicial power. Knowledge thus has an even more important consequence than is ordinarily recognized.

IV. The Impact of Court Decisions on Public Opinion

Institutional legitimacy provides judicial institutions the political capital they require in order to make decisions running contrary to the preferences of the majority. Legitimacy encourages citizens to accept decisions with which they disagree.

Scholars have also considered the hypothesis that courts are capable of changing the substantive policy views of citizens, thereby rendering the palliative effects of legitimacy unnecessary (see Franklin and Kosaki, 1989, regarding abortion; and Stoutenborough et al., 2006, regarding gay civil rights). To the extent that a court can persuade citizens to change their policy views in accordance with a ruling of the court, no objection precondition exists and the court need not mobilize its legitimacy to induce citizen acceptance (under the assumption that citizens routinely accept decisions with which they *agree*). Thus, a handful of research projects, conducted almost exclusively in the U.S., have been reported assessing the impact of court rulings on the distribution of public opinion on policy germane to the court ruling.

The general finding of this research is that courts are persuasive under some conditions and only with some citizens. Two factors seem to influence the degree of success courts have in shaping opinions. First, to the extent that a court is ruling on an established policy, citizens are likely to have crystallized attitudes that are resistant to change. It is unlikely, for instance, that a court decision could do much to alter the established attitudes of citizens toward issues such as the use of the death penalty, abortion, the right to carry guns, etc. Persuasion is most likely to occur when a court is ruling on a novel issue, such as the land rights of Aboriginal Australians (see Myers and Sheehan, 2009).

Second, court decisions are unlikely to be judged as authoritative by the entire population. We know, for instance, that the legitimacy of high courts varies considerably (see above) and that without legitimacy a court is unlikely to be viewed as a credible source by citizens. To the extent that a citizen views a court decision as grounded in politics, not legal reasoning, it is unlikely that the decision will generate attitude change (see Baird and Gangl, 2006; Gibson et al., 2005).

This theory of judicial influence is ultimately a theory of individual-level attitude change. Unfortunately, however, the bulk of the research on this question has been forced to rely upon aggregate-level data that make detailed understanding of change difficult. Moreover, studies typically do not include variables indicating the degree of crystallization of preexisting attitudes (see Johnson and Martin, 1998), the degree of legitimacy the citizen attributes to the court, or even measures of awareness of the decision hypothesized to cause attitude change. Consequently, research findings are inconsistent and bedeviled by difficult questions of causality. To the extent that courts can protect their authority by getting citizens to change their attitudes on substantive matters, legitimacy is less essential to courts. A great deal more research, however, must be conducted before the hypothesis of attitude change can be accepted.

V. THE EXPECTATIONS CITIZENS HOLD OF JUSTICES

Legitimacy is one of the most highly valued forms of political capital. Legitimacy, however, typically turns on institutional decision-makers satisfying expectations regarding the procedural components of their decision-making (see Tyler, 2006; Gibson et al., 2005). Citizens expect judges to make decisions in a fair and impartial way and when they do so, that process of decision-making, when it is made known to ordinary people, virtually automatically generates a sense of obligation to comply. Thus, the satisfaction of expectations is crucial to legitimacy.

We typically think of courts as subject to some defining sets of expectations, particularly the requirement that they be fair and impartial (Gibson, 2009). It seems quite reasonable to assume that the vast majority of citizens in a democratic polity expect their judges to make decisions in a fair and impartial way on the basis of the rule of law.

But these are of course not the only expectations citizens might hold of judges. They might, for instance, expect judges to make decisions that are fair and just, but it may very well be that in some instances fairness and the rule of law battle with one another.[2] In the instance of conflict between justice and legality, some may prefer that fairness trump legality; others prefer that legality be deemed superior to fairness. The expectations citizens hold matter (Gibson and Caldeira, 2009a).

Furthermore, in many instances, the technical aspects of legal decisions are nearly irrelevant to rendering conclusions. Under such conditions—the condition under which law is not dispositive and broad discretion exists on how decisions should be made (e.g., in imposing criminal sentences, or in dealing with novel issues of law, conflicting legal precedents, or ambiguous statutory language)—citizens may expect that judges take into account the wider values of the society in making their decisions, something that can be seen in the post-war evolution of family law in the United States in response to changing cultural values (see Jacob, 1988). Of course, not all citizens will agree that judges should make such decisions; some may believe that decisions ought to be made only on the basis of the intent of those creating the legislation and constitutions. If citizens understand decision-making to be discretionary in the sense that judges must choose their course of action rather than deduce it, then it follows that law cannot be the only legitimate basis of decision-making. But again, citizens likely differ on these issues. The essential point here is that expectations matter and that expectations vary across citizens.

I have presented here a simple theory of expectations. It is doubtful, however, that expectations are themselves quite so simple. Citizens may expect many things from their judicial institutions and the things they expect may not be internally coherent or consistent. Some citizens may understand the judiciary as "just another political institution," whereas others may view the judiciary as a unique institution that should act in a fashion quite distinct from other political institutions. Citizens vary on this score. In a society in which courts are well-defined, quite salient public institutions, often rendering important public-policy decisions (such as in the United States), citizens may have reasonably well developed but diverse understandings and expectations of courts.

Institutional legitimacy is ultimately grounded in the satisfaction of the expectations of the citizenry. In the case of courts (but perhaps more broadly as well), the expectations primarily concern processes of decision-making inasmuch as courts are the most procedurally self-conscious and constrained of all political institutions. It is crucial, therefore, to understand the nature of these expectations.

Scholars of the legislative process have paid significant attention to citizens' expectations (e.g., Kimball and Patterson, 1997) but only a handful of studies have seriously considered the expectations citizens hold of judges and courts. Focusing on public attitudes toward the German Federal Constitutional Court, Baird (2001)

---

[2] Throughout this Chapter I treat "fairness" and "justice" as synonyms.

shows that the nature of the expectations citizens hold of the FCC, and especially expectations of legalistic styles of decision-making, is related to the willingness to attribute legitimacy to the institution—legalism enhances legitimacy and acquiescence (see also Baird and Gangl, 2006).

Gibson and Caldeira (2009a) report an analysis of Americans' expectations of courts based on the responses of a representative sample to the following question: "Now I would like you to focus on thinking about the characteristics of a good Supreme Court judge, that is, what a good judge ought to be like. First, how important would you say it is for a good Supreme Court judge to [INSERT ITEM]?" The attributes about which they queried the respondents are reported in Table 3, along with the importance the American people ascribe to these characteristics.

The data clearly reveal that Americans expect their Supreme Court Justices to maintain the appearance of fairness and impartiality (75.5%) (and also, no doubt, to

Table 3: Expectations of the Characteristics of a Good Supreme Court Justice

Characteristic	% Rating It Very Important	Mean[a]	Std. Dev.	N
Appear fair & impartial	75.5	3.66	.70	334
Protect people without power	71.7	3.62	.69	334
Uphold constitutional values	67.4	3.59	.68	335
Strictly follow the law	61.7	3.47	.80	334
Independent of president and government	60.9	3.47	.77	334
Respect existing decisions	37.3	3.11	.89	334
Represent the majority	36.0	2.84	1.10	334
Give my ideology a voice	32.9	2.95	.95	335
Base decisions on party affiliations	17.8	2.08	1.12	333

The items read:

"Now I would like you to focus on thinking about the characteristics of a good Supreme Court judge, that is, what a good judge ought to be like. First, how important would you say it is for a good Supreme Court judge to...

Try to maintain the appearance of being fair and impartial no matter what the cost.

Be especially concerned about protecting people without power from people and groups with power.

Uphold the values of those who wrote our constitution two hundred years ago.

Strictly follow the law no matter what people in the country may want.

Stay entirely independent of the president and the government.

Respect existing Supreme Court decisions by changing the law as little as possible.

Be involved in politics, since ultimately they should represent the majority.

Give (conservatives/liberals) a strong voice in how the constitution is interpreted.

Base their decisions on whether they are a Republican or a Democrat.

[a] The response varies from (1) Not at all important/Don't know to (4) Very important. Thus, higher mean scores indicate greater ascribed importance to the characteristic.

act in a fair and impartial way, inasmuch as few citizens prefer unfairness and bias to fairness and impartiality, and in the sense that it is reasonable to assume that if citizens prefer the *appearance* of impartiality they also prefer the *actuality* of impartiality), to be especially concerned about protecting people without power from those with power (71.7%), and to uphold long-standing constitutional values (67.4%). Perhaps the most surprising finding in these data is the relatively small weight that Americans give to respecting existing Supreme Court decisions (only 37.3% rate it as very important). Across the set of items, the average number of characteristics judged to be extremely important is 3.7 (with a median of 4). Virtually all respondents found something on our list to rate as very important.

Perhaps the most notable finding from Table 3 is that a sizable constituency exists in favor of a relatively politicized mode of judging. Nearly one-third of the respondents want judges who will give their ideologies a voice on the bench; nearly one-fifth want decisions based on partisanship. There can be no doubt that these expectations are complicated. But it is clear that Americans are not united in the expectation that judges engage in some form of mechanical jurisprudence. Many Americans seem to recognize and accept the inherently political nature of courts.

VI. CONCLUDING COMMENTS

Social science interest in the questions of how knowledgeable ordinary people are about law and politics is being rekindled, with the result that a significant revisionist group has emerged centered on the view that earlier studies both underestimated political knowledge and emphasized a particular type of knowledge that is actually of limited value when it comes to citizens in a democracy discharging their duties. The new thinking about knowledge is still emerging, but its most important attribute is that it views the acquisition and use of information as dynamic. Citizens learn, but they also unlearn, they forget. Moreover, citizens acquire knowledge when it is useful to do so, and, since political and legal activity is often seasonal, it matters exactly when pollsters are inquiring about levels of information. Citizens use political information; when it is no longer useful, they often discard it.

Previous research on knowledge has focused a great deal on political personalities and the ability to recall the names of people occupying specific political positions. When given a list of names and asked to associate those names with positions, ordinary people do vastly better on knowledge tests. Unfortunately, methodological questions about how best to measure political knowledge are crucial to understanding substantive results, and, at present, many methodological questions remain unanswered.

Knowledge is important because it is a strong contributor to perceptions of institutional legitimacy. It may be that information per se is not so important, but rather that in the process of acquiring information, people are exposed to and accept the symbols of judicial authority. From this viewpoint, it is not so essential that people acquire discrete bits of information; more important is that they pay attention to and engage with judicial institutions.

No aspect of the interconnections between courts and ordinary people is as important as the willingness to attribute legitimacy to the judiciary. Without legitimacy, courts are impotent. Available evidence indicates that national high courts differ greatly in the legitimacy they have acquired. Future research should focus on the processes through which courts become salient to ordinary people and how interactions with courts, especially judicial symbols, contribute to institutional legitimacy.

Finally, researchers are only beginning to investigate the expectations citizens hold of the third branch. Much additional work needs to be done, but at a minimum there is variability in what citizens want from courts and a significant minority seems to prefer a fairly politicized model of judging.

The most general conclusion to be drawn from this analysis is that the views of ordinary people are increasingly recognized by scholars as important for the effective functioning of the judiciary. In the past, scholars were dismissive of research on the attitudes and views of the mass public. Given the emerging findings on political and judicial knowledge and the connection of knowledge and perceived legitimacy, that view can no longer be justified.

REFERENCES

Baird, V.A. (2001). "Building Institutional Legitimacy: The Role of Procedural Justice," *Political Research Quarterly* 54(2) June: 333–54.

Baird, V.A. and Gangl, A. (2006). "Shattering the Myth of Legality: The Impact of the Media's Framing on Supreme Court Procedures on Perceptions of Fairness," *Political Psychology* 27(4) (August): 597–614.

Benesh, S.C. (2006). "Understanding Public Confidence in American Courts," *Journal of Politics* 68: 697–707.

Benesh, S.C., Steigerwalt, A., and Scherer, N. (2009). "Public Perceptions of the Lower Federal Courts," (#3, August), available at <http://ssrn.com/abstract=1443434>.

Brandenburg, B. and Schotland, R.A. (2008). "Keeping Courts Impartial Amid Changing Judicial Elections," *Daedalus* 137(4) (Fall): 102–9.

Caldeira, G.A. and Gibson, J.L. (1992). "The Etiology of Public Support for the Supreme Court," *American Journal of Political Science* 36(3) (August): 635–64.

Caldeira, G.A. and Gibson, J.L. (1995). "The Legitimacy of the Court of Justice in the European Union: Models of Institutional Support," *American Political Science Review* 89(2) (June): 356–76.

Caldeira, G.A. and McGuire, K.T. (2005). "What Americans Know About the Courts and Why It Matters," in K.L. Hall and K.T. McGuire (eds.), *Institutions of American Democracy: The Judiciary*, New York: Oxford University Press: 262–79.

Dean, J.W. (2001). *The Rehnquist Choice: The Untold Story of the Nixon Appointment That Redefined the Supreme Court*, New York: The Free Press.

Easton, D. (1953). *The Political System, An Inquiry into the State of Political Science*, New York: A. Knopf.

Easton, D. (1965). *A Systems Analysis of Political Life*, New York: John Wiley & Son, Inc.

Farnsworth, W. (2004). *The Regulation of Turnover on the Supreme Court*, Boston University School of Law, Working Paper Series, Public Law & Legal Theory, Working Paper No. 04–18.

Franklin, C. and Kosaki, L.C. (1989). "Republican Schoolmaster: The US Supreme Court, Public Opinion, and Abortion," *American Political Science Review* 83 (3, September): 751–73.

Friedman, B. (2005). "The Politics of Judicial Review," *Texas Law Review* 84 (2, December): 257–337.

Geyh, C.G. (2006). *When Courts & Congress Collide: The Struggle for Control of America's Judicial System*. Ann Arbor: The University of Michigan Press.

Gibson, J.L. (2004). *Overcoming Apartheid: Can Truth Reconcile a Divided Nation?*, New York: Russell Sage Foundation.

Gibson, J.L. (2007). "The Legitimacy of the US Supreme Court in a Polarized Polity," *Journal of Empirical Legal Studies* 4(3) (November): 507–38.

Gibson, J.L. (2008a). "Challenges to the Impartiality of State Supreme Courts: Legitimacy Theory and "New-Style" Judicial Campaigns," *American Political Science Review* 102(1) February: 59–75.

Gibson, J.L. (2008b). "The Evolving Legitimacy of the South African Constitutional Court," in F. du Bois and A. du Bois-Pedain (eds.), *Justice and Reconciliation in Post-Apartheid South Africa*, New York: Cambridge University Press, 229–66.

Gibson, J.L. (2009). "Judging the Politics of Judging: Are Politicians in Robes Inevitably Illegitimate?," Paper presented at the *What's Law Got To Do With It?* conference, Bloomington: Indiana University School of Law, March 27–29, 2009.

Gibson, J.L. and Caldeira, G.A. (2003). "Defenders of Democracy? Legitimacy, Popular Acceptance, and the South African Constitutional Court," *The Journal of Politics* 65(1) February: 1–30.

Gibson, J.L. and Caldeira, G.A. (2009a). *Citizens, Courts, and Confirmations: Positivity Theory and the Judgments of the American People*, Princeton, NJ: Princeton University Press.

Gibson, J.L. and Caldeira, G.A. (2009b). "Knowing the Supreme Court? A Reconsideration of Public Ignorance of the High Court," *The Journal of Politics* 71(2) April: 429–41.

Gibson, J.L. and Caldeira, G.A. (2009c). "Confirmation Politics and the Legitimacy of the US Supreme Court: Institutional Loyalty, Positivity Bias, and the Alito Nomination," *American Journal of Political Science* 53(1) (January): 139–55.

Gibson, J.L., Caldeira, G.A., and Baird, V. (1998). "On the Legitimacy of National High Courts," *American Political Science Review* 92 (2, June): 343–58.

Gibson, J.L., Caldeira, G.A., and Spence, L.K. (2003a). "The Supreme Court and the US Presidential Election of 2000: Wounds, Self-Inflicted or Otherwise?' *British Journal of Political Science* 33 (#4, October): 535–56.

Gibson, J.L., Caldeira, G.A., and Spence, L.K. (2003b). "Measuring Attitudes toward the United States Supreme Court," *American Journal of Political Science* 47(2) (April): 354–67.

Gibson, J.L., Caldeira, G.A., and Spence, L.K. (2005). "Why Do People Accept Public Policies They Oppose? Testing Legitimacy Theory with a Survey-Based Experiment," *Political Research Quarterly* 58(2) (June): 187–201.

Gimpel, J.G. and Wolpert, R.M. (1996). "Opinion-Holding and Public Attitudes toward Controversial Supreme Court Nominees," *Political Research Quarterly* 49 (#1, March): 163–76.

Jacob, H. (1988). *Silent Revolution: The Transformation of Divorce Law in the United States*, Chicago: University of Chicago Press.

Johnson, T.R. and Martin, A.D. (1998). "The Public's Conditional Response to the Supreme Court," *American Political Science Review* 92 (#2, June): 299–304.

Kimball, D.C. and Patterson, S.C. (1997). "Living Up to Expectations: Public Attitudes Toward Congress," *The Journal of Politics* 59(3) (August): 701–28.

Kritzer, H.M. (2001). "The Impact of Bush v. Gore on Public Perceptions and Knowledge of the Supreme Court," *Judicature* 85(1) (July–August): 32–8.

Kritzer, H.M. (2005). "The American Public's Assessment of the Rehnquist Court," *Judicature* 89(3) November–December: 168–76.

Kritzer, H.M. (2007). "Law Is the Mere Continuation of Politics by Different Means: American Judicial Selection in the Twenty-First Century," *DePaul Law Review* 56(2) Winter: 423–67.

Mate, M. and Wright, M. (2006). "*Bush v. Gore* and the Micro-foundations of Public Support for the Supreme Court," Paper presented at the 2006 Annual Meeting of the American Political Science Association, September 2, 2006, Philadelphia, PA.

Mondak, J.J. (2001). "Developing Valid Knowledge Scales," *American Journal of Political Science* 45(1) (January): 224–38.

Morin, R. (1989). "Wapner v. Rehnquist: No Contest; TV Judge Vastly Outpolls Justices in Test of Public Recognition," *The Washington Post* (June 23): A21.

Myers, W. and Sheehan, R.S. (2009). "The Australian High Court and Attitudes Toward Aborigines: A Test of Court Influence on Australian Public Opinion," Paper delivered at the 2009 Annual Meeting of the American Political Science Association, September 3–6, Toronto, Ontario.

Schwartz, H. (2000). *The Struggle for Constitutional Justice in Post-Communist Europe*, Chicago: University of Chicago Press.

Spitz, R. and Chaskalson, M. (2000). *The Politics of Transition: A Hidden History of South Africa's Negotiated Settlement*, Johannesburg: Witwatersrand University Press.

Stoutenborough, J.W., Haider-Markel, D.P., and Allen, M.D. (2006). "Reassessing the Impact of Supreme Court Decisions on Public Opinion: Gay Civil Rights Cases," *Political Research Quarterly* 59(3) (September): 419–33.

Sunstein, C.R., Schkade, D., Ellman, L.M., and Andres Sawicki, A. (2006). *Are Judges Political? An Empirical Analysis of the Federal Judiciary*, Washington, DC: Brookings Institution Press.

Toharia, J.J. (2003). "Judicial Systems in Western Europe: Comparative Indicators of Legal Professionals, Courts, Litigation, and Budgets in the 1990s," in E.G. Jensen and T.C. Heller (eds.), *Beyond Common Knowledge: Empirical Approaches to the Rule of Law*, Stanford, CA: Stanford University Press: 21–62.

Tyler, T.R. (1990). *Why People Follow the Law: Procedural Justice, Legitimacy, and Compliance*, New Haven: Yale University Press.

Tyler, T.R. (2006). "Psychological Perspectives on Legitimacy and Legitimation," *Annual Review of Psychology* 57: 375–400.

Whittington, K.E. (2003). "Legislative Sanctions and the Strategic Environment of Judicial Review," *International Journal of Constitutional Law* 1(3): 446–74.

35

LEGAL EDUCATION AND THE LEGAL ACADEMY

FIONA COWNIE

I. INTRODUCTION

ALTHOUGH many legal academics are deeply involved in researching legal phenomena, relatively few of them have chosen to research aspects of the law schools in which they work, or the way in which law is taught, either theoretically or empirically. This is not unusual in the academy; observers have long noted that academics tend to study everything but themselves (Clark, 1987: 2).

Examining empirical research on legal education reveals a story of increasing sophistication in both the methods and the analysis used in this area. Early work was often small-scale in nature; many of the studies were not methodologically sophisticated and the results obtained were thus of limited interest. Although there is much of practical utility for law teachers in learning about the classroom practices of colleagues that would otherwise go unnoticed, legal education research suffered from a tendency to be rather descriptive and narrow in focus. This is no longer true of the best work in the area, which is as methodologically and analytically sophisticated as empirical research in other areas of law.

Another noticeable feature of research into legal education is that it is predominantly found in common law jurisdictions, such as the UK, U.S., Australia, Canada, New Zealand, and South Africa. There is very little research into legal education in civil law jurisdictions, such as those on continental Europe, or in other parts of the world. This is partly because of the different cultures of academic law which exist in the different jurisdictions. In common law jurisdictions it is more acceptable to research aspects of legal education, as opposed to a substantive area of law, such as company law or international law. In other countries, however, such research is frequently regarded as the province of the discipline of education, not law, and academic lawyers are not encouraged to research the pedagogical aspects of their discipline. The different standing of legal education research is clearly reflected, for instance, in the history of academic journals on legal education: in the United States, the first issue of the *Journal of Legal Education* was published in 1948, while the first issue of *The Law Teacher* was published in the UK in 1967 and the first issue of the Australian *Legal Education Review* in 1989. However, the first issue of the *European Journal of Legal Education* was only published in 2004. Many other jurisdictions have no specialist legal education journals at all.

Such empirical research on legal education and the legal academy as has been undertaken by a relatively small cohort of researchers can be divided into three main categories: work on legal pedagogy, focusing on the ways in which law is taught, including surveys of the teaching of individual subjects, such as company law (for example, Snaith, 1990); work on the legal academy as an institution, such as the periodic surveys of UK law schools which started in 1966 and have continued to the present day (see, for example, Harris and Jones, 1997) and work on the students and staff who populate the law school, such as Thornton's study of the changing higher education environment as experienced by Australian legal academics (Thornton, 2007).

When considering empirical research into the legal academy, it is important to be aware of the variations in contexts within which law schools operate in different jurisdictions. In some places, university legal education includes not only the education of students in an academic sense, involving study of the content of the law, theoretical analysis of legal phenomena and so on, but also the vocational education of students, training them in the skills which they will need to become practicing lawyers, such as advocacy and drafting. In some jurisdictions, such as England and Wales, the academic stage of legal education and the vocational stage are clearly separated, and only a minority of university law schools are involved in the delivery of vocational training. Vocational training in England and Wales is delivered by the College of Law and a limited number of universities (for intending solicitors) or by the Inns of Court School of Law and some universities (for intending barristers). In the U.S. the law degree is a graduate program which contains more vocational elements than is the case in England and Wales, such as courses in professional responsibility (Perry, 2008: 160). However, in almost all American states law graduates must also pass state licensing examinations before they can practice law, which is a significant hurdle (Rush and Matsuo, 2007: 225). The significance of these different emphases for empirical research in legal education is that such work may include studies both of the academic and of the vocational aspects of legal education.

Due to the differing kinds of legal education which may be offered in different countries around the world, it is particularly important to remember that law schools, the legal academics who work in them, the students who study the law, and the curricula that they study frequently differ, not just in minor details, but in fundamental ways, including, for example, the relationship that law schools have with the legal professions in the jurisdiction in which they are situated. In some jurisdictions, such as England and Wales, the legal professions have played a decreasing role in regulating the content of academic legal education, giving university law schools correspondingly more independence (Cownie and Cocks, 2009: Ch. 10). Although the profession sets out requirements which university law schools must satisfy if their students are to be able to use their law degrees as a qualification to move on to the vocational stage of their training, the requirements which must be satisfied have become less detailed over time, so that they now comprise a series of broad statements rather than detailed curricula (Boon and Webb, 2008: 80). In other jurisdictions the legal profession plays a major role in regulating legal education. In the United States, for example, the American Bar Association has a considerable influence on the legal education through, for instance, the formal accreditation of law schools. All this means that comparisons among aspects of legal education in different jurisdictions can be made but, if they are to be accurate, they need to be sensitive to the cultural context to the matters being discussed (Bradney, 2007).

II. Exploring Legal Pedagogy

Pedagogy has been one of the most popular areas for those undertaking empirical research on legal education. Law teachers, faced with challenges such as teaching law to non-lawyers, or the introduction of a new method of assessment, and wishing to discover more about the process in which they are engaged, have embarked on empirical research, often primarily for their own purposes as reflective practitioners, and have then published the results. Early work in this area tended to be somewhat descriptive and parochial, although this was not true of all such work, and some of the earlier empirical studies relating to legal education have provided interesting information about a range of aspects of law teaching. In the UK a number of surveys relating to the teaching of particular subjects offered the opportunity for law teachers to reflect on their own practice in the light of comprehensive information about what others were doing. Today, these surveys remain of interest because they provide historical data which can afford interesting insights into law teaching then and now. Cotterrell and Woodliffe's survey of jurisprudence teaching revealed that in the early 1970s in the UK jurisprudence was a compulsory subject in the vast majority of universities (Cotterrell and Woodliffe, 1974: 78). Although Hart and Austin featured in most courses, there was usually an attempt to balance the teaching of traditional forms of jurisprudence with other more modern approaches, often informed by sociology. Frequently, students were taught by experts in other disciplines, such as philosophy, and this interdisciplinary approach was underpinned by the fact that many jurisprudence teachers themselves had qualifications or experience in disciplines other than law (ibid). Harris and Beinart's much more recent survey of UK law schools shows that by the academic year 2002–2003 jurisprudence (or legal theory) was a compulsory subject in just under half of the law schools responding (with a response rate of 71% of all UK law schools), although more than three times as many "new" universities reported no coverage at all, as compared with "old" universities[1] (Harris and Beinart, 2005: 311). Comparing the two sets of data reveals a marked decline in the compulsory status of jurisprudence in the past 30 years. Similarly, Lynch et al.'s survey of English Legal System and Legal Method courses, carried out from 1991–1993, uncovered the fact that there was a high degree of consensus in UK law schools about the need for foundational legal instruction which provided not only basic information about the legal system, but instruction in the skills necessary to use legal materials (Lynch et al., 1992). This finding continues to be of interest, given that the teaching of legal skills was not highly developed at the time of that survey, in contrast to the situation today when publishers offer large numbers of textbooks focusing on the whole range of legal skills needed by law students for the effective study of academic law from analyzing legal materials, such as case reports or statutes, to writing legal essays and exam technique (see, for example, Bradney et al., 2005; Carr et al., 2009; Finch and Fafinski, 2009). Lynch et al.'s work

---

[1] "New" universities are those which became universities after the abolition of the "binary divide" between universities and polytechnics by the Further and Higher Education Act 1992.

serves to remind us of the speed with which legal skills as a distinct subject has entered the academic legal curriculum in the UK.

More recently, more of the empirical studies of legal pedagogy have begun to exhibit a greater awareness of the need to adopt a rigorous approach to methodology and also to situate findings within the relevant theoretical literature. This approach is reflected in the research carried out by Fisher et al. (2007) in Australia on the teaching of Alternative Dispute Resolution (ADR). ADR features increasingly in law school curricula in Australia, reflecting the increasing role of ADR in the legal system. Importantly, practicing lawyers in Australia have a duty to advise their clients of ADR options, so that, the authors argue, "Most lawyers are exposed to ADR in some way and are called upon to use their skills as collaborative problem solvers rather than 'hired guns'" (ibid: 68). The question which interested the researchers was whether the teaching of ADR results in any attitudinal change on the part of law students, who are otherwise mostly exposed to a traditional, adversarial approach to lawyering. The empirical project undertaken was a pilot study of teaching ADR as a compulsory subject to first-year law students at La Trobe University in 2005. Its broad conclusion was that the students exhibited a significant movement away from the view that lawyers' negotiations must be adversarial, accompanied by a shift toward client empowerment and away from lawyer intervention, thus valuing broader client needs over narrow legal entitlements (ibid: 82–4). However, what sets this article apart from earlier empirical work on legal pedagogy is its extensive discussion of methodology, and the willingness of the authors to be self-critical when reflecting on the method they used; the limitations of the study, both in terms of the overall formulation of the survey instrument and of individual questions, are openly discussed in a way which would have been unthinkable in early empirical studies of legal education (ibid: 93–5).

In contrast to other jurisdictions, there has been a large quantity of empirical research focused on legal pedagogy carried out in the United States, much of it published in the *Journal of Legal Education*, as well as in monographs. One of the most impressive recent studies is that carried out by Elizabeth Mertz, in which she examines the intellectual transformation process experienced by first-year law students when they begin to learn to "think like a lawyer" (Mertz, 2007). This process has been much criticized over the years, including in a very well-known article by Duncan Kennedy ("Legal Education and the Reproduction of Hierarchy") in which Kennedy drew attention to the way in which legal education traditionally taught students to separate the legal and moral aspects of conflicts and to exclude any concern with equity, fairness and so on from their analyses of legal problems on the basis that as lawyers, their concern was solely with the legal aspects of a conflict, not with the moral aspects (Kennedy, 1982). While many others have studied the phenomenon of "thinking like a lawyer," what is impressive about Mertz's study is the detailed nature of her data, obtained from observations and interviews with students and staff in a range of law schools of varying status, mission and location (Mertz, 2007: Ch. 3). Mertz argues that legal education involves students being initiated into distinctively legal ways of approaching knowledge, so that they begin to talk and think in new ways about conflicts; it is an initiation into a particular linguistic and textual tradition (Mertz, 2007: 4).

In her analysis of the ways in which law teachers educate their students, Mertz provides us with detailed evidence about precisely what goes on in law school classrooms: analyzing how students are taught to read legal materials in a particular way, she points out that a crucial aspect of a legal reading is the selection of what lawyers call "the facts" (i.e., the *legal* narrative of what happened). When students are called upon to recite "the facts," they are learning to create a new, legally defined narrative of what occurred, and once they have mastered this, they will know how to create versions of conflict stories that are acceptable to courts and judges (ibid: 67). In analyzing her data, Mertz gives us examples of classroom exchanges between teachers and students which demonstrate how fact-construction is learned.

[P]rofessors will push students to enunciate details that seem picky in the extreme. In the following exchange, an otherwise well-prepared student bogs down when asked for such a detail, one that is important to the resolution of the case, but that might easily escape the eye of an average lay reader attempting to tell the story of a conflict between people:

Transcript 4.4 [3/3/7]

Prof: Wait, wait, was there a contract for the delivery of wheat! No, for the sale of wheat, right? A contract for the sale of wheat?

Student: Right.

Prof: Okay, and so what was the price of wheat?

Student: Well, the delivery to (price at the) time of delivery.

Prof: When was the time of delivery?

Student: Specifically? Ah (pause).

Mertz draws our attention to the repeated questioning, with its minute attention to detail, and the message the professor is trying to get across—that a good legal reading of facts might entail some background investigation of pertinent legally-relevant features. "It is not good enough to simply gloss over or guess at the meaning of key features of important facts" (ibid: 69). Mertz's study thus provides new insights into the significance of language in the process of learning to "think like a lawyer," arguing that the students' transformation is as much a shift in how they approach language—how they talk and read and write—as in how they "think" (ibid: Ch. 9). This study represents the best of research in legal education, bringing new insights to a fundamental feature of the law school experience which has interested researchers for many years.

III. PEOPLE IN THE LAW SCHOOL

In many jurisdictions there is a surprisingly modest amount of empirical research which examines aspects of the law student experience and the lived experience of being a legal academic. This may be because the primary interests of the majority of legal academics lie solely within their chosen area of law, be that tax or civil liberties, medical law or environmental law, rather than in the way that law is taught or researched. For educationalists and other researchers outside the discipline of law, legal education, with its image as relating to the technical subject of law, often strongly connected to the legal profession, has been of little interest. Whatever the reason, in many jurisdictions, this is an area which is greatly under-researched. As with research into legal pedagogy, however, this is not true of the United States, where a significant body of literature exists, both about the student experience and about university law teachers.

Despite the general lack of research in this area outside the United States, the experience of female law teachers has generated a significant amount of interest from researchers around the world. In 1999 the Association of American Law Schools ran a workshop for women in legal education entitled "Getting Unstuck—Without Coming Unglued" for which Robbins and Okonska (1999) compiled a 35-page bibliography, the majority of which is composed of material specifically relating to the legal academy. Much, though not all, of the work cited in that bibliography is empirical, and it remains true that the position of women in the legal academy has excited the interest of empirical researchers in a number of jurisdictions. In Australia, Margaret Thornton's empirically based book on women in the legal profession, *Dissonance and Distrust*, included a chapter on women in the legal academy, in which she drew attention to the "benchmark men" who represent the "core of the university club" (Thornton, 1996: 108). She argued that the legal academy is particularly resistant to the idea of women as purveyors of legal knowledge, embracing instead the idea that men, as the "knowers," create knowledge while women teach it, thus contributing to the effacement of the feminine within the constitution of legal knowledge (ibid: 111). Female academics are tolerated by the institution provided that they adopt one of a limited range of subject positions, all of which are characterized by conventional notions of the feminine, in that they emphasize qualities such as deference, docility, diligence, care, and self-sacrifice. Essentially, their role is to be "dutiful daughters"; the pastoral care of students is one of the "appropriate" roles which women are allocated. Resistance to such stereotyping is met with criticism. One of Thornton's respondents commented that women do not have access to the same networks as men, nor are they invited to lunch with senior academics; if they wish to further their career they have to seek these things out: "Then, if you do look after yourself, you get the kind of response that I got from one of the deans: 'You know, why are you so interested in yourself, you should think of the law school for a change'" (ibid: 113). Thornton also argued that women legal academics are discriminated against by being denied access to permanent positions and promotion on the same terms as their male colleagues, noting a comment from one of her respondents that: "The dean told me that the senior tutorship had been downgraded to a tutorship, which I found out afterwards must have been a lie and that I was simply being hired at the lowest possible salary in order to free up some money for other purposes in the law school" (ibid: 116). Thornton concluded that:

the expansion in higher education and the demand for legal services have accommodated the "letting in" of women as a class. However, the technocratic mechanisms of bureaucracy, the new managerialism, and economic rationality, in conjunction with a dramatic increase in the number of students, have been utilised in an endeavour to maintain women academics as a docile labour force... (ibid: 128).

Some of Thornton's findings were echoed by those of McGlynn (1998), in her examination of the UK legal academy, also contained in a book which was primarily about women in the legal profession. McGlynn's survey of all UK university law schools, carried out in 1997, obtained a 93% response rate, giving her sound data. At that time, women formed 46% of lecturers, but only 14% of professors; 63% of law schools had no women professors at all (ibid: 41). McGlynn adopted Thornton's analysis of the marginalization of women in the law school, pointing to empirical evidence of inequality of pay and differential promotion practices (ibid: 47–8). In considering the position of women in the legal academy, however, McGlynn sounds a slightly more positive note, arguing that although many academics may be inclined to resist the increased scrutiny and quality assessment which have been introduced to higher education, such scrutiny may bring with it exactly the sort of transparency which many feminists have been calling for in an attempt to overcome the marginalization of women in the academy (ibid: 56).

More recently, Wells's study of women law professors in the UK focused on the effect of gender on the careers of those women who have achieved "success" within the law school. Wells was particularly interested in discovering whether women's experiences changed as they became more senior members of the academy (Wells, 2002: 2). One of the things to which she draws attention is the way in which although a substantial majority of the cohort of 37 women thought that gender had affected their career, or their relationships with colleagues and students, there was a distinct tendency for the respondents to think that gender was relevant, but not a real disadvantage (ibid: 11). However, several of those who reported that gender had not affected their career drew attention, when interviewed, to instances in their careers when they had experienced gender-related problems. Wells comments "They perhaps did not see or want to see themselves as victims (especially as they were objectively 'successful'). It appeared important to these women to emphasise that they had not received any special treatment, which may have reflected an overall political value system which assumes that appointments and promotion are the result of meritocratic processes" (ibid, 12). Yet instances of stereotyping abounded: one of Wells's respondents commented "Years ago I remember complaining at a union meeting about how few women there were on a university committee. Within a week, someone rang to ask if I'd like to be on the committee which supervised the university nursery" (ibid: 15).

One of the things that Wells noted was the increased tendency of her respondents to relate "gender stories" when the subject of promotion was mentioned. Several of the women had experienced difficulties with promotion, including one respondent who decided, after several attempts at internal promotion had been unsuccessful, to apply for posts in other institutions: "The last time I was rejected for promotion I was on the shortlist for three chairs. The man who was promoted was not shortlisted for the only one of these posts he applied for and remains an SL [senior lecturer] 10 years later" (ibid: 21). Those female professors who had been head of their law school reported that gender affected their performance of this role as well: "I think it is easier to be seen as weak because I am not aggressive or vindictive" (Wells, 2002: 31). Overall, Wells found that women law professors did think that gender was a significant factor affecting their careers, although she uncovered a complex picture, with a diversity of perceptions of gender effects, and significant variations between institutions. Organizational cultures emerged as an important dimension, with those who had worked in more than one law school often having quite different experiences in different institutions (ibid: 35). Wells's research illustrates clearly the potential of more focused studies to throw light on taken-for-granted aspects of the lived experience of the legal academy; as Wells herself points out, much more remains to be discovered.

Turning to studies of the legal academy as a whole, Thornton's study of legal academics in 25 Australian universities places the legal academy in the context of a higher education sector which she characterizes as moving from social liberalism (in which higher education was seen as a public good) to neo-liberalism (which espouses market values). Thornton argues that these political changes have been accompanied by a move from elite to mass higher education, where "the focus is on applied and vocational knowledge." Accompanying changes have included the charging of high fees, transformation of the teacher-student relationship into one of "customer" and "service provider," and a narrowing of the law school curriculum "in a way that supports the market" (Thornton, 2007: 1). In addition, underfunding of higher education has caused a move away from innovative teaching methods (which are generally more resource-intensive) to a much more traditional approach. Thornton's respondents commented adversely on the changes they were experiencing:

I'm used to teaching legal theory in a seminar context. Here, the class is going to be 300 and there's going to be two lecture groups—two lectures a week and one tutorial, and I'm quite alarmed about teaching legal theory by pontificating from the front....

[Lectures of 2–3 hours are] exhausting, and by the end of yesterday, I had covered too much material, but I felt I had to get the material covered for the purposes of the course (ibid: 13–14).

Thornton argues that assessment has been similarly affected, with greater use of traditional unseen examinations, "a mode that is peculiarly suited to the cramming and regurgitation of doctrine" (ibid: 16). One of her respondents reflected that:

Instead of 60 pieces of work to mark, we've now got 100 ... We might have a theoretical piece in the first session of property, but I'm going to have to do away with that now. I'm marking them all, and there will just have to be a problem that I can mark quickly rather than a theoretical piece that takes longer to mark (ibid: 17).

Thornton comments that "as a result of abolishing essays altogether, or making them optional, it is now possible for a student to go through law school without having done a single research paper" (ibid: 17). Overall, she is not optimistic about the future of legal education in Australia. Her only hope is that the pendulum might swing back toward social liberalism again, though she sees no sign of that happening unaided, and urges legal academics to "stand up and start pushing before even more depredations occur" (ibid: 26).

In the UK there has been a growing interest in empirical work exploring aspects of legal academic life. Vick et al.'s research (1998) on the Research Assessment Exercise in the UK provides some interesting empirical evidence about a key aspect of the working lives of those legal academics who are involved in research. The Research Assessment Exercise (the most recent version of which is called the Research Excellence Framework) is a periodic exercise carried out on behalf of the UK Government by the Higher Education Funding Councils, which assesses the quality of the research submitted by academics (see, for example, <http://www .hefce.ac.uk>). Vick et al.'s research, in keeping with the modern trend, provides detailed analysis of the methodology used; such transparency increases the reader's confidence in the findings. A significant proportion of legal academics in the study (representing a 40% response rate from a random sample of 993 academics) were unconvinced that the RAE provided an objective assessment of their research, but believed that their departments valued their research on the basis of how they were perceived to perform in the context of the RAE (Vick et al., 1998: 546). The significance of the RAE could also be seen in appointment and promotion practices. Unpromoted staff perceived the exercise in significantly more negative terms than professors, and women were particularly likely to perceive the RAE as discouraging departmental cohesiveness and having a negative impact on relationships with colleagues, as well as causing stress (ibid: 552). Despite comments by members of the RAE panel to the contrary, there was a strong perception that publication in a relatively small number of "high-quality" journals would be rewarded in the RAE exercise (ibid: 556). This article was followed by another, focused on the question of journals, which had proved to be so significant in the first survey (Campbell et al., 1999). This additional research, based on empirical data gained from a comprehensive survey of legal academics in the UK found that not only was there a widely-held belief that success in the RAE depended upon publication in a "high quality" journal, but that there was considerable consensus about which journals fell into this category, with journals such as the *Harvard Law Review*, the *Oxford Journal of Legal Studies*, and the *Modern Law Review* identified as some of the most desirable in which to publish, though many specialist journals were also highly regarded by those working in specific sub-disciplines (ibid: 486).

Spencer and Kent focused on another research-related aspect of the UK legal academy when they investigated sabbaticals (Spencer and Kent, 2007). It was perhaps not surprising that they discovered differences in sabbatical policies as between "old" and "new" universities, suggesting that sabbatical leave is one way in which differences between these types of institutions are perpetuated; although the situation was complex, with some research-active new university departments providing sabbaticals in an effort to increase research output in much the same way as old universities (ibid: 673). However, more interesting in many ways was their finding that there may be limits to the effects on individual academic lives of what is commonly called "the new managerialism." Heads of Department reported that sabbaticals were rarely refused, leading the researchers to comment that this was counter to the rigidly enforced, target-driven policies which they would have expected to see in a strongly mangerialist culture (ibid: 665).

Cownie's extended study of English legal academics, based on in-depth interviews with 54 law teachers of varying levels of seniority and experience, found, as Thornton did, a strong perception that the higher education context within which they work had become more bureaucratic, with those working in new universities expressing particular concerns about an increasingly "managerial" environment, focusing on "results," "performance," and "outcomes" (Cownie, 2004: 107). This response from a mid-career female lecturer in a new university succinctly expresses the attitude of many respondents:

I dislike the fact that, it all ties in with management, with internal politics, with a lack of apparent awareness on the part of many senior people about how the rest of us work, about different workloads.... We seem to have a whole host of people in management positions now, and fewer and fewer people doing teaching, and yet still the place isn't brilliantly managed (ibid: 108).

However, the academics in Cownie's study remained wedded to delivering a liberal education in law. Their main aim was to teach their students to think, and if that was achieved, it was up to the students to decide whether or not they wished to use their legal skills and knowledge to become practicing lawyers:

I'm probably trying to get them to think. That's the main thing I'm trying to do. I'm trying to get them to develop the thinking processes which are necessary to help them to approach any material (Lecturer, early-career, female, new university) (ibid: 76).

Unlike the academics Thornton interviewed in Australia, Cownie's respondents were not returning to a traditional, doctrinal approach to teaching and researching law. On the contrary, it appeared that they were part of a discipline which is becoming more socio-legal and less practitioner-oriented, and which is taking UK academic lawyers ever closer to the heart of the university (ibid: 58).

Work on law students, as opposed to law teachers, has covered a range of topics. In the UK a relatively early study by Sherr and Webb (1989) explored the socialization effects of undergraduate legal education at the University of Warwick. Their finding that students wanted the curriculum to be practical rather than theoretical, with an emphasis on "thinking like a lawyer" (ibid: 246) anticipated the results of a much larger longitudinal study of law students in England and Wales carried out by the Law Society's Research and Policy Planning Unit. In the first report arising out of that study, published in 1994, the data clearly showed that undergraduate law students had a much more vocationally oriented approach to their degrees than did the legal academics who taught them. This was particularly the case at Oxford and Cambridge, and in other "old" universities (Halpern, 1994: 37). Meanwhile, Rochette and Pue's survey of law students' curriculum choices at the University of British Columbia during the 1990s discovered that, contrary to the views of some practicing lawyers, law graduates in Canada selected the overwhelming majority of their courses from traditional "core" subjects, suggesting that students' actual experience of contemporary Canadian legal education (as opposed to the education they have the opportunity to receive) may be narrower and more traditional than had been thought (Rochette and Pue, 2001: 190).

Unsurprisingly, there is a large amount of research on law students in the United States. An interesting example of the American work on students is the large body of empirical research into the impact of law school on student values. Such studies have consistently shown that while a substantial proportion of students entering law school are interested in careers in "public interest law," serving disadvantaged sectors of society, that interest wanes significantly during their time in law school (see, e.g., Erlanger, 1978; Granfield, 1992; Erlanger et al., 1996). Guinier et al.'s (1994) study "Becoming Gentlemen" is a classic example of the best type of research into legal education. Carried out in the early 1990s at the University of Pennsylvania Law School (described as "typical, if elite"), this study drew on a wide range of data, including academic performance data, self-reported survey data, written narratives and group interviews, to examine the ways in which the law school experience of female law students differed markedly from that of their male peers (ibid: 2). One of the reasons this research has become a much-cited classic is that it went beyond earlier research, both in being more methodologically sophisticated and in adopting a critical, analytical approach as opposed to merely describing what was found. Starting with quantitative data on academic performance, the researchers found that women and men began their career at Pennsylvania (Penn) law school "with equally stellar credentials," but that women graduated with "significantly less distinguished academic credentials" (ibid: 21). During the second and third years of study, men were twice as likely to reach the top 10% of the cohort, and as a consequence of their disproportionately low rankings women were underrepresented in the Law School's prestigious positions and extracurricular activities, many of which were allocated on the basis of academic performance (ibid: 26–8). One of the researchers, a former student at Penn, related how some of her male colleagues selected classes based on the number of women enrolled in each class, believing (correctly, as the researchers discovered) that their own chances of getting higher grades increased as the number of women enrolled in the class increased, because the women would absorb a disproportionate number of the lower grades (ibid: 32–3).

The researchers also discovered that female law students were significantly less likely than male students to ask questions or volunteer answers in class, and that the male students received more attention from their teachers, both in class and post-class "follow-up" (ibid: 33). These differences were particularly acute in the first year of study; by the third year, the women were either more tolerant of what they had regarded as offensive incidents of sexism, or the number of such incidents had diminished (ibid: 38). This apparent change in women's attitudes was accompanied by others. The researchers noted that many more women than men came to law school expressing a commitment to public interest law; but over the three years, the gender differences reduced, so that by the third year women students came to sound more like their male classmates and significantly less like their first-year "selves." The researchers comment: "One could conclude that women become more 'like men' over time.... Yet women's academic performance does not mirror that of men.... Attitudinally they become closer to men; academically they move apart" (ibid: 41). The qualitative data reflected women's profoundly negative experience of law school, especially in the first year; they expressed profound alienation from the law school, and also from their former selves, the people they used to be. The use of the Socratic method of teaching in large first-year classes (which involves the teacher asking students questions in front of the whole group) reinforced feelings of alienation and inadequacy. This method can easily be used to intimidate or establish a hierarchy within large classes and women often reported that they could not learn in such an intimidating environment, especially when contributions made by women were treated with derision or disrespect:

Women's sexuality becomes the focus for keeping us in our place. If someone was rumoured to be a woman who speaks too much, she was a lesbian.... Now I'm in a room with 120 frat boys, a mass of faces that say nothing when you speak. No feedback from professors. No one cares what you did, and who you were, people hiss, laugh, and there is rarely an interruption of that from other students or professors. We need to change class size and how classes are taught so that men and women can speak publicly, and not self-consciously, in front of others (ibid: 52).

The researchers concluded that "becoming gentlemen" exacts an academic cost for many women, pointing out that it is likely that there is a psychological link between self-confidence and academic performance; students who are alienated by the learning process are arguably not well prepared psychologically to succeed in examinations (ibid: 62). Socratic teaching, in particular, was seen as disabling for women, especially if it is designed to intimidate. Overall, some women disengage from the law school because they find its adversarial nature, its focus on argumentation and its emphasis on abstract as opposed to contextual reasoning to be unappealing (ibid: 65). The research thus forms the basis for a strong conclusion that since traditional methods of legal education clearly disadvantage a significant group of students (most, but not all, female) there is reason to change educational practices in law schools, for instance by introducing more diverse teaching styles, and more emphasis on cooperative approaches to problem-solving rather than adversarial approaches (ibid: 93–8). Overall, this article illustrates how the best empirical research in legal education can address fundamental issues of great significance, not only accurately recording "what actually goes on," but also grounding those findings in the relevant literature, drawing on other theoretical research (in education and psychology, for example) to explain and analyze what has been discovered.

IV. THE LAW SCHOOL AND LEGAL EDUCATION

The UK is fortunate in having a large set of data about legal education which has been gathered intermittently but quite regularly, since 1966, when the Society of Public Teachers of Law (now the Society of Legal Scholars) was prompted by the Chair of its Legal Education Sub-Committee, Professor Montrose, of Queen's University Belfast, to undertake a comprehensive survey of legal education to provide concrete evidence with which to inform contemporary debates (Cownie and Cocks, 2009: 93). Introducing the report of the first survey, its author, J.F. Wilson, noted that there was "an almost total lack of information concerning the present organization of law schools and the opinions of those teaching law" (Wilson, 1966: 5). The first survey now offers fascinating insights into law teaching and legal education as it was over 40 years ago, drawing our attention to the comparatively small number of law schools and law students, and a curriculum which, in contrast to the situation in many contemporary law schools, largely consisted of compulsory subjects (ibid: 8, 44). More recently, the surveys have charted the changing range of subjects on offer, with media law, insolvency law, and gender and the law appearing, while courses which had at one time been compulsory in many law schools, such as Roman law, have declined in popularity (see Harris and Jones, 1997: 51). In the most recent survey (Harris and Beinart, 2005), undertaken in 2002, subjects such as planning law, housing law and welfare law appear to be on the decline, while gender and the law is holding its own, and new subjects include sport law and child law (ibid:

314). As compared with the previous survey, the number of students graduating with first or upper second class degrees increased from 27% to 41%, particularly in "old" universities, reflecting the general trend in UK universities (Universities UK, 2007: 24) while on average 60% of students in single honors law degrees courses are female, reflecting the growing numbers of women participating in higher education (ibid: 332–34). As well as documenting changes in the landscape of legal education, these surveys provide a rich source of data for the legal historian, which arguably has yet to be fully exploited.

In Canada, the highly influential "Arthurs Report" on legal education, *Law and Learning*, with its emphasis on the concept of "humane professionalism" as being the fundamental aim of legal education, included data which was specifically collected for the Consultative Group on Law and Learning, which then published The Arthurs Committee Report (Arthurs, 1983). The Committee commissioned several research reports, and two of these in particular throw light on law schools and legal academics in Canada (McKennirey, 1982a, 1982b). While the research for the Arthurs Report found a variety of views about the purposes of legal education, overall, Canadian legal academics exhibited a strong desire to offer a liberal education in law, and saw themselves as producing humane professionals rather than technocrats.

Our knowledge of American legal education has recently been informed by an investigation undertaken, under the aegis of the Carnegie Foundation, as part of a series of comparative studies which examine how the members of different professions are educated (Sullivan et al., 2007). Members of the research team visited 16 law schools in America and Canada, chosen to be geographically diverse, with different missions, including one historically black school as well as others distinctive for their attention to Native American and First Nation peoples and their concerns, and others which represented innovations in legal education judged by the researchers to be important (ibid: 16). The authors of the study were interested in the ways in which law schools develop legal understanding and form professional identities (ibid: 3). An important context of their analysis was an awareness of the balance between two competing influences on law schools—the community of practitioners, focused on the craft of lawyering, and the modern research university, with its emphasis on theory and abstract ideas; and an acknowledgment that the position of the law school, poised between these two ideologies, has often led to conflict between defenders of theoretical legal learning and champions of a legal education that includes training in the actual practice of law (ibid: 8). One of the significant findings of the study was the efficiency with which law schools were able to impart a distinctive way of thinking to their students. "Within months of their arrival in law school, students demonstrate new capacities for understanding legal processes, for seeing both sides of legal arguments, for sifting through facts and precedents in search of the more plausible account, for using precise language, and for understanding the applications and conflicts of legal rules" (ibid: 186). Another interesting finding, particularly in the light of the other studies discussed in this section, was that the process of enabling students to learn to "think like a lawyer" "took place primarily through the medium of a single form of teaching—the case-dialogue method" (ibid). The researchers found that legal pedagogy is remarkably homogeneous, and is accompanied by a remarkably standardized first-year curriculum and a standard system of grading. As the researchers comment: "In particular, the academic setting of most law school training emphasises the priority of analytical thinking in which students learn to categorize and discuss persons and events in highly generalised terms. This emphasis on analysis and system has profound effects in shaping a legal frame of mind. It conveys at a deep, largely uncritical level an understanding of the law as a formal and rational system, however much its doctrines and rules may diverge from the commonsense understandings of the layperson" (ibid). The authors of the report are very keen to put forward what they call an "integrative strategy" for legal education. They support the fusion of the academic and vocational aspects of legal education, recommending that all aspects of what they term "the legal apprenticeship" should be given equal weight by law schools, in contrast to the current model of legal education in which cognitive (or academic) education dominates the law school, and the other practical aspects of the apprenticeship are tacitly thought of as adjuncts (ibid: 191). This is a vision of legal education which is very clearly tied to a professional model.

A major review of Australian legal education was undertaken by a committee of legal education specialists appointed by the Commonwealth Government who published their report (the Pearce Report) in 1987. The focus of this enquiry was on the efficient delivery and the quality of legal education; but in common with reports in other jurisdictions, there was also mention of more theoretical concerns, with a suggestion that "all law schools should examine the adequacy of their attention to theoretical and critical perspectives, including the study of law in operation and the study of relations between law and other social forces" (Pearce et al., 1987: 149). In the early 1990s, empirical data was gathered from Australian law schools in an effort to assess the impact of the Pearce Report (McInnes and Marginson, 1994). It found that the Pearce Report appeared to have had some significant effects—for example, all law schools had "embraced aspects of theory, reflection, and law in action" and that law schools were paying much more attention to skills teaching than they had previously (ibid: 155).

In 2000, as part of its review of the federal civil justice system, the Australian Law Reform Commission examined educational changes necessary to give effect to its reform proposals for civil litigation. *Inter alia* it recommended that serious consideration should be given to commissioning another national discipline review of legal education in Australia (ALRC, 2000: 145, para 2.100). This recommendation was implemented when research into legal education was commissioned by the Australian Universities Teaching Committee. The resulting report (Johnstone and Vignaendra, 2003) aimed to capture the changes in Australian legal education in the previous 15 years or so. Drawing on data from all but one of the Australian university law schools, the report draws attention to some of the significant changes in Australian legal education during that time. One of the main developments was a significant trend toward the teaching of legal skills. Until the late 1980s, Australian law schools did little to teach practical legal skills (those needed for legal practice), such as drafting and negotiation, but there has been a considerable change in more recent times, and now the majority of Australian law schools have a commitment to covering the major areas of law relevant to practice. They also consciously encourage the development of ethical legal practice and legal ethics commonly forms part of the curriculum. However, the researchers report that law schools appear to be divided on the *importance* of practical legal skills, with about a third of schools taking a low-key approach to their inclusion in the curriculum (ibid: Ch. 18). While there does not appear to be any greater engagement in the scholarship of teaching by Australian law teachers as compared with law teachers in other jurisdictions, the researchers found that Australian law teachers displayed a much greater concern with student-focused teaching than they had done previously, and (in contrast to the situation in America) Australian law teachers are increasingly turning to the use of discussion-based teaching methods and small group work to supplement, or in some cases to replace, traditional lectures. These new methods of teaching are supported by a much greater variety of teaching materials than was the case a decade ago, many of them available on the Web (ibid: Ch. 18). Like other examples of the best of empirical research in legal education, this report provides a range of information about Australian law teaching which can inform debates and discussion about legal education not just in Australia, but also in other jurisdictions.

V. RESEARCH IN LEGAL EDUCATION

While the quantity of empirical research in legal education is not great, it is an area which has developed exponentially in recent years in terms of sophistication and rigor. It is no longer sufficient merely to describe a "clever little idea" about a new way to teach students the law of contract or EU law. The best researchers in legal education draw on a wide variety of disciplines to analyze the data they uncover in new and original ways. They are sophisticated in their use of methodology, and continue to look for new perspectives to throw light on all aspects of the law school and legal education.

REFERENCES

Arthurs, H.W. (1983). *Law and Learning*, Report to the Social Sciences and Humanities Research Council of Canada by the Consultative Group on Research and Education in Law (H.W. Arthurs, Chairman), Ottawa: SSHRCC.

Australian Law Reform Commission (2000). *Managing Justice: A Review of the Federal Civil Justice System* (Report No 89) Canberra, AGPS.

Boon, A. and Webb, J. (2008). "Legal Education and Training in England and Wales: Back to the Future?," *Journal of Legal Education* 58: 79.

Bradney, A. (2007). "Can There Be Commensurability in Comparative Legal Education? *Canadian Legal Education Annual Review/Revue de l'enseignment de droit au Canada* 1: 67–84.

Bradney, A., Cownie, F., Masson, J., Neal, A., and Newell, D. (2005). *How To Study Law* (5th edn.), London: Sweet and Maxwell.

Campbell, K., Vick, D.W., Murray, A.D., and Little, G.F. (1999). "Journal Publishing, Journal Reputation and the United Kingdom's Research Assessment Exercise," *Journal of Law and Society* 26: 470.

Carr, H., Carter, S., and Horsey, K. (2009). *Skills for Law Students*, Oxford: Oxford University Press.

Clark, B.R. (1987). *The Academic Life. Small Worlds, Different Worlds*, Princeton: Carnegie Foundation.

Cotterrell, R.B.M. and Woodliffe, J.C. (1974). "The Teaching of Jurisprudence in British Universities," *Journal of the Society of Public Teachers of Law (NS)* 13: 73.

Cownie, F. (2004). *Legal Academics: culture and identities*, Oxford: Hart Publishing.

Cownie, F. and Cocks, R. (2009). *A Great and Noble Occupation! The History of the Society of Legal Scholars*, Oxford: Hart Publishing.

Erlanger, H. (1978). "Young Lawyers and Work in the Public Interest," *American Bar Foundation Research Journal* 83.

Erlanger, H., Epp, C., Cahill, M., and Haines, K. (1996). "Law Student Idealism and Job Choice: Some New Data on an Old Question," *Law and Society Review* 8: 95.

Finch, E. and Fafinski, S. (2009). *Legal Skills* (2nd edn.), Oxford: Oxford University Press.

Fisher, T., Gutman, J., and Martens, E. (2007). "Why Teach ADR to Law Students? Part 2: An Empirical Survey," *Legal Education Review* 17: 67.

Granfield, R. (1992). *Making Elite Lawyers: Visions of Law at Harvard and Beyond*, New York: Routledge.

Guinier, L., Fine, M., Balin, J., with Bartow, A. and Stachel, D.L. (1994). "Becoming Gentlemen: Women's Experiences At One Ivy League Law School," *University of Pennsylvania Law Review* 143: 1.

Halpern, D. (1994). *Entry Into The Legal Profession: The Law Student Cohort Study Years 1 and 2*, London: The Law Society.

Harris, P. and Beinart, S. (2005). "A Survey of Law Teachers in the United Kingdom, 2004," *The Law Teacher* 39(3): 299.

Harris, P. and Jones, M. (1997). "A Survey of Law Schools in the United Kingdom, 1996," *The Law Teacher* 31(1): 38.

Johnstone, R. and Vignaendra, S. (2003). *Learning Outcomes and Curriculum Development in Law*, Canberra: AUTC.

Kennedy, D. (1982). "Legal Education and the Reproduction of Hierarchy," *Journal of Legal Education* 32: 591.

Lynch, B., Moodie, P., and Salter, D. (1992). "The Teaching of Foundational Legal Instruction," *The Law Teacher* 216.

McGlynn, C. (1998). *The Woman Lawyer: Making the Difference*, London: Butterworths.

McInnes, C. and Marginson, S. (1994). *Australian Law Schools After the Pearce Report*, Canberra, AGPS.

McKennirey, J.S. (1982a). *Canadian Law Professors: A report to the Consultative Group on Research and Education in Law, based on the 1981 survey of full-time professors in Canada*, Ottawa: SSHRCC.

McKennirey, J.S. (1982b). *Canadian Law Faculties: A report to the Consultative Group on Research and Education in Law, based on the 1981 survey of law faculties and statistics of the Canadian Deans of Law*, Ottawa: SSHRCC.

Mertz, E. (2007). *The Language of Law School: learning to "Think Like A Lawyer,"* New York: Oxford University Press.

Ormrod, R. Lord Justice (1971). *Report of the Committee on Legal Education*, Cmnd 4595, London: HMSO.

Pearce, D., Campbell, E., and Harding, D. (1987). *Australian Law Schools: A Discipline Assessment for the Commonwealth Tertiary Education Commission*, Canberra: AGPS.

Perry, J. (2008). "Thinking Like A Professional," *Journal of Legal Education* 58: 159.

Robbins, S. and Okonska, M. (1999). *Bibliography on Women in Legal Education*, available at <http://www.aals.org/wle99/biblio.html>.

Rochette, A. and Pue, W. (2001). "'Back to Basics?' University Legal Education and 21st Century Professionalism," *Windsor Yearbook of Access to Justice* 20: 167.

Rush, D.K. and Matsuo, H. (2007). "Does Law School Curriculum Affect Bar Examination Passage? An Empirical Analysis of Factors Related to Bar Examination Passage During the Years 2001 Through 2006 at a Midwestern Law School," *Journal of Legal Education* 57: 224.

Sherr, A. and Webb, J. (1989). "Law Students, the External Market and Socialization: Do We Make Them Turn to the City?," *Journal of Law and Society* 16(2): 225.

Snaith, I. (1990). "Company Law on Degree Courses: Survey Report," *The Company Lawyer* 11(9): 177.

Spencer, M. and Kent, P. (2007). "Perpetuating Difference: law school sabbaticals in the era of performativity," *Legal Studies* 27: 649.

Sullivan, W.M., Colby, A., Welch Wegner, J., Bond, L., and Shulman, L. (2007). *Educating Lawyers: Preparation for the Profession of Law*, San Francisco: Jossey-Bass.

Thornton, M. (1996). *Dissonance and Distrust: Women in the Legal Profession*, Melbourne: Oxford University Press.

Thornton, M. (2007). "The Law School, the Market and the New Knowledge Economy," *Legal Education Review* 17(2): 1.

Universities UK (2007). *Beyond the Honours Degree Classification*, Burgess Group Final Report London: Universities UK.

Vick, D.W., Murray, A.D., Little, G.F., and Campbell, K. (1998). "The Perceptions of Academic Lawyers Concerning the Effects of the United Kingdom Research Assessment Exercise," *Journal of Law and Society* 25: 536.

Wells, C. (2002). "Women Law Professors—Negotiating and Transcending Gender Identities at Work," *Feminist Legal Studies* 10: 1.

Wilson, J.F. (1966). "A Survey of Legal Education in the United Kingdom," *Journal of the Society of Public Teachers of Law (NS)* 9: 1.

PART II

DOING AND USING EMPIRICAL LEGAL RESEARCH

THE (NEARLY) FORGOTTEN EARLY EMPIRICAL LEGAL RESEARCH

HERBERT M. KRITZER

I. Introduction

In 2008, one of the leading American scholars of bankruptcy law and practice published a co-authored article presenting an empirical analysis of the high fees charged by professionals involved in handling bankruptcy cases in the U.S. bankruptcy court (LoPucki and Doherty, 2008). The findings reported probably did not come as a great surprise to anyone who has paid significant attention to the bankruptcy process. However, that same attentive audience for empirical research on modern bankruptcy practice may be surprised to learn that there is a substantial body of *empirical* scholarship on the bankruptcy process—including costs, duration, outcomes—that preceded this contemporary study by about 80 years.

More generally, most of those in the community of scholars engaged in the empirical study of legal phenomena are probably aware of the major studies of the 1950s and 1960s—the American jury project, the commercial arbitration study, the court delay study, studies of Supreme Court decision-making, studies of the legal profession, studies of compensation for auto accidents, and studies of various types of trial courts. Many of these studies from the post-World War II period have framed research agendas that continue to this day. However, few contemporary empirical legal research (ELR) scholars are familiar with the empirical research on law conducted prior to World War II. A search of early law reviews and other sources reveals empirically oriented research on such disparate law-related topics as appellate court decision-making, criminal courts, auto injury compensation, divorce, debt, grand juries, judicial personnel, and legal education.

This Chapter provides a sketch of early empirical research related to law.[1] The first section discusses what explains the burst of research in the United States in the 1920s and 1930s as well as the smattering of such research prior to 1920. Three brief sections then consider the funding dilemmas that confronted those undertaking this research, why the research was found almost exclusively in the United States, and the methodologies that the research employed. The largest section of the Chapter discusses a variety of themes found in the early empirical legal research with a particular focus on projects and findings that presage debates and concerns in contemporary empirical legal research. The Chapter concludes with a discussion of why empirical work seemed to fade out in the late 1930s and then began to be revived in the 1950s.

---

[1] See Kritzer (2009) for a bibliography and a more extensive review of this early literature.

II. The Impetus Behind Early Empirical Legal Studies: Three "Starters"

What might explain the development of empirical legal research in the first third of the twentieth century? Arguably many of the same factors that account for the burst of such research that we have seen in recent years also account for it in that early period. First was the growing availability of information that made empirical analyses possible. Second were concerns about social problems of the period. And, third were interests of academic institutions that sought to distinguish themselves through supporting and encouraging distinctive research that was allied with a new intellectual movement.

A. Development of judicial statistics

Collecting data is time-consuming and costly. Governmental statistical reports provide a basic source that can be used by empirically-oriented researchers. Even when the data reported are shallow—providing only aggregate counts of cases, dispositions, and the like—they can serve as the basis of research on time trends. If government reports include information on geographic variations, the data reported can be the basis for trying to determine what might account for those variations. For example, in the 1820s France began assembling a variety of national and regional level statistics concerning crime, including at least some information regarding disposition of criminal cases, which later in the nineteenth century became the basis of analyses of factors that might explain the patterns in those statistics.

In England, the first regular judicial statistics began to appear in 1858 and included statistics related to both criminal and civil cases. The system of judicial statistics was revised in the 1890s, and again in 1922. In the intervening years, the English civil justice statistical reports have changed in only relatively minor ways, typically reflecting changes to institutional structure and/or jurisdiction.

In the United States, judicial statistics for the federal courts first appeared as part of the annual report of the Attorney General for the fiscal year 1872. Initially, the statistics covered only cases in which the federal government was a party, but were soon expanded to include all federal civil cases. Over time, the statistics became more detailed, and by 1922 about 50 categories were reported for both civil and criminal cases. In the late 1930s and early 1940s responsibility for collecting the data shifted to the newly created Administrative Office for the United States Courts (Shafroth, 1948). Some rudimentary data on criminals and those with criminal records were collected as part of the 1850, 1860, and 1870 censuses, and in 1907 the Bureau of the Census published a special report entitled, *Prisoners and Juvenile Delinquents* (Robinson, 1911: 12–13). Statistics collected by the states in the nineteenth century were very spotty and focused largely on crime, criminal cases, and prison populations (ibid: 43–65). By approximately 1930, there had been substantial increases in the amount of statistical information available in the form of various reports, although there were no consistent definitions or reporting standards. Despite the problem with the then-extant statistics (e.g., they were generally spotty, often limited in detail, and not standardized), their existence provided at least some basis for research on key legal phenomena.

B. Concerns about crime, crime commissions, and judicial councils

Empirical criminology goes back into the nineteenth century. However, the focus in this early research was on the causes of crime, and reflected even then the debate between those who saw crime as having social roots and those who saw it as inherent in individual character. During the 1920s, and in a few cases even earlier, a number of states and localities in the U.S. established crime commissions to study the then-current crime problem and to come up with recommendations that would reduce crime and improve how police, prosecutors, and courts handled criminal cases. Many of these commissions undertook what became known as "crime surveys" which were comprehensive studies of the criminal justice system.

The first of the crime surveys was carried out in Cleveland under the leadership of Roscoe Pound and Felix Frankfurter (see Pound and Frankfurter, 1922). Crime surveys were ultimately carried out in approximately 20 states and cities. Nationally, the Wickersham Commission, formally the National Commission on Law Observance and Enforcement, was established to assess the problems of law enforcement related to prohibition; it expanded its purview to include criminal justice issues more broadly. The Commission was to inspire some significant early empirical research, in particular the studies of criminal and civil cases in the federal courts overseen by Charles Clark.

In the late 1920s and into the 1930s, a number of states established judicial councils. These councils were often charged with studying the operation of the courts including caseloads, outcomes, and the like. The Ohio Judicial Council, in collaboration with the Institute of Law at Johns Hopkins University, organized a three-year study of judicial administration in Ohio; some of the specific studies from that endeavor are discussed below.

In England, various government bodies considered a number of issues related to criminal justice. As part of the work of these government bodies, some analyses of existing statistics were conducted, and in several cases additional data were collected and discussed. It is not clear whether there was a particular concern about crime in England during this period; there certainly was nothing equivalent to the problems created by prohibition enforcement in the United States although there was considerable political unrest surrounding both labor and economic issues in the mid-1920s and Ireland's drive for independence during and immediately after World War I.

C. The legal realism movement

The third element leading to empirical legal research in the United States during the pre-World War II period was the rise of legal realism, and the empirical orientation of some of the legal academics associated with legal realism (see Schlegel, 1995). As noted above, Roscoe Pound and Felix Frankfurter led the Cleveland Crime Survey effort. Frankfurter went on to author, with James Landis, a study of the work of the Supreme Court, published (starting in 1925) as a series in the *Harvard Law Review* and then as *The Business of the Supreme Court* (Frankfurter and Landis, 1928). This work in turn spawned the annual compilation of statistics on the work of the Supreme Court published by the *Harvard Law Review* since 1929 (Frankfurter and Landis serving as authors initially, and Frankfurter continuing with various co-authors until he himself joined the Supreme Court in 1939). Meanwhile, a study of the work of civil trial courts in Connecticut was undertaken by Charles Clark at Yale (Clark and Shulman, 1937), studies of debt and bankruptcy were led by William Douglas at Yale (Douglas, 1932, 1933; Douglas and Marshall, 1932), and studies of divorce in Ohio and Maryland were led by Leon Marshall at Johns Hopkins (Marshall et al., 1932, 1933).

As described by Schlegel (1995), reform was a significant motivator for at least some of the legal realists. For example, bankruptcy was one major area of research, which was not surprising given the surge caused by the depression. More generally, much of the research was directed to documenting problems in how courts handled various types of cases ranging from criminal cases through divorce to tort. One interesting question, which I will not seek to answer (but see Schlegel, 1995, *passim*) is whether legal realism led to an interest in empirical approaches or, conversely, empirical research led to a legal realist outlook? What Schlegel does make clear is that institutions saw empirical research as a distinctive enterprise through which they could create or maintain their leadership within the competitive academic world of the period.

III. FUNDING

While there were many reasons why researchers decided to undertake empirical work, that work would not have been possible without funding for the considerable expense involved. As is true today, that funding came largely from a combination of government, foundations, and internal resources of academic institutions.

The crime surveys of the 1920s and 1930s typically took a census of cases for some period of time. They variously included analyses of police actions, prosecutors' decisions, trial court proceedings, flows in and out of penal institutions, and appellate processes for criminal cases, although not all surveys included all elements. Some of the crime surveys were funded by government, either directly or through crime commissions. Others, such as the first of the crime surveys done in Cleveland, were funded by local foundations sometimes in partnership with governments.

In his study of the empirical research associated with the legal realism movement, Schlegel (1995) discusses many of the funding struggles. Two of the key universities involved, Yale and Johns Hopkins, set up institutes where the empirical research was based. The universities seeded these institutes with some funding, but the expectation was that the researchers and institutes would be able to raise outside funds to sustain their research programs once the value of those programs had been established. For example, Clark's study of justice administration in Connecticut (Clark and Shulman, 1937), which was an effort to extend the crime survey approach to include civil cases as well as criminal cases, was started in 1926 with sufficient funding from Yale University to allow him to hire four research assistants. Using the initial funds, Clark collected data on 9,300 cases. By producing these results, Clark was able to secure another grant of $55,000 from the Laura Spelman Rockefeller Foundation to extend the study (eventually collecting data on about 28,000 civil cases and 4,000 criminal cases). Clark then secured government funding through the Wickersham Commission to undertake a similar study of cases in the federal district courts; when the Commission's funds ran out, Clark obtained funds from the Rockefeller Foundation to finish the analysis of the data he had in hand (Schlegel, 1995: 84–90).

Another study in which Charles Clark played a significant role (even though it was not based at Yale) examined compensation to those injured in auto accidents. This study was funded by a $72,000 Rockefeller Foundation grant to the Columbia University Council for Research in the Social Sciences in 1929 but was conducted under the auspices of the Committee to Study Compensation for Automobile Accidents (1932). The research team collected data regarding almost 9,000 accidents from 10 localities in six states. The funding was fairly quickly exhausted, and the team was not able to secure supplemental funding; the result was that the researchers had to produce a report that was much less extensive than leaders of the project had hoped (Schlegel, 1995: 108–09).

The second major center of empirical legal research around 1930 was Johns Hopkins University. In the late 1920s Hopkins, where there was and still is no law school, moved to create a non-teaching research institute for law. Schlegel (1995: 160–8) details the struggles of the Institute of Law that came into being in 1928. A request to the Rockefeller Foundation for up to $5 million was unsuccessful.

The University nonetheless committed substantial sums to the Institute and that funding allowed several major research projects to get underway in 1929, including studies of courts in Ohio and Maryland that ultimately produced numerous monographs and reports. However, because the Institute never generated significant outside funding to support its research program and as a result of major hits to the University's endowment which had supported the Institute's initial years, the Institute itself quickly ran out of steam and folded in 1933 (Schlegel, 1995: 189–95).[2]

A third institution that played a significant role in empirical research on law in the 1930s was the University of Wisconsin. Much of the research conducted at Wisconsin in the 1930s was funded through New Deal programs such as the Civil Works Administration (CWA). The CWA funding allowed several members of the law school faculty to engage law students and recent law graduates to go out and collect data from court files, insurance company files, and admission-to-practice records held by local courts. In one study the CWA funding made possible an observational study where research staff were paid to sit in court and observe what was happening in the courtroom (Berkanovic et al., 1934). However, while Wisconsin would later become known as a center of empirical research in the "law and society" tradition, this early work was short-lived, and ended when the CWA funding ran out.

IV. WHY WAS EARLY EMPIRICAL
RESEARCH ON LAW SO U.S.-CENTRIC?

As briefly noted in the introduction, most pre-World War II empirical legal research was carried out in the United States. What accounts for the dearth of research in other English-speaking countries?[3] My search for early empirical research focused initially on academic journals related to law, which largely consist of legal journals published by law schools. Such journals first flourished in the United States, and only developed later in other English-speaking countries. For example, two of the

---

[2] Schlegel (1995) notes that the Institute did secure at least one outside grant, $75,000 from Andrew Mellon. Schlegel argues that funding was not the primary reason for the Institute's short life; rather, he asserts that in the end the Institute was not central to the University's self-image and in the absence of a major benefactor the University preferred to devote its resources elsewhere. It is hard to see why this is not an issue of money and resources.

[3] Due to the limitations of the author, the search for empirically oriented legal research in the pre-World War II period did not extend beyond English-speaking countries.

leading English law journals of today, the *Cambridge Law Journal* and *Modern Law Review*, first appeared in 1933 and 1937 respectively, although the Oxford-based *Law Quarterly Review* dates from 1885.[4] More importantly, the role of academic institutions in preparing future practitioners came much later in England, Canada, and Australia than was true in the U.S. which meant that the legal academy outside the United States was a less significant part of university communities. The result was that while legal academics in the U.S. turned to empirical work in very limited numbers in the pre-World War II period, such work was virtually unheard of among legal academics outside the U.S.

Also relevant is that fact that in countries such as England, relationships among legal academics, legal practitioners, and legal policy-makers remained much more distant than they were in the United States. A number of American law professors moved into prominent positions of legal and political authority, including some who had been active in carrying out empirical research (i.e., Felix Frankfurter and William Douglas to the Supreme Court, Charles Clark to the Court of Appeals, and Wayne Morse to Congress). In contrast, the legal academy in England was not a path into the upper reaches of government office or the senior judiciary.

More generally, the university as a center of research in the social sciences and humanities developed strongly in the U.S. in the early twentieth century. Departments of sociology and political science began to appear.[5] Academic research journals came into being: the *Political Science Quarterly* was founded in 1886, the *American Journal of Sociology* was founded in 1895, the *American Political Science Review* in 1906, and the *Journal of Criminal Law and Criminology* in 1910. In contrast, *Political Quarterly* started publication in England in 1930, the *British Journal of Sociology* around 1950, *Political Studies* in 1952, the *British Journal of Political Science* in 1971, and the *British Journal of Criminology* in 1971.[6] In Britain, the *Howard Journal of Criminal Justice* was started in 1921 by the Howard League for Penal Reform, but contained virtually no empirical research during its first two decades. More generally, in the early twentieth century British interest in criminology came not from the academy but

---

[4] An editorial in the very first issue of the *Modern Law Review* published in 1937 observed: "English legal periodicals have hitherto dealt almost exclusively with the technical aspects of the law treated from such varying points of view as the historical, analytical, or descriptive."

[5] American political scientists included law and courts within their purview more or less from the start of that profession. Discussions of constitutional decisions of both the U.S. Supreme Court and the various state supreme courts are a regular feature appearing from some the earliest volumes of the *American Political Science Review* (*APSR*). Starting in the 1920s one sees intermittently in the *APSR* a section entitled "Judicial Organization and Procedure" which includes brief reports on developments in the courts along with mentions of research being done.

[6] While the major British academic journals in sociology, political science, and criminology did not start publishing until after World War II, journals in the fields of psychology and economics had appeared by early in the twentieth century (*Economic Journal* in 1891 preceding the *American Economic Review* by 20 years; *British Journal of Psychology* in 1909).

from criminal justice professionals working inside the criminal justice system and particularly within the prison system. A brief sketch of political science in Great Britain in the 1920s, while noting some prominent scholars as exceptions, observed that most research work on government problems in that country was done by governmental bodies.

As noted earlier, there was a strong linkage between the legal realism movement in the United States and early empirical research on law. Importantly, legal realism did not gain a foothold in other common law jurisdictions; it was largely a phenomenon of the American legal academy. For example, while at least some legal academics in England may have looked longingly at the intellectual developments within the American legal academy, and perhaps advocated some changes that might have facilitated a move in that direction, little actually happened and what did happen came late in the 1930s (Glasser, 1987: 695–7). In fact when studies in the tradition of legal realism—one on plea bargaining and one on the political influences on judges— were published in the 1970s in England, they were highly controversial, producing outcries from judges and senior members of the legal profession.[7] Some of this probably reflected how strongly the leading figures in the English legal system clung to a positivist view of law and legal process.

While empirical legal research during the pre-World War II period came largely from U.S. sources, there was at least some such research done outside the U.S. In the discussion that follows, I make reference to some of that research.

V. Methodologies

The distinctive feature of empirical legal research is the use of systematically collected data, either qualitative or quantitative, to describe or otherwise analyze some legal phenomenon. While many people equate empirical with quantitative or statistical analysis, this need not be the case. Work that is qualitative and systematic is also empirical. Still, as with contemporary empirical legal studies, the empirical legal research of the early twentieth century was largely quantitative in character.

One challenge to researchers of the period before World War II was that training in formal statistical methods was not widespread. Most of those conducting empirical studies related to law in this period had training in neither statistics

---

[7] In an effort to suppress one of the studies, the head of the organization of barristers wrote to a government official, "In my view it would be directly contrary to the public interest that the book be published in its proposed form at this stage."

nor social science more generally. There was little in the way of interdisciplinary cross-over, and few social scientists undertook empirical research related to law. While today American political scientists are major producers of empirical research related to law (particularly judicial behavior), it was not until the early 1940s that the first such research appeared. Much of the empirical legal research at Yale was tied both to the law school and the Institute of Human Relations, the latter intended to foster interdisciplinary connections; and through this connection some social scientists became involved in the empirical legal research conducted at Yale. One actually taught a seminar in empirical legal research (see Schlegel, 1995: 113). However, this type of collaboration was infrequent during this period

Many of the kinds of statistics that are common today were just being developed during this period. Even the use of extant statistical methods was limited by the large amount of labor involved in computing such statistics on mechanical calculators in the pre-computer era. Many studies do use percentages and graphical displays such as time plots or bar graphs. However, there was virtually no use of inferential statistics; in fact, very few studies employed anything as sophisticated as correlation coefficients. One problem that arises from the absence of inferential statistics is that conclusions about differences are sometimes drawn even though the actual differences are very small and could easily be due to chance.

The rudimentary nature of statistical analysis was very evident in the understanding of methods of sampling. While there was an understanding of random assignment in experimental settings, there was little understanding of what was necessary to obtain representativeness when drawing a sample from a population. This was evident in the early Gallup polls, which in seeking to obtain representative samples of voters, relied on samples of 100,000 or more. Hence, it is not surprising that in the early empirical legal studies one often sees massive samples, many numbering in the tens of thousands. In contrast, modern studies of court cases and similar phenomena typically rely upon probability samples of several thousand or fewer cases.

While the use of statistics and probability samples was rudimentary, the sophistication of early methods of data collection is quite impressive. For example, a number of the studies collected information on court cases by coding information found in court records. Central to such data collection work is the need to develop a coding form. Many of the monographs reproduced the forms used by the research staff that coded the court records. Some of the forms became the basis of the early court information systems, elements of which are still in use today.

Also impressive is the range of data collection methods employed. In addition to coding from institutional records, researchers sought to use key informants, such as judges, who were asked to provide information on cases they oversaw; they also sought out and interviewed accident victims and bankrupts; they organized clinics through which they could see how people dealt with legal issues; they sought to trace business transactions; and they sat, observed, and recorded what went on in court. In some areas they were able to take advantage of quasi-experiments, as laws changed or methods of doing things changed; and there were several examples of what would be labeled "field experiments."

VI. Major Findings of Early Empirical Legal Studies of Continuing Contemporary Significance and Commentary

My search for early empirical legal research located about 150 publications or reports discussing something more than 100 different studies (see Kritzer, 2009). In the following discussion, I focus on aspects of that research that continue to be relevant today, either in showing patterns that we continue to find or in providing important comparisons to contemporary patterns.

A. Criminal justice

Some of the earliest empirical legal research focused on the operation of the criminal justice system reflecting in part the founding of the American Institute of Criminal Law and Criminology in 1909 and the journal it started in 1910 which we know today as the *Journal of Criminal Law and Criminology*. The first study traceable to the Institute's founding appeared in 1912. Oliver Rundell, an instructor at the University of Wisconsin Law School, carried out a study of the duration of criminal cases in Wisconsin. This study, which may have been the first based on data collected from court files, examines cases from three counties. Rundell discovered that relatively few cases actually went to trial before a jury, and while there could be considerable delay in getting to trial, the actual trial of cases consumed "comparatively little time" and "protracted trials [were] a rare occurrence" (Rundell, 1912: 59). Rundell's research was replicated and greatly extended in the crime surveys of the 1920s, a central focus of which was the disposition of cases. These studies typically highlighted tables, often labeled "mortality tables," showing that seldom more than half, and often a much smaller proportion of felony arrests (as low as 18% in one study) resulted in convictions, that most of the convictions that did occur followed guilty pleas, and that jury trials constituted a small fraction of dispositions.

A team from Johns Hopkins University conducted extensive studies of criminal courts in Ohio and Maryland, producing multiple volumes of analyses, some statewide (Gehlke, 1936), some focused on particular communities (Blackburn, 1935), and some focused on the lowest level of courts (Douglass, 1932). One intriguing finding was a difference between patterns of disposition in Ohio and patterns in Maryland (or at least Baltimore). Maryland dispositions were much more likely to follow from trials, although most trials were bench trials. Specifically, in Maryland, 62% of convictions resulted from guilty pleas with 38% following trials; however, a mere 17% of trials were before juries, the rest having been bench trials (Marshall, 1932: 10–11). Moreover, of those cases not resulting in convictions (27% of all dispositions), 58% were formal acquittals, 84% of which followed bench trials (ibid: 15). Overall, 49.5% of dispositions in Maryland followed trials. In contrast, in Ohio 87% of convictions followed a guilty plea, and overall only 11% of dispositions followed trials, mostly jury trials (Gehlke, 1936: 34, 89–91). What makes this contrast particularly interesting is the dominance of bench trials in Maryland, a finding highlighted in a study conducted 40 years later comparing criminal court patterns in Baltimore, Detroit, and Chicago; the authors of the three-city study titled their chapter on Baltimore "A City of Trials" (Eisenstein and Jacob, 1977).

In contemporary discussions of criminal justice processes, it is often asserted that high rates of guilty pleas reflect the pressures of heavy caseloads in urban courts. In a 1978 essay, Malcolm Feeley showed that guilty-plea rates did not reflect urban-non-urban differences. In fact, Raymond Moley (1928: 105–6) reported the same thing 50 years earlier. Twenty of 24 cities for which he found data had guilty-plea rates of 70% or more; the same was true of four out of five counties without large urban centers, some of which were rural and others partially rural. Moreover, the study of federal criminal cases conducted for the Wickersham Commission by Charles Clark produced the interesting finding that while the vast majority of convictions in federal court followed guilty pleas (78% in non-liquor cases and over 90% in liquor cases) the high guilty-plea rate did not exist prior to 1915 (when only about half of federal convictions followed guilty pleas). Importantly, the increase *preceded* the sharp increase in caseloads that came with prohibition, most of the change coming between 1915 and 1918 (American Law Institute, 1934: 52, 76).[8]

Another contemporary issue found in the early research is the impact on outcomes of the type of representation. The issue appears in a number of the studies of the period. For example, the section on criminal courts in the Cleveland crime survey report shows virtually identical rates of guilty pleas for different types of

[8] The prohibition amendment was ratified in 1919 and came into effect in 1920.

representation, although appointed counsel are somewhat less successful in securing acquittals than are retained counsel (Pound and Frankfurter, 1922: 311). In a study of waiver of juries in Michigan, Abraham Goldberg (1929: 168–9) found minimal difference in the likelihood of waiver between appointed and retained counsel; however, retained counsel were much more likely to obtain acquittals at trial than were appointed counsel.

B. Civil justice

1. *Divorce*

There were at least four studies of divorce cases during the period under consideration: in California (Warner, 1921), Maryland (Marshall et al., 1932), Ohio (Marshall et al., 1933), and Wisconsin (Feinsinger, 1932). The California, Maryland, and Ohio studies all involved collection of information from court records; the Wisconsin study relied on a combination of court records and interviews with lawyers and judges. While this was a time when divorce was almost universally fault-based, a finding central to all of the studies was that most divorces were effectively consensual. The studies typically discussed the need to confront the reality of the divorce process and adopt procedures consistent with that reality. While the nature of the divorce process from the perspective of the husband and wife was consistent across localities (i.e., the requirement of finding fault on the part of one party), the actual handling of the divorce did vary, reflecting differences in law and practice.

2. *Auto accident litigation and compensation*

The early twentieth century saw the emergence of litigation over injuries resulting from auto accidents. General studies of litigation (e.g., Clark and Shulman, 1937) showed the significant portions of courts' civil caseloads made up by such cases. During the period there were at least four studies focused specifically on compensation for injuries suffered in automobile accidents, a multi-state study done by the Committee to Study Compensation for Automobile Accidents (CSCAA) (1932), a study in California (May, 1932), and two studies in Wisconsin, one of court cases (Brown, 1935) and another of insurance company files (Feinsinger, 1934). A major finding was that compensation, as a percentage of loss, declined as loss increased (CSCAA, 1932: 62, 91), a theme that continues to be widely discussed today with regard to the American tort system. In a period prior to mandatory insurance laws and before the development of "uninsured motorist" coverage (under which tort victims can be compensated by their own insurance company if the tortfeasor is uninsured), a key finding in two of the studies (CSCAA, 1932; May, 1932) was the relationship between insurance and receipt of compensation: compensation was much more likely to be obtained when there was insurance available to pay the claim. The studies showed that very few cases went to trial, and those that did produced plaintiffs' verdicts in about two-thirds of the cases; the median award in most locations was less than $1,000 (CSCAA, 1932: 62, 91; Brown, 1935: 177).[9]

One of the studies included an intensive examination of compensation from all sources in Connecticut accidents, including employer-provided insurance, life insurance, and the victim's own insurance. A number of modern studies have similarly sought to examine compensation broadly, although such studies have not typically been limited to auto accidents. The Connecticut analysis shows that in two-thirds of cases, part or all of the cost of the accident was borne directly by the victim or the victim's family. This finding, combined with the central role of insurance and the inverse relationship between size of loss and compensation, led the authors of the study to propose that auto accident injuries be compensated by a no-fault plan similar to workers' compensation The theme of the need for some alternative system for compensating injuries arising from automobile accidents recurs in the other studies of those accidents conducted during this period, often drawing comparisons to the systems then in place for compensating injured workers (see particularly CSCAA, 1932; May, 1932); although only the California study (May, 1932) actually involved an empirical comparison between auto accident injuries handled through tort and workplace injuries handled through a no-fault system.

3. Civil juries

One theme in recent empirical work has been the "vanishing trial," particularly in civil cases. In the 1920s and 1930s, one finds discussions of the vanishing jury, both in the United States and in England. Silas Harris (1930) showed decline in jury requests in Connecticut in the wake of the imposition of a fee for requesting a jury. In one of the very few empirical studies in England, Robert Jackson (1937) tracked the drop in civil jury trials in England in the wake of changes in 1918 and 1925 that allowed most such jury trials solely at the discretion of the judge.[10]

---

[9] The Wisconsin study found that the median verdict in Milwaukee County was about $3,000, the equivalent of $40,869 in 2001 dollars (Brown, 1935: 177). A study of jury verdicts from large U.S. counties in 2001 reported a median for auto accident cases of $16,000, and a median of $27,000 for all cases with plaintiffs' verdicts. The median of all tort awards (97 cases) in Milwaukee County was $19,000; for the 36 auto injury cases, the median in 2001 was only $10,500. Thus, adjusting for inflation, it appears that tort awards in Milwaukee County are today only about one quarter of what they were around 1930.

[10] Given the scarcity of empirical legal research outside the United States, it is worth taking note of one other jury-related study conducted by Jackson that appeared in an article on eligibility for jury duty. Jackson (1938) looked at eligibility among the residents of one ward in Cambridge. About 5,000 residents were eligible to vote in Parliamentary elections and 3,500 in local elections; of those, only

A contemporary issue about the civil jury in the United States is how juries decide cases in contrast to how judges do. Back in the 1920s, Dunbar Carpenter (1929) looked at this same question. He found that in two of four jurisdictions with sufficient bench trials for comparison, jury trials yielded higher average awards, but bench trials were more likely than jury trials to yield plaintiffs' verdicts in two of seven jurisdictions. He also compared appeal and reversal rates depending on whether there had been a jury or a bench trial and found no difference after controlling for type of case. In their seminal study of the American jury, Kalven and Zeisel (1971: 521–2) briefly discuss a study by Judge Philip J. McCook of the New York Supreme Court, who tracked jury verdicts in 114 cases tried in his courtroom over 10 trial terms and compared them with how he would have decided the cases himself. According to Kalven and Zeisel, McCook reported that he disagreed with the jury's verdict in 28% of cases, 23% in which he would have found for the defendant while the jury found for the plaintiff and 5% in which he would have found for the plaintiff while the jury found for the defendant. He also was reported as observing that in 32 of the cases where he agreed with the jury in finding for the plaintiff, he disagreed with the amount of damages awarded, and in two thirds of those cases he would have awarded more. Contemporary research comparing decisions by civil juries to decisions of judges has produced results that are largely consistent with these early studies.

C. Debt and bankruptcy

It should not be surprising that there was a flurry of research related to bankruptcy and debt in the late 1920s and early 1930s. Some of American legal history authored some of this research: William Douglas as a law professor at Yale and Abe Fortas (1933) as a Yale law student. Douglas headed up a study based at Yale Law School. The project, initiated soon after Douglas arrived at Yale in 1928, was planned to focus on business failures, but evolved into a broader study of bankruptcy (see Schlegel, 1995: 98–105). Studies of debt and bankruptcy were part of the Johns Hopkins Institute of Law study of judicial administration in Ohio (Billig, 1932), and others were linked to specific reform efforts (Thacher, 1932). At the opening of this Chapter I cited a contemporary study reporting the high cost of bankruptcy administration; one early study reported that the administration costs of a bankruptcy-type proceeding consumed 30–40% or more of assets of the estates (Billig, 1932: 138–40).

187 met the qualifications to serve on a jury, 5 of whom were known to be Labour Party supporters, 62 Conservative Party supporters, with the rest unknown as to their political preference.

While some of the bankruptcy research concerned businesses, there was also research specifically focused on the debt and bankruptcy problems of "wage earners" (Douglas, 1933; Fortas, 1933; Nehemkis, 1933; Sturges and Cooper, 1933). Two themes that came out of these studies are echoed in the credit and banking crisis of 2008–09: the problem of individuals who abuse credit opportunities and the abuse of consumers by certain types of credit providers. Other important factors of the period included medical bills, unemployment, tort judgments against the debtor, and real estate speculation.

One of the innovations of the early part of the twentieth century in the United States was the creation of small claims courts that followed simplified procedures to allow unrepresented litigants to obtain redress in small damage cases. Contemporary observers have noted that such courts seem to be primarily used for debt collection. What is probably the first empirical study of a small claims court found precisely this. Charles Clark assembled data on the first 19 months of operation of the Hartford small claims court. During that time the court disposed of about 5,200 cases, 92% of which appear to have involved debts. There were judgments in about 2,500 of the likely debt cases, all but 73 of which were for the plaintiff; over 1,900 were default judgments (Clark and O'Connell, 1929).

D. Legal needs

Yet another contemporary topic that one finds addressed in the early empirical legal work, some of which appears before 1920, is that of legal needs, particularly the legal needs of those with low incomes. In 1916, Walton Wood, then the public defender in Los Angeles County, published an analysis of the work of his office (Wood, 1916). Most of that study focused on criminal cases, but Wood includes a brief analysis of civil cases. According to Wood, in 1914 there were 7,872 applicants for aid, 55% of whom sought only advice (the majority of these were women in domestic trouble). Thirty percent were claims that the office accepted for "adjustment," two-thirds of which were adjusted out of court. Of the claims accepted for adjustment, 70% were wage claims. Only a few of the one-third of claims not adjusted out of court resulted in lawsuits, often because the claimant could not pay filing and court fees. Only 115 suits were filed, 76 of which were wage claims. Reginald Heber Smith (1919) drew on and extended Wood's analysis by looking at the work of a number legal aid organizations, including the disposition of over 8,000 cases handled by such organizations in six cities.

The first study that resembles the modern "legal needs" or "justiciable problems" survey was conducted by Charles Clark and social scientist Emma Corstvet (1938). Using support from the Federal Emergency Relief Administration, they hired young unemployed lawyers, professionals, and students in need of financial assistance, to conduct interviews with both individuals and small business owners. The authors looked at the likelihood of consulting an "advisor" (not necessarily a lawyer, although only 14% of those seeking advice consulted someone who was not a lawyer) by problem type. Looking only at those needs occurring at least 10 times, the percentage consulting such an advisor varied from under 10% to 70% or more; such advice was more often sought for contentious matters (45%) than for transactional matters (19%). The authors sought to compare the use of advisors by those with incomes up to $2,000 with their use by those with higher incomes; they found slightly greater use by the higher-income group in contentious matters, but in transactional matters, the lower-income group was more likely to seek advice. However, the samples were small and the differences not large, leading the authors to be cautious about drawing conclusions from their analysis.

E. Appellate courts

Perhaps the best known empirical study of the pre-World War II period is Frankfurter and Landis's *The Business of the Supreme Court* (1928).[11] The focus of this book is on how the jurisdiction of the Supreme Court evolved and how both the volume and the content of the caseload shifted with the jurisdictional changes and changes in both the law and the country as a whole, topics of continuing interest today. While Frankfurter and Landis focused largely on the Supreme Court, they also considered other appellate courts, showing how the volume of cases heard by the federal Courts of Appeals had increased since their creation in 1891, and comparing the caseloads of selected state supreme courts to those of the UK House of Lords and English Privy Council.[12]

   Empirical research on appellate courts during this period was by no means limited to the federal courts, or to docket profiles. Political scientist Rodney Mott (1936) anticipated a variety of modern studies of state supreme courts in a study of "judicial influence." He employed a survey of law professors to rate the reputation of the supreme courts of the then-48 states, an analysis of case books to determine the number of opinions of each state's supreme court appearing in such books, and a

---

[11]   Most of the material in the book had previously appeared in an eight-part series under the same title in volumes 38–40 of the *Harvard Law Review.*

[12]   As noted previously, Frankfurter's empirical work on the Supreme Court did not end with the publication of *The Business of the Supreme Court.* Rather, in 1929, one finds the first of what became annual statistical reports of the work of the Supreme Court that have continued to this day to appear in annually in the *Harvard Law Review.* The annual statistical reports concerning the work of the Supreme Court in the *Harvard Law Review* inspired similar reports for at least one state. Starting in 1933, and continuing until the late 1940s, the *Wisconsin Law Review* published a brief statistical report on the work of the Wisconsin Supreme Court covering dispositions, topics covered, who on the Court wrote opinions on which topics, and the frequency of dissent by individual justices

count of citations to opinions of each state's court by other state supreme courts and by the United States Supreme Court. Mott combined his various measures to produce an overall prestige ranking. Mott's prestige ratings correlated 0.52 with a set of prestige ratings created about 50 years later.

There were at least three studies of the disposition of criminal appeals by state supreme courts, in California (Vernier and Selig, 1928), Illinois, and Missouri (the latter two appeared as parts of the crime surveys for those two states). The California study assembled data for the period between 1850 and 1926, and showed that the rate of reversal had declined over that period (from about 50% to around 15%) at the same time that the number of such appeals grew sharply (from about 100 in the first decade to over 1,000 in the last seven years considered). The decline in reversal rates was particularly sharp in the last 16 years considered, a pattern the authors attribute to a constitutional change in 1911 limiting reversals to situations where "error in light of all the evidence resulted in a miscarriage of justice." The analyses in the crime surveys focused on shorter periods, and document the types of crimes involved and reversal rates and patterns. The broadest study of a state appellate court was an analysis of five years of the Maryland Court of Appeals (Brune and Strahorn, 1940). Of particular interest in this study were analyses of dissent and concurrence patterns for individual justices, as well as the decision-writing patterns for the justices. Contemporary studies of state supreme courts cover these very same issues: docket profiles, reversal patterns, dissent and concurrence. What is missing in the early studies of appellate courts, which has become common today, are statistical analyses of the decisions of individual justices. The first such analysis did not appear until 1941.

F. Legal profession and legal education

1. *Legal profession*

Today it is common for state bars in the various U.S. states to do periodic surveys of their members, often focused on the economic issues facing legal practitioners.[13] The first such survey I found was done by the New York County Lawyers' Association in 1934 (Committee on Professional Economics of the New York County Lawyers' Association, 1936). Questionnaires were sent to 19,000 persons, with 5,000 responses received from what was estimated post hoc to be a population of about 15,000. Using

---

[13] Such studies are also regularly done by lawyers' organizations in other countries. The late Cyril Glasser told me of such a survey done by the Law Society of England and Wales in the late 1930s which was entitled "National Service: Report of the Special Committee." According to Glasser, the report, which was ostensibly to assess the potential contribution of solicitors to the war effort that was thought to be imminent, has never been made public. Glasser speculated that part of the Law Society's purpose was to obtain the technology needed to compile statistical information on the profession.

these data a report was prepared profiling the local bar along a variety of dimensions: gender (2% women), years in practice (58% 10 years or less), income (median $2,990), practice organization (38% solo, 41% firm or equivalent, 21% employed by a firm), type of legal education (55% full-time law school), pre-law education (53% college graduates), practice overheads (average of about 35%), race (one half of one percent "Negro"), and place of birth (81% born in the U.S.). In addition, tables examined variation in income by training, length of time in practice, and the like, and there was a discussion of the change in income over time (the median had dropped about 25% since the stock market crash).

The first academic study of the profession was focused on the Wisconsin bar and was carried out by Lloyd Garrison (1935). While the article is described as a "survey of the Wisconsin bar," no survey of lawyers was carried out. Instead Garrison dispatched his assistants (who were funded by the CWA) to every courthouse in Wisconsin to come up with figures showing the numbers of lawyers practicing in each county in each year since the state's founding in 1848. One question he sought to answer was whether the bar was "overcrowded." A second question was whether lawyers who had performed better in law school than other members of the bar had higher incomes. To answer this latter question, Garrison was somehow able to access income tax information for individuals and to match those data with information on performance in law school (limited to University of Wisconsin Law School graduates); Garrison concluded that while there was a tendency for those with stronger law school records to have higher incomes, not all those with a good record had high incomes and some of those with weak records nonetheless did achieve high incomes.

2. Legal education

Related to research on the legal profession was a body of work on legal education. Much of this work focused on methods of selecting students for admission—that is, what were the best predictors of success in law school and whether additional predictors, such as general or specialized tests, could be devised?[14] Articles in various law reviews attempted to show that such tests either did (e.g., Gaudet and Marryott, 1930), or did not (e.g., Wigmore, 1929), improve upon other predictors. Other studies focused on the predictive quality of traditional indicators such as number of years of undergraduate education and undergraduate grade point averages. Some of these studies employed what are now standard statistical tools such as correlation and regression.

A second issue concerning legal education that appeared in the empirical literature concerned grading. One study (Grant, 1929) focusing on grade distributions in law school courses showed that those distributions differed substantially

---

[14] At least three, and probably more, such tests were developed.

by course. While the study did not provide information on variation by instructors, the author argued that the differences reflected differing standards applied by individual instructors. The article concluded with a proposal that contemporary American law faculties will find very familiar: law schools should adopt a standard grade distribution to insure comparability across courses, and that distribution should approximate a normal distribution. Another area of concern was the reliability of evaluation and the form of grading. A study conducted at Columbia Law School (Wood, 1924) showed that the correlation of the marking of exams by two professors was usually in the range of 0.50, and that the average correlation of grades across courses was only 0.50. The study also estimated the reliability of grades using a standard measure and found it to be 0.70, which was not inconsistent with the reliability found for essay exam grading in other fields. Interestingly, the author was able to conduct a small experiment where exams included a combination of true-false questions and essay questions; the correlation between the two parts ranged from 0.39 to 0.57; the average reliability for the true-false was 0.66 compared to 0.54 for the essay.

G. Judicial staffing and selection

A contemporary controversy in the United States concerns methods of selecting and retaining judges and what if any difference selection and retention methods make either in the backgrounds of those who get selected or in behavior on the bench. This is by no means a new issue; it has been a point of debate periodically throughout American history. Several empirical studies related to this debate appeared in the 1930s. Edward Martin (1936) looked at judicial elections in Chicago, with a particular focus on what impact the bar had on outcomes of those elections; Martin concluded that the bar influenced a minority of voters, at most 30% and often much less. A second study (Mott et al., 1933) focused on the characteristics and reputations of state supreme court judges and federal trial and appellate judges, and how they might vary by selection system. The researchers assembled a variety of factors for over 1,000 judges, including demographics (nature of education, marital status, age at attainment of office, number of children, religion, wealth, and military service), years of judicial service, organizational memberships, political experience, and a rating of legal ability from a published source. Sixteen pieces of information were combined to create a "personnel index" for each state, and the states were ranked with Massachusetts highest and Kentucky lowest. While the authors report a slightly higher average personnel index for states with justices appointed by the governor compared to states using elections, either popular or legislative, the difference (92 vs. 91) was so small that it is nothing more than a statistical artifact.

One of the major themes in Martin's study of judicial elections in Chicago was the role of political patronage. Interestingly, one of the few empirical legal studies from Britain (albeit originally published in a U.S. law journal) during this period also focused on the role of patronage in judicial selection. Harold Laski (1926) examined the backgrounds of English judges appointed between 1832 and 1906, a total of 139 judges. He found that 80 were members of Parliament at the time of appointment and 11 others had been candidates for Parliament; 66 (82.5%) of those appointed from Parliament were members of the party in power at the time of their appointment. Thirty-six (45%) of those who had served in Parliament had held office as Attorney General or Solicitor General, and every Chief Justice in the preceding 60 years, save one, had previously served as Attorney General.

VII. Conclusion

A. Decline of empirical legal research in the late 1930s

Early empirical legal studies peaked in the period 1925 to 1935. At all three academic centers of such research—Yale, Johns Hopkins, and Wisconsin—the energy that marked the start of this project faded. At the same time the empirical work sponsored by crime commissions and judicial councils also seemed to fade from view. Why was this endeavor not sustained? Why was there a gap of about 20 years before a renewed interest in empirical legal studies in the mid-1950s?

One reason for the decline can be found in the difficulties and complexities of the work undertaken, particularly given the absence of technologies that were to come later. As noted above, many of the data collection efforts were massive. In significant part the large samples probably reflected the rudimentary nature of sampling theory as it then existed; researchers simply did not understand that valid and reliable conclusions could be drawn using probability samples of 1,000 or fewer observations. The belief that very large samples were needed made data collection, which was and still is labor-intensive, very costly. As noted above, some of the data collection during the 1930s was done using funding provided as part of depression relief efforts. The academic institutions themselves did not have the resources to provide long-term support that went beyond faculty salaries. Even with the data in hand, analyzing those data in the pre-computer era was labor-intensive. By the 1930s, counter-sorter technology was available; however, calculations beyond simple counting had to be done using mechanical calculators. Something as simple as a single correlation coefficient would take hours to compute from the large samples that were being collected.

Virtually none of the scholars who undertook empirical legal research in the 1920s and 1930s were trained as social scientists. While a small number of social scientists were brought in as collaborators, I suspect that the legal academics who led the projects never acquired much in the way of the technical skills needed to do the nitty-gritty of the work. Moreover, to the extent that those scholars did get their "hands dirty," they probably discovered that the work was a lot more tedious and time consuming than the traditional legal scholarship that most had previously undertaken (and which was probably adequate to secure and maintain their academic positions). It might also have been the case that the empiricists' law school colleagues did not look favorably on this type of work, at least in part because the linkage between that research and the training of lawyers was not readily apparent to most legal academics. The Institute of Law at law-school-less Johns Hopkins "was closed because of animosity to its members on the part of the arts and sciences faculty at Hopkins and that institution's President, all of whom saw the group at the Institute as an overpaid distraction from the central part of a university that was under severe financial strain as a result of the Depression" (Schlegel, 1995: 10).

The projects undertaken by the early practitioners of empirical legal research were largely motivated by a desire to devise ways to make the courts and the broader legal system work better. What their research revealed was that the world of law and courts was extremely complex, and that world was often only vaguely like what legal scholars, previously concerned largely with doctrine, probably thought they would find. Moreover, the complexity they uncovered seldom made for clear or easy paths to reform.

Many of the leaders of the early empirical movement moved on to other things. Felix Frankfurter and William Douglas became immersed in advising or working within the New Deal, and both were then appointed to the Supreme Court. Charles Clark, drawing on his empirical work, became a leader in the development of the Federal Rules of Civil Procedure, and was then appointed as a federal appellate judge. Nathan Feinsinger, who conducted studies of divorce and insurance settlements at the University of Wisconsin, moved on to become a prominent scholar (and arbitrator) in the area of labor law. Sam Bass Warner, who conducted one of the very earliest empirical studies in California, moved to Harvard, became the head attorney of the War Production Board during World War II, and in 1945 was appointed Register of Copyrights. Wayne Morse, who led major studies at the University of Oregon in the early 1930s, also became involved in a variety of New Deal activities, and in 1944 was elected to the United States Senate. He is probably best remembered as one of only two senators who voted against the Tonkin Gulf Resolution, which was then used to justify American escalation of the war in Vietnam.

B. The reemergence of empirical legal research, 1950–1975

In the 1950s, one begins to see the reemergence of empirical research on law. The best known of such work is probably the jury study led by Harry Kalven and Hans Zeisel that produced *The American Jury*. This was not the only study during this period; as noted at the beginning of this Chapter, studies were also undertaken on the legal profession, arbitration, court delay, and topics related to crime and criminal justice. By the 1960s, one began to see a growing research community with a focus on this type of research; the Law and Society Association was founded in 1964 and its journal, the *Law & Society Review*, first appeared in 1967. With support from the Russell Sage Foundation, several programs developed that introduced social scientists to law and social science to legal academics. The behavioral turn in American political science led a growing number of scholars to undertake empirical research on courts and judicial behavior. By the 1970s in England, one saw the use of systematic research by several royal commissions into legal processes and issues (e.g., the Royal Commission on Legal Services and the Royal Commission on Civil Liability and Compensation for Personal Injury). The Centre for Socio-Legal Studies was founded at Oxford in 1972. These institutional developments facilitated cross-disciplinary contacts and collaborations.

The reemergence of empirical legal research in the 1950s and 1960s was probably facilitated in part by advances in technology that made possible the computation of statistics by mainframe computers. It is likely that the blossoming of modern empirical legal research starting in the mid-1990s, is related to the development of desktop computing and relatively low cost statistical software. The availability of electronic legal research tools such as Westlaw and Lexis has made it possible for scholars to undertake empirical research that would have been virtually impossible 50, or even 30, years ago. The development of data archives and the increasing availability of data on the Internet allow scholars to undertake empirical analyses of a wide range of legal phenomena without having to devote extensive time and resources to the collection of data from raw materials. In the United States the growing phenomenon of law school faculty members who have both JDs and PhDs in social sciences means that many legal academics now have the methodological training to carry out sophisticated empirical studies.

While modern empirical legal research covers a broad, and rapidly growing, range of subjects, and often deals with subjects that did not exist in the first third of the twentieth century, the cursory review presented in this Chapter shows that many of the contemporary ELR subjects, and many of the findings about those subjects, are not new. Today's practitioners of empirical legal research are able to bring to bear sophisticated methodologies and technologies, and have access to data resources and tools (data archives, online government data, electronic case reports that allow subsets of cases to be identified for coding, etc.) that those undertaking such work in the 1920s and 1930s could not even imagine. Both government and private funding sources now recognize the value of empirical research on a wide range of legal topics. Yet, even with modern techniques, greatly expanded data resources, and access to research funding, today's researchers looking at the questions considered in the 1920s and 1930s often arrive at answers that are essentially the same as found by the early researchers. Still, the data, methods, and technologies available today do make possible more in-depth considerations of the issues which in turn provide a better understanding of why the answers to the questions are what they are.

REFERENCES

American Law Institute (1934). *A Study of the Business of the Federal Courts: Part I, Criminal Cases*, Philadelphia: American Law Institute.

Berkanovic, E., Connolly, C.D., Harvey, R.G., Jr., Heller, N.W., Mooberry, W., Porter, J.D., and Tonjes, J.C. (1934). "Congestion in the Milwaukee Circuit Court: A Study of the Reasons for the Excessive Delays in Reaching Trial, with Suggested Remedies," *Wisconsin Law Review* 9: 325–41.

Billig, T.C. (1932). *Equity Receiverships in the Common Pleas Court of Franklin County, Ohio in the Years 1927 and 1928*, Baltimore: Johns Hopkins Press.

Blackburn, W.J., Jr. (1935). *The Administration of Criminal Justice in Franklin County, Ohio*, Baltimore: Johns Hopkins Press.

Brown, R.A. (1935). "Automobile Accident Litigation in Wisconsin: A Factual Study," *Wisconsin Law Review* 10: 170–91.

Brune, H.M., Jr. and Strahorn, J.S., Jr. (1940). "The Court of Appeals of Maryland, a Five Year Case Study," *Maryland Law Review* 4: 343–89.

Carpenter, D.F. (1929). "The Jury's Manifest Destiny [Letter]," *ABA Journal* 15: 581.

Clark, C.E. and Corstvet, E. (1938). "The Lawyer and the Public: An A.A.L.S. Survey," *Yale Law Journal* 47: 1272–93.

Clark, C.E. and O'Connell, R.D. (1929). "The Working of the Hartford Small Claims court," *Connecticut Bar Journal* 3: 123–9.

Clark, C.E. and Shulman, H. (1937). *A Study of Law Administration in Connecticut: A Report of an Investigation of the Activities of Certain Trial Courts of the State*, New Haven: Yale University Press.

Committee on Professional Economics of the New York County Lawyers' Association (1936). *Survey of the Legal Profession in New York County with Conclusions and Recommendations*, New York: New York County Lawyers' Association.

CSCAA (1932). *Report to the Columbia University Council for Research in the Social Sciences*, Philadelphia: Press of International Printing.

Douglas, W.O. (1932). "Some Functional Aspects of Bankruptcy," *Yale Law Journal* 41: 329–64.

Douglas, W.O. (1933). "Wage Earner Bankruptcies," *Yale Law Journal* 42: 591–642.

Douglas, W.O. and Marshall, J. H. (1932). "A Factual Study of Bankruptcy," *Columbia Law Review* 32: 25–59.

Douglass, P.F. (1932). *The Justice of the Peace Courts of Hamilton County, Ohio*, Baltimore: Johns Hopkins Press.

Eisenstein, J. and Jacob, H. (1977). *Felony Justice: An Organizational Analysis of Criminal Courts*, Boston: Little, Brown & Company.

Feeley, M.M. (1978). "The Effects of Heavy Caseloads," in S. Goldman and A. Sarat (eds.), *American Court Systems: Readings in Judical Process and Behavior*, San Francisco: W.H. Freeman: 125–33.

Feinsinger, N.P. (1932). "Observations on Judicial Administration of Divorce Law in Wisconsin," *Wisconsin Law Review* 9: 26–48.

Feinsinger, N.P. (1934). "Financial Responsibility Laws and Compulsory Insurance: The Problem in Wisconsin," *Wisconsin Law Review* 10: 191–222.

Fortas, A. (1933). "Wage Assignment in Chicago," *Yale Law Journal* 42: 540–60.

Frankfurter, F. and Landis, J.M. (1928). *The Business of the Supreme Court: A Study in the Federal Judicial System*, New York: Macmillan.

Garrison, L.K. (1935). "A Survey of the Wisconsin Bar," *Wisconsin Law Review* 10: 131–69.

Gaudet, F.J. and Marryott, F.J. (1930). "Predictive Value of the Ferson-Stoddard Law Aptitude Examination," *American Law School Review* 7: 27–32.

Gehlke, C.E. (1936). *Criminal Actions in the Common Pleas Court of Ohio*, Baltimore: Johns Hopkins Press.

Glasser, C. (1987). "Radicals and Refugees: The Foundation of the *Modern Law Review* and English Legal Scholarship," *Modern Law Review* 50: 688–708.

Goldberg, W.A. (1929). "Waiver of Jury in Felony Trials," *Michigan Law Review* 28: 163–78.

Grant, J. (1929). "The Single Standard in Grading," *Columbia Law Review* 29: 920–55.

Harris, S.A. (1930). "Is the Jury Vanishing?," *Connecticut Bar Journal* 4: 74–94.

Jackson, R.M. (1937). "The Incidence of Jury Trial During the Past Century," *Modern Law Review* 1: 132–44.

Jackson, R.M. (1938). "Jury Trial To-Day," *Cambridge Law Journal* 6: 367–80.

Kalven, H. and Zeisel, H. (1971). *The American Jury*, Chicago: University of Chicago Press.

Kritzer, H.M. (2009). "Empirical Legal Studies before 1940: A Bibliographic Essay," *Journal of Empirical Legal Studies* 6: 925–68.

Laski, H. J. (1926). "The Technique of Judicial Appointment," *Michigan Law Review* 24: 529–43.

LoPucki, L.M. and Doherty, J.W. (2008). "Professional Overcharging in Large Bankruptcy Reorganization Cases," *Journal of Empirical Legal Studies* 5: 983–1017.

Marshall, L.C. (1932). *Judicial Criminal Statistics in Maryland*, Baltimore: Johns Hopkins University Institute of Law.

Marshall, L.C., May, G., Marquard, E. L., and Reticker, R. (1932). *The Divorce Court Volume One: Maryland*, Baltimore, MD: Johns Hopkins Press.

Marshall, L.C., May, G., Marquard, E. L., and Reticker, R. (1933). *The Divorce Court Volume Two: Ohio*, Baltimore, MD: Johns Hopkins Press.

Martin, E.M. (1936). *The Role of the Bar in Electing the Bench in Chicago*, Chicago: University of Chicago Press.

May, S.C. (1932). "Personal Injury Litigation: A Report of the Research Service of the Commonwealth Club of California," *Transactions of the commonwealth Club of California* 26: 453–67.

Moley, R. (1928). "The Vanishing Jury Trial," *Southern California Law Review* 2: 97–127.

Mott, R.L. (1936). "Judicial Influence," *American Political Science Review* 30: 295–315.

Mott, R.L., Albright, S.D. and Semmerling, H.R. (1933). "Judicial Personnel," *Annals of the American Academy of Political and Social Science* 167: 145–55.

Nehemkis, P. (1933). "The Boston Poor Debtor Court—A Study in Collection Procedure," *Yale Law Journal* 42: 562–90.

Pound, R. and Frankfurter, F. (eds.) (1922). *Criminal Justice in Cleveland*, Cleveland: The Cleveland Foundation.

Robinson, L.N. (1911). *History and Organization of Criminal Statistics in the United States*, Boston: Houghton Mifflin Company.

Rundell, O. (1912). "The Time Element in Criminal Prosecutions in Wisconsin," *Bulletin of the University of Wisconsin* (512).

Schlegel, J. H. (1995). *American Legal Realism & Empirical Social Science*, Chapel Hill: University of North Carolina Press.

Shafroth, W. (1948). "Federal Judicial Statistics," *Law and Contemporary Problems* 13: 200–11.

Smith, R.H. (1919). *Justice and the Poor*, New York: Carnegie Endowment for the Advancement of Teaching.

Sturges, W.A. and Cooper, D.E. (1933). "Credit Administration and Wage Earner Bankruptcies," *Yale Law Journal* 42: 487–525.

Thacher, T.D. (1932). "Report of the Attorney General on Bankruptcy Law and Practice," *Strengthening of Procedure in the Judicial System*, Washington: Government Printing Office.

Vernier, C.G. and Selig, P., Jr. (1928). "The Reversal of Criminal Cases in the Supreme Court of California," *Southern California Law Review* 2: 21–52.

Warner, S.B. (1921). "San Francisco Divorce Suits," *California Law Review* 9: 175–85.

Wigmore, J.H. (1929). "[Editorial] Juristic Psychopoyemetrology—Or, How to Find Out Whether a Boy Has the Making of a Lawyer," *Illinois Law Review* 24: 454–65.

Wood, B.D. (1924). "The Measurement of Law School Work," *Columbia Law Review* 24: 224–65.

Wood, W.J. (1916). "Necessity of Public Defender Established by Statistics," *Journal of the American Institute of Criminal Law & Criminology* 7: 230–44.

37

QUANTITATIVE APPROACHES TO EMPIRICAL LEGAL RESEARCH

LEE EPSTEIN AND ANDREW D. MARTIN[1]

[1] For research support, we thank the National Science Foundation, Northwestern University School of Law, and the Center for Empirical Research in the Law at Washington University. For their very helpful comments, we thank the editors of this volume. We adapt some of the material in this Chapter from Epstein and King (2002); Epstein and Martin (2005); Epstein, Martin, and Boyd (2007); Epstein, Martin, and Schneider (2006); and Epstein and Martin's annual workshop, *Conducting Empirical Legal Research*.

THE title of this Chapter seems too wordy. Why call it doing "empirical *legal* research," and not simply doing "empirical research"? After all, regardless of whether empirical researchers are addressing a legal question or any other, they follow the same rules—the rules that enable them to draw inferences from the data they have collected (Epstein and King, 2002; King et al., 1994). What's more, because empirical research in law has methodological concerns that overlap with those in Biology, Chemistry, Economics, Medicine and Public Health, Political Science, Psychology, and Sociology, empirical legal researchers can adopt methods from these other disciplines to suit their own purposes.

On the other hand, in virtually every discipline that has developed a serious empirical research program—law not excepted—scholars discover methodological problems that are unique to the special concerns in that area. Each new data source often requires at least some adaptation of existing methods, and sometimes the development of new methods altogether. There is bioinformatics within Biology, biostatistics and epidemiology within Medicine and Public Health, econometrics within Economics, chemometrics within Chemistry, political methodology within Political Science, psychometrics within Psychology, sociological methodology within Sociology, and so on. As of this writing, there is no "legalmetrics" but that should happen soon enough (though probably not before this Chapter appears in print).

In short, with a few wording substitutions here and there, much of what follows pertains to all empirical research. But *much* is not *all*. Recognizing that empirical legal work is unique in various ways, as we describe the research process we also outline some of the field's distinct challenges—most notably, how to communicate complex statistical results to a community lacking in statistical training.

We begin by describing the research process. Then, in sections II–V, we flesh out the various components of the process: designing research, collecting and coding data, analyzing data, and presenting results.

I. CONDUCTING EMPIRICAL LEGAL RESEARCH: AN OVERVIEW

How do scholars implement quantitative empirical research? What challenges do they confront? To begin to formulate responses, consider a legal question at the center of hundreds, perhaps thousands, of lawsuits each year: do employers pay men more than women solely because of their gender? Next consider how researchers who faced absolutely no constraints—i.e., researchers with more powers than

Batman, Superman, and Wonder Woman combined—would address this question. If we were the researchers, we would begin by creating a workplace, randomly drawing a worker from the workforce population, randomly assigning a sex (say, male) to the worker, instructing him to enter the workplace, and observing his wage.[2] Next, we would reverse time, and assign the same worker the other sex (female), send her into exactly the same workplace, and observe her wage. If we observed a difference in the wages of our two workers—such that the same employer paid the male version less than the female version—then we might conclude that, yes, gender causes pay inequities.

Unfortunately, researchers aren't superheroes; they usually don't have the power to create a workplace and assign a sex. And they certainly don't have the power to rerun history. This is known as *fundamental problem of causal inference* (Holland, 1986: 947). It simply means that researchers can only observe the factual (e.g., a female worker's salary, if in fact the worker was a female) and not the counterfactual (e.g., a male worker's salary, if in fact the worker was female).[3]

This is a problem without a solution but scholars have developed various fixes. The gold standard along these lines is a proper experiment—that is, an experiment in which the researcher randomly selects subjects from the population of interest and then randomly assigns the subjects to treatment and control conditions (see Ho et al., 2007). Very few experiments in empirical legal studies actually meet the first condition (random selection from the population) but some scholars have tried to meet the second. Jeffrey J. Rachlinski and his colleagues (2006), for example, recruited 113 bankruptcy court judges to participate in an experiment designed to detect whether the race of a party affected the judges' decisions.[4] They asked the judges to read the same case materials but unbeknownst to the judges, the researchers randomly assigned them to a control or treatment group. Those judges in the control group were led to believe that the debtor was white; those in the treatment group were led to believe that the debtor was black. (It turned out that race did not affect the judges' decisions.)

This is a reasonable approach to the fundamental problem of causal inference. But, sadly, it is infeasible for many empirical legal projects—including studies of pay equity (no experiment can assign a sex to workers). It is not even feasible for most analyses of judicial behavior (the Rachlinski et al. study is a notable exception). To provide but one example, suppose we wanted to investigate the extent to which female judges affect the decisions of their male colleagues. No U.S. Court of Appeals would allow us to manipulate the composition of panels so that we could identify

[2] Though it should be obvious, for this hypothetical we are assuming that the employer is assigning wages intentionally, not randomly.
[3] For a more formal accounting of this type of analysis, many scholars have adopted a potential outcomes framework—posited by Neyman (1935) and Rubin (1973, 1974), thoroughly reviewed in Holland (1986), and recently applied in the social sciences by Imai (2005), Epstein et al. (2005), and Boyd, et al. (2010).   [4] Their research tested for other biases as well, including anchoring and framing.

a possible gender effect. We could say the same of the other institutions of government. Can you imagine the President of the United States agreeing to nominate two judicial candidates identical in all respects except that one is highly qualified and the other highly unqualified just to enable us to learn whether qualifications affect the confirmation votes of U.S. senators? We can't.

The upshot is that most empirical legal researchers simply do not have the luxury of analyzing data they developed in an experiment (i.e., experimental data). Instead, they must make use of data the world—not they—generated (i.e., observational data): salaries paid to workers by real companies; the decisions of judges in concrete cases; the votes cast by senators over the president's nominee to the federal courts. And this, of course, substantially complicates the task empirical legal researchers confront. While experimental data—generated by random assignment to treatment and control groups—effectively minimize the confounding effects of other variables, the same cannot be said of observational data. For those data, researchers must invoke statistical techniques (discussed below) to accomplish the same thing.

Because observational datasets are so much more common in quantitative empirical legal research, in what follows we focus on strategies for working with them. It is important to keep in mind, however, that other than issues of data generation and control (statistical versus experimental), experimental and observational studies are not altogether different for our purposes. Either way, scholars tend to execute them in four steps: they design their projects, collect and code data, conduct analyses, and present results.[5]

Research design largely (though not exclusively) involves the process of moving from the conceptual to the concrete. To return to our example of pay equity, suppose the researcher hypothesizes that once she takes into account the experience of the workers, males earn no more than females. However plausible this hypothesis, the researcher confronts a non-trivial problem in assessing it: how to operationally define the concept of "experience." Is it years from degree? Years in the workforce? Months in the same job? More generally, before researchers can answer empirical legal questions—actually before they can even collect the first

---

[5] These are indeed the key components, and in the Sections to follow we describe them in order, from designing research to conducting analyses. Nonetheless, empirical legal scholars rarely regard their research as following a singular, mechanical process from which they can never deviate. Quite the opposite: scholars must have the flexibility of mind to overturn old ways of looking at the world, to ask new questions, to revise their blueprints as necessary, and to collect more (or different) data than they might have intended. On the other hand, being flexible does not mean that researchers do or should do ad or post hoc adjustment of theories to fit idiosyncrasies. Adjustments made to harmonize theory with data, of course, do not constitute any confirmation of the theory at all. While it is fine to use data to create theory, investigators know they must consult a brand new data set, or completely different and previously unanticipated testable consequences of the theory in the same data set, before concluding that data confirm their theory. For more on the idea of research as a "dynamic process conforming to fixed standards," see Epstein and King (2001).

piece of data—they must devise ways to clarify concepts such as experience so that they can observe them. All of this and more appear on that first (metaphorical) slide.

Data collection and coding entails translating information in a way that researchers can make use of it. For a study of pay equity, the researcher may have piles of pay stubs and employee records. Unless the researcher can transform the piles into data she can analyze the study cannot proceed.

Data analysis typically consists of two activities. First, researchers often summarize the data they have collected. If, for example, we collect information on a sample of 50 workers' salaries in a firm with 500 workers, it may be interesting to know the average salary for the men in our sample and the average salary for the women. Second, analysts use data to make inferences—to use facts they know (about the salaries, gender, experience, and so on of the 50 workers in their sample) to learn about facts they do not know (the salaries, gender, experience, and so on of the 500 workers). To perform inference in quantitative studies, researchers employ various statistical methods. Worth noting, though is that use of statistics presupposes that the study is well designed and the data are of a sufficiently high quality. If either the design is poor or the data inadequate, researchers will be unable to reach inferences of high quality. In other words, without a proper research design no statistical method can provide reliable answers; not even the best statistician cannot make lemonade without lemons.

Finally, once empirical legal analysts have drawn inferences from their data, they must be able to communicate their results to a community that may have little (or no) knowledge of even simple statistics. Doing so effectively blends both art and science, and requires careful consideration of both the project and the intended audience.

These are the contours of the research process. Let us now flesh them out to the extent possible given space constraints.

II. Designing Research

It should go without saying that before researchers can design their project, they must have one. To "have a project" usually means that the analyst has a *question* she wishes to answer and has *theorized* about possible responses.

Research questions in empirical legal studies come from everywhere and anywhere. Perhaps scholars see a gap in the existing literature or perhaps they think the literature is incomplete or even wrong. Sometimes questions come from current events—whether a new law is having the desired (or any) effect or whether a court decision is efficacious—and sometimes they come from history. A perusal of any socio-legal journal would provide evidence of these and other motivations.

The variation is not unexpected. Empirical legal scholars are a diverse lot, with equally diverse interests. What their questions have in common, though, may be just as important: virtually all are quite conceptual. Consider a variation on the question we asked at the onset:

Do males and females who have the same level of experience earn the same amount of money?

However important this question, it is not one that even the best empirical legal project can ever address. Rather, the question the study will actually answer comes closer to this:

Do males and females who have been in the workforce for the same number of years net the same salary per month?

Note that the first form of the question contains several concepts—"earn" and "experience"—which researchers cannot directly observe. Only by clarifying these concepts, as the second form does, can the researcher empirically answer the question. Because this is more or less true of every empirical project, a major research challenge is to tighten the fit between the question asked and the question actually answered. If it is too loose the researcher cannot, at the end of the day, claim to have answered the question she initially posed.[6]

Once analysts have settled on a research question, they usually begin *theorizing* about possible answers they can use to develop *observable implications* (sometimes called hypotheses or expectations).[7] A theory is simply a reasonable and precise answer to the research question. An observable implication is a claim about what we would expect to observe in the real world if our theory is right—typically, a claim that specifies a relationship between (or among) a dependent variable (what we are trying to explain) and an independent variable(s) (what our theory suggests explains the dependent variable) (Epstein and King, 2002: 61–2).

Theorizing is a big topic, one to which we can hardly do justice in this short Chapter. So two observations will have to suffice. First, theorizing in empirical legal scholarship comes in many different forms: in some projects theories are quite big

---

[6] How to ensure a good fit? We turn to this question when we tackle the subject of measurement.

[7] Some might argue that these steps are unnecessary in research motivated purely by policy concerns. Not so. Because the statistical methods we describe momentarily are designed to test hypotheses, the researcher should, well, develop some hypotheses to test.

and grand, seeking to provide insight into a wide range of phenomena (e.g., rational choice theory in law and economics); others are simple, small, or tailored to fit particular situations. For the purposes of conducting an empirical study, this distinction may not be very important.

What is important—and this takes us to the second key point—is that the researcher extract observable implications from the theory. The reason is simple. Just as analysts almost never actually answer the question they pose, they almost never directly test their theory. Rather, they only indirectly assess it by evaluating the observable implications that follow from it.

To see the point, return to our question about pay equity between males and females, and consider the following theories and their observable implications.

Difference Theory
Owing to discriminatory judgments about worth, employers pay females less than comparable males.

Observable Implication
All else being equal (e.g., experience), if my theory is correct, we should observe females earning less than males.

Efficiency Theory
Because labor markets are efficient, any observed differences between male and female workers are a product of experience, quality, productivity, and so on.

Observable Implication
All else being equal (e.g., experience), if my theory is correct, we should observe females and males earning the same

Note that in neither instance—no matter how good their design, their data, and their methods—will the researchers be able to conclude that their theory is right or wrong (that discriminatory judgments lead to pay inequity or that efficient markets lead to pay equity). All they will be able to say is whether their data are *consistent* with the observable implications following from their theory.

And even saying that involves hard work. The problem, yet again, is that observable implications are *conceptual* claims about the relationship between (or among) variables. To evaluate these, researchers must delineate how they actually can observe them in the real world. They must, in short, move from the abstract to the concrete—a task that forms the core of research design and that Figure 1 depicts.
Note that in the clarification process the researcher translates abstract notions, such as "experience" and "earnings," into the far more concrete "years in the workforce" and "gross annual income." Unlike the abstractions, researchers can observe and measure "years in the workforce" and so on.

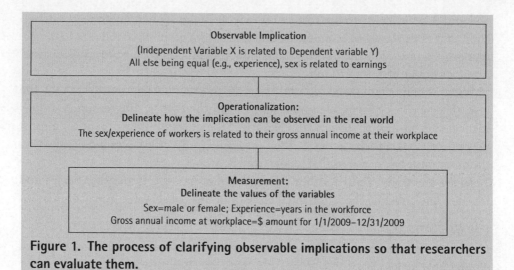

Figure 1. The process of clarifying observable implications so that researchers can evaluate them.

Note that in the clarification process the researcher translates abstract notions, such as "experience" and "earnings," into the far more concrete "years in the workforce" and "gross annual income." Unlike the abstractions, researchers can observe and measure "years in the workforce" and so on.

But how do analysts evaluate their choices and procedures? Why "years in the workforce" and not "years from degree," "months in the same position," or any of the other many plausible measures of experience? Typically, researchers look to the reliability and validity of their measures. Reliability is the extent to which it is possible to replicate a measure, reproducing the same value (regardless of whether it is the right one) on the same standard for the same subject at the same time. Measures of high reliability are preferable to those with lower levels of reliability. Validity is the extent to which a reliable measure reflects the underlying concept being measured. Along these lines, we might consider whether the measure is facially valid, that is, whether it comports with prior evidence or existing knowledge, among other criteria.

There is another test to which many researchers put their measures: robustness checks. Suppose we settled on "years in the workforce" as our measure of experience but believed that "months in the same position" was plausible as well. In our statistical work, we might try both hoping to obtain consistent results regardless of the particular measure. This procedure does not tell us whether "years in the workforce" is a better measure than "years in the same position" but it does help to anticipate a question put to many empirical legal scholars: "what if you had used measure Y instead of measure X? Would your results have been the same?"

III. COLLECTING DATA AND CODING VARIABLES

Once researchers have designed their project—that is, they have filled out the first slide—they typically turn to *collecting* and *coding* their data—the makings of the second slide. By this point, it should go without saying, though we shall say it anyway, that we can hardly scratch the surface of either; both deserve Chapters of their own.

What we can do instead is offer some brief counsel, beginning with data collection—actually, with a crucial step before data collection: determining whether the data the researcher needs already exist in the form she needs it. For decades now, empirical legal scholars have been amassing datasets—some for particular projects and others, the so-called "multi-user" datasets, designed for application to a wide range of problems. Either way, it is entirely possible (even probable in some areas of empirical legal studies) that researchers can locate suitable data without having to invest in costly from-scratch data-collection efforts.

A few examples suffice to make the point. If analysts are interested in cases decided by the U.S. Supreme Court, they should proceed directly to the U.S. Supreme Court Database (<http://supremecourtdatabase.org>). This remarkable resource houses scores of variables on Supreme Court cases decided since 1953, including the legal provisions under analysis, the identity of the majority opinion writer, and the votes of the justices. A similar dataset, the U.S. Courts of Appeals Database, exists for cases decided by the U.S. circuit courts (at: http://www.cas.sc.edu/poli/juri/). For the researcher interested in public opinion, the General Social Survey and the American National Election Study (both available via an intuitive interface at: <http://sda.berkeley.edu/archive.htm>) are natural places to look for relevant data. For other types of projects, we recommend visiting the websites of the Inter-University Consortium for Political and Social Research (<http://www.icpsr.umich.edu/>) and the IQSS Dataverse Network <http://dvn.iq.harvard.edu/dvn/>), both of which serve as repositories for (or have links to) existing datasets. Federal and state governments and agencies too retain enormous amounts of information of interest to empirical legal scholars, including data on population demographics, economic indicators, and court caseloads. Last but not least, experience has taught us that a well-formulated Internet search can unearth datasets that scholars maintain on their own websites.

If the data simply do not exist in an analyzable form, empirical legal researchers can and do make use of a wide variety of data-generation mechanisms. They amass numerical data from structured interviews or surveys, from field research, from public sources, from private papers, and on and on. Each has its strengths and weaknesses (as do archived datasets) and it is the researchers' job to learn, understand, and convey them.

Still, within all this variation, two principles governing the data-collection process apply to most empirical legal research projects. One is simple enough: as a general rule, researchers should collect as much data as resources and time allow because basing inferences on more data rather than less is almost always preferable. To see the point, think about a study designed to study gender pay equity in academia. The more professors included in the study, the more certain the conclusions the analyst can reach. As a practical matter, however, diminishing returns kick in and settling on a sample size (as opposed to including all professors) is good enough. For example, one can estimate a proportion with ±2% margin of error with a random sample of approximately 2400 observations; the number increases dramatically to 9,600 for ±1%. This is why most public opinion surveys query, at most, a couple thousand respondents. As discussed in more detail below, this "margin of error" is sometimes referred to as the "sampling error" or the "confidence interval" (e.g., "CI ±3%" in examples below).

Second, if researchers cannot collect data on all members of the population of interest (e.g., all professors)—and they rarely can—they must invoke selection mechanisms that avoid selection bias (mechanisms that don't bias their sample for or against their theory). For large-n studies (where n = number of participants) only *random probability sampling* meets this criterion.[8] A random probability sample involves identifying the population of interest (all professors) and selecting a subset (the sample) according to known probabilistic rules. To perform these tasks, the researcher must assign each member of the population a selection probability and select each person into the observed sample according to these probabilities. (Collecting all the observations is a special case of random selection with a selection probability of 1.0 for every element in the population.)[9]

Researchers can implement random sampling in various ways depending on the nature of the problem. For a study of pay equity in the academy, for example, we could draw an equal probability sample—a sample in which all professors have an equal chance of being selected. If, on the other hand, we wanted to include all racial and ethnic groups in our study and worried that our sample, by chance, might not include, say, any American Indians, stratified random sampling may be a better strategy. The idea is to draw separate equal-probability-of-selection random samples within each category of a variable (here, race/ethnicity).

---

[8] For advice on small-n studies, see Epstein and King (2002: 112–13); King et al. (1994: 124–8).

[9] Dealing with data collected on a population raises some foundational statistical issues. One approach is to argue that an observed population is a "sample" from possible histories, and as such, traditional inferential statistics can be used. Another option is to simply summarize the data and not report measures of uncertainty. The ideal approach, from our perspective, is to adopt a Bayesian approach and treat the parameters as random variables, not the data.

Whatever the procedure (so long as it involves random selection for large-*n* samples!), the legal researcher will typically end up with piles or computer files of questionnaires, field notes, court cases, and so on. *Coding variables* is the process of translating the relevant properties or attributes of the world (i.e., variables) housed in the piles and files into a form that the researcher can then analyze systematically (presumably after they have chosen appropriate measures to tap the underlying variables of interest).

Coding is a near-universal task in empirical legal studies. No matter whether their data are quantitative or qualitative, from where their data come, or how they plan to analyze the information they have collected, researchers seeking to make claims or inferences based on observations of the real world must code their data. And yet, despite the common and fundamental role it plays in research, coding typically receives only the briefest mention in most volumes on empirical research; it has received almost no attention in empirical legal studies.

Why this is the case is a question on which we can only speculate, but an obvious response centers on the seemingly idiosyncratic nature of the undertaking. For some projects researchers may be best off coding inductively, that is, collecting their data, drawing a representative sample, examining the data in the sample, and then developing their coding scheme. For others, investigators proceed in a deductive manner, that is, they develop their schemes first and then collect/code their data. For still a third set, a combination of inductive and deductive coding may be most appropriate.[10]

Nonetheless, we believe it is possible to offer three generalizations about the process of coding variables. First, regardless of the type of data they collect, the variables they intend to code, or even of whether they plan to code inductively or deductively, at some point empirical legal researchers require a coding schema, that is, a detailing of each variable of interest, along with the values of each variable. For example, in a study of the effect of female judges on the votes of their male colleagues, the variable Vote of the Judge would obviously figure prominently; for this variable we might code three values: the judge voted to "affirm," to "reverse," or "other." With this sort of information in hand, investigators can prepare codebooks—or guides they employ to code their data and that others can use to replicate, reproduce, update, or build on the variables the resulting database contains and any analyses generated from it.

Second, depending on the type of data and variables, developing schema and creating codebooks are not always easy or straightforward tasks. To see this, reconsider the seemingly simple example of the variable Vote of the Judge. We just listed three

---

[10] Some writers associate inductive coding with research that primarily relies on qualitative data and deductive coding, with quantitative research. Given the [typically] dynamic nature of the processes of collecting data and coding, however, these associations do not always or perhaps even usually hold. Indeed, it is probably the case that most researchers, regardless of whether their data are qualitative or quantitative, invoke some combination of deductive and inductive coding.

values (affirm, reverse, and other) but what of a vote "affirming in part and reversing in part"? Should we code this as "other," even if the judge gave the plaintiff some
relief? For that matter, what should we make of the "other" category? Depending
on the subjects under analysis, it may be appropriate (meaning that it would be an
option exercised infrequently) or not. But our more general point should not be
missed: accounting for the values of the variables of interest, even of seemingly simple ones, may be tricky.[11]

To be sure, following best practices can help; for example, ensuring that the
values of the variables are exhaustive, creating more (rather than fewer) values,
establishing that the values of the variables are mutually exclusive, and more generally, pretesting the schema (for more details, see Epstein and Martin, 2005). But
there is one assumption that all the rules and guidelines make—and this brings
us to our third point: researchers must have a strong sense of their project, particularly about the piece of the legal world they are studying and how that piece
generated the data they will be coding, as well as the observable implications of the
theory that they will be assessing (see, e.g., Babbie, 2007: 384; Frankfort-Nachmias
and Nachmias, 2007). Even adhering to simple rules will be difficult, if not impossible, if the researcher lacks a deep understanding of the objects of her study and
an underlying theory about whatever feature(s) of their behavior for she wishes to
account.

IV. ANALYZING DATA

If research design is the first overhead slide and collecting and coding data, the
second, then data analysis enables researchers to compare their overlap. When the
overlap between the observable implications and data is substantial, analysts may
conclude that the real world confirms their hunches; if the overlap is negligible, they
may go back to the drawing board or even abandon the project altogether.

How do empirical legal scholars perform this task? The answer depends in no
small part on their goals. If the goal is to summarize the data they have collected (say,
the salaries of all male and female professors at their school), then some simple measures of central tendency (e.g., means, medians) and dispersion (e.g., standard deviations, ranges) might suffice. These will give researchers a feel for the distributions

---

[11] More generally, the relative ease (or difficulty) of the coding task varies according to the types of
data with which the researcher is working, the level of detail for which the coding scheme calls, and
the amount of pretesting the analyst has conducted.

of their variables that, depending on the number of cases, they could not possibly develop from looking at a column of data.

For the vast majority of empirical legal projects, however, making inferences—using facts we know to learn about facts we do not know—is the goal. Rarely do we care much about the, say, 50 individuals or 100 cases in our sample. Rather, we care about what those 50 individuals or 100 cases can tell us about all the employees of the corporation or all the cases. In quantitative research, inferences come in two flavors: *descriptive* and *causal*. Descriptive claims themselves can take several forms but some seem quite a kin to data summaries. Suppose, for example, that we collected data on 100 court cases involving employment discrimination and learned that, on average, appellate court panels held for the plaintiff in 40% of the cases. In and of itself this figure of 40% (a summary of the data), probably isn't all that interesting to our readers or us. What we want to learn about is the fraction of *all* employment discrimination cases in which all courts held for the plaintiff. That is, we want to use what we know (the 100 cases we have collected) to learn about what we do not know (the cases we haven't collected). This is the task of drawing a descriptive inference. We do not perform it by summarizing facts; we make it by using facts we know—the small part of the world we have studied—to learn about facts we do not observe (the rest of the world). Researchers call the "small part" a sample and the "world" a population. (An important part of performing descriptive inference is *quantifying* the uncertainty we have about that inference. We discuss this in greater detail below.) It is important to keep in mind that when dealing with data coming from a non-probability sampling neither descriptive nor causal inferences can be drawn.

Causal inference too is about using facts we do know to learn about facts we do not know. In fact, *a causal inference is the difference between two descriptive inferences*—the average value the dependent variable (for example, the fraction of cases decided in favor of the plaintiff) takes on when a "treatment" is applied (for example, a female judge serves on the panel) and the average value the dependent variable takes on when a "control" is applied (for example, if no female judge sits on the panel). The *causal effect*—the goal of the process of causal inference—is this difference, the amount the fraction of decisions in favor of the plaintiff increases or decreases when we move from all-male panels to panels with a female.

How do quantitative empirical researchers go about making descriptive or causal claims? Assuming they have appropriately designed their projects and appropriately amassed and coded their data, they make use of *statistical inference*, which entails examining a small piece of the world (the sample) to learn about the entire world (the population), along with evaluating the quality of the inference they reach. Conceptually, statistical inference is not all that hard to understand; actually we confront such inferences almost every day. When we open a newspaper, we might find the results of a survey showing that 70% (± 5% margin of error) of American voters have confidence in the US president. Or when we read about a scientific study indicating that a daily dose of aspirin helps 60% (95% CI ± 3%) of

Americans with heart disease. (95% CI and ± X% are explained below.) In neither of these instances, of course, did *all* Americans participate. The pollsters did not survey every voter, and the scientists did not study every person with heart problems. They rather made an inference (in these examples, a descriptive inference) about all voters and all those stricken with heart disease by drawing a sample of voters and of ill people.

But how do the researchers go about making the statistical inference (for example, 70% of all American voters have confidence in the president) and assess its quality (that is, indicate how *un*certain they are about the 70% figure, as indicated by the ± 5%)? It is one thing to say that 70% of the voters in the sample have confidence in the president (this is summarizing or describing the data); but it is quite another to say that 70% of *all* voters have confidence (this is the descriptive inference).

To support the first claim, all analysts need do is tally (i.e., *summarize*) the responses to their survey. To support (and evaluate) the second, they must (1) draw a random probability sample of the population of interest and (2) determine how certain (or uncertain) they are that the value they observe from their sample of voters (70%), called the *sample statistic,* reflects the population of voters, the *population parameter.*

We already have discussed (1)—drawing a random sample—so we only need reiterate here that this step is crucial. If a sample is biased (for instance, if Democrats had a better chance of being in the pollsters' sample than Republicans), researchers cannot draw accurate conclusions.

Assuming researchers draw a random probability sample, they can move to (2) and make a (descriptive) inference about how well their sample reflects the population. Or, to put it another way, they can convey their *degree of uncertainty* about the sample statistic. Surveys reported in the press, for example, typically convey this degree of uncertainty as "the margin of error," which is usually a 95% confidence interval (or 95% CI). When pollsters report the results of a survey— that 70% of the respondents have confidence in the president with a ±5 margin of error—they are supplying the level of uncertainty they have about the sample statistic of 70%. That is, the true fraction of voters who have confidence in the president will be captured in the stated confidence interval in 95 out of 100 applications of the same sampling procedure. The fact that the data come from a random sample is what makes it possible to use the rules of probability to compute these margins of error.

Note that this information does not say exactly where, or whether, the population (parameter) lies within this range. (In fact, the parameter either falls within the interval or not; only an all-knowing researcher would ever know.) What is critical, however, is that if the researcher continues to draw samples from a population of voters, the mean of the samples of voters will eventually equal the mean of the population, and if the researcher creates a specialized bar graph called a histogram showing the distribution of the individual sample means, the resulting shape would resemble a

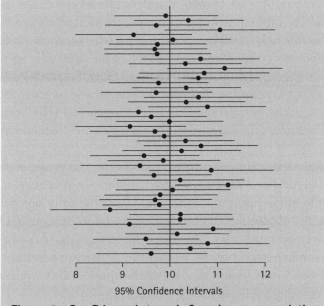

8   9   10   11   12

95% Confidence Intervals

Figure 2. Confidence intervals for a known population mean ten for fifty random samples from a population.

normal distribution. This is what enables researchers to make an inference—here, in the form of a sample statistic and a margin of error—about how all voters (the population) feel about the president by observing a single sample statistic. For the sake of illustration, consider Figure 2. Here we show the confidence intervals computed from 50 random samples from a population where the known parameter of interest is ten. The 95% confidence intervals are constructed to contain the true parameter 95% of the time. Here in all but two samples the horizontal confidence intervals contain the known parameter value. Of course, in any application we do not know the parameter value (if we did we would not need to perform inference!), but we use confidence intervals that over repeated samples will return the right answer a high percentage of the time.

This pertains to descriptive claims but it is important to draw a statistical inference when performing causal inference as well. Suppose that the average monthly income for the male professors in our sample of employees was $4,200, while for the females it was $3,900, yielding a difference of $300 in this sample. There are two possible explanations for the $300 difference (assuming *all else is constant*, a phrase we explain below). It might be the case that it is due solely to the particular sample we randomly drew; in other samples from the population the difference might only be $10, or women might make, on average, $250 more than men. It is also possible that in the population, men actually earn more than women.

The process researchers use to make this determination is called *hypothesis testing*. A hypothesis test tells us whether differences across groups are simply an artifact of sampling (the first possible explanation), or whether meaningful differences exist in the population (the second possibility). In the latter case we would say the difference is *statistically significant*. All statistical significance means is that sampling alone cannot explain the observed difference, and as such, it is likely that differences exist in the population. One would conclude a relationship is statistically insignificant when the difference in the sample can be explained by sampling alone.

In addition to statistical significance, it is important to consider the *substantive significance* of any finding. A $1,000 per month difference in salary is certainly large; an $8 per month difference is not. Both could be statistically significant, but only the first would be substantively significant. Accordingly, it is crucial for empirical researchers to compute and report the size of the differences—in addition to reporting the results of hypothesis tests—so that the reader can ascertain whether the findings are substantively important. In the following section we recommend using graphics to report these differences.

But before turning to data displays, one final topic deserves some attention: the assumption of "all else being constant" or "all things being equal." This assumption takes us back to a point we made at the onset; namely, when working with data generated by the world, most of the time "all else is constant" or "all things being equal" is untenable. It is quite possible, for example, that male professors in our sample do not have the same experience as females. Thus, just naïvely comparing the average salaries across the two groups would not provide a reliable causal inference.

Today, there are two approaches commonly used for making causal inferences from observational data. One type of analysis is *multiple regression* analysis, and related regression models (such as logistic regression). Regression models work by allowing the researcher to hold all other measured variables constant while assessing the relationship of interest. In this example, we could see whether the difference in salaries persisted by controlling for experience. Regression models have been used for decades and are the most common tool in empirical legal research. For many types of research they work quite well, but they do require some strong assumptions about the relationship between the key causal variable and the outcome variable of interest (see Imai, 2005).

Another set of methods called *matching methods* is becoming more popular in applied statistics. These cutting-edge tools are making their way into empirical legal studies (Epstein et al. 2005; Greiner 2008), and for many reasons we predict that their use will increase in the coming decades. The idea, to return to the example of pay equity, is to match most-similar male and female professors, and then compute differences between the matched observations. Once researchers have made the matches, these methods allow them to treat observational data as if it were experimental.

Regardless of whether one uses regression analysis or matching to control for alternative explanations, a causal inference is just a statistical inference about a difference. At bottom what researchers want to know is whether observed differences in a sample represent the same differences in a population.

V. THE LAST STEP: PRESENTING THE RESULTS OF EMPIRICAL LEGAL RESEARCH[12]

Just as scholars have been improving methods for causal inference, they have been working on approaches to convey the results of their studies. These developments should be of particular interest to quantitative empirical legal scholars who often must communicate their findings to judges, lawyers, and policy-makers—in other words, to audiences who have little or no training in statistics. Too often, though, analysts fail to take advantage of the new developments thus missing an opportunity to speak accessibly to their community.

To see the problem, consider an example adapted from a study that seeks to explain the votes cast by U.S. senators on Supreme Court nominees (Epstein et al., 2006).[13] Briefly, the authors operate under the assumption that electorally minded senators vote on the basis of their constituents' "principal concerns in the nomination process" (Cameron et al., 1990: 528). These concerns primarily (though not exclusively) center on whether a candidate for the Court is (1) qualified for office and (2) ideologically proximate to the senator (i.e., to his or her constituents). Consequently, the two key causal variables in their statistical model are (1) the degree to which a senator perceives the candidate as *qualified* for office and (2) the *ideological distance* between the senator and the candidate, such that the more qualified the nominee and the closer the nominee is to the senator on the ideological spectrum, the more likely the senator is to cast a yea vote. Also following from the extant literature, the researchers control for two other possible determinants of senators' votes: whether the president was "strong" in the sense that his party controlled the Senate and he was not in his fourth year of office; and whether a senator is of the same political party as the president.

To assess the extent to which these variables help account for senators' votes, the researchers employed logistic regression, a common tool in legal scholarship when

---

[12] We draw material in this section from Epstein et al. (2007); Epstein et al. (2006); Gelman, et al. (2002); King et al. (2000).

[13] Since publication of their study, Epstein et al. have updated their dataset (available at: <http://epstein.law.northwestern.edu/research/Bork.html>). We rely on the updated data.

Table 1. The "Ugly" Table. Logistic regression analysis of the effects on individual senators' votes on 41 Supreme Court nominees (Black through Alito). Cell entries are logit coefficients and robust standard errors. *p <.01.

Variable	Coefficient	Standard Error
Lack of Qualifications	−4.11*	0.22
Ideological Distance	−3.92*	0.23
Strong President	1.01*	0.13
Same Party	1.45*	0.15
Constant	3.32*	0.15
N	3809	
Log-likelihood	−916.91	
$X^2_{(4)}$	632.68	

the dependent variable is binary. Table 1 displays the results, and they seem to lend support to the researchers' hypothesis. For example, the * on the coefficient for lack of qualifications variable tells us that a statistically significant relationship exists between qualifications and voting: the lower a nominee's qualifications, the higher the likelihood that a senator will vote against the nominee.

On the other hand, tables of this sort (which run rampant in empirical legal scholarship) are not just ugly and off-putting to most readers; they communicate virtually no information of value either to the audience or even to the researchers themselves. Most lawyers, judges, and even law professors do not understand terms such as "statistical significance," much less "logit coefficient."

How might empirical legal scholars improve their data presentations? Adhering to three general principles would be a good start. First, we recommend that analysts communicate substance, and not only statistics. Reconsider this statement:

In looking at Table 1, we see that the coefficient on the variable lack of qualifications of -4.11 is "statistically significant."

This is not wrong but the emphasis on the coefficient is more than off-putting; it fails to convey useful information. In fact, all we learn from the -4.11 coefficient on lack of qualifications is that, controlling for all other factors, as we move from the most qualified to the most unqualified nominee we move down 4.11 on a logit scale. To make matters worse, because the logit scale is non-linear, moving down 4.11 units will result in different probabilities of a yea vote depending on where we start on the scale.

Because few of their readers would understand what any of this means, it is no wonder many empirical legal scholars simply say "the coefficient on lack of qualifications is statistically significant at the.01 level." But this too isn't an informative statement to many readers; it isn't even informative to readers with statistical training (a very small fraction of the legal community). It tells us is that qualified candidates are more likely to receive a yea vote than unqualified candidates but not how much more likely. 0.2 times more likely? 2 times? Or perhaps even 4 times? We probably wouldn't be very impressed, for example, if all else being equal, the predicted probability of a senator voting for a very qualified candidate was 0.11 and for a very unqualified candidate was 0.14. Certainly, a quantity such as a predicted probability is what matter most to readers of empirical legal scholarship. But it is not one that they can learn from a tabular display of logit coefficients.

This is why we recommend supplying readers with a quantity of interest; that is, replace "In looking at Table 1, we see that the coefficient on the variable lack of quali-fications of -4.11 is statistically significant" with:

Other things being equal,[14] when a nominee is perceived as highly unqualified the likeli-hood of a senator casting a yea vote is only about **0.24**. That probability increases to **0.92** when the nominee is highly qualified.

Statements of this sort are easy to understand even by the most statistically chal-lenged members of the legal community.

Second, we suggest that when they perform inference, researchers convey their uncertainty. To see the point, think about the statement above—that the likelihood of a senator casting a yea vote is only about 0.24 when the candidate is unqualified. This figure of 0.24 represents the researchers' "best guess" about the likelihood of a senator voting yea based on qualifications. But we know that error or uncer-tainty exists around that best guess. It is simply a fact of statistical analysis that we can never be certain about our guesses because they themselves are based on estimates.

Most quantitative empirical legal scholars appreciate this fact and supply the error surrounding their *estimated coefficients*. Statements such as this are not uncommon:

In looking at Table 1, the coefficient on the variable lack of qualifications (-4.11 with a stand-ard error of 0.22) is statistically significant at the.01 level.

True, this conveys uncertainty in the form of a standard error around the estimate but of what value is it? None, it turns out, because all the error value supplies is an estimate of the standard deviation of the estimated coefficient—which, standing alone, is of interest to no one, readers and scientists alike.[15]

One possible fix is for empirical legal scholars to follow other disciplines and report far-more-meaningful 95% (or even 99%) confidence intervals rather than (or

---

[14] We use the term "other things being equal" to signify that all variables in the model (other than the variable interest, here qualifications) are fixed at particular values. In this example, we set ideologi-cal distance at its mean and strong president and same party at o.

[15] Its value, rather, lies in computing confidence intervals.

in addition to) standard errors. In the case of lack of qualifications, the values of that interval are a lower bound of -4.54 and an upper bound of -3.69.

This interval comes closer than the standard error to conveying useful information: the researchers' best guess about the coefficient on lack of qualifications is -4.11 but they are "95% certain" that it is in the range of -4.54 to -3.69. Because 0 is not in this range (the confidence interval), the researchers and their readers can safely reject the null hypothesis of no relationship between the nominees' qualifications and senators' votes.

But even denoting the confidence interval around a coefficient would not be making the most of the model's results. When researchers say they are "95% certain" that the true logit coefficient lies between -4.54 to -3.69, they lose half their audience. What we recommend instead is combining the lesson here of relating uncertainty with the first principle of conveying substantive information:

Other things being equal, when a nominee is perceived as highly unqualified the likelihood of a senator casting a yea vote is only about 0.24 (±0.05). That predicted probability increases to 0.93, (±0.02) when the nominee is highly qualified.

Now readers need no specialized knowledge about standard errors or even confidence intervals to understand the results of the study—including uncertainty about the results. They can easily see that the researchers' best guess about the predicted probability of yea vote for a highly unqualified candidate is 0.24, though it could be as low as 0.19 or as high 0.29. Such accessible communication creates a win-win for empirical legal researchers and their audience: both are now in a far better position to evaluate the study's conclusions.

Our final recommendation is that analysts graph their data and results. With this, we are trying to convey two ideas. One is just a general point: if the goal is to give readers a feel for patterns or trends in the data, graphs are superior to tables—even for small amounts of data. Figure 3 provides an example from the project on Supreme Court nominees.

To be sure, if we looked at the table long enough some of the patterns we observe in the figure would emerge but it takes a lot more cognitive work on the part of the reader. Plus, it is unlikely that readers of empirical legal studies need such specific, precise information as in the table. So in most instances graphic displays can convey the right information without losing much.

The second idea, more relevant to the communication of results (rather than data, as in Figure 3), is that figures enable analysts to combine the first two principles we set out above (substance and uncertainty) across *many* values. Think about it this way: while substantive claims of the form "When a nominee is perceived as highly unqualified the likelihood of a senator casting a yea vote is only about 0.24 (±0.05)" may be informative, they exclude a lot of information—the values in between "highly unqualified" and "highly qualified." To provide these quantities, we could generate

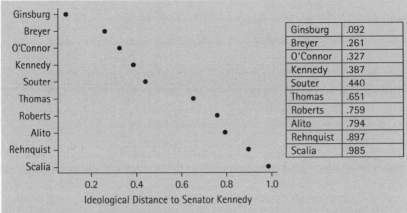

Ginsburg	.092
Breyer	.261
O'Connor	.327
Kennedy	.387
Souter	.440
Thomas	.651
Roberts	.759
Alito	.794
Rehnquist	.897
Scalia	.985

Ideological Distance to Senator Kennedy

Figure 3. Tables versus Figures.

Both the table and the figure provide information on the ideological distance between Senator Edward Kennedy (D-Mass.) and ten recent Supreme Court nominees. Juxtaposed against the table, the dot plot provides a more visually and cognitively appealing solution to the problem of providing the reader with information about variables of interest.

a long series of statements such as

- Other things being equal, when a nominee is perceived as highly unqualified the likelihood of a senator casting a yea vote is 0.24 (±0.05).
- Other things being equal, when a nominee is perceived as about average on the qualifications scale, the likelihood of a senator casting a yea vote is 0.83 (±0.03).
- Other things being equal, when a nominee is perceived as highly qualified the likelihood of a senator casting a yea vote is 0.93 (±0.02).

But graphing the results is a far more parsimonious, pleasing, and, for the readers of empirical legal work, cognitively less demanding approach. Underscoring these points is Figure 4. Here the reader gets a real sense of the (1) results and (2) uncertainty across the values of qualifications without having to sift through a long series of claims.

Even better, and usually necessary in multivariate analysis, is to bring in other variables of interest, as Figure 5 does. Here, we've juxtaposed qualifications against another variable: ideology, when senators and nominees are ideologically very close and when they are very distant. Specifically, in the two panels we show the probability of a senator casting a yea vote across the range of lack of qualifications and when we set ideological distance at its minimum and maximum levels. In both panels we depict our uncertainty, in the form of 95% confidence intervals, with vertical lines.

This display, we believe, is a good example of what we mean by parsimony. It conveys a great deal of information—actually it encodes 66 pieces of information—quite

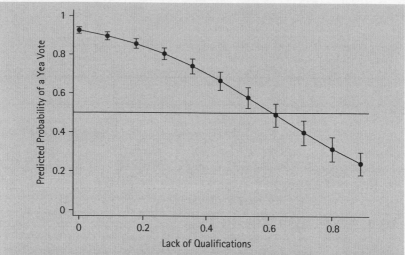

Figure 4. The effect of qualifications on Senate votes over Supreme Court nominees, from Black (1937) through Alito (2006).

The figure shows the predicted probability of a senator casting a yea vote over the range of lack of qualifications (0 is the most qualified), when we set ideological distance at its mean and the other variables in the statistical model at 0. The small vertical bars are 95% confidence intervals. Created using S-Post.

efficiently or at least more efficiently than the 66 sentences it would have taken to describe each and every result depicted in the two panels and certainly more accessibly than a table of logit coefficients.

Little more than a decade ago, implementing a graph of the sort depicted in Figure 4 would have been quite the chore: estimating the confidence intervals, in particular, was not possible for most empirical legal scholars. But now, because contemporary software packages use simulations (repeated sampling of the model parameters from their sampling distribution) to produce estimates of quantities of interest (e.g., predicted probabilities), generating assessments of error (e.g., confidence intervals) is quite easy.[16] Moreover, using the software requires no additional assumptions beyond those the researcher already has made to perform statistical inference.

Once researchers have prepared their results for presentation (and, ultimately, publication), their work would seem to be done. And, for the most part it is. But we in the empirical legal community should demand that they take one final step: archive their data and documentation. So doing ensures that empirical legal scholars adhere to the *replication standard*: Another researcher should be able to understand, evaluate, build on, and reproduce the research without any additional information from the author (King, 1995). This rule does not actually require anyone to replicate the results of an article or book; it only requires that researchers provide information—in

---

[16] King et al.'s (2000) Clarify is an example. It uses the Monte Carlo algorithm for the simulations, and can be implemented via the Clarify plug-in for Stata.

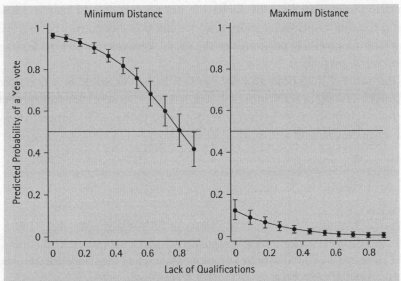

Figure 5. The effect of qualifications on Senate votes over Supreme Court nominees, from Black (1937) through Alito (2006), when the ideological distance between the Senator and nominee is very close (minimum) and very distant (maximum) and all other variables in the statistical model are set at 0.

the article or book or in some other publicly available or accessible form—sufficient to replicate the results in principle.

Why is such documentation a requisite step in conducting empirical research (regardless of whether the work is qualitative or quantitative in nature)? Epstein and King (2002) supply two answers. The first centers on the ability of outsiders to evaluate the research and its conclusions. In a broad sense, the point of the replication standard is to ensure that a published work stands alone so that readers can consume what it has to offer without any necessary connection with, further information from, or beliefs about the status or reputation of the author. The replication standard keeps empirical inquiry above the level of ad hominum attacks on or unquestioning acceptance of arguments by authority figures. The second reason is straightforward enough: as this Chapter has (hopefully!) made clear, the analyst's procedures may, and in most instances do, influence the outcomes they report. Readers deserve an opportunity to evaluate the researchers' choices, not to mention their data.

* * *

Designing research, collecting and coding data, analyzing data, and presenting results represent the four chief tasks of quantitative empirical legal scholarship, and we have tried to explain some of the basics. But readers should keep in mind that mastering the four requires far more than we can possibly convey here; it requires training. That is why PhD programs in the social sciences offer (at the least) a one-semester course on each.

Reading some of the books and articles we cite below would be a good start for legal scholars wishing to learn more—but only a start. To develop a full appreciation for the research process, we strongly recommend that readers contact their local social science departments.

References

Babbie, E. (2007). *The Practice of Social Research*, (11th edn.), Belmont, CA: Thomson.

Boyd, C.L., Epstein, L., and Martin, A.D. (2010). "Untangling the Causal Effects of Sex and Judging," *American Journal of Political Science* 54: 389–411.

Cameron, C.M., Cover, A.D., and Segal, J.A. (1990). "Senate Voting on Supreme Court Nominees: A Neo-Institutional Model," *American Political Science Review* 85: 525–34.

Epstein, L. and King, G. (2002). "The Rules of Inference," *University of Chicago Law Review* 69: 191–209.

Epstein, L. and Martin, A.D. (2005). "Coding Variables," in K. Kempf-Leonard (ed.), *The Encyclopedia of Social Measurement*, San Diego: Academic Press.

Epstein, L., Ho, D.E., King, G., and Segal, J.A. (2005). "The Supreme Court During Crisis," *NYU Law Review* 80: 1–116.

Epstein, L., Lindstadt, R., Segal, J.A., and Westerland, C. (2006). "The Changing Dynamics of Senate Voting on Supreme Court Nominees," *Journal of Politics* 68: 296–307.

Epstein, L., Martin, A.D., and Schneider, M. (2006). "On the Effective Communication of the Results of Empirical Studies, Part I," *Vanderbilt Law Review* 59: 1811–71.

Epstein, L., Martin, A.D., and Boyd, C. (2007). "On the Effective Communication of the Results of Empirical Studies, Part II," *Vanderbilt Law Review* 60: 798–846.

Frankfort-Nachmias, C. and Nachmias, D. (2007). *Research Methods in the Social Sciences*, New York: Worth.

Gelman, A. et al. (2002). "Let's Practice What We Preach: Turning Tables into Graphs," *The American Statistician* 56: 121.

Greiner, D.J. (2008). "Causal Inference in Civil Rights Litigation," *Harvard Law Review* 122: 533.

Ho, D.E. et al. (2007). "Matching as Nonparametric Preprocessing for Reducing Model Dependence in Parametric Causal Inference," *Political Analysis* 15: 199.

Holland, P.W. (1986). "Statistics and Causal Inference," *Journal of American Statistical Association* 81: 945–70.

Imai, K. (2005). "Do Get-Out-The-Vote Calls Reduce Turnout: The Importance of Statistical Methods for Field Experiments," *American Political Science Review* 99: 283–300.

King, G. (1995). "Replication, Replication, Replication," *PS: Political Science and Politics* 28: 443–99.

King, G., Keohane, R.O., and Verba, S. (1994). *Designing Social Inquiry*, Princeton University Press.

King, G., Tomz, M., and Wittenberg, J. (2000). "Making the Most of Statistical Analyses," *American Journal of Political Science* 44: 50.

Neyman, J. (1935). "Statistical Problems in Agricultural Experimentation," *Journal of the Royal Statistical Society* 2: 107–154.

Rachlinski, J.A., Guthrie, C., and Wistrich, A.J. (2006). "Inside the Bankruptcy Judge's Mind," *Boston University Law Review* 86: 1227–65.

Rubin, D.B. (1973). "Matching to Remove Bias in Observational Studies," *Biometrics* 29: 159–83.

Rubin, D.B. (1974). "Estimating Causal Effects of Treatments in Randomized and Nonrandomized Studies," *Journal of Educational Psychology* 6: 688–701.

3 8

QUALITATIVE APPROACHES TO EMPIRICAL LEGAL RESEARCH

LISA WEBLEY

I. Introduction and Background

QUALITATIVE research methods are often identified with the social sciences and humanities more generally than with the discipline of law in particular. That is not to say that lawyers do not make use of qualitative research methods in their own practice. Many common law practitioners are unaware that they undertake qualitative empirical legal research on a regular basis—the case-based method of establishing the law through analysis of precedent is in fact a form of qualitative research using documents as source material. But qualitative empirical legal research goes far beyond this kind of research. This Chapter will not focus on common law legal analysis of cases but instead provide an insight into different qualitative methods, many of which have been used in studies examining people's perception of law and justice (see, for example, Genn's *Paths to Justice*, 1999); lawyer-client interactions (see, for example, Sarat and Felstiner's study of divorce lawyers and their clients, 1995); alternative dispute resolution mechanisms and their relationship with the legal system (see, for example, Davis et al.'s study of the family mediation legal aid pilot in England and Wales, 2000, and Dingwall and Greatbatch's observation of family mediation sessions, 1991); gender, the legal profession, and professional identity (for example, Duff and Webley's study of women solicitors and career breaks, 2004); and legal aid and access to justice (see, for example, Moorhead et al.'s study of legal aid models and quality of legal service delivery, 2001).

It may be helpful to begin with a basic definition of qualitative research. Kirk and Miller (1986: 9) suggest that qualitative research

fundamentally depends on watching people in their own territory and interacting with them in their own language, on their own terms. As identified with sociology, cultural anthropology, and political science, among other disciplines, qualitative research has been seen to be "naturalistic," "ethnographic," and participatory."

By naturalistic Kirk and Miller mean that the research is conducted in its natural context (often "the field") rather than in an environment constructed by the researcher. By ethnographic they mean holistic (in an anthropological sense) and by participatory they mean that the research subject plays an active part in the process. The latter is, however, a contested point, as we shall examine later in the Chapter when we consider analysis of "traces"—documents constructed by those other than the researcher for a non-research purpose, such as a media report or a policy document.

Qualitative approaches are distinct from quantitative ones in that: "Technically, a 'qualitative observation' identifies the presence or absence of something, in contrast to 'quantitative observation,' which involves measuring the degree to which some feature is present...." (Kirk and Miller, 1986: 9). Consequently, qualitative research does not depend on statistical quantification, but attempts to capture and categorize social phenomena and their meanings. Bauer et al. (2000: 9) explain that:

One needs to have a notion of qualitative distinctions between social categories before one can measure how many people belong to one or the other category. If one wants to know the colour distribution in a field of flowers, one first needs to establish the set of colours that are in the field; then one can start counting the flowers of a particular colour. The same is true for social facts.

It is not possible to measure the frequency of a "social fact" until it has been identified and defined.

In qualitative research, the data are usually collected through three main methods, used singly or in combination: direct observation, in-depth interviews and analysis of documents (for a discussion, see May, 2001: 138–73; Punch, 1998: 139–68; or Patton, 2002: 4–5). The data may take a number of forms. It may include notes made by the researcher that provide a detailed description of what, where, and how people did what they did, their interactions, processes, etc., or a description of the researcher's observations and reactions to text-based sources, sounds, video, or images. Data may also be in the form of a transcript or verbatim quotes of what was said by the research participants and the researcher, or what was written in the text sources that s/he is examining. Consequently data may be derived from the research participants or texts and images directly (in the form of quotes) or via the researcher in the form of his or her reaction to or understanding of what was said or written.

There are misconceptions about when qualitative and quantitative research, and different modes of data collection within those approaches, should be used. Some have argued that qualitative methods should be used for exploratory research (research that is designed to examine whether an issue, situation, or problem exists and if so to define it) and quantitative research methods for explanatory research (research designed to determine why or how an issue, situation, or problem is as it is), but that both types may be used for descriptive studies (research designed to describe an issue, situation, problem or set of attitudes). These "rules" contain an element of truth, in that different forms of research design and different data collection methods lend themselves more readily to different types of research question. But the "rules" are by no means determinative. It is possible to use qualitative research for exploratory, explanatory, and descriptive research and to draw causal inferences from the data—assuming of course that the researcher develops an appropriate research design, and adopts an appropriate data collection method and mode(s) of data analysis in order to answer the research questions posed. We shall consider each of these later in the Chapter.

The discussion that follows is sub-divided into six sections. The first section considers the theoretical context and development of qualitative research. It has not been possible to look at any of the issues in detail, or to give in-depth answers to all the theoretical criticisms of qualitative methods. The second section provides a brief overview of aspects of qualitative research design including sampling, validity and dependability. The third section examines a range of data collection methods employed in qualitative empirical legal research, and the fourth section outlines three key modes of data analysis: classical content analysis, discourse analysis, and grounded theory method. The fifth section provides a case study to illustrate many of the themes discussed in the previous sections from research design to research method and data analysis. The final section offers some conclusions about qualitative research in the context of empirical legal studies.

II. Qualitative Research—Assumptions and Theoretical Underpinning

It is difficult to provide a precise or widely accepted definition of qualitative research and the theory underpinning it because so much of the terrain is contested. Most researchers who conduct qualitative research would agree that it is socially concerned, examines phenomena in their social settings (if field work is being undertaken) and considers those phenomena in context. Some argue that epistemological and ontological differences are at the heart of the divide between qualitative and quantitative research, and also at the heart of the definitional difficulties within the qualitative research literature. Epistemology, one's understanding of the nature of knowledge, and ontology, one's understanding of the nature of being or reality (is there one reality or several, or does each person construct their own reality?) affect the way in which one conducts research, interprets data, and reports findings. The two methodological traditions rest on different epistemologies—quantitative methods are often associated with deductive reasoning while qualitative methods often rely heavily on inductive reasoning. Deductive reasoning is based on a general hypotheses posed before data collection begins whereas inductive reasoning seeks to derive general themes or patterns from the data collected as the research progresses. But even those generalizations are not without their problems.

The focus of quantitative researchers on rigorous data-collection and modes of data-analysis is progressively being picked up by qualitative researchers intent on increasing the acceptability of qualitative research findings. But despite the similarities between quantitative research and at least some qualitative research, the basis upon which judgments are made in the two traditions respectively is often viewed as being very different. Many purely quantitative researchers argue that quantitative research enquires into observable, measurable, independent facts whereas many purely qualitative researchers argue that they enquire into socially constructed facts that do not have independence beyond the meaning ascribed to them by people. This has been explained as an objective/subjective divide, or in terms of a distinction between positivist and intepretivist (or "constructivist") epistemological approaches. However, there are other ways to categorize and delineate different forms of qualitative research. Patton (2002: Ch. 3) provides an extremely crisp and useful summary of these and May (2001: Ch. 1) outlines the main points of departure for the various modes of qualitative inquiry. Positivism considers people as the products of their environment and the researcher attempts to be an objective observer. The researcher examines the environment and people's reactions to it so as to understand the environment far better. Interpretivism also considers people as the products of their environment but additionally as those who construct the environment through their understandings of it. Researchers from the intepretivist tradition are more inclined to focus on an individual's inner world, their understanding of the world and as such are less concerned about researcher objectivity as they believe that we all construct our own reality.

Broadly researchers have tended to divide into one of two research traditions: positivism and interpretivism. Positivism has tended to be linked to quantitative research and intepretivism to qualitative research although there is no necessary link between interpretivism and qualitative research and indeed there are qualitative researchers (as discussed above) who undertake research from a positivist standpoint. King et al. (1994: 3), for example, appear to be more closely associated with the positivist conception of qualitative research than the interpretivist. One of the difficulties of linking positivism to quantitative research and interpretivism to qualitative research is that it may suggest that quantitative data speak for themselves because they are objective and that qualitative data require interpretation and lack of objectivity and thus validity. Quantitative data (statistical data) require human interpretation to give them meaning (see Kritzer, 1996); qualitative data sometimes need to be quantified to provide some understanding of how frequently particular themes emerge within the data.

Natural science is grounded in positivism and researcher objectivity and social science research has much in common with the natural sciences in this regard. Durkheim prescribes, first, that assumptions should not be made in advance of the research process and all preconceptions should be discarded. Secondly, he stipulates that the phenomena to be investigated, and the way they should be examined, must be determined before the research is undertaken but after previous research findings have been considered. He claims that the research process should be objective in the sense of being value-neutral and capable of revealing the truth about a given proposition. This is in keeping with the hypothesis-testing quantitative tradition in social science research, which is redolent of natural science. Some qualitative researchers adhere to these tenets and thus consider that if done well, both qualitative and quantitative forms of research can be systematic and produce valid, dependable findings.

King et al. argue that qualitative research is just as capable as quantitative research of producing valid descriptive and causal inferences (1994: 3), both being underpinned by the same logic of inference even though the two styles and techniques of research may be different.

However, researchers allied to interpretivism argue that positivist approaches to research may fall short when it comes to understanding and revealing the layers of social meaning and context that underpin social behavior and practices, which in turn produce and reproduce structural relations over time. The method of understanding people's meaning, whether it is the meaning that they attach to their own actions or the meaning they attach to other people's actions, Max Weber called *verstehen*. He considered this to be the method that all social sciences should follow. Many qualitative methods draw upon this understanding of social research. But if people construct their own meaning, where does that leave the researcher who seeks to understand others' meanings? Lofland (1971) argues that the role of a qualitative researcher is not to interject one's own view but instead to describe accurately another's experience so as to elicit what the research participant believes or understands, and to provide quotes as evidence, rather than to judge through one's own lens what that person must think or feel. This requires empathy rather than distance, even if that empathy should be derived from a place of neutrality (Patton (2002) coined the phrase "emphatic neutrality": p. 50). Some argue that stripping away the context in an attempt to achieve objectivity may in fact undermine the research, the analysis and the findings (see, for example, Bourdieu, 1992, and Goffman, 1981: 122). What does that mean in practice? It means that in order to really learn from others, one may need to interact with them rather than to remain entirely distanced. The researcher collects data by way of describing what she has heard or witnessed in a neutral way and without personal judgment. An intepretivist researcher would argue that her analysis will always reflect her own frame of reference, because no one is capable of being objective, all meaning being socially constructed. She would argue that to deny this is to deny the opportunity for the researcher to uncover and to critique her own understanding, which is an important part of interpretivist research.

Interestingly, at the same time as qualitative research has become more complex and divided in its theoretical underpinnings and understandings, a less clearly theoretically defined method of qualitative research has become increasingly popular and appears to appeal to researchers from different traditions. This is known as grounded theory. The grounded theory research method seeks to collect and analyze data in such a way so as to generate theory from data sources using a constant comparative method. It requires the researcher to revisit her descriptions of phenomena to examine whether they have continued validity or need amendment. The method appears to be broadly positivist in its underpinnings. However, the way in which the researcher extracts data from the data sources appears to have more in common with interpretivism, at least in the practice of some researchers (as discussed below). Grounded theory thus appears to skirt around many of the theoretical debates on epistemology, although they are hidden under the surface.

III. Research Design

Research design is a fundamentally important factor in any research project, including qualitative studies. However, research design may need to be more flexible and adaptive to changing circumstances and understandings when research is conducted in situ—for example, when observing a mediation meeting or a client meeting taking place in a solicitor's office. In design terms, qualitative research unfolds—it develops as the researcher learns more; in other words the experiment is not usually set up and then allowed to run along a predetermined course. Instead, the research may be redesigned to meet changing conditions, perceptions and findings. This means that the research design may be relatively fluid; the parameters of the study and the approach and methods adopted may have to be amended to accommodate altered understandings and changing dynamics. Different researchers embrace such change more or less willingly. Some will consider a fluid method to be a positive benefit, indicating the responsiveness of the research and the researcher, while others may experience rising panic that they are losing their grip on the study.

There are five basic aspects of designing a qualitative empirical research study once the researcher has framed the question to be posed in the research. First, the researcher needs to determine the methodology that is the most appropriate to answer the question within any constraints, such as limited access to data, ethical considerations, etc. A researcher will consider whether a case-study method, surveys and interviews, participant observation and ethnography, documentary analysis, or a combination of such methods is likely to answer the question most effectively. Data may be generated by examining documents that are already in existence, through interview transcripts, through audio or visual recordings or pictures, through observation notes, or through survey instruments or a number of sources in combination. Secondly, the researcher will need to consider how to select her research subjects or documents and how many to select, in keeping with the data collection methods that she has chosen to adopt. The third aspect concerns how the data are to be analyzed. Will the researcher use a grounded-theory method, content analysis, discourse analysis, thematic coding, historical or linguistic analysis, or statistical analysis? Will this be done using pen and paper or with the aid of a computer? Fourth, ethical considerations must be at the forefront of the researcher's mind, as the first rule is to try to do no harm to participants and if possible to do some good. Finally, the researcher may need to take into account whether they are working alone or in a team, as this may have an impact on various aspects of the research design. In order to answer the research question as fully and reliably as possible, it is important that all five aspects dovetail and are in tune with each other.

There are a number of research strategies, including experiments (in empirical legal research these will often take the form of simulated situations), historical analyses, interviews and surveys used to determine views and perceptions, case studies, documentary analysis (which could include historical analysis) and analysis of researcher-generated or extant statistics such as cost/benefit analyses. At one time it was thought that particular types of data were more appropriate for different types of research question: qualitative data was thought more useful the more exploratory the research, while quantitative data was thought more useful the more descriptive or explanatory the research. Particular research methods became allied with particular types of inquiry: interviews and case studies became linked with exploratory research, and experiments and surveys with descriptive and explanatory research. Yin (1994: 3) argues that over time these assumptions have been replaced by a more nuanced appreciation of the relative merits of the different research strategies and research methods. He argues that more important than the type of research being undertaken is the fit between the strategy (case study, archival analysis, survey, etc.) the form of the research question (why, who, what, where, when, how, etc.?), whether the research focuses on contemporary or historical events, and whether the researcher needs to have control over participant behavior or events or, by contrast, is operating in a naturalistic setting in which lack of control poses few if any problems (ibid: 6). Genn indicates that some researchers may consider a "quant sandwich" more appropriate, combining qualitative exploratory work, followed by a quantitative survey, which is then followed up with in-depth interviews (2009: 231). Kritzer considers that it may be useful to undertake qualitative research after quantitative research, so that the nuances of and mechanisms underlying the themes that have emerged during the quantitative phase may be examined in more detail (2009: 272).

A. Sampling

All researchers need to consider whom to interview, or what to observe or analyze, and how many participants or data sources are necessary to elicit findings in which one may have confidence. In other words, has the researcher interviewed a sufficient number of people or observed sufficient instances in order to capture a spectrum of viewpoints and experiences and to be able to report findings that report the nuances of experience rather than a narrow perspective? As a rule of thumb, quantitative methods rely heavily on the collection of large quantities of data from an entire population, or a random or representative sample, in a systematic fashion. Such data are analyzed statistically so that conclusions may be drawn to prove or disprove one or more defined hypotheses. If the data do not cover an entire population, it is important that they are from a sufficiently large and representative or random sample of that population, if the researcher wishes to argue that conclusions can be drawn from the data about the entire population. This is what political opinion polls are intended to do. Pollsters hope that by selecting a representative or random sample of the population of interest, asking respondents carefully worded, unambiguous questions in a consistent way, and analyzing that data using appropriate statistical techniques, they will be able to generalize to the entire population of interest. Quantitative studies that have been well designed and well executed should produce findings that are generalizable to the population if an appropriate sample has been drawn from that population (see Black, 1999: 27–139).

In contrast, qualitative research tends to focus on a smaller number of "observations" or "data sources," whether people or events or documents, which are considered to be data rich and thus worthy of study, and to examine them in-depth. There are various sampling techniques that may be employed. Some qualitative researchers may adopt versions of representative or random sampling used by quantitative researchers. Others may adopt an intentionally stratified sampling method in which they ensure that the research sample includes (for instance) people or documents in key categories. For example, if the research concerns the views of legal professionals, the sample may include a certain number of judges, a certain number of advocates, and a certain number of transactional lawyers in order to capture a full range of views among legal professionals. The researcher may opt for a snowball sampling technique, meaning that she will begin with a group of research participants known to her (or otherwise identified in advance in some way), and then ask each to provide details of someone else whom they consider to be a good research subject for the purposes of the study, and in that way gradually build up a larger sample of participants. Alternatively the researcher may seek out key people or events that are likely to provide rich sources of information or data. Patton describes this as "purposeful sampling" (2002: 45).

Qualitative researchers are not (usually) concerned that these people or situations should be statistically representative because they do not seek to reach findings that are generalizable to an entire population. Instead, focused, in-depth studies are designed to go beyond description to find meaning, even if that meaning is related to an individual's experiences of the justice system (for instance), or the perceptions of a small number of people on access to justice (for instance). In-depth research affords the researcher the opportunity to learn how research participants understand the world and interact with each other. A well designed study will usually also provide findings that capture a broad range of experiences rather than those from only a few people or situations. The findings will be representative in the sense of capturing the range or variation in a phenomenon, but not in the sense of allowing for the estimation of the distribution of the phenomenon in the population as a whole. The extent to which the researcher truly gets to grips with, say, model clients' experiences of the quality of the work undertaken by their solicitors (see Moorhead et al., 2001) will depend to a great extent on the research method employed, the rigor with which it is executed and also one's epistemological perspective. Once again, if the study has been well designed and well executed then the findings should be valid and dependable, but that does not mean that they will be generalizable. The findings should provide insight into a phenomenon and the extent to which it is present or absent; but unlike quantitative research, qualitative findings rarely provide a measure of frequency of occurrence.

B. Validity, reliability, and dependability of qualitative research

As discussed above, quantitative research methods have been closely linked to the natural sciences, and judgments about the quality of research have tended to adopt this perspective. Validity and reliability are both terms used extensively in respect of studies that make use of quantitative data. Validity is a measure of the extent to which the researcher has captured an accurate reflection of a phenomenon. Reliability refers to the extent to which the measurement procedure or instrument (such as a survey) would produce the same data were it to be administered at a different time or by someone else (Kirk and Miller, 1986: 41–42). Taken together, reliability and validity determine the extent to which the research, if done by someone else or in slightly different conditions, would lead to similar data (reliability) and whether the findings that flow from that data would provide an accurate reflection of the phenomenon being researched (validity). The terminology of validity and reliability are derived from positivist rather than interpretivist conceptions of data and data analysis. Interpretivist researchers argue that there are some difficulties with applying positivist interpretations of reliability to qualitative research, which is less concerned with quantity and distribution and more with people's understandings of the meaning of social facts.

In addition, in much qualitative research the researcher is the data collection tool, as well as the one who analyzes the data. In other research the researcher may construct a data collection tool (such as a survey), which captures the data at one step removed from the researcher. The extent to which the researcher is a stable and reliable data collection tool depends on his or her training and experience. Also important are the extent to which she is willing to pilot her method, to make adjustments in the light of the pilot, to be reflexive and to report on the strengths and weaknesses of her research, to be specific rather than too sweeping in her findings, and to provide evidence in support of points to allow others to check the extent to which she has drawn acceptable conclusions from the evidence. Rather than using the concepts "validity" and "reliability," some researchers prefer to assess the dependability and integrity (some would say trustworthiness or the extent to which the research and its findings are free from bias) of qualitative studies in terms of the questions posed, the methods used, data generated, triangulation (the combination of methods and data types), modes of analysis, and whether the evidence supports the findings. Some argue that qualitative research has much to learn from quantitative conceptions, and others such as Kritzer (1996) argue that quantitative research has much to learn from qualitative research. However, both traditions' tests for quality encompass an assessment of the research design, the data collection method and the data analysis in order to judge validity and dependability/reliability of the findings and thus are essentially similar. The next section will consider data generation and collection methods.

IV. Qualitative Data Generation and Collection Methods

Well done qualitative research should add to our understanding of individuals' experiences and behavior, or of structures and organizations, or of other social phenomena. Various research methods will support different types of findings, because different methods provide different insights. This section will consider some key data collection and/or data generation methods, concentrating on those that are more widely used in qualitative empirical legal research. Selection of data-collection methods is largely dependent on the research question, leading to the research strategy (design) that best fits the research objectives, the availability of or access to particular data sources and the resources available to conduct the study. Ethical issues also play an important role in choice of research subject and research method. The following sub-sections will focus on individual and group interviews; observation and participant observation; document analysis; and case study research.

A. Individual and group interviews

Individual and group interviews provide researchers with access to others' (memories of) experiences and perceptions. Interviews may be conducted face-to-face or remotely (via telephone or video link). Individual interviews are used extensively by qualitative researchers examining legal phenomena, and perceptions of law and the legal profession (see for example: Sommerlad, 2007; Thornton, 1996). Focus groups (group interviews) are one of a range of qualitative data collection methods that may lead to both useful data and truly participatory interviewer-interviewee interaction. "Groups are not just a convenient way to accumulate the individual knowledge of their members. They give rise synergistically to insights and solutions that would not come about without them" (Brown et al., 1989: 40). They are used less frequently in empirical legal research than are individual interviews, probably in part because of the negative connotations associated with their use in the party political arena, and in part because they are logistically more difficult to organize and require a skilled facilitator (for an example, see Duff and Webley, 2004).

Some general rules apply to qualitative interviews. For instance, they should be either very loosely structured (the researcher may make use of prompts to steer the discussion through a series of issues deemed important by the researcher) or only semi-structured (the researcher will have some set questions to ask but the majority of questions will be open-ended rather than closed). If the respondent consents, interviews are generally taped where possible to allow the researcher to analyze the full transcript. Interviews are extremely effective at garnering data on individuals' perceptions or views and on the reasoning underlying the responses. They also provide an insight into individuals' experiences. However, they do not provide good data on the interviewee's behavior (other than behavior in an interview setting) because of problems of memory and selective recall. Having the interview observed by a third party may assist the researcher, if the study is to examine behavior or interactions between research participants (Dingwall and Greatbatch, 1991).

B. Third party and participant observation

Observation research is fraught with methodological and ethical difficulties—if people know that they are being observed then they may consciously or subconsciously alter their behavior (known as the Hawthorne effect). But covert research poses significant ethical problems. Some researchers, principally ethnographers, may immerse themselves in a situation for an extended period of weeks, or even months or years, and keep a journal to note their observations. The researcher may even participate in the environment rather than observe as a bystander. This form of research has the benefit that research participants over time become less affected by researcher presence and revert to more usual patterns of behavior. However, it is also argued by others that research derived through participant observation may be tainted by the lack of critical reflection. Many ethnographers would argue that "going native" is a positive rather than a negative of this type of research, as it yields far better data, as long as the researcher remains reflexive (she examines critically her assumptions and motives). Becker and Geer state:

The most complete form of the sociological datum, after all, is the form in which the participant observer gathers it: an observation of some social event, the events which precede and follow it, and explanations of its meaning by participants and spectators, before, during and after its occurrence. Such a datum gives us more information about the event under study than data gathered by any other sociological method (1970: 133).

Dingwall argues that observation provides data that cannot be collected via interviews (Dingwall, 1997). One study that drew upon participant observation in the empirical legal arena is Flood's research on barristers' clerks (Flood, 1983).

Others prefer to observe from a more independent standpoint, as an outsider rather than as a participant. This form of observation is more likely to be episodic rather than continuous, in that the researcher observes a specific event or events for a relatively short period. Advocates of this research method consider that it combines some distance with a wealth of opportunities to collect contextualized, rich, description of the setting and quotes from those being observed. Eekelaar et al.'s (2000) study of divorce solicitors employed this form of observation along with other data collection methods (discussed in detail below). Observation notes seek to capture the detail of the scenes observed, along with researcher perceptions of those scenes. They should be sufficiently detailed to form the basis of reports that take the reader into the scene observed, and allow him or her to share the experience and learn from it as much as is possible through the written word. But access can be difficult, and the skill of writing field notes requires considerable practice (see Flood, 2005). Some researchers choose instead to tape record the interaction among research subjects (with consent) as well as to make observation notes (see Sarat and Felstiner, 1995).

C. Qualitative document analysis

Documentary analysis can provide a wealth of data, ranging from the official to the personal, the text-based and the image based. Documentary sources, other than primary legal sources such as cases and statutes, are relatively under-utilized in empirical legal research even though they provide a rich source of data (for an example, see Webley, 2008). May notes that

[d]ocuments, as the sedimentations of social practices, have the potential to inform and structure the decisions which people make on a daily and longer-term basis; they also constitute particular readings of social events. They tell us about the aspirations and intentions of the period to which they refer and describe places and social relationships at a time when we may not have been born, or were simply not present (2001: 157–8).

The apparent reluctance of empirical legal researchers to use non-legal documents as sources of data may in part be explained by the many differing conceptions of what constitutes appropriate method and about the reliance that can be placed on documents as sources of data. It may also indicate that researchers have not found documents that they consider useful data sources for their research.

There are many approaches to document analysis, and there is insufficient space to discuss them here. The mode of analysis (the way in which data are extracted from the documents) will in part depend on the nature of the documents, for example whether they are formal communications (case reports, legislation, newspaper articles, or policy documents) or informal communications (solicitor file notes, private letters, etc.). Some researchers may consider the context within which the documents were written and their intended audience. Others may examine the substance of the document but not its context. Some researchers have developed a checklist of questions that they believe the researcher should ask before documents or images are selected, reviewed and analyzed (see, for example, Finnegan's list of eight questions, 1996: 146–9).

Documentary analysis has been criticized on a number of grounds. Some argue that documents are not susceptible to scientific, systematic analysis in keeping with positivist traditions. To what extent can one draw conclusions from these documents? For some, documents reflect or report reality, describing an event, a perception, or an understanding (May, 2001: 158). An alternative view is that documents represent the practical requirements for which they were created or, in other words the purpose of the document. A third conception is that documents do not report social reality as such but are a source of meanings, "we now utilize our own cultural understanding in order to 'engage' with 'meanings' which are embedded in the document itself" (May, 2001: 163). This conception requires the researcher to elicit the meaning of the words as used in the document rather than to use the researcher's own understanding of the words and their meanings. However, this approach can lead to the conclusion that the document represents nothing but the words and meanings within it. For many researchers, documents provide evidence of policy directions, legislative intent, understandings of perceived shortcomings or best practice in the legal system, and agenda for change (see Bloch, 1992, for a discussion).

D. Case studies

The case study may be either an umbrella strategy that combines a range of data (for example survey data, interviews, documentary or historical analysis) or a distinct method of undertaking research. Yin describes a case study as "an empirical study that investigates a contemporary phenomenon within its real-life context, especially when the boundaries between the phenomenon and context are not clearly evident" (1994: 13). A case study may use either qualitative or quantitative methods or both. Yin argues that case studies come in three types—explanatory, exploratory and descriptive. He considers that they are best used to answer "how" and "why" questions through in-depth analysis of one situation, event or location. They are useful when the researcher has little control over the situation that she wishes to interrogate or when the researcher wishes to test a hypothesis that has been based on a broadly accepted theory (i.e., when the theoretical underpinning of the hypothesis is not itself the subject of the inquiry). However, case studies are far from an easy option. Although only one event, or case, or organization, or situation may be considered, it must be examined in great detail, relying on as many data sources as possible. The use of different data sources collected using a range of research methods assists in reducing the possibility that the research will lead to misleading findings based on an incomplete picture. The process of using multiple data sources to reach well rounded conclusions is known as triangulation. This adds weight to any findings. Researchers may choose to examine more than one event, situation, case or organization using a case-study format, although because the research must focus in depth on each one, it may be prohibitively time consuming to undertake case studies for a large number of situations or events (see Yin, 1994). The single case study has its roots in anthropology whereas multiple case studies have been more usual in sociological research (see Hamel et al., 1993: Ch. 1). Case-study research is designed to focus in detail on a given situation rather than to provide findings that are generalizable to other situations. However, it may be possible to reach a general conclusion by testing the findings of one case study by undertaking another, or if the specific case represents what Yin has referred to as a "critical case."

The next section will consider three of the main methods used to analyze the data, whether the researcher's own field notes, observation journals, interview transcripts, and so on, or documents developed by others.

V. Qualitative Research—Analyzing the Data and Finding Meaning

Data analysis and the drawing of conclusions and findings from the data are among the more contentious aspects of qualitative research. How can one derive valid and dependable findings from reams of observation notes, interview transcripts, or documents? As Miles explains:

[t]he most serious and central difficulty in the use of qualitative data is that methods of analysis are not well formulated. For quantitative data, there are clear conventions the researcher can use. But the analyst faced with a bank of qualitative data has very few guidelines for protection against self-delusion, let alone the presentation of unreliable or invalid conclusions to scientific or policy-making audiences. How can we be sure that an "earthy," "undeniable," "serendipitous" finding is not, in fact, wrong? (1979: 591)

We shall consider three relatively widely used modes of analysis in this section: classical content analysis, discourse analysis and the grounded-theory method. All rely on coding, which, as Gibbs states:

involves identifying and recording one or more passages of text or other data items such as the parts of pictures that, in some sense, exemplify the same theoretical or descriptive idea. Usually several passages are identified and they are then linked with a name for that idea—the code (2007: 38).

But, each method seeks to develop codes and to use codes in slightly different ways. These will be discussed below.

A. Classical content analysis

Classical content analysis is used to examine text or images, either documents that have been developed for other purposes (newspaper articles, case reports, etc.) or research-generated texts such as interview transcripts. It sits at the cusp of the quantitative and qualitative divide in that it often involves thematic categorization or coding, as well as counting the frequency with which those themes or codes appear. Content analysis has wide application. It can be used to examine the nature and frequency of particular types of legal phenomena within press reports or legal cases, or to consider the content of interviews or policy documents. It reduces text to codes by categorizing items in the text and then counting occurrences of those items to allow inferences to be drawn from the document. It facilitates analysis of longitudinal change over time—for example how use of the term "terrorist" has changed over time in case law. Content analysis can be descriptive, delineating the codes and the relationships between them, but it may also be used to explain or to develop a theory or theories. Researchers using classical content analysis rather than more qualitative forms of content analysis may be careful to ensure that they have drawn a random or representative sample of documents or research participants to interview, in this respect drawing on the quantitative sampling tradition rather than on qualitative methods. They will also be concerned with validity and reliability in the sense that those terms are used by quantitative researchers because their codes (units of measurement) and the inferences that they draw from them are broadly quantitative in nature. Researchers will keep a code-book that provides an exact, detailed description of each code in order to enable others to review their analysis and to reach judgments about the validity and reliability of the data analysis and findings.

However, some content analysts are more inclined toward a qualitative interpretation and may use purposive sampling, less quantification and more interpretation in their development of codes and their treatment of those codes. Code selection and development are a matter of researcher interpretation and researcher judgment. The researcher will develop an index of descriptors with labels that summarize the essence of the description (a code) to allow the data to be categorized. These indices are known as coding frames and may have more in common with forms of grounded theory than quasi-quantitative classical content analysis. Researchers read the text to pull out emerging themes, attempting to make them as specific as possible by analyzing how they are used, the limits of their use, the context within which they appear, and so on. Once these themes solidify, they become "codes" which may then be counted and considered in relationship with other codes.

Some researchers may code using pen and paper, while others may use computer software such as NVivo and Atlas to assist them in their work. Computer-assisted analysis may help to systematize coding, but it is still reliant on the researcher's selection of codes and her interpretation of the relationships between them. As such, content analysis can be a relatively highly systematized mode of qualitative data analysis, with relatively well-developed rules of sampling, selection of codes, analysis of those codes and reporting of findings. However, it remains interpretive, and the researcher must be able to justify the sampling method, and the validity of her coding frame, to a greater degree than in many other forms of qualitative analysis. In addition, as Bauer argues, the subject of content analysis is content present in the material being analyzed rather than what the material does not contain. The researcher can make few claims about material that is not found in the text, by comparison with material that is present, unless she has a prior hypothesis that she tests with reference to the presence or absence of particular content in the documents. Content analysis is reliant on a relatively large data set, which allows the researcher to interrogate the content of a range of documents to draw conclusions relating to a theme or themes, or a group or groups (such as solicitors, or judges, or the police). It thus focuses on collectives rather than individuals. Also, the context of communications may be (partly) lost when examining the text or the image in question.

B. Discourse analysis

Discourse analysis is a genre rather than a single mode of data analysis—there are a number of approaches underneath the umbrella term. Discourse analysis focuses on texts and examines the use of language, syntax, grammar, pauses, hesitations, repetitions, and so on, in the discourse being studied. It is an extremely detailed method that analyzes the text word by word, pause by pause, coupling description with evaluation. In the case of interviews, discourse analysis relies on extraordinarily detailed transcripts. Gill considers that there are four main themes in discourse analysis (2000: 174): "a concern with the discourse itself; a view of language as constructive and constructed; an emphasis upon discourse as a form of action; and a conviction in the rhetorical organization of discourse." All forms of text may be analyzed, and it is the structure of the discourse, rather than the meaning behind the text that is the key object of study. The organization of the text and its content are the subject of the inquiry. This form of analysis does not attempt to uncover objective facts. Indeed discourse analysts view discourse as socially constructed and as a way in which the speaker or writer can establish a particular version of the world. This may seem relatively straightforward, but the explanation of how discourse analysts go about their work is far more amorphous:

> Somewhere between "transcription" and "writing up," the essence of doing discourse analysis seems to slip away: ever elusive, it is never quite captured by descriptions of coding schemes, hypotheses and analytical schemata. However, just because the skills of discourse analysis do not lend themselves to procedural description, there is no need for them to be deliberately mystified and placed beyond the reach of all but the cognoscenti. Discourse analysis is similar to many other tasks: journalists, for example, are not given formal training in identifying what makes an event news, and yet after a short time in the profession their sense of "news values" is hard to shake. There really is no substitute for learning by doing (Gill, 2000: 177).

As with other forms of qualitative data analysis, data must be coded or categorized so as to reveal meanings contained within the data. The researcher will seek to develop labels that capture different phenomena present in the transcript. In discourse analysis the researcher will seek to uncover phenomena as understood by the research subject, rather than phenomena that they can read into the transcript from their own experience. Gill suggests that coding should be as open and inclusive as possible in the early stages, but over time, as differences emerge, the researcher will find patterns that require the codes to be refined, rethought, or rejected. Unlike classical content analysts, discourse analysts will consider what is not present as well as what is present. But, how does a researcher know that she has developed sound codes, particularly when she believes that all discourse, including her own, is constructed? Potter (1996) argues that codes should be subjected to deviant case analysis, meaning that data that appears to contradict codes should be subject to special scrutiny so as to assist with refining codes to a greater level of specificity. In addition, although not unique to discourse analysis, it may be useful to check how the research participants view the analysis; the extent to which later studies have agreed with or have deviated from the findings; and the extent to which readers have evaluated the study. Many discourse analysts will include the text that they have analyzed as part of the publication process, so that others too may subject it to analysis. Researchers must constantly review their codes to examine whether the codes accurately describe phenomena as viewed through the eyes of the speaker or writer rather than as viewed from the researcher's standpoint.

C. Grounded theory method

In keeping with much qualitative research, grounded theory involves developing theory as the research proceeds rather than testing a hypothesis posited in advance. Grounded theory has an appeal to many qualitative researchers because it follows the natural pattern of human inquiry. It allows the researcher to seek an understanding of an area, by developing and refining a theory as more is learned about the area. It is pragmatic and yet theoretical (Glaser and Strauss, 1967). In other words, grounded theory provides a framework for the whole research process and not simply a means of extracting data. It is a theory of research, a data collection method, a mode of analysis and a way of generating theory.

It would, perhaps be useful, to explain the actual research process by way of illustration. A well established theory is formed after three stages of analysis, although the stages are not necessarily consecutive, and the researcher could be undertaking different stages simultaneously as she adds more texts or documents to the sample she is analyzing. Stage one is to analyze documents, interview transcripts, or observation notes to discover conceptual categories from the data—basic codes. This is done by reading a document line by line, and "memoing" (a systematic form of note-taking) phenomena that are important in each sentence or paragraph, to come up with concepts. The researcher should note anything that strikes her as she is reading each line of text. This goes beyond describing what she has read and includes any reactions that she has to the text, or any associations that spring to mind. This stage is known as "open coding" because of its breadth. Over time, the researcher should refine her concepts: those concepts that continue to hold solid as she reads through the documents should be kept, and things that are not sustained in later documents should be rejected. The researcher constantly compares what she has found, line by line, document by document to ensure that her observations are producing replicable concepts rather than one-off observations.

In the second coding phase the relationships between the ever more specific concepts are examined to produce theoretical categories with reference to the memos developed in stage one. This is known as the axial coding stage. If one follows Strauss's and Corbin's view, the researcher needs to undertake this phase in the light of a particular theory. On the other hand, Glaser criticizes this standpoint and considers that true grounded theory requires the researcher to take his or her lead from the data rather than trying to impose a particular theoretical approach on the process (Glaser, 1992). The third and final stage of data analysis is to use the stage two theoretical categories to develop a core concept, theory, or conclusion. Each stage of data analysis leads to a higher level of abstraction from the original data. Because of the cyclical design, data could be collected for the second data cycle at the same time as the data from the previous cycle are being analyzed. These constant comparisons continue until the researcher considers that no further refinements can be made by examining more data—until nothing new is added, nothing more is rejected, and the theory or conclusion has crystallized. Grounded theory analysis is reliant on both what the researcher observes as she reads through the documents and her reactions to what she has observed.

Many criticisms have been leveled at the grounded theory approach. Commentators such as Denzin note that grounded theory only goes part way to meeting the needs of some interpretivist researchers because grounded theory is a product of an empirical research genre which seeks to systematize the research process to allow for replication of findings as required by positivist research theory (Denzin and Lincoln, 2000: 509–35). However, this assumes that the researcher considers that the core concept she has abstracted into theory is an objective truth that has been discovered in much the same way as that in which scientific principles may be established. On the contrary, the grounded theory methodology can be understood as offering a method of undertaking research as well as a systematic approach to qualitative analysis, a strategy for research rather than as method to generate more positivist findings. Like most modes of qualitative analysis, it is broadly inductive and thus seeks to draw out concepts from the data, to organize them and to theorize them, but to do so in a structured and considered fashion.

VI. Qualitative Research in Practice: A Case Study of Lawyer-Client Interactions in a Divorce Context

In order to illustrate some of the issues raised in the general discussion above, this section considers a qualitative empirical legal study conducted by Eekelaar, Maclean, and Beinart (2000). The study examined the work of solicitors in divorce cases in England and Wales (Davis et al. (1994) conducted similar research in England and Wales, and Sarat and Felstiner (1995) in the U.S.). Eekelaar et al.'s study is informative, because it used a mixed method in two distinct phases (principally observation and interviews, with some documentary research), and content analysis to analyze the interview transcripts.

The background to the study was a set of assumptions about solicitor adversarialism in divorce matters seemingly widely held by the media, policy-makers, and politicians around the passage of a new Family Law Bill in the UK. In a previous study Lewis had examined government policy-makers' perceptions of adversarialism through a qualitative study of policy documents (Lewis, 2000: 6–7) and found these assumptions to be widespread and influential in the policy and legislative agenda in the UK at the time. There was little systematic evidence underpinning these perceptions, and yet they were prevalent and were regularly referred to in political and media discourse as well. Eekelaar et al.'s study sought to consider whether these assumptions had any empirical validity, by examining the primary data source—the way in which solicitors interacted with their divorce clients and with other solicitors—through observation of interactions and through the traces of their interactions in the form of letters and file notes on their case files. They also asked solicitors to explain their interactions and their approach to clients and to other solicitors.

This was a micro level study, examining the work of a sample of individual solicitors. The researchers used a three-fold methodology. In the first instance they observed ten partner-level solicitors at work for a day (14 days' observation in total as two researchers observed some of the solicitors), recording what the solicitors did in descriptive terms. They explained that, "The purpose of this exercise was to acquire evidence of the business context in which the lawyers operated, how they prioritised and responded to issues as they arose, and the details of their interaction with clients" (2000: 31). The second mode of data collection was to conduct interviews with 40 solicitors who were asked to talk about pre-selected cases from the beginning of the case to the present position. These solicitors were from four regions in England and Wales and were chosen from solicitors listing family work as an area of practice in the Law Society Regional Directories (2000: 34). Because of the qualitative nature of the study and the size of the sample, the researchers could not claim that the findings were representative of all divorce solicitors in England and Wales; but the research methods deployed provided a depth of understanding that could not have been gained by quantitative methods. The range of solicitors that were interviewed provided a variety of experiences that were considered to be representative of different types of family law solicitors even if not representative in quantitative terms.

The dual approach to data collection (observation and interviews linked to case files) provided a more rounded data set and more in-depth findings than would have been possible using a single method alone. The observation allowed the researchers to watch solicitor-client interaction (behavior), as well as to experience their working day. The interviews provided evidence of solicitor perceptions, their reasoning and their approach to clients and to other solicitors. The researchers asked the solicitor to pull out the file prior to the interview and to talk through the case. The discussion of the case files provided insights into solicitor-client and solicitor-solicitor interactions. After the pilot the researchers drew up a list of prompts, open questions that acted as a means to begin discussions on particular issues, which they could use in interviewing solicitors to ensure that key information was not missed and yet discussions were not unduly choreographed by the interviewer. Once all the data had been collected, the interview transcripts were analyzed using content analysis, and illustrative quotes were included in the write-up of their findings as evidence of what they had observed and heard. The quotes also allow the reader to see some of the raw data, allowing the reader to travel to the solicitors' offices to sit with the researchers and reach conclusions of their own.

Eekelaar et al.'s findings have done much to challenge pervasive perceptions, among law-makers, some academics and even some family mediators, that divorce solicitors adopt an adversarial posture. They found little evidence of adversarialism, only coming across two cases in which there was any evidence of "point scoring" by one or both of the solicitors—and this appeared to be driven by the clients rather than originating from the solicitors. They found a plethora of examples of solicitors providing practical support, guidance, assistance with third parties, assistance over and above what would be expected of a solicitor acting as adviser and champion in the adversarial paradigm. Solicitors tried to encourage their clients to negotiate between themselves in relation to children and household issues and items; they did not encourage a complete break in communication that would have allowed them to "handle" the case in all respects (Eekelaar et al., 2000: 184). The team found that, if anything, solicitors tried to take measures to reduce tension between the couple rather than increase it. Solicitors did not see tension as an effective tool to resolve disputes between the parties in a divorce context. In addition, this research provides some evidence indicating that solicitors, in England and Wales at least, do not attempt to maximize the outcome for their clients, at the expense of the other party and other interested parties, regardless of applicable legal norms. These findings did not support the policy-makers' and media's perceptions of adversarialism, and provide an alternative, evidence-based picture of divorce practice in England and Wales.

VII. Conclusions

As I hope this Chapter has illustrated, there are a number of understandings of qualitative research, research design and strategy, the methods that may be adopted to undertake such studies, the data that may be collected and the ways in which they may be analyzed. Many of these understandings are held in common by qualitative and quantitative researchers, even if sampling and measures of validity and reliability/dependability may differ between the two traditions. Before choosing a method, standpoint, or mode of analysis, a researcher needs to consider the purpose of her study, the access that she may be given to potential participants and places, the extent of her resources, the research time frame, the intended audience, the use to which she hopes that the research will be put, her view on research and its meaning, and her training and expertise. Then she should choose a research strategy, and all that flows from it, which is suited to the research question and the study's aims.

Qualitative research is particularly good for examining whether or not a particular social phenomenon exists and if so, the nature of the phenomenon. It is less use for assessing the extent and distribution of a phenomenon, something that is better left to quantitative research. Qualitative research usually yields extensive data, much of it descriptive in its initial stages, from which the researcher often seeks to derive an understanding of key patterns or themes. It is not unusual to discover that one's findings are actually relatively modest in scope, if insightful. Qualitative studies may not (usually) provide systematic generalizable findings, but often problems within the legal system, best practice insights and the effect of policy shifts can only be examined using in-depth, qualitative methods. Just as the common lawyer learns to understand the law by focusing on a small number of important and relevant precedent-bearing cases, so the qualitative researcher sets out to understand individuals' experiences of law, legal meaning, and the justice system and their relationship with it.

REFERENCES

Bauer, M.W. (2000). "Classical Content Analysis: A Review," in M.W. Bauer, G. Gaskell, and N.C. Allum (eds.), *Qualitative Researching with Text, Image and Sound: A Practical Handbook*, London: Sage Publications.

Becker, H. and Geer, B. (1970). "Participant Observation and Interviewing: A Comparison," in W.J. Filstead (ed.), *Qualitative Methodology Firsthand Involvement with the Social World*, Chicago: Markham Publishing, 133–42.

Black, T. (1999). *Doing Quantitative Research in the Social Sciences: An Integrated Approach to Research Design, Measurement and Statistics*, London: Sage Publications.

Bloch, M. (1992). *The Historian's Craft*, P. Putnam (transl.), Manchester: Manchester University Press.

Bourdieu, P. (1992). *Language and Symbolic Power*, J. Thompson (ed.), and G. Raymond and M. Adamson (transl.), Cambridge: Polity Press.

Brown, J., Collins, A., and Duguid, P. (1989). "Situated Cognition and the Culture of Learning," *Educational Researcher* 18: 32–42.

Bryman, A. (2004). *Social Research Methods*, (2nd edn.), Oxford: Oxford University Press.

Burgess R. (1990). *In the Field: An Introduction to Field Research* (4th edn.), London: George Allen and Unwin.

Chalmers, A. (1982). *What Is This Thing Called Science?*, Milton Keynes: Open University Press.

Davis, G., Bevan, G., Dingwall, R., Finch, S. Fitzgerald, R., and James, A. (2000). Monitoring Publicly Funded Family Mediation: Final Report to the Legal Services Commission, Legal Services Commission.

Davis, G., Cretney, S., and Collins, J. (1994). *Simple Quarrels: Negotiations and Adjudication in Divorce*, New York: Oxford University Press: chapter 3.

Denzin, N. and Lincoln, Y. (eds.) (2000). *Handbook of Qualitative Research* (2nd edn.), Thousand Oaks, CA: Sage Publishing.

Dingwall, R. (1997). "Accounts, Interviews and Observations," in G. Miller and R. Dingwall (eds.), *Context and Method in Qualitative Research*, London: Sage Publications.

Dingwall, R. and Greatbatch, D. (1991). "Behind Closed Doors. A Preliminary Report on Mediator/Client Interaction in England," *Family Court Review* 29(3): 291.

Duff, L. and Webley, L. (2004). *Equality and Diversity: Women Solicitors Research Study 48 Volume II*, Law Society Research Study Series, London: The Law Society.

Durkheim, E. (1982). *The Rules of Sociological Method And Selected Texts on Sociology and Its Method*, New York: Free Press.

Eekelaar, J., Maclean, M., and Beinart, S. (2000). *Family Lawyers: The Divorce Work of Solicitors*, Oxford: Hart Publishing.

Finnegan, R. (1996). "Using Documents," in R. Sapsford and V. Jupp (eds.), *Data Collection and Analysis*, London: Sage Publications Ltd, 146–9.

Flood, J. (1983). *Barristers' Clerks: The Law's Middlemen*, Manchester: Manchester University Press.

Flood, J. (2005). "Socio-Legal Ethnography," in R. Banakar and M. Travers (eds.), *Theory and Method in Socio-Legal Research*, Oxford: Hart Publishing, 33–48.

Genn, H. (1999). *Paths to Justice: What Do People Think About Going To Law?*, Oxford: Hart Publishing.

Genn, H. (2009). "Hazel Genn and Paths to Justice," in S. Halliday and P. Schmidt (eds.), *Conducting Law and Society Research: Reflections on Methods and Practices*, New York: Cambridge University Press: 227–39.

Gibbs, G.R. (2007). *Analyzing Qualitative Data*, London, Thousand Oaks CA: Sage Publications.

Giddens, A. (1993). *Sociology*, Cambridge: Polity Press.

Gill, R. (2000). "Discourse Analysis," in M.W Bauer, G. Gaskell, and N.C. Allum (eds.), *Qualitative Researching with Text, Image and Sound A Practical Handbook*, London: Thousand Oaks, CA: Sage Publications.

Glaser, B. (1992). *Basics of Grounded Theory Analysis: Emergence vs. Forcing*, Mill Valley, CA: Sociology Press.

Glaser, B. (2002). "Constructivist Grounded Theory?," *Qualitative Sozialforschung/Forum: Qualitative Social Research* 3(3), available at <http://www.qualitative-research.net/fqs/fqs-eng.htm>.

Glaser, B. and Strauss, A. (1967). *The Discovery of Grounded Theory: Strategies for Qualitative Research*, Chicago: Aldine.

Goffman, E. (1981). *Forms of Talk*, Philadelphia: University of Pennsylvania Press.

Gubrium, J. and Holstein, J. (2000). "Analyzing Interpretive Practice," in N. Denzin and Y. Lincoln (eds.), *Handbook of Qualitative Research* (2nd edn.), Thousand Oaks, CA: Sage Publications: 487–508.

Hamel, J. with Dufour, S. and Fortin, D. (1993). *Qualitative Research Methods Volume 2*, Newbury Park: Sage Publications.

King, G., Keohane, R.O., and Verba, S. (1994). *Designing Social Inquiry Scientific Inference in Qualitative Research*, Princeton, NJ: Princeton University Press.

Kirk, J. and Miller, M.L. (1986). *Reliability and Validity in Qualitative Research*, Beverly Hills: Sage Publications.

Kritzer, H.M. (1996). "The Data Puzzle: The Nature of Interpretation in Quantitative Research," *American Journal of Political Science* 40: 1–32.

Kritzer, H.M. (2009). "Conclusion: 'Research Is a Messy Business' An Archeology of the Craft of Socio-Legal Research," in S. Halliday and P. Schmidt (eds.), *Conducting Law and Society Research: Reflections on Methods and Practices*, New York: Cambridge University Press: 264–85.

Lewis, P. (2000). *Assumptions about Lawyers in Policy Statements: A Survey of Relevant Research No. 1/2000*, London: The Lord Chancellor's Department.

Lofland, J. (1971). *Analyzing Social Settings*, Belmont, CA: Wadsworth.

May, T. (2001). Social *Research: Issues, Methods and Practices* (2nd edn.), Buckingham: Open University Press.

Miles, M. (1979). "Qualitative Data as an Attractive Nuisance: The Problem of Analysis," *Administrative Science Quarterly* 24: 590.

Miles, M. and Huberman, A. (1994). *Qualitative Data Analysis* (2nd edn.) Thousand Oaks, CA: Sage Publications.

Moorhead, R., Sherr, A., Webley, L., Rogers, S., Sherr, L., Paterson, A., and Domberger, S. (2001). *Quality and Cost: Final Report on the Contracting of Civil Non-Family Advice and Assistance Pilot*, Norwich: The Stationery Office.

Patton, M.Q. (2002). *Qualitative Research and Evaluation Methods* (3rd edn.), London: Sage Publications.

Platt, J. (1981). "Evidence and Proof in Documentary Research: Some Specific Problems of Documentary Research," *Sociological Review* 29(1): 31.

Potter, J. (1996). *Representing Reality: Discourse, Rhetoric and Social Construction*, London: Sage Publishing.

Punch, K. (1998). *Introduction to Social Research*, London: Sage Publications.

Roberts, S. (1979). *Order and Dispute: An Introduction to Legal Anthropology*, Harmondsworth: Penguin.

Sarat, A. and Felstiner, W.L.F. (1995). *Divorce Lawyers and Their Clients: Power and Meaning in the Legal Process*, New York: Oxford University Press.

Schwandt, T. (2007). *Dictionary of Qualitative Inquiry* (3rd edn.), Thousand Oaks, CA: Sage Publications.

Scott, J. (1990). *A Matter of Record: Documentary Sources in Social Research*, Cambridge: Polity Press.

Sommerlad, H. (2007). "Researching and Theorising the Processes of Professional Identity Formation," *Journal of Law and Society* 34(2): 190.

Strauss, A. and Corbin, J. (1998). *Basics of Qualitative Research: Techniques and Procedures for Developing Grounded Theory* (2nd edn.), Thousand Oaks, CA: Sage Publications.

Thornton, M. (1996). *Dissonance and Distrust—Women and the Legal Profession*, Oxford: Oxford University Press.

Weber, M. (1949). *The Methodology of the Social Sciences*, E. Shils and H. Finch (transl.), New York: Free Press.

Webley, L. (2008). *Adversarialism and Consensus? The Messages Professional Bodies Transmit About Professional Approach and Professional Identity to Solicitors and Family Mediators Undertaking Divorce Matters*, IALS: London.

Yin, R. K. (1994). *Case Study Research Design and Methods* (2nd edn.), Thousand Oaks, CA: Sage Publications.

39

THE NEED FOR MULTI-METHOD APPROACHES IN EMPIRICAL LEGAL RESEARCH

LAURA BETH NIELSEN

I. INTRODUCTION

AN Indian parable (which has Buddhist, Jain, and Sufi variations) describes blind men (or men in the dark) feeling (empirically researching) an elephant. The man who feels the tail reports that the elephant is like a brush, the man who feels the tusk says the elephant is like a spear, the man who touches the side reports that the elephant is like a wall, and the man who feels the ear describes the elephant as resembling a fan. The lesson of multiple perspectives—indeed multiple truths—is often borne out in empirical legal research. Like the men in the dark, we often study a phenomenon using one approach. That approach may lead us to accurate information about some part of the phenomenon, but as researchers, we typically want to study the whole elephant. How can we do that? How do we turn on the lights? In this essay I propose multi-method research as a comprehensive approach for empirical legal studies.

Empirical research in the Law and Society tradition (which I take to include various schools of research known as "Sociolegal Research," "New Legal Realism," and now "Empirical Legal Studies") has long embraced multi-method research to better understand the relationship of law and the social world. Some of the most enduring findings about important aspects of the legal system come from projects employing multi-method approaches. I suggest that the reason is that the phenomenon of law itself consists of individuals, organizational settings, institutional fields, and the interactions among them. Law is practiced by individuals as plaintiffs, defendants, lawyers, and judges. These individuals operate within organizations like workplaces, law firms, schools, to name just a few. These organizations can obfuscate, constrain, and empower individual actors, and therefore play a mediating role in how law operates. Finally, law operates in various institutional contexts. Social institutions like race, gender, and class affect legal processes, as well. As a result, fully understanding law demands research conducted using multiple approaches.

Not only does the complexity of the social world in which law operates make multiple research methods appropriate, but the empirical study of law almost always is in fact multi-method. Even when a project does not systematically employ multiple methods, empirically oriented scholars of law and legal institutions are almost always using multiple methods whether or not they recognize that fact. For example, reading a case or a set of cases may inspire questions about how business is (or is not) reacting to a body of law (Macaulay, 1963). Or, reading newspaper accounts of a "litigation explosion" may lead us to wonder about rates of litigation over time (Galanter, 1983). Empirical observations from our own practice of law or anecdotes from our lawyer-friends may lead to questions about how regulatory agencies make decisions or how courts interpret legal doctrine. We may not always conduct *systematic* multi-methodological research, but the very process of research necessarily involves gathering information in a variety of ways.

This Chapter examines the multi-method tradition in empirical legal research, defines some basic concepts, discusses when and why multi-method research is useful, and how the different actions of research (reading, counting, and interacting) can provide unique approaches to the same questions. I explore three examples of projects to demonstrate how the combination of research methods can lead to findings unanticipated or impossible using only one approach. I conclude with a cautionary note about projects using multi-method design.

II. What is Multi-method Research?

Put most simply, multi-method research is any research that uses more than one research technique or strategy to study one or several closely related phenomena. Research that employs multiple tactics for observing and understanding is more reliable than a single study if the studies are of comparable quality. The term "triangulation" is often used to describe deployment of multiple methods (Bachman and Schutt, 2007) although triangulation may seem to require three different studies or methods whereas a researcher may conduct multi-method research using two or more than three methods (Brewer and Hunter, 2006).[1]

Given the variety of useful research methodologies described in this volume and elsewhere, why might it be necessary to do multi-method research? As this volume demonstrates, every methodology provides a technique for studying how law works in the world but each methodology comes with important caveats. *Experimental designs* have substantial internal validity, meaning that the design assesses whether the experimental treatment has an effect because the researcher employs strict controls on manipulated conditions. Internal validity can come at the expense of external validity because the very conditions for an experimental design may not reflect the variety of conditions in the social world. *Surveys* provide a snapshot of a system or population at a particular moment in time and thus can supply comprehensive measurement of attitudes and demographic characteristics. Yet surveys are less able to adequately explain processes and mechanisms. *Qualitative in-depth interviews* provide insight into processes and subjectivities, but often at the expense of representativeness. Systematic and critical *document analysis and historiography* (using court opinions, court documents, newspaper

---

[1] While the term "triangulation" seems to suggest three perspectives, it actually comes from the idea that one can locate a point by viewing it from two locations, thus creating a triangle.

clippings, and other primary archival materials) provide important knowledge about formal processes; but some of these kinds of documents (e.g., materials in court files) are constructed as part of an adversarial process, or according to the norms of other professions such as the media. Such documents are themselves artifacts and must be understood in context rather than as representing some sort of neutral lens on the truth. Each research strategy is appropriate for certain kinds of questions, but we may wonder what we are missing by employing a single strategy when we seek to understand complex interactions, organizations, and institutions that make up our legal systems.

Kim Scheppele describes the strategies of research as falling into three basic categories: reading; interacting; and counting (Scheppele, 2009). Scheppele's typology is designed to aid the researcher's focus on what they are doing. "Reading" methodologies include document analysis, historiography, archival work, content analysis of newspapers, photographs, or movies and the like. "Interacting" research includes interviews, ethnography, surveys, and case studies. Finally, "counting" can occur in quantitative research and includes use of surveys, and official statistics collected by the researcher or by a third party like the Department of Justice or the FBI. Each category of methodologies is appropriate for different kinds of questions and research collected in one way can be analyzed in other ways. Put differently: "if you are asking 'how many, or how much?' questions, then you have to collect quantitative data. But when you get to 'Why do people do the things that they do?' or 'What are the factors that influence choices?' . . . if you actually want to understand it, you have to do it qualitatively" (Genn, 2009). Scholars who employ multiple methods have the luxury of being able to do reading and interacting or counting and interacting. In other words, a multi-method approach allows us to understand "how many" and "how come?"

Consider a well-known focus of socio-legal research: crime rates. Scholars use all sorts of methods to understand crime rates. A crime rate seems to be the quintessential "how much?" question. "How often does a particular crime occur?" seems best answered using quantitative methods. For example, the FBI regularly collects survey data about a variety of crimes from local, state, and federal police departments (Federal Bureau of Investigation, 2007). A survey that asks a nationally representative sample of police forces to disclose reported rapes and murders would produce a "crime rate" for both crimes. The murder rate likely would be fairly accurate (assuming the survey was easy to understand and had a respectable response rate) but might include some over-counting (perhaps a natural death ruled a murder) and some undercounting (perhaps bodies never found of people never reported missing). Rape, on the other hand, is notoriously under-reported (Clay-Warner and Burt, 2005); and so while a survey of law enforcement would provide an accurate count of *reported* rapes, that rate's relationship to the underlying number of *actual* rapes is far less straightforward than in the example of murder. The quantitative or counting approach might be a good place to start, but interactive methods provide important further information about the rape crime rate.

To come closer to counting actual rapes, a researcher may conduct in-person interviews with a random sample of women in which interviewer and interviewee establish a level of rapport required for discussion of such matters. Other scholars of rape have conducted ethnography in rape-crisis centers both to understand the process by which women who believe they have been raped decide whether or not to report the incident to the police (an interactive method) and to try to determine the ratio of reported rapes to actual rapes. When the qualitative and quantitative data converge and researchers arrive at a level of consistency about the ratio of unreported to reported rape, we may then be able to estimate the number of actual rapes based on the numbers reported. There is voluminous research on how to accurately count rapes, but the point here is to provide a concrete example of how—as in the case of our men studying the elephant—counting, interacting, and reading provide different "realities." And, when used together, multiple approaches to research can lead to better information.

The best kinds of research then, often involve some combination of methods. Preliminary interviews and exploratory data collection may lead us to theory generation (Fenno, 1986). For some researchers, this phase of qualitative investigation at the start of a project—talking to lawyers, judges, reading, and observing—is a crucial first step in identifying the kinds of questions to ask. It leads to the kinds of "how much" or "how many" questions best answered with quantitative or counting research. Quantitative results then often raise new questions that the researcher goes on to answer using systematic qualitative analysis. This kind of staged research, which begins with "theory generating" qualitative work, followed by quantitative work, which in turn raises new questions that are explored qualitatively, has been referred to as the "quant sandwich" (Genn, 2009). One can also easily imagine a "qual sandwich," where quantitative research raises process questions, which are explored qualitatively and the themes that emerge are then operationalized[2] for additional quantitative analysis.

Either way, the revelations from the different sources are best understood when they are in conversation with one another. The best research uses a variety of methodologies to provide a more nuanced understanding of law, legal institutions, and legal processes than can be provided by any one methodology alone due to the complex nature of the social world in which they operate. And when different methodologies are used together in ways that are interactive and linked, research can have more explanatory power (Brewer and Hunter, 2006)

---

[2] Operationalization refers to the process by which non-specific concepts are translated into discrete variables that can be measured. For example, if "length" is the concept, its operationalized form could be centimeters, inches, or meters.

The next section of this Chapter describes multi-method research projects in three different fields of law-related research. Each project has different theoretical underpinnings, descriptive findings, and explanatory analysis. And yet, through the combination of research methods, each reveals something that would not have been revealed using a single method.

III. Exemplars of Multi-Method Research in Empirical Legal Studies

While "empirical legal studies" as an intellectual movement may be relatively new, the empirical study of law, legal institutions, and legal processes has quite a long history (see Chapter 36 in this volume). Whether conducted under the banner of sociological jurisprudence, legal realism, law and society, socio-legal studies, new legal realism, jurisprudence and social policy, or empirical legal studies, legal scholarship long has been improved and influenced by empirical studies of law. In this section of the Chapter, I will examine three completed multi-method studies discussing (1) why a multi-method design was theoretically important; (2) what the multi-method design was like; (3) highlights of what was learned that could not have been learned without multi-method; and (4) the further research such quality research spawns.

A. Studying civil litigation in the United States: the Civil Litigation Research Project

The Civil Litigation Research Project (CLRP) provides some of the most enduring truths about citizens' use of law. Spearheaded by David Trubek and his colleagues at the University of Wisconsin and funded by the United States Department of Justice, CLRP is a study of households conducted in 1980. The survey was conducted in five federal judicial districts in the United States (Eastern Wisconsin, Eastern Pennsylvania, South Carolina, New Mexico, and Central California) to study claiming behavior of individuals involved in disputes that might have become lawsuits. The survey inquired about consumer problems, problems related to injuries, discrimination problems, debt problems (both debts owed to the respondent and debts owed by the respondent), property-related problems, landlord-tenant problems, problems with government benefits, and post-divorce problems.

Growing out of observations from the emerging literature on unmet legal needs (Curran, 1977) the CLRP team set out to better understand the costs of litigation and its alternatives. The research addressed how many people with potential legal claims used the system and why. The quantitative household survey demonstrated a fundamental empirical truth repeatedly borne out in law and society scholarship—that very few of the *perceived injurious experiences* which make up the base of the dispute pyramid actually become *disputes,* and fewer still become *legal cases* in the form of filings or trials (Felstiner et al., 1980; Miller and Sarat, 1981). The quantitative data demonstrated unquestionably that there is a pyramid of disputes and that only a tiny proportion of disputes rise to the highest level of the dispute process—trial and appeal. The research also demonstrated that various factors affect whether a case ends up settling early or going all the way to trial. While some of the variation across cases could be explained (the "how many?" questions), the mechanisms that produced this variation were not well understood. In other words, the "how come?" questions—"how come some people have lawyers and others don't?"; "how come some people are willing to settle while others with similar cases go forward to trial?"; "how do lawyers explain these processes to their clients?"—remained to be answered. Marc Galanter used the quantitative data from CLRP (along with a wide range of other data) to show that the so-called "litigation explosion" being lamented by conservative lawyers in the late 1970s and early 1980s was more a social construction for political purposes than something that had a basis in actual reality (Galanter, 1983, 1986). Galanter (1983) is now a law and society classic but it too, left unanswered "how come" questions about mechanisms.

CLRP documented crucial facts about the U.S. litigation system but spawned more questions for the research team. For example, Felstiner and Sarat wondered how disputes were transformed as they proceeded in the litigation system. How did ordinary people understand what was happening? Kristin Bumiller wondered why some people made the decision to forsake law altogether and simply "lump it" or deal with the problem in some way other than litigation. How did ordinary people make the decision about whether to turn to law? Herbert Kritzer wondered about the role of lawyers as gatekeepers and brokers in ordinary civil litigation. All of these process-oriented questions led to more research—primarily qualitative—which, when combined with the quantitative research, paints a more nuanced picture of civil litigation in the United States; and such research has been replicated and extended in Great Britain and elsewhere (Eisenberg, 1989, 1990; Genn, 1987, 2009; Nielsen et al., 2010).

Each of these scholars undertook new research to answer their process questions. Felstiner and Sarat studied divorce lawyers and their clients; Bumiller interviewed ordinary citizens who reported they had been discriminated against in the workplace but had taken no formal action; and Kritzer observed lawyers and non-lawyers in a variety of advocacy settings. The combination of high quality quantitative data and explanatory research based on qualitative data produced insights about the justice system that would not have been possible without multi-method research.

1. *Studying individuals in civil litigation*

Kristin Bumiller was interested in why some people who understood that they had justiciable claims failed to use the law at all. To better understand why individuals may or may not turn to the law, Bumiller generated a sample of the individuals, who had participated in the survey and had (or believed they had) legal grievances with their employers, but took no formal legal action (Bumiller, 1987, 1988). Bumiller's groundbreaking work involved qualitative interviews which demonstrated that there are many reasons why individuals do not pursue legal claims. Respondents mentioned not just financial barriers to turning to the law for redress of grievances but also that they rejected defining themselves as "victims," as the law would effectively require. So while the legal needs studies of the 1970s focused quite a bit on people's inability to afford a lawyer, Bumiller's qualitative research uncovered complex psychological and structural barriers to using law.

Although based on (and criticized for) reliance on a fairly small sample of respondents (this is a common critique of time and resource-intensive qualitative research like interviews and ethnography), Bumiller's qualitative analysis inspired an entire subfield of law and society mobilization research that presumes that meanings, ideologies, rights, conceptions of rights, law, and social relationships are not static categories, but are continually being constructed, negotiated, altered, and resisted (Ewick and Silbey, 1992, 1998; Harrington and Yngvesson, 1990). Starting with Bumiller, we begin to understand that calculations about exercising rights formally do not depend simply on whether or not individuals understand that they have a right and whether they can afford a lawyer (although these are, of course really important factors). Rather, this research is (in part) responsible for a whole new field of research to examine who invokes rights, when rights claims are made, and when they are successful, looking for both intended and unintended consequences of rights. This literature teaches us that legal rights are affected by the organizational settings in which they are applied, the nature of the competing claims being made by using rights, and the different social locations of the individual rights claims (Merry, 1990; Nielsen, 2000; Sarat, 1990; Sarat and Kearns, 1995; Yngvesson, 1985).

Bumiller's emphasis on rights in the workplace also revealed that people's understanding of their problems is a product not just of the law itself, but also of location; of how the problems are defined by court actors such as judges (Merry, 1990), court clerks (Yngvesson, 1988), friends and neighbors (Albiston, 2005; Ewick and Silbey, 1998; Nielsen, 2000); and of past experiences with law and legal actors (Macaulay, 1963; Merry, 1990; Nielsen, 2000; Sarat and Kearns, 1995).

Like other aspects of the CLRP research, the quantitative data opened a field of research which now fundamentally shapes empirical legal studies. Although we may approach questions about hesitation to use the law through our own disciplinary frame, Bumiller's work demonstrates that we have to be open to the possibility that it is a result not simply of finance or psychology or organization, but of a complex mix of all of them. There is important variation among individuals in their willingness to pursue a legal claim. For example, some individuals may not know the law; others may eschew the category of "victim"; many individuals prefer to maintain relationships rather than assert legal rights; and all individuals exist in socio-economic, race, and gender hierarchies that affect their ability and willingness to pursue legal claims.

What we know about the process by which people identify themselves as victims runs counter to what psychologists call the "just world view" (Major et al., 2002; Major and Kaiser, 2005)—i.e. the idea that people have a strong psychological need to perceive the world as fair and just. In the face of discrimination, individuals often prefer to blame negative outcomes on their own failings rather than concluding that the world has operated unfairly. The "right" to experience a discrimination-free workplace, for example, often is not vindicated because individuals do not know that what happened to them is legally actionable (Bumiller, 1988) (failure to "name"), or because those who know they are victims may be reluctant to turn to the law for redress for a variety of reasons (ibid).

Even when individuals understand that they have a legal right that has been breached and they know who is responsible, they may not choose to pursue it for a variety of reasons. They may fear retaliation (Ewick and Silbey, 1998), they may have become accustomed, due to their social location, to being harmed without redress (Sarat, 1990), or they may lack confidence that legal actors will believe their claims or be responsive to them (Taub and Schneider, 1998).

Individuals come to the law (and the law often comes to individuals) with a body of knowledge, assumptions, ideology, and experience with the law and legal actors that affects whether or not they will assert their legal rights. Perfect legal knowledge does not automatically spring into the minds of individuals; individuals often do not know what rights they enjoy and when they have been breached (Ewick and Silbey, 1998). As a corollary, ideology about rights is important because people may have an inflated idea of what their rights are, turning everything into a discussion of "rights" where none truly exist (Glendon, 1991). It is not just "law" that informs decisions about when and where to look for assistance when one has been wronged, but also competing ideologies about law, self-sufficiency, and gender roles to name just a few (Nielsen, 2000).

However, Bumiller was not the only researcher who started with the quantitative data from CLRP and found new and different questions about how the claiming process works. The combination of qualitative and quantitative data ultimately used by scholars who had worked on CLRP inspired mobilization research in law and society. In addition to important findings about unmet legal needs of the public, the addition of the qualitative component contributed to and inspired decades of research that has provided important insights into legal mobilization which would not have been possible without the multi-methodological approach that embedded interesting qualitative research within a larger quantitative research design.

2. Comparing lawyers and non-lawyers as advocates

Ordinary people are important in the study of civil litigation. Bumiller's research helped us understand how ordinary people related to one sphere of civil litigation and why some people choose not to file claims even when they understand they have been legally wronged. CLRP also stimulated interest into the roles of lawyers in civil litigation. The CLRP data showed profound effects on outcomes in civil cases if a plaintiff had legal representation, but Bumiller's findings revealed little about what lawyers did to produce these effects. Herbert Kritzer, drawing on the mass of data collected by CLRP, analyzed the telephone interviews with nearly 1,500 lawyers in five judicial districts. Kritzer explored a wide range of issues about the lawyer's role in civil litigation: client control and lawyer autonomy, the actual tasks lawyers carried out, the impact of how lawyers are paid, and the results the lawyers achieved for their clients and themselves in the litigation process. His conclusion raised the intriguing question of whether laypersons could effectively conduct much, perhaps most, of the work done by lawyers in ordinary cases (Kritzer, 1990: 168–76).

This led Kritzer to pursue a follow-up project that explicitly compared lawyers and non-lawyers in four settings where both were permitted to appear as advocates (social security disability appeals, unemployment compensation appeals, tax appeals, and labor grievance arbitration) (Kritzer, 1998). This new project employed multiple methods, including observation of hearings, interviews of advocates and adjudicators, statistical analyses of case records, and a small-scale experiment conducted by mail. He posited that advocacy involved a combination of substantive and process expertise, and that both lawyers and non-lawyers could possess the necessary knowledge to be effective advocates. In fact, his analysis confirmed his core hypotheses, showing that lawyers lacking specific process expertise (i.e., who were unfamiliar with a particular advocacy setting) were less effective than non-lawyers experienced in a particular setting, and that lawyers and non-lawyers with similar levels of specific expertise did not generally differ in effectiveness. In some settings lawyers were more effective: in one venue (tax appeals) because the non-lawyers lacked process expertise (even though they typically had substantive expertise) and in another (social security disability appeals) because the lawyers' incentive structure for success was stronger (lawyers were paid only if they were successful). The differing types of data revealed different aspects of the study's findings. The quantitative data were used to confirm broad patterns of relative success of different types of advocates while the qualitative data, particularly the observational data, provided insights that accounted for the differences in the patterns of relative success.

3. Studying lawyer/client interactions in one type of litigation

Intrigued by the nature of the dispute pyramid (Engel and Steele, 1979; Miller and Sarat, 1981) and their own observations that how disputes are transformed depends on who the parties spoke to, the type of lawyers used, and other things that we think of as exogenous to the lawsuit itself, Felstiner and Sarat wanted to study how disputes are transformed over the course of a lawsuit. They chose to examine divorce lawyers because divorce disputes mix emotions—about the dissolution of marriage and custody of children—with simple asset allocation and financial matters (Sarat and Felstiner, 1995). They found that emotion-management was a large part of divorce lawyers' work, at least in the no-fault states where they conducted their research.

These findings about a particular disputing context came from ethnographic and qualitative research. Sarat and Felstiner show that because divorce disputes typically end in a negotiated settlement and rarely in trial, lawyers had to play a role in helping their clients re-imagine the divorce not as a battle of wills in which the court acts as moral arbiter, but as a financial and parenting transaction which dissolves the marriage and puts financial and custody matters to rest. Because the typical case is not resolved by a court, formal law will usually not declare which partner was unfaithful or somehow otherwise tainted the marriage, or whether one spouse was emotionally distant.

How do lawyers help their clients make the transition from an emotional dispute to a transaction? Of course, a divorce nearly always involves emotion, but lawyers have to help their clients understand that the legal sphere is not where such matters are going to be resolved. Sarat and Felstiner were able to observe 115 lawyer-client meetings which they combined with 130 interviews, both conducted over the course of about two years, representing a level of researcher access that remains arguably unequalled (Sarat and Felstiner, 1995: 8). They found that lawyers engaged in sympathetic complaining about the "faults" of the divorce system, not because they necessarily agreed, but in order to be able to say something like, "it stinks that the courts don't do what they really should, but this is all the courts can provide." By sympathizing with their clients, the lawyers were helping the clients transform how they viewed their disputes. Thus the processes which lead to the resolution of a case are not simply negotiation, but also include efforts by lawyers to persuade their clients to reframe their goals and expectations, often by denigrating the legal process of divorce.

CLRP and the projects that came from it provided the cornerstone for a new understanding of the civil justice system and of the role of representatives in that process. Now I turn to an example of multi-method research in criminology that advances criminological theory and public policy questions in important ways.

B. Multi-methodological research in criminology: *Darfur and the Crime of Genocide*

In their influential and already-heralded book, *Darfur and the Crime of Genocide*, John Hagan and Wenona Rymond-Richmond (2009) ask why the discipline of criminology has for so long ignored genocide and the ways in which states and militias work together to dehumanize particular social groups leading to the rape of the women and the murder of the men. The authors' creative use of multiple sources of data and multiple methodologies leads to significant new understanding about the crime of genocide in general, as well as new understandings of some basic facts about Darfur in particular. In Darfur, the (Islamic) Sudanese army and the (Islamic) militia, known as the Janjaweed, together carried out two violent waves of murder and rape against Black Africans, which led to massive refugee migrations of survivors into nearby Chad. A significant question posed by the authors is whether these crimes amount to genocide.

Hagan and Rymond-Richmond explain that "[t]he US charge of genocide in Darfur includes an assertion of racial intent…[and] that the Sudanese government has intentionally used…racism to collectively motivate the death and destruction of a legally protected group (or groups) in Darfur" (2009: 108). *Darfur and the Crime of Genocide* is part criminal indictment, part compelling narrative account of how the genocide was experienced by surviving refugees, and part ingenious multi-methodological empirical legal research. "Both the qualitative and quantitative evidence are essential to providing a criminological description and explanation of genocide and holding the architects of genocide responsible" (Hagan and Rymond-Richmond, 2009: 3). Hagan and Rymond-Richmond rely on the qualitative and quantitative data in the "Atrocities Documentation Survey" (ADS) collected by the U.S. State Department in 2004 in Chad about refugees from Darfur. They use these data to demonstrate (1) that the mass murders in Darfur were committed not only by the Janjaweed militia (non-state actors) and that the most serious atrocities (murder and rape) occurred under Sudanese army attack alone or when the Sudanese army and the Janjaweed attacked together; and (2) that the crimes of rape and murder were racially motivated. If both propositions are true, the crime is one of genocide, which would engage the machinery of the international criminal law.

The authors use a statistical technique called Hierarchical Linear Modeling (HLM) to locate the geographic sites of the most significant crime scenes. The UN High Commission on Refugees placed refugees in sectors based on their former villages, which allowed the researchers to locate crime scenes in Darfur based on the refugee camp where the interviewee was living. Using witness accounts that were cross-verified with other witness accounts, the authors coded a set of variables describing the attacks including whether the attack was conducted by Sudanese military only, Janjaweed militia only, or Sudanese military and Janjaweed combined; whether or not explicit racial epithets accompanied the attack; frequency of murder, and frequency of rape; to name just a few.

The results demonstrate that the most atrocious criminal activity occurred in attacks perpetrated by the Sudanese army and Janjaweed militia together. The geocoding allows body counts from mass graves to be associated with eyewitness accounts of the raids so that the murderers (killers)[3] are identified. Some commander-murderers are individually identified. Equally important is the identification of the murderers and rapists as state actors who were following orders given by army commanders.

Hagan and Rymond-Richmond use the quantitative data to firmly establish a military presence in the most violent raids; but there remains the question of whether or not the raids were racially motivated. To draw conclusions about this issue, the authors rely on the words of the killers and rapists as reported by witnesses. Again, it is important to note that the researchers cross-verified witness accounts. During the attacks, Sudanese army and Janjaweed militia members said things like, "This is the last day for blacks," "Kill all the blacks," "We will destroy all the black-skinned people" (Hagan and Rymond-Richmond, 2009: 132); "You donkey, you slave, we must get rid of you;" (p. 9); and the definitive genocidal quote, "We will kill all the men and rape all the women. We want to change the color."' (p. 10).

My goal in this Chapter is not to convince the reader that genocide occurred in Darfur (although I think Hagan and Rymond-Richmond go a long way toward demonstrating this). Rather, here I use this study as an exemplar of the power of combining sophisticated quantitative modeling techniques to estimate the number of killings and to identify the perpetrators of those killings, with in-depth qualitative analysis of the events on the ground to demonstrate the racialized nature of the crimes that took place. Either set of data would be powerful in its own right and would tell us a lot about what happened, but together the two data sets paint a picture that is vastly more compelling than either alone could produce.

C. Ongoing multi-method research

My own current multi-method research concerns employment civil-rights complaints and litigation.[4] The project involves an interdisciplinary team of lawyers, sociologists and economists, and we have sought advice from social psychologists, anthropologists and others. I am interested in how ordinary citizens think of (or don't think of) law as a possible solution to their everyday problems, and

[3] The Sudanese government claims that it is battling an insurrection of Black Africans. The question is: are these (1) killings in the course of a civil war (no one in the world community really believes this to be true), (2) murders conducted largely by non-state actors (Janjaweed militia), or (3) state-driven, racially motivated murders (and therefore genocide, as Hagan and Rymond-Richmond authors argue)?

[4] This work is being conducted with my colleague and collaborator, Robert L. Nelson.

the process by which they begin to think of a problem as merely an annoyance or, by contrast, as something about which the law may be able to help. My prior research on offensive public speech demonstrated that while people viewed offensive speech as part of a continuum of race and sex subordination, and as a personal and social problem, they did not favor the use of law to restrict such speech. Different people had different reasons for disfavoring the use of law, but there was broad consensus that the law should not be used to regulate offensive public speech (Nielsen, 2000, 2004). This research was conducted using interactive approaches (ethnography and interviews) and counting (standardized questions asked during the interview).

After studying public places (where almost no one thinks there should be speech restriction), I wanted to turn my attention to how people begin to define discrimination as a legal problem in the workplace (where most Americans agree that law has a legitimate role of prohibiting discrimination). This research is multi-methodological and includes reading, interacting, and counting methodologies. With John Donohue, Peter Siegleman, Ryon Lancaster, and Robert Nelson, I have completed a multi-phased study of federal employment discrimination litigation that combines three large empirical projects (see Nielsen et al., 2010).[5] We are "counting" and analyzing a confidential data set of 1.6 million Equal Employment Opportunity Commission (EEOC) complaints filed between 1988 and 2003. A second way that we are "counting" is by conducting a quantitative analysis of a national random sample of 1,850 employment civil-rights cases filed in federal courts in seven federal judicial districts across seven states in the same time period. Before we can "count" however, a certain amount of documentary analysis is needed (more on that below). Finally, we have conducted qualitative analyses of a subset of cases including in-depth interviews with parties and lawyers in those cases.

1. *Reading and counting*

The filings-study part of the project had us read and analyze court documents which include state human-rights agencies' complaint forms, federal EEOC complaint forms, pleadings and responses made in federal court, rulings on evidence, expert witness reports, full texts of transcribed depositions, medical reports, and judicial decrees. We analyzed all the documents in the first wave of analysis, but it had to be done in the courthouses and records centers because these public documents are not available to "check out" and the expense of copying the full case files meant that

---

[5] The United States has a variety of mechanisms designed to prevent workplace discrimination, but the primary statutory mechanisms rely at the federal level on a government agency, the Equal Employment Opportunity Commission (EEOC). The EEOC is supposed to investigate and conciliate disputes but it has become overwhelmed by the volume of complaints. If the EEOC cannot investigate and resolve the issue in a timely way, the person who believes they were discriminated against may pursue the claim in the court system. There are similar systems in most states.

we had to determine what pieces of information from the files were relevant to our analysis. We began by counting and categorizing from court documents. Using an extensive coding form, researchers read the case documents and then classified cases by their date, type of claim, plaintiffs' and defendants' demographic characteristics, the size of the file in inches, outcome, and more than 100 other variables. The coding process necessarily means extracting some and not other information. Researchers read the entire file and the coding form provided ample room for narrative description of the case so that researchers could provide context; but this process necessarily reduces the volume of information from a case file into a set of variables one can count. At this point, the research necessarily becomes easier in some ways (for example, statistical analysis software can be used to determine how many claims are race claims), but the data may become less rich than the entirety of its file: much detail about a case is lost when the information must be collapsed onto a coding form (even if it is a 13-page coding form).

Developing a coding form, while seemingly a banal part of research, actually is a critical methodological moment in which theory and method intersect profoundly. There has to be theorizing about the data the researcher needs from the documents. Some of the items of data we needed were obvious: What are the outcomes in these cases? What is the cause of action in civil rights litigation? But some issues were theoretically driven and descriptive. For example, a staple of sexual harassment theory is that sexual harassment is less about sex and more about power. As such, we were interested in whether harassment situations occur more often between supervisors and subordinates or if peer sexual harassment is equally common. And, perhaps more importantly, does the relationship between the parties have any effect on the outcome of the case? These are just a few examples to make the point that if you cannot readily return to the documents (and in this case they are spread all over the United States) the researcher must recognize that whatever is not captured during the coding process is lost to the analysis. So before the counting, there has to be careful and systematic reading of the case files in their entirety.

2. *Counting to interacting*

Reading the full case files led to key insights about what to code and count. As we read case files, new questions emerged which we simply could not answer from the case files or by analyzing the quantitative data we extracted from the case filings. Together, our reading and counting informed our approach to the interviews (interacting). At this stage of the research, results garnered from one methodology informed another phase of the research in critical ways.

In the United States, it is illegal to make employment decisions based on a worker's age, race, sex, pregnancy status, religion, ethnicity, or disability, but there is no easy mechanism for differentiating the basis of federal employment discrimination cases easily. An important descriptive question that no one tracks is how many such cases are brought on the basis of race, sex, national origin, and religion respectively. Scholars of civil rights can *estimate* using EEOC data to make an educated guess about what proportion of cases fall into the various categories, but it is not at all certain if the proportions are the same in Federal Courts as at the EEOC (Nielsen and Nelson, 2005). So this is one of the first things we set about to measure. Our analysis of the case filings shows that the four most common bases of employment civil rights claims made in federal court are race, sex, age, and disability (Nielsen et al., 2008). But what are the outcomes of such cases?

From general discussions with experienced litigators, we determined that there are four theoretically important outcomes in such cases: dismissal, settlement which occurs early in the process, settlement that occurs later in the process, and trial. In federal court, early dismissals may be a very significant category of outcomes, but they also are the least observable because they seldom generate appeals or opinions. As is generally true in the American civil justice system, settlements make up the vast majority of outcomes in employment discrimination cases; nonetheless, we sought to provide more detail about this category by distinguishing between cases that settled early and those that survived until later in the process. We classified settled cases according to whether they settled before or after the filing of a motion for summary judgment. While not a perfect (or perhaps even good) proxy for the quality of the case, surviving a motion for summary judgment means that a judge determined that there is a claim that, if proven, amounts to discrimination, and that there is a material issue of fact as to whether the illegal activity occurred. Surviving motion for summary judgment also typically means the plaintiff had a lawyer. Very few unrepresented plaintiffs can successfully respond to a motion for summary judgment. Finally, we were interested in the cases that made it to trial and reach a judgment, knowing that this is the most unlikely outcome of all.

Our quantitative "counting" and our study of the case files (reading) led us to a systematic process for choosing the cases for which we were going to conduct in-depth interviews. We sought cases that fit into one of 16 categories in the four by four table formed by cross-classifying the four major types of discrimination claim with the four major categories of case outcome. Thus, we placed each of the 1,850 closed cases from our sample into one of the 16 categories and then randomly drew from within each category to create a sample of cases to study in greater detail. For each of the cases in this sample, our team located and contacted the plaintiff and asked if the person was willing to participate in the research. If so, we scheduled an interview. Because we sought multiple perspectives in each case, we also tried to interview the plaintiff's lawyer (if there was one), the defendant (typically a representative of a business or government office), and the defense lawyer (if the defendant used outside counsel). In this way, the qualitative data can be located within a representative sample of cases. It allows us to probe the individual circumstances of cases while at the same time examining how particular cases relate to the system as a whole.

3. *The payoffs*

How do the qualitative, quantitative, and documentary data speak to one another and speak to us as researchers to help us provide better answers to our theoretical questions? Quality multi-method projects integrate data and allow the insights from one methodological approach to speak to the insights of others. In the words of Brewer and Hunter (2006), the goal is to "synthesize styles" for a better appreciation of our object of study rather than just presenting the qualitative data and the quantitative data as separate projects. One of the primary benefits of embedding high-quality qualitative research into a framework of systematic quantitative analysis is the synthetic approach that takes into account the various forces—individual (e.g., identity, consciousness), organizational (e.g., workplace, social movement groups), and institutional (e.g., gender, work, race)—that affect litigation. Moreover, embedded qualitative analysis does not draw attention away from broader patterns in the way that can happen with some qualitative research (di Leonardo, 1998). Thus, embedding brings to light the organizational and institutional forces that shape civil rights disputes. We know that legal rights and individuals' willingness to pursue them within the EEOC or federal courts are affected by the organizational settings in which those rights are applied, by the nature of the competing institutional claims to rights, and by the different social locations of the individuals making rights claims (Merry, 1990; Nielsen, 2004; Sarat, 1990; Sarat and Kearns, 1995; Selznick, 1969; Yngvesson, 1985).

For our research, the payoffs of a multi-methodological approach were impressive. As I indicated, summary judgment is of significant theoretical interest for our approach. And, it turns out that each of our methodologies presented us with very different pictures of the role of this legal hurdle, providing an important example of the value of multiple methods.

A common theme among plaintiff and defense lawyers was that summary judgment rates have changed over time. This defense attorney's analysis is not unusual:

I: So you mentioned summary judgment a few minutes ago; how many of your cases, how many cases in employment are you filing motion for summary judgment? Do you think it's changed over time and how successful are you with it?

R: Well I think it's changed over time. I don't think the judges like these cases so I think they're more willing to find no issues of material fact which is the standard.

I: Right.

R: And especially here in the seventh circuit where it's like a dream come true. I like to say the Seventh Circuit has other standards in sexual harassment cases as, "what can't you take a joke?" [laughs] You know it's a great place to be a defense attorney. I have a woman here who was a plaintiff's attorney and said you don't want to be a plaintiff's attorney in the Seventh Circuit. The Fourth Circuit is another great place to be a defense attorney, the Seventh Circuit is probably just a little better nowadays though. And the Ninth Circuit's a terrible place to be a defense attorney because everything goes to trial. Most cases, probably 90% of the cases we get, are summary judgment cases.[6]

This assertion happens to come from a defense attorney, but plaintiffs' lawyers also commonly claimed that summary judgment rates had changed over time (not in their favor) and that rates of summary judgment vary across judicial district. Of course there are many possible ways to study how summary judgment works. One easy way to begin to understand summary judgment is to conduct research on PACER (the online case file service available through the federal courts)[7] or other online databases, such as Lexis or Westlaw. However, PACER is expensive and digitized files are incomplete for the period we wanted to study, making a reliable analysis of data over time more difficult or even impossible. Quantitative analysis based on Lexis or Westlaw searches would skew the results to appealed cases, which we know are not representative of filed cases in general (Siegelman and Donohue, 1990).

Our quantitative analysis of case filings demonstrates that all three empirical assertions made by the defense lawyer quoted above are incorrect. Sixty-nine percent of filings exit the system through dismissal for the plaintiff's failure to state a valid claim, or through early settlement before reaching the filing of a motion for summary judgment (Nielsen et al., 2008). Summary judgments against plaintiffs make up only 18% of total case outcomes. If we look only at the 31% of cases that are not settled at an early stage, more than one-half (299 of 522, or 57%) end in summary judgment against the plaintiff. The defense attorney is closer to correct about the defendant success rate at summary judgment, but even for this stage is off by 30%. The rate at which cases end in summary judgment remained largely unchanged over the time period of the survey. In fact summary judgment outcomes declined somewhat in the last few years of the time series, but dismissals grew to make up the difference (Nielsen et al., 2010). Nor does the rate of summary judgment against plaintiffs vary significantly across the seven jurisdictions. (The Eastern District of Pennsylvania is an outlier, with fewer summary judgment outcomes and more settlement outcomes (Nielsen et al., 2008).) These data are consistent with other recent empirical analysis of summary judgment over time (Cecil et al., 2007).

In this instance, the quantitative data directly tests the impression of lawyers' wisdom captured through in-depth interviewing. The strategy of sampling filings and carefully coding their outcomes makes visible a large class of cases that is invisible even to the professionals working in this subfield. As has been shown in other empirical research, our research demonstrates that actors in the legal system do not always accurately perceive what happens in a typical case even though they are active participants in the system (see also, Feeley, 1983).

---

[6] ED-73 DLR CL page 10.   [7] <http://pacer.psc.uscourts.gov/>.

In-depth interviews illuminate how plaintiffs experience the litigation process, a phenomenon not captured in the kind of counting we did in this project. A plaintiff by the pseudonym of Sam Grayson offered these comments about the outcome of his case, which was a late settlement in our typology of outcomes.

RN: Are you free to discuss the settlement, is it done?

SG: It wasn't anything big. It was a hundred thousand dollars, but you know obviously it goes for the attorney and it wasn't anything and like my attorney said if I hadn't quit and I had just sat, it could have been more. But it cost the City more than a hundred thousand with all the—

LB: Did that surprise you? Had your attorney prepared you for what the outcome might be or was that in the ball park that you were thinking, did you think it was fair?

SG: Well you know what I didn't want any money, I wanted my job back. I didn't want the money, I wanted my job back and I actually to be completely honest with you, I cried and left and felt like I lost because it wasn't about the money.

RN: So even at that point you were still hoping to get your job back?

SG: Yeah.

This quote, when taken in combination with other interviews and quantitative results (Nielsen and Beim, 2004), reveals much about plaintiffs' expectations in discrimination cases. What Grayson does not know is that his settlement of $100,000 makes him one of the more financially successful plaintiffs in our sample, where the median settlement result is $30,000. What we learn is that Grayson considers the settlement a failure. He, like many plaintiffs who had lost their jobs, would prefer to have their jobs back. It is only through systematic coding of cases that we can put Grayson's outcome in economic context. Grayson's interview, and the interviews with many other plaintiffs and attorneys, make the point that plaintiffs frequently enter the litigation process with unrealistic expectations, such as regaining jobs that they believe they had lost due to illegal actions by their former employers.

One of the few plaintiffs who did get his job back, only to lose it a year later during a reduction in force, offers another unique, if depressing, insight into the fate of plaintiffs who pursue discrimination claims. Gerry Handley was subjected to racial harassment on the job, including questions by a foreman about whether Handley had practiced incest with his daughters as the foreman said he had heard was common among slaves. Despite his legal success, Handley concluded the following:

GH: I mean, it was like these 10 people that were supporting me in the department, they like ruined their lives. They like had to move and lost their jobs and had to relocate, and I could tell you, it was just horrible. It poisoned the whole environment. If I had to do it over again, I wouldn't do it because I lost everything.

LB: So what would you do if you had to do it over again?

GH: I would have took it. When he said that, you know, about my daughter, I would have just took it and kept my mouth shut and not tell anybody. Keep your mouth shut and just take it, you know, because if you fight back, it ain't worth it. The legal system and the justice, it ain't there.

Gerry Handley's narrative about his experience with discrimination and with the litigation process was provided to us through a telephone interview. It was only by interacting with Handley, by asking not only about the facts of the case but also how it affected his life, that we learned about the life-effects of discrimination law. If we had counted Gerry Handley's case only as an early settlement win in a race discrimination case, we would not have learned nearly as much about the nature of workplace discrimination or the difficulties plaintiffs encounter when they press a case.

IV. Cautionary Notes

Multi-method research allows us to observe the elephant in its entirety or, if not in its entirety, more completely than a research project that employs only one method. At the same time, multi-method research comes with great costs and risks that must be considered at the outset of such a project as well as during the project itself.

The kinds of research described in this Chapter are costly. Different projects follow different paths, but generally speaking most multi-method research involves conducting exploratory research to develop theory (using qualitative or quantitative methods), developing reliable quantitative instruments to measure and count, and then following up with a qualitative or document-analysis phase to better understand the processes that produce the outcomes analyzed in the quantitative data. Such research takes years. For pre-tenure academics, the long time horizon of such research may make it professionally costly to pursue. One way to mitigate the problems associated with the need to publish is to plan opportunities to publish initial, theoretically informed, empirical findings. A researcher's "plan" is often interrupted by the real-world messiness of data collection and analysis (Kritzer, 2009), so the initial publications may not be exactly what was foreseen at the outset. Nonetheless, it is important to be mindful of the possible need to produce research products before the information from all of the phases of research are complete.

A second cost is financial. Research that involves collection (or even just use) of multiple data sets is expensive. It is more expensive if the researcher determines that she must collect original data. Of course, collecting original data allows the researcher to ask precisely the kinds of questions he or she would like, but it is costly and messy (Kritzer, 2009). Moreover, even when we think we are asking precisely the question we want answered, our projects evolve. What we thought was going to be crucial often turns out to be far less important than we thought. Other factors emerge requiring new strategies for data collection.

A further risk of multi-method research is that the length of the project and the sheer quantity of data make it easy to lose sight of the initial theoretical motivations of the project. And, one has to be careful to ensure that each phase of the research stays relevant to the theoretical motivations that undergird the project. Even if a researcher alone is not collecting all the data, the simple abundance of data can be overwhelming. Moreover, where the different types of data lead to conflicting conclusions, the researcher must figure out how to resolve those conflicts.

Methodology is a tool for testing theory, and choices among methodologies must be theoretically driven. As empirical research on law becomes more popular, there is a danger that we will lose sight of the importance of theory in designing research. The full potential of social research on law is best realized when our theoretical questions inform our choice of methods. Research that seeks to relate the use of law by individuals, institutions, and organizations requires both a theoretical account of the relationships among those entities and a set of methods that can capture those relationships.

V. Conclusion

Social research, especially in interdisciplinary fields, such as empirical research on law, is very diverse. Traditions, assumptions, and approaches vary among psychologists, sociologists, anthropologists, and economists. Various approaches have different strengths and weaknesses. When a researcher employs multiple approaches to answer questions, the results are likely to be more reliable and contribute more to the theoretical development of our understanding of law and society.

The examples discussed here are certainly not the only multi-method studies in law and society or other types of empirical legal research. However, these studies illustrate nicely how different approaches to asking the same question can yield different (complementary or contradictory) findings which can lead to whole new areas of research (as in the case of CLRP), can verify information given by parties (as in the employment discrimination example), and can demonstrate motive (Darfur). Each of these studies began with descriptive, policy-driven, and theoretical questions. The answers to those questions would have been incomplete and in some circumstances incorrect if the researchers had relied on only one methodology. With CLRP, the qualitative follow-up studies provided extensive context about civil litigation that would not have been possible using only the original data. This context included the important and varied roles of lawyers in civil litigation (Kritzer, 1998); how plaintiffs' worldviews affected their willingness to litigate (Bumiller, 1987, 1988); and how lawyers and clients co-construct the meaning of the litigation process itself (Sarat and Felstiner, 1995).

Without the qualitative data collected in the Darfur case, we would be left wondering if the atrocities perpetrated on the Blacks by the state and the militias were mass murder or genocide. Since the mass killings were carried out in secret, the research provides important quantitative findings (how many people were killed); but also the qualitative interviews (in which surviving victims told their stories in narrative form) reveal that racism was, at root, the motivation for the murders. The true nature of the crimes in Darfur could only be understood using a mixed method approach.

Finally, in the employment discrimination context, our qualitative in-depth interviews with parties round out our understanding of our quantitative analyses of case filings. The random draw of employment civil rights cases and analysis of the quantitative data helped shape our qualitative questions to plaintiffs ("why did you drop your case?"), the answers to which revealed fundamental misunderstandings of the civil justice process. On the defense side, we were able to identify some of the more difficult-to-quantify costs that these lawsuits impose on employing organizations; and this resulted in a fuller understanding of the true costs imposed by the employment discrimination system on those organizations.

The recent reinvigoration of the empirical study of law and its new importance in more law schools is encouraging. To be effective, the law must be empirically examined in the real world and insights gleaned must inform law-makers through some sort of feedback mechanism. Although multi-method research is costly, rigorous empirical research (be it mixed or single method) is always better than theoretical speculation or armchair empiricism based on anecdote.

As I suggested at the start of this Chapter, multi-method research is perhaps the most effective way to understand the relationship between law and society. I argued that because the phenomenon of law itself consists of individuals, organizational settings, institutional fields, and the interactions among them, fully understanding law demands research conducted using multiple approaches.

REFERENCES

Albiston, C.R. (2005). "Bargaining in the Shadow of Social Institutions: Competing Discourses and Social Change in Workplace Mobilization of Civil Rights," *Law & Society Review* 39: 11–49.

Bachman, R. and Schutt, R.K. (2007). *The Practice of Research in Criminology and Criminal Justice*, (3rd. edn.), London: Sage Publications.

Brewer, J. and Hunter, A. (2006). *Foundations of Multimethod Research: Synthesizing Styles*, Thousand Oaks, CA: Sage Publications.

Bumiller, K. (1987). "Victims in the Shadow of the Law: A Critique of the Model of Legal Protection," *Signs: Journal of Women and Culture in Society* 12: 421–534.

Bumiller, K. (1988). *The Civil Rights Society: The Social Construction of Victims*, Baltimore: John Hopkins University Press.

Cecil, J.S., Eyre, R.N., Miletich, D., and Rindskopf, D. (2007). "A Quarter-Century of Summary Judgment Practice in Six Federal District Courts," *Journal of Empirical Legal Studies* 4: 861–907.

Clay-Warner, J. and Burt, C.H. (2005). "Rape Reporting after Reforms: Have Times Really Changed?," *Violence against Women* 11: 150–76.

Curran, B.A. (1977). *The Legal Needs of the Public: The Final Report of a National Survey*, Chicago: American Bar Foundation.

di Leonardo, M. (1998). *Exotics at Home: Anthropologies, Other, and American Modernity*, Chicago: University of Chicago Press.

Eisenberg, T. (1989). "Litigation Models and Trial Outcomes in Civil Rights and Prisoner Cases," *Georgetown Law Journal* 77: 1567–602.

Eisenberg, T. (1990). "Testing the Selection Effect: A New Theoretical Framework with Empirical Tests," *Journal of Legal Studies* 19: 337–58.

Engel, D.M. and Steele, E.H. (1979). "Civil Cases and Society: Process and Order in the Civil Justice System," *American Bar Foundation Research Journal*: 295–346.

Ewick, P. and Silbey, S.S. (1992). "Conformity, Contestation, and Resistance: An Account of Legal Consciousness," *New England Law Review* 26: 731–49.

Ewick, P. and Silbey, S.S. (1998). *The Common Place of Law: Stories From Everyday Life*, Chicago: University of Chicago Press.

Federal Bureau of Investigation (2007). "Crime in the United States, 2007," Washington, DC: U.S. Department of Justice.

Feeley, M. (1983). *Court Reform on Trial: Why Simple Solutions Fail*, New York: Basic Books.

Felstiner, W., Abel, R., and Sarat, A. (1980). "The Emergence and Transformation of Disputes: Naming, Blaming, and Claiming," *Law and Society Review* 15: 631–55.

Fenno, R. (1986). "Observation, Context, and Sequence in the Study of Politics," *American Political Science Review* 80: 3–15.

Galanter, M.S. (1983). "Reading the Landscape of Disputes: What We Know and Don't Know (and Think We Know) About Our Allegedly Contentious and Litigious Society," *UCLA Law Review* 31(4): 31–71.

Galanter. M.S. (1986). "The Day After the Litigation Explosion," *University of Maryland Law Review* 46: 3.

Genn, H. (1987). *Hard Bargaining: Out of Court Settlement in Personal Injury Actions*, New York: Oxford University Press.

Genn, H. (2009). "Hazel Genn and Paths to Justice," in S. Halliday and P. Schmidt (eds.), *Conducting Law and Society Research: Reflections on Methods and Practices*, New York: Cambridge University Press.

Glendon, M.A. (1991). *Rights Talk: The Impoverishment of Political Discourse*, New York: The Free Press.

Hagan, J. and Rymond-Richmond, W. (2009). *Darfur and the Crime of Genocide*, New York: Cambridge University Press.

Halliday, S. and Schmidt, P. (eds.) (2009). *Conducting Law and Society Research: Reflections on Methods and Practices*, New York: Cambridge University Press.

Harrington, C.B. and Yngvesson, B. (1990). "Interpretive Sociolegal Research," *Law and Social Inquiry* 15: 135–48.

Kritzer, H.M. (1990). *The Justice Broker: Lawyers and Ordinary Litigation*, New York: Oxford University Press.

Kritzer, H.M. (1998). *Legal Advocacy: Lawyers and Nonlawyers at Work*, Ann Arbor: University of Michigan Press.

Kritzer, H.M. (2009). "Conclusion: Research is Messy Business—An Archeology of the Craft of Sociolegal Research," in S. Halliday and P. Schmidt (eds), *Conducting Law and Society Research: Reflections on Methods and Practices*, New York: Cambridge University Press.

Macaulay, S. (1963). "Non-Contractual Relations in Business: A Preliminary Study," *American Sociological Review* 28: 55–67.

Major, B., Gramzow, R.H., McCoy, S.K., Levin, S., Schmader, T., and Sidanius, J. (2002). "Perceiving Personal Discrimination: The Role of Group States and Legitimizing Ideology," *Journal of Personality and Social Psychology* 82: 269–82.

Major, B. and Kaiser, C. (2005). "Perceiving and Claiming Discrimination," in Laura Beth Nielsen and Robert L. Nelson (eds.), *Handbook of Employment Discrimination Research: Rights and Realities*, Dordrecht: Springer.

Merry, S.E. (1990). *Getting Justice and Getting Even: Legal Consciousness among Working-Class Americans*, Chicago: University of Chicago Press.

Miller, R.E. and Sarat, A. (1981). "Grievances, Claims, and Disputes: Assessing the Adversary Culture," *Law and Society Review* 15: 525–66.

Nielsen, L.B. (2000). "Situating Legal Consciousness: Experiences and Attitudes of Ordinary Citizens about Law and Street Harassment," *Law and Society Review* 34: 201–36.

Nielsen, L.B. (2004). "The Work of Rights and the Work Rights Do: A Critical Empirical Approach," in A. Sarat (ed.), *The Blackwell Companion to Law and Society*, Oxford: Blackwell Publishing.

Nielsen, L.B. (2004). *License to Harass: Law, Hierarchy, and Offensive Public Speech*, Princeton: Princeton University Press.

Nielsen, L.B. and Beim, A. (2004). "Media Misrepresentation: Title VII, Print Media, and Public Perceptions of Discrimination Litigation," *Stanford Law and Policy Review* 15: 101–130.

Nielsen, L.B. and Nelson, R.L. (2005). "Rights Realized? An Empirical Analysis of Employment Discrimination Litigation as a Claiming System," *Wisconsin Law Review* 663–711.

Nielsen, L.B., Lancaster, R., Nelson, R.L., and Pedriana, N. (2008). *Characteristics and Outcomes of Federal Employment Discrimination in Courts 1987–2003*, Chicago: American Bar Foundation.

Nielsen, L.B., Nelson, R.L., and Lancaster, R. (2010). "Individual Justice or Collective Legal Mobilization? Employment Discrimination Litigation in the Post-Civil Rights United States" *Journal of Empirical Legal Studies* 7(2): 175–201.

Sarat, A. (1990). "The Law is All Over: Power, Resistance, and the Legal Consciousness of the Welfare Poor," *Yale Journal of Law and Humanities* 3: 343–79.

Sarat, A. and Felstiner, W. (1995). *Divorce Lawyers and Their Clients: Power and Meaning in the Legal Process*, New York: Oxford University Press.

Sarat, A. and Kearns, T.R. (1995). *Law in Everyday Life,* Ann Arbor: University of Michigan Press.

Scheppele, K.L. (2009). "Counting, Reading, Interacting: Focusing on the Activities of the Researcher in Thinking about Methods," Paper presented at the Law and Society Association Early Career Workshop, Denver.

Selznick, P. (1969). *Law, Society, and Industrial Justice,* New York: Russell Sage Foundation.

Siegelman, P. and Donohue, J.J. (1990). "Studying the Iceberg from Its Tip: A Comparison of Published and Unpublished Employment Discrimination Cases," *Law and Society Review* 21: 165–74.

Taub, N. and Schneider, E. (1998). "Women's Subordination and the Role of Law," in D. Kairys (ed.), *The Politics of Law: A Progressive Critique* (3rd edn.), New York: Basic Books: 328–55.

Yngvesson, B. (1985). "Law, Private Governance, and Continuing Relationships," *Wisconsin Law Review* 1985: 623–46.

Yngvesson, B. (1988). "Making Law at the Doorway: The Clerk, the Court, and the Construction of Community in a New England Town," *Law and Society Review* 22: 409–48.

LEGAL THEORY
AND EMPIRICAL
RESEARCH

D.J. GALLIGAN[1]

I. INTRODUCTION[2]

LEGAL theory and empirical research into law are conducted independently of each other, each asking its own questions, using its own methods, and drawing its own

[1] The author wishes to thank the editors, Peter Cane and Herbert Kritzer, for their very helpful comments during the course of writing this Chapter; also colleagues at the Oxford Centre for Socio-Legal Studies: Fernanda Pirie, William Twining, Marina Kurkchiyan, David Erdos, and Julian Semphill.
[2] The analysis here develops that advanced in Galligan, 2007.

conclusions. The aim of this Chapter is to examine the links between them and whether each could be of more use to the other than is now the case. Legal theory takes different forms, appears under different names, and varies as to subject matter. The analysis here is confined to legal theory that is philosophical in method and descriptive in aim, and since that is just one of numerous types of theory, an explanation of what it means and why it is singled out for consideration is the starting point.

Jurisprudence, until recently the usual term for theoretical approaches to law, is now often replaced by legal theory, the dominant strand of which aligns itself with philosophy, hence encouraging use of the term legal philosophy. Behind the terminology is the notion that questions as to the nature of law and legal systems are to be answered by the methods of philosophical reasoning. The association between legal theory and philosophy is of recent origin, owing much to the publication in 1961 of H.L.A. Hart's *The Concept of Law*. Legal theory includes more than legal philosophy: its perspective can be disciplinary, based on anthropology, sociology, or other social sciences; it can be inspired by ideology, such as Marxism and its offspring critical legal studies, or by a normative standard, as in the case of race theory, or gender theory; and finally legal theory may reflect an epistemology, as illustrated by post-modernism. Another variation is socio-legal theory, which I touch on at the end of this Chapter. A further distinction is that between legal theory as general jurisprudence, which examines the general nature of law and legal systems, and special jurisprudence, which concentrates on the theoretical analysis of an area of law, such as criminal law, torts, or contract. This Chapter deals only with general jurisprudence.

A distinction is also made between legal theory as descriptive of law and legal systems as they occur in the world, and ideal accounts,[3] which are part of normative political theory and which begin with the premise that law has certain purposes and should satisfy certain values if it is to be in the full sense law. Ideal theories focus on what those purposes and values are rather than the nature of actual legal systems, although the reality of law ought to be both a guide and a constraint if ideal accounts are to be credible (Miller, 1999). Whether a clear line can be drawn between the descriptive and the ideal is a matter of debate among legal philosophers (e.g., Finnis, 1978; Dworkin, 2007), which we need not enter here, except to say that in my view they are distinct, although the distinction can be fine and the line between them easily crossed. My reason for limiting this Chapter to philosophical theory is that it asks the most basic questions about the nature of law and is often the foundation on which to construct other theories and perspectives, even if their purpose is to

---

[3] Precisely what that means is considered later in this Chapter. As descriptive theorists I shall have in mind in this essay mainly H.L.A. Hart, J. Raz, and H. Kelsen, while mention is made of J.W. Harris, M. Kramer, T. Morawetz, and E. Bodenheimer.

question certain of its tenets.[4] Since Hart's *The Concept of Law* makes a notable contribution to legal theory of this kind, I use it as a point of reference.

The usual aim of empirical research is to examine how law works in practice, covering such matters as: how laws are made; what functions they have; how legal institutions work, including the application and implementation of laws; how and to what extent law influences the actions, attitudes, and expectations of officials and non-officials; and what people think the law is and their attitudes toward it. A few examples illustrate the kinds of issues investigated and their breadth: how lobster fishing inspectors interpret and implement a complex set of regulatory rules (McMullan and Perrier, 2002); why victims of accidents fail to pursue remedies for damages in the courts (Harris et al., 1984); how court decisions affect the actions of those to whom they are directed (Garth and Sarat, 1998); why the ranchers of Shasta County ignore the law and adopt their own social rules (Ellickson, 1991); and what the inhabitants of two Russian towns understand the law to be, what they think of it, and how they use it (Kurkchiyan, 2009).

The differences between legal theory and empirical research are brought out by considering their subject matters, aims, and methods of research. The subject matter of legal theory is, for Hart "the general framework of legal thought" (Hart, 1961), and for Thomas Morawetz, echoing Hans Kelsen, the presuppositions "that go unquestioned by practitioners and are implicit in their activity" (Morawetz, 1980; Kelsen, 1967). Law means state law in whose making, interpretation, and implementation state officials play a prominent part. The aim is to formulate a theory "true of all legal systems' whose features must of necessity be general and abstract" (Raz, 1979: 104). Those features, according to Joseph Raz, pertain to: the existence, identity, structure, and content of a legal system. The method is to identify, develop, and refine the concepts implicit in law and legal systems.

In order to identify such concepts, theorists must have some evidence of law and legal systems in operation, of how law is practiced and how practitioners understand what they are doing. The information theorists rely on is not that obtained by empirical research; common sense and intuitions about law, what some call folk knowledge, is considered enough. They are enough for two reasons. One is that legal theory is interested only in the features both common and essential to legal systems or a defined group of them. Since common and essential features are likely to be few and easily identified, the range of information about law and legal systems needed for a theory of law is limited. The other reason is that legal theory is concerned only with the "legal," which means a judgment has to be made as to what is distinctively legal and what is not. Legal theorists differ in that judgment, but they are united in excluding from consideration the social environment around law (Harris, 1979). Whether law can be separated so clearly from its social environment is questionable, and a matter to consider later on. The

---

[4] Future references to legal theory are to be taken in this sense.

point for the moment is that legal theory of the philosophical kind is based on the separation.

Empirical research means collecting and analyzing data about law. It is a method of research rather than an end in itself and may be conducted with different aims in mind: simply to know more about some aspect of law, or to lay the groundwork for reform, or to build a set of generalizations about law. Another aim could be to contribute to legal theory, although as we shall see this is rarely the motivation for empirical research. Whether there is a strict line between law and other social phenomena is not important for empirical research; indeed empirical researchers are likely to count themselves among those who question whether there are precise boundaries between the two. Since empirical research is concerned with how law works in practice, it is to be expected that law's interaction with other social factors is often one of its subjects. Empirical research is not restricted to state law, but investigates law and legal experience of all kinds, of which state law is just one kind.

The method of empirical research is: to pose questions about an aspect of law; to gather evidence; to interpret the evidence; and then draw conclusions. An understanding of how law works in the circumstances is the first, and often the only, objective. A second step may be taken to relate the findings to wider issues, or to compare them across different legal systems, or to place them in a broader framework of generalizations about law. For example, an understanding of the failure of Japan's equal opportunity laws points to causal factors likely to be present in other equal opportunity situations. Another approach is to begin with a general idea, expressed in an hypothesis or a model, and then set out to test it by empirical evidence. Max Weber pioneered this approach with *ideal types,* by which he meant theoretical models for understanding and interpreting evidence of what happens in practice (Weber, 1968: 19–22). Generalizations based on evidence of what happens in particular cases are contingent and potentially falsifiable, and therefore different from those of legal theory, which purport to be general truths about law.

Despite the differences between them, legal theory and empirical research have some common features. Both aim at understanding law and legal systems (MacCormick, 1978). Legal theory, while philosophical in method, still has as its subject a social phenomenon, created and practiced for social ends. It must, then, have a footing in social reality and be true to the social practices about which it theorizes. Since empirical research is essentially a means for obtaining and analyzing information about law, it should be a useful source of information for legal theory. Yet in acquiring knowledge of law, legal theorists tend to rely on what they know from common sense and perhaps their own experience of law. Empirical research is not considered relevant and is rarely cited. Hart's approach illustrates the point: he relies on "familiar" facts about law and criticizes other theorists whom he claims overlook or misunderstand the facts (Hart, 1961). It seems strange at first sight that legal theorists do not see empirical research as potentially useful, perhaps in providing a fuller understanding of familiar facts or unearthing less familiar ones. In deepening our understanding of law, empirical research has the potential to stimu-late new insights and understandings of use in developing legal theories or correcting mistakes. However, more information about law, more analysis and understanding of how it works in practice, are not necessarily of use to legal theory, and so one of the issues to consider here is when and under what conditions legal theory could benefit from empirical research.

Empirical researchers display a range of attitudes toward legal theory. Some are unfamiliar with it, while those who have some knowledge appear united in holding it marginal to their research. Lip service is sometimes paid to its importance for empirical research and occasional reference is made to juris-prudential writings, such as those of Hart and Dworkin.[5] Some researchers are wary of legal theory because of its unduly narrow understanding of law and the negative implications of that for the scope of empirical research. Whatever the reason, empirical studies utilizing ideas from legal theory or investigating those ideas are rare. Both omissions call for explanation. The failure of empirical researchers to utilize legal theory needs explaining because, in gathering and analyzing evidence, they need to have ideas, concepts, and insights as to the nature of law of the kind legal theory provides. The other omission also invites inquiry, for the empirical foundations on which legal theories are based may be wrong, incomplete, or defective in some other way. Suppose that, after extensive empirical research, Hart's claim, that law consists essentially of actions on the part of officials and others who are best understood as accepting and applying rules, turns out to be false. This might have resulted from Hart's lacking enough evidence of what officials are doing, or misunderstanding the evidence he had, with the result that the concept of a rule no longer matches the evidence. The same could be said of many other empirical claims implicit in legal theory, as we shall see shortly. Yet rarely are such claims tested by empirical research. Robert Ellickson's study of the ranchers of Shasta County, and his reflections on the claims of legal theory concerning the functions of law, is one of the few to do so (Ellickson, 1991).

My purpose in this Chapter is to examine relations between legal theory and empirical research, and to assess to what extent empirical research both does and could make use of legal theory, and vice versa. The essay divides into two sections. The first considers the use of legal theory in empirical research, offers an explanation of why it has been marginal, and considers whether it could be of more use. The ques-tion is reversed in the second section where the focus is on legal theory, on analyzing its components, and then considering why empirical research has been marginal to it and how it could potentially be less so.

---

[5] Dworkin's account of discretion, for example, is often referred to in a collection of studies of discretion: Hawkins, 1992.

II. Empirical Research and the Use of Legal Theory

There are two main ways legal theory could be relevant to empirical research: one would be the use of empirical research to test the factual basis on which theories are based, the other to rely on the ideas and concepts of legal theory in framing questions for empirical research. Empirical research has not embraced legal theory in either way. Researchers have not seen legal theory as a source of research questions and it is hard to find examples of its tenets being directly examined empirically. Some empirical research, although not directed at testing legal theory, is nevertheless indirectly and perhaps unintentionally relevant to it, as we shall see. The failure of researchers to use legal theory as an aid to their research also raises interesting questions: why have the ideas and concepts of legal theory not performed a service similar to that of ideal types or theoretical models? Hart thought they could and offered his ideas to social scientists, who have been on the whole unreceptive.

A. Legal theory as the source of subjects for empirical research

The observation that with few exceptions legal theory has not been a source of empirical research projects prompts several questions: what subjects for empirical projects could be drawn from legal theory? what have been the subjects of empirical research? and to what extent is such research, although not directed at the claims of legal theory, of potential significance for them? One way of seeing what research subjects can be drawn from theories of law is to consider the five elements around which theories are based: *structure, identity, existence, authority,* and *content*.[6]

Structure. A legal system, according to Hart, consists of rules. Rules are duty-imposing or power-conferring, and clusters of rules constitute institutions of a legislative, administrative, and adjudicative kind. Hart adds as "a salient fact of social life" that on important matters there are usually legal rules, and they are usually clear and determinate. Possible issues for research are: the character and composition of social rules; whether law is made up of rules and whether rules capture the full scope of law; the variety of rules; how rules work and are applied in practice; whether Hart's salient feature of social life is correct.

---

[6] I am following Raz's analysis with the addition of *authority*: Raz, 1972.

Identity. Hart defines the identity of a legal system in terms of a rule of recognition which consists of conventions as to what counts as a source of law. Legal rules are identified as law by the rule of recognition, and are different and separate from other kinds of social rules. The main issue is whether there is a master test for identifying law and, if so, what it consists of and whether it is capable of separating law from other social norms.

Existence. Hart says that the existence of a legal system depends on officials accepting the law as binding, while it is enough that the people, in the sense of non-officials, obey.[7] Hart's account of acceptance and obedience is much debated by legal philosophers, one set of questions concerning its conceptual coherence, another set whether the concepts express accurately the respective relationship to law of the two categories, officials and the people.

Authority. The authority of law refers to its claim to be binding and to be final with respect to society. The main issues are what it means for law to be binding, and in what sense it has final authority over other rule-governed arenas, some of which may claim also to be law and to be binding and final.

Content. Content refers to the notion that laws must have certain content in order to discharge their function of providing social goods, such as order, stability of relationships, security of property, and protection of the person. Hart contends that society could not survive without laws securing social goods of these kinds. The content of law ties into questions about its social functions: whether it has certain distinctive functions; if so, what they are; and what law adds to other, non-legal mechanisms for achieving social goods.

B. Subjects of empirical research

This agenda of potential questions has not caught the attention of empirical researchers, whose research interests lie elsewhere and cover three main subjects. The way state legal systems work is the most common and divides into two main lines of inquiry. One studies the actions of officials within legal institutions, such as, administrative bodies, regulatory agencies, or courts, in interpreting, implementing, and enforcing the law. The other studies the actions of non-officials—individual persons, groups, and enterprises—in relation to law, including how they use, exploit, or avoid law and legal institutions, and what effect law has on their behavior. Research into the actions of welfare officials deciding on the distribution of benefits is a good example of the first (e.g., Baldwin et al., 1992, Halliday, 2004), how studies of private enterprises comply with legal standards, what measures and mechanisms they

---

[7] "People" is used throughout the Chapter to mean non-officials; this should not be taken to mean officials are not people.

adopt, in such matters as equal opportunity in the workplace, illustrates the second (e.g., Parkinson 1989).

The common aim of such studies is to understand how law and legal institutions work in practice, how law is experienced by officials and the people, and how it influences their behavior. Law as it is written is one thing, how it works in reality another. What occurs in the interpretation and application of law in the welfare department, the magistrates' court, or the licensing agency, until recently has been fairly much unknown and yet of considerable social importance. The same can be said of how people use law and legal institutions, raising questions such as whether the rights they have on paper are upheld in practice and, if not, what obstacles impede fuller implementation and enforcement. An early and influential study conducted by the Oxford Centre for Socio-Legal Studies asks simple questions such as: what happens to the victims of accidents? to what extent do they pursue and obtain remedies? what deters them from doing so? (Harris et al., 1984). A main impetus for empirical research has been to find out how law works, how people use it, and how they are treated by it.

That natural curiosity is buttressed by a concern for social justice, which has been the impetus for some of the most significant empirical research, particularly within the discipline of socio-legal studies. If law is not working as it is supposed to, people are not being treated as they should be, and issues of justice arise. As new groups seek advantage and protection, their expectations of law as an instrument for achieving social justice strengthen. Empirical research is the means for testing how successful law is in achieving its own goals and, at times, for exposing its failures. There are of course other reasons besides a concern for social justice for conducting empirical research, but the point of present interest is that a desire to investigate the foundations of legal theory has not been among them. Nor have legal theorists, such as Kelsen, Hart, Raz, and others, encouraged empirical investigation of their ideas, presenting them as philosophical truths rather than models or hypotheses to be tested. The position may be changing as some theorists now advocate a role for empirical research in legal theory (Twining, 2009; Leiter, 2007).

Apart from the workings of the state legal order, two other themes are prominent in empirical research. One concerns the functions of law, whether certain functions are essential to society, and, if so, whether laws must have certain content in order to perform those functions. The role of state law is, of course, central in examining law's functions; but the inquiry includes other social rules and institutions which perform similar functions, and relations between the two. Durkheim's relegation of social norms to a minor role in social solidarity, and by implication in meeting the needs of society, and his corresponding promotion of law as effective, may need to be revised in the light of recent research (Galligan and Kurkchiyan, 2003). Of particular interest is Robert Ellickson's study of the ranchers of Shasta County and why they adopted their own social rules to govern the daily affairs of a farming community, despite the existence of state laws on the subject (Ellickson,

1991). In another celebrated study, Stewart Macaulay shows how the laws of contract have a limited place in contractual relations among businesses (Macaulay, 1963). Both studies raise questions about the functions of law and, in turn, the content of specific laws, subjects which have long been of interest to anthropologists, who begin their enquiries with a wider notion of law than state law, and for whom legal rules tend to merge into and become inseparable from social rules (Moore, 2005).

The other strand of empirical research, and the most recent, is how and to what extent law and legal ideas enter into people's understandings, attitudes, and activities. The approach, often framed as legal consciousness, at first emphasized how and to what extent people adopt ideas and concepts from state law and apply them in their actions. The approach has now expanded to include wider questions, such as, what people think law is, the sources of their ideas of law, and how they use them in daily life (e.g., Ewick and Silbey, 1998; Kurkchiyan, 2009). Widening the scope of research in this way shifts the emphasis from officials to the people, and to some degree from state law to other more informal senses and sources of law. This is a significant development in empirical research and opens up a number of questions about the nature of law, and whether the people share the same view of state law as officials, or perhaps think about it in quite different ways. Legal theory for its part shows little interest in either the people (as opposed to officials) or the notion of non-state law.[8]

C. Empirical research of potential relevance to legal theory

Although empirical research has not been directed at testing the factual basis of theories of law, some of its findings may be indirectly relevant, as the following examples show. Whether such findings are actually of use to legal theorists, and whether they could be used to develop or improve theories of law, is considered later in the Chapter.

With respect to *structure,* studies of how laws are interpreted and applied by officials, especially administrative bodies, regulatory agencies, and courts, show that rules come in different forms, some precise, some with open standards, others authorizing discretion. They show that interpretation and application occur in a social context of attitudes, practices, and norms, which guide and influence the process. Research into these matters could be brought to bear on Hart's claim that as a "salient feature of social life—the life of the law consists to a very large extent of the guidance both of officials and private individuals by determinate

---

[8]   A valuable exception is a recent essay by Gerald Postema: Postema, 2008.

rules" (Hart, 1961). It is also relevant to his contention that rules have a settled core of meaning with indeterminacy only at the margins. Empirical research raises questions about the very nature of social rules as guides to action, and hence about the claim that law consists of social rules. Empirical studies certainly support the idea that, while rules guide and structure the legal environment, their application involves other social factors, elsewhere described as contextual contingencies, entering into and forming part of that environment (Galligan, 2007: 47–102).

The same research encourages skepticism as to the centrality of rules in a legal order. If the decisive variables in legal decisions are external to the legal rules, then describing law in terms of rules is questionable. If, as David Robertson concludes from his study of the House of Lords in its judicial capacity, judges of the highest court have discretion whether or not to apply a legal rule, the skepticism may be well-founded (Robertson, 1998; see also Galligan, 2007: 47–65). The opposite may also be the case: judges sometimes apply the rules in the narrowest way, as a recent study of adjudication in the Polish administrative courts shows. Here judges preferred a literal reading of the statutes, declining even to refer to binding constitutional and European Law standards (Galligan and Matczak, 2007). A different line of research, familiar to anthropologists casts doubt on whether laws are rules at all. Max Gluckman found that court-like bodies among the Lozi of Rhodesia judge actions according to standards such as "reasonableness" or "the right course of action" rather than definite legal rules (Gluckman, 1955; see also Bohannan, 1957, and Pospisil, 1971). John Baker reaches a similar conclusion in his study of the early common law (Baker, 2002).

Empirical studies relevant to the *identity* of legal systems and the notion of a unifying rule are not so common although some recent work may be relevant to the issue (e.g., La Porta et al., 2008). Studies questioning the role of rules lead to reflection on whether the rule of recognition is subject to indeterminacy and dependence on contextual contingencies in the same way as other legal rules. If interpretation of the master rule depends on social factors and requires resort to moral, political, and social considerations, then the question could be asked whether law is capable of being identified adequately by resort to a master rule. Doubts are likely to increase when the notion of "officials" is prised apart to find not a united body of individual office-holders but a plurality of institutions and organizations, each cultivating distinct social environments where diverse views are held as to what law is, what it is for, and how to recognize it. When the focus shifts from officials to the people, a quite different perspective emerges as to the identity of a legal system: the interest in legal consciousness, in studying what people understand the law to be, how they render it manageable, and resolve conflicts between it and their beliefs, values, and norms, could stimulate a fresh approach to what counts as law (Ewick and Silbey, 1998; Kurkchiyan, 2009).

These issues are also relevant to the *existence* of a legal system, which, according to Hart, depends on the officials accepting the law as binding and the people obeying.

Legal philosophers are troubled by both aspects of this claim and debate what it means and whether it is true. If acceptance by officials means regarding law as binding and giving it priority over competing norms, values, and interests, then there are ample studies of how officials marginalize, selectively enforce, or ignore law because of such factors. Empirical studies of governmental bodies present a more realistic and nuanced account of officials' attitudes to law and how they balance it against competing demands (e.g., Lempert, 1992; Richardson et al., 1982).

From the perspective of the people, empirical research shows that obedience is too crude a notion to capture the complexity of their attitudes and behavior toward law (Parkinson, 1989; McBarnet, 2004; He, 2005). The mute and minor role legal theory assigns to them, where obedience is all that is necessary, plainly needs revisiting. An analysis of different areas of law shows how the attitudes and actions of the people vary according to whether the law concerns private relations, crime, regulation of legitimate activities, and so on. The concept of obedience has its place, but, if legal theory is to take account of this fuller range of attitudes and actions, it also needs other concepts and perhaps more empirical evidence on which to base them. In another line of research, the notion of compliance has replaced obedience on the ground that, being wider and looser, it is better able to express the social processes involved in people's conforming to law (discussed in Galligan, 2007: 331 ff). Studies of the new democracies of Eastern Europe move in another direction and show how low levels of compliance do not necessarily undermine the existence of a legal system (Galligan and Kurkchiyan, 2003; Kurkchiyan, 2009). And finally, legal consciousness, as we saw earlier, is emerging as a fertile way of expressing the way the people use, rely on, or reject law in their everyday affairs.

The *authority* of law has two elements. One is the notion of authority and what it means for officials and the people to accept law as binding. The notion of legal authority gained prominence after Max Weber, who tied authority to legitimacy and then proposed different kinds of legitimate authority and the social conditions on which they rely (Weber, 1968). Weber shows that the authority and legitimacy of law are not all-or-nothing, are not a matter of officials and the people either accepting or not accepting, as Hart's account seems to suggest. The degree of acceptance of a legal system, and therefore its authority, is a variable, so that law's authority can be high or low or somewhere in between. Also, we should distinguish between the authority of a legal system as a whole and the authority of particular laws. This adds to the variability of authority, for officials may accept the authority of law as a whole and yet concede varying degrees of authority to particular laws. A further complication is that attitudes among officials, as well as among the people, are likely to vary; the judge, the police officer, and the welfare official all accept the authority of law in a general way, but differ as to the intensity of their acceptance of both the system and specific laws within it (Galligan, 2007: 94 ff). The differences in attitudes among the people to the authority of law are even more varied. One way of assessing empirically the authority of law would be to study how officials and the people deal with laws in practice, subjects on which there is much empirical research, including studies of compliance with law by officials and citizens, the clash of law and social norms, and how laws are creatively interpreted, selectively applied, marginalized, or ignored (e.g., Hawkins, 1984; Halliday, 2004; McBarnet, 2004).

State law's claim to final authority over society generally and other sets of social rules in particular could be the subject of empirical investigation, although I have not found studies which do so directly. Studies of the relationship between state law and other social rules abound, but none focuses on the issue of the two competing for authority. There are studies showing how social relations are settled within the shadow of the law (Mnookin and Kornhauser, 1979); how ranchers build an informal order of social rules within the framework of state law (Ellickson, 1991); and how businessmen negotiate contracts with little reference to the law (Macaulay, 1963). Activities such as these, while normally conducted within the law, may sometimes stray beyond the law, but generally without challenging its final authority.

Links can be made with legal pluralism, a loose term, ranging from the idea of several legal orders existing together, as in medieval Europe (Berman, 1983), colonial South America, New South Wales, and Georgia (Benton, 2002; Ford 2010), or post-apartheid South Africa (Mnisi, 2009), to more questionable claims that state law is only one form of law and that a wide range of rule-governed arenas constitute legal orders (Griffith, 1986). One set of studies show how legal orders exist in parallel, sometimes each having distinct jurisdiction over defined matters, at other times arranged hierarchically. Empirical studies also show how parallel legal orders intersect and overlap, and how the boundaries between them are prone to become blurred and hard to locate. One conclusion could be that, in circumstances of such entanglement, the claim of state law to final authority has little significance. Stronger forms of legal pluralism, in claiming legal status for various rule-governed arenas, do seem to challenge the final authority of state law. If society is made up of a plurality of legal orders, then the claim of one to have final authority over the others becomes questionable. Until the theoretical and empirical bases of extended legal pluralism are developed further, it is difficult to assess how real is the threat it poses to state law's claim of final authority.

Consideration of the *content* of law is closely connected to the social functions of law. One way of reading studies which portray ranchers, businessmen, or divorcing couples conducting their affairs according to informal social norms rather than the law is that the content of the law is inadequate or unsuitable for the tasks in hand and the interests involved. The relationship between the two has stimulated some of the best research (Macaulay, 1963; Ellickson, 1991; Kurkchiyan, 2009). Another issue is whether law has essential functions to perform in maintaining order and stability, and whether, as Hart claims, laws with certain contents are necessary for that purpose. Both have been the subject of considerable empirical research, as well as theoretical speculation, from Durkheim onwards (Durkheim, 1984).

D. Potential use of legal theory in empirical research

Another set of questions is why empirical researchers, in studying law, have not found legal theory useful, either in the design of research or the analysis of data. The ability to recognize laws, to perceive the differences between different types of law, to grasp their significance as rules, to separate legal rules from the non-legal, to identify an institution as legal, to understand the relations between law and morality, and between state law and social norms—the very subject matter of legal theory—all seem a necessary foundation for empirical research. The same applies to the analysis of data and conclusions based on the analysis, where we would expect the ideas and concepts of legal theory to be of use. It is surely desirable that anyone conducting empirical research into law should have a working knowledge of theories of law, in the same way one would expect political scientists to be familiar with political theory and sociologists with sociological theory, although perhaps nowadays such expectations are unduly idealistic. I have drawn attention elsewhere to the difficulty social scientists often have in grasping the complexity of a legal order and its architecture, and the resulting over-simplification that results (Galligan, 2007).

The point is easily overstated: from the simple truth that a researcher must have some idea of the nature of law, it does not follow that it need be the fruit of assiduous study of legal theory. Apart from the fact that legal theorists are divided in their views of the nature of law and even the methodology for studying it, we ought to ask whether anything more than a broad familiarity with the main elements is necessary. Naivety with respect to legal theory need not mar empirical work, depending of course on the subjects of research, and I have not been able to find a project that positively would have benefited from theoretical insights. Weber, a master empirical researcher, was content with a simple idea of law as a coercive order. He found no need for the purposes of empirical projects to entertain the finer distinctions of legal theory, positing instead a different set of concepts or ideal types for analyzing the evidence. He goes further, pointing out the differences between a sociological approach and that of legal theory, and explaining why the latter is too restrictive for a social understanding of law (Weber, 1968). Weber could be the model for contemporary researchers, who are likely to have some idea of what law is, without necessarily being aware of legal theory or feeling the need to be better acquainted with it. To the extent that the ideas and concepts of legal theory are relevant to empirical research, they are likely to have seeped into the general consciousness, or at least the tutored consciousness of empirical researchers. Dworkin, who is not an empirical researcher, in suggesting that a stipulative and, by implication, rough definition of law is enough for empirical research, apparently belongs to the same school of thought (Dworkin, 2007).

Could empirical research better utilize legal theory? Hart as a legal theorist was confident of the utility of his analysis for empirical purposes, a confidence that has proved more controversial than it deserves and which remains unfulfilled in practice (Twining, 2009; Lacey, 2006). The point, made briefly in the Preface of *The Concept of Law*, where Hart refers to its being also an "essay in descriptive sociology," is not developed, so we have to reconstruct what could be useful. The main potential "sociological concepts" in *The Concept of Law* are those expressed in describing the five elements of a theory of law considered earlier.[9] Hart's point is that the ideas and concepts he analyzes are the same as those used by officials and citizens in the social practice of law and are implicit in practical thought and action. If, for example, researchers do not understand the activity of following rules, they will miss a range of legal activity or misinterpret it; similar consequences will follow from failure to distinguish between laws and other types of rules. If the ideas and concepts of legal theory accurately reflect the reality of law, it follows they ought to be useful in research concerning that reality, in designing projects and interpreting the evidence, just as Weber's ideal types and the models of social scientists are useful. Their usefulness is shown in Damaška's comparative study of the rules of evidence and court procedures, where he creates two models of state authority, which then serve as a lens through which to view and classify the adversarial and inquisitorial systems of evidence (Damaška, 1986).[10]

Yet Hart's ideas and concepts have not, to my knowledge, been significant in empirical research. Among possible explanations, two are telling. One is that his generalizations about the nature of law are already known by empirical researchers. An aspiring researcher, untutored and inexperienced in law, would find *The Concept of Law* useful, while to the experienced the ideas will be familiar. The notion of a rule, which is the foundation of Hart's account and the subject of his most valuable insights, is integral to social life without reference to law. His explication of the internal point of view, and its connotations for rule-following, while new and illuminating for legal theory, long ago entered the canon of social science by way of Weber's analysis of social action, which has influenced social science literature and research ever since (Weber, 1968: 4–28).[11] The transfer of such knowledge to the empirical study of law does not need the mediation of legal theory. As guides to empirical research, Hart's other main ideas have fared no better.

---

[9] Compare Harris (1979) who interprets Hart differently on this point.

[10] Damaška writes: "Systematic study of features impressed on the legal process by state officialdom requires a scheme to identify and describe different modes of organizing procedural authority" (1986: 16).

[11] Hart arguably derived the notion of the internal view of rules from Weber.

E. More serious limitations on the use of legal theory in empirical research

A more fundamental reason why Hart's account of law (and philosophical legal theory generally) is of marginal use to empirical researchers is that the ideas and concepts are too narrow, too elementary, and too general to be useful in investigating law empirically. In showing how laws and legal institutions work in diverse social contexts, empirical research is outward-looking, drawing attention to the other social factors with which law interacts and how the interaction is managed. Rules provide a good example: legal theory tells us what a rule is, that law is made up of rules, and that rules have a core of settled meaning. Empirical researchers accept all three but only as starting points, for their interest is in seeing how legal rules are interpreted, how they relate to, are dependent on, and are compromised by social factors. Legal rules, then, are part, but only part, of the fuller social process of interest to empirical researchers. Research might prompt reconsideration of the concept of a rule; but, whether or not that would be justified, rules in theory and rules in practice are very different things.

Hart's claims are also too elementary: they may be of use at a preliminary stage of inquiry in identifying law and legal institutions, but as the investigation confronts specific, detailed, and local issues, it is likely to outgrow his categories. Issues may have to be decided without the guidance of rules and left to unstructured discretion; clear rules may be the tips of complex social situations; and the sources of law may be clouded in history and tradition rather than springing from a master rule. This is not to say Hart's account is wrong, which is a different issue; it is just to say that empirical research of local and specific issues is liable to find a general legal theory too restrictive to deal with law in practice. It may provide an initial framework, a way of getting started, but soon will be left behind in the wake of the evidence.

Empirical researchers could go on the offensive, contending that ignorance, even scepticism, of legal theory is a strength rather than a weakness, the point of empirical research being to understand how law works in diverse situations, letting the evidence speak for itself, without the pre-conceptions of legal theory. Too much reliance on fixed ideas and concepts risks evidence falling outside them and being overlooked or rejected for irrelevance, when properly examined it could reveal something novel. A lesson should be learned from anthropologists, who grapple with the question of to what extent the ideas and concepts of developed western societies are either useful or legitimate in studying the social life of traditional societies. Those who approach the unfamiliar with a conceptual framework of law and legal institutions firmly in mind risk interpreting local practices in accordance with them, while overlooking evidence indicating new lines of inquiry and potentially revealing new concepts. The approach likely to be most fruitful in understanding such unfamiliar societies requires a mind relatively open to the ideas and concepts implicit in their practices (Winch, 1958). The issue is not, of course, so cut and dried; the researcher setting out to study law in such societies has to have some elementary concepts and questions in mind, some indicators of what constitutes law, legal relationships, and legal institutions; and since these are not innate or natural types, the ideas must come from practical experience of legal systems. It is then a matter of drawing a line between settled ideas and concepts on the one hand, and a clean slate on the other hand; somewhere between the two lies a balance between having a notion of what law is, yet being receptive to the signs of diversity and novelty.

III. Relevance of Empirical Research for Legal Theory

A. Assumptions of legal theory and the empirical challenge

Just as empirical researchers have tended to ignore legal theory, legal theorists have shown little interest in empirical research. This may be attributable, in part, to the lack of research directly engaging the claims of legal theory, although we have seen the potential relevance of some research. The more likely reason is that legal theorists do not think empirical research on law is either necessary to their discipline or especially useful. Legal philosophy consists of identifying the concepts and methods "that enable us to describe and think about what we observe" and is a quite different activity from empirical research (Nagel, 2005, Raz, 2009).[12] This is to concede, at least implicitly, that a theory of law has an empirical part: since a theory of law is about the social phenomenon of law, the theorist needs information about the phenomenon. The theorist's task is then to find the concepts that best fit the social phenomenon, "fit" in making the most sense of what is observed. By following the five points of inquiry suggested earlier—structure, identity, existence, authority, and content—the legal theorist should arrive at concepts, which taken together constitute a theory of law.

Theorists occasionally need pulling up with a reminder of the facts, or correction from the standpoint of practice and experience, and Hart was adept at correcting other theories for failing to fit the facts. "Facts" must be used with caution since legal phenomena have to be interpreted and different

---

[12] In commenting on Hart's moving from a pre-legal to a legal order, P. Hacker writes: "It is important to understand that this revealing analysis is not a piece of armchair anthropology, but is a conceptual analysis" (Hacker, 1977: 12).

interpretations are open. The point is that legal theorists assume that the features of law relevant to legal theory are known or easily ascertained, though not ruling out the possibility of new aspects being discovered. There is no sign among legal theorists that their theories suffer due to a lack of information about legal systems; their debates are about how best to interpret and understand the familiar features of law. Austin thought the concept of sovereign commands to be the best fit; Hart pointed out its shortcomings and proposed instead the concept of a rule; Dworkin insists rules are not enough and adds principles. Some legal theorists limit their theory to mature or developed legal systems with which they are familiar, and so avoid having to obtain information about other, less familiar systems (Hart, 1961; Raz, 1972).

We now see how empirical research is potentially of use to legal theory: it reveals features of law which are not known by common sense and limited experience and which might be of use in identifying and refining theoretical concepts. That potential is limited by two additional factors. One is that legal theories normally purport to be general theories, which means they must hold true for all or a defined group of legal systems. The very idea of a general theory of law raises philosophical questions which need not be considered here; it is enough to keep in mind that philosophical legal theories are presented as general theories of law. The more general a theory is, the fewer the features of law it will include, and the less it will be concerned with deep and detailed knowledge of any one legal system. Accordingly, empirical studies investigating aspects of one or even several legal systems do not necessarily provide information of use in formulating a theory for all legal systems. The other limitation is that legal theory is concerned only with the essential features of legal systems (Raz, 2009). Again putting aside the philosophical questions raised by this claim, we see how legal theorists, by limiting legal theory to the essential features of legal systems, reduce further the usefulness of the detailed knowledge obtained by empirical investigation of one or a few legal systems.

This approach to legal theory has drawn criticism on two main grounds, one philosophical, the other pragmatic. The philosophical point is that all claims to knowledge are answerable to experience, yet legal theory allegedly consists of a type of knowledge that is not (Leiter, 2007; Twining, 2009). This is an issue for legal theorists which I shall not enter into beyond asking whether the criticism is valid. It is true that the formation and refinement of concepts, the task of legal theory, is not a matter of drawing inferences from evidence, since concepts are abstract entities reached by reasoning rather than proof or disproof by evidence. Nevertheless, since their purpose is to understand a social phenomenon, concepts must reflect accurately its features. It follows that legal theories are open to correction or development on the basis of evidence, subject to certain conditions being met. This leads to the more pragmatic criticism that legal theories fail to take account of empirical research of legal systems, either to develop and make them more complete (Bodenheimer, 1956), or as a corrective to claims based on unsound empirical foundations (Tamanaha, 1997; Lyons, 2008).

According to this critique, legal theory, in order to develop and progress, must go beyond the elucidation of legal concepts and provide "a thorough consideration of social factors" (Bodenheimer, 1956) and of "institutional and social aspects" (Lacey, 2006: 955). Legal theory, and here reference is made to Hart's in particular, is said to rest on empirical assumptions "at the most abstract level" (Lacey, 2006: 955). The claim seems to be that Hart's theory of law, purporting to be based on social reality, does not take account of enough social reality, the result being an unduly narrow theory. The trouble with such criticisms is that they do not say exactly what the additional elements should have been or how a theory, Hart's for instance, would be different, beyond calling for "a far richer conception of the social functions of law and its institutional base" (Lacey, 2006: 957). The argument concludes that empirical research, to which Hart paid no attention, is the key to unlocking the fuller social reality of law and leading to a more complete legal theory.[13]

Empirical research might also be of use in correcting theoretical errors. Brian Tamanaha, in his search for a general socio-legal theory of law, eliminated both the claim that law must be effective and that it performs certain social functions, on the ground that neither is supported by the facts. He drew on experience of a Micronesian society, which apparently has a legal system which the people by-and-large ignore, rendering it inefficacious. This is said to be contrary to the basic tenet of legal theory that, in order to exist, a legal system must be efficacious (Tamanaha, 1997). David Lyons describes a case, in the post-bellum southern states of the United States, of unlawful actions becoming entrenched in the attitudes of officials toward freed slaves, and so casting doubt on Hart's claim of the centrality of officials' acceptance of law as binding (Lyons, 2008).[14] Such cases are said to undermine legal theory or at least provoke "theoretical reflection."

B. Bridging the gap: the conditions for empirical research being of use to legal theory

It is not enough to urge fuller consideration of law's social aspects, or to encourage legal philosophers to rise from their armchairs and find out what other disciplines "can tell us about the social practices in and around law" (Leiter, 2007: 134), without showing how that new information would make a difference to legal theory. Nor is it enough to claim that a legal theory is wrong because a counter example

---

[13] It is not entirely clear whether the aim of such criticisms is: (i) to improve philosophical legal theories by taking account of wider social factors, or (ii) to suggest a quite different kind of theory of theory of law. For present purposes, I take the aim to be (i).

[14] Lyons concludes, after close analysis of Hart's claims, that there is, after all, no incompatibility.

or exceptional case is found. Nevertheless, the underlying intuition that empirical research can contribute to legal theory is correct, and my purpose in the rest of this Chapter is to show how it can contribute and under what conditions.

To enquire into the conditions by which empirical research may be of use to legal theory is to enquire as to what information legal theorists need about legal systems and how much. Hart's approach illustrates the point. He observed that a lot of law-related actions involve the application of rules. The concept of a rule is well-established in language and in understanding the social world, and so putting the two together—what he observed and the concept of a rule—Hart concludes that law is a system of rules; that is to say, the concept of a rule is the basis for understanding what is happening in practice. He goes on to refine the concept and to distinguish different kinds of rules, surmising, probably correctly but without reference to evidence, that what he observes in the legal systems he knows is true of other developed systems. But is the case so clear-cut, so straightforward? Does a social phenomenon as complex and variable as law turn on a few basic features and fit so easily into a few simple concepts? It is surely possible that by gathering more information about how law and legal systems work, by paying more attention to empirical research, Hart might have encountered other features which would have led to further development of his theory, or possibly suggested corrections or modifications. On further probing, several points emerge at which more information about law, the very sort of information empirical evidence provides, might have been of use.

Hart's limiting his theory to developed or mature municipal legal systems illustrates the point in a general way. The contrast he makes is not with actual, under-developed legal systems but with a theoretical model of a "pre-legal system." Hart learns what is distinctive about a developed legal system by reflecting on how it differs from the model of a pre-legal system. The trouble is that the pre-legal model is not based on actual legal systems; it is a device created by way of contrast to a notion of a developed legal system, whose features Hart had already identified. Being an artificial device, the pre-legal model tells us nothing about actual legal systems. By relying on the model, Hart misses the opportunity of learning from other actual legal systems, which we know about from different kinds of empirical research, including comparative, anthropological, historical, and sociological. Had he considered the variety of legal systems as revealed by such research, Hart might have found two aspects useful. It would have been plain that the features he ascribes to mature systems, in particular a structure of rules, a rule of recognition, and institutions for making, applying, and adjudicating law, are common features of other legal systems that do not qualify as mature in his terms. More importantly, he would have discovered that some of the features he considers essential to a legal system—a structure based on rules and an identity based on a rule of recognition, for instance—are in fact contingent. For as we saw earlier, there is ample evidence of viable systems which neither are based on rules nor have a rule of recognition, at least not in Hart's sense. Whether information about other legal systems would have led to any changes in Hart's theory is conjecture, but at least it might have prompted a more thorough justification for selecting some features rather than others as the core of a legal system.

Let us now consider more closely how empirical research has the potential to contribute to legal theory. A thorough account would examine each of the five issues that legal theory addresses, but we shall have to be content with discussing just two, one regarding structure, the other existence. The structure of a legal system, according to Hart, comprises legal rules. Empirical research shows how legal rules are interpreted and applied by administrative bodies, regulatory agencies, and courts in different situations. A reasonable conclusion to be drawn from such research is that legal rules interact with other social factors to such an extent, and in so many different ways, that understanding the interaction is essential to understanding the nature of rules, and hence the nature of law (e.g., Eisenberg and Johnson, 1990–1991; Robertson, 1998). The significance of the interaction is acknowledged in less philosophically and more socially inclined theories of law, but does it matter for philosophical legal theory? Is the interaction of laws and their environment a necessary dimension of the structure of a legal system? If it is, a theory of law which describes the structure of a legal system in terms of rules should include that dimension.

This is not to challenge the significance of legal rules. The argument acknowledges them as components of a legal system, but contends that an account of rules is incomplete unless it includes the way they function in practice, by which is meant their interaction with the social environment. The result may be that, in order to take account of this dimension of rules revealed by empirical research, the concept of a rule needs to be re-formulated and refined, or perhaps other concepts invoked or invented. The result would be a fuller account of the structure of a legal system and recognition of the role empirical research can have in building a legal theory. However, the relationship between the two, while clear enough in principle, is not so easy or straightforward to apply in practice for reasons we shall now see.

An initial obstacle is the claim that law is one thing, its application in practice another. Language reinforces the point, for it is common to distinguish between law on the one hand, and its application in practice on the other hand. The distinction is crucial to legal theories of the kind advanced by Hans Kelsen and J.W. Harris, who define the subject matter of "legal science" as the "normative field" of law (Kelsen, 1967; Harris, 1979). On this view, anything outside the strict analysis of legal norms is irrelevant to legal theory. Luhmann, interestingly, in formulating a sociological theory of law, adopts the same approach, arguing that a sociological theory is concerned only with the essential legal "operations," not the environment around them (Luhmann, 2004). Hart's approach is different and yet ends in the same way. In proposing a theory more receptive to the social dimensions of law, he focuses instead on law as social rules. Yet his analysis concentrates on what are best described as the formal qualities of rules; and, just as Kelsen draws a line between the philosophical analysis of legal norms and all other questions about law, Hart distinguishes between legal rules, which are essential components of a legal order, and their interpretation and application in practice, which are not. Interpretation is a necessary feature of legal rules and so warrants philosophical attention; but the variable factors influencing interpretation and application in practice, and connecting law to other factors and influences, are not of philosophical interest. On this approach, empirical studies devoted to understanding the process of interpretation and application of law appear to be of no use to legal theorists.

An alternative would be to suggest that what constitutes the legal element of a set of social practices is the very matter in issue and cannot be preempted by definitional decree. If theorists start with open minds as to what are the essential features of law, and if they are receptive to empirical research on the application of laws, they would realize that the interaction of laws and their social environment is a genuine part of legal experience and should be included in a theory of law. The upshot is two different views as to what is the proper subject matter of legal theory, one narrow and relying mainly on intuition, the other expansive and responsive to empirical evidence. This is not the place to try to show how the more expansive view could be developed; but at least we see the direction such a theory could take and how empirical research on the interpretation and application of laws would be relevant to it.

Another obstacle to the use of empirical studies in identifying the structure of a legal system is the requirement of generality. Here the question is whether the interaction of legal rules with social factors is so widespread among legal systems, so necessary to the functioning of any legal system, that it forms part of the structure of law. A substantial body of research of different kinds of legal institutions across a selection of legal systems suggests the interaction, far from being particular to some legal systems, is common to all, and so the generality condition is met. That is just the first step: the second is to find concepts to express this aspect of a legal system. Legal theories acknowledge "interpretation" as a necessary aspect of rules and much has been written about the concept (e.g., MacCormick, 1978). The philosophical accounts, however, emphasize the analytical features of interpretation and take no account of the social aspects. If the philosophical focus is to expand to include the social aspects, in particular the interaction of law and its environment, what concepts are there adequate to the task? The challenge is to find concepts which are general enough to capture variation from one set of laws to another, and which, at the same time, have explanatory value. Given both such variation and the need for generality, it may be that legal theories can do more than acknowledge, without detailed elaboration, that social factors enter into the interpretation and application of legal rules. That would hardly be a theoretical break-through. But it may be there are no concepts both more explanatory and of adequate generality. We need not pursue the matter further here for the lessons are clear: first, the findings of empirical research, no matter how interesting and illuminating of an aspect of law, are of use to legal theorists only if they pass the generality test; and, secondly, even if they do, their contribution to the conceptual framework of legal theory may be marginal.

The issue of contingency presents a third obstacle: theories of law, according to legal theorists, include only elements that are essential features of a legal system. Since knowledge of the interaction between rules and their social environment comes from empirical studies that are local, particular, and by no means comprehensive, it is not clear that their findings satisfy the test of necessity. Empirical evidence provides the basis for hypotheses as to the nature of law, but does not prove them, since there is always the possibility of counter examples. Here the different methods of social science and legal theory are revealing: in social science generalizations normally are reached by induction from empirical investigation of particular cases, while legal theory claims to identify general and essential truths about law.

A possible response to the problem of contingency would be to claim that, although empirical research is local and piecemeal, it is reasonable to assume that the interaction between legal rules and their environment is a necessary feature of all legal systems. In support of that assumption it may be argued that philosophical legal theories, though purporting to be truths about law, are in fact based on limited knowledge of a few legal systems. On the basis of such limited knowledge, judgments are made that certain features are essential rather than contingent. One might ask how it can be legitimate to make claims about the essential features of law based on such contingent and selective information; but that would be to provoke another debate. The point for present purposes is that the condition of necessity or essentiality should not be taken too literally and may not be as exacting as it first appears. And from that we may conclude that empirical investigation, despite being local and particular, has the potential to reveal new and essential features of law.

My purpose in examining the interaction of laws and their environments has been to show that information revealed by empirical research has obstacles to overcome and conditions to meet, if it is to be of use to legal theory. Despite such impediments, there is always the potential that the findings of an empirical research project will stimulate fresh insights into the nature of law of such significance that current concepts will need to be modified or new ones added. Theories of law are not static and settled for all time, as Hart demonstrated in challenging the orthodox and long-held view that the essence of law is best expressed by the concepts of sovereign commands, sanctions, and habits of obedience. His correction of earlier theories came from paying attention to the facts, to the empirical realities, and then finding suitable concepts to express them. That account now has been subjected to similar refinement and revision as legal theorists continue to search for the essence of law. And although legal theorists tend to assume the relevant features of law are those familiar to them, it may be that less familiar facts, of the kind empirical research is good at uncovering, have a part to play.

By way of final illustration, I conclude the Chapter with two issues which seem ripe for reconsideration in the light of empirical research. They both relate to the conditions of existence of a legal system: acceptance by officials and popular obedience. The post-civil war case in the United States, where officials "systematically disapprove of or violate the law" (Lyons, 2008: 39), to allow discrimination against the black population, ties in with a large body of empirical research, adverted to earlier, showing the attitudes of officials to law in different situations. Their attitudes to law are not uniform but vary according to several factors, including the institutional setting, their roles within it, and the informal norms and practices accepted as binding. We know that officials, particularly but not only, those at the lower end of the legal chain, such as police, welfare officers, prison warders, even magistrates and regulators, have to interpret the law as they see fit, decide how to apply it, and even whether to apply it. We also know that officials work within institutional settings with distinctive understandings, purposes, and norms, which shape and determine how they approach and deal with law. As evidence mounts of variation in the way different sets of officials view the law, Hart's concept of acceptance, on which much of his theory depends and which is itself far from clear, becomes less and less adequate as a generalization of the social reality to which it refers and needs revising.

Revision is needed also to Hart's claims about general obedience. The case of Micronesia, of a legal system appearing to exist despite being largely ignored by the people, is not unlike that of Russia and its neighbors during the communist period (Kurkchiyan, 2009). Reflection on such cases leads one to question the concept of general obedience and its capacity to express the way the people, as opposed to officials, relate to law. Gerald Postema's recent analysis of what it means for law to be used by the people is a step toward more suitable concepts (Postema, 2008), while empirical research could contribute by showing what happens in different situations. One set of issues which is obvious to anyone with the barest knowledge of law is that people's attitudes and actions differ according to different types of law. Criminal law, by reason of its nature and purpose, induces patterns of response in marked contrast to those of welfare law, which in turn differ from private law or regulatory law (Galligan, 2007). Empirical research could help in mapping the different attitudes and providing a deeper understanding of them.

A more fundamental matter is what the people consider to be law. Theories of law such as Hart's assume that the people share the view of officials as to what is law. Yet we learn from the studies of Californian ranchers and Wisconsin businessmen, and many others, that communities, associations, and professions tend to reject laws which do not serve their purposes. We know from research that strong social norms or self-interest, or the two combined, lead to laws being creatively complied with, subtly marginalized, discreetly ignored, or simply rejected. The range of attitudes toward law shown in studies like these may be linked to the growing interest among empirical researchers in the people and the law. Further reflection on the general issue of the people and law might lead to a paradigm shift in the social understanding of law. Instead of beginning with state law and the prominence of officials, an alternative would be to begin with the people, to ask what they understand by law and how it features in their actions. As empirical research investigates further, it is possible that general features will emerge which require radical revision of some of the basic concepts of philosophical legal theory.

My conclusion is that empirical research about law may be relevant to philosophical legal theory. In providing evidence of the workings of legal systems and the way officials and the people understand and use law, empirical research can stimulate theoretical reflection and perhaps contribute to better legal theory. The conditions imposed by the very nature of philosophical legal theory are exacting and will not easily or often be met. Nevertheless, theoretical understanding of the social world is constantly changing and to imagine that legal philosophers have already unearthed all relevant features of law and legal systems is implausible. It is, after all, not so long ago that H.L.A. Hart, on a reassessment of the evidence, overturned the philosophical certainties of his era, which must have seemed as immutable as those of today.

This is not to suggest that empirical researchers should necessarily change direction and address their enquiries to the foundations of legal theory; they have broader aims to pursue and should continue to pursue them. What is missing from those aims is attention to a different kind of legal theory, one more at ease with, indeed a natural companion of, empirical research. That kind of legal theory is implicit in the criticisms of philosophical theories referred to above but neither made explicit nor properly and publicly declared. Instead of trying to infuse legal philosophy with socio-legal research, the idea here is to exploit the intuition that that kind of theory is not the only kind of general legal theory. The alternative would be to develop a different kind of legal theory, one concentrating on the social aspects of law and building piece-by-piece from empirical studies a set of generalizations, contingent and defeasible though they will be, about law in society. This would bring empirical research about law more into line with the normal approach of the social sciences toward the building of theories; it would also put to good use the great range of empirical research projects conducted in recent years and, in the process, give them a new lease of life. Most of all it would increase the understanding of law and legal systems as they occur in contemporary societies.

REFERENCES

Baert, P. (2005). *Philosophy of the Social Sciences,* Cambridge: Cambridge University Press.

Baker, J. H. (2002). *An Introduction to English Legal History*, London: Butterworths.

Baldwin, J., Whiteley, N., and Young, R. (1992). *Judging Social Security*, Oxford: Oxford University Press.

Benton, L. (2002). *Law and Colonial Cultures: Legal Regimes in World History*, Cambridge: Cambridge University Press.

Berman, H. (1983). *Law and Revolution: The Formation of the Western Legal Tradition*, Cambridge, MA: Harvard University Press.

Bodenheimer, E. (1956). "Modern Analytical Jurisprudence and the Limits of Its Usefulness," *University of Pennsylvania Law Review* 104: 1080–6.

Bohannan, P. (1957). *Justice and Judgment Among the Tiv*, Oxford: Oxford University Press.

Damaška, M. (1986). *The Faces of Justice and State Authority*, New Haven: Yale University Press.

Durkheim, E. (1984). *The Division of Labour in Society*, New York: Free Press.

Dworkin, R. (2007). *Justice in Robes*, Cambridge, MA: Harvard University Press.

Eisenberg, T. and Johnson, S.L., (1990–1991). "The Effects of Intent: Do We Know How Legal Standards Work?," *Cornell Law Review* 76: 1151–97.

Ellickson, R. (1991). *Order Without Law*, Cambridge MA, Harvard University Press.

Ewick, P.E. and Silbey, S. (1998). *The Common Place of Law*, Chicago: Chicago University Press.

Finnis, J. (1978). *Natural Law and Natural Rights*, Oxford: Oxford University Press.

Ford, L. (2010). *Settler Sovereignty*, Cambridge, MA: Harvard University Press.

Galligan, D.J. (2007). *Law in Modern Society*, Oxford: Oxford University Press.

Galligan, D.J. and Kurkchiyan M. (2003). *Law and Informal Practices: The Post-Communist Experience*, Oxford: Oxford University Press.

Galligan, D.J. and Matczak, M. (2007). "Formalism in Post-Communist Courts: Empirical Study of Judicial Discretion in Polish Administrative Courts Deciding Business Cases," in R. Coman, and J.-M. De Wade (eds.), *Judicial Reforms in Central and Eastern European Countries*, Brugge: Vanden Broele: 226–50.

Garth, B. and Sarat, A. (eds) (1998). *How Does Law Matter?*, Evanston: Northwestern University Press.

Geertz, C. (2000). *Available Light: Anthropological Reflections on Philosophical Topics*, Princeton: Princeton University Press.

Gluckman, M. (1955). *The Judicial Process Among the Barotse of Northern Rhodesia*, Manchester: Manchester University Press.

Griffith, J. (1986). "What Is Legal Pluralism?," *Journal of Legal Pluralism* 24: 1–55.

Hacker, P. (1977). "Hart's Philosophy of Law," in P. Hacker and J. Raz (eds.), *Law, Morality and Society*, Oxford: Oxford University Press.

Halliday, S. (2004). *Judicial Review and Compliance with Administrative Law*, Oxford: Hart Publishing.

Harris, D., Maclean, M., Genn, H., Lloyd-Bostock, S., Fenn, P., Corfield, P., and Brittan, Y. (1984). *Compensation and Support for Illness and Injury*, Oxford: Oxford University Press.

Harris, J.W. (1979). *Law and Legal Science*, Oxford: Oxford University Press.

Hart, H.L.A. (1961). *The Concept of Law*, Oxford: Clarendon Press.

Hawkins, K. (1984). *Environment and Enforcement*, Oxford: Oxford University Press.

Hawkins, K. (ed.) (1992). *The Uses of Discretion*, Oxford: Oxford University Press.

He, X. (2005). "Why Do They Not Comply With Law?," *Law and Society Review* 39: 527–62

Kelsen, H. (1967). *Pure Theory of Law*, New York: Free Press.

Kurkchiyan, M. (2009). "Russian Legal Culture: An Analysis of Adaptive Response to an Institutional Transplant," *Law and Social Inquiry* 34: 337–64.

Kurkchiyan, M. and Galligan, D.J. (eds.) (2003). *Law and Informal Practices: The Post-Communist Experience*, Oxford: Oxford University Press.

Lacey, N. (2006). "Analytical Jurisprudence versus Descriptive Sociology Revisited," *University of Texas Law Review* 84: 944–82.

La Porta R., Lopez-de-Silanes, F., and Shleifer, A. (2008). "The Economic Consequences of Legal Origins," *Journal of Economic Literature* 46: 285–332.

Leiter, B. (2007). *Naturalizing Jurisprudence*, Oxford: Oxford University Press.

Lempert, R. (1992). "Discretion in a Behavioural Perspective," in K. Hawkins (ed.), *The Uses of Discretion*, Oxford: Clarendon Press.

Luhmann, N. (2004). *Law as a Social System*, (English edn.), Oxford: Oxford University Press.

Lyons, D. (2008). "The Legal Entrenchment of Illegality," in M. Kramer, C. Grant, B. Coulburn, and A. Hatzistavrou, (eds.), *The Legacy of H.L.A. Hart*, Oxford: Oxford University Press.

Macaulay, S. (1963). "Non-Contractual Relations in Business: A Preliminary Study," *American Sociological Review* 28: 59–76.

MacCormick, N. (1978). *Legal Reasoning and Legal Theory*, Oxford: Clarendon Press.

McBarnet, D. (2004). *Crime, Compliance, and Control*, Farnham: Ashgate.

McMullan, J.L. and Perrier, D. (2002). "Poaching and the Ironies of Law Enforcement," *Law and Society Review* 36(4): 679–717.

Miller, D. (1999). *Principles of Social Justice*, Cambridge, MA: Harvard University Press.

Mnisi, S. (2009). *The Interface Between Living Customary Law(s) of Succession and South African State Law*, PhD Dissertation, Oxford University.

Mnookin, R. and Kornhauser, L. (1979). "Bargaining in the Shadow of the Law: The Case of Divorce," *Yale Law Journal* 88: 950–97.

Moore, S.F. (2005). *Law and Anthropology: A Reader*, Oxford: Blackwell.

Morawetz, T. (1980). *The Philosophy of Law*, New York: Macmillan.

Nagel, T. (2005). "The Central Questions," *London Review of Books* (3rd February): 27.

Parkinson, L. (1989). "Japan's Equal Employment Opportunity Law: An Alternative Approach to Social Change," *Columbia Law Review* 89: 604–61.

Pospisil, L. (1971). *Anthropology of Law: A Comparative Theory*, New York: Harper and Rowe.

Postema, G. (2008). "Conformity, Custom, Congruence: Rethinking the Efficacy of Law," in M. Kramer, C. Grant, B. Colburn, and A. Hatzistavrou (eds.) *The Legacy of H. L.A. Hart*, Oxford: Oxford University Press.

Raz, J. (1972). *The Concept of a Legal System*, Oxford: Oxford University Press.

Raz, J. (1979). *The Authority of Law*, Oxford: Oxford University Press.

Raz, J. (2009). *Between Authority and Interpretation*, Oxford: Oxford University Press.

Richardson, G., Ogus, A., and Burrows, P. (1982). *Policing Pollution*, Oxford: Clarendon Press.

Robertson, D. (1998). *Judicial Discretion in the House of Lords*, Oxford: Clarendon Press.

Tamanaha, B. (1997). *Realistic Socio-Legal Theory: Pragmatism and a Social Theory of Law*, Oxford: Oxford University Press.

Twining, W. (2009). *General Jurisprudence: Understanding Law from a Global Perspective*, Cambridge: Cambridge University Press.

Weber, M. (1968). *Economy and Society*, G. Roth and C. Wittick (eds.), Berkeley: University of California Press.

Winch, P. (1958). *The Idea of a Social Science and Its Relation to Philosophy*, London: Routledge.

4 1

EMPIRICAL LEGAL RESEARCH AND POLICY-MAKING

MARTIN PARTINGTON[1]

---

[1] Comments on this chapter may be sent to martin.partington@bris.ac.uk.

I. INTRODUCTION

EMPIRICAL research on law (ELR) seeks to understand and explain how law works in the real world. This volume demonstrates clearly that empirical research on law has become a recognized part of the social science research environment. The results of empirical research on law are (or should be) central to the concerns of the academic analysis of law (McCrudden, 2006) as well as more generally to understanding the role of law in modern society.

However, given that law is the principal tool used by modern governments to deliver social and economic policy, the lessons to be drawn from empirical research on law should not be of academic interest only. They should also be of considerable value to those working in government and other policy-making contexts. Lawmakers should want to understand how law may be used to deliver policy objectives and how the laws they have promoted are impacting on the challenges arising in the societies they seek to govern.

There are at least two reasons why policy-makers could benefit from a clearer understanding of the contribution of empirical legal studies to policy-making.

1. Empirical evidence can reveal gaps in current legal provision, or weaknesses in the ways in which current law works. It can help identify new strategies for dispute resolution and more generally for increasing the impact of law on society. In short, empirical legal research can assist policy-makers in defining changes needed in law or legal process.
2. Empirical research on law can also be used to address policy areas where problems are not likely to be assisted by more legislation. Empirical research can challenge assumptions about the effectiveness of law as a regulatory tool. Those with experience of doing empirical research in law, who understand both the substance of current law and why it does not work, are well placed to suggest how sensible policy-making might not require the introduction of new law, but rather seek better use of existing legal provisions (See, for example, Law Commission, 2008)

The argument in this Chapter is that, notwithstanding the enormous amount of empirical research on law that has been published over recent decades, much of which is reviewed in Part 2 of this book, the impact of such empirical research on the policy-making process is still not as significant as it should be.

This Chapter starts by offering some general reflections on the relationship between research and government. It then considers a number of examples of empirical research on law influencing policy-making and reflects briefly on what these case studies suggest about the relationship between empirical research on law and the policy-making process. It then seeks to identify the factors that need to be addressed to ensure that the research-policy-making process is as strong and integrated as possible.

II. Research and Government — the Need for an Evidence Base

Most people agree that, to a greater or lesser extent, the key social and economic problems facing the modern world have to be addressed by government intervention. And, there is increasing recognition that the really big challenges arising from globalization and environmental degradation can only be solved by governmental action on an international scale.

In identifying the issues to be addressed and shaping responses to them, many governments now seek to take into account research findings from both the physical and the social sciences. It is argued that, in principle, "evidence-based" policy-making is likely to be better than policy-making shaped by anecdote or personal preference.

There are various ways in which governments seek to promote and use research results in policy-making. These can be grouped under two broad headings: *investment* and *knowledge transfer*.

On the investment side, many countries fund substantial research activity, either through in-house research facilities, or by providing resources for research undertaken by third parties, principally university research departments but also other private sector research organizations. Thus, by way of examples only, in New Zealand, the government has established a Foundation for Research, Science and Technology which provides funds for a program of research[2] set by the Ministry for Research, Science & Technology.[3] In Australia, the Australian Research Council has a mission "to deliver policy and programs that advance Australian research and innovation globally and benefit the community."[4] The National Research Council of Canada similarly funds research which contributes "to Canada and all Canadians" that (among other objectives) uncovers "solutions to national challenges in health, climate change, the environment, clean energy and other fields."[5] In the United States, the National Science Foundation spends over $6 billion a year on research—about a fifth of all federally funded research.[6] The UK has a network of research funding councils,[7] and many government departments also invest directly in research. The European Union invests heavily in research under the leadership of a Commissioner for Science and Research.[8] A review of the websites of research funding in other

---

[2] Reports on the success of the program can be found at <http://www.frst.govt.nz/results/success-stories>.

[3] See <http://www.morst.govt.nz/funding/how/>.

[4] See <http://www.arc.gov.au/>.

[5] See <http://www.nrc-cnrc.gc.ca/eng/index.html>.

[6] See <http://www.nsf.gov/about/>.

[7] An overview of the seven research councils is available at <http://www.rcuk.ac.uk/default.htm>.

[8] An introduction to the research activities of the EU can be found at <http://ec.europa.eu/research/index.cfm?lg=en>.

countries would reveal myriad examples of public agencies investing in research, the bulk of which is of policy relevance.

In order to promote knowledge transfer, research funders now frequently require researchers to set out their plans for sharing knowledge about the research they have completed.[9] Many governments have created ways for those who work in government to gain access to information about, and to participate in, a wide range of research activity. Leading academics and other research professionals may be hired to work within government as researchers or policy advisors, either generally within their area of expertise or for specific projects.

In some countries more formal, longer-term arrangements have been instituted. For example, in the UK, the government employs a Chief Scientific Advisor, (currently Professor John Beddington)[10] who, among other tasks, oversees a network of other Scientific Advisors and research advisory groups based in various government departments. All these have created bridges between the worlds of research and government. In addition, UK government social research falls under the umbrella of the Government Social Research Unit.[11] All these activities are underpinned by a Council for Science and Technology, an independent research advisory group for all the UK governments.[12]

The vast bulk of the research funded by governments falls under the broad umbrella of the natural sciences. This research is directed at the acquisition of the technological and other scientific knowledge that is seen as being at the heart of modern economies. There is a more limited focus on the social science research needed for governments to understand and attempt to resolve the key social problems of the age.

From the specific point of view of this Chapter, what is striking about the outlines of government research priorities which appear on the relevant websites is the almost total lack of reference to research into issues relating to questions of law and justice. (The Scottish government provides a remarkable exception to this generalization. It includes both crime and justice within its published lists of research interests, perhaps because these are areas in which the Scottish Parliament has legislative competence).[13]

This is not to suggest that governments neither invest nor take an interest in the outcomes of empirical research in law. We consider below examples of how such research has influenced policy. But empirical research on law is regarded within governments as being at best of secondary importance, found within the specialist

---

[9] See generally, for the UK, <http://www.rcuk.ac.uk/innovation/ktportal/default.htm>.

[10] For an introduction to the Government Office for Science, see <http://www.dius.gov.uk/partner_organizations/office_for_science>.

[11] See <http://www.civilservice.gov.uk/networks/professional/gsr/index.aspx>. For operational research, see <http://www.operational-research.gov.uk/recruitment/>.

[12] For information about the Council, see <http://www.cst.gov.uk/>.

[13] See <http://www.scotland.gov.uk/topics/research>.

interests of departments of state concerned with law and the legal system. It is not seen as relevant to government as a whole.

However, as noted above, given that whenever governments decide to implement policy, the principal tool that they use for providing themselves with the authority for their interventions is law, it seems logical to suggest that policy-makers should have as much understanding as possible of how law works in the real world.

There are all kinds of question which empirical research results could help to answer: what kind of regulatory structures work best and in what contexts? When is direct regulation by government to be preferred to, say, regulation by newly created agencies, or self-regulation by industry? Who should determine regulatory standards? What enforcement strategies work best? Is enforcement best achieved by individuals taking proceedings in courts or being required to use alternative dispute resolution procedures? Is it by government or other public agencies taking proceedings? What should be the relationship between the use of formal and informal processes? How can access to justice be best promoted: by public legal services; by private finance? How can justice systems be resourced and encouraged to work with greater efficiency? These are questions which affect all aspects of government. One could think of many other examples.

Nevertheless, despite their dependence on law, governments do not currently appreciate as fully as they might how empirical research on law (with the possible exception of criminological research) might enable them to develop more successful legislative strategies and outcomes.

Notwithstanding this tentative conclusion, I consider in the next section a number of cases where empirical research on law clearly has had an impact, both positive and negative, upon policy-making and implementation, before going on to ask how relationships between researchers and policy-makers might be enhanced.

II. Case Studies: the Impact of Empirical Legal Research

In an essay of this kind, I can do no more than offer instances of empirical research influencing policy-makers. A full analysis requires its own empirical study. The examples I have chosen are selected mainly from projects with which I have had some association during my professional life. (While about 75% of my professional career was spent as a legal academic, my more recent experience has been working closer to government as a law reformer in the Law Commission for England and Wales and as consultant to or member of a number of government committees.)[14] Thus notwithstanding the international character of this book, they reveal a clear Anglo-centric bias. However, the examples mentioned here should be read in conjunction with those discussed in Part 2 of this volume. The Chapters there offer many other examples of empirical legal research undertaken in a wide variety of jurisdictions, many of which have made an impact on policy-making.

A. Legal aid and legal services

The area of legal policy-making, outside the area of crime control and criminal justice, that has arguably been most influenced by empirical research is that relating to the development of legal aid and the provision of legal services. Many countries have used empirical research to map the provision of legal services, to define the extent to which there is unmet need for legal services and to consider ways in which new models for the delivery of legal services might be promoted.

In the UK, it is nearly 40 years since Abel-Smith, Zander, and Brooke undertook their pioneering research on unmet legal need (1973). More recently, the work led by Genn (1999) revealed the extent to which those with potential causes of action failed to pursue their legal entitlements. This study was replicated in Scotland (Paterson and Genn, 2001).

The importance of empirical research to the development and delivery of legal aid is evidenced by the creation in 1996 of the Legal Services Research Centre.[15] Although funded by the Legal Services Commission—the agency currently responsible for delivering legal services—the center operates independently of the Commission. It uses its resources not only to undertake its own research (see, e.g., Pleasence et al., 2006) but also to commission research from outside researchers. It also facilitates contact between researchers and policy-makers through its biannual research conferences. Its work (and work upon which it is based) has served as a model for similar research in many other countries (including Canada, Scotland, New Zealand, Hong Kong, and the Netherlands)

B. Civil justice reform

In the common law world, much effort has been expended by policy-makers in recent years trying to create a civil justice system that is not exclusively available

---

[14] I write here in a purely personal capacity. My views are not to be taken as representative of any of the bodies with which I have been associated.

[15] Originally the Legal Aid Board Research Unit. See: <http://www.lsrc.org.uk/index2.htm>.

to either the very rich or (in those situations where legal aid is available) the very poor. Despite this, the empirical evidence on which proposals for reform might be based has historically been very patchy. Nevertheless in recent years policy relating to the reshaping of civil justice systems has been influenced, at least in part, by the outcomes of empirical research.

For example, in England and Wales, Lord Woolf's Report *Access to Justice* (Woolf, 1996) contained an empirical analysis of the costs of litigation (Genn, 1996). Following the introduction of the Woolf reforms, the newly created Civil Justice Council has been instrumental in promoting a number of research projects which have led to further policy development. For example, empirical research, sponsored by the Council, was central to the development of a new approach to the use of fixed fees to be charged by lawyers acting for clients in relation to certain classes of civil proceedings, notably low-value road traffic accidents where liability is admitted (Fenn and Rickman, 2003).[16] More recently it sponsored empirical research on collective legal actions (Mulheron, 2008),[17] which fed into policy recommendations on the issue made to government by the Council.[18]

The Australian Law Reform Commission's report on the Australian Federal Justice system (ALRC, 2000) similarly commissioned and used empirical research to assist it in its thinking on reform of the Australian Federal justice system, and called for greater investment in empirical research on law and the justice system. Recommendations from this report were incorporated into an (undated) policy paper, *Civil Justice Strategy*, published by the Australian Attorney-General's department.[19]

C. Alternative dispute resolution

Another policy issue closely related to reform of court process is alternative dispute resolution. A considerable body of empirical work, from a large number of jurisdictions, seeks to analyse the advantages and disadvantages of different forms of non-court dispute resolution procedures. For example, in the UK, a series of empirical studies of particular mediation schemes were commissioned, from the mid-1990s, by the (then) Lord Chancellor's Department/Department for Constitutional Affairs. These have been drawn together in a major report by Genn et al. (2007). The principal conclusion of this research was that while those who used mediation generally liked the process, it was not greatly used.

---

[16] See <http://www.justice.gov.uk/about/docs/personal-injury-claims-road.pdf>.

[17] Available at <http://www.civiljusticecouncil.gov.uk/files/collective_redress.pdf>.

[18] See: <http://www.civiljusticecouncil.gov.uk/files/Improving_Access__to_Justice_through_Collective_Actions.pdf> (2008)

[19] See *Executive Summary* in <http://www.clrc.gov.au/www/agd/agd.nsf/Page/Publications_FederalCivilJusticeSystemStrategyPaper-December2003>.

This is a possible example of empirical research having an indirect, rather than a direct, impact on policy-making. The government remains committed to encouragement of the use of mediation, possibly more than the research might suggest is warranted. But the research is nonetheless important for policy-makers in that is identifies the issues that need to be addressed by government if greater use of ADR is to be achieved in England.

D. Developing administrative justice

One of the great changes that occurred in many countries during the twentieth century has been the creation of specialist forums for the resolution of disputes between citizen and the state. Myriad tribunals offering (arguably) more informal justice than courts have been established, especially in the common law world. These specialist fora have been the subject of a good deal of empirical research, much of which has influenced administrative justice policy (for an early study, see Robson, 1951).

In the UK, studies by the late Professor Kathleen Bell in the 1970s (Bell et al., 1974; Bell, 1975) led directly to policy initiatives involving, first the training of social security tribunal chairs and secondly, structural changes to the social security tribunal system introduced in 1983 (Partington, 1986). Empirical work on tribunals also influenced more recent policy-making related to the creation in 2007 of the new Tribunals Service. This was the outcome of a review of Administrative Tribunals, led by Sir Andrew Leggatt (Leggatt, 2001). Although the review itself commissioned only a modest empirical study, the thinking in the report was influenced by a great deal of empirical work (Partington and Harris, 1999; Partington, 2001).

In developing the new service, the Senior President of Tribunals Lord Justice Carnwath, anxious to ensure that lessons from research should not be lost, commissioned a review of empirical work on tribunals (Partington et al., 2007).[20] The newly created Administrative Justice and Tribunals Council has, as part of its statutory remit, the promotion of research into the operation of the administrative justice system in the UK (though no budget for achieving this goal).[21] This statutory requirement would have been unthinkable a few years ago. Its first report on research indicates a variety of ways in which it hopes to bring researchers and funders together to undertake further research on the work of tribunals and other institutions in the administrative justice system.[22]

---

[20] Published online by the Administrative Justice and Tribunals Council at <http://www.ajtc.gov.uk/publications/179.htm>.

[21] Tribunals, Courts and Enforcement Act 2007, sched 7 para 13(1)(e).

[22] See AJTC, 2008. In 2007, the Nuffield Foundation committed itself to sponsoring a program of research into administrative justice which, among other objectives, it hopes will

E. Family justice

Many developments in family law and the administration of family justice have been influenced by empirical research. This was a priority area for empirical research in the UK right from the start of the government's investment in empirical research on law.[23] Given the often extremely emotive terms in which debates on developments in family justice are conducted, empirical research has played an important role in ensuring that policy is not wholly driven by emotional argument.

A recent example has been debate on the extent to which courts that hear cases about children should be open—especially to reporting by the press. There was a clear division of opinion between those—notably fathers' groups—who felt that injustice resulted from secrecy and those who felt that confidentiality was necessary to protect the interests of the parties, particularly the children. The issue generated a considerable amount of press attention driven by a number of individual stories of alleged injustice. This in turn led to significant political pressure. The initial government response was to propose a very open policy; but empirical research suggested that such a policy response might not be the best way forward (Brophy and Roberts, 2009). The outcome was that changes to the ways in which family court proceedings can be reported in the press were introduced at the end of April 2009, but they were more nuanced than had originally been proposed.[24]

More generally, the sensitivity of the work of family courts and the impact of court decisions on individuals is such that a number of jurisdictions have both sponsored and used empirical investigations in relation to different aspects of family justice policy. At the time of writing this Chapter, for example, the Australian Institute of Family Studies has undertaken a major empirical evaluation of family law reforms for the Australian Attorney General's Department, which is likely to be of considerable importance to the future development of family justice policy there.[25]

F. Equal treatment

A dramatic example of the impact on policy-making of empirical research on law occurred in the mid-1990s. Empirical research on the criminal courts raised

---

influence policy-making. See <http://www.nuffieldfoundation.org/go/grants/accesstojustice/page_480.html>.

[23] The research reports from the former Department for Constitutional Affairs are all available at <http://www.dca.gov.uk/research/resrep.htm>.

[24] See <http://www.justice.gov.uk/consultations/docs/family-justice-in-view.pdf>.

[25] See <http://www.aifs.gov.au/familylawevaluation/>.

controversial questions about whether members of ethnic minorities received equal sentencing treatment in criminal trials (Hood, 1992; see also Shute et al., 2005). This research had two major impacts.

First, the Judicial Studies Board embarked on a program of compulsory judicial training on equal treatment—as direct an impact on policy-making as could be imagined. Second, the Lord Chancellor's Department, the Department for Constitutional Affairs and the Ministry of Justice commissioned further empirical studies on equal treatment in other areas of the justice system. (The most recent report is Mason et al., 2009.) It remains an issue that concerns policy-makers, to which empirical research has had a significant input.

G. Law reform agencies

When law reform agencies enquire into a subject, they are heavily reliant on published research to inform their thinking. Until recently, the bulk of that research focussed on the black-letter analysis of case and statute law and was designed to identify ways in which existing law could be improved or rationalized.

However, many law reform agencies have increasingly come to realize that they must use, and in some cases commission, empirical research to facilitate their work. (See the view of the Australian Law Reform Commission considered above.) One important reason for this is that, although lawyers in the main see the purpose and value of law reform, others in the political system may not share those views. Law reform agencies need to make the case for reform to the governments for whom they work; empirical research on law can help to make that case.

Three very different examples from the Law Commission for England and Wales include work on: personal injury compensation (Genn, 1994), the effect of evidence of bad character on magistrates (Lloyd-Bostock, 2001) and the use of trustee exemption clauses (Dunn, 2002). While all three studies had a direct impact on the Law Commission's reports and recommendations on the subject in question, only the bad character study had further impact on subsequent legislation.[26] The commissioning and use of empirical research by law reform agencies, while expanding, is not as widespread as might be expected, not least because of the costs involved in undertaking such research.

---

[26] Criminal Justice Act 2003, Part 11.

H. Observations

The above examples lead to the following observations. First, there is greater awareness among policy-makers of the potential value of empirical research on law than there was even 20 years ago. However, this understanding is found largely in those departments of government directly concerned with the administration of justice. Policy-makers in other parts of government have not developed similar awareness.

Second, this awareness is now also found among leading members of the judiciary. Leading judges now understand much better the potential value of empirical research on law to provide information about the work of the courts, access to justice, problems of costs, and the like. Empirical legal research has also helped to identify issues on which there needs to be judicial training (for a recent example, see Moorhead and Sefton, 2005).

Third, there is an increasing number of government advisory bodies who understand the value of and are anxious to promote relevant empirical research on law. Currently, most lack the funding to commission it directly, though some work with private foundations to commission new studies.

Fourth, by no means all empirical work leads to identifiable policy outcomes, even where it has been commissioned by a government department or agency. In particular, research findings implying significant increases in public expenditure or the costs of litigation are in general less likely to lead to policy implementation than research indicating how things might be done more cost-effectively.

Fifth, coverage of the issues that have been the subject of empirical research on law remains patchy. There is comparatively more research on issues affecting the poor and disadvantaged than on those affecting the better-off (including commerce and business).

These observations—reflecting the current position in England and Wales—will find some resonance in other countries, in particular other common law countries where empirical legal research has also been developed.

The one exception is the U.S. Despite the fact that scholars in the U.S. have conducted major empirical investigations on law and legal process, the impact of this work on policy-makers seems to be relatively modest. Institutional arrangements in the U.S. seem to work against the ability of empirical legal researchers to influence policy-makers. This argument has been made both in the context of civil justice (Galanter, 1993) and criminal justice (Feeley, 1984). While there are government agencies, such as the Social Security Administration, that have research capacity, the outcomes of that research do not appear to be used in ways in which empirical research on law has been utilized in the examples given above. This raises a number of questions—which cannot be examined here—as to why this should be the case. It reinforces the point that the impact of empirical research on law on policy-making should itself be the subject of empirical study.

IV. Integrating Empirical Research on Law and Policy-making

Some may argue that the piecemeal approach to empirical research on law and its impact on policy-making—exemplified by the examples given above—is the best that can be achieved. This Chapter argues for a more ambitious view—that researchers and policy-makers should be more consciously working toward the development of a strategic program of empirical research on law, justified both for its own intrinsic interest and also for its wider potential impact on society. The question remains: how could this more ambitious vision be realized?

It is suggested here that a number of interlinking factors need consideration if a strategy for improving the ELR–policy-making environment is to be developed. For the sake of analysis, these are divided into macro and micro issues.

A. Macro issues

Two issues are fundamental to the greater integration of empirical research on law and policy-making: funding, and the shaping of disciplinary boundaries

1. Funding

An ambitious strategy for promoting empirical research on law cannot be delivered without adequate funding. It is true that in many countries research-funders—both governmental and private—have for many years supported projects in empirical research in law. In some cases, the effects of such investment are clear. For example, many countries have made significant investment in criminological research.

For well over 50 years, the UK Government's Home Office Research Unit funded research that enabled a number of universities to build up critical masses of researchers able to develop sustainable research programs.[27] (Though that Unit no longer

---

[27] The Cambridge Institute for Criminology was founded in 1959: see <http://www.crim.cam.ac.uk/>. The Oxford Centre for Criminology also has a history going back over 50 years; see <http://www.crim.ox.ac.uk/welcome/index.htm>.

exists as such, its functions continue in the Research Development and Statistics Directorate of the Home Office.)[28] In the U.S., there are annual programs of funding for the collection and analysis of data on crime run by the Bureau of Justice Statistics,[29] and the State Justice Institute has a program of grants that sometimes include research funding. The list of research reports published by the Canadian Department of Justice, going back to 2000, indicates a central concern with crime.[30] As a consequence, many countries have well established criminology research groups working in the universities.

On the civil justice side, major investments in empirical research on law have been made in the U.S. by bodies such as the RAND Corporation, which has long funded a major program of research on civil justice and has also created its own Institute for Civil Justice, employing a team of 40 researchers.[31] The National Center for State Courts regularly conducts research and produces statistical reports related to civil justice issues. There are now a number of well-established empirical law research centers in leading U.S. universities, including Cornell,[32] University of Wisconsin-Madison, University of California-Berkeley, and Georgetown. The American Bar Foundation has, for more than 50 years, also been providing empirical research "fundamental to the understanding of legal institutions and legal processes."[33]

In the UK, the Economic and Social Research Council (ESRC) provided core funding for a number of years to the Oxford Centre for Socio-Legal Studies.[34] This was a key development, both in terms of the path-breaking research the Centre undertook, but also because it trained a cadre of researchers, many of whom have gone on to establish significant research careers, and who have been the backbone of empirical legal research on law in the UK for the last 30 years. But by comparison with the United States, large centers of empirical research on law have not emerged in the UK. Once core funding for the Oxford Centre dried up in the 1990s, levels of funding for empirical research outside the criminal justice field have been more modest. The ESRC continued to include socio-legal research in its portfolio of activities for which funding would be provided, and this has been supplemented in recent years by some funding from the Arts and Humanities Research Council. However, the take-up of available resources by researchers has been relatively modest.

---

[28] See <http://rds.homeoffice.gov.uk/rds/index.html>. An overview of other Home Office research activity, including science research, is at <http://scienceandresearch.homeoffice.gov.uk/>.
[29] See <http://www.ojp.usdoj.gov/bjs/funding.htm>.
[30] See <http://www.justice.gc.ca/eng/pi/rs/date.cfm>.
[31] See <http://www.rand.org/icj/about/>.
[32] From where the Journal of Empirical Legal Studies is edited.
[33] See <http://www.americanbarfoundation.org/index.html>.
[34] See <http://www.csls.ox.ac.uk/>.

In addition, from the mid-1990s, the UK Lord Chancellor's Department, which historically had commissioned empirical research on an ad hoc basis for the purpose of particular projects, established a modest research team, with equally modest funds.[35] This has expanded with the creation of the Ministry of Justice. A number of research foundations, most notably the Nuffield Foundation,[36] have funded empirical research in law (see further Genn et al., 2006).

Perhaps because of its separate legal system, combined in part with the relatively small size of the academic community in Scotland, the Scottish government has made a (comparatively) significant investment in empirical research in law over many years. While much of this research was done in-house, the government also sponsored research by empirical legal researchers working in the universities.[37]

In other jurisdictions, a number of Law Foundations have been established, funded by the interest payments received by lawyers on money held in their client accounts. These Foundations use their resources to sponsor a range of activities including empirical research on law.[38] This has enabled a number of researchers to undertake empirical research in law. But the resource has never been sufficient for the creation of the infrastructure needed to build capacity for undertaking empirical legal research. Outside the United States, empirical research on law is mostly carried out by relatively small groups working on specific projects. There are no well-established civil justice research centers of the kind found in the U.S.[39]

2. Shaping disciplinary boundaries

It is not, however, purely a question of funding. Universities play a central role in the shaping of disciplinary boundaries. There have been at least three trends which appear to have militated against the emergence of empirical research on law as a distinct disciplinary area, central to the academic enterprise.

First, on the legal side, while over the last 30 to 40 years the scope of law as a discipline has greatly expanded, with traditional "black-letter" approaches to legal scholarship being supplemented by "socio-legal" or "law and society" approaches which embrace insights from a number of social science disciplines, these developments do not appear—except possibly in some law schools in the U.S.—to have

---

[35] The early research reports are at <http://www.dca.gov.uk/research/resrep.htm>; current project reports are at <http://www.justice.gov.uk/publications/research.htm>.

[36] See <http://www.nuffieldfoundation.org/>.

[37] See <http://www.scotland.gov.uk/Topics/Research/by-topic/crime-and-justice> for information about their research on crime and justice (including civil justice) and an archive of published empirical research on law.

[38] See, for example, the Law and Justice Foundation of New South Wales—<http://www.lawfoundation.net.au/>, or the Law Foundation of Ontario—<http://www.lawfoundation.on.ca/>. In the current economic climate this does not represent a significant source of income.

[39] The Centre for Empirical Research in Law at University College London may start to change this: see <http://www.ucl.ac.uk/laws/socio-legal/index.shtml>.

led to a proportionate increase of empirical research on law. The Nuffield review of the field in the UK (Genn et al., 2006) showed that comparatively little attention has been given to the development and provision of the intellectual skills needed for evaluating and perhaps ultimately undertaking empirical research on law. Even in those countries such as Canada and the United States, where law is a post-graduate subject studied by those who already have undergraduate degrees in other subjects, there seem to be only a limited number of contexts in which lessons from undergraduate programs of study, especially in subjects in the social sciences which include an introduction to empirical research methods, are brought into the law curriculum (see further Chapter 42 below). The undertaking or even analysis of empirical research on law is still not generally regarded as a central part of the discipline of law.

Secondly, on the social science side, it appears that law is no longer seen as an important focus for social research. In some countries, there also appears to be a reluctance to do empirical research in the social sciences. While this is not universally true—in the U.S. there is a strong empirical research effort in political science for example—this does seem to be the case in the UK.

Thirdly, although much lip-service is paid to the desirability of encouraging interdisciplinary research in universities—fundamental to the promotion of high quality empirical research on law—there are increasing institutional pressures working against those who want to develop intellectual collaborations. Whatever forward-thinking college presidents or university vice-chancellors may say, other pressures, such as the need to produce research papers published in refereed journals, still encourage researchers to stay within the comfort of familiar disciplinary boundaries.

Apart from criminology, where, as noted earlier, there is a number of well established research centers, these trends make it hard for those interested in empirical research on law to build the inter-disciplinary research groups and centers needed to enable this area of research activity to develop its full potential, both as an area of research in its own right and as a resource of value to the policy-making process. Those who currently undertake such research should ask how it can be developed into a clearly defined disciplinary area, analogous to criminology. There is a fundamental need for academic leadership on this issue.

Of course, these two macro issues are interrelated. Academic disciplines are not shaped by pure academic analysis. New financial incentives would undoubtedly help the academic community to reshape disciplinary boundaries in ways that would promote empirical research on law. But to argue that this is essential does not mean that the required resources will be made available. There is intense argument in the academic community about how available resources should be divided. Investment in empirical research on law will only be provided if a compelling case for investment is made to those responsible for funding decisions. Absent new money, funding for empirical research on law can only be secured at the expense of some other current area(s) of research activity.

Even if these two macro issues are resolved, however, this would not necessarily mean that the ELR-policy-making environment would be strengthened. Other micro issues also need to be addressed if that environment is to be as fruitful and as dynamic as it could be.

B. Micro issues

1. *Applied versus pure research*

Tensions exist in many parts of the academic community about the relative merits of pure as opposed to applied research. Many academics argue that academic freedom should mean freedom to set personal research goals, untrammelled by questions of practical utility and social impact. They regard pure research as having higher status and more value than applied research. Others want to do applied research which seeks to address known problems in innovative ways. They want to work with industry and government to try to ensure that their research outputs have practical outcomes.

While the distinction between pure and applied research is not in practice as cut and dried as suggested in the previous paragraph—there is a continuum of activity that goes on within these parameters—nevertheless tensions arise when those who engage in pure research fear that those who fund research are trying to set research agendas more at the applied end of the spectrum. Fears for the future of "pure" research lead practitioners to assert the importance of pure research, thereby—if only by implication—devaluing the contribution of applied research. This can undermine the confidence of those who wish to do applied empirical research.[40]

Thus those who wish to enrich the ELR-policy-making environment must build their confidence in the importance of high quality empirical research and recognize that it is of value not just to policy-makers but for the development of legal theory and legal scholarship generally. The impact of empirical legal studies on policy-making will be the greater if those who do the work are confident about their work and its contribution to learning.

2. *The "branding" of empirical research on law*

Although criminology has established itself as a clear academic disciplinary area, outside of criminal justice there is no comparable "civilology" brand. Instead,

---

[40] One of the principal reasons for establishing the Legal Empirical Research Support Network—an Internet support facility for empirical legal researchers—was to provide new researchers with a support network of scholars with whom they could share concerns and experience: see <http://www.lersnet.ac.uk/>.

non-criminological empirical research on law has become caught up in the more generic and less readily comprehensible label of "socio-legal studies" (Twining, 2009: Ch. 8). The concepts of socio-legal studies or "law in society" may be relatively well understood within universities but not outside the academy. For example, in the 1990s, in the UK the ESRC conducted a review of socio-legal research chaired by the late Mary Tuck, herself a distinguished criminologist working in the Home Office. She took a long time to understand what socio-legal studies were and why they would be worth supporting; once she did, however, she became an enthusiastic supporter and powerful advocate.

The ELR-policy-making environment is unlikely to the strengthened unless this question of the branding of empirical research on law is addressed by the academic community—a key recommendation of the UK Nuffield Review (Genn et al., 2006). Otherwise, it is likely that those in government will continue to have only a limited understanding of how empirical research on law might help them with the development and effective delivery of their social and economic policies.

3. *Lawyers in government*

Within government, lawyers are hired primarily for their specialist expertise in law, and only secondarily, if at all, for any wider knowledge they may have about how law works. This is certainly the case in the UK. In part this reflects how lawyers see themselves, with the focus being on their technical legal skills rather than any wider contribution that might derive from a broader vision of their potential role. This is in turn fostered by the perception of the discipline of law developed in the universities, discussed above. If lawyers are educated without any introduction to a wider range of social sciences, including empirical research on law, it is not surprising if they are unable to consider, other than in a somewhat amateurish way, how law works in the real world. Equally it is no surprise that policy-makers have not considered that those in government with a disciplinary background in law might have something more to offer than technical legal skills.

There have been some notable exceptions to this generalization. For example, for a number of years in the UK the Lord Chancellor's Department/Ministry of Justice employed, on a consultancy basis, a very experienced and well-established empirical legal researcher who both advised on and engaged in research sponsored by the department on various aspects of family law and family justice.[41] This work directly helped to shape a number of important policy initiatives. However, it will however be hard to improve the ELR-policy-making environment without a broader under-

---

[41]   Mavis Maclean, formerly of the Centre for Socio-Legal Studies in the University of Oxford, more recently director of the Oxford Centre of Family Law and Policy: see <http://www.spsw.ox.ac.uk/research/groups/oxflap.html>.

standing within government of the insights that the empirical researcher on law can bring to the policy-making process.

4. *Communication*

Certainly in the UK, perhaps to a lesser extent in other countries, many researchers seem extraordinarily reluctant to communicate the results of their research beyond the narrow world of their academic colleagues. This is not an issue that exclusively affects legal researchers; there is a general problem of how academics communicate with the public, both generally and in more specialist contexts. In the UK, the Research Councils and Higher Education Funding Councils all have programs to encourage "knowledge transfer." There is increasing political pressure to ensure that the public at large benefits from the investments government makes in research activity.

In the context of legal research generally, not just empirical legal studies, some senior legal academics are clearly very concerned about this. For example, the 2008 conference of the Society of Legal Scholars adopted, as its main theme, the "communication of legal scholarship."[42] Strikingly, although most keynote speakers urged scholars to be more open with their research findings, many of those speaking from the floor insisted that the only audience worth communicating with was that of fellow academics. For a subject, such as law, which plays such a key role in everyone's life, this seems to reflect an extraordinarily modest ambition for the legal scholar (see Twining, 1994).

There is evidence that the research community is taking steps to address the communication issue. The creation of the Social Science Research Network may be cited as an example.[43] But any idea that research output speaks for itself is wishful thinking; scholars must actively promote their ideas if they are to gain the recognition they deserve in the societies in which they work.

Of course, there are individual scholars who over the years have communicated their research findings to a wider public clearly and effectively; their impact on society has, as a consequence, been significant. But so long as scholars, including those engaged in empirical research in law, remain reluctant to communicate the outcomes of their research to a wider public, the ELR-policy-making environment will be impoverished.

5. *Building relationships between policy-makers and researchers*

In the early years, when empirical research in law was in its infancy, there was some antipathy among policy-makers toward researchers, particularly toward

---

[42] For details, see <http://www.lse.ac.uk/collections/law/sls/sls.htm>.
[43] See <http://www.ssrn.com/>.

academics working in universities. They were perceived as difficult to work with; their research reports were said to be too long and complicated; they were thought not to deliver their reports on time.

Whatever may have been the case in the past, the current generation of researchers is much more professional in its approach. Nonetheless, insofar as such negative views are still held, this inevitably sours the ELR-policy-making environment. It is essential to devise constructive ways for facilitating contact and building trust between researchers and policy-makers.

Most obvious is by making informal contact at research conferences and briefings. In such contexts it is important that both researchers and policy-makers can speak and debate freely. A current concern must be that, in a period of extreme public financial austerity, the opportunities for such communication will be reduced. Specific policy areas benefit from detailed collaboration between researchers and policy-makers. In addition, more formal channels of communication are required. Adapting what happens in the UK, governments should consider the appointment of a legally focussed Scientific Advisor or the establishment of a powerful advisory committee focussed on empirical legal research.

V. Concluding Remarks

Despite the potential for empirical research in law to influence policy-making, it is not argued here that the sole function of empirical research in law is to provide a background against which policy-making is to be conducted. Good scientific empirical research in law is to be justified for its own sake and for the contribution it makes generally to our understanding of the impact of law on society. The idea that law in the books is not the same as law in practice is not, of course, a new one. The basic theory of legal realism has been articulated and accepted for many years. But if the idea of legal realism is to be based on something more scientific than anecdote, empirical research is essential to analyze the differences between the theory and practice of law and legal institutions. Many empirical legal studies will have no impact on policy-making nor will they seriously challenge existing or potential policy developments.

Nonetheless, it is clear that some empirical research on law has had a major impact on the policy-making environment. The precise extent of this impact (which as suggested earlier itself deserves empirical investigation) is hard to measure. It also varies from country to country.

While the achievements of empirical research in law have already been significant it could potentially have even greater impact on policy-making. If this potential is to be achieved, a number of fundamental issues need to be addressed. These issues include research funding, facilitating the crossing of disciplinary boundaries, and providing the means for researchers and policy-makers to interact effectively.

Notwithstanding the positive examples discussed earlier, some areas of empirical research on law have not yet had the impact on policy-making one might expect. For example, although governments are more concerned about the nature and extent of regulation than they once were, such concern appears to focus on the economic impacts of regulation, rather than the legal effectiveness of different forms of regulatory strategy. Thus there is an extensive body of empirical legal work which has shown that theories of legislative impact based on the idea of "command and control" (which assumes that government acts and people respond) simply do not reflect the empirical reality of what happens in the real world. This was one of the principal streams of work undertaken in the early years of the Oxford Centre for Socio-Legal Studies (see Hawkins, 1997, 2003). It has been developed by other research groups both in the UK (e.g., LSE[44]) and elsewhere, notably by the group at the Australian National University in Canberra.[45] This work has not yet had the impact on legal policy-making that it deserves.

This Chapter has not considered the possibility of empirical research on law impacting on social policy-making at the international level, which seems to be a particularly undeveloped area for empirical research. A wonderful study on intellectual property rights might however serve as a model for future developments in this context (Whatmore, 2002).

Not all empirical research on law can lead directly to policy development. There will always be policy decisions that do not derive from and are not even influenced by, research outcomes. Indeed, in some cases, policy choices will be made that positively fly in the face of published research. Policy-makers, particularly those who are dependent on the popular vote for their power, often find that to adopt policies that might seem to arise logically from research findings would lead to measures that are politically unacceptable.

In cases where empirical research findings might suggest the development of policies which would require significant additional public expenditure, governments—particularly in an age of austerity—will inevitably resist. In such cases, the results of empirical research may have indirect rather than direct impact by leading to alternative policy outcomes designed to avoid additional public expenditure. For example, in the mid-1980s the then-Lord Chancellor's Department commissioned Hazel and Yvette Genn to study the impact of representation on the outcomes of cases heard by a range of administrative tribunals (Genn and Genn, 1989). The report demonstrated

[44] Centre for Analysis of Risk and Regulation: see <http://www.lse.ac.uk/collections/CARR/aboutUs/Default.htm>.
[45] The Regulatory Institutions Network within the ANU College of Asia and the Pacific: <http://regnet.anu.edu.au/program/aboutus/>.

clearly that there was a correlation between representation and outcome—appellants with representation had better outcomes at hearings than appellants without representation. The report noted that such representation did not have to be provided by qualified lawyers—lay representatives were also very successful on behalf of their clients. Nonetheless, there was a clear policy implication that there should be more public expenditure on the provision of representation services. However, the government was not willing to find the additional resources that were required. Although the direct effect of this research was limited, it nevertheless had significant indirect effects. Those who ran tribunals became conscious of the need to develop what came to be known as "the enabling role" (see Leggatt, 2001: Ch. 7). In other words, tribunals were encouraged themselves to give as much assistance as possible to the unrepresented in putting their case. Preliminary findings from more recent research suggest that this alternative strategy may have had some success (Adler, 2009).

None of these arguments, however, reduces the importance to government of empirical research on law. What is currently lacking in any jurisdiction is acceptance of the view that empirical research on law is relevant to the whole of government and not just to those parts of government dealing with the legal system and justice issues. The ELR-policy-making environment needs both academic leadership and governmental support to enable ELR on law to achieve its full potential and to maximize its contribution to society.

REFERENCES

Abel-Smith, B., Zander, M., and Brooke, R. (1973). *Legal Problems and the Citizen: A Study in Three London Boroughs*, London: Heinemann Educational.

Adler, M. (2009). "Self-representation, just outcomes and fair procedures in Tribunal Hearings: Some inferences from recently completed research," unpublished paper presented at Senior Presidents Conference for Tribunal Judges, Birmingham Exhibition Center, 20 May.

AJTC (2008). *Developing Administrative Justice Research*, London: Administrative Justice and Tribunals Council.

ALRC (2000). *Managing Justice: A review of the federal civil justice system* (Report No 89), Canberra: ALRC.

Bell, K. (1975). *Research Study on Supplementary Benefit Appeal Tribunals—Review of Main Findings: Conclusions: Recommendations*, London: HMSO.

Bell, K. et al. (1974). "National Insurance Local Tribunals: A research study," Part 1 *Journal of Social Policy* 3: 289. (Part 2 in (1975) *Journal of Social Policy* 4: 1).

Brophy, J. and Roberts, C. (2009). *Openness and transparency in family courts: what the experience in other countries tells us about reform in England and Wales*, Oxford: Department of Social Policy and Social Work.

Dunn, A. (2002). *Study of the Use of Trustee Exemption Clauses, discussed in Trustee Exemption Clauses: A Consultation Paper* (CP 171), London: HMSO.

Feeley, M. (1984). *Court reform on trial: Why simple solutions fail*, New York: Basic Books.

Fenn, P. and Rickman, N. (2003). *Costs of low value RTA claims 1997–2002: A report prepared for the Civil Justice Council, UK*, available at <http://www.justice.gov.uk/about/docs/personal-injury-claims-road.pdf>.

Galanter, M. (1993). "News from nowhere: the debased debate on civil justice," *Denver University Law Review* 71(1): 77.

Genn, H. (1994). *How much is enough? A study of the compensation experiences of victims of personal injury* (LawCom 225), London: HMSO.

Genn, H. (1996). *Survey of Litigation Costs: Summary of Main Findings*, in Woolf, Lord, *Access to justice: final report to the Lord Chancellor on the civil justice system in England and Wales*, (Annex 3), London: HMSO.

Genn, H. (1999). *Paths to justice: what people do and think about going to law*, Oxford: Hart.

Genn, H. and Genn, Y. (1989). *The effectiveness of representation at tribunals: report to the Lord Chancellor*, London: Queen Mary College, Faculty of Laws.

Genn, H., Fenn, P., Mason, M., Lane, A., Bechai, N., Gray, L., and Vencappa, D. (2007). *Twisting arms: court referred and court linked mediation under judicial pressure*, London: Ministry of Justice.

Genn, H., Partington, M., and Wheeler, S. (2006). *Law in the Real World: the Nuffield Inquiry on Empirical Research on Law*, London: Nuffield Foundation.

Hawkins, K. (ed.) (1997). *The Human Face of Law: Essays in Honour of Donald Harris*, Oxford: Clarendon Press.

Hawkins, K. (2003). *Law as Last Resort: Prosecution Decision-Making in a Regulatory Agency*, Oxford: Oxford University Press.

Hood, R., in collaboration with Cordovil, G. (1992). *Race and Sentencing: a Study in the Crown Court: a Report for the Commission for Racial Equality*, Oxford: Clarendon Press.

Law Commission (2008). *Encouraging Responsible Renting*, London: Law Commission.

Leggatt, Sir A. (2001). *Tribunals for Users—One System, One Service Report of the Review of Tribunals*, London: Department for Constitutional Affairs.

Lloyd-Bostock, S. (2001). "The Effect on Magistrates of Knowing a Defendant's Criminal Record," *Evidence of Bad Character in Criminal Proceedings*, (Appendix A), (LawCom 273), London: HMSO.

Mason, P., Hughes, N., with Hek, R., Spalek, B., and Ward, N. (2009). *Access to Justice: a review of existing evidence of the experiences of minority groups based on ethnicity, identity and sexuality*, London: Ministry of Justice.

McCrudden, C. (2006). "Legal Research and the Social Sciences," *Law Quarterly Review* 122: 632–50

Moorhead, R. and Sefton, M. (2005). *Litigants in person: Unrepresented litigants in first instance proceedings*, London: Department for Constitutional Affairs.

Mulheron, R. (2008). *Reform of Collective Redress in England and Wales: A Perspective of Need*, London: Civil Justice Council.

Partington, M. (1986). "The Restructuring of Social Security Appeal Tribunals: a Personal View," in C. Harlow (ed.) *Public law and politics: Essays in Honour of Prof. J.A.G. Griffith*, London: Sweet and Maxwell.

Partington, M. (ed.) (2001). *The Leggatt Review of Tribunals: academic seminar papers*, Bristol: Bristol Centre for the Study of Administrative Justice.

Partington, M. and Harris, M. (eds.) (1999). *Administrative justice in the 21st century*, Oxford: Hart.

Partington., M., Kirton-Darling, E., and McClenaghan, F. (2007). *Empirical Research on Tribunals: An Annotated Review of Research Published between 1992 and 2007*, London: Administrative Justice and Tribunals Council.

Paterson, A. and Genn, H. (2001). *Paths to Justice: Scotland*, Oxford: Hart.

Pleasence, P. with Balmer, N. and Buck, A. (2006). *Causes of action: civil law and social justice, incorporating findings from the 2004 English and Welsh Civil and Social Justice Survey* (2nd edn.), London: Stationery Office.

Robson, W.A. (1951). *Justice and administrative law: a study of the British constitution* (3rd edn.), London: Stevens and Sons.

Shute, S., Hood, R., and Seemungal, F. (2005). *A fair hearing?: ethnic minorities in the criminal courts*, Uffculme: Willan Publishing.

Twining, W. (1994). *Blackstone's Tower: Discipline of Law*, London: Sweet and Maxwell.

Twining, W. (2009). *General Jurisprudence: Understanding Law from a Global Perspective*, Cambridge: Cambridge University Press.

Whatmore, S. (2002). *Hybrid Geographies: Natures Cultures Spaces*, Newbury Park, CA: Sage.

Woolf, Lord H. (1996). *Access to justice: final report to the Lord Chancellor on the civil justice system in England and Wales*, London: HMSO.

4 2

THE PLACE OF EMPIRICAL LEGAL RESEARCH IN THE LAW SCHOOL CURRICULUM

ANTHONY BRADNEY

I. Introduction

EMPIRICAL legal research is defined in a number of different ways. These differences in definition are important when considering the place that empirical legal studies does or should have in the law school curriculum. Thus, for example, King and Epstein have a very broad definition of the term, including even doctrinal analysis, leading them to conclude that "virtually all legal scholars" conduct empirical research (King and Epstein, 2002: 18). Using this definition it would be true to say that virtually all law school curricula that currently exist or that can be envisaged for the future involve the study of empirical legal material. However, most definitions of empirical legal research are much more restricted than that formulated by King and Epstein.

The editor's introduction to the first volume of the *Journal of Empirical Legal Studies* states that the "JELS's editorial board is committed to providing expert statistical evaluation of manuscripts with the goal of raising the level of statistical sophistication in empirical legal scholarship" (Eisenberg et al., 2004: v). This focus on quantitative methods is characteristic of the relatively new empirical legal studies movement in the United States that has found concrete expression in the *Journal of Empirical Legal Studies*, first published in 2004, the Annual Conference on Empirical Legal Studies, first held in 2006, and the Society for Empirical Legal Studies. However, this definition of empirical legal research has little resonance outside the United States, where empirical legal research is usually understood to encompass both quantitative and qualitative studies of legal phenomena. Thus, for example, Baldwin and Davis begin their study of empirical legal research by writing that the term "is not a synonym for 'statistical' or 'factual'..." (Baldwin and Davis, 2003: 881). In this Chapter, because the definition has greatest global currency, empirical legal research will be taken to be studies conducted at least partly by quantitative or qualitative methods of data collection and analysis. The questions for this Chapter are the extent to which such research is or should be found in law school curricula.

Consideration of the place of empirical legal research in law school curricula needs to begin with two caveats. First, law school curricula, like law students, law schools, legal academics, and anything else related to university legal education, are not uniform in their nature throughout the world. The differences between them are frequently structural in their form. They relate, among other things, to the relationship that law schools have with their parent universities and the legal professions in their jurisdiction. Comparisons between curricula from different jurisdictions can be made but, if they are to be accurate, they need to be sensitive to the cultural context of the teaching and learning being discussed (Bradney, 2007). These general observations about the difficulty of comparative work in legal education are particularly pertinent to the subject-matter of this Chapter. Thus, for example, in the U.S.

the case for expanding the place of empirical legal research in law school curricula is largely made on the basis that students, once they have graduated, "will need the [empirical] skills to evaluate such [empirical] research, whether for clients, senior members of their law firms, or judges…" (Epstein and King, 2003: 313). Implicit in this argument are the notions that graduates from the law school are going to be lawyers and that the role of the law school is to educate them for that profession. Both these positions are rarely contested in the U.S. and form the basis for most evaluations of law schools and their pedagogy (see, for example, Sullivan et al., 2007). However these propositions are plainly not applicable to England and Wales where only a minority of law graduates go on to qualify as lawyers and where the vast majority of legal academics in academic law schools do not see themselves as educating students for the legal professions (Cownie, 2004: 75–8). A different case for the place of empirical legal studies in the curricula of English and Welsh university law schools thus needs to be made out. Other jurisdictions will have their own views on the role of the legal curriculum, which will in turn have an effect on the place of empirical legal studies within that curriculum.

The curricula that are specifically referred to in this essay are, in the main, those found in law schools in the United States and the United Kingdom. This is because reliable data about legal education is in short supply. Rochette and Pue note of Canadian law schools,

[l]awyers, law students and legal academics hold tenaciously—furiously even—to opinions about legal education. So too do university administrators, politicians, law society benchers, media pundits and others, but virtually no scholarly research focuses on what *actually* happens in legal education. Opinion in these fields is undisciplined, entirely unconstrained by reliable verifiable data or evidence of any sort (Rochette and Pue, 2001: 167–8).

As with Canada so with the rest of the world. Even in the U.S. and the UK, where the study of legal education is relatively well developed, there are comparatively few surveys or other studies that give a clear picture of the practice of legal education, writing instead tending to focus on issues of policy and pedagogy. Again this is general observation is particularly relevant to this essay. A questionnaire about empirical legal research in the curriculum sent out in 2009 by the Socio-Legal Studies Association in the United Kingdom begins by noting the paucity of information about this matter (<http://www.york.ac.uk/law/LERSNet/empirical_research .htm>). A second caveat is therefore that the observations in this Chapter are necessarily tentative.

Finally, one further definitional point needs to be noted. Curricula in law schools cover a wide variety of courses. Law is taught at undergraduate and postgraduate levels and what this distinction means varies from country to country. Law can be taught as an academic or a professional subject and, again, what this distinction means varies from country to country. Law can be taught in isolation or as part of a joint course of study, combined with some other academic discipline. Law can be a single module within a course that focuses on something else. This Chapter refers to curricula for academic law degree courses which provide the student's first exposure to the systematic study of law, whether or not they also lead to professional qualification, because it is these courses that are usually the focus for teaching and learning within the law school. Even when specified in this manner the curricula to be analyzed still encompass a variety of academic programs including undergraduate degrees taught to students first entering university and law degrees taught to students all of whom have previously undertaken undergraduate studies in other academic disciplines. Some have argued that empirical legal material should be included in a much broader range of law school curricula than those that are considered in this Chapter. Thus, for example, one might consider the place of empirical legal research in the curricula of Masters courses or other programs offered by law schools (see, for example, Genn et al., 2006: 40–1). Looking at the place of empirical legal studies in curricula other than those considered in this Chapter changes the detail of the argument but does not change its general direction.

II. THE PRESENT PLACE OF EMPIRICAL LEGAL STUDIES IN THE CURRICULUM

Law school teaching and learning is largely part of the private life of universities. What goes on in seminars and lectures is mainly hidden from the outside world. There have been few surveys of law school curricula and those that have been conducted provide little detail about the content of individual modules (see, for example, Johnstone and Vignaedra, 2003). Even studies of individual subjects taught within the law curriculum do not supply information about precisely what course materials are used or do so only anecdotally (see, for example, Lynch et al., 1993: 225–35, and Burton et al., 1999: 111–13). Notwithstanding the lack of any reliable empirical data on this matter, it is clear that empirical legal studies are largely absent from law school curricula. Given their purpose, student textbooks can serve as accurate proxies for the content of individual courses. Reference to empirical legal research, no matter which jurisdiction is being considered, is largely missing from such works. In part this reflects the paucity of such research. However, even where empirical legal research has been done, most textbooks continue to focus on doctrinal material and fail to mention empirical data.

In jurisdictions such as the U.S. the lack of impact of empirical legal studies on the curriculum might seem unsurprising, given the well-documented failure of non-doctrinal approaches of whatever kind to have any significant impact in the law school (see, for example, Austin, 1998). The continued dominance of Socratic teaching and the case-book model allied with the marginal place of non-doctrinal scholars in American law schools leads almost inevitably to the general invisibility of empirical legal research within law school curricula (Mertz, 2007). Of course, not all law schools in the U.S. take a purely doctrinal approach to their curriculum, as is illustrated by, for example, the "Law-in-Action" method used at the University of Wisconsin (<http://www.law.wisc.edu/law-in-action/davislawinactionessay.html>). Where alternative approaches in curricula are to be found they may be more hospitable to the use of empirical material. Equally, even law schools that take a mainly traditional approach to the curriculum may put on some courses that feature empirical work. Merlino et al.'s recent study (2008) shows both that some such courses exist and that institutions that had students with higher LSAT scores were more likely to offer such courses than those institutions whose students had lower scores. American textbooks with empirical content do exist and they have some influence on some law school curricula. In 2005, for example, *Contracts: Law in Action*, then edited by Macaulay, Kidwell, and Whitford, first published in 1995 with a slightly different authorial team, was used in 20 law schools (Macaulay, 2005: 402). Empirical legal research does exist and has long existed in the curricula of American law schools, and there is currently, as there has been on occasions in the past, a flurry of enthusiasm for it. Nonetheless, its present place in the curriculum remains marginal. This is arguably unsurprising since it mirrors the place that doing empirical legal research has had in law schools in the U.S. Schlegel has written that "[t]he impetus to do empirical legal research never really died out in at least the elite [American] law schools" (Schlegel, 1995: 238). However, he also suggests that the history of empirical legal research in American law schools is one of "a recurrence of cases of modest success followed by ... well ... nothing" (Schlegel, 1995: 211).

The neglect of empirical work in student textbooks is more puzzling in England and Wales than in the United States. On the face of it, conditions for the reception of empirical legal studies are much more propitious in England and Wales than they are in the U.S. Purely doctrinal analysis is no longer central to what is being done by legal academics. An ethnographic study of academics in English law schools suggests that only half of all full-time legal academics in contemporary English law schools see themselves as being doctrinal lawyers and only 20% describe themselves without qualification as being doctrinal in their approach (Cownie, 2004: 54–8). Cownie's conclusion was that the majority of legal scholars in her study were in fact socio-legal in their approach in that they drew on, at least in part, a range of disciplines in the humanities and social sciences in their work (p. 58). The value of using methods and concepts from academic disciplines other than law is now widely accepted within most United Kingdom law schools. Many scholars in British law schools who would describe their work as being socio-legal hold prominent positions within academic life as, for example, heads of law schools, leading members of professional bodies for academics working in law schools and members of external audit bodies such as the Research Assessment panels (Bradney, 2003: 9–11). If the majority of legal academics value the use of non-doctrinal material in the study of law and if at least some of those scholars are in positions of academic influence why is it that empirical legal research does not find its way into textbooks?

The current absence of empirical legal studies in contemporary curricula in England and Wales results from a number of factors. First, an acceptance of the importance of the use of methods and concepts from outside the law school does not necessarily lead on to a desire to engage personally in empirical legal research, unless such research is conceived very broadly. The Nuffield-funded enquiry into empirical legal research in the United Kingdom noted that it was "clear that empirical study of the operation of law and legal processes represents only a modest part of the body of socio-legal literature" (Genn et al., 2006: 3). Many socio-legal scholars in the United Kingdom use empirical work without themselves frequently, if ever, undertaking such research. Other British socio-legal scholars pursue work that is theoretical in its nature and touches lightly, if at all, upon empirical work. Theoretical work can itself be regarded as being empirical legal research (Twining, 2009: 226). Hart described *The Concept of Law* as "an essay in descriptive sociology" (Hart, 1961: viii). However, it is empirical only in a much wider and looser sense than is normally understood. While scholars who are mainly engaged in theoretical work may accept the legitimacy of empirical legal research as understood for the purposes of this Chapter and, in principle, see a place for it in the law school curriculum, they will not necessarily be at the forefront of introducing it into the curriculum. The pre-eminence of socio-legal studies in the law school does not therefore necessarily lead to the presence of empirical work in the curriculum.

Although socio-legal studies now dominate the legal academy in the UK, this is a relatively recent phenomenon. Doctrinal law had ascendency within British university law schools for much of the twentieth century and textbooks published during that period reflected that fact. Many of these textbooks continue to be in print and while their authors change with time, the structure of the textbooks changes more slowly. Moreover these longstanding textbooks set a pattern that newer books continue to emulate. The importance of this should not be underestimated when considering the nature of learning. A textbook recommended for a course has considerable authority for the students who use it. Other reading recommended by an academic that falls outside the compass of the textbook may, because of that fact, be regarded as less compelling by students. From the student's perspective doctrinal learning may still have a superior status, given the textbook that is recommended, even though those teaching the course do not themselves take a purely doctrinal stance.

It is possible for a textbook to strike out in a new direction. Thus, for example, Tillotson's textbook on contract law, *Contract Law in Perspective*, which was first published in 1981, set out to relate contract law to a range of non-legal material including some empirical matter. The "Law in Context" series, first published by Weidenfeld and Nicolson and now published by Cambridge University Press, was intended to bring material from the social sciences and other academic disciplines into the analysis of law, with its first volume in 1970 being Atiyah's *Accidents, Compensation and the Law*. It now includes textbooks, research monographs, and books that fall between the two. In books of this kind there is often some reference to empirical data. Nevertheless, in the mainstream of textbooks and teaching it remains the case that very little if any reference to empirical research is made. This, however, is not true for all subjects taught within English law schools.

Some subjects such as law-and-economics and criminology do include significant amounts of empirical work. However, these subjects are only taught in a minority of law schools and have had relatively little impact on more mainstream subjects such as criminal law. In several areas of legal study commonly taught within England and Wales empirical work has taken on a greater prominence in teaching than is to be found elsewhere. Two of the more obvious examples of this are family law and legal system. In both of these areas most of the leading textbooks now make regular if not frequent use of empirical data in their analyses. Moreover, this is not just a recent innovation. For example, Cretney's *Principles of Family Law*, now in its eighth edition, was first published in 1974, while Smith and Bailey's *The Modern English Legal System*, now *Smith, Bailey, and Gunn on the Modern English Legal System*, was first published in 1984. Both books are and always have been firmly socio-legal in their approach, and empirical data has always been part of their content. Why there is greater interest in empirical research in these areas of teaching is not clear. Family law is a relatively new sub-discipline within English law schools and may therefore not be so affected by the history of doctrinal study as some other law sub-disciplines. On the other hand, legal system textbooks have a much longer history that takes them back to the first half of the twentieth century, when doctrinal approaches were dominant. Both these areas have been the subject of considerable reforms in the past few decades and both relate to important areas of public policy. However, this could also be said of other areas of legal study where textbooks do not engage with empirical research. There does not appear to be any compelling reason why empirical legal research should be found in textbooks in these areas and not in other areas. The fortuitous intellectual interests of a small number of individual textbook writers may be the most important explanation for this phenomenon.

Even in areas such as family law and legal system, where empirical legal research is found in the curriculum in England and Wales, its presence should not be overstated. Empirical legal research has a small place in the curriculum compared with doctrinal analysis and policy arguments that rely only lightly on empirical evidence.

The use of empirical research in teaching is the exception rather than the norm in both the U.S. and England and Wales. Individual courses, individual textbooks and sometimes individual law schools belie this generalization. Nevertheless, in both places the use of empirical research in teaching is unusual. Other jurisdictions do not deviate from this pattern. Thus, for example, Rochette and Pue's study of the University of British Columbia's law curriculum found that 73% of student time was devoted to doctrinal study or skills acquisition (Rochette and Pue, 2001: 185). Any other approach, including the use of empirical legal research, had to find its place in the small minority of the student's time that remained. Of Canadian law schools generally Macdonald observes that, notwithstanding the fact that "law and society and socio-legal programmes have proliferated throughout the university," "most faculties... reinforce a court-centric, anti-intellectual, remedial perception of law" (MacDonald, 2003: 6 and 16). Empirical work does not seem to have achieved any prominence. Shanahan's study of English-speaking Ontario law schools found that while doctrinal scholarship was denigrated by academics that she interviewed, in practice it was the second most common approach to scholarship, theoretical work being slightly more favored, with less than 3% of academics producing empirical research (Shanahan, 2006: 36). She concludes that in their teaching "[academics] are clearly closely connected to the profession" (p. 49). In Australia, Johnstone and Vignaendra's 2003 report on legal education noted the strong commitment to teaching basic legal principles in Australian university law schools whilst also stressing the fact that many, if not most, newer law schools set out to offer an alternative to traditional forms of legal education (2003: 29 and chapter 2 *passim*). Cowley argues that "[l]aw is now largely taught by legal academics with postgraduate qualifications, whose teaching is informed by wide-ranging and in-depth research.... The reality is...that in the 21st century, an LLB is not a narrow vocational degree program" (Cowley, 2008: 284). However other commentators have stressed the hold that doctrinal and professional approaches still have on the practice of legal education in Australian law schools (see, for example, James, 2004). Thornton's description of the replacement of socio-legal academics with "professionally-oriented" academics at La Trobe University, in the context of a general analysis of the corporatizing tendencies of Australian universities, does not suggest that Australia is particularly hospitable to the idea of using empirical legal studies in the curriculum (Thornton, 2006). Johnstone and Vignaendra's survey noted that while two Australian law schools thought it was very important that students learnt how to conduct empirical research, five thought that it was not at all important (Johnstone and Vignaendra, 2003: 29). In New Zealand, Chart reports the centrality of doctrinal law to the curriculum, while, in South Africa, Lenta writes of the "emerging consensus that practical legal skills are to be elevated at the expense of theory and theoretical disciplines," the study of empirical work seeming to not even have a place in the debate (Chart, 2000: 191–2; Lenta, 2002: 846).

Law schools in each jurisdiction have their own unique answer to the question of what the curriculum should contain. These answers reflect the law schools' response to the various different pressures that they are under from government, the legal professions, students and others. However, it would appear to be the case that almost every one of those unique answers includes the proposition that there is very little need for the presence in the curriculum of anything other than the most limited amount of empirical legal research.

III. What Place Should Empirical Legal Studies Have in the Curriculum?

One indispensable pre-condition for any law school curriculum is that it must reflect what those teaching it believe to be true. No other criterion of what should be included in the curriculum can trump the importance of individual academic freedom (Russell, 1993). This is so even where, as is the case in the U.S., law schools see themselves as having a responsibility to educate students for the legal professions. If academics cease to teach what they believe to be true and instead teach what others think is important they cease to be academics, becoming involved in training rather than education. As Fiss put it in the interchange which followed the publication of Carrington's "Of Law and the River":

[l]aw professors are not paid to train lawyers, but to study law and to teach their students what they happen to discover. The law school . . . is an integral part of the university, and by virtue of that membership and all the commitments it entails must be pure in its academic obligations (Martin, 1985: 26).

Academic freedom in teaching is in this sense a duty not a right. This freedom is broad and rules out (among other things) demanding that an academic take an approach to the curriculum that they do not accept is warranted. It would be no more correct to insist on an individual academic incorporating empirical legal research in their teaching than it would be to seek to make a doctrinal lawyer take a socio-legal approach to their course. This having been said, there are good arguments that might persuade some academics that empirical legal research has utility in the curriculum.

Quantitative and qualitative empirical research into law and legal processes provides not just more information about law; it provides information of a different character from that which can be obtained through other methods of research. It answers questions about law that cannot be answered in any other way. To ignore empirical legal research is thus to ignore some of the things that can be said about law and thereby decrease our potential knowledge of law. It is this unique character of empirical legal research that provides the prima facie justification for its presence in the curriculum. This is not to suggest that empirical legal research will always be the appropriate way of answering questions about law. Other research methodologies also have their own unique character. However, none of them, individually or together, can replicate what empirical legal research can do.

Arguments about the content of the law school curriculum are, first, about the degree to which it should be vocationally and professionally oriented as against the degree to which it should be academic and concerned with a liberal education. Secondly such arguments are about the extent to which the law school should focus on the analysis of legal rules or, instead, look at a range of other questions about legal phenomena such as the efficacy of law, the realities of the operation of the legal system or the nature of law. However, no matter what choice is made as regards these issues, arguments for the place of empirical legal research in the curriculum can be made. Empirical legal research can find a proper place in curricula that are designed to serve the needs of law schools that seek to prepare students to be lawyers and also those that seek to provide a liberal education in law. However, the nature of the curriculum does have an impact on the type of empirical legal research that is appropriately included in it.

If a law school curriculum's purpose is simply to allow students to learn about law, empirical legal research has, for the reasons above, a place in it; failing to include empirical legal research in the curriculum, is to exclude a distinctive form of learning from the curriculum thus impoverishing the student experience. However, not all school curricula are so broadly conceived. In such instances, more specific arguments for the place of empirical legal research are needed. Where, for example, a law school's curriculum is narrowly doctrinal, concerned only with examining the content of legal rules and the primary authorities for those rules, then empirical research is only relevant if it can be shown to be pertinent to those authorities. Danner contends that this is precisely the case in the U.S., arguing that "throughout the twentieth century, U.S. courts have considered and cited increasing amounts of legislative history, social science data, scientific research, and other types of information in addition to the cases and statutes, the traditional authorities cited in judicial opinions" (Danner, 2003: 192). Whether Danner is correct and whether his observations are also valid for other jurisdictions is a matter for both empirical investigation and debate. If a law school's curricular concerns are professional, focusing on training its students to be lawyers, empirical legal research is relevant only if it can be shown to be useful for lawyers. A law school such as this is not concerned with enhancing its students' knowledge of law per se. Its interests are instrumental. Again, whether knowledge of empirical legal research is of benefit to practicing lawyers is a matter for investigation and debate. Jackson argues that "[l]awyers—whether corporate counsel or public interest advocates—must work in a world in which arguments are phrased in quantitative terms and presentation of data are critical to effective advocacy" (Jackson, 2003: 321–2). An ability to understand at least some forms of empirical legal research would therefore seem relevant to the skills involved in presenting and analyzing quantitative material. However, in a study of English solicitors, Bermingham and Hodgson report that numeracy ranks only 12th out of 16 skills and attributes that solicitors seek in trainee lawyers (2001: 22), the solicitors ranking analytical skills and literacy most highly, suggesting that a knowledge of quantitative empirical legal work might not be perceived to be relevant to practice. Empirical legal research may also be appropriate to the professional curriculum where it is concerned with examining the working lives of lawyers or the institutions in which they work.

The more a law school aspires to offer a liberal education the more important empirical legal research becomes. At first sight this proposition seems to be counter-intuitive. Providing new and more precise information about law and legal pro-cesses is exactly what lies at the heart of empirical legal research. However, in a liberal education it is knowledge not information that is sought; knowledge, in this sense, being

something intellectual, something which grasps what it perceives through the senses; some-thing which takes a view of things; which sees more than the senses convey; which reasons upon what it sees, and while it sees; which invest it with an idea (Newman, 1960: 85).

Like skeptical enquiry and awareness of individual autonomy in learning, ideas are more central to the liberal curriculum than the accumulation of facts (Bradney, 2003: Ch. 2). Empiricism and the concept of a liberal education, on the face of it, therefore, appear to contradict each other. However, a liberal education is an educa-tion about the world. If a liberal education enables us to "call...[our] minds...[our] own" and puts "the mind above the influence of chance and necessity, above anxiety, suspense, unsettlement and superstition" it does so, in part, by enabling us to com-prehend the corporeal world around us (Nussbaum, 1997: 293; Newman, 1960: 104); knowledge, for this reason, "requires a great deal of reading, or a wide range of infor-mation" (Newman, 1960: 97). In the case of law schools that aim to provide a liberal education, information about law, all types of information about law, must be part of the basis for achieving understanding. In such schools, empirical legal research is important not for its own sake but for how it can potentially assist analysis.

All of this having been said, some of the information provided by empirical legal research is not necessarily of utility in any law school curriculum at all. Empiricism can be "crass" or "mindless" (Suchman, 2006: 3; Chambliss, 2008: 37). Factual infor-mation, even factual information that has been accurately gathered, can be trivial in itself and of little import in understanding law or legal processes. It is also the case that some empirical legal research has been the subject of persistent criticism. Questions have been raised about methodological quality and objectivity, among other things (Chambliss, 2008: 20–1). One of the self-stated aims of the empirical legal studies movement in the United States is to address some of these perceived failings and to produce more valid findings. However the work of this movement is itself regarded with suspicion by some because it is seen as being too focussed on state law, ignoring law that emanates from other sources, and too resistant to social theory (ibid: 2008: 37–8). For some, empirical legal research into law is, or can be, a "scientific" way of researching law and meritorious because of this (Ulen, 2004). Yet, for others, skepticism about the nature and value of science should be part of the process of research (Erlanger et al., 2005: 342–3). "[U]nlike most social scientists," writes George, "ELS scholars generally offer some connection between their positive results and normative alternatives" (George, 2006: 146). However, this connection between doing research and making policy suggestions, a source of pride for those within the empirical legal studies movement, can itself be seen as a failing if it becomes too much concerned with the prompting of social change and too little concerned with understanding what New Legal Realism describes as the "multicausal, nonlinear, reciprocating, recursive interactions between law, the environment in which it works, and the ideas that people have about it" (McEvoy, 2005: 434).

Empirical legal research is thus not always valuable in the curriculum. Only good empirical legal research is valuable; but the notion of what is good and bad empirical legal research is itself contested. Moreover it is not enough for academics, acting as gatekeepers, to incorporate good empirical legal research into the curriculum. In a doctrinal context student learning fails if students can do no more than recite legal rules without being able to trace the reasoning that results in the rules. Similarly, with empirical legal research, students need to be alive to potential methodological and theoretical failings in such studies as well as conversant with the conclusions drawn by them. Traditionally law schools have been a place where students learn how to distinguish bad doctrinal arguments from good doctrinal arguments. If empirical legal studies are to have a full place within a curriculum, students must themselves be able to debate what is good and bad research.

IV. CAN EMPIRICAL LEGAL RESEARCH BE INCORPORATED INTO THE CURRICULUM?

Empirical legal studies can only be properly incorporated into the law school curriculum if students not only use and understand such studies but also understand the methods used and the theories upon which they are based. Otherwise they will be encouraged to take a surface rather than a deep approach to their learning (Ramsden, 1992: Ch. 4). However, this creates an immediate resource problem for law schools. First, students will best learn such methods and theories if they have time in the curriculum when they focus on the methods and theories and the problems that surround them as opposed to the studies that result from the use of the methods and theories. Secondly they then need regular opportunities to apply that learning to particular empirical studies. Repetition is vital to the learning of most students. In these respects, best pedagogical practice in relation the empirical study of law is no different from that relevant to the doctrinal legal approach that has traditionally dominated law schools. Doctrinal learning is best done when it involves repetition and is supplemented by courses devoted to legal method; as with doctrine so with empirical legal research.

Providing courses on methods in empirical legal research is problematic for law schools. The curricula in law schools are already crowded and providing a course in empirical research methods, which logically has to be compulsory since it lies at the base of student learning, would further exacerbate this difficulty. Moreover, while there is the same intellectual justification for such a course as there is for a course in doctrinal method, the use that students will make of the material they cover will, in almost all law schools, be much more limited than is the case with doctrine. Teaching depends upon the research material available and tends to lag behind that material. Even if law schools want to make more use of empirical legal research in their teaching, the shortage of it means that there are severe limits to what they can do within the foreseeable future. Doctrine infuses many courses in the law school but empirical research is found far less often in the curriculum. It is thus harder to justify the time spent on a course that is likely subsequently only to be irregularly used by students in their studies. These pragmatic arguments suggest that law schools may find it difficult to create the space in the curriculum for a complete course, still less a range of courses, on empirical research methods and theories. An alternative solution would be to change existing courses on legal method so that they covered not just doctrinal method but also the other approaches that legal scholars now take to legal research.

Empirical legal research draws upon a diverse range of methods and theories. George suggests that even the empirical legal studies movement, which has coalesced round the Society for Empirical Legal Studies and the *Journal for Empirical Legal Studies*, with its relatively narrow definition of what constitutes empirical legal research, covers (among other things) "behavioral law and economics, judicial politics, positive political theory [and] experimental economics" (George, 2006: 146). Chambliss notes that the founding members of the Society for Empirical Legal Studies have PhDs in a range of disciplines including economics, education and social policy, psychology, and political science (Chambliss, 2008: 32–3). The wider definitions of empirical legal research noted at the beginning of this chapter include an even greater range of methods and theories. What can be put into a methods course and what can safely be left are therefore fraught questions. These questions are made even more problematic by the fact that the appropriateness of various empirical legal research methods is itself subject to intense and inconclusive debate. When King and Epstein set out the "rules of inference" that they thought ought to underlie empirical legal research and called for all law schools to set up a research methods course in quantitative and qualitative research methods, they were met with the immediate rejoinder that their account of those rules was itself fundamentally flawed (King and Epstein, 2002: 116; Goldsmith and Vermeule, 2002: 159–60).

In part the problems outlined above are familiar in the law school. While some scholars have clear views on what constitutes doctrinal method, those views are contested by others. The debates about doctrine are sometimes about matters of detail and nuance. However, they can also be about matters fundamental to the nature and application of doctrine. For example, the views of Critical Legal Scholars on the nature of doctrine are at a polar extreme from those that were traditional in the legal academy in most of the common law world for much of the twentieth century and which continue to be supported by some in the twenty-first century. It is nothing new to note that the academy is riven with disagreement and that courses offered to students, if they are to be educationally appropriate, have to give those students access to the arguments that are taking place within a discipline. However, with regard to empirical legal studies the problem is one of scale. To give students access to debates about method and theory within one discipline is one thing; to give them access to debates that are occurring in the very large number of disciplines that legal scholarship now draws upon is a completely different undertaking. "[I]n virtually every [academic] discipline that has begun to develop a serious empirical research program, scholars discover methodological problems that are unique to the special concerns in that area" (King and Epstein, 2002: 117). Because of this, a general course in methods and theory runs the risk of being so superficial as to lead to a misunderstanding of the nature of the research enterprise being considered, thus thwarting the fundamental aims of the course.

What a course in empirical legal research methods should contain is one pressing problem for a law school. Another equally intractable problem is the question of who is to teach whatever course is offered. Only a minority of legal academics in any jurisdiction frequently engage in empirical legal research and therefore have even possibly have the competence to teach such a course. Moreover, when they do undertake such research their knowledge may be limited to those methods and theories that they themselves use. It is certainly unlikely to cover the whole area of empirical legal studies. There are, of course, academics in other disciplines in the university who will have knowledge of research methods and theory. However, whether they will have the range of knowledge that is necessary in the field of empirical legal research taken as a whole or whether they will have the disposition to teach law students is another matter. Moreover, even when the focus of the course is on issues of method, law students will need to see its potential relevance to their law studies if they are to engage with it. Academics from outside the law school may find engaging students even harder than do academics from inside the law school. Courses taught by those in law schools or academics from outside the law schools are not the only options. Courses can also be taught by a combination of staff drawn from both within and outside the law school, but this may come at the expense of coherence in the course.

In areas of substantive law, law schools will expect to staff their courses with academics who regard these areas as part of the mainstay of their research or at least their teaching. Few law schools seem likely to be able to do the same if they attempt to put on a course in empirical legal research methods and theory. If this is the case, student perception that empirical legal studies are marginal in the law school may in fact be further enhanced by their experience of a course on method.

The final problem for a course on empirical methods in the law school lies with the students in the law school. As was noted above, once the decision to include empirical legal studies in the curriculum is made, and once it is accepted that a methods course is a prerequisite to such a course, it becomes necessary for the student body as whole. However, students have their own expectations of what law school will entail. Those expectations do not necessarily chime with what the law school sees as its mission (Cownie, 2004: 76–8; Bradney, 2003: 71; Thornton, 2006). Given the history of legal education, most law students are likely to come to law school with the belief that it will be a text-based education concerned with the analysis of words. The fact that they wish to enrol in such a course suggests that they believe that they will be competent in that form of learning. The further a methods course moves from text-based data the more resistant students are likely to be to engaging with it. The fact that law students might not wish to see a course on empirical legal methods in the curriculum does not mean that it should not be there. A disjunction between law school mission and student expectation does not necessarily lead to the conclusion that there needs to be a change to that mission, unless a purely commodified view is taken of legal education. Law students rarely, if ever, have the necessary knowledge to judge what will constitute the most effective curriculum. However, student expectation has to be taken into account when constructing courses. Law students do not explicitly elect to study empirical, and in particular quantitative, methods in the way that, for example, economics students do. This has to be taken into account in course design. Students on such courses may be recalcitrant and anxious about their ability to use material that lies outside what they had expected to be exposed to.

While a methods course on empirical legal research is highly desirable, it is not in itself enough if students are going to be properly introduced to empirical legal research. First, a methods course, no matter how well planned and executed, can provide no more than an introduction to understanding what good empirical legal research is. Regular and frequent practice is necessary before students will become accomplished in the application of the knowledge that they will have acquired on such a course. Secondly, for a variety of different reasons depending on the nature of the curricula, a law school will be trying to show students how empirical research improves their learning in a various areas of the curriculum. A long-term aim for the law school would therefore be for empirical legal studies to have a pervasive presence in the curriculum, thus both allowing students the frequent practice that they need in assessing whether research is good or not and also showing them how such research can add to their knowledge. However, it seems unlikely that this will happen in either the short or medium term. In many areas of the curriculum such research is in short supply. Moreover, in many jurisdictions the dominance of doctrinal approaches to law means that a large number of academics will not wish to use such empirical material as there is. In this context, how can students be given the opportunities that they need to study empirical material?

In their study of the place of empirical legal research in the academy Genn, Partington, and Wheeler suggest that law schools should offer either an option in "law in society" or some other course where empirical studies have a place, so that students can learn about the value of such studies (Genn et al., 2006: 43). The suggestion that such a course should be optional is an implicit acceptance of the congested nature of existing law school curricula. However, if empirical legal research is to be taken seriously in law schools, the value of an optional course is questionable. That which is merely optional can be seen as therefore being marginal. The argument that has been put above is that knowledge of empirical legal research is, at least in the context of the aims of some law school curricula, now a necessity for students. If this is so then an element of such study needs to be compulsory. In some jurisdictions, certain courses already seem to be an appropriate vehicle by which students can learn the value of empirical legal research. In England and Wales, for example, legal system courses might fulfill this function because, as is noted above, empirical legal studies already have a place in most legal system textbooks. In addition to this, the course is already compulsory in most law schools (Lynch et al., 1993: 222). Alternatively it might be possible to offer a course that combined method and theory and showed how empirical legal research could be used to advance knowledge of a particular legal area.

V. Conclusion

This Chapter has considered the place of empirical legal studies in the curriculum without looking at the wider context of the nature of the legal academy. However, this context is relevant to the arguments put forward above. A number of commentators in different jurisdictions have noted the changing nature of the legal academy. In England and Wales, Cownie describes "a discipline in transition, moving away from traditional doctrinal analysis toward a more contextual, interdisciplinary approach" (Cownie, 2004: 196). In the United States Ulen writes about an increasing "schizophrenia ... between one's teaching life and one's scholarly life" as academics in law schools become more concerned with non-doctrinal approaches to research (Ulen, 2004: 248). The move to include more empirical legal research in the curricula of law schools is only part of broader changes in the law school. These changes are not uniform in their nature as Thornton's account of the politics of La Trobe law school, with its description of a move away from contextual scholarship in favor of doctrine and practice, illustrates (Thornton, 2006). While there is much to indicate that many law schools are becoming more academically oriented, at least in relation to their research agenda, and less concerned with the needs of legal professions, in some cases the reverse is true. Empirical legal research has to compete for the attention of academics in law schools with a number of other areas of research that are becoming more popular, particularly legal theory conceived in an ever-increasing number of ways. That which is true for academics is also true for law students. Even in jurisdictions where doctrine still holds sway it is not just empirical legal studies that offer alternative approaches. The calls for more empirical legal research come in different ways. In the United States there is the evangelical enthusiasm of the empirical legal studies movement; in the United Kingdom the concern is both that there is not sufficient present capacity to sustain empirical legal research and that many of those academics who do engage in such research are coming to the end of their careers (Genn et al., 2006: 2). Law schools throughout the world are in a state of flux. What place empirical legal studies will find in future law school curricula depends not just on how academics react to such studies but also on how they react to other opportunities that are now opening.

REFERENCES

Atiyah, P. (1970). *Accidents, Compensation and the Law*, London: Weidenfeld and Nicolson.

Austin, A. (1998). *The Empire Strikes Back Outsiders and the Struggle over Legal Education*, New York: New York University Press.

Bailey, S., Gunn, M., Taykor, N., and Ormerod, D. (2007). *Smith, Bailey and Gunn on the Modern English Legal System*, London: Sweet and Maxwell.

Baldwin, J. and Davis, G. (2003). "Empirical research in Law," in P. Cane and M. Tushnet (eds.), *The Oxford Handbook of Legal Studies*, Oxford: Oxford University Press.

Bermingham, V. and Hodgson, J. (2001). "Desiderata: What Lawyers Want from Their Recruits," *The Law Teacher* 35: 1–32.

Bradney, A. (2003). *Conversations, Choices and Chances: The Liberal Law School in the Twenty-First Century*, Oxford: Hart Publishing.

Bradney, A. (2007). "Can There Be Commensurability in Comparative Legal Education?," *Canadian Legal Education Annual Review/Revue de l'enseignment de droit au Canada* 1: 67–84.

Burton, F., Clement, N., Standley, K., and Williams, C. (1999). *Teaching Family Law*, Coventry: National Centre for Legal Education, University of Warwick.

Chambliss, E. (2008). "When Do Facts Persuade? Some Thoughts on the Market for 'Empirical Legal Studies'," *Law and Contemporary Problems* 71(2): 17–40.

Chart, J. (2000). "Lawyers' Work and Legal Education: Getting a Better Fit," *New Zealand Universities Law Review* 19: 177–205.

Cowley, J. (2008). "Recognising and Valuing Excellence in Law Schools and Teaching Intensive Appointments," *Journal of the Australasian Law Teachers Association* 1: 275–85.

Cownie, F. (2004). *Legal Academics: Culture and Identities*, Oxford: Hart Publishing.

Cretney, S. (1974). *Principles of Family Law*, London: Sweet and Maxwell.

Danner, R. (2003). "Contemporary and Future Directions in American Legal Research: Responding to the Threat of the Available," *International Journal of Legal Information* 31: 179–204.

Eisenberg, T., Rachlinski, J., Schwab, S., and Wells, M. "Editors' Introduction". *Journal of Empirical Legal Studies* 1: v–vi.

Eisenberg, T., Rachlinski, J., Schwab, S., and Wells, M.

Epstein, L. and King, G. (2003). "Building an Infrastructure for Empirical Research in Law," *Journal of Legal Education* 53: 311–20.

Erlanger, H., Garth, B., Carson, J., and Mertz, E. (2005). "Is It Time for a New Legal Realism?," *Wisconsin Law Review* 335–65.

Genn, H., Partington, M., and Wheeler, S. (2006). *Law in the Real World: Improving Our Understanding of How Law Works*, London: The Nuffield Foundation.

George, T. (2006). "An Empirical Study of Empirical Legal Scholarship: The Top Law Schools," *Indiana Law Journal* 81: 141–61.

Goldsmith, J. and Vermeule, A. (2002). "Empirical Methodology and Legal Scholarship," *Chicago Law Review* 69: 153–67.

Hart, H. (1961). *The Concept of Law*, Oxford: Clarendon Press.

Jackson, H. (2003). "Analytical Methods for Lawyers," *Journal of Legal Education* 53: 321–7.

James, N. (2004). "Australian Legal Education and the Instability of Critique," *Melbourne University Law Review* 28: 375–405.

Johnstone, R. and Vignaedra, S. (2003). *Learning Outcomes and Curriculum Development in Law*, Canberra: Higher Education Group, Department of Education, Science and Training.

King, G. and Epstein, L. (2002). "The Rules of Inference," *University of Chicago Law Review* 69: 1–133.

Lenta, P. (2002). "Is There a Class in This Text? Law and Literature in Legal Education," *South African Law Journal* 119: 841–65.

Lynch, B., Moodie, P., and Salter, D. (1993). "The Teaching of Foundation Legal Instruction," *The Law Teacher* 27: 216–43.

Macaulay, S., Kidwell, J., and Whitford, W. (2003). *Contracts: Law in Action*, Newark, NJ: LexisNexis.

Macaulay, S. (2005). "New Versus the Old Legal Realism: Things Ain't What They Used to Be," *Wisconsin Law Review* 365–402.

Macaulay, S., Kidwell, J., and Whitford, W. (2003). *Contracts: Law in Action*, Newark, NJ: LexisNexis.

MacDonald, R. (2003). "Still 'Law' and 'Learning'? Quel 'droit' et quell 'savoir'?," *Canadian Journal of Law and Society* 18(1): 5–31.

Martin, P. (ed.). (1985). "Of Law and the River and of Nihilism and Academic Freedom," *Journal of Legal Education* 35: 1–26.

Masson, J., Baliey-Harris, R., and Probert, R. (2008). *Cretney: Principles of Family Law*, London: Sweet and Maxwell.

McEvoy, A. (2005). "New Realism for Legal Studies," *Wisconsin Law Review* 433–54.

Merlino, M., Richardson, J., Chamberlain, J. and Springer, V. (2008). "Science in the Classroom: A Snapshot of the Legal Education Landscape," *Journal of Legal Education* 58: 190–213.

Mertz, E. (2007). *The Language of Law School: Learning to "Think Like a Lawyer,"* New York: Oxford University Press.

Newman, J (1960). *The Idea of a University*, New York: Holt, Rinehart and Winston.

Nussbaum, M. (1997). *Cultivating Humanity: A Classical Defense of Reform in Liberal Education*, Cambridge: Harvard University Press.

Ramsden, P. (1992). *Learning to Teach in Higher Education*, London: Routledge.

Rochette, A. and Pue, W. (2001). "'Back to Basics'? University Legal Education and 21st Century Professionalism," *Windsor Yearbook of Access to Justice* 20: 167–90.

Russell, C. (1993). *Academic Freedom*, London: Routledge.

Schlegel, J. (1995). *American Legal Realism and Empirical Social Science*, Chapel Hill: University of North Carolina Press.

Shanahan, T. (2006). "Legal Scholarship in Ontario English-Speaking Law Schools," *Canadian Journal of Law and Society* 26(2): 25–50.

Smith, P. and Bailey, S. (1984). *The Modern English Legal System*, London: Sweet and Maxwell.

Suchman, M. (2006). "Empirical Legal Studies: Sociology of Law or Something ELS Entirely?," *Amici* 13(1): 1–4.

Sullivan, W., Colby, A., Wegner, J., Bond, L., and Shulman, L. (2007). *Educating Lawyers: Preparation for the Profession of Law*, San Francisco: John Wiley and Sons.

Thornton, M. (2006). "The Dissolution of the Social in the Legal Academy," *The Australian Feminist Law Journal* 25: 3–18.

Tillotson, J. (1981). *Contract Law in Perspective*, London: Butterworths.

Twining, W. (2009). *General Jurisprudence: Understanding Law from a Global Perspective*, Cambridge: Cambridge University Press.

Ulen, T. (2004). "The Unexpected Guest: Law and Economics, Law and Other Cognate Disciplines, and the Future of Legal Scholarship," *Chicago-Kent Law Review* 79: 403–29.

43

EMPIRICAL LEGAL TRAINING IN THE U.S. ACADEMY

CHRISTINE B. HARRINGTON AND SALLY ENGLE MERRY

OVER the past three decades, as empirical legal research has moved to examine the role of law in everyday life, particularly its role in constituting identities, relationships, legal entitlements, consciousness, and even spatial relationships, the importance of the legal dimension to social analysis has become ever more critical. However, to bring the legal dimension into an empirical framework requires processes of translation between the modes of thought and analysis in the legal academy and those of empirical research.

What is taken for granted in legal reasoning is treated as a concept in empirical legal studies—a concept that can have various values (e.g., degrees of "freedom of speech" that may vary by historical context and in relationship to the content of the speech). Empirical legal scholars approach what is taken to be "the law" in the legal academy, as well as in legal institutions, as a social construction to be explained by empirically testing causal and non-causal hypotheses. Meaning-making and interpretations by lawyers, judges, clerks, and other state legal actors are, for empirical legal scholars, the "antecedent conditions"[1] that may (or may not) condition the formation of independent variables like everyday legal consciousness, a phenomenon hypothesized as playing an important role in explaining varying levels of support for social reform and public policies (the dependent variable in this illustration). Empirical legal scholars, thus operate from the perspective that what counts as "law" can be continually, and to varying degrees, struggled over. Therefore, identifying what factors (variables) are significant (predictive) in the processes of determining "what counts as law" is central in empirical legal theory. It is at this juncture—testing for significant relationships—where applying, developing and honing empirical legal methods happens. Traversing the divide between internal, implicit understandings about "the legal form" (e.g., doctrinal and institutional) on the one hand, and the performance of law under particular conditions (e.g., mobilization of law by social movements) on the other, is where we, the authors of this Chapter, engage the next generation of scholars in the logic of empirical legal inquiry.

This Chapter is based on the experience of the authors in training New York University graduate students in methods for conducting empirical legal research. The first part of the Chapter discusses challenges encountered while managing the epistemology of legal modes of thinking and social science, and the limits, as we see them, of relying on discipline-based (social sciences) methodologies for the advancement of empirical legal scholarship. In the second part of the Chapter we discuss two approaches to empirical legal training we employ in New York University's PhD and JD/PhD Law and Society Program [herein LSP]: 1) the LSP Practicum; and 2) supervised field research. Here we seek to demonstrate the strengths of collaborative research with illustrations of a cross-national collaboration (the LSP Practicum) and a research collaboration in our neighborhood—ethnography in New York City.

---

[1] For a discussion of C.G. Hempel's (1965) definition of "antecedent" in this context, see Van Evera (1997: 9), who describes it as the "condition's presence precedes the casual process that it activates or magnified." The casual process would in this instance be the interpretative process through which "law" is given meaning, if not "force."

I. Disciplinary and Multi-Transdisciplinary Empirical Legal Training

At present, in the United States, empirical legal scholars are negotiating empirical methods for the next generation largely by directing them to study the methodological canons and approaches of social science disciplines—the disciplines that *best fit* what students need to learn in order to acquire general empirical literacy on the one hand, and the specific skills or tools they will need to conduct their research on the other hand. This *best-fit approach* to negotiating the translation process may work well for students who want to acquire the capacity to judge the validity of methods employed in disciplinary studies, such as those in anthropology, economics, history, political science, psychology, and sociology.

The limits of the best-fit approach, however, are not always evident until it becomes clear that disciplinary canons in the social sciences, as well as the humanities, rarely comprehend law as a distinctive social phenomenon—distinctive in the sense of being relatively autonomous from partisan politics (the lens through which the discipline of political science tends to view law) and at the same time as a social phenomenon that is constituted (though selectively) by cultural, economic, historical, political, psychological, and social forces. Without academic programs structured to train students in the research methods that empirical *legal* researchers employ and develop in their own work,[2] students tend to learn methods *in translation*. That is, they learn methods designed for disciplines, including traditional legal analysis, that, in general, do not grasp the social, economic, political, psychological, and cultural dimensions *of* law itself. Students report that they often find themselves *acting as if* non-law, disciplinary methods, such as those used by political scientists to study elections, by sociologists to study stratification, or by psychologists to study cognitive development, were readily translatable to processes that empirical legal scholars study, such as litigation and disputing. And if students attempting to do empirical legal research cannot fill in the knowledge gap, as it were, they are left to work out the *best fit* for themselves. This situation produces an additional methodological challenge for students. In the end, the best-fit approach may create problems rather than remove hurdles, making it cumbersome and at times confusing.

---

[2] The oldest empirical legal studies graduate program in the United States is the University of California-Berkeley, Jurisprudence and Social Policy Program (founded in 1977), <http://www.law .berkeley.edu/636.htm>; Arizona State University, Justice Studies Program, <http://justice.clas.asu. edu/phd>; University of California-Irvine, Department of Criminology Law & Society, <http://cls .soceco.uci.edu/>; New York University, Law and Society Program (founded in 1996), <http://www1 .law.nyu.edu/ils/faculty.html>.

The best-fit approach to training in empirical methods has another inefficiency: empirical legal scholars have to do all the translating from the non-law disciplines to their own field. To be clear, we base our insights on the fact of where most empirical legal research in the United States has been rooted—either in the multi- and trans-disciplinary graduate programs (see note 2, *supra*) or, as was more the case in the past, in social science departments with significant faculty resources for sub-disciplinary research in areas such as public law in political science, the sociology of law, law and psychology, legal history, legal anthropology, and law and economics. While this situation is far from ideal, there is no question that empirical legal training in the United States is currently constrained by non-law, social science disciplinary canons. In the UK and Australia, in contrast, most empirical legal researchers are trained in law and few have PhDs in social science disciplines. Yet, as the Nuffield Inquiry on Empirical Legal Research notes, "the disciplines of sociology and, to a lesser degree, philosophy, psychology, and economics have entered into and enriched the study of law" (Genn et al., 2006: 1, quoting Baldwin and Davis, 2003).

We are not yet at the stage where the "problem of crossing boundaries" (Shapiro, 2008) is behind us.[3] Differences between modes of thought and analysis of traditional legal scholarship on the one hand, and empirical legal research on the other, coupled with shortcomings of the best-fit approach to methods training, currently present challenges we need to address so that the theoretical fruits of empirical theory will better inform our methodological practices. Empirical legal scholarship has developed into a professional practice over the past 100 years in the United States largely on the basis of empirical *theory* about law. Over the past century, the "sociological movement in law"[4] has been focused mainly on empirical theory as represented by sociological jurisprudence, legal realism, judicial decision-making and process, feminist jurisprudence, critical legal studies, critical legal race theory, constitutive socio-legal theory, law and economics, historical-institutional legal theory, strategic and formal modeling, and ethnographic and interpretative legal theory. It is now time to draw this knowledge base together as a foundation for developing distinctively legal *empirical* methods.

Indeed, as we thought through the processes of empirical legal inquiry and the current practices of empirical legal researchers for this Chapter we became more aware of the need for formal training in methods. In *Conducting Law and Society Research: Reflections on Methods and Practices* (2009), Simon Halliday and Patrick Schmidt bring together methodological and theoretical insights from 28 empirical legal scholars that provide evidence for arguing that there are common empirical

---

[3] The crossing boundaries problem Shapiro discusses is between the law and politics, which has its own particular legacy that does surface at times in empirical legal studies debates.

[4] See A. Hunt's book by this title (1978); also see H.P. Stumpf (1998), chapters 1 and 2 and R. Cotterrell (1995) for an intellectual survey of the socio-legal "schools of thought."

methods in this field and intriguing puzzles yet to figure out as the object of study—law and legal institutions—broadens.

We make choices, even in the programs and departments that award PhDs in Law and Society, Jurisprudence and Social Policy, or Justice Studies. What are those choices? What are their advantages and weakness? At NYU (where both authors teach), the three general substantive areas of empirical legal training at the graduate level are: 1) Socio-legal Theory; 2) Law and Policy; and 3) Comparative and Global Perspectives on Law. Broadly speaking the more contemporary literature in these three areas reveals a combination of disciplinary, cross-disciplinary and trans-disciplinary approaches to research. Studying empirical research is an important way of providing instruction in methodology and we use the literature as part of how we teach methods.

Lynn Mather and Barbara Yngvesson's (1980–1981) study of how institutional actors (lawyers, court officials) frame problems and shape conflicts that come to courts is a good representation of how cross-disciplinary research contributes to methodological training. It pairs ethnographic and judicial-process methodologies to reveal a process of transformations of the definition and understanding of problems that take place in courts between lay complainants and court officials. Building on judicial process research by political scientists and the concept of disputing in anthropology, Mather and Yngvesson's work shifted attention to the importance of studying how the meaning of law is produced in encounters between legal actors and disputing parties. Their study provides students with empirical training as it formulates a theory based on empirical data—dispute transformation and the politics of framing disputes—and a set of quantitative and qualitative empirical methods.

The early trans-disciplinary research produced by the Civil Litigation Research Project (CLRP) at the University of Wisconsin-Madison emphasizes the importance of treating "dispute" as the unit of analysis.[5] This work not only established an alternative to the then-dominant decision-making approach to studying courts, but it also expanded our understanding of adjudication processes to incorporate alternative dispute processing, as well as the disputants and their lawyers. By turning some of our attention to "disputes," rather than focusing on legal doctrine or judicial voting behavior alone, CLRP expanded our thinking about theory-testing possibilities and the empirical methods that would later produce measures like the propensity to sue (Kritzer, 1991). Among other things, CLRP found that whether a grievance becomes a claim depends on the type of dispute (e.g., tort, post-divorce, discrimination) and the type of access claimants have to various dispute processes. These findings inspired quantitative and qualitative empirical research on disputing patterns across multiple legal jurisdictions; both within and outside the United States.

Similarly, Anthony Paik, Ann Southworth, and John Heinz's study of "Lawyers of the Right: Networks and Organization," demonstrates the value of using network

---

[5] For a bibliography of reports, monographs, and articles from this project, see <http://users .polisci.wisc.edu/kritzer/research/clrpbib.htm>.

analysis to analyze interview data (2007; see also Heinz et al., 2003; Southworth, 2008). They find that lawyers representing politically conservative organizations and causes "are divided into segments or blocks that are identified with particular constituencies, but that a distinct set of actors with an extensive range of relationships serves to bridge the constituencies." This method identifies the structure of ideological coalitions within neo-conservative legal movements, while "measures of centrality and brokerage confirm the structural importance of these actors in the network, and a search of references in news media confirms their prominence or prestige." Paik et al.'s analysis is one example of how to do co-relational analysis of ties within a network for the purpose of empirically articulating the dynamics of power operating within this movement.

One might question whether there is anything particular to legal interest groups and actors that would not apply to other policy areas? The answer is "yes." Empirical research on the influence of lawyers in national policy-making found that lawyers more often than not have a relatively specialized niche in the system of interest-representation that allows them to command substantial economic rewards, while limiting their influence in policy-formation, which is compatible with another goal of these lawyers of maintaining a measure of independence and autonomy in their work (Nelson and Heinz, 1988).[6]

Statistical methods employed to address theoretical debates about issues, such as the relative weight of partisan preferences and legal precedent in explaining judicial decisions, have made significant headway in opening up a sub-field of empirical research on legal doctrine. In particular, Richards and Kritzer formulate the concept of a "jurisprudential regime," set out criteria for empirically determining the existence or absence of such a regime, and apply the model in four distinct areas of law—freedom of expression (Richards and Kritzer, 2002), establishment clause (Kritzer and Richards, 2003), search and seizure (Kritzer and Richards, 2005), and judicial deference to administrative agencies (Richards et al., 2006), thus demonstrating that their methodology is replicable across areas of law.[7] Because they are transparent about both their analytical and empirical strategy for testing what is a compelling concept, graduate students learn the logic of applying these statistical methods to socio-legal questions. In turn, students are asked to subject a wider-range of conceptual work to statistical examination.

John Hagan and Wenona Rymond-Richmond's path-breaking study, *Darfur and the Crime of Genocide* (2009) is a particularly important work for students studying empirical methods in what we call the field of "Comparative and Global Perspectives

[6] In their study of U.S. tort reform, Haltom and McCann (2004) also found that lawyers behave differently in the media than insurance companies, with the American Trial Lawyers Association limiting their media role because, as lawyers, they did not want the political exposure.

[7] As mentioned in a recent rebuttal to a critique of their statistical approach, Kritzer and Richards (2010) also tried to operationalizing the jurisprudential regime concept in obscenity, commercial speech, and right to counsel cases, but got nonsense patterns for the results.

on Law." This study provides the opportunity to teach students about multi-methods research design in the context of collecting empirical evidence to make the case in the ICJ that rape in Darfur constituted a "war crime." Their research methodology uses macro and micro data and methodological analyses to address a national and transnational problem.

In addition to learning empirical theory and methods while mastering the literatures in the three substantive areas, graduate training for empirical legal research requires at least two methods courses. Given the value placed on quantitative methods, graduate students interested in conducting empirical legal research are required to take an introductory quantitative methods course in the social science discipline that has the "best-fit" with their substantive intellectual orientation and research project. Typically economics, political science, psychology, and sociology departments all offer quantitative survey courses. The second methods course that students in NYU's LSP are required to take is one closely tailored to the methods they intend to use in their doctoral research. For example, students who will use and collect interview, participation/observation, and/or ethnographic data in their fieldwork will typically take a quantitative methods course in sociology. Below we discuss in more detail translating between "law" and "culture" though the empirical process of ethnography. Students who choose either to analyze existing survey research data or develop their own survey instrument will take a methods course in a sociology—or psychology program that deals with survey techniques. Short courses on Geographical Information Systems (GIS) and computational text analysis are primarily focused on the software, and should our students have a research question that is appropriate for either of these programs, they will study them. Very few students who are getting PhDs or JD/PhDs in Law and Society use formal models or game theory in their doctoral research. Nonetheless, NYU's Wilf Department of Politics has an extraordinary number of faculty members who use these tools and they are available to our students as well. Whether graduate students continue to develop their quantitative skills, or pursue more in-depth qualitative empirical training in their second methods course, they must translate non-law, disciplinary focused research methods that are taught without reference to theoretical or empirical knowledge of law and legal institutions.

II. Toward Developing Methods for Doing Empirical Legal Research

In the LSP, we supplement the *best-fit approach* with an intensive, four-part professional development program. First, students take workshops on research design where they examine the strengths and weakness of previous and existing studies carried out by LSP faculty. Secondly, students study the legislative history and current regulations in the United States on human subjects research, anticipating the impact of government and university regulations affecting data acquisition and data access as well as alternative strategies to deal with these regulations (Feeley, 2007). A third aspect of LSP professional development is the "Grants Writing Workshop," which is critical in this multi-disciplinary and trans-disciplinary field where grants and thematic post-doctoral fellowships are often not primarily identified as encompassing law. In the workshop we teach students how to translate grant headings such as "immigration," "climate change," or "digital archives" into "guest-worker regulatory regimes," "water refugees," or "access to information," respectively. We also have students read peer reviews that faculty members and more advanced graduate students have received on grant submissions and on subsequent, revised proposals. They then read the proposals that have been revised and re-submitted after taking into account comments from the blind reviews. Finally, almost all LSP students submit pre-dissertation grant proposals (in-house and outside of NYU) seeking funds to launch a pilot study for their dissertation research. The purpose of the pilot study is to bring together research design with grant writing; and if the study is successful, it enables the student to get into the field before she commits to a dissertation project, and to probe on a smaller scale their hunches about sources and the utility of a multi-method research design.

Empirical research is embedded in theoretical questions, and in the absence of broader theoretical training, the techniques of various research approaches can only be taught in a superficial way. Training in methods must be done in conjunction with the study of relevant policy questions. Empirical research on law has adopted a range of methods from in-depth ethnographic work to large-sample statistical analyses. Multi-method studies are fairly common in this field. Multi-method approaches (see Chapter 39) enrich the insights a research project provides but require a sophisticated knowledge of several methodologies. For example, Michael McCann's classic study, *Rights at Work* (1994), relies on ethnographic observations of activist groups, interviews with leaders and participants, quantitative and qualitative analysis of media reporting, analysis of legal cases, and an examination of the symbolic and discursive meanings of law for social movements (see also Gilliom, 2001; Scheingold, 1974; Silverstein, 1996). Patricia Ewick and Susan Silbey's study of legal consciousness, *The Common Place of Law* (1998), uses an extensive set of interviews with ordinary people as the basis for their analysis of narratives about law commonly deployed in this population. The study is based on the narrative as a unit of analysis. Through comparison of a large number of narratives and the stories they provide about the law, Ewick and Silbey develop a typology of forms of legal consciousness. Although their research focuses on the narratives, some of their methodology relied on a statistical analysis of the appearance of various words and discursive forms.

Stewart Macaulay's classic article on "Non-Contractual Relations in Business" relies both on interviews with contractors and on an examination, over a period of time, of contract documents and their terms and conditions to see how they were framed (1963). Malcom Feeley's study of plea bargaining, *The Process is the Punishment* (1979), is a study of the misdemeanor court in New Haven, Connecticut, in its political context, the phenomenon of plea bargaining in historical context through an observational analysis of the everyday practices of the courtroom and a quantitative analysis of court cases by type and by outcome. Clearly, being able to move nimbly among methodologies commonly thought of as quantitative, qualitative, and archival is fundamental to good empirical legal scholarship.

A. Pedagogy in empirical legal research

In the NYU Law & Society Program, graduate students who expect to do research in the field for their dissertation have opportunities to do such work prior to undertaking their dissertation in order to gradually acquire and test out a wide range of skills they may need for a multiple-methods study. Ideally, graduate students will co-teach with a faculty member or will conduct an undergraduate seminar that has a field-research component. We call this the "Law & Society Practicum." In addition, graduate students may have the opportunity to do field-work with a faculty member who serves as a mentor and ultimately co-author, as we describe below.

The LSP Practicum, which is encouraged but not required, enables graduate students to design a project with research and teaching elements. The goal of the practicum is to incorporate aspects of "clinical work," as a law student might do, in a field-research setting while teaching field-research and methods to undergraduates. Through their participation in a cross-culturally designed LSP Practicum created by NYU Professor Christine Harrington and LSP graduate student Cesar Rodriguez, NYU undergraduate students found that the NAFTA-induced growth in global sweatshops has taken a significant toll on factory workers, the environment, and transnational labor practices. The practicum, devoted to an examination of the effects of globalization on law, politics, and economics, provided students from various academic disciplines with first-hand experience of investigating the impact of NAFTA on *maquiladoras*—assembly plants operating mainly in the textile, electronic, and automobile industries—in the Puebla region of Mexico and on sweatshops in the fashion world of New York City. Seventeen NYU students traveled to Puebla and joined with eighteen students from Mexico's Universidad de las Americas (UDLA). Together they conducted on-site investigation of Puebla's *maquiladoras*, which have proliferated since the passage of NAFTA in 1994. US transnational corporations (TNCs) operate some of the "legal" *maquiladoras* in Mexico. But students also toured smaller, non-regulated factories where workers, mainly young women, provide sub-contract labor for the larger factories that need to hire out jobs to fill U.S. orders on time. While in Mexico, students spoke with scholars, workers, activists, and government officials. They also interviewed lawyers in Mexico City hired to represent the United States before the NAFTA panel; interviewed indigenous people opposed to "*maquiladora* culture"; and investigated environmental effects of *maquiladoras* on towns and neighborhoods. Students found evidence of pollution in the Puebla region, including dye-stained rivers and loss of vegetation. In addition, they found that some 90% of the workers they interviewed had been left uninformed about the union that represented them, and that conversation between workers is strictly prohibited in most *maquiladoras*.

Next, the students explored working conditions in New York City's Garment District and Chinatown areas, interviewing sweatshop employees and day workers. They also explored the coalition of American and Mexican human rights organizations and unions that oppose sweatshops, and the trans-national communities of immigrants from Puebla in NYC. The final report of the students' findings, including a video produced by Elizabeth Chan, was made electronically accessible on the Institute for Law and Society website.

Commonly used methodologies in field research are surveys, archival work in historical records, more-or-less structured interviews, and ethnography. As noted above, LSP requires students to take a quantitative methods course in statistics and a qualitative methods course in historical, interviewing, or ethnographic methods, and recommends advanced courses in both areas. While a course can teach the techniques of quantitative data management, teaching observational and ethnographic skills is less easily done in a course format. There are no straightforward guides to this kind of research; it depends instead on paying attention to what one sees and what people say in terms of a set of questions the observer carries in her head. Indeed, anthropologists have coined the term "head notes" to describe the ongoing process by which an ethnographer makes observations and stitches them together into an analysis that combines attention to social relationships, interactions, discourse and meaning, and power. Each situation needs to be interpreted through an extensive understanding of the context of the scene and its history. Head notes are the interpretations that an ethnographer makes as he or she is working to make sense of a situation in a theoretical framework.

It is not easy to teach these skills. Teaching the researcher to attend to subtle cues and to be open to multiple interpretations is, in some ways, like teaching a person to drive: the new driver must attend not only to the obvious stop signs and road markers, but also to the ball rolling across the street which may well be followed by a running child. Or it may not, but the driver must keep open that interpretive possibility.

One key strategy is to pay attention to the categories used by the actors in the scene under scrutiny. For example, in her study of New England lower courts, Sally Engle Merry confronted the question of how to sort the wide array of cases brought to the court into a coherent typology. She noticed that court clerks, mediation program staff, attorneys, and judges routinely divided them into a few categories based on the nature of the relationship between the parties: family, neighbor, boyfriend/girlfriend, for example (1990). These categories became the lens through which cases were interpreted and sorted in the courthouse. Thus, they provided a valuable way to analyze the differences viewed as significant in the court. Moreover, once in the sphere of the law, court personnel separated these different views into those primarily concerned respectively with emotional issues, moral considerations, and legal claims. The first two kinds of cases were readily dismissed by the court. Only the legal cases were treated as warranting sustained attention. Thus, the actors in this situation used a set of categories to divide up the world and decide how to act. Recognizing the categories and the way they frame action is a critical step in gaining ethnographic knowledge.

An ideal way to teach ethnography is through the experience of locating a field site, negotiating access, developing relationships, and figuring out what to ask and what to learn from it. The opportunity to do ethnographic research in an ongoing project offers an ideal training situation. In 2005–2006, for example, two NYU Law and Society PhD students, Mihaela Serban and Diana Yoon, worked with Merry for about ten months, in between their other academic work, on a project examining the way international women's rights ideas were appropriated and translated into terms that made sense in local contexts. They each focused on a different NGO in New York City, but they also collaborated with each other, a situation facilitated by the fact that the two organizations were connected. They also participated in two conferences with the other three teams in the research project and together wrote a paper on their work for a special issue of *Global Networks* (Levitt and Merry, 2009) that features the work of all four groups, from Beijing, Baroda (India), Lima, and New York City. A second paper, co-authored with Peggy Levitt, the other principal investigator, and Mihaela Serban and Diana Yoon, appeared in the *Law and Society Review* (Merry et al., 2010). Both students described this experience as a very valuable way to learn to do ethnography.

There are several features of this research experience that were particularly valuable for learning ethnography. First, the students entered an ongoing project in which they did not have to figure out the question being addressed. Doing so is one of the major challenges of a dissertation, so to begin with a field experience that did not require a decision about the topic made it easier for the students to move into the research itself. Second, they learned how to find a research site. Even though the broad question—how are global human rights translated into local contexts?—was already established, it was still necessary to find an appropriate research site, negotiate permission to study it, and find a way to get involved. The students and faculty members worked together on this project, using a variety of networks and suggestions. It was not easy, since many organizations in New York City have experienced waves of researchers and are understandably reluctant to take on more. However, with patience and persistence, they located two wonderful examples of the phenomenon they wanted to study. The students were part of this searching and exploration process, and clearly saw the difficulties and challenges of identifying an appropriate research site.

Third, they carried out several interviews together, so that they could watch and participate in the interview process. A faculty member at another law school generously agreed to be interviewed both by her own students and by Merry's as part of a training exercise for both groups. Sometimes Merry took the lead in the interview and at other times the students did. Learning by watching and doing is an invaluable dimension of field research.

Fourth, the students had many meetings to discuss what they were learning. Part of the challenge of ethnographic field research is becoming aware of things that seem taken for granted. For example, as Diana Yoon was describing the discussions and strategies for handling conflicts in the women's NGO she was working with, she realized that this organization uses the language and techniques of the battered women's movement and only adopts human rights as a superficial overlay to this older, well-established discourse. In these discussions, faculty members and students learned a great deal from their observations and insights because they were involved in a fully collaborative process. Since this was a comparative study of the work of women's NGOs around the world, the team was able to make comparisons with work currently being done by the other three teams.

Fifth, the graduate students then worked together to write a paper based on their field research. They worked productively together and shared their drafts with the faculty, so that we had ongoing theoretical debate. They talked about what they had seen, what they made of it, and how they interpreted what they saw. Although the final analysis was clearly developed by the students, it was the result of long, sustained discussions among faculty members and students. Although, as an ethnographer with considerable experience, Merry felt more in control of the methodology than the graduate students, they each brought their expertise to the discussion.

In sum, teaching ethnography requires collaborative strategies, much along the lines of those outlined in this paper. Lifting the burden of coming up with the overarching theoretical question is an important contribution. Collaboratively negotiating the field site is also constructive. Sharing insights and interpretive frameworks, and finally working together to make sense of the observations and turn them into a publishable manuscript, are all enormously important to developing ethnographic skills. Ideally, ethnography should be taught in this way.

Teaching quantitative skills similarly requires hands-on learning, ideally in a participatory form. Moving from a theoretical question to a set of specific, measurable ways to answer it is a challenging part of empirical research. Debating ways to address and quantify theoretical issues with a team provides excellent training in how to do this kind of research and underscores the fact that there are multiple possible approaches, several of which could be effective. Conversations between a faculty member and a student engaged in working through similar problems encourage students to weigh and compare the benefits of various approaches. Such collaborative work also emphasizes the interpretive dimension of quantitative research, showing how numerical findings require analysis in terms of theoretical frameworks and qualitative information (see Kritzer, 1996). While quantitative and archival methods can be learned autonomously, as can ethnographic ones, in each case a collaborative research project is an invaluable learning opportunity.

III. Conclusion

In sum, providing students with training in methods is one of the most challenging parts of graduate training in the empirical legal research field. This is an eclectic field that draws on a wide array of methodologies ranging from quantitative approaches (that require knowledge about how to manipulate existing data sets or assemble new ones for the purpose of doing statistical analysis of relationships and patterns observed overtime) to interpretive, qualitative methods (that map the formation of legal consciousness, its stability or change over time, and the discursive meanings of law). Ideally, empirical legal training provides students with a background they need to be literate in a broad range of social science methods and develop mastery over a set of methods they can ultimately triangulate or juxtapose in order to capture the factors that explain and or give meaning to law as a social phenomenon. As they do so, they translate among a variety of empirical methodologies and bodies of scholarship that together provide the optimum way of doing empirical legal studies.

References

Baldwin, J. and Davis, G. (2003). "Empirical Research in Law," in P. Cane and M. Tushnet, *The Oxford Handbook of Legal Studies*, Oxford: Oxford University Press, 880–901.

Cotterrell, R. (1995). *Law's Community: Legal Ideas in Sociological Perspective*, Oxford: Clarendon Press.

Ewick, P. and Silbey, S. (1998). *The Common Place of Law*, Chicago: University of Chicago Press.

Feeley, M. (1979). *The Process is the Punishment: Handling Cases in a Lower Criminal Court*, New York: Russell Sage.

Feeley, M. (2007). "Legality, Social Research, and the Challenge of Institutional Review Boards," *Law & Society Review* 41: 757–76.

Genn, H., Partington, M., and Wheeler, S. (2006). *Law in the Real World: Improving Our Understanding of How Law Works,* Nuffield Inquiry on Empirical Legal Research, London: Nuffield Foundation.

Gilliom, J. (2001). *Overseers of the Poor: Surveillance, Resistance, and the Limits of Privacy,* Chicago: University of Chicago Press.

Hagan, J. and Rymond-Richmond, W. (2009). *Darfur and the Crime of Genocide,* New York: Cambridge University Press.

Halliday, S. and Schmidt, P. (2009). *Conducting Law and Society Research: Reflections on Methods and Practices,* New York: Cambridge University Press.

Haltom, W. and McCann, M. (2004). *Distorting the Law: Politics, Media and the Litigation Crisis,* Chicago: University of Chicago Press.

Hempel, C.G. (1965). *Aspects of Scientific Explanation and Other Essays in the Philosophy of Science,* New York: Free Press.

Heinz, J. P., Paik, A., and Southworth, A. (2003). "Lawyers for Conservative Causes: Clients, Ideology, and Social Distance," *Law and Society Review* 37: 5–50.

Hunt, A. (1978). *The Sociological Movement in Law,* London: Macmillan.

Kritzer, H.M. (1991). "Propensity to Sue in England and the United States: Blaming and Claiming in Tort Cases," *Journal of Law and Society* 18: 400–27.

Kritzer, H.M. (1996). "The Data Puzzle: The Nature of Interpretation in Quantitative Research," *American Journal of Political Science* 40: 1–32.

Kritzer, H.M. and Richards, M.J. (2003). "Jurisprudential Regimes and Supreme Court Decisionmaking: The *Lemon* Regime and Establishment Clause Cases," *Law & Society Review* 37: 827–40.

Kritzer, H.M. and Richards, M.J. (2005). "The Influence of Law in the Supreme Court's Search-and-Seizure Jurisprudence," *American Politics Research* 33: 33–55.

Kritzer, H.M. and Richards, M.J. (2010). "Taking and Testing Jurisprudential Regimes Seriously: A Response to Lax and Rader," *Journal of Politics* 72: 285–8.

Levitt, P. and Merry, S.E. (2009). "Vernacularization on the Ground: Local Uses of Global Women's Rights in Peru, China, India and the United States," *Global Networks* 9(4): 441–61.

Macaulay, S. (1963). "Non-Contractual Relations in Business: A Preliminary Study," *American Sociological Review* 28: 59–76.

Mather, L.M. and Yngvesson, B. (1980–1981). "Language, Audience, and the Transformation of Disputes," *Law & Society Review* 15: 775–821.

McCann, M. (1994). *Rights at Work: Pay Equity Reform and the Politics of Legal Mobilization,* Chicago: University of Chicago Press.

Merry, S.E. (1990). *Getting Justice and Getting Even: Legal Consciousness Among Working-Class Americans,* Chicago: University of Chicago Press.

Merry, S.E., Levitt, P., Rosen, M.S., and Yoon, D.H. (2010). "Law from Below: Women's Human Rights and Social Movements in New York City," *Law & Society Review* 44: 101–28.

Nelson, R.L. and Heinz, J.P. (1988). "Lawyers and the Structure of Influence in Washington," *Law & Society Review* 22: 237–300.

Paik, A., Southworth, A., and Heinz, J.P. (2007). "Lawyers of the Right: Networks and Organization," *Law and Social Inquiry* 32: 883–917.

Richards, M.J. and Kritzer, H.M. (2002). "Jurisprudential Regimes in Supreme Court Decision Making," *American Political Science Review* 96: 305–20.

Richards, M.J., Smith, J., and Kritzer, H.M. (2006). "Does Chevron Matter?," *Law and Policy* 28: 444–69.

Scheingold, S. (1974). *The Politics of Rights*, New Haven: Yale University Press.

Shapiro, M. (2008). "Law and Politics: The Problem of Boundaries," in K. Whittington, R.D. Kelemen, and G. Caldeira (eds.), *The Oxford Handbook of Law and Politics*, New York: Oxford University Press, 767–74.

Silverstein, H. (1996). *Unleashing Rights: Law, Meaning, and the Animal Rights Movement*, Ann Arbor: University of Michigan Press.

Southworth, A. (2008). *Lawyers of the Right: Professionalizing the Conservative Coalition*, Chicago: University of Chicago Press.

Stumpf, H.P. (1998). *American Judicial Politics* (2nd edn.), Englewood Cliffs, NJ: Prentice Hall.

Van Evera, S. (1997). *Guide to Methods for Students of Political Science*, Ithaca, NY: Cornell University Press.

INDEX

....

THE OXFORD HANDBOOK OF

EMPIRICAL LEGAL RESEARCH

Edited by

PETER CANE

HERBERT M. KRITZER

OXFORD
UNIVERSITY PRESS

OXFORD

UNIVERSITY PRESS

Great Clarendon Street, Oxford OX2 6DP
United Kingdom

Oxford University Press is a department of the University of Oxford.
It furthers the University's objective of excellence in research, scholarship,
and education by publishing worldwide. Oxford is a registered trade mark of
Oxford University Press in the UK and in certain other countries

First published 2010
First published in paperback 2012
Reprinted 2013

British Library Cataloguing in Publication Data
Data available

Library of Congress Cataloging in Publication Data
Data available

ISBN 978-0-19-965994-4

CONTENTS

······························